A GENEALOGICAL CHART OF GREEK MYTHOLOGY

A Genealogical Chart of Greek Mythology

COMPRISING 3,673 NAMED FIGURES OF GREEK MYTHOLOGY,

ALL RELATED TO EACH OTHER WITHIN A SINGLE FAMILY OF 20 GENERATIONS

COMPILED BY HAROLD NEWMAN AND JON O. NEWMAN

The University of North Carolina Press

Chapel Hill and London

© 2003 The University of North Carolina Press
All rights reserved
Manufactured in China

Library of Congress Cataloging-in-Publication Data
Newman, Harold.
A genealogical chart of Greek mythology: comprising 3,673 named figures of Greek mythology, all related to each other within a single family of 20 generations / compiled by Harold Newman and Jon O. Newman.
p. cm. Includes bibliographical references (p.) and index.
ISBN 0-8078-2790-8 (cloth: alk. paper)
1. Mythology, Greek—Charts, diagrams, etc. I. Newman, Jon O. (Jon Ormond) II. Title.
BL785 .N44 2003 292.1'3—dc21 2002043574

07 06 05 04 03 5 4 3 2

NOTE ON TYPOGRAPHY AND THE CONSTRUCTION OF THE CHART

The Complete Chart and the Master Chart are set in Helvetica, except for capital I's, which are in Times to distinguish them from lowercase l's. The text uses Times only. The charts and text were created on a Macintosh® computer, using the PageMaker® desktop publishing program.

It would have been nearly impossible to create the charts without a computer. The reason has nothing to do with the availability of genealogy programs. These are useful for constructing family trees but are not suitable for the complexity of the 72 segments of the Complete Chart, and such programs were not used. What a computer and PageMaker crucially made possible were two aspects of chart construction. First, they facilitated the placement of thousands of horizontal and vertical lines at precisely the correct location so that figures in the same generation appear at the same depth on all segments and the horizontal lines that connect between two segments continue laterally from one to the next. Second, and even more important, they made it possible instantly to add or move figures as additional research identified relationships that could be verified in ancient sources. The computer also facilitated making the innumerable changes that had to be made in the Index as figures were added, their segment locations were changed, and earlier sources were identified.

The computer also facilitated searching the Index, the creation of searchable lists of ancient sources, and examination of several online library catalogues.

Contents

Preface

I hope this book will be a useful and intriguing reference work for all who have an interest in Greek mythology, from serious scholars to curious amateurs. It should be of special interest to students, affording an opportunity to see at a glance that nearly all the figures they will be reading about in the *Iliad*, the *Odyssey*, the Greek tragedies, and other accounts of Greek mythology can be shown to have been related to each other.

As more fully explained in the Introduction, the Complete Chart, which is the core of this book, reflects only one version of the ancestry and family relationships of each figure, although several alternate versions of the parentage of many figures are listed in the Index. Necessarily in constructing a genealogical chart, numerous choices have to be made among the various versions reported by recognized mythographers. The responsibility for these choices is the compilers'. Any comments from readers, either pointing out errors or simply arguing the case for selecting a different version of the relationships of some of the figures, will be appreciated.

Appropriately for a work of genealogy, this has been a father-son project. Harold Newman, my father, conceived the project and constructed the initial version of the Complete Chart, hand-lettering the names of the figures on large cardboard sheets. I completed the project, adding about 1,000 names to the Complete Chart, constructing the Master Chart, compiling the Index and the appendices, and typesetting the book on a computer.

The identification of ancient sources confirming every relationship shown was performed by several classics scholars. The principal researcher was Dr. Maria-Viktoria Abricka, whose advice on many of the subtleties of Greek mythology is much appreciated. Graduate students, especially James Goodwin and Jessica Clark, assisted. Their research has confirmed that each relationship shown in the Index is reported by the author and work listed for that relationship. However, the connections shown on the Complete Chart include some relationships that are a matter of inference, rather than confirmation in an ancient source. For example, a source might confirm the name of a child's father, and another source might confirm a woman as the wife of that father, but not confirm that the wife is the mother of that child. In many instances, unless a different mother can be confirmed, the chart often shows the child as the offspring of both the father and his spouse. Relationships shown in that manner are the responsibility of the compilers, not the researchers. The Index is more authoritative than the Complete Chart, since an ancient source is provided whenever a wife or paramour has been confirmed as the mother of a child. Ultimately, all responsibility for any errors is mine.

I express special appreciation to Dr. Jeffrey Kaimowitz and the staff of the Watkinson Library at Trinity College, Hartford, Conn., for locating many obscure sources and responding helpfully to my many questions.

The project was begun in 1964 and completed in 2002. Harold Newman died in 1993 at the age of 93.

Throughout the project the compilers benefited from the helpful advice, encouragement, and patience of our wives, Martha Newman and the late Wendy Newman.

Jon O. Newman
West Hartford, Conn.

Foreword

At the beginning of Book 6 of the *Iliad*, Homer has Diomedes (after a very successful session of carnage in Book 5) shrewdly inquire of his next opponent as to the opponent's ancestors (hoping to discover whether the person in question might be a god, and thus to be avoided). The Trojan ally Glaucus responds with the famous speech observing that men are like leaves on a tree: after but a brief time they fall, and the next generation replaces them. But having thus advised us on the vanity of human genealogy, Glaucus does not scruple to expend the next fifty-seven lines describing his own ancestry in considerable detail, and we are reminded that ancient Greeks did after all set great store by whom they could claim relations: the fact that Diomedes and Glaucus exchange friendship gifts (armor) rather than fight is entirely due to the discovery that Diomedes' grandfather Oeneus once played host to Glaucus' grandfather Bellerophon. Connections are everything.

As time went on, Greek mythographers (beginning perhaps with the six-century BC Catalogue Poet, author of the Hesiodic *Catalogue of Women*, but probably much earlier) began to systematize these connections, reporting them where they had already been attested and creating new genealogicial structures to fill in the gaps in cases where they had not. Already at this point Greeks of the aristocratic ranks were tracing their ancestry back to the heroes of Greek mythology, and thus the ability to convincingly map the pedigree of the mythological family one wished to be adopted by took on special importance. The *Bibliotheke*, or handbook of the Greek mythographer we know as Apollodorus (most likely writing in the second century AD) represents the most systematic effort to bring the various genealogies created into line, with a remarkable degree of organization. With its primary interest in narrative, however, this work does not attempt to actually create a large-scale picture of the genealogical relationships, even though Apollodorus had at his disposal the evidence with which to construct such a picture.

Apollodorus, to be fair, working with pen and papyrus (or parchment), lacked the resources to produce such a chart (or at least a readable one). Armed with modern computer technology, I once thought that I might be able to do what he did not as an appendix to my own *Early Greek Myth* (Baltimore 1993). It was not long before, confronted with the complexity of the enterprise and the magnitude of the labor involved, I settled for generating a few very simple one-page tables of the kind one finds in any handbook of mythology, and decided that someone else would have to tackle the larger task. Jon Newman has done so, and having seen the length of the chart required to do it properly, I am more than ever thankful that I folded my tent and slipped away.

Any reader interested in the author's qualifications will no doubt have observed that Mr. Newman is not a trained Classicist, and normally this is in my field grounds for a bit of skepticism. But he and his father before him have dedicated nearly forty years to their project, and while perhaps someone with the appropriate degree (and an academic post allowing serious opportunities for research) could have managed it in a bit less time, the results seem to me no less professional. Not only have all the usual suspects been consulted, but the (vitally important in this line of endeavor) really obscure ones as well: sources like Lycophron, Parthenaeus, and yes, even Stephanus of Byzantium, as well as of course anonymous scholia, have been pressed into service where appropriate. I make no claim to have checked all the citations (they have been reviewed by a highly qualified Classicist whom I will leave to the author to identify and thank in his acknowledgements) but the whole has I think been done right.

Admittedly, the complete chart that has been produced, extending as it does over seventy-two pages, is at times hard to follow (it could hardly have been otherwise). But the identifications within the chart of the sources for the relationships are an important value-added factor, and the 92-page index of the 3,673 named figures is not simply an essential guide to the chart, but a highly valuable free-standing piece of research which I will likely consult in years to come even more than the chart itself: it names names, pins down exactly who is the source for what, and tells Classicists with the precision they need where to find the original texts proffering this wealth of information. The fact that the author is by vocation a federal appellate judge may perhaps explain why this work presents us with such a substantial body of witnesses and their evidence, rather than simply relying on those well-known poets and mythographers who are so often the only ones called upon to testify. In any case, this is a major contribution to our understanding of how ancient Greeks organized the vast corpus of figures constituting what we call Greek mythology; there is (certainly to my knowledge) nothing like it, and I am quite grateful to have it at my disposal.

Timothy Gantz
Professor of Classics
University of Georgia
Athens, Georgia

Introduction

1. Though Greek mythology has been recounted by hundreds of writers throughout the world over the course of nearly three thousand years, this book endeavors to make a new contribution to the field—a comprehensive genealogical chart that displays one version of the relationships among virtually all the figures from the Greek myths who can be linked together in a single "family tree." Many books display separate family trees of small groups of well-known mythological figures, but this is the first attempt to present a genealogical chart that connects 3,673 related figures named by the leading mythographers, with citations to an ancient source for each relationship shown.

2. This project makes visually apparent a remarkable aspect of Greek mythology: there are 3,673 named figures all of whom can be shown to be related to each other. They marry, sometimes more than once. They have extra-marital liaisons. They have children. Many ancient writers mentioned genealogical relationships in their verses, plays, and narratives, and Hesiod in the *Theogony,* the poet of the *Catalogue of Women*, and later Apollodorus recounted an extensive number of relationships. But it is unlikely that the early Greeks thought of all the figures shown on the Chart in this book as related within one comprehensive "family." The oral tradition in which these myths originated generated accounts of relationships among relatively small numbers of figures, and as the stories were retold, different versions of a figure's parentage emerged. As a result, there is no one authoritative version of the genealogy of the figures of Greek mythology. That is why this work is called "A Genealogical Chart of Greek Mythology," not "The Genealogical Chart of Greek Mythology." Nevertheless, from careful examination of numerous ancient writings, a comprehensive chart can be constructed that connects together a vast number of named figures, many of whom are not generally thought to have been related. This Chart and the accompanying Index, with its citations to all the relationships shown on the Chart and to many alternate versions of parentage, provide an innovative and useful framework to assist the reader in exploring Greek mythology, reviewing known relationships, and discovering relationships that might not have been known.

3. The total of 3,673 linked figures shown on the Chart comprises only named figures. Groups of related but unnamed figures, such as the 50 daughters of Endymion and *Selene* (throughout the book, female names appear in italic type) or the 50 sons of Pallas[6] (throughout the book, superscript numbers distinguish different figures with the same name), are shown on the Chart, but the number of unnamed figures in such groups has not been included in the total number of linked figures.

4. Of course, some of the ancient writers named mythical figures who are not related to the extensive group of figures shown on this Chart. For example, Homer mentioned various warriors who fought at Troy, but whose parents or wives are not identified. Without such information, they cannot be linked to the network of figures charted in this book.

5. The figures appearing in this book span the entire cast of Greek mythology—Titans, gods and goddesses, kings, heroes, mortals, giants, monsters, centaurs, horses, rivers, winds, stars, and personifications of abstract conceptions. Twenty generations are included, displayed in an orderly arrangement that maintains each generation in a consistent position across all 72 segments of the Chart.

6. The book consists of three components:

(a) **The Complete Chart**: 72 segments that connect horizontally to form one continuous genealogical chart containing all 3,673 named figures.

(b) **The Master Chart**: two pages containing the principal figures from the Complete Chart and the number of the segment on which they appear. The Master Chart enables the reader to see at a glance how the figures on any one of the 72 segments of the Complete Chart connect to figures appearing on all of the other segments.

(c) **The Index**: a list of each of the 3,673 named figures, together with a citation to an ancient source confirming each relationship of the figure, identifying information about the figure, and a reference to each location where the figure appears on any of the 72 segments of the Complete Chart. For many figures, the entry also includes alternative versions of the figure's parentage, with a citation to an ancient source reporting these versions.

A "Guide to the Master Chart and the Complete Chart" explains their structure and symbols, and a separate "Guide to the Index" explains its entries.

7. An undertaking of this sort cannot claim to be "accurate." There was no registry of births and marriages on Mt. Olympus, or at Athens or Troy. The early writers who first recounted the myths told different versions of the same stories, often attributing different parents to the same figure and different sets of children to the same parents. Some modern mythographers have perpetuated these differences. Indeed, they have often compounded confusion by failing to recognize that many different figures bore the same name. Just as there are several people named John Smith in most English-speaking communities, it should not be surprising that in Greek mythology there are, for example, several men named Lycus and several women named *Merope*. Yet many writers have attributed to one figure the spouses and children of a different figure who has the same name. Confusion also arises from typographical errors occurring with similarly spelled names. Some writers have referred to *Pyrene* when they meant *Cyrene* (and vice-versa), or to Lamedon when they meant Laomedon. Sometimes the same figure is rendered with two different spellings, *e.g.*, the son of Hippocoon[1] is called Tebrus in Apollodorus *Bibl.* 3.10.5, and Sebrus in Pausanius 3.15.1-2.

8. Constructing a genealogical chart from such conflicting and, on occasion, erroneous information obviously requires that choices be made. These are the principal choices reflected in this book and the reasons for them:

(a) Only one version of the ancestry of each figure is shown on the Complete Chart. A genealogical chart showing even the two or three most widely reported versions of the ancestry of each figure would be hopelessly confusing. However, alternate versions of the parentage of the principal figures, as reported by leading mythographers, are set forth in the Index.

(b) Although it would have been possible to construct a limited genealogical chart based on the writings of a single mythographer, this book draws upon the accounts of many ancient poets, playwrights, and other writers in order to construct a comprehensive chart. However, an effort has been made to maintain consistency of traditions by reflecting primarily the versions of relationships as reported by the earliest writers. Hesiod's *Theogony* is used for the relationships that concern the creation of the world and the parentage of the first figures, starting with Chaos (which may be more a concept than a figure). Homer is the principal source for relationships in later generations. If the relationship is not confirmed by Hesiod or Homer, other ancient sources are used, usually the earliest known source (see "A Note on Sources").

(c) Uncertainty frequently arises as to whether mythographers are writing about two different versions of the parentage of the same figure or two different figures who had the same name. Sometimes, it is reasonably apparent from the different stories told about the figures, or from the different locales or periods in which the figures lived, that they were two different figures. In other situations, however, there is an insufficient basis for decision. In this book, such doubts have usually been resolved in favor of two different figures with the same name. Where it is reasonably clear that different writers are reporting different versions of the parentage of the same figure, one version of the figure's parentage, usually as reported by the earliest writer, is shown on the Master Chart and on the Complete Chart, and the alternate version or versions are shown in the Index. To distinguish different figures who have the same name, superscript numbers are used, *e.g.*, Lycus[1], Lycus[2], Lycus[3]. The same superscript number consistently identifies a figure each time that figure is shown. The particular number selected has no significance.

9. In some instances, this book might err by representing as two figures with the same name (but with different superscript numbers) what is really one figure. This might occur for either of two reasons:

(a) Some writers have reported inconsistent family relationships, suggesting that they are describing two different figures. For example, one Lycus is described as the son of Poseidon and *Celaeno*[1] while another Lycus is described as the son of Ares. Although these might be different versions of the same figure, this book treats them as two figures, Lycus[7] and Lycus[8].

(b) Other writers have reported two family relationships that could be consistent for a single figure, but have provided no reason for concluding that they are describing the same figure. For example, one *Merope* is described as the daughter of Atlas and *Pleione*, while another *Merope* is described as the wife of Megareus[1]. Although the daughter and the wife might be the same figure, in the absence of a confirming source, this book treats them as two figures, *Merope*[1] and *Merope*[8].

10. In some instance, this book might err by representing as one figure what are really two figures with the same name. For example, Haemon[1] is shown on segment 55 of the Complete Chart as the son of Creon[2] and *Eurydice*[9] and as the husband of *Antigone*[1]. It is possible that these are two different figures.

11. A line must be drawn between Greek and Roman mythology. Of course, many figures of Roman mythology are simply the Roman counterparts of figures in Greek mythology, and these have been identified in Appendix A (together with a listing of the Greek counterparts of figures in Roman mythology in Appendix B). But many figures who belong in Greek mythology have children whose primary significance is in Roman mythology. Odysseus, for example, has a relationship with *Circe*, and among their children is Latinus[1], the father of *Lavinia*[2]. The Complete Chart includes the Roman children and sometimes the Roman grandchildren of Greek figures, but goes no further into Roman mythology.

12. An equally arbitrary line separates myth from reality. Many of the early kings of the Greek states are referred to by mythographers as "legendary kings." Yet for some of them, precise dates of birth and death have been reported, strongly suggesting that they were real people. These figures, however, were said to be the descendants of mythic figures, often one of the gods or goddesses. It seems likely that many of them were real, but claimed mythological ancestry, perhaps to enhance their authority. This book includes them whenever they are reported as mythic figures by a recognized ancient source. That seems to be a reasonable way to resolve a matter of considerable uncertainty. (Besides, their claims might be correct, and one ought not to risk the wrath of the gods.)

To whatever extent some of the figures of Greek mythology might have been real people, one may speculate about the time period in which they might have lived. Since 1184 B.C. is often accepted as the likely date of the Trojan War, and since many of the figures reported to have participated in that war appear in either the 12th or 13th generation of the Complete Chart, it may be surmised that any "real figures" who are shown on the Complete Chart lived somewhere during a 600-year span from 1500 B.C. to 900 B.C.

13. Children are often shown on the Complete Chart in both their paternal and maternal chains. Sometimes, because of space limitations, they are shown only in their maternal chains, but a cross-reference indicates where the ancestors of their fathers are located. The placement of a figure in either the paternal or the maternal chain often has a significant effect upon the generation in which the figure is located. That is because some male figures married or had extra-marital relations with female figures of different generations. The gods, being immortal, appear as the fathers of children by female figures who were born in widely separated generations. Placing such children in the paternal chain locates them in the sixth generation, whereas placing them in the maternal chain often locates them in a much later generation.

14. A remarkable aspect of Greek mythology, visible from the Complete Chart, is the high degree of generational consistency, sometimes referred to as chronicity. Many figures who shared common exploits, such as the Trojan War, and all of the Seven against Thebes appear within just two generations of each other.

A Note on Sources

Hesiod and Homer are the principal sources for figures reported by these writers. For figures not reported by these writers, principal sources are the *Catalogue of Women*, the *Homeric Hymns*, Bacchylides, Pherecydes, Pindar, and the early playwrights, such as Aeschylus, Euripides, and Sophocles. Relationships not confirmed in these sources are as reported primarily by later mythographers, such as Apollodorus, Apollonius Rhodius, Diodorus Siculus, Hyginus, Pausanias, and Stephanus of Byzantium.

In addition to the ancient writers, whose works are cited in the Index for every relationship shown, the works of many modern writers have been consulted, including those of Thomas Bulfinch, Michael

Grant, Robert Graves, Edith Hamilton, Sir Paul Harvey, David Kravitz, Sabine Oswalt, H. J. Rose, William Smith, Edward Tripp, M. L. West, and J. E. Zimmerman. The writings of all of these mythographers have been examined and relied upon to some extent, but the five principal "modern" compilations of Greek mythography that have been helpful are the Reverend Jean Lempriere's *Classical Dictionary*, first published in France in 1788, Pierre Grimal's *Dictionary of Classical Mythology*, first published in France in 1951, Robert E. Bell's *Women of Classical Mythology*, published in the United States in 1991, Carlos Parada's *Genealogical Guide to Greek Mythology*, published in Sweden in 1993, and especially Timothy Gantz's *Early Greek Myth—A Guide to Literary and Artistic Sources*, published in the United States in 1993. All of these compilations have provided guidance, but all citations in the Index are to ancient sources.

A Note on Spelling

The spelling of names throughout the book is generally a combination of transliteration from the Greek and Latin versions of well known names. Adjustments have been made to promote identification of familiar figures. The changes from precise transliteration include the following:

(a) "k" has been changed to "c." Cyclops and Heracles seem more recognizable than Kyklops and Herakles. However, "k" has been retained for *Dike* and *Nike*.

(b) "os" endings have generally been changed to "us," *e.g.*, Danaus instead of Danaos. However, the "os" ending has been retained for some names, *e.g.*, Helios and Hypnos, which are more familiar.

(c) "i" has been changed to "j" and "s" to "x" in a few instances, *e.g.*, Ajax instead of Aias.

(d) "i" has been changed to "e" in a few instances, *e.g.*, *Gaea* instead of *Gaia*.

(e) "e" has been changed to "a" in a few instances, *e.g.*, *Eudora* instead of *Eudore*.

(f) "i" has been omitted from the "eia" ending for some female names to promote recognition, *e.g.*, *Medea* instead of *Medeia*.

Guide to the Master Chart and the Complete Chart

This "Guide to the Master Chart and the Complete Chart" explains, on this page, the structure of each chart and, on the next four pages, the type styles, line arrangements, and symbols used to indicate the relationships of figures on both charts. In this Guide, and throughout the book, male names appear in roman type, female names appear in italic type, and superscript numbers are used to distinguish figures with the same name (see paragraphs 9 and 10).

Structure

1. The Complete Chart contains all of the 3,673 figures of the genealogy connected together to form one family tree. The Master Chart is a summary of the Complete Chart, showing the principal figures from the Complete Chart.

2. The Master Chart, located on pages 10 and 11, consists of two segments that connect horizontally to form one continuous summary chart. The Complete Chart, located on the 142 pages that follow page 13, consists of 72 segments that connect horizontally to form one continuous chart. Each segment of the Complete Chart is prominently numbered with a large number in the upper right-hand corner of the segment. Except for the first and last segments, each segment appears twice, once on the right-hand page and again (with the same segment number) on the immediately following left-hand page. This duplication should assist the reader in following the connections as each segment joins horizontally with the next segment. To avoid confusion, page numbers do not appear at the bottom of the pages of the Complete Chart. Only the segment numbers appear, 1 through 72. The page numbering of the book resumes on page 157.

3. All cross-references on the segments of the Complete Chart and all references in the Index are to the large-type segment numbers in the upper right-hand corner of each segment. All references contain both a segment number and a letter, either a, b, c, or d. These letters correspond to the four quadrants of a segment, *viz.*,

a	b
c	d

Thus, a reference to 55b means the upper right-hand quadrant of segment 55. *No lines appear on the segments of the Complete Chart to divide them into the four quadrants; the reader will have to visualize the quadrants.*

4. The numbers on the Master Chart below each figure indicate the segment on which the figure appears in the particular relationship that is shown on that segment.

5. The Master Chart enables the reader, when examining any one of the 72 segments of the Complete Chart, to see at a glance (a) how the principal figures shown on that segment relate to the principal figures shown on all of the other segments, and (b) how that segment relates to all of the other segments:

(a) To illustrate use of the Master Chart to see the relationships *among principal figures*, a reader looking at Ares and his immediate relatives on segment 7 of the Complete Chart can turn to the first page of the Master Chart and locate, on the upper left side of page 10, the name *Hebe* above the number 5. The reader can then see the relationship of *Hebe* to her ultimate ancestor, Chaos, by moving up the Master Chart from *Hebe* to Zeus, Cronus, Uranus, *Gaea*, and ultimately to Chaos. Similarly, the reader can see the relationship between Hebe and Deucalion[1], her second cousin, by moving up the Master Chart from *Hebe* to her father, Zeus, and to her grandfather, Cronus, then across to the right to Cronus's brother, Iapetus, then down to Iapetus's son, Prometheus[1], and to Iapetus's grandson, Deucalion[1], located in the upper right portion of page 10, above the number 16. Or, as another example, Sisyphus, located on the middle left side of page 10, above the number 18, can be seen to be the fourth cousin of Agamemnon, located on the same generational line on the middle right side of page 10, above the number 36, since both Sisyphus and Agamemnon are descended, after four generations, from the sons of Iapetus, who is located on the upper right side of page 10, above the number 16.

This feature of the Master Chart enables the reader to confirm at a glance some of the significant generational relationships of Greek mythology. For example, in *Prometheus Bound*, Aeschylus tells of the prophecy by Prometheus[1] to *Io* that he will be freed by one of her direct descendants in the thirteenth generation of her line. The reader can locate *Io* in the upper center area of page 11, above the number 55, and then, starting with *Io*, count down twelve more generations in her line through Epaphus[1], *Libya*[1], Belus[1], Danaus[1], *Hypermnestra*[1], Abas[1], Acrisius, *Danae*, Perseus[1], Electryon[1], *Alcmene*, and finally to Heracles[1], whose feats included the freeing of Prometheus[1].

(b) To illustrate use of the Master Chart to see relationships *among the segments of the Complete Chart*, a reader looking at segment 15 of the Complete Chart can turn to the first page of the Master Chart (p. 10) and locate, on the left side of this page, several figures identified as appearing on segment 15. The reader can then notice that these figures have immediate relatives who are identified on this first page of the Master Chart as appearing on nearby segments. For example, Aetolus[1] (segment 15) has a brother, Paeon[1] (segment 16); *Protogeneia*[1] (segment 15) has a brother, Hellen(us)[1] (segment 17) and a nephew, Aeolus[1] (segment 18). Having thus seen the relationship of figures on segment 15 to figures on segments 16, 17, and 18, the reader can then move across the entire Master Chart to see the relationship of segment 15 (including all figures identified on the Master Chart above the number 15) to all of the other segments of the Complete Chart.

6. The Master Chart enables the reader to see at a glance that the placement of a figure in a particular generation depends on the relationship being shown. The three appearances of Achilles on the Master Chart illustrate the point. He first appears on the upper left side of page 10, above the number 24. Here he is shown in his paternal chain, where he is seen to be the great-grandson of Zeus and in the eighth generation (counting down from Chaos). Achilles also appears on the upper right side of page 11, above the number 65. Here he is shown in his maternal chain, where he is seen to be in the seventh

generation (counting down from Chaos). Finally, Achilles also appears in the lower middle portion of page 10, above the number 24. Here he is shown in his paternal chain, but he appears in the thirteenth generation (counting down from Chaos) because his paternal great-grandmother, *Aegina*, appears in the tenth generation as the wife of Actor^3.

7. The Master Chart shows most of the important figures that appear on the 72 segments of the Complete Chart. The Master Chart also contains at least one figure from almost all of the 72 segments of the Complete Chart, together with the number of the segment, so that a reader examining any one of the 72 segments can locate the number of that segment on the Master Chart and see where that segment fits in the overall arrangement of all 72 segments.

8. The numbers of the 72 segments of the Complete Chart appear on the Master Chart in roughly ascending order, with the low numbers generally on the left-hand side of page 10 and the high numbers generally on the right-hand side of page 11.

Type Styles, Line Arrangements, and Symbols

9. All male figures are shown in roman type, all female figures in italic type, in large type on the Complete Chart, *e.g.*,

Zeus *Hera*

and in slightly smaller type on the Master Chart, *e.g.*,

Zeus *Hera*

10. Different figures with the same name are distinguished by a numerical superscript, which is used every time the figures appear on the Master Chart, the Complete Chart, and in the Index, *e.g.*,

Lycus^1 Lycus^2 Lycus^3

11. In a few instances, different figures with the same name are distinguished by roman numerals if they were rulers who were usually identified in that manner, *e.g.*,

Pandion I Pandion II Cecrops I Cecrops II

12. Only the principal name of a figure is indicated on the Master Chart and the Complete Chart; alternate names of a figure, used by some mythographers, are shown in the Index.

13. Principal spelling variations of a name are indicated by placing in parentheses the letter or syllable that some mythographers use in spelling the name, *e.g.*,

Asty(a)dameia^1 Bellerephon(tes)

Although this practice might lead to occasional awkwardness in typography, it is more economical visually than listing all the possible variations separately.

14. Groups of figures known only by their designation (without a name) are shown in brackets, *e.g.*,

[satyrs] [three virgins]

Designations that are English words are in roman type, even if the figures are female.

15. On the Complete Chart, the name of a group of named figures appears in small type in parentheses above the names of the figures; the designation of what the figures in a group are appears in brackets, *e.g.*,

(Dioscuri) (Erinyes) [seasons] [centaurs]

16. Relationships among the figures are indicated by horizontal and vertical lines. For marital and extra-marital relationships, the basic format is to show the male figure with his wife or paramour usually to his right, a dash between them, and a line underneath both names, *e.g.*,

Zeus – *Hera* Zeus – *Alcmene*

to indicate Zeus and his wife, *Hera*, and Zeus and his paramour, *Alcmene*. Throughout this book, "paramour" is used to refer to any unmarried male or female mate, whether the extra-marital relationship results from a love affair, a dalliance, or even a rape. The charts do not distinguish between spouse and paramour. Sometimes a paramour is shown even though the report of a relationship is very likely false, *e.g.*, Peleus and *Hippolyte*^{2}.

17. Where a male figure has two wives or paramours, or a female figure has two husbands or paramours, divided lines underneath the names are used, *e.g.*,

Philyra – Cronus – *Rhea*

to indicate that *Rhea* is the wife and *Philyra* is the paramour of Cronus.

18. Where a male or female figure has more than two spouses or paramours, the marital or extra-marital relationship with each additional spouse or paramour is indicated by a colon, a dash, and a line underneath the colon and the name of the spouse or paramour; the figure with which the additional spouse or paramour has a relationship is the first figure of the opposite gender located away from the colon, *e.g.*,

Cleola – Atreus – *Aeropē* : – *Pelopeia*^{2}

to indicate that *Pelopeia*^{2} is an additional paramour of Atreus. In some instances, additional paramours appear on the left side of a figure and sometimes on both sides. The placement of multiple paramours often indicates alternate versions of different writers, not necessarily implying that one figure had all of the relationships shown.

19. In some situations, a figure, whether male or female, has so many paramours that space limitations prevent placing all of them on the same line. Where this occurs, the name of the principal figure is repeated below the figure's first location, enclosed in braces, and a carat points downward (or occasionally upward) to where the principal figure again appears, *e.g.*,

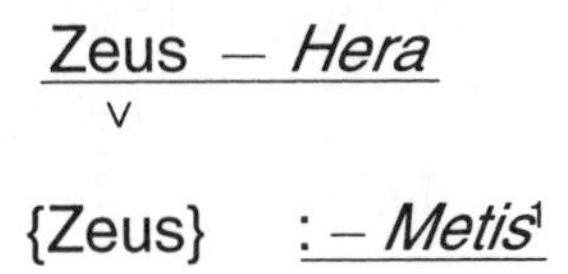

to indicate that *Metis*[1] is an additional paramour of Zeus, listed below *Hera* because of space limitations, but not indicating a subsequent generation.

20. Paramours are usually placed in alphabetical order, but not always.

21. A homosexual relationship is indicated by a tilde between the names and a line underneath both names, or, where there are several relationships, by a colon, a tilde, and a line underneath the colon and the name of the companion, *e.g.*,

to indicate that Apollo had homosexual relationships with Hyacinthus[1] and Hymen(aeus)[1].

22. The relationship of parents to their child is indicated slightly differently on the Master Chart and the Complete Chart. On both charts the parent-child relationship is indicated by a vertical line connecting the line underneath the name of one or both parents with the line above the child's name, but **on the Master Chart** the vertical line is sometimes placed directly underneath the dash between the names of both parents and sometimes underneath the name of only one parent, usually the father, *e.g.*,

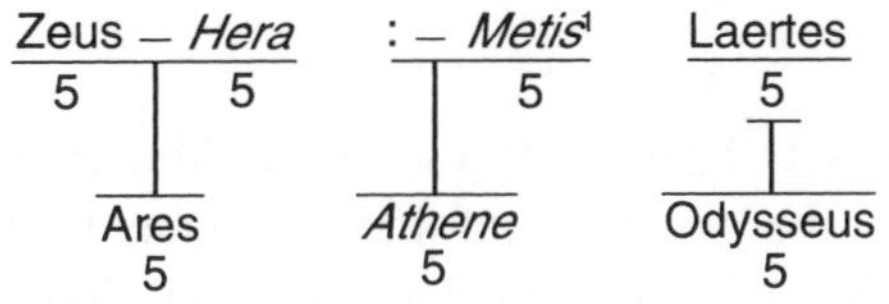

to indicate that **on the Master Chart** Ares is the son of Zeus and his wife, *Hera*, all appearing on segment 5; that *Athene* is the daughter of Zeus and his paramour, *Metis*, both appearing on segment 5; and that Odysseus is the son of Laertes, both appearing on segment 5. However, **on the Complete Chart** the vertical line is always placed directly under the dash between the names of both parents, *e.g.*,

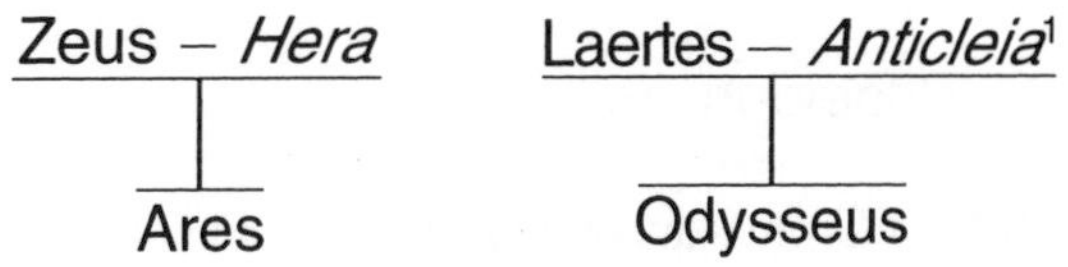

to indicate that Ares is the son of Zeus and his wife, *Hera* , and that Odysseus is the son of Laertes and *Anticleia*[1]. *In some instances where a child is shown below the dash between the names of a male and female figure, only the parentage of the father has been confirmed; the relation of the female to the male has also been confirmed, but not necessarily the maternal relationship of the child.* If the maternal relationship has been confirmed, a citation for that relationship appears in the Index entry for the child.

23. In the few situations **on the Complete Chart** where a child was born of only a mother (parthenogenesis), the vertical line connecting with the child's name is placed directly under the name of the mother, *e.g.*,

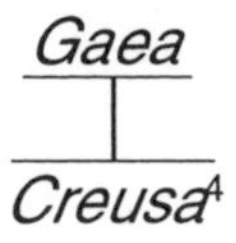

to indicate that *Creusa*[4] is the child of *Gaea* alone.

24. For relationships where some mythographers report an alternate version of the parentage of a figure, different from the parentage shown on the Master Chart and the Complete Chart, the line underneath the parents' name is connected to the line above the child's name by a double vertical line, *e.g.*,

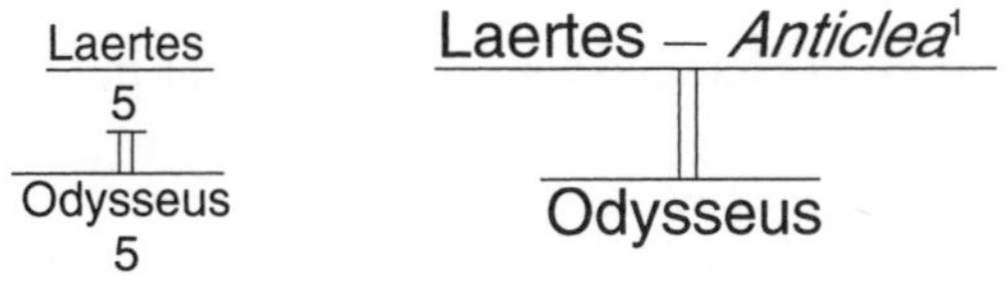

to indicate that **on the Master Chart** Laertes in shown as the father of Odysseus and **on the Complete Chart** Laertes and *Anticlea*[1] are shown as the parents of Odysseus, but that some mythographers report at least one alternate version of the parentage of Odysseus. A citation to an ancient source for each alternate parentage shown is included in the Index.

25. On the Complete Chart, an abbreviation of the author relied on as the source that confirms the paternal relationship of the figure shown on the chart appears in small type in brackets below the name of the figure, and an abbreviation for the author relied on as the source that confirms the relationship of a wife or paramour appears in small type in brackets below the name of the wife or paramour, *e.g.*,

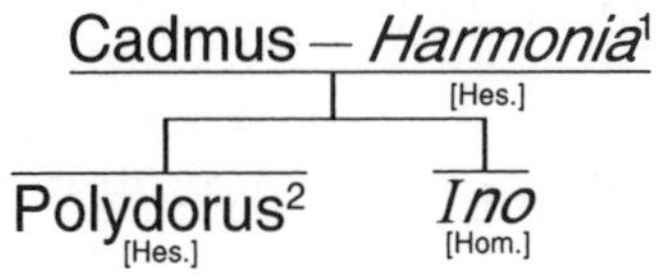

to indicate that Hesiod is the source reporting that Polydorus[2] is the son of Cadmus, Homer is the source stating that *Ino* is the daughter of Cadmus, and Hesiod is the source stating that *Harmonia* is the wife or paramour of Cadmus. The full citation (book, chapter, and verse) appears in the Index. *The source shown on the Complete Chart is only for the paternal relationship. If a source is known for the maternal relationship, that source appears in the Index.* Abbreviations of the sources are explained at the end of the Guide to the Index on page 159.

26. Many children are shown in both their paternal chain, *i.e.*, at the location where their father appears as the child of *his* parents, and in their maternal chain, *i.e.*, at the location where their mother appears as the child of *her* parents, *e.g.*,

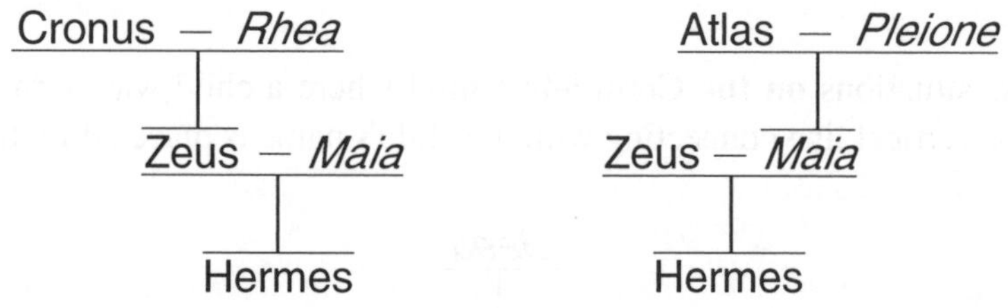

to show Hermes in both his paternal and maternal chains.

27. Because of space limitations, children are not always shown in both their paternal and maternal chains; instead, a cross-reference is sometimes used to indicate where the children of a marriage or an extra-marital relationship may be found, *e.g.*,

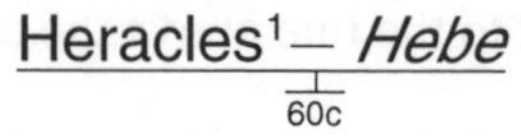

to indicate that the children of Heracles[1] and *Hebe* appear in the lower left-hand quadrant of segment 60 of the Complete Chart.

28. In some situations, a cross-reference appears below only one name to indicate where the family (wives, paramours, and children) of that figure is located, *e.g.*,

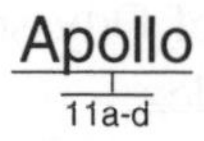

to indicate that the family of Apollo appears in all four quadrants of segment 11 of the Complete Chart.

29. Where parents have more than one child, the vertical line underneath the parents' names connects with a long horizontal line, called a "generational line," from which vertical lines connect with the lines above the names of the children, *e.g.*,

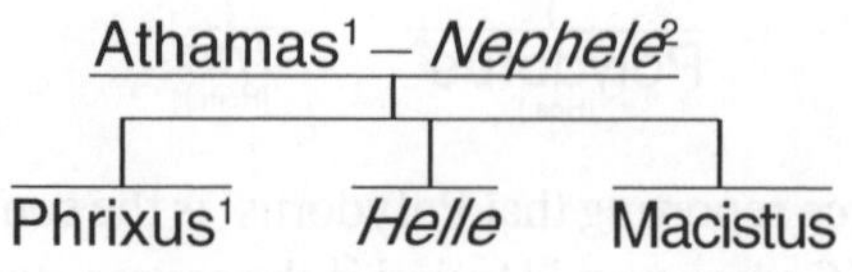

to indicate the three children of Athamas[1] and *Nephele*[2]. Even more often than with one child, the maternal relationship to all of the children shown has not necessarily been confirmed, but the paternal relationship has been confirmed. The Index entry of each child indicates whether only one or both parental relationships have been confirmed.

30. Where some children of one set of parents form an identifiable group, a short vertical line connects their generational line with a horizontal line to which the children of the group are connected, *e.g.*,

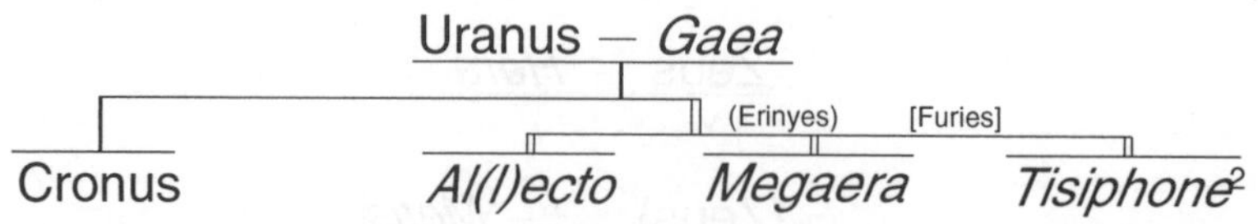

to indicate that the children of Uranus and *Gaea* include Cronus and a group consisting of *Al(l)lecto*, *Megaera*, and *Tisiphone*[2], who are the Furies and are called Erinyes.

31. In some situations, one set of parents has more children than can be placed on the generational line to which their children's names are connected. Where this occurs, the vertical line descending below the parents' names is thicker than the usual line, and two or more horizontal lines extend across that thicker vertical line, *e.g.*,

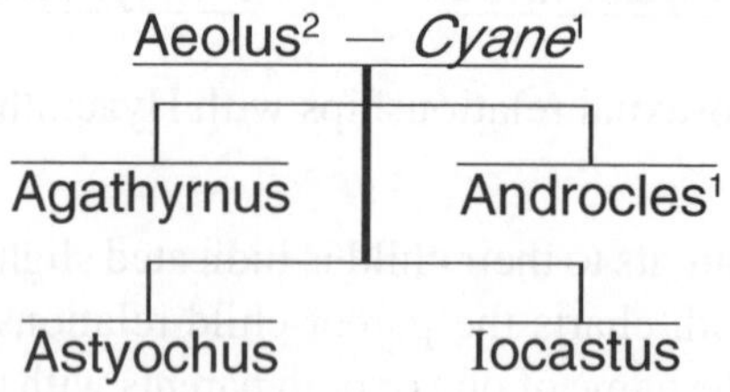

to indicate that Agathyrnus, Androcles[1], Astyochus, and Iocastus are all children of Aeolus[2] and *Cyane*[1]. The use of the thickened vertical line should alert the reader that all the children branching from this line are in the same generation, even though some names are placed below others.

32. In some situations, one set of parents has so many children that they cannot all be shown on one segment. Where this occurs, the generational line continues horizontally from one segment to another. The parents are shown above the continued generational line in angle brackets, with a double angle bracket pointing in the direction of the segment where the parents are located, usually in the paternal chain of the father, *e.g.*,

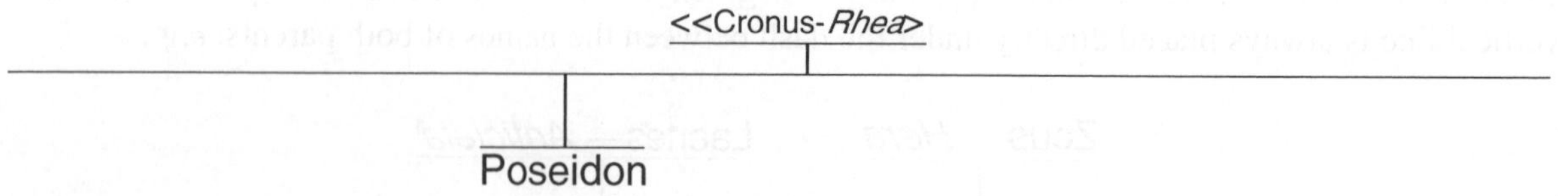

to indicate that Poseidon, a child of Cronus and *Rhea*, appears beneath a generational line that continues beyond the segment on which Cronus appears in his paternal chain. In this example, the double angle bracket indicates that the segment on which Cronus appears in his paternal chain is located one or more segments to the left of the segment on which Poseidon appears.

33. In some instances, a generational line continues across several segments on which no children of the parents in the angle brackets appear, *e.g.*,

<<Cronus-*Rhea*>

to indicate that the generational line continues to adjacent segments, to the left and right of the segment being read, on which more children of Cronus and *Rhea* are shown.

34. Children of each set of parents are usually placed in alphabetical order, but not always. Children are not placed in the order of their birth.

35. If the parents of a spouse or paramour of a figure are known, the parents (*i.e.*, the figure's in-laws) are shown on the Complete Chart in small type above the name of the spouse or paramour, *e.g.*,

Tantalus[1]-*Dione*[3]
Amphion[1]– *Niobe*[1]

to indicate that the parents of *Niobe*[1], the wife of Amphion[1], are Tantalus[1] and *Dione*[3]. This should assist the reader in identifying the spouse or paramour, especially in distinguishing the spouse or paramour from other figures with the same name, in this example, to distinguish her from *Niobe*[2], whose parents are Phoroneus and *Teledice*.

36. A question mark indicates that the name of a spouse, paramour, or child is not known, *e.g.*,

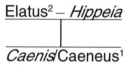

Pylas – ?
Pandion II - *Pylia*
Sciron[1] – ?

to indicate that Pylas and a wife, whose name is unknown, had a son, Sciron[1], who married a daughter, whose name is unknown, of Pandion II and *Pylia. Where one question mark is used to indicate an unnamed wife or paramour of a figure who fathered several children, e.g.,* Priam[1] *or* Lycaon[1], *the question mark does not necessarily mean that one women was the mother of all the children; it simply means that the mother of these children, or, more likely, their mothers, are unknown.*

37. Figures who at one time were male and at another time in their lives were female are shown in both roman type and italic type (and with the spellings of their male and female names, if different) at the location that indicates their birth, *e.g.*,

Elatus[2] – *Hippeia*
Caenis/Caeneus[1]

to indicate that the child of Elatus[2] and *Hippeia* was at one time a female called *Caenis* and at a later time a male called Caeneus[1]. Where such figures have a relationship with a spouse or paramour on a segment other than the segment that indicates their birth, only the type and spelling for the appropriate gender is shown. The figure Agdistis began life with both genders but became entirely female and was thereafter known primarily as *Cybele*. This figure is shown at the location that indicates its birth as Agdistis/*Cybele*[2]. In relationships with paramours, the appropriate name, Agdistis or *Cybele*[2], is shown, including the "relationship" of Agdistis with *Nana* on the occasion when *Nana* became pregnant from the almond that fell from the tree that grew from the seed of Agdistis.

The Master Chart

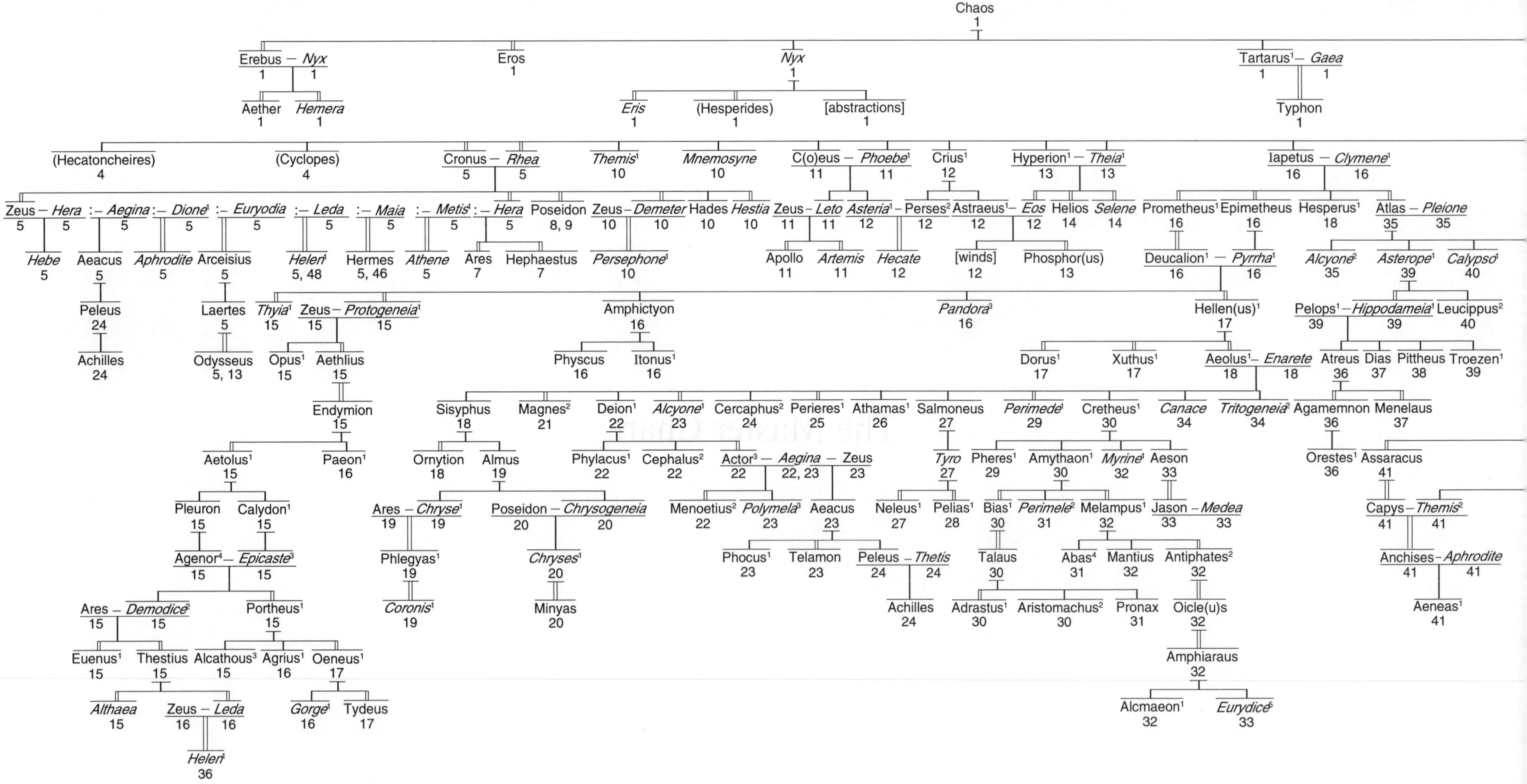

A guide to this Master Chart
is located at pages 5-9

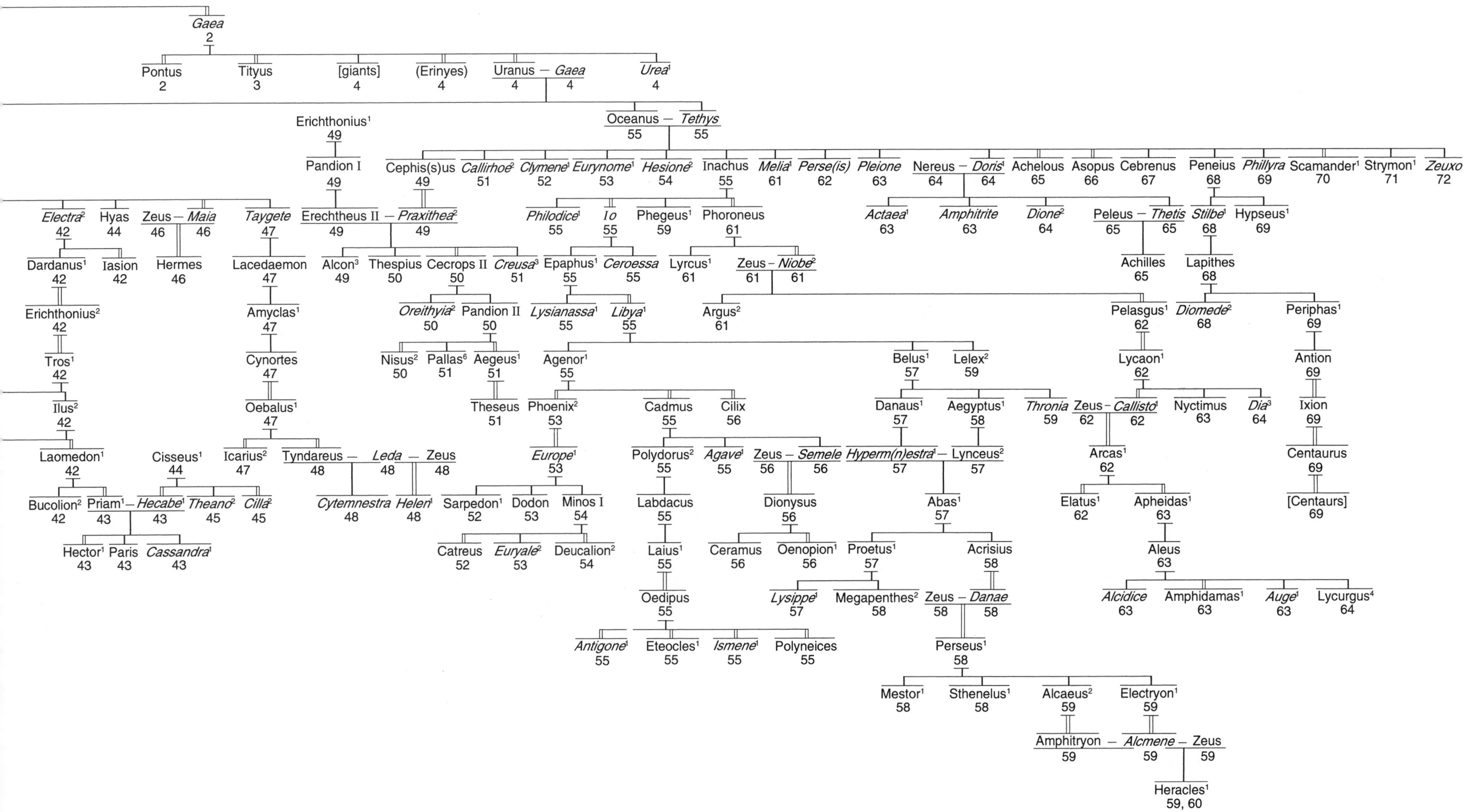
Gaea 2
Pontus 2
Tityus 3
[giants] 4
(Erinyes) 4
Uranus – Gaea 4 4
Urea[1] 4
Erichthonius[1] 49
Oceanus – Tethys 55 55
Pandion I 49
Cephis(s)us 49
Callirhoe[2] 51
Clymene[1] 52
Eurynome[1] 53
Hesione[2] 54
Inachus 55
Melia[1] 61
Perse(is) 62
Pleione 63
Nereus – Doris[1] 64 64
Achelous 65
Asopus 66
Cebrenus 67
Peneius 68
Phillyra 69
Scamander[1] 70
Strymon[1] 71
Zeuxo 72
Electra[2] 42
Hyas 44
Zeus – Maia 46 46
Taygete 47
Erechtheus II – Praxithea[2] 49 49
Philodice[1] 55
Io 55
Phegeus[1] 59
Phoroneus 61
Actaea[1] 63
Amphitrite 63
Dione[2] 64
Peleus – Thetis 65 65
Stilbe[1] 68
Hypseus[1] 69
Dardanus[1] 42
Iasion 42
Hermes 46
Lacedaemon 47
Alcon[3] 49
Thespius 50
Cecrops II 50
Creusa[3] 51
Epaphus[1] 55
Ceroessa 55
Lyrcus[1] 61
Zeus – Niobe[2] 61 61
Achilles 65
Lapithes 68
Erichthonius[2] 42
Amyclas[1] 47
Oreithyia[2] 50
Pandion II 50
Lysianassa[1] 55
Libya[1] 55
Argus[2] 61
Pelasgus[1] 62
Diomede[2] 68
Periphas[1] 69
Tros[1] 42
Cynortes 47
Nisus[2] 50
Pallas[6] 51
Aegeus[1] 51
Agenor[1] 55
Belus[1] 57
Lelex[2] 59
Lycaon[1] 62
Antion 69
Ilus[2] 42
Oebalus[1] 47
Theseus 51
Phoenix[2] 53
Cadmus 55
Cilix 56
Danaus[1] 57
Aegyptus[1] 58
Thronia 59
Zeus – Callisto[1] 62 62
Nyctimus 63
Dia[3] 64
Ixion 69
Laomedon[1] 42
Cisseus[1] 44
Icarius[2] 47
Tyndareus – Leda – Zeus 48 48 48
Europe[1] 53
Polydorus[2] 55
Agave[1] 55
Zeus – Semele 56 56
Hyperm(n)estra[1] – Lynceus[2] 57 57
Arcas[1] 62
Centaurus 69
Bucolion[2] 42
Priam[1] – Hecabe[1] 43 43
Theano[2] 45
Cilla[2] 45
Cytemnestra 48
Helen[1] 48
Sarpedon[1] 52
Dodon 53
Minos I 54
Labdacus 55
Dionysus 56
Abas[1] 57
Elatus[1] 62
Apheidas[1] 63
[Centaurs] 69
Hector[1] 43
Paris 43
Cassandra[1] 43
Catreus 52
Euryale[2] 53
Deucalion[2] 54
Laius[1] 55
Ceramus 56
Oenopion[1] 56
Proetus[1] 57
Acrisius 58
Aleus 63
Oedipus 55
Lysippe[1] 57
Megapenthes[2] 58
Zeus – Danae 58 58
Alcidice 63
Amphidamas[1] 63
Auge[1] 63
Lycurgus[4] 64
Antigone[1] 55
Eteocles[1] 55
Ismene[1] 55
Polyneices 55
Perseus[1] 58
Mestor[1] 58
Sthenelus[1] 58
Alcaeus[2] 59
Electryon[1] 59
Amphitryon – Alcmene – Zeus 59 59 59
Heracles[1] 59, 60

The Complete Chart

Segments 1 - 72

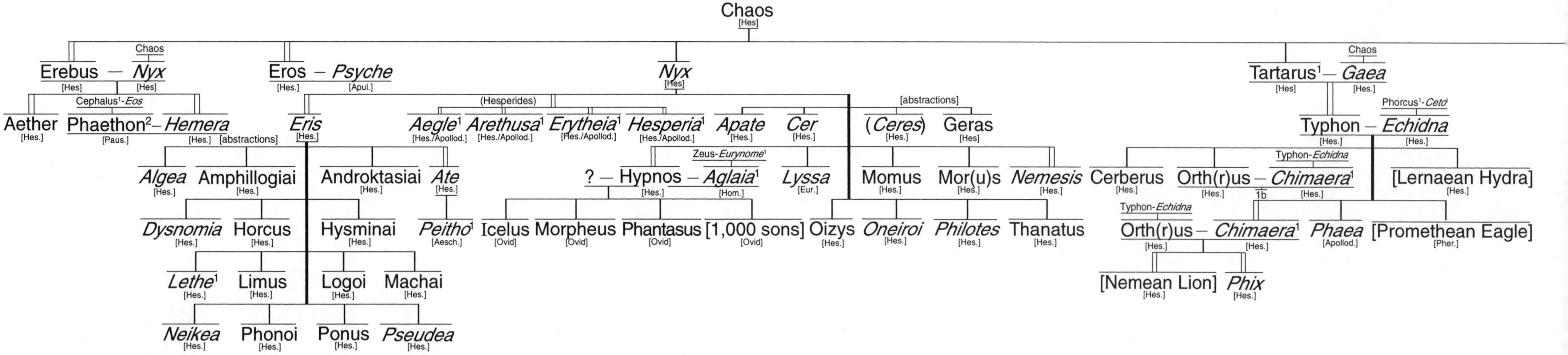

Chaos
[Hes]
Chaos
Erebus – Nyx
[Hes] [Hes]
Eros – Psyche
[Hes.] [Apul.]
Nyx
[Hes]
Chaos
Tartarus1 – Gaea
[Hes] [Hes.]
Cephalus1-Eos
Aether
[Hes.]
Phaethon2 – Hemera
[Paus.] [Hes.]
[abstractions]
Eris
[Hes.]
(Hesperides)
Aegle1
[Hes./Apollod.]
Arethusa1
[Hes./Apollod.]
Erytheia1
[Hes./Apollod.]
Hesperia1
[Hes./Apollod.]
Apate
[Hes.]
Cer
[Hes.]
[abstractions]
(Ceres)
[Hes.]
Geras
[Hes]
Phorcus1-Ceto1
Typhon – Echidna
[Hes.] [Hes.]
Algea
[Hes.]
Amphillogiai
[Hes.]
Androktasiai
[Hes.]
Ate
[Hes.]
Zeus-Eurynome1
? – Hypnos – Aglaia1
[Hes.] [Hom.]
Lyssa
[Eur.]
Momus
[Hes.]
Mor(u)s
[Hes.]
Nemesis
[Hes.]
Cerberus
[Hes.]
Typhon-Echidna
Orth(r)us – Chimaera1
[Hes.] [Hes.]
1b
[Lernaean Hydra]
[Hes.]
Dysnomia
[Hes.]
Horcus
[Hes.]
Hysminai
[Hes.]
Peitho1
[Aesch.]
Icelus
[Ovid]
Morpheus
[Ovid]
Phantasus
[Ovid]
[1,000 sons]
[Ovid]
Oizys
[Hes.]
Oneiroi
[Hes.]
Philotes
[Hes.]
Thanatus
[Hes.]
Typhon-Echidna
Orth(r)us – Chimaera1
[Hes.] [Hes.]
Phaea
[Apollod.]
[Promethean Eagle]
[Pher.]
Lethe1
[Hes.]
Limus
[Hes.]
Logoi
[Hes.]
Machai
[Hes.]
[Nemean Lion]
[Hes.]
Phix
[Hes.]
Neikea
[Hes.]
Phonoi
[Hes.]
Ponus
[Hes.]
Pseudea
[Hes.]

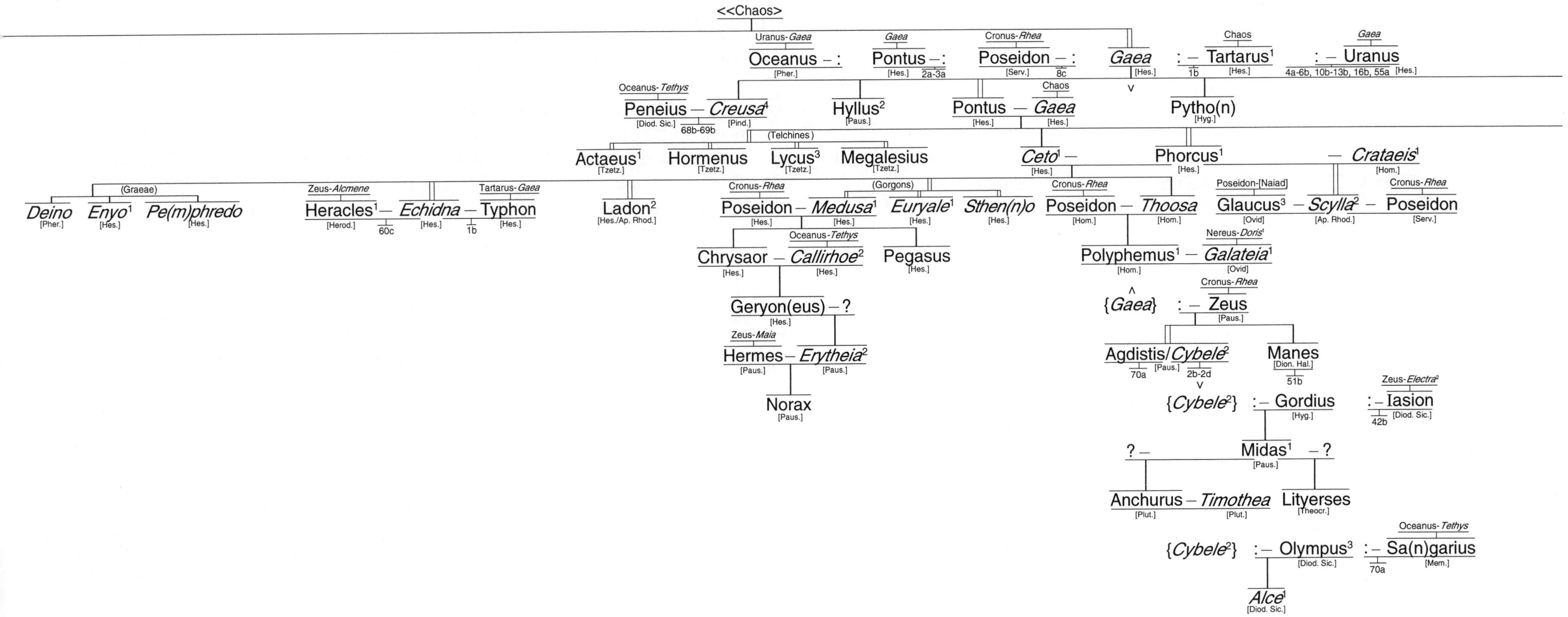

<<Chaos>
Uranus-Gaea
Oceanus – :
[Pher.]
Gaea
Pontus – :
[Hes.]
2a-3a
Cronus-Rhea
Poseidon – :
[Serv.]
8c
Gaea
[Hes.]
Chaos
: – Tartarus¹
1b
[Hes.]
Gaea
: – Uranus
4a-6b, 10b-13b, 16b, 55a [Hes.]
Oceanus-Tethys
Peneius – Creusa⁴
[Diod. Sic.]
68b-69b
[Pind.]
Hyllus²
[Paus.]
Chaos
Pontus – Gaea
[Hes.]
[Hes.]
Pytho(n)
[Hyg.]
(Telchines)
Actaeus¹
[Tzetz.]
Hormenus
[Tzetz.]
Lycus³
[Tzetz.]
Megalesius
[Tzetz.]
Ceto¹ –
[Hes.]
Phorcus¹
[Hes.]
– Crataeis¹
[Hom.]
(Graeae)
Deino
[Pher.]
Enyo¹
[Hes.]
Pe(m)phredo
[Hes.]
Zeus-Alcmene
Heracles¹ – Echidna – Typhon
[Herod.]
60c
[Hes.]
1b
Tartarus-Gaea
[Hes.]
Ladon²
[Hes./Ap. Rhod.]
Cronus-Rhea
Poseidon – Medusa¹
[Hes.]
[Hes.]
(Gorgons)
Euryale¹
[Hes.]
Sthen(n)o
[Hes.]
Cronus-Rhea
Poseidon – Thoosa
[Hom.]
[Hom.]
Poseidon-[Naiad]
Glaucus³ – Scylla² – Poseidon
[Ovid]
[Ap. Rhod.]
Cronus-Rhea
[Serv.]
Oceanus-Tethys
Chrysaor – Callirhoe²
[Hes.]
[Hes.]
Pegasus
[Hes.]
Nereus-Doris¹
Polyphemus¹ – Galateia¹
[Hom.]
[Ovid]
Geryon(eus) – ?
[Hes.]
Cronus-Rhea
{Gaea} : – Zeus
[Paus.]
Zeus-Maia
Hermes – Erytheia²
[Paus.]
[Paus.]
Agdistis/Cybele²
70a
[Paus.]
2b-2d
Manes
[Dion. Hal.]
51b
Norax
[Paus.]
{Cybele²} : – Gordius
[Hyg.]
Zeus-Electra²
: – Iasion
42b
[Diod. Sic.]
? –
Midas¹ – ?
[Paus.]
Anchurus – Timothea
[Plut.]
[Plut.]
Lityerses
[Theocr.]
Oceanus-Tethys
{Cybele²} : – Olympus³ : – Sa(n)garius
[Diod. Sic.]
70a
[Mem.]
Alce¹
[Diod. Sic.]

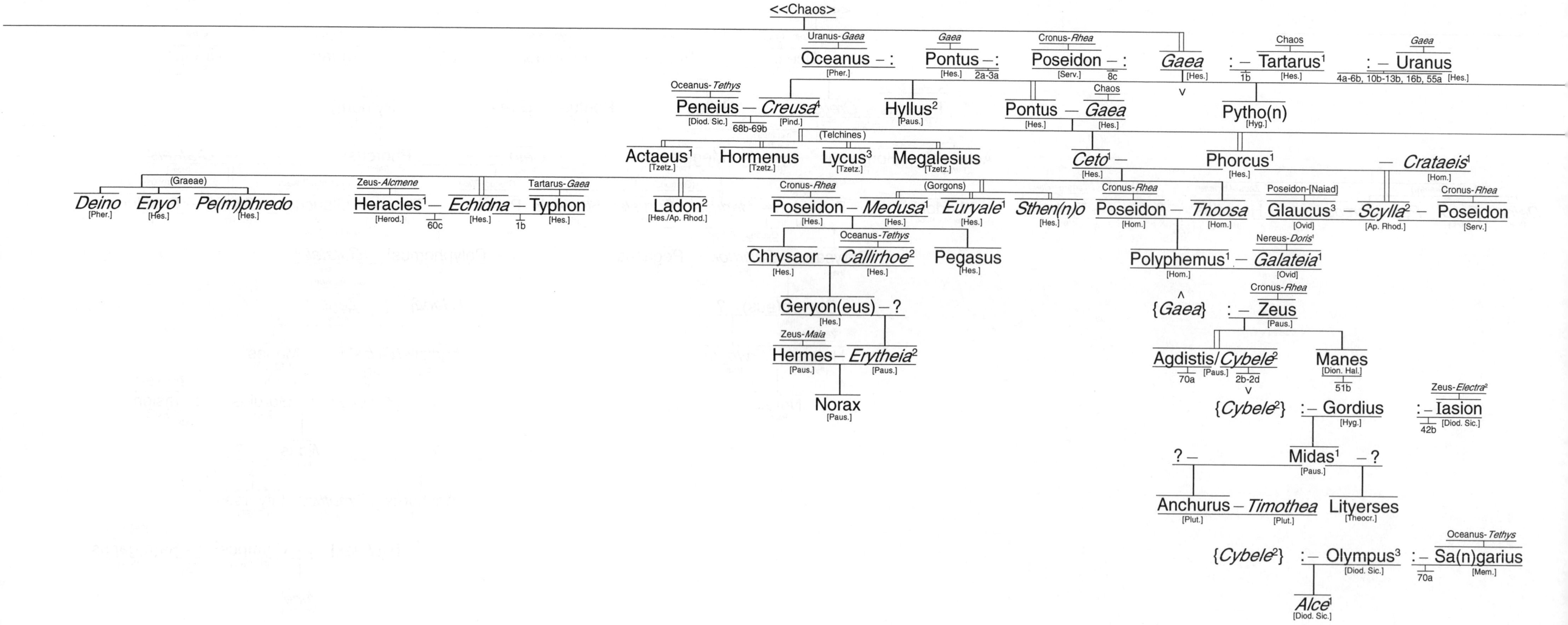
<<Chaos>
Uranus-Gaea
Oceanus – :
[Pher.]
Gaea
Pontus – :
[Hes.] 2a-3a
Cronus-Rhea
Poseidon – :
[Serv.] 8c
Gaea
[Hes.]
v
: – Tartarus[1]
Chaos
1b [Hes.]
Gaea
: – Uranus
4a-6b, 10b-13b, 16b, 55a [Hes.]
Oceanus-Tethys
Peneius – Creusa[1]
[Diod. Sic.] 68b-69b [Pind.]
Hyllus[2]
[Paus.]
Pontus – Gaea
Chaos
[Hes.] [Hes.]
Pytho(n)
[Hyg.]
(Telchines)
Actaeus[1]
[Tzetz.]
Hormenus
[Tzetz.]
Lycus[3]
[Tzetz.]
Megalesius
[Tzetz.]
Ceto[1] –
[Hes.]
Phorcus[1]
[Hes.]
– Crataeis[1]
[Hom.]
(Graeae)
Deino
[Pher.]
Enyo[1]
[Hes.]
Pe(m)phredo
[Hes.]
Zeus-Alcmene
Heracles[1] – Echidna – Typhon
Tartarus-Gaea
[Herod.] 60c [Hes.] 1b [Hes.]
Ladon[2]
[Hes./Ap. Rhod.]
Cronus-Rhea
Poseidon – Medusa[1]
[Hes.] [Hes.]
(Gorgons)
Euryale[1]
[Hes.]
Sthen(n)o
[Hes.]
Cronus-Rhea
Poseidon – Thoosa
[Hom.] [Hom.]
Poseidon-[Naiad]
Glaucus[3] – Scylla[2] – Poseidon
[Ovid] [Ap. Rhod.] [Serv.]
Cronus-Rhea
Oceanus-Tethys
Chrysaor – Callirhoe[2]
[Hes.] [Hes.]
Pegasus
[Hes.]
Nereus-Doris[1]
Polyphemus[1] – Galateia[1]
[Hom.] [Ovid]
Geryon(eus) – ?
[Hes.]
^
{Gaea} : – Zeus
Cronus-Rhea
[Paus.]
Zeus-Maia
Hermes – Erytheia[2]
[Paus.] [Paus.]
Agdistis/Cybele[2]
70a [Paus.] 2b-2d
v
Manes
[Dion. Hal.]
51b
Norax
[Paus.]
{Cybele[2]} : – Gordius
[Hyg.]
Zeus-Electra[2]
: – Iasion
42b [Diod. Sic.]
? –
Midas[1] – ?
[Paus.]
Anchurus – Timothea
[Plut.] [Plut.]
Lityerses
[Theocr.]
Oceanus-Tethys
{Cybele[2]} : – Olympus[3] : – Sa(n)garius
[Diod. Sic.] 70a [Mem.]
Alce[1]
[Diod. Sic.]

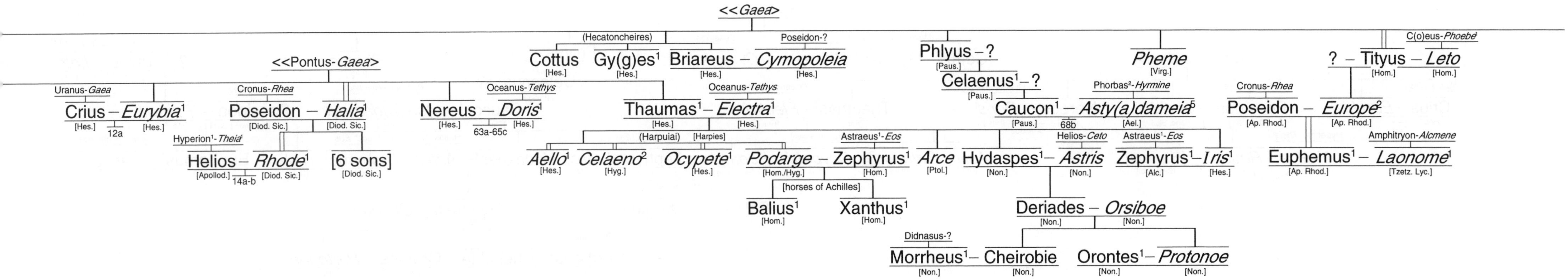

<<Gaea>
(Hecatoncheires)
Cottus [Hes.]
Gy(g)es¹ [Hes.]
Poseidon-?
Briareus [Hes.] – Cymopoleia [Hes.]
Phlyus – ? [Paus.]
Celaenus¹ – ? [Paus.]
Phorbas²-Hyrmine
Caucon¹ [Paus.] – Asty(a)dameia⁵ [Ael.]
68b
Pheme [Virg.]
C(o)eus-Phoebe¹
? – Tityus [Hom.] – Leto [Hom.]
Cronus-Rhea
Poseidon [Ap. Rhod.] – Europe² [Ap. Rhod.]
Amphitryon-Alcmene
Euphemus¹ [Ap. Rhod.] – Laonome¹ [Tzetz. Lyc.]
<<Pontus-Gaea>
Uranus-Gaea
Crius [Hes.] – Eurybia¹ [Hes.]
12a
Cronus-Rhea
Poseidon [Diod. Sic.] – Halia¹ [Diod. Sic.]
Hyperion¹-Theia¹
Helios [Apollod.] – Rhode¹ [Diod. Sic.]
14a-b
[6 sons] [Diod. Sic.]
Oceanus-Tethys
Nereus [Hes.] – Doris¹ [Hes.]
63a-65c
Oceanus-Tethys
Thaumas¹ [Hes.] – Electra¹ [Hes.]
(Harpuiai) [Harpies]
Aello¹ [Hes.]
Celaeno² [Hyg.]
Ocypete¹ [Hes.]
Astraeus¹-Eos
Podarge [Hom./Hyg.] – Zephyrus¹ [Hom.]
[horses of Achilles]
Balius¹ [Hom.]
Xanthus¹ [Hom.]
Arce [Ptol.]
Helios-Ceto
Hydaspes¹ [Non.] – Astris [Non.]
Astraeus¹-Eos
Zephyrus¹ [Alc.] – Iris¹ [Hes.]
Deriades [Non.] – Orsiboe [Non.]
Didnasus-?
Morrheus¹ [Non.] – Cheirobie [Non.]
Orontes¹ [Non.] – Protonoe [Non.]

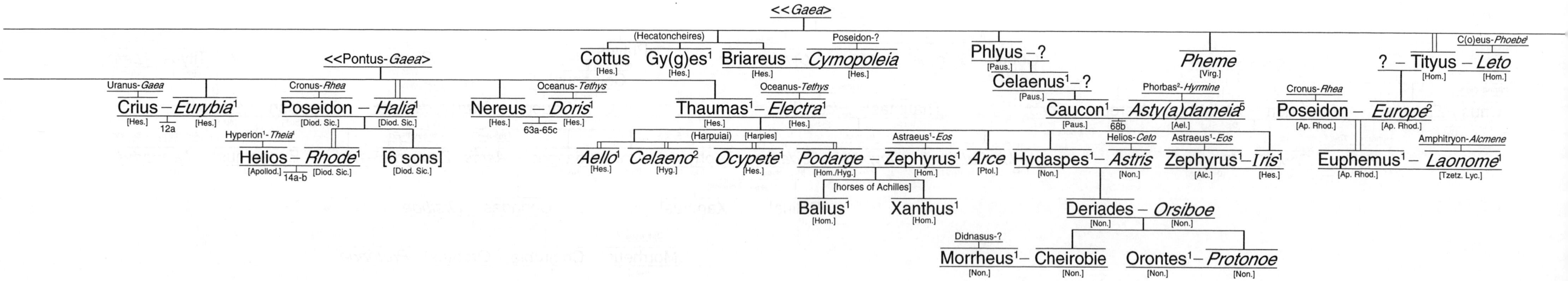

<<*Gaea*>
(Hecatoncheires)
Cottus
[Hes.]
Gy(g)es[1]
[Hes.]
Briareus – *Cymopoleia*
[Hes.] [Hes.]
Poseidon-?
Phlyus – ?
[Paus.]
Celaenus[1] – ?
[Paus.]
Pheme
[Virg.]
C(o)eus-*Phoebe*[1]
? – Tityus – *Leto*
[Hom.] [Hom.]
<<Pontus-*Gaea*>
Uranus-*Gaea*
Crius – *Eurybia*[1]
[Hes.] 12a [Hes.]
Cronus-*Rhea*
Poseidon – *Halia*[1]
[Diod. Sic.] [Diod. Sic.]
Hyperion[1]-*Theia*[1]
Helios – *Rhode*[1]
[Apollod.] 14a-b [Diod. Sic.]
[6 sons]
[Diod. Sic.]
Nereus – *Doris*[1]
[Hes.] 63a-65c [Hes.]
Oceanus-*Tethys*
Thaumas[1] – *Electra*[1]
[Hes.] [Hes.]
Oceanus-*Tethys*
(Harpuiai) [Harpies]
Aello[1]
[Hes.]
Celaeno[2]
[Hyg.]
Ocypete[1]
[Hes.]
Podarge – Zephyrus[1]
[Hom./Hyg.] [Hom.]
Astraeus[1]-*Eos*
[horses of Achilles]
Balius[1]
[Hom.]
Xanthus[1]
[Hom.]
Arce
[Ptol.]
Hydaspes[1] – *Astris*
[Non.] [Non.]
Helios-*Ceto*
Zephyrus[1] – *Iris*[1]
[Alc.] [Hes.]
Astraeus[1]-*Eos*
Phorbas[2]-*Hyrmine*
Caucon[1] – *Asty(a)dameia*[5]
[Paus.] 68b [Ael.]
Deriades – *Orsiboe*
[Non.] [Non.]
Didnasus-?
Morrheus[1] – Cheirobie
[Non.] [Non.]
Orontes[1] – *Protonoe*
[Non.] [Non.]
Cronus-*Rhea*
Poseidon – *Europe*[2]
[Ap. Rhod.] [Ap. Rhod.]
Amphitryon-*Alcmene*
Euphemus[1] – *Laonome*[1]
[Ap. Rhod.] [Tzetz. Lyc.]

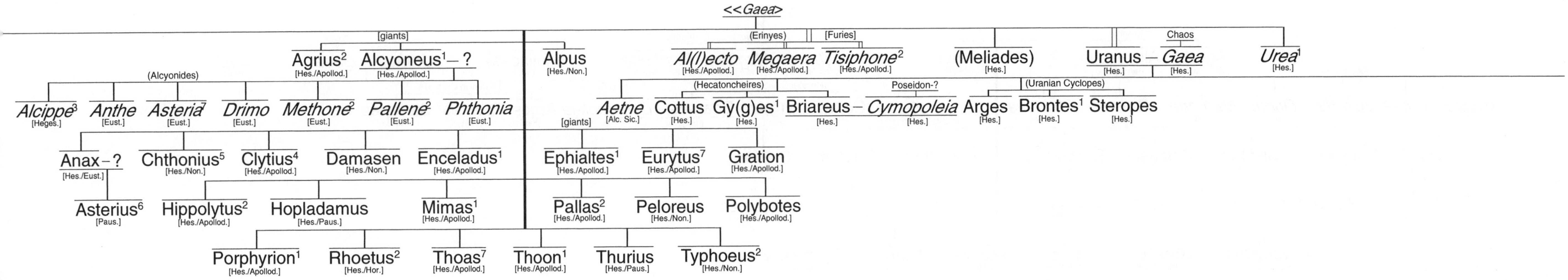

<<Gaea>
[giants]
Agrius[2] [Hes./Apollod.]
Alcyoneus[1] – ? [Hes./Apollod.]
(Alcyonides)
Alcippe[3] [Heges.]
Anthe [Eust.]
Asteria[7] [Eust.]
Drimo [Eust.]
Methone[2] [Eust.]
Pallene[2] [Eust.]
Phthonia [Eust.]
Anax – ? [Hes./Eust.]
Chthonius[5] [Hes./Non.]
Clytius[4] [Hes./Apollod.]
Damasen [Hes./Non.]
Enceladus[1] [Hes./Apollod.]
Asterius[6] [Paus.]
Hippolytus[2] [Hes./Apollod.]
Hopladamus [Hes./Paus.]
Mimas[1] [Hes./Apollod.]
Porphyrion[1] [Hes./Apollod.]
Rhoetus[2] [Hes./Hor.]
Thoas[7] [Hes./Apollod.]
Thoon[1] [Hes./Apollod.]
Thurius [Hes./Paus.]
Typhoeus[2] [Hes./Non.]
Alpus [Hes./Non.]
[giants]
Ephialtes[1] [Hes./Apollod.]
Eurytus[7] [Hes./Apollod.]
Gration [Hes./Apollod.]
Pallas[2] [Hes./Apollod.]
Peloreus [Hes./Non.]
Polybotes [Hes./Apollod.]
(Erinyes) [Furies]
Al(l)ecto [Hes./Apollod.]
Megaera [Hes./Apollod.]
Tisiphone[2] [Hes./Apollod.]
(Meliades) [Hes.]
Chaos
Uranus [Hes.] – Gaea [Hes.]
Urea[1] [Hes.]
Aetne [Alc. Sic.]
(Hecatoncheires)
Cottus [Hes.]
Gy(g)es[1] [Hes.]
Briareus [Hes.] – Cymopoleia [Hes.]
Poseidon-?
(Uranian Cyclopes)
Arges [Hes.]
Brontes[1] [Hes.]
Steropes [Hes.]

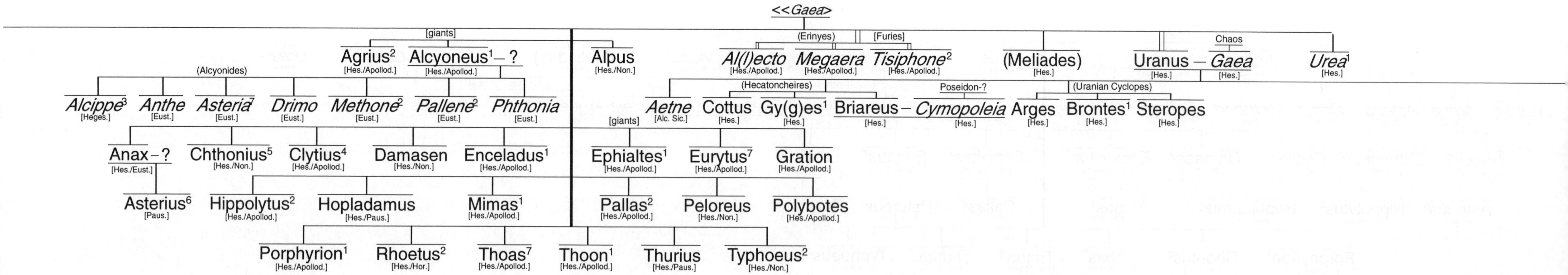
<<Gaea>
[giants]
Agrius[2] [Hes./Apollod.]
Alcyoneus[1] – ? [Hes./Apollod.]
Alpus [Hes./Non.]
(Erinyes)
[Furies]
Al(l)ecto [Hes./Apollod.]
Megaera [Hes./Apollod.]
Tisiphone[2] [Hes./Apollod.]
(Meliades) [Hes.]
Chaos
Uranus [Hes.] – Gaea [Hes.]
Urea[1] [Hes.]
(Alcyonides)
Alcippe[3] [Heges.]
Anthe [Eust.]
Asteria[7] [Eust.]
Drimo [Eust.]
Methone[2] [Eust.]
Pallene[2] [Eust.]
Phthonia [Eust.]
[giants]
Aetne [Alc. Sic.]
(Hecatoncheires)
Cottus [Hes.]
Gy(g)es[1] [Hes.]
Briareus [Hes.] – Cymopoleia [Hes.]
Poseidon-?
(Uranian Cyclopes)
Arges [Hes.]
Brontes[1] [Hes.]
Steropes [Hes.]
Anax – ? [Hes./Eust.]
Chthonius[5] [Hes./Non.]
Clytius[4] [Hes./Apollod.]
Damasen [Hes./Non.]
Enceladus[1] [Hes./Apollod.]
Ephialtes[1] [Hes./Apollod.]
Eurytus[7] [Hes./Apollod.]
Gration [Hes./Apollod.]
Asterius[6] [Paus.]
Hippolytus[2] [Hes./Apollod.]
Hopladamus [Hes./Paus.]
Mimas[1] [Hes./Apollod.]
Pallas[2] [Hes./Apollod.]
Peloreus [Hes./Non.]
Polybotes [Hes./Apollod.]
Porphyrion[1] [Hes./Apollod.]
Rhoetus[2] [Hes./Hor.]
Thoas[7] [Hes./Apollod.]
Thoon[1] [Hes./Apollod.]
Thurius [Hes./Paus.]
Typhoeus[2] [Hes./Non.]

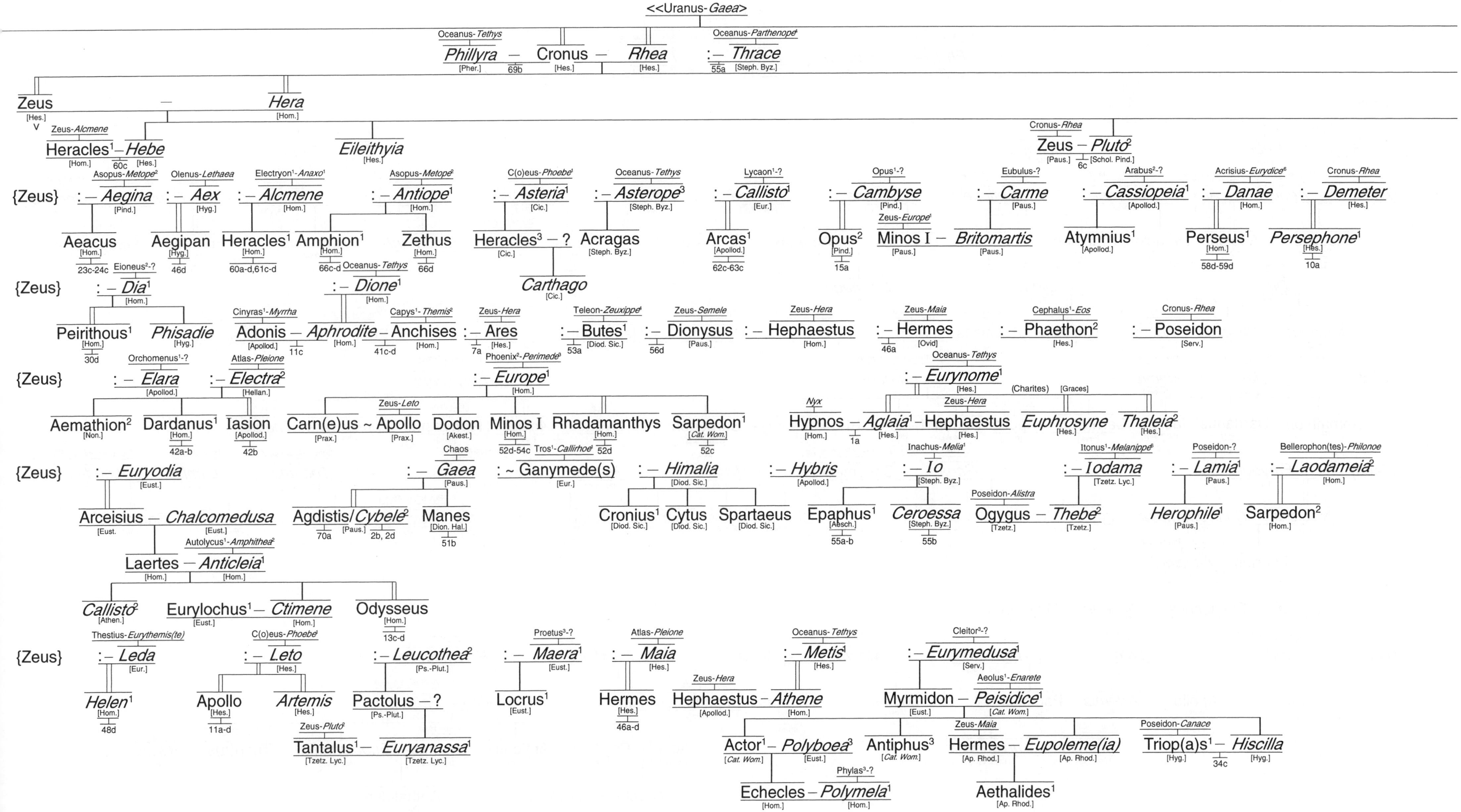

<<Uranus-Gaea>
Oceanus-Tethys
Phillyra [Pher.] — 69b — Cronus [Hes.] — Rhea [Hes.]
Oceanus-Parthenope[4]
:— Thrace [Steph. Byz.] 55a
Zeus [Hes.] — Hera [Hom.]
V
Zeus-Alcmene
Heracles[1] — Hebe [Hom.] 60c [Hes.]
Eileithyia [Hes.]
Cronus-Rhea
Zeus — Pluto[2] [Paus.] 6c [Schol. Pind.]
{Zeus}
Asopus-Metope[2] :— Aegina [Pind.]
Olenus-Lethaea :— Aex [Hyg.]
Electryon[1]-Anaxo[1] :— Alcmene [Hom.]
Asopus-Metope[2] :— Antiope[1] [Hom.]
C(o)eus-Phoebe[1] :— Asteria[1] [Cic.]
Oceanus-Tethys :— Asterope[3] [Steph. Byz.]
Lycaon[1]-? :— Callisto[1] [Eur.]
Opus[1]-? :— Cambyse [Pind.]
Eubulus-? :— Carme [Paus.]
Arabus[2]-? :— Cassiopeia[1] [Apollod.]
Acrisius-Eurydice[6] :— Danae [Hom.]
Cronus-Rhea :— Demeter [Hes.]
Aeacus [Hom.] 23c-24c
Aegipan [Hyg.] 46d
Heracles[1] [Hom.] 60a-d,61c-d
Amphion[1] [Hom.] 66c-d
Zethus [Hom.] 66d
Heracles[3] [Cic.] — ?
Carthago [Cic.]
Acragas [Steph. Byz.]
Arcas[1] [Apollod.] 62c-63c
Opus[2] [Pind.] 15a
Zeus-Europe[1]
Minos I [Paus.] — Britomartis [Paus.]
Atymnius[1] [Apollod.]
Perseus[1] [Hom.] 58d-59d
Persephone[1] [Hes.] 10a
{Zeus}
Eioneus[2]-? :— Dia[1] [Hom.]
Oceanus-Tethys :— Dione[1] [Hom.]
Peirithous[1] [Hom.] 30d
Phisadie [Hyg.]
Cinyras[1]-Myrrha
Adonis [Apollod.] — Aphrodite [Hom.] 11c
Capys[1]-Themis[2]
Anchises [Hom.] 41c-d
Zeus-Hera :— Ares [Hes.] 7a
Teleon-Zeuxippe[1] :— Butes[1] [Diod. Sic.] 53a
Zeus-Semele :— Dionysus [Paus.] 56d
Zeus-Hera :— Hephaestus [Hom.]
Zeus-Maia :— Hermes [Ovid] 46a
Cephalus[1]-Eos :— Phaethon[2] [Hes.]
Cronus-Rhea :— Poseidon [Serv.]
{Zeus}
Orchomenus[1]-? :— Elara [Apollod.]
Atlas-Pleione :— Electra[2] [Hellan.]
Phoenix[2]-Perimede[3] :— Europe[1] [Hom.]
Oceanus-Tethys :— Eurynome[1] [Hes.]
(Charites) [Graces]
Aemathion[2] [Non.]
Dardanus[1] [Hom.] 42a-b
Iasion [Apollod.] 42b
Zeus-Leto
Carn(e)us [Prax.] ~ Apollo [Prax.]
Dodon [Akest.]
Minos I [Hom.] 52d-54c
Rhadamanthys [Hom.] 52d
Sarpedon[1] [Cat. Wom.] 52c
Nyx
Hypnos [Hom.] — Aglaia[1] [Hes.] 1a
Zeus-Hera
Hephaestus [Hes.]
Euphrosyne [Hes.]
Thaleia[2] [Hes.]
{Zeus}
:— Euryodia [Eust.]
Chaos :— Gaea [Paus.]
Tros[1]-Callirhoe[1] :~ Ganymede(s) [Eur.]
:— Himalia [Diod. Sic.]
:— Hybris [Apollod.]
Inachus-Melia[1] :— Io [Steph. Byz.]
Itonus[1]-Melanippe[5] :— Iodama [Tzetz. Lyc.]
Poseidon-? :— Lamia[1] [Paus.]
Bellerophon(tes)-Philonoe :— Laodameia[2] [Hom.]
Arceisius [Eust.] — Chalcomedusa [Eust.]
Agdistis/Cybele[2] [Paus.] 70a 2b, 2d
Manes [Dion. Hal.] 51b
Cronius[1] [Diod. Sic.]
Cytus [Diod. Sic.]
Spartaeus [Diod. Sic.]
Epaphus[1] [Aesch.] 55a-b
Ceroessa [Steph. Byz.] 55b
Poseidon-Alistra
Ogygus [Tzetz.] — Thebe[2] [Tzetz.]
Herophile[1] [Paus.]
Sarpedon[2] [Hom.]
Autolycus[1]-Amphithea[2]
Laertes [Hom.] — Anticleia[1] [Hom.]
Callisto[2] [Athen.]
Eurylochus[1] [Eust.] — Ctimene [Hom.]
Odysseus [Hom.] 13c-d
{Zeus}
Thestius-Eurythemis(te) :— Leda [Eur.]
C(o)eus-Phoebe[1] :— Leto [Hes.]
:— Leucothea[2] [Ps.-Plut.]
Proetus[3]-? :— Maera[1] [Eust.]
Atlas-Pleione :— Maia [Hes.]
Oceanus-Tethys :— Metis[1] [Hes.]
Cleitor[3]-? :— Eurymedusa[1] [Serv.]
Helen[1] [Hom.] 48d
Apollo [Hes.] 11a-d
Artemis [Hes.]
Pactolus [Ps.-Plut.] — ?
Zeus-Pluto[2]
Tantalus[1] [Tzetz. Lyc.] — Euryanassa[1] [Tzetz. Lyc.]
Locrus[1] [Eust.]
Hermes [Hes.] 46a-d
Zeus-Hera
Hephaestus [Apollod.] — Athene [Hom.]
Aeolus[1]-Enarete
Myrmidon [Eust.] — Peisidice[1] [Cat. Wom.]
Actor[1] [Cat. Wom.] — Polyboea[3] [Eust.]
Antiphus[3] [Cat. Wom.]
Zeus-Maia
Hermes [Ap. Rhod.] — Eupoleme(ia) [Ap. Rhod.]
Poseidon-Canace
Triop(a)s[1] [Hyg.] — Hiscilla [Hyg.] 34c
Phylas[3]-?
Echecles [Hom.] — Polymela[1] [Hom.]
Aethalides[1] [Ap. Rhod.]

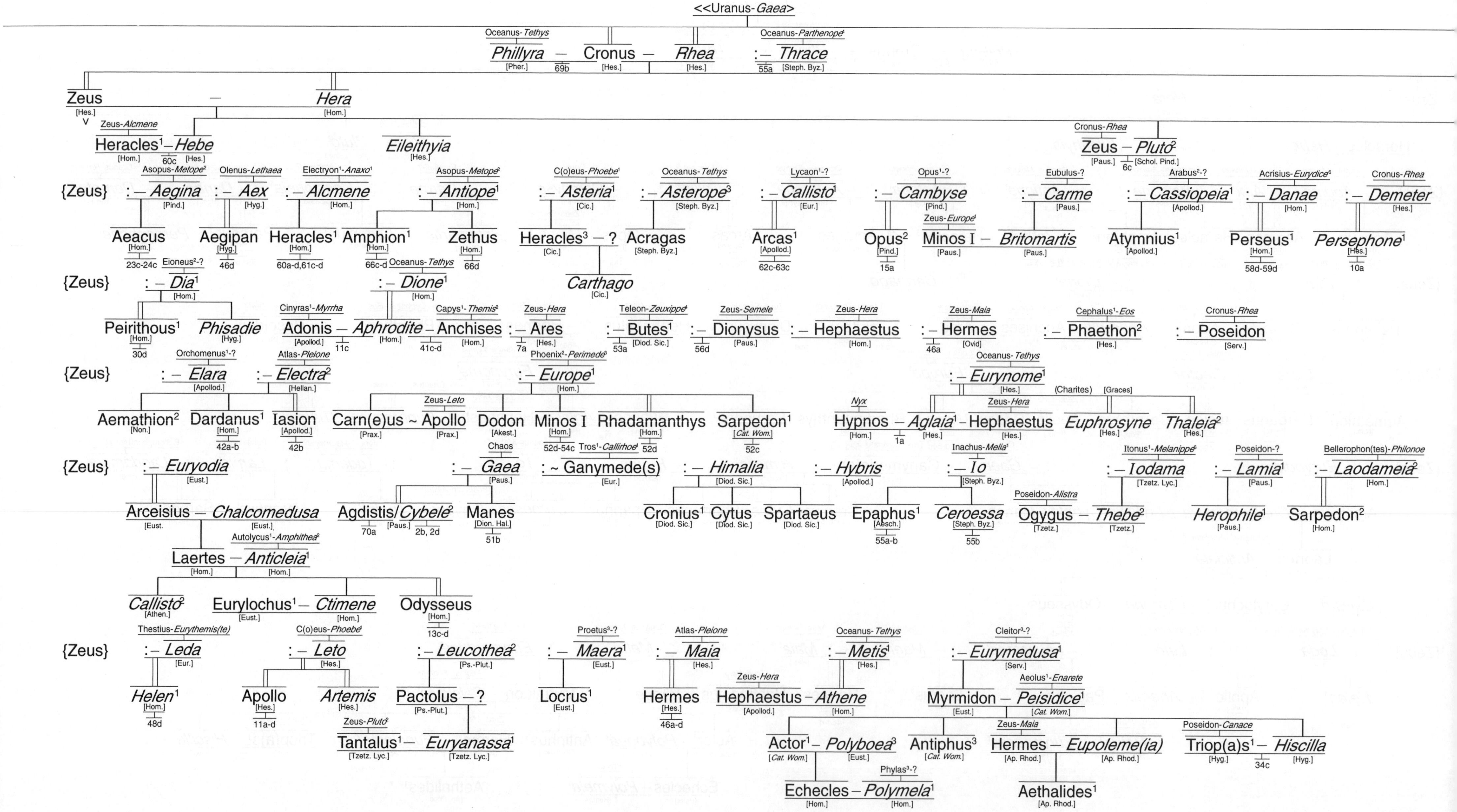

<<Uranus-Gaea>
Oceanus-Tethys
Phillyra – Cronus – Rhea
[Pher.] 69b [Hes.] [Hes.]
Oceanus-Parthenope[4]
:– Thrace
55a [Steph. Byz.]
Zeus – Hera
[Hes.] [Hom.]
V
Zeus-Alcmene
Heracles[1] – Hebe
[Hom.] 60c [Hes.]
Eileithyia
[Hes.]
Cronus-Rhea
Zeus – Pluto[2]
[Paus.] 6c [Schol. Pind.]
{Zeus}
Asopus-Metope[2]
:– Aegina
[Pind.]
Aeacus
[Hom.]
23c-24c
Olenus-Lethaea
:– Aex
[Hyg.]
Aegipan
[Hyg.]
46d
Electryon[1]-Anaxo[1]
:– Alcmene
[Hom.]
Heracles[1]
[Hom.]
60a-d,61c-d
Asopus-Metope[2]
:– Antiope[1]
[Hom.]
Amphion[1]
[Hom.]
66c-d
Zethus
[Hom.]
66d
C(o)eus-Phoebe[1]
:– Asteria[1]
[Cic.]
Heracles[3] – ?
[Cic.]
Carthago
[Cic.]
Oceanus-Tethys
:– Asterope[3]
[Steph. Byz.]
Acragas
[Steph. Byz.]
Lycaon[1]-?
:– Callisto[1]
[Eur.]
Arcas[1]
[Apollod.]
62c-63c
Opus[1]-?
:– Cambyse
[Pind.]
Opus[2]
[Pind.]
15a
Zeus-Europe[1]
Minos I – Britomartis
[Paus.] [Paus.]
Eubulus-?
:– Carme
[Paus.]
Arabus[2]-?
:– Cassiopeia[1]
[Apollod.]
Atymnius[1]
[Apollod.]
Acrisius-Eurydice[6]
:– Danae
[Hom.]
Perseus[1]
[Hom.]
58d-59d
Cronus-Rhea
:– Demeter
[Hes.]
Persephone[1]
[Hes.]
10a
{Zeus}
Eioneus[2]-?
:– Dia[1]
[Hom.]
Peirithous[1]
[Hom.]
30d
Phisadie
[Hyg.]
Oceanus-Tethys
:– Dione[1]
[Hom.]
Cinyras[1]-Myrrha
Adonis – Aphrodite – Anchises
[Apollod.] 11c [Hom.] 41c-d [Hom.]
Capys[1]-Themis[2]
Zeus-Hera
:– Ares
7a [Hes.]
Teleon-Zeuxippe[4]
:– Butes[1]
53a [Diod. Sic.]
Zeus-Semele
:– Dionysus
56d [Paus.]
Zeus-Hera
:– Hephaestus
[Hom.]
Zeus-Maia
:– Hermes
46a [Ovid]
Cephalus[1]-Eos
:– Phaethon[2]
[Hes.]
Cronus-Rhea
:– Poseidon
[Serv.]
{Zeus}
Orchomenus[1]-?
:– Elara
[Apollod.]
Aemathion[2]
[Non.]
Atlas-Pleione
:– Electra[2]
[Hellan.]
Dardanus[1]
[Hom.]
42a-b
Iasion
[Apollod.]
42b
Phoenix[2]-Perimede[3]
:– Europe[1]
[Hom.]
Zeus-Leto
Carn(e)us ~ Apollo
[Prax.] [Prax.]
Dodon
[Akest.]
Minos I
[Hom.]
52d-54c
Rhadamanthys
[Hom.]
52d
Sarpedon[1]
[Cat. Wom.]
52c
Oceanus-Tethys
:– Eurynome[1]
[Hes.]
Nyx
Hypnos – Aglaia[1] – Hephaestus
[Hom.] 1a [Hes.] [Hes.]
Zeus-Hera
(Charites) [Graces]
Euphrosyne
[Hes.]
Thaleia[2]
[Hes.]
{Zeus}
:– Euryodia
[Eust.]
Arceisius – Chalcomedusa
[Eust.] [Eust.]
Autolycus[1]-Amphithea[2]
Laertes – Anticleia[1]
[Hom.] [Hom.]
Callisto[2]
[Athen.]
Eurylochus[1] – Ctimene
[Eust.] [Hom.]
Odysseus
[Hom.]
13c-d
Chaos
:– Gaea
[Paus.]
Agdistis/Cybele[2]
70a [Paus.] 2b, 2d
Manes
[Dion. Hal.]
51b
Tros[1]-Callirhoe[1]
:~ Ganymede(s)
[Eur.]
:– Himalia
[Diod. Sic.]
Cronius[1]
[Diod. Sic.]
Cytus
[Diod. Sic.]
Spartaeus
[Diod. Sic.]
:– Hybris
[Apollod.]
Inachus-Melia[1]
:– Io
[Steph. Byz.]
Epaphus[1]
[Aesch.]
55a-b
Ceroessa
[Steph. Byz.]
55b
Poseidon-Alistra
Ogygus – Thebe[2]
[Tzetz.] [Tzetz.]
Itonus[1]-Melanippe[6]
:– Iodama
[Tzetz. Lyc.]
Poseidon-?
:– Lamia[1]
[Paus.]
Herophile[1]
[Paus.]
Bellerophon(tes)-Philonoe
:– Laodameia[2]
[Hom.]
Sarpedon[2]
[Hom.]
{Zeus}
Thestius-Eurythemis(te)
:– Leda
[Eur.]
Helen[1]
[Hom.]
48d
C(o)eus-Phoebe[1]
:– Leto
[Hes.]
Apollo
[Hes.]
11a-d
Artemis
[Hes.]
:– Leucothea[2]
[Ps.-Plut.]
Pactolus – ?
[Ps.-Plut.]
Zeus-Pluto[2]
Tantalus[1] – Euryanassa[1]
[Tzetz. Lyc.] [Tzetz. Lyc.]
Proetus[3]-?
:– Maera[1]
[Eust.]
Locrus[1]
[Eust.]
Atlas-Pleione
:– Maia
[Hes.]
Hermes
[Hes.]
46a-d
Zeus-Hera
Hephaestus – Athene
[Apollod.] [Hom.]
Oceanus-Tethys
:– Metis[1]
[Hes.]
Cleitor[3]-?
:– Eurymedusa[1]
[Serv.]
Aeolus[1]-Enarete
Myrmidon – Peisidice[1]
[Eust.] [Cat. Wom.]
Actor[1] – Polyboea[3]
[Cat. Wom.] [Eust.]
Phylas[3]-?
Echecles – Polymela[1]
[Hom.] [Hom.]
Antiphus[3]
[Cat. Wom.]
Zeus-Maia
Hermes – Eupoleme(ia)
[Ap. Rhod.] [Ap. Rhod.]
Aethalides[1]
[Ap. Rhod.]
Poseidon-Canace
Triop(a)s[1] – Hiscilla
[Hyg.] 34c [Hyg.]

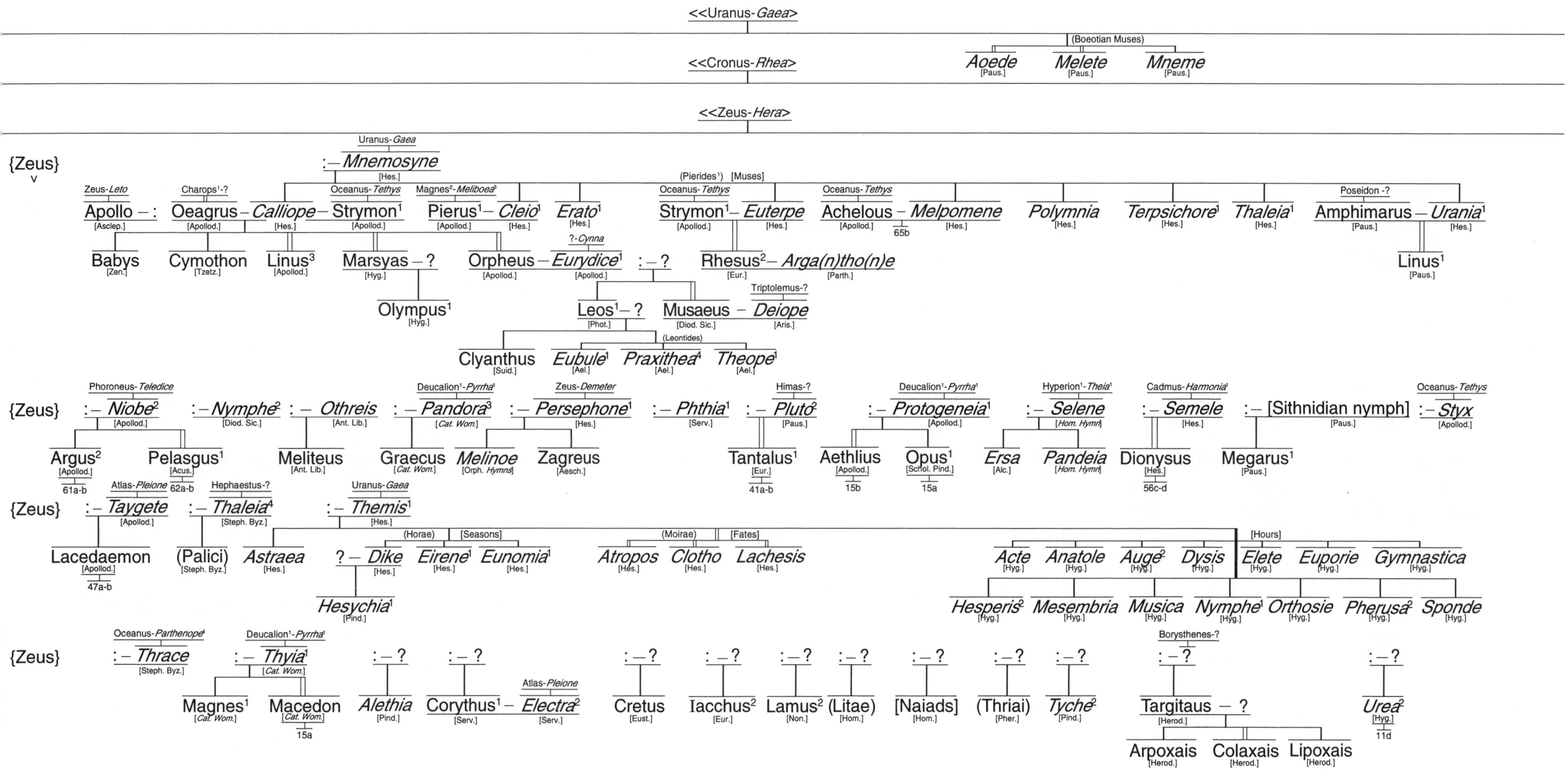
<<Uranus-Gaea>
<<Cronus-Rhea>
(Boeotian Muses)
Aoede [Paus.]
Melete [Paus.]
Mneme [Paus.]
<<Zeus-Hera>
{Zeus}
v
Uranus-Gaea
:— Mnemosyne [Hes.]
(Pierides[1]) [Muses]
Zeus-Leto
Apollo — : [Asclep.]
Charops[1]-?
Oeagrus [Apollod.]
Calliope [Hes.]
Oceanus-Tethys
Strymon[1] [Apollod.]
Magnes[2]-Meliboea[3]
Pierus[1] [Apollod.]
Cleio[1] [Hes.]
Erato[1] [Hes.]
Oceanus-Tethys
Strymon[1] [Apollod.]
Euterpe [Hes.]
Oceanus-Tethys
Achelous [Apollod.]
65b
Melpomene [Hes.]
Polymnia [Hes.]
Terpsichore[1] [Hes.]
Thaleia[1] [Hes.]
Poseidon -?
Amphimarus [Paus.]
Urania[1] [Hes.]
Babys [Zen.]
Cymothon [Tzetz.]
Linus[3] [Apollod.]
Marsyas — ? [Hyg.]
Orpheus [Apollod.]
?-Cynna
Eurydice[1] [Apollod.]
: — ?
Rhesus[2] [Eur.]
Arga(n)tho(n)e [Parth.]
Linus[1] [Paus.]
Olympus[1] [Hyg.]
Leos[1] — ? [Phot.]
Triptolemus-?
Musaeus [Diod. Sic.]
Deiope [Aris.]
(Leontides)
Clyanthus [Suid.]
Eubule[1] [Ael.]
Praxithea[4] [Ael.]
Theope[1] [Ael.]
{Zeus}
Phoroneus-Teledice
:— Niobe[2] [Apollod.]
:— Nymphe[2] [Diod. Sic.]
:— Othreis [Ant. Lib.]
Deucalion[1]-Pyrrha[1]
:— Pandora[3] [Cat. Wom.]
Zeus-Demeter
:— Persephone[1] [Hes.]
:— Phthia[1] [Serv.]
Himas-?
:— Pluto[2] [Paus.]
Deucalion[1]-Pyrrha[1]
:— Protogeneia[1] [Apollod.]
Hyperion[1]-Theia[1]
:— Selene [Hom. Hymn]
Cadmus-Harmonia[1]
:— Semele [Hes.]
:— [Sithnidian nymph] [Paus.]
Oceanus-Tethys
:— Styx [Apollod.]
Argus[2] [Apollod.]
61a-b
Pelasgus[1] [Acus.]
62a-b
Meliteus [Ant. Lib.]
Graecus [Cat. Wom.]
Melinoe [Orph. Hymns]
Zagreus [Aesch.]
Tantalus[1] [Eur.]
41a-b
Aethlius [Apollod.]
15b
Opus[1] [Schol. Pind.]
15a
Ersa [Alc.]
Pandeia [Hom. Hymn]
Dionysus [Hes.]
56c-d
Megarus[1] [Paus.]
{Zeus}
Atlas-Pleione
:— Taygete [Apollod.]
Hephaestus-?
:— Thaleia[4] [Steph. Byz.]
Uranus-Gaea
:— Themis[1] [Hes.]
(Horae) [Seasons]
(Moirae) [Fates]
[Hours]
Lacedaemon [Apollod.]
47a-b
(Palici) [Steph. Byz.]
Astraea [Hes.]
? — Dike [Hes.]
Eirene[1] [Hes.]
Eunomia[1] [Hes.]
Atropos [Hes.]
Clotho [Hes.]
Lachesis [Hes.]
Acte [Hyg.]
Anatole [Hyg.]
Auge[2] [Hyg.]
Dysis [Hyg.]
Elete [Hyg.]
Euporie [Hyg.]
Gymnastica [Hyg.]
Hesychia[1] [Pind.]
Hesperis[2] [Hyg.]
Mesembria [Hyg.]
Musica [Hyg.]
Nymphe[1] [Hyg.]
Orthosie [Hyg.]
Pherusa[2] [Hyg.]
Sponde [Hyg.]
{Zeus}
Oceanus-Parthenope[1]
:— Thrace [Steph. Byz.]
Deucalion[1]-Pyrrha[1]
:— Thyia[1] [Cat. Wom.]
:— ?
:— ?
Atlas-Pleione
:— ?
:— ?
:— ?
:— ?
:— ?
:— ?
:— ?
Borysthenes-?
:— ?
:— ?
Magnes[1] [Cat. Wom.]
Macedon [Cat. Wom.]
15a
Alethia [Pind.]
Corythus[1] [Serv.]
Electra[2] [Serv.]
Cretus [Eust.]
Iacchus[2] [Eur.]
Lamus[2] [Non.]
(Litae) [Hom.]
[Naiads] [Hom.]
(Thriai) [Pher.]
Tyche[2] [Pind.]
Targitaus — ? [Herod.]
Urea[2] [Hyg.]
11d
Arpoxais [Herod.]
Colaxais [Herod.]
Lipoxais [Herod.]

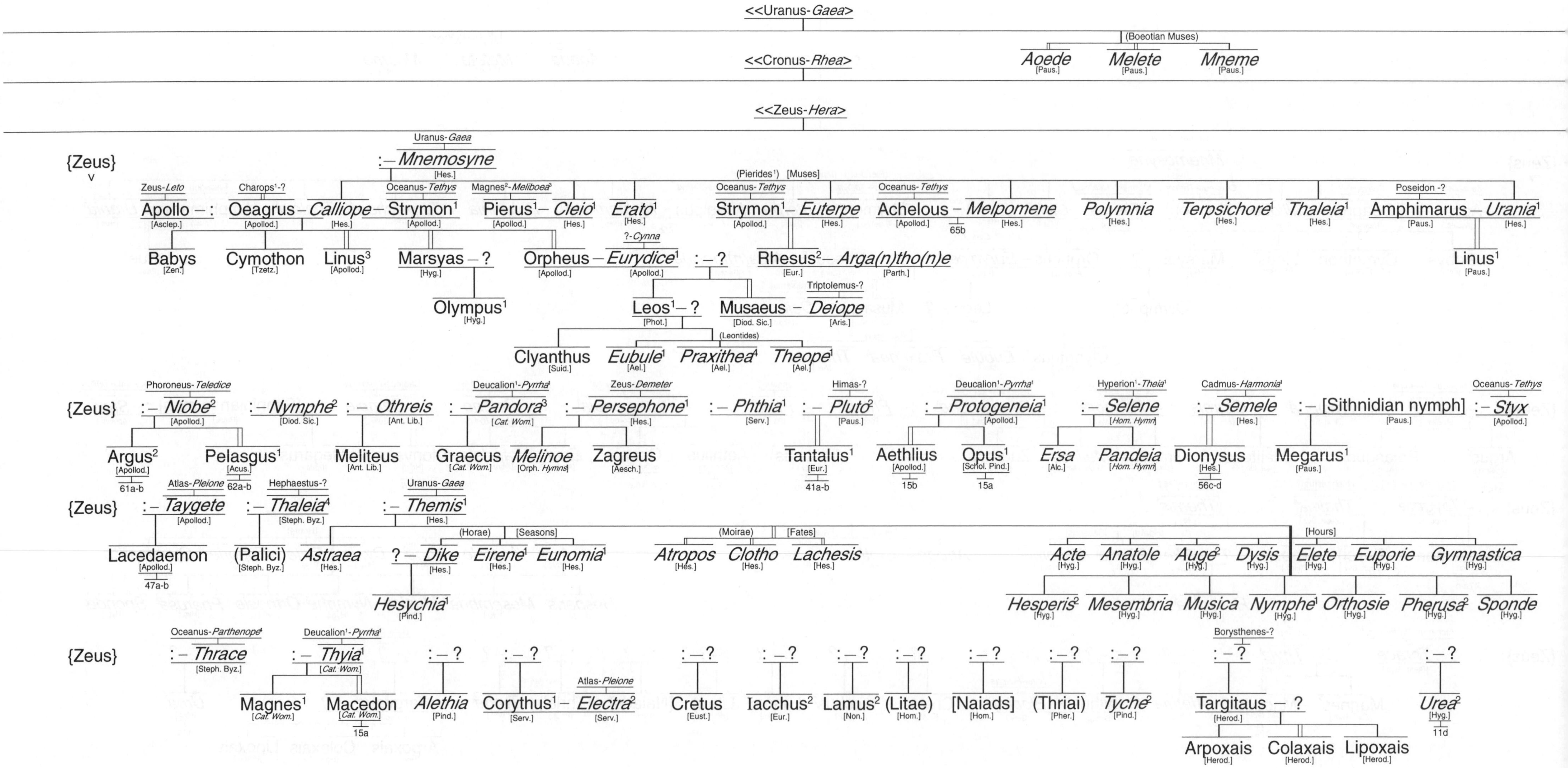
<<Uranus-Gaea>
(Boetian Muses)
<<Cronus-Rhea>
Aoede [Paus.]
Melete [Paus.]
Mneme [Paus.]
<<Zeus-Hera>
{Zeus}
Uranus-Gaea
:– Mnemosyne [Hes.]
(Pierides[1]) [Muses]
Zeus-Leto
Apollo –: [Asclep.]
Charops[1]-?
Oeagrus – [Apollod.]
Oceanus-Tethys
Calliope – [Hes.]
Strymon[1] [Apollod.]
Magnes[2]-Meliboea[3]
Pierus[1] – [Apollod.]
Cleio[1] [Hes.]
Erato[1] [Hes.]
Oceanus-Tethys
Strymon[1] – [Apollod.]
Euterpe [Hes.]
Oceanus-Tethys
Achelous – [Apollod.]
Melpomene [Hes.]
65b
Polymnia [Hes.]
Terpsichore[1] [Hes.]
Thaleia[1] [Hes.]
Poseidon -?
Amphimarus – [Paus.]
Urania[1] [Hes.]
Babys [Zen.]
Cymothon [Tzetz.]
Linus[3] [Apollod.]
Marsyas – ? [Hyg.]
?-Cynna
Orpheus – [Apollod.]
Eurydice[1] [Apollod.]
:– ?
Rhesus[2] – [Eur.]
Arga(n)tho(n)e [Parth.]
Linus[1] [Paus.]
Olympus[1] [Hyg.]
Triptolemus-?
Leos[1] – ? [Phot.]
Musaeus – [Diod. Sic.]
Deiope [Aris.]
(Leontides)
Clyanthus [Suid.]
Eubule[1] [Ael.]
Praxithea[4] [Ael.]
Theope[1] [Ael.]
{Zeus}
Phoroneus-Teledice
:– Niobe[2] [Apollod.]
:– Nymphe[2] [Diod. Sic.]
:– Othreis [Ant. Lib.]
Deucalion[1]-Pyrrha[1]
:– Pandora[3] [Cat. Wom.]
Zeus-Demeter
:– Persephone[1] [Hes.]
:– Phthia[1] [Serv.]
Himas-?
:– Pluto[2] [Paus.]
Deucalion[1]-Pyrrha[1]
:– Protogeneia[1] [Apollod.]
Hyperion[1]-Theia[1]
:– Selene [Hom. Hymn]
Cadmus-Harmonia[1]
:– Semele [Hes.]
:– [Sithnidian nymph] [Paus.]
Oceanus-Tethys
:– Styx [Apollod.]
Argus[2] [Apollod.]
61a-b
Pelasgus[1] [Acus.]
62a-b
Meliteus [Ant. Lib.]
Graecus [Cat. Wom.]
Melinoe [Orph. Hymns]
Zagreus [Aesch.]
Tantalus[1] [Eur.]
41a-b
Aethlius [Apollod.]
15b
Opus[1] [Schol. Pind.]
15a
Ersa [Alc.]
Pandeia [Hom. Hymn]
Dionysus [Hes.]
56c-d
Megarus[1] [Paus.]
{Zeus}
Atlas-Pleione
:– Taygete [Apollod.]
Hephaestus-?
:– Thaleia[4] [Steph. Byz.]
Uranus-Gaea
:– Themis[1] [Hes.]
(Horae) [Seasons]
(Moirae) [Fates]
[Hours]
Lacedaemon [Apollod.]
47a-b
(Palici) [Steph. Byz.]
Astraea [Hes.]
? – Dike [Hes.]
Eirene[1] [Hes.]
Eunomia[1] [Hes.]
Atropos [Hes.]
Clotho [Hes.]
Lachesis [Hes.]
Acte [Hyg.]
Anatole [Hyg.]
Auge[2] [Hyg.]
Dysis [Hyg.]
Elete [Hyg.]
Euporie [Hyg.]
Gymnastica [Hyg.]
Hesychia[1] [Pind.]
Hesperis[2] [Hyg.]
Mesembria [Hyg.]
Musica [Hyg.]
Nymphe[1] [Hyg.]
Orthosie [Hyg.]
Pherusa[2] [Hyg.]
Sponde [Hyg.]
{Zeus}
Oceanus-Parthenope[1]
:– Thrace [Steph. Byz.]
Deucalion[1]-Pyrrha[1]
:– Thyia[1] [Cat. Wom.]
:– ?
:– ?
:– ?
:– ?
:– ?
:– ?
:– ?
:– ?
:– ?
Borysthenes-?
:– ?
:– ?
Magnes[1] [Cat. Wom.]
Macedon [Cat. Wom.]
15a
Alethia [Pind.]
Atlas-Pleione
Corythus[1] – [Serv.]
Electra[2] [Serv.]
Cretus [Eust.]
Iacchus[2] [Eur.]
Lamus[2] [Non.]
(Litae) [Hom.]
[Naiads] [Hom.]
(Thriai) [Pher.]
Tyche[2] [Pind.]
Targitaus – ? [Herod.]
Urea[2] [Hyg.]
11d
Arpoxais [Herod.]
Colaxais [Herod.]
Lipoxais [Herod.]

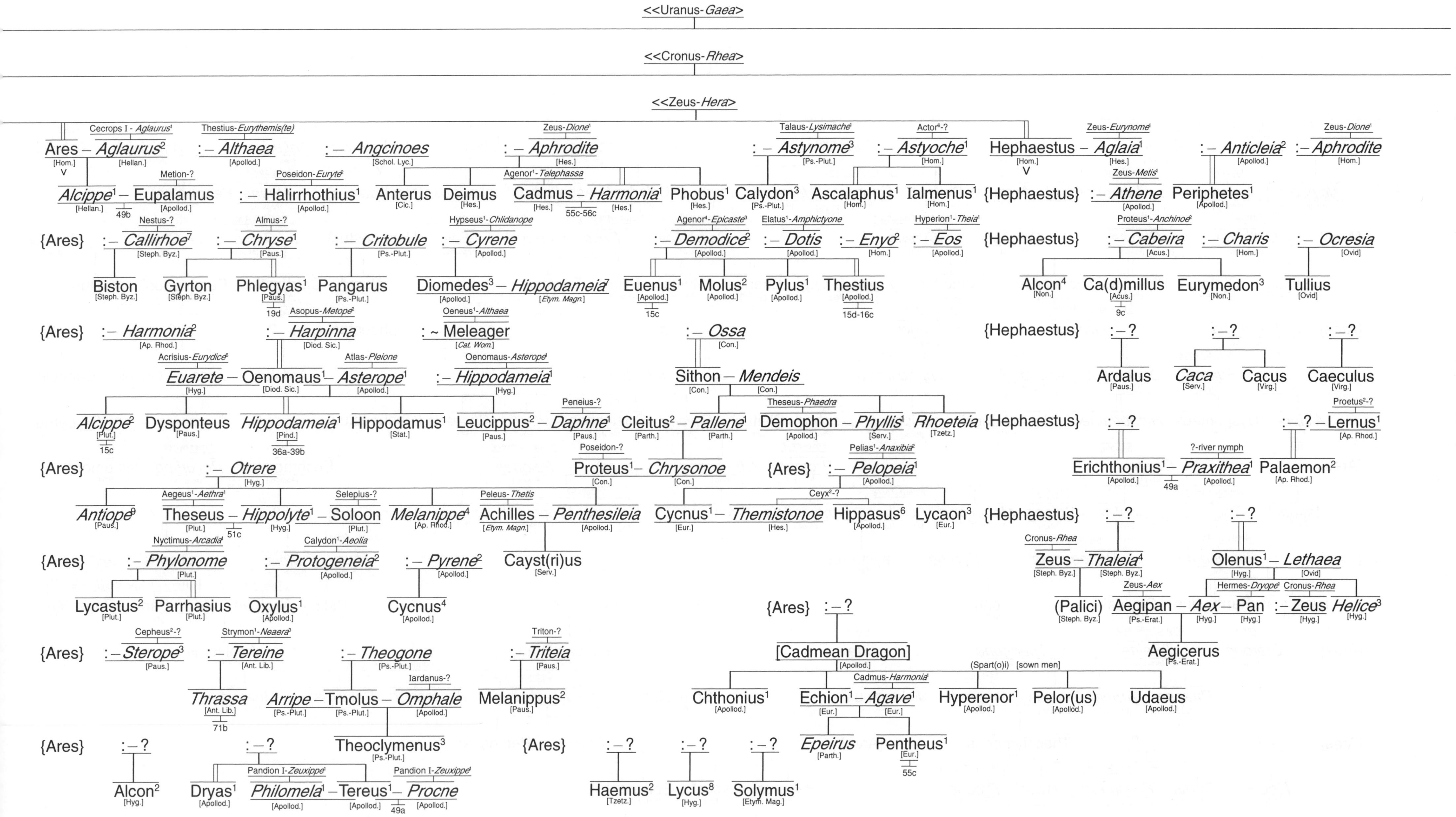

<<Uranus-Gaea>
<<Cronus-Rhea>
<<Zeus-Hera>
Cecrops I - Aglaurus1
Ares – Aglaurus2 [Hom.] [Hellan.]
Thestius-Eurythemis(te)
:– Althaea [Apollod.]
:– Angcinoes [Schol. Lyc.]
Zeus-Dione1
:– Aphrodite [Hes.]
Talaus-Lysimache1
:– Astynome3 [Ps.-Plut.]
Actor6-?
:– Astyoche1 [Hom.]
Hephaestus – Aglaia1 [Hom.] [Hes.]
Zeus-Eurynome1
:– Anticleia2 [Apollod.]
Zeus-Dione1
:– Aphrodite [Hom.]
Metion-?
Alcippe1 – Eupalamus [Hellan.] [Apollod.]
49b
Poseidon-Euryte2
:– Halirrhothius1 [Apollod.]
Anterus [Cic.]
Deimus [Hes.]
Agenor1-Telephassa
Cadmus – Harmonia1 [Hes.] [Hes.]
55c-56c
Phobus1 [Hes.]
Calydon3 [Ps.-Plut.]
Ascalaphus1 [Hom.]
Ialmenus1 [Hom.]
{Hephaestus}
Zeus-Metis1
:– Athene [Apollod.]
Periphetes1 [Apollod.]
Nestus-?
Almus-?
Hypseus1-Chlidanope
Agenor4-Epicaste3
Elatus1-Amphictyone
Hyperion1-Theia1
Proteus1-Anchinoe3
{Ares} :– Callirhoe7 [Steph. Byz.]
:– Chryse1 [Paus.]
:– Critobule [Ps.-Plut.]
:– Cyrene [Apollod.]
:– Demodice2 [Apollod.]
:– Dotis [Apollod.]
:– Enyo2 [Hom.]
:– Eos [Apollod.]
{Hephaestus}
:– Cabeira [Acus.]
:– Charis [Hom.]
:– Ocresia [Ovid]
Biston [Steph. Byz.]
Gyrton [Steph. Byz.]
Phlegyas1 [Paus.]
19d
Pangarus [Ps.-Plut.]
Diomedes3 – Hippodameia7 [Apollod.] [Etym. Magn.]
Euenus1 [Apollod.]
15c
Molus2 [Apollod.]
Pylus1 [Apollod.]
Thestius [Apollod.]
15d-16c
Alcon4 [Non.]
Ca(d)millus [Acus.]
9c
Eurymedon3 [Non.]
Tullius [Ovid]
Asopus-Metope2
Oeneus1-Althaea
{Ares} :– Harmonia2 [Ap. Rhod.]
:– Harpinna [Diod. Sic.]
:~ Meleager [Cat. Wom.]
:– Ossa [Con.]
{Hephaestus} :–? :–? :–?
Acrisius-Eurydice6
Atlas-Pleione
Oenomaus-Asterope1
Euarete – Oenomaus1 – Asterope1 [Hyg.] [Diod. Sic.] [Apollod.]
:– Hippodameia1 [Hyg.]
Sithon – Mendeis [Con.] [Con.]
Ardalus [Paus.]
Caca [Serv.]
Cacus [Virg.]
Caeculus [Virg.]
Peneius-?
Theseus-Phaedra
Proetus2-?
Alcippe2 [Plut.]
15c
Dysponteus [Paus.]
Hippodameia1 [Pind.]
36a-39b
Hippodamus1 [Stat.]
Leucippus2 – Daphne1 [Paus.] [Paus.]
Cleitus2 – Pallene1 [Parth.] [Parth.]
Demophon – Phyllis1 [Apollod.] [Serv.]
Rhoeteia [Tzetz.]
{Hephaestus} :–?
:– ? – Lernus1 [Ap. Rhod.]
Poseidon-?
Pelias1-Anaxibia2
?-river nymph
{Ares} :– Otrere [Hyg.]
Proteus1 – Chrysonoe [Con.] [Con.]
{Ares} :– Pelopeia1 [Apollod.]
Erichthonius1 – Praxithea1 [Apollod.] [Apollod.]
49a
Palaemon2 [Ap. Rhod.]
Aegeus1-Aethra1
Selepius-?
Peleus-Thetis
Ceyx2-?
Antiope9 [Paus.]
Theseus – Hippolyte1 – Soloon [Plut.] [Hyg.] [Plut.]
51c
Melanippe4 [Ap. Rhod.]
Achilles – Penthesileia [Etym. Magn.] [Apollod.]
Cycnus1 – Themistonoe [Eur.] [Hes.]
Hippasus6 [Apollod.]
Lycaon3 [Eur.]
{Hephaestus} :–? :–?
Nyctimus-Arcadia1
Calydon1-Aeolia
Cronus-Rhea
{Ares} :– Phylonome [Plut.]
:– Protogeneia2 [Apollod.]
:– Pyrene2 [Apollod.]
Cayst(ri)us [Serv.]
Zeus – Thaleia4 [Steph. Byz.] [Steph. Byz.]
Olenus1 – Lethaea [Hyg.] [Ovid]
Zeus-Aex
Hermes-Dryope1
Cronus-Rhea
Lycastus2 [Plut.]
Parrhasius [Plut.]
Oxylus1 [Apollod.]
Cycnus4 [Apollod.]
{Ares} :–?
(Palici) [Steph. Byz.]
Aegipan – Aex – Pan [Ps.-Erat.] [Hyg.] [Hyg.]
:– Zeus [Hyg.]
Helice3 [Hyg.]
Cepheus2-?
Strymon1-Neaera3
Triton-?
{Ares} :– Sterope3 [Paus.]
:– Tereine [Ant. Lib.]
:– Theogone [Ps.-Plut.]
:– Triteia [Paus.]
[Cadmean Dragon] [Apollod.]
Aegicerus [Ps.-Erat.]
Iardanus-?
(Spart(o)i) [sown men]
Cadmus-Harmonia1
Thrassa [Ant. Lib.]
71b
Arripe – Tmolus – Omphale [Ps.-Plut.] [Ps.-Plut.] [Apollod.]
Melanippus2 [Paus.]
Chthonius1 [Apollod.]
Echion1 – Agave1 [Eur.] [Eur.]
Hyperenor1 [Apollod.]
Pelor(us) [Apollod.]
Udaeus [Apollod.]
{Ares} :–?
:–?
Theoclymenus3 [Ps.-Plut.]
{Ares} :–? :–? :–?
Epeirus [Parth.]
Pentheus1 [Eur.]
55c
Pandion I-Zeuxippe1
Pandion I-Zeuxippe1
Alcon2 [Hyg.]
Dryas1 [Apollod.]
Philomela1 – Tereus1 – Procne [Apollod.] [Apollod.] [Apollod.]
49a
Haemus2 [Tzetz.]
Lycus8 [Hyg.]
Solymus1 [Etym. Mag.]

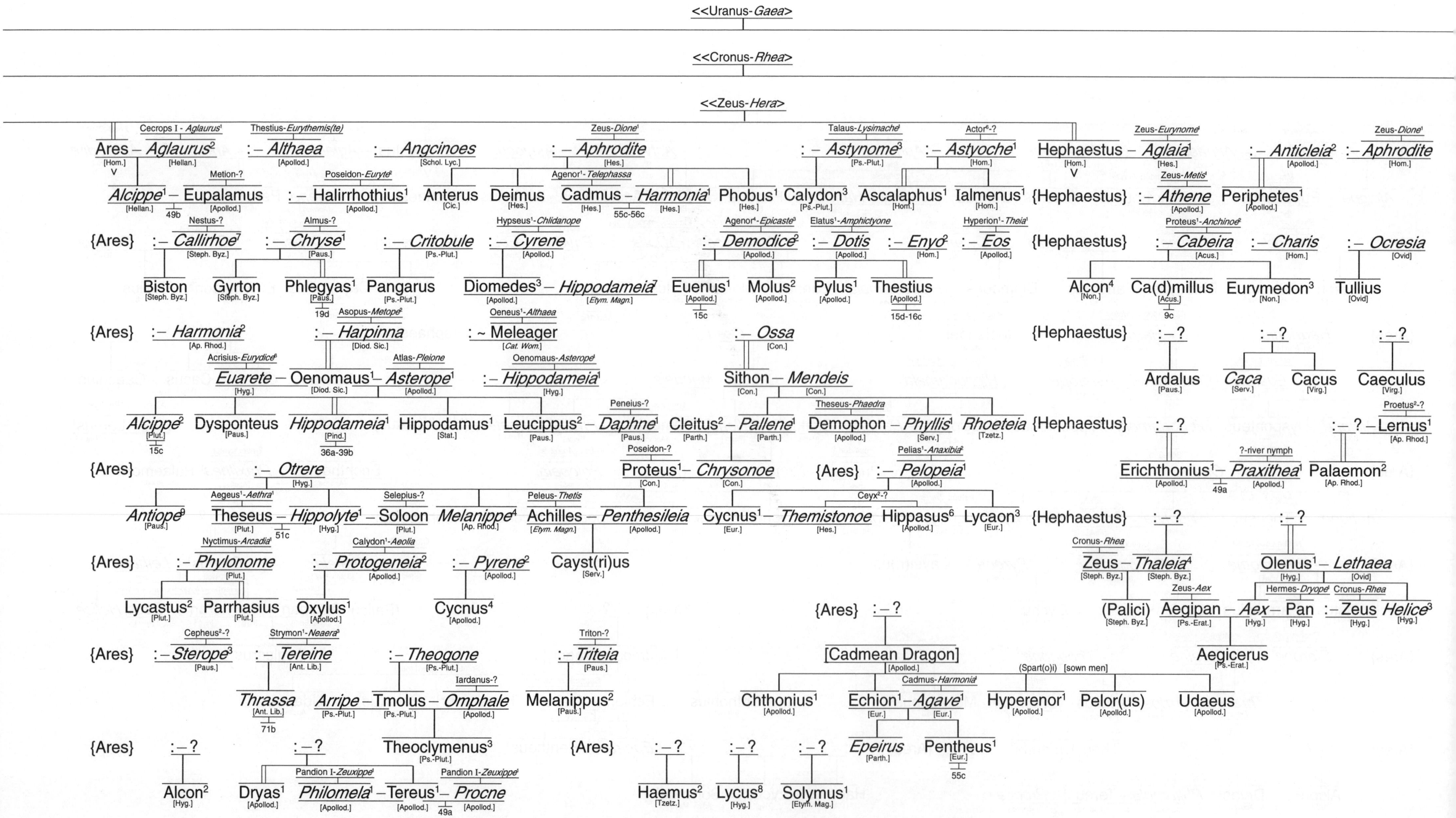

<<Uranus-Gaea>
<<Cronus-Rhea>
<<Zeus-Hera>
Cecrops I - Aglaurus¹ | Thestius-Eurythemis(te) | Zeus-Dione¹ | Talaus-Lysimache¹ | Actor⁶-? | Zeus-Eurynome¹ | Zeus-Dione¹
Ares – Aglaurus² [Hom.] [Hellan.] | :– Althaea [Apollod.] | :– Angcinoes [Schol. Lyc.] | :– Aphrodite [Hes.] | :– Astynome³ [Ps.-Plut.] | :– Astyoche¹ [Hom.] | Hephaestus – Aglaia¹ [Hom.] [Hes.] | :– Anticleia² [Apollod.] | :– Aphrodite [Hom.]
Metion-? | Poseidon-Euryte² | Agenor¹-Telephassa | Zeus-Metis¹
Alcippe¹ – Eupalamus [Hellan.] [Apollod.] 49b | :– Halirrhothius¹ [Apollod.] | Anterus [Cic.] | Deimus [Hes.] | Cadmus – Harmonia¹ [Hes.] [Hes.] 55c-56c | Phobus¹ [Hes.] | Calydon³ [Ps.-Plut.] | Ascalaphus¹ [Hom.] | Ialmenus¹ [Hom.] | {Hephaestus} :– Athene [Apollod.] | Periphetes¹ [Apollod.]
Nestus-? | Almus-? | Hypseus¹-Chlidanope | Agenor⁴-Epicaste³ | Elatus¹-Amphictyone | Hyperion¹-Theia¹ | Proteus¹-Anchinoe²
{Ares} :– Callirhoe⁷ [Steph. Byz.] | :– Chryse¹ [Paus.] | :– Critobule [Ps.-Plut.] | :– Cyrene [Apollod.] | :– Demodice² [Apollod.] | :– Dotis [Apollod.] | :– Enyo² [Hom.] | :– Eos [Apollod.] | {Hephaestus} :– Cabeira [Acus.] | :– Charis [Hom.] | :– Ocresia [Ovid]
Biston [Steph. Byz.] | Gyrton [Steph. Byz.] | Phlegyas¹ [Paus.] 19d | Pangarus [Ps.-Plut.] | Diomedes³ – Hippodameia⁷ [Apollod.] [Etym. Magn.] | Euenus¹ [Apollod.] 15c | Molus² [Apollod.] | Pylus¹ [Apollod.] | Thestius [Apollod.] 15d-16c | Alcon⁴ [Non.] | Ca(d)millus [Acus.] 9c | Eurymedon³ [Non.] | Tullius [Ovid]
Asopus-Metope² | Oeneus¹-Althaea
{Ares} :– Harmonia² [Ap. Rhod.] | :– Harpinna [Diod. Sic.] | :~ Meleager [Cat. Wom.] | :– Ossa [Con.] | {Hephaestus} :– ? | :– ? | :– ?
Acrisius-Eurydice⁶ | Atlas-Pleione | Oenomaus-Asterope¹
Euarete – Oenomaus¹ – Asterope¹ [Hyg.] [Diod. Sic.] [Apollod.] | :– Hippodameia¹ [Hyg.] | Sithon – Mendeis [Con.] [Con.] | Ardalus [Paus.] | Caca [Serv.] | Cacus [Virg.] | Caeculus [Virg.]
Peneius-? | Theseus-Phaedra | Proetus²-?
Alcippe² [Plut.] 15c | Dysponteus [Paus.] | Hippodameia¹ [Pind.] 36a-39b | Hippodamus¹ [Stat.] | Leucippus² – Daphne¹ [Paus.] [Paus.] | Cleitus² – Pallene¹ [Parth.] [Parth.] | Demophon – Phyllis¹ [Apollod.] [Serv.] | Rhoeteia [Tzetz.] | {Hephaestus} :– ? | :– ? – Lernus¹ [Ap. Rhod.]
Poseidon-? | Pelias¹-Anaxibia² | ?-river nymph
{Ares} :– Otrere [Hyg.] | Proteus¹ – Chrysonoe [Con.] [Con.] | {Ares} :– Pelopeia¹ [Apollod.] | Erichthonius¹ – Praxithea¹ [Apollod.] [Apollod.] 49a | Palaemon² [Ap. Rhod.]
Aegeus¹-Aethra¹ | Selepius-? | Peleus-Thetis | Ceyx²-?
Antiope⁸ [Paus.] | Theseus – Hippolyte¹ – Soloon [Plut.] [Hyg.] [Plut.] 51c | Melanippe⁴ [Ap. Rhod.] | Achilles – Penthesileia [Etym. Magn.] [Apollod.] | Cycnus¹ – Themistonoe [Eur.] [Hes.] | Hippasus⁶ [Apollod.] | Lycaon³ [Eur.] | {Hephaestus} :– ? | :– ?
Nyctimus-Arcadia¹ | Calydon¹-Aeolia | Cronus-Rhea
{Ares} :– Phylonome [Plut.] | :– Protogeneia² [Apollod.] | :– Pyrene² [Apollod.] | Cayst(ri)us [Serv.] | Zeus – Thaleia⁴ [Steph. Byz.] [Steph. Byz.] | Olenus¹ – Lethaea [Hyg.] [Ovid]
Zeus-Aex | Hermes-Dryope¹ | Cronus-Rhea
Lycastus² [Plut.] | Parrhasius [Plut.] | Oxylus¹ [Apollod.] | Cycnus⁴ [Apollod.] | {Ares} :– ? | (Palici) [Steph. Byz.] | Aegipan – Aex – Pan [Ps.-Erat.] [Hyg.] [Hyg.] | :– Zeus Helice³ [Hyg.] [Hyg.]
Cepheus²-? | Strymon¹-Neaera³ | Triton-?
{Ares} :– Sterope³ [Paus.] | :– Tereine [Ant. Lib.] | :– Theogone [Ps.-Plut.] | :– Triteia [Paus.] | [Cadmean Dragon] [Apollod.] | Aegicerus [Ps.-Erat.]
Iardanus-? | (Spart(o)i) [sown men] | Cadmus-Harmonia¹
Thrassa [Ant. Lib.] 71b | Arripe – Tmolus – Omphale [Ps.-Plut.] [Ps.-Plut.] [Apollod.] | Melanippus² [Paus.] | Chthonius¹ [Apollod.] | Echion¹ – Agave¹ [Eur.] [Eur.] | Hyperenor¹ [Apollod.] | Pelor(us) [Apollod.] | Udaeus [Apollod.]
{Ares} :– ? | :– ? | Theoclymenus³ [Ps.-Plut.] | {Ares} :– ? | :– ? | :– ? | Epeirus [Parth.] | Pentheus¹ [Eur.] 55c
Pandion I-Zeuxippe¹ | Pandion I-Zeuxippe¹
Alcon² [Hyg.] | Dryas¹ [Apollod.] | Philomela¹ – Tereus¹ – Procne [Apollod.] [Apollod.] [Apollod.] 49a | Haemus² [Tzetz.] | Lycus⁸ [Hyg.] | Solymus¹ [Etym. Mag.]

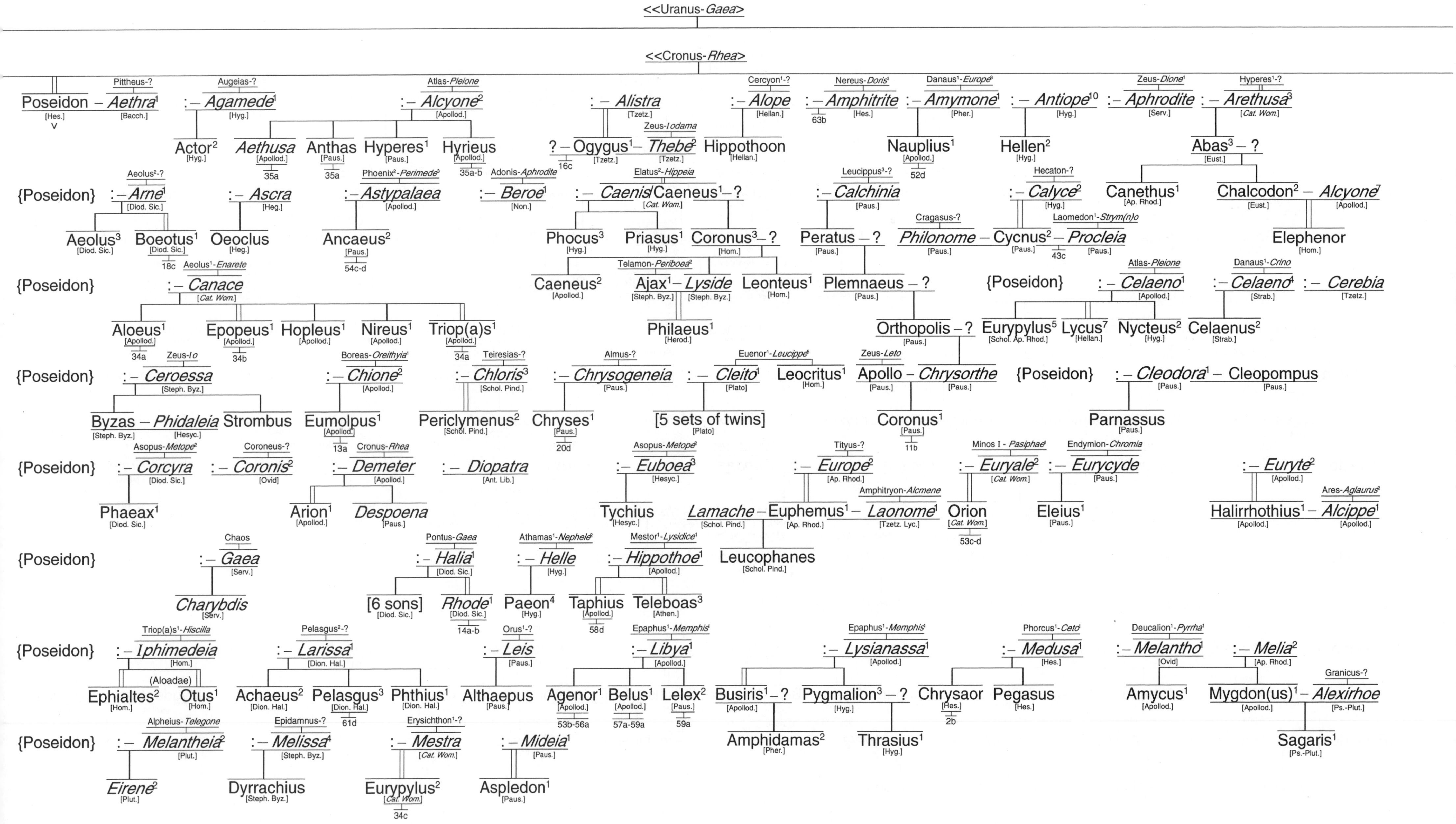
<<Uranus-Gaea>
<<Cronus-Rhea>
Pittheus-?
Poseidon – Aethra[1]
[Hes.] [Bacch.]
V
Augeias-?
:– Agamede[1]
[Hyg.]
Actor[2] [Hyg.]
Atlas-Pleione
:– Alcyone[2]
[Apollod.]
Aethusa [Apollod.] 35a
Anthas [Paus.] 35a
Hyperes[1] [Paus.]
Hyrieus [Apollod.] 35a-b
:– Alistra
[Tzetz.]
? – Ogygus[1] – Thebe[2]
[Tzetz.] [Tzetz.]
Zeus-Iodama
16c
Cercyon[1]-?
:– Alope
[Hellan.]
Hippothoon [Hellan.]
Nereus-Doris[1]
:– Amphitrite
[Hes.]
63b
Danaus[1]-Europe[3]
:– Amymone[1]
[Pher.]
Nauplius[1] [Apollod.] 52d
:– Antiope[10]
[Hyg.]
Hellen[2] [Hyg.]
Zeus-Dione[1]
:– Aphrodite
[Serv.]
Hyperes[1]-?
:– Arethusa[3]
[Cat. Wom.]
Abas[3] – ?
[Eust.]
Canethus[1] [Ap. Rhod.]
Chalcodon[2] – Alcyone[7]
[Eust.] [Apollod.]
Elephenor [Hom.]
Aeolus[2]-?
{Poseidon} :– Arne[1]
[Diod. Sic.]
Aeolus[3] [Diod. Sic.]
Boeotus[1] [Diod. Sic.] 18c
:– Ascra
[Heg.]
Oeoclus [Heg.]
Phoenix[2]-Perimede[3]
:– Astypalaea
[Apollod.]
Ancaeus[2] [Paus.] 54c-d
Adonis-Aphrodite
:– Beroe[1]
[Non.]
Elatus[2]-Hippeia
:– Caenis/Caeneus[1] – ?
[Cat. Wom.]
Phocus[3] [Hyg.]
Priasus[1] [Hyg.]
Coronus[3] – ? [Hom.]
Caeneus[2] [Apollod.]
Telamon-Periboea[2]
Ajax[1] – Lyside
[Steph. Byz.] [Steph. Byz.]
Philaeus[1] [Herod.]
Leonteus[1] [Hom.]
Leucippus[3]-?
:– Calchinia
[Paus.]
Peratus – ?
[Paus.]
Plemnaeus – ?
[Paus.]
Orthopolis – ?
[Paus.]
Cragasus-?
Hecaton-?
:– Calyce[2]
[Hyg.]
Laomedon[1]-Strym(n)o
Philonome – Cycnus[2] – Procleia
[Paus.] [Paus.] [Paus.]
43c
Aeolus[1]-Enarete
{Poseidon} :– Canace
[Cat. Wom.]
Aloeus[1] [Apollod.] 34a
Epopeus[1] [Apollod.] 34b
Hopleus[1] [Apollod.]
Nireus[1] [Apollod.]
Triop(a)s[1] [Apollod.] 34a
Atlas-Pleione
{Poseidon} :– Celaeno[1]
[Apollod.]
Eurypylus[5] [Schol. Ap. Rhod.]
Lycus[7] [Hellan.]
Nycteus[2] [Hyg.]
Danaus[1]-Crino
:– Celaeno[4]
[Strab.]
Celaenus[2] [Strab.]
:– Cerebia
[Tzetz.]
Zeus-Io
{Poseidon} :– Ceroessa
[Steph. Byz.]
Byzas – Phidaleia
[Steph. Byz.] [Hesyc.]
Strombus
Boreas-Oreithyia[1]
:– Chione[2]
[Apollod.]
Eumolpus[1] [Apollod.] 13a
Teiresias-?
:– Chloris[3]
[Schol. Pind.]
Periclymenus[2] [Schol. Pind.]
Almus-?
:– Chrysogeneia
[Paus.]
Chryses[1] [Paus.] 20d
Euenor[1]-Leucippe[5]
:– Cleito[1]
[Plato]
[5 sets of twins] [Plato]
Leocritus[1] [Hom.]
Zeus-Leto
Apollo – Chrysorthe
[Paus.] [Paus.]
Coronus[1] [Paus.] 11b
{Poseidon} :– Cleodora[1] – Cleopompus
[Paus.] [Paus.]
Parnassus [Paus.]
Asopus-Metope[2]
{Poseidon} :– Corcyra
[Diod. Sic.]
Phaeax[1] [Diod. Sic.]
Coroneus-?
:– Coronis[2]
[Ovid]
Cronus-Rhea
:– Demeter
[Apollod.]
Arion[1] [Apollod.]
Despoena [Paus.]
:– Diopatra
[Ant. Lib.]
Asopus-Metope[2]
:– Euboea[3]
[Hesyc.]
Tychius [Hesyc.]
Tityus-?
:– Europe[2]
[Ap. Rhod.]
Amphitryon-Alcmene
Lamache – Euphemus[1] – Laonome[1]
[Schol. Pind.] [Ap. Rhod.] [Tzetz. Lyc.]
Leucophanes [Schol. Pind.]
Minos I - Pasiphae[1]
:– Euryale[2]
[Cat. Wom.]
Orion [Cat. Wom.] 53c-d
Endymion-Chromia
:– Eurycyde
[Paus.]
Eleius[1] [Paus.]
:– Euryte[2]
[Apollod.]
Ares-Aglaurus[2]
Halirrhothius[1] – Alcippe[1]
[Apollod.] [Apollod.]
Chaos
{Poseidon} :– Gaea
[Serv.]
Charybdis [Serv.]
Pontus-Gaea
:– Halia[1]
[Diod. Sic.]
[6 sons] [Diod. Sic.]
Rhode[1] [Diod. Sic.] 14a-b
Athamas[1]-Nephele[2]
:– Helle
[Hyg.]
Paeon[4] [Hyg.]
Mestor[1]-Lysidice[1]
:– Hippothoe[1]
[Apollod.]
Taphius [Apollod.] 58d
Teleboas[3] [Athen.]
Triop(a)s[1]-Hiscilla
{Poseidon} :– Iphimedeia
[Hom.]
(Aloadae)
Ephialtes[2] [Hom.]
Otus[1] [Hom.]
Pelasgus[2]-?
:– Larissa[1]
[Dion. Hal.]
Achaeus[2] [Dion. Hal.]
Pelasgus[3] [Dion. Hal.] 61d
Phthius[1] [Dion. Hal.]
Orus[1]-?
:– Leis
[Paus.]
Althaepus [Paus.]
Epaphus[1]-Memphis[1]
:– Libya[1]
[Apollod.]
Agenor[1] [Apollod.] 53b-56a
Belus[1] [Apollod.] 57a-59a
Lelex[2] [Paus.] 59a
Epaphus[1]-Memphis[1]
:– Lysianassa[1]
[Apollod.]
Busiris[1] – ?
[Apollod.]
Amphidamas[2] [Pher.]
Pygmalion[3] – ?
[Hyg.]
Thrasius[1] [Hyg.]
Phorcus[1]-Ceto[1]
:– Medusa[1]
[Hes.]
Chrysaor [Hes.] 2b
Pegasus [Hes.]
Deucalion[1]-Pyrrha[1]
:– Melantho[1]
[Ovid]
Amycus[1] [Apollod.]
:– Melia[2]
[Ap. Rhod.]
Granicus-?
Mygdon(us)[1] – Alexirhoe
[Apollod.] [Ps.-Plut.]
Sagaris[1] [Ps.-Plut.]
Alpheius-Telegone
{Poseidon} :– Melantheia[2]
[Plut.]
Eirene[2] [Plut.]
Epidamnus-?
:– Melissa[4]
[Steph. Byz.]
Dyrrachius [Steph. Byz.]
Erysichthon[1]-?
:– Mestra
[Cat. Wom.]
Eurypylus[2] [Cat. Wom.] 34c
:– Mideia[1]
[Paus.]
Aspledon[1] [Paus.]

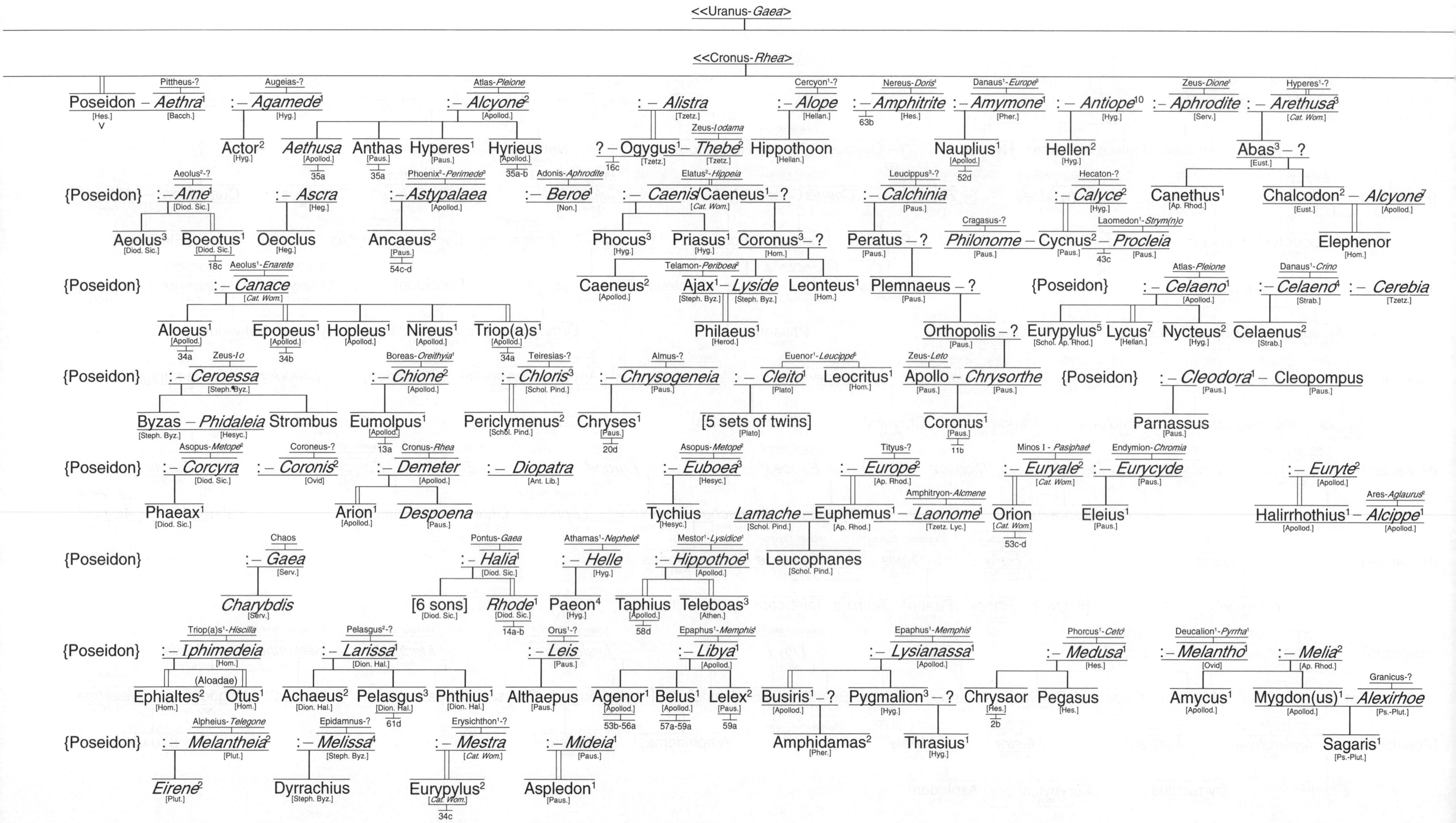

<<Uranus-Gaea>
<<Cronus-Rhea>
Pittheus-? Augeias-? Atlas-Pleione Cercyon¹-? Nereus-Doris¹ Danaus¹-Europe³ Zeus-Dione¹ Hyperes¹-?
Poseidon – Aethra¹ [Hes.] [Bacch.] V
:– Agamede¹ [Hyg.]
:– Alcyone² [Apollod.]
:– Alistra [Tzetz.]
:– Alope [Hellan.]
:– Amphitrite [Hes.] 63b
:– Amymone¹ [Pher.]
:– Antiope¹⁰ [Hyg.]
:– Aphrodite [Serv.]
:– Arethusa³ [Cat. Wom.]
Actor² [Hyg.] Aethusa [Apollod.] 35a Anthas [Paus.] 35a Hyperes¹ [Paus.] Hyrieus [Apollod.] 35a-b
Zeus-Iodama
? – Ogygus¹ – Thebe² [Tzetz.] [Tzetz.] 16c Hippothoon [Hellan.] Nauplius¹ [Apollod.] 52d Hellen² [Hyg.] Abas³ – ? [Eust.]
Aeolus²-? Phoenix²-Perimede³ Adonis-Aphrodite Elatus²-Hippeia Leucippus³-? Hecaton-?
{Poseidon} :– Arne¹ [Diod. Sic.] :– Ascra [Heg.] :– Astypalaea [Apollod.] :– Beroe¹ [Non.] :– Caenis/Caeneus¹ – ? [Cat. Wom.] :– Calchinia [Paus.] :– Calyce² [Hyg.] Canethus¹ [Ap. Rhod.] Chalcodon² – Alcyone⁷ [Eust.] [Apollod.]
Cragasus-? Laomedon¹-Strym(n)o
Aeolus³ [Diod. Sic.] Boeotus¹ [Diod. Sic.] 18c Oeoclus [Heg.] Ancaeus² [Paus.] 54c-d Phocus³ [Hyg.] Priasus¹ [Hyg.] Coronus³ – ? [Hom.] Peratus – ? [Paus.] Philonome – Cycnus² – Procleia [Paus.] [Paus.] 43c [Paus.] Elephenor [Hom.]
Aeolus¹-Enarete Telamon-Periboea² Atlas-Pleione Danaus¹-Crino
{Poseidon} :– Canace [Cat. Wom.] Caeneus² [Apollod.] Ajax¹ – Lyside [Steph. Byz.] [Steph. Byz.] Leonteus¹ [Hom.] Plemnaeus – ? [Paus.] {Poseidon} :– Celaeno¹ [Apollod.] :– Celaeno⁴ [Strab.] :– Cerebia [Tzetz.]
Aloeus¹ [Apollod.] 34a Epopeus¹ [Apollod.] 34b Hopleus¹ [Apollod.] Nireus¹ [Apollod.] Triop(a)s¹ [Apollod.] 34a Philaeus¹ [Herod.] Orthopolis – ? [Paus.] Eurypylus⁵ [Schol. Ap. Rhod.] Lycus⁷ [Hellan.] Nycteus² [Hyg.] Celaenus² [Strab.]
Zeus-Io Boreas-Oreithyia¹ Teiresias-? Almus-? Euenor¹-Leucippe⁶ Zeus-Leto
{Poseidon} :– Ceroessa [Steph. Byz.] :– Chione² [Apollod.] :– Chloris³ [Schol. Pind.] :– Chrysogeneia [Paus.] :– Cleito¹ [Plato] Leocritus¹ [Hom.] Apollo – Chrysorthe [Paus.] [Paus.] {Poseidon} :– Cleodora¹ – Cleopompus [Paus.] [Paus.]
Byzas – Phidaleia [Steph. Byz.] [Hesyc.] Strombus Eumolpus¹ [Apollod.] 13a Periclymenus² [Schol. Pind.] Chryses¹ [Paus.] 20d [5 sets of twins] [Plato] Coronus¹ [Paus.] 11b Parnassus [Paus.]
Asopus-Metope² Coroneus-? Cronus-Rhea Asopus-Metope² Tityus-? Minos I - Pasiphae¹ Endymion-Chromia
{Poseidon} :– Corcyra [Diod. Sic.] :– Coronis² [Ovid] :– Demeter [Apollod.] :– Diopatra [Ant. Lib.] :– Euboea³ [Hesyc.] :– Europe² [Ap. Rhod.] :– Euryale² [Cat. Wom.] :– Eurycyde [Paus.] :– Euryte² [Apollod.]
Amphitryon-Alcmene Ares-Aglaurus²
Phaeax¹ [Diod. Sic.] Arion¹ [Apollod.] Despoena [Paus.] Tychius [Hesyc.] Lamache – Euphemus¹ – Laonome¹ [Schol. Pind.] [Ap. Rhod.] [Tzetz. Lyc.] Orion [Cat. Wom.] 53c-d Eleius¹ [Paus.] Halirrhothius¹ – Alcippe¹ [Apollod.] [Apollod.]
Chaos Pontus-Gaea Athamas¹-Nephele² Mestor¹-Lysidice¹
{Poseidon} :– Gaea [Serv.] :– Halia¹ [Diod. Sic.] :– Helle [Hyg.] :– Hippothoe¹ [Apollod.] Leucophanes [Schol. Pind.]
Charybdis [Serv.] [6 sons] [Diod. Sic.] Rhode¹ [Diod. Sic.] 14a-b Paeon⁴ [Hyg.] Taphius [Apollod.] 58d Teleboas³ [Athen.]
Triop(a)s¹-Hiscilla Pelasgus²-? Orus¹-? Epaphus¹-Memphis¹ Epaphus¹-Memphis¹ Phorcus¹-Ceto¹ Deucalion¹-Pyrrha¹
{Poseidon} :– Iphimedeia [Hom.] :– Larissa¹ [Dion. Hal.] :– Leis [Paus.] :– Libya¹ [Apollod.] :– Lysianassa¹ [Apollod.] :– Medusa¹ [Hes.] :– Melantho¹ [Ovid] :– Melia² [Ap. Rhod.]
(Aloadae) Granicus-?
Ephialtes² [Hom.] Otus¹ [Hom.] Achaeus² [Dion. Hal.] Pelasgus³ [Dion. Hal.] 61d Phthius¹ [Dion. Hal.] Althaepus [Paus.] Agenor¹ [Apollod.] 53b-56a Belus¹ [Apollod.] 57a-59a Lelex² [Paus.] 59a Busiris¹ – ? [Apollod.] Pygmalion³ – ? [Hyg.] Chrysaor [Hes.] 2b Pegasus [Hes.] Amycus¹ [Apollod.] Mygdon(us)¹ – Alexirhoe [Apollod.] [Ps.-Plut.]
Alpheius-Telegone Epidamnus-? Erysichthon¹-?
{Poseidon} :– Melantheia² [Plut.] :– Melissa⁴ [Steph. Byz.] :– Mestra [Cat. Wom.] :– Mideia¹ [Paus.] Amphidamas² [Pher.] Thrasius¹ [Hyg.] Sagaris¹ [Ps.-Plut.]
Eirene² [Plut.] Dyrrachius [Steph. Byz.] Eurypylus² [Cat. Wom.] 34c Aspledon¹ [Paus.]

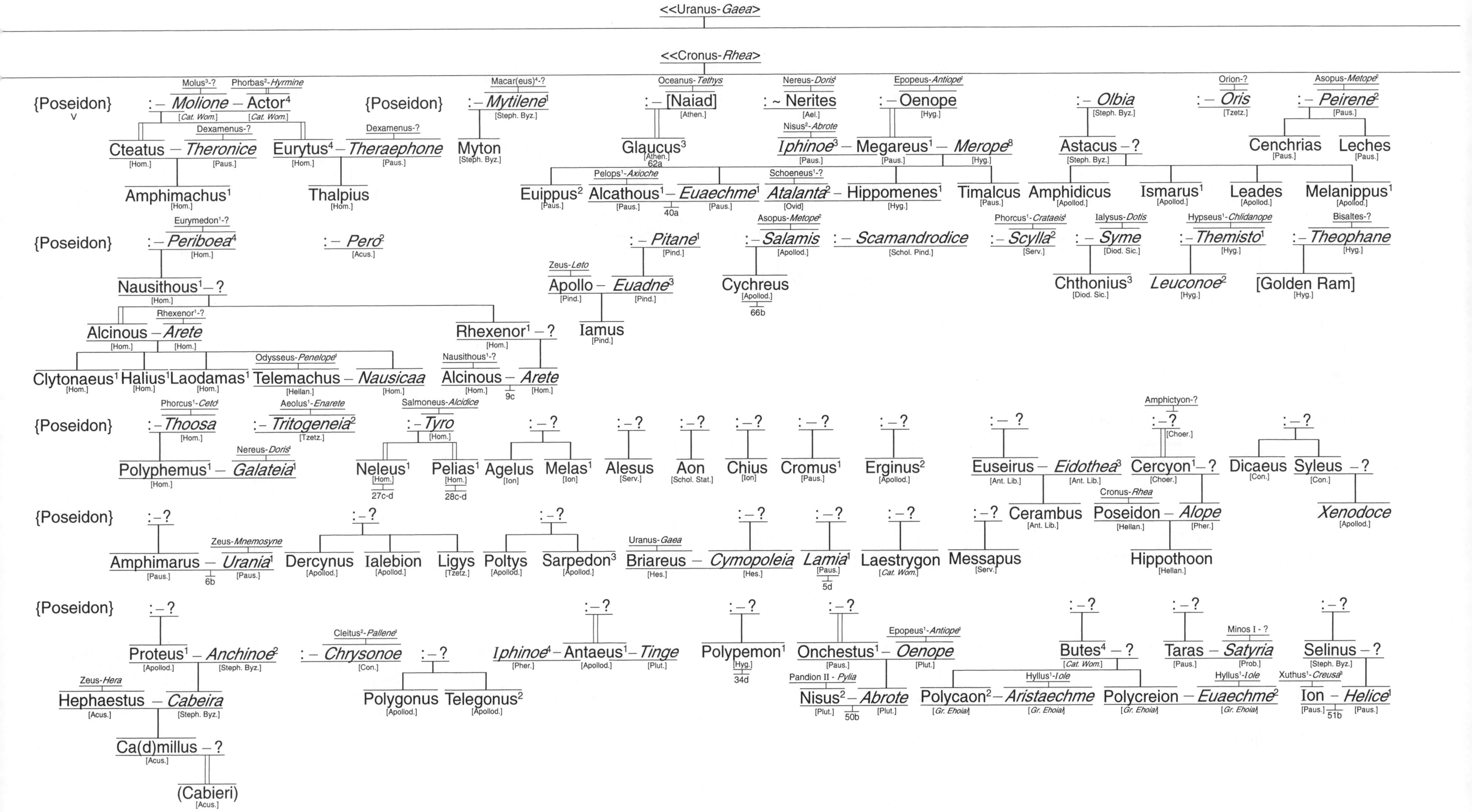

<<Uranus-Gaea>
<<Cronus-Rhea>
{Poseidon}
Molus[3]-? Phorbas[2]-Hyrmine
:– Molione – Actor[4]
[Cat. Wom.] [Cat. Wom.]
Dexamenus-?
Cteatus – Theronice
[Hom.] [Paus.]
Dexamenus-?
Eurytus[4] – Theraephone
[Hom.] [Paus.]
Amphimachus[1]
[Hom.]
Thalpius
[Hom.]
{Poseidon}
Macar(eus)[4]-?
:– Mytilene[1]
[Steph. Byz.]
Myton
[Steph. Byz.]
Oceanus-Tethys
:– [Naiad]
[Athen.]
Glaucus[3]
[Athen.]
62a
Nereus-Doris[1]
: ~ Nerites
[Ael.]
Nisus[2]-Abrote
Iphinoe[3] – Megareus[1] – Merope[8]
[Paus.] [Paus.] [Hyg.]
Epopeus-Antiope[1]
:– Oenope
[Hyg.]
:– Olbia
[Steph. Byz.]
Astacus – ?
[Steph. Byz.]
Orion-?
:– Oris
[Tzetz.]
Asopus-Metope[2]
:– Peirene[2]
[Paus.]
Cenchrias
[Paus.]
Leches
[Paus.]
Euippus[2]
[Paus.]
Pelops[1]-Axioche
Alcathous[1] – Euaechme[1]
[Paus.] [Paus.]
40a
Schoeneus[1]-?
Atalanta[2] – Hippomenes[1]
[Ovid] [Hyg.]
Timalcus
[Paus.]
Amphidicus
[Apollod.]
Ismarus[1]
[Apollod.]
Leades
[Apollod.]
Melanippus[1]
[Apollod.]
{Poseidon}
Eurymedon[1]-?
:– Periboea[4]
[Hom.]
:– Pero[2]
[Acus.]
Nausithous[1] – ?
[Hom.]
:– Pitane[1]
[Pind.]
Zeus-Leto
Apollo – Euadne[3]
[Pind.] [Pind.]
Iamus
[Pind.]
Asopus-Metope[2]
:– Salamis
[Apollod.]
Cychreus
[Apollod.]
66b
:– Scamandrodice
[Schol. Pind.]
Phorcus[1]-Crataeis[1]
:– Scylla[2]
[Serv.]
Ialysus-Dotis
:– Syme
[Diod. Sic.]
Chthonius[3]
[Diod. Sic.]
Hypseus[1]-Chlidanope
:– Themisto[1]
[Hyg.]
Leuconoe[2]
[Hyg.]
Bisaltes-?
:– Theophane
[Hyg.]
[Golden Ram]
[Hyg.]
Rhexenor[1]-?
Alcinous – Arete
[Hom.] [Hom.]
Rhexenor[1] – ?
[Hom.]
Clytonaeus[1]
[Hom.]
Halius[1]
[Hom.]
Laodamas[1]
[Hom.]
Odysseus-Penelope[1]
Telemachus – Nausicaa
[Hellan.] [Hom.]
Nausithous[1]-?
Alcinous – Arete
[Hom.] [Hom.]
9c
{Poseidon}
Phorcus[1]-Ceto[1]
:– Thoosa
[Hom.]
Polyphemus[1] – Galateia[1]
[Hom.]
Nereus-Doris[1]
Aeolus[1]-Enarete
:– Tritogeneia[2]
[Tzetz.]
Salmoneus-Alcidice
:– Tyro
[Hom.]
Neleus[1]
[Hom.]
27c-d
Pelias[1]
[Hom.]
28c-d
:– ?
Agelus
[Ion]
Melas[1]
[Ion]
:– ?
Alesus
[Serv.]
:– ?
Aon
[Schol. Stat.]
:– ?
Chius
[Ion]
:– ?
Cromus[1]
[Paus.]
:– ?
Erginus[2]
[Apollod.]
:– ?
Euseirus – Eidothea[3]
[Ant. Lib.] [Ant. Lib.]
Cerambus
[Ant. Lib.]
Amphictyon-?
:– ?
[Choer.]
Cercyon[1] – ?
[Choer.]
Cronus-Rhea
Poseidon – Alope
[Hellan.] [Pher.]
Hippothoon
[Hellan.]
:– ?
Dicaeus
[Con.]
Syleus – ?
[Con.]
Xenodoce
[Apollod.]
{Poseidon}
:– ?
Amphimarus – Urania[1]
[Paus.] [Paus.]
Zeus-Mnemosyne
6b
:– ?
Dercynus
[Apollod.]
Ialebion
[Apollod.]
Ligys
[Tzetz.]
:– ?
Poltys
[Apollod.]
Sarpedon[3]
[Apollod.]
Uranus-Gaea
Briareus – Cymopoleia
[Hes.] [Hes.]
:– ?
Lamia[1]
[Paus.]
5d
:– ?
Laestrygon
[Cat. Wom.]
:– ?
Messapus
[Serv.]
{Poseidon}
:– ?
Proteus[1] – Anchinoe[2]
[Apollod.] [Steph. Byz.]
Zeus-Hera
Hephaestus – Cabeira
[Acus.] [Steph. Byz.]
Ca(d)millus – ?
[Acus.]
(Cabieri)
[Acus.]
Cleitus[2]-Pallene[1]
:– Chrysonoe
[Con.]
:– ?
Polygonus
[Apollod.]
Telegonus[2]
[Apollod.]
:– ?
Iphinoe[4] – Antaeus[1] – Tinge
[Pher.] [Apollod.] [Plut.]
:– ?
Polypemon[1]
[Hyg.]
34d
:– ?
Onchestus[1] – Oenope
[Paus.] [Plut.]
Epopeus[1]-Antiope[1]
Pandion II - Pylia
Nisus[2] – Abrote
[Plut.] [Plut.]
50b
:– ?
Butes[4] – ?
[Cat. Wom.]
Hyllus[1]-Iole
Polycaon[2] – Aristaechme
[Gr. Ehoiai] [Gr. Ehoiai]
Polycreion – Euaechme[2]
[Gr. Ehoiai] [Gr. Ehoiai]
Hyllus[1]-Iole
:– ?
Taras – Satyria
[Paus.] [Prob.]
Minos I - ?
:– ?
Selinus – ?
[Steph. Byz.]
Xuthus[1]-Creusa[3]
Ion – Helice[1]
[Paus.] [Paus.]
51b

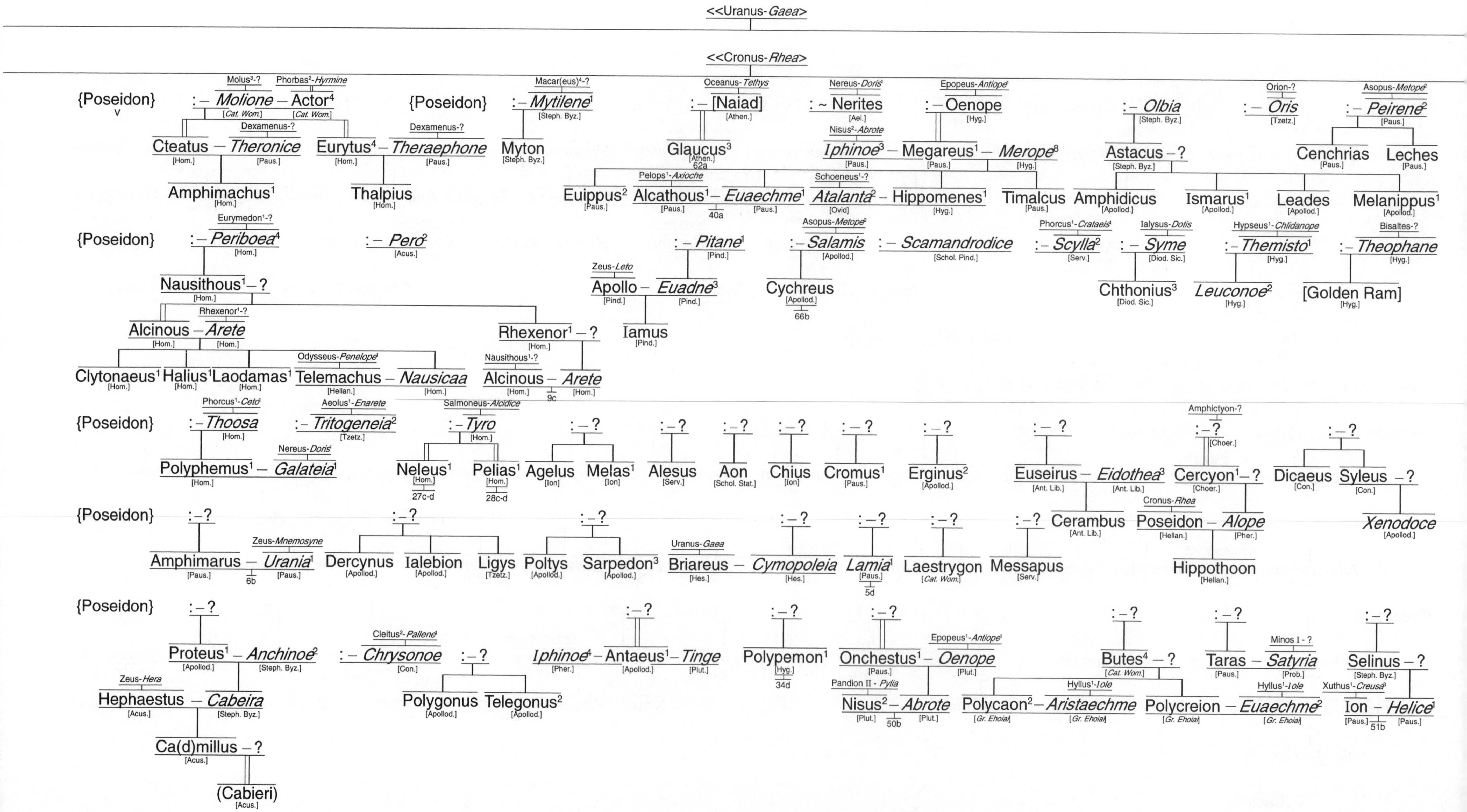

<<Uranus-Gaea>
<<Cronus-Rhea>
{Poseidon}
Molus³-?
Phorbas²-Hyrmine
:– Molione – Actor⁴
[Cat. Wom.]
[Cat. Wom.]
Dexamenus-?
Cteatus – Theronice
[Hom.]
[Paus.]
Eurytus⁴ – Theraephone
[Hom.]
[Paus.]
Amphimachus¹
[Hom.]
Thalpius
[Hom.]
{Poseidon}
Macar(eus)⁴-?
:– Mytilene¹
[Steph. Byz.]
Myton
[Steph. Byz.]
Oceanus-Tethys
:– [Naiad]
[Athen.]
Glaucus³
[Athen.]
62a
Nereus-Doris⁴
:~ Nerites
[Ael.]
Nisus²-Abrote
Iphinoe³ – Megareus¹ – Merope⁸
[Paus.]
[Paus.]
[Hyg.]
Epopeus-Antiope¹
:– Oenope
[Hyg.]
:– Olbia
[Steph. Byz.]
Astacus – ?
[Steph. Byz.]
Orion-?
:– Oris
[Tzetz.]
Asopus-Metope²
:– Peirene²
[Paus.]
Cenchrias
[Paus.]
Leches
[Paus.]
Pelops¹-Axioche
Schoeneus¹-?
Euippus²
[Paus.]
Alcathous¹ – Euaechme¹
[Paus.]
[Paus.]
40a
Atalanta² – Hippomenes¹
[Ovid]
[Hyg.]
Timalcus
[Paus.]
Amphidicus
[Apollod.]
Ismarus¹
[Apollod.]
Leades
[Apollod.]
Melanippus¹
[Apollod.]
{Poseidon}
Eurymedon¹-?
:– Periboea⁴
[Hom.]
:– Pero²
[Acus.]
:– Pitane¹
[Pind.]
Asopus-Metope²
:– Salamis
[Apollod.]
:– Scamandrodice
[Schol. Pind.]
Phorcus¹-Crataeis⁴
:– Scylla²
[Serv.]
Ialysus-Dotis
:– Syme
[Diod. Sic.]
Hypseus¹-Chlidanope
:– Themisto¹
[Hyg.]
Bisaltes-?
:– Theophane
[Hyg.]
Zeus-Leto
Apollo – Euadne³
[Pind.]
[Pind.]
Iamus
[Pind.]
Cychreus
[Apollod.]
66b
Chthonius³
[Diod. Sic.]
Leuconoe²
[Hyg.]
[Golden Ram]
[Hyg.]
Nausithous¹ – ?
[Hom.]
Rhexenor¹-?
Alcinous – Arete
[Hom.]
[Hom.]
Rhexenor¹ – ?
[Hom.]
Nausithous¹-?
Odysseus-Penelope¹
Clytonaeus¹
[Hom.]
Halius¹
[Hom.]
Laodamas¹
[Hom.]
Telemachus – Nausicaa
[Hellan.]
[Hom.]
Alcinous – Arete
[Hom.]
[Hom.]
9c
{Poseidon}
Phorcus¹-Ceto¹
:– Thoosa
[Hom.]
Aeolus¹-Enarete
:– Tritogeneia²
[Tzetz.]
Salmoneus-Alcidice
:– Tyro
[Hom.]
Nereus-Doris⁴
Polyphemus¹ – Galateia¹
[Hom.]
Neleus¹
[Hom.]
27c-d
Pelias¹
[Hom.]
28c-d
:– ?
Agelus
[Ion]
Melas¹
[Ion]
:– ?
Alesus
[Serv.]
:– ?
Aon
[Schol. Stat.]
:– ?
Chius
[Ion]
:– ?
Cromus¹
[Paus.]
:– ?
Erginus²
[Apollod.]
:– ?
Euseirus – Eidothea³
[Ant. Lib.]
[Ant. Lib.]
Cerambus
[Ant. Lib.]
Amphictyon-?
:– ?
[Choer.]
Cercyon¹ – ?
[Choer.]
Cronus-Rhea
Poseidon – Alope
[Hellan.]
[Pher.]
Hippothoon
[Hellan.]
:– ?
Dicaeus
[Con.]
Syleus – ?
[Con.]
Xenodoce
[Apollod.]
{Poseidon}
:– ?
Zeus-Mnemosyne
Amphimarus – Urania¹
[Paus.]
6b
[Paus.]
:– ?
Dercynus
[Apollod.]
Ialebion
[Apollod.]
Ligys
[Tzetz.]
:– ?
Poltys
[Apollod.]
Sarpedon³
[Apollod.]
Uranus-Gaea
Briareus – Cymopoleia
[Hes.]
[Hes.]
:– ?
:– ?
Lamia¹
[Paus.]
5d
:– ?
Laestrygon
[Cat. Wom.]
:– ?
Messapus
[Serv.]
{Poseidon}
:– ?
Proteus¹ – Anchinoe²
[Apollod.]
[Steph. Byz.]
Zeus-Hera
Hephaestus – Cabeira
[Acus.]
[Steph. Byz.]
Ca(d)millus – ?
[Acus.]
(Cabieri)
[Acus.]
Cleitus²-Pallene¹
:– Chrysonoe
[Con.]
:– ?
Polygonus
[Apollod.]
Telegonus²
[Apollod.]
:– ?
Iphinoe⁴ – Antaeus¹ – Tinge
[Pher.]
[Apollod.]
[Plut.]
:– ?
Polypemon¹
[Hyg.]
34d
:– ?
Epopeus¹-Antiope¹
Onchestus¹ – Oenope
[Paus.]
[Plut.]
Pandion II - Pylia
Nisus² – Abrote
[Plut.]
50b
[Plut.]
:– ?
Butes⁴ – ?
[Cat. Wom.]
Hyllus¹-Iole
Polycaon² – Aristaechme
[Gr. Ehoiai]
[Gr. Ehoiai]
Polycreion – Euaechme²
[Gr. Ehoiai]
[Gr. Ehoiai]
:– ?
Minos I - ?
Taras – Satyria
[Paus.]
[Prob.]
Hyllus¹-Iole
:– ?
Selinus – ?
[Steph. Byz.]
Xuthus¹-Creusa³
Ion – Helice¹
[Paus.]
51b
[Paus.]

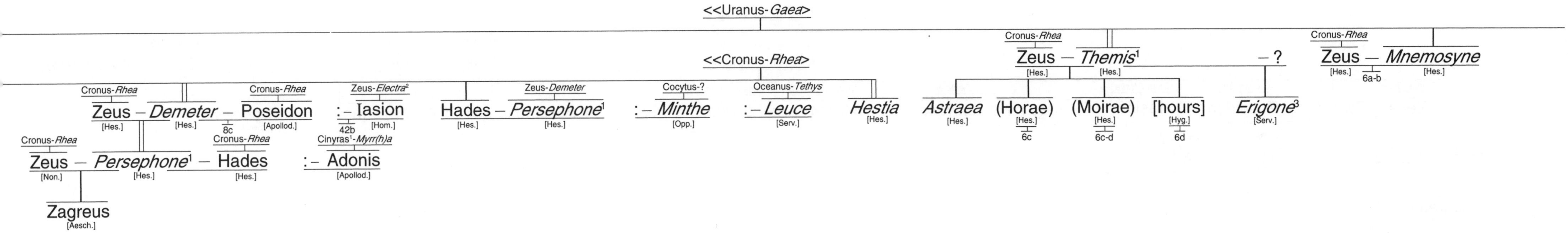

<<Uranus-Gaea>
<<Cronus-Rhea>
Cronus-Rhea
Zeus – Demeter – Poseidon
[Hes.]
[Hes.]
8c
[Apollod.]
Cronus-Rhea
Zeus – Persephone[1] – Hades
[Non.]
[Hes.]
Cronus-Rhea
[Hes.]
Zagreus
[Aesch.]
Zeus-Electra[2]
:– Iasion
42b
[Hom.]
Cinyras[1]-Myrr(h)a
:– Adonis
[Apollod.]
Hades – Persephone[1]
[Hes.]
Zeus-Demeter
[Hes.]
Cocytus-?
:– Minthe
[Opp.]
Oceanus-Tethys
:– Leuce
[Serv.]
Hestia
[Hes.]
Cronus-Rhea
Zeus – Themis[1]
[Hes.]
[Hes.]
– ?
Astraea
[Hes.]
(Horae)
[Hes.]
6c
(Moirae)
[Hes.]
6c-d
[hours]
[Hyg.]
6d
Erigone[3]
[Serv.]
Cronus-Rhea
Zeus – Mnemosyne
[Hes.]
6a-b
[Hes.]

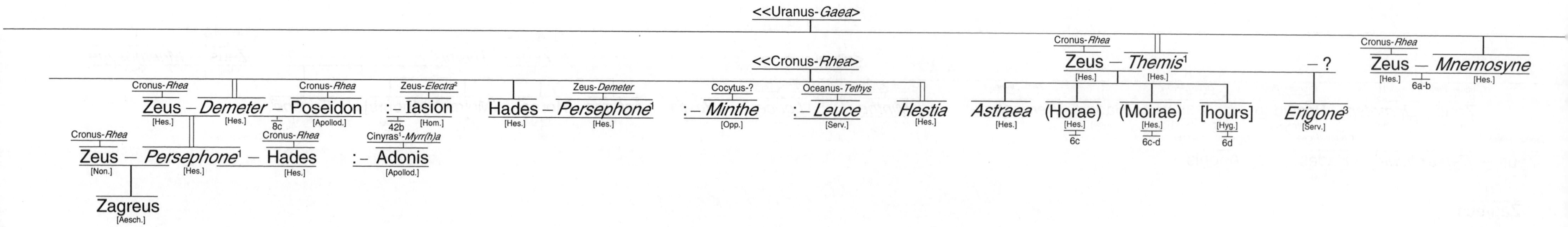
<<Uranus-Gaea>
<<Cronus-Rhea>
Cronus-Rhea
Zeus – Demeter – Poseidon
[Hes.] [Hes.] 8c [Apollod.]
Zeus-Electra2
: – Iasion
42b [Hom.]
Hades – Persephone1
[Hes.] [Hes.]
Zeus-Demeter
Cocytus-?
: – Minthe
[Opp.]
Oceanus-Tethys
: – Leuce
[Serv.]
Hestia
[Hes.]
Cronus-Rhea
Zeus – Persephone1 – Hades
[Non.] [Hes.] [Hes.]
Zagreus
[Aesch.]
Cinyras1-Myrr(h)a
: – Adonis
[Apollod.]
Zeus – Themis1
[Hes.] [Hes.]
Astraea
[Hes.]
(Horae)
[Hes.]
6c
(Moirae)
[Hes.]
6c-d
[hours]
[Hyg.]
6d
– ?
Erigone3
[Serv.]
Zeus – Mnemosyne
[Hes.] 6a-b [Hes.]

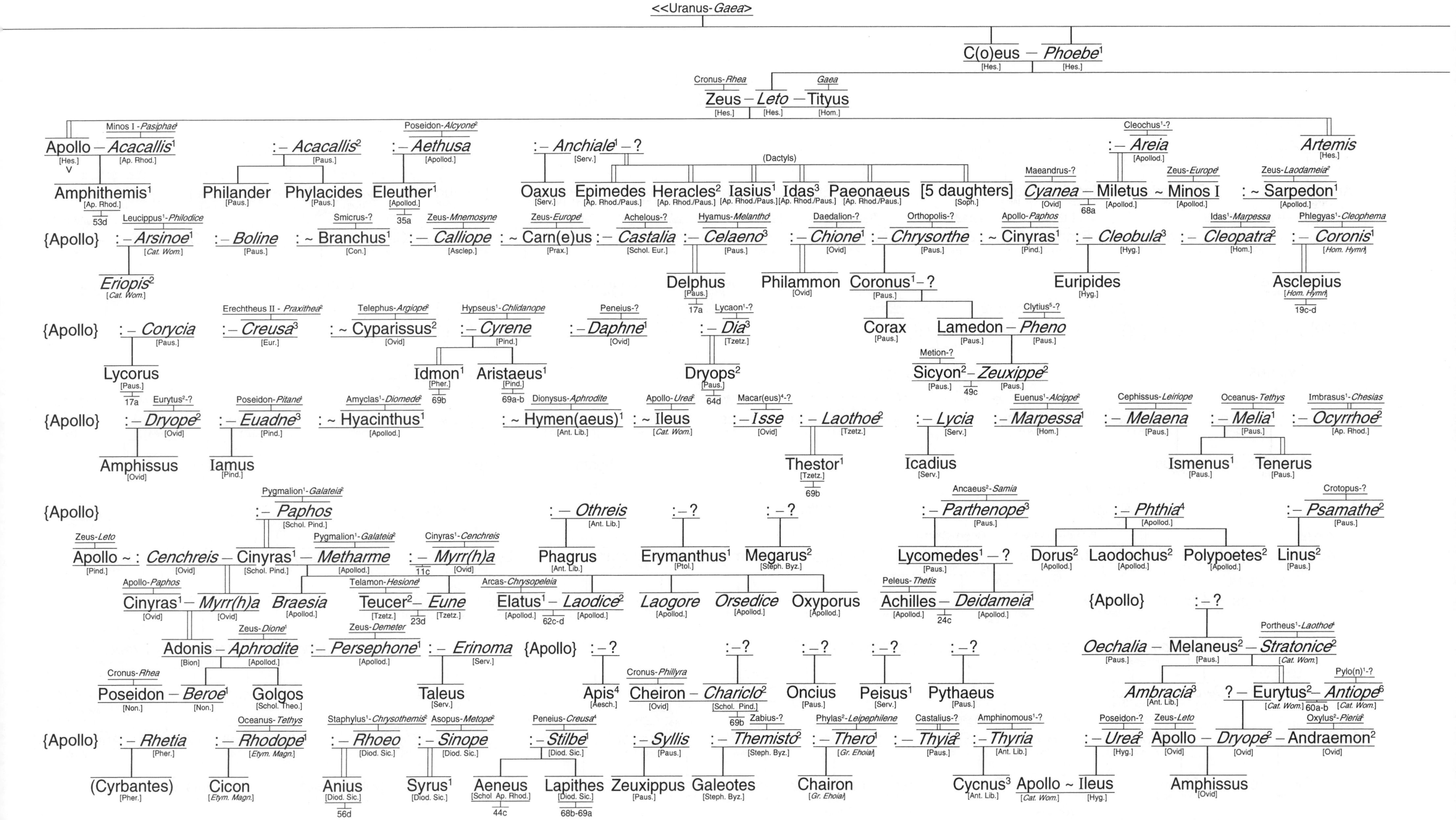

<<Uranus-*Gaea*>
C(o)eus – *Phoebe*[1]
[Hes.] [Hes.]
Cronus-*Rhea* *Gaea*
Zeus – *Leto* – Tityus
[Hes.] [Hes.] [Hom.]
Minos I -*Pasiphae*
Apollo – *Acacallis*[1]
[Hes.] [Ap. Rhod.]
V
Amphithemis[1]
[Ap. Rhod.]
53d
:– *Acacallis*[2]
[Paus.]
Philander [Paus.]
Phylacides [Paus.]
Poseidon-*Alcyone*
:– *Aethusa*
[Apollod.]
Eleuther[1]
[Apollod.]
35a
:– *Anchiale*[1] – ?
[Serv.]
(Dactyls)
Oaxus [Serv.]
Epimedes [Ap. Rhod./Paus.]
Heracles[2] [Ap. Rhod./Paus.]
Iasius[1] [Ap. Rhod./Paus.]
Idas[3] [Ap. Rhod./Paus.]
Paeonaeus [Ap. Rhod./Paus.]
[5 daughters] [Soph.]
Cleochus[1]-?
:– *Areia*
[Apollod.]
Maeandrus-?
Cyanea – Miletus ~ Minos I
[Ovid] [Apollod.] [Apollod.]
68a
Zeus-*Europe*
Artemis
[Hes.]
Zeus-*Laodameia*
: ~ Sarpedon[1]
[Apollod.]
{Apollo}
Leucippus[1]-*Philodice*
:– *Arsinoe*[1]
[*Cat. Wom.*]
Eriopis[2]
[*Cat. Wom.*]
:– *Boline*
[Paus.]
Smicrus-?
: ~ Branchus[1]
[Con.]
Zeus-*Mnemosyne*
:– *Calliope*
[Asclep.]
Zeus-*Europe*
: ~ Carn(e)us
[Prax.]
Achelous-?
:– *Castalia*
[Schol. Eur.]
Hyamus-*Melantho*
:– *Celaeno*[3]
[Paus.]
Delphus
[Paus.]
17a
Daedalion-?
:– *Chione*[1]
[Ovid]
Philammon
[Ovid]
Orthopolis-?
:– *Chrysorthe*
[Paus.]
Coronus[1] – ?
[Paus.]
Apollo-*Paphos*
: ~ Cinyras[1]
[Pind.]
:– *Cleobula*[3]
[Hyg.]
Euripides
[Hyg.]
Idas[1]-*Marpessa*
:– *Cleopatra*[2]
[Hom.]
Phlegyas[1]-*Cleophema*
:– *Coronis*[1]
[*Hom. Hymn*]
Asclepius
[*Hom. Hymn*]
19c-d
{Apollo}
:– *Corycia*
[Paus.]
Lycorus
[Paus.]
17a
Erechtheus II - *Praxithea*
:– *Creusa*[3]
[Eur.]
Telephus-*Argiope*
: ~ Cyparissus[2]
[Ovid]
Hypseus[1]-*Chlidanope*
:– *Cyrene*
[Pind.]
Idmon[1]
[Pher.]
69b
Aristaeus[1]
[Pind.]
69a-b
Peneius-?
:– *Daphne*[1]
[Ovid]
Lycaon[1]-?
:– *Dia*[3]
[Tzetz.]
Dryops[2]
[Paus.]
64d
Corax
[Paus.]
Clytius[5]-?
Lamedon – *Pheno*
[Paus.] [Paus.]
Metion-?
Sicyon[2] – *Zeuxippe*[2]
[Paus.] [Paus.]
49c
{Apollo}
Eurytus[2]-?
:– *Dryope*[2]
[Ovid]
Amphissus
[Ovid]
Poseidon-*Pitane*
:– *Euadne*[3]
[Pind.]
Iamus
[Pind.]
Amyclas[1]-*Diomede*
: ~ Hyacinthus[1]
[Apollod.]
Dionysus-*Aphrodite*
: ~ Hymen(aeus)[1]
[Ant. Lib.]
Apollo-*Urea*
: ~ Ileus
[*Cat. Wom.*]
Macar(eus)[4]-?
:– *Isse*
[Ovid]
:– *Laothoe*[2]
[Tzetz.]
Thestor[1]
[Tzetz.]
69b
:– *Lycia*
[Serv.]
Icadius
[Serv.]
Euenus[1]-*Alcippe*
:– *Marpessa*[1]
[Hom.]
Cephissus-*Leiriope*
:– *Melaena*
[Paus.]
Oceanus-*Tethys*
:– *Melia*[1]
[Paus.]
Ismenus[1]
[Paus.]
Tenerus
[Paus.]
Imbrasus[1]-*Chesias*
:– *Ocyrrhoe*[2]
[Ap. Rhod.]
{Apollo}
Pygmalion[1]-*Galateia*
:– *Paphos*
[Schol. Pind.]
:– *Othreis*
[Ant. Lib.]
Phagrus
[Ant. Lib.]
:– ?
Erymanthus[1]
[Ptol.]
:– ?
Megarus[2]
[Steph. Byz.]
Ancaeus[2]-*Samia*
:– *Parthenope*[3]
[Paus.]
Lycomedes[1] – ?
[Paus.]
:– *Phthia*[4]
[Apollod.]
Dorus[2]
[Apollod.]
Laodochus[2]
[Apollod.]
Polypoetes[2]
[Apollod.]
Crotopus-?
:– *Psamathe*[2]
[Paus.]
Linus[2]
[Paus.]
Zeus-*Leto*
Apollo ~ : *Cenchreis* – Cinyras[1] – *Metharme*
[Pind.] [Ovid] [Schol. Pind.] [Apollod.]
Pygmalion[1]-*Galateia*
Cinyras[1]-*Cenchreis*
:– *Myrr(h)a*
11c [Ovid]
Apollo-*Paphos*
Cinyras[1] – *Myrr(h)a*
[Ovid] [Ovid]
Braesia
[Apollod.]
Telamon-*Hesione*
Teucer[2] – *Eune*
[Tzetz.] [Tzetz.]
23d
Arcas-*Chrysopeleia*
Elatus[1] – *Laodice*[2]
[Apollod.] [Apollod.]
62c-d
Laogore
[Apollod.]
Orsedice
[Apollod.]
Oxyporus
[Apollod.]
Peleus-*Thetis*
Achilles – *Deidameia*[1]
[Apollod.] [Apollod.]
24c
{Apollo}
:– ?
Zeus-*Dione*
Adonis – *Aphrodite*
[Bion] [Apollod.]
Zeus-*Demeter*
:– *Persephone*[1]
[Apollod.]
:– *Erinoma*
[Serv.]
Taleus
[Serv.]
{Apollo}
:– ?
Apis[4]
[Aesch.]
:– ?
Cronus-*Phillyra*
Cheiron – *Chariclo*[2]
[Ovid] [Schol. Pind.]
69b
:– ?
Oncius
[Paus.]
:– ?
Peisus[1]
[Serv.]
:– ?
Pythaeus
[Paus.]
Portheus[1]-*Laothoe*
Oechalia – Melaneus[2] – *Stratonice*[2]
[Paus.] [Paus.] [*Cat. Wom.*]
Ambracia[3]
[Ant. Lib.]
Pylo(n)[1]-?
? – Eurytus[2] – *Antiope*[6]
[*Cat. Wom.*] 60a-b [*Cat. Wom.*]
Cronus-*Rhea*
Poseidon – *Beroe*[1]
[Non.] [Non.]
Golgos
[Schol. Theo.]
{Apollo}
:– *Rhetia*
[Pher.]
(Cyrbantes)
[Pher.]
Oceanus-*Tethys*
:– *Rhodope*[1]
[*Etym. Magn.*]
Cicon
[*Etym. Magn.*]
Staphylus[1]-*Chrysothemis*
:– *Rhoeo*
[Diod. Sic.]
Anius
[Diod. Sic.]
56d
Asopus-*Metope*
:– *Sinope*
[Diod. Sic.]
Syrus[1]
[Diod. Sic.]
Peneius-*Creusa*
:– *Stilbe*[1]
[Diod. Sic.]
Aeneus
[Schol. Ap. Rhod.]
44c
Lapithes
[Diod. Sic.]
68b-69a
:– *Syllis*
[Paus.]
Zeuxippus
[Paus.]
Zabius-?
:– *Themisto*[2]
[Steph. Byz.]
Galeotes
[Steph. Byz.]
Phylas[2]-*Leipephilene*
:– *Thero*[1]
[*Gr. Ehoiai*]
Chairon
[*Gr. Ehoiai*]
Castalius-?
:– *Thyia*[2]
[Paus.]
Amphinomous[1]-?
:– *Thyria*
[Ant. Lib.]
Cycnus[3]
[Ant. Lib.]
Apollo ~ Ileus
[*Cat. Wom.*] [Hyg.]
Poseidon-?
:– *Urea*[2]
[Hyg.]
Zeus-*Leto*
Apollo – *Dryope*[2] – Andraemon[2]
[Ovid] [Ovid] [Ovid]
Oxylus[2]-*Pieria*
Amphissus
[Ovid]

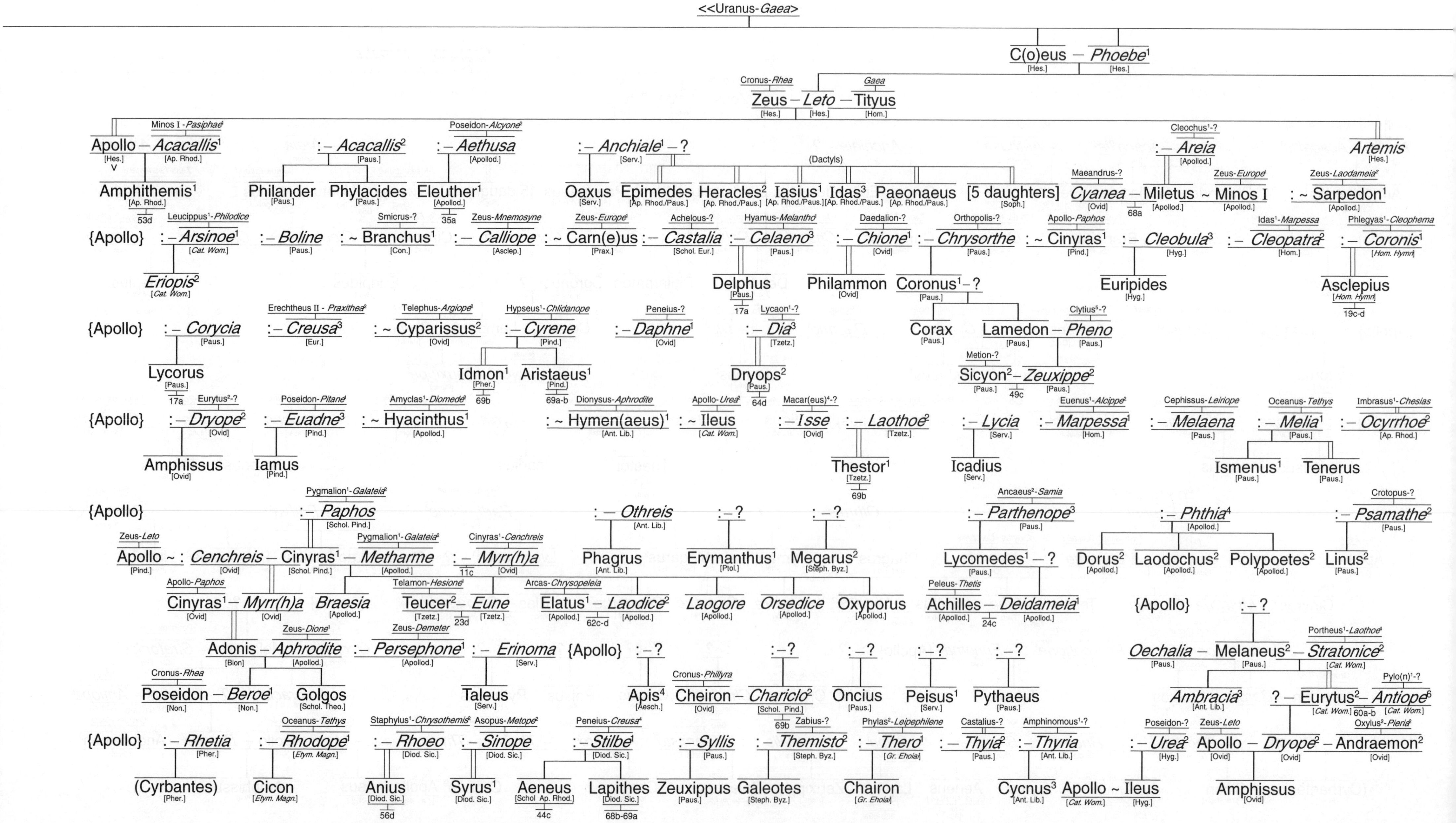

<<Uranus-Gaea>
C(o)eus – Phoebe[1]
[Hes.] [Hes.]
Cronus-Rhea
Gaea
Zeus – Leto – Tityus
[Hes.] [Hes.] [Hom.]
Minos I -Pasiphae[1]
Apollo – Acacallis[1]
[Hes.] [Ap. Rhod.]
:– Acacallis[2]
[Paus.]
Poseidon-Alcyone[2]
:– Aethusa
[Apollod.]
:– Anchiale[1] – ?
[Serv.]
(Dactyls)
Cleochus[1]-?
:– Areia
[Apollod.]
Artemis
[Hes.]
Amphithemis[1]
[Ap. Rhod.]
53d
Philander
[Paus.]
Phylacides
[Paus.]
Eleuther[1]
[Apollod.]
35a
Oaxus
[Serv.]
Epimedes
[Ap. Rhod./Paus.]
Heracles[2]
[Ap. Rhod./Paus.]
Iasius[1]
[Ap. Rhod./Paus.]
Idas[3]
[Ap. Rhod./Paus.]
Paeonaeus
[Ap. Rhod./Paus.]
[5 daughters]
[Soph.]
Maeandrus-?
Cyanea – Miletus ~ Minos I
[Ovid] [Apollod.] [Apollod.]
68a
Zeus-Europe[1]
Zeus-Laodameia[2]
:~ Sarpedon[1]
[Apollod.]
{Apollo}
Leucippus[1]-Philodice
:– Arsinoe[1]
[Cat. Wom.]
:– Boline
[Paus.]
Smicrus-?
:~ Branchus[1]
[Con.]
Zeus-Mnemosyne
:– Calliope
[Asclep.]
Zeus-Europe[1]
:~ Carn(e)us
[Prax.]
Achelous-?
:– Castalia
[Schol. Eur.]
Hyamus-Melantho[1]
:– Celaeno[3]
[Paus.]
Daedalion-?
:– Chione[1]
[Ovid]
Orthopolis-?
:– Chrysorthe
[Paus.]
Apollo-Paphos
:~ Cinyras[1]
[Pind.]
:– Cleobula[3]
[Hyg.]
Idas[1]-Marpessa
:– Cleopatra[2]
[Hom.]
Phlegyas[1]-Cleophema
:– Coronis[1]
[Hom. Hymn]
Eriopis[2]
[Cat. Wom.]
Delphus
[Paus.]
17a
Philammon
[Ovid]
Coronus[1] – ?
[Paus.]
Euripides
[Hyg.]
Asclepius
[Hom. Hymn]
19c-d
{Apollo}
:– Corycia
[Paus.]
Erechtheus II - Praxithea[2]
:– Creusa[3]
[Eur.]
Telephus-Argiope[2]
:~ Cyparissus[2]
[Ovid]
Hypseus[1]-Chlidanope
:– Cyrene
[Pind.]
Peneius-?
:– Daphne[1]
[Ovid]
Lycaon[1]-?
:– Dia[3]
[Tzetz.]
Corax
[Paus.]
Lamedon – Pheno
[Paus.] [Paus.]
Clytius[5]-?
Lycorus
[Paus.]
17a
Idmon[1]
[Pher.]
69b
Aristaeus[1]
[Pind.]
69a-b
Dryops[2]
[Paus.]
64d
Metion-?
Sicyon[2] – Zeuxippe[2]
[Paus.] [Paus.]
49c
{Apollo}
Eurytus[2]-?
:– Dryope[2]
[Ovid]
Poseidon-Pitane[1]
:– Euadne[3]
[Pind.]
Amyclas[1]-Diomede[2]
:~ Hyacinthus[1]
[Apollod.]
Dionysus-Aphrodite
:~ Hymen(aeus)[1]
[Ant. Lib.]
Apollo-Urea[2]
:~ Ileus
[Cat. Wom.]
Macar(eus)[4]-?
:– Isse
[Ovid]
:– Laothoe[2]
[Tzetz.]
:– Lycia
[Serv.]
Euenus[1]-Alcippe[2]
:– Marpessa[1]
[Hom.]
Cephissus-Leiriope
:– Melaena
[Paus.]
Oceanus-Tethys
:– Melia[1]
[Paus.]
Imbrasus[1]-Chesias
:– Ocyrrhoe[2]
[Ap. Rhod.]
Amphissus
[Ovid]
Iamus
[Pind.]
Thestor[1]
[Tzetz.]
69b
Icadius
[Serv.]
Ismenus[1]
[Paus.]
Tenerus
[Paus.]
{Apollo}
Pygmalion[1]-Galateia[2]
:– Paphos
[Schol. Pind.]
:– Othreis
[Ant. Lib.]
:– ?
:– ?
Ancaeus[2]-Samia
:– Parthenope[3]
[Paus.]
:– Phthia[4]
[Apollod.]
Crotopus-?
:– Psamathe[2]
[Paus.]
Zeus-Leto
Apollo ~ : Cenchreis – Cinyras[1] – Metharme
[Pind.] [Ovid] [Schol. Pind.] [Apollod.]
Pygmalion[1]-Galateia[2]
Cinyras[1]-Cenchreis
:– Myrr(h)a
11c [Ovid]
Phagrus
[Ant. Lib.]
Erymanthus[1]
[Ptol.]
Megarus[2]
[Steph. Byz.]
Lycomedes[1] – ?
[Paus.]
Dorus[2]
[Apollod.]
Laodochus[2]
[Apollod.]
Polypoetes[2]
[Apollod.]
Linus[2]
[Paus.]
Apollo-Paphos
Cinyras[1] – Myrr(h)a
[Ovid] [Ovid]
Braesia
[Apollod.]
Telamon-Hesione[1]
Teucer[2] – Eune
[Tzetz.] [Tzetz.]
23d
Arcas-Chrysopeleia
Elatus[1] – Laodice[2]
[Apollod.] [Apollod.]
62c-d
Laogore
[Apollod.]
Orsedice
[Apollod.]
Oxyporus
[Apollod.]
Peleus-Thetis
Achilles – Deidameia[1]
[Apollod.] [Apollod.]
24c
{Apollo}
:– ?
Zeus-Dione[1]
Adonis – Aphrodite
[Bion] [Apollod.]
Zeus-Demeter
:– Persephone[1]
[Apollod.]
:– Erinoma
[Serv.]
{Apollo}
:– ?
:– ?
:– ?
:– ?
:– ?
Portheus[1]-Laothoe[4]
Oechalia – Melaneus[2] – Stratonice[2]
[Paus.] [Paus.] [Cat. Wom.]
Cronus-Rhea
Poseidon – Beroe[1]
[Non.] [Non.]
Golgos
[Schol. Theo.]
Taleus
[Serv.]
Apis[4]
[Aesch.]
Cronus-Phillyra
Cheiron – Chariclo[2]
[Ovid] [Schol. Pind.]
69b
Oncius
[Paus.]
Peisus[1]
[Serv.]
Pythaeus
[Paus.]
Ambracia[3]
[Ant. Lib.]
Pylo(n)[1]-?
? – Eurytus[2] – Antiope[6]
[Cat. Wom.] 60a-b [Cat. Wom.]
{Apollo}
:– Rhetia
[Pher.]
Oceanus-Tethys
:– Rhodope[1]
[Etym. Magn.]
Staphylus[1]-Chrysothemis[2]
:– Rhoeo
[Diod. Sic.]
Asopus-Metope[2]
:– Sinope
[Diod. Sic.]
Peneius-Creusa[4]
:– Stilbe[1]
[Diod. Sic.]
:– Syllis
[Paus.]
Zabius-?
:– Themisto[2]
[Steph. Byz.]
Phylas[2]-Leipephilene
:– Thero[1]
[Gr. Ehoiai]
Castalius-?
:– Thyia[2]
[Paus.]
Amphinomous[1]-?
:– Thyria
[Ant. Lib.]
Poseidon-?
:– Urea[2]
[Hyg.]
Zeus-Leto
Apollo – Dryope[2] – Andraemon[2]
[Ovid] [Ovid] [Ovid]
Oxylus[2]-Pieria[2]
(Cyrbantes)
[Pher.]
Cicon
[Etym. Magn.]
Anius
[Diod. Sic.]
56d
Syrus[1]
[Diod. Sic.]
Aeneus
[Schol Ap. Rhod.]
44c
Lapithes
[Diod. Sic.]
68b-69a
Zeuxippus
[Paus.]
Galeotes
[Steph. Byz.]
Chairon
[Gr. Ehoiai]
Cycnus[3]
[Ant. Lib.]
Apollo ~ Ileus
[Cat. Wom.] [Hyg.]
Amphissus
[Ovid]

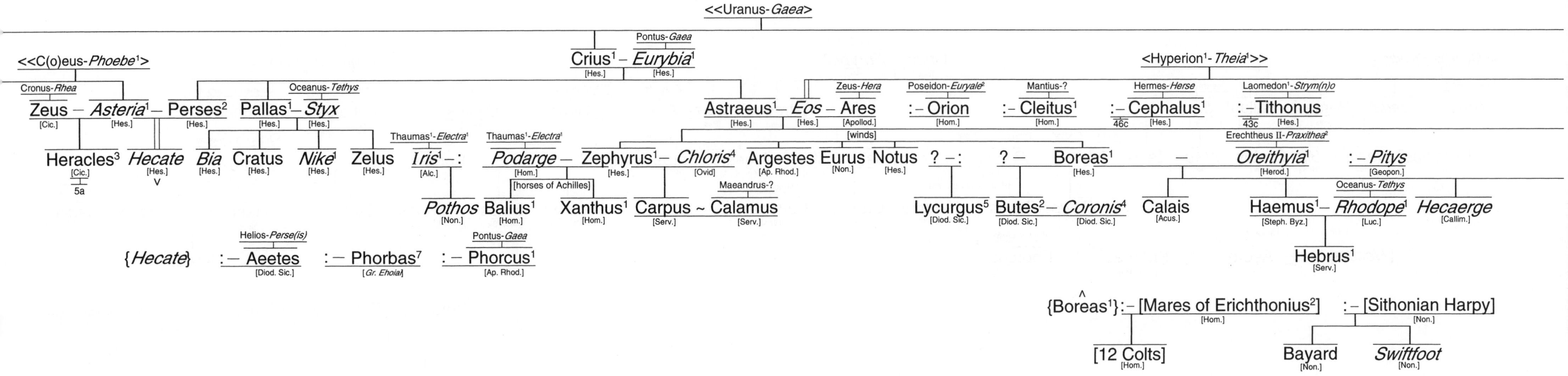
<<Uranus-Gaea>
<<C(o)eus-Phoebe[1]>
Pontus-Gaea
Crius[1] – Eurybia[1]
[Hes.] [Hes.]
<Hyperion[1]-Theia[1]>>
Cronus-Rhea
Zeus – Asteria[1] – Perses[2]
[Cic.] [Hes.] [Hes.]
Oceanus-Tethys
Pallas[1] – Styx
[Hes.] [Hes.]
Astraeus[1] – Eos – Ares
[Hes.] [Hes.] [Apollod.]
Zeus-Hera
Poseidon-Euryale[2]
:– Orion
[Hom.]
Mantius-?
:– Cleitus[1]
[Hom.]
Hermes-Herse
:– Cephalus[1]
46c [Hes.]
Laomedon[1]-Strym(n)o
:– Tithonus
43c [Hes.]
Thaumas[1]-Electra[1]
Thaumas[1]-Electra[1]
[winds]
Erechtheus II-Praxithea[2]
Heracles[3] Hecate Bia Cratus Nike[1] Zelus
[Cic.] [Hes.] [Hes.] [Hes.] [Hes.] [Hes.]
5a
Iris[1] –:
[Alc.]
Podarge – Zephyrus[1] – Chloris[4]
[Hom.] [Hes.] [Ovid]
Argestes Eurus Notus
[Ap. Rhod.] [Non.] [Hes.]
? –:
? – Boreas[1] – Oreithyia[1]
[Hes.] [Herod.]
:– Pitys
[Geopon.]
[horses of Achilles]
Maeandrus-?
Oceanus-Tethys
Pothos Balius[1] Xanthus[1] Carpus ~ Calamus
[Non.] [Hom.] [Hom.] [Serv.] [Serv.]
Lycurgus[5] Butes[2] – Coronis[4]
[Diod. Sic.] [Diod. Sic.] [Diod. Sic.]
Calais
[Acus.]
Haemus[1] – Rhodope[1] Hecaerge
[Steph. Byz.] [Luc.] [Callim.]
Hebrus[1]
[Serv.]
Helios-Perse(is)
Pontus-Gaea
{Hecate} :– Aeetes :– Phorbas[7] :– Phorcus[1]
[Diod. Sic.] [Gr. Ehoiai] [Ap. Rhod.]
{Boreas[1]}:– [Mares of Erichthonius[2]] :– [Sithonian Harpy]
[Hom.] [Non.]
[12 Colts] Bayard Swiftfoot
[Hom.] [Non.] [Non.]

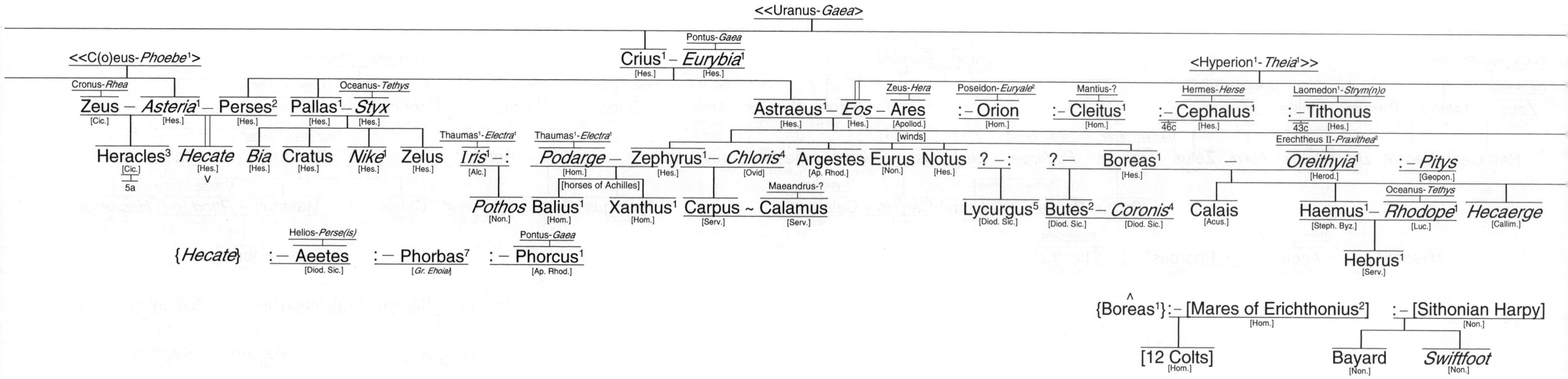

<<Uranus-Gaea>
Pontus-Gaea
<<C(o)eus-Phoebe1>
Crius1 - Eurybia1
[Hes.] [Hes.]
<Hyperion1-Theia1>>
Cronus-Rhea
Oceanus-Tethys
Zeus-Hera
Poseidon-Euryale2
Mantius-?
Hermes-Herse
Laomedon1-Strym(n)o
Zeus - Asteria1 - Perses2 Pallas1 - Styx
[Cic.] [Hes.] [Hes.] [Hes.] [Hes.]
Astraeus1 - Eos - Ares
[Hes.] [Hes.] [Apollod.]
:- Orion
[Hom.]
:- Cleitus1
[Hom.]
:- Cephalus1
46c [Hes.]
:- Tithonus
43c [Hes.]
Thaumas1-Electra1
Thaumas1-Electra1
[winds]
Erechtheus II-Praxithea2
Heracles3 Hecate Bia Cratus Nike1 Zelus
[Cic.] [Hes.] [Hes.] [Hes.] [Hes.] [Hes.]
5a V
Iris1 -:
[Alc.]
Podarge - Zephyrus1 - Chloris4
[Hom.] [Hes.] [Ovid]
Argestes Eurus Notus
[Ap. Rhod.] [Non.] [Hes.]
? -:
? -
Boreas1
[Hes.]
Oreithyia1
[Herod.]
:- Pitys
[Geopon.]
[horses of Achilles]
Maeandrus-?
Oceanus-Tethys
Pothos
[Non.]
Balius1
[Hom.]
Xanthus1
[Hom.]
Carpus ~ Calamus
[Serv.] [Serv.]
Lycurgus5
[Diod. Sic.]
Butes2 - Coronis4
[Diod. Sic.] [Diod. Sic.]
Calais
[Acus.]
Haemus1 - Rhodope1
[Steph. Byz.] [Luc.]
Hecaerge
[Callim.]
Helios-Perse(is)
Pontus-Gaea
{Hecate}
:- Aeetes
[Diod. Sic.]
:- Phorbas7
[Gr. Ehoiai]
:- Phorcus1
[Ap. Rhod.]
Hebrus1
[Serv.]
{Boreas1}:- [Mares of Erichthonius2]
[Hom.]
:- [Sithonian Harpy]
[Non.]
[12 Colts]
[Hom.]
Bayard
[Non.]
Swiftfoot
[Non.]

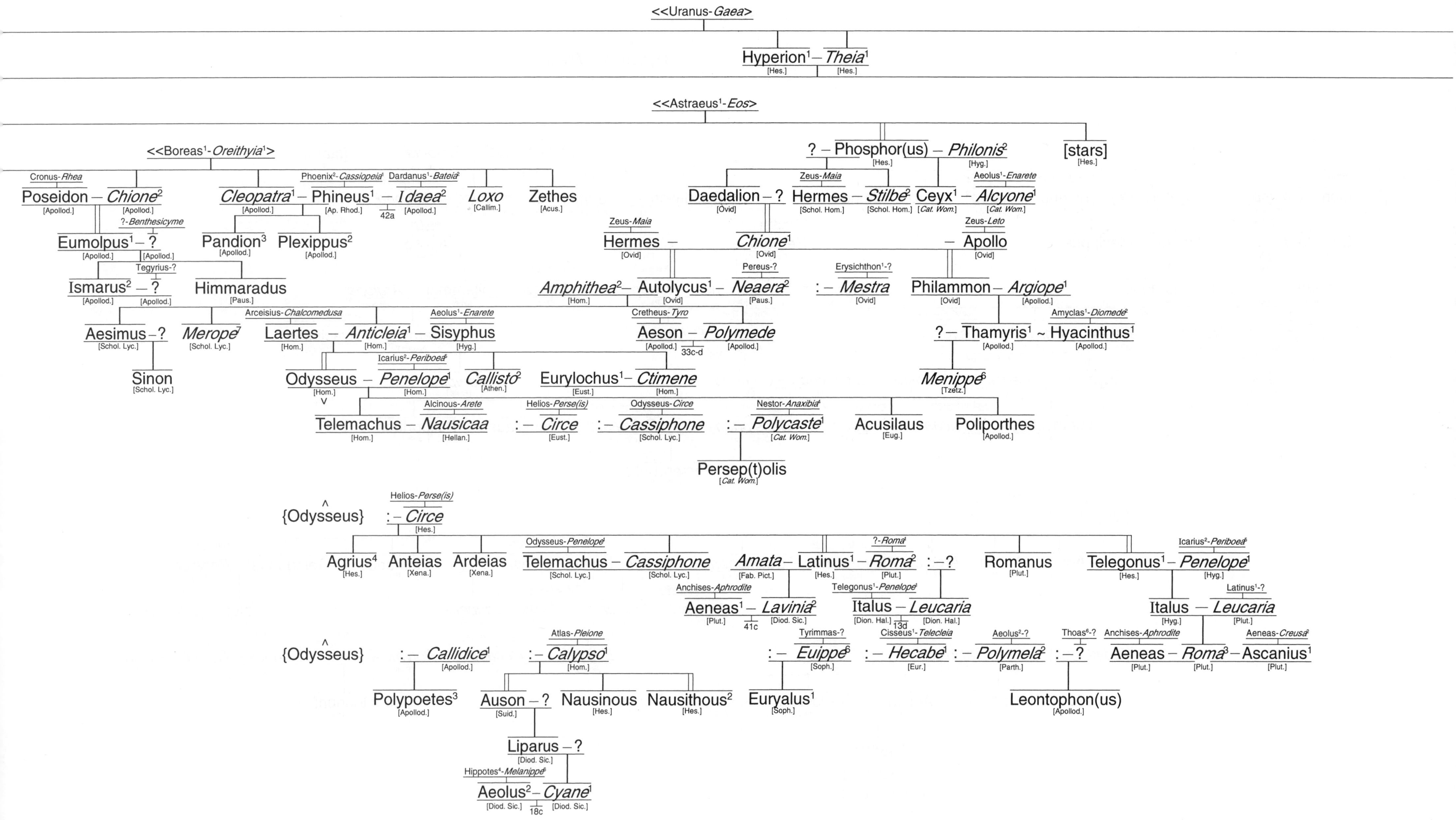

<<Uranus-Gaea>
Hyperion¹ – Theia¹
[Hes.] [Hes.]
<<Astraeus¹-Eos>
<<Boreas¹-Oreithyia¹>
? – Phosphor(us) – Philonis²
[Hes.] [Hyg.]
[stars]
[Hes.]
Cronus-Rhea
Poseidon – Chione²
[Apollod.] [Apollod.]
Phoenix²-Cassiopeia¹ Dardanus¹-Bateia²
Cleopatra¹ – Phineus¹ – Idaea²
[Apollod.] [Ap. Rhod.] [Apollod.]
42a
Loxo
[Callim.]
Zethes
[Acus.]
Daedalion – ?
[Ovid]
Zeus-Maia
Hermes – Stilbe²
[Schol. Hom.] [Schol. Hom.]
Aeolus¹-Enarete
Ceyx¹ – Alcyone¹
[Cat. Wom.] [Cat. Wom.]
?-Benthesicyme
Eumolpus¹ – ?
[Apollod.] [Apollod.]
Pandion³
[Apollod.]
Plexippus²
[Apollod.]
Zeus-Maia
Hermes –
[Ovid]
Chione¹
[Ovid]
Zeus-Leto
– Apollo
[Ovid]
Tegyrius-?
Ismarus² – ?
[Apollod.] [Apollod.]
Himmaradus
[Paus.]
Amphithea² – Autolycus¹ – Neaera²
[Hom.] [Ovid] [Paus.]
Pereus-?
Erysichthon¹-?
: – Mestra
[Ovid]
Philammon – Argiope¹
[Ovid] [Apollod.]
Aesimus – ?
[Schol. Lyc.]
Merope⁷
[Schol. Lyc.]
Arceisius-Chalcomedusa
Laertes – Anticleia¹ – Sisyphus
[Hom.] [Hom.] [Hyg.]
Aeolus¹-Enarete
Cretheus-Tyro
Aeson – Polymede
[Apollod.] [Apollod.]
33c-d
Amyclas¹-Diomede²
? – Thamyris¹ ~ Hyacinthus¹
[Apollod.] [Apollod.]
Sinon
[Schol. Lyc.]
Icarius²-Periboea⁶
Odysseus – Penelope¹
[Hom.] [Hom.]
Callisto²
[Athen.]
Eurylochus¹ – Ctimene
[Eust.] [Hom.]
Menippe⁶
[Tzetz.]
Alcinous-Arete
Telemachus – Nausicaa
[Hom.] [Hellan.]
Helios-Perse(is)
: – Circe
[Eust.]
Odysseus-Circe
: – Cassiphone
[Schol. Lyc.]
Nestor-Anaxibia⁴
: – Polycaste¹
[Cat. Wom.]
Acusilaus
[Eug.]
Poliporthes
[Apollod.]
Persep(t)olis
[Cat. Wom.]
Helios-Perse(is)
{Odysseus}
: – Circe
[Hes.]
Agrius⁴
[Hes.]
Anteias
[Xena.]
Ardeias
[Xena.]
Odysseus-Penelope¹
Telemachus – Cassiphone
[Schol. Lyc.] [Schol. Lyc.]
?-Roma¹
Amata – Latinus¹ – Roma²
[Fab. Pict.] [Hes.] [Plut.]
: – ?
Romanus
[Plut.]
Icarius²-Periboea⁶
Telegonus¹ – Penelope¹
[Hes.] [Hyg.]
Anchises-Aphrodite
Aeneas¹ – Lavinia²
[Plut.] [Diod. Sic.]
41c
Telegonus¹-Penelope¹
Italus – Leucaria
[Dion. Hal.] [Dion. Hal.]
13d
Latinus¹-?
Italus – Leucaria
[Hyg.] [Plut.]
Atlas-Pleione
{Odysseus}
: – Callidice¹
[Apollod.]
: – Calypso¹
[Hom.]
Tyrimmas-?
: – Euippe⁶
[Soph.]
Cisseus¹-Telecleia
: – Hecabe¹
[Eur.]
Aeolus²-?
: – Polymela²
[Parth.]
Thoas⁶-?
: – ?
Anchises-Aphrodite
Aeneas-Creusa²
Aeneas – Roma³ – Ascanius¹
[Plut.] [Plut.] [Plut.]
Polypoetes³
[Apollod.]
Auson – ?
[Suid.]
Nausinous
[Hes.]
Nausithous²
[Hes.]
Euryalus¹
[Soph.]
Leontophon(us)
[Apollod.]
Liparus – ?
[Diod. Sic.]
Hippotes⁴-Melanippe⁶
Aeolus² – Cyane¹
[Diod. Sic.] [Diod. Sic.]
18c

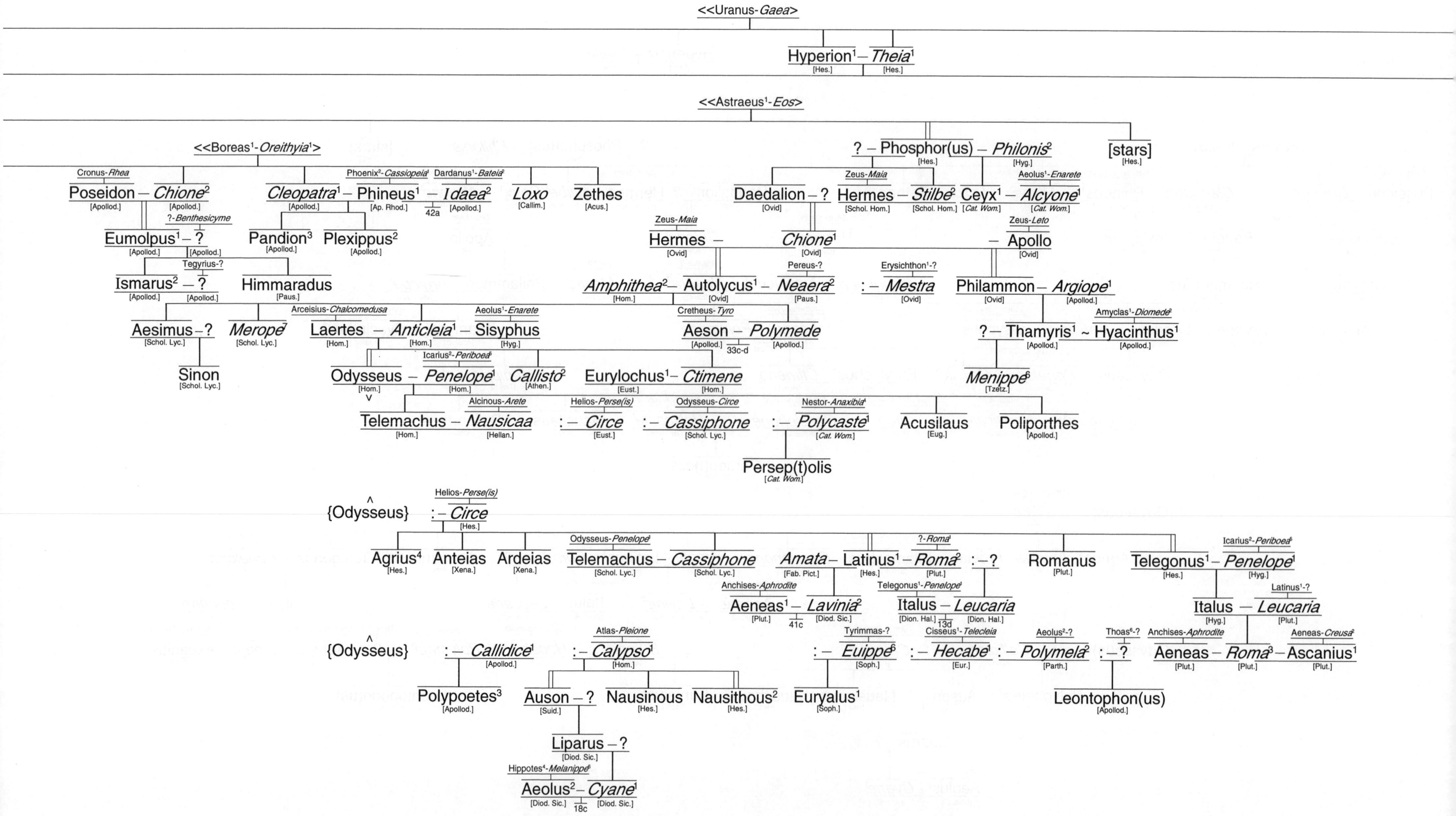

<<Uranus-Gaea>
Hyperion[1] – Theia[1]
[Hes.] [Hes.]
<<Astraeus[1]-Eos>
<<Boreas[1]-Oreithyia[1]>
? – Phosphor(us) – Philonis[2]
[Hes.] [Hyg.]
[stars]
[Hes.]
Cronus-Rhea
Poseidon – Chione[2]
[Apollod.] [Apollod.]
?-Benthesicyme
Phoenix[2]-Cassiopeia[1]
Dardanus[1]-Bateia[2]
Cleopatra[1] – Phineus[1] – Idaea[2]
[Apollod.] [Ap. Rhod.] [Apollod.]
42a
Loxo
[Callim.]
Zethes
[Acus.]
Eumolpus[1] – ?
[Apollod.] [Apollod.]
Pandion[3] Plexippus[2]
[Apollod.] [Apollod.]
Tegyrius-?
Ismarus[2] – ?
[Apollod.] [Apollod.]
Himmaradus
[Paus.]
Aesimus – ?
[Schol. Lyc.]
Merope[7]
[Schol. Lyc.]
Sinon
[Schol. Lyc.]
Zeus-Maia
Daedalion – ? Hermes – Stilbe[2] Ceyx[1] – Alcyone[1]
[Ovid] [Schol. Hom.] [Schol. Hom.] [Cat. Wom.] [Cat. Wom.]
Aeolus[1]-Enarete
Zeus-Maia
Hermes – Chione[1] – Apollo
[Ovid] [Ovid] [Ovid]
Zeus-Leto
Pereus-?
Erysichthon[1]-?
Amphithea[2] – Autolycus[1] – Neaera[2]
[Hom.] [Ovid] [Paus.]
: – Mestra
[Ovid]
Philammon – Argiope[1]
[Ovid] [Apollod.]
Amyclas[1]-Diomede[2]
? – Thamyris[1] ~ Hyacinthus[1]
[Apollod.] [Apollod.]
Menippe[6]
[Tzetz.]
Arceisius-Chalcomedusa
Aeolus[1]-Enarete
Laertes – Anticleia[1] – Sisyphus
[Hom.] [Hom.] [Hyg.]
Cretheus-Tyro
Aeson – Polymede
[Apollod.] [Apollod.]
33c-d
Icarius[2]-Periboea[2]
Odysseus – Penelope[1] Callisto[2] Eurylochus[1] – Ctimene
[Hom.] [Hom.] [Athen.] [Eust.] [Hom.]
v
Alcinous-Arete
Helios-Perse(is)
Odysseus-Circe
Nestor-Anaxibia[1]
Telemachus – Nausicaa
[Hom.] [Hellan.]
: – Circe
[Eust.]
: – Cassiphone
[Schol. Lyc.]
: – Polycaste[1]
[Cat. Wom.]
Acusilaus
[Eug.]
Poliporthes
[Apollod.]
Persep(t)olis
[Cat. Wom.]
^
{Odysseus}
Helios-Perse(is)
: – Circe
[Hes.]
Agrius[4] Anteias Ardeias
[Hes.] [Xena.] [Xena.]
Odysseus-Penelope[1]
Telemachus – Cassiphone
[Schol. Lyc.] [Schol. Lyc.]
?-Roma[1]
Amata – Latinus[1] – Roma[2] : – ?
[Fab. Pict.] [Hes.] [Plut.]
Romanus
[Plut.]
Icarius[2]-Periboea[2]
Telegonus[1] – Penelope[1]
[Hes.] [Hyg.]
Anchises-Aphrodite
Aeneas[1] – Lavinia[2]
[Plut.] [Diod. Sic.]
41c
Telegonus[1]-Penelope[1]
Italus – Leucaria
[Dion. Hal.] [Dion. Hal.]
13d
Latinus[1]-?
Italus – Leucaria
[Hyg.] [Plut.]
^
{Odysseus}
: – Callidice[1]
[Apollod.]
Atlas-Pleione
: – Calypso[1]
[Hom.]
Tyrimmas-?
: – Euippe[6]
[Soph.]
Cisseus[1]-Telecleia
: – Hecabe[1]
[Eur.]
Aeolus[2]-?
: – Polymela[2]
[Parth.]
Thoas[6]-?
: – ?
Anchises-Aphrodite
Aeneas-Creusa[2]
Aeneas – Roma[3] – Ascanius[1]
[Plut.] [Plut.] [Plut.]
Polypoetes[3]
[Apollod.]
Auson – ?
[Suid.]
Nausinous
[Hes.]
Nausithous[2]
[Hes.]
Euryalus[1]
[Soph.]
Leontophon(us)
[Apollod.]
Liparus – ?
[Diod. Sic.]
Hippotes[4]-Melanippe[6]
Aeolus[2] – Cyane[1]
[Diod. Sic.] [Diod. Sic.]
18c

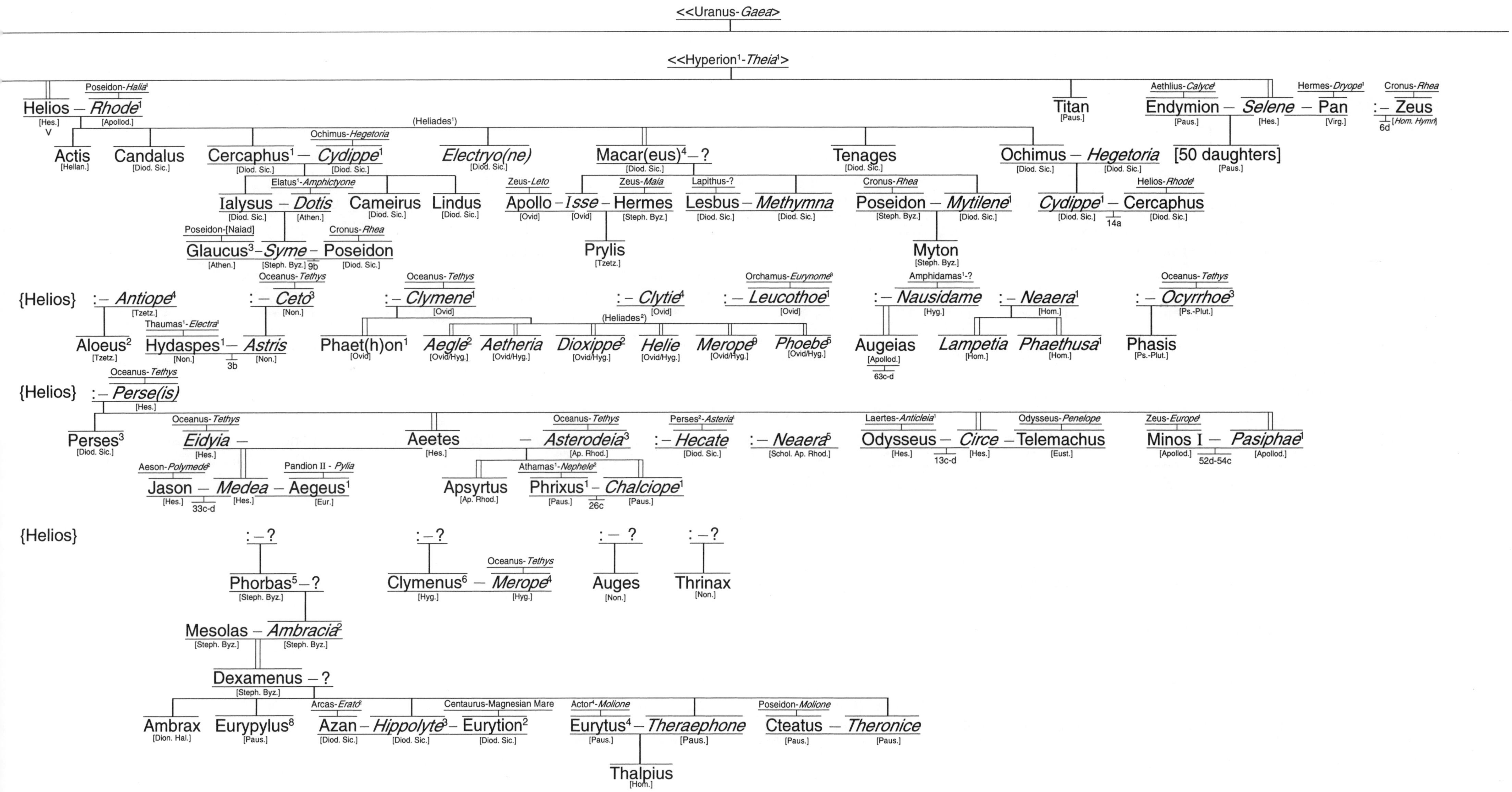

<<Uranus-Gaea>
<<Hyperion1-Theia1>
Poseidon-Halia1
Helios – Rhode1
[Hes.] [Apollod.]
V
Titan
[Paus.]
Aethlius-Calyce1
Endymion – Selene – Pan
[Paus.] [Hes.] [Virg.]
Hermes-Dryope1
Cronus-Rhea
: – Zeus
6d [Hom. Hymn]
(Heliades1)
Actis
[Hellan.]
Candalus
[Diod. Sic.]
Ochimus-Hegetoria
Cercaphus1 – Cydippe1
[Diod. Sic.] [Diod. Sic.]
Electryo(ne)
[Diod. Sic.]
Macar(eus)4 – ?
[Diod. Sic.]
Tenages
[Diod. Sic.]
Ochimus – Hegetoria
[Diod. Sic.] [Diod. Sic.]
[50 daughters]
[Paus.]
Elatus1-Amphictyone
Ialysus – Dotis
[Diod. Sic.] [Athen.]
Cameirus
[Diod. Sic.]
Lindus
[Diod. Sic.]
Zeus-Leto
Apollo – Isse – Hermes
[Ovid] [Ovid] [Steph. Byz.]
Zeus-Maia
Lapithus-?
Lesbus – Methymna
[Diod. Sic.] [Diod. Sic.]
Cronus-Rhea
Poseidon – Mytilene1
[Steph. Byz.] [Diod. Sic.]
Helios-Rhode1
Cydippe1 – Cercaphus
[Diod. Sic.] 14a [Diod. Sic.]
Poseidon-[Naiad]
Cronus-Rhea
Glaucus3 – Syme – Poseidon
[Athen.] [Steph. Byz.] 9b [Diod. Sic.]
Prylis
[Tzetz.]
Myton
[Steph. Byz.]
{Helios} : – Antiope4
[Tzetz.]
Aloeus2
[Tzetz.]
Thaumas1-Electra1
Hydaspes1 – Astris
[Non.] 3b [Non.]
Oceanus-Tethys
: – Ceto3
[Non.]
Oceanus-Tethys
: – Clymene1
[Ovid]
(Heliades2)
Phaet(h)on1
[Ovid]
Aegle2
[Ovid/Hyg.]
Aetheria
[Ovid/Hyg.]
Dioxippe2
[Ovid/Hyg.]
Helie
[Ovid/Hyg.]
Merope9
[Ovid/Hyg.]
Phoebe5
[Ovid/Hyg.]
: – Clytie4
[Ovid]
Orchamus-Eurynome3
: – Leucothoe1
[Ovid]
Amphidamas1-?
: – Nausidame
[Hyg.]
Augeias
[Apollod.]
63c-d
: – Neaera1
[Hom.]
Lampetia
[Hom.]
Phaethusa1
[Hom.]
Oceanus-Tethys
: – Ocyrrhoe3
[Ps.-Plut.]
Phasis
[Ps.-Plut.]
Oceanus-Tethys
{Helios} : – Perse(is)
[Hes.]
Perses3
[Diod. Sic.]
Oceanus-Tethys
Eidyia –
[Hes.]
Aeetes
[Hes.]
Oceanus-Tethys
– Asterodeia3
[Ap. Rhod.]
Perses2-Asteria1
: – Hecate
[Diod. Sic.]
: – Neaera5
[Schol. Ap. Rhod.]
Laertes-Anticleia1
Odysseus – Circe – Telemachus
[Hes.] 13c-d [Hes.] [Eust.]
Odysseus-Penelope
Zeus-Europe1
Minos I – Pasiphae1
[Apollod.] 52d-54c [Apollod.]
Aeson-Polymede2
Pandion II - Pylia
Jason – Medea – Aegeus1
[Hes.] 33c-d [Hes.] [Eur.]
Apsyrtus
[Ap. Rhod.]
Athamas1-Nephele2
Phrixus1 – Chalciope1
[Paus.] 26c [Paus.]
{Helios}
: – ?
Phorbas5 – ?
[Steph. Byz.]
Mesolas – Ambracia2
[Steph. Byz.] [Steph. Byz.]
Dexamenus – ?
[Steph. Byz.]
: – ?
Clymenus6 – Merope4
[Hyg.] [Hyg.]
Oceanus-Tethys
: – ?
Auges
[Non.]
: – ?
Thrinax
[Non.]
Ambrax
[Dion. Hal.]
Eurypylus8
[Paus.]
Arcas-Erato2
Azan – Hippolyte3 – Eurytion2
[Diod. Sic.] [Diod. Sic.] [Diod. Sic.]
Centaurus-Magnesian Mare
Actor4-Molione
Eurytus4 – Theraephone
[Paus.] [Paus.]
Thalpius
[Hom.]
Poseidon-Molione
Cteatus – Theronice
[Paus.] [Paus.]

14

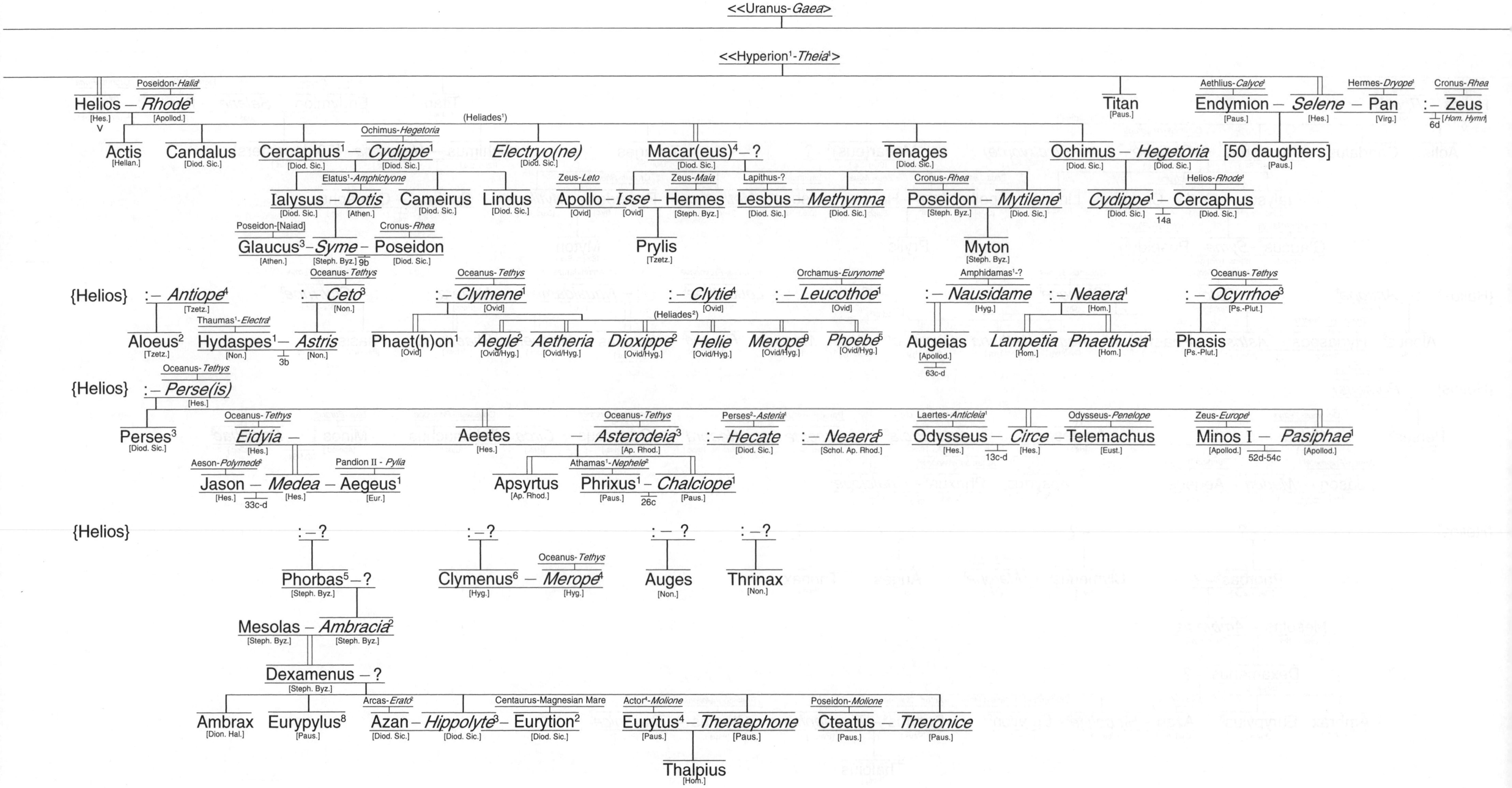

<<Uranus-Gaea>
<<Hyperion[1]-Theia[1]>
Poseidon-Halia[1]
Helios – Rhode[1]
[Hes.] [Apollod.]
V
Titan
[Paus.]
Aethlius-Calyce[1]
Endymion – Selene – Pan
[Paus.] [Hes.] [Virg.]
Hermes-Dryope[1]
Cronus-Rhea
:– Zeus
[Hom. Hymn]
6d
(Heliades[1])
Actis
[Hellan.]
Candalus
[Diod. Sic.]
Ochimus-Hegetoria
Cercaphus[1] – Cydippe[1]
[Diod. Sic.] [Diod. Sic.]
Electryo(ne)
[Diod. Sic.]
Macar(eus)[4] – ?
[Diod. Sic.]
Tenages
[Diod. Sic.]
Ochimus – Hegetoria
[Diod. Sic.] [Diod. Sic.]
[50 daughters]
[Paus.]
Elatus[1]-Amphictyone
Ialysus – Dotis
[Diod. Sic.] [Athen.]
Cameirus
[Diod. Sic.]
Lindus
[Diod. Sic.]
Zeus-Leto
Apollo – Isse – Hermes
[Ovid] [Ovid] [Steph. Byz.]
Zeus-Maia
Lapithus-?
Lesbus – Methymna
[Diod. Sic.] [Diod. Sic.]
Cronus-Rhea
Poseidon – Mytilene[1]
[Steph. Byz.] [Diod. Sic.]
Cydippe[1] – Cercaphus
[Diod. Sic.] 14a [Diod. Sic.]
Helios-Rhode[1]
Poseidon-[Naiad]
Glaucus[3] – Syme – Poseidon
[Athen.] [Steph. Byz.] 9b [Diod. Sic.]
Cronus-Rhea
Prylis
[Tzetz.]
Myton
[Steph. Byz.]
{Helios} :– Antiope[4]
[Tzetz.]
Oceanus-Tethys
:– Ceto[3]
[Non.]
Oceanus-Tethys
:– Clymene[1]
[Ovid]
:– Clytie[4]
[Ovid]
Orchamus-Eurynome[3]
:– Leucothoe[1]
[Ovid]
Amphidamas[1]-?
:– Nausidame
[Hyg.]
:– Neaera[1]
[Hom.]
Oceanus-Tethys
:– Ocyrrhoe[3]
[Ps.-Plut.]
Aloeus[2]
[Tzetz.]
Thaumas[1]-Electra[1]
Hydaspes[1] – Astris
[Non.] 3b [Non.]
(Heliades[2])
Phaet(h)on[1]
[Ovid]
Aegle[2]
[Ovid/Hyg.]
Aetheria
[Ovid/Hyg.]
Dioxippe[2]
[Ovid/Hyg.]
Helie
[Ovid/Hyg.]
Merope[9]
[Ovid/Hyg.]
Phoebe[5]
[Ovid/Hyg.]
Augeias
[Apollod.]
63c-d
Lampetia
[Hom.]
Phaethusa[1]
[Hom.]
Phasis
[Ps.-Plut.]
Oceanus-Tethys
{Helios} :– Perse(is)
[Hes.]
Perses[3]
[Diod. Sic.]
Oceanus-Tethys
Eidyia –
[Hes.]
Aeetes
[Hes.]
Oceanus-Tethys
– Asterodeia[3]
[Ap. Rhod.]
Perses[2]-Asteria[1]
:– Hecate
[Diod. Sic.]
:– Neaera[5]
[Schol. Ap. Rhod.]
Laertes-Anticleia[1]
Odysseus – Circe – Telemachus
[Hes.] 13c-d [Hes.] [Eust.]
Odysseus-Penelope
Zeus-Europe[1]
Minos I – Pasiphae[1]
[Apollod.] 52d-54c [Apollod.]
Aeson-Polymede[2]
Jason – Medea – Aegeus[1]
[Hes.] 33c-d [Hes.] [Eur.]
Pandion II - Pylia
Apsyrtus
[Ap. Rhod.]
Athamas[1]-Nephele[2]
Phrixus[1] – Chalciope[1]
[Paus.] 26c [Paus.]
{Helios}
:– ?
:– ?
:– ?
:– ?
Phorbas[5] – ?
[Steph. Byz.]
Clymenus[6] – Merope[4]
[Hyg.] [Hyg.]
Oceanus-Tethys
Auges
[Non.]
Thrinax
[Non.]
Mesolas – Ambracia[2]
[Steph. Byz.] [Steph. Byz.]
Dexamenus – ?
[Steph. Byz.]
Ambrax
[Dion. Hal.]
Eurypylus[8]
[Paus.]
Arcas-Erato[3]
Azan – Hippolyte[3] – Eurytion[2]
[Diod. Sic.] [Diod. Sic.] [Diod. Sic.]
Centaurus-Magnesian Mare
Actor[4]-Molione
Eurytus[4] – Theraephone
[Paus.] [Paus.]
Poseidon-Molione
Cteatus – Theronice
[Paus.] [Paus.]
Thalpius
[Hom.]

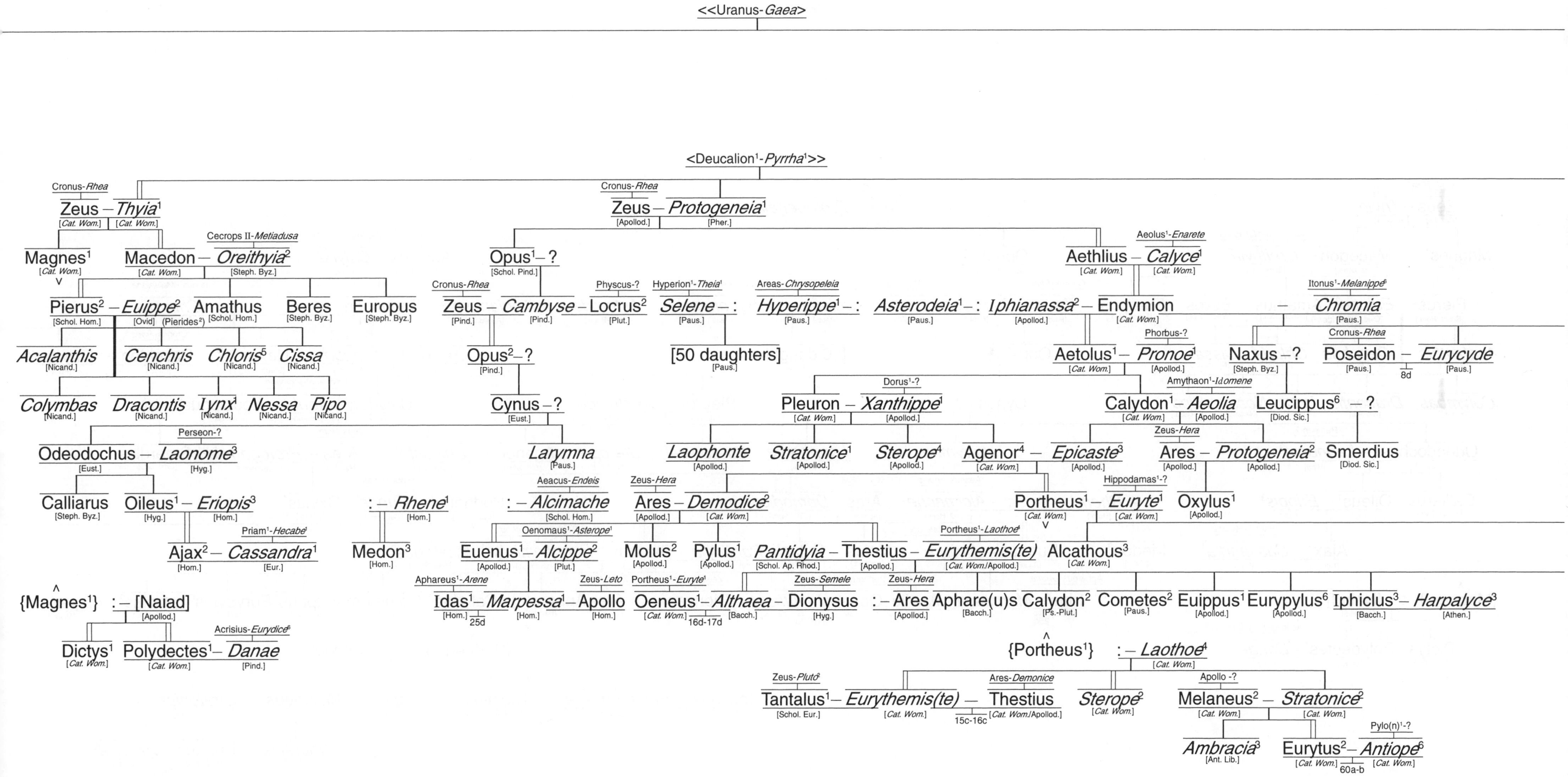

<<Uranus-Gaea>
<Deucalion¹-Pyrrha¹>>
Cronus-Rhea
Zeus – Thyia¹
[Cat. Wom.] [Cat. Wom.]
Cronus-Rhea
Zeus – Protogeneia¹
[Apollod.] [Pher.]
Magnes¹
[Cat. Wom.]
Cecrops II-Metiadusa
Macedon – Oreithyia²
[Cat. Wom.] [Steph. Byz.]
Opus¹ – ?
[Schol. Pind.]
Aeolus¹-Enarete
Aethlius – Calyce¹
[Cat. Wom.] [Cat. Wom.]
Pierus² – Euippe²
[Schol. Hom.] [Ovid] (Pierides²)
Amathus
[Schol. Hom.]
Beres
[Steph. Byz.]
Europus
[Steph. Byz.]
Cronus-Rhea
Zeus – Cambyse – Locrus²
[Pind.] [Pind.] [Plut.]
Physcus-?
Hyperion¹-Theia¹
Selene – :
[Paus.]
Areas-Chrysopeleia
Hyperippe¹ – :
[Paus.]
Asterodeia¹ – :
[Paus.]
Iphianassa² – Endymion
[Apollod.] [Cat. Wom.]
Itonus¹-Melanippe⁶
– Chromia
[Paus.]
Acalanthis
[Nicand.]
Cenchris
[Nicand.]
Chloris⁵
[Nicand.]
Cissa
[Nicand.]
Opus² – ?
[Pind.]
[50 daughters]
[Paus.]
Phorbus-?
Aetolus¹ – Pronoe¹
[Cat. Wom.] [Apollod.]
Naxus – ?
[Steph. Byz.]
Cronus-Rhea
Poseidon – Eurycyde
[Paus.] 8d [Paus.]
Colymbas
[Nicand.]
Dracontis
[Nicand.]
Iynx¹
[Nicand.]
Nessa
[Nicand.]
Pipo
[Nicand.]
Cynus – ?
[Eust.]
Dorus¹-?
Pleuron – Xanthippe¹
[Cat. Wom.] [Apollod.]
Amythaon¹-Idomene
Calydon¹ – Aeolia
[Cat. Wom.] [Apollod.]
Leucippus⁶ – ?
[Diod. Sic.]
Perseon-?
Odeodochus – Laonome³
[Eust.] [Hyg.]
Larymna
[Paus.]
Laophonte
[Apollod.]
Stratonice¹
[Apollod.]
Sterope⁴
[Apollod.]
Agenor⁴ – Epicaste³
[Cat. Wom.] [Apollod.]
Zeus-Hera
Ares – Protogeneia²
[Apollod.] [Apollod.]
Smerdius
[Diod. Sic.]
Calliarus
[Steph. Byz.]
Oileus¹ – Eriopis³
[Hyg.] [Hom.]
: – Rhene¹
[Hom.]
Aeacus-Endeis
: – Alcimache
[Schol. Hom.]
Zeus-Hera
Ares – Demodice²
[Apollod.] [Cat. Wom.]
Hippodamas¹-?
Portheus¹ – Euryte¹
[Cat. Wom.] [Cat. Wom.]
Oxylus¹
[Apollod.]
Priam¹-Hecabe¹
Ajax² – Cassandra¹
[Hom.] [Eur.]
Medon³
[Hom.]
Oenomaus¹-Asterope¹
Euenus¹ – Alcippe²
[Apollod.] [Plut.]
Molus²
[Apollod.]
Pylus¹
[Apollod.]
Pantidyia – Thestius – Eurythemis(te)
[Schol. Ap. Rhod.] [Apollod.] [Cat. Wom./Apollod.]
Portheus¹-Laothoe⁴
Alcathous³
[Cat. Wom.]
{Magnes¹} : – [Naiad]
[Apollod.]
Aphareus¹-Arene
Idas¹ – Marpessa¹ – Apollo
[Hom.] 25d [Hom.] [Hom.]
Zeus-Leto
Portheus¹-Euryte¹
Oeneus¹ – Althaea – Dionysus
[Cat. Wom.] 16d-17d [Bacch.] [Hyg.]
Zeus-Semele
Zeus-Hera
: – Ares
[Apollod.]
Aphare(u)s
[Bacch.]
Calydon²
[Ps.-Plut.]
Cometes²
[Paus.]
Euippus¹
[Apollod.]
Eurypylus⁶
[Apollod.]
Iphiclus³ – Harpalyce³
[Bacch.] [Athen.]
Acrisius-Eurydice⁶
Dictys¹
[Cat. Wom.]
Polydectes¹ – Danae
[Cat. Wom.] [Pind.]
{Portheus¹} : – Laothoe⁴
[Cat. Wom.]
Zeus-Pluto²
Tantalus¹ – Eurythemis(te) – Thestius
[Schol. Eur.] [Cat. Wom.] 15c-16c [Cat. Wom./Apollod.]
Ares-Demonice
Sterope²
[Cat. Wom.]
Apollo -?
Melaneus² – Stratonice²
[Cat. Wom.] [Cat. Wom.]
Ambracia³
[Ant. Lib.]
Pylo(n)¹-?
Eurytus² – Antiope⁶
[Cat. Wom.] 60a-b [Cat. Wom.]

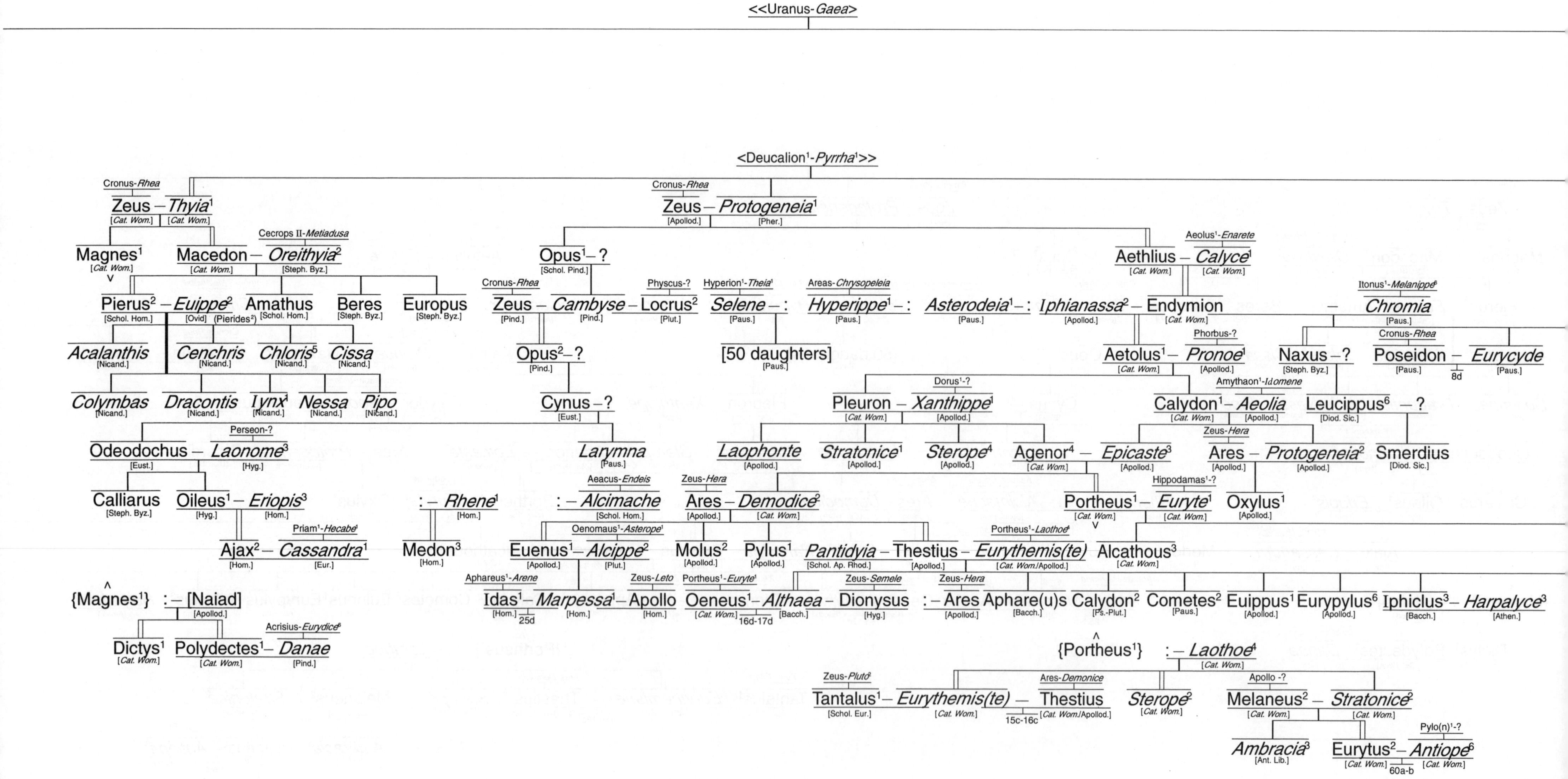

<<Uranus-Gaea>
<Deucalion[1]-Pyrrha[1]>>
Cronus-Rhea
Zeus – Thyia[1]
[Cat. Wom.] [Cat. Wom.]
Cronus-Rhea
Zeus – Protogeneia[1]
[Apollod.] [Pher.]
Cecrops II-Metiadusa
Aeolus[1]-Enarete
Magnes[1]
[Cat. Wom.]
Macedon – Oreithyia[2]
[Cat. Wom.] [Steph. Byz.]
Opus[1] – ?
[Schol. Pind.]
Aethlius – Calyce[1]
[Cat. Wom.] [Cat. Wom.]
Cronus-Rhea
Physcus-?
Hyperion[1]-Theia[1]
Areas-Chrysopeleia
Itonus[1]-Melanippe[6]
Pierus[2] – Euippe[2]
[Schol. Hom.] [Ovid] (Pierides[2])
Amathus
[Schol. Hom.]
Beres
[Steph. Byz.]
Europus
[Steph. Byz.]
Zeus – Cambyse – Locrus[2]
[Pind.] [Pind.] [Plut.]
Selene – :
[Paus.]
Hyperippe[1] – :
[Paus.]
Asterodeia[1] – :
[Paus.]
Iphianassa[2] – Endymion
[Apollod.] [Cat. Wom.]
– Chromia
[Paus.]
Phorbus-?
Cronus-Rhea
Acalanthis
[Nicand.]
Cenchris
[Nicand.]
Chloris[5]
[Nicand.]
Cissa
[Nicand.]
Opus[2] – ?
[Pind.]
[50 daughters]
[Paus.]
Aetolus[1] – Pronoe[1]
[Cat. Wom.] [Apollod.]
Naxus – ?
[Steph. Byz.]
Poseidon – Eurycyde
[Paus.] 8d [Paus.]
Dorus[1]-?
Amythaon[1]-Idomene
Colymbas
[Nicand.]
Dracontis
[Nicand.]
Iynx[1]
[Nicand.]
Nessa
[Nicand.]
Pipo
[Nicand.]
Cynus – ?
[Eust.]
Pleuron – Xanthippe[1]
[Cat. Wom.] [Apollod.]
Calydon[1] – Aeolia
[Cat. Wom.] [Apollod.]
Leucippus[6] – ?
[Diod. Sic.]
Perseon-?
Zeus-Hera
Odeodochus – Laonome[3]
[Eust.] [Hyg.]
Larymna
[Paus.]
Laophonte
[Apollod.]
Stratonice[1]
[Apollod.]
Sterope[4]
[Apollod.]
Agenor[4] – Epicaste[3]
[Cat. Wom.] [Apollod.]
Ares – Protogeneia[2]
[Apollod.] [Apollod.]
Smerdius
[Diod. Sic.]
Aeacus-Endeis
Zeus-Hera
Hippodamas[1]-?
Calliarus
[Steph. Byz.]
Oileus[1] – Eriopis[3]
[Hyg.] [Hom.]
: – Rhene[1]
[Hom.]
: – Alcimache
[Schol. Hom.]
Ares – Demodice[2]
[Apollod.] [Cat. Wom.]
Portheus[1] – Euryte[1]
[Cat. Wom.] [Cat. Wom.]
Oxylus[1]
[Apollod.]
Priam[1]-Hecabe[1]
Oenomaus[1]-Asterope[1]
Portheus[1]-Laothoe[4]
Ajax[2] – Cassandra[1]
[Hom.] [Eur.]
Medon[3]
[Hom.]
Euenus[1] – Alcippe[2]
[Apollod.] [Plut.]
Molus[2]
[Apollod.]
Pylus[1]
[Apollod.]
Pantidyia – Thestius – Eurythemis(te)
[Schol. Ap. Rhod.] [Apollod.] [Cat. Wom./Apollod.]
Alcathous[3]
[Cat. Wom.]
Aphareus[1]-Arene
Zeus-Leto
Portheus[1]-Euryte[1]
Zeus-Semele
Zeus-Hera
{Magnes[1]} : – [Naiad]
[Apollod.]
Idas[1] – Marpessa[1] – Apollo
[Hom.] 25d [Hom.] [Hom.]
Oeneus[1] – Althaea – Dionysus
[Cat. Wom.] 16d-17d [Bacch.] [Hyg.]
: – Ares
[Apollod.]
Aphare(u)s
[Bacch.]
Calydon[2]
[Ps.-Plut.]
Cometes[2]
[Paus.]
Euippus[1]
[Apollod.]
Eurypylus[6]
[Apollod.]
Iphiclus[3] – Harpalyce[3]
[Bacch.] [Athen.]
Acrisius-Eurydice[6]
Dictys[1]
[Cat. Wom.]
Polydectes[1] – Danae
[Cat. Wom.] [Pind.]
{Portheus[1]} : – Laothoe[4]
[Cat. Wom.]
Zeus-Pluto[3]
Ares-Demonice
Apollo -?
Tantalus[1] – Eurythemis(te) – Thestius
[Schol. Eur.] [Cat. Wom.] 15c-16c [Cat. Wom./Apollod.]
Sterope[2]
[Cat. Wom.]
Melaneus[2] – Stratonice[2]
[Cat. Wom.] [Cat. Wom.]
Pylo(n)[1]-?
Ambracia[3]
[Ant. Lib.]
Eurytus[2] – Antiope[6]
[Cat. Wom.] 60a-b [Cat. Wom.]

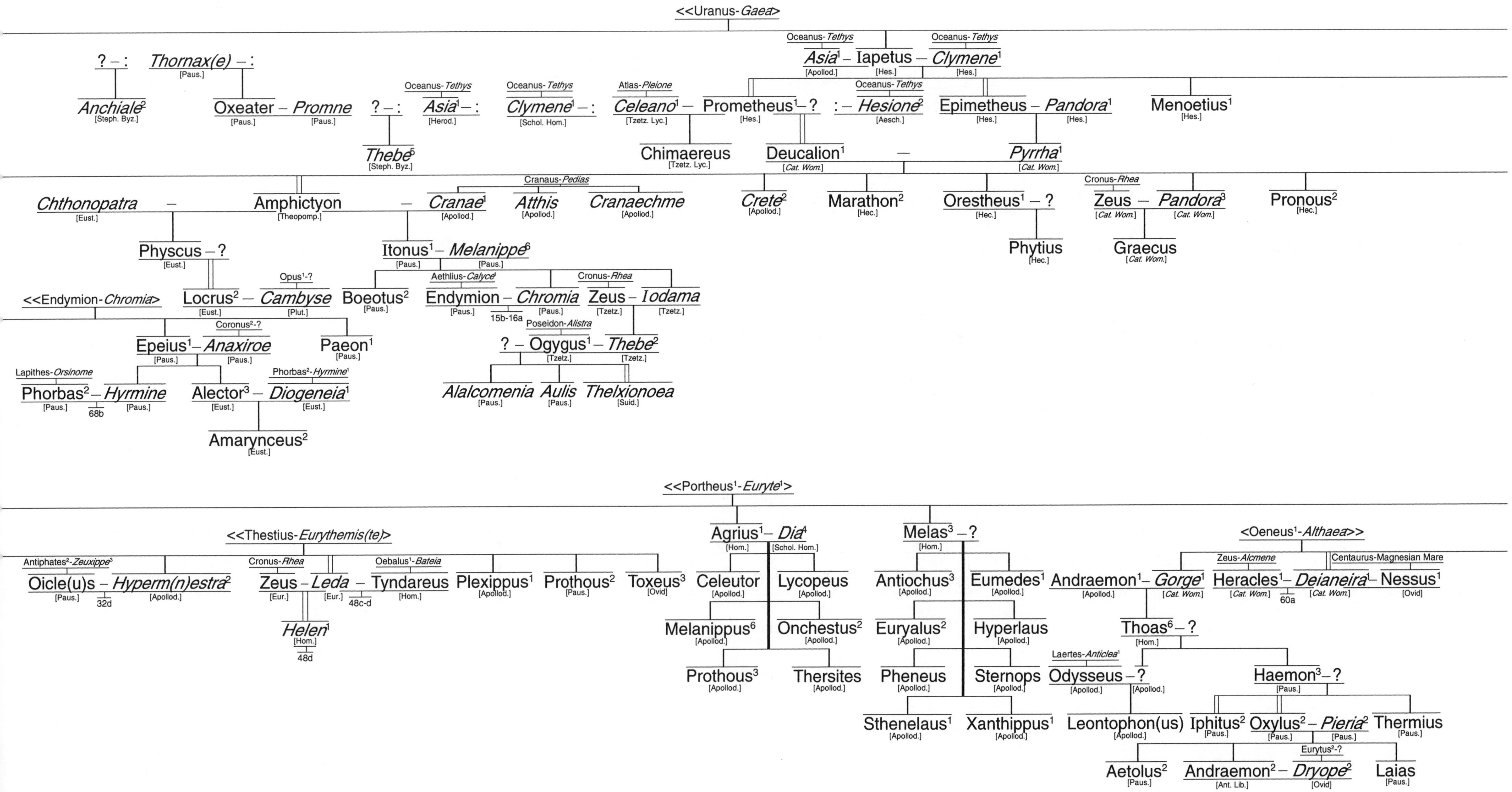

<<Uranus-Gaea>
Oceanus-Tethys
Asia[1] – Iapetus – Clymene[1]
[Apollod.] [Hes.] [Hes.]
Oceanus-Tethys
?–: Thornax(e) –:
[Paus.]
Anchiale[2]
[Steph. Byz.]
Oxeater – Promne
[Paus.] [Paus.]
?–:
Thebe[5]
[Steph. Byz.]
Oceanus-Tethys
Asia[1] –:
[Herod.]
Oceanus-Tethys
Clymene[1] –:
[Schol. Hom.]
Atlas-Pleione
Celeano[1] – Prometheus[1] – ?
[Tzetz. Lyc.] [Hes.]
Oceanus-Tethys
: – Hesione[2]
[Aesch.]
Epimetheus – Pandora[1]
[Hes.] [Hes.]
Menoetius[1]
[Hes.]
Chimaereus
[Tzetz. Lyc.]
Deucalion[1] – Pyrrha[1]
[Cat. Wom.] [Cat. Wom.]
Chthonopatra – Amphictyon – Cranae[1]
[Eust.] [Theopomp.] [Apollod.]
Cranaus-Pedias
Atthis
[Apollod.]
Cranaechme
[Apollod.]
Crete[2]
[Apollod.]
Marathon[2]
[Hec.]
Orestheus[1] – ?
[Hec.]
Cronus-Rhea
Zeus – Pandora[3]
[Cat. Wom.] [Cat. Wom.]
Pronous[2]
[Hec.]
Physcus – ?
[Eust.]
Itonus[1] – Melanippe[6]
[Paus.] [Paus.]
Phytius
[Hec.]
Graecus
[Cat. Wom.]
Opus[1]-?
<<Endymion-Chromia>
Locrus[2] – Cambyse
[Eust.] [Plut.]
Boeotus[2]
[Paus.]
Aethlius-Calyce[1]
Endymion – Chromia
[Paus.] [Paus.]
15b-16a
Cronus-Rhea
Zeus – Iodama
[Tzetz.] [Tzetz.]
Coronus[2]-?
Epeius[1] – Anaxiroe
[Paus.] [Paus.]
Paeon[1]
[Paus.]
Poseidon-Alistra
? – Ogygus[1] – Thebe[2]
[Tzetz.] [Tzetz.]
Lapithes-Orsinome
Phorbas[2] – Hyrmine
[Paus.] [Paus.]
68b
Phorbas[2]-Hyrmine[1]
Alector[3] – Diogeneia[1]
[Eust.] [Eust.]
Alalcomenia
[Paus.]
Aulis
[Paus.]
Thelxionoea
[Suid.]
Amarynceus[2]
[Eust.]
<<Portheus[1]-Euryte[1]>
<<Thestius-Eurythemis(te)>
Agrius[1] – Dia[4]
[Hom.] [Schol. Hom.]
Melas[3] – ?
[Hom.]
<Oeneus[1]-Althaea>>
Antiphates[2]-Zeuxippe[3]
Oicle(u)s – Hyperm(n)estra[2]
[Paus.] [Apollod.]
32d
Cronus-Rhea
Zeus – Leda – Tyndareus
[Eur.] [Eur.] [Hom.]
48c-d
Oebalus[1]-Bateia
Plexippus[1]
[Apollod.]
Prothous[2]
[Paus.]
Toxeus[3]
[Ovid]
Celeutor
[Apollod.]
Lycopeus
[Apollod.]
Antiochus[3]
[Apollod.]
Eumedes[1]
[Apollod.]
Andraemon[1] – Gorge[1]
[Apollod.] [Cat. Wom.]
Zeus-Alcmene
Heracles[1] – Deianeira[1] – Nessus[1]
[Cat. Wom.] [Cat. Wom.] [Ovid]
60a
Centaurus-Magnesian Mare
Helen[1]
[Hom.]
48d
Melanippus[6]
[Apollod.]
Onchestus[2]
[Apollod.]
Euryalus[2]
[Apollod.]
Hyperlaus
[Apollod.]
Thoas[6] – ?
[Hom.]
Laertes-Anticlea[1]
Prothous[3]
[Apollod.]
Thersites
[Apollod.]
Pheneus
[Apollod.]
Sternops
[Apollod.]
Odysseus – ?
[Apollod.] [Apollod.]
Haemon[3] – ?
[Paus.]
Sthenelaus[1]
[Apollod.]
Xanthippus[1]
[Apollod.]
Leontophon(us)
[Apollod.]
Iphitus[2]
[Paus.]
Oxylus[2] – Pieria[2]
[Paus.] [Paus.]
Thermius
[Paus.]
Eurytus[2]-?
Aetolus[2]
[Paus.]
Andraemon[2] – Dryope[2]
[Ant. Lib.] [Ovid]
Laias
[Paus.]

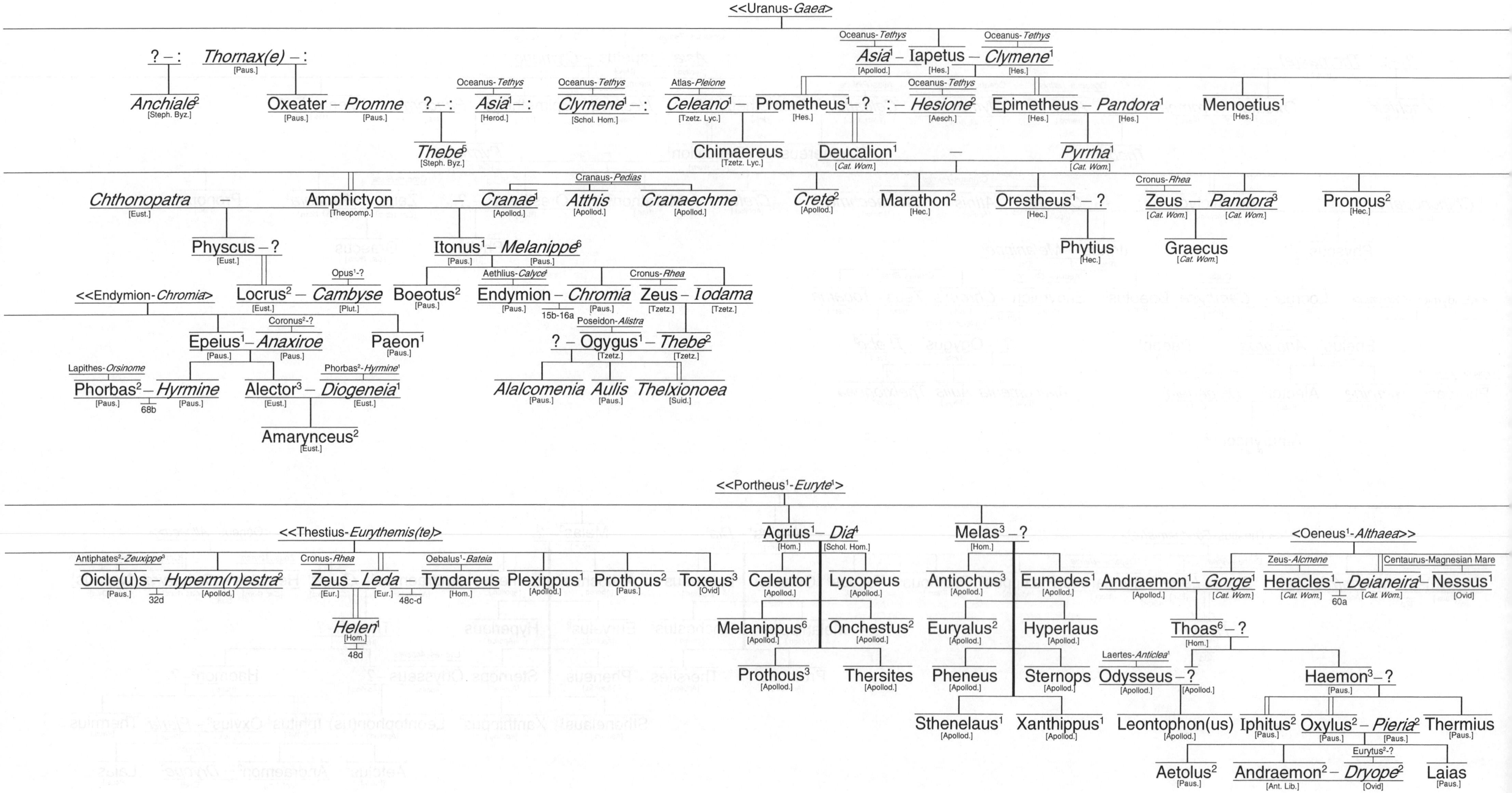

<<Uranus-Gaea>
?–: Thornax(e)–: [Paus.]
Anchiale[2] [Steph. Byz.]
Oxeater [Paus.] – Promne [Paus.]
?–:
Oceanus-Tethys
Asia[1]–: [Herod.]
Thebe[5] [Steph. Byz.]
Oceanus-Tethys
Clymene[1]–: [Schol. Hom.]
Atlas-Pleione
Celeano[1] [Tzetz. Lyc.] – Prometheus[1] [Hes.] – ?
Chimaereus [Tzetz. Lyc.]
Oceanus-Tethys
Asia[1] [Apollod.] – Iapetus [Hes.] – Clymene[1] [Hes.]
Oceanus-Tethys
:– Hesione[2] [Aesch.]
Deucalion[1] [Cat. Wom.] – Pyrrha[1] [Cat. Wom.]
Epimetheus [Hes.] – Pandora[1] [Hes.]
Menoetius[1] [Hes.]
Chthonopatra [Eust.] – Amphictyon [Theopomp.] –
Cranaus-Pedias
Cranae[1] [Apollod.]
Atthis [Apollod.]
Cranaechme [Apollod.]
Crete[2] [Apollod.]
Marathon[2] [Hec.]
Orestheus[1] [Hec.] – ?
Phytius [Hec.]
Cronus-Rhea
Zeus [Cat. Wom.] – Pandora[3] [Cat. Wom.]
Graecus [Cat. Wom.]
Pronous[2] [Hec.]
Physcus [Eust.] – ?
Itonus[1] [Paus.] – Melanippe[6] [Paus.]
Opus[1]-?
Locrus[2] [Eust.] – Cambyse [Plut.]
Boeotus[2] [Paus.]
Aethlius-Calyce[1]
Endymion [Paus.] – Chromia [Paus.]
15b-16a
Cronus-Rhea
Zeus [Tzetz.] – Iodama [Tzetz.]
<<Endymion-Chromia>
Coronus[2]-?
Epeius[1] [Paus.] – Anaxiroe [Paus.]
Paeon[1] [Paus.]
Poseidon-Alistra
? – Ogygus[1] [Tzetz.] – Thebe[2] [Tzetz.]
Alalcomenia [Paus.]
Aulis [Paus.]
Thelxionoea [Suid.]
Lapithes-Orsinome
Phorbas[2] [Paus.] – Hyrmine [Paus.]
68b
Alector[3] [Eust.] – Diogeneia[1] [Eust.]
Phorbas[2]-Hyrmine[1]
Amarynceus[2] [Eust.]
<<Portheus[1]-Euryte[1]>
<<Thestius-Eurythemis(te)>
Antiphates[2]-Zeuxippe[3]
Oicle(u)s [Paus.] – Hyperm(n)estra[2] [Apollod.]
32d
Cronus-Rhea
Zeus [Eur.] – Leda [Eur.] – Tyndareus [Hom.]
Oebalus[1]-Bateia
48c-d
Helen[1] [Hom.]
48d
Plexippus[1] [Apollod.]
Prothous[2] [Paus.]
Toxeus[3] [Ovid]
Agrius[1] [Hom.] – Dia[4] [Schol. Hom.]
Celeutor [Apollod.]
Lycopeus [Apollod.]
Melanippus[6] [Apollod.]
Onchestus[2] [Apollod.]
Prothous[3] [Apollod.]
Thersites [Apollod.]
Melas[3] [Hom.] – ?
Antiochus[3] [Apollod.]
Eumedes[1] [Apollod.]
Euryalus[2] [Apollod.]
Hyperlaus [Apollod.]
Pheneus [Apollod.]
Sternops [Apollod.]
Sthenelaus[1] [Apollod.]
Xanthippus[1] [Apollod.]
<Oeneus[1]-Althaea>>
Andraemon[1] [Apollod.] – Gorge[1] [Cat. Wom.]
Zeus-Alcmene
Heracles[1] [Cat. Wom.] – Deianeira[1] [Cat. Wom.] – Nessus[1] [Ovid]
60a
Centaurus-Magnesian Mare
Thoas[6] [Hom.] – ?
Laertes-Anticlea[1]
Odysseus [Apollod.] – ? [Apollod.]
Haemon[3] [Paus.] – ?
Leontophon(us) [Apollod.]
Iphitus[2] [Paus.]
Oxylus[2] [Paus.] – Pieria[2] [Paus.]
Thermius [Paus.]
Eurytus[2]-?
Aetolus[2] [Paus.]
Andraemon[2] [Ant. Lib.] – Dryope[2] [Ovid]
Laias [Paus.]

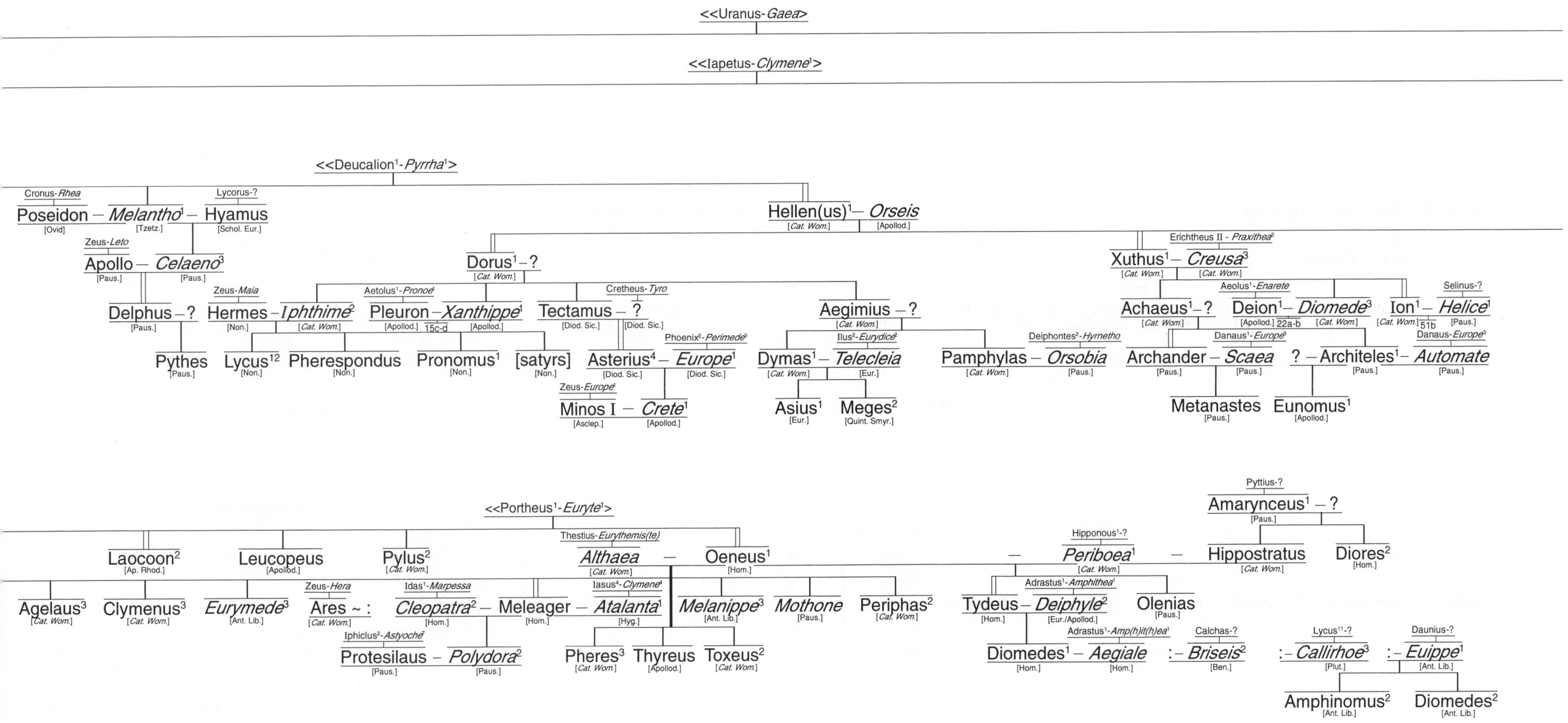
<<Uranus-Gaea>
<<Iapetus-Clymene[1]>
<<Deucalion[1]-Pyrrha[1]>
Cronus-Rhea
Poseidon – Melantho[1] – Hyamus
[Ovid] [Tzetz.] [Schol. Eur.]
Lycorus-?
Zeus-Leto
Apollo – Celaeno[3]
[Paus.] [Paus.]
Delphus – ?
[Paus.]
Pythes
[Paus.]
Hellen(us)[1] – Orseis
[Cat. Wom.] [Apollod.]
Dorus[1] – ?
[Cat. Wom.]
Zeus-Maia
Hermes – Iphthime[2]
[Non.] [Cat. Wom.]
Aetolus[1]-Pronoe[1]
Pleuron – Xanthippe[1]
[Apollod.] 15c-d [Apollod.]
Cretheus-Tyro
Tectamus – ?
[Diod. Sic.] [Diod. Sic.]
Lycus[12]
[Non.]
Pherespondus
[Non.]
Pronomus[1]
[Non.]
[satyrs]
[Non.]
Phoenix[2]-Perimede[3]
Asterius[4] – Europe[1]
[Diod. Sic.] [Diod. Sic.]
Zeus-Europe[1]
Minos I – Crete[1]
[Asclep.] [Apollod.]
Aegimius – ?
[Cat. Wom.]
Ilus[2]-Eurydice[3]
Dymas[1] – Telecleia
[Cat. Wom.] [Eur.]
Asius[1]
[Eur.]
Meges[2]
[Quint. Smyr.]
Deiphontes[2]-Hyrnetho
Pamphylas – Orsobia
[Cat. Wom.] [Paus.]
Erichtheus II - Praxithea[2]
Xuthus[1] – Creusa[3]
[Cat. Wom.] [Cat. Wom.]
Aeolus[1]-Enarete
Achaeus[1] – ?
[Cat. Wom.]
Deion[1] – Diomede[3]
[Apollod.] 22a-b [Cat. Wom.]
Selinus-?
Ion[1] – Helice[1]
[Cat. Wom.] 51b [Paus.]
Danaus[1]-Europe[3]
Archander – Scaea
[Paus.] [Paus.]
Danaus-Europe[3]
? – Architeles[1] – Automate
[Paus.] [Paus.]
Metanastes
[Paus.]
Eunomus[1]
[Apollod.]
<<Portheus[1]-Euryte[1]>
Laocoon[2]
[Ap. Rhod.]
Leucopeus
[Apollod.]
Pylus[2]
[Cat. Wom.]
Thestius-Eurythemis(te)
Althaea – Oeneus[1] – Periboea[1] – Hippostratus
[Cat. Wom.] [Hom.] [Cat. Wom.] [Cat. Wom.]
Hipponous[1]-?
Pyttius-?
Amarynceus[1] – ?
[Paus.]
Diores[2]
[Hom.]
Agelaus[3]
[Cat. Wom.]
Clymenus[3]
[Cat. Wom.]
Eurymede[3]
[Ant. Lib.]
Zeus-Hera
Ares ~ :
[Cat. Wom.]
Idas[1]-Marpessa
Cleopatra[2] – Meleager – Atalanta[1]
[Hom.] [Hom.] [Hyg.]
Iasus[4]-Clymene[4]
Iphiclus[2]-Astyoche[7]
Protesilaus – Polydora[2]
[Paus.] [Paus.]
Pheres[3]
[Cat. Wom.]
Thyreus
[Apollod.]
Toxeus[2]
[Cat. Wom.]
Melanippe[3]
[Ant. Lib.]
Mothone
[Paus.]
Periphas[2]
[Cat. Wom.]
Adrastus[1]-Amphithea[1]
Tydeus – Deiphyle[2]
[Hom.] [Eur./Apollod.]
Olenias
[Paus.]
Adrastus[1]-Amp(h)it(h)ea[1]
Diomedes[1] – Aegiale
[Hom.] [Hom.]
Calchas-?
:– Briseis[2]
[Ben.]
Lycus[11]-?
:– Callirhoe[3]
[Plut.]
Daunius-?
:– Euippe[1]
[Ant. Lib.]
Amphinomus[2]
[Ant. Lib.]
Diomedes[2]
[Ant. Lib.]

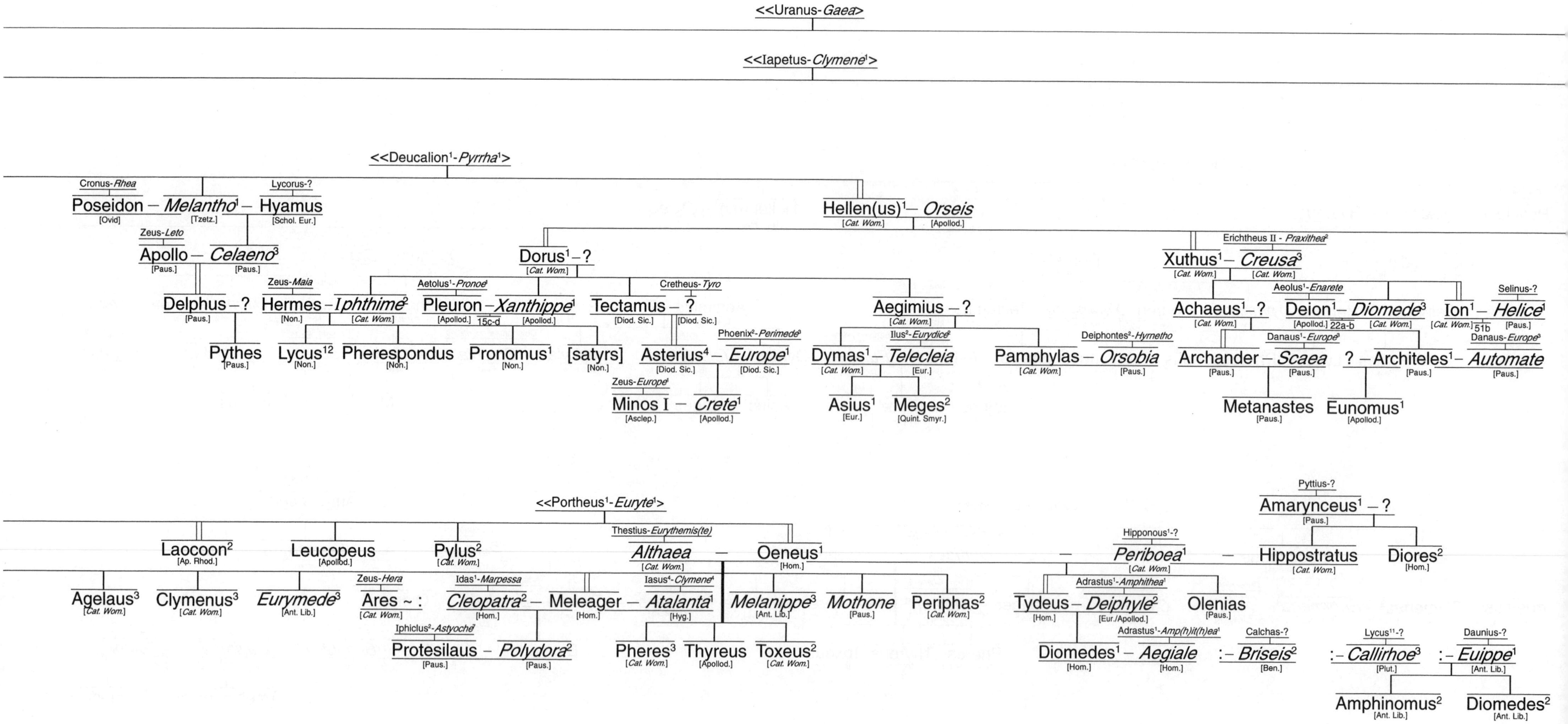

<<Uranus-*Gaea*>
<<Iapetus-*Clymene*[1]>
<<Deucalion[1]-*Pyrrha*[1]>
Cronus-*Rhea*
Poseidon – *Melantho*[1] – Hyamus
[Ovid] [Tzetz.] [Schol. Eur.]
Lycorus-?
Zeus-*Leto*
Apollo – *Celaeno*[3]
[Paus.] [Paus.]
Delphus – ?
[Paus.]
Pythes
[Paus.]
Zeus-*Maia*
Hermes – *Iphthime*[2]
[Non.] [Cat. Wom.]
Lycus[12]
[Non.]
Pherespondus
[Non.]
Aetolus[1]-*Pronoe*[1]
Pleuron – *Xanthippe*[1]
[Apollod.] 15c-d [Apollod.]
Pronomus[1]
[Non.]
[satyrs]
[Non.]
Hellen(us)[1] – *Orseis*
[Cat. Wom.] [Apollod.]
Dorus[1] – ?
[Cat. Wom.]
Tectamus – ?
[Diod. Sic.] [Diod. Sic.]
Cretheus-*Tyro*
Asterius[4] – *Europe*[1]
[Diod. Sic.] [Diod. Sic.]
Phoenix[2]-*Perimede*[3]
Zeus-*Europe*[1]
Minos I – *Crete*[1]
[Asclep.] [Apollod.]
Aegimius – ?
[Cat. Wom.]
Ilus[2]-*Eurydice*[2]
Dymas[1] – *Telecleia*
[Cat. Wom.] [Eur.]
Asius[1]
[Eur.]
Meges[2]
[Quint. Smyr.]
Pamphylas – *Orsobia*
[Cat. Wom.] [Paus.]
Deiphontes[2]-*Hyrnetho*
Erichtheus II - *Praxithea*[2]
Xuthus[1] – *Creusa*[3]
[Cat. Wom.] [Cat. Wom.]
Aeolus[1]-*Enarete*
Achaeus[1] – ?
[Cat. Wom.]
Deion[1] – *Diomede*[3]
[Apollod.] 22a-b [Cat. Wom.]
Selinus-?
Ion[1] – *Helice*[1]
[Cat. Wom.] 51b [Paus.]
Danaus[1]-*Europe*[3]
Archander – *Scaea*
[Paus.] [Paus.]
Danaus-*Europe*[3]
? – Architeles[1] – *Automate*
[Paus.] [Paus.]
Metanastes
[Paus.]
Eunomus[1]
[Apollod.]
<<Portheus[1]-*Euryte*[1]>
Laocoon[2]
[Ap. Rhod.]
Leucopeus
[Apollod.]
Pylus[2]
[Cat. Wom.]
Thestius-*Eurythemis(te)*
Althaea – Oeneus[1] – *Periboea*[1] – Hippostratus
[Cat. Wom.] [Hom.] [Cat. Wom.] [Cat. Wom.]
Hipponous[1]-?
Pyttius-?
Amarynceus[1] – ?
[Paus.]
Diores[2]
[Hom.]
Agelaus[3]
[Cat. Wom.]
Clymenus[3]
[Cat. Wom.]
Eurymede[3]
[Ant. Lib.]
Zeus-*Hera*
Ares ~ :
[Cat. Wom.]
Idas[1]-*Marpessa*
Cleopatra[2] – Meleager – *Atalanta*[1]
[Hom.] [Hom.] [Hyg.]
Iasus[4]-*Clymene*[4]
Iphiclus[2]-*Astyoche*[2]
Protesilaus – *Polydora*[2]
[Paus.] [Paus.]
Pheres[3]
[Cat. Wom.]
Thyreus
[Apollod.]
Toxeus[2]
[Cat. Wom.]
Melanippe[3]
[Ant. Lib.]
Mothone
[Paus.]
Periphas[2]
[Cat. Wom.]
Adrastus[1]-*Amphithea*[1]
Tydeus – *Deiphyle*[2]
[Hom.] [Eur./Apollod.]
Olenias
[Paus.]
Adrastus[1]-*Amp(h)it(h)ea*[1]
Diomedes[1] – *Aegiale*
[Hom.] [Hom.]
Calchas-?
:– *Briseis*[2]
[Ben.]
Lycus[11]-?
:– *Callirhoe*[3]
[Plut.]
Daunius-?
:– *Euippe*[1]
[Ant. Lib.]
Amphinomus[2]
[Ant. Lib.]
Diomedes[2]
[Ant. Lib.]

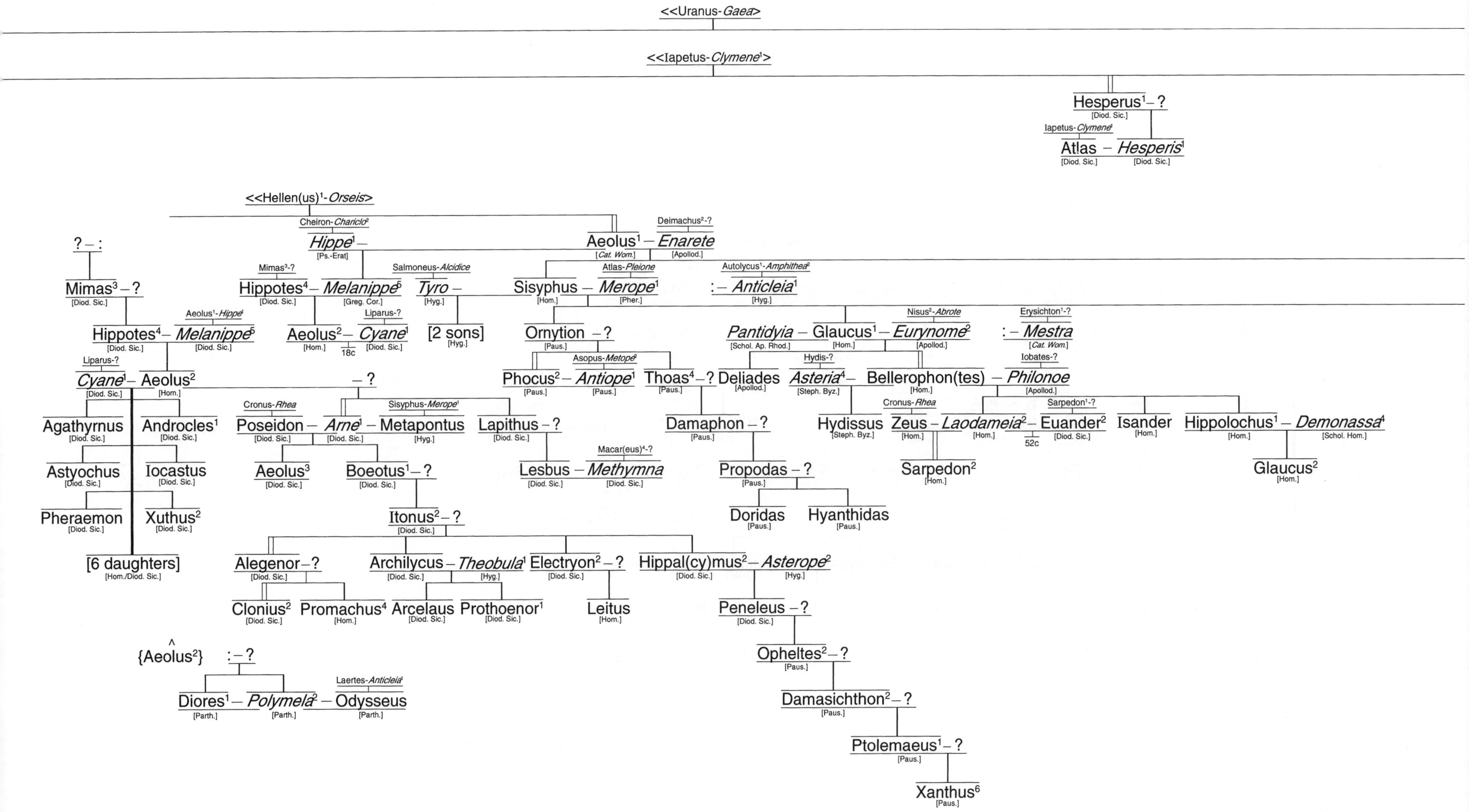

<<Uranus-Gaea>
<<Iapetus-Clymene[1]>
Hesperus[1] – ? [Diod. Sic.]
Iapetus-Clymene[1]
Atlas [Diod. Sic.] – Hesperis[1] [Diod. Sic.]
<<Hellen(us)[1]-Orseis>
Cheiron-Chariclo[2]
Hippe[1] – [Ps.-Erat]
Deimachus[2]-?
Aeolus[1] [Cat. Wom.] – Enarete [Apollod.]
?–:
Mimas[3] – ? [Diod. Sic.]
Mimas[3]-?
Hippotes[4] [Diod. Sic.] – Melanippe[5] [Greg. Cor.]
Salmoneus-Alcidice
Tyro – [Hyg.]
Atlas-Pleione
Sisyphus [Hom.] – Merope[1] [Pher.]
Autolycus[1]-Amphithea[2]
:– Anticleia[1] [Hyg.]
Aeolus[1]-Hippe[1]
Hippotes[4] [Diod. Sic.] – Melanippe[5] [Diod. Sic.]
Liparus-?
Aeolus[2] [Hom.] – Cyane[1] [Diod. Sic.]
18c
[2 sons] [Hyg.]
Ornytion – ? [Paus.]
Nisus[2]-Abrote
Pantidyia [Schol. Ap. Rhod.] – Glaucus[1] [Hom.] – Eurynome[2] [Apollod.]
Erysichton[1]-?
:– Mestra [Cat. Wom.]
Liparus-?
Cyane[1] [Diod. Sic.] – Aeolus[2] [Hom.]
– ?
Asopus-Metope[2]
Phocus[2] [Paus.] – Antiope[1] [Paus.]
Thoas[4] – ? [Paus.]
Deliades [Apollod.]
Hydis-?
Asteria[4] [Steph. Byz.] –
Bellerophon(tes) [Hom.] – Philonoe [Apollod.]
Iobates-?
Agathyrnus [Diod. Sic.]
Androcles[1] [Diod. Sic.]
Cronus-Rhea
Poseidon [Diod. Sic.] – Arne[1] [Diod. Sic.] – Metapontus [Hyg.]
Sisyphus-Merope[1]
Lapithus – ? [Diod. Sic.]
Damaphon – ? [Paus.]
Hydissus [Steph. Byz.]
Cronus-Rhea
Zeus [Hom.] – Laodameia[2] [Hom.] – Euander[2] [Diod. Sic.]
52c
Sarpedon[1]-?
Isander [Hom.]
Hippolochus[1] [Hom.] – Demonassa[4] [Schol. Hom.]
Astyochus [Diod. Sic.]
Iocastus [Diod. Sic.]
Aeolus[3] [Diod. Sic.]
Boeotus[1] – ? [Diod. Sic.]
Macar(eus)[4]-?
Lesbus [Diod. Sic.] – Methymna [Diod. Sic.]
Propodas – ? [Paus.]
Sarpedon[2] [Hom.]
Glaucus[2] [Hom.]
Pheraemon [Diod. Sic.]
Xuthus[2] [Diod. Sic.]
Itonus[2] – ? [Diod. Sic.]
Doridas [Paus.]
Hyanthidas [Paus.]
[6 daughters] [Hom./Diod. Sic.]
Alegenor – ? [Diod. Sic.]
Archilycus [Diod. Sic.] – Theobula[1] [Hyg.]
Electryon[2] – ? [Diod. Sic.]
Hippal(cy)mus[2] [Diod. Sic.] – Asterope[2] [Hyg.]
Clonius[2] [Diod. Sic.]
Promachus[4] [Hom.]
Arcelaus [Diod. Sic.]
Prothoenor[1] [Diod. Sic.]
Leitus [Hom.]
Peneleus – ? [Diod. Sic.]
{Aeolus[2]}
:– ?
Opheltes[2] – ? [Paus.]
Laertes-Anticleia[1]
Diores[1] [Parth.] – Polymela[2] [Parth.] – Odysseus [Parth.]
Damasichthon[2] – ? [Paus.]
Ptolemaeus[1] – ? [Paus.]
Xanthus[6] [Paus.]

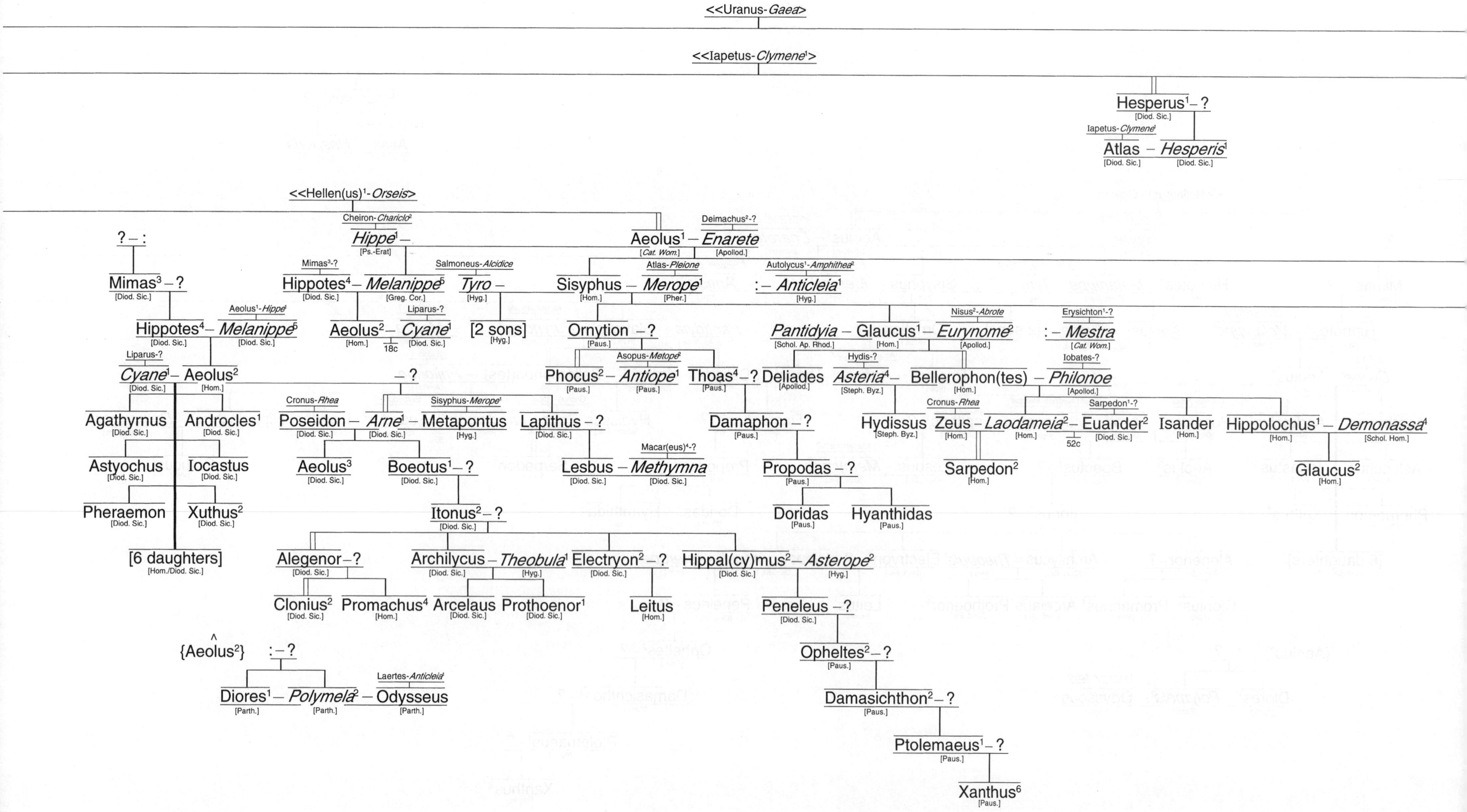

<<Uranus-Gaea>
<<Iapetus-Clymene[1]>
Hesperus[1] – ?
[Diod. Sic.]
Iapetus-Clymene[1]
Atlas – Hesperis[1]
[Diod. Sic.] [Diod. Sic.]
<<Hellen(us)[1]-Orseis>
Cheiron-Chariclo[2]
Hippe[1] –
[Ps.-Erat]
Deimachus[2]-?
Aeolus[1] – Enarete
[Cat. Wom.] [Apollod.]
? – :
Mimas[3] – ?
[Diod. Sic.]
Mimas[3]-?
Hippotes[4] – Melanippe[5]
[Diod. Sic.] [Greg. Cor.]
Salmoneus-Alcidice
Tyro –
[Hyg.]
Atlas-Pleione
Sisyphus – Merope[1]
[Hom.] [Pher.]
Autolycus[1]-Amphithea[2]
: – Anticleia[1]
[Hyg.]
Aeolus[1]-Hippe[1]
Hippotes[4] – Melanippe[5]
[Diod. Sic.] [Diod. Sic.]
Liparus-?
Aeolus[2] – Cyane[1]
[Hom.] 18c [Diod. Sic.]
[2 sons]
[Hyg.]
Ornytion – ?
[Paus.]
Pantidyia – Glaucus[1] – Eurynome[2]
[Schol. Ap. Rhod.] [Hom.] [Apollod.]
Nisus[2]-Abrote
Erysichton[1]-?
: – Mestra
[Cat. Wom.]
Liparus-?
Cyane[1] – Aeolus[2]
[Diod. Sic.] [Hom.]
– ?
Asopus-Metope[2]
Phocus[2] – Antiope[1]
[Paus.] [Paus.]
Thoas[4] – ?
[Paus.]
Deliades
[Apollod.]
Hydis-?
Asteria[4] –
[Steph. Byz.]
Iobates-?
Bellerophon(tes) – Philonoe
[Hom.] [Apollod.]
Cronus-Rhea
Poseidon – Arne[1] – Metapontus
[Diod. Sic.] [Diod. Sic.] [Hyg.]
Sisyphus-Merope[1]
Lapithus – ?
[Diod. Sic.]
Damaphon – ?
[Paus.]
Hydissus
[Steph. Byz.]
Cronus-Rhea
Zeus – Laodameia[2] – Euander[2]
[Hom.] [Hom.] 52c [Diod. Sic.]
Sarpedon[1]-?
Isander
[Hom.]
Hippolochus[1] – Demonassa[4]
[Hom.] [Schol. Hom.]
Agathyrnus
[Diod. Sic.]
Androcles[1]
[Diod. Sic.]
Astyochus
[Diod. Sic.]
Iocastus
[Diod. Sic.]
Aeolus[3]
[Diod. Sic.]
Boeotus[1] – ?
[Diod. Sic.]
Macar(eus)[4]-?
Lesbus – Methymna
[Diod. Sic.] [Diod. Sic.]
Propodas – ?
[Paus.]
Sarpedon[2]
[Hom.]
Glaucus[2]
[Hom.]
Pheraemon
[Diod. Sic.]
Xuthus[2]
[Diod. Sic.]
Itonus[2] – ?
[Diod. Sic.]
Doridas
[Paus.]
Hyanthidas
[Paus.]
[6 daughters]
[Hom./Diod. Sic.]
Alegenor – ?
[Diod. Sic.]
Archilycus – Theobula[1]
[Diod. Sic.] [Hyg.]
Electryon[2] – ?
[Diod. Sic.]
Hippal(cy)mus[2] – Asterope[2]
[Diod. Sic.] [Hyg.]
Clonius[2]
[Diod. Sic.]
Promachus[4]
[Hom.]
Arcelaus
[Diod. Sic.]
Prothoenor[1]
[Diod. Sic.]
Leitus
[Hom.]
Peneleus – ?
[Diod. Sic.]
^
{Aeolus[2]}
: – ?
Laertes-Anticleia[1]
Diores[1] – Polymela[2] – Odysseus
[Parth.] [Parth.] [Parth.]
Opheltes[2] – ?
[Paus.]
Damasichthon[2] – ?
[Paus.]
Ptolemaeus[1] – ?
[Paus.]
Xanthus[6]
[Paus.]

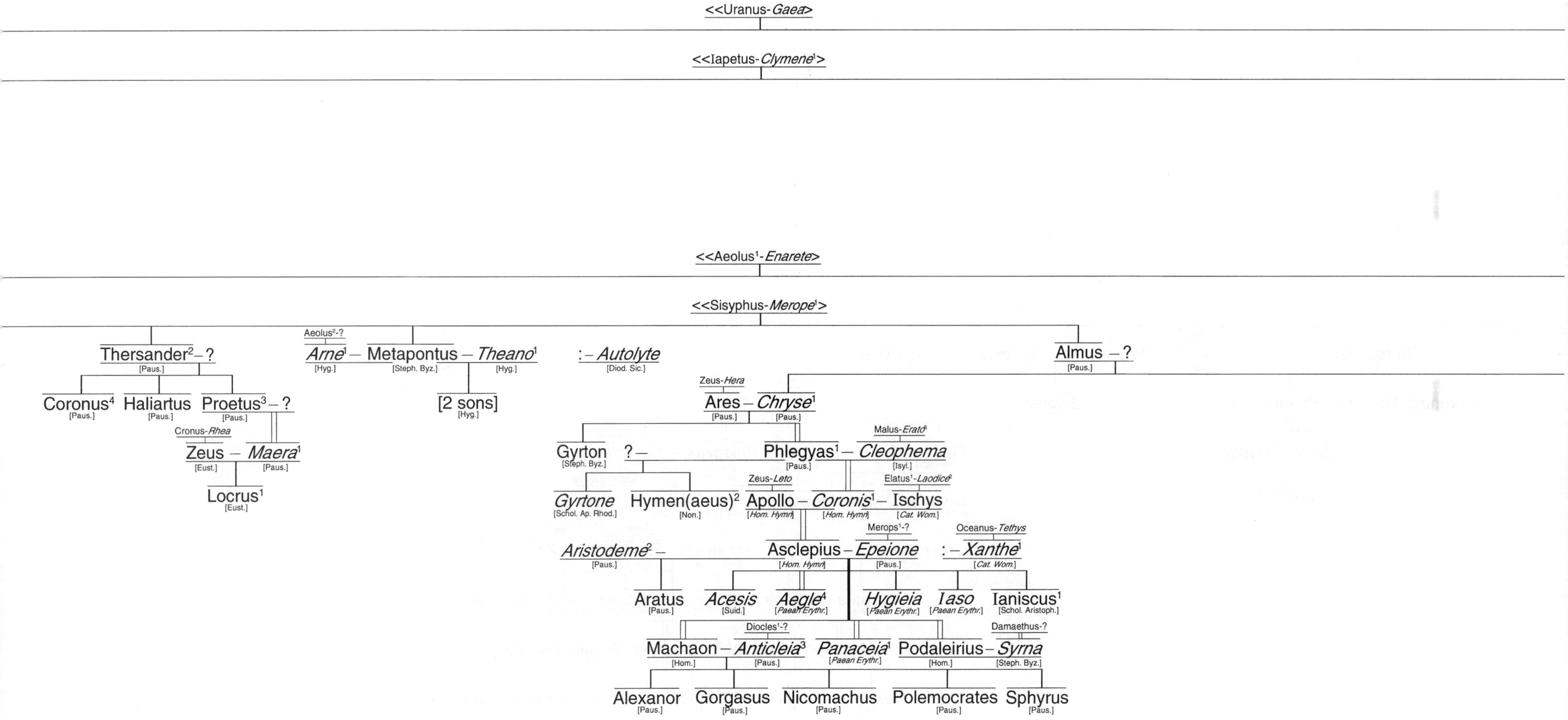
<<Uranus-*Gaea*>
<<Iapetus-*Clymene*¹>
<<Aeolus¹-*Enarete*>
<<Sisyphus-*Merope*¹>
Thersander²–?
[Paus.]
Coronus⁴
[Paus.]
Haliartus
[Paus.]
Proetus³–?
[Paus.]
Cronus-*Rhea*
Zeus – *Maera*¹
[Eust.]
[Paus.]
Locrus¹
[Eust.]
Aeolus²-?
*Arne*¹ – Metapontus – *Theano*¹
[Hyg.]
[Steph. Byz.]
[Hyg.]
[2 sons]
[Hyg.]
: – *Autolyte*
[Diod. Sic.]
Zeus-*Hera*
Ares – *Chryse*¹
[Paus.]
[Paus.]
Gyrton
[Steph. Byz.]
? –
Malus-*Erato*⁶
Phlegyas¹ – *Cleophema*
[Paus.]
[Isyl.]
Gyrtone
[Schol. Ap. Rhod.]
Hymen(aeus)²
[Non.]
Zeus-*Leto*
Apollo – *Coronis*¹ – Ischys
[Hom. Hymn]
[Hom. Hymn]
Elatus¹-*Laodice*²
[Cat. Wom.]
*Aristodeme*² –
[Paus.]
Merops¹-?
Asclepius – *Epeione*
[Hom. Hymn]
[Paus.]
Oceanus-*Tethys*
: – *Xanthe*¹
[Cat. Wom.]
Aratus
[Paus.]
Acesis
[Suid.]
*Aegle*⁴
[Paean Erythr.]
Hygieia
[Paean Erythr.]
Iaso
[Paean Erythr.]
Ianiscus¹
[Schol. Aristoph.]
Diocles¹-?
Machaon – *Anticleia*³
[Hom.]
[Paus.]
*Panaceia*¹
[Paean Erythr.]
Damaethus-?
Podaleirius – *Syrna*
[Hom.]
[Steph. Byz.]
Alexanor
[Paus.]
Gorgasus
[Paus.]
Nicomachus
[Paus.]
Polemocrates
[Paus.]
Sphyrus
[Paus.]
Almus – ?
[Paus.]

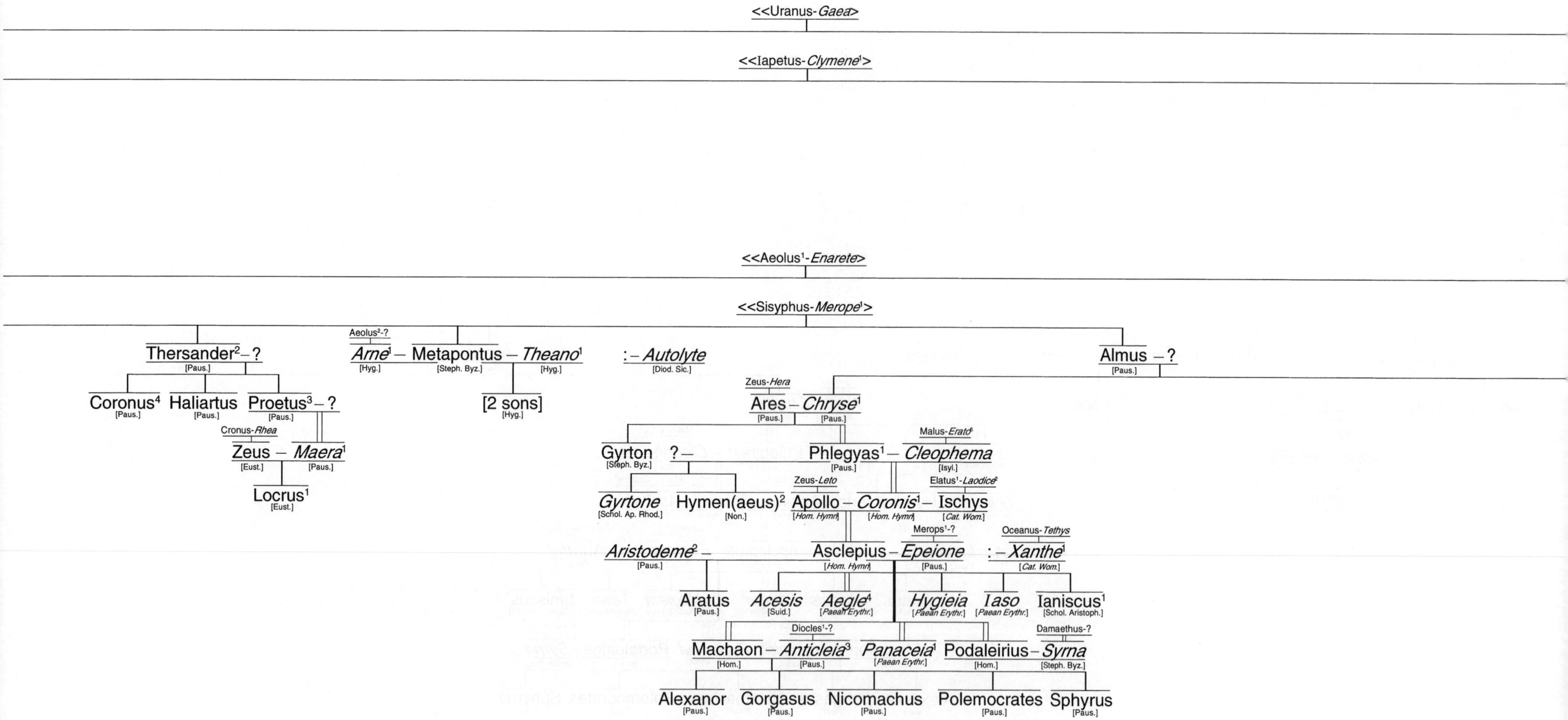
<<Uranus-*Gaea*>
<<Iapetus-*Clymene*[1]>
<<Aeolus[1]-*Enarete*>
<<Sisyphus-*Merope*[1]>
Thersander[2] – ? [Paus.]
Aeolus[2]-?
Arne[1] – Metapontus – *Theano*[1]
[Hyg.] [Steph. Byz.] [Hyg.]
: – *Autolyte* [Diod. Sic.]
Almus – ? [Paus.]
Coronus[4] [Paus.]
Haliartus [Paus.]
Proetus[3] – ? [Paus.]
[2 sons] [Hyg.]
Zeus-*Hera*
Ares – *Chryse*[1]
[Paus.] [Paus.]
Cronus-*Rhea*
Zeus – *Maera*[1]
[Eust.] [Paus.]
Locrus[1] [Eust.]
Gyrton [Steph. Byz.]
? –
Malus-*Erato*[6]
Phlegyas[1] – *Cleophema*
[Paus.] [Isyl.]
Zeus-*Leto*
Elatus[1]-*Laodice*[2]
Gyrtone [Schol. Ap. Rhod.]
Hymen(aeus)[2] [Non.]
Apollo – *Coronis*[1] – Ischys
[*Hom. Hymn*] [*Hom. Hymn*] [*Cat. Wom.*]
Merops[1]-?
Oceanus-*Tethys*
Aristodeme[2] – [Paus.]
Asclepius – *Epeione*
[*Hom. Hymn*] [Paus.]
: – *Xanthe*[1] [*Cat. Wom.*]
Aratus [Paus.]
Acesis [Suid.]
Aegle[4] [*Paean Erythr.*]
Hygieia [*Paean Erythr.*]
Iaso [*Paean Erythr.*]
Ianiscus[1] [Schol. Aristoph.]
Diocles[1]-?
Damaethus-?
Machaon – *Anticleia*[3]
[Hom.] [Paus.]
Panaceia[1] [*Paean Erythr.*]
Podaleirius – *Syrna*
[Hom.] [Steph. Byz.]
Alexanor [Paus.]
Gorgasus [Paus.]
Nicomachus [Paus.]
Polemocrates [Paus.]
Sphyrus [Paus.]

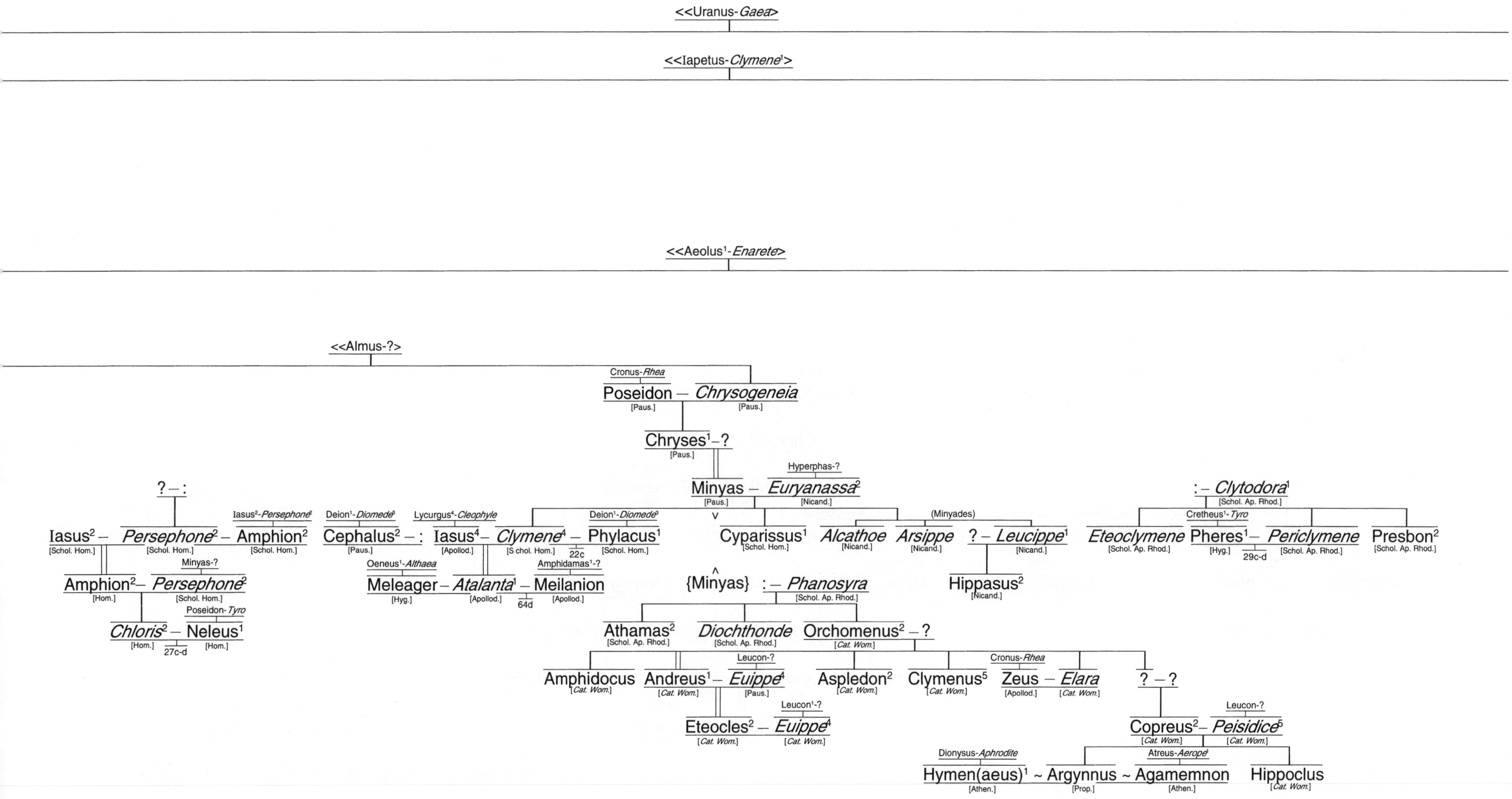
<<Uranus-*Gaea*>
<<Iapetus-*Clymene*[1]>
<<Aeolus[1]-*Enarete*>
<<Almus-?>
Cronus-*Rhea*
Poseidon – *Chrysogeneia*
[Paus.] [Paus.]
Chryses[1]–?
[Paus.]
Hyperphas-?
Minyas – *Euryanassa*[2]
[Paus.] [Nicand.]
?–:
Iasus[2]-*Persephone*[2]
Iasus[2] – *Persephone*[2] – Amphion[2]
[Schol. Hom.] [Schol. Hom.] [Schol. Hom.]
Minyas-?
Amphion[2]– *Persephone*[2]
[Hom.] [Schol. Hom.]
Poseidon-*Tyro*
Chloris[2] – Neleus[1]
[Hom.] 27c-d [Hom.]
Deion[1]-*Diomede*[3]
Cephalus[2] – :
[Paus.]
Lycurgus[4]-*Cleophyle*
Iasus[4]– *Clymene*[4] – Phylacus[1]
[Apollod.] [S chol. Hom.] 22c [Schol. Hom.]
Deion[1]-*Diomede*[3]
Oeneus[1]-*Althaea*
Amphidamas[1]-?
Meleager – *Atalanta*[1] – Meilanion
[Hyg.] [Apollod.] 64d [Apollod.]
v
(Minyades)
Cyparissus[1] *Alcathoe* *Arsippe* ? – *Leucippe*[1]
[Schol. Hom.] [Nicand.] [Nicand.] [Nicand.]
Hippasus[2]
[Nicand.]
^
{Minyas} : – *Phanosyra*
[Schol. Ap. Rhod.]
Athamas[2] *Diochthonde* Orchomenus[2] – ?
[Schol. Ap. Rhod.] [Schol. Ap. Rhod.] [*Cat. Wom.*]
Leucon-?
Amphidocus Andreus[1]– *Euippe*[4]
[*Cat. Wom.*] [*Cat. Wom.*] [Paus.]
Aspledon[2] Clymenus[5]
[*Cat. Wom.*] [*Cat. Wom.*]
Cronus-*Rhea*
Zeus – *Elara*
[Apollod.] [*Cat. Wom.*]
? – ?
Leucon[1]-?
Eteocles[2] – *Euippe*[4]
[*Cat. Wom.*] [*Cat. Wom.*]
Leucon-?
Copreus[2]– *Peisidice*[5]
[*Cat. Wom.*] [*Cat. Wom.*]
Dionysus-*Aphrodite*
Atreus-*Aerope*[1]
Hymen(aeus)[1] ~ Argynnus ~ Agamemnon
[Athen.] [Prop.] [Athen.]
Hippoclus
[*Cat. Wom.*]
: – *Clytodora*[1]
[Schol. Ap. Rhod.]
Cretheus[1]-*Tyro*
Eteoclymene Pheres[1]– *Periclymene* Presbon[2]
[Schol. Ap. Rhod.] [Hyg.] 29c-d [Schol. Ap. Rhod.] [Schol. Ap. Rhod.]

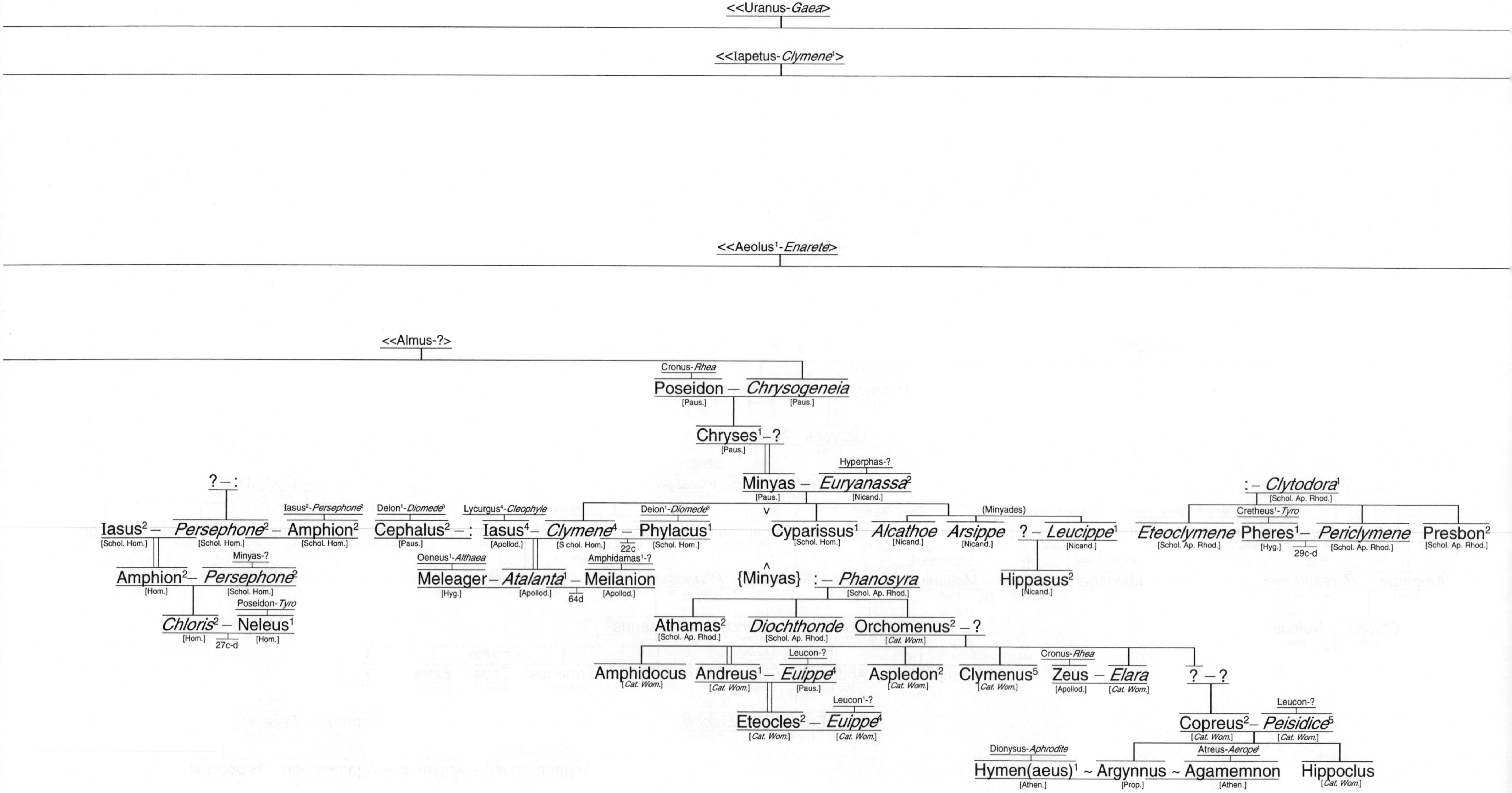

<<Uranus-Gaea>
<<Iapetus-Clymene1>
<<Aeolus1-Enarete>
<<Almus-?>
Cronus-Rhea
Poseidon – Chrysogeneia
[Paus.] [Paus.]
Chryses1–?
[Paus.]
Hyperphas-?
Minyas – Euryanassa2
[Paus.] [Nicand.]
?–:
Iasus2-Persephone2
Iasus2 – Persephone2 – Amphion2
[Schol. Hom.] [Schol. Hom.] [Schol. Hom.]
Minyas-?
Amphion2– Persephone2
[Hom.] [Schol. Hom.]
Poseidon-Tyro
Chloris2 – Neleus1
[Hom.] 27c-d [Hom.]
Deion1-Diomede3
Cephalus2 – :
[Paus.]
Lycurgus4-Cleophyle
Iasus4– Clymene4
[Apollod.] [S chol. Hom.]
22c
Deion1-Diomede3
Phylacus1
[Schol. Hom.]
Oeneus1-Althaea
Amphidamas1-?
Meleager – Atalanta1 – Meilanion
[Hyg.] [Apollod.] 64d [Apollod.]
Cyparissus1
[Schol. Hom.]
(Minyades)
Alcathoe Arsippe
[Nicand.] [Nicand.]
? – Leucippe1
[Nicand.]
Hippasus2
[Nicand.]
{Minyas} : – Phanosyra
[Schol. Ap. Rhod.]
Athamas2
[Schol. Ap. Rhod.]
Diochthonde
[Schol. Ap. Rhod.]
Orchomenus2 – ?
[Cat. Wom.]
Amphidocus
[Cat. Wom.]
Leucon-?
Andreus1 – Euippe4
[Cat. Wom.] [Paus.]
Leucon1-?
Eteocles2 – Euippe4
[Cat. Wom.] [Cat. Wom.]
Aspledon2
[Cat. Wom.]
Clymenus5
[Cat. Wom.]
Cronus-Rhea
Zeus – Elara
[Apollod.] [Cat. Wom.]
? – ?
Leucon-?
Copreus2– Peisidice5
[Cat. Wom.] [Cat. Wom.]
Dionysus-Aphrodite
Hymen(aeus)1 ~ Argynnus ~ Agamemnon
[Athen.] [Prop.] [Athen.]
Atreus-Aerope1
Hippoclus
[Cat. Wom.]
: – Clytodora1
[Schol. Ap. Rhod.]
Cretheus1-Tyro
Eteoclymene
[Schol. Ap. Rhod.]
Pheres1– Periclymene
[Hyg.] 29c-d [Schol. Ap. Rhod.]
Presbon2
[Schol. Ap. Rhod.]

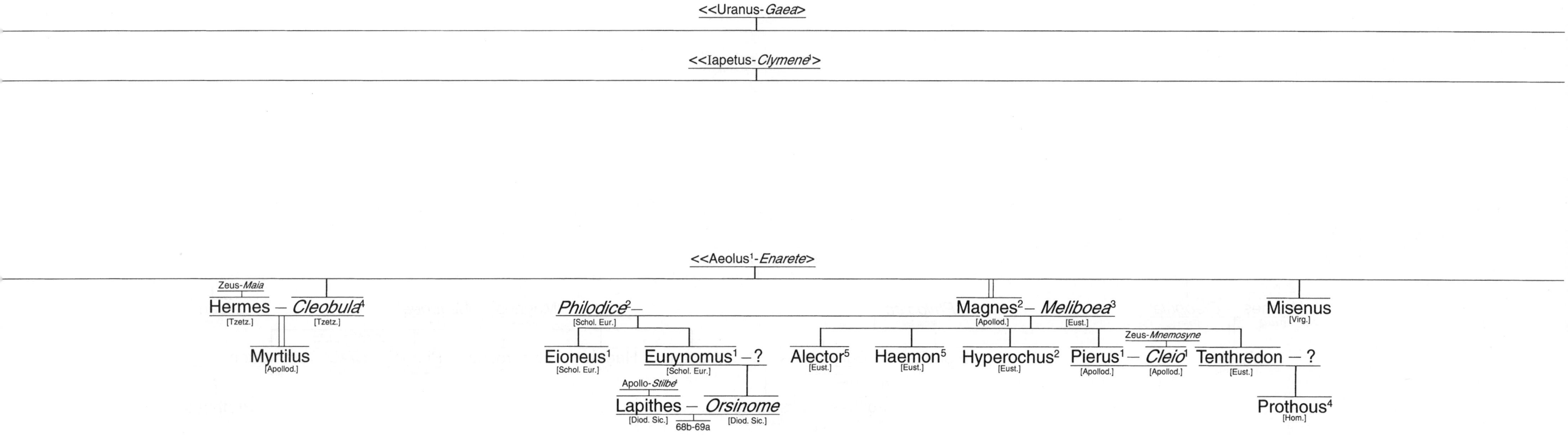
<<Uranus-Gaea>
<<Iapetus-Clymene[1]>
<<Aeolus[1]-Enarete>
Zeus-Maia
Hermes – Cleobula[4]
[Tzetz.]
[Tzetz.]
Myrtilus
[Apollod.]
Philodice[2] –
[Schol. Eur.]
Eioneus[1]
[Schol. Eur.]
Eurynomus[1] – ?
[Schol. Eur.]
Apollo-Stilbe[1]
Lapithes – Orsinome
[Diod. Sic.]
68b-69a
[Diod. Sic.]
Magnes[2] – Meliboea[3]
[Apollod.]
[Eust.]
Alector[5]
[Eust.]
Haemon[5]
[Eust.]
Hyperochus[2]
[Eust.]
Zeus-Mnemosyne
Pierus[1] – Cleio[1]
[Apollod.]
[Apollod.]
Tenthredon – ?
[Eust.]
Prothous[4]
[Hom.]
Misenus
[Virg.]

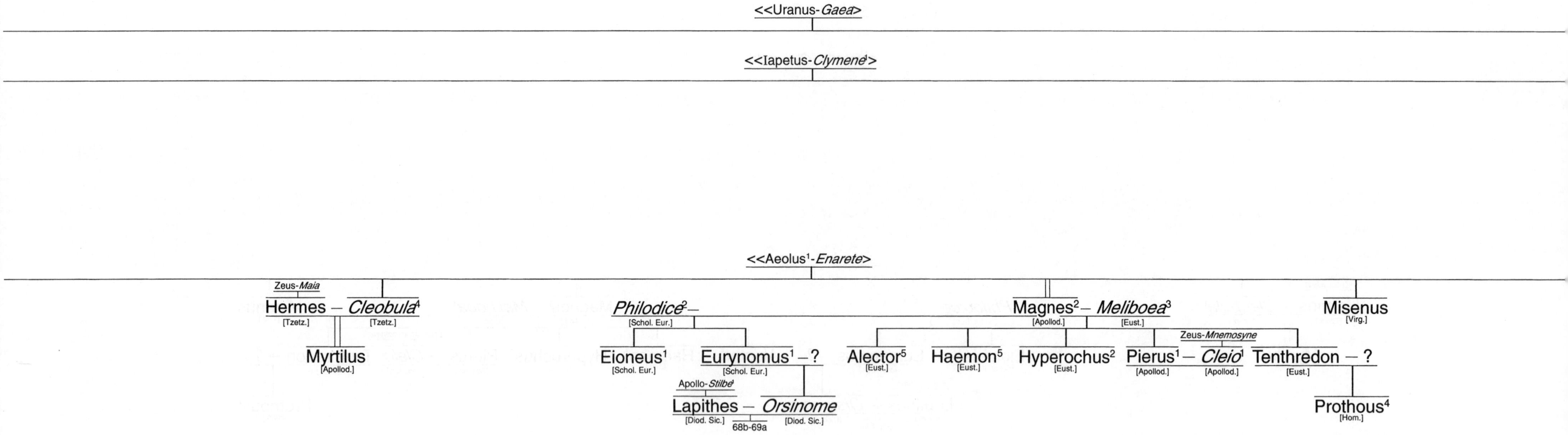
<<Uranus-*Gaea*>
<<Iapetus-*Clymene*[1]>
<<Aeolus[1]-*Enarete*>
Zeus-*Maia*
Hermes – *Cleobula*[4]
[Tzetz.]
[Tzetz.]
Myrtilus
[Apollod.]
Philodice[2] –
[Schol. Eur.]
Eioneus[1]
[Schol. Eur.]
Eurynomus[1] – ?
[Schol. Eur.]
Apollo-*Stilbe*[1]
Lapithes – *Orsinome*
[Diod. Sic.]
68b-69a
[Diod. Sic.]
Magnes[2] – *Meliboea*[3]
[Apollod.]
[Eust.]
Alector[5]
[Eust.]
Haemon[5]
[Eust.]
Hyperochus[2]
[Eust.]
Zeus-*Mnemosyne*
Pierus[1] – *Cleio*[1]
[Apollod.]
[Apollod.]
Tenthredon – ?
[Eust.]
Prothous[4]
[Hom.]
Misenus
[Virg.]

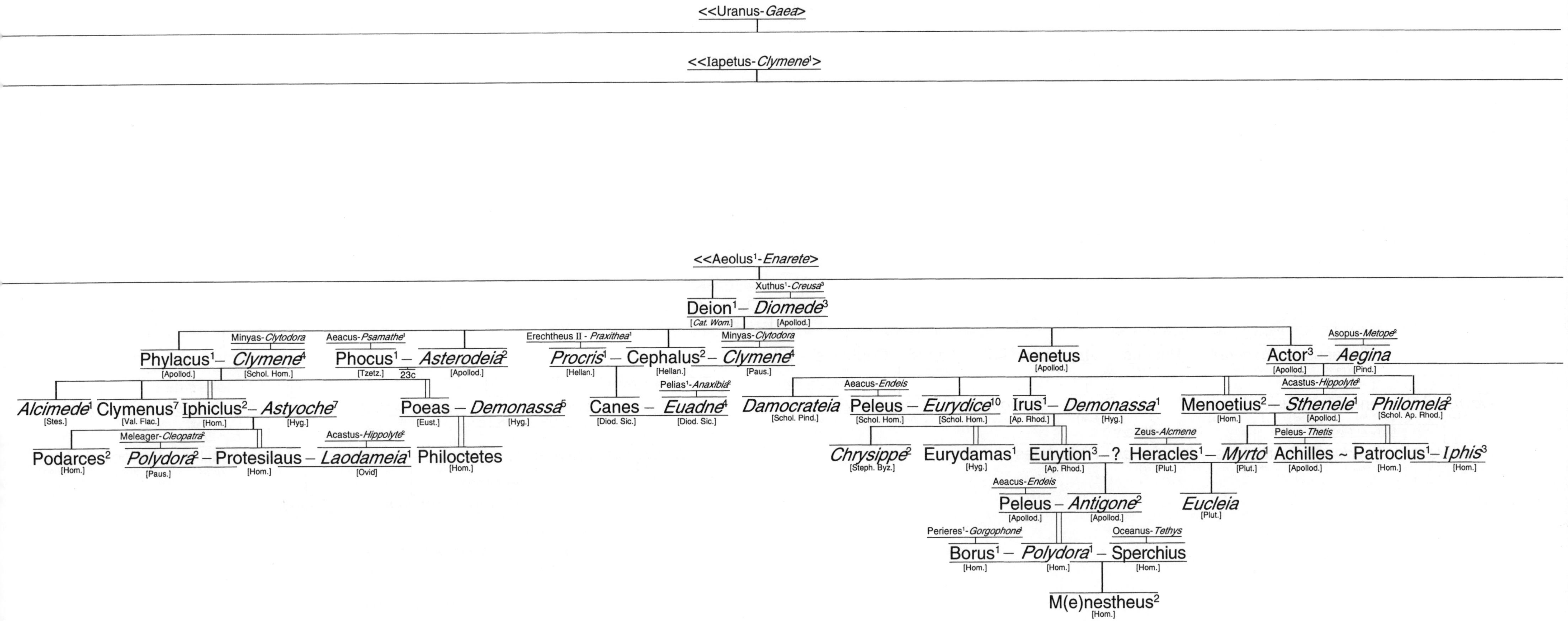

<<Uranus-Gaea>
<<Iapetus-Clymene1>
<<Aeolus1-Enarete>
Xuthus1-Creusa3
Deion1 – Diomede3
[Cat. Wom.]
[Apollod.]
Minyas-Clytodora
Aeacus-Psamathe1
Erechtheus II - Praxithea1
Minyas-Clytodora
Asopus-Metope2
Phylacus1 – Clymene4
[Apollod.]
[Schol. Hom.]
Phocus1 – Asterodeia2
[Tzetz.]
23c
[Apollod.]
Procris1 – Cephalus2 – Clymene4
[Hellan.]
[Hellan.]
[Paus.]
Aenetus
[Apollod.]
Actor3 – Aegina
[Apollod.]
[Pind.]
Alcimede1
[Stes.]
Clymenus7
[Val. Flac.]
Iphiclus2 – Astyoche7
[Hom.]
[Hyg.]
Poeas – Demonassa5
[Eust.]
[Hyg.]
Pelias1-Anaxibia2
Canes – Euadne4
[Diod. Sic.]
[Diod. Sic.]
Damocrateia
[Schol. Pind.]
Aeacus-Endeis
Peleus – Eurydice10
[Schol. Hom.]
[Schol. Hom.]
Irus1 – Demonassa1
[Ap. Rhod.]
[Hyg.]
Menoetius2 – Sthenele1
[Hom.]
Acastus-Hippolyte2
[Apollod.]
Philomela2
[Schol. Ap. Rhod.]
Meleager-Cleopatra2
Acastus-Hippolyte2
Podarces2
[Hom.]
Polydora2 – Protesilaus – Laodameia1
[Paus.]
[Hom.]
[Ovid]
Philoctetes
[Hom.]
Chrysippe2
[Steph. Byz.]
Eurydamas1
[Hyg.]
Eurytion3 – ?
[Ap. Rhod.]
Zeus-Alcmene
Heracles1 – Myrto1
[Plut.]
[Plut.]
Peleus-Thetis
Achilles ~ Patroclus1 – Iphis3
[Apollod.]
[Hom.]
[Hom.]
Aeacus-Endeis
Peleus – Antigone2
[Apollod.]
[Apollod.]
Eucleia
[Plut.]
Perieres1-Gorgophone1
Oceanus-Tethys
Borus1 – Polydora1 – Sperchius
[Hom.]
[Hom.]
[Hom.]
M(e)nestheus2
[Hom.]

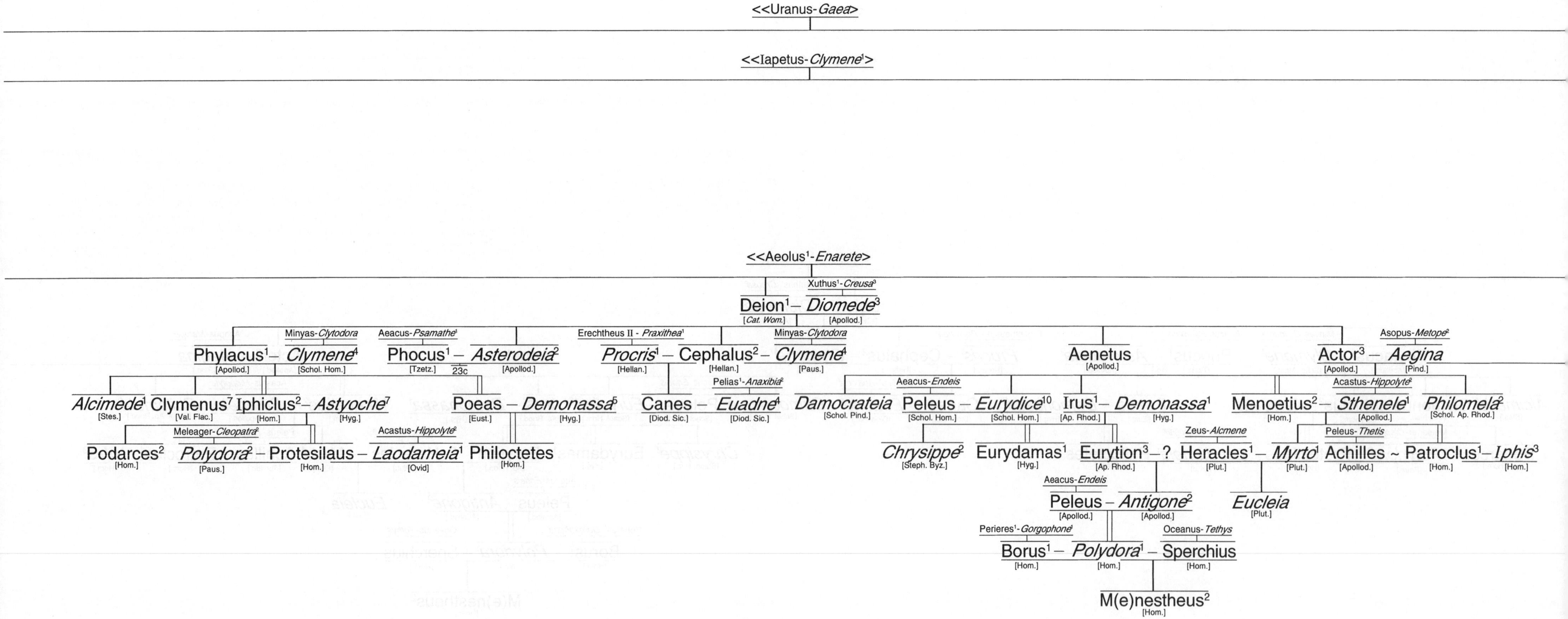

<<Uranus-Gaea>
<<Iapetus-Clymene1>
<<Aeolus1-Enarete>
Xuthus1-Creusa3
Deion1 – Diomede3
[Cat. Wom.]
[Apollod.]
Minyas-Clytodora
Aeacus-Psamathe1
Erechtheus II - Praxithea1
Minyas-Clytodora
Asopus-Metope2
Phylacus1 – Clymene4
[Apollod.]
[Schol. Hom.]
Phocus1 – Asterodeia2
[Tzetz.]
23c
[Apollod.]
Procris1 – Cephalus2 – Clymene4
[Hellan.]
[Hellan.]
[Paus.]
Aenetus
[Apollod.]
Actor3 – Aegina
[Apollod.]
[Pind.]
Pelias1-Anaxibia2
Aeacus-Endeis
Acastus-Hippolyte2
Alcimede1
[Stes.]
Clymenus7
[Val. Flac.]
Iphiclus2 – Astyoche7
[Hom.]
[Hyg.]
Poeas – Demonassa5
[Eust.]
[Hyg.]
Canes – Euadne4
[Diod. Sic.]
[Diod. Sic.]
Damocrateia
[Schol. Pind.]
Peleus – Eurydice10
[Schol. Hom.]
[Schol. Hom.]
Irus1 – Demonassa1
[Ap. Rhod.]
[Hyg.]
Menoetius2 – Sthenele1
[Hom.]
[Apollod.]
Philomela2
[Schol. Ap. Rhod.]
Meleager-Cleopatra2
Acastus-Hippolyte2
Zeus-Alcmene
Peleus-Thetis
Podarces2
[Hom.]
Polydora2 – Protesilaus – Laodameia1
[Paus.]
[Hom.]
[Ovid]
Philoctetes
[Hom.]
Chrysippe2
[Steph. Byz.]
Eurydamas1
[Hyg.]
Eurytion3 – ?
[Ap. Rhod.]
Heracles1 – Myrto1
[Plut.]
[Plut.]
Achilles ~ Patroclus1 – Iphis3
[Apollod.]
[Hom.]
[Hom.]
Aeacus-Endeis
Peleus – Antigone2
[Apollod.]
[Apollod.]
Eucleia
[Plut.]
Perieres1-Gorgophone1
Oceanus-Tethys
Borus1 – Polydora1 – Sperchius
[Hom.]
[Hom.]
[Hom.]
M(e)nestheus2
[Hom.]

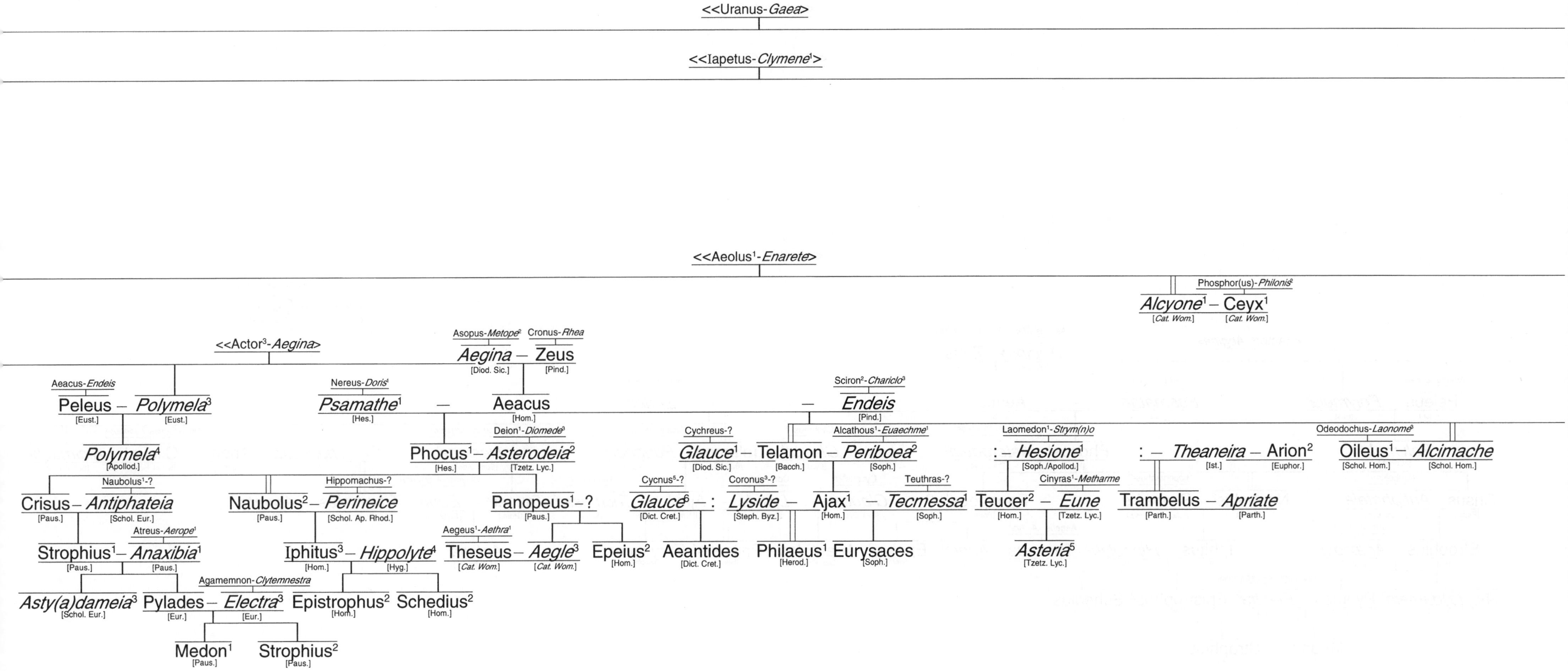

<<Uranus-Gaea>
<<Iapetus-Clymene[1]>
<<Aeolus[1]-Enarete>
Phosphor(us)-Philonis[2]
Alcyone[1] – Ceyx[1]
[Cat. Wom.]
[Cat. Wom.]
<<Actor[3]-Aegina>
Asopus-Metope[2]
Cronus-Rhea
Aegina – Zeus
[Diod. Sic.]
[Pind.]
Aeacus-Endeis
Peleus – Polymela[3]
[Eust.]
[Eust.]
Nereus-Doris[1]
Psamathe[1] – Aeacus
[Hes.]
[Hom.]
Sciron[2]-Chariclo[3]
– Endeis
[Pind.]
Polymela[4]
[Apollod.]
Deion[1]-Diomede[3]
Phocus[1] – Asterodeia[2]
[Hes.]
[Tzetz. Lyc.]
Cychreus-?
Glauce[1] – Telamon – Periboea[2]
[Diod. Sic.]
[Bacch.]
[Soph.]
Alcathous[1]-Euaechme[1]
Laomedon[1]-Strym(n)o
: – Hesione[1]
[Soph./Apollod.]
: – Theaneira – Arion[2]
[Ist.]
[Euphor.]
Odeodochus-Laonome[3]
Oileus[1] – Alcimache
[Schol. Hom.]
[Schol. Hom.]
Naubolus[1]-?
Crisus – Antiphateia
[Paus.]
[Schol. Eur.]
Hippomachus-?
Naubolus[2] – Perineice
[Paus.]
[Schol. Ap. Rhod.]
Panopeus[1] – ?
[Paus.]
Cycnus[5]-?
Glauce[6] – :
[Dict. Cret.]
Coronus[3]-?
Lyside – Ajax[1] – Tecmessa[1]
[Steph. Byz.]
[Hom.]
[Soph.]
Teuthras-?
Cinyras[1]-Metharme
Teucer[2] – Eune
[Hom.]
[Tzetz. Lyc.]
Trambelus – Apriate
[Parth.]
[Parth.]
Atreus-Aerope[1]
Strophius[1] – Anaxibia[1]
[Paus.]
[Paus.]
Iphitus[3] – Hippolyte[4]
[Hom.]
[Hyg.]
Aegeus[1]-Aethra[1]
Theseus – Aegle[3]
[Cat. Wom.]
[Cat. Wom.]
Epeius[2]
[Hom.]
Aeantides
[Dict. Cret.]
Philaeus[1]
[Herod.]
Eurysaces
[Soph.]
Asteria[5]
[Tzetz. Lyc.]
Agamemnon-Clytemnestra
Asty(a)dameia[3]
[Schol. Eur.]
Pylades – Electra[3]
[Eur.]
[Eur.]
Epistrophus[2]
[Hom.]
Schedius[2]
[Hom.]
Medon[1]
[Paus.]
Strophius[2]
[Paus.]

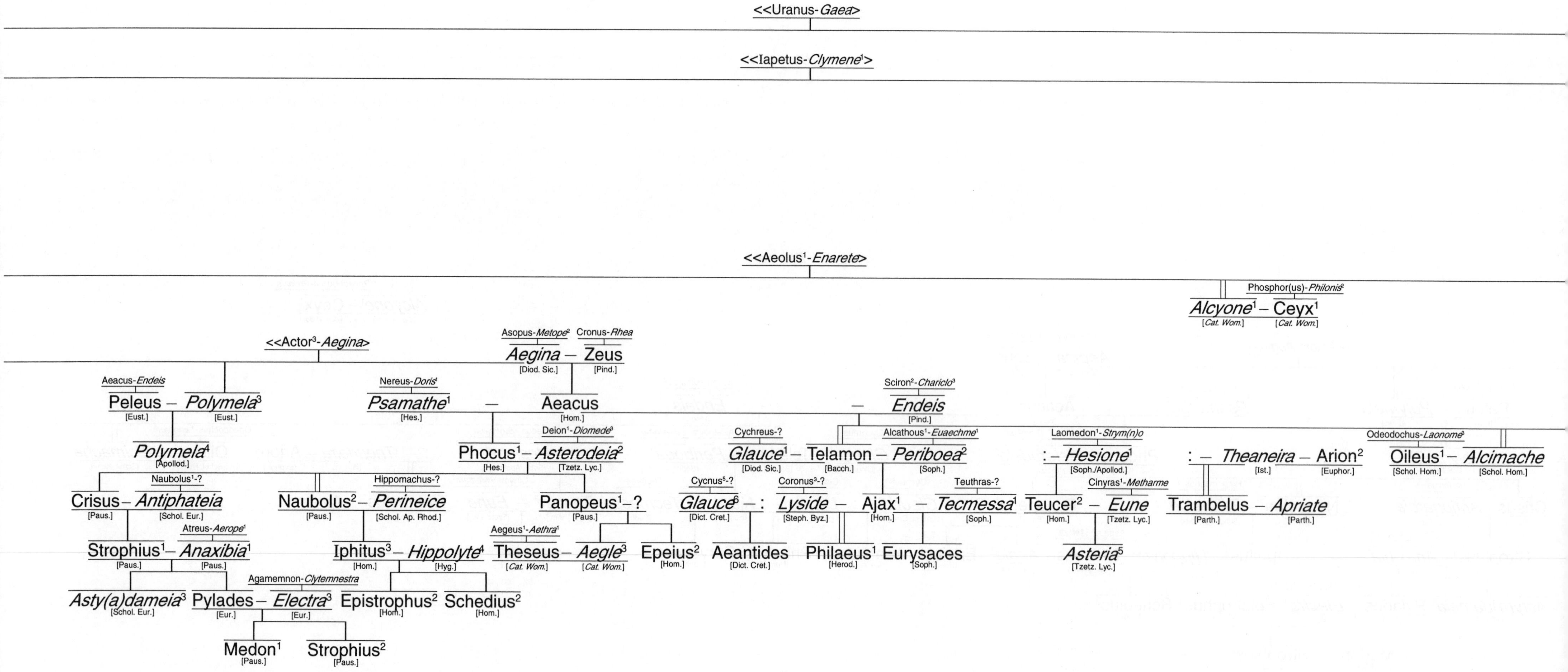

<<Uranus-Gaea>
<<Iapetus-Clymene1>
<<Aeolus1-Enarete>
Phosphor(us)-Philonis2
Alcyone1 – Ceyx1
[Cat. Wom.] [Cat. Wom.]
<<Actor3-Aegina>
Asopus-Metope2 Cronus-Rhea
Aegina – Zeus
[Diod. Sic.] [Pind.]
Aeacus-Endeis
Peleus – Polymela3
[Eust.] [Eust.]
Nereus-Doris1
Psamathe1 – Aeacus
[Hes.] [Hom.]
Sciron2-Chariclo3
– Endeis
[Pind.]
Polymela4
[Apollod.]
Deion1-Diomede3
Phocus1 – Asterodeia2
[Hes.] [Tzetz. Lyc.]
Cychreus-?
Glauce1 – Telamon – Periboea2
[Diod. Sic.] [Bacch.] [Soph.]
Alcathous1-Euaechme1
Laomedon1-Strym(n)o
: – Hesione1
[Soph./Apollod.]
: – Theaneira – Arion2
[Ist.] [Euphor.]
Odeodochus-Laonome3
Oileus1 – Alcimache
[Schol. Hom.] [Schol. Hom.]
Naubolus1-?
Crisus – Antiphateia
[Paus.] [Schol. Eur.]
Hippomachus-?
Naubolus2 – Perineice
[Paus.] [Schol. Ap. Rhod.]
Panopeus1 – ?
[Paus.]
Cycnus5-?
Glauce6 – :
[Dict. Cret.]
Coronus3-?
Lyside – Ajax1 – Tecmessa1
[Steph. Byz.] [Hom.] [Soph.]
Teuthras-?
Cinyras1-Metharme
Teucer2 – Eune
[Hom.] [Tzetz. Lyc.]
Trambelus – Apriate
[Parth.] [Parth.]
Atreus-Aerope1
Strophius1 – Anaxibia1
[Paus.] [Paus.]
Iphitus3 – Hippolyte4
[Hom.] [Hyg.]
Aegeus1-Aethra1
Theseus – Aegle3
[Cat. Wom.] [Cat. Wom.]
Epeius2
[Hom.]
Aeantides
[Dict. Cret.]
Philaeus1 Eurysaces
[Herod.] [Soph.]
Asteria5
[Tzetz. Lyc.]
Agamemnon-Clytemnestra
Asty(a)dameia3
[Schol. Eur.]
Pylades – Electra3
[Eur.] [Eur.]
Epistrophus2 Schedius2
[Hom.] [Hom.]
Medon1 Strophius2
[Paus.] [Paus.]

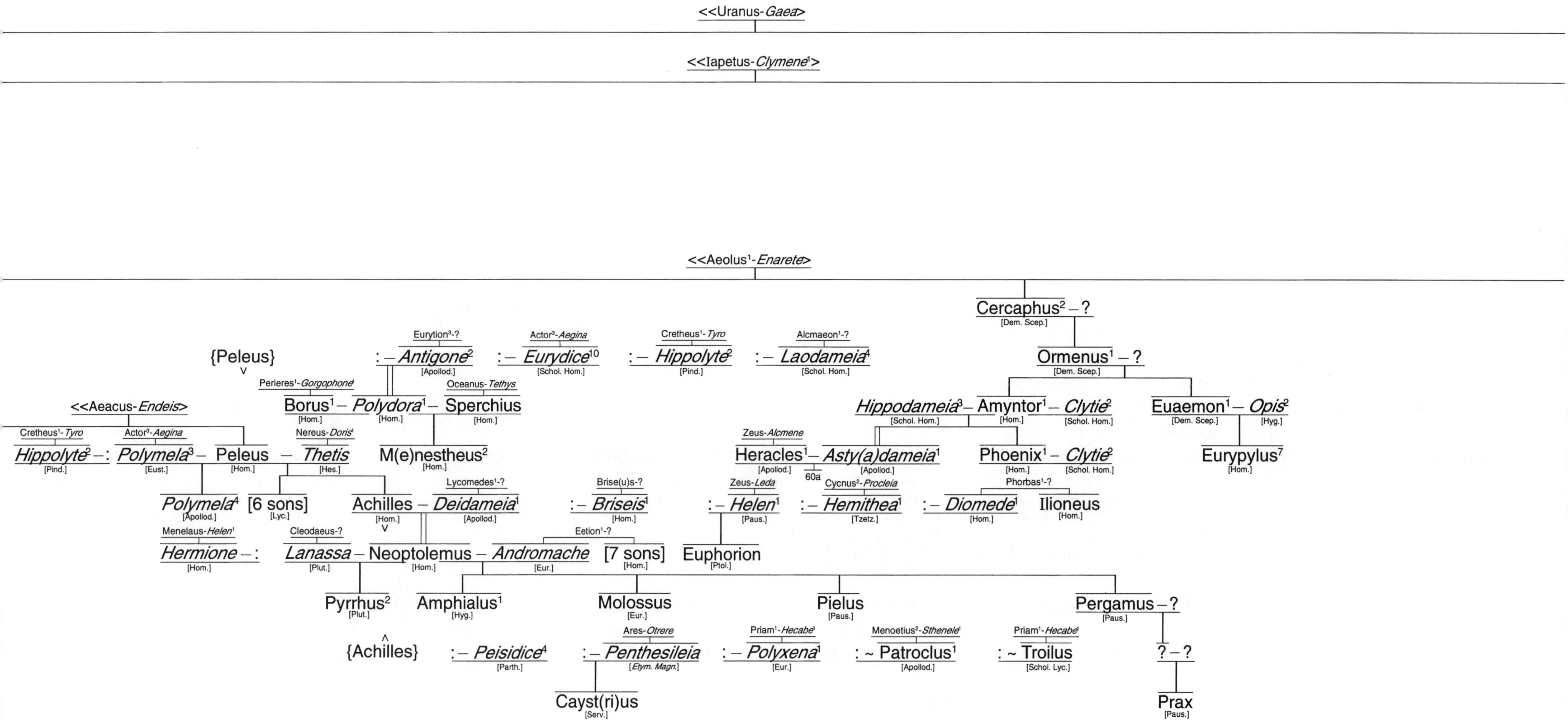

<<Uranus-Gaea>
<<Iapetus-Clymene1>
<<Aeolus1-Enarete>
Cercaphus2 – ?
[Dem. Scep.]
Eurytion3-?
: – Antigone2
[Apollod.]
Actor3-Aegina
: – Eurydice10
[Schol. Hom.]
Cretheus1-Tyro
: – Hippolyte2
[Pind.]
Alcmaeon1-?
: – Laodameia4
[Schol. Hom.]
Ormenus1 – ?
[Dem. Scep.]
{Peleus}
Perieres1-Gorgophone1
Oceanus-Tethys
Borus1 – Polydora1 – Sperchius
[Hom.]
[Hom.]
[Hom.]
<<Aeacus-Endeis>
Hippodameia3 – Amyntor1 – Clytie2
[Schol. Hom.]
[Hom.]
[Schol. Hom.]
Euaemon1 – Opis2
[Dem. Scep.]
[Hyg.]
Cretheus1-Tyro
Actor3-Aegina
Nereus-Doris1
Zeus-Alcmene
Hippolyte2 –: Polymela3 – Peleus – Thetis
[Pind.]
[Eust.]
[Hom.]
[Hes.]
M(e)nestheus2
[Hom.]
Heracles1 – Asty(a)dameia1
[Apollod.]
[Apollod.]
60a
Phoenix1 – Clytie2
[Hom.]
[Schol. Hom.]
Eurypylus7
[Hom.]
Lycomedes1-?
Brise(u)s-?
Zeus-Leda
Cycnus2-Procleia
Phorbas1-?
Polymela4 [6 sons]
[Apollod.]
[Lyc.]
Achilles – Deidameia1
[Hom.]
[Apollod.]
: – Briseis1
[Hom.]
: – Helen1
[Paus.]
: – Hemithea1
[Tzetz.]
: – Diomede1
[Hom.]
Ilioneus
[Hom.]
Menelaus-Helen1
Cleodaeus-?
Eetion1-?
Hermione –:
[Hom.]
Lanassa – Neoptolemus – Andromache [7 sons]
[Plut.]
[Hom.]
[Eur.]
[Hom.]
Euphorion
[Ptol.]
Pyrrhus2
[Plut.]
Amphialus1
[Hyg.]
Molossus
[Eur.]
Pielus
[Paus.]
Pergamus – ?
[Paus.]
{Achilles}
: – Peisidice4
[Parth.]
Ares-Otrere
: – Penthesileia
[Etym. Magn.]
Priam1-Hecabe1
: – Polyxena1
[Eur.]
Menoetius2-Sthenele1
: ~ Patroclus1
[Apollod.]
Priam1-Hecabe1
: ~ Troilus
[Schol. Lyc.]
? – ?
Cayst(ri)us
[Serv.]
Prax
[Paus.]

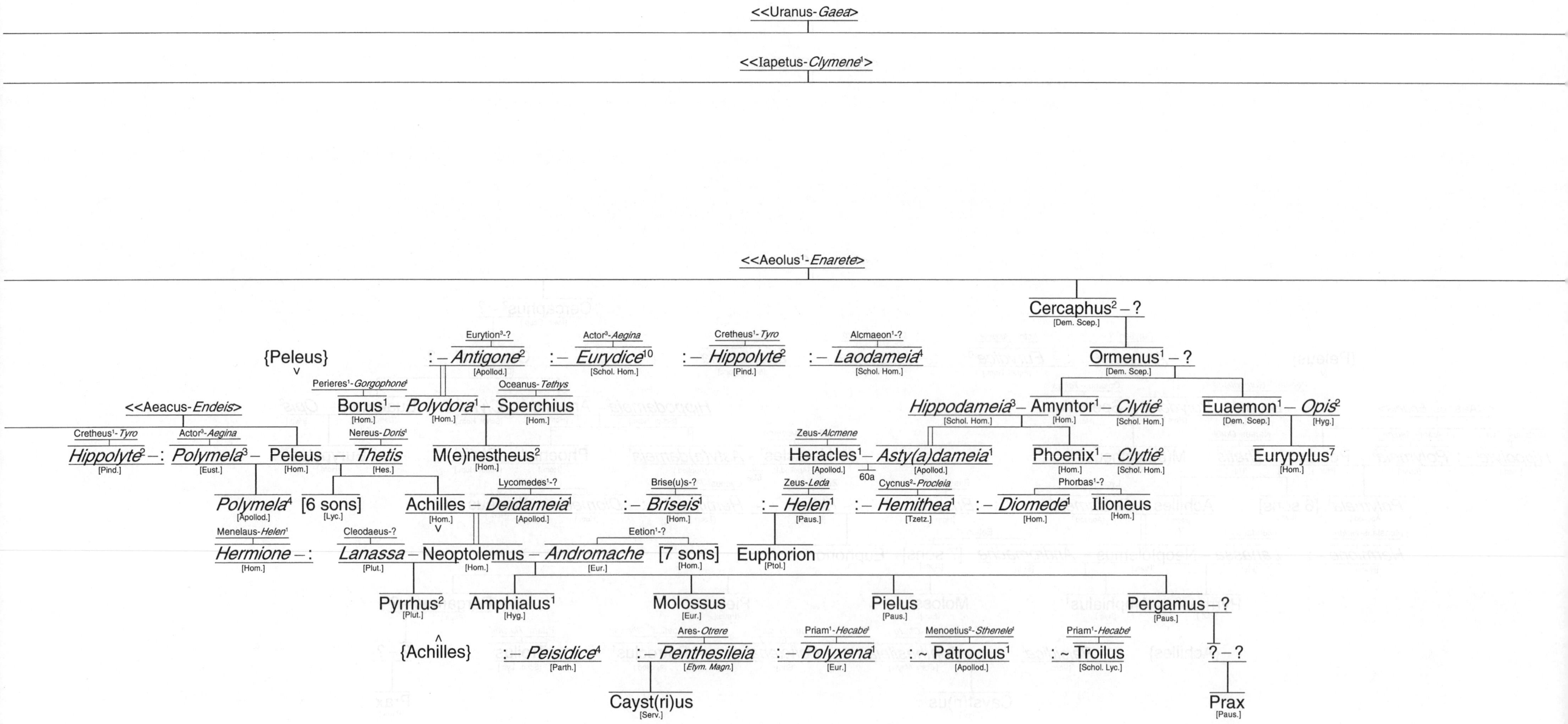

<<Uranus-*Gaea*>
<<Iapetus-*Clymene*[1]>
<<Aeolus[1]-*Enarete*>
Cercaphus[2] – ?
[Dem. Scep.]
Ormenus[1] – ?
[Dem. Scep.]
Eurytion[3]-?
: – *Antigone*[2]
[Apollod.]
Actor[3]-*Aegina*
: – *Eurydice*[10]
[Schol. Hom.]
Cretheus[1]-*Tyro*
: – *Hippolyte*[2]
[Pind.]
Alcmaeon[1]-?
: – *Laodameia*[4]
[Schol. Hom.]
{Peleus}
Perieres[1]-*Gorgophone*[1]
Oceanus-*Tethys*
<<Aeacus-*Endeis*>
Borus[1] – *Polydora*[1] – Sperchius
[Hom.] [Hom.] [Hom.]
Hippodameia[3] – Amyntor[1] – *Clytie*[2]
[Schol. Hom.] [Hom.] [Schol. Hom.]
Euaemon[1] – *Opis*[2]
[Dem. Scep.] [Hyg.]
Cretheus[1]-*Tyro*
Actor[3]-*Aegina*
Nereus-*Doris*[1]
Zeus-*Alcmene*
Hippolyte[2] – : *Polymela*[3] – Peleus – *Thetis*
[Pind.] [Eust.] [Hom.] [Hes.]
M(e)nestheus[2]
[Hom.]
Heracles[1] – *Asty(a)dameia*[1]
[Apollod.] [Apollod.]
60a
Phoenix[1] – *Clytie*[2]
[Hom.] [Schol. Hom.]
Eurypylus[7]
[Hom.]
Lycomedes[1]-?
Brise(u)s-?
Zeus-*Leda*
Cycnus[2]-*Procleia*
Phorbas[1]-?
Polymela[4]
[Apollod.]
[6 sons]
[Lyc.]
Achilles – *Deidameia*[1]
[Hom.] [Apollod.]
: – *Briseis*[1]
[Hom.]
: – *Helen*[1]
[Paus.]
: – *Hemithea*[1]
[Tzetz.]
: – *Diomede*[1]
[Hom.]
Ilioneus
[Hom.]
Menelaus-*Helen*[1]
Cleodaeus-?
Eetion[1]-?
Hermione – :
[Hom.]
Lanassa – Neoptolemus – *Andromache*
[Plut.] [Hom.] [Eur.]
[7 sons]
[Hom.]
Euphorion
[Ptol.]
Pyrrhus[2]
[Plut.]
Amphialus[1]
[Hyg.]
Molossus
[Eur.]
Pielus
[Paus.]
Pergamus – ?
[Paus.]
Ares-*Otrere*
Priam[1]-*Hecabe*[1]
Menoetius[2]-*Sthenele*[1]
Priam[1]-*Hecabe*[1]
{Achilles}
: – *Peisidice*[4]
[Parth.]
: – *Penthesileia*
[*Etym. Magn.*]
: – *Polyxena*[1]
[Eur.]
: ~ Patroclus[1]
[Apollod.]
: ~ Troilus
[Schol. Lyc.]
? – ?
Cayst(ri)us
[Serv.]
Prax
[Paus.]

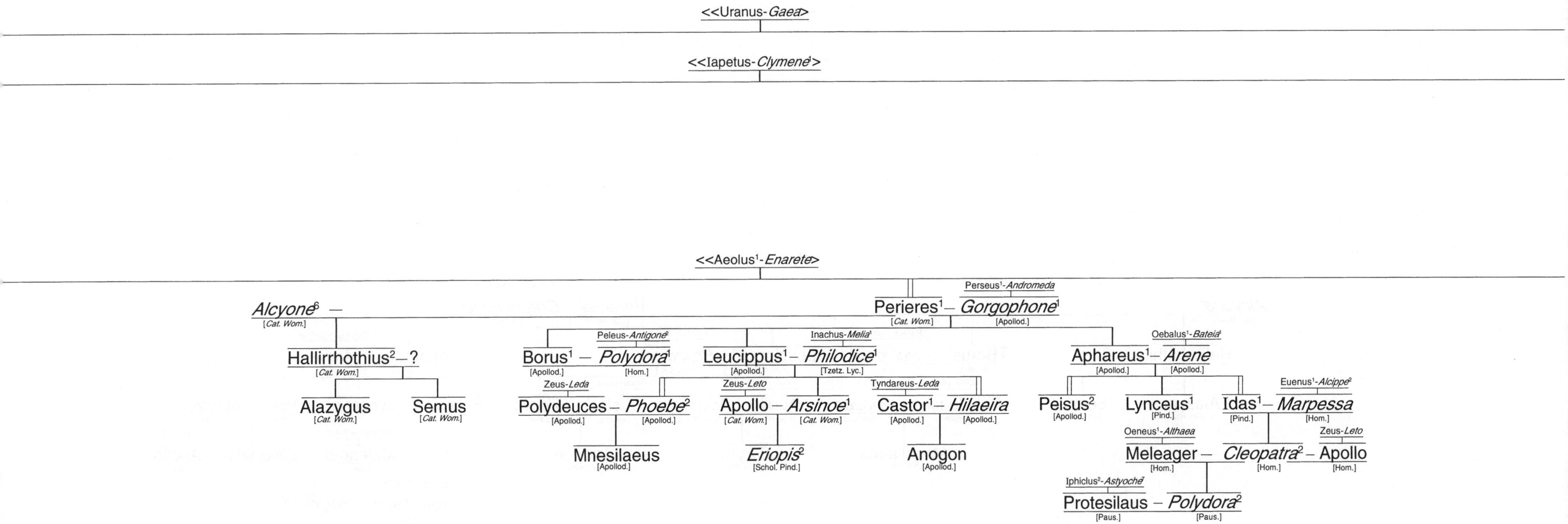
<<Uranus-Gaea>
<<Iapetus-Clymene[1]>
<<Aeolus[1]-Enarete>
Alcyone[6] –
[Cat. Wom.]
Hallirrhothius[2]–?
[Cat. Wom.]
Alazygus
[Cat. Wom.]
Semus
[Cat. Wom.]
Perseus[1]-Andromeda
Perieres[1]– Gorgophone[1]
[Cat. Wom.]
[Apollod.]
Peleus-Antigone[2]
Borus[1] – Polydora[1]
[Apollod.]
[Hom.]
Inachus-Melia[1]
Leucippus[1]– Philodice[1]
[Apollod.]
[Tzetz. Lyc.]
Oebalus[1]-Bateia[1]
Aphareus[1]– Arene
[Apollod.]
[Apollod.]
Zeus-Leda
Polydeuces– Phoebe[2]
[Apollod.]
[Apollod.]
Zeus-Leto
Apollo – Arsinoe[1]
[Cat. Wom.]
[Cat. Wom.]
Tyndareus-Leda
Castor[1]– Hilaeira
[Apollod.]
[Apollod.]
Peisus[2]
[Apollod.]
Lynceus[1]
[Pind.]
Euenus[1]-Alcippe[2]
Idas[1]– Marpessa
[Pind.]
[Hom.]
Mnesilaeus
[Apollod.]
Eriopis[2]
[Schol. Pind.]
Anogon
[Apollod.]
Oeneus[1]-Althaea
Zeus-Leto
Meleager – Cleopatra[2] – Apollo
[Hom.]
[Hom.]
[Hom.]
Iphiclus[2]-Astyoche[3]
Protesilaus – Polydora[2]
[Paus.]
[Paus.]

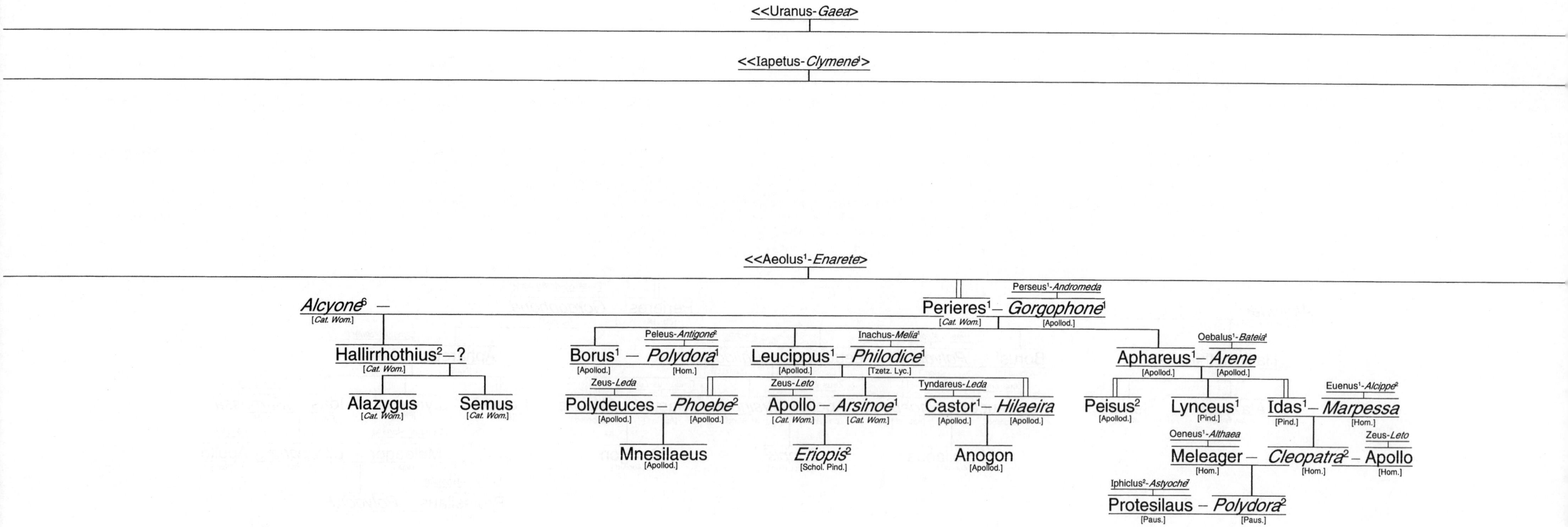

<<Uranus-Gaea>
<<Iapetus-Clymene1>
<<Aeolus1-Enarete>
Alcyone6 –
[Cat. Wom.]
Perseus1-Andromeda
Perieres1 – Gorgophone1
[Cat. Wom.]
[Apollod.]
Hallirrhothius2 – ?
[Cat. Wom.]
Peleus-Antigone2
Borus1 – Polydora1
[Apollod.]
[Hom.]
Inachus-Melia1
Leucippus1 – Philodice1
[Apollod.]
[Tzetz. Lyc.]
Oebalus1-Bateia1
Aphareus1 – Arene
[Apollod.]
[Apollod.]
Alazygus
[Cat. Wom.]
Semus
[Cat. Wom.]
Zeus-Leda
Polydeuces – Phoebe2
[Apollod.]
[Apollod.]
Zeus-Leto
Apollo – Arsinoe1
[Cat. Wom.]
[Cat. Wom.]
Tyndareus-Leda
Castor1 – Hilaeira
[Apollod.]
[Apollod.]
Peisus2
[Apollod.]
Lynceus1
[Pind.]
Euenus1-Alcippe2
Idas1 – Marpessa
[Pind.]
[Hom.]
Mnesilaeus
[Apollod.]
Eriopis2
[Schol. Pind.]
Anogon
[Apollod.]
Oeneus1-Althaea
Meleager – Cleopatra2 – Apollo
[Hom.]
[Hom.]
Zeus-Leto
[Hom.]
Iphiclus2-Astyoche2
Protesilaus – Polydora2
[Paus.]
[Paus.]

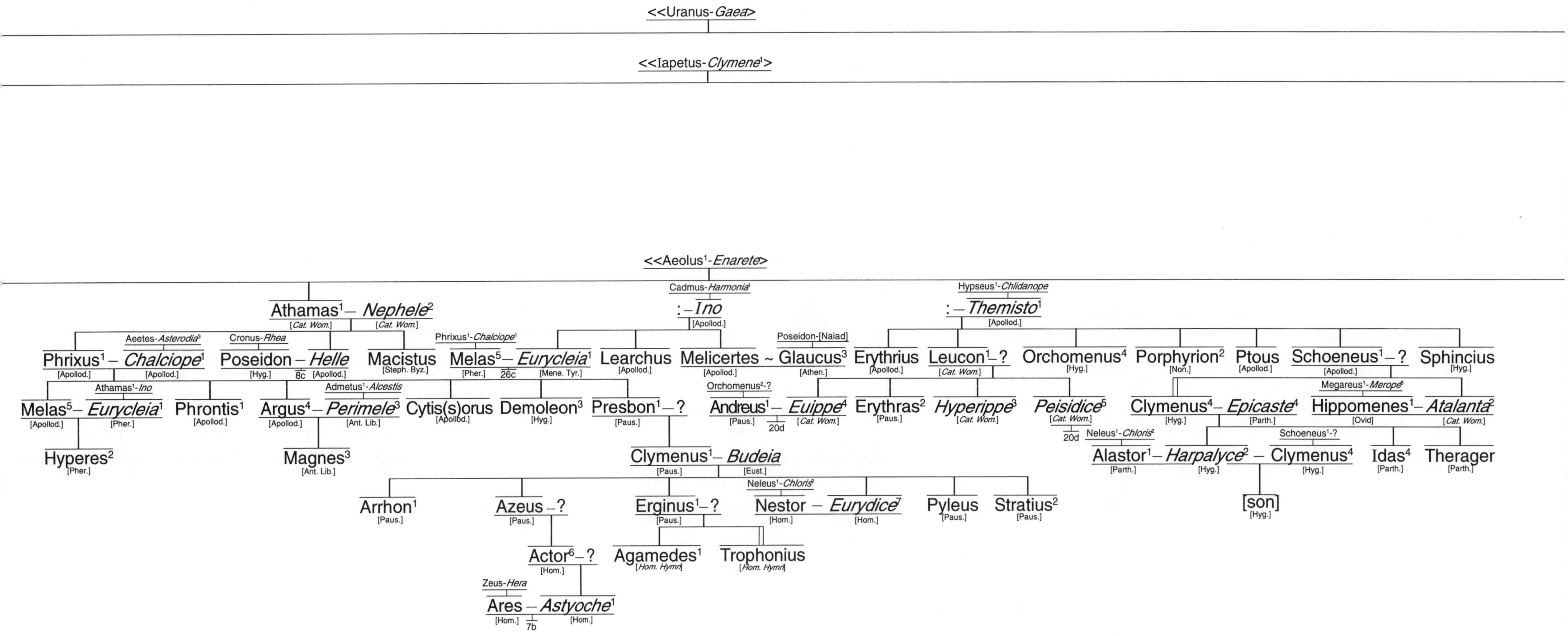

<<Uranus-Gaea>
<<Iapetus-Clymene1>
<<Aeolus1-Enarete>
Athamas1 – Nephele2
[Cat. Wom.] [Cat. Wom.]
Cadmus-Harmonia1
: – Ino
[Apollod.]
Hypseus1-Chlidanope
: – Themisto1
[Apollod.]
Aeetes-Asterodia3
Cronus-Rhea
Phrixus1-Chalciope1
Poseidon-[Naiad]
Phrixus1 – Chalciope1
[Apollod.] [Apollod.]
Poseidon – Helle
[Hyg.] 8c [Apollod.]
Macistus
[Steph. Byz.]
Melas5 – Eurycleia1
[Pher.] 26c [Mene. Tyr.]
Learchus
[Apollod.]
Melicertes ~ Glaucus3
[Apollod.] [Athen.]
Erythrius
[Apollod.]
Leucon1 – ?
[Cat. Wom.]
Orchomenus4
[Hyg.]
Porphyrion2
[Non.]
Ptous
[Apollod.]
Schoeneus1 – ?
[Apollod.]
Sphincius
[Hyg.]
Athamas1-Ino
Admetus1-Alcestis
Orchomenus2-?
Megareus1-Merope6
Melas5 – Eurycleia1
[Apollod.] [Pher.]
Phrontis1
[Apollod.]
Argus4 – Perimele3
[Apollod.] [Ant. Lib.]
Cytis(s)orus
[Apollod.]
Demoleon3
[Hyg.]
Presbon1 – ?
[Paus.]
Andreus1 – Euippe4
[Paus.] 20d [Cat. Wom.]
Erythras2
[Paus.]
Hyperippe3
[Cat. Wom.]
Peisidice5
[Cat. Wom.]
20d
Clymenus4 – Epicaste4
[Hyg.] [Parth.]
Hippomenes1 – Atalanta2
[Ovid] [Cat. Wom.]
Neleus1-Chloris2
Schoeneus1-?
Hyperes2
[Pher.]
Magnes3
[Ant. Lib.]
Clymenus1 – Budeia
[Paus.] [Eust.]
Alastor1 – Harpalyce2 – Clymenus4
[Parth.] [Hyg.] [Hyg.]
Idas4
[Parth.]
Therager
[Parth.]
Neleus1-Chloris2
Arrhon1
[Paus.]
Azeus – ?
[Paus.]
Erginus1 – ?
[Paus.]
Nestor – Eurydice7
[Hom.] [Hom.]
Pyleus
[Paus.]
Stratius2
[Paus.]
[son]
[Hyg.]
Actor6 – ?
[Hom.]
Agamedes1
[Hom. Hymn]
Trophonius
[Hom. Hymn]
Zeus-Hera
Ares – Astyoche1
[Hom.] 7b [Hom.]

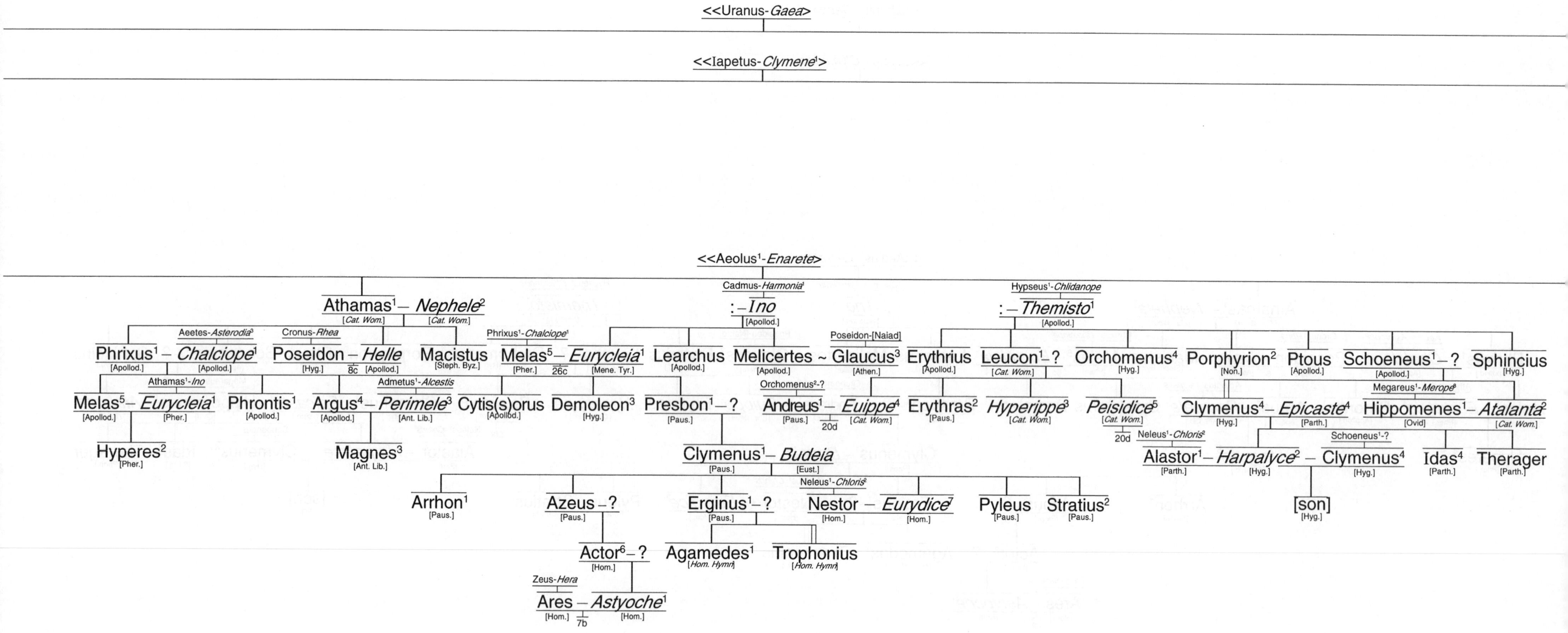

<<Uranus-Gaea>
<<Iapetus-Clymene1>
<<Aeolus1-Enarete>
Athamas1 – Nephele2
[Cat. Wom.] [Cat. Wom.]
Cadmus-Harmonia1
: – Ino
[Apollod.]
Hypseus1-Chlidanope
: – Themisto1
[Apollod.]
Aeetes-Asterodia3
Cronus-Rhea
Phrixus1-Chalciope1
Poseidon-[Naiad]
Phrixus1 – Chalciope1
[Apollod.] [Apollod.]
Poseidon – Helle
[Hyg.] 8c [Apollod.]
Macistus
[Steph. Byz.]
Melas5 – Eurycleia1
[Pher.] 26c [Mene. Tyr.]
Learchus
[Apollod.]
Melicertes ~ Glaucus3
[Apollod.] [Athen.]
Erythrius
[Apollod.]
Leucon1 – ?
[Cat. Wom.]
Orchomenus4
[Hyg.]
Porphyrion2
[Non.]
Ptous
[Apollod.]
Schoeneus1 – ?
[Apollod.]
Sphincius
[Hyg.]
Athamas1-Ino
Admetus1-Alcestis
Orchomenus2-?
Megareus1-Merope
Melas5 – Eurycleia1
[Apollod.] [Pher.]
Phrontis1
[Apollod.]
Argus4 – Perimele3
[Apollod.] [Ant. Lib.]
Cytis(s)orus
[Apollod.]
Demoleon3
[Hyg.]
Presbon1 – ?
[Paus.]
Andreus1 – Euippe4
[Paus.] 20d [Cat. Wom.]
Erythras2
[Paus.]
Hyperippe3
[Cat. Wom.]
Peisidice5
[Cat. Wom.]
20d
Clymenus4 – Epicaste4
[Hyg.] [Parth.]
Hippomenes1 – Atalanta2
[Ovid] [Cat. Wom.]
Hyperes2
[Pher.]
Magnes3
[Ant. Lib.]
Clymenus1 – Budeia
[Paus.] [Eust.]
Neleus1-Chloris2
Alastor1 – Harpalyce2 – Clymenus4
[Parth.] [Hyg.] [Hyg.]
Schoeneus1-?
Idas4
[Parth.]
Therager
[Parth.]
Neleus1-Chloris2
Arrhon1
[Paus.]
Azeus – ?
[Paus.]
Erginus1 – ?
[Paus.]
Nestor – Eurydice7
[Hom.] [Hom.]
Pyleus
[Paus.]
Stratius2
[Paus.]
[son]
[Hyg.]
Actor6 – ?
[Hom.]
Agamedes1
[Hom. Hymn]
Trophonius
[Hom. Hymn]
Zeus-Hera
Ares – Astyoche1
[Hom.] 7b [Hom.]

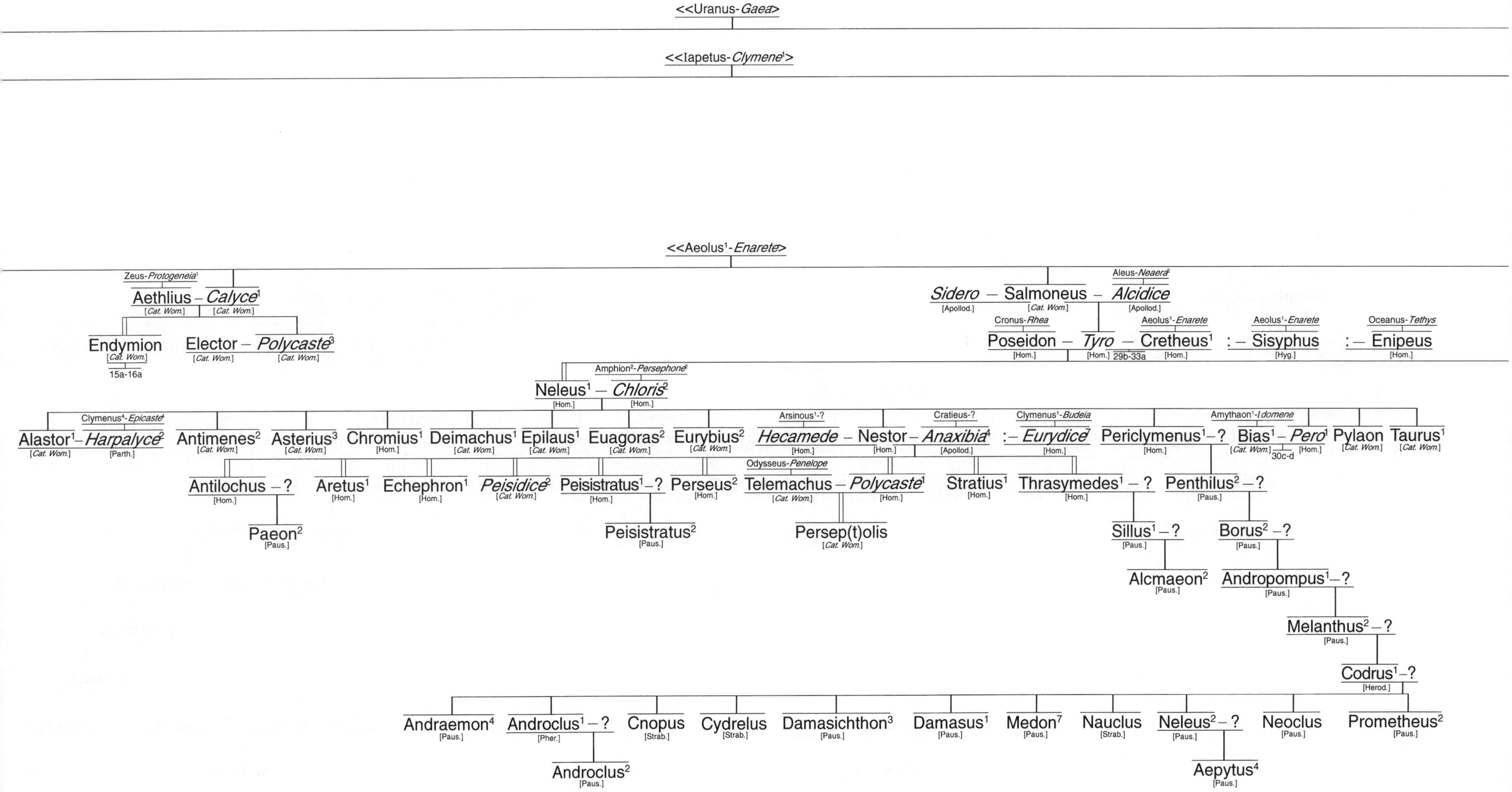

<<Uranus-*Gaea*>
<<Iapetus-*Clymene*¹>
<<Aeolus¹-*Enarete*>
Zeus-*Protogeneia*¹
Aethlius – *Calyce*¹
[Cat. Wom.] [Cat. Wom.]
Endymion
[Cat. Wom.]
15a-16a
Elector – *Polycaste*³
[Cat. Wom.] [Cat. Wom.]
Sidero – Salmoneus – *Alcidice*
[Apollod.] [Cat. Wom.] [Apollod.]
Aleus-*Neaera*²
Cronus-*Rhea*
Poseidon – *Tyro* – Cretheus¹
[Hom.] [Hom.] 29b-33a [Hom.]
Aeolus¹-*Enarete*
: – Sisyphus
[Hyg.]
Aeolus¹-*Enarete*
Oceanus-*Tethys*
: – Enipeus
[Hom.]
Amphion²-*Persephone*²
Neleus¹ – *Chloris*²
[Hom.] [Hom.]
Clymenus⁴-*Epicaste*⁴
Alastor¹ – *Harpalyce*²
[Cat. Wom.] [Parth.]
Antimenes²
[Cat. Wom.]
Asterius³
[Cat. Wom.]
Chromius¹
[Hom.]
Deimachus¹
[Cat. Wom.]
Epilaus¹
[Cat. Wom.]
Euagoras²
[Cat. Wom.]
Eurybius²
[Cat. Wom.]
Arsinous¹-?
Hecamede – Nestor – *Anaxibia*⁴
[Hom.] [Hom.] [Apollod.]
Cratieus-?
Clymenus¹-*Budeia*
: – *Eurydice*⁷
[Hom.]
Periclymenus¹ – ?
[Hom.]
Amythaon¹-*Idomene*
Bias¹ – *Pero*¹
[Cat. Wom.] 30c-d [Hom.]
Pylaon
[Cat. Wom.]
Taurus¹
[Cat. Wom.]
Antilochus – ?
[Hom.]
Paeon²
[Paus.]
Aretus¹
[Hom.]
Echephron¹
[Hom.]
*Peisidice*²
[Cat. Wom.]
Peisistratus¹ – ?
[Hom.]
Peisistratus²
[Paus.]
Perseus²
[Hom.]
Odysseus-*Penelope*
Telemachus – *Polycaste*¹
[Cat. Wom.] [Hom.]
Persep(t)olis
[Cat. Wom.]
Stratius¹
[Hom.]
Thrasymedes¹ – ?
[Hom.]
Sillus¹ – ?
[Paus.]
Alcmaeon²
[Paus.]
Penthilus² – ?
[Paus.]
Borus² – ?
[Paus.]
Andropompus¹ – ?
[Paus.]
Melanthus² – ?
[Paus.]
Codrus¹ – ?
[Herod.]
Andraemon⁴
[Paus.]
Androclus¹ – ?
[Pher.]
Androclus²
[Paus.]
Cnopus
[Strab.]
Cydrelus
[Strab.]
Damasichthon³
[Paus.]
Damasus¹
[Paus.]
Medon⁷
[Paus.]
Nauclus
[Strab.]
Neleus² – ?
[Paus.]
Aepytus⁴
[Paus.]
Neoclus
[Paus.]
Prometheus²
[Paus.]

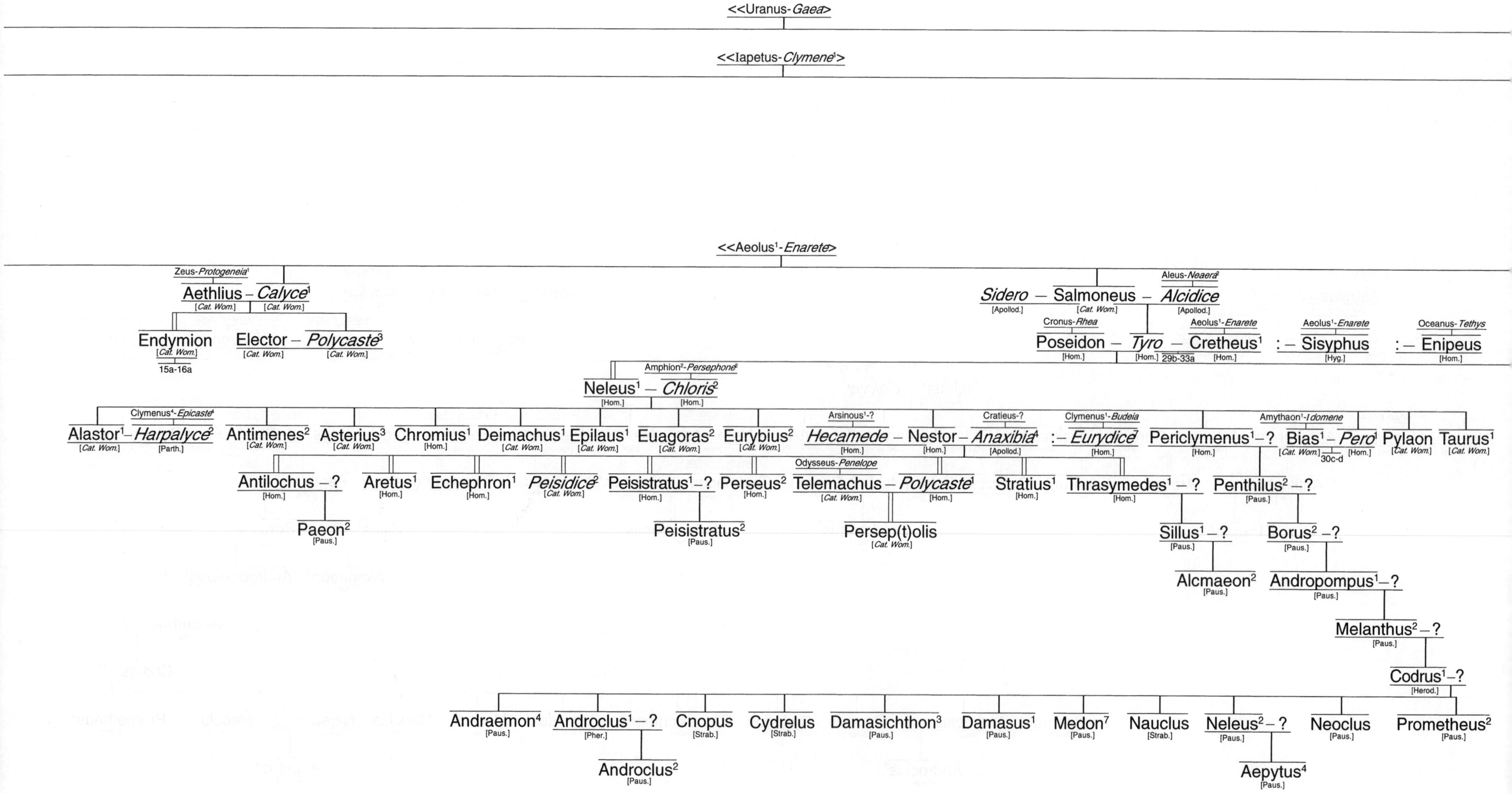

<<Uranus-*Gaea*>
<<Iapetus-*Clymene*¹>
<<Aeolus¹-*Enarete*>
Zeus-*Protogeneia*¹
Aethlius – *Calyce*¹
[Cat. Wom.] [Cat. Wom.]
Endymion
[Cat. Wom.]
15a-16a
Elector – *Polycaste*³
[Cat. Wom.] [Cat. Wom.]
Aleus-*Neaera*²
Sidero – Salmoneus – *Alcidice*
[Apollod.] [Cat. Wom.] [Apollod.]
Cronus-*Rhea*
Poseidon – *Tyro* – Cretheus¹
[Hom.] [Hom.] 29b-33a [Hom.]
Aeolus¹-*Enarete*
Aeolus¹-*Enarete*
: – Sisyphus
[Hyg.]
Oceanus-*Tethys*
: – Enipeus
[Hom.]
Amphion²-*Persephone*²
Neleus¹ – *Chloris*²
[Hom.] [Hom.]
Clymenus⁴-*Epicaste*⁴
Alastor¹ – *Harpalyce*²
[Cat. Wom.] [Parth.]
Antimenes²
[Cat. Wom.]
Asterius³
[Cat. Wom.]
Chromius¹
[Hom.]
Deimachus¹
[Cat. Wom.]
Epilaus¹
[Cat. Wom.]
Euagoras²
[Cat. Wom.]
Eurybius²
[Cat. Wom.]
Arsinous¹-?
Hecamede – Nestor – *Anaxibia*⁴
[Hom.] [Hom.] [Apollod.]
Cratieus-?
Clymenus¹-*Budeia*
: – *Eurydice*⁷
[Hom.]
Periclymenus¹ – ?
[Hom.]
Amythaon¹-*Idomene*
Bias¹ – *Pero*¹
[Cat. Wom.] 30c-d [Hom.]
Pylaon
[Cat. Wom.]
Taurus¹
[Cat. Wom.]
Antilochus – ?
[Hom.]
Aretus¹
[Hom.]
Echephron¹
[Hom.]
*Peisidice*²
[Cat. Wom.]
Peisistratus¹ – ?
[Hom.]
Perseus²
[Hom.]
Odysseus-*Penelope*
Telemachus – *Polycaste*¹
[Cat. Wom.] [Hom.]
Stratius¹
[Hom.]
Thrasymedes¹ – ?
[Hom.]
Penthilus² – ?
[Paus.]
Paeon²
[Paus.]
Peisistratus²
[Paus.]
Persep(t)olis
[Cat. Wom.]
Sillus¹ – ?
[Paus.]
Borus² – ?
[Paus.]
Alcmaeon²
[Paus.]
Andropompus¹ – ?
[Paus.]
Melanthus² – ?
[Paus.]
Codrus¹ – ?
[Herod.]
Andraemon⁴
[Paus.]
Androclus¹ – ?
[Pher.]
Cnopus
[Strab.]
Cydrelus
[Strab.]
Damasichthon³
[Paus.]
Damasus¹
[Paus.]
Medon⁷
[Paus.]
Nauclus
[Strab.]
Neleus² – ?
[Paus.]
Neoclus
[Paus.]
Prometheus²
[Paus.]
Androclus²
[Paus.]
Aepytus⁴
[Paus.]

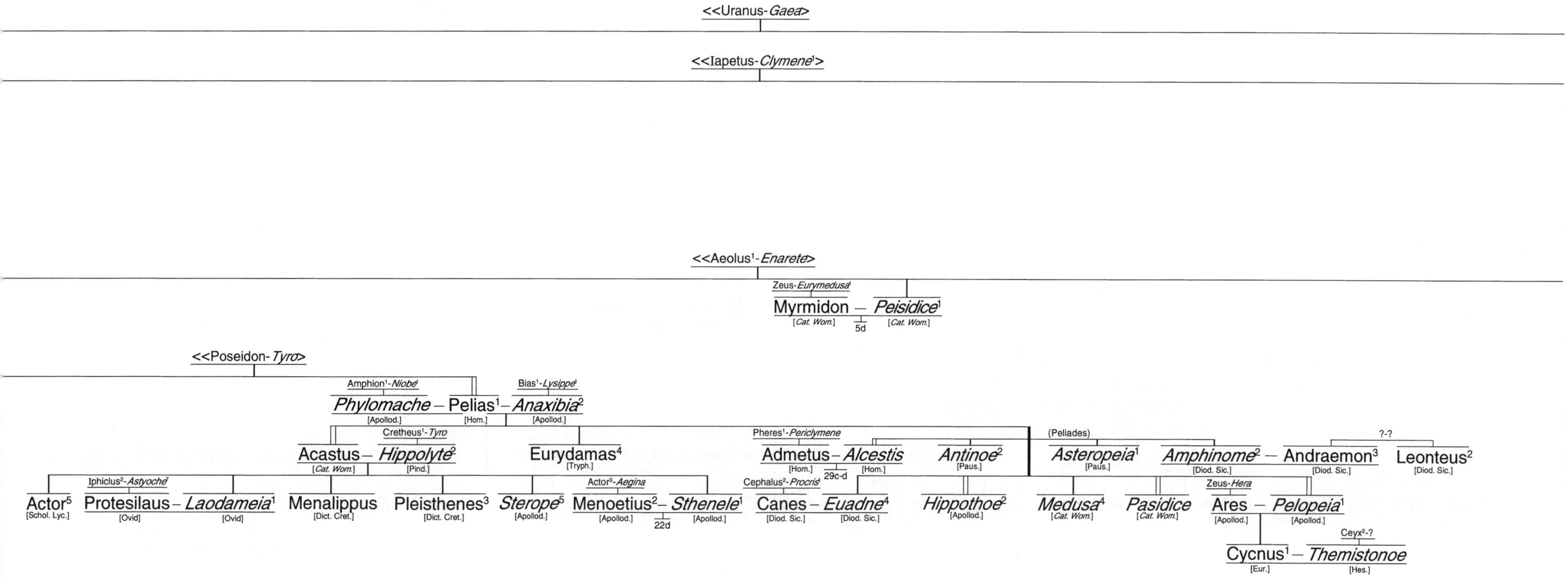
<<Uranus-Gaea>
<<Iapetus-Clymene[1]>
<<Aeolus[1]-Enarete>
Zeus-Eurymedusa[1]
Myrmidon – Peisidice[1]
[Cat. Wom.]
5d
[Cat. Wom.]
<<Poseidon-Tyro>
Amphion[1]-Niobe[1]
Bias[1]-Lysippe[1]
Phylomache – Pelias[1] – Anaxibia[2]
[Apollod.]
[Hom.]
[Apollod.]
Cretheus[1]-Tyro
Acastus – Hippolyte[2]
[Cat. Wom.]
[Pind.]
Eurydamas[4]
[Tryph.]
Pheres[1]-Periclymene
Admetus – Alcestis
[Hom.]
29c-d
[Hom.]
Antinoe[2]
[Paus.]
(Peliades)
Asteropeia[1]
[Paus.]
Amphinome[2] – Andraemon[3]
[Diod. Sic.]
[Diod. Sic.]
?-?
Leonteus[2]
[Diod. Sic.]
Iphiclus[2]-Astyoche[2]
Actor[5]
[Schol. Lyc.]
Protesilaus – Laodameia[1]
[Ovid]
[Ovid]
Menalippus
[Dict. Cret.]
Pleisthenes[3]
[Dict. Cret.]
Sterope[5]
[Apollod.]
Actor[3]-Aegina
Menoetius[2] – Sthenele[1]
[Apollod.]
22d
[Apollod.]
Cephalus[2]-Procris[1]
Canes – Euadne[4]
[Diod. Sic.]
[Diod. Sic.]
Hippothoe[2]
[Apollod.]
Medusa[4]
[Cat. Wom.]
Pasidice
[Cat. Wom.]
Zeus-Hera
Ares – Pelopeia[1]
[Apollod.]
[Apollod.]
Ceyx[2]-?
Cycnus[1] – Themistonoe
[Eur.]
[Hes.]

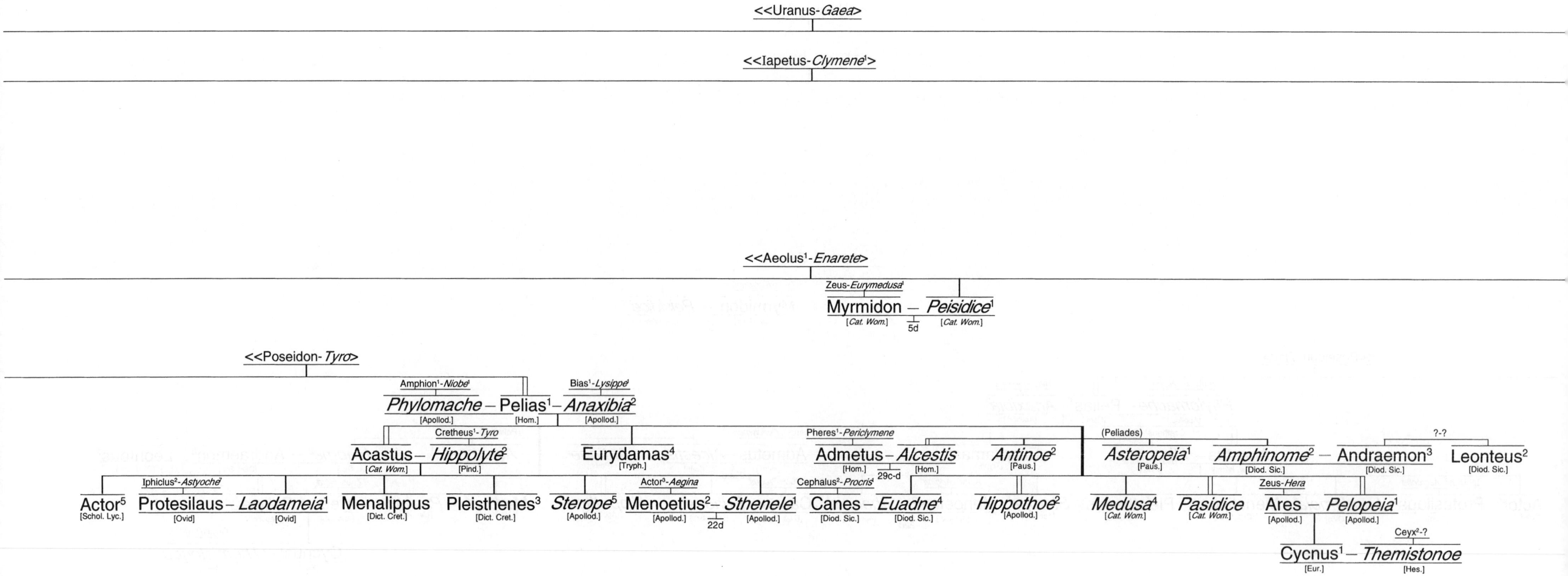

<<Uranus-Gaea>
<<Iapetus-Clymene[1]>
<<Aeolus[1]-Enarete>
Zeus-Eurymedusa[1]
Myrmidon – Peisidice[1]
[Cat. Wom.]
5d
[Cat. Wom.]
<<Poseidon-Tyro>
Amphion[1]-Niobe[1]
Bias[1]-Lysippe[1]
Phylomache – Pelias[1] – Anaxibia[2]
[Apollod.]
[Hom.]
[Apollod.]
Cretheus[1]-Tyro
Pheres[1]-Periclymene
(Peliades)
?-?
Acastus – Hippolyte[2]
[Cat. Wom.]
[Pind.]
Eurydamas[4]
[Tryph.]
Admetus – Alcestis
[Hom.]
29c-d
[Hom.]
Antinoe[2]
[Paus.]
Asteropeia[1]
[Paus.]
Amphinome[2] – Andraemon[3]
[Diod. Sic.]
[Diod. Sic.]
Leonteus[2]
[Diod. Sic.]
Iphiclus[2]-Astyoche[2]
Actor[3]-Aegina
Cephalus[2]-Procris[1]
Zeus-Hera
Actor[5]
[Schol. Lyc.]
Protesilaus – Laodameia[1]
[Ovid]
[Ovid]
Menalippus
[Dict. Cret.]
Pleisthenes[3]
[Dict. Cret.]
Sterope[5]
[Apollod.]
Menoetius[2] – Sthenele[1]
[Apollod.]
22d
[Apollod.]
Canes – Euadne[4]
[Diod. Sic.]
[Diod. Sic.]
Hippothoe[2]
[Apollod.]
Medusa[4]
[Cat. Wom.]
Pasidice
[Cat. Wom.]
Ares – Pelopeia[1]
[Apollod.]
[Apollod.]
Ceyx[2]-?
Cycnus[1] – Themistonoe
[Eur.]
[Hes.]

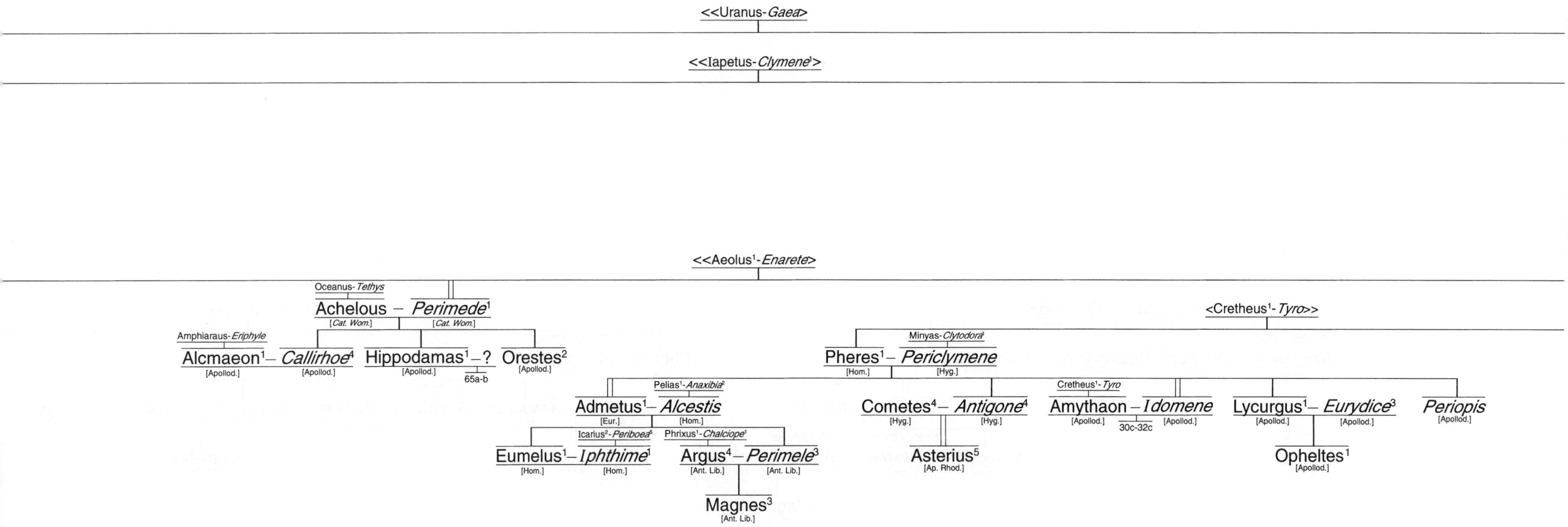

<<Uranus-Gaea>
<<Iapetus-Clymene1>
<<Aeolus1-Enarete>
Oceanus-Tethys
Achelous – Perimede1
[Cat. Wom.]
[Cat. Wom.]
<Cretheus1-Tyro>>
Amphiaraus-Eriphyle
Alcmaeon1– Callirhoe4
[Apollod.]
[Apollod.]
Hippodamas1–?
[Apollod.]
65a-b
Orestes2
[Apollod.]
Minyas-Clytodora1
Pheres1– Periclymene
[Hom.]
[Hyg.]
Pelias1-Anaxibia2
Admetus1– Alcestis
[Eur.]
[Hom.]
Icarius2-Periboea5
Eumelus1–Iphthime1
[Hom.]
[Hom.]
Phrixus1-Chalciope1
Argus4–Perimele3
[Ant. Lib.]
[Ant. Lib.]
Magnes3
[Ant. Lib.]
Cometes4– Antigone4
[Hyg.]
[Hyg.]
Asterius5
[Ap. Rhod.]
Cretheus1-Tyro
Amythaon – Idomene
[Apollod.]
30c-32c
[Apollod.]
Lycurgus1– Eurydice3
[Apollod.]
[Apollod.]
Opheltes1
[Apollod.]
Periopis
[Apollod.]

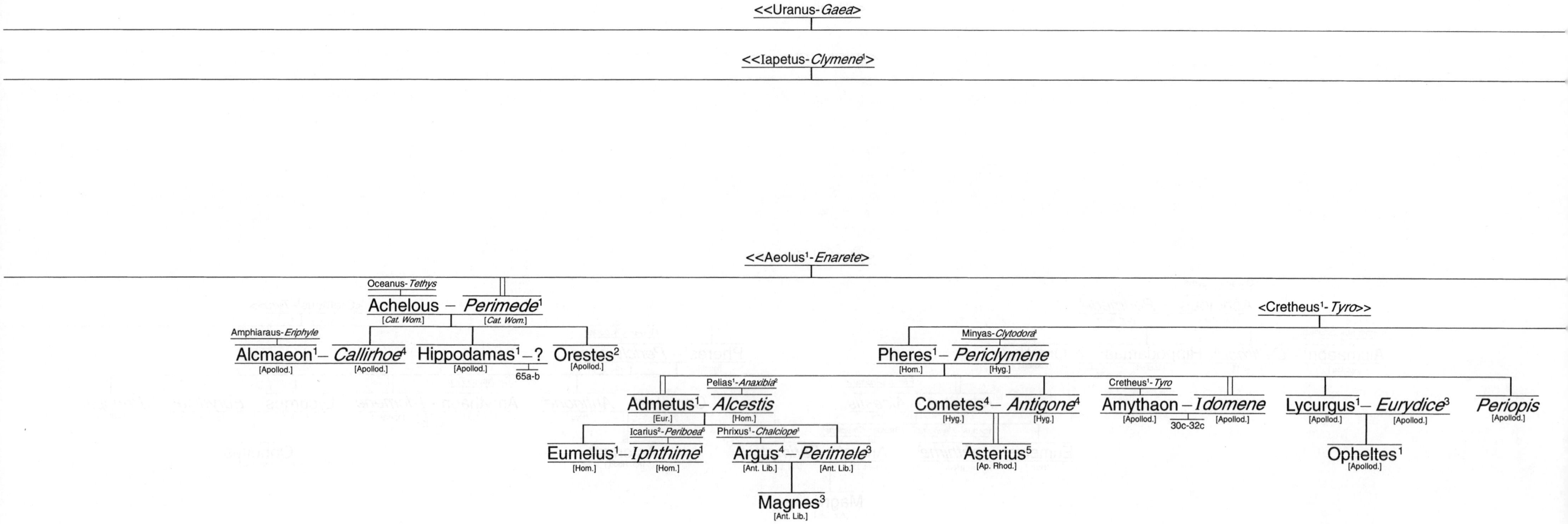

<<Uranus-Gaea>
<<Iapetus-Clymene[1]>
<<Aeolus[1]-Enarete>
Oceanus-Tethys
Achelous – Perimede[1]
[Cat. Wom.]
[Cat. Wom.]
Amphiaraus-Eriphyle
Alcmaeon[1]– Callirhoe[4]
[Apollod.]
[Apollod.]
Hippodamas[1]–?
[Apollod.]
65a-b
Orestes[2]
[Apollod.]
<Cretheus[1]-Tyro>>
Minyas-Clytodora[1]
Pheres[1]– Periclymene
[Hom.]
[Hyg.]
Pelias[1]-Anaxibia[2]
Admetus[1]– Alcestis
[Eur.]
[Hom.]
Icarius[2]-Periboea[5]
Phrixus[1]-Chalciope[1]
Eumelus[1]– Iphthime[1]
[Hom.]
[Hom.]
Argus[4]– Perimele[3]
[Ant. Lib.]
[Ant. Lib.]
Magnes[3]
[Ant. Lib.]
Cometes[4]– Antigone[4]
[Hyg.]
[Hyg.]
Asterius[5]
[Ap. Rhod.]
Cretheus[1]- Tyro
Amythaon – Idomene
[Apollod.]
30c-32c
[Apollod.]
Lycurgus[1]– Eurydice[3]
[Apollod.]
[Apollod.]
Opheltes[1]
[Apollod.]
Periopis
[Apollod.]

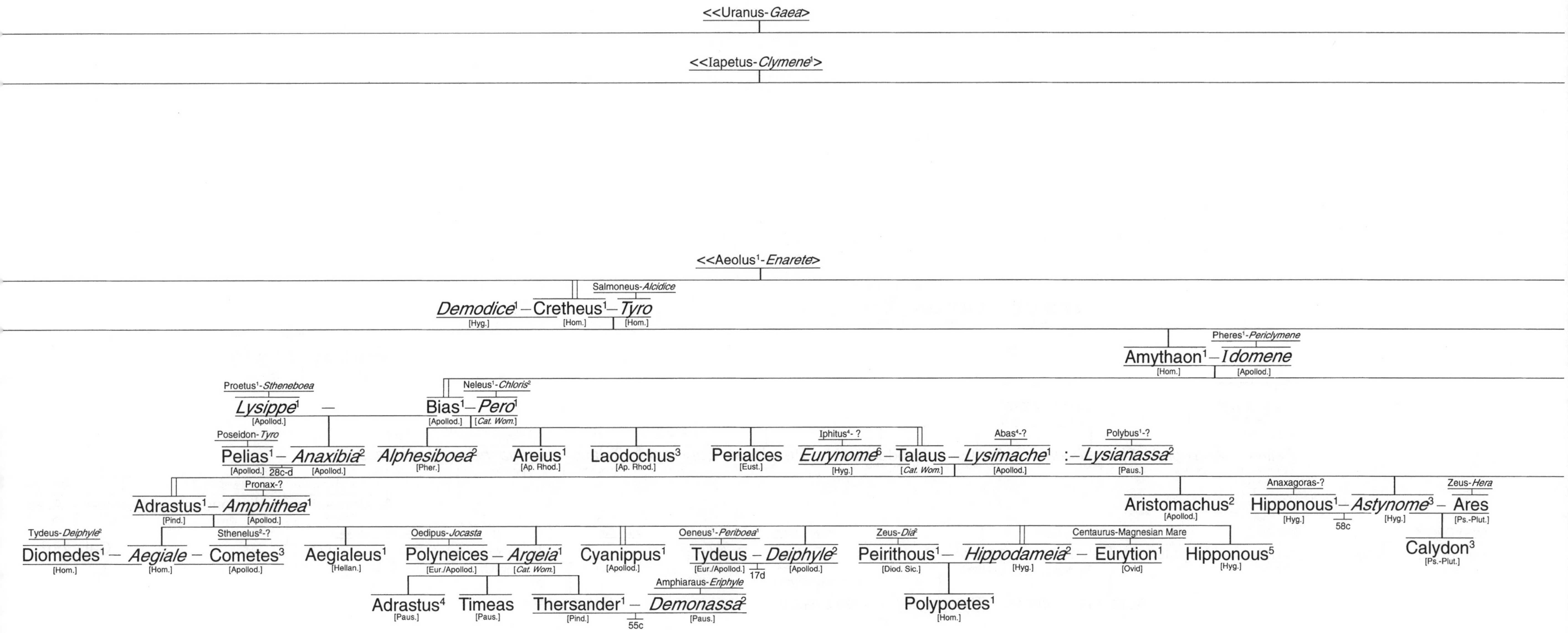

<<Uranus-Gaea>
<<Iapetus-Clymene[1]>
<<Aeolus[1]-Enarete>
Salmoneus-Alcidice
Demodice[1] – Cretheus[1] – Tyro
[Hyg.] [Hom.] [Hom.]
Pheres[1]-Periclymene
Amythaon[1] – Idomene
[Hom.] [Apollod.]
Proetus[1]-Stheneboea
Neleus[1]-Chloris[2]
Lysippe[1] – Bias[1] – Pero[1]
[Apollod.] [Apollod.] [Cat. Wom.]
Poseidon-Tyro
Iphitus[4]-?
Abas[4]-?
Polybus[1]-?
Pelias[1] – Anaxibia[2]
[Apollod.] 28c-d [Apollod.]
Alphesiboea[2]
[Pher.]
Areius[1]
[Ap. Rhod.]
Laodochus[3]
[Ap. Rhod.]
Perialces
[Eust.]
Eurynome[6] – Talaus – Lysimache[1] :– Lysianassa[2]
[Hyg.] [Cat. Wom.] [Apollod.] [Paus.]
Pronax-?
Adrastus[1] – Amphithea[1]
[Pind.] [Apollod.]
Aristomachus[2]
[Apollod.]
Anaxagoras-?
Zeus-Hera
Hipponous[1] – Astynome[3] – Ares
[Hyg.] 58c [Hyg.] [Ps.-Plut.]
Tydeus-Deiphyle[2]
Sthenelus[2]-?
Oedipus-Jocasta
Oeneus[1]-Periboea[1]
Zeus-Dia[2]
Centaurus-Magnesian Mare
Diomedes[1] – Aegiale – Cometes[3]
[Hom.] [Hom.] [Apollod.]
Aegialeus[1]
[Hellan.]
Polyneices – Argeia[1]
[Eur./Apollod.] [Cat. Wom.]
Cyanippus[1]
[Apollod.]
Tydeus – Deiphyle[2]
[Eur./Apollod.] 17d [Apollod.]
Peirithous[1] – Hippodameia[2] – Eurytion[1]
[Diod. Sic.] [Hyg.] [Ovid]
Hipponous[5]
[Hyg.]
Calydon[3]
[Ps.-Plut.]
Amphiaraus-Eriphyle
Adrastus[4]
[Paus.]
Timeas
[Paus.]
Thersander[1] – Demonassa[2]
[Pind.] 55c [Paus.]
Polypoetes[1]
[Hom.]

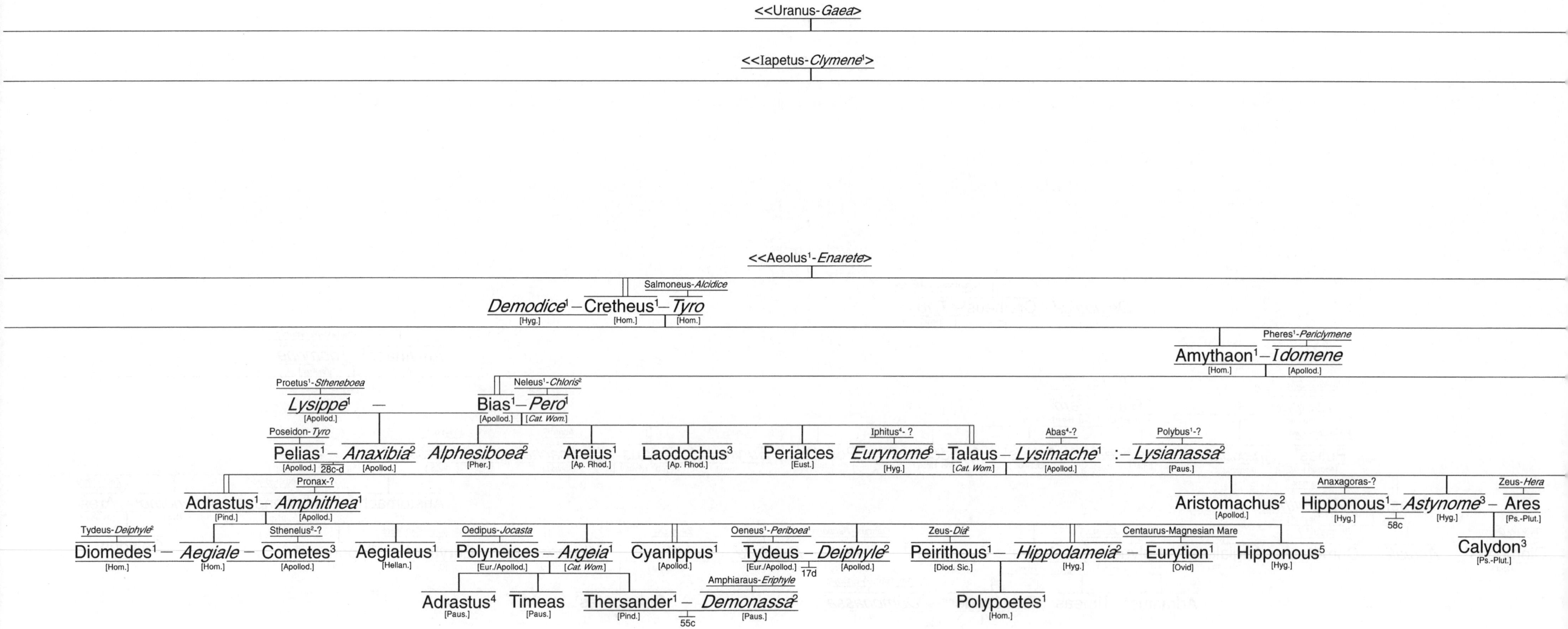

<<Uranus-*Gaea*>
<<Iapetus-*Clymene*[1]>
<<Aeolus[1]-*Enarete*>
Salmoneus-*Alcidice*
Demodice[1] – Cretheus[1] – *Tyro*
[Hyg.]
[Hom.]
[Hom.]
Pheres[1]-*Periclymene*
Amythaon[1] – *Idomene*
[Hom.]
[Apollod.]
Proetus[1]-*Stheneboea*
Lysippe[1] –
[Apollod.]
Neleus[1]-*Chloris*[2]
Bias[1] – *Pero*[1]
[Apollod.]
[*Cat. Wom.*]
Poseidon-*Tyro*
Pelias[1] – *Anaxibia*[2]
[Apollod.]
28c-d
[Apollod.]
Alphesiboea[2]
[Pher.]
Areius[1]
[Ap. Rhod.]
Laodochus[3]
[Ap. Rhod.]
Perialces
[Eust.]
Iphitus[4]-?
Eurynome[6] – Talaus – *Lysimache*[1]
[Hyg.]
[*Cat. Wom.*]
Abas[4]-?
[Apollod.]
Polybus[1]-?
:– *Lysianassa*[2]
[Paus.]
Pronax-?
Adrastus[1] – *Amphithea*[1]
[Pind.]
[Apollod.]
Aristomachus[2]
[Apollod.]
Anaxagoras-?
Hipponous[1] – *Astynome*[3] – Ares
[Hyg.]
58c
[Hyg.]
Zeus-*Hera*
[Ps.-Plut.]
Tydeus-*Deiphyle*[2]
Diomedes[1] – *Aegiale* – Cometes[3]
[Hom.]
[Hom.]
Sthenelus[2]-?
[Apollod.]
Aegialeus[1]
[Hellan.]
Oedipus-*Jocasta*
Polyneices – *Argeia*[1]
[Eur./Apollod.]
[*Cat. Wom.*]
Cyanippus[1]
[Apollod.]
Oeneus[1]-*Periboea*[1]
Tydeus – *Deiphyle*[2]
[Eur./Apollod.]
17d
[Apollod.]
Zeus-*Dia*[2]
Peirithous[1] – *Hippodameia*[2] – Eurytion[1]
[Diod. Sic.]
[Hyg.]
Centaurus-Magnesian Mare
[Ovid]
Hipponous[5]
[Hyg.]
Calydon[3]
[Ps.-Plut.]
Adrastus[4]
[Paus.]
Timeas
[Paus.]
Amphiaraus-*Eriphyle*
Thersander[1] – *Demonassa*[2]
[Pind.]
55c
[Paus.]
Polypoetes[1]
[Hom.]

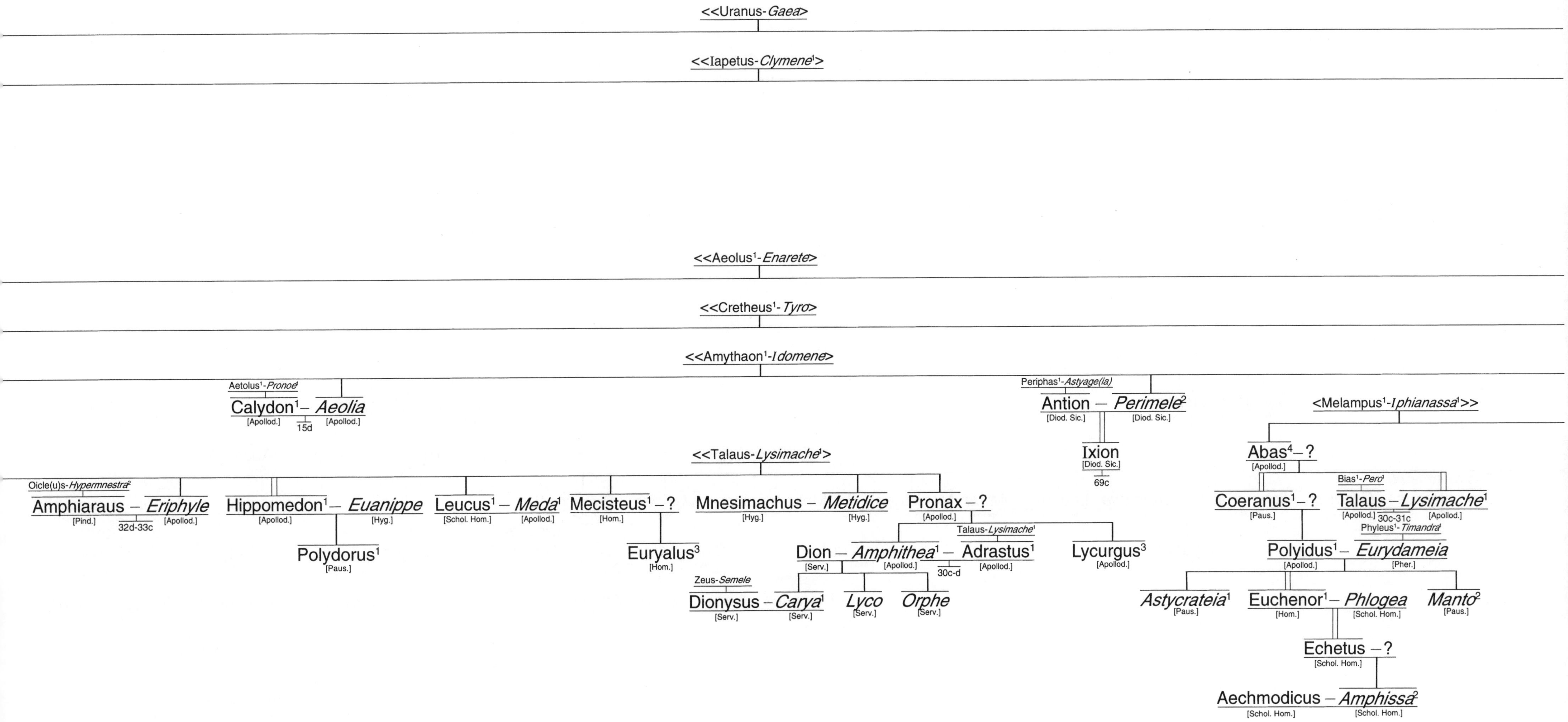

<<Uranus-Gaea>
<<Iapetus-Clymene[1]>
<<Aeolus[1]-Enarete>
<<Cretheus[1]-Tyro>
<<Amythaon[1]-Idomene>
Aetolus[1]-Pronoe
Calydon[1] – Aeolia
[Apollod.]
15d
[Apollod.]
Periphas[1]-Astyage(ia)
Antion – Perimele[2]
[Diod. Sic.]
[Diod. Sic.]
Ixion
[Diod. Sic.]
69c
<Melampus[1]-Iphianassa[1]>>
Abas[4] – ?
[Apollod.]
<<Talaus-Lysimache[1]>
Oicle(u)s-Hypermnestra[2]
Amphiaraus – Eriphyle
[Pind.]
32d-33c
[Apollod.]
Hippomedon[1] – Euanippe
[Apollod.]
[Hyg.]
Polydorus[1]
[Paus.]
Leucus[1] – Meda[1]
[Schol. Hom.]
[Apollod.]
Mecisteus[1] – ?
[Hom.]
Euryalus[3]
[Hom.]
Mnesimachus – Metidice
[Hyg.]
[Hyg.]
Pronax – ?
[Apollod.]
Talaus-Lysimache[1]
Dion – Amphithea[1] – Adrastus[1]
[Serv.]
[Apollod.]
30c-d
[Apollod.]
Lycurgus[3]
[Apollod.]
Zeus-Semele
Dionysus – Carya[1]
[Serv.]
[Serv.]
Lyco
[Serv.]
Orphe
[Serv.]
Bias[1]-Pero[1]
Coeranus[1] – ?
[Paus.]
Talaus – Lysimache[1]
[Apollod.]
30c-31c
[Apollod.]
Phyleus[1]-Timandra[1]
Polyidus[1] – Eurydameia
[Apollod.]
[Pher.]
Astycrateia[1]
[Paus.]
Euchenor[1] – Phlogea
[Hom.]
[Schol. Hom.]
Manto[2]
[Paus.]
Echetus – ?
[Schol. Hom.]
Aechmodicus – Amphissa[2]
[Schol. Hom.]
[Schol. Hom.]

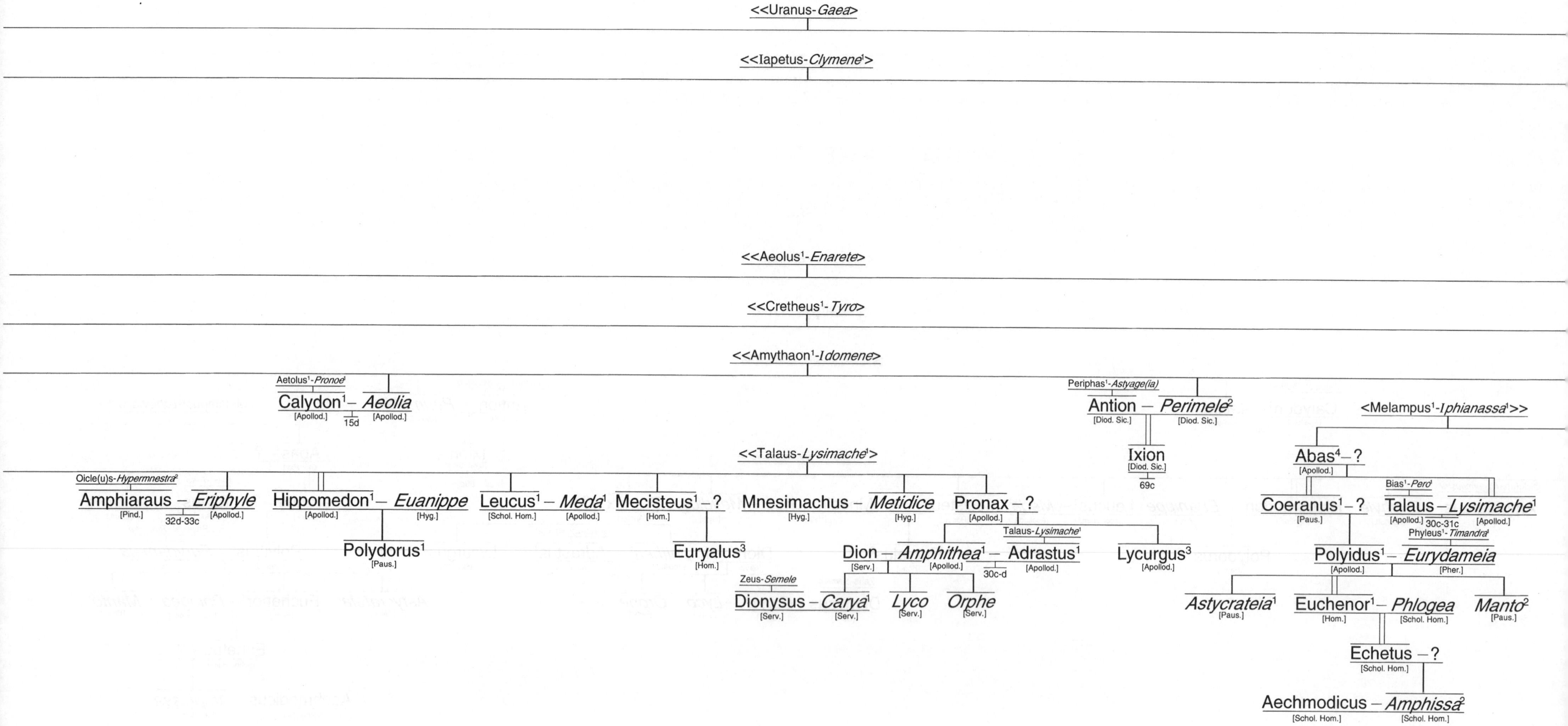
<<Uranus-Gaea>
<<Iapetus-Clymene[1]>
<<Aeolus[1]-Enarete>
<<Cretheus[1]-Tyro>
<<Amythaon[1]-Idomene>
Aetolus[1]-Pronoe[1]
Calydon[1] – Aeolia
[Apollod.]
15d
[Apollod.]
Periphas[1]-Astyage(ia)
Antion – Perimele[2]
[Diod. Sic.]
[Diod. Sic.]
Ixion
[Diod. Sic.]
69c
<Melampus[1]-Iphianassa[1]>>
<<Talaus-Lysimache[1]>
Oicle(u)s-Hypermnestra[2]
Amphiaraus – Eriphyle
[Pind.]
32d-33c
[Apollod.]
Hippomedon[1] – Euanippe
[Apollod.]
[Hyg.]
Polydorus[1]
[Paus.]
Leucus[1] – Meda[1]
[Schol. Hom.]
[Apollod.]
Mecisteus[1] – ?
[Hom.]
Euryalus[3]
[Hom.]
Mnesimachus – Metidice
[Hyg.]
[Hyg.]
Pronax – ?
[Apollod.]
Talaus-Lysimache[1]
Dion – Amphithea[1] – Adrastus[1]
[Serv.]
[Apollod.]
30c-d
[Apollod.]
Lycurgus[3]
[Apollod.]
Zeus-Semele
Dionysus – Carya[1]
[Serv.]
[Serv.]
Lyco
[Serv.]
Orphe
[Serv.]
Abas[4] – ?
[Apollod.]
Coeranus[1] – ?
[Paus.]
Bias[1]-Pero[1]
Talaus – Lysimache[1]
[Apollod.]
30c-31c
[Apollod.]
Phyleus[1]-Timandra[1]
Polyidus[1] – Eurydameia
[Apollod.]
[Pher.]
Astycrateia[1]
[Paus.]
Euchenor[1] – Phlogea
[Hom.]
[Schol. Hom.]
Manto[2]
[Paus.]
Echetus – ?
[Schol. Hom.]
Aechmodicus – Amphissa[2]
[Schol. Hom.]
[Schol. Hom.]

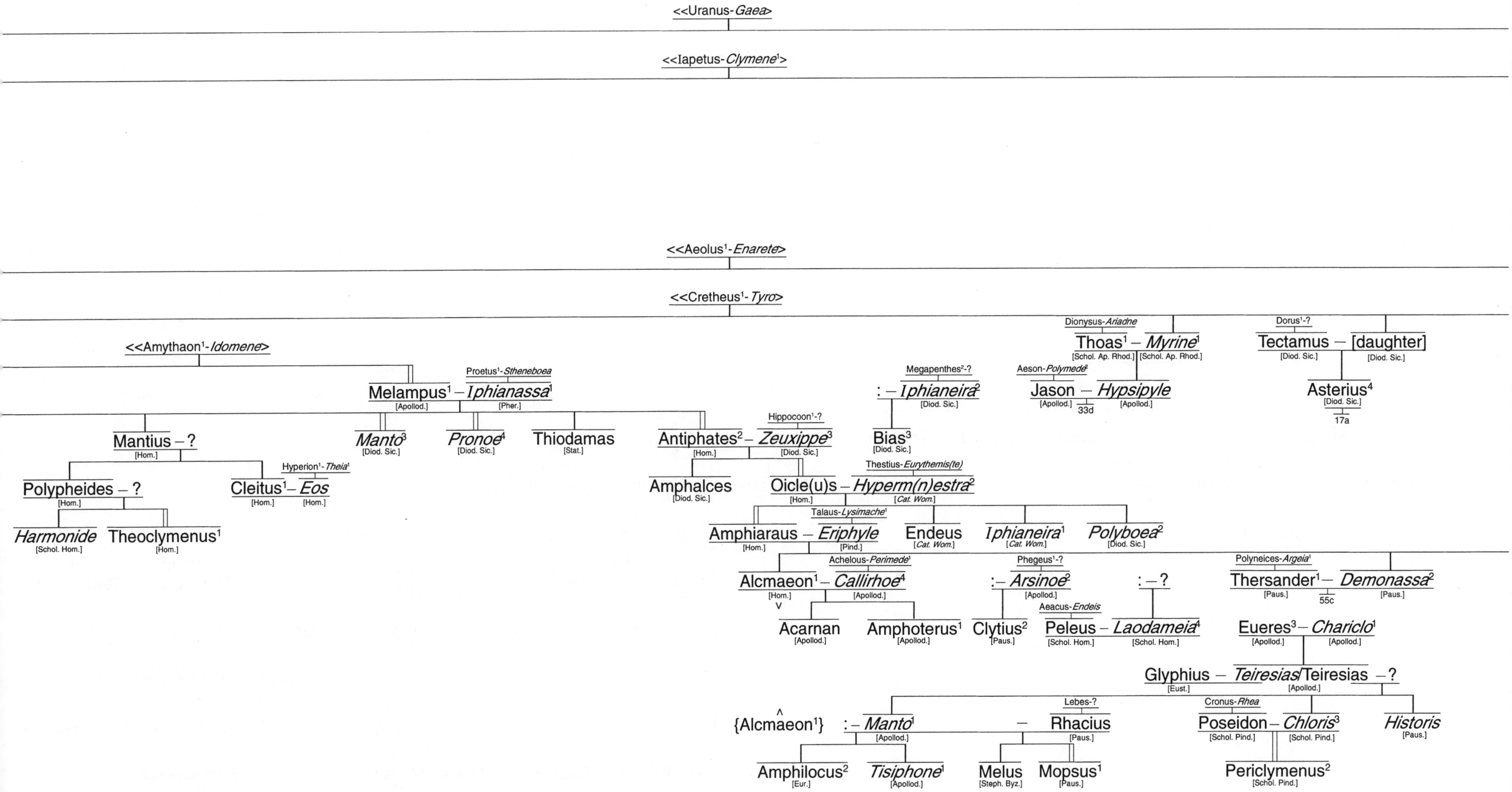
<<Uranus-Gaea>
<<Iapetus-Clymene[1]>
<<Aeolus[1]-Enarete>
<<Cretheus[1]-Tyro>
<<Amythaon[1]-Idomene>
Proetus[1]-Stheneboea
Melampus[1] – Iphianassa[1]
[Apollod.] [Pher.]
Mantius – ?
[Hom.]
Manto[3]
[Diod. Sic.]
Pronoe[4]
[Diod. Sic.]
Thiodamas
[Stat.]
Hippocoon[1]-?
Antiphates[2] – Zeuxippe[3]
[Hom.] [Diod. Sic.]
Polypheides – ?
[Hom.]
Hyperion[1]-Theia[1]
Cleitus[1] – Eos
[Hom.] [Hom.]
Harmonide
[Schol. Hom.]
Theoclymenus[1]
[Hom.]
Amphalces
[Diod. Sic.]
Thestius-Eurythemis(te)
Oicle(u)s – Hyperm(n)estra[2]
[Hom.] [Cat. Wom.]
Talaus-Lysimache[1]
Amphiaraus – Eriphyle
[Hom.] [Pind.]
Endeus
[Cat. Wom.]
Iphianeira[1]
[Cat. Wom.]
Polyboea[2]
[Diod. Sic.]
Megapenthes[2]-?
: – Iphianeira[2]
[Diod. Sic.]
Bias[3]
[Diod. Sic.]
Dionysus-Ariadne
Thoas[1] – Myrine[1]
[Schol. Ap. Rhod.] [Schol. Ap. Rhod.]
Aeson-Polymede[2]
Jason – Hypsipyle
[Apollod.] 33d [Apollod.]
Dorus[1]-?
Tectamus – [daughter]
[Diod. Sic.] [Diod. Sic.]
Asterius[4]
[Diod. Sic.]
17a
Achelous-Perimede[1]
Alcmaeon[1] – Callirhoe[4]
[Hom.] [Apollod.]
V
Acarnan
[Apollod.]
Amphoterus[1]
[Apollod.]
Phegeus[1]-?
:– Arsinoe[2]
[Apollod.]
Clytius[2]
[Paus.]
: – ?
Aeacus-Endeis
Peleus – Laodameia[4]
[Schol. Hom.] [Schol. Hom.]
Polyneices-Argeia[1]
Thersander[1] – Demonassa[2]
[Paus.] 55c [Paus.]
Eueres[3] – Chariclo[1]
[Apollod.] [Apollod.]
Glyphius – Teiresias/Teiresias – ?
[Eust.] [Apollod.]
^
{Alcmaeon[1]} : – Manto[1]
[Apollod.]
Lebes-?
– Rhacius
[Paus.]
Cronus-Rhea
Poseidon – Chloris[3]
[Schol. Pind.] [Schol. Pind.]
Historis
[Paus.]
Amphilocus[2]
[Eur.]
Tisiphone[1]
[Apollod.]
Melus
[Steph. Byz.]
Mopsus[1]
[Paus.]
Periclymenus[2]
[Schol. Pind.]

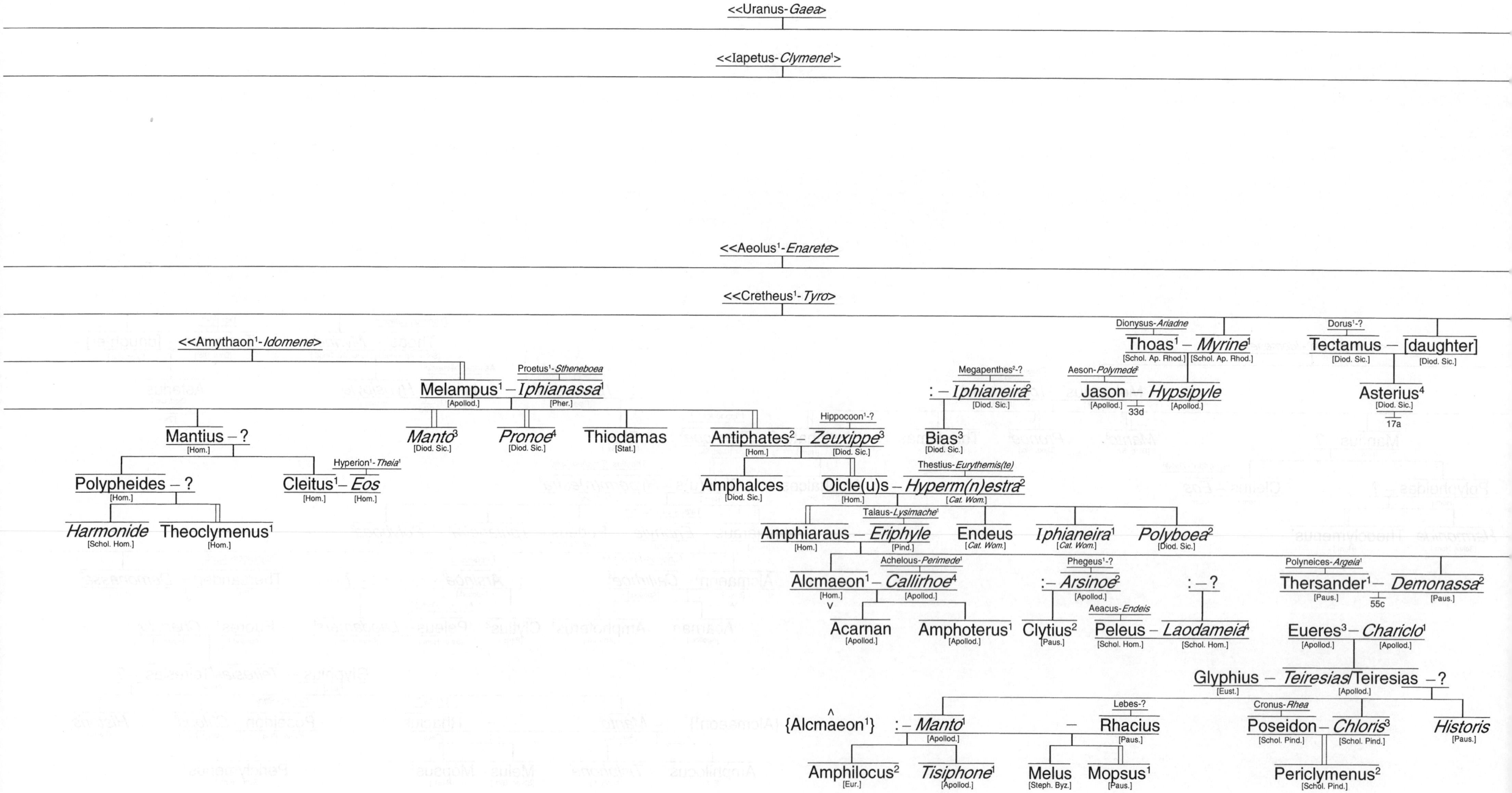

<<Uranus-Gaea>
<<Iapetus-Clymene¹>
<<Aeolus¹-Enarete>
<<Cretheus¹-Tyro>
<<Amythaon¹-Idomene>
Dionysus-Ariadne
Thoas¹ – Myrine¹
[Schol. Ap. Rhod.] [Schol. Ap. Rhod.]
Dorus¹-?
Tectamus – [daughter]
[Diod. Sic.] [Diod. Sic.]
Proetus¹-Stheneboea
Melampus¹ – Iphianassa¹
[Apollod.] [Pher.]
Megapenthes²-?
: – Iphianeira²
[Diod. Sic.]
Aeson-Polymede²
Jason – Hypsipyle
[Apollod.] [Apollod.]
33d
Asterius⁴
[Diod. Sic.]
17a
Hippocoon¹-?
Mantius – ?
[Hom.]
Manto³
[Diod. Sic.]
Pronoe⁴
[Diod. Sic.]
Thiodamas
[Stat.]
Antiphates² – Zeuxippe³
[Hom.] [Diod. Sic.]
Bias³
[Diod. Sic.]
Hyperion¹-Theia¹
Thestius-Eurythemis(te)
Polypheides – ?
[Hom.]
Cleitus¹ – Eos
[Hom.] [Hom.]
Amphalces
[Diod. Sic.]
Oicle(u)s – Hyperm(n)estra²
[Hom.] [Cat. Wom.]
Talaus-Lysimache¹
Harmonide
[Schol. Hom.]
Theoclymenus¹
[Hom.]
Amphiaraus – Eriphyle
[Hom.] [Pind.]
Endeus
[Cat. Wom.]
Iphianeira¹
[Cat. Wom.]
Polyboea²
[Diod. Sic.]
Achelous-Perimede¹
Phegeus¹-?
Polyneices-Argeia¹
Alcmaeon¹ – Callirhoe⁴
[Hom.] [Apollod.]
:– Arsinoe²
[Apollod.]
: – ?
Thersander¹ – Demonassa²
[Paus.] [Paus.]
55c
Aeacus-Endeis
Acarnan
[Apollod.]
Amphoterus¹
[Apollod.]
Clytius²
[Paus.]
Peleus – Laodameia⁴
[Schol. Hom.] [Schol. Hom.]
Eueres³ – Chariclo¹
[Apollod.] [Apollod.]
Glyphius – Teiresias/Teiresias – ?
[Eust.] [Apollod.]
Lebes-?
Cronus-Rhea
{Alcmaeon¹}
: – Manto¹
[Apollod.]
Rhacius
[Paus.]
Poseidon – Chloris³
[Schol. Pind.] [Schol. Pind.]
Historis
[Paus.]
Amphilocus²
[Eur.]
Tisiphone¹
[Apollod.]
Melus
[Steph. Byz.]
Mopsus¹
[Paus.]
Periclymenus²
[Schol. Pind.]

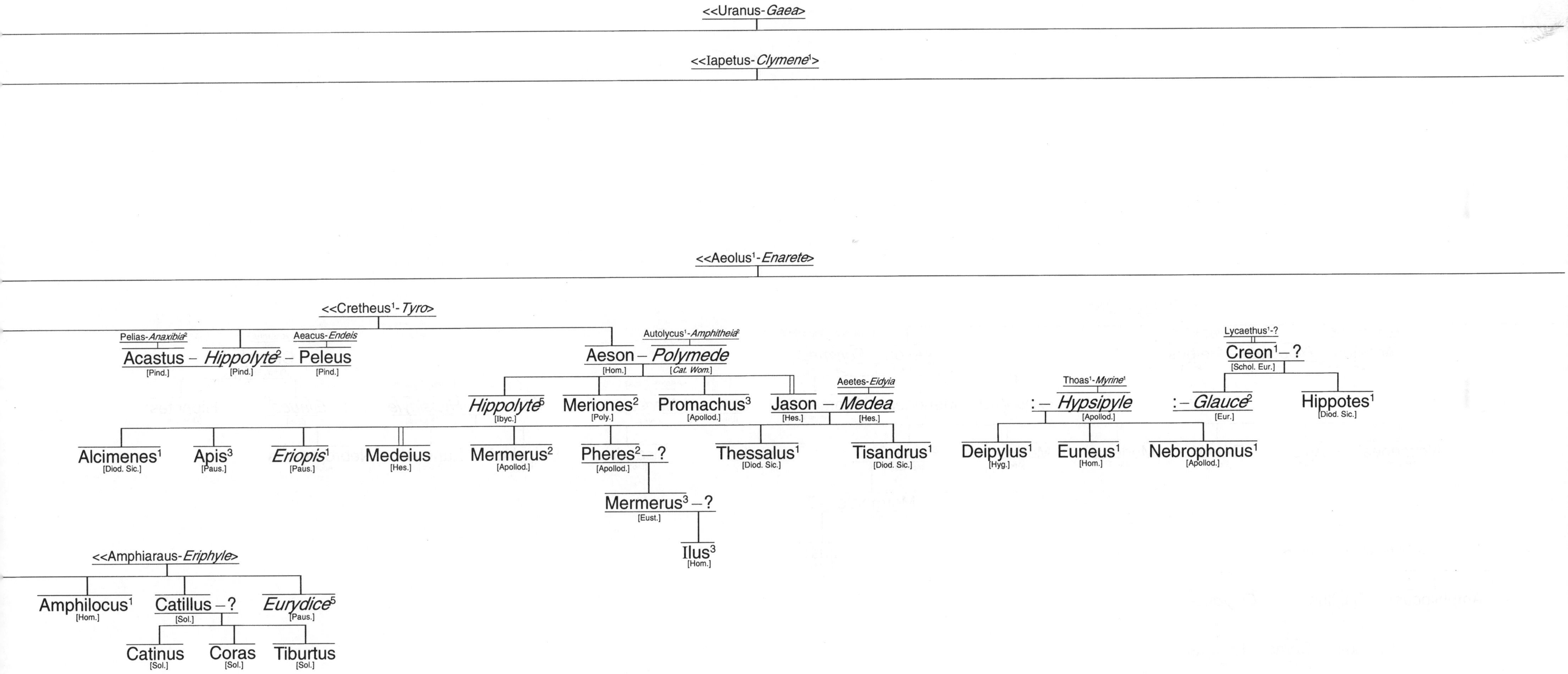

<<Uranus-*Gaea*>
<<Iapetus-*Clymene*1>
<<Aeolus1-*Enarete*>
<<Cretheus1-*Tyro*>
Pelias-*Anaxibia*2
Acastus – *Hippolyte*2 – Peleus
[Pind.] [Pind.] [Pind.]
Aeacus-*Endeis*
Autolycus1-*Amphitheia*2
Aeson – *Polymede*
[Hom.] [*Cat. Wom.*]
*Hippolyte*5 [Ibyc.]
Meriones2 [Poly.]
Promachus3 [Apollod.]
Aeetes-*Eidyia*
Jason – *Medea*
[Hes.] [Hes.]
Alcimenes1 [Diod. Sic.]
Apis3 [Paus.]
*Eriopis*1 [Paus.]
Medeius [Hes.]
Mermerus2 [Apollod.]
Pheres2 – ? [Apollod.]
Mermerus3 – ? [Eust.]
Ilus3 [Hom.]
Thessalus1 [Diod. Sic.]
Tisandrus1 [Diod. Sic.]
Thoas1-*Myrine*1
:– *Hypsipyle* [Apollod.]
Deipylus1 [Hyg.]
Euneus1 [Hom.]
Nebrophonus1 [Apollod.]
Lycaethus1-?
Creon1 – ? [Schol. Eur.]
:– *Glauce*2 [Eur.]
Hippotes1 [Diod. Sic.]
<<Amphiaraus-*Eriphyle*>
Amphilocus1 [Hom.]
Catillus – ? [Sol.]
*Eurydice*5 [Paus.]
Catinus [Sol.]
Coras [Sol.]
Tiburtus [Sol.]

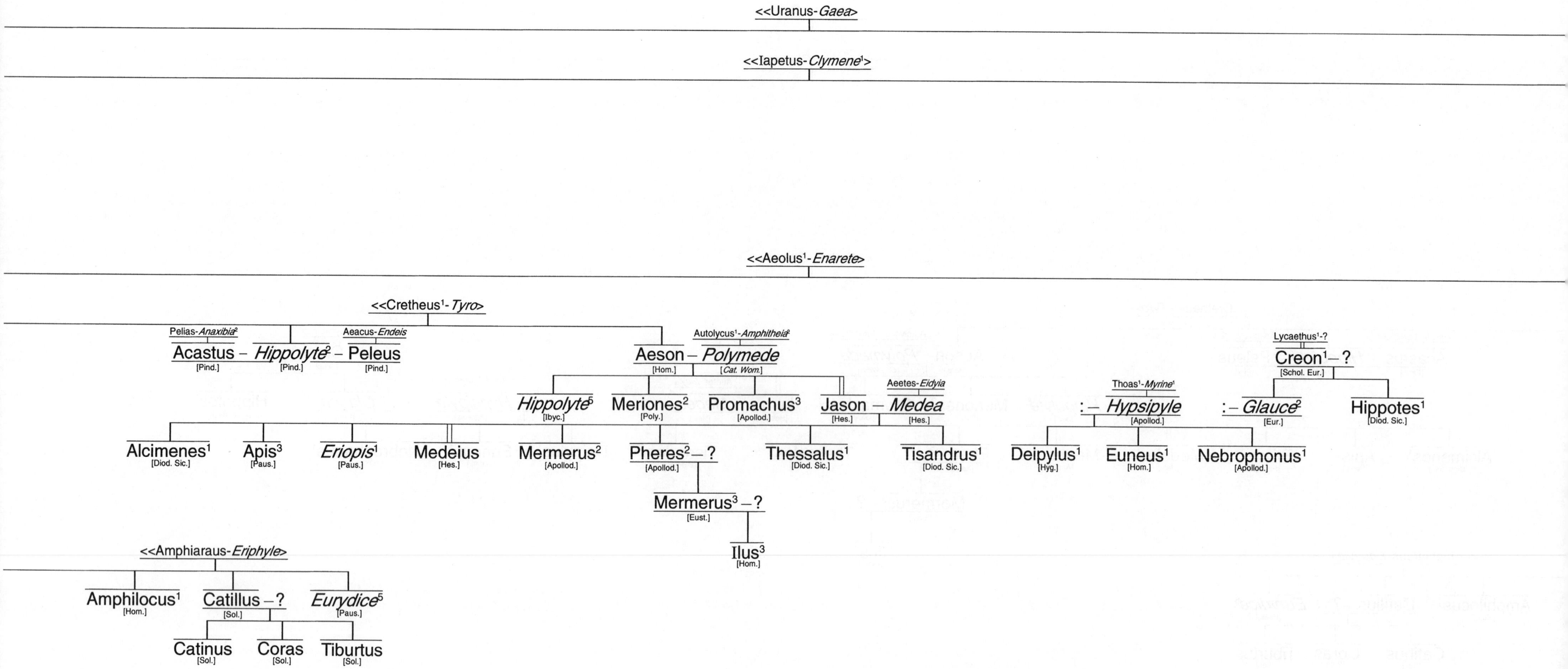
<<Uranus-Gaea>
<<Iapetus-Clymene[1]>
<<Aeolus[1]-Enarete>
<<Cretheus[1]-Tyro>
Pelias-Anaxibia[2]
Aeacus-Endeis
Acastus – Hippolyte[2] – Peleus
[Pind.] [Pind.] [Pind.]
Autolycus[1]-Amphithea[2]
Aeson – Polymede
[Hom.] [Cat. Wom.]
Hippolyte[5] [Ibyc.]
Meriones[2] [Poly.]
Promachus[3] [Apollod.]
Aeetes-Eidyia
Jason – Medea
[Hes.] [Hes.]
Thoas[1]-Myrine[1]
:– Hypsipyle [Apollod.]
Lycaethus[1]-?
Creon[1] – ?
[Schol. Eur.]
:– Glauce[2] [Eur.]
Hippotes[1] [Diod. Sic.]
Alcimenes[1] [Diod. Sic.]
Apis[3] [Paus.]
Eriopis[1] [Paus.]
Medeius [Hes.]
Mermerus[2] [Apollod.]
Pheres[2] – ? [Apollod.]
Thessalus[1] [Diod. Sic.]
Tisandrus[1] [Diod. Sic.]
Deipylus[1] [Hyg.]
Euneus[1] [Hom.]
Nebrophonus[1] [Apollod.]
Mermerus[3] – ? [Eust.]
Ilus[3] [Hom.]
<<Amphiaraus-Eriphyle>
Amphilocus[1] [Hom.]
Catillus – ? [Sol.]
Eurydice[5] [Paus.]
Catinus [Sol.]
Coras [Sol.]
Tiburtus [Sol.]

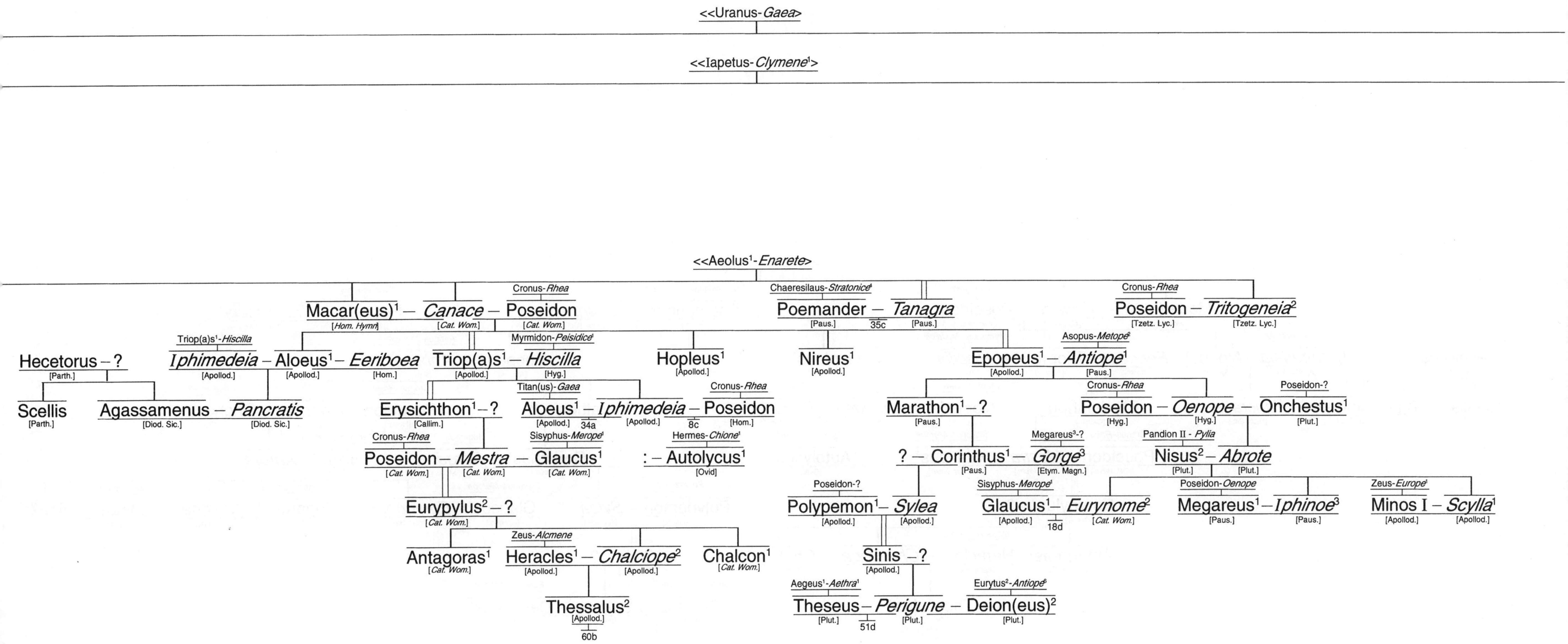
<<Uranus-Gaea>
<<Iapetus-Clymene[1]>
<<Aeolus[1]-Enarete>
Cronus-Rhea
Macar(eus)[1] – Canace – Poseidon
[Hom. Hymn] [Cat. Wom.] [Cat. Wom.]
Chaeresilaus-Stratonice[1]
Poemander – Tanagra
[Paus.] 35c [Paus.]
Cronus-Rhea
Poseidon – Tritogeneia[2]
[Tzetz. Lyc.] [Tzetz. Lyc.]
Triop(a)s[1]-Hiscilla
Myrmidon-Peisidice[1]
Asopus-Metope[2]
Hecetorus – ?
[Parth.]
Iphimedeia – Aloeus[1] – Eeriboea
[Apollod.] [Apollod.] [Hom.]
Triop(a)s[1] – Hiscilla
[Apollod.] [Hyg.]
Hopleus[1]
[Apollod.]
Nireus[1]
[Apollod.]
Epopeus[1] – Antiope[1]
[Apollod.] [Paus.]
Scellis
[Parth.]
Agassamenus – Pancratis
[Diod. Sic.] [Diod. Sic.]
Erysichthon[1] – ?
[Callim.]
Titan(us)-Gaea
Aloeus[1] – Iphimedeia – Poseidon
[Apollod.] 34a [Apollod.] 8c [Hom.]
Cronus-Rhea
Marathon[1] – ?
[Paus.]
Cronus-Rhea
Poseidon – Oenope – Onchestus[1]
[Hyg.] [Hyg.] [Plut.]
Poseidon-?
Cronus-Rhea
Poseidon – Mestra – Glaucus[1]
[Cat. Wom.] [Cat. Wom.] [Cat. Wom.]
Sisyphus-Merope[1]
Hermes-Chione[1]
: – Autolycus[1]
[Ovid]
Megareus[3]-?
? – Corinthus[1] – Gorge[3]
[Paus.] [Etym. Magn.]
Pandion II - Pylia
Nisus[2] – Abrote
[Plut.] [Plut.]
Eurypylus[2] – ?
[Cat. Wom.]
Poseidon-?
Polypemon[1] – Sylea
[Apollod.] [Apollod.]
Sisyphus-Merope[1]
Glaucus[1] – Eurynome[2]
[Apollod.] 18d [Cat. Wom.]
Poseidon-Oenope
Megareus[1] – Iphinoe[3]
[Paus.] [Paus.]
Zeus-Europe[1]
Minos I – Scylla[1]
[Apollod.] [Apollod.]
Zeus-Alcmene
Antagoras[1]
[Cat. Wom.]
Heracles[1] – Chalciope[2]
[Apollod.] [Apollod.]
Chalcon[1]
[Cat. Wom.]
Sinis – ?
[Apollod.]
Aegeus[1]-Aethra[1]
Eurytus[2]-Antiope[3]
Theseus – Perigune – Deion(eus)[2]
[Plut.] 51d [Plut.] [Plut.]
Thessalus[2]
[Apollod.]
60b

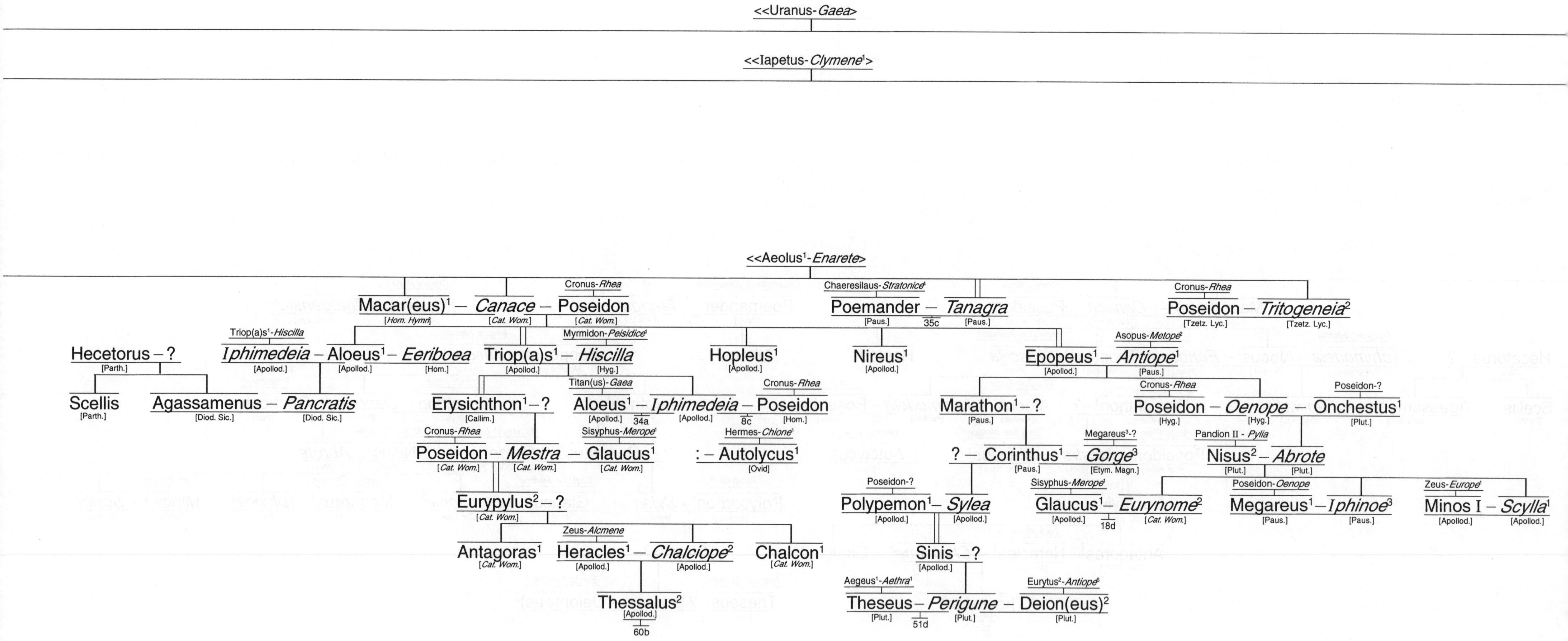

<<Uranus-Gaea>
<<Iapetus-Clymene¹>
<<Aeolus¹-Enarete>
Cronus-Rhea
Chaeresilaus-Stratonice
Cronus-Rhea
Macar(eus)¹ – Canace – Poseidon
[Hom. Hymn] [Cat. Wom.] [Cat. Wom.]
Poemander – Tanagra
[Paus.] 35c [Paus.]
Poseidon – Tritogeneia²
[Tzetz. Lyc.] [Tzetz. Lyc.]
Triop(a)s¹-Hiscilla
Myrmidon-Peisidice
Asopus-Metope
Hecetorus – ?
[Parth.]
Iphimedeia – Aloeus¹ – Eeriboea
[Apollod.] [Apollod.] [Hom.]
Triop(a)s¹ – Hiscilla
[Apollod.] [Hyg.]
Hopleus¹
[Apollod.]
Nireus¹
[Apollod.]
Epopeus¹ – Antiope¹
[Apollod.] [Paus.]
Titan(us)-Gaea
Cronus-Rhea
Cronus-Rhea
Poseidon-?
Scellis
[Parth.]
Agassamenus – Pancratis
[Diod. Sic.] [Diod. Sic.]
Erysichthon¹ – ?
[Callim.]
Aloeus¹ – Iphimedeia – Poseidon
[Apollod.] 34a [Apollod.] 8c [Hom.]
Marathon¹ – ?
[Paus.]
Poseidon – Oenope – Onchestus¹
[Hyg.] [Hyg.] [Plut.]
Cronus-Rhea
Sisyphus-Merope¹
Hermes-Chione¹
Megareus³-?
Pandion II - Pylia
Poseidon – Mestra – Glaucus¹
[Cat. Wom.] [Cat. Wom.] [Cat. Wom.]
: – Autolycus¹
[Ovid]
? – Corinthus¹ – Gorge³
[Paus.] [Etym. Magn.]
Nisus² – Abrote
[Plut.] [Plut.]
Poseidon-?
Sisyphus-Merope¹
Poseidon-Oenope
Zeus-Europe¹
Eurypylus² – ?
[Cat. Wom.]
Polypemon¹ – Sylea
[Apollod.] [Apollod.]
Glaucus¹ – Eurynome²
[Apollod.] 18d [Cat. Wom.]
Megareus¹ – Iphinoe³
[Paus.] [Paus.]
Minos I – Scylla¹
[Apollod.] [Apollod.]
Zeus-Alcmene
Antagoras¹
[Cat. Wom.]
Heracles¹ – Chalciope²
[Apollod.] [Apollod.]
Chalcon¹
[Cat. Wom.]
Sinis – ?
[Apollod.]
Aegeus¹-Aethra¹
Eurytus²-Antiope⁶
Thessalus²
[Apollod.]
60b
Theseus – Perigune – Deion(eus)²
[Plut.] 51d [Plut.] [Plut.]

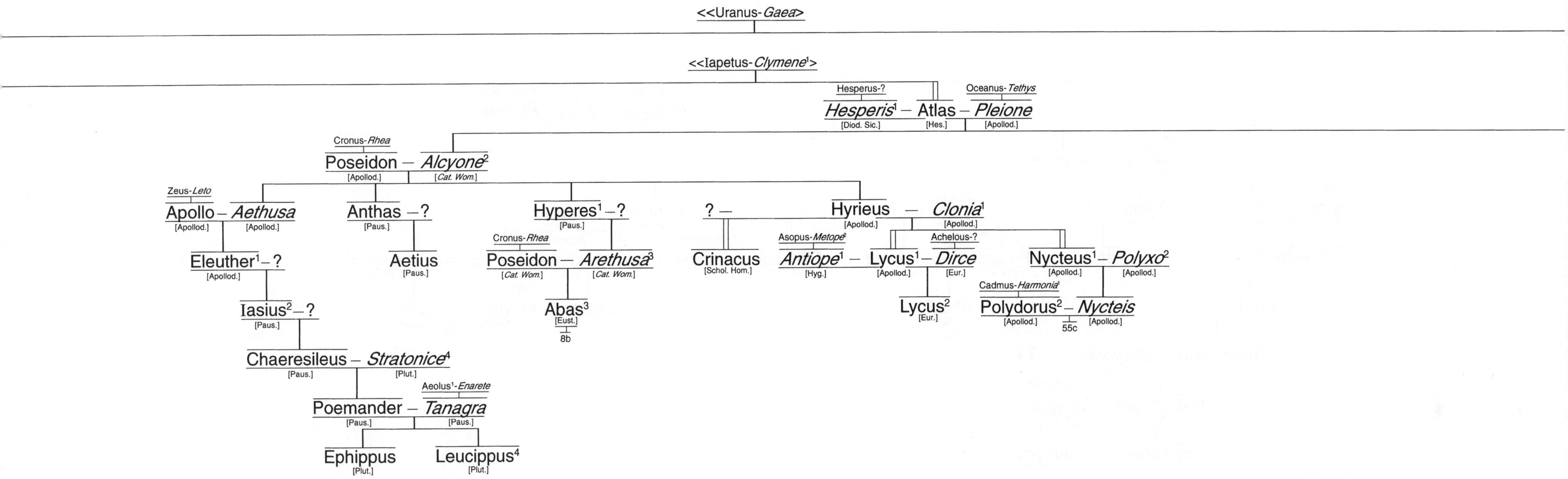
<<Uranus-*Gaea*>
<<Iapetus-*Clymene*[1]>
Hesperus-?
Hesperis[1] – Atlas – *Pleione*
[Diod. Sic.] [Hes.] [Apollod.]
Oceanus-*Tethys*
Cronus-*Rhea*
Poseidon – *Alcyone*[2]
[Apollod.] [*Cat. Wom.*]
Zeus-*Leto*
Apollo – *Aethusa*
[Apollod.] [Apollod.]
Anthas – ?
[Paus.]
Aetius
[Paus.]
Hyperes[1] – ?
[Paus.]
Cronus-*Rhea*
Poseidon – *Arethusa*[3]
[*Cat. Wom.*] [*Cat. Wom.*]
Abas[3]
[Eust.]
8b
? –
Crinacus
[Schol. Hom.]
Hyrieus – *Clonia*[1]
[Apollod.] [Apollod.]
Asopus-*Metope*[2]
Antiope[1] – Lycus[1] – *Dirce*
[Hyg.] [Apollod.] [Eur.]
Achelous-?
Lycus[2]
[Eur.]
Nycteus[1] – *Polyxo*[2]
[Apollod.] [Apollod.]
Cadmus-*Harmonia*[1]
Polydorus[2] – *Nycteis*
[Apollod.] [Apollod.]
55c
Eleuther[1] – ?
[Apollod.]
Iasius[2] – ?
[Paus.]
Chaeresileus – *Stratonice*[4]
[Paus.] [Plut.]
Aeolus[1]-*Enarete*
Poemander – *Tanagra*
[Paus.] [Paus.]
Ephippus
[Plut.]
Leucippus[4]
[Plut.]

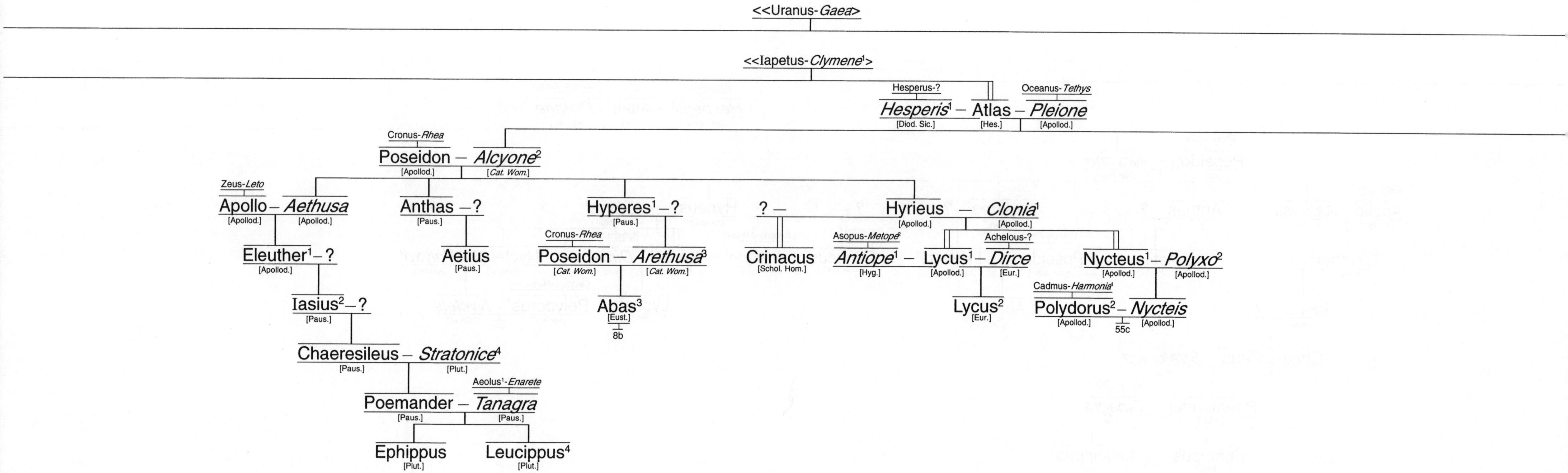
<<Uranus-Gaea>
<<Iapetus-Clymene[1]>
Hesperus-?
Hesperis[1] – Atlas – Pleione
[Diod. Sic.] [Hes.] [Apollod.]
Oceanus-Tethys
Cronus-Rhea
Poseidon – Alcyone[2]
[Apollod.] [Cat. Wom.]
Zeus-Leto
Apollo – Aethusa
[Apollod.] [Apollod.]
Anthas – ?
[Paus.]
Hyperes[1] – ?
[Paus.]
? –
Hyrieus – Clonia[1]
[Apollod.] [Apollod.]
Eleuther[1] – ?
[Apollod.]
Aetius
[Paus.]
Cronus-Rhea
Poseidon – Arethusa[3]
[Cat. Wom.] [Cat. Wom.]
Crinacus
[Schol. Hom.]
Asopus-Metope[2]
Antiope[1] –
[Hyg.]
Lycus[1] – Dirce
[Apollod.] [Eur.]
Achelous-?
Nycteus[1] – Polyxo[2]
[Apollod.] [Apollod.]
Iasius[2] – ?
[Paus.]
Abas[3]
[Eust.]
8b
Lycus[2]
[Eur.]
Cadmus-Harmonia[1]
Polydorus[2] – Nycteis
[Apollod.] [Apollod.]
55c
Chaeresileus – Stratonice[4]
[Paus.] [Plut.]
Aeolus[1]-Enarete
Poemander – Tanagra
[Paus.] [Paus.]
Ephippus
[Plut.]
Leucippus[4]
[Plut.]

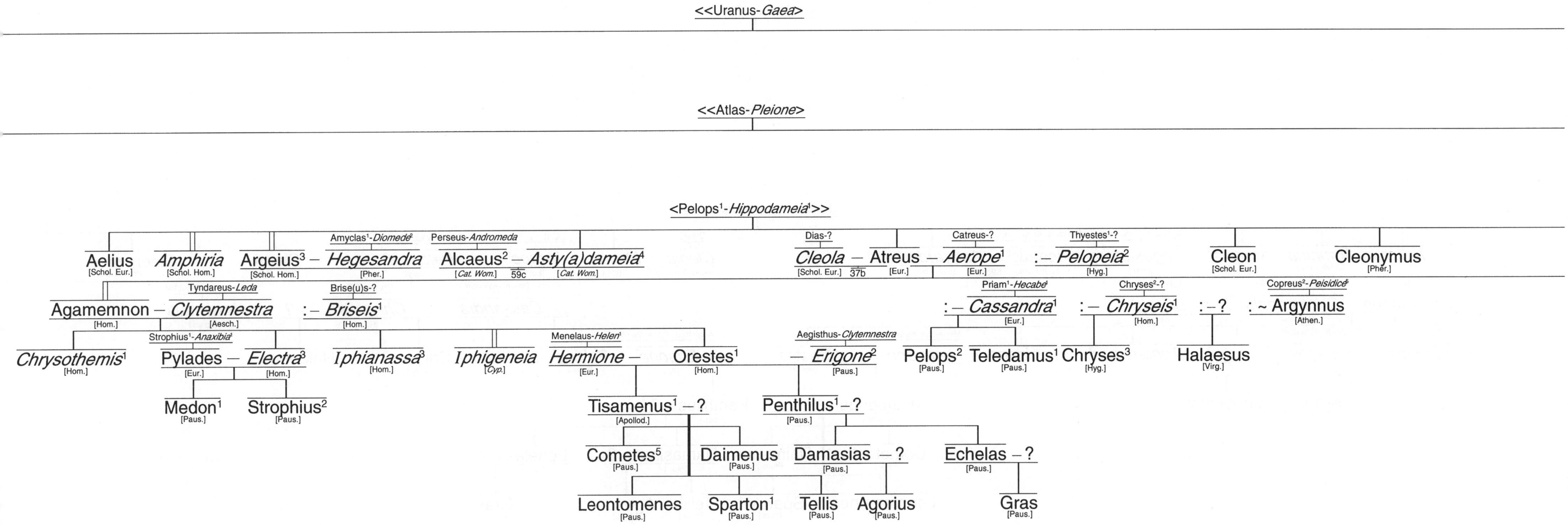

<<Uranus-Gaea>
<<Atlas-Pleione>
<Pelops¹-Hippodameia¹>>
Aelius [Schol. Eur.]
Amphiria [Schol. Hom.]
Argeius³ – Hegesandra [Schol. Hom.] [Pher.]
Amyclas¹-Diomede²
Perseus-Andromeda
Alcaeus² – Asty(a)dameia⁴ [Cat. Wom.] 59c [Cat. Wom.]
Dias-?
Cleola – Atreus – Aerope¹ [Schol. Eur.] 37b [Eur.] [Eur.]
Catreus-?
Thyestes¹-?
:– Pelopeia² [Hyg.]
Cleon [Schol. Eur.]
Cleonymus [Pher.]
Tyndareus-Leda
Agamemnon – Clytemnestra [Hom.] [Aesch.]
Brise(u)s-?
:– Briseis¹ [Hom.]
Priam¹-Hecabe¹
:– Cassandra¹ [Eur.]
Chryses²-?
:– Chryseis¹ [Hom.]
:–?
Copreus²-Peisidice⁵
:~ Argynnus [Athen.]
Chrysothemis¹ [Hom.]
Strophius¹-Anaxibia¹
Pylades – Electra³ [Eur.] [Hom.]
Iphianassa³ [Hom.]
Iphigeneia [Cyp.]
Menelaus-Helen¹
Hermione – [Eur.]
Orestes¹ [Hom.]
Aegisthus-Clytemnestra
– Erigone² [Paus.]
Pelops² [Paus.]
Teledamus¹ [Paus.]
Chryses³ [Hyg.]
Halaesus [Virg.]
Medon¹ [Paus.]
Strophius² [Paus.]
Tisamenus¹ – ? [Apollod.]
Penthilus¹ – ? [Paus.]
Cometes⁵ [Paus.]
Daimenus [Paus.]
Damasias – ? [Paus.]
Echelas – ? [Paus.]
Leontomenes [Paus.]
Sparton¹ [Paus.]
Tellis [Paus.]
Agorius [Paus.]
Gras [Paus.]

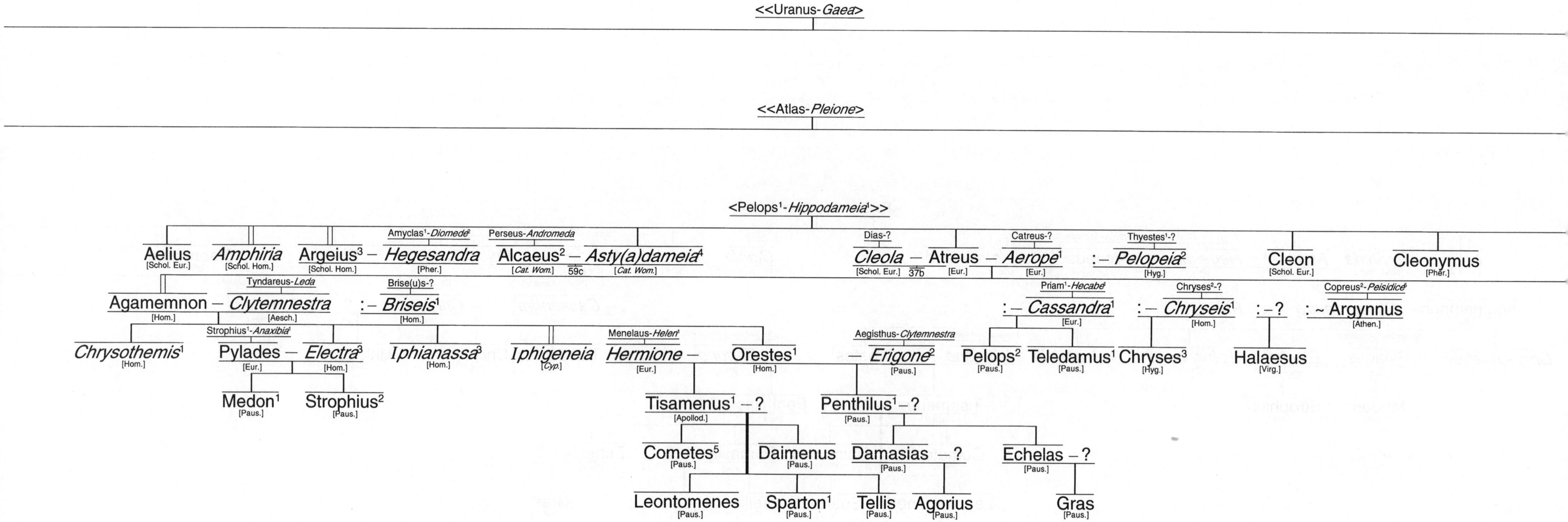

<<Uranus-Gaea>
<<Atlas-Pleione>
<Pelops1-Hippodameia1>>
Aelius [Schol. Eur.]
Amphiria [Schol. Hom.]
Amyclas1-Diomede2
Argeius3 – Hegesandra [Schol. Hom.] [Pher.]
Perseus-Andromeda
Alcaeus2 – Asty(a)dameia4 [Cat. Wom.] 59c [Cat. Wom.]
Dias-?
Cleola – Atreus [Schol. Eur.] 37b [Eur.]
Catreus-?
Aerope1 [Eur.]
Thyestes1-?
:– Pelopeia2 [Hyg.]
Cleon [Schol. Eur.]
Cleonymus [Pher.]
Tyndareus-Leda
Agamemnon – Clytemnestra [Hom.] [Aesch.]
Brise(u)s-?
:– Briseis1 [Hom.]
Priam1-Hecabe1
:– Cassandra1 [Eur.]
Chryses2-?
:– Chryseis1 [Hom.]
:–?
Copreus2-Peisidice5
:~ Argynnus [Athen.]
Chrysothemis1 [Hom.]
Strophius1-Anaxibia1
Pylades – Electra3 [Eur.] [Hom.]
Iphianassa3 [Hom.]
Iphigeneia [Cyp.]
Menelaus-Helen1
Hermione – [Eur.]
Orestes1 [Hom.]
Aegisthus-Clytemnestra
– Erigone2 [Paus.]
Pelops2 [Paus.]
Teledamus1 [Paus.]
Chryses3 [Hyg.]
Halaesus [Virg.]
Medon1 [Paus.]
Strophius2 [Paus.]
Tisamenus1 – ? [Apollod.]
Penthilus1 – ? [Paus.]
Cometes5 [Paus.]
Daimenus [Paus.]
Damasias – ? [Paus.]
Echelas – ? [Paus.]
Leontomenes [Paus.]
Sparton1 [Paus.]
Tellis [Paus.]
Agorius [Paus.]
Gras [Paus.]

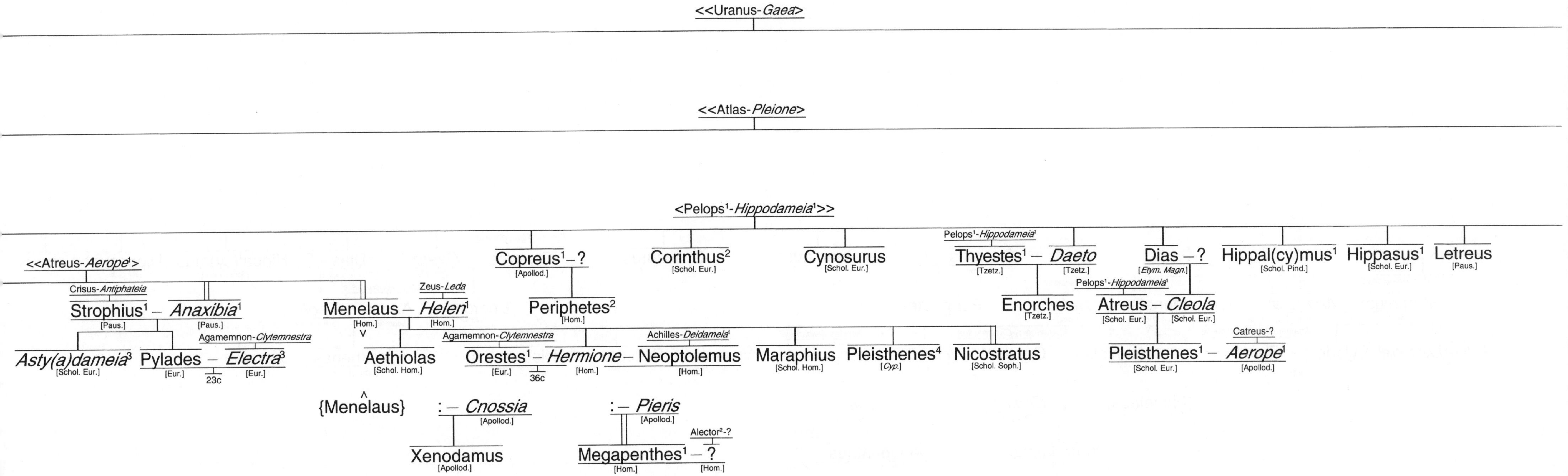

<<Uranus-*Gaea*>
<<Atlas-*Pleione*>
<Pelops¹-*Hippodameia*¹>>
<<Atreus-*Aerope*¹>
Copreus¹ – ?
[Apollod.]
Corinthus²
[Schol. Eur.]
Cynosurus
[Schol. Eur.]
Pelops¹-*Hippodameia*¹
Thyestes¹ – *Daeto*
[Tzetz.]
[Tzetz.]
Dias – ?
[*Etym. Magn.*]
Hippal(cy)mus¹
[Schol. Pind.]
Hippasus¹
[Schol. Eur.]
Letreus
[Paus.]
Crisus-*Antiphateia*
Strophius¹ – *Anaxibia*¹
[Paus.]
[Paus.]
Zeus-*Leda*
Menelaus – *Helen*¹
[Hom.]
[Hom.]
Periphetes²
[Hom.]
Enorches
[Tzetz.]
Pelops¹-*Hippodameia*¹
Atreus – *Cleola*
[Schol. Eur.]
[Schol. Eur.]
Agamemnon-*Clytemnestra*
Agamemnon-*Clytemnestra*
Achilles-*Deidameia*¹
Catreus-?
*Asty(a)dameia*³
[Schol. Eur.]
Pylades – *Electra*³
[Eur.]
[Eur.]
23c
Aethiolas
[Schol. Hom.]
Orestes¹ – *Hermione* – Neoptolemus
[Eur.]
36c
[Hom.]
[Hom.]
Maraphius
[Schol. Hom.]
Pleisthenes⁴
[*Cyp.*]
Nicostratus
[Schol. Soph.]
Pleisthenes¹ – *Aerope*¹
[Schol. Eur.]
[Apollod.]
{Menelaus}
: – *Cnossia*
[Apollod.]
: – *Pieris*
[Apollod.]
Alector²-?
Xenodamus
[Apollod.]
Megapenthes¹ – ?
[Hom.]
[Hom.]

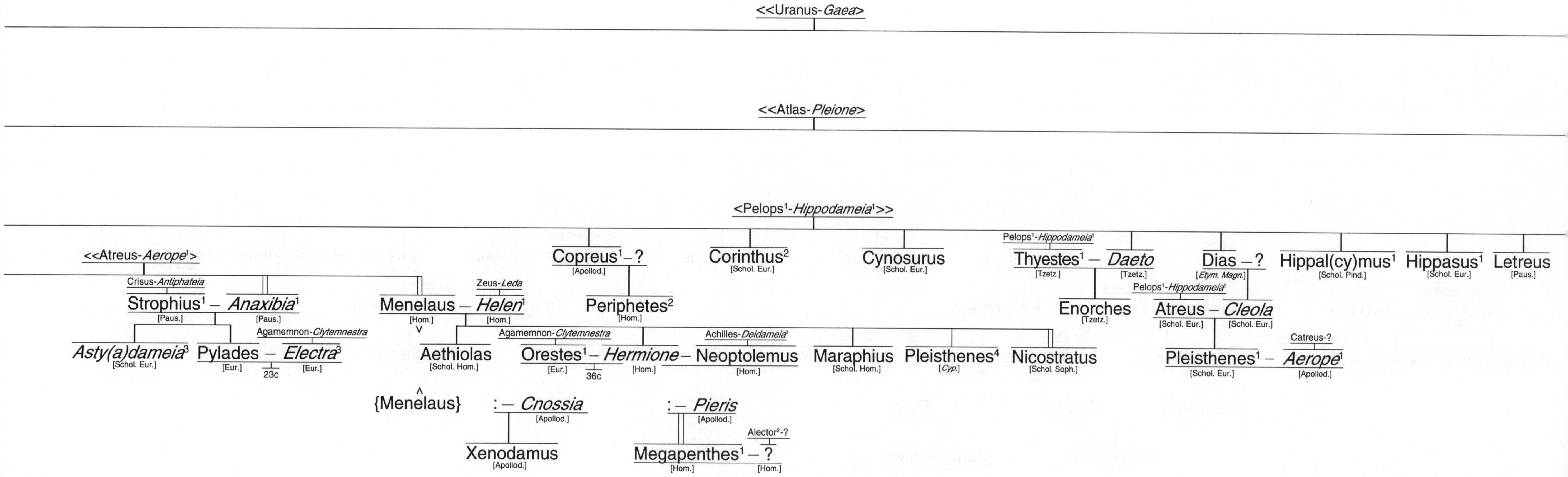

<<Uranus-Gaea>
<<Atlas-Pleione>
<Pelops¹-Hippodameia¹>>
<<Atreus-Aerope¹>
Crisus-Antiphateia
Strophius¹ – Anaxibia¹
[Paus.] [Paus.]
Agamemnon-Clytemnestra
Asty(a)dameia³ [Schol. Eur.]
Pylades – Electra³
[Eur.] 23c [Eur.]
Menelaus – Helen¹
Zeus-Leda
[Hom.] [Hom.]
Aethiolas [Schol. Hom.]
{Menelaus}
: – Cnossia [Apollod.]
Xenodamus [Apollod.]
Copreus¹ – ? [Apollod.]
Periphetes² [Hom.]
Agamemnon-Clytemnestra
Orestes¹ – Hermione – Neoptolemus
[Eur.] 36c [Hom.] [Hom.]
Achilles-Deidameia¹
: – Pieris [Apollod.]
Alector²-?
Megapenthes¹ – ?
[Hom.] [Hom.]
Corinthus² [Schol. Eur.]
Cynosurus [Schol. Eur.]
Maraphius [Schol. Hom.]
Pleisthenes⁴ [Cyp.]
Nicostratus [Schol. Soph.]
Pelops¹-Hippodameia¹
Thyestes¹ – Daeto
[Tzetz.] [Tzetz.]
Enorches [Tzetz.]
Dias – ? [Etym. Magn.]
Pelops¹-Hippodameia¹
Atreus – Cleola
[Schol. Eur.] [Schol. Eur.]
Catreus-?
Pleisthenes¹ – Aerope¹
[Schol. Eur.] [Apollod.]
Hippal(cy)mus¹ [Schol. Pind.]
Hippasus¹ [Schol. Eur.]
Letreus [Paus.]

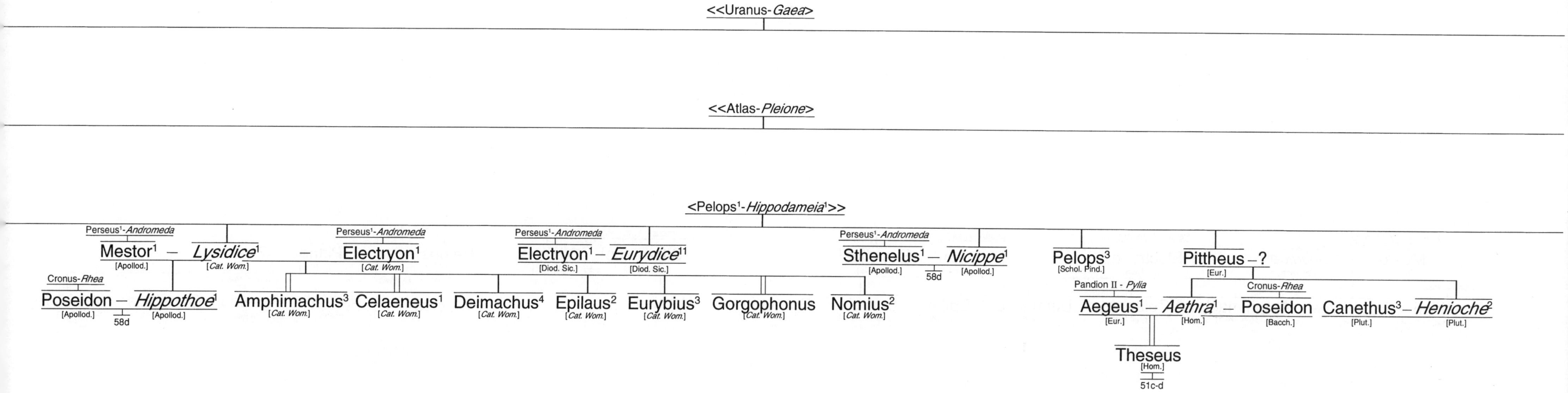

<<Uranus-Gaea>
<<Atlas-Pleione>
<Pelops1-Hippodameia1>>
Perseus1-Andromeda
Mestor1 – Lysidice1 – Electryon1
[Apollod.]
[Cat. Wom.]
[Cat. Wom.]
Perseus1-Andromeda
Perseus1-Andromeda
Electryon1 – Eurydice11
[Diod. Sic.]
[Diod. Sic.]
Perseus1-Andromeda
Sthenelus1 – Nicippe1
[Apollod.]
58d
[Apollod.]
Pelops3
[Schol. Pind.]
Pittheus – ?
[Eur.]
Cronus-Rhea
Poseidon – Hippothoe1
[Apollod.]
58d
[Apollod.]
Amphimachus3
[Cat. Wom.]
Celaeneus1
[Cat. Wom.]
Deimachus4
[Cat. Wom.]
Epilaus2
[Cat. Wom.]
Eurybius3
[Cat. Wom.]
Gorgophonus
[Cat. Wom.]
Nomius2
[Cat. Wom.]
Pandion II - Pylia
Cronus-Rhea
Aegeus1 – Aethra1 – Poseidon
[Eur.]
[Hom.]
[Bacch.]
Canethus3 – Henioche2
[Plut.]
[Plut.]
Theseus
[Hom.]
51c-d

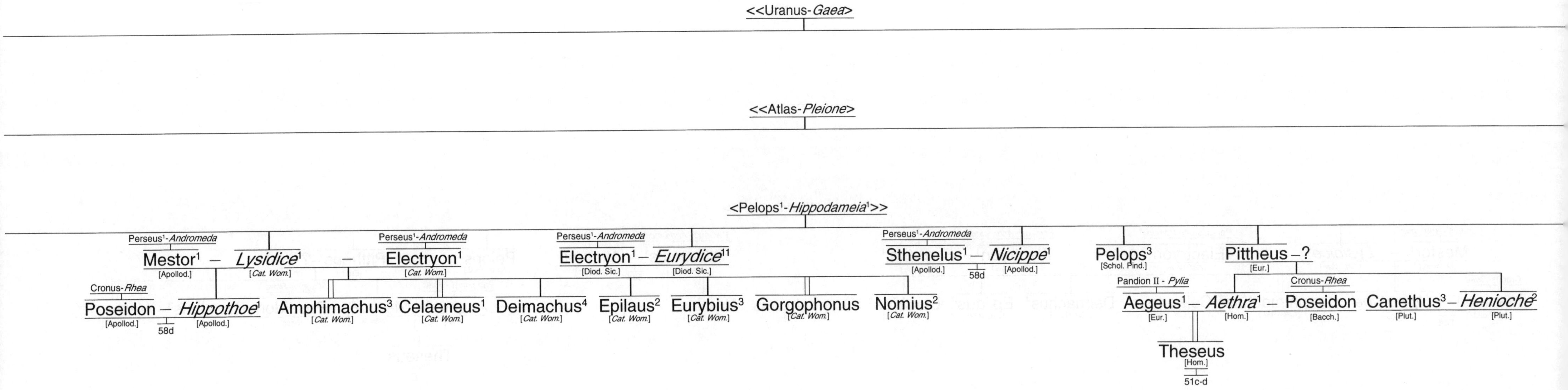

<<Uranus-*Gaea*>
<<Atlas-*Pleione*>
<Pelops[1]-*Hippodameia*[1]>>
Perseus[1]-*Andromeda*
Mestor[1] – *Lysidice*[1] – Electryon[1]
[Apollod.]
[Cat. Wom.]
Perseus[1]-*Andromeda*
[Cat. Wom.]
Perseus[1]-*Andromeda*
Electryon[1] – *Eurydice*[11]
[Diod. Sic.]
[Diod. Sic.]
Perseus[1]-*Andromeda*
Sthenelus[1] – *Nicippe*[1]
[Apollod.]
58d
[Apollod.]
Pelops[3]
[Schol. Pind.]
Pittheus – ?
[Eur.]
Cronus-*Rhea*
Poseidon – *Hippothoe*[1]
[Apollod.]
58d
[Apollod.]
Amphimachus[3]
[Cat. Wom.]
Celaeneus[1]
[Cat. Wom.]
Deimachus[4]
[Cat. Wom.]
Epilaus[2]
[Cat. Wom.]
Eurybius[3]
[Cat. Wom.]
Gorgophonus
[Cat. Wom.]
Nomius[2]
[Cat. Wom.]
Pandion II - *Pylia*
Aegeus[1] – *Aethra*[1] – Poseidon
[Eur.]
[Hom.]
Cronus-*Rhea*
[Bacch.]
Canethus[3] – *Henioche*[2]
[Plut.]
[Plut.]
Theseus
[Hom.]
51c-d

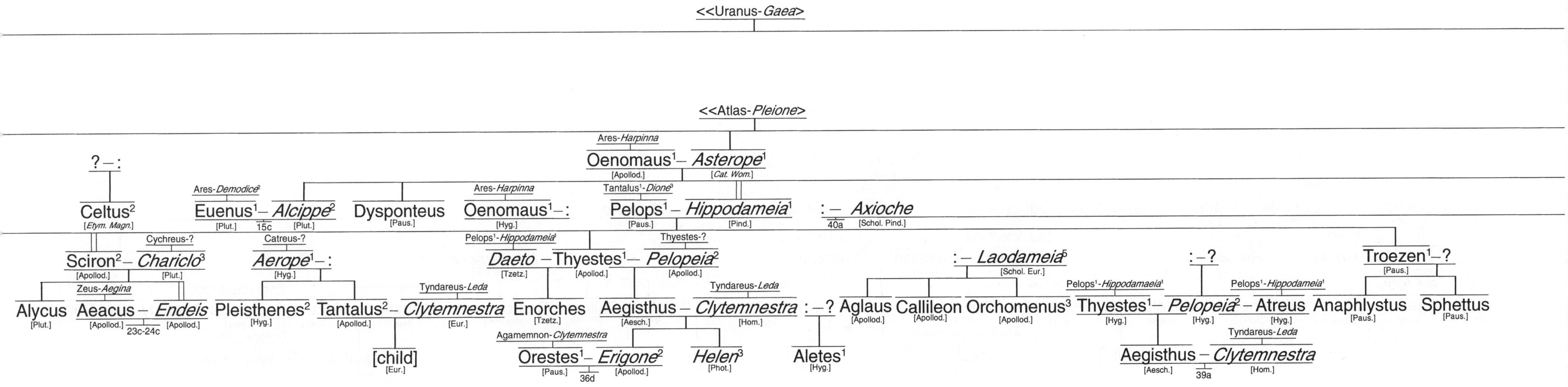

<<Uranus-Gaea>
<<Atlas-Pleione>
Ares-Harpinna
Oenomaus[1]– Asterope[1]
[Apollod.]
[Cat. Wom.]
?–:
Celtus[2]
[Etym. Magn.]
Ares-Demodice[2]
Euenus[1]– Alcippe[2]
[Plut.]
15c
[Plut.]
Dysponteus
[Paus.]
Ares-Harpinna
Oenomaus[1]–:
[Hyg.]
Tantalus[1]-Dione[3]
Pelops[1] – Hippodameia[1]
[Paus.]
[Pind.]
:– Axioche
40a
[Schol. Pind.]
Cychreus-?
Sciron[2]– Chariclo[3]
[Apollod.]
[Plut.]
Catreus-?
Aerope[1]–:
[Hyg.]
Pelops[1]-Hippodameia[1]
Daeto –Thyestes[1]– Pelopeia[2]
[Tzetz.]
[Apollod.]
Thyestes-?
[Apollod.]
:– Laodameia[5]
[Schol. Eur.]
:–?
Troezen[1]–?
[Paus.]
Zeus-Aegina
Alycus
[Plut.]
Aeacus– Endeis
[Apollod.]
23c-24c
[Apollod.]
Pleisthenes[2]
[Hyg.]
Tyndareus-Leda
Tantalus[2]– Clytemnestra
[Apollod.]
[Eur.]
Enorches
[Tzetz.]
Tyndareus-Leda
Aegisthus – Clytemnestra
[Aesch.]
[Hom.]
:–?
Aglaus
[Apollod.]
Callileon
[Apollod.]
Orchomenus[3]
[Apollod.]
Pelops[1]-Hippodamaeia[1]
Thyestes[1]– Pelopeia[2]
[Hyg.]
[Hyg.]
Pelops[1]-Hippodameia[1]
– Atreus
[Hyg.]
Anaphlystus
[Paus.]
Sphettus
[Paus.]
[child]
[Eur.]
Agamemnon-Clytemnestra
Orestes[1]– Erigone[2]
[Paus.]
36d
[Apollod.]
Helen[3]
[Phot.]
Aletes[1]
[Hyg.]
Tyndareus-Leda
Aegisthus – Clytemnestra
[Aesch.]
39a
[Hom.]

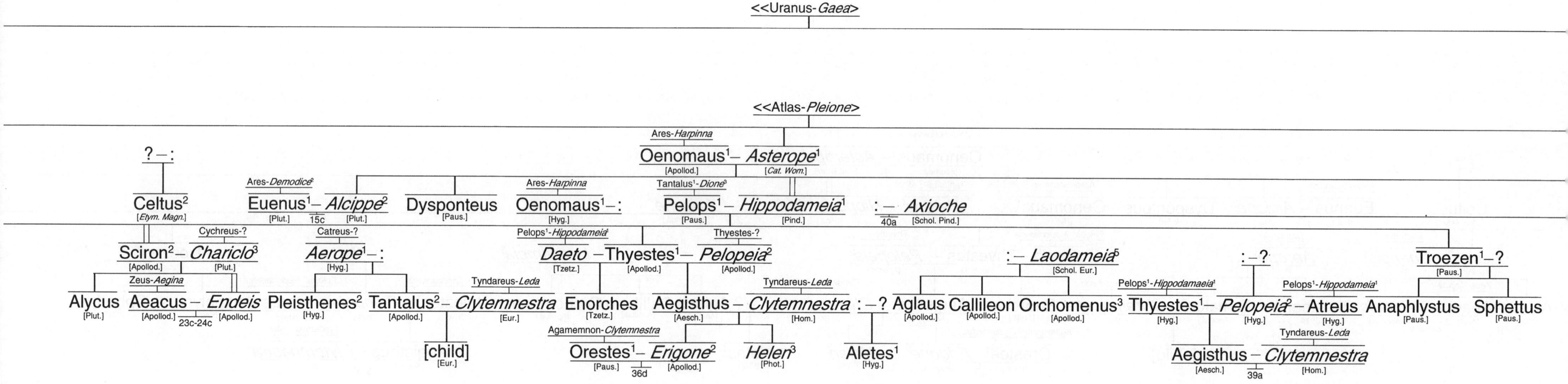

<<Uranus-Gaea>
<<Atlas-Pleione>
Ares-Harpinna
Oenomaus¹– Asterope¹
[Apollod.]
[Cat. Wom.]
?–:
Celtus²
[Etym. Magn.]
Ares-Demodice²
Euenus¹– Alcippe²
[Plut.]
15c
[Plut.]
Dysponteus
[Paus.]
Ares-Harpinna
Oenomaus¹–:
[Hyg.]
Tantalus¹-Dione³
Pelops¹– Hippodameia¹
[Paus.]
[Pind.]
:– Axioche
40a
[Schol. Pind.]
Cychreus-?
Sciron²– Chariclo³
[Apollod.]
[Plut.]
Catreus-?
Aerope¹–:
[Hyg.]
Pelops¹-Hippodameia¹
Daeto –Thyestes¹– Pelopeia²
[Tzetz.]
[Apollod.]
[Apollod.]
Thyestes-?
:– Laodameia⁵
[Schol. Eur.]
:–?
Troezen¹–?
[Paus.]
Zeus-Aegina
Alycus
[Plut.]
Aeacus– Endeis
[Apollod.]
23c-24c
[Apollod.]
Pleisthenes²
[Hyg.]
Tyndareus-Leda
Tantalus²– Clytemnestra
[Apollod.]
[Eur.]
Enorches
[Tzetz.]
Tyndareus-Leda
Aegisthus – Clytemnestra
[Aesch.]
[Hom.]
:–?
Aglaus
[Apollod.]
Callileon
[Apollod.]
Orchomenus³
[Apollod.]
Pelops¹-Hippodamaeia¹
Thyestes¹– Pelopeia² – Atreus
[Hyg.]
[Hyg.]
[Hyg.]
Pelops¹-Hippodameia¹
Anaphlystus
[Paus.]
Sphettus
[Paus.]
[child]
[Eur.]
Agamemnon-Clytemnestra
Orestes¹– Erigone²
[Paus.]
36d
[Apollod.]
Helen³
[Phot.]
Aletes¹
[Hyg.]
Tyndareus-Leda
Aegisthus – Clytemnestra
[Aesch.]
39a
[Hom.]

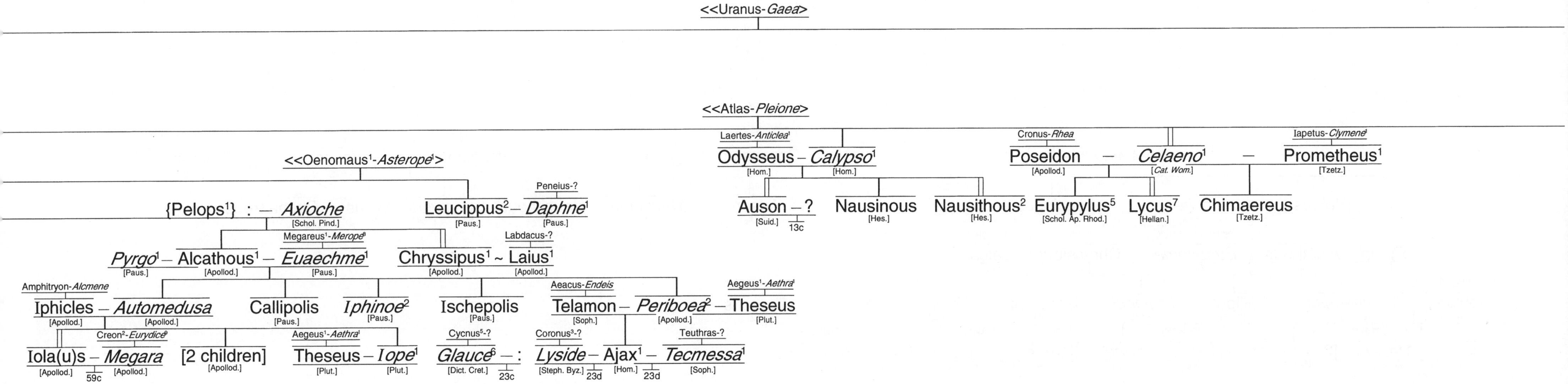

<<Uranus-Gaea>
<<Atlas-Pleione>
Laertes-Anticlea
Odysseus – Calypso
[Hom.]
[Hom.]
Cronus-Rhea
Poseidon – Celaeno – Prometheus
[Apollod.]
[Cat. Wom.]
Iapetus-Clymene
[Tzetz.]
Auson – ?
[Suid.]
13c
Nausinous
[Hes.]
Nausithous
[Hes.]
Eurypylus
[Schol. Ap. Rhod.]
Lycus
[Hellan.]
Chimaereus
[Tzetz.]
<<Oenomaus-Asterope>
{Pelops} : – Axioche
[Schol. Pind.]
Peneius-?
Leucippus – Daphne
[Paus.]
[Paus.]
Megareus-Merope
Labdacus-?
Pyrgo – Alcathous – Euaechme
[Paus.]
[Apollod.]
[Paus.]
Chryssipus ~ Laius
[Apollod.]
[Apollod.]
Amphitryon-Alcmene
Iphicles – Automedusa
[Apollod.]
[Apollod.]
Callipolis
[Paus.]
Iphinoe
[Paus.]
Ischepolis
[Paus.]
Aeacus-Endeis
Telamon – Periboea – Theseus
[Soph.]
[Apollod.]
[Plut.]
Aegeus-Aethra
Creon-Eurydice
Iola(u)s – Megara
[Apollod.]
59c
[Apollod.]
[2 children]
[Apollod.]
Aegeus-Aethra
Theseus – Iope
[Plut.]
[Plut.]
Cycnus-?
Glauce – :
[Dict. Cret.]
23c
Coronus-?
Lyside – Ajax – Tecmessa
[Steph. Byz.]
23d
[Hom.]
23d
Teuthras-?
[Soph.]

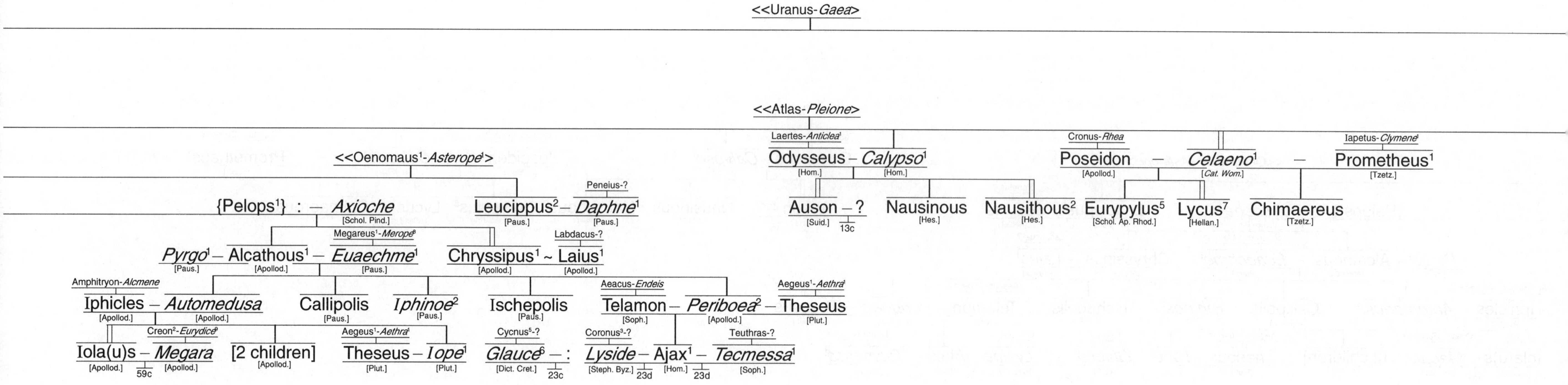
<<Uranus-Gaea>
<<Atlas-Pleione>
<<Oenomaus[1]-Asterope[1]>
Laertes-Anticlea[1]
Odysseus - Calypso[1]
[Hom.] [Hom.]
Cronus-Rhea
Poseidon - Celaeno[1] - Prometheus[1]
[Apollod.] [Cat. Wom.] [Tzetz.]
Iapetus-Clymene[1]
{Pelops[1]} : - Axioche
[Schol. Pind.]
Peneius-?
Leucippus[2] - Daphne[1]
[Paus.] [Paus.]
Auson - ?
[Suid.] 13c
Nausinous
[Hes.]
Nausithous[2]
[Hes.]
Eurypylus[5]
[Schol. Ap. Rhod.]
Lycus[7]
[Hellan.]
Chimaereus
[Tzetz.]
Megareus[1]-Merope[8]
Labdacus-?
Pyrgo[1] - Alcathous[1] - Euaechme[1]
[Paus.] [Apollod.] [Paus.]
Chryssipus[1] ~ Laius[1]
[Apollod.] [Apollod.]
Amphitryon-Alcmene
Iphicles - Automedusa
[Apollod.] [Apollod.]
Callipolis
[Paus.]
Iphinoe[2]
[Paus.]
Ischepolis
[Paus.]
Aeacus-Endeis
Telamon - Periboea[2] - Theseus
[Soph.] [Apollod.] [Plut.]
Aegeus[1]-Aethra[1]
Creon[2]-Eurydice[9]
Iola(u)s - Megara
[Apollod.] 59c [Apollod.]
[2 children]
[Apollod.]
Aegeus[1]-Aethra[1]
Theseus - Iope[1]
[Plut.] [Plut.]
Cycnus[5]-?
Glauce[6] - :
[Dict. Cret.] 23c
Coronus[3]-?
Lyside - Ajax[1] - Tecmessa[1]
[Steph. Byz.] 23d [Hom.] 23d [Soph.]
Teuthras-?

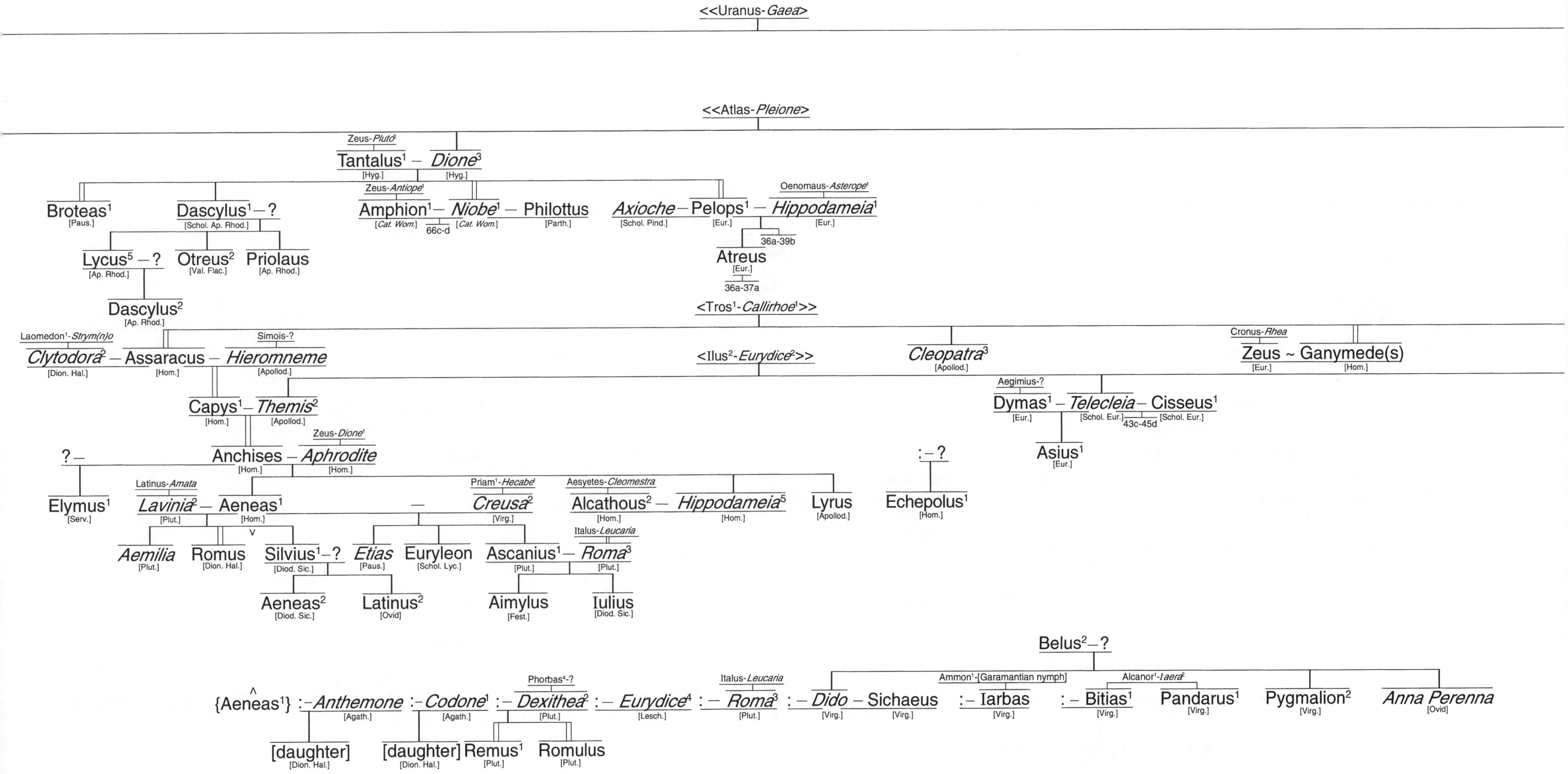

<<Uranus-Gaea>
<<Atlas-Pleione>
Zeus-Pluto
Tantalus¹ – Dione³
[Hyg.] [Hyg.]
Zeus-Antiope¹
Broteas¹ [Paus.]
Dascylus¹ – ? [Schol. Ap. Rhod.]
Amphion¹ – Niobe¹ – Philottus
[Cat. Wom.] 66c-d [Cat. Wom.] [Parth.]
Axioche – Pelops¹ – Hippodameia¹
[Schol. Pind.] [Eur.] [Eur.]
Oenomaus-Asterope¹
36a-39b
Lycus⁵ – ? [Ap. Rhod.]
Otreus² [Val. Flac.]
Priolaus [Ap. Rhod.]
Atreus [Eur.]
36a-37a
Dascylus² [Ap. Rhod.]
<Tros¹-Callirhoe¹>>
Laomedon¹-Strym(n)o
Simois-?
Clytodora² – Assaracus – Hieromneme
[Dion. Hal.] [Hom.] [Apollod.]
<Ilus²-Eurydice²>>
Cleopatra³ [Apollod.]
Cronus-Rhea
Zeus ~ Ganymede(s)
[Eur.] [Hom.]
Aegimius-?
Dymas¹ – Telecleia – Cisseus¹
[Eur.] [Schol. Eur.] 43c-45d [Schol. Eur.]
Capys¹ – Themis²
[Hom.] [Apollod.]
Zeus-Dione¹
? –
Anchises – Aphrodite
[Hom.] [Hom.]
:– ?
Asius¹ [Eur.]
Latinus-Amata
Priam¹-Hecabe¹
Aesyetes-Cleomestra
Elymus¹ [Serv.]
Lavinia² – Aeneas¹
[Plut.] [Hom.]
–
Creusa² [Virg.]
Alcathous² – Hippodameia⁵
[Hom.] [Hom.]
Lyrus [Apollod.]
Echepolus¹ [Hom.]
Italus-Leucaria
Aemilia [Plut.]
Romus [Dion. Hal.]
Silvius¹ – ? [Diod. Sic.]
Etias [Paus.]
Euryleon [Schol. Lyc.]
Ascanius¹ – Roma³
[Plut.] [Plut.]
Aeneas² [Diod. Sic.]
Latinus² [Ovid]
Aimylus [Fest.]
Iulius [Diod. Sic.]
Belus² – ?
Phorbas⁴-?
Italus-Leucaria
Ammon¹-[Garamantian nymph]
Alcanor¹-Iaera²
{Aeneas¹} :– Anthemone :– Codone¹ :– Dexithea² :– Eurydice⁴ :– Roma³ :– Dido – Sichaeus :– Iarbas :– Bitias¹
[Agath.] [Agath.] [Plut.] [Lesch.] [Plut.] [Virg.] [Virg.] [Virg.] [Virg.]
Pandarus¹ [Virg.]
Pygmalion² [Virg.]
Anna Perenna [Ovid]
[daughter] [Dion. Hal.]
[daughter] [Dion. Hal.]
Remus¹ [Plut.]
Romulus [Plut.]

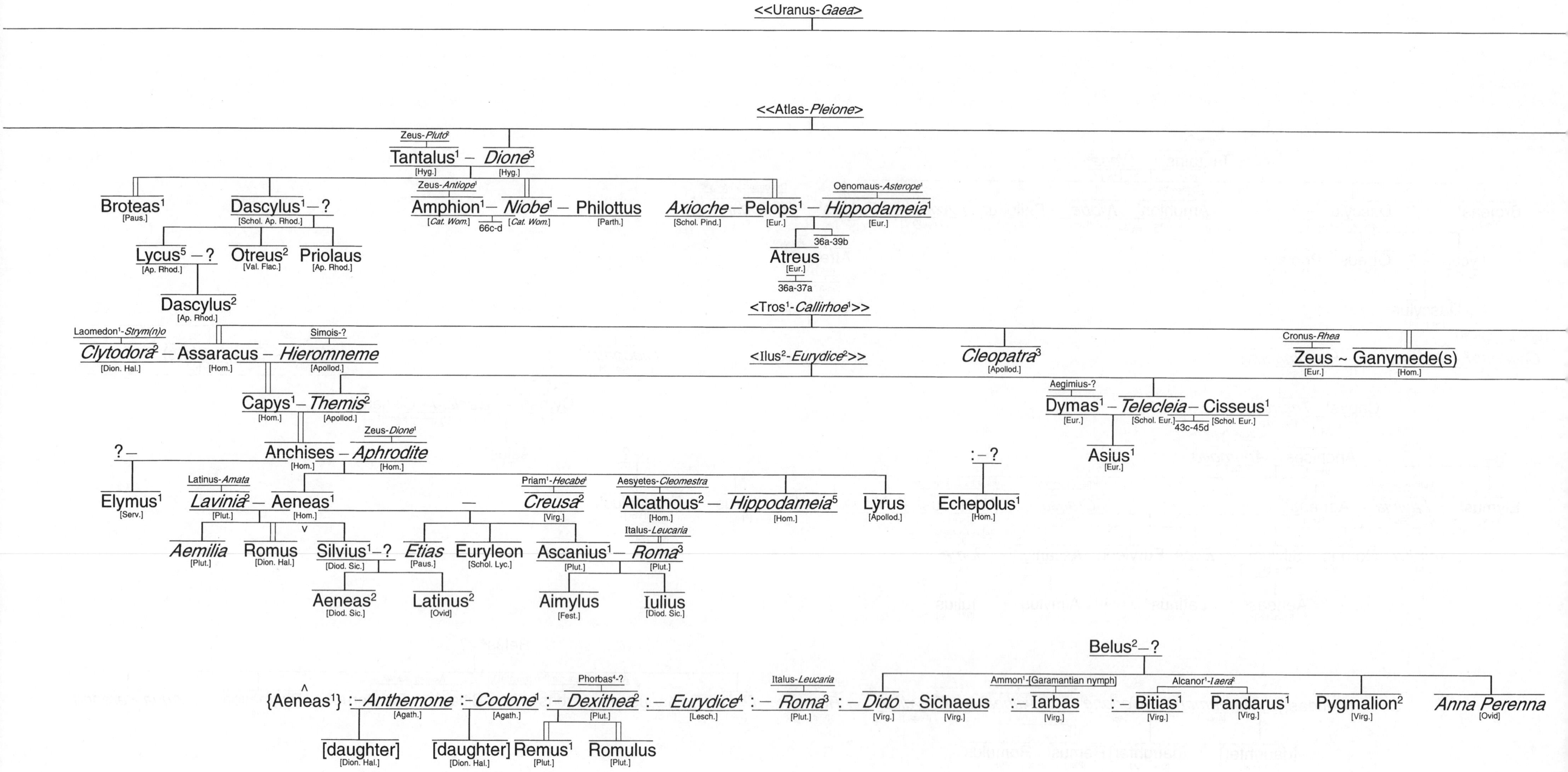

<<Uranus-*Gaea*>
<<Atlas-*Pleione*>
Zeus-*Pluto*[2]
Tantalus[1] – *Dione*[3]
[Hyg.] [Hyg.]
Broteas[1]
[Paus.]
Dascylus[1] – ?
[Schol. Ap. Rhod.]
Zeus-*Antiope*[1]
Amphion[1] – *Niobe*[1] – Philottus
[*Cat. Wom.*] 66c-d [*Cat. Wom.*] [Parth.]
Axioche – Pelops[1] – *Hippodameia*[1]
[Schol. Pind.] [Eur.] [Eur.]
Oenomaus-*Asterope*[1]
36a-39b
Lycus[5] – ?
[Ap. Rhod.]
Otreus[2]
[Val. Flac.]
Priolaus
[Ap. Rhod.]
Atreus
[Eur.]
36a-37a
Dascylus[2]
[Ap. Rhod.]
<Tros[1]-*Callirhoe*[1]>>
Laomedon[1]-*Strym(n)o*
Simois-?
Clytodora[2] – Assaracus – *Hieromneme*
[Dion. Hal.] [Hom.] [Apollod.]
<Ilus[2]-*Eurydice*[2]>>
Cleopatra[3]
[Apollod.]
Cronus-*Rhea*
Zeus ~ Ganymede(s)
[Eur.] [Hom.]
Capys[1] – *Themis*[2]
[Hom.] [Apollod.]
Aegimius-?
Dymas[1] – *Telecleia* – Cisseus[1]
[Eur.] [Schol. Eur.] 43c-45d [Schol. Eur.]
Zeus-*Dione*[1]
? –
Anchises – *Aphrodite*
[Hom.] [Hom.]
:– ?
Asius[1]
[Eur.]
Latinus-*Amata*
Priam[1]-*Hecabe*[1]
Aesyetes-*Cleomestra*
Elymus[1]
[Serv.]
Lavinia[2] – Aeneas[1] –
[Plut.] [Hom.]
Creusa[2]
[Virg.]
Alcathous[2] – *Hippodameia*[5]
[Hom.] [Hom.]
Lyrus
[Apollod.]
Echepolus[1]
[Hom.]
Italus-*Leucaria*
Aemilia
[Plut.]
Romus
[Dion. Hal.]
Silvius[1] – ?
[Diod. Sic.]
Etias
[Paus.]
Euryleon
[Schol. Lyc.]
Ascanius[1] – *Roma*[3]
[Plut.] [Plut.]
Aeneas[2]
[Diod. Sic.]
Latinus[2]
[Ovid]
Aimylus
[Fest.]
Iulius
[Diod. Sic.]
Belus[2] – ?
Phorbas[4]-?
Italus-*Leucaria*
Ammon[1]-[Garamantian nymph]
Alcanor[1]-*Iaera*[2]
{Aeneas[1]} :– *Anthemone* :– *Codone*[1] :– *Dexithea*[2] :– *Eurydice*[4] :– *Roma*[3] :– *Dido* – Sichaeus :– Iarbas :– Bitias[1]
[Agath.] [Agath.] [Plut.] [Lesch.] [Plut.] [Virg.] [Virg.] [Virg.] [Virg.]
Pandarus[1]
[Virg.]
Pygmalion[2]
[Virg.]
Anna Perenna
[Ovid]
[daughter]
[Dion. Hal.]
[daughter]
[Dion. Hal.]
Remus[1]
[Plut.]
Romulus
[Plut.]

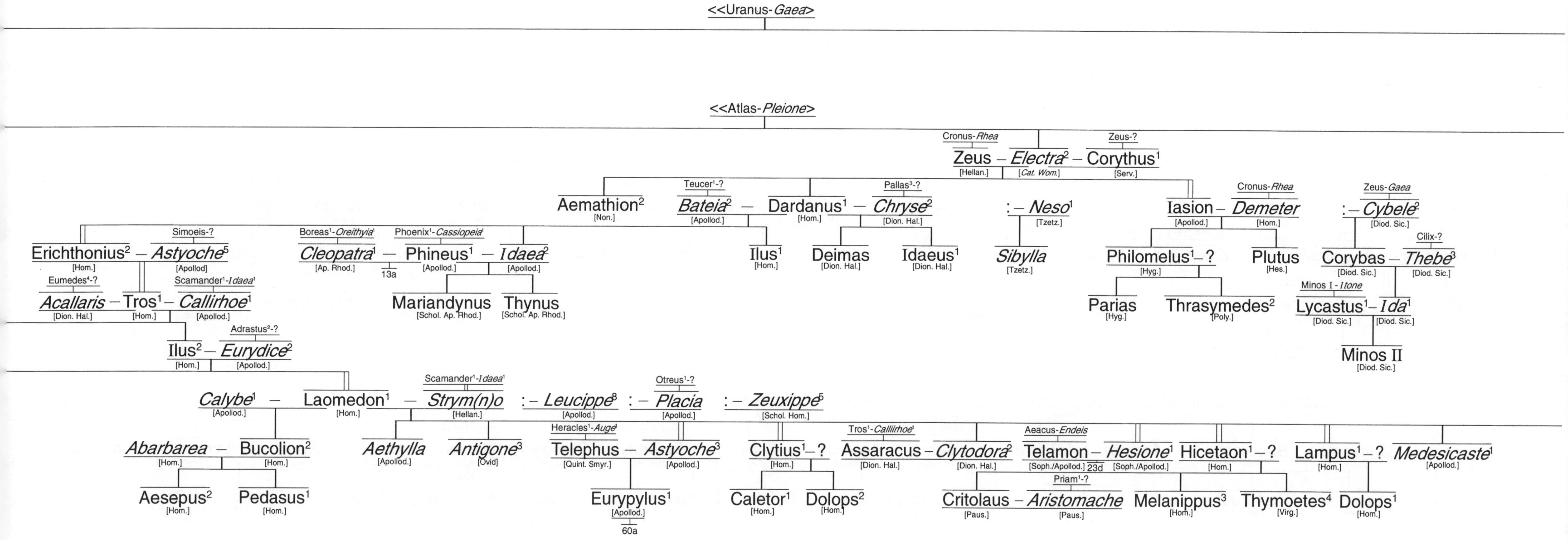

<<Uranus-*Gaea*>
<<Atlas-*Pleione*>
Cronus-*Rhea*
Zeus-?
Zeus – *Electra*2 – Corythus1
[Hellan.] [*Cat. Wom.*] [Serv.]
Aemathion2
[Non.]
Teucer1-?
*Bateia*2 – Dardanus1 – *Chryse*2
[Apollod.] [Hom.] [Dion. Hal.]
Pallas3-?
:– *Neso*1
[Tzetz.]
Iasion – *Demeter*
[Apollod.] [Hom.]
Cronus-*Rhea*
Zeus-*Gaea*
:– *Cybele*2
[Diod. Sic.]
Simoeis-?
Erichthonius2 – *Astyoche*5
[Hom.] [Apollod]
Boreas1-*Oreithyia*1
Phoenix1-*Cassiopeia*1
*Cleopatra*1 – Phineus1 – *Idaea*2
[Ap. Rhod.] [Apollod.] [Apollod.]
13a
Ilus1
[Hom.]
Deimas
[Dion. Hal.]
Idaeus1
[Dion. Hal.]
Sibylla
[Tzetz.]
Philomelus1 – ?
[Hyg.]
Plutus
[Hes.]
Cilix-?
Corybas – *Thebe*3
[Diod. Sic.] [Diod. Sic.]
Eumedes4-?
Scamander1-*Idaea*1
Acallaris – Tros1 – *Callirhoe*1
[Dion. Hal.] [Hom.] [Apollod.]
Mariandynus
[Schol. Ap. Rhod.]
Thynus
[Schol. Ap. Rhod.]
Parias
[Hyg.]
Thrasymedes2
[Poly.]
Minos I - *Itone*
Lycastus1 – *Ida*1
[Diod. Sic.] [Diod. Sic.]
Adrastus2-?
Ilus2 – *Eurydice*2
[Hom.] [Apollod.]
Minos II
[Diod. Sic.]
Scamander1-*Idaea*1
Otreus1-?
*Calybe*1 – Laomedon1 – *Strym(n)o* :– *Leucippe*8 :– *Placia* :– *Zeuxippe*5
[Apollod.] [Hom.] [Hellan.] [Apollod.] [Apollod.] [Schol. Hom.]
Heracles1-*Auge*1
Tros1-*Callirhoe*1
Aeacus-*Endeis*
Abarbarea – Bucolion2
[Hom.] [Hom.]
Aethylla
[Apollod.]
*Antigone*3
[Ovid]
Telephus – *Astyoche*3
[Quint. Smyr.] [Apollod.]
Clytius1 – ?
[Hom.]
Assaracus – *Clytodora*2
[Dion. Hal.] [Dion. Hal.]
Telamon – *Hesione*1
[Soph./Apollod.] [Soph./Apollod.]
23d
Hicetaon1 – ?
[Hom.]
Lampus1 – ?
[Hom.]
*Medesicaste*1
[Apollod.]
Priam1-?
Aesepus2
[Hom.]
Pedasus1
[Hom.]
Eurypylus1
[Apollod.]
60a
Caletor1
[Hom.]
Dolops2
[Hom.]
Critolaus – *Aristomache*
[Paus.] [Paus.]
Melanippus3
[Hom.]
Thymoetes4
[Virg.]
Dolops1
[Hom.]

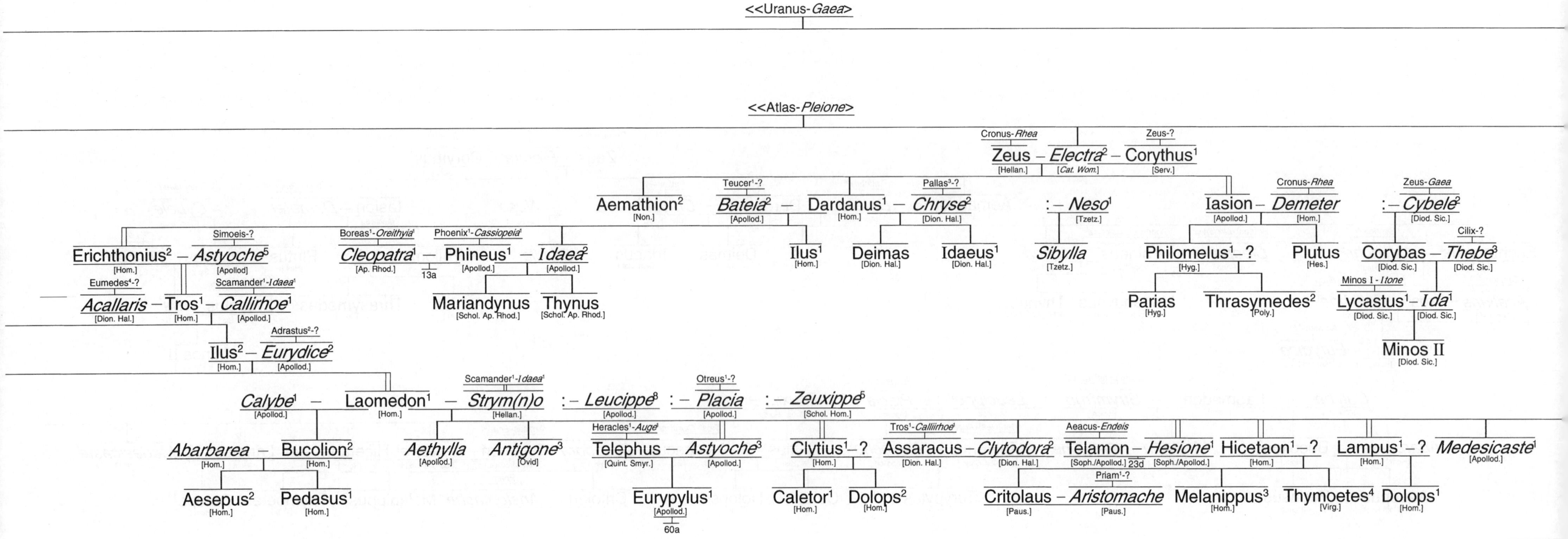

<<Uranus-Gaea>
<<Atlas-Pleione>
Cronus-Rhea
Zeus - Electra[2] - Corythus[1]
[Hellan.] [Cat. Wom.] [Serv.]
Zeus-?
Teucer[1]-?
Pallas[3]-?
Aemathion[2]
[Non.]
Bateia[2] - Dardanus[1] - Chryse[2]
[Apollod.] [Hom.] [Dion. Hal.]
:- Neso[1]
[Tzetz.]
Iasion - Demeter
[Apollod.] [Hom.]
Cronus-Rhea
Zeus-Gaea
:- Cybele[2]
[Diod. Sic.]
Simoeis-?
Boreas[1]-Oreithyia[1]
Phoenix[1]-Cassiopeia[1]
Erichthonius[2] - Astyoche[5]
[Hom.] [Apollod]
Cleopatra[1] - Phineus[1] - Idaea[2]
[Ap. Rhod.] [Apollod.] [Apollod.]
13a
Ilus[1]
[Hom.]
Deimas
[Dion. Hal.]
Idaeus[1]
[Dion. Hal.]
Sibylla
[Tzetz.]
Philomelus[1] - ?
[Hyg.]
Plutus
[Hes.]
Cilix-?
Corybas - Thebe[3]
[Diod. Sic.] [Diod. Sic.]
Eumedes[4]-?
Scamander[1]-Idaea[1]
Acallaris - Tros[1] - Callirhoe[1]
[Dion. Hal.] [Hom.] [Apollod.]
Mariandynus
[Schol. Ap. Rhod.]
Thynus
[Schol. Ap. Rhod.]
Parias
[Hyg.]
Thrasymedes[2]
[Poly.]
Minos I - Itone
Lycastus[1] - Ida[1]
[Diod. Sic.] [Diod. Sic.]
Adrastus[2]-?
Ilus[2] - Eurydice[2]
[Hom.] [Apollod.]
Minos II
[Diod. Sic.]
Scamander[1]-Idaea[1]
Otreus[1]-?
Calybe[1] - Laomedon[1] - Strym(n)o :- Leucippe[8] :- Placia :- Zeuxippe[5]
[Apollod.] [Hom.] [Hellan.] [Apollod.] [Apollod.] [Schol. Hom.]
Heracles[1]-Auge
Tros[1]-Callirhoe[1]
Aeacus-Endeis
Abarbarea - Bucolion[2]
[Hom.] [Hom.]
Aethylla
[Apollod.]
Antigone[3]
[Ovid]
Telephus - Astyoche[3]
[Quint. Smyr.] [Apollod.]
Clytius[1] - ?
[Hom.]
Assaracus - Clytodora[2]
[Dion. Hal.] [Dion. Hal.]
Telamon - Hesione[1]
[Soph./Apollod.] 23d [Soph./Apollod.]
Hicetaon[1] - ?
[Hom.]
Lampus[1] - ?
[Hom.]
Medesicaste[1]
[Apollod.]
Priam[1]-?
Aesepus[2]
[Hom.]
Pedasus[1]
[Hom.]
Eurypylus[1]
[Apollod.]
60a
Caletor[1]
[Hom.]
Dolops[2]
[Hom.]
Critolaus - Aristomache
[Paus.] [Paus.]
Melanippus[3]
[Hom.]
Thymoetes[4]
[Virg.]
Dolops[1]
[Hom.]

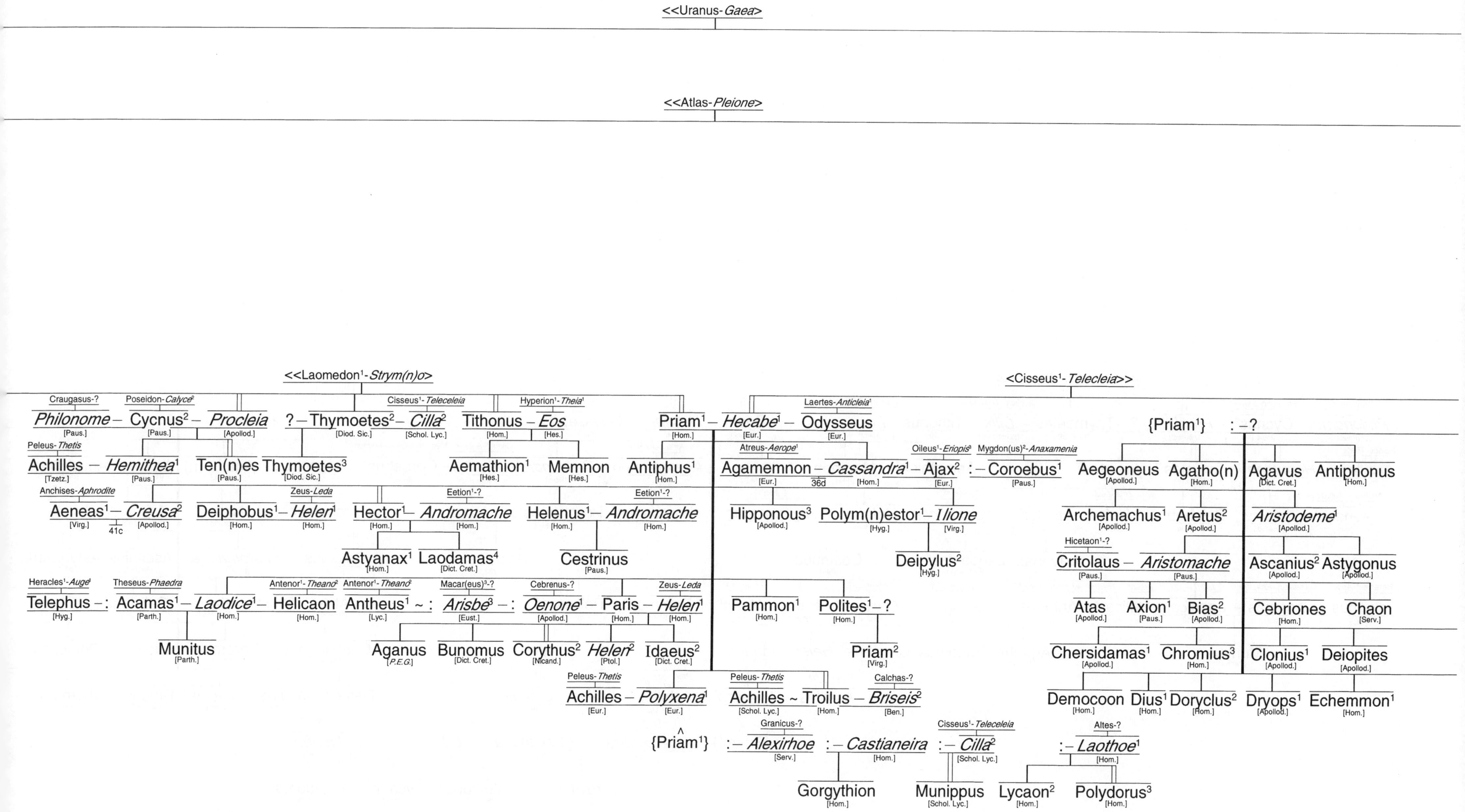

<<Uranus-Gaea>
<<Atlas-Pleione>
<<Laomedon¹-Strym(n)o>
<Cisseus¹-Telecleia>>
Craugasus-?
Philonome [Paus.]
Poseidon-Calyce²
Cycnus² [Paus.]
Procleia [Apollod.]
? – Thymoetes² [Diod. Sic.]
Cisseus¹-Teleceleia
Cilla² [Schol. Lyc.]
Tithonus [Hom.]
Hyperion¹-Theia¹
Eos [Hes.]
Priam¹ [Hom.]
Hecabe¹ [Eur.]
Laertes-Anticleia¹
Odysseus [Eur.]
{Priam¹} :–?
Peleus-Thetis
Achilles [Tzetz.]
Hemithea¹ [Paus.]
Ten(n)es [Paus.]
Thymoetes³ [Diod. Sic.]
Aemathion¹ [Hes.]
Memnon [Hes.]
Antiphus¹ [Hom.]
Atreus-Aerope¹
Agamemnon [Eur.]
36d
Cassandra¹ [Hom.]
Oileus¹-Eriopis¹
Ajax² [Eur.]
Mygdon(us)²-Anaxamenia
:– Coroebus¹ [Paus.]
Aegeoneus [Apollod.]
Agatho(n) [Hom.]
Agavus [Dict. Cret.]
Antiphonus [Hom.]
Anchises-Aphrodite
Aeneas¹ [Virg.]
41c
Creusa² [Apollod.]
Deiphobus¹ [Hom.]
Zeus-Leda
Helen¹ [Hom.]
Hector¹ [Hom.]
Eetion¹-?
Andromache [Hom.]
Helenus¹ [Hom.]
Eetion¹-?
Andromache [Hom.]
Hipponous³ [Apollod.]
Polym(n)estor¹ [Hyg.]
Ilione [Virg.]
Archemachus¹ [Apollod.]
Aretus² [Apollod.]
Aristodeme¹ [Apollod.]
Astyanax¹ [Hom.]
Laodamas⁴ [Dict. Cret.]
Cestrinus [Paus.]
Deipylus² [Hyg.]
Hicetaon¹-?
Critolaus [Paus.]
Aristomache [Paus.]
Ascanius² [Apollod.]
Astygonus [Apollod.]
Heracles¹-Auge¹
Telephus [Hyg.]
Theseus-Phaedra
Acamas¹ [Parth.]
Laodice¹ [Hom.]
Antenor¹-Theano²
Helicaon [Hom.]
Antenor¹-Theano²
Antheus¹ [Lyc.]
Macar(eus)³-?
Arisbe³ [Eust.]
Cebrenus-?
Oenone¹ [Apollod.]
Paris [Hom.]
Zeus-Leda
Helen¹ [Hom.]
Pammon¹ [Hom.]
Polites¹ – ? [Hom.]
Atas [Apollod.]
Axion¹ [Paus.]
Bias² [Apollod.]
Cebriones [Hom.]
Chaon [Serv.]
Munitus [Parth.]
Aganus [P.E.G.]
Bunomus [Dict. Cret.]
Corythus² [Nicand.]
Helen² [Ptol.]
Idaeus² [Dict. Cret.]
Priam² [Virg.]
Chersidamas¹ [Apollod.]
Chromius³ [Hom.]
Clonius¹ [Apollod.]
Deiopites [Apollod.]
Peleus-Thetis
Achilles [Eur.]
Polyxena¹ [Eur.]
Peleus-Thetis
Achilles [Schol. Lyc.]
Troilus [Hom.]
Calchas-?
Briseis² [Ben.]
Democoon [Hom.]
Dius¹ [Hom.]
Doryclus² [Hom.]
Dryops¹ [Apollod.]
Echemmon¹ [Hom.]
{Priam¹}
Granicus-?
:– Alexirhoe [Serv.]
:– Castianeira [Hom.]
Cisseus¹-Teleceleia
:– Cilla² [Schol. Lyc.]
Altes-?
:– Laothoe¹ [Hom.]
Gorgythion [Hom.]
Munippus [Schol. Lyc.]
Lycaon² [Hom.]
Polydorus³ [Hom.]

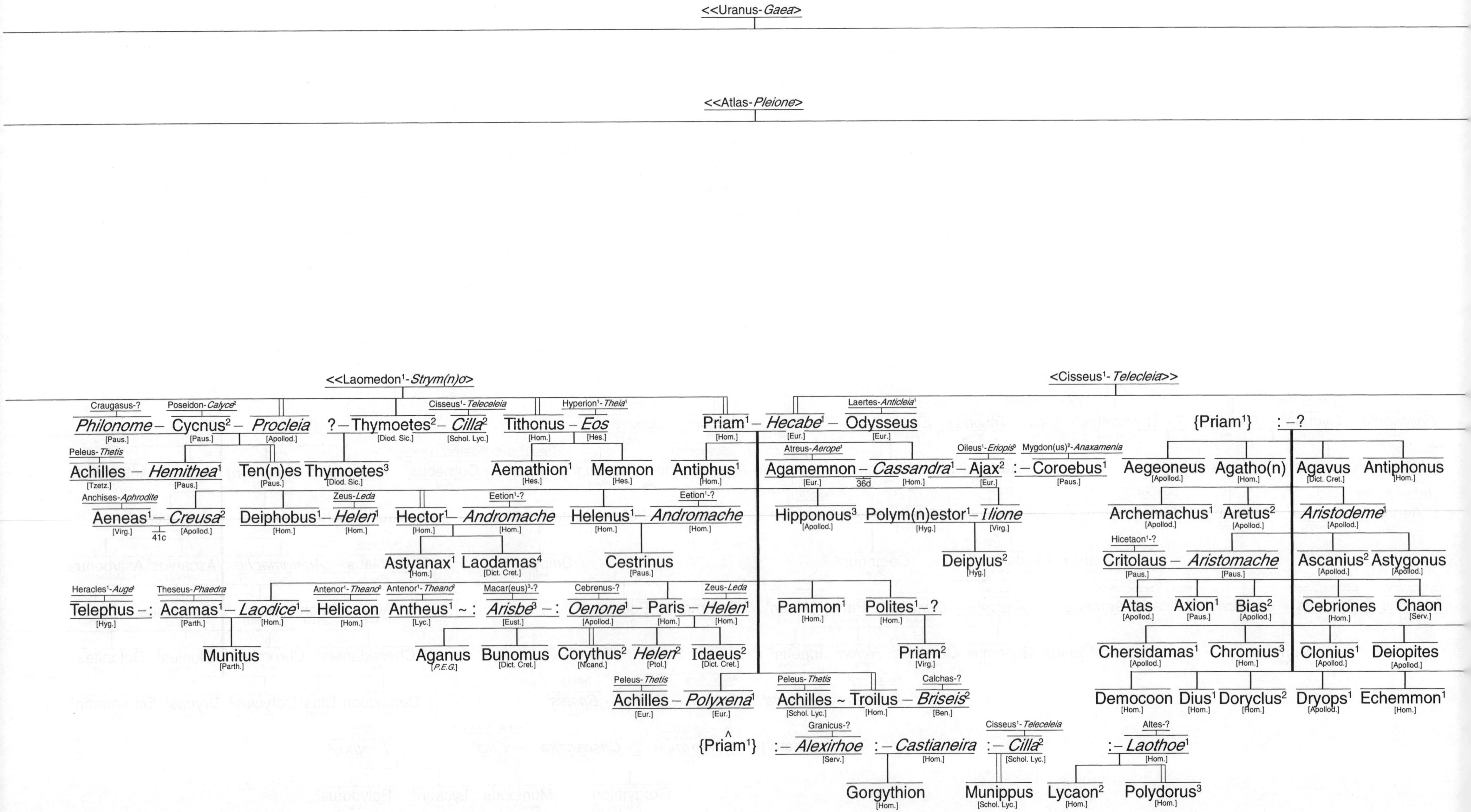

<<Uranus-*Gaea*>
<<Atlas-*Pleione*>
<<Laomedon[1]-*Strym(n)o*>
<Cisseus[1]-*Telecleia*>>
Craugasus-? Poseidon-*Calyce*[2] Cisseus[1]-*Teleceleia* Hyperion[1]-*Theia*[1]
Philonome – Cycnus[2] – *Procleia* ?–Thymoetes[2]– *Cilla*[2] Tithonus – *Eos*
[Paus.] [Paus.] [Apollod.] [Diod. Sic.] [Schol. Lyc.] [Hom.] [Hes.]
Priam[1] – *Hecabe*[1] – Odysseus
[Hom.] [Eur.] [Eur.]
Laertes-*Anticleia*[1]
{Priam[1]} :–?
Peleus-*Thetis*
Achilles – *Hemithea*[1] Ten(n)es Thymoetes[3] Aemathion[1] Memnon Antiphus[1]
[Tzetz.] [Paus.] [Paus.] [Diod. Sic.] [Hes.] [Hes.] [Hom.]
Atreus-*Aerope*[1] Oileus[1]-*Eriopis*[1] Mygdon(us)[2]-*Anaxamenia*
Agamemnon – *Cassandra*[1] – Ajax[2] :– Coroebus[1]
[Eur.] 36d [Hom.] [Eur.] [Paus.]
Aegeoneus Agatho(n) Agavus Antiphonus
[Apollod.] [Hom.] [Dict. Cret.] [Hom.]
Anchises-*Aphrodite* Zeus-*Leda* Eetion[1]-? Eetion[1]-?
Aeneas[1] – *Creusa*[2] Deiphobus[1] – *Helen*[1] Hector[1] – *Andromache* Helenus[1] – *Andromache*
[Virg.] 41c [Apollod.] [Hom.] [Hom.] [Hom.] [Hom.] [Hom.] [Hom.]
Hipponous[3] Polym(n)estor[1] – *Ilione*
[Apollod.] [Hyg.] [Virg.]
Archemachus[1] Aretus[2] *Aristodeme*[1]
[Apollod.] [Apollod.] [Apollod.]
Astyanax[1] Laodamas[4] Cestrinus Deipylus[2]
[Hom.] [Dict. Cret.] [Paus.] [Hyg.]
Hicetaon[1]-?
Critolaus – *Aristomache* Ascanius[2] Astygonus
[Paus.] [Paus.] [Apollod.] [Apollod.]
Heracles[1]-*Auge*[1] Theseus-*Phaedra* Antenor[1]-*Theano*[2] Antenor[1]-*Theano*[2] Macar(eus)[3]-? Cebrenus-? Zeus-*Leda*
Telephus –: Acamas[1] – *Laodice*[1] – Helicaon Antheus[1] ~ : *Arisbe*[3] –: *Oenone*[1] – Paris – *Helen*[1]
[Hyg.] [Parth.] [Hom.] [Hom.] [Lyc.] [Eust.] [Apollod.] [Hom.] [Hom.]
Pammon[1] Polites[1]–?
[Hom.] [Hom.]
Atas Axion[1] Bias[2] Cebriones Chaon
[Apollod.] [Paus.] [Apollod.] [Hom.] [Serv.]
Munitus Aganus Bunomus Corythus[2] *Helen*[2] Idaeus[2] Priam[2]
[Parth.] [P.E.G.] [Dict. Cret.] [Nicand.] [Ptol.] [Dict. Cret.] [Virg.]
Chersidamas[1] Chromius[3] Clonius[1] Deiopites
[Apollod.] [Hom.] [Apollod.] [Apollod.]
Peleus-*Thetis* Peleus-*Thetis* Calchas-?
Achilles – *Polyxena*[1] Achilles ~ Troilus – *Briseis*[2]
[Eur.] [Eur.] [Schol. Lyc.] [Hom.] [Ben.]
Democoon Dius[1] Doryclus[2] Dryops[1] Echemmon[1]
[Hom.] [Hom.] [Hom.] [Apollod.] [Hom.]
Granicus-? Cisseus[1]-*Teleceleia* Altes-?
{Priam[1]} :– *Alexirhoe* :– *Castianeira* :– *Cilla*[2] :– *Laothoe*[1]
[Serv.] [Hom.] [Schol. Lyc.] [Hom.]
Gorgythion Munippus Lycaon[2] Polydorus[3]
[Hom.] [Schol. Lyc.] [Hom.] [Hom.]

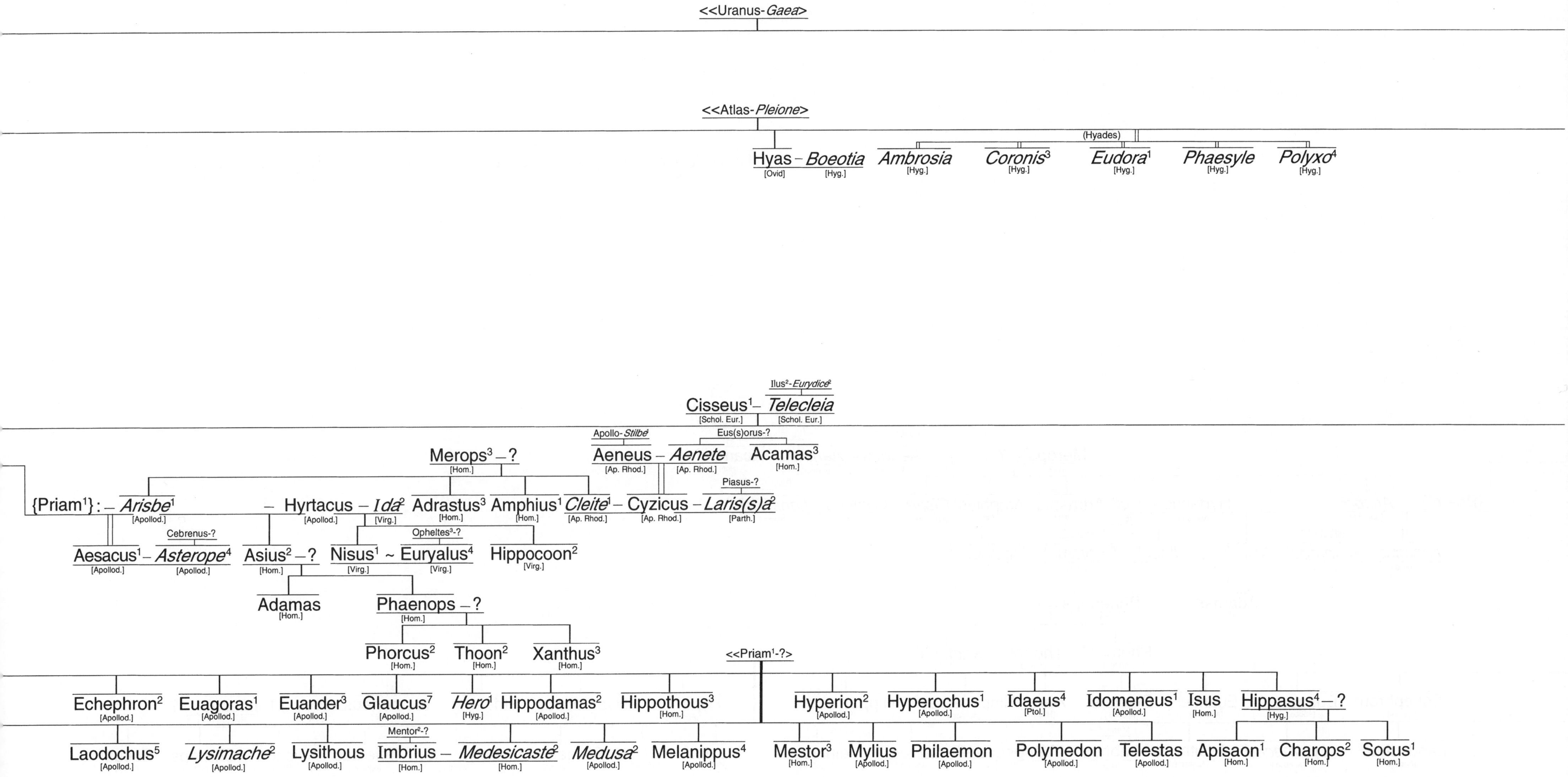

<<Uranus-Gaea>
<<Atlas-Pleione>
(Hyades)
Hyas – Boeotia
[Ovid] [Hyg.]
Ambrosia [Hyg.]
Coronis[3] [Hyg.]
Eudora[1] [Hyg.]
Phaesyle [Hyg.]
Polyxo[4] [Hyg.]
Ilus[2]-Eurydice[2]
Cisseus[1] – Telecleia
[Schol. Eur.] [Schol. Eur.]
Apollo-Stilbe
Eus(s)orus-?
Merops[3] – ?
[Hom.]
Aeneus – Aenete
[Ap. Rhod.] [Ap. Rhod.]
Acamas[3]
[Hom.]
Piasus-?
{Priam[1]}: – Arisbe[1]
[Apollod.]
– Hyrtacus – Ida[2]
[Apollod.] [Virg.]
Adrastus[3]
[Hom.]
Amphius[1]
[Hom.]
Cleite[1] – Cyzicus – Laris(s)a[2]
[Ap. Rhod.] [Ap. Rhod.] [Parth.]
Cebrenus-?
Opheltes[3]-?
Aesacus[1] – Asterope[4]
[Apollod.] [Apollod.]
Asius[2] – ?
[Hom.]
Nisus[1] ~ Euryalus[4]
[Virg.] [Virg.]
Hippocoon[2]
[Virg.]
Adamas
[Hom.]
Phaenops – ?
[Hom.]
Phorcus[2] [Hom.]
Thoon[2] [Hom.]
Xanthus[3] [Hom.]
<<Priam[1]-?>
Echephron[2] [Apollod.]
Euagoras[1] [Apollod.]
Euander[3] [Apollod.]
Glaucus[7] [Apollod.]
Hero[1] [Hyg.]
Hippodamas[2] [Apollod.]
Hippothous[3] [Hom.]
Hyperion[2] [Apollod.]
Hyperochus[1] [Apollod.]
Idaeus[4] [Ptol.]
Idomeneus[1] [Apollod.]
Isus [Hom.]
Hippasus[4] – ?
[Hyg.]
Mentor[2]-?
Laodochus[5] [Apollod.]
Lysimache[2] [Apollod.]
Lysithous [Apollod.]
Imbrius – Medesicaste[2]
[Hom.] [Hom.]
Medusa[2] [Apollod.]
Melanippus[4] [Apollod.]
Mestor[3] [Hom.]
Mylius [Apollod.]
Philaemon [Apollod.]
Polymedon [Apollod.]
Telestas [Apollod.]
Apisaon[1] [Hom.]
Charops[2] [Hom.]
Socus[1] [Hom.]

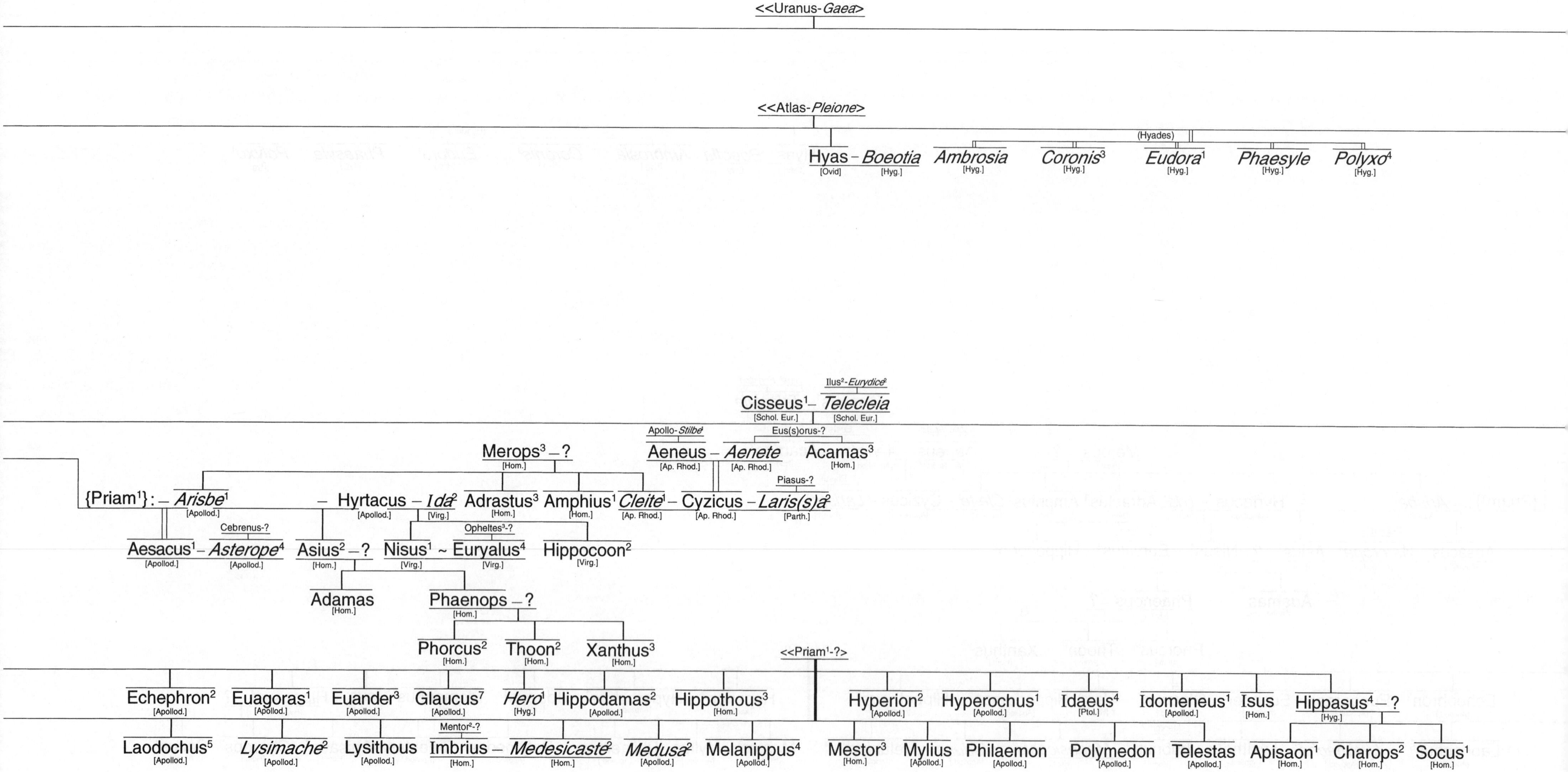
<<Uranus-*Gaea*>
<<Atlas-*Pleione*>
(Hyades)
Hyas [Ovid] - *Boeotia* [Hyg.]
Ambrosia [Hyg.]
Coronis[3] [Hyg.]
Eudora[1] [Hyg.]
Phaesyle [Hyg.]
Polyxo[4] [Hyg.]
Ilus[2]-*Eurydice*[3]
Cisseus[1] [Schol. Eur.] – *Telecleia* [Schol. Eur.]
Apollo-*Stilbe*[1]
Eus(s)orus-?
Aeneus [Ap. Rhod.] – *Aenete* [Ap. Rhod.]
Acamas[3] [Hom.]
Merops[3] [Hom.] – ?
Piasus-?
{Priam[1]}: – *Arisbe*[1] [Apollod.]
– Hyrtacus [Apollod.] – *Ida*[2] [Virg.]
Adrastus[3] [Hom.]
Amphius[1] [Hom.]
Cleite[1] [Ap. Rhod.] – Cyzicus [Ap. Rhod.] – *Laris(s)a*[2] [Parth.]
Cebrenus-?
Opheltes[3]-?
Aesacus[1] [Apollod.] – *Asterope*[4] [Apollod.]
Asius[2] [Hom.] – ?
Nisus[1] [Virg.] ~ Euryalus[4] [Virg.]
Hippocoon[2] [Virg.]
Adamas [Hom.]
Phaenops [Hom.] – ?
Phorcus[2] [Hom.]
Thoon[2] [Hom.]
Xanthus[3] [Hom.]
<<Priam[1]-?>
Echephron[2] [Apollod.]
Euagoras[1] [Apollod.]
Euander[3] [Apollod.]
Glaucus[7] [Apollod.]
Hero[1] [Hyg.]
Hippodamas[2] [Apollod.]
Hippothous[3] [Hom.]
Hyperion[2] [Apollod.]
Hyperochus[1] [Apollod.]
Idaeus[4] [Ptol.]
Idomeneus[1] [Apollod.]
Isus [Hom.]
Hippasus[4] [Hyg.] – ?
Mentor[2]-?
Laodochus[5] [Apollod.]
Lysimache[2] [Apollod.]
Lysithous [Apollod.]
Imbrius [Hom.] – *Medesicaste*[2] [Hom.]
Medusa[2] [Apollod.]
Melanippus[4] [Apollod.]
Mestor[3] [Hom.]
Mylius [Apollod.]
Philaemon [Apollod.]
Polymedon [Apollod.]
Telestas [Apollod.]
Apisaon[1] [Hom.]
Charops[2] [Hom.]
Socus[1] [Hom.]

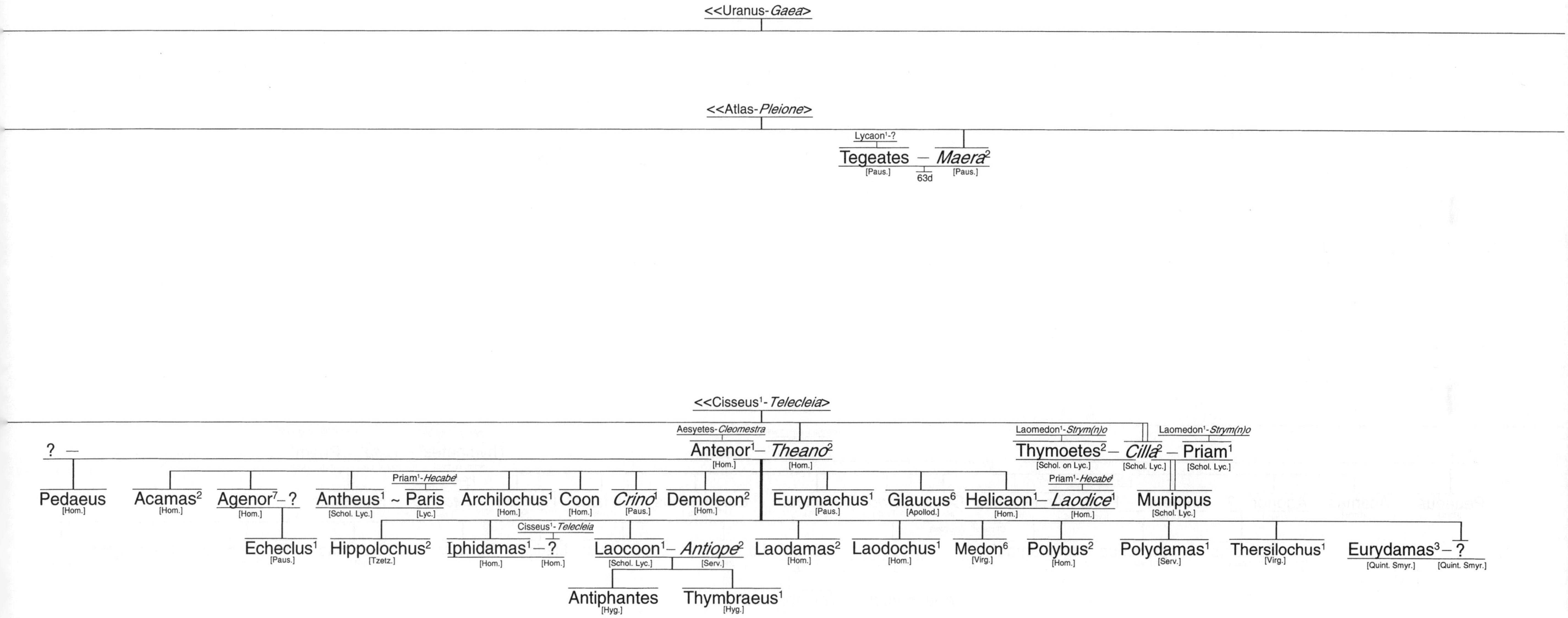

<<Uranus-*Gaea*>
<<Atlas-*Pleione*>
Lycaon¹-?
Tegeates – *Maera*²
[Paus.]
63d
[Paus.]
<<Cisseus¹-*Telecleia*>
Aesyetes-*Cleomestra*
Antenor¹– *Theano*²
[Hom.]
[Hom.]
Laomedon¹-*Strym(n)o*
Thymoetes²– *Cilla*² – Priam¹
[Schol. on Lyc.]
[Schol. Lyc.]
Laomedon¹-*Strym(n)o*
[Schol. Lyc.]
? –
Pedaeus
[Hom.]
Acamas²
[Hom.]
Agenor⁷– ?
[Hom.]
Priam¹-*Hecabe*¹
Antheus¹ ~ Paris
[Schol. Lyc.]
[Lyc.]
Archilochus¹
[Hom.]
Coon
[Hom.]
*Crino*¹
[Paus.]
Demoleon²
[Hom.]
Eurymachus¹
[Paus.]
Glaucus⁶
[Apollod.]
Priam¹-*Hecabe*¹
Helicaon¹– *Laodice*¹
[Hom.]
[Hom.]
Munippus
[Schol. Lyc.]
Echeclus¹
[Paus.]
Hippolochus²
[Tzetz.]
Cisseus¹-*Telecleia*
Iphidamas¹ – ?
[Hom.]
[Hom.]
Laocoon¹– *Antiope*²
[Schol. Lyc.]
[Serv.]
Laodamas²
[Hom.]
Laodochus¹
[Hom.]
Medon⁶
[Virg.]
Polybus²
[Hom.]
Polydamas¹
[Serv.]
Thersilochus¹
[Virg.]
Eurydamas³ – ?
[Quint. Smyr.]
[Quint. Smyr.]
Antiphantes
[Hyg.]
Thymbraeus¹
[Hyg.]

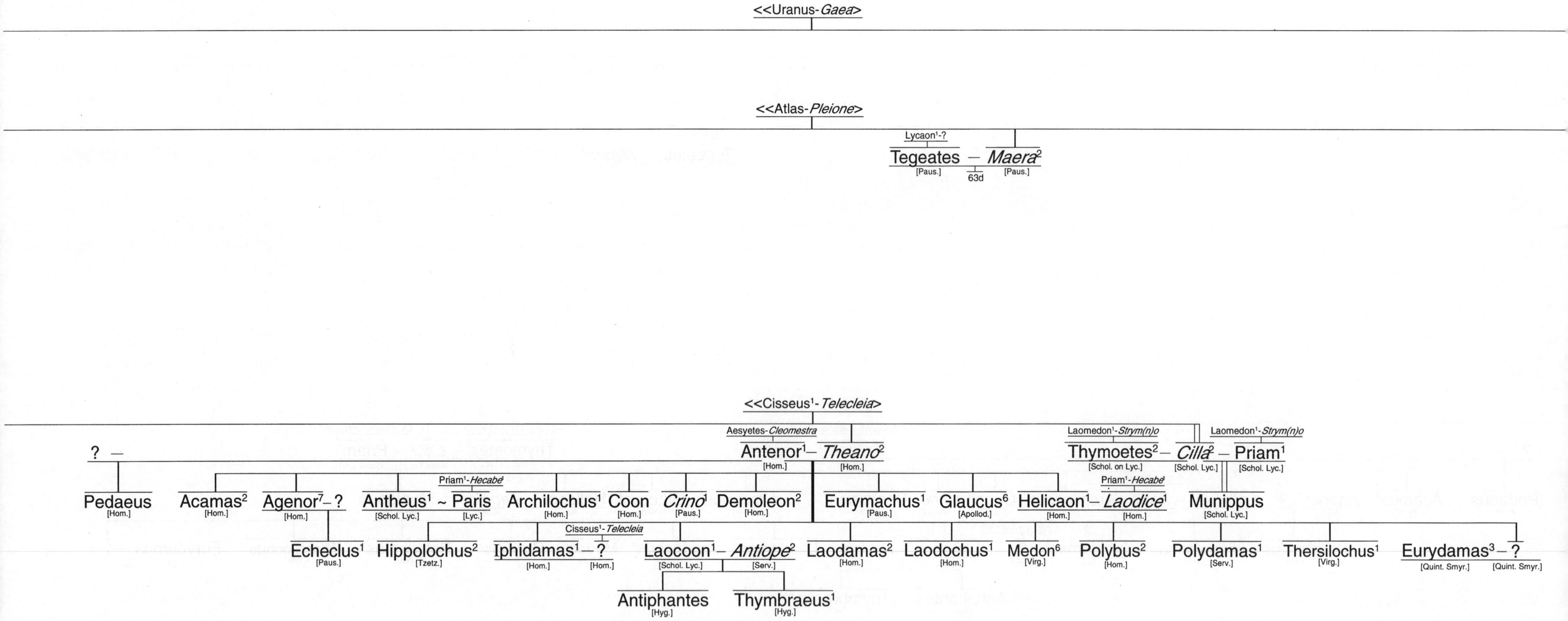

<<Uranus-*Gaea*>
<<Atlas-*Pleione*>
Lycaon¹-?
Tegeates [Paus.] – *Maera*² [Paus.]
63d
<<Cisseus¹-*Telecleia*>
Aesyetes-*Cleomestra*
Antenor¹ [Hom.] – *Theano*² [Hom.]
Laomedon¹-*Strym(n)o*
Thymoetes² [Schol. on Lyc.] – *Cilla*² [Schol. Lyc.] – Priam¹ [Schol. Lyc.]
Laomedon¹-*Strym(n)o*
? –
Pedaeus [Hom.]
Acamas² [Hom.]
Agenor⁷ [Hom.] – ?
Priam¹-*Hecabe*¹
Antheus¹ [Schol. Lyc.] ~ Paris [Lyc.]
Archilochus¹ [Hom.]
Coon [Hom.]
*Crino*¹ [Paus.]
Demoleon² [Hom.]
Eurymachus¹ [Paus.]
Glaucus⁶ [Apollod.]
Priam¹-*Hecabe*¹
Helicaon¹ [Hom.] – *Laodice*¹ [Hom.]
Munippus [Schol. Lyc.]
Echeclus¹ [Paus.]
Hippolochus² [Tzetz.]
Cisseus¹-*Telecleia*
Iphidamas¹ [Hom.] – ? [Hom.]
Laocoon¹ [Schol. Lyc.] – *Antiope*² [Serv.]
Laodamas² [Hom.]
Laodochus¹ [Hom.]
Medon⁶ [Virg.]
Polybus² [Hom.]
Polydamas¹ [Serv.]
Thersilochus¹ [Virg.]
Eurydamas³ [Quint. Smyr.] – ? [Quint. Smyr.]
Antiphantes [Hyg.]
Thymbraeus¹ [Hyg.]

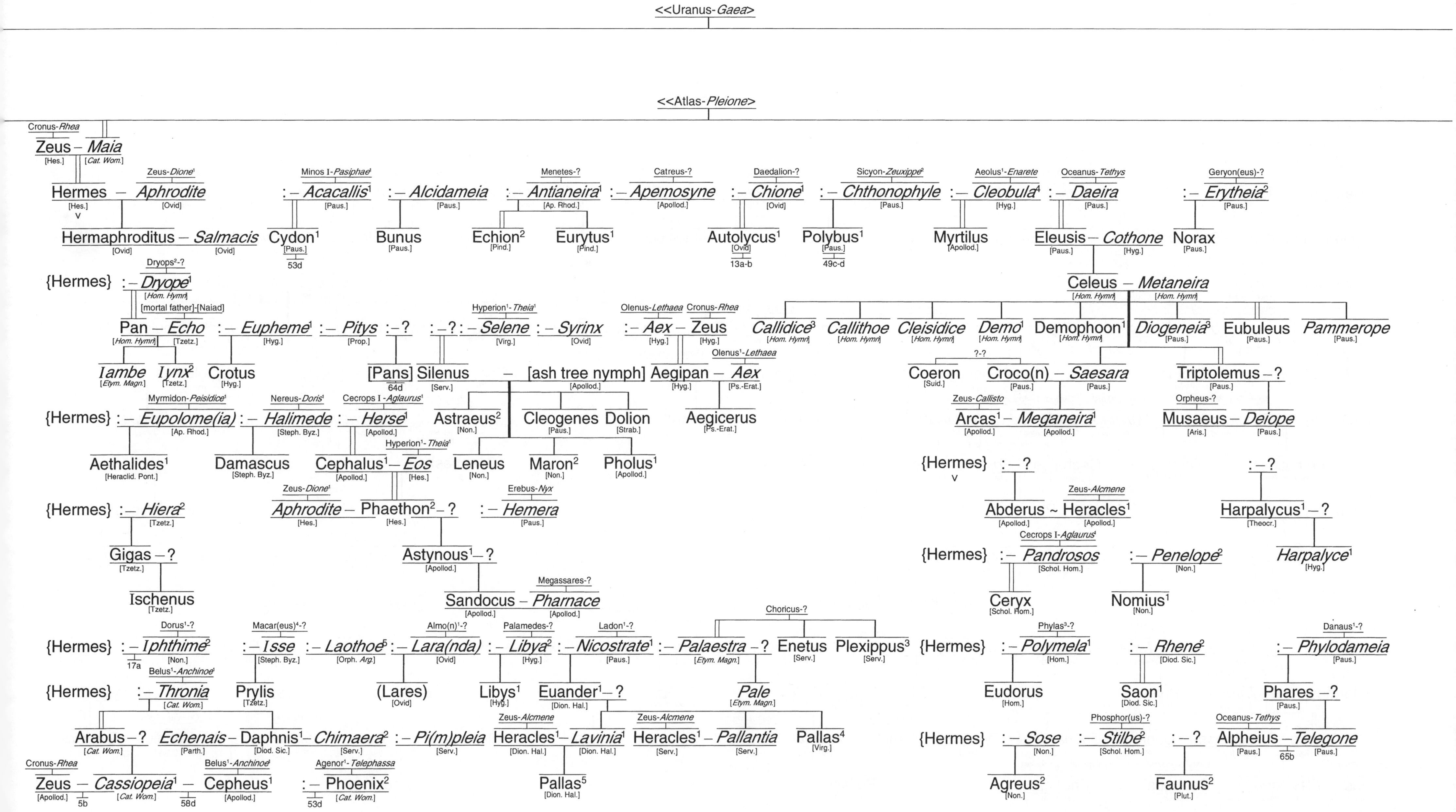
<<Uranus-Gaea>
<<Atlas-Pleione>
Cronus-Rhea
Zeus – Maia
[Hes.]
[Cat. Wom.]
Zeus-Dione[1]
Hermes – Aphrodite
[Hes.]
[Ovid]
Hermaphroditus – Salmacis
[Ovid]
[Ovid]
Minos I-Pasiphae[1]
:– Acacallis[1]
[Paus.]
Cydon[1]
[Paus.]
53d
:– Alcidameia
[Paus.]
Bunus
[Paus.]
Menetes-?
:– Antianeira[1]
[Ap. Rhod.]
Echion[2]
[Pind.]
Eurytus[1]
[Pind.]
Catreus-?
:– Apemosyne
[Apollod.]
Daedalion-?
:– Chione[1]
[Ovid]
Autolycus[1]
[Ovid]
13a-b
Sicyon-Zeuxippe[2]
:– Chthonophyle
[Paus.]
Polybus[1]
[Paus.]
49c-d
Aeolus[1]-Enarete
:– Cleobula[4]
[Hyg.]
Myrtilus
[Apollod.]
Oceanus-Tethys
:– Daeira
[Paus.]
Eleusis – Cothone
[Paus.]
[Hyg.]
Geryon(eus)-?
:– Erytheia[2]
[Paus.]
Norax
[Paus.]
Dryops[2]-?
{Hermes} :– Dryope[1]
[Hom. Hymn]
[mortal father]-[Naiad]
Pan – Echo
[Hom. Hymn]
[Tzetz.]
Iambe
[Etym. Magn.]
Iynx[2]
[Tzetz.]
:– Eupheme[1]
[Hyg.]
Crotus
[Hyg.]
:– Pitys
[Prop.]
:– ?
[Pans]
64d
Hyperion[1]-Theia[1]
:– ? :– Selene
[Virg.]
:– Syrinx
[Ovid]
Silenus – [ash tree nymph]
[Serv.]
[Apollod.]
Astraeus[2]
[Non.]
Cleogenes
[Paus.]
Dolion
[Strab.]
Leneus
[Non.]
Maron[2]
[Non.]
Pholus[1]
[Apollod.]
Olenus-Lethaea
Cronus-Rhea
:– Aex – Zeus
[Hyg.]
[Hyg.]
Olenus[1]-Lethaea
Aegipan – Aex
[Hyg.]
[Ps.-Erat.]
Aegicerus
[Ps.-Erat.]
Celeus – Metaneira
[Hom. Hymn]
[Hom. Hymn]
Callidice[3]
[Hom. Hymn]
Callithoe
[Hom. Hymn]
Cleisidice
[Hom. Hymn]
Demo[1]
[Hom. Hymn]
Demophoon[1]
[Hom. Hymn]
Diogeneia[3]
[Paus.]
Eubuleus
[Paus.]
Pammerope
[Paus.]
?-?
Coeron
[Suid.]
Croco(n) – Saesara
[Paus.]
[Paus.]
Triptolemus – ?
[Paus.]
Zeus-Callisto
Arcas[1] – Meganeira[1]
[Apollod.]
[Apollod.]
Orpheus-?
Musaeus – Deiope
[Aris.]
[Paus.]
Myrmidon-Peisidice[1]
{Hermes} :– Eupolome(ia)
[Ap. Rhod.]
Aethalides[1]
[Heraclid. Pont.]
Nereus-Doris[1]
:– Halimede
[Steph. Byz.]
Damascus
[Steph. Byz.]
Cecrops I-Aglaurus[1]
:– Herse[1]
[Apollod.]
Hyperion[1]-Theia[1]
Cephalus[1] – Eos
[Apollod.]
[Hes.]
Zeus-Dione[1]
Aphrodite – Phaethon[2] – ?
[Hes.]
[Hes.]
Astynous[1] – ?
[Apollod.]
Megassares-?
Sandocus – Pharnace
[Apollod.]
[Apollod.]
Erebus-Nyx
:– Hemera
[Paus.]
{Hermes} :– Hiera[2]
[Tzetz.]
Gigas – ?
[Tzetz.]
Ischenus
[Tzetz.]
{Hermes} :– ?
Zeus-Alcmene
Abderus ~ Heracles[1]
[Apollod.]
[Apollod.]
:– ?
Harpalycus[1] – ?
[Theocr.]
Harpalyce[1]
[Hyg.]
Cecrops I-Aglaurus[1]
{Hermes} :– Pandrosos
[Schol. Hom.]
Ceryx
[Schol. Hom.]
:– Penelope[2]
[Non.]
Nomius[1]
[Non.]
Dorus[1]-?
{Hermes} :– Iphthime[2]
[Non.]
17a
Macar(eus)[4]-?
:– Isse
[Steph. Byz.]
Prylis
[Tzetz.]
:– Laothoe[5]
[Orph. Arg.]
Almo(n)[1]-?
:– Lara(nda)
[Ovid]
(Lares)
[Ovid]
Palamedes-?
:– Libya[2]
[Hyg.]
Libys[1]
[Hyg.]
Ladon[1]-?
:– Nicostrate[1]
[Paus.]
Euander[1] – ?
[Dion. Hal.]
Choricus-?
:– Palaestra – ?
[Etym. Magn.]
Pale
[Etym. Magn.]
Enetus
[Serv.]
Plexippus[3]
[Serv.]
Belus[1]-Anchinoe[1]
{Hermes} :– Thronia
[Cat. Wom.]
Arabus – ?
[Cat. Wom.]
Echenais – Daphnis[1] – Chimaera[2]
[Parth.]
[Diod. Sic.]
[Serv.]
:– Pi(m)pleia
[Serv.]
Zeus-Alcmene
Heracles[1] – Lavinia[1]
[Dion. Hal.]
[Dion. Hal.]
Pallas[5]
[Dion. Hal.]
Zeus-Alcmene
Heracles[1] – Pallantia
[Serv.]
[Serv.]
Pallas[4]
[Virg.]
Cronus-Rhea
Zeus – Cassiopeia[1] – Cepheus[1]
[Apollod.]
5b
[Cat. Wom.]
58d
Belus[1]-Anchinoe[1]
[Apollod.]
Agenor[1]-Telephassa
:– Phoenix[2]
53d
[Cat. Wom.]
Phylas[3]-?
{Hermes} :– Polymela[1]
[Hom.]
Eudorus
[Hom.]
:– Rhene[2]
[Diod. Sic.]
Saon[1]
[Diod. Sic.]
Danaus[1]-?
:– Phylodameia
[Paus.]
Phares – ?
[Paus.]
{Hermes} :– Sose
[Non.]
Agreus[2]
[Non.]
Phosphor(us)-?
:– Stilbe[2]
[Schol. Hom.]
:– ?
Faunus[2]
[Plut.]
Oceanus-Tethys
Alpheius – Telegone
[Paus.]
65b
[Paus.]

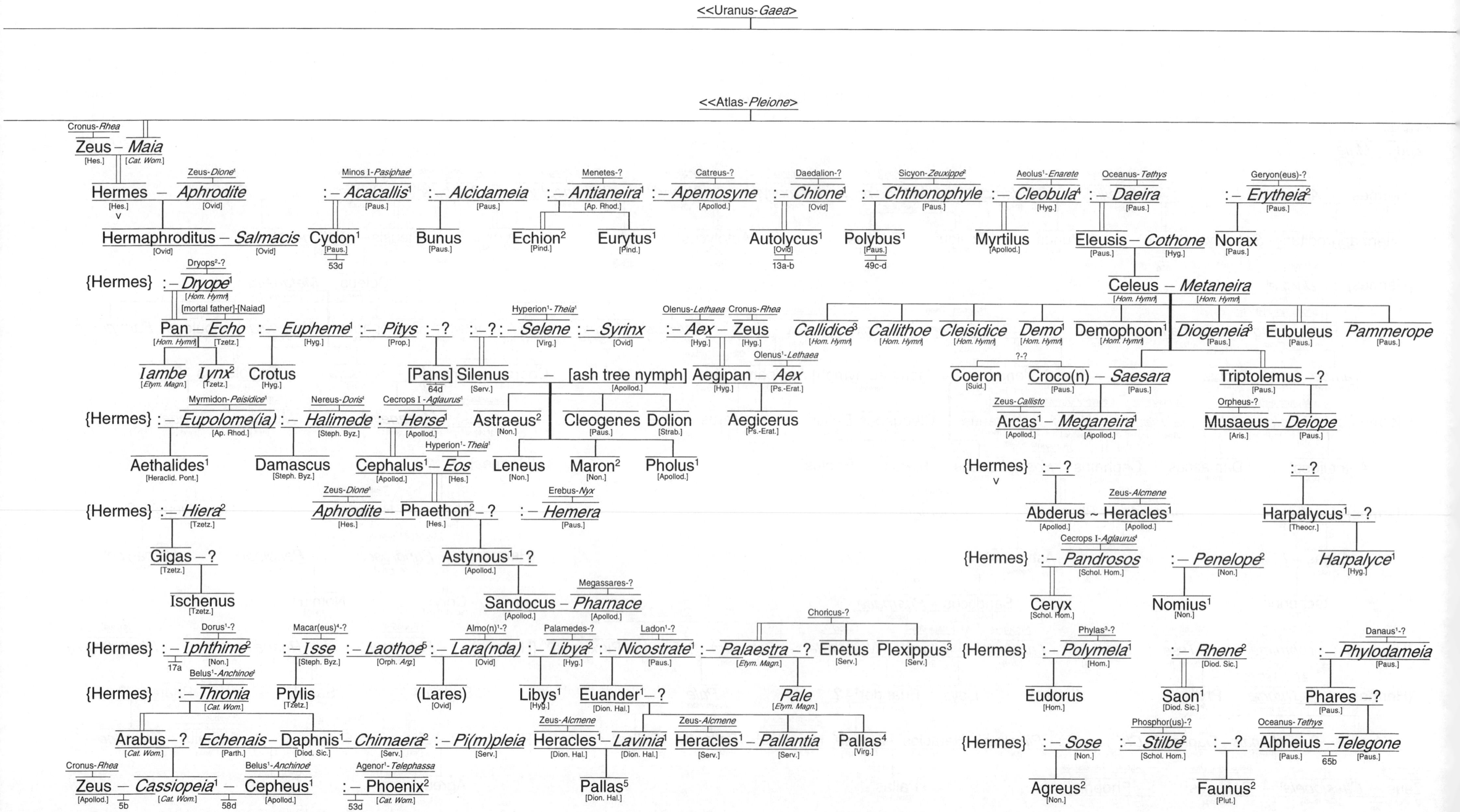

<<Uranus-Gaea>
<<Atlas-Pleione>
Cronus-Rhea
Zeus – Maia
[Hes.] [Cat. Wom.]
Zeus-Dione¹
Hermes – Aphrodite
[Hes.] [Ovid]
Hermaphroditus – Salmacis
[Ovid] [Ovid]
Minos I-Pasiphae¹
:– Acacallis¹ [Paus.]
Cydon¹ [Paus.] 53d
:– Alcidameia [Paus.]
Bunus [Paus.]
Menetes-?
:– Antianeira¹ [Ap. Rhod.]
Echion² [Pind.]
Eurytus¹ [Pind.]
Catreus-?
:– Apemosyne [Apollod.]
Daedalion-?
:– Chione¹ [Ovid]
Autolycus¹ [Ovid] 13a-b
Sicyon-Zeuxippe²
:– Chthonophyle [Paus.]
Polybus¹ [Paus.] 49c-d
Aeolus¹-Enarete
:– Cleobula⁴ [Hyg.]
Myrtilus [Apollod.]
Oceanus-Tethys
:– Daeira [Paus.]
Eleusis – Cothone
[Paus.] [Hyg.]
Geryon(eus)-?
:– Erytheia² [Paus.]
Norax [Paus.]
Dryops²-?
{Hermes} :– Dryope¹ [Hom. Hymn]
[mortal father]-[Naiad]
Pan – Echo
[Hom. Hymn] [Tzetz.]
Iambe [Etym. Magn.]
Iynx² [Tzetz.]
:– Eupheme¹ [Hyg.]
Crotus [Hyg.]
:– Pitys [Prop.]
:–?
[Pans] 64d
Hyperion¹-Theia¹
:–? :– Selene [Virg.]
:– Syrinx [Ovid]
Silenus [Serv.] – [ash tree nymph] [Apollod.]
Astraeus² [Non.]
Cleogenes [Paus.]
Dolion [Strab.]
Leneus [Non.]
Maron² [Non.]
Pholus¹ [Apollod.]
Olenus-Lethaea
Cronus-Rhea
:– Aex – Zeus
[Hyg.] [Hyg.]
Olenus¹-Lethaea
Aegipan – Aex
[Hyg.] [Ps.-Erat.]
Aegicerus [Ps.-Erat.]
Celeus – Metaneira
[Hom. Hymn] [Hom. Hymn]
Callidice³ [Hom. Hymn]
Callithoe [Hom. Hymn]
Cleisidice [Hom. Hymn]
Demo¹ [Hom. Hymn]
Demophoon¹ [Hom. Hymn]
Diogeneia³ [Paus.]
Eubuleus [Paus.]
Pammerope [Paus.]
?-?
Coeron [Suid.]
Croco(n) – Saesara
[Paus.] [Paus.]
Zeus-Callisto
Arcas¹ – Meganeira¹
[Apollod.] [Apollod.]
Triptolemus –? [Paus.]
Orpheus-?
Musaeus – Deiope
[Aris.] [Paus.]
Myrmidon-Peisidice¹
{Hermes} :– Eupolome(ia) [Ap. Rhod.]
Aethalides¹ [Heraclid. Pont.]
Nereus-Doris¹
:– Halimede [Steph. Byz.]
Damascus [Steph. Byz.]
Cecrops I-Aglaurus¹
:– Herse¹ [Apollod.]
Hyperion¹-Theia¹
Cephalus¹ – Eos
[Apollod.] [Hes.]
Zeus-Dione¹
Aphrodite – Phaethon² –?
[Hes.] [Hes.]
Erebus-Nyx
:– Hemera [Paus.]
Astynous¹ –? [Apollod.]
Megassares-?
Sandocus – Pharnace
[Apollod.] [Apollod.]
{Hermes} :– Hiera² [Tzetz.]
Gigas –? [Tzetz.]
Ischenus [Tzetz.]
{Hermes} :–?
Zeus-Alcmene
Abderus ~ Heracles¹
[Apollod.] [Apollod.]
:–?
Harpalycus¹ –? [Theocr.]
Harpalyce¹ [Hyg.]
Cecrops I-Aglaurus¹
{Hermes} :– Pandrosos [Schol. Hom.]
Ceryx [Schol. Hom.]
:– Penelope² [Non.]
Nomius¹ [Non.]
Dorus¹-?
{Hermes} :– Iphthime² [Non.] 17a
Macar(eus)⁴-?
:– Isse [Steph. Byz.]
Prylis [Tzetz.]
:– Laothoe⁵ [Orph. Arg.]
Almo(n)¹-?
:– Lara(nda) [Ovid]
(Lares) [Ovid]
Palamedes-?
:– Libya² [Hyg.]
Libys¹ [Hyg.]
Ladon¹-?
:– Nicostrate¹ [Paus.]
Euander¹ –? [Dion. Hal.]
Choricus-?
:– Palaestra –? [Etym. Magn.]
Enetus [Serv.]
Plexippus³ [Serv.]
Pale [Etym. Magn.]
Phylas³-?
{Hermes} :– Polymela¹ [Hom.]
Eudorus [Hom.]
:– Rhene² [Diod. Sic.]
Saon¹ [Diod. Sic.]
Danaus¹-?
:– Phylodameia [Paus.]
Phares –? [Paus.]
Belus¹-Anchinoe¹
{Hermes} :– Thronia [Cat. Wom.]
Arabus –? [Cat. Wom.]
Echenais – Daphnis¹ – Chimaera²
[Parth.] [Diod. Sic.] [Serv.]
:– Pi(m)pleia [Serv.]
Zeus-Alcmene
Heracles¹ – Lavinia¹
[Dion. Hal.] [Dion. Hal.]
Zeus-Alcmene
Heracles¹ – Pallantia
[Serv.] [Serv.]
Pallas⁴ [Virg.]
Pallas⁵ [Dion. Hal.]
Cronus-Rhea
Zeus – Cassiopeia¹ – Cepheus¹
[Apollod.] 5b [Cat. Wom.] 58d [Apollod.]
Belus¹-Anchinoe¹
Agenor¹-Telephassa
:– Phoenix² [Cat. Wom.] 53d
{Hermes} :– Sose [Non.]
Agreus² [Non.]
Phosphor(us)-?
:– Stilbe² [Schol. Hom.]
:–?
Faunus² [Plut.]
Oceanus-Tethys
Alpheius – Telegone
[Paus.] 65b [Paus.]

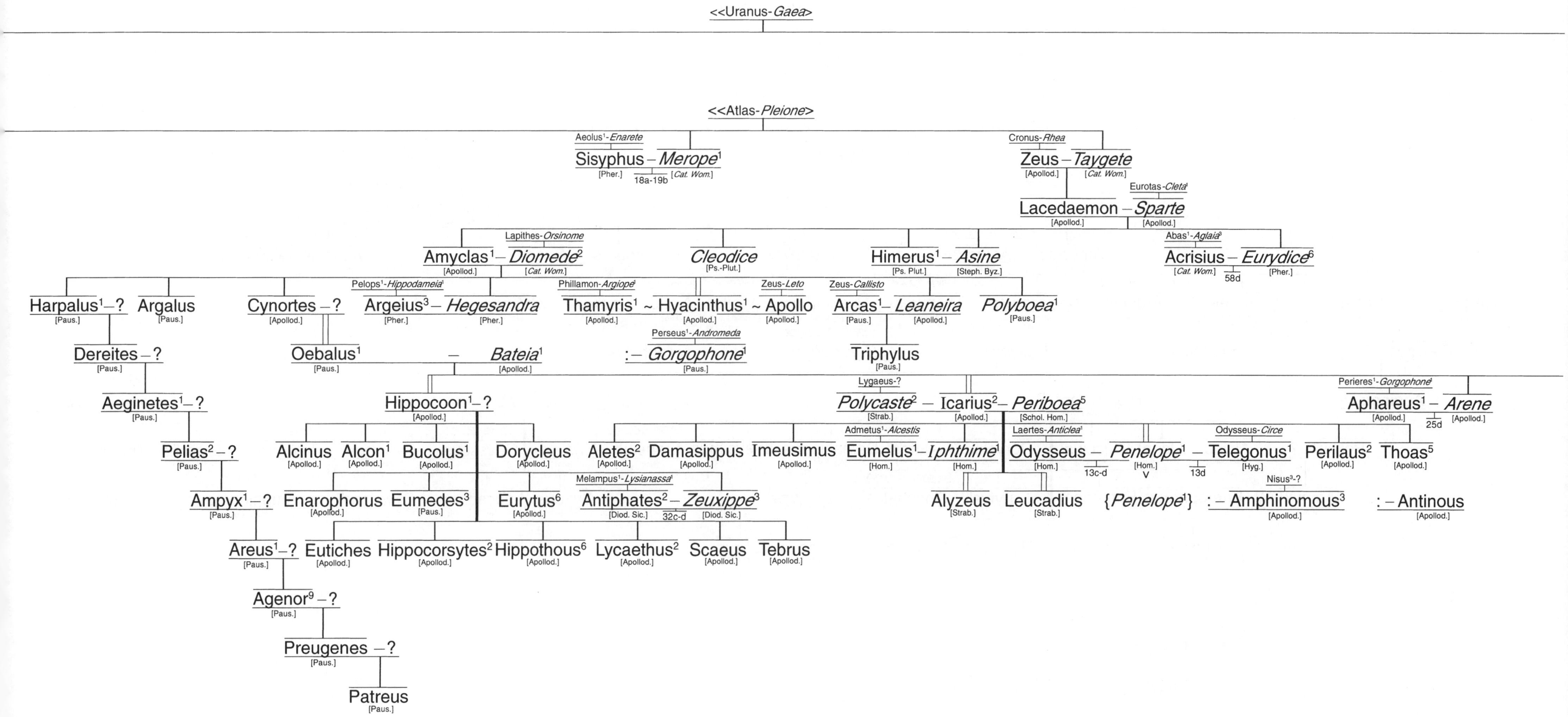
<<Uranus-*Gaea*>
<<Atlas-*Pleione*>
Aeolus[1]-*Enarete*
Sisyphus – *Merope*[1]
[Pher.] 18a-19b [*Cat. Wom.*]
Cronus-*Rhea*
Zeus – *Taygete*
[Apollod.] [*Cat. Wom.*]
Eurotas-*Cleta*[1]
Lacedaemon – *Sparte*
[Apollod.] [Apollod.]
Lapithes-*Orsinome*
Amyclas[1] – *Diomede*[2]
[Apollod.] [*Cat. Wom.*]
Cleodice
[Ps.-Plut.]
Himerus[1] – *Asine*
[Ps. Plut.] [Steph. Byz.]
Abas[1]-*Aglaia*[3]
Acrisius – *Eurydice*[6]
[*Cat. Wom.*] 58d [Pher.]
Harpalus[1] – ? Argalus
[Paus.] [Paus.]
Cynortes – ?
[Apollod.]
Pelops[1]-*Hippodameia*[1]
Argeius[3] – *Hegesandra*
[Pher.] [Pher.]
Phillamon-*Argiope*[1]
Thamyris[1] ~ Hyacinthus[1] ~ Apollo
[Apollod.] [Apollod.] [Apollod.]
Zeus-*Leto*
Zeus-*Callisto*
Arcas[1] – *Leaneira*
[Paus.] [Apollod.]
Polyboea[1]
[Paus.]
Dereites – ?
[Paus.]
Oebalus[1] – *Bateia*[1]
[Paus.] [Apollod.]
Perseus[1]-*Andromeda*
:– *Gorgophone*[1]
[Paus.]
Triphylus
[Paus.]
Aeginetes[1] – ?
[Paus.]
Hippocoon[1] – ?
[Apollod.]
Lygaeus-?
Polycaste[2] – Icarius[2] – *Periboea*[5]
[Strab.] [Apollod.] [Schol. Hom.]
Perieres[1]-*Gorgophone*[1]
Aphareus[1] – *Arene*
[Apollod.] 25d [Apollod.]
Pelias[2] – ?
[Paus.]
Alcinus Alcon[1] Bucolus[1] Dorycleus
[Apollod.] [Apollod.] [Apollod.] [Apollod.]
Aletes[2] Damasippus Imeusimus
[Apollod.] [Apollod.] [Apollod.]
Admetus[1]-*Alcestis*
Eumelus[1] – *Iphthime*[1]
[Hom.] [Hom.]
Laertes-*Anticlea*[1]
Odysseus – *Penelope*[1] – Telegonus[1]
[Hom.] 13c-d [Hom.] V 13d [Hyg.]
Odysseus-*Circe*
Perilaus[2] Thoas[5]
[Apollod.] [Apollod.]
Ampyx[1] – ?
[Paus.]
Enarophorus Eumedes[3]
[Apollod.] [Paus.]
Eurytus[6]
[Apollod.]
Melampus[1]-*Lysianassa*[1]
Antiphates[2] – *Zeuxippe*[3]
[Diod. Sic.] 32c-d [Diod. Sic.]
Alyzeus Leucadius
[Strab.] [Strab.]
{*Penelope*[1]}
Nisus[3]-?
:– Amphinomous[3]
[Apollod.]
:– Antinous
[Apollod.]
Areus[1] – ?
[Paus.]
Eutiches Hippocorsytes[2] Hippothous[6] Lycaethus[2] Scaeus Tebrus
[Apollod.] [Apollod.] [Apollod.] [Apollod.] [Apollod.] [Apollod.]
Agenor[9] – ?
[Paus.]
Preugenes – ?
[Paus.]
Patreus
[Paus.]

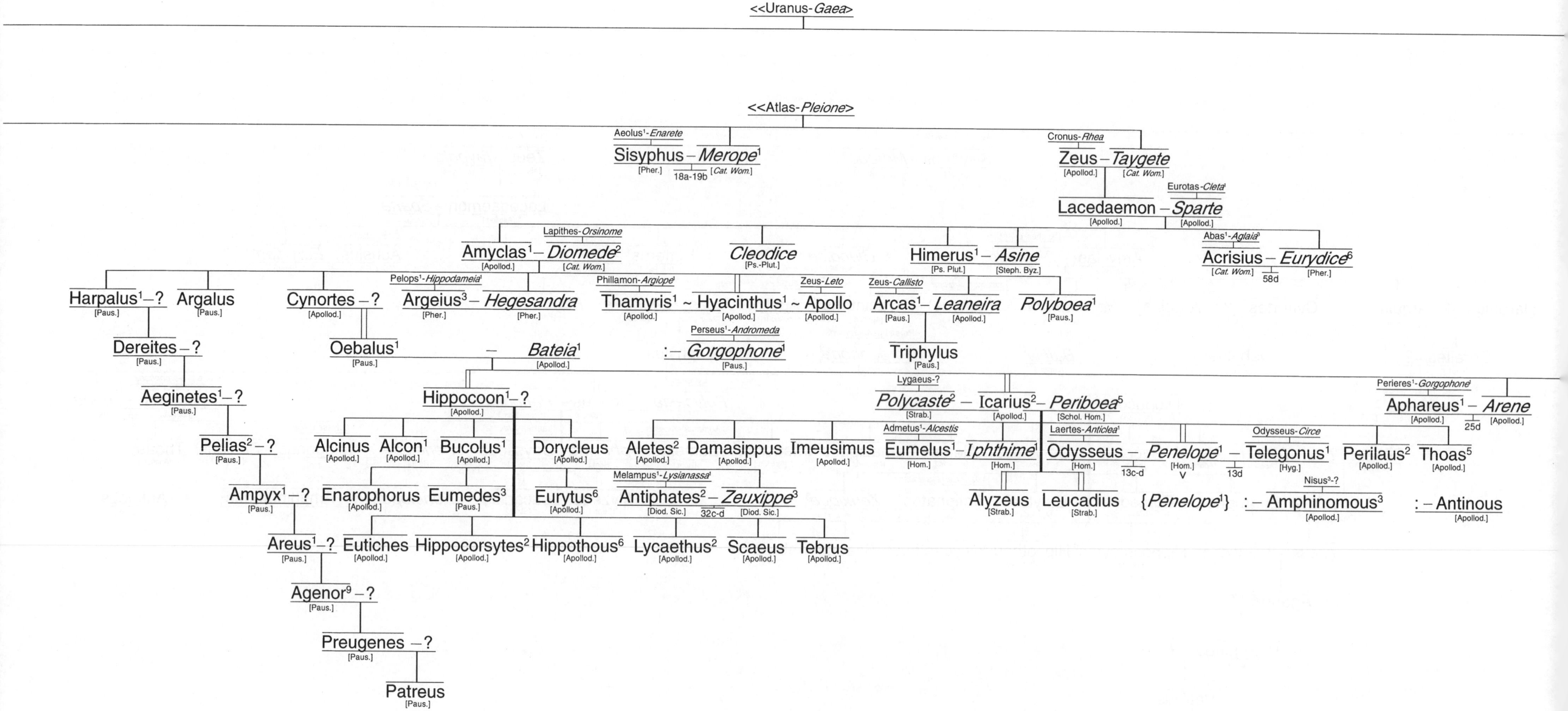

<<Uranus-Gaea>
<<Atlas-Pleione>
Aeolus¹-Enarete
Sisyphus – Merope¹
[Pher.] 18a-19b [Cat. Wom.]
Cronus-Rhea
Zeus – Taygete
[Apollod.] [Cat. Wom.]
Eurotas-Cleta¹
Lacedaemon – Sparte
[Apollod.] [Apollod.]
Lapithes-Orsinome
Amyclas¹ – Diomede²
[Apollod.] [Cat. Wom.]
Cleodice
[Ps.-Plut.]
Himerus¹ – Asine
[Ps. Plut.] [Steph. Byz.]
Abas¹-Aglaia³
Acrisius – Eurydice⁶
[Cat. Wom.] 58d [Pher.]
Harpalus¹ – ? Argalus
[Paus.] [Paus.]
Cynortes – ?
[Apollod.]
Pelops¹-Hippodameia¹
Argeius³ – Hegesandra
[Pher.] [Pher.]
Phillamon-Argiope¹
Thamyris¹ ~ Hyacinthus¹ ~ Apollo
[Apollod.] [Apollod.] [Apollod.]
Zeus-Leto
Zeus-Callisto
Arcas¹ – Leaneira
[Paus.] [Apollod.]
Polyboea¹
[Paus.]
Dereites – ?
[Paus.]
Oebalus¹ – Bateia¹
[Paus.] [Apollod.]
Perseus¹-Andromeda
:– Gorgophone¹
[Paus.]
Triphylus
[Paus.]
Aeginetes¹ – ?
[Paus.]
Hippocoon¹ – ?
[Apollod.]
Lygaeus-?
Polycaste² – Icarius² – Periboea⁵
[Strab.] [Apollod.] [Schol. Hom.]
Perieres¹-Gorgophone¹
Aphareus¹ – Arene
[Apollod.] 25d [Apollod.]
Pelias² – ?
[Paus.]
Alcinus Alcon¹ Bucolus¹ Dorycleus
[Apollod.] [Apollod.] [Apollod.] [Apollod.]
Aletes² Damasippus Imeusimus
[Apollod.] [Apollod.] [Apollod.]
Admetus¹-Alcestis
Eumelus¹ – Iphthime¹
[Hom.] [Hom.]
Laertes-Anticlea¹
Odysseus – Penelope¹ – Telegonus¹
[Hom.] 13c-d [Hom.] V 13d [Hyg.]
Odysseus-Circe
Perilaus² Thoas⁵
[Apollod.] [Apollod.]
Ampyx¹ – ?
[Paus.]
Enarophorus Eumedes³
[Apollod.] [Paus.]
Eurytus⁶
[Apollod.]
Melampus¹-Lysianassa¹
Antiphates² – Zeuxippe³
[Diod. Sic.] 32c-d [Diod. Sic.]
Alyzeus Leucadius
[Strab.] [Strab.]
{Penelope¹}
Nisus³-?
:– Amphinomous³
[Apollod.]
:– Antinous
[Apollod.]
Areus¹ – ?
[Paus.]
Eutiches Hippocorsytes² Hippothous⁶ Lycaethus² Scaeus Tebrus
[Apollod.] [Apollod.] [Apollod.] [Apollod.] [Apollod.] [Apollod.]
Agenor⁹ – ?
[Paus.]
Preugenes – ?
[Paus.]
Patreus
[Paus.]

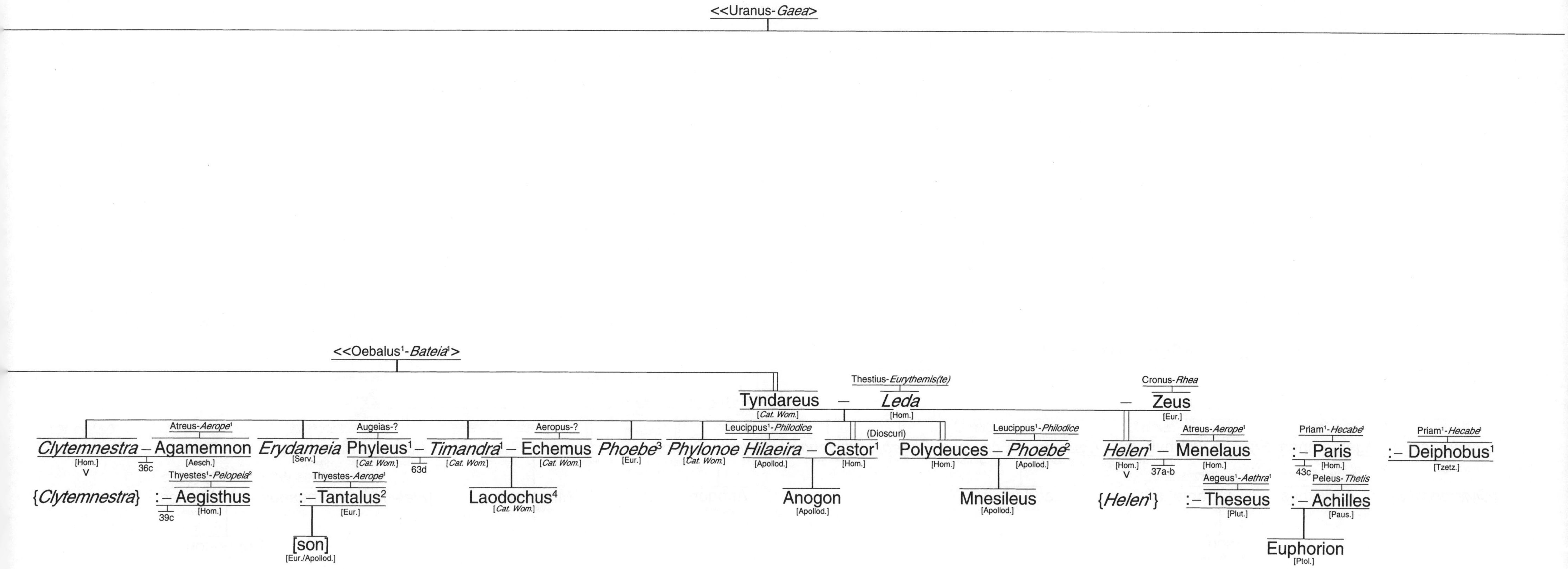

<<Uranus-*Gaea*>
<<Oebalus[1]-*Bateia*[1]>
Thestius-*Eurythemis(te)*
Tyndareus – *Leda* – Zeus
[Cat. Wom.]
[Hom.]
Cronus-*Rhea*
[Eur.]
Atreus-*Aerope*[1]
Clytemnestra – Agamemnon
[Hom.]
[Aesch.]
36c
{*Clytemnestra*}
Thyestes[1]-*Pelopeia*[2]
:– Aegisthus
[Hom.]
39c
Erydameia
[Serv.]
Augeias-?
Phyleus[1] – *Timandra*[1] – Echemus
[Cat. Wom.]
63d
Aeropus-?
Thyestes-*Aerope*[1]
:–Tantalus[2]
[Eur.]
[son]
[Eur./Apollod.]
Laodochus[4]
[Cat. Wom.]
Phoebe[3]
[Eur.]
Phylonoe
[Cat. Wom.]
Leucippus[1]-*Philodice*
Hilaeira – Castor[1]
[Apollod.]
[Hom.]
(Dioscuri)
Anogon
[Apollod.]
Polydeuces – *Phoebe*[2]
[Hom.]
[Apollod.]
Leucippus[1]-*Philodice*
Mnesileus
[Apollod.]
Helen[1] – Menelaus
[Hom.]
37a-b
{*Helen*[1]}
Atreus-*Aerope*[1]
Aegeus[1]-*Aethra*[1]
:–Theseus
[Plut.]
Priam[1]-*Hecabe*[1]
:– Paris
[Hom.]
43c
Peleus-*Thetis*
:– Achilles
[Paus.]
Euphorion
[Ptol.]
Priam[1]-*Hecabe*[1]
:– Deiphobus[1]
[Tzetz.]

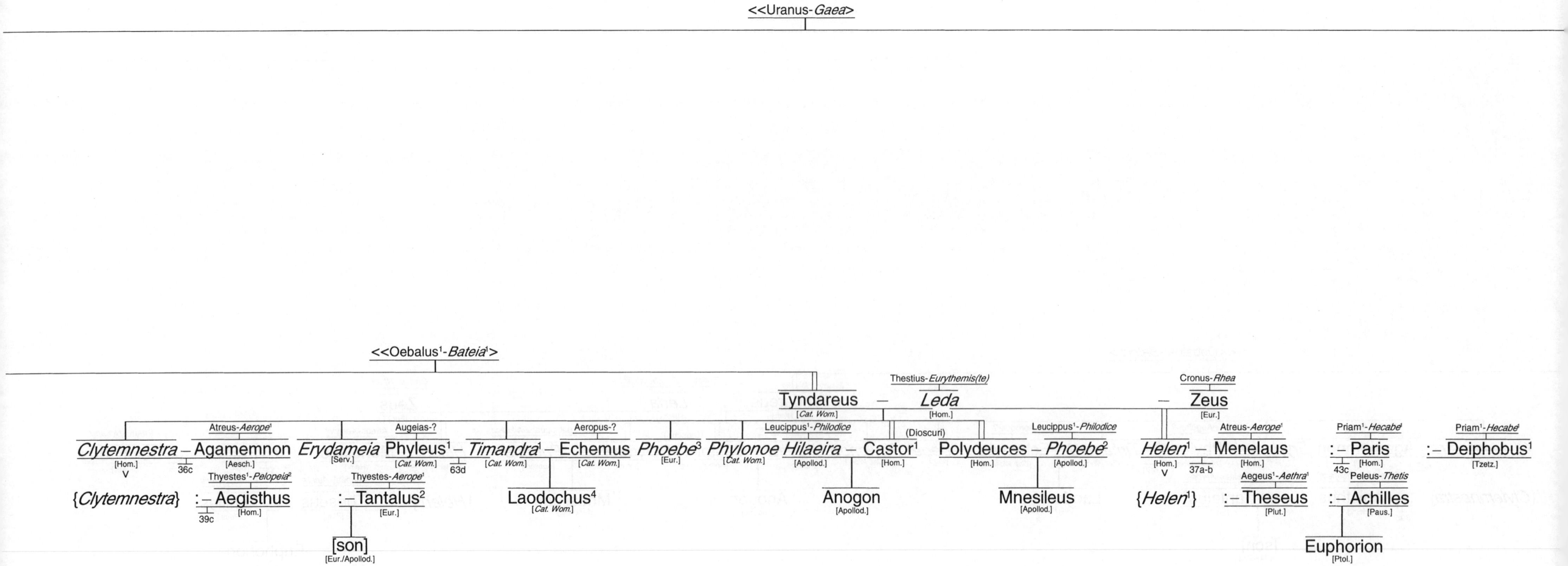

<<Uranus-Gaea>
<<Oebalus[1]-Bateia[1]>
Thestius-Eurythemis(te)
Cronus-Rhea
Tyndareus – Leda – Zeus
[Cat. Wom.]
[Hom.]
[Eur.]
Atreus-Aerope[1]
Augeias-?
Aeropus-?
Leucippus[1]-Philodice
(Dioscuri)
Leucippus[1]-Philodice
Atreus-Aerope[1]
Priam[1]-Hecabe[1]
Priam[1]-Hecabe[1]
Clytemnestra – Agamemnon
[Hom.]
[Aesch.]
V
36c
Erydameia
[Serv.]
Phyleus[1] – Timandra[1] – Echemus
[Cat. Wom.]
63d
[Cat. Wom.]
[Cat. Wom.]
Phoebe[3]
[Eur.]
Phylonoe
[Cat. Wom.]
Hilaeira – Castor[1]
[Apollod.]
[Hom.]
Polydeuces – Phoebe[2]
[Hom.]
[Apollod.]
Helen[1] – Menelaus
[Hom.]
V
37a-b
[Hom.]
:– Paris
43c
[Hom.]
:– Deiphobus[1]
[Tzetz.]
Thyestes[1]-Pelopeia[2]
Thyestes-Aerope[1]
Aegeus[1]-Aethra[1]
Peleus-Thetis
{Clytemnestra}
:– Aegisthus
39c
[Hom.]
:– Tantalus[2]
[Eur.]
Laodochus[4]
[Cat. Wom.]
Anogon
[Apollod.]
Mnesileus
[Apollod.]
{Helen[1]}
:– Theseus
[Plut.]
:– Achilles
[Paus.]
[son]
[Eur./Apollod.]
Euphorion
[Ptol.]

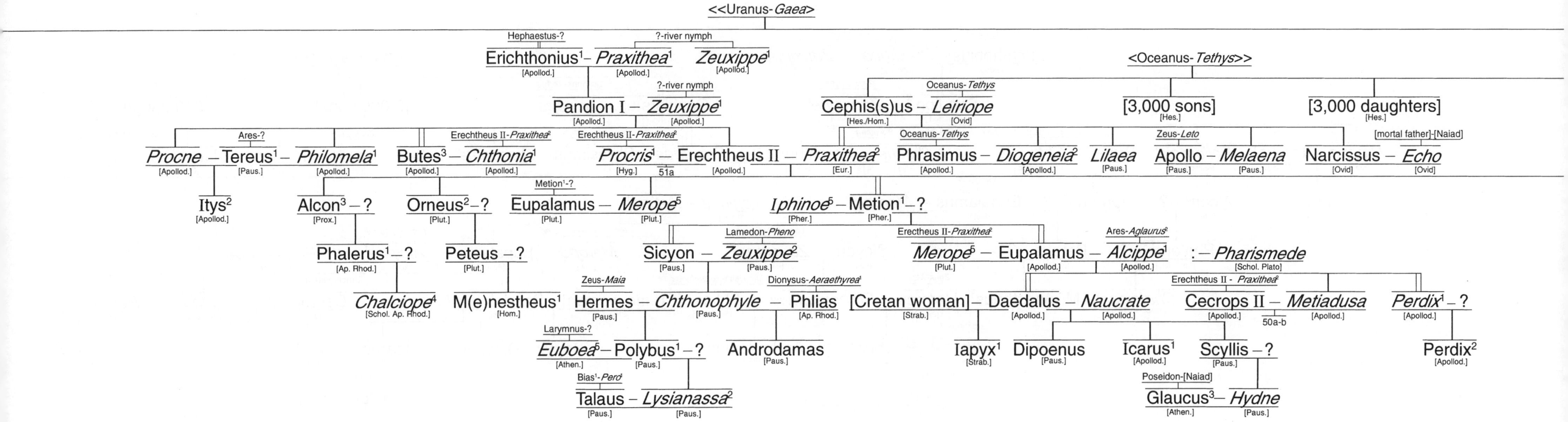

<<Uranus-Gaea>
Hephaestus-?
?-river nymph
Erichthonius1- Praxithea1 [Apollod.] [Apollod.]
Zeuxippe1 [Apollod.]
<Oceanus-Tethys>>
?-river nymph
Pandion I – Zeuxippe1 [Apollod.] [Apollod.]
Oceanus-Tethys
Cephis(s)us – Leiriope [Hes./Hom.] [Ovid]
[3,000 sons] [Hes.]
[3,000 daughters] [Hes.]
Ares-?
Erechtheus II-Praxithea2
Erechtheus II-Praxithea2
Oceanus-Tethys
Zeus-Leto
[mortal father]-[Naiad]
Procne – Tereus1 – Philomela1 [Apollod.] [Paus.] [Apollod.]
Butes3 – Chthonia1 [Apollod.] [Apollod.]
Procris1 – Erechtheus II – Praxithea2 [Hyg.] 51a [Apollod.] [Eur.]
Phrasimus – Diogeneia2 [Apollod.] [Apollod.]
Lilaea [Paus.]
Apollo – Melaena [Paus.] [Paus.]
Narcissus – Echo [Ovid] [Ovid]
Metion1-?
Itys2 [Apollod.]
Alcon3 – ? [Prox.]
Orneus2 – ? [Plut.]
Eupalamus – Merope5 [Plut.] [Plut.]
Iphinoe5 – Metion1 – ? [Pher.] [Pher.]
Lamedon-Pheno
Erectheus II-Praxithea2
Ares-Aglaurus2
Phalerus1 – ? [Ap. Rhod.]
Peteus – ? [Plut.]
Sicyon – Zeuxippe2 [Paus.] [Paus.]
Merope5 – Eupalamus – Alcippe1 [Plut.] [Apollod.] [Apollod.]
:– Pharismede [Schol. Plato]
Zeus-Maia
Dionysus-Aeraethyrea1
Erechtheus II - Praxithea2
Chalciope4 [Schol. Ap. Rhod.]
M(e)nestheus1 [Hom.]
Hermes – Chthonophyle – Phlias [Paus.] [Paus.] [Ap. Rhod.]
[Cretan woman] – Daedalus – Naucrate [Strab.] [Apollod.] [Apollod.]
Cecrops II – Metiadusa [Apollod.] 50a-b [Apollod.]
Perdix1 – ? [Apollod.]
Larymnus-?
Euboea5 – Polybus1 – ? [Athen.] [Paus.]
Androdamas [Paus.]
Iapyx1 [Strab.]
Dipoenus [Paus.]
Icarus1 [Apollod.]
Scyllis – ? [Paus.]
Perdix2 [Apollod.]
Bias1-Pero1
Poseidon-[Naiad]
Talaus – Lysianassa2 [Paus.] [Paus.]
Glaucus3 – Hydne [Athen.] [Paus.]

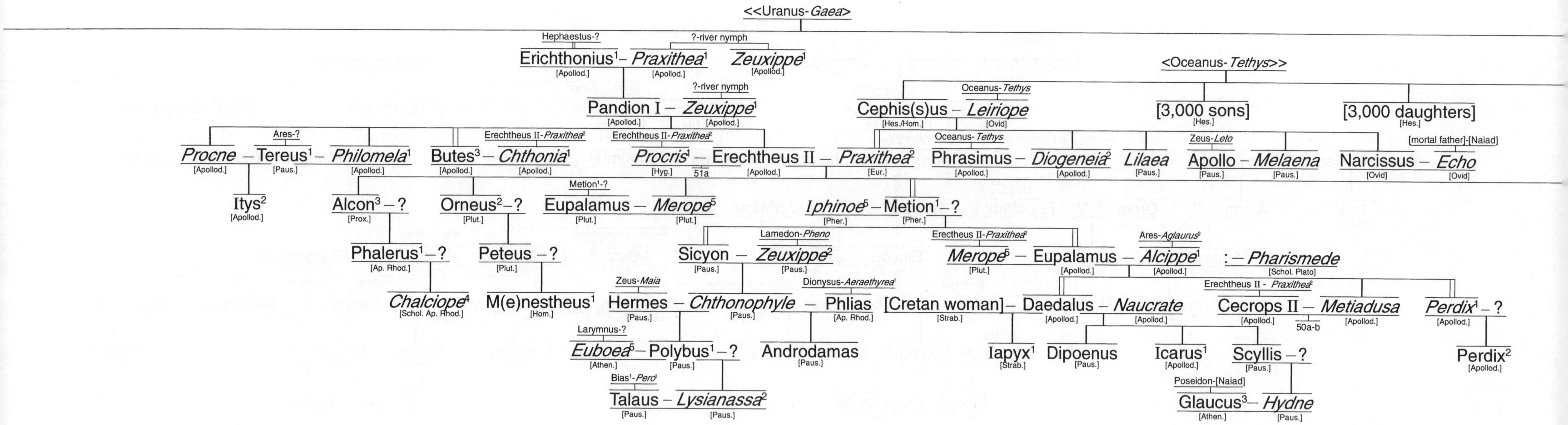

<<Uranus-Gaea>
Hephaestus-?
?-river nymph
Erichthonius[1] – Praxithea[1]
[Apollod.]
[Apollod.]
Zeuxippe[1]
[Apollod.]
<Oceanus-Tethys>>
?-river nymph
Pandion I – Zeuxippe[1]
[Apollod.]
[Apollod.]
Oceanus-Tethys
Cephis(s)us – Leiriope
[Hes./Hom.]
[Ovid]
[3,000 sons]
[Hes.]
[3,000 daughters]
[Hes.]
Ares-?
Erechtheus II-Praxithea[2]
Erechtheus II-Praxithea[2]
Oceanus-Tethys
Zeus-Leto
[mortal father]-[Naiad]
Procne – Tereus[1] – Philomela[1]
[Apollod.]
[Paus.]
[Apollod.]
Butes[3] – Chthonia[1]
[Apollod.]
[Apollod.]
Procris[1] – Erechtheus II – Praxithea[2]
[Hyg.]
51a
[Apollod.]
[Eur.]
Phrasimus – Diogeneia[2]
[Apollod.]
[Apollod.]
Lilaea
[Paus.]
Apollo – Melaena
[Paus.]
[Paus.]
Narcissus – Echo
[Ovid]
[Ovid]
Metion[1]-?
Itys[2]
[Apollod.]
Alcon[3] – ?
[Prox.]
Orneus[2] – ?
[Plut.]
Eupalamus – Merope[5]
[Plut.]
[Plut.]
Iphinoe[5] – Metion[1] – ?
[Pher.]
[Pher.]
Lamedon-Pheno
Erectheus II-Praxithea[2]
Ares-Aglaurus[2]
Phalerus[1] – ?
[Ap. Rhod.]
Peteus – ?
[Plut.]
Sicyon – Zeuxippe[2]
[Paus.]
[Paus.]
Merope[5] – Eupalamus – Alcippe[1] : – Pharismede
[Plut.]
[Apollod.]
[Apollod.]
[Schol. Plato]
Zeus-Maia
Dionysus-Aeraethyrea[1]
Erechtheus II - Praxithea[2]
Chalciope[4]
[Schol. Ap. Rhod.]
M(e)nestheus[1]
[Hom.]
Hermes – Chthonophyle – Phlias
[Paus.]
[Paus.]
[Ap. Rhod.]
[Cretan woman] – Daedalus – Naucrate
[Strab.]
[Apollod.]
[Apollod.]
Cecrops II – Metiadusa
[Apollod.]
50a-b
[Apollod.]
Perdix[1] – ?
[Apollod.]
Larymnus-?
Euboea[5] – Polybus[1] – ?
[Athen.]
[Paus.]
Androdamas
[Paus.]
Iapyx[1]
[Strab.]
Dipoenus
[Paus.]
Icarus[1]
[Apollod.]
Scyllis – ?
[Paus.]
Perdix[2]
[Apollod.]
Bias[1]-Pero[1]
Poseidon-[Naiad]
Talaus – Lysianassa[2]
[Paus.]
[Paus.]
Glaucus[3] – Hydne
[Athen.]
[Paus.]

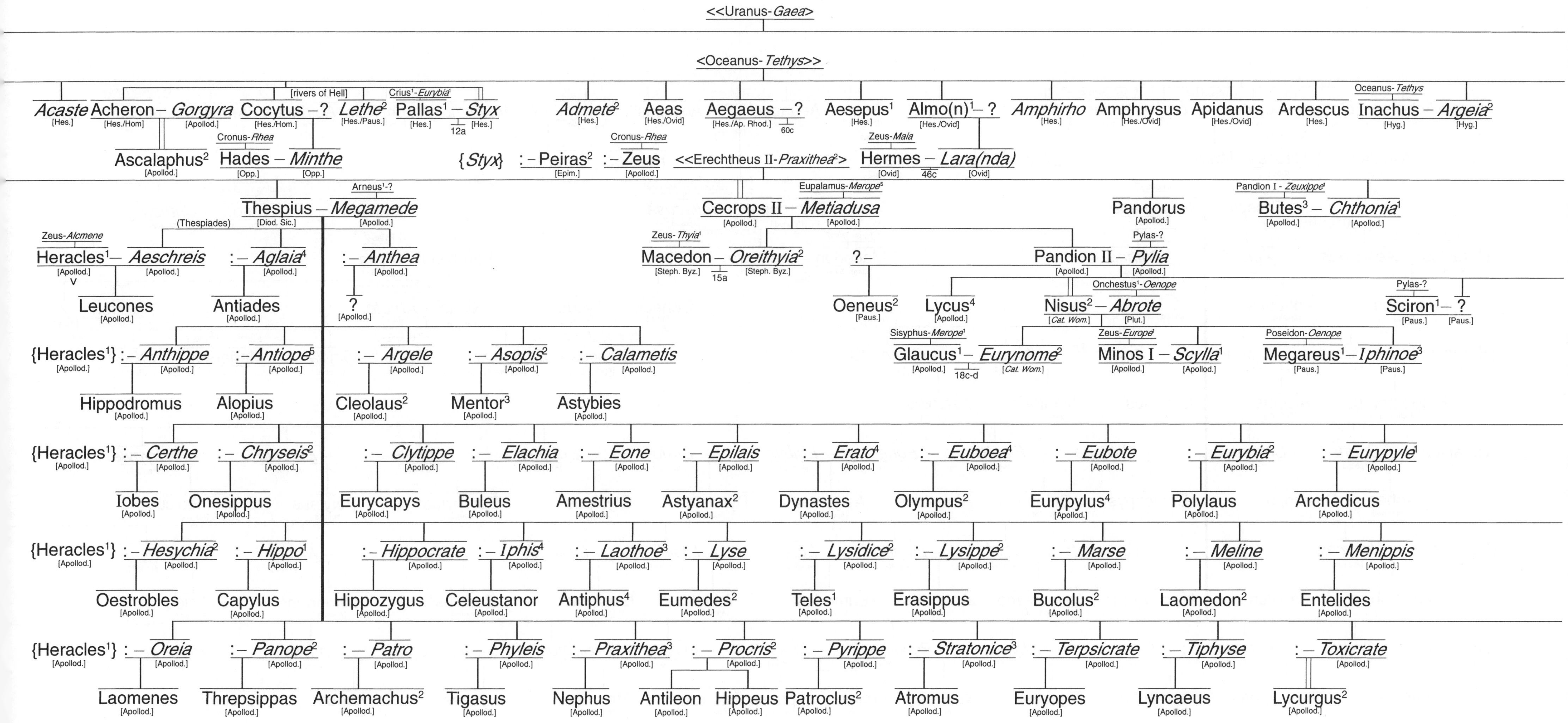
<<Uranus-Gaea>
<Oceanus-Tethys>>
[rivers of Hell] Crius[1]-Eurybia[1] Oceanus-Tethys
Acaste [Hes.] Acheron [Hes./Hom] – Gorgyra [Apollod.] Cocytus [Hes./Hom.] – ? Lethe[2] [Hes./Paus.] Pallas[1] [Hes.] – Styx [Hes.] 12a Admete[2] [Hes.] Aeas [Hes./Ovid] Aegaeus [Hes./Ap. Rhod.] – ? 60c Aesepus[1] [Hes.] Almo(n)[1] [Hes./Ovid] – ? Amphirho [Hes.] Amphrysus [Hes./Ovid] Apidanus [Hes./Ovid] Ardescus [Hes.] Inachus [Hyg.] – Argeia[2] [Hyg.]
Cronus-Rhea Cronus-Rhea Zeus-Maia
Ascalaphus[2] [Apollod.] Hades [Opp.] – Minthe [Opp.] {Styx} :– Peiras[2] [Epim.] :– Zeus [Apollod.] <<Erechtheus II-Praxithea[2]> Hermes [Ovid] – Lara(nda) [Ovid] 46c
Arneus[1]-? Eupalamus-Merope[5] Pandion I - Zeuxippe[1]
Thespius [Diod. Sic.] – Megamede [Apollod.] Cecrops II [Apollod.] – Metiadusa [Apollod.] Pandorus [Apollod.] Butes[3] [Apollod.] – Chthonia[1] [Apollod.]
(Thespiades)
Zeus-Alcmene Zeus-Thyia[1] Pylas-?
Heracles[1] [Apollod.] v – Aeschreis [Apollod.] :– Aglaia[4] [Apollod.] :– Anthea [Apollod.] Macedon [Steph. Byz.] – Oreithyia[2] [Steph. Byz.] 15a ?– Pandion II [Apollod.] – Pylia [Apollod.]
Onchestus[1]-Oenope Pylas-?
Leucones [Apollod.] Antiades [Apollod.] ? [Apollod.] Oeneus[2] [Paus.] Lycus[4] [Apollod.] Nisus[2] [Cat. Wom.] – Abrote [Plut.] Sciron[1] [Paus.] – ? [Paus.]
Sisyphus-Merope[1] Zeus-Europe[1] Poseidon-Oenope
{Heracles[1]} [Apollod.] :– Anthippe [Apollod.] :– Antiope[5] [Apollod.] :– Argele [Apollod.] :– Asopis[2] [Apollod.] :– Calametis [Apollod.] Glaucus[1] [Apollod.] – Eurynome[2] [Cat. Wom.] 18c-d Minos I [Apollod.] – Scylla[1] [Apollod.] Megareus[1] [Paus.] – Iphinoe[3] [Paus.]
Hippodromus [Apollod.] Alopius [Apollod.] Cleolaus[2] [Apollod.] Mentor[3] [Apollod.] Astybies [Apollod.]
{Heracles[1]} [Apollod.] :– Certhe [Apollod.] :– Chryseis[2] [Apollod.] :– Clytippe [Apollod.] :– Elachia [Apollod.] :– Eone [Apollod.] :– Epilais [Apollod.] :– Erato[4] [Apollod.] :– Euboea[4] [Apollod.] :– Eubote [Apollod.] :– Eurybia[2] [Apollod.] :– Eurypyle[1] [Apollod.]
Iobes [Apollod.] Onesippus [Apollod.] Eurycapys [Apollod.] Buleus [Apollod.] Amestrius [Apollod.] Astyanax[2] [Apollod.] Dynastes [Apollod.] Olympus[2] [Apollod.] Eurypylus[4] [Apollod.] Polylaus [Apollod.] Archedicus [Apollod.]
{Heracles[1]} [Apollod.] :– Hesychia[2] [Apollod.] :– Hippo[1] [Apollod.] :– Hippocrate [Apollod.] :– Iphis[4] [Apollod.] :– Laothoe[3] [Apollod.] :– Lyse [Apollod.] :– Lysidice[2] [Apollod.] :– Lysippe[2] [Apollod.] :– Marse [Apollod.] :– Meline [Apollod.] :– Menippis [Apollod.]
Oestrobles [Apollod.] Capylus [Apollod.] Hippozygus [Apollod.] Celeustanor [Apollod.] Antiphus[4] [Apollod.] Eumedes[2] [Apollod.] Teles[1] [Apollod.] Erasippus [Apollod.] Bucolus[2] [Apollod.] Laomedon[2] [Apollod.] Entelides [Apollod.]
{Heracles[1]} [Apollod.] :– Oreia [Apollod.] :– Panope[2] [Apollod.] :– Patro [Apollod.] :– Phyleis [Apollod.] :– Praxithea[3] [Apollod.] :– Procris[2] [Apollod.] :– Pyrippe [Apollod.] :– Stratonice[3] [Apollod.] :– Terpsicrate [Apollod.] :– Tiphyse [Apollod.] :– Toxicrate [Apollod.]
Laomenes [Apollod.] Threpsippas [Apollod.] Archemachus[2] [Apollod.] Tigasus [Apollod.] Nephus [Apollod.] Antileon [Apollod.] Hippeus [Apollod.] Patroclus[2] [Apollod.] Atromus [Apollod.] Euryopes [Apollod.] Lyncaeus [Apollod.] Lycurgus[2] [Apollod.]

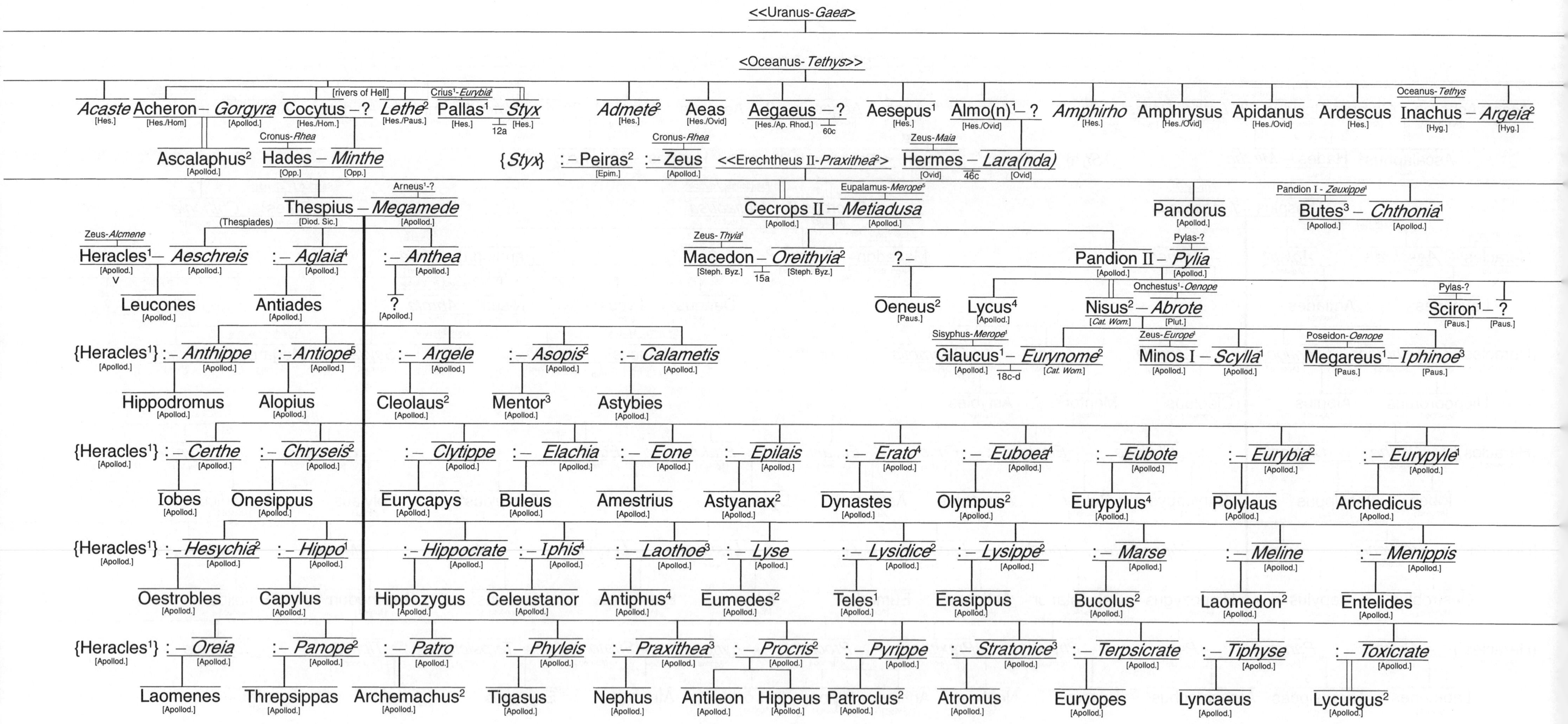

<<Uranus-Gaea>
<Oceanus-Tethys>>
Acaste [Hes.]
Acheron – Gorgyra [Hes./Hom] [Apollod.]
[rivers of Hell]
Cocytus – ? [Hes./Hom.]
Lethe² [Hes./Paus.]
Crius¹-Eurybia¹
Pallas¹ – Styx [Hes.] [Hes.] 12a
Admete² [Hes.]
Aeas [Hes./Ovid]
Aegaeus – ? [Hes./Ap. Rhod.] 60c
Aesepus¹ [Hes.]
Almo(n)¹ – ? [Hes./Ovid]
Amphirho [Hes.]
Amphrysus [Hes./Ovid]
Apidanus [Hes./Ovid]
Ardescus [Hes.]
Oceanus-Tethys
Inachus – Argeia² [Hyg.] [Hyg.]
Ascalaphus² [Apollod.]
Cronus-Rhea
Hades – Minthe [Opp.] [Opp.]
{Styx} :– Peiras² [Epim.]
Cronus-Rhea
:– Zeus [Apollod.]
<<Erechtheus II-Praxithea²>
Zeus-Maia
Hermes – Lara(nda) [Ovid] 46c [Ovid]
Arneus¹-?
Thespius – Megamede [Diod. Sic.] [Apollod.]
(Thespiades)
Eupalamus-Merope⁵
Cecrops II – Metiadusa [Apollod.] [Apollod.]
Pandorus [Apollod.]
Pandion I - Zeuxippe¹
Butes³ – Chthonia¹ [Apollod.] [Apollod.]
Zeus-Alcmene
Heracles¹ – Aeschreis [Apollod.] v [Apollod.]
:– Aglaia⁴ [Apollod.]
:– Anthea [Apollod.]
Zeus-Thyia¹
Macedon – Oreithyia² [Steph. Byz.] 15a [Steph. Byz.]
? –
Pylas-?
Pandion II – Pylia [Apollod.] [Apollod.]
Leucones [Apollod.]
Antiades [Apollod.]
? [Apollod.]
Oeneus² [Paus.]
Lycus⁴ [Apollod.]
Onchestus¹-Oenope
Nisus² – Abrote [Cat. Wom.] [Plut.]
Pylas-?
Sciron¹ – ? [Paus.] [Paus.]
Sisyphus-Merope¹
Glaucus¹ – Eurynome² [Apollod.] 18c-d [Cat. Wom.]
Zeus-Europe¹
Minos I – Scylla¹ [Apollod.] [Apollod.]
Poseidon-Oenope
Megareus¹ – Iphinoe³ [Paus.] [Paus.]
{Heracles¹} :– Anthippe [Apollod.] [Apollod.]
:– Antiope⁵ [Apollod.]
:– Argele [Apollod.]
:– Asopis² [Apollod.]
:– Calametis [Apollod.]
Hippodromus [Apollod.]
Alopius [Apollod.]
Cleolaus² [Apollod.]
Mentor³ [Apollod.]
Astybies [Apollod.]
{Heracles¹} :– Certhe [Apollod.] [Apollod.]
:– Chryseis² [Apollod.]
:– Clytippe [Apollod.]
:– Elachia [Apollod.]
:– Eone [Apollod.]
:– Epilais [Apollod.]
:– Erato⁴ [Apollod.]
:– Euboea⁴ [Apollod.]
:– Eubote [Apollod.]
:– Eurybia² [Apollod.]
:– Eurypyle¹ [Apollod.]
Iobes [Apollod.]
Onesippus [Apollod.]
Eurycapys [Apollod.]
Buleus [Apollod.]
Amestrius [Apollod.]
Astyanax² [Apollod.]
Dynastes [Apollod.]
Olympus² [Apollod.]
Eurypylus⁴ [Apollod.]
Polylaus [Apollod.]
Archedicus [Apollod.]
{Heracles¹} :– Hesychia² [Apollod.] [Apollod.]
:– Hippo¹ [Apollod.]
:– Hippocrate [Apollod.]
:– Iphis⁴ [Apollod.]
:– Laothoe³ [Apollod.]
:– Lyse [Apollod.]
:– Lysidice² [Apollod.]
:– Lysippe² [Apollod.]
:– Marse [Apollod.]
:– Meline [Apollod.]
:– Menippis [Apollod.]
Oestrobles [Apollod.]
Capylus [Apollod.]
Hippozygus [Apollod.]
Celeustanor [Apollod.]
Antiphus⁴ [Apollod.]
Eumedes² [Apollod.]
Teles¹ [Apollod.]
Erasippus [Apollod.]
Bucolus² [Apollod.]
Laomedon² [Apollod.]
Entelides [Apollod.]
{Heracles¹} :– Oreia [Apollod.] [Apollod.]
:– Panope² [Apollod.]
:– Patro [Apollod.]
:– Phyleis [Apollod.]
:– Praxithea³ [Apollod.]
:– Procris² [Apollod.]
:– Pyrippe [Apollod.]
:– Stratonice³ [Apollod.]
:– Terpsicrate [Apollod.]
:– Tiphyse [Apollod.]
:– Toxicrate [Apollod.]
Laomenes [Apollod.]
Threpsippas [Apollod.]
Archemachus² [Apollod.]
Tigasus [Apollod.]
Nephus [Apollod.]
Antileon [Apollod.]
Hippeus [Apollod.]
Patroclus² [Apollod.]
Atromus [Apollod.]
Euryopes [Apollod.]
Lyncaeus [Apollod.]
Lycurgus² [Apollod.]

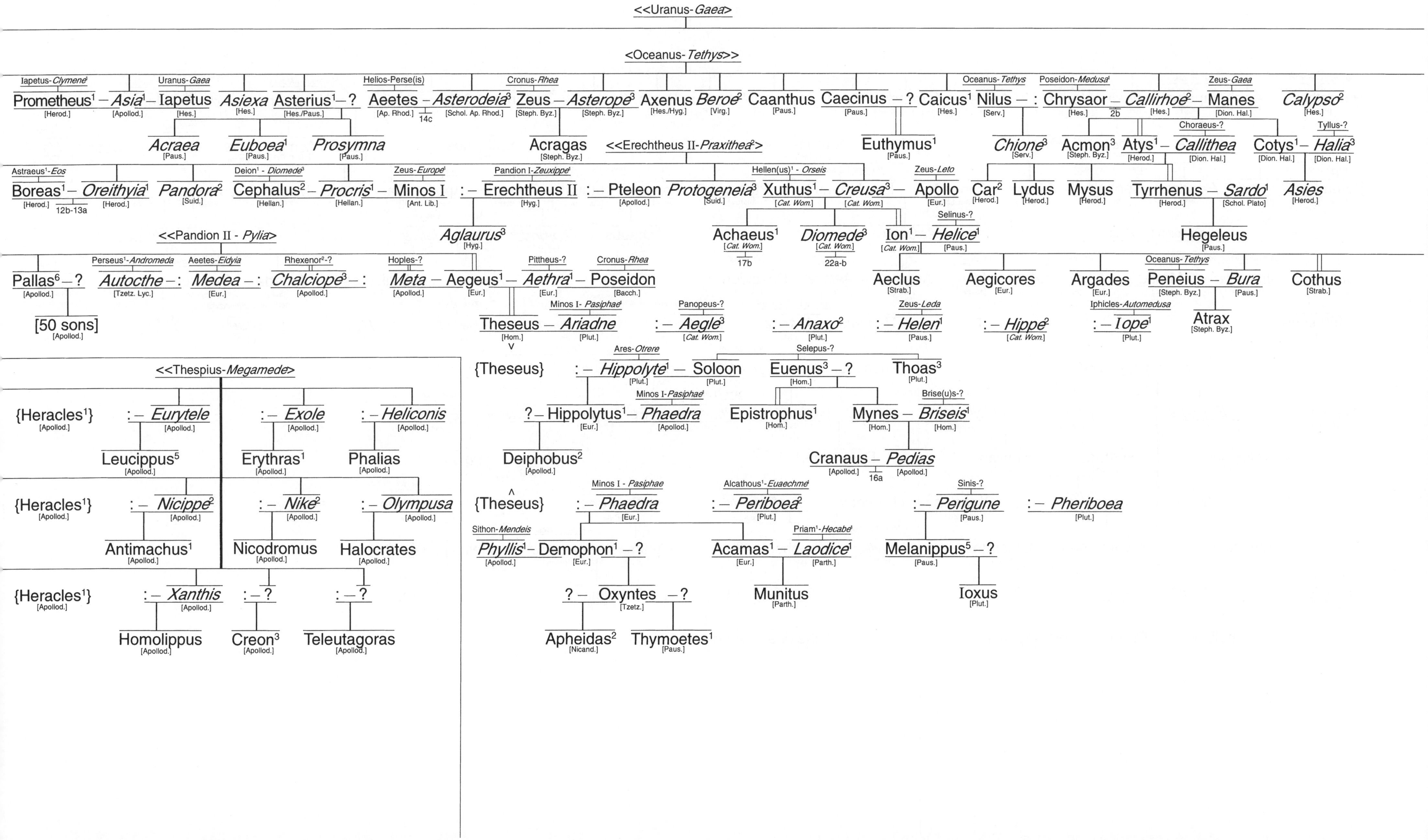
<<Uranus-Gaea>
<Oceanus-Tethys>>
Iapetus-Clymene[1]
Uranus-Gaea
Helios-Perse(is)
Cronus-Rhea
Oceanus-Tethys
Poseidon-Medusa[1]
Zeus-Gaea
Prometheus[1] – Asia[1] – Iapetus
[Herod.] [Apollod.] [Hes.]
Asiexa [Hes.]
Asterius[1] – ? [Hes./Paus.]
Aeetes – Asterodeia[3]
[Ap. Rhod.] 14c [Schol. Ap. Rhod.]
Zeus – Asterope[3]
[Steph. Byz.] [Steph. Byz.]
Axenus [Hes./Hyg.]
Beroe[2] [Virg.]
Caanthus [Paus.]
Caecinus – ? [Paus.]
Caicus[1] [Hes.]
Nilus – : [Serv.]
Chrysaor – Callirhoe[2] – Manes
[Hes.] 2b [Hes.] [Dion. Hal.]
Calypso[2] [Hes.]
Acraea [Paus.]
Euboea[1] [Paus.]
Prosymna [Paus.]
Acragas [Steph. Byz.]
<<Erechtheus II-Praxithea[2]>
Euthymus[1] [Paus.]
Chione[3] [Serv.]
Acmon[3] [Steph. Byz.]
Choraeus-?
Atys[1] – Callithea
[Herod.] [Dion. Hal.]
Tyllus-?
Cotys[1] – Halia[3]
[Dion. Hal.] [Dion. Hal.]
Astraeus[1]-Eos
Deion[1] - Diomede[3]
Zeus-Europe[1]
Pandion I-Zeuxippe[1]
Hellen(us)[1] - Orseis
Zeus-Leto
Boreas[1] – Oreithyia[1]
[Herod.] 12b-13a [Herod.]
Pandora[2] [Suid.]
Cephalus[2] – Procris[1] – Minos I
[Hellan.] [Hellan.] [Ant. Lib.]
: – Erechtheus II [Hyg.]
: – Pteleon [Apollod.]
Protogeneia[3] [Suid.]
Xuthus[1] – Creusa[3] – Apollo
[Cat. Wom.] [Cat. Wom.] [Eur.]
Car[2] [Herod.]
Lydus [Herod.]
Mysus [Herod.]
Tyrrhenus – Sardo[1]
[Herod.] [Schol. Plato]
Asies [Herod.]
<<Pandion II - Pylia>
Aglaurus[3] [Hyg.]
Achaeus[1] [Cat. Wom.] 17b
Diomede[3] [Cat. Wom.] 22a-b
Selinus-?
Ion[1] – Helice[1]
[Cat. Wom.] [Paus.]
Hegeleus [Paus.]
Perseus[1]-Andromeda
Aeetes-Eidyia
Rhexenor[2]-?
Hoples-?
Pittheus-?
Cronus-Rhea
Oceanus-Tethys
Pallas[6] – ? [Apollod.]
Autocthe – : [Tzetz. Lyc.]
Medea – : [Eur.]
Chalciope[3] – : [Apollod.]
Meta – Aegeus[1] – Aethra[1] – Poseidon
[Apollod.] [Eur.] [Eur.] [Bacch.]
Aeclus [Strab.]
Aegicores [Eur.]
Argades [Eur.]
Peneius – Bura
[Steph. Byz.] [Paus.]
Cothus [Strab.]
[50 sons] [Apollod.]
Minos I- Pasiphae[1]
Panopeus-?
Zeus-Leda
Iphicles-Automedusa
Theseus – Ariadne
[Hom.] [Plut.]
: – Aegle[3] [Cat. Wom.]
: – Anaxo[2] [Plut.]
: – Helen[1] [Paus.]
: – Hippe[2] [Cat. Wom.]
: – Iope[1] [Plut.]
Atrax [Steph. Byz.]
<<Thespius-Megamede>
Ares-Otrere
Selepus-?
{Theseus}
: – Hippolyte[1] – Soloon
[Plut.] [Plut.]
Euenus[3] – ? [Hom.]
Thoas[3] [Plut.]
Minos I-Pasiphae[1]
Brise(u)s-?
{Heracles[1]} [Apollod.]
: – Eurytele [Apollod.]
: – Exole [Apollod.]
: – Heliconis [Apollod.]
? – Hippolytus[1] – Phaedra
[Eur.] [Apollod.]
Epistrophus[1] [Hom.]
Mynes – Briseis[1]
[Hom.] [Hom.]
Leucippus[5] [Apollod.]
Erythras[1] [Apollod.]
Phalias [Apollod.]
Deiphobus[2] [Apollod.]
Cranaus – Pedias
[Apollod.] 16a [Apollod.]
Minos I - Pasiphae
Alcathous[1]-Euaechme[1]
Sinis-?
{Heracles[1]} [Apollod.]
: – Nicippe[2] [Apollod.]
: – Nike[2] [Apollod.]
: – Olympusa [Apollod.]
{Theseus}
: – Phaedra [Eur.]
: – Periboea[2] [Plut.]
: – Perigune [Paus.]
: – Pheriboea [Plut.]
Sithon-Mendeis
Priam[1]-Hecabe[1]
Antimachus[1] [Apollod.]
Nicodromus [Apollod.]
Halocrates [Apollod.]
Phyllis[1] – Demophon[1] – ?
[Apollod.] [Eur.]
Acamas[1] – Laodice[1]
[Eur.] [Parth.]
Melanippus[5] – ? [Paus.]
{Heracles[1]} [Apollod.]
: – Xanthis [Apollod.]
: – ?
: – ?
? – Oxyntes – ? [Tzetz.]
Munitus [Parth.]
Ioxus [Plut.]
Homolippus [Apollod.]
Creon[3] [Apollod.]
Teleutagoras [Apollod.]
Apheidas[2] [Nicand.]
Thymoetes[1] [Paus.]

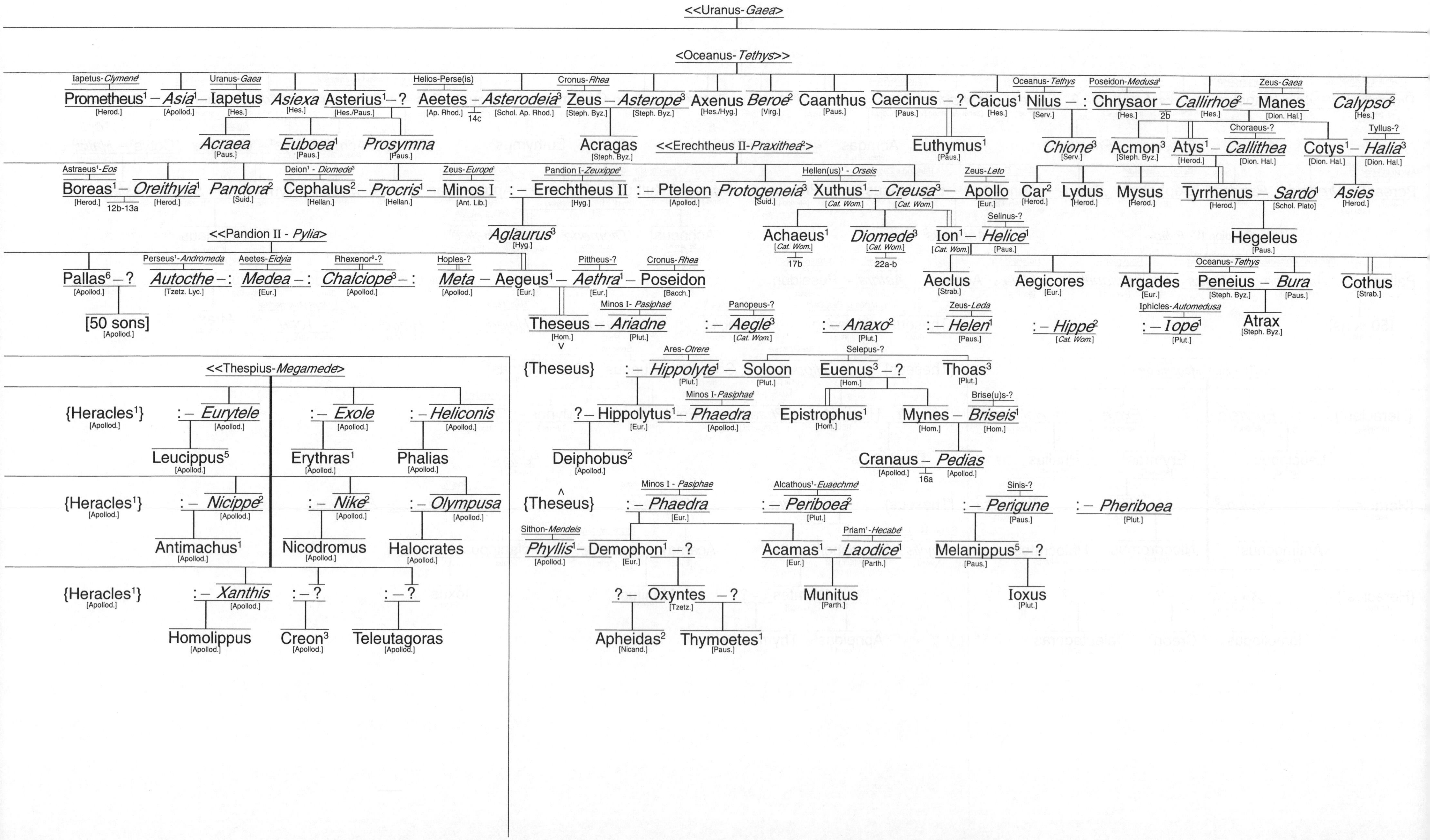

<<Uranus-Gaea>
<Oceanus-Tethys>>
Iapetus-Clymene
Prometheus[1] – Asia[1] – Iapetus
[Herod.] [Apollod.] [Hes.]
Uranus-Gaea
Asiexa [Hes.]
Asterius[1] – ? [Hes./Paus.]
Helios-Perse(is)
Aeetes – Asterodeia[3] [Ap. Rhod.] [Schol. Ap. Rhod.]
14c
Cronus-Rhea
Zeus – Asterope[3] [Steph. Byz.] [Steph. Byz.]
Axenus [Hes./Hyg.]
Beroe[2] [Virg.]
Caanthus [Paus.]
Caecinus – ? [Paus.]
Caicus[1] [Hes.]
Oceanus-Tethys
Nilus – : [Serv.]
Poseidon-Medusa
Chrysaor – Callirhoe[2] – Manes [Hes.] [Hes.] [Dion. Hal.]
2b
Zeus-Gaea
Calypso[2] [Hes.]
Acraea [Paus.]
Euboea[1] [Paus.]
Prosymna [Paus.]
Acragas [Steph. Byz.]
<<Erechtheus II-Praxithea[2]>
Euthymus[1] [Paus.]
Chione[3] [Serv.]
Acmon[3] [Steph. Byz.]
Choraeus-?
Atys[1] – Callithea [Herod.] [Dion. Hal.]
Tyllus-?
Cotys[1] – Halia[3] [Dion. Hal.] [Dion. Hal.]
Astraeus[1]-Eos
Boreas[1] – Oreithyia[1] [Herod.] [Herod.]
12b-13a
Pandora[2] [Suid.]
Deion[1] - Diomede[3]
Cephalus[2] – Procris[1] – [Hellan.] [Hellan.]
Zeus-Europe
Minos I [Ant. Lib.]
Pandion I-Zeuxippe
: – Erechtheus II [Hyg.]
: – Pteleon [Apollod.]
Protogeneia[3] [Suid.]
Hellen(us)[1] - Orseis
Xuthus[1] – Creusa[3] – [Cat. Wom.] [Cat. Wom.]
Zeus-Leto
Apollo [Eur.]
Car[2] [Herod.]
Lydus [Herod.]
Mysus [Herod.]
Tyrrhenus – Sardo[1] [Herod.] [Schol. Plato]
Asies [Herod.]
Aglaurus[3] [Hyg.]
<<Pandion II - Pylia>
Achaeus[1] [Cat. Wom.]
17b
Diomede[3] [Cat. Wom.]
22a-b
Selinus-?
Ion[1] – Helice[1] [Cat. Wom.] [Paus.]
Hegeleus [Paus.]
Pallas[6] – ? [Apollod.]
Perseus[1]-Andromeda
Autocthe – : [Tzetz. Lyc.]
Aeetes-Eidyia
Medea – : [Eur.]
Rhexenor[2]-?
Chalciope[3] – : [Apollod.]
Hoples-?
Meta – Aegeus[1] – [Apollod.] [Eur.]
Pittheus-?
Aethra[1] – [Eur.]
Cronus-Rhea
Poseidon [Bacch.]
Aeclus [Strab.]
Aegicores [Eur.]
Argades [Eur.]
Oceanus-Tethys
Peneius – Bura [Steph. Byz.] [Paus.]
Cothus [Strab.]
[50 sons] [Apollod.]
Minos I- Pasiphae
Theseus – Ariadne [Hom.] [Plut.]
v
Panopeus-?
: – Aegle[3] [Cat. Wom.]
: – Anaxo[2] [Plut.]
Zeus-Leda
: – Helen[1] [Paus.]
: – Hippe[2] [Cat. Wom.]
Iphicles-Automedusa
: – Iope[1] [Plut.]
Atrax [Steph. Byz.]
<<Thespius-Megamede>
{Theseus}
Ares-Otrere
: – Hippolyte[1] – Soloon [Plut.] [Plut.]
Selepus-?
Euenus[3] – ? [Hom.]
Thoas[3] [Plut.]
{Heracles[1]} [Apollod.]
: – Eurytele [Apollod.]
: – Exole [Apollod.]
: – Heliconis [Apollod.]
Minos I-Pasiphae
? – Hippolytus[1] – Phaedra [Eur.] [Apollod.]
Epistrophus[1] [Hom.]
Brise(u)s-?
Mynes – Briseis[1] [Hom.] [Hom.]
Leucippus[5] [Apollod.]
Erythras[1] [Apollod.]
Phalias [Apollod.]
Deiphobus[2] [Apollod.]
Cranaus – Pedias [Apollod.] [Apollod.]
16a
^
{Heracles[1]} [Apollod.]
: – Nicippe[2] [Apollod.]
: – Nike[2] [Apollod.]
: – Olympusa [Apollod.]
{Theseus}
Minos I - Pasiphae
: – Phaedra [Eur.]
Alcathous[1]-Euaechme
: – Periboea[2] [Plut.]
Sinis-?
: – Perigune [Paus.]
: – Pheriboea [Plut.]
Antimachus[1] [Apollod.]
Nicodromus [Apollod.]
Halocrates [Apollod.]
Sithon-Mendeis
Phyllis[1] – Demophon[1] – ? [Apollod.] [Eur.]
Priam[1]-Hecabe
Acamas[1] – Laodice[1] [Eur.] [Parth.]
Melanippus[5] – ? [Paus.]
{Heracles[1]} [Apollod.]
: – Xanthis [Apollod.]
: – ?
: – ?
? – Oxyntes – ? [Tzetz.]
Munitus [Parth.]
Ioxus [Plut.]
Homolippus [Apollod.]
Creon[3] [Apollod.]
Teleutagoras [Apollod.]
Apheidas[2] [Nicand.]
Thymoetes[1] [Paus.]

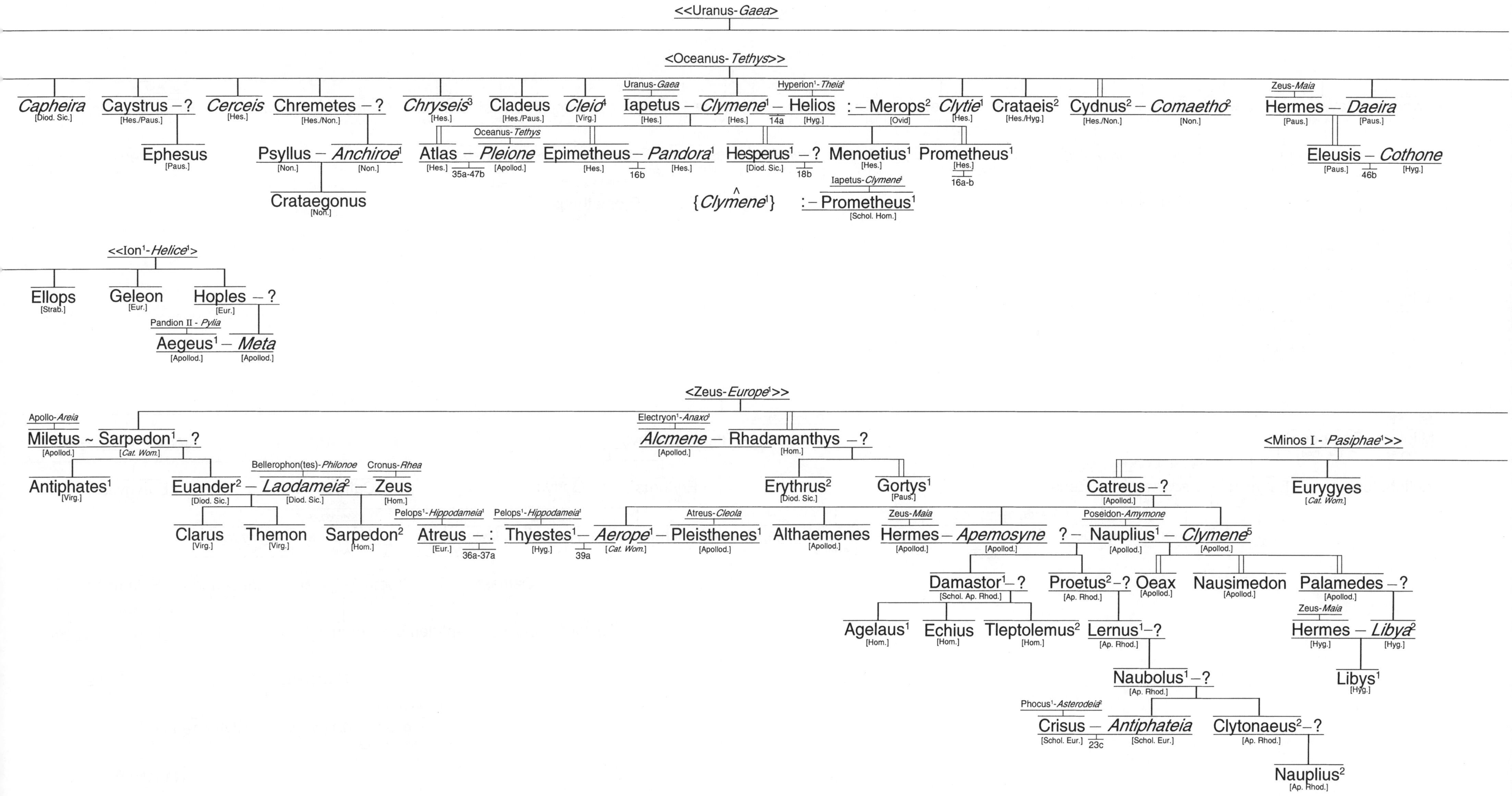

<<Uranus-Gaea>
<Oceanus-Tethys>>
Capheira [Diod. Sic.]
Caystrus – ? [Hes./Paus.]
Ephesus [Paus.]
Cerceis [Hes.]
Chremetes – ? [Hes./Non.]
Psyllus – Anchiroe¹ [Non.] [Non.]
Crataegonus [Non.]
Chryseis³ [Hes.]
Cladeus [Hes./Paus.]
Cleio⁴ [Virg.]
Uranus-Gaea
Iapetus – Clymene¹ [Hes.] [Hes.]
Hyperion¹-Theia¹
– Helios 14a [Hyg.]
: – Merops² [Ovid]
Clytie¹ [Hes.]
Crataeis² [Hes./Hyg.]
Cydnus² – Comaetho² [Hes./Non.] [Non.]
Zeus-Maia
Hermes – Daeira [Paus.] [Paus.]
Eleusis – Cothone [Paus.] 46b [Hyg.]
Oceanus-Tethys
Atlas – Pleione [Hes.] 35a-47b [Apollod.]
Epimetheus – Pandora¹ [Hes.] 16b [Hes.]
Hesperus¹ – ? [Diod. Sic.] 18b
{Clymene¹}
Menoetius¹ [Hes.]
Prometheus¹ [Hes.] 16a-b
Iapetus-Clymene¹
: – Prometheus¹ [Schol. Hom.]
<<Ion¹-Helice¹>
Ellops [Strab.]
Geleon [Eur.]
Hoples – ? [Eur.]
Pandion II - Pylia
Aegeus¹ – Meta [Apollod.] [Apollod.]
<Zeus-Europe¹>>
Apollo-Areia
Miletus ~ Sarpedon¹ – ? [Apollod.] [Cat. Wom.]
Antiphates¹ [Virg.]
Bellerophon(tes)-Philonoe
Cronus-Rhea
Euander² – Laodameia² – Zeus [Diod. Sic.] [Diod. Sic.] [Hom.]
Clarus [Virg.]
Themon [Virg.]
Sarpedon² [Hom.]
Pelops¹-Hippodameia¹
Atreus – : [Eur.] 36a-37a
Pelops¹-Hippodameia¹
Thyestes¹ – Aerope¹ – Pleisthenes¹ [Hyg.] 39a [Cat. Wom.] [Apollod.]
Atreus-Cleola
Electryon¹-Anaxo¹
Alcmene – Rhadamanthys – ? [Apollod.] [Hom.]
Erythrus² [Diod. Sic.]
Gortys¹ [Paus.]
<Minos I - Pasiphae¹>>
Catreus – ? [Apollod.]
Eurygyes [Cat. Wom.]
Althaemenes [Apollod.]
Zeus-Maia
Hermes – Apemosyne [Apollod.] [Apollod.]
Poseidon-Amymone
? – Nauplius¹ – Clymene⁵ [Apollod.] [Apollod.]
Damastor¹ – ? [Schol. Ap. Rhod.]
Proetus² – ? [Ap. Rhod.]
Oeax [Apollod.]
Nausimedon [Apollod.]
Palamedes – ? [Apollod.]
Agelaus¹ [Hom.]
Echius [Hom.]
Tleptolemus² [Hom.]
Lernus¹ – ? [Ap. Rhod.]
Zeus-Maia
Hermes – Libya² [Hyg.] [Hyg.]
Libys¹ [Hyg.]
Naubolus¹ – ? [Ap. Rhod.]
Phocus¹-Asterodeia²
Crisus – Antiphateia [Schol. Eur.] 23c [Schol. Eur.]
Clytonaeus² – ? [Ap. Rhod.]
Nauplius² [Ap. Rhod.]

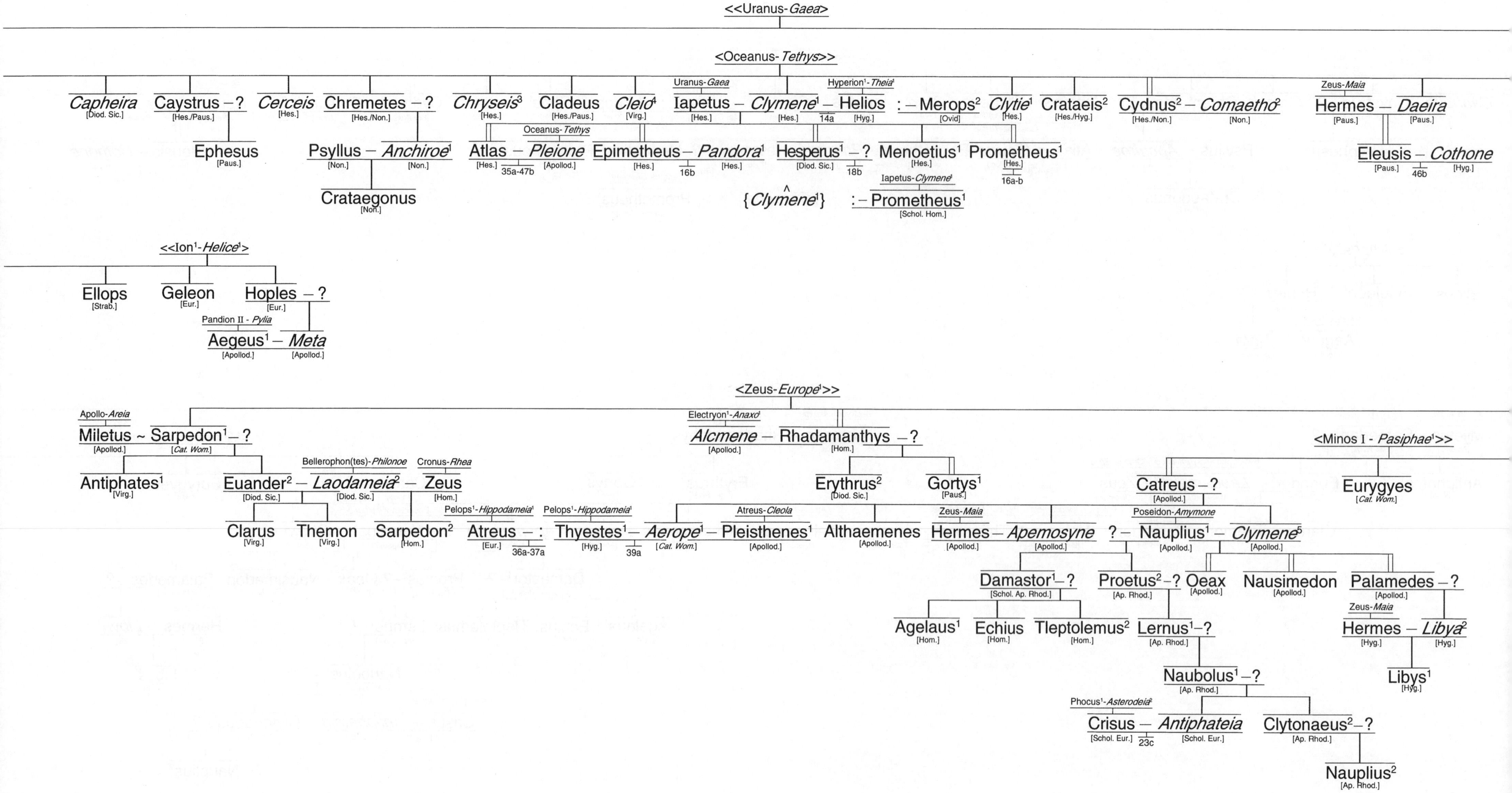
<<Uranus-Gaea>
<Oceanus-Tethys>>
Capheira [Diod. Sic.]
Caystrus – ? [Hes./Paus.]
Ephesus [Paus.]
Cerceis [Hes.]
Chremetes – ? [Hes./Non.]
Psyllus – Anchiroe[1] [Non.] [Non.]
Crataegonus [Non.]
Chryseis[3] [Hes.]
Cladeus [Hes./Paus.]
Cleio[4] [Virg.]
Uranus-Gaea
Iapetus – Clymene[1] – Helios [Hes.] [Hes.] 14a [Hyg.]
Hyperion[1]-Theia[1]
:– Merops[2] [Ovid]
Clytie[1] [Hes.]
Crataeis[2] [Hes./Hyg.]
Cydnus[2] – Comaetho[2] [Hes./Non.] [Non.]
Zeus-Maia
Hermes – Daeira [Paus.] [Paus.]
Eleusis – Cothone [Paus.] 46b [Hyg.]
Oceanus-Tethys
Atlas – Pleione [Hes.] 35a-47b [Apollod.]
Epimetheus – Pandora[1] [Hes.] 16b [Hes.]
Hesperus[1] – ? [Diod. Sic.] 18b
Menoetius[1] [Hes.]
Prometheus[1] [Hes.] 16a-b
^
{Clymene[1]}
Iapetus-Clymene[1]
:– Prometheus[1] [Schol. Hom.]
<<Ion[1]-Helice[1]>
Ellops [Strab.]
Geleon [Eur.]
Hoples – ? [Eur.]
Pandion II - Pylia
Aegeus[1] – Meta [Apollod.] [Apollod.]
<Zeus-Europe[1]>>
Apollo-Areia
Miletus ~ Sarpedon[1] – ? [Apollod.] [Cat. Wom.]
Antiphates[1] [Virg.]
Bellerophon(tes)-Philonoe
Cronus-Rhea
Euander[2] – Laodameia[2] – Zeus [Diod. Sic.] [Diod. Sic.] [Hom.]
Clarus [Virg.]
Themon [Virg.]
Sarpedon[2] [Hom.]
Pelops[1]-Hippodameia[1]
Atreus – : [Eur.] 36a-37a
Pelops[1]-Hippodameia[1]
Thyestes[1] – Aerope[1] – Pleisthenes[1] [Hyg.] 39a [Cat. Wom.] [Apollod.]
Atreus-Cleola
Electryon[1]-Anaxo[1]
Alcmene – Rhadamanthys – ? [Apollod.] [Hom.]
Erythrus[2] [Diod. Sic.]
Gortys[1] [Paus.]
Althaemenes [Apollod.]
Zeus-Maia
Hermes – Apemosyne [Apollod.] [Apollod.]
<Minos I - Pasiphae[1]>>
Catreus – ? [Apollod.]
Eurygyes [Cat. Wom.]
Poseidon-Amymone
? – Nauplius[1] – Clymene[5] [Apollod.] [Apollod.]
Damastor[1] – ? [Schol. Ap. Rhod.]
Agelaus[1] [Hom.]
Echius [Hom.]
Tleptolemus[2] [Hom.]
Proetus[2] – ? [Ap. Rhod.]
Lernus[1] – ? [Ap. Rhod.]
Naubolus[1] – ? [Ap. Rhod.]
Phocus[1]-Asterodeia[2]
Crisus – Antiphateia [Schol. Eur.] 23c [Schol. Eur.]
Clytonaeus[2] – ? [Ap. Rhod.]
Nauplius[2] [Ap. Rhod.]
Oeax [Apollod.]
Nausimedon [Apollod.]
Palamedes – ? [Apollod.]
Zeus-Maia
Hermes – Libya[2] [Hyg.] [Hyg.]
Libys[1] [Hyg.]

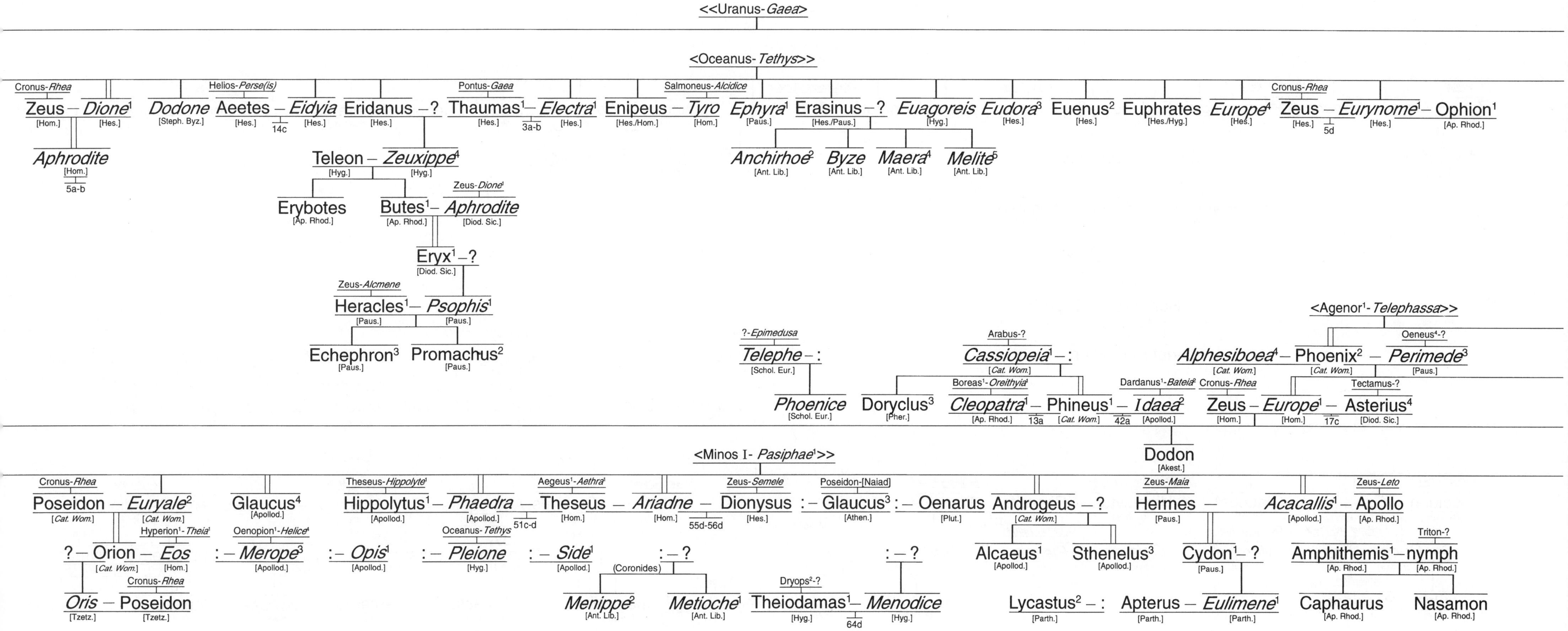

<<Uranus-Gaea>
<Oceanus-Tethys>>
Cronus-Rhea
Zeus – Dione[1]
[Hom.] [Hes.]
Aphrodite
[Hom.]
5a-b
Dodone
[Steph. Byz.]
Helios-Perse(is)
Aeetes – Eidyia
[Hes.] 14c [Hes.]
Eridanus – ?
[Hes.]
Teleon – Zeuxippe[4]
[Hyg.] [Hyg.]
Erybotes
[Ap. Rhod.]
Zeus-Dione[1]
Butes[1] – Aphrodite
[Ap. Rhod.] [Diod. Sic.]
Eryx[1] – ?
[Diod. Sic.]
Zeus-Alcmene
Heracles[1] – Psophis[1]
[Paus.] [Paus.]
Echephron[3]
[Paus.]
Promachus[2]
[Paus.]
Pontus-Gaea
Thaumas[1] – Electra[1]
[Hes.] 3a-b [Hes.]
Enipeus – Tyro
[Hes./Hom.] [Hom.]
Salmoneus-Alcidice
Ephyra[1]
[Paus.]
Erasinus – ?
[Hes./Paus.]
Anchirhoe[2]
[Ant. Lib.]
Byze
[Ant. Lib.]
Maera[4]
[Ant. Lib.]
Melite[5]
[Ant. Lib.]
Euagoreis
[Hyg.]
Eudora[3]
[Hes.]
Euenus[2]
[Hes.]
Euphrates
[Hes./Hyg.]
Europe[4]
[Hes.]
Cronus-Rhea
Zeus – Eurynome[1] – Ophion[1]
[Hes.] 5d [Hes.] [Ap. Rhod.]
?-Epimedusa
Telephe – :
[Schol. Eur.]
Phoenice
[Schol. Eur.]
Arabus-?
Cassiopeia[1] – :
[Cat. Wom.]
Doryclus[3]
[Pher.]
Boreas[1]-Oreithyia[1]
Cleopatra[1] – Phineus[1] – Idaea[2]
[Ap. Rhod.] 13a [Cat. Wom.] 42a [Apollod.]
Dardanus[1]-Bateia[2]
<Agenor[1]-Telephassa>>
Alphesiboea[4] – Phoenix[2] – Perimede[3]
[Cat. Wom.] [Cat. Wom.] [Paus.]
Oeneus[4]-?
Cronus-Rhea
Zeus – Europe[1] – Asterius[4]
[Hom.] [Hom.] 17c [Diod. Sic.]
Tectamus-?
Dodon
[Akest.]
<Minos I- Pasiphae[1]>>
Cronus-Rhea
Poseidon – Euryale[2]
[Cat. Wom.] [Cat. Wom.]
? – Orion – Eos
[Cat. Wom.] [Hom.]
Hyperion[1]-Theia[1]
Cronus-Rhea
Oris – Poseidon
[Tzetz.] [Tzetz.]
Glaucus[4]
[Apollod.]
Oenopion[1]-Helice[4]
: – Merope[3]
[Apollod.]
: – Opis[1]
[Apollod.]
Theseus-Hippolyte[1]
Hippolytus[1] – Phaedra – Theseus – Ariadne – Dionysus
[Apollod.] [Apollod.] 51c-d [Hom.] [Hom.] 55d-56d [Hes.]
Aegeus[1]-Aethra[1]
Zeus-Semele
Oceanus-Tethys
: – Pleione
[Hyg.]
: – Side[1]
[Apollod.]
: – ?
(Coronides)
Menippe[2]
[Ant. Lib.]
Metioche[1]
[Ant. Lib.]
Poseidon-[Naiad]
: – Glaucus[3] : – Oenarus
[Athen.] [Plut.]
Dryops[2]-?
Theiodamas[1] – Menodice
[Hyg.] 64d [Hyg.]
: – ?
Androgeus – ?
[Cat. Wom.]
Alcaeus[1]
[Apollod.]
Sthenelus[3]
[Apollod.]
Lycastus[2] – :
[Parth.]
Zeus-Maia
Hermes – Acacallis[1] – Apollo
[Paus.] [Apollod.] [Ap. Rhod.]
Zeus-Leto
Cydon[1] – ?
[Paus.]
Apterus – Eulimene[1]
[Parth.] [Parth.]
Triton-?
Amphithemis[1] – nymph
[Ap. Rhod.] [Ap. Rhod.]
Caphaurus
[Ap. Rhod.]
Nasamon
[Ap. Rhod.]

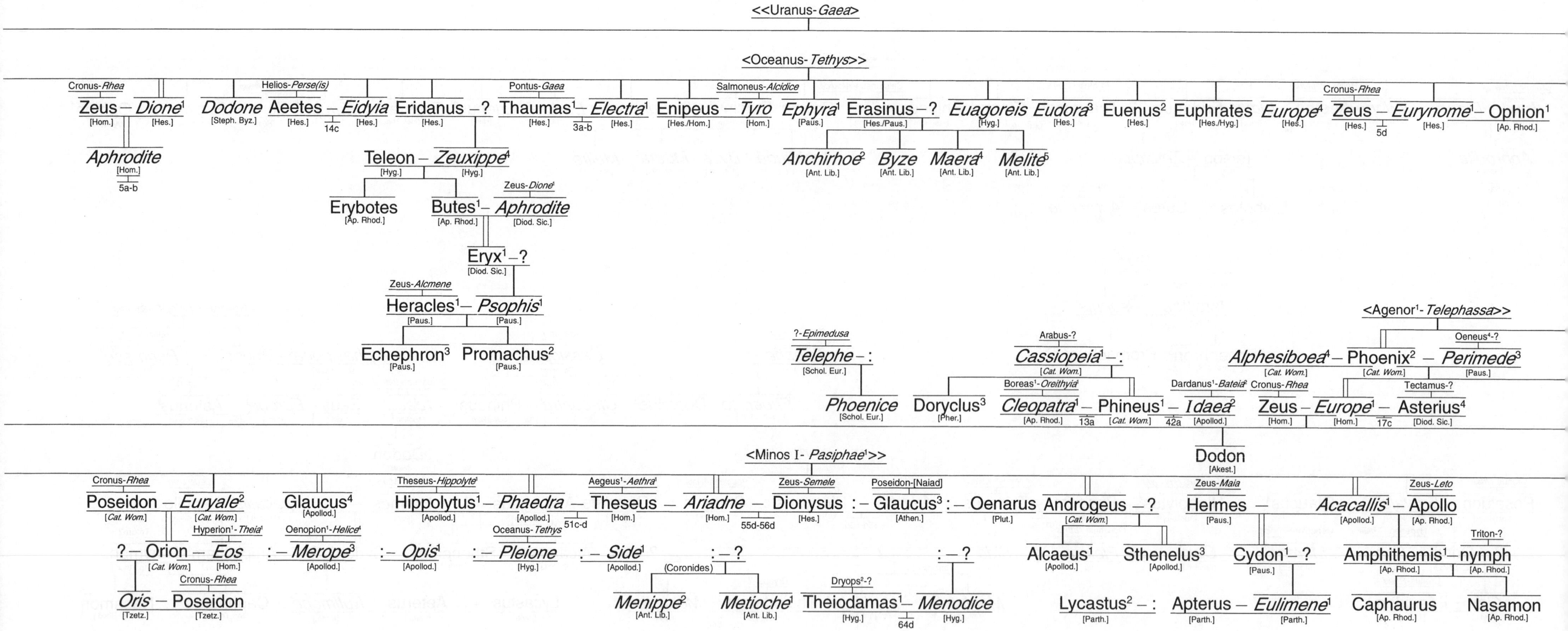

<<Uranus-*Gaea*>
<Oceanus-*Tethys*>>
Cronus-*Rhea*
Zeus – *Dione*[1]
[Hom.] [Hes.]
Aphrodite
[Hom.]
5a-b
Dodone
[Steph. Byz.]
Helios-*Perse(is)*
Aeetes – *Eidyia*
[Hes.] 14c [Hes.]
Eridanus – ?
[Hes.]
Teleon – *Zeuxippe*[4]
[Hyg.] [Hyg.]
Erybotes
[Ap. Rhod.]
Butes[1] – *Aphrodite*
[Ap. Rhod.] [Diod. Sic.]
Zeus-*Dione*[1]
Eryx[1] – ?
[Diod. Sic.]
Zeus-*Alcmene*
Heracles[1] – *Psophis*[1]
[Paus.] [Paus.]
Echephron[3] Promachus[2]
[Paus.] [Paus.]
Pontus-*Gaea*
Thaumas[1] – *Electra*[1]
[Hes.] 3a-b [Hes.]
Salmoneus-*Alcidice*
Enipeus – *Tyro*
[Hes./Hom.] [Hom.]
Ephyra[1]
[Paus.]
Erasinus – ?
[Hes./Paus.]
Anchirhoe[2] *Byze* *Maera*[4] *Melite*[5]
[Ant. Lib.] [Ant. Lib.] [Ant. Lib.] [Ant. Lib.]
Euagoreis
[Hyg.]
Eudora[3]
[Hes.]
Euenus[2]
[Hes.]
Euphrates
[Hes./Hyg.]
Europe[4]
[Hes.]
Cronus-*Rhea*
Zeus – *Eurynome*[1] – Ophion[1]
[Hes.] 5d [Hes.] [Ap. Rhod.]
<Agenor[1]-*Telephassa*>>
?-*Epimedusa*
Telephe – :
[Schol. Eur.]
Phoenice
[Schol. Eur.]
Arabus-?
Cassiopeia[1] – :
[Cat. Wom.]
Doryclus[3]
[Pher.]
Boreas[1]-*Oreithyia*
Cleopatra[1] – Phineus[1] – *Idaea*[2]
[Ap. Rhod.] 13a [Cat. Wom.] 42a [Apollod.]
Dardanus[1]-*Bateia*[2]
Oeneus[4]-?
Alphesiboea[4] – Phoenix[2] – *Perimede*[3]
[Cat. Wom.] [Cat. Wom.] [Paus.]
Cronus-*Rhea*
Zeus – *Europe*[1] – Asterius[4]
[Hom.] [Hom.] 17c [Diod. Sic.]
Tectamus-?
Dodon
[Akest.]
<Minos I- *Pasiphae*[1]>>
Cronus-*Rhea*
Poseidon – *Euryale*[2]
[Cat. Wom.] [Cat. Wom.]
Hyperion[1]-*Theia*[1]
? – Orion – *Eos*
[Cat. Wom.] [Hom.]
Cronus-*Rhea*
Oris – Poseidon
[Tzetz.] [Tzetz.]
Glaucus[4]
[Apollod.]
Oenopion[1]-*Helice*[4]
: – *Merope*[3]
[Apollod.]
Theseus-*Hippolyte*[1]
Hippolytus[1] – *Phaedra* – Theseus – *Ariadne* – Dionysus : – Glaucus[3] : – Oenarus
[Apollod.] [Apollod.] 51c-d [Hom.] [Hom.] 55d-56d [Hes.] [Athen.] [Plut.]
Aegeus[1]-*Aethra*[1]
Zeus-*Semele*
Poseidon-[Naiad]
: – *Opis*[1]
[Apollod.]
Oceanus-*Tethys*
: – *Pleione*
[Hyg.]
: – *Side*[1]
[Apollod.]
: – ?
(Coronides)
Menippe[2] *Metioche*[1]
[Ant. Lib.] [Ant. Lib.]
Dryops[2]-?
Theiodamas[1] – *Menodice*
[Hyg.] 64d [Hyg.]
: – ?
Androgeus – ?
[Cat. Wom.]
Alcaeus[1] Sthenelus[3]
[Apollod.] [Apollod.]
Lycastus[2] – :
[Parth.]
Zeus-*Maia*
Hermes –
[Paus.]
Cydon[1] – ?
[Paus.]
Apterus – *Eulimene*[1]
[Parth.] [Parth.]
Zeus-*Leto*
Acacallis[1] – Apollo
[Apollod.] [Ap. Rhod.]
Triton-?
Amphithemis[1] – nymph
[Ap. Rhod.] [Ap. Rhod.]
Caphaurus Nasamon
[Ap. Rhod.] [Ap. Rhod.]

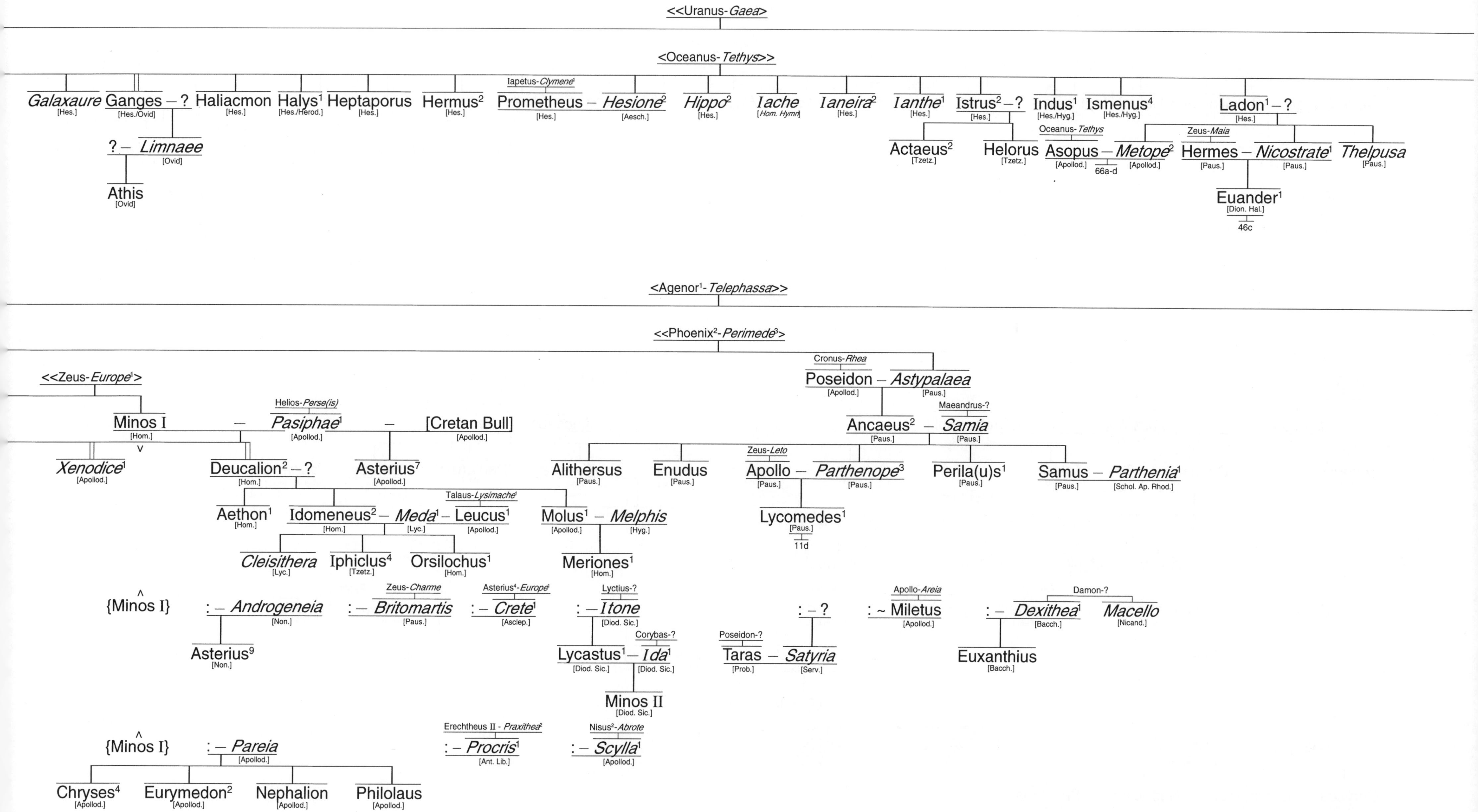
<<Uranus-*Gaea*>>
<Oceanus-*Tethys*>>
Galaxaure [Hes.]
Ganges – ? [Hes./Ovid]
? – *Limnaee* [Ovid]
Athis [Ovid]
Haliacmon [Hes.]
Halys[1] [Hes./Herod.]
Heptaporus [Hes.]
Hermus[2] [Hes.]
Iapetus-*Clymene*[1]
Prometheus [Hes.] – *Hesione*[2] [Aesch.]
Hippo[2] [Hes.]
Iache [Hom. Hymn]
Ianeira[2] [Hes.]
Ianthe[1] [Hes.]
Istrus[2] – ? [Hes.]
Actaeus[2] [Tzetz.]
Helorus [Tzetz.]
Indus[1] [Hes./Hyg.]
Ismenus[4] [Hes./Hyg.]
Oceanus-*Tethys*
Asopus [Apollod.] – *Metope*[2] [Apollod.]
66a-d
Ladon[1] – ? [Hes.]
Zeus-*Maia*
Hermes [Paus.] – *Nicostrate*[1] [Paus.]
Thelpusa [Paus.]
Euander[1] [Dion. Hal.]
46c
<Agenor[1]-*Telephassa*>>
<<Phoenix[2]-*Perimede*[3]>
<<Zeus-*Europe*[1]>
Minos I [Hom.]
Helios-*Perse(is)*
– *Pasiphae*[1] [Apollod.] – [Cretan Bull] [Apollod.]
Xenodice[1] [Apollod.]
Deucalion[2] – ? [Hom.]
Asterius[7] [Apollod.]
Aethon[1] [Hom.]
Idomeneus[2] [Hom.] – *Meda*[1] [Lyc.]
Talaus-*Lysimache*[1]
– Leucus[1] [Apollod.]
Molus[1] [Apollod.] – *Melphis* [Hyg.]
Cleisithera [Lyc.]
Iphiclus[4] [Tzetz.]
Orsilochus[1] [Hom.]
Meriones[1] [Hom.]
Cronus-*Rhea*
Poseidon [Apollod.] – *Astypalaea* [Paus.]
Maeandrus-?
Ancaeus[2] [Paus.] – *Samia* [Paus.]
Alithersus [Paus.]
Enudus [Paus.]
Zeus-*Leto*
Apollo [Paus.] – *Parthenope*[3] [Paus.]
Lycomedes[1] [Paus.]
11d
Perila(u)s[1] [Paus.]
Samus [Paus.] – *Parthenia*[1] [Schol. Ap. Rhod.]
{Minos I}
: – *Androgeneia* [Non.]
Asterius[9] [Non.]
Zeus-*Charme*
: – *Britomartis* [Paus.]
Asterius[4]-*Europe*[1]
: – *Crete*[1] [Asclep.]
Lyctius-?
: – *Itone* [Diod. Sic.]
Corybas-?
Lycastus[1] [Diod. Sic.] – *Ida*[1] [Diod. Sic.]
Minos II [Diod. Sic.]
Poseidon-?
Taras [Prob.] – *Satyria* [Serv.]
: – ?
Apollo-*Areia*
: ~ Miletus [Apollod.]
Damon-?
: – *Dexithea*[1] [Bacch.]
Macello [Nicand.]
Euxanthius [Bacch.]
{Minos I}
: – *Pareia* [Apollod.]
Chryses[4] [Apollod.]
Eurymedon[2] [Apollod.]
Nephalion [Apollod.]
Philolaus [Apollod.]
Erechtheus II - *Praxithea*[2]
: – *Procris*[1] [Ant. Lib.]
Nisus[2]-*Abrote*
: – *Scylla*[1] [Apollod.]

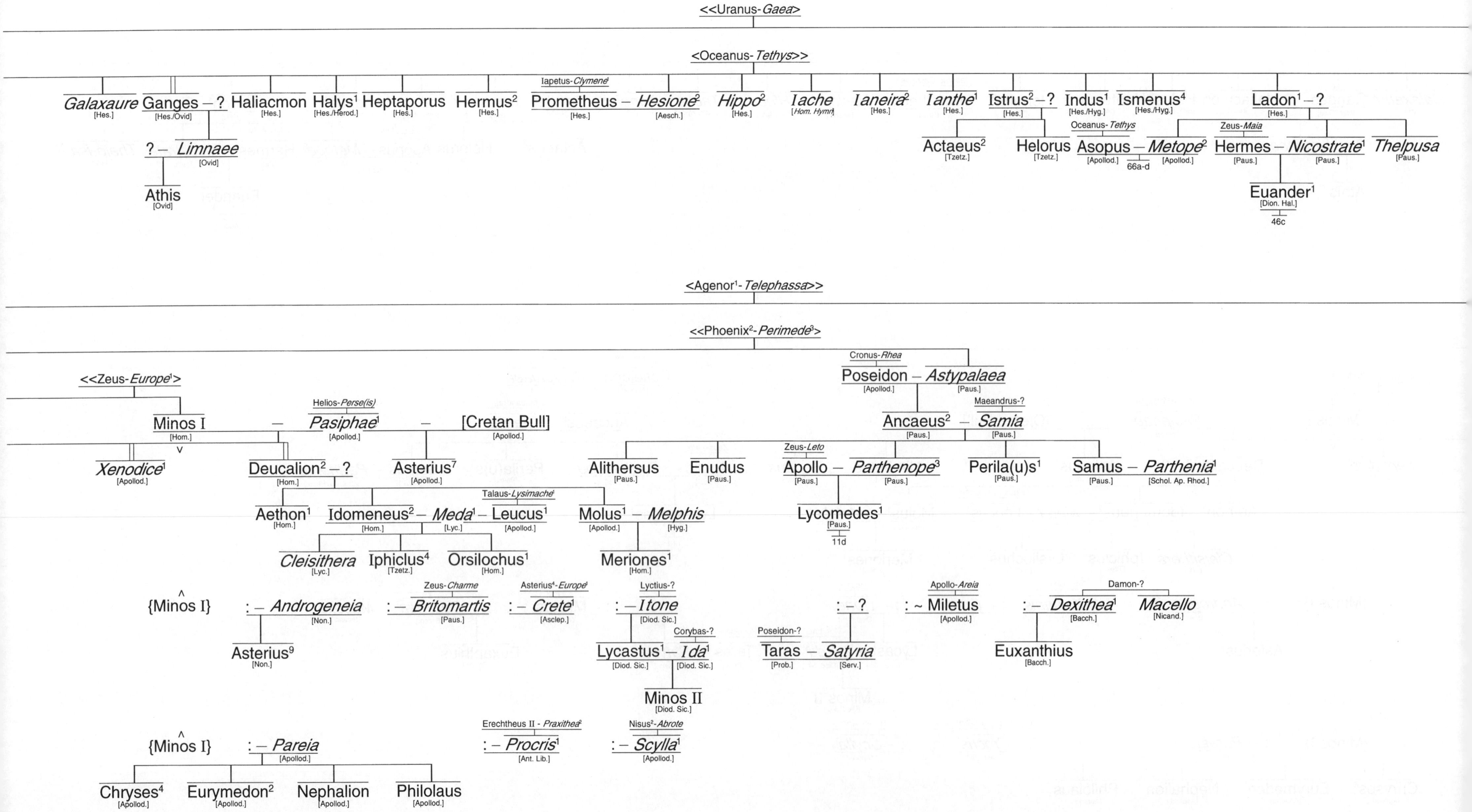

<<Uranus-Gaea>
<Oceanus-Tethys>>
Galaxaure [Hes.]
Ganges – ? [Hes./Ovid]
? – Limnaee [Ovid]
Athis [Ovid]
Haliacmon [Hes.]
Halys[1] [Hes./Herod.]
Heptaporus [Hes.]
Hermus[2] [Hes.]
Iapetus-Clymene
Prometheus [Hes.] – Hesione[2] [Aesch.]
Hippo[2] [Hes.]
Iache [Hom. Hymn]
Ianeira[2] [Hes.]
Ianthe[1] [Hes.]
Istrus[2] – ? [Hes.]
Actaeus[2] [Tzetz.]
Helorus [Tzetz.]
Indus[1] [Hes./Hyg.]
Ismenus[4] [Hes./Hyg.]
Oceanus-Tethys
Asopus [Apollod.] – Metope[2] [Apollod.]
66a-d
Ladon[1] – ? [Hes.]
Zeus-Maia
Hermes [Paus.] – Nicostrate[1] [Paus.]
Thelpusa [Paus.]
Euander[1] [Dion. Hal.]
46c
<Agenor[1]-Telephassa>>
<<Phoenix[2]-Perimede[3]>
<<Zeus-Europe[1]>
Minos I [Hom.]
Helios-Perse(is)
Pasiphae[1] [Apollod.]
[Cretan Bull] [Apollod.]
Xenodice[1] [Apollod.]
Deucalion[2] – ? [Hom.]
Asterius[7] [Apollod.]
Aethon[1] [Hom.]
Idomeneus[2] [Hom.] – Meda[1] [Lyc.] – Leucus[1] [Apollod.]
Talaus-Lysimache[1]
Molus[1] [Apollod.] – Melphis [Hyg.]
Cleisithera [Lyc.]
Iphiclus[4] [Tzetz.]
Orsilochus[1] [Hom.]
Meriones[1] [Hom.]
Cronus-Rhea
Poseidon [Apollod.] – Astypalaea [Paus.]
Maeandrus-?
Ancaeus[2] [Paus.] – Samia [Paus.]
Alithersus [Paus.]
Enudus [Paus.]
Zeus-Leto
Apollo [Paus.] – Parthenope[3] [Paus.]
Perila(u)s[1] [Paus.]
Samus [Paus.] – Parthenia[1] [Schol. Ap. Rhod.]
Lycomedes[1] [Paus.]
11d
{Minos I}
: – Androgeneia [Non.]
Asterius[9] [Non.]
Zeus-Charme
: – Britomartis [Paus.]
Asterius[4]-Europe[1]
: – Crete[1] [Asclep.]
Lyctius-?
: – Itone [Diod. Sic.]
Corybas-?
Lycastus[1] [Diod. Sic.] – Ida[1] [Diod. Sic.]
Minos II [Diod. Sic.]
: – ?
Poseidon-?
Taras [Prob.] – Satyria [Serv.]
Apollo-Areia
: ~ Miletus [Apollod.]
Damon-?
: – Dexithea[1] [Bacch.]
Macello [Nicand.]
Euxanthius [Bacch.]
{Minos I}
: – Pareia [Apollod.]
Chryses[4] [Apollod.]
Eurymedon[2] [Apollod.]
Nephalion [Apollod.]
Philolaus [Apollod.]
Erechtheus II - Praxithea[2]
: – Procris[1] [Ant. Lib.]
Nisus[2]-Abrote
: – Scylla[1] [Apollod.]

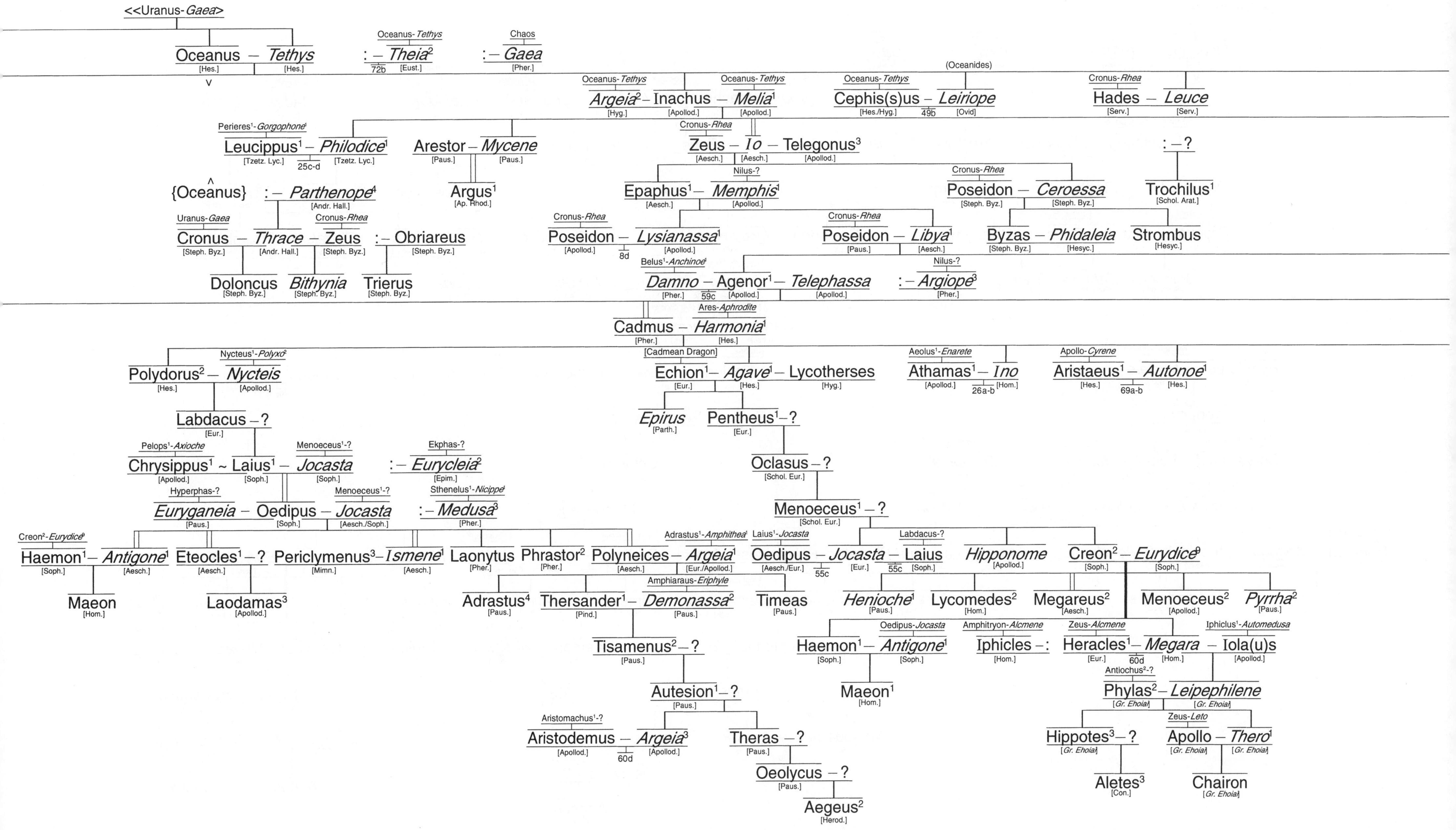

<<Uranus-Gaea>
Oceanus – Tethys [Hes.] [Hes.]
Oceanus-Tethys
: – Theia² 72b [Eust.]
Chaos
: – Gaea [Pher.]
(Oceanides)
Oceanus-Tethys
Argeia² – Inachus – Melia¹ [Hyg.] [Apollod.] [Apollod.]
Oceanus-Tethys
Oceanus-Tethys
Cephis(s)us – Leiriope [Hes./Hyg.] 49b [Ovid]
Cronus-Rhea
Hades – Leuce [Serv.] [Serv.]
Perieres¹-Gorgophone¹
Leucippus¹ – Philodice¹ [Tzetz. Lyc.] 25c-d [Tzetz. Lyc.]
Arestor – Mycene [Paus.] [Paus.]
Cronus-Rhea
Zeus – Io – Telegonus³ [Aesch.] [Aesch.] [Apollod.]
: – ?
{Oceanus}
: – Parthenope⁴ [Andr. Hall.]
Argus¹ [Ap. Rhod.]
Nilus-?
Epaphus¹ – Memphis¹ [Aesch.] [Apollod.]
Cronus-Rhea
Poseidon – Ceroessa [Steph. Byz.] [Steph. Byz.]
Trochilus¹ [Schol. Arat.]
Uranus-Gaea
Cronus-Rhea
Cronus – Thrace – Zeus : – Obriareus [Steph. Byz.] [Andr. Hall.] [Steph. Byz.] [Steph. Byz.]
Cronus-Rhea
Poseidon – Lysianassa¹ [Apollod.] 8d [Apollod.]
Cronus-Rhea
Poseidon – Libya¹ [Paus.] [Aesch.]
Byzas – Phidaleia [Steph. Byz.] [Hesyc.]
Strombus [Hesyc.]
Doloncus [Steph. Byz.]
Bithynia [Steph. Byz.]
Trierus [Steph. Byz.]
Belus¹-Anchinoe¹
Damno – Agenor¹ – Telephassa [Pher.] 59c [Apollod.] [Apollod.]
Nilus-?
: – Argiope³ [Pher.]
Ares-Aphrodite
Cadmus – Harmonia¹ [Pher.] [Hes.]
Nycteus¹-Polyxo²
Polydorus² – Nycteis [Hes.] [Apollod.]
[Cadmean Dragon]
Echion¹ – Agave¹ – Lycotherses [Eur.] [Hes.] [Hyg.]
Aeolus¹-Enarete
Athamas¹ – Ino [Apollod.] 26a-b [Hom.]
Apollo-Cyrene
Aristaeus¹ – Autonoe¹ [Hes.] 69a-b [Hes.]
Labdacus – ? [Eur.]
Epirus [Parth.]
Pentheus¹ – ? [Eur.]
Pelops¹-Axioche
Menoeceus¹-?
Chrysippus¹ ~ Laius¹ – Jocasta [Apollod.] [Soph.] [Soph.]
Ekphas-?
: – Eurycleia² [Epim.]
Oclasus – ? [Schol. Eur.]
Hyperphas-?
Menoeceus¹-?
Euryganeia – Oedipus – Jocasta [Paus.] [Soph.] [Aesch./Soph.]
Sthenelus¹-Nicippe¹
: – Medusa³ [Pher.]
Menoeceus¹ – ? [Schol. Eur.]
Creon²-Eurydice⁹
Haemon¹ – Antigone¹ [Soph.] [Aesch.]
Eteocles¹ – ? [Aesch.]
Periclymenus³ – Ismene¹ [Mimn.] [Aesch.]
Laonytus [Pher.]
Phrastor² [Pher.]
Adrastus¹-Amphithea¹
Polyneices – Argeia¹ [Aesch.] [Eur./Apollod.]
Laius¹-Jocasta
Oedipus – Jocasta – Laius [Aesch./Eur.] 55c [Eur.] 55c [Soph.]
Labdacus-?
Hipponome [Apollod.]
Creon² – Eurydice⁹ [Soph.] [Soph.]
Maeon [Hom.]
Laodamas³ [Apollod.]
Adrastus⁴ [Paus.]
Amphiaraus-Eriphyle
Thersander¹ – Demonassa² [Pind.] [Paus.]
Timeas [Paus.]
Henioche¹ [Paus.]
Lycomedes² [Hom.]
Megareus² [Aesch.]
Menoeceus² [Apollod.]
Pyrrha² [Paus.]
Oedipus-Jocasta
Haemon¹ – Antigone¹ [Soph.] [Soph.]
Amphitryon-Alcmene
Iphicles – : [Hom.]
Zeus-Alcmene
Heracles¹ – Megara [Eur.] 60d [Hom.]
Iphiclus¹-Automedusa
– Iola(u)s [Apollod.]
Tisamenus² – ? [Paus.]
Maeon¹ [Hom.]
Antiochus²-?
Phylas² – Leipephilene [Gr. Ehoiai] [Gr. Ehoiai]
Autesion¹ – ? [Paus.]
Aristomachus¹-?
Aristodemus – Argeia³ [Apollod.] 60d [Apollod.]
Theras – ? [Paus.]
Hippotes³ – ? [Gr. Ehoiai]
Zeus-Leto
Apollo – Thero¹ [Gr. Ehoiai] [Gr. Ehoiai]
Oeolycus – ? [Paus.]
Aletes³ [Con.]
Chairon [Gr. Ehoiai]
Aegeus² [Herod.]

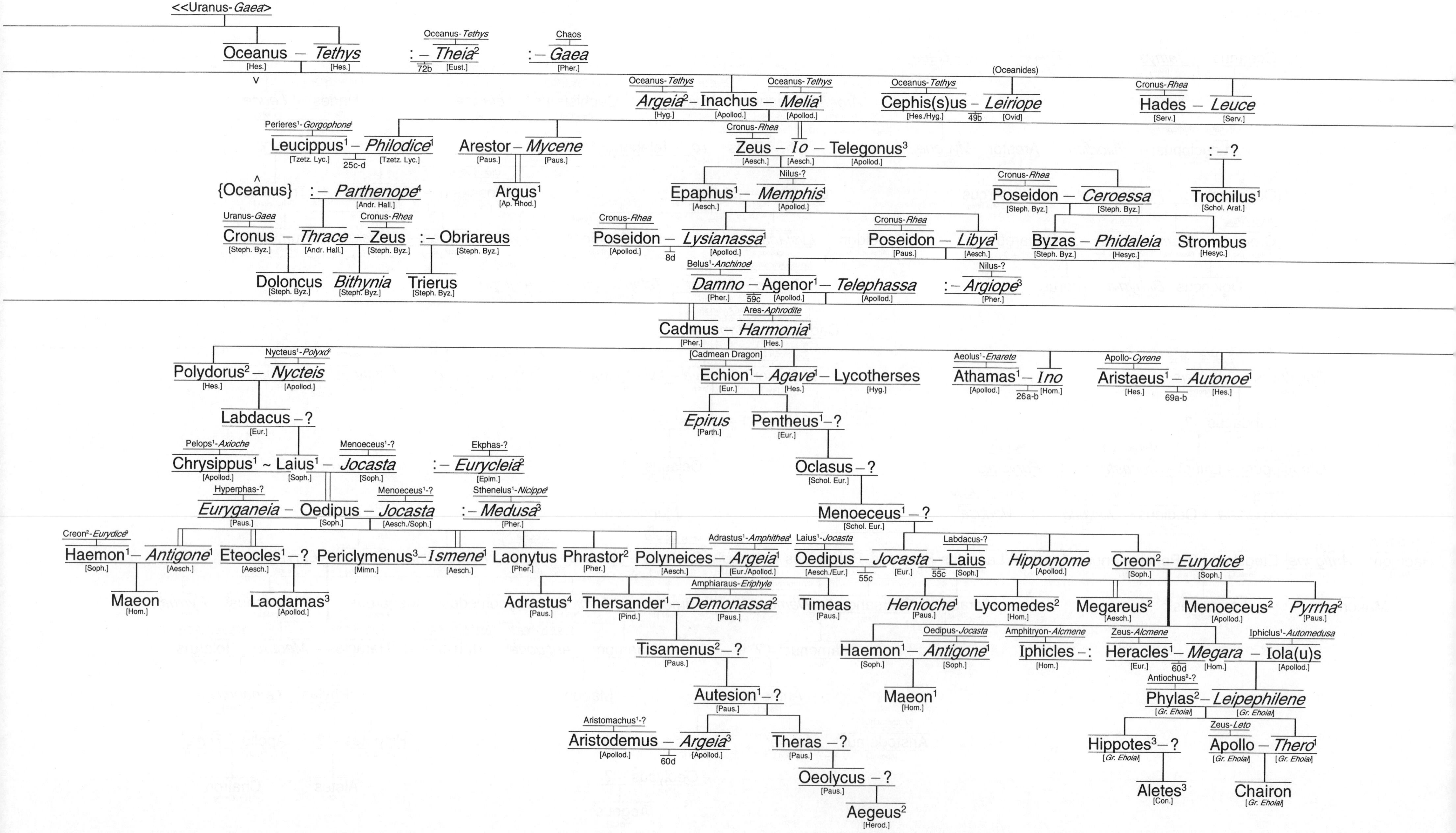

<<Uranus-Gaea>
Oceanus – Tethys
[Hes.] [Hes.]
Oceanus-Tethys
: – Theia[2]
72b [Eust.]
Chaos
: – Gaea
[Pher.]
(Oceanides)
Oceanus-Tethys
Argeia[2] – Inachus – Melia[1]
[Hyg.] [Apollod.] [Apollod.]
Oceanus-Tethys
Cephis(s)us – Leiriope
[Hes./Hyg.] 49b [Ovid]
Cronus-Rhea
Hades – Leuce
[Serv.] [Serv.]
Perieres[1]-Gorgophone[1]
Leucippus[1] – Philodice[1]
[Tzetz. Lyc.] 25c-d [Tzetz. Lyc.]
Arestor – Mycene
[Paus.] [Paus.]
Cronus-Rhea
Zeus – Io – Telegonus[3]
[Aesch.] [Aesch.] [Apollod.]
: – ?
{Oceanus} : – Parthenope[4]
[Andr. Hall.]
Argus[1]
[Ap. Rhod.]
Nilus-?
Epaphus[1] – Memphis[1]
[Aesch.] [Apollod.]
Cronus-Rhea
Poseidon – Ceroessa
[Steph. Byz.] [Steph. Byz.]
Trochilus[1]
[Schol. Arat.]
Uranus-Gaea
Cronus – Thrace – Zeus
[Steph. Byz.] [Andr. Hall.] [Steph. Byz.]
Cronus-Rhea
: – Obriareus
[Steph. Byz.]
Cronus-Rhea
Poseidon – Lysianassa[1]
[Apollod.] 8d [Apollod.]
Cronus-Rhea
Poseidon – Libya[1]
[Paus.] [Aesch.]
Byzas – Phidaleia
[Steph. Byz.] [Hesyc.]
Strombus
[Hesyc.]
Doloncus
[Steph. Byz.]
Bithynia
[Steph. Byz.]
Trierus
[Steph. Byz.]
Belus[1]-Anchinoe[1]
Damno – Agenor[1] – Telephassa
[Pher.] 59c [Apollod.] [Apollod.]
Nilus-?
: – Argiope[3]
[Pher.]
Ares-Aphrodite
Cadmus – Harmonia[1]
[Pher.] [Hes.]
[Cadmean Dragon]
Nycteus[1]-Polyxo[2]
Polydorus[2] – Nycteis
[Hes.] [Apollod.]
Echion[1] – Agave[1] – Lycotherses
[Eur.] [Hes.] [Hyg.]
Aeolus[1]-Enarete
Athamas[1] – Ino
[Apollod.] 26a-b [Hom.]
Apollo-Cyrene
Aristaeus[1] – Autonoe[1]
[Hes.] 69a-b [Hes.]
Labdacus – ?
[Eur.]
Epirus
[Parth.]
Pentheus[1] – ?
[Eur.]
Pelops[1]-Axioche
Chrysippus[1] ~ Laius[1] – Jocasta
[Apollod.] [Soph.] [Soph.]
Menoeceus[1]-?
Ekphas-?
: – Eurycleia[2]
[Epim.]
Oclasus – ?
[Schol. Eur.]
Hyperphas-?
Euryganeia – Oedipus – Jocasta
[Paus.] [Soph.] [Aesch./Soph.]
Menoeceus[1]-?
Sthenelus[1]-Nicippe[1]
: – Medusa[3]
[Pher.]
Menoeceus[1] – ?
[Schol. Eur.]
Creon[2]-Eurydice[9]
Haemon[1] – Antigone[1]
[Soph.] [Aesch.]
Eteocles[1] – ?
[Aesch.]
Periclymenus[3] – Ismene[1]
[Mimn.] [Aesch.]
Laonytus
[Pher.]
Phrastor[2]
[Pher.]
Adrastus[1]-Amphithea[1]
Polyneices – Argeia[1]
[Aesch.] [Eur./Apollod.]
Laius[1]-Jocasta
Oedipus – Jocasta – Laius
[Aesch./Eur.] 55c [Eur.] 55c [Soph.]
Labdacus-?
Hipponome
[Apollod.]
Creon[2] – Eurydice[9]
[Soph.] [Soph.]
Maeon
[Hom.]
Laodamas[3]
[Apollod.]
Amphiaraus-Eriphyle
Adrastus[4]
[Paus.]
Thersander[1] – Demonassa[2]
[Pind.] [Paus.]
Timeas
[Paus.]
Henioche[1]
[Paus.]
Lycomedes[2]
[Hom.]
Megareus[2]
[Aesch.]
Menoeceus[2]
[Apollod.]
Pyrrha[2]
[Paus.]
Oedipus-Jocasta
Haemon[1] – Antigone[1]
[Soph.] [Soph.]
Amphitryon-Alcmene
Iphicles – :
[Hom.]
Zeus-Alcmene
Heracles[1] – Megara – Iola(u)s
[Eur.] 60d [Hom.] [Apollod.]
Iphiclus[1]-Automedusa
Tisamenus[2] – ?
[Paus.]
Antiochus[2]-?
Phylas[2] – Leipephilene
[Gr. Ehoiai] [Gr. Ehoiai]
Autesion[1] – ?
[Paus.]
Maeon[1]
[Hom.]
Aristomachus[1]-?
Aristodemus – Argeia[3]
[Apollod.] 60d [Apollod.]
Theras – ?
[Paus.]
Hippotes[3] – ?
[Gr. Ehoiai]
Zeus-Leto
Apollo – Thero[1]
[Gr. Ehoiai] [Gr. Ehoiai]
Oeolycus – ?
[Paus.]
Aletes[3]
[Con.]
Chairon
[Gr. Ehoiai]
Aegeus[2]
[Herod.]

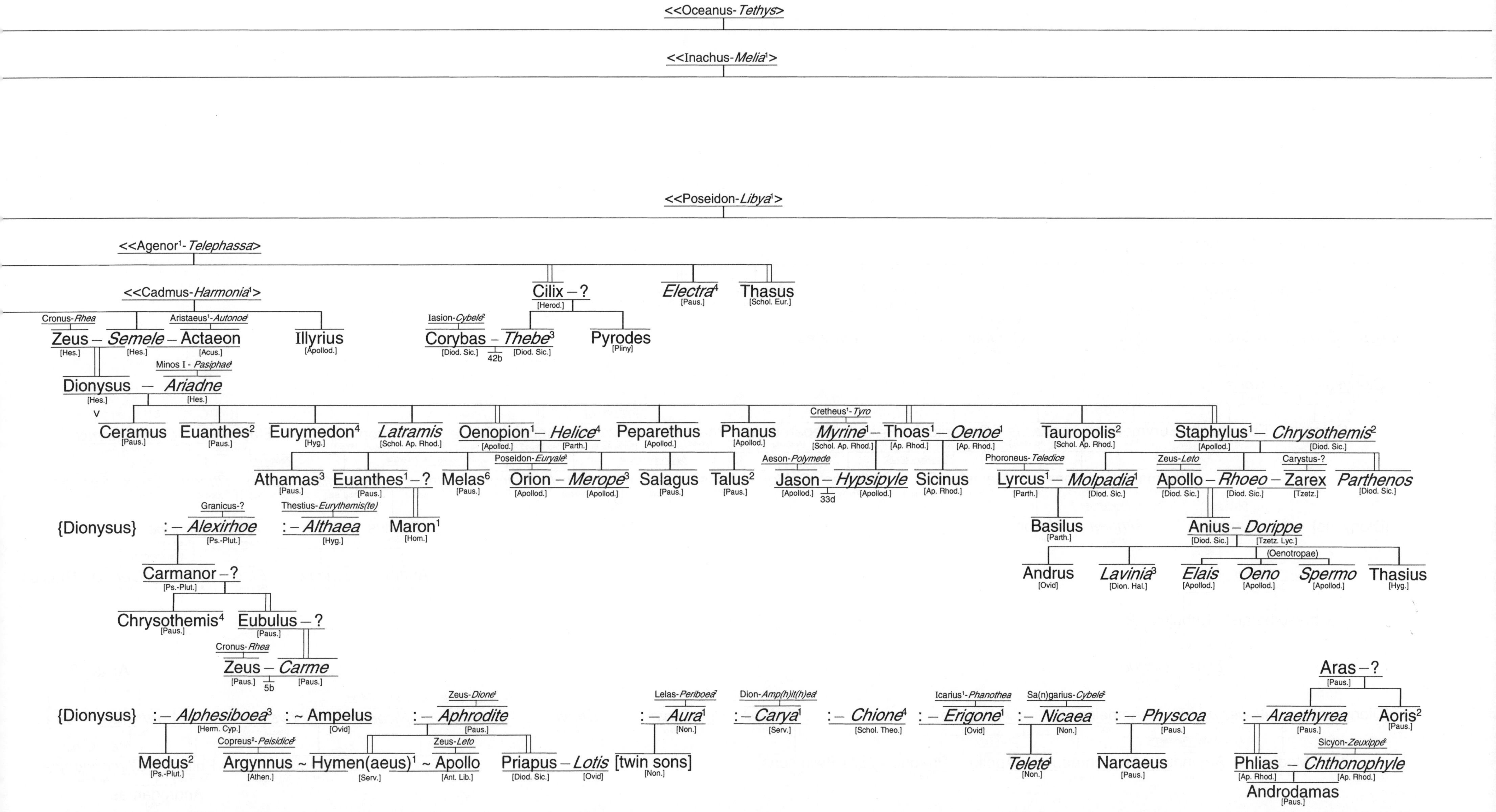

<<Oceanus-Tethys>
<<Inachus-Melia¹>
<<Poseidon-Libya¹>
<<Agenor¹-Telephassa>
<<Cadmus-Harmonia¹>
Cilix – ? [Herod.]
Electra⁴ [Paus.]
Thasus [Schol. Eur.]
Cronus-Rhea
Zeus – Semele – Actaeon
[Hes.] [Hes.] [Acus.]
Aristaeus¹-Autonoe¹
Illyrius [Apollod.]
Iasion-Cybele²
Corybas – Thebe³ [Diod. Sic.] 42b [Diod. Sic.]
Pyrodes [Pliny]
Minos I - Pasiphae¹
Dionysus – Ariadne [Hes.] [Hes.]
v
Ceramus [Paus.]
Euanthes² [Paus.]
Eurymedon⁴ [Hyg.]
Latramis [Schol. Ap. Rhod.]
Oenopion¹ – Helice⁴ [Apollod.] [Parth.]
Peparethus [Apollod.]
Phanus [Apollod.]
Cretheus¹-Tyro
Myrine¹ – Thoas¹ – Oenoe¹ [Schol. Ap. Rhod.] [Ap. Rhod.] [Ap. Rhod.]
Tauropolis² [Schol. Ap. Rhod.]
Staphylus¹ – Chrysothemis² [Apollod.] [Diod. Sic.]
Athamas³ [Paus.]
Euanthes¹ – ? [Paus.]
Melas⁶ [Paus.]
Poseidon-Euryale²
Orion – Merope³ [Apollod.] [Apollod.]
Salagus [Paus.]
Talus² [Paus.]
Aeson-Polymede
Jason – Hypsipyle [Apollod.] 33d [Apollod.]
Sicinus [Ap. Rhod.]
Phoroneus-Teledice
Lyrcus¹ – Molpadia¹ [Parth.] [Diod. Sic.]
Zeus-Leto
Apollo – Rhoeo – Zarex [Diod. Sic.] [Diod. Sic.] [Tzetz.]
Carystus-?
Parthenos [Diod. Sic.]
Granicus-?
{Dionysus} : – Alexirhoe [Ps.-Plut.]
Thestius-Eurythemis(te)
: – Althaea [Hyg.]
Maron¹ [Hom.]
Basilus [Parth.]
Anius – Dorippe [Diod. Sic.] [Tzetz. Lyc.]
(Oenotropae)
Andrus [Ovid]
Lavinia³ [Dion. Hal.]
Elais [Apollod.]
Oeno [Apollod.]
Spermo [Apollod.]
Thasius [Hyg.]
Carmanor – ? [Ps.-Plut.]
Chrysothemis⁴ [Paus.]
Eubulus – ? [Paus.]
Cronus-Rhea
Zeus – Carme [Paus.] 5b [Paus.]
Aras – ? [Paus.]
{Dionysus} : – Alphesiboea³ [Herm. Cyp.]
: ~ Ampelus [Ovid]
Zeus-Dione¹
: – Aphrodite [Paus.]
Lelas-Periboea⁷
: – Aura¹ [Non.]
Dion-Amp(h)it(h)ea¹
: – Carya¹ [Serv.]
: – Chione⁴ [Schol. Theo.]
Icarius¹-Phanothea
: – Erigone¹ [Ovid]
Sa(n)garius-Cybele²
: – Nicaea [Non.]
: – Physcoa [Paus.]
: – Araethyrea [Paus.]
Aoris² [Paus.]
Medus² [Ps.-Plut.]
Copreus²-Peisidice⁵
Argynnus ~ Hymen(aeus)¹ ~ Apollo [Athen.] [Serv.] [Ant. Lib.]
Zeus-Leto
Priapus – Lotis [Diod. Sic.] [Ovid]
[twin sons] [Non.]
Telete¹ [Non.]
Narcaeus [Paus.]
Sicyon-Zeuxippe²
Phlias – Chthonophyle [Ap. Rhod.] [Ap. Rhod.]
Androdamas [Paus.]

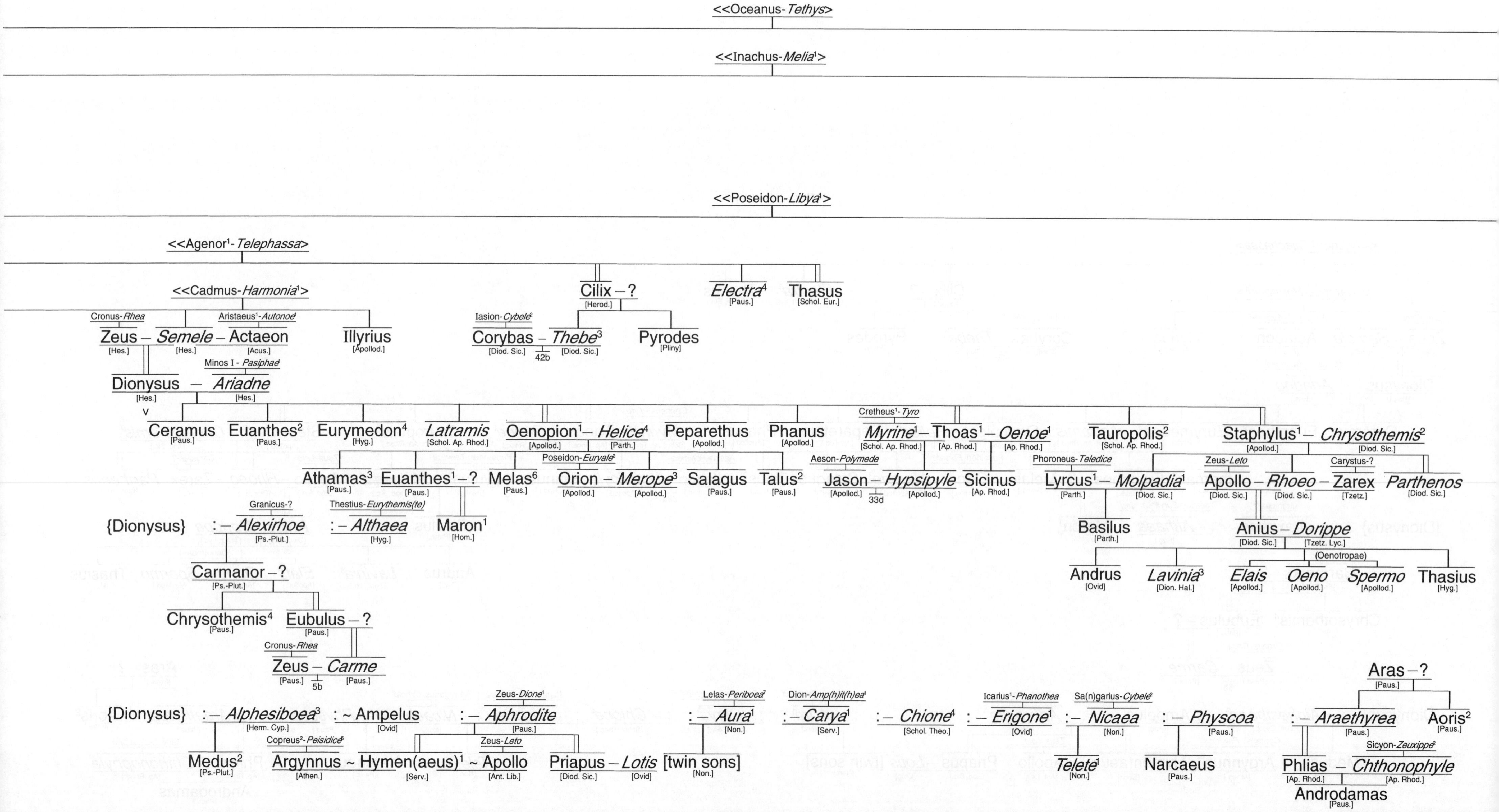

<<Oceanus-Tethys>
<<Inachus-Melia1>
<<Poseidon-Libya1>
<<Agenor1-Telephassa>
<<Cadmus-Harmonia1>
Cilix – ?
[Herod.]
Electra4
[Paus.]
Thasus
[Schol. Eur.]
Cronus-Rhea
Zeus – Semele – Actaeon
[Hes.] [Hes.] [Acus.]
Aristaeus1-Autonoe1
Illyrius
[Apollod.]
Iasion-Cybele2
Corybas – Thebe3
[Diod. Sic.] [Diod. Sic.]
42b
Pyrodes
[Pliny]
Minos I - Pasiphae1
Dionysus – Ariadne
[Hes.] [Hes.]
Ceramus
[Paus.]
Euanthes2
[Paus.]
Eurymedon4
[Hyg.]
Latramis
[Schol. Ap. Rhod.]
Oenopion1 – Helice4
[Apollod.] [Parth.]
Peparethus
[Apollod.]
Phanus
[Apollod.]
Cretheus1-Tyro
Myrine1 – Thoas1 – Oenoe1
[Schol. Ap. Rhod.] [Ap. Rhod.] [Ap. Rhod.]
Tauropolis2
[Schol. Ap. Rhod.]
Staphylus1 – Chrysothemis2
[Apollod.] [Diod. Sic.]
Athamas3
[Paus.]
Euanthes1 – ?
[Paus.]
Melas6
[Paus.]
Poseidon-Euryale2
Orion – Merope3
[Apollod.] [Apollod.]
Salagus
[Paus.]
Talus2
[Paus.]
Aeson-Polymede
Jason – Hypsipyle
[Apollod.] [Apollod.]
33d
Sicinus
[Ap. Rhod.]
Phoroneus-Teledice
Lyrcus1 – Molpadia1
[Parth.] [Diod. Sic.]
Zeus-Leto
Apollo – Rhoeo – Zarex
[Diod. Sic.] [Diod. Sic.] [Tzetz.]
Carystus-?
Parthenos
[Diod. Sic.]
Granicus-?
{Dionysus} : – Alexirhoe
[Ps.-Plut.]
Thestius-Eurythemis(te)
: – Althaea
[Hyg.]
Maron1
[Hom.]
Basilus
[Parth.]
Anius – Dorippe
[Diod. Sic.] [Tzetz. Lyc.]
(Oenotropae)
Andrus
[Ovid]
Lavinia3
[Dion. Hal.]
Elais
[Apollod.]
Oeno
[Apollod.]
Spermo
[Apollod.]
Thasius
[Hyg.]
Carmanor – ?
[Ps.-Plut.]
Chrysothemis4
[Paus.]
Eubulus – ?
[Paus.]
Cronus-Rhea
Zeus – Carme
[Paus.] [Paus.]
5b
Aras – ?
[Paus.]
{Dionysus} : – Alphesiboea3
[Herm. Cyp.]
: ~ Ampelus
[Ovid]
Zeus-Dione1
: – Aphrodite
[Paus.]
Lelas-Periboea7
: – Aura1
[Non.]
Dion-Amp(h)it(h)ea1
: – Carya1
[Serv.]
: – Chione4
[Schol. Theo.]
Icarius1-Phanothea
: – Erigone1
[Ovid]
Sa(n)garius-Cybele2
: – Nicaea
[Non.]
: – Physcoa
[Paus.]
: – Araethyrea
[Paus.]
Aoris2
[Paus.]
Medus2
[Ps.-Plut.]
Copreus2-Peisidice6
Argynnus ~ Hymen(aeus)1 ~ Apollo
[Athen.] [Serv.] [Ant. Lib.]
Zeus-Leto
Priapus – Lotis
[Diod. Sic.] [Ovid]
[twin sons]
[Non.]
Telete1
[Non.]
Narcaeus
[Paus.]
Sicyon-Zeuxippe2
Phlias – Chthonophyle
[Ap. Rhod.] [Ap. Rhod.]
Androdamas
[Paus.]

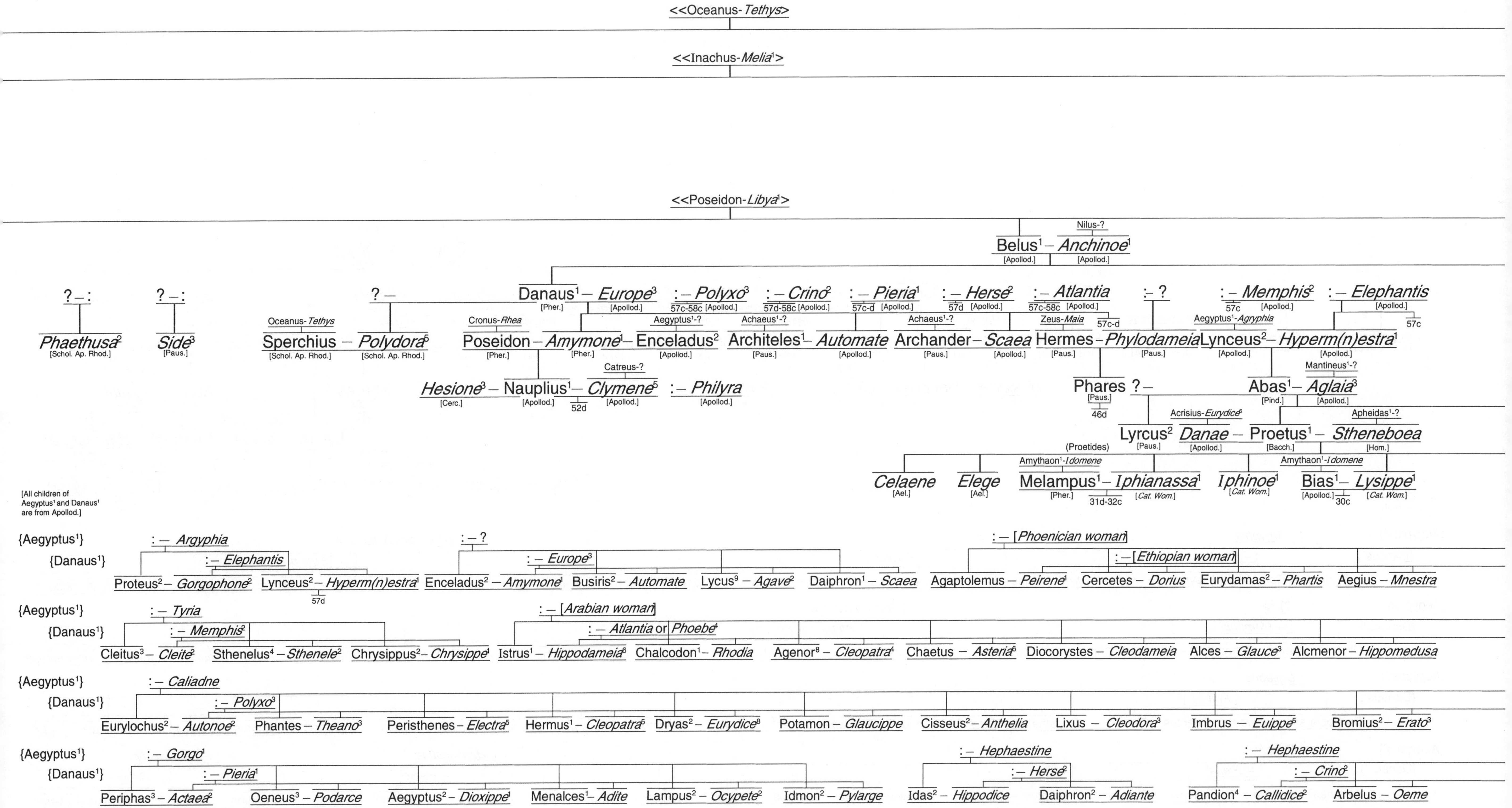

<<Oceanus-Tethys>
<<Inachus-Melia[1]>
<<Poseidon-Libya[1]>
Nilus-?
Belus[1] – Anchinoe[1]
[Apollod.] [Apollod.]
Danaus[1] – Europe[3] [Pher.] [Apollod.]
:– Polyxo[3] 57c-58c [Apollod.]
:– Crino[2] 57d-58c [Apollod.]
:– Pieria[1] 57c-d [Apollod.]
:– Herse[2] 57d [Apollod.]
:– Atlantia 57c-58c [Apollod.] 57c-d
:– ?
:– Memphis[2] 57c [Apollod.]
:– Elephantis [Apollod.] 57c
?–:
Phaethusa[2] [Schol. Ap. Rhod.]
?–:
Side[3] [Paus.]
?–
Oceanus-Tethys
Sperchius – Polydora[5]
[Schol. Ap. Rhod.] [Schol. Ap. Rhod.]
Cronus-Rhea
Poseidon – Amymone[1] – Enceladus[2]
[Pher.] [Pher.] [Apollod.]
Aegyptus[1]-?
Achaeus[1]-?
Architeles[1] – Automate
[Paus.] [Apollod.]
Achaeus[1]-?
Archander – Scaea
[Paus.] [Apollod.]
Zeus-Maia
Hermes – Phylodameia
[Paus.] [Paus.]
Aegyptus[1]-Agryphia
Lynceus[2] – Hyperm(n)estra[1]
[Apollod.] [Apollod.]
Catreus-?
Hesione[3] – Nauplius[1] – Clymene[5] :– Philyra
[Cerc.] [Apollod.] 52d [Apollod.] [Apollod.]
Phares ?–
[Paus.] 46d
Mantineus[1]-?
Abas[1] – Aglaia[3]
[Pind.] [Apollod.]
Acrisius-Eurydice[6]
Apheidas[1]-?
Lyrcus[2] Danae – Proetus[1] – Stheneboea
[Paus.] [Apollod.] [Bacch.] [Hom.]
(Proetides)
Amythaon[1]-Idomene
Amythaon[1]-Idomene
Celaene [Ael.]
Elege [Ael.]
Melampus[1] – Iphianassa[1]
[Pher.] 31d-32c [Cat. Wom.]
Iphinoe[1] [Cat. Wom.]
Bias[1] – Lysippe[1]
[Apollod.] 30c [Cat. Wom.]
[All children of Aegyptus[1] and Danaus[1] are from Apollod.]
{Aegyptus[1]}
{Danaus[1]}
:– Argyphia
:– Elephantis
Proteus[2] – Gorgophone[2]
Lynceus[2] – Hyperm(n)estra[1] 57d
:– ?
:– Europe[3]
Enceladus[2] – Amymone[1]
Busiris[2] – Automate
Lycus[9] – Agave[2]
Daiphron[1] – Scaea
:– [Phoenician woman]
:– [Ethiopian woman]
Agaptolemus – Peirene[1]
Cercetes – Dorius
Eurydamas[2] – Phartis
Aegius – Mnestra
{Aegyptus[1]}
{Danaus[1]}
:– Tyria
:– Memphis[2]
Cleitus[3] – Cleite[2]
Sthenelus[4] – Sthenele[2]
Chrysippus[2] – Chrysippe[1]
:– [Arabian woman]
:– Atlantia or Phoebe[4]
Istrus[1] – Hippodameia[5]
Chalcodon[1] – Rhodia
Agenor[8] – Cleopatra[4]
Chaetus – Asteria[6]
Diocorystes – Cleodameia
Alces – Glauce[3]
Alcmenor – Hippomedusa
{Aegyptus[1]}
{Danaus[1]}
:– Caliadne
:– Polyxo[3]
Eurylochus[2] – Autonoe[2]
Phantes – Theano[3]
Peristhenes – Electra[5]
Hermus[1] – Cleopatra[5]
Dryas[2] – Eurydice[8]
Potamon – Glaucippe
Cisseus[2] – Anthelia
Lixus – Cleodora[3]
Imbrus – Euippe[5]
Bromius[2] – Erato[3]
{Aegyptus[1]}
{Danaus[1]}
:– Gorgo[1]
:– Pieria[1]
Periphas[3] – Actaea[2]
Oeneus[3] – Podarce
Aegyptus[2] – Dioxippe[1]
Menalces[1] – Adite
Lampus[2] – Ocypete[2]
Idmon[2] – Pylarge
:– Hephaestine
:– Herse[2]
Idas[2] – Hippodice
Daiphron[2] – Adiante
:– Hephaestine
:– Crino[2]
Pandion[4] – Callidice[2]
Arbelus – Oeme

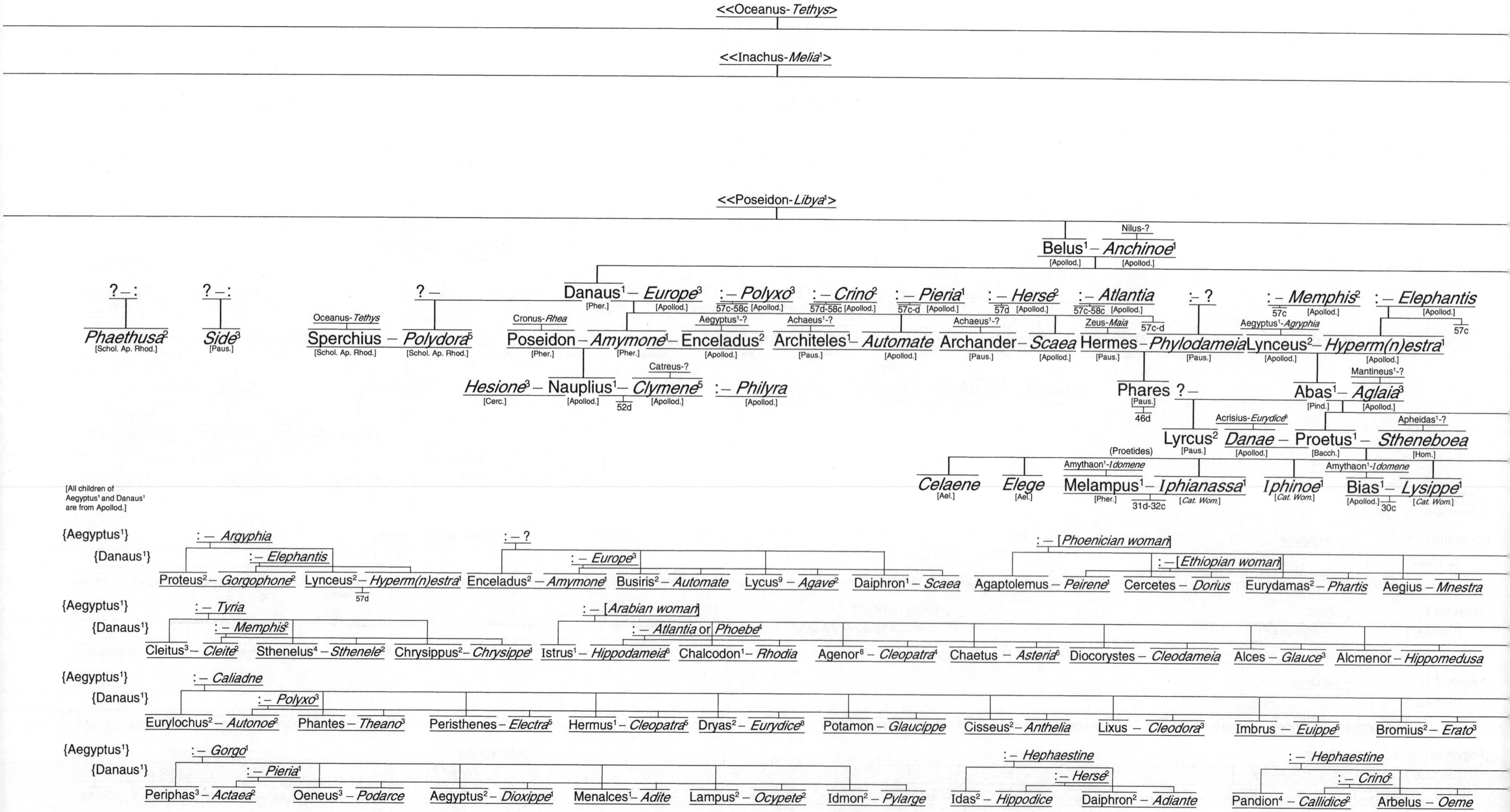

<<Oceanus-*Tethys*>
<<Inachus-*Melia*[1]>
<<Poseidon-*Libya*[1]>
Nilus-?
Belus[1] – *Anchinoe*[1]
[Apollod.] [Apollod.]
? – :
Phaethusa[2]
[Schol. Ap. Rhod.]
? – :
Side[3]
[Paus.]
? –
Oceanus-*Tethys*
Sperchius – *Polydora*[5]
[Schol. Ap. Rhod.] [Schol. Ap. Rhod.]
Danaus[1] – *Europe*[3]
[Pher.] [Apollod.]
: – *Polyxo*[3]
57c-58c [Apollod.]
: – *Crino*[2]
57d-58c [Apollod.]
: – *Pieria*[1]
57c-d [Apollod.]
: – *Herse*[2]
57d [Apollod.]
: – *Atlantia*
57c-58c [Apollod.]
: – ?
: – *Memphis*[2]
57c [Apollod.]
: – *Elephantis*
[Apollod.]
57c
Cronus-*Rhea*
Poseidon – *Amymone*[1]
[Pher.] [Pher.]
Aegyptus[1]-?
Enceladus[2]
[Apollod.]
Achaeus[1]-?
Architeles[1] – *Automate*
[Paus.] [Apollod.]
Achaeus[1]-?
Archander – *Scaea*
[Paus.] [Apollod.]
Zeus-*Maia*
Hermes – *Phylodameia*
[Paus.] [Paus.]
57c-d
Aegyptus[1]-*Agryphia*
Lynceus[2] – *Hyperm(n)estra*[1]
[Apollod.] [Apollod.]
Catreus-?
Hesione[3] – Nauplius[1] – *Clymene*[5]
[Cerc.] [Apollod.] 52d [Apollod.]
: – *Philyra*
[Apollod.]
Phares
[Paus.]
46d
? –
Mantineus[1]-?
Abas[1] – *Aglaia*[3]
[Pind.] [Apollod.]
Acrisius-*Eurydice*[6]
Lyrcus[2]
[Paus.]
Danae – Proetus[1]
[Apollod.] [Bacch.]
Apheidas[1]-?
Stheneboea
[Hom.]
(Proetides)
Amythaon[1]-*Idomene*
Celaene
[Ael.]
Elege
[Ael.]
Melampus[1] – *Iphianassa*[1]
[Pher.] 31d-32c [Cat. Wom.]
Iphinoe[1]
[Cat. Wom.]
Amythaon[1]-*Idomene*
Bias[1] – *Lysippe*[1]
[Apollod.] 30c [Cat. Wom.]
[All children of Aegyptus[1] and Danaus[1] are from Apollod.]
{Aegyptus[1]}
{Danaus[1]}
: – *Argyphia*
: – *Elephantis*
Proteus[2] – *Gorgophone*[2]
Lynceus[2] – *Hyperm(n)estra*[1]
57d
: – ?
: – *Europe*[3]
Enceladus[2] – *Amymone*[1]
Busiris[2] – *Automate*
Lycus[9] – *Agave*[2]
Daiphron[1] – *Scaea*
: – [*Phoenician woman*]
: – [*Ethiopian woman*]
Agaptolemus – *Peirene*[1]
Cercetes – *Dorius*
Eurydamas[2] – *Phartis*
Aegius – *Mnestra*
{Aegyptus[1]}
{Danaus[1]}
: – *Tyria*
: – *Memphis*[2]
Cleitus[3] – *Cleite*[2]
Sthenelus[4] – *Sthenele*[2]
Chrysippus[2] – *Chrysippe*[1]
: – [*Arabian woman*]
: – *Atlantia* or *Phoebe*[4]
Istrus[1] – *Hippodameia*[5]
Chalcodon[1] – *Rhodia*
Agenor[8] – *Cleopatra*[4]
Chaetus – *Asteria*[6]
Diocorystes – *Cleodameia*
Alces – *Glauce*[3]
Alcmenor – *Hippomedusa*
{Aegyptus[1]}
{Danaus[1]}
: – *Caliadne*
: – *Polyxo*[3]
Eurylochus[2] – *Autonoe*[2]
Phantes – *Theano*[3]
Peristhenes – *Electra*[5]
Hermus[1] – *Cleopatra*[5]
Dryas[2] – *Eurydice*[8]
Potamon – *Glaucippe*
Cisseus[2] – *Anthelia*
Lixus – *Cleodora*[3]
Imbrus – *Euippe*[5]
Bromius[2] – *Erato*[3]
{Aegyptus[1]}
{Danaus[1]}
: – *Gorgo*[1]
: – *Pieria*[1]
Periphas[3] – *Actaea*[2]
Oeneus[3] – *Podarce*
Aegyptus[2] – *Dioxippe*[1]
Menalces[1] – *Adite*
Lampus[2] – *Ocypete*[2]
Idmon[2] – *Pylarge*
: – *Hephaestine*
: – *Herse*[2]
Idas[2] – *Hippodice*
Daiphron[2] – *Adiante*
: – *Hephaestine*
: – *Crino*[2]
Pandion[4] – *Callidice*[2]
Arbelus – *Oeme*

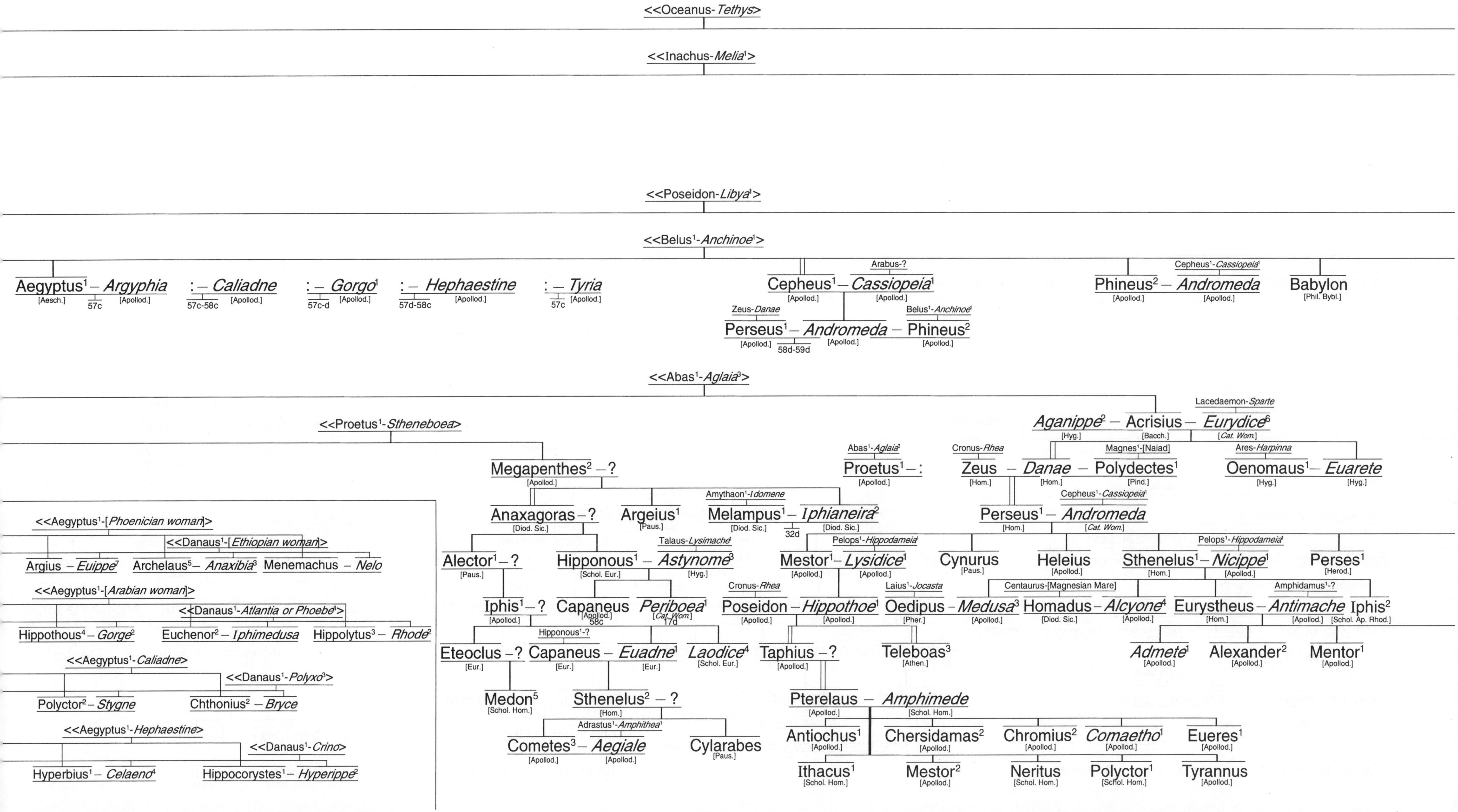

<<Oceanus-Tethys>
<<Inachus-Melia[1]>
<<Poseidon-Libya[1]>
<<Belus[1]-Anchinoe[1]>
Aegyptus[1] – Argyphia
[Aesch.] 57c [Apollod.]
: – Caliadne
57c-58c [Apollod.]
: – Gorgo[1]
57c-d [Apollod.]
: – Hephaestine
57d-58c [Apollod.]
: – Tyria
57c [Apollod.]
Arabus-?
Cepheus[1] – Cassiopeia[1]
[Apollod.] [Apollod.]
Zeus-Danae
Belus[1]-Anchinoe[1]
Perseus[1] – Andromeda – Phineus[2]
[Apollod.] 58d-59d [Apollod.] [Apollod.]
Cepheus[1]-Cassiopeia[1]
Phineus[2] – Andromeda
[Apollod.] [Apollod.]
Babylon
[Phil. Bybl.]
<<Abas[1]-Aglaia[3]>
<<Proetus[1]-Stheneboea>
Lacedaemon-Sparte
Aganippe[2] – Acrisius – Eurydice[6]
[Hyg.] [Bacch.] [Cat. Wom.]
Megapenthes[2] – ?
[Apollod.]
Abas[1]-Aglaia[3]
Proetus[1] – :
[Apollod.]
Cronus-Rhea
Zeus – Danae – Polydectes[1]
[Hom.] [Hom.] [Pind.]
Magnes[1]-[Naiad]
Ares-Harpinna
Oenomaus[1] – Euarete
[Hyg.] [Hyg.]
Amythaon[1]-Idomene
Anaxagoras – ?
[Diod. Sic.]
Argeius[1]
[Paus.]
Melampus[1] – Iphianeira[2]
[Diod. Sic.] 32d [Diod. Sic.]
Cepheus[1]-Cassiopeia[1]
Perseus[1] – Andromeda
[Hom.] [Cat. Wom.]
<<Aegyptus[1]-[Phoenician woman]>
<<Danaus[1]-[Ethiopian woman]>
Argius – Euippe[7]
Archelaus[5] – Anaxibia[3]
Menemachus – Nelo
<<Aegyptus[1]-[Arabian woman]>
<<Danaus[1]-Atlantia or Phoebe[4]>
Hippothous[4] – Gorge[2]
Euchenor[2] – Iphimedusa
Hippolytus[3] – Rhode[2]
<<Aegyptus[1]-Caliadne>
<<Danaus[1]-Polyxo[3]>
Polyctor[2] – Stygne
Chthonius[2] – Bryce
<<Aegyptus[1]-Hephaestine>
<<Danaus[1]-Crino>
Hyperbius[1] – Celaeno[4]
Hippocorystes[1] – Hyperippe[2]
Alector[1] – ?
[Paus.]
Talaus-Lysimache[1]
Hipponous[1] – Astynome[3]
[Schol. Eur.] [Hyg.]
Pelops[1]-Hippodameia[1]
Mestor[1] – Lysidice[1]
[Apollod.] [Apollod.]
Cynurus
[Paus.]
Heleius
[Apollod.]
Pelops[1]-Hippodameia[1]
Sthenelus[1] – Nicippe[1]
[Hom.] [Apollod.]
Perses[1]
[Herod.]
Iphis[1] – ?
[Apollod.]
Capaneus
[Apollod.] 58c
Periboea[1]
[Cat. Wom.] 17d
Cronus-Rhea
Poseidon – Hippothoe[1]
[Apollod.] [Apollod.]
Laius[1]-Jocasta
Oedipus – Medusa[3]
[Pher.] [Apollod.]
Centaurus-[Magnesian Mare]
Homadus – Alcyone[4]
[Diod. Sic.] [Apollod.]
Amphidamus[1]-?
Eurystheus – Antimache
[Hom.] [Apollod.]
Iphis[2]
[Schol. Ap. Rhod.]
Hipponous[1]-?
Eteoclus – ?
[Eur.]
Capaneus – Euadne[1]
[Eur.] [Eur.]
Laodice[4]
[Schol. Eur.]
Taphius – ?
[Apollod.]
Teleboas[3]
[Athen.]
Admete[1]
[Apollod.]
Alexander[2]
[Apollod.]
Mentor[1]
[Apollod.]
Medon[5]
[Schol. Hom.]
Sthenelus[2] – ?
[Hom.]
Pterelaus – Amphimede
[Apollod.] [Schol. Hom.]
Adrastus[1]-Amphithea[1]
Cometes[3] – Aegiale
[Apollod.] [Apollod.]
Cylarabes
[Paus.]
Antiochus[1]
[Apollod.]
Chersidamas[2]
[Apollod.]
Chromius[2]
[Apollod.]
Comaetho[1]
[Apollod.]
Eueres[1]
[Apollod.]
Ithacus[1]
[Schol. Hom.]
Mestor[2]
[Apollod.]
Neritus
[Schol. Hom.]
Polyctor[1]
[Schol. Hom.]
Tyrannus
[Apollod.]

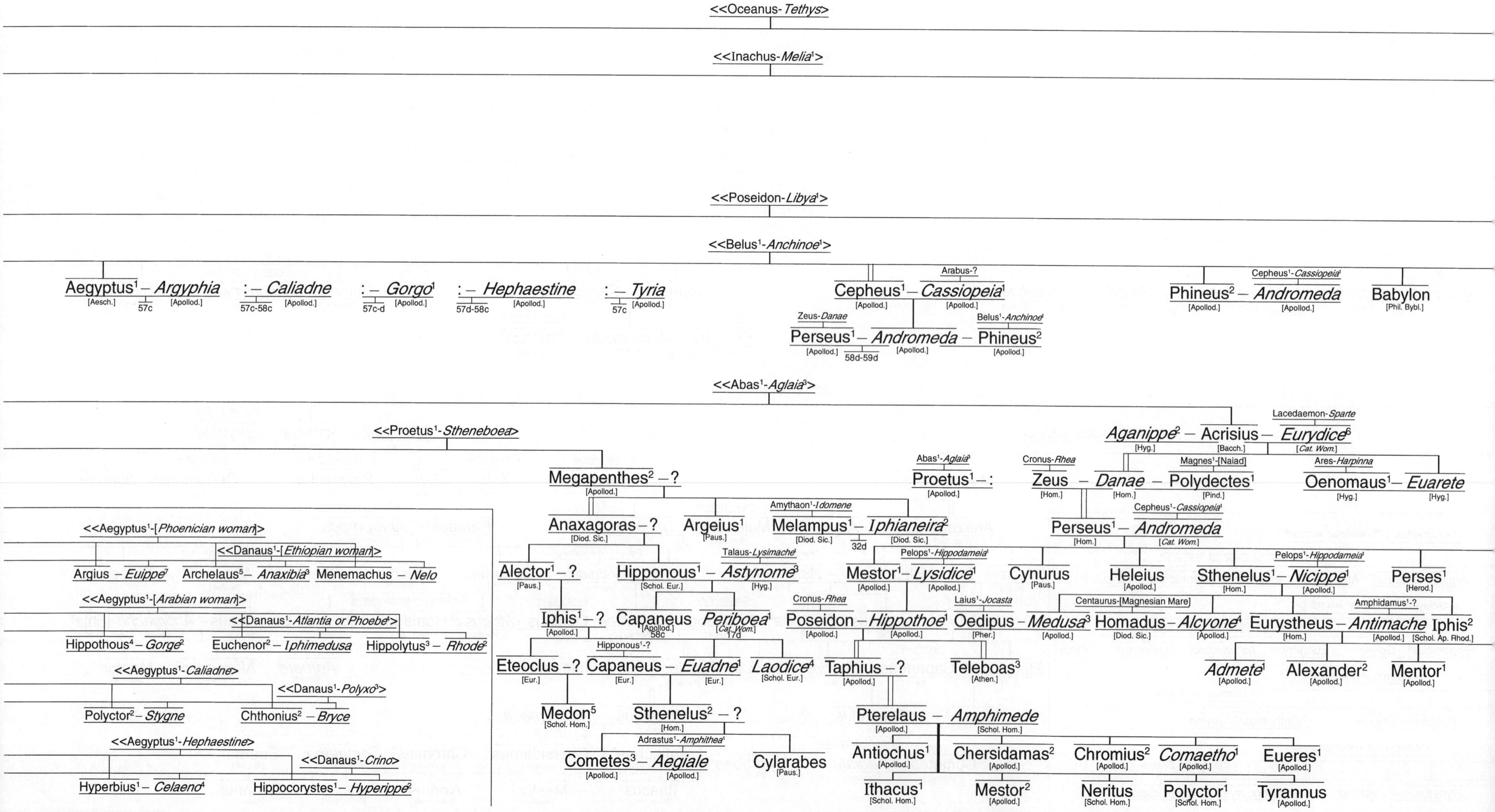

<<Oceanus-*Tethys*>
<<Inachus-*Melia*1>
<<Poseidon-*Libya*1>
<<Belus1-*Anchinoe*1>
Aegyptus1 – *Argyphia* [Aesch.] 57c [Apollod.]
: – *Caliadne* 57c-58c [Apollod.]
: – *Gorgo*1 57c-d [Apollod.]
: – *Hephaestine* 57d-58c [Apollod.]
: – *Tyria* 57c [Apollod.]
Arabus-?
Cepheus1 – *Cassiopeia*1 [Apollod.] [Apollod.]
Zeus-*Danae*
Belus1-*Anchinoe*1
Perseus1 – *Andromeda* – Phineus2 [Apollod.] 58d-59d [Apollod.] [Apollod.]
Cepheus1-*Cassiopeia*1
Phineus2 – *Andromeda* [Apollod.] [Apollod.]
Babylon [Phil. Bybl.]
<<Abas1-*Aglaia*3>
<<Proetus1-*Stheneboea*>
Megapenthes2 – ? [Apollod.]
Lacedaemon-*Sparte*
*Aganippe*2 – Acrisius – *Eurydice*6 [Hyg.] [Bacch.] [*Cat. Wom.*]
Abas1-*Aglaia*3
Proetus1 – : [Apollod.]
Cronus-*Rhea*
Magnes1-[Naiad]
Ares-*Harpinna*
Zeus – *Danae* – Polydectes1 [Hom.] [Hom.] [Pind.]
Oenomaus1 – *Euarete* [Hyg.] [Hyg.]
Amythaon1-*Idomene*
Cepheus1-*Cassiopeia*1
Anaxagoras – ? [Diod. Sic.]
Argeius1 [Paus.]
Melampus1 – *Iphianeira*2 [Diod. Sic.] 32d [Diod. Sic.]
Perseus1 – *Andromeda* [Hom.] [*Cat. Wom.*]
<<Aegyptus1-[*Phoenician woman*]>
<<Danaus1-[*Ethiopian woman*]>
Argius – *Euippe*7
Archelaus5 – *Anaxibia*3
Menemachus – *Nelo*
Talaus-*Lysimache*1
Pelops1-*Hippodameia*1
Pelops1-*Hippodameia*1
Alector1 – ? [Paus.]
Hipponous1 – *Astynome*3 [Schol. Eur.] [Hyg.]
Mestor1 – *Lysidice*1 [Apollod.] [Apollod.]
Cynurus [Paus.]
Heleius [Apollod.]
Sthenelus1 – *Nicippe*1 [Hom.] [Apollod.]
Perses1 [Herod.]
<<Aegyptus1-[*Arabian woman*]>
<<Danaus1-*Atlantia or Phoebe*1>
Hippothous4 – *Gorge*2
Euchenor2 – *Iphimedusa*
Hippolytus3 – *Rhode*2
Cronus-*Rhea*
Laius1-*Jocasta*
Centaurus-[Magnesian Mare]
Amphidamus1-?
Iphis1 – ? [Apollod.]
Capaneus [Apollod.] 58c
*Periboea*1 [*Cat. Wom.*] 17d
Poseidon – *Hippothoe*1 [Apollod.] [Apollod.]
Oedipus – *Medusa*3 [Pher.] [Apollod.]
Homadus – *Alcyone*4 [Diod. Sic.] [Apollod.]
Eurystheus – *Antimache* [Hom.] [Apollod.]
Iphis2 [Schol. Ap. Rhod.]
Hipponous1-?
<<Aegyptus1-*Caliadne*>
<<Danaus1-*Polyxo*3>
Eteoclus – ? [Eur.]
Capaneus – *Euadne*1 [Eur.] [Eur.]
*Laodice*4 [Schol. Eur.]
Taphius – ? [Apollod.]
Teleboas3 [Athen.]
*Admete*1 [Apollod.]
Alexander2 [Apollod.]
Mentor1 [Apollod.]
Polyctor2 – *Stygne*
Chthonius2 – *Bryce*
Medon5 [Schol. Hom.]
Sthenelus2 – ? [Hom.]
Pterelaus – *Amphimede* [Apollod.] [Schol. Hom.]
<<Aegyptus1-*Hephaestine*>
Adrastus1-*Amphithea*1
<<Danaus1-*Crino*>
Cometes3 – *Aegiale* [Apollod.] [Apollod.]
Cylarabes [Paus.]
Antiochus1 [Apollod.]
Chersidamas2 [Apollod.]
Chromius2 [Apollod.]
*Comaetho*1 [Apollod.]
Eueres1 [Apollod.]
Hyperbius1 – *Celaeno*4
Hippocorystes1 – *Hyperippe*2
Ithacus1 [Schol. Hom.]
Mestor2 [Apollod.]
Neritus [Schol. Hom.]
Polyctor1 [Schol. Hom.]
Tyrannus [Apollod.]

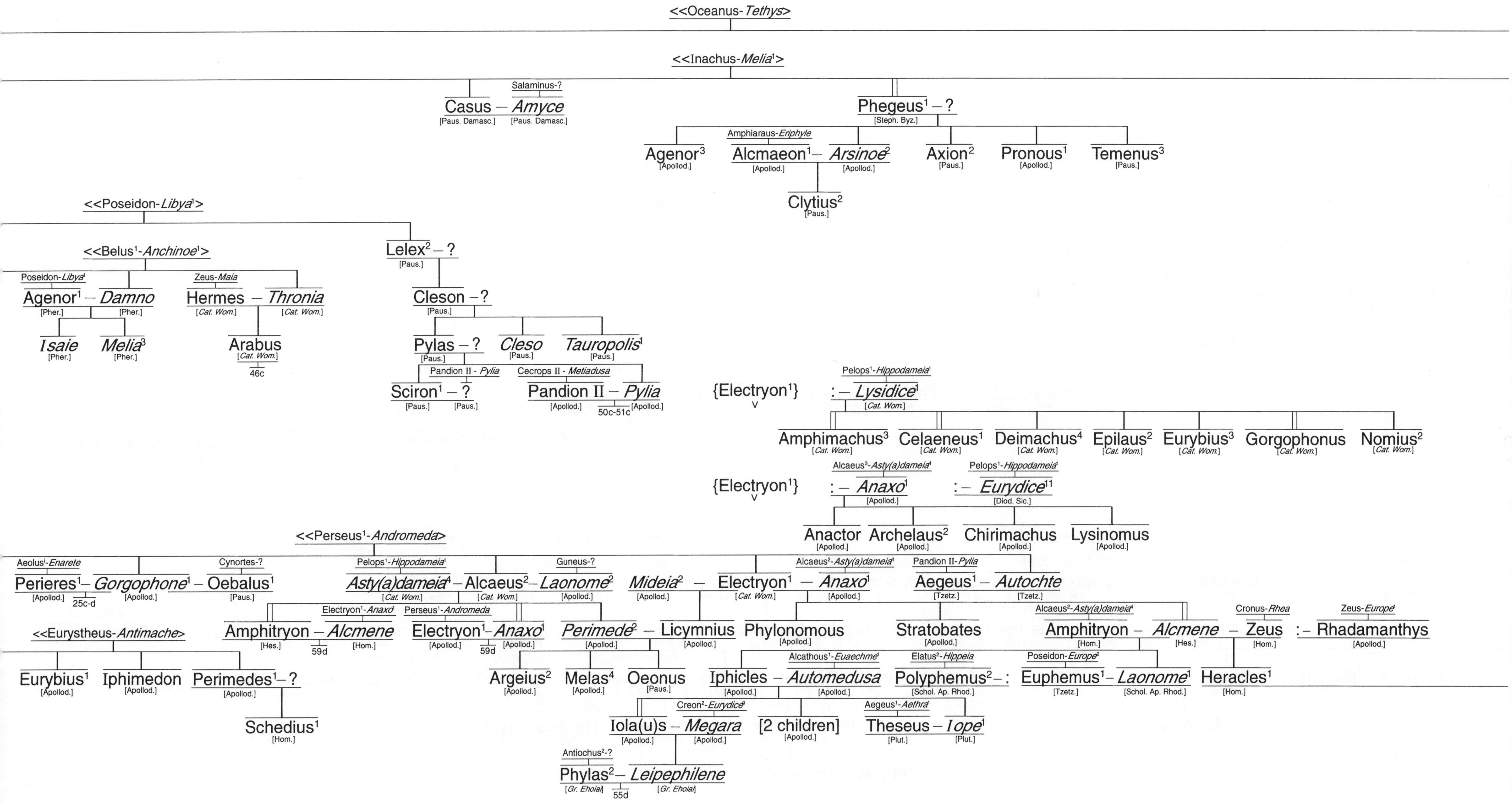

<<Oceanus-Tethys>
<<Inachus-Melia^1>
Salaminus-?
Casus – Amyce
[Paus. Damasc.] [Paus. Damasc.]
Phegeus^1 – ?
[Steph. Byz.]
Amphiaraus-Eriphyle
Agenor^3 [Apollod.]
Alcmaeon^1 – Arsinoe^2
[Apollod.] [Apollod.]
Axion^2 [Paus.]
Pronous^1 [Apollod.]
Temenus^3 [Paus.]
Clytius^2 [Paus.]
<<Poseidon-Libya^1>
<<Belus^1-Anchinoe^1>
Lelex^2 – ? [Paus.]
Poseidon-Libya^1
Zeus-Maia
Agenor^1 – Damno
[Pher.] [Pher.]
Hermes – Thronia
[Cat. Wom.] [Cat. Wom.]
Cleson – ? [Paus.]
Isaie [Pher.]
Melia^3 [Pher.]
Arabus [Cat. Wom.]
46c
Pylas – ? [Paus.]
Cleso [Paus.]
Tauropolis^1 [Paus.]
Pandion II - Pylia
Cecrops II - Metiadusa
Sciron^1 – ?
[Paus.] [Paus.]
Pandion II – Pylia
[Apollod.] 50c-51c [Apollod.]
{Electryon^1}
Pelops^1-Hippodameia^1
: – Lysidice^1 [Cat. Wom.]
Amphimachus^3 [Cat. Wom.]
Celaeneus^1 [Cat. Wom.]
Deimachus^4 [Cat. Wom.]
Epilaus^2 [Cat. Wom.]
Eurybius^3 [Cat. Wom.]
Gorgophonus [Cat. Wom.]
Nomius^2 [Cat. Wom.]
{Electryon^1}
Alcaeus^3-Asty(a)dameia^4
: – Anaxo^1 [Apollod.]
Pelops^1-Hippodameia^1
: – Eurydice^{11} [Diod. Sic.]
Anactor [Apollod.]
Archelaus^2 [Apollod.]
Chirimachus [Apollod.]
Lysinomus [Apollod.]
<<Perseus^1-Andromeda>
Aeolus^1-Enarete
Cynortes-?
Pelops^1-Hippodameia^1
Guneus-?
Alcaeus^2-Asty(a)dameia^4
Pandion II-Pylia
Perieres^1 – Gorgophone^1 – Oebalus^1
[Apollod.] 25c-d [Apollod.] [Paus.]
Asty(a)dameia^4 – Alcaeus^2 – Laonome^2
[Cat. Wom.] [Cat. Wom.] [Apollod.]
Mideia^2 – Electryon^1 – Anaxo^1
[Apollod.] [Cat. Wom.] [Apollod.]
Aegeus^1 – Autochte
[Tzetz.] [Tzetz.]
<<Eurystheus-Antimache>
Electryon^1-Anaxo^1
Perseus^1-Andromeda
Amphitryon – Alcmene
[Hes.] 59d [Hom.]
Electryon^1 – Anaxo^1
[Apollod.] 59d [Apollod.]
Perimede^2 – Licymnius
[Apollod.] [Apollod.]
Phylonomous [Apollod.]
Stratobates [Apollod.]
Alcaeus^2-Asty(a)dameia^4
Cronus-Rhea
Zeus-Europe^1
Amphitryon – Alcmene – Zeus : – Rhadamanthys
[Hom.] [Hes.] [Hom.] [Apollod.]
Eurybius^1 [Apollod.]
Iphimedon [Apollod.]
Perimedes^1 – ? [Apollod.]
Schedius^1 [Hom.]
Argeius^2 [Apollod.]
Melas^4 [Apollod.]
Oeonus [Paus.]
Alcathous^1-Euaechme^1
Elatus^2-Hippeia
Poseidon-Europe^2
Iphicles – Automedusa
[Apollod.] [Apollod.]
Polyphemus^2 – :
[Schol. Ap. Rhod.]
Euphemus^1 – Laonome^1
[Tzetz.] [Schol. Ap. Rhod.]
Heracles^1 [Hom.]
Creon^2-Eurydice^3
Aegeus^1-Aethra^1
Iola(u)s – Megara
[Apollod.] [Apollod.]
[2 children] [Apollod.]
Theseus – Iope^1
[Plut.] [Plut.]
Antiochus^2-?
Phylas^2 – Leipephilene
[Gr. Ehoiai] 55d [Gr. Ehoiai]

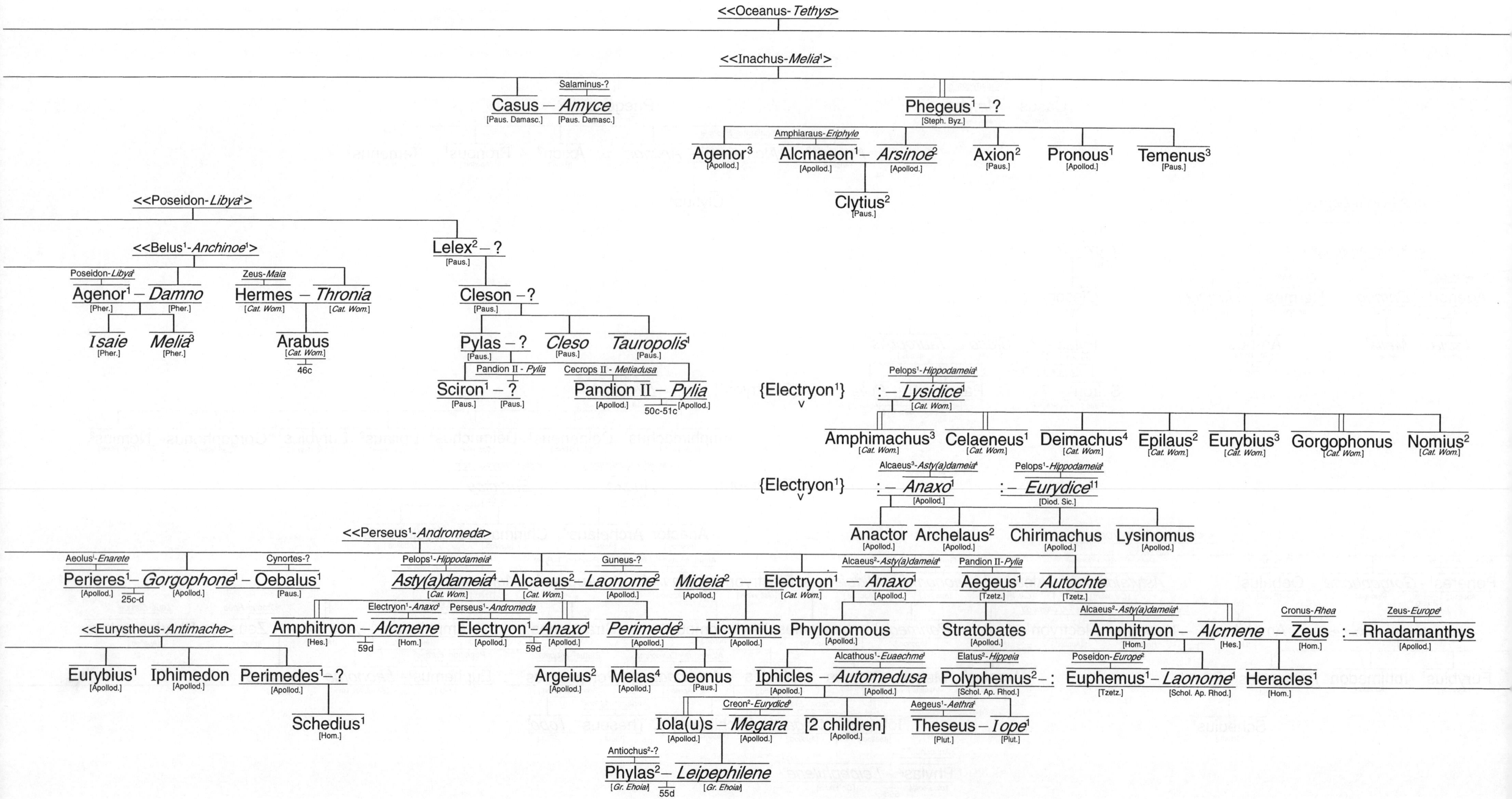

<<Oceanus-Tethys>
<<Inachus-Melia¹>
Salaminus-?
Casus – Amyce
[Paus. Damasc.] [Paus. Damasc.]
Phegeus¹ – ?
[Steph. Byz.]
Amphiaraus-Eriphyle
Agenor³ [Apollod.]
Alcmaeon¹ – Arsinoe² [Apollod.] [Apollod.]
Axion² [Paus.]
Pronous¹ [Apollod.]
Temenus³ [Paus.]
Clytius² [Paus.]
<<Poseidon-Libya¹>
<<Belus¹-Anchinoe¹>
Lelex² – ? [Paus.]
Poseidon-Libya¹
Agenor¹ – Damno [Pher.] [Pher.]
Zeus-Maia
Hermes – Thronia [Cat. Wom.] [Cat. Wom.]
Isaie [Pher.]
Melia³ [Pher.]
Arabus [Cat. Wom.] 46c
Cleson – ? [Paus.]
Pylas – ? [Paus.]
Cleso [Paus.]
Tauropolis¹ [Paus.]
Pandion II - Pylia
Cecrops II - Metiadusa
Sciron¹ – ? [Paus.] [Paus.]
Pandion II – Pylia [Apollod.] 50c-51c [Apollod.]
Pelops¹-Hippodameia¹
{Electryon¹} :– Lysidice¹ [Cat. Wom.]
Amphimachus³ [Cat. Wom.]
Celaeneus¹ [Cat. Wom.]
Deimachus⁴ [Cat. Wom.]
Epilaus² [Cat. Wom.]
Eurybius³ [Cat. Wom.]
Gorgophonus [Cat. Wom.]
Nomius² [Cat. Wom.]
Alcaeus³-Asty(a)dameia⁴
Pelops¹-Hippodameia¹
{Electryon¹} :– Anaxo¹ [Apollod.] :– Eurydice¹¹ [Diod. Sic.]
Anactor [Apollod.]
Archelaus² [Apollod.]
Chirimachus [Apollod.]
Lysinomus [Apollod.]
<<Perseus¹-Andromeda>
Aeolus¹-Enarete
Cynortes-?
Pelops¹-Hippodameia¹
Guneus-?
Alcaeus²-Asty(a)dameia⁴
Pandion II-Pylia
Perieres¹ – Gorgophone¹ – Oebalus¹ [Apollod.] 25c-d [Apollod.] [Paus.]
Asty(a)dameia⁴ – Alcaeus² – Laonome² [Cat. Wom.] [Cat. Wom.] [Apollod.]
Mideia² – Electryon¹ – Anaxo¹ [Apollod.] [Cat. Wom.] [Apollod.]
Aegeus¹ – Autochte [Tzetz.] [Tzetz.]
Electryon¹-Anaxo¹
Perseus¹-Andromeda
Alcaeus²-Asty(a)dameia⁴
Cronus-Rhea
Zeus-Europe¹
<<Eurystheus-Antimache>
Amphitryon – Alcmene [Hes.] 59d [Hom.]
Electryon¹ – Anaxo¹ [Apollod.] 59d [Apollod.]
Perimede² – Licymnius [Apollod.] [Apollod.]
Phylonomous [Apollod.]
Stratobates [Apollod.]
Amphitryon – Alcmene – Zeus :– Rhadamanthys [Hom.] [Hes.] [Hom.] [Apollod.]
Eurybius¹ [Apollod.]
Iphimedon [Apollod.]
Perimedes¹ – ? [Apollod.]
Argeius² [Apollod.]
Melas⁴ [Apollod.]
Oeonus [Paus.]
Alcathous¹-Euaechme¹
Elatus²-Hippeia
Poseidon-Europe²
Iphicles – Automedusa [Apollod.] [Apollod.]
Polyphemus² – : [Schol. Ap. Rhod.]
Euphemus¹ – Laonome¹ [Tzetz.] [Schol. Ap. Rhod.]
Heracles¹ [Hom.]
Schedius¹ [Hom.]
Creon²-Eurydice⁹
Aegeus¹-Aethra¹
Iola(u)s – Megara [Apollod.] [Apollod.]
[2 children] [Apollod.]
Theseus – Iope¹ [Plut.] [Plut.]
Antiochus²-?
Phylas² – Leipephilene [Gr. Ehoiai] 55d [Gr. Ehoiai]

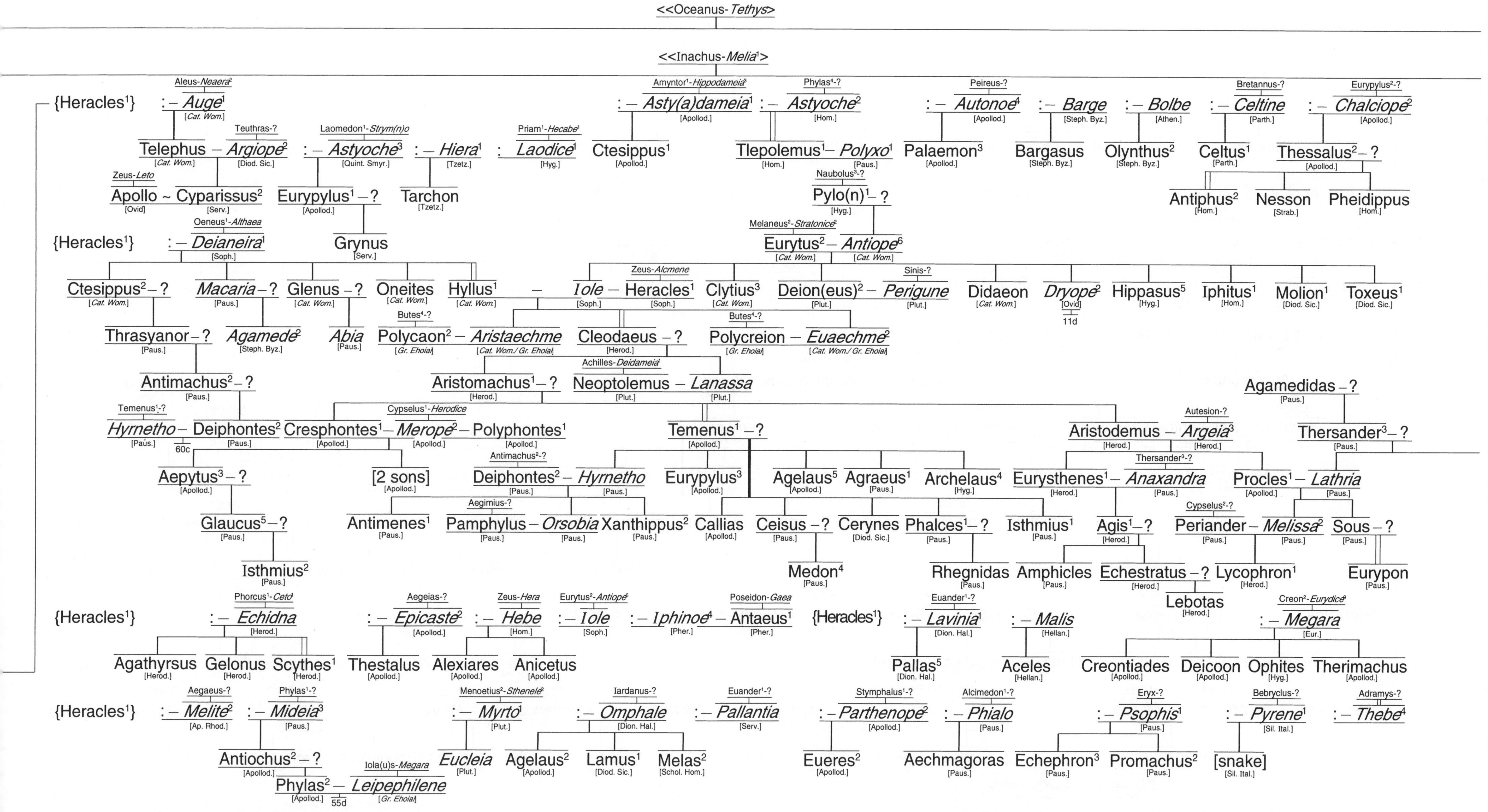

<<Oceanus-Tethys>
<<Inachus-Melia1>
{Heracles1}
Aleus-Neaera2
: – Auge1 [Cat. Wom.]
Telephus [Cat. Wom.] – Argiope2 [Diod. Sic.]
Teuthras-?
Zeus-Leto
Apollo [Ovid] ~ Cyparissus2 [Serv.]
Laomedon1-Strym(n)o
: – Astyoche3 [Quint. Smyr.]
Eurypylus1 – ? [Apollod.]
Grynus [Serv.]
: – Hiera1 [Tzetz.]
Tarchon [Tzetz.]
Priam1-Hecabe1
: Laodice1 [Hyg.]
Amyntor1-Hippodameia3
: – Asty(a)dameia1 [Apollod.]
Ctesippus1 [Apollod.]
Phylas4-?
: – Astyoche2 [Hom.]
Tlepolemus1 [Hom.] – Polyxo1 [Paus.]
Naubolus3-?
Pylo(n)1 – ? [Hyg.]
Peireus-?
: – Autonoe4 [Apollod.]
Palaemon3 [Apollod.]
: – Barge [Steph. Byz.]
Bargasus [Steph. Byz.]
: – Bolbe [Athen.]
Olynthus2 [Steph. Byz.]
Bretannus-?
: – Celtine [Parth.]
Celtus1 [Parth.]
Eurypylus2-?
: – Chalciope2 [Apollod.]
Thessalus2 – ? [Apollod.]
Antiphus2 [Hom.]
Nesson [Strab.]
Pheidippus [Hom.]
{Heracles1}
Oeneus1-Althaea
: – Deianeira1 [Soph.]
Melaneus2-Stratonice2
Eurytus2 [Cat. Wom.] – Antiope6 [Cat. Wom.]
Ctesippus2 – ? [Cat. Wom.]
Macaria – ? [Paus.]
Glenus – ? [Cat. Wom.]
Oneites [Cat. Wom.]
Hyllus1 [Cat. Wom.]
Zeus-Alcmene
Iole [Soph.] – Heracles1 [Soph.]
Clytius3 [Cat. Wom.]
Sinis-?
Deion(eus)2 [Plut.] – Perigune [Plut.]
Didaeon [Cat. Wom.]
Dryope2 [Ovid]
11d
Hippasus5 [Hyg.]
Iphitus1 [Hom.]
Molion1 [Diod. Sic.]
Toxeus1 [Diod. Sic.]
Thrasyanor – ? [Paus.]
Agamede2 [Steph. Byz.]
Abia [Paus.]
Butes4-?
Polycaon2 [Gr. Ehoiai] – Aristaechme [Cat. Wom./Gr. Ehoiai]
Cleodaeus – ? [Herod.]
Butes4-?
Polycreion [Gr. Ehoiai] – Euaechme2 [Cat. Wom./Gr. Ehoiai]
Antimachus2 – ? [Paus.]
Aristomachus1 – ? [Herod.]
Achilles-Deidameia1
Neoptolemus [Plut.] – Lanassa [Plut.]
Agamedidas – ? [Paus.]
Temenus1-?
Hyrnetho [Paus.] – Deiphontes2 [Paus.]
60c
Cypselus1-Herodice
Cresphontes1 [Apollod.] – Merope2 [Apollod.] – Polyphontes1 [Apollod.]
Temenus1 – ? [Apollod.]
Aristodemus [Herod.] – Argeia3 [Herod.]
Autesion-?
Thersander3 – ? [Paus.]
Aepytus3 – ? [Apollod.]
[2 sons] [Apollod.]
Antimachus2-?
Deiphontes2 [Paus.] – Hyrnetho [Paus.]
Eurypylus3 [Apollod.]
Agelaus5 [Apollod.]
Agraeus1 [Paus.]
Archelaus4 [Hyg.]
Thersander3-?
Eurysthenes1 [Herod.] – Anaxandra [Paus.]
Procles1 [Apollod.] – Lathria [Paus.]
Glaucus5 – ? [Paus.]
Antimenes1 [Paus.]
Aegimius-?
Pamphylus [Paus.] – Orsobia [Paus.]
Xanthippus2 [Paus.]
Callias [Apollod.]
Ceisus – ? [Paus.]
Cerynes [Diod. Sic.]
Phalces1 – ? [Paus.]
Isthmius1 [Paus.]
Agis1 – ? [Herod.]
Cypselus2-?
Periander [Paus.] – Melissa2 [Paus.]
Sous – ? [Paus.]
Isthmius2 [Paus.]
Medon4 [Paus.]
Rhegnidas [Paus.]
Amphicles [Paus.]
Echestratus – ? [Herod.]
Lycophron1 [Herod.]
Eurypon [Paus.]
Lebotas [Herod.]
{Heracles1}
Phorcus1-Ceto1
: – Echidna [Herod.]
Agathyrsus [Herod.]
Gelonus [Herod.]
Scythes1 [Herod.]
Aegeias-?
: – Epicaste2 [Apollod.]
Thestalus [Apollod.]
Zeus-Hera
: – Hebe [Hom.]
Alexiares [Apollod.]
Anicetus [Apollod.]
Eurytus2-Antiope6
: – Iole [Soph.]
Poseidon-Gaea
: – Iphinoe4 [Pher.] – Antaeus1 [Pher.]
{Heracles1}
Euander1-?
: – Lavinia1 [Dion. Hal.]
Pallas5 [Dion. Hal.]
: – Malis [Hellan.]
Aceles [Hellan.]
Creon2-Eurydice6
: – Megara [Eur.]
Creontiades [Apollod.]
Deicoon [Apollod.]
Ophites [Hyg.]
Therimachus [Apollod.]
{Heracles1}
Aegaeus-?
: – Melite2 [Ap. Rhod.]
Phylas1-?
: – Mideia3 [Paus.]
Antiochus2 – ? [Apollod.]
Iola(u)s-Megara
Phylas2 [Apollod.] – Leipephilene [Gr. Ehoiai]
55d
Menoetius2-Sthenele2
: – Myrto1 [Plut.]
Eucleia [Plut.]
Iardanus-?
: – Omphale [Dion. Hal.]
Agelaus2 [Apollod.]
Lamus1 [Diod. Sic.]
Melas2 [Schol. Hom.]
Euander1-?
: – Pallantia [Serv.]
Stymphalus1-?
: – Parthenope2 [Apollod.]
Eueres2 [Apollod.]
Alcimedon1-?
: – Phialo [Paus.]
Aechmagoras [Paus.]
Eryx-?
: – Psophis1 [Paus.]
Echephron3 [Paus.]
Promachus2 [Paus.]
Bebryclus-?
: – Pyrene1 [Sil. Ital.]
[snake] [Sil. Ital.]
Adramys-?
: – Thebe4

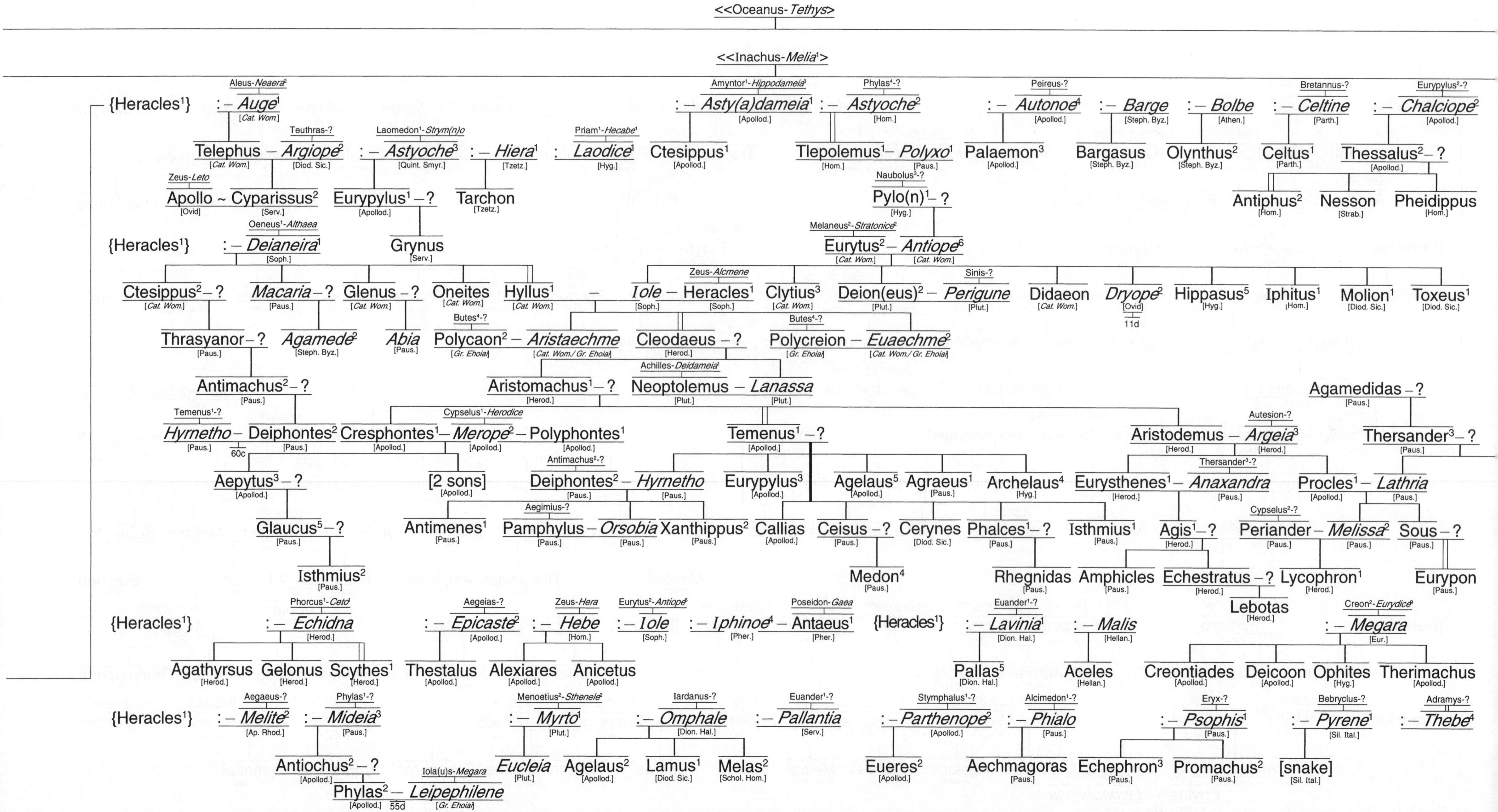

<<Oceanus-Tethys>
<<Inachus-Melia1>
{Heracles1}
Aleus-Neaera2
:– Auge1 [Cat. Wom.]
Teuthras-?
Telephus – Argiope2 [Cat. Wom.] [Diod. Sic.]
Zeus-Leto
Apollo ~ Cyparissus2 [Ovid] [Serv.]
Laomedon1-Strym(n)o
:– Astyoche3 [Quint. Smyr.]
Eurypylus1 – ? [Apollod.]
Grynus [Serv.]
:– Hiera1 [Tzetz.]
Tarchon [Tzetz.]
Priam1-Hecabe1
: Laodice1 [Hyg.]
Amyntor1-Hippodameia3
:– Asty(a)dameia1 [Apollod.]
Ctesippus1 [Apollod.]
Phylas4-?
:– Astyoche2 [Hom.]
Tlepolemus1 – Polyxo1 [Hom.] [Paus.]
Naubolus3-?
Pylo(n)1 – ? [Hyg.]
Peireus-?
:– Autonoe4 [Apollod.]
Palaemon3 [Apollod.]
:– Barge [Steph. Byz.]
Bargasus [Steph. Byz.]
:– Bolbe [Athen.]
Olynthus2 [Steph. Byz.]
Bretannus-?
:– Celtine [Parth.]
Celtus1 [Parth.]
Eurypylus2-?
:– Chalciope2 [Apollod.]
Thessalus2 – ? [Apollod.]
Antiphus2 [Hom.]
Nesson [Strab.]
Pheidippus [Hom.]
{Heracles1}
Oeneus1-Althaea
:– Deianeira1 [Soph.]
Ctesippus2 – ? [Cat. Wom.]
Thrasyanor – ? [Paus.]
Antimachus2 – ? [Paus.]
Macaria – ? [Paus.]
Agamede2 [Steph. Byz.]
Glenus – ? [Cat. Wom.]
Abia [Paus.]
Oneites [Cat. Wom.]
Hyllus1 [Cat. Wom.]
Melaneus2-Stratonice2
Eurytus2 – Antiope6 [Cat. Wom.] [Cat. Wom.]
Zeus-Alcmene
Iole – Heracles1 [Soph.] [Soph.]
Clytius3 [Cat. Wom.]
Sinis-?
Deion(eus)2 – Perigune [Plut.] [Plut.]
Didaeon [Cat. Wom.]
Dryope2 [Ovid]
11d
Hippasus5 [Hyg.]
Iphitus1 [Hom.]
Molion1 [Diod. Sic.]
Toxeus1 [Diod. Sic.]
Butes4-?
Polycaon2 – Aristaechme [Gr. Ehoiai] [Cat. Wom./Gr. Ehoiai]
Cleodaeus – ? [Herod.]
Butes4-?
Polycreion – Euaechme2 [Gr. Ehoiai] [Cat. Wom./Gr. Ehoiai]
Achilles-Deidameia1
Aristomachus1 – ? [Herod.]
Neoptolemus – Lanassa [Plut.] [Plut.]
Temenus1-?
Hyrnetho – Deiphontes2 [Paus.] [Paus.]
60c
Aepytus3 – ? [Apollod.]
Glaucus5 – ? [Paus.]
Isthmius2 [Paus.]
Cypselus1-Herodice
Cresphontes1 – Merope2 – Polyphontes1 [Apollod.] [Apollod.]
[2 sons] [Apollod.]
Antimachus2-?
Deiphontes2 – Hyrnetho [Paus.] [Paus.]
Antimenes1 [Paus.]
Aegimius-?
Pamphylus – Orsobia [Paus.] [Paus.]
Xanthippus2 [Paus.]
Temenus1 – ? [Apollod.]
Eurypylus3 [Apollod.]
Agelaus5 [Apollod.]
Agraeus1 [Paus.]
Archelaus4 [Hyg.]
Callias [Apollod.]
Ceisus – ? [Paus.]
Medon4 [Paus.]
Cerynes [Diod. Sic.]
Phalces1 – ? [Paus.]
Rhegnidas [Paus.]
Isthmius1 [Paus.]
Agamedidas – ? [Paus.]
Thersander3 – ? [Paus.]
Autesion-?
Aristodemus – Argeia3 [Herod.] [Herod.]
Thersander3-?
Eurysthenes1 – Anaxandra [Herod.] [Paus.]
Agis1 – ? [Herod.]
Amphicles [Paus.]
Echestratus – ? [Herod.]
Lebotas [Herod.]
Procles1 – Lathria [Apollod.] [Paus.]
Cypselus2-?
Periander – Melissa2 [Paus.] [Paus.]
Lycophron1 [Herod.]
Sous – ? [Paus.]
Eurypon [Paus.]
{Heracles1}
Phorcus1-Ceto1
:– Echidna [Herod.]
Agathyrsus [Herod.]
Gelonus [Herod.]
Scythes1 [Herod.]
Aegeias-?
:– Epicaste2 [Apollod.]
Thestalus [Apollod.]
Zeus-Hera
:– Hebe [Hom.]
Alexiares [Apollod.]
Anicetus [Apollod.]
Eurytus2-Antiope6
:– Iole [Soph.]
:– Iphinoe4 – Antaeus1 [Pher.] [Pher.]
{Heracles1}
Euander1-?
:– Lavinia1 [Dion. Hal.]
Pallas5 [Dion. Hal.]
:– Malis [Hellan.]
Aceles [Hellan.]
Creon2-Eurydice8
:– Megara [Eur.]
Creontiades [Apollod.]
Deicoon [Apollod.]
Ophites [Hyg.]
Therimachus [Apollod.]
{Heracles1}
Aegaeus-?
:– Melite2 [Ap. Rhod.]
Phylas1-?
:– Mideia3 [Paus.]
Antiochus2 – ? [Apollod.]
Iola(u)s-Megara
Phylas2 – Leipephilene [Apollod.] [Gr. Ehoiai]
55d
Menoetius2-Sthenele2
:– Myrto1 [Plut.]
Eucleia [Plut.]
Iardanus-?
:– Omphale [Dion. Hal.]
Agelaus2 [Apollod.]
Lamus1 [Diod. Sic.]
Melas2 [Schol. Hom.]
Euander1-?
:– Pallantia [Serv.]
Stymphalus1-?
:– Parthenope2 [Apollod.]
Eueres2 [Apollod.]
Alcimedon1-?
:– Phialo [Paus.]
Aechmagoras [Paus.]
Eryx-?
:– Psophis1 [Paus.]
Echephron3 [Paus.]
Promachus2 [Paus.]
Bebryclus-?
:– Pyrene1 [Sil. Ital.]
[snake] [Sil. Ital.]
Adramys-?
:– Thebe4

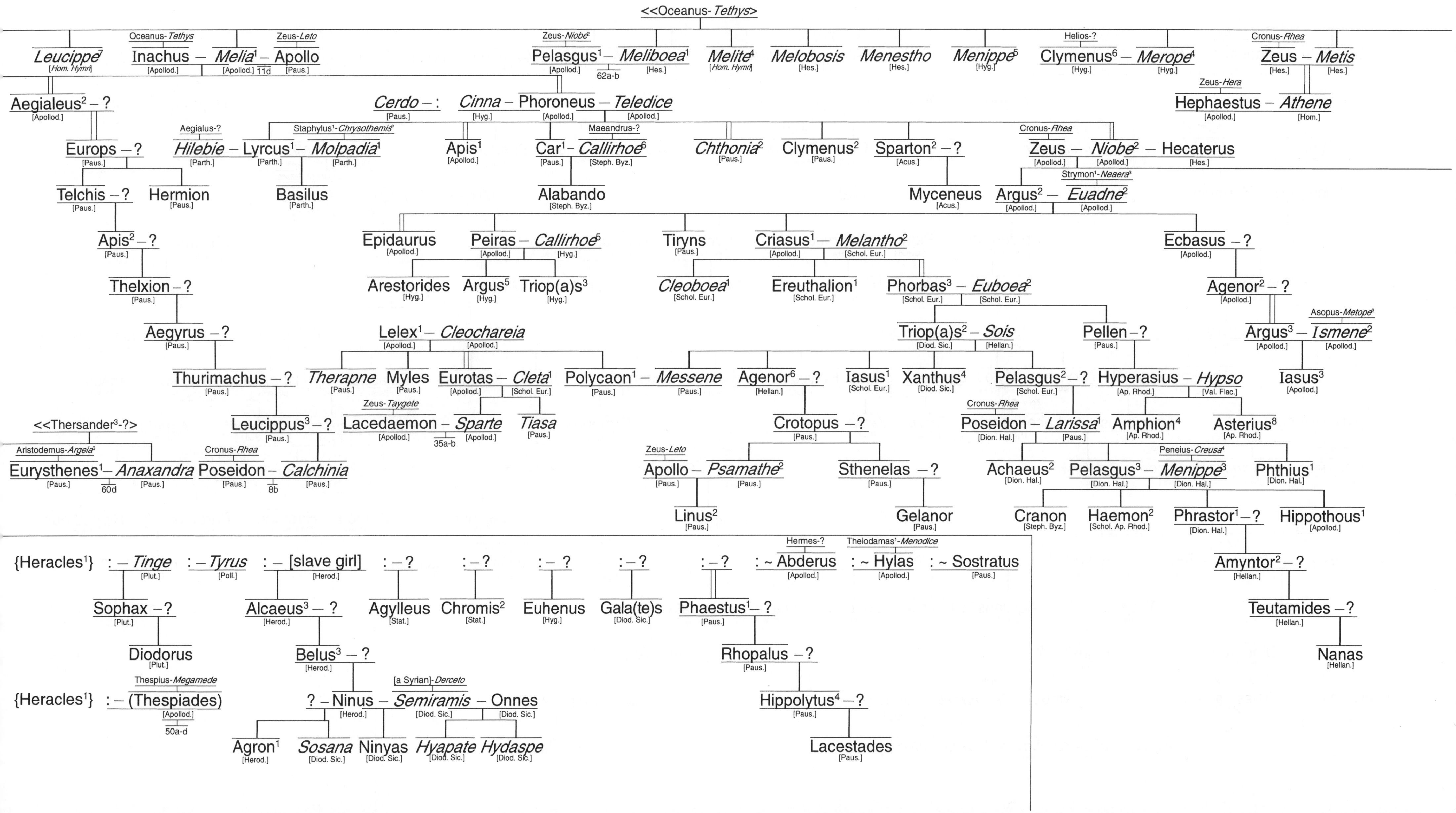
<<Oceanus-Tethys>
Oceanus-Tethys
Zeus-Leto
Zeus-Niobe2
Helios-?
Cronus-Rhea
Leucippe7 [Hom. Hymn]
Inachus [Apollod.]
Melia1 [Apollod.]
Apollo [Paus.]
11d
Pelasgus1 [Apollod.]
62a-b
Meliboea1 [Hes.]
Melite4 [Hom. Hymn]
Melobosis [Hes.]
Menestho [Hes.]
Menippe5 [Hyg.]
Clymenus6 [Hyg.]
Merope4 [Hyg.]
Zeus [Hes.]
Metis [Hes.]
Zeus-Hera
Aegialeus2 – ? [Apollod.]
Cerdo – : [Paus.]
Cinna [Hyg.]
Phoroneus [Apollod.]
Teledice [Apollod.]
Hephaestus [Apollod.]
Athene [Hom.]
Aegialus-?
Staphylus1-Chrysothemis2
Maeandrus-?
Cronus-Rhea
Europs – ? [Paus.]
Hilebie [Parth.]
Lyrcus1 [Parth.]
Molpadia1 [Parth.]
Apis1 [Apollod.]
Car1 [Paus.]
Callirhoe6 [Steph. Byz.]
Chthonia2 [Paus.]
Clymenus2 [Paus.]
Sparton2 – ? [Acus.]
Zeus [Apollod.]
Niobe2 [Apollod.]
Hecaterus [Hes.]
Strymon1-Neaera3
Telchis – ? [Paus.]
Hermion [Paus.]
Basilus [Parth.]
Alabando [Steph. Byz.]
Myceneus [Acus.]
Argus2 [Apollod.]
Euadne2 [Apollod.]
Apis2 – ? [Paus.]
Epidaurus [Apollod.]
Peiras [Apollod.]
Callirhoe5 [Hyg.]
Tiryns [Paus.]
Criasus1 [Apollod.]
Melantho2 [Schol. Eur.]
Ecbasus – ? [Apollod.]
Thelxion – ? [Paus.]
Arestorides [Hyg.]
Argus5 [Hyg.]
Triop(a)s3 [Hyg.]
Cleoboea1 [Schol. Eur.]
Ereuthalion1 [Schol. Eur.]
Phorbas3 [Schol. Eur.]
Euboea2 [Schol. Eur.]
Agenor2 – ? [Apollod.]
Asopus-Metope2
Aegyrus – ? [Paus.]
Lelex1 [Apollod.]
Cleochareia [Apollod.]
Triop(a)s2 [Diod. Sic.]
Sois [Hellan.]
Pellen – ? [Paus.]
Argus3 [Apollod.]
Ismene2 [Apollod.]
Thurimachus – ? [Paus.]
Therapne [Paus.]
Myles [Paus.]
Eurotas [Apollod.]
Cleta1 [Schol. Eur.]
Polycaon1 [Paus.]
Messene [Paus.]
Agenor6 – ? [Hellan.]
Iasus1 [Schol. Eur.]
Xanthus4 [Diod. Sic.]
Pelasgus2 – ? [Schol. Eur.]
Hyperasius [Ap. Rhod.]
Hypso [Val. Flac.]
Iasus3 [Apollod.]
Zeus-Taygete
Cronus-Rhea
<<Thersander3-?>
Leucippus3 – ? [Paus.]
Lacedaemon [Apollod.]
Sparte [Apollod.]
35a-b
Tiasa [Paus.]
Crotopus – ? [Paus.]
Poseidon [Dion. Hal.]
Larissa1 [Paus.]
Amphion4 [Ap. Rhod.]
Asterius8 [Ap. Rhod.]
Aristodemus-Argeia3
Cronus-Rhea
Zeus-Leto
Peneius-Creusa4
Eurysthenes1 [Paus.]
60d
Anaxandra [Paus.]
Poseidon [Paus.]
8b
Calchinia [Paus.]
Apollo [Paus.]
Psamathe2 [Paus.]
Sthenelas – ? [Paus.]
Achaeus2 [Dion. Hal.]
Pelasgus3 [Dion. Hal.]
Menippe3 [Dion. Hal.]
Phthius1 [Dion. Hal.]
Linus2 [Paus.]
Gelanor [Paus.]
Cranon [Steph. Byz.]
Haemon2 [Schol. Ap. Rhod.]
Phrastor1 – ? [Dion. Hal.]
Hippothous1 [Apollod.]
Hermes-?
Theiodamas1-Menodice
{Heracles1}
: – Tinge [Plut.]
: – Tyrus [Poll.]
: – [slave girl] [Herod.]
: – ?
: – ?
: – ?
: – ?
: – ?
: ~ Abderus [Apollod.]
: ~ Hylas [Apollod.]
: ~ Sostratus [Paus.]
Amyntor2 – ? [Hellan.]
Sophax – ? [Plut.]
Alcaeus3 – ? [Herod.]
Agylleus [Stat.]
Chromis2 [Stat.]
Euhenus [Hyg.]
Gala(te)s [Diod. Sic.]
Phaestus1 – ? [Paus.]
Teutamides – ? [Hellan.]
Diodorus [Plut.]
Belus3 – ? [Herod.]
Rhopalus – ? [Paus.]
Nanas [Hellan.]
Thespius-Megamede
[a Syrian]-Derceto
{Heracles1}
: – (Thespiades) [Apollod.]
50a-d
? – Ninus [Herod.]
Semiramis [Diod. Sic.]
Onnes [Diod. Sic.]
Hippolytus4 – ? [Paus.]
Agron1 [Herod.]
Sosana [Diod. Sic.]
Ninyas [Diod. Sic.]
Hyapate [Diod. Sic.]
Hydaspe [Diod. Sic.]
Lacestades [Paus.]

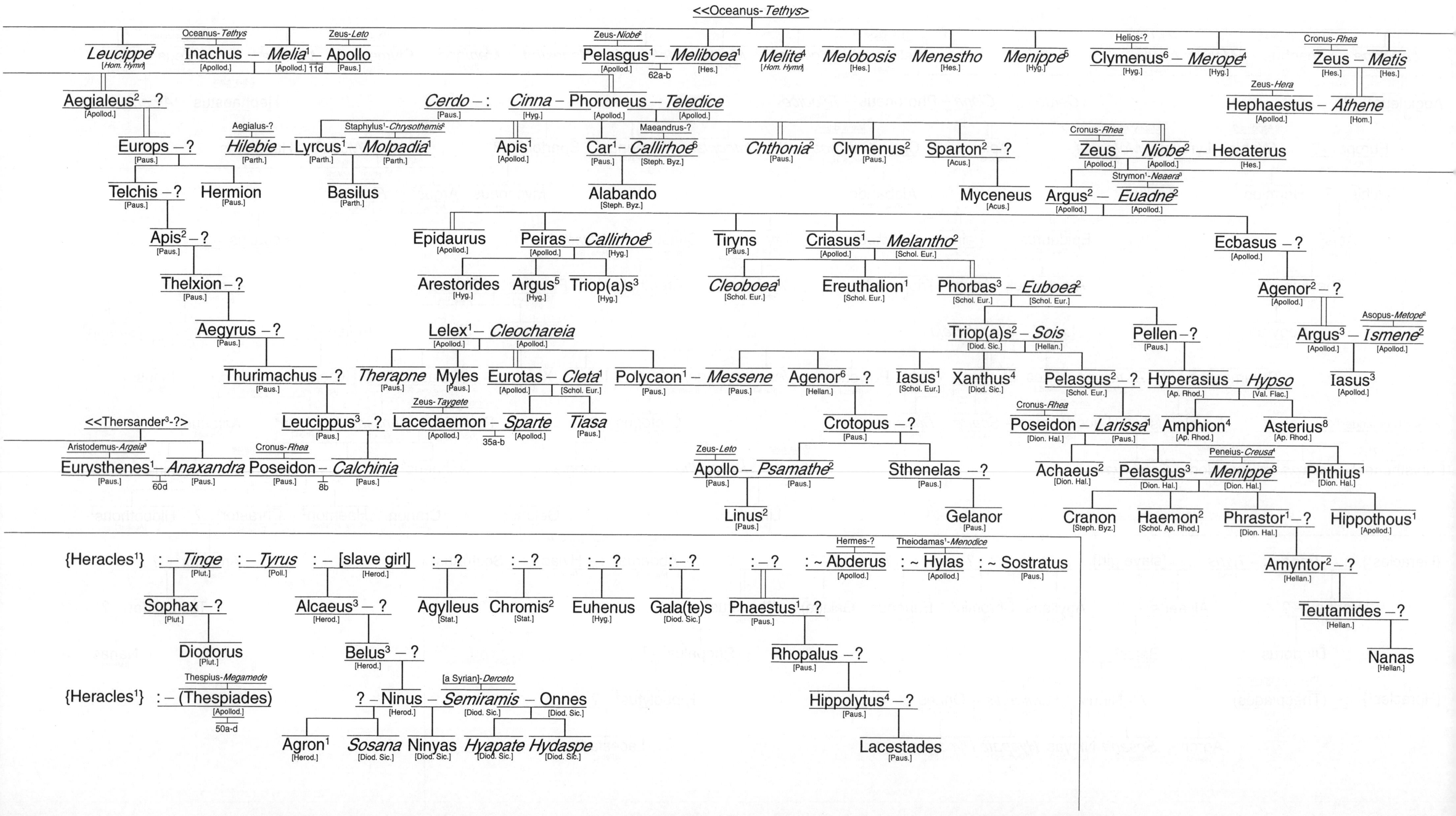

<<Oceanus- Tethys>
Leucippe7 [Hom. Hymn]
Oceanus- Tethys
Inachus – Melia1 – Apollo
[Apollod.] [Apollod.] 11d [Paus.]
Zeus-Leto
Zeus-Niobe2
Pelasgus1 – Meliboea1
[Apollod.] 62a-b [Hes.]
Melite4 [Hom. Hymn]
Melobosis [Hes.]
Menestho [Hes.]
Menippe5 [Hyg.]
Helios-?
Clymenus6 – Merope4
[Hyg.] [Hyg.]
Cronus-Rhea
Zeus – Metis
[Hes.] [Hes.]
Zeus-Hera
Hephaestus – Athene
[Apollod.] [Hom.]
Aegialeus2 – ?
[Apollod.]
Cerdo – :
[Paus.]
Cinna – Phoroneus – Teledice
[Hyg.] [Apollod.] [Apollod.]
Europs – ?
[Paus.]
Aegialus-?
Hilebie – Lyrcus1 – Molpadia1
[Parth.] [Parth.] [Parth.]
Staphylus1-Chrysothemis2
Apis1
[Apollod.]
Maeandrus-?
Car1 – Callirhoe6
[Paus.] [Steph. Byz.]
Chthonia2 [Paus.]
Clymenus2 [Paus.]
Sparton2 – ?
[Acus.]
Cronus-Rhea
Zeus – Niobe2 – Hecaterus
[Apollod.] [Apollod.] [Hes.]
Telchis – ?
[Paus.]
Hermion
[Paus.]
Basilus
[Parth.]
Alabando
[Steph. Byz.]
Myceneus
[Acus.]
Strymon1-Neaera3
Argus2 – Euadne2
[Apollod.] [Apollod.]
Apis2 – ?
[Paus.]
Epidaurus
[Apollod.]
Peiras – Callirhoe5
[Apollod.] [Hyg.]
Tiryns
[Paus.]
Criasus1 – Melantho2
[Apollod.] [Schol. Eur.]
Ecbasus – ?
[Apollod.]
Thelxion – ?
[Paus.]
Arestorides [Hyg.]
Argus5 [Hyg.]
Triop(a)s3 [Hyg.]
Cleoboea1 [Schol. Eur.]
Ereuthalion1 [Schol. Eur.]
Phorbas3 – Euboea2
[Schol. Eur.] [Schol. Eur.]
Agenor2 – ?
[Apollod.]
Aegyrus – ?
[Paus.]
Lelex1 – Cleochareia
[Apollod.] [Apollod.]
Triop(a)s2 – Sois
[Diod. Sic.] [Hellan.]
Pellen – ?
[Paus.]
Asopus-Metope2
Argus3 – Ismene2
[Apollod.] [Apollod.]
Thurimachus – ?
[Paus.]
Therapne [Paus.]
Myles [Paus.]
Eurotas – Cleta1
[Apollod.] [Schol. Eur.]
Polycaon1 – Messene
[Paus.] [Paus.]
Agenor6 – ?
[Hellan.]
Iasus1 [Schol. Eur.]
Xanthus4 [Diod. Sic.]
Pelasgus2 – ?
[Schol. Eur.]
Hyperasius – Hypso
[Ap. Rhod.] [Val. Flac.]
Iasus3 [Apollod.]
<<Thersander3-?>
Leucippus3 – ?
[Paus.]
Zeus-Taygete
Lacedaemon – Sparte
[Apollod.] 35a-b [Apollod.]
Tiasa [Paus.]
Crotopus – ?
[Paus.]
Cronus-Rhea
Poseidon – Larissa1
[Dion. Hal.] [Paus.]
Amphion4 [Ap. Rhod.]
Asterius8 [Ap. Rhod.]
Aristodemus-Argeia3
Eurysthenes1 – Anaxandra
[Paus.] 60d [Paus.]
Cronus-Rhea
Poseidon – Calchinia
[Paus.] 8b [Paus.]
Zeus-Leto
Apollo – Psamathe2
[Paus.] [Paus.]
Sthenelas – ?
[Paus.]
Achaeus2 [Dion. Hal.]
Peneius-Creusa4
Pelasgus3 – Menippe3
[Dion. Hal.] [Dion. Hal.]
Phthius1 [Dion. Hal.]
Linus2 [Paus.]
Gelanor [Paus.]
Cranon [Steph. Byz.]
Haemon2 [Schol. Ap. Rhod.]
Phrastor1 – ?
[Dion. Hal.]
Hippothous1 [Apollod.]
{Heracles1} : – Tinge [Plut.] : – Tyrus [Poll.] : – [slave girl] [Herod.] : – ? : – ? : – ? : – ? : – ?
Hermes-?
: ~ Abderus [Apollod.]
Theiodamas1-Menodice
: ~ Hylas [Apollod.]
: ~ Sostratus [Paus.]
Amyntor2 – ?
[Hellan.]
Sophax – ?
[Plut.]
Alcaeus3 – ?
[Herod.]
Agylleus [Stat.]
Chromis2 [Stat.]
Euhenus [Hyg.]
Gala(te)s [Diod. Sic.]
Phaestus1 – ?
[Paus.]
Teutamides – ?
[Hellan.]
Diodorus
[Plut.]
Belus3 – ?
[Herod.]
Rhopalus – ?
[Paus.]
Nanas
[Hellan.]
Thespius-Megamede
{Heracles1} : – (Thespiades)
[Apollod.]
50a-d
[a Syrian]-Derceto
? – Ninus – Semiramis – Onnes
[Herod.] [Diod. Sic.] [Diod. Sic.]
Hippolytus4 – ?
[Paus.]
Agron1 [Herod.]
Sosana [Diod. Sic.]
Ninyas [Diod. Sic.]
Hyapate [Diod. Sic.]
Hydaspe [Diod. Sic.]
Lacestades
[Paus.]

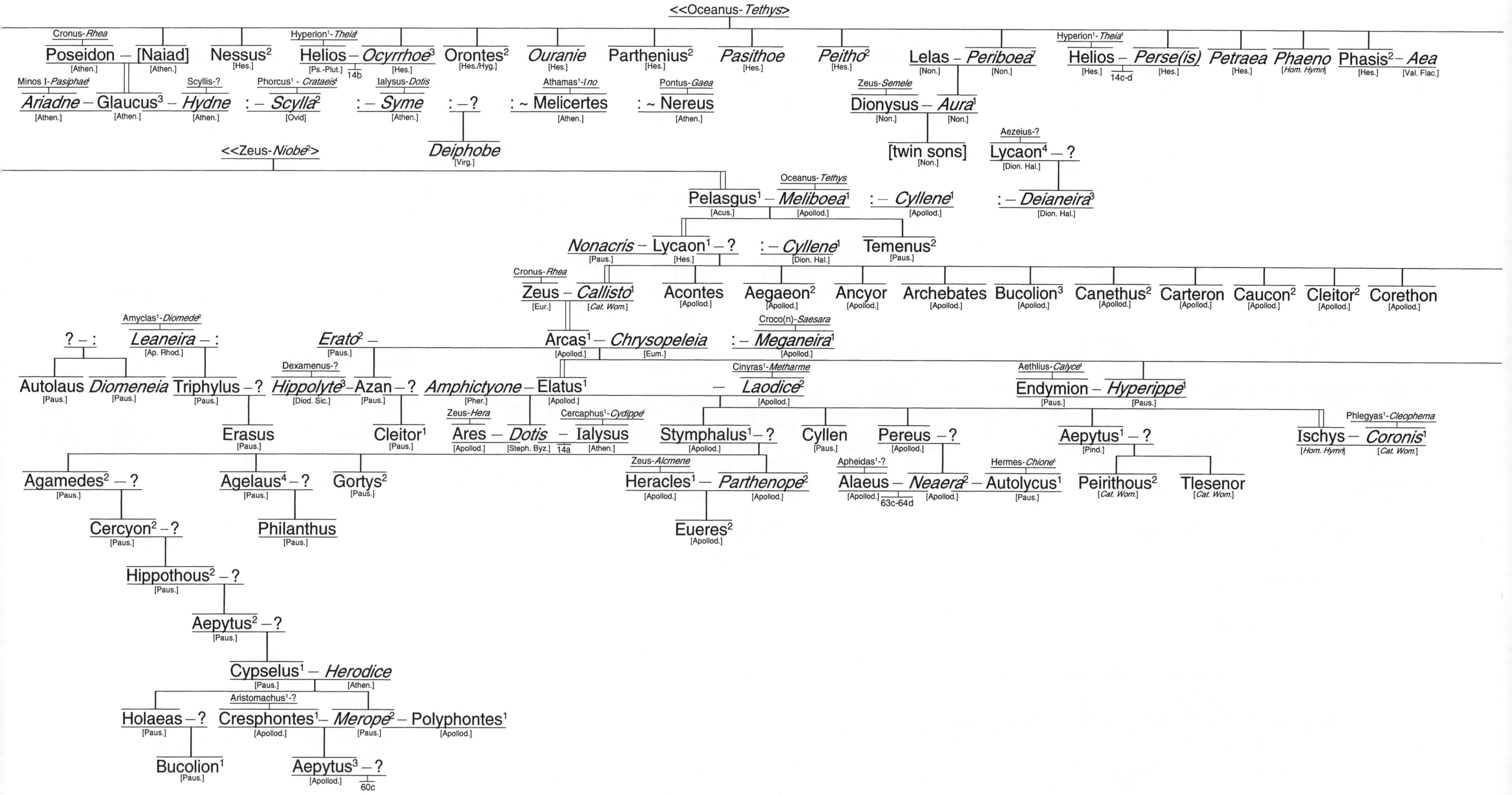

<<Oceanus-Tethys>
Cronus-Rhea
Poseidon – [Naiad]
[Athen.] [Athen.]
Nessus2
[Hes.]
Hyperion1-Theia2
Helios – Ocyrrhoe3
[Ps.-Plut.] 14b [Hes.]
Orontes2
[Hes./Hyg.]
Ouranie
[Hes.]
Parthenius2
[Hes.]
Pasithoe
[Hes.]
Peitho2
[Hes.]
Lelas – Periboea7
[Non.] [Non.]
Hyperion1-Theia1
Helios – Perse(is)
[Hes.] 14c-d [Hes.]
Petraea
[Hes.]
Phaeno
[Hom. Hymn]
Phasis2 – Aea
[Hes.] [Val. Flac.]
Minos I-Pasiphae1
Ariadne – Glaucus3 – Hydne
[Athen.] [Athen.] [Athen.]
Scyllis-?
Phorcus1 - Crataeis1
: – Scylla2
[Ovid]
Ialysus-Dotis
: – Syme
[Athen.]
: – ?
Deiphobe
[Virg.]
Athamas1-Ino
: ~ Melicertes
[Athen.]
Pontus-Gaea
: ~ Nereus
[Athen.]
Zeus-Semele
Dionysus – Aura1
[Non.] [Non.]
[twin sons]
[Non.]
Aezeius-?
Lycaon4 – ?
[Dion. Hal.]
: – Deianeira3
[Dion. Hal.]
<<Zeus-Niobe2>
Oceanus-Tethys
Pelasgus1 – Meliboea1
[Acus.] [Apollod.]
: – Cyllene1
[Apollod.]
Nonacris – Lycaon1 – ?
[Paus.] [Hes.]
: – Cyllene1
[Dion. Hal.]
Temenus2
[Paus.]
Cronus-Rhea
Zeus – Callisto1
[Eur.] [Cat. Wom.]
Acontes
[Apollod.]
Aegaeon2
[Apollod.]
Ancyor
[Apollod.]
Archebates
[Apollod.]
Bucolion3
[Apollod.]
Canethus2
[Apollod.]
Carteron
[Apollod.]
Caucon2
[Apollod.]
Cleitor2
[Apollod.]
Corethon
[Apollod.]
Amyclas1-Diomede2
? – :
Leaneira – :
[Ap. Rhod.]
Erato2 –
[Paus.]
Arcas1 – Chrysopeleia
[Apollod.] [Eum.]
Croco(n)-Saesara
: – Meganeira1
[Apollod.]
Autolaus
[Paus.]
Diomeneia
[Paus.]
Triphylus – ?
[Paus.]
Dexamenus-?
Hippolyte3 – Azan – ?
[Diod. Sic.] [Paus.]
Amphictyone – Elatus1
[Pher.] [Apollod.]
Cinyras1-Metharme
– Laodice2
[Apollod.]
Aethlius-Calyce1
Endymion – Hyperippe1
[Paus.] [Paus.]
Erasus
[Paus.]
Cleitor1
[Paus.]
Zeus-Hera
Ares – Dotis
[Apollod.] [Steph. Byz.]
Cercaphus1-Cydippe1
– Ialysus
14a [Athen.]
Stymphalus1 – ?
[Apollod.]
Cyllen
[Paus.]
Pereus – ?
[Apollod.]
Aepytus1 – ?
[Pind.]
Phlegyas1-Cleophema
Ischys – Coronis1
[Hom. Hymn] [Cat. Wom.]
Agamedes2 – ?
[Paus.]
Agelaus4 – ?
[Paus.]
Gortys2
[Paus.]
Zeus-Alcmene
Heracles1 – Parthenope2
[Apollod.] [Apollod.]
Apheidas1-?
Alaeus – Neaera2 – Autolycus1
[Apollod.] 63c-64d [Apollod.] [Paus.]
Hermes-Chione1
Peirithous2
[Cat. Wom.]
Tlesenor
[Cat. Wom.]
Cercyon2 – ?
[Paus.]
Philanthus
[Paus.]
Eueres2
[Apollod.]
Hippothous2 – ?
[Paus.]
Aepytus2 – ?
[Paus.]
Cypselus1 – Herodice
[Paus.] [Athen.]
Aristomachus1-?
Holaeas – ?
[Paus.]
Cresphontes1 – Merope2 – Polyphontes1
[Apollod.] [Paus.] [Apollod.]
Bucolion1
[Paus.]
Aepytus3 – ?
[Apollod.] 60c

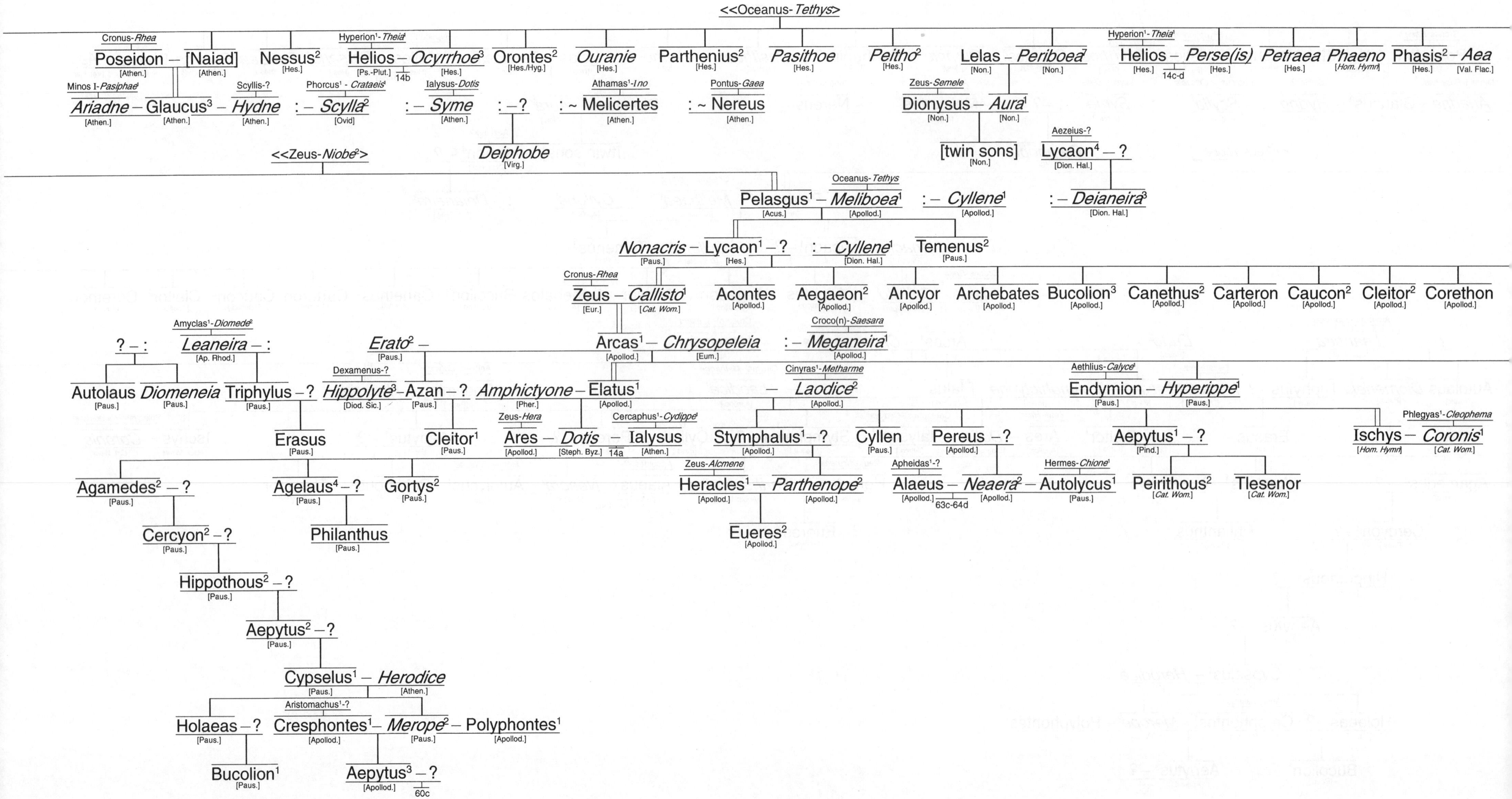
<<Oceanus-Tethys>
Cronus-Rhea
Poseidon – [Naiad]
[Athen.] [Athen.]
Nessus[2]
[Hes.]
Hyperion[1]-Theia[1]
Helios – Ocyrrhoe[3]
[Ps.-Plut.] [Hes.]
14b
Orontes[2]
[Hes./Hyg.]
Ouranie
[Hes.]
Parthenius[2]
[Hes.]
Pasithoe
[Hes.]
Peitho[2]
[Hes.]
Lelas – Periboea[7]
[Non.] [Non.]
Hyperion[1]-Theia[1]
Helios – Perse(is)
[Hes.] [Hes.]
14c-d
Petraea
[Hes.]
Phaeno
[Hom. Hymn]
Phasis[2] – Aea
[Hes.] [Val. Flac.]
Minos I-Pasiphae[1]
Ariadne – Glaucus[3] – Hydne
[Athen.] [Athen.] [Athen.]
Scyllis-?
Phorcus[1] - Crataeis[1]
: – Scylla[2]
[Ovid]
Ialysus-Dotis
: – Syme
[Athen.]
: – ?
Deiphobe
[Virg.]
Athamas[1]-Ino
: ~ Melicertes
[Athen.]
Pontus-Gaea
: ~ Nereus
[Athen.]
Zeus-Semele
Dionysus – Aura[1]
[Non.] [Non.]
[twin sons]
[Non.]
Aezeius-?
Lycaon[4] – ?
[Dion. Hal.]
: – Deianeira[3]
[Dion. Hal.]
<<Zeus-Niobe[2]>
Oceanus-Tethys
Pelasgus[1] – Meliboea[1]
[Acus.] [Apollod.]
: – Cyllene[1]
[Apollod.]
Nonacris – Lycaon[1] – ?
[Paus.] [Hes.]
: – Cyllene[1]
[Dion. Hal.]
Temenus[2]
[Paus.]
Cronus-Rhea
Zeus – Callisto[1]
[Eur.] [Cat. Wom.]
Acontes
[Apollod.]
Aegaeon[2]
[Apollod.]
Ancyor
[Apollod.]
Archebates
[Apollod.]
Bucolion[3]
[Apollod.]
Canethus[2]
[Apollod.]
Carteron
[Apollod.]
Caucon[2]
[Apollod.]
Cleitor[2]
[Apollod.]
Corethon
[Apollod.]
Amyclas[1]-Diomede[2]
? – :
Leaneira – :
[Ap. Rhod.]
Erato[2] –
[Paus.]
Arcas[1] – Chrysopeleia
[Apollod.] [Eum.]
Croco(n)-Saesara
: – Meganeira[1]
[Apollod.]
Autolaus
[Paus.]
Diomeneia
[Paus.]
Triphylus – ?
[Paus.]
Dexamenus-?
Hippolyte[3] – Azan – ?
[Diod. Sic.] [Paus.]
Amphictyone – Elatus[1]
[Pher.] [Apollod.]
Cinyras[1]-Metharme
Laodice[2]
[Apollod.]
Aethlius-Calyce[1]
Endymion – Hyperippe[1]
[Paus.] [Paus.]
Erasus
[Paus.]
Cleitor[1]
[Paus.]
Zeus-Hera
Ares – Dotis
[Apollod.] [Steph. Byz.]
Cercaphus[1]-Cydippe[1]
– Ialysus
14a
[Athen.]
Stymphalus[1] – ?
[Apollod.]
Cyllen
[Paus.]
Pereus – ?
[Apollod.]
Aepytus[1] – ?
[Pind.]
Phlegyas[1]-Cleophema
Ischys – Coronis[1]
[Hom. Hymn] [Cat. Wom.]
Agamedes[2] – ?
[Paus.]
Agelaus[4] – ?
[Paus.]
Gortys[2]
[Paus.]
Zeus-Alcmene
Heracles[1] – Parthenope[2]
[Apollod.] [Apollod.]
Apheidas[1]-?
Alaeus – Neaera[2] – Autolycus[1]
[Apollod.] [Apollod.] [Paus.]
63c-64d
Hermes-Chione[1]
Peirithous[2]
[Cat. Wom.]
Tlesenor
[Cat. Wom.]
Cercyon[2] – ?
[Paus.]
Philanthus
[Paus.]
Eueres[2]
[Apollod.]
Hippothous[2] – ?
[Paus.]
Aepytus[2] – ?
[Paus.]
Cypselus[1] – Herodice
[Paus.] [Athen.]
Aristomachus[1]-?
Holaeas – ?
[Paus.]
Cresphontes[1] – Merope[2] – Polyphontes[1]
[Apollod.] [Paus.] [Apollod.]
Bucolion[1]
[Paus.]
Aepytus[3] – ?
[Apollod.]
60c

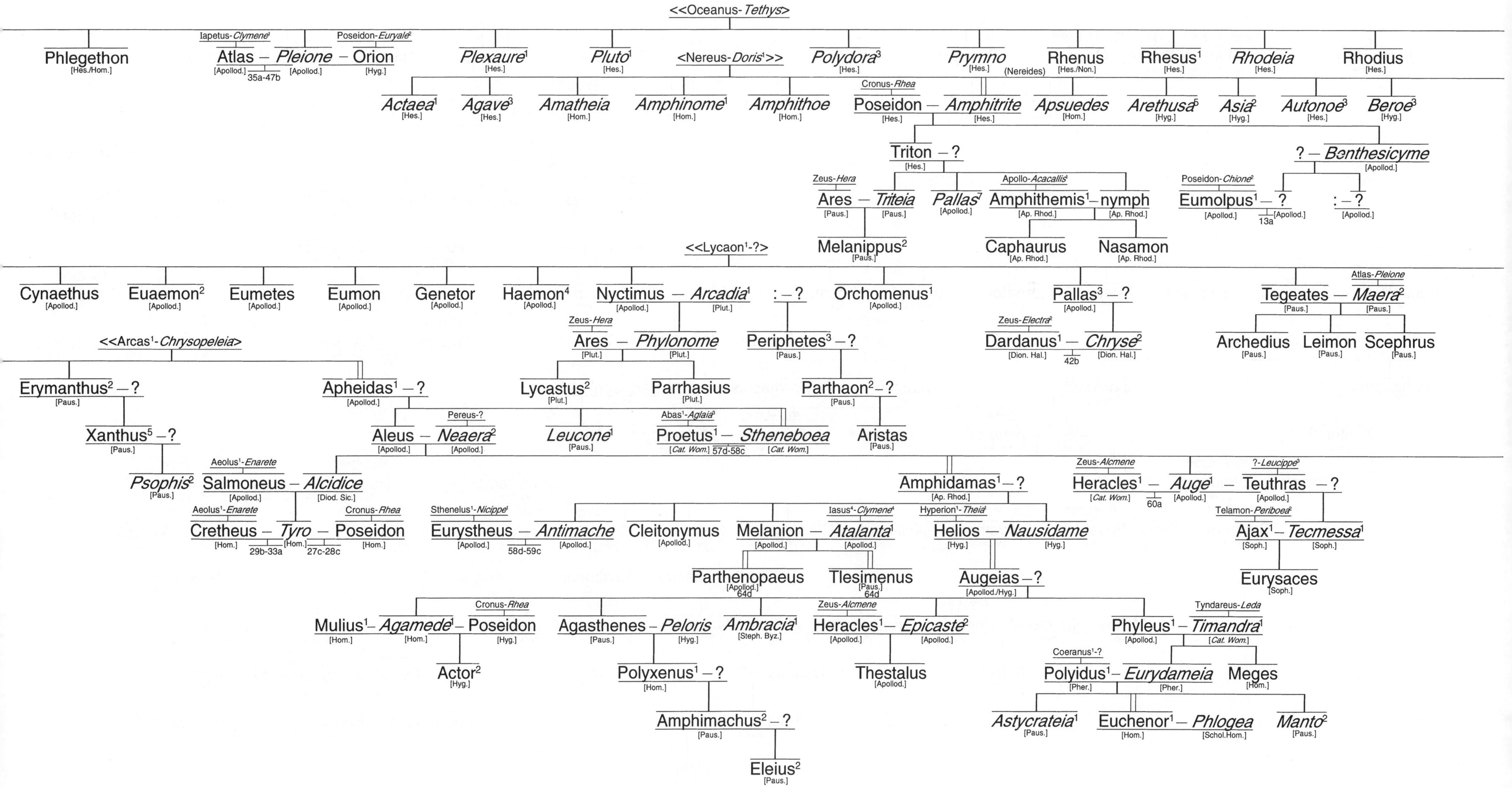
<<Oceanus-*Tethys*>
Phlegethon [Hes./Hom.]
Iapetus-*Clymene*[1]
Atlas [Apollod.]
35a-47b
Pleione [Apollod.]
Poseidon-*Euryale*[2]
Orion [Hyg.]
Plexaure[1] [Hes.]
Pluto[1] [Hes.]
<Nereus-*Doris*[1]>>
Polydora[3] [Hes.]
Prymno [Hes.]
(Nereides)
Rhenus [Hes./Non.]
Rhesus[1] [Hes.]
Rhodeia [Hes.]
Rhodius [Hes.]
Actaea[1] [Hes.]
Agave[3] [Hes.]
Amatheia [Hom.]
Amphinome[1] [Hom.]
Amphithoe [Hom.]
Cronus-*Rhea*
Poseidon [Hes.]
Amphitrite [Hes.]
Apsuedes [Hom.]
Arethusa[5] [Hyg.]
Asia[2] [Hyg.]
Autonoe[3] [Hes.]
Beroe[3] [Hyg.]
Triton – ? [Hes.]
? – *Benthesicyme* [Apollod.]
Zeus-*Hera*
Ares [Paus.]
Triteia [Paus.]
Pallas[7] [Apollod.]
Apollo-*Acacallis*[1]
Amphithemis[1] [Ap. Rhod.]
nymph [Ap. Rhod.]
Poseidon-*Chione*[2]
Eumolpus[1] [Apollod.]
– ? [Apollod.]
13a
: – ? [Apollod.]
Melanippus[2] [Paus.]
Caphaurus [Ap. Rhod.]
Nasamon [Ap. Rhod.]
<<Lycaon[1]-?>
Cynaethus [Apollod.]
Euaemon[2] [Apollod.]
Eumetes [Apollod.]
Eumon [Apollod.]
Genetor [Apollod.]
Haemon[4] [Apollod.]
Nyctimus [Apollod.]
Arcadia[1] [Plut.]
: – ?
Orchomenus[1] [Apollod.]
Pallas[3] – ? [Apollod.]
Atlas-*Pleione*
Tegeates [Paus.]
Maera[2] [Paus.]
Zeus-*Hera*
Ares [Plut.]
Phylonome [Plut.]
Periphetes[3] – ? [Paus.]
Zeus-*Electra*[2]
Dardanus[1] [Dion. Hal.]
42b
Chryse[2] [Dion. Hal.]
Archedius [Paus.]
Leimon [Paus.]
Scephrus [Paus.]
<<Arcas[1]-*Chrysopeleia*>
Erymanthus[2] – ? [Paus.]
Apheidas[1] – ? [Apollod.]
Lycastus[2] [Plut.]
Parrhasius [Plut.]
Parthaon[2] – ? [Paus.]
Xanthus[5] – ? [Paus.]
Aleus [Apollod.]
Pereus-?
Neaera[2] [Apollod.]
Leucone[1] [Paus.]
Abas[1]-*Aglaia*[3]
Proetus[1] [*Cat. Wom.*]
57d-58c
Stheneboea [*Cat. Wom.*]
Aristas [Paus.]
Psophis[2] [Paus.]
Aeolus[1]-*Enarete*
Salmoneus [Apollod.]
Alcidice [Diod. Sic.]
Amphidamas[1] – ? [Ap. Rhod.]
Zeus-*Alcmene*
Heracles[1] [*Cat. Wom.*]
60a
Auge[1] [Apollod.]
?-*Leucippe*[3]
Teuthras – ? [Apollod.]
Aeolus[1]-*Enarete*
Cretheus [Hom.]
29b-33a
Tyro [Hom.]
27c-28c
Cronus-*Rhea*
Poseidon [Hom.]
Sthenelus[1]-*Nicippe*[1]
Eurystheus [Apollod.]
58d-59c
Antimache [Apollod.]
Cleitonymus [Apollod.]
Melanion [Apollod.]
Iasus[4]-*Clymene*[4]
Atalanta[1] [Apollod.]
Hyperion[1]-*Theia*[1]
Helios [Hyg.]
Nausidame [Hyg.]
Telamon-*Periboea*[2]
Ajax[1] [Soph.]
Tecmessa[1] [Soph.]
Parthenopaeus [Apollod.] 64d
Tlesimenus [Paus.] 64d
Augeias – ? [Apollod./Hyg.]
Eurysaces [Soph.]
Cronus-*Rhea*
Mulius[1] [Hom.]
Agamede[1] [Hom.]
Poseidon [Hyg.]
Agasthenes [Paus.]
Peloris [Hyg.]
Ambracia[1] [Steph. Byz.]
Zeus-*Alcmene*
Heracles[1] [Apollod.]
Epicaste[2] [Apollod.]
Tyndareus-*Leda*
Phyleus[1] [Apollod.]
Timandra[1] [*Cat. Wom.*]
Actor[2] [Hyg.]
Polyxenus[1] – ? [Hom.]
Thestalus [Apollod.]
Coeranus[1]-?
Polyidus[1] [Pher.]
Eurydameia [Pher.]
Meges [Hom.]
Amphimachus[2] – ? [Paus.]
Astycrateia[1] [Paus.]
Euchenor[1] [Hom.]
Phlogea [Schol.Hom.]
Manto[2] [Paus.]
Eleius[2] [Paus.]

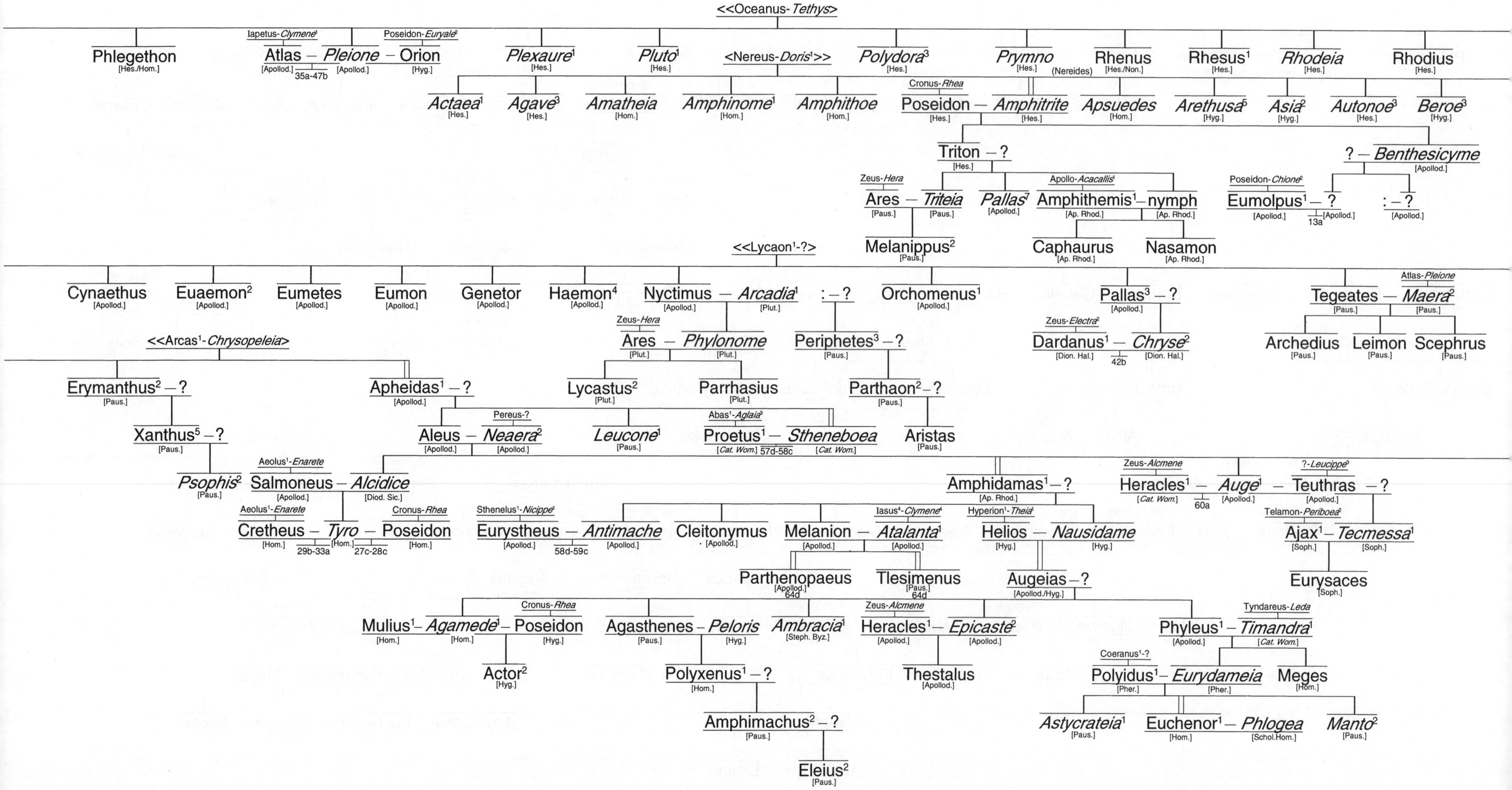
<<Oceanus-Tethys>
Phlegethon [Hes./Hom.]
Iapetus-Clymene[1]
Atlas [Apollod.] – Pleione [Apollod.] – Orion [Hyg.]
35a-47b
Poseidon-Euryale[2]
Plexaure[1] [Hes.]
Pluto[1] [Hes.]
<Nereus-Doris[1]>>
Polydora[3] [Hes.]
Prymno [Hes.]
(Nereides)
Rhenus [Hes./Non.]
Rhesus[1] [Hes.]
Rhodeia [Hes.]
Rhodius [Hes.]
Actaea[1] [Hes.]
Agave[3] [Hes.]
Amatheia [Hom.]
Amphinome[1] [Hom.]
Amphithoe [Hom.]
Cronus-Rhea
Poseidon [Hes.] – Amphitrite [Hes.]
Apsuedes [Hom.]
Arethusa[5] [Hyg.]
Asia[2] [Hyg.]
Autonoe[3] [Hes.]
Beroe[3] [Hyg.]
Triton – ? [Hes.]
? – Benthesicyme [Apollod.]
Zeus-Hera
Ares [Paus.] – Triteia [Paus.]
Pallas[7] [Apollod.]
Apollo-Acacallis[1]
Amphithemis[1] [Ap. Rhod.] – nymph [Ap. Rhod.]
Poseidon-Chione[2]
Eumolpus[1] [Apollod.] – ? [Apollod.]
13a
: – ? [Apollod.]
Melanippus[2] [Paus.]
Caphaurus [Ap. Rhod.]
Nasamon [Ap. Rhod.]
<<Lycaon[1]-?>
Cynaethus [Apollod.]
Euaemon[2] [Apollod.]
Eumetes [Apollod.]
Eumon [Apollod.]
Genetor [Apollod.]
Haemon[4] [Apollod.]
Nyctimus [Apollod.] – Arcadia[1] [Plut.]
: – ?
Orchomenus[1] [Apollod.]
Pallas[3] – ? [Apollod.]
Atlas-Pleione
Tegeates [Paus.] – Maera[2] [Paus.]
<<Arcas[1]-Chrysopeleia>
Zeus-Hera
Ares [Plut.] – Phylonome [Plut.]
Periphetes[3] – ? [Paus.]
Zeus-Electra[2]
Dardanus[1] [Dion. Hal.] – Chryse[2] [Dion. Hal.]
42b
Archedius [Paus.]
Leimon [Paus.]
Scephrus [Paus.]
Erymanthus[2] – ? [Paus.]
Apheidas[1] – ? [Apollod.]
Lycastus[2] [Plut.]
Parrhasius [Plut.]
Parthaon[2] – ? [Paus.]
Xanthus[5] – ? [Paus.]
Pereus-?
Aleus [Apollod.] – Neaera[2] [Apollod.]
Leucone[1] [Paus.]
Abas[1]-Aglaia[3]
Proetus[1] [Cat. Wom.] – Stheneboea [Cat. Wom.]
57d-58c
Aristas [Paus.]
Aeolus[1]-Enarete
Psophis[2] [Paus.]
Salmoneus [Apollod.] – Alcidice [Diod. Sic.]
Amphidamas[1] – ? [Ap. Rhod.]
Zeus-Alcmene
Heracles[1] [Cat. Wom.] – Auge[1] [Apollod.]
60a
?-Leucippe[3]
– Teuthras – ? [Apollod.]
Aeolus[1]-Enarete
Cretheus [Hom.] – Tyro [Hom.] – Poseidon [Hom.]
29b-33a
27c-28c
Cronus-Rhea
Sthenelus[1]-Nicippe[1]
Eurystheus [Apollod.] – Antimache [Apollod.]
58d-59c
Cleitonymus [Apollod.]
Iasus[4]-Clymene[4]
Melanion [Apollod.] – Atalanta[1] [Apollod.]
Hyperion[1]-Theia[1]
Helios [Hyg.] – Nausidame [Hyg.]
Telamon-Periboea[2]
Ajax[1] [Soph.] – Tecmessa[1] [Soph.]
Parthenopaeus [Apollod.] 64d
Tlesimenus [Paus.] 64d
Augeias – ? [Apollod./Hyg.]
Eurysaces [Soph.]
Cronus-Rhea
Mulius[1] [Hom.] – Agamede[1] [Hom.] – Poseidon [Hyg.]
Agasthenes [Paus.] – Peloris [Hyg.]
Ambracia[1] [Steph. Byz.]
Zeus-Alcmene
Heracles[1] [Apollod.] – Epicaste[2] [Apollod.]
Tyndareus-Leda
Phyleus[1] [Apollod.] – Timandra[1] [Cat. Wom.]
Actor[2] [Hyg.]
Polyxenus[1] – ? [Hom.]
Thestalus [Apollod.]
Coeranus[1]-?
Polyidus[1] [Pher.] – Eurydameia [Pher.]
Meges [Hom.]
Amphimachus[2] – ? [Paus.]
Astycrateia[1] [Paus.]
Euchenor[1] [Hom.] – Phlogea [Schol.Hom.]
Manto[2] [Paus.]
Eleius[2] [Paus.]

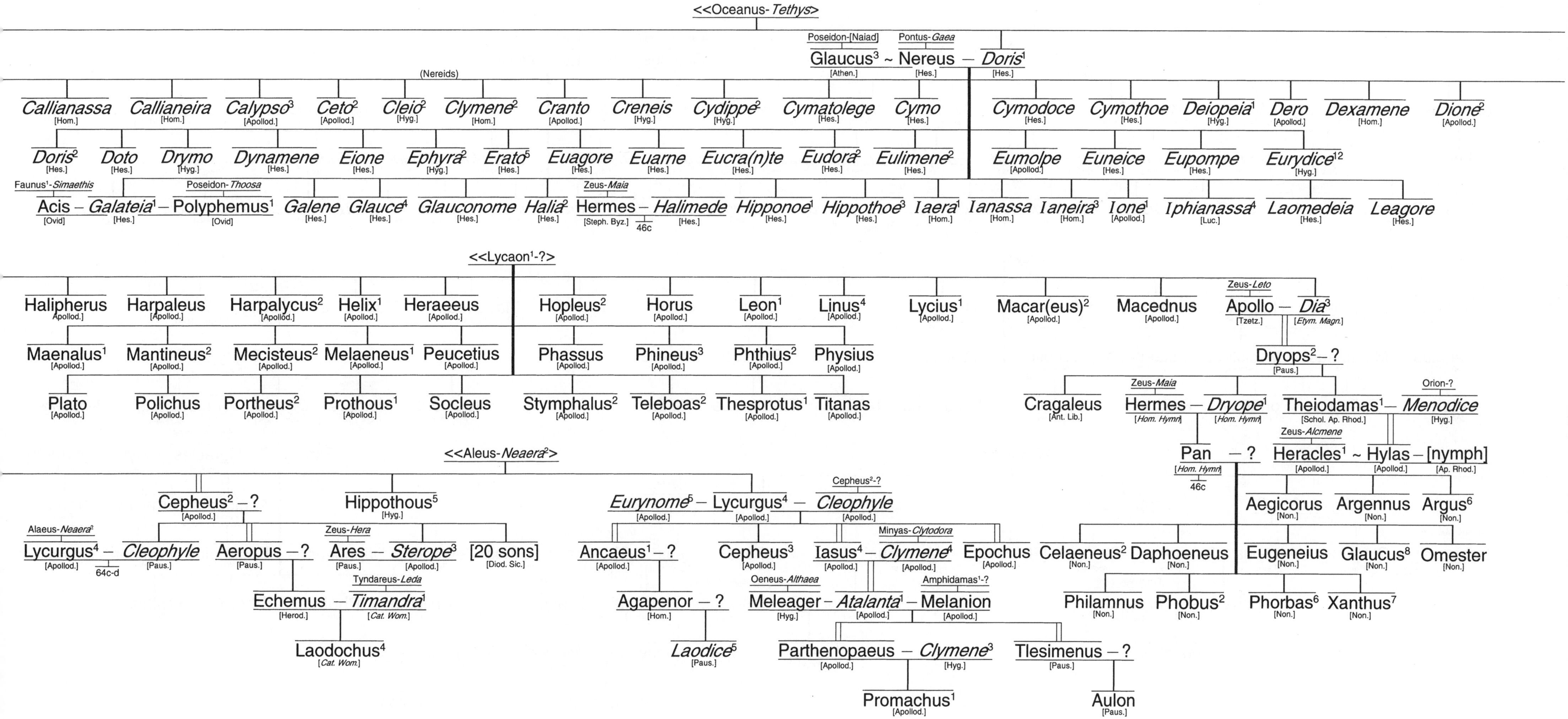

<<Oceanus-Tethys>
Poseidon-[Naiad]
Pontus-Gaea
Glaucus3 ~ Nereus – Doris1
[Athen.] [Hes.] [Hes.]
(Nereids)
Callianassa [Hom.]
Callianeira [Hom.]
Calypso3 [Apollod.]
Ceto2 [Apollod.]
Cleio2 [Hyg.]
Clymene2 [Hom.]
Cranto [Apollod.]
Creneis [Hyg.]
Cydippe2 [Hyg.]
Cymatolege [Hes.]
Cymo [Hes.]
Cymodoce [Hes.]
Cymothoe [Hes.]
Deiopeia1 [Hyg.]
Dero [Apollod.]
Dexamene [Hom.]
Dione2 [Apollod.]
Doris2 [Hes.]
Doto [Hes.]
Drymo [Hyg.]
Dynamene [Hes.]
Eione [Hes.]
Ephyra2 [Hyg.]
Erato5 [Hes.]
Euagore [Hes.]
Euarne [Hes.]
Eucra(n)te [Hes.]
Eudora2 [Hes.]
Eulimene2 [Hes.]
Eumolpe [Apollod.]
Euneice [Hes.]
Eupompe [Hes.]
Eurydice12 [Hyg.]
Faunus1-Simaethis
Poseidon-Thoosa
Zeus-Maia
Acis – Galateia1 – Polyphemus1
[Ovid] [Hes.] [Ovid]
Galene [Hes.]
Glauce4 [Hes.]
Glauconome [Hes.]
Halia2 [Hes.]
Hermes – Halimede
[Steph. Byz.] [Hes.]
46c
Hipponoe1 [Hes.]
Hippothoe3 [Hes.]
Iaera1 [Hom.]
Ianassa [Hom.]
Ianeira3 [Hom.]
Ione1 [Apollod.]
Iphianassa4 [Luc.]
Laomedeia [Hes.]
Leagore [Hes.]
<<Lycaon1-?>
Halipherus [Apollod.]
Harpaleus [Apollod.]
Harpalycus2 [Apollod.]
Helix1 [Apollod.]
Heraeeus [Apollod.]
Hopleus2 [Apollod.]
Horus [Apollod.]
Leon1 [Apollod.]
Linus4 [Apollod.]
Lycius1 [Apollod.]
Macar(eus)2 [Apollod.]
Macednus [Apollod.]
Zeus-Leto
Apollo – Dia3
[Tzetz.] [Etym. Magn.]
Maenalus1 [Apollod.]
Mantineus2 [Apollod.]
Mecisteus2 [Apollod.]
Melaeneus1 [Apollod.]
Peucetius [Apollod.]
Phassus [Apollod.]
Phineus3 [Apollod.]
Phthius2 [Apollod.]
Physius [Apollod.]
Dryops2 – ?
[Paus.]
Plato [Apollod.]
Polichus [Apollod.]
Portheus2 [Apollod.]
Prothous1 [Apollod.]
Socleus [Apollod.]
Stymphalus2 [Apollod.]
Teleboas2 [Apollod.]
Thesprotus1 [Apollod.]
Titanas [Apollod.]
Cragaleus [Ant. Lib.]
Zeus-Maia
Hermes – Dryope1
[Hom. Hymn] [Hom. Hymn]
Orion-?
Theiodamas1 – Menodice
[Schol. Ap. Rhod.] [Hyg.]
Pan – ?
[Hom. Hymn]
46c
Zeus-Alcmene
Heracles1 ~ Hylas – [nymph]
[Apollod.] [Apollod.] [Ap. Rhod.]
<<Aleus-Neaera2>
Cepheus2 – ?
[Apollod.]
Hippothous5 [Hyg.]
Cepheus2-?
Eurynome5 – Lycurgus4 – Cleophyle
[Apollod.] [Apollod.] [Apollod.]
Aegicorus [Non.]
Argennus [Non.]
Argus6 [Non.]
Alaeus-Neaera2
Lycurgus4 – Cleophyle
[Apollod.] [Paus.]
64c-d
Aeropus – ?
[Paus.]
Zeus-Hera
Ares – Sterope3
[Paus.] [Apollod.]
[20 sons] [Diod. Sic.]
Ancaeus1 – ?
[Apollod.]
Cepheus3 [Apollod.]
Minyas-Clytodora
Iasus4 – Clymene4
[Apollod.] [Apollod.]
Epochus [Apollod.]
Celaeneus2 [Non.]
Daphoeneus [Non.]
Eugeneius [Non.]
Glaucus8 [Non.]
Omester [Non.]
Tyndareus-Leda
Echemus – Timandra1
[Herod.] [Cat. Wom.]
Agapenor – ?
[Hom.]
Oeneus-Althaea
Amphidamas1-?
Meleager – Atalanta1 – Melanion
[Hyg.] [Apollod.] [Apollod.]
Philamnus [Non.]
Phobus2 [Non.]
Phorbas6 [Non.]
Xanthus7 [Non.]
Laodochus4 [Cat. Wom.]
Laodice5 [Paus.]
Parthenopaeus – Clymene3
[Apollod.] [Hyg.]
Tlesimenus – ?
[Paus.]
Promachus1 [Apollod.]
Aulon [Paus.]

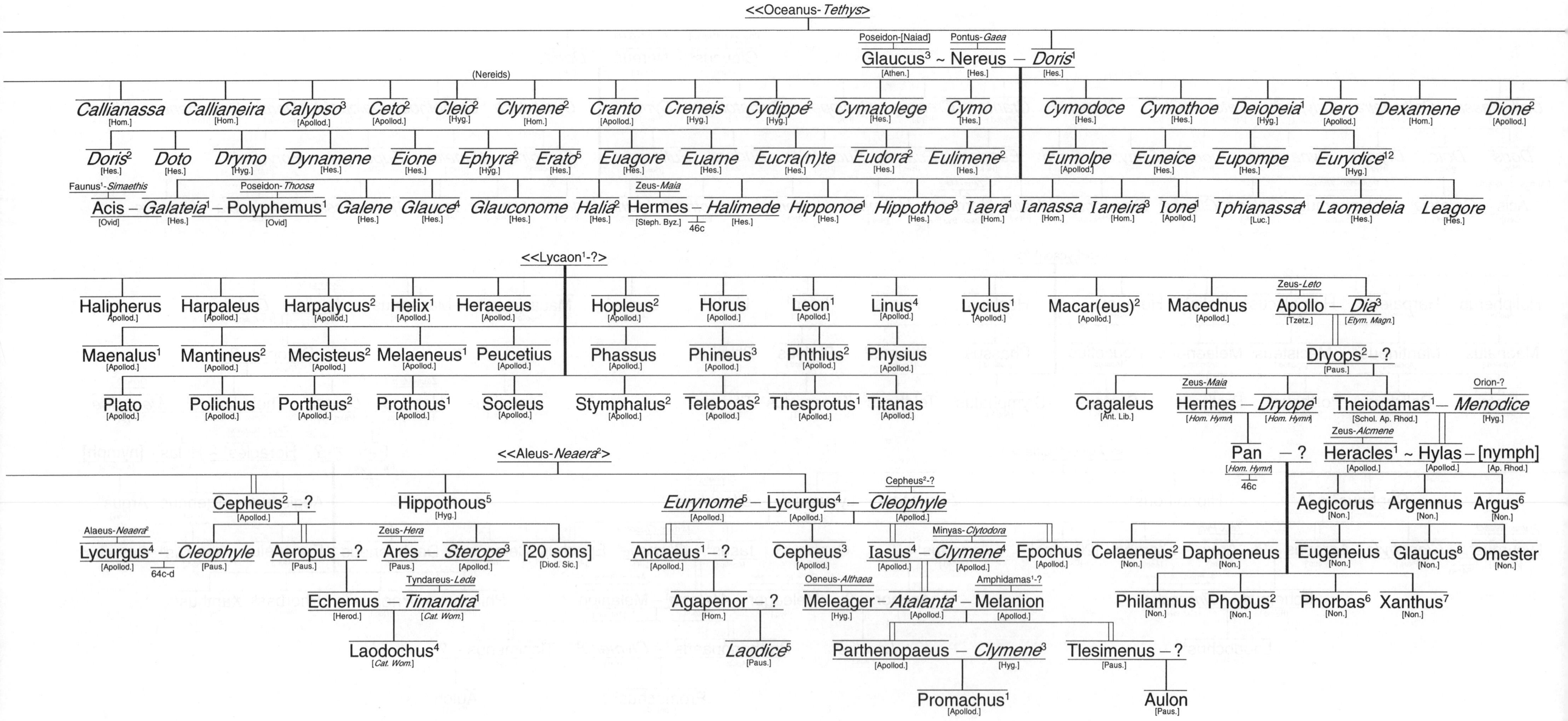
<<Oceanus-*Tethys*>
Poseidon-[Naiad]
Pontus-*Gaea*
Glaucus³ ~ Nereus – *Doris*¹
[Athen.] [Hes.] [Hes.]
(Nereids)
Callianassa [Hom.]
Callianeira [Hom.]
*Calypso*³ [Apollod.]
*Ceto*² [Apollod.]
*Cleio*² [Hyg.]
*Clymene*² [Hom.]
Cranto [Apollod.]
Creneis [Hyg.]
*Cydippe*² [Hyg.]
Cymatolege [Hes.]
Cymo [Hes.]
Cymodoce [Hes.]
Cymothoe [Hes.]
*Deiopeia*¹ [Hyg.]
Dero [Apollod.]
Dexamene [Hom.]
*Dione*² [Apollod.]
*Doris*² [Hes.]
Doto [Hes.]
Drymo [Hyg.]
Dynamene [Hes.]
Eione [Hes.]
*Ephyra*² [Hyg.]
*Erato*⁵ [Hes.]
Euagore [Hes.]
Euarne [Hes.]
Eucra(n)te [Hes.]
*Eudora*² [Hes.]
*Eulimene*² [Hes.]
Eumolpe [Apollod.]
Euneice [Hes.]
Eupompe [Hes.]
*Eurydice*¹² [Hyg.]
Faunus¹-*Simaethis*
Poseidon-*Thoosa*
Zeus-*Maia*
Acis – *Galateia*¹ – Polyphemus¹
[Ovid] [Hes.] [Ovid]
Galene [Hes.]
*Glauce*⁴ [Hes.]
Glauconome [Hes.]
*Halia*² [Hes.]
Hermes – *Halimede*
[Steph. Byz.] 46c [Hes.]
*Hipponoe*¹ [Hes.]
*Hippothoe*³ [Hes.]
*Iaera*¹ [Hom.]
Ianassa [Hom.]
*Ianeira*³ [Hom.]
*Ione*¹ [Apollod.]
*Iphianassa*⁴ [Luc.]
Laomedeia [Hes.]
Leagore [Hes.]
<<Lycaon¹-?>
Halipherus [Apollod.]
Harpaleus [Apollod.]
Harpalycus² [Apollod.]
Helix¹ [Apollod.]
Heraeeus [Apollod.]
Hopleus² [Apollod.]
Horus [Apollod.]
Leon¹ [Apollod.]
Linus⁴ [Apollod.]
Lycius¹ [Apollod.]
Macar(eus)² [Apollod.]
Macednus [Apollod.]
Zeus-*Leto*
Apollo – *Dia*³
[Tzetz.] [*Etym. Magn.*]
Maenalus¹ [Apollod.]
Mantineus² [Apollod.]
Mecisteus² [Apollod.]
Melaeneus¹ [Apollod.]
Peucetius [Apollod.]
Phassus [Apollod.]
Phineus³ [Apollod.]
Phthius² [Apollod.]
Physius [Apollod.]
Dryops² – ?
[Paus.]
Plato [Apollod.]
Polichus [Apollod.]
Portheus² [Apollod.]
Prothous¹ [Apollod.]
Socleus [Apollod.]
Stymphalus² [Apollod.]
Teleboas² [Apollod.]
Thesprotus¹ [Apollod.]
Titanas [Apollod.]
Cragaleus [Ant. Lib.]
Zeus-*Maia*
Hermes – *Dryope*¹
[*Hom. Hymn*] [*Hom. Hymn*]
Orion-?
Theiodamas¹ – *Menodice*
[Schol. Ap. Rhod.] [Hyg.]
Zeus-*Alcmene*
Pan – ?
[*Hom. Hymn*]
46c
Heracles¹ ~ Hylas – [nymph]
[Apollod.] [Apollod.] [Ap. Rhod.]
<<Aleus-*Neaera*²>
Cepheus² – ?
[Apollod.]
Hippothous⁵
[Hyg.]
Cepheus²-?
*Eurynome*⁵ – Lycurgus⁴ – *Cleophyle*
[Apollod.] [Apollod.] [Apollod.]
Aegicorus [Non.]
Argennus [Non.]
Argus⁶ [Non.]
Alaeus-*Neaera*²
Lycurgus⁴ – *Cleophyle*
[Apollod.] 64c-d [Paus.]
Aeropus – ?
[Paus.]
Zeus-*Hera*
Ares – *Sterope*³
[Paus.] [Apollod.]
[20 sons]
[Diod. Sic.]
Ancaeus¹ – ?
[Apollod.]
Cepheus³ [Apollod.]
Minyas-*Clytodora*
Iasus⁴ – *Clymene*⁴
[Apollod.] [Apollod.]
Epochus [Apollod.]
Celaeneus² [Non.]
Daphoeneus [Non.]
Eugeneius [Non.]
Glaucus⁸ [Non.]
Omester [Non.]
Tyndareus-*Leda*
Echemus – *Timandra*¹
[Herod.] [*Cat. Wom.*]
Agapenor – ?
[Hom.]
Oeneus-*Althaea*
Amphidamas¹-?
Meleager – *Atalanta*¹ – Melanion
[Hyg.] [Apollod.] [Apollod.]
Philamnus [Non.]
Phobus² [Non.]
Phorbas⁶ [Non.]
Xanthus⁷ [Non.]
Laodochus⁴
[*Cat. Wom.*]
*Laodice*⁵
[Paus.]
Parthenopaeus – *Clymene*³
[Apollod.] [Hyg.]
Tlesimenus – ?
[Paus.]
Promachus¹
[Apollod.]
Aulon
[Paus.]

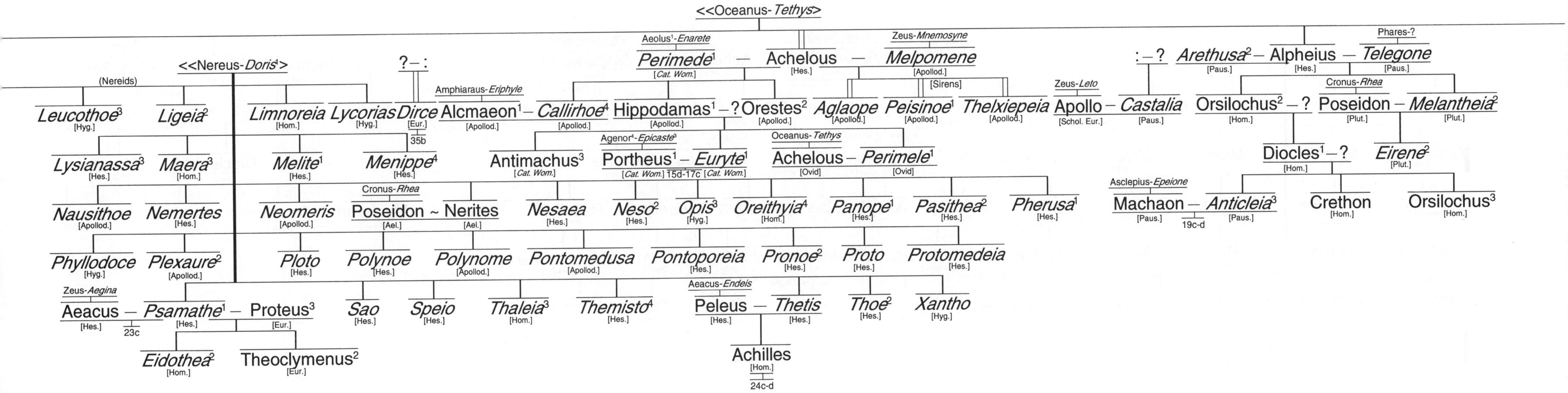

<<Oceanus-Tethys>
Aeolus¹-Enarete
Perimede¹ [Cat. Wom.]
Achelous [Hes.]
Zeus-Mnemosyne
Melpomene [Apollod.]
[Sirens]
Phares-?
:–? Arethusa² – Alpheius – Telegone
[Paus.] [Hes.] [Paus.]
<<Nereus-Doris¹>
(Nereids)
?–:
Leucothoe³ [Hyg.]
Ligeia²
Limnoreia [Hom.]
Lycorias [Hyg.]
Dirce [Eur.]
35b
Amphiaraus-Eriphyle
Alcmaeon¹ – Callirhoe⁴ [Apollod.] [Apollod.]
Hippodamas¹ – ? [Apollod.]
Orestes² [Apollod.]
Aglaope [Apollod.]
Peisinoe¹ [Apollod.]
Thelxiepeia [Apollod.]
Zeus-Leto
Apollo – Castalia [Schol. Eur.] [Paus.]
Cronus-Rhea
Orsilochus² – ? [Hom.]
Poseidon – Melantheia² [Plut.] [Plut.]
Lysianassa³ [Hes.]
Maera³ [Hom.]
Melite¹ [Hes.]
Menippe⁴ [Hes.]
Antimachus³ [Cat. Wom.]
Agenor⁴-Epicaste³
Portheus¹ – Euryte¹ [Cat. Wom.] 15d-17c [Cat. Wom.]
Oceanus-Tethys
Achelous – Perimele¹ [Ovid] [Ovid]
Diocles¹ – ? [Hom.]
Eirene² [Plut.]
Nausithoe [Apollod.]
Nemertes [Hes.]
Neomeris [Apollod.]
Cronus-Rhea
Poseidon ~ Nerites [Ael.] [Ael.]
Nesaea [Hes.]
Neso² [Hes.]
Opis³ [Hyg.]
Oreithyia⁴ [Hom.]
Panope¹ [Hes.]
Pasithea² [Hes.]
Pherusa¹ [Hes.]
Asclepius-Epeione
Machaon – Anticleia³ [Paus.] 19c-d [Paus.]
Crethon [Hom.]
Orsilochus³ [Hom.]
Phyllodoce [Hyg.]
Plexaure² [Apollod.]
Ploto [Hes.]
Polynoe [Hes.]
Polynome [Apollod.]
Pontomedusa [Apollod.]
Pontoporeia [Hes.]
Pronoe² [Hes.]
Proto [Hes.]
Protomedeia [Hes.]
Zeus-Aegina
Aeacus – Psamathe¹ – Proteus³ [Hes.] 23c [Hes.] [Eur.]
Sao [Hes.]
Speio [Hes.]
Thaleia³ [Hom.]
Themisto⁴ [Hes.]
Aeacus-Endeis
Peleus – Thetis [Hes.] [Hes.]
Thoe² [Hes.]
Xantho [Hyg.]
Eidothea² [Hom.]
Theoclymenus² [Eur.]
Achilles [Hom.]
24c-d

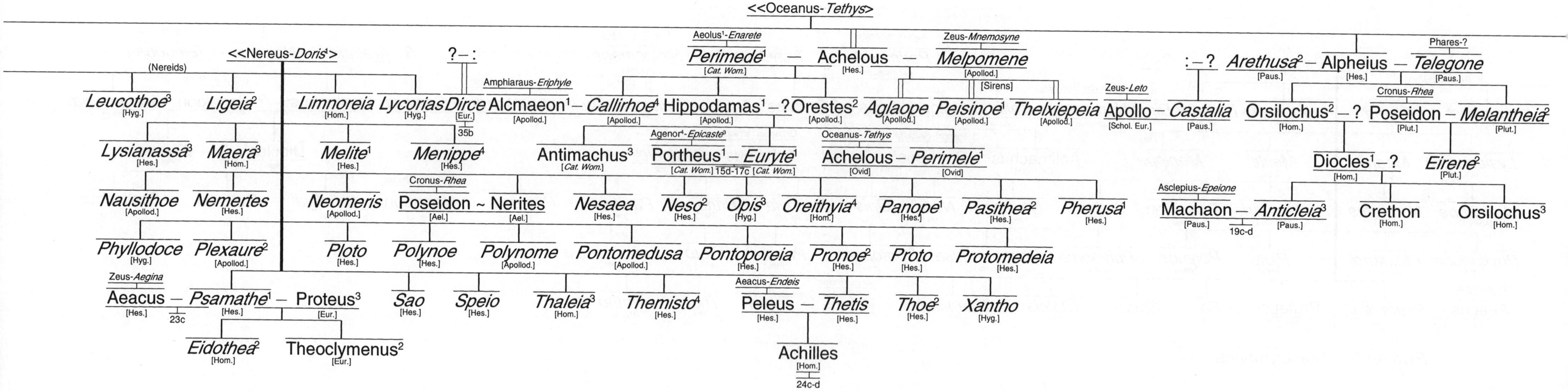
<<Oceanus-*Tethys*>
Aeolus1-*Enarete*
*Perimede*1 — Achelous — *Melpomene*
[*Cat. Wom.*]
[Hes.]
Zeus-*Mnemosyne*
[Apollod.]
<<Nereus-*Doris*1>
(Nereids)
?—:
*Leucothoe*3 [Hyg.]
*Ligeia*2
Limnoreia [Hom.]
Lycorias [Hyg.]
Dirce [Eur.]
35b
Amphiaraus-*Eriphyle*
Alcmaeon1 — *Callirhoe*4
[Apollod.]
[Apollod.]
Hippodamas1 — ? Orestes2
[Apollod.]
[Apollod.]
[Sirens]
Aglaope [Apollod.]
*Peisinoe*1 [Apollod.]
Thelxiepeia [Apollod.]
Zeus-*Leto*
Apollo — *Castalia*
[Schol. Eur.]
[Paus.]
:—? *Arethusa*2 — Alpheius — *Telegone*
[Paus.]
[Hes.]
[Paus.]
Phares-?
Cronus-*Rhea*
Orsilochus2 — ? Poseidon — *Melantheia*2
[Hom.]
[Plut.]
[Plut.]
*Lysianassa*3 [Hes.]
*Maera*3 [Hom.]
*Melite*1 [Hes.]
*Menippe*4 [Hes.]
Antimachus3 [*Cat. Wom.*]
Agenor4-*Epicaste*3
Portheus1 — *Euryte*1
[*Cat. Wom.*] 15d-17c [*Cat. Wom.*]
Oceanus-*Tethys*
Achelous — *Perimele*1
[Ovid]
[Ovid]
Diocles1 — ?
[Hom.]
*Eirene*2 [Plut.]
Nausithoe [Apollod.]
Nemertes [Hes.]
Neomeris [Apollod.]
Cronus-*Rhea*
Poseidon ~ Nerites
[Ael.]
[Ael.]
Nesaea [Hes.]
*Neso*2 [Hes.]
*Opis*3 [Hyg.]
*Oreithyia*4 [Hom.]
*Panope*1 [Hes.]
*Pasithea*2 [Hes.]
*Pherusa*1 [Hes.]
Asclepius-*Epeione*
Machaon — *Anticleia*3
[Paus.]
19c-d
[Paus.]
Crethon [Hom.]
Orsilochus3 [Hom.]
Phyllodoce [Hyg.]
*Plexaure*2 [Apollod.]
Ploto [Hes.]
Polynoe [Hes.]
Polynome [Apollod.]
Pontomedusa [Apollod.]
Pontoporeia [Hes.]
*Pronoe*2 [Hes.]
Proto [Hes.]
Protomedeia [Hes.]
Zeus-*Aegina*
Aeacus — *Psamathe*1 — Proteus3
[Hes.]
23c
[Hes.]
[Eur.]
Sao [Hes.]
Speio [Hes.]
*Thaleia*3 [Hom.]
*Themisto*4 [Hes.]
Aeacus-*Endeis*
Peleus — *Thetis*
[Hes.]
[Hes.]
*Thoe*2 [Hes.]
Xantho [Hyg.]
*Eidothea*2 [Hom.]
Theoclymenus2 [Eur.]
Achilles [Hom.]
24c-d

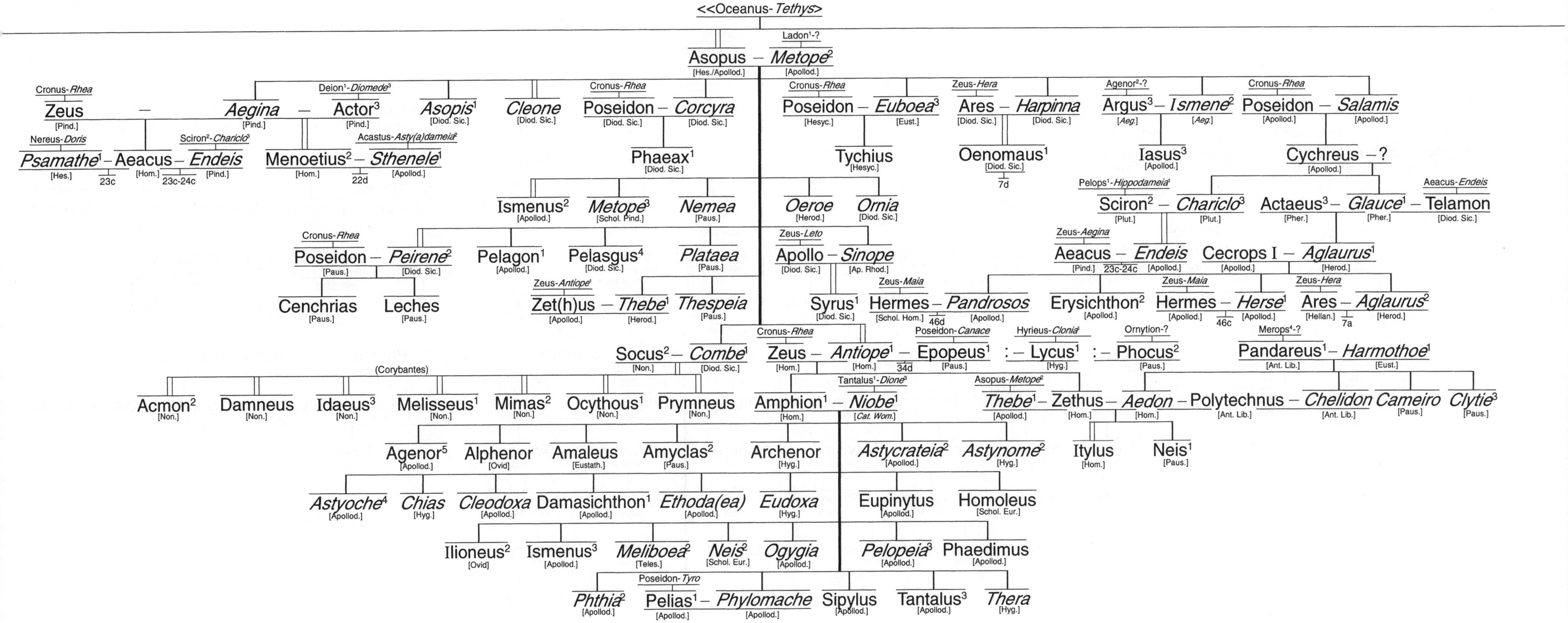

<<Oceanus-Tethys>
Ladon¹-?
Asopus – Metope²
[Hes./Apollod.] [Apollod.]
Cronus-Rhea
Zeus – Aegina – Actor³
[Pind.] [Pind.] [Pind.]
Deion¹-Diomede³
Asopis¹ [Diod. Sic.]
Cleone [Diod. Sic.]
Cronus-Rhea
Poseidon – Corcyra
[Diod. Sic.] [Diod. Sic.]
Cronus-Rhea
Poseidon – Euboea³
[Hesyc.] [Eust.]
Zeus-Hera
Ares – Harpinna
[Diod. Sic.] [Diod. Sic.]
Agenor²-?
Argus³ – Ismene²
[Aeg.] [Aeg.]
Cronus-Rhea
Poseidon – Salamis
[Apollod.] [Apollod.]
Nereus-Doris
Psamathe¹ – Aeacus – Endeis
[Hes.] [Hom.] [Pind.]
23c 23c-24c
Sciron²-Chariclo³
Menoetius² – Sthenele¹
[Hom.] [Apollod.]
22d
Acastus-Asty(a)dameia²
Phaeax¹ [Diod. Sic.]
Tychius [Hesyc.]
Oenomaus¹ [Diod. Sic.]
7d
Iasus³ [Apollod.]
Cychreus – ? [Apollod.]
Ismenus² [Apollod.]
Metope³ [Schol. Pind.]
Nemea [Paus.]
Oeroe [Herod.]
Ornia [Diod. Sic.]
Pelops¹-Hippodameia¹
Sciron² – Chariclo³
[Plut.] [Plut.]
Actaeus³ – Glauce¹ – Telamon
[Pher.] [Pher.] [Diod. Sic.]
Aeacus-Endeis
Cronus-Rhea
Poseidon – Peirene²
[Paus.] [Diod. Sic.]
Pelagon¹ [Apollod.]
Pelasgus⁴ [Diod. Sic.]
Plataea [Paus.]
Zeus-Leto
Apollo – Sinope
[Diod. Sic.] [Ap. Rhod.]
Zeus-Aegina
Aeacus – Endeis
[Pind.] 23c-24c [Apollod.]
Cecrops I – Aglaurus¹
[Apollod.] [Herod.]
Cenchrias [Paus.]
Leches [Paus.]
Zeus-Antiope¹
Zet(h)us – Thebe¹
[Apollod.] [Herod.]
Thespeia [Paus.]
Syrus¹ [Diod. Sic.]
Zeus-Maia
Hermes – Pandrosos
[Schol. Hom.] 46d [Apollod.]
Erysichthon² [Apollod.]
Zeus-Maia
Hermes – Herse¹
[Apollod.] 46c [Apollod.]
Zeus-Hera
Ares – Aglaurus²
[Hellan.] 7a [Herod.]
Cronus-Rhea
Socus² – Combe¹
[Non.] [Diod. Sic.]
Zeus – Antiope¹ – Epopeus¹
[Hom.] [Hom.] 34d [Paus.]
Poseidon-Canace
Hyrieus-Clonia¹
: – Lycus¹ [Hyg.]
Ornytion-?
: – Phocus² [Paus.]
Merops⁴-?
Pandareus¹ – Harmothoe¹
[Ant. Lib.] [Eust.]
(Corybantes)
Acmon² [Non.]
Damneus [Non.]
Idaeus³ [Non.]
Melisseus¹ [Non.]
Mimas² [Non.]
Ocythous¹ [Non.]
Prymneus [Non.]
Tantalus¹-Dione³
Amphion¹ – Niobe¹
[Hom.] [Cat. Wom.]
Asopus-Metope²
Thebe¹ – Zethus – Aedon – Polytechnus – Chelidon
[Apollod.] [Hom.] [Hom.] [Ant. Lib.] [Ant. Lib.]
Cameiro [Paus.]
Clytie³ [Paus.]
Agenor⁵ [Apollod.]
Alphenor [Ovid]
Amaleus [Eustath.]
Amyclas² [Paus.]
Archenor [Hyg.]
Astycrateia² [Apollod.]
Astynome² [Hyg.]
Itylus [Hom.]
Neis¹ [Paus.]
Astyoche⁴ [Apollod.]
Chias [Hyg.]
Cleodoxa [Apollod.]
Damasichthon¹ [Apollod.]
Ethoda(ea) [Apollod.]
Eudoxa [Hyg.]
Eupinytus [Apollod.]
Homoleus [Schol. Eur.]
Ilioneus² [Ovid]
Ismenus³ [Apollod.]
Meliboea² [Teles.]
Neis² [Schol. Eur.]
Ogygia [Apollod.]
Pelopeia³ [Apollod.]
Phaedimus [Apollod.]
Phthia² [Apollod.]
Poseidon-Tyro
Pelias¹ – Phylomache
[Apollod.] [Apollod.]
Sipylus [Apollod.]
Tantalus³ [Apollod.]
Thera [Hyg.]

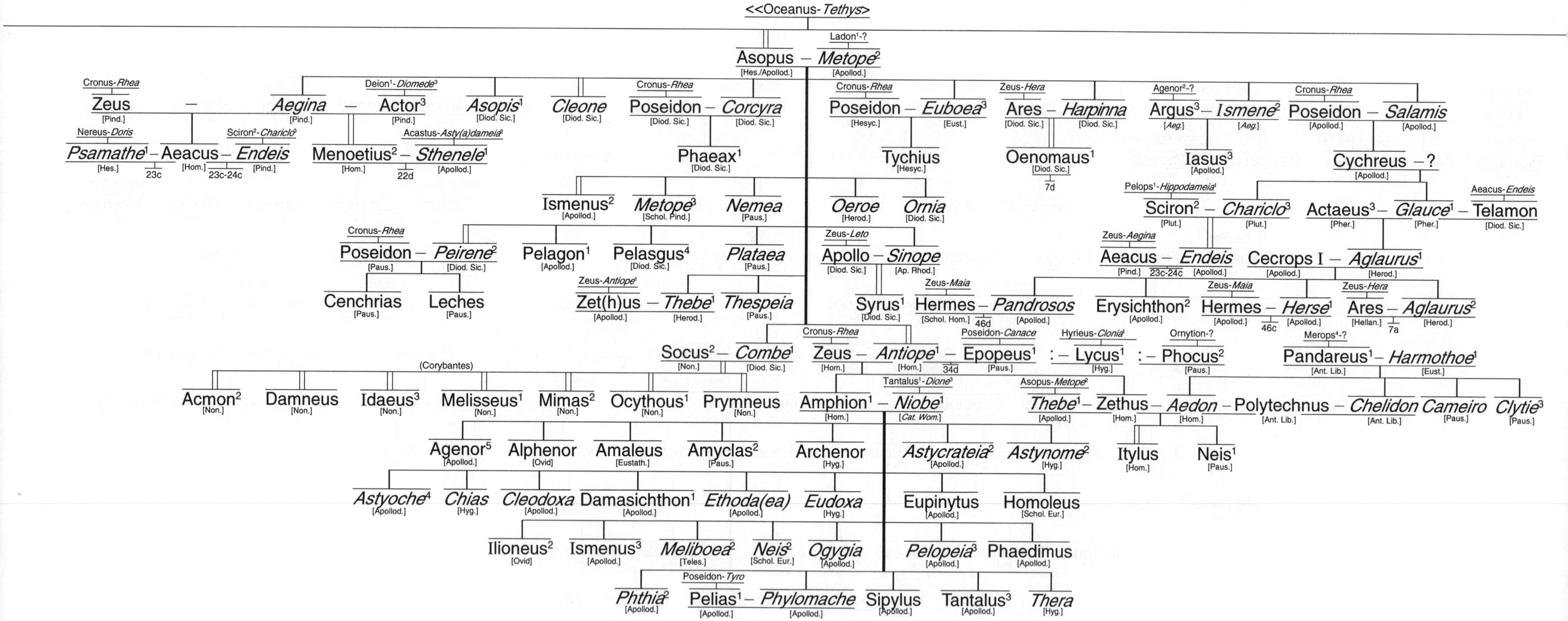

<<Oceanus-Tethys>
Ladon¹-?
Asopus – Metope²
[Hes./Apollod.] [Apollod.]
Cronus-Rhea
Zeus [Pind.]
Aegina [Pind.]
Deion¹-Diomede³
Actor³ [Pind.]
Asopis¹ [Diod. Sic.]
Cleone [Diod. Sic.]
Cronus-Rhea
Poseidon – Corcyra [Diod. Sic.] [Diod. Sic.]
Cronus-Rhea
Poseidon – Euboea³ [Hesyc.] [Eust.]
Zeus-Hera
Ares – Harpinna [Diod. Sic.] [Diod. Sic.]
Agenor²-?
Argus³ – Ismene² [Aeg.] [Aeg.]
Cronus-Rhea
Poseidon – Salamis [Apollod.] [Apollod.]
Nereus-Doris
Psamathe¹ – Aeacus – Endeis [Hes.] [Hom.] [Pind.]
Sciron²-Chariclo³
23c 23c-24c
Acastus-Asty(a)dameia²
Menoetius² – Sthenele¹ [Hom.] [Apollod.]
22d
Phaeax¹ [Diod. Sic.]
Tychius [Hesyc.]
Oenomaus¹ [Diod. Sic.]
7d
Iasus³ [Apollod.]
Cychreus – ? [Apollod.]
Ismenus² [Apollod.]
Metope³ [Schol. Pind.]
Nemea [Paus.]
Oeroe [Herod.]
Ornia [Diod. Sic.]
Pelops¹-Hippodameia¹
Sciron² – Chariclo³ [Plut.] [Plut.]
Actaeus³ – Glauce¹ – Telamon [Pher.] [Pher.] [Diod. Sic.]
Aeacus-Endeis
Cronus-Rhea
Poseidon – Peirene² [Paus.] [Diod. Sic.]
Pelagon¹ [Apollod.]
Pelasgus⁴ [Diod. Sic.]
Plataea [Paus.]
Zeus-Leto
Apollo – Sinope [Diod. Sic.] [Ap. Rhod.]
Zeus-Aegina
Aeacus – Endeis [Pind.] 23c-24c [Apollod.]
Cecrops I – Aglaurus¹ [Apollod.] [Herod.]
Cenchrias [Paus.]
Leches [Paus.]
Zeus-Antiope¹
Zet(h)us – Thebe¹ [Apollod.] [Herod.]
Thespeia [Paus.]
Syrus¹ [Diod. Sic.]
Zeus-Maia
Hermes – Pandrosos [Schol. Hom.] 46d [Apollod.]
Erysichthon² [Apollod.]
Zeus-Maia
Hermes – Herse¹ [Apollod.] 46c [Apollod.]
Zeus-Hera
Ares – Aglaurus² [Hellan.] 7a [Herod.]
Cronus-Rhea
Poseidon-Canace
Hyrieus-Clonia¹
Ornytion-?
Merops⁴-?
Socus² – Combe¹ [Non.] [Diod. Sic.]
Zeus – Antiope¹ – Epopeus¹ [Hom.] [Hom.] 34d [Paus.]
: – Lycus¹ [Hyg.]
: – Phocus² [Paus.]
Pandareus¹ – Harmothoe¹ [Ant. Lib.] [Eust.]
(Corybantes)
Acmon² [Non.]
Damneus [Non.]
Idaeus³ [Non.]
Melisseus¹ [Non.]
Mimas² [Non.]
Ocythous¹ [Non.]
Prymneus [Non.]
Tantalus¹-Dione³
Amphion¹ – Niobe¹ [Hom.] [Cat. Wom.]
Asopus-Metope²
Thebe¹ – Zethus – Aedon – Polytechnus – Chelidon [Apollod.] [Hom.] [Hom.] [Ant. Lib.] [Ant. Lib.]
Cameiro [Paus.]
Clytie³ [Paus.]
Agenor⁵ [Apollod.]
Alphenor [Ovid]
Amaleus [Eustath.]
Amyclas² [Paus.]
Archenor [Hyg.]
Astycrateia² [Apollod.]
Astynome² [Hyg.]
Itylus [Hom.]
Neis¹ [Paus.]
Astyoche⁴ [Apollod.]
Chias [Hyg.]
Cleodoxa [Apollod.]
Damasichthon¹ [Apollod.]
Ethoda(ea) [Apollod.]
Eudoxa [Hyg.]
Eupinytus [Apollod.]
Homoleus [Schol. Eur.]
Ilioneus² [Ovid]
Ismenus³ [Apollod.]
Meliboea² [Teles.]
Neis² [Schol. Eur.]
Ogygia [Apollod.]
Pelopeia³ [Apollod.]
Phaedimus [Apollod.]
Poseidon-Tyro
Phthia² [Apollod.]
Pelias¹ – Phylomache [Apollod.] [Apollod.]
Sipylus [Apollod.]
Tantalus³ [Apollod.]
Thera [Hyg.]

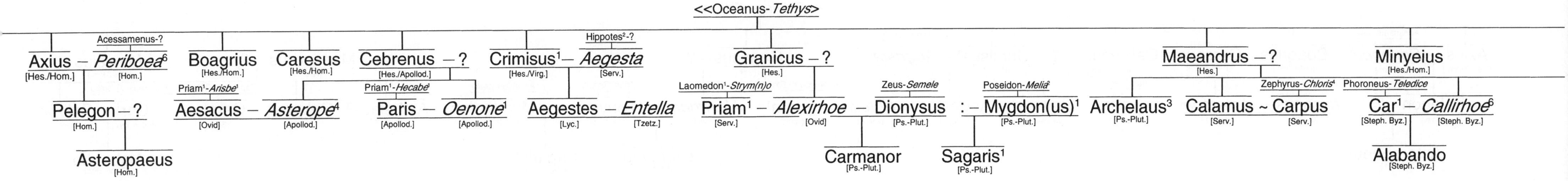

<<Oceanus- *Tethys*>
Acessamenus-?
Axius – *Periboea*[6]
[Hes./Hom.]
[Hom.]
Pelegon – ?
[Hom.]
Asteropaeus
[Hom.]
Boagrius
[Hes./Hom.]
Priam[1]-*Arisbe*[1]
Aesacus – *Asterope*[4]
[Ovid]
[Apollod.]
Caresus
[Hes./Hom.]
Cebrenus – ?
[Hes./Apollod.]
Priam[1]-*Hecabe*[1]
Paris – *Oenone*[1]
[Apollod.]
[Apollod.]
Hippotes[2]-?
Crimisus[1] – *Aegesta*
[Hes./Virg.]
[Serv.]
Aegestes – *Entella*
[Lyc.]
[Tzetz.]
Granicus – ?
[Hes.]
Laomedon[1]-*Strym(n)o*
Priam[1] – *Alexirhoe* – Dionysus
[Serv.]
[Ovid]
Zeus-*Semele*
[Ps.-Plut.]
Carmanor
[Ps.-Plut.]
Poseidon-*Melia*[2]
: – Mygdon(us)[1]
[Ps.-Plut.]
Sagaris[1]
[Ps.-Plut.]
Maeandrus – ?
[Hes.]
Archelaus[3]
[Ps.-Plut.]
Zephyrus-*Chloris*[4]
Calamus ~ Carpus
[Serv.]
[Serv.]
Minyeius
[Hes./Hom.]
Phoroneus-*Teledice*
Car[1] – *Callirhoe*[6]
[Steph. Byz.]
[Steph. Byz.]
Alabando
[Steph. Byz.]

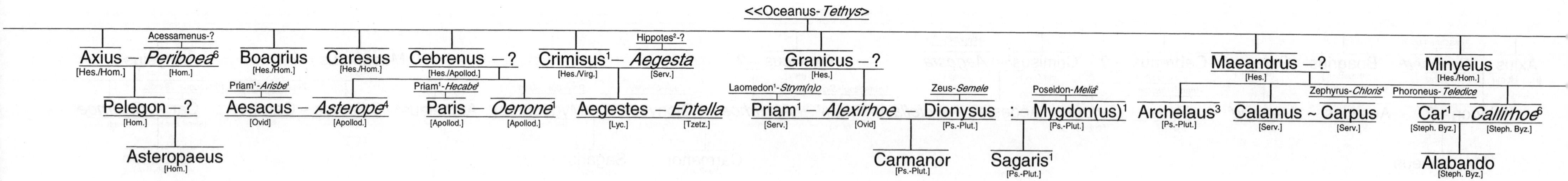

<<Oceanus- Tethys>
Acessamenus-?
Axius – Periboea[6]
[Hes./Hom.]
[Hom.]
Pelegon – ?
[Hom.]
Asteropaeus
[Hom.]
Boagrius
[Hes./Hom.]
Priam[1]-Arisbe[1]
Aesacus – Asterope[4]
[Ovid]
[Apollod.]
Caresus
[Hes./Hom.]
Cebrenus – ?
[Hes./Apollod.]
Priam[1]-Hecabe[1]
Paris – Oenone[1]
[Apollod.]
[Apollod.]
Hippotes[2]-?
Crimisus[1]– Aegesta
[Hes./Virg.]
[Serv.]
Aegestes – Entella
[Lyc.]
[Tzetz.]
Granicus – ?
[Hes.]
Laomedon[1]-Strym(n)o
Priam[1] – Alexirhoe
[Serv.]
[Ovid]
Zeus-Semele
– Dionysus
[Ps.-Plut.]
Carmanor
[Ps.-Plut.]
Poseidon-Melia[2]
: – Mygdon(us)[1]
[Ps.-Plut.]
Sagaris[1]
[Ps.-Plut.]
Maeandrus – ?
[Hes.]
Archelaus[3]
[Ps.-Plut.]
Calamus ~ Carpus
[Serv.]
Zephyrus-Chloris[4]
[Serv.]
Minyeius
[Hes./Hom.]
Phoroneus- Teledice
Car[1] – Callirhoe[6]
[Steph. Byz.]
[Steph. Byz.]
Alabando
[Steph. Byz.]

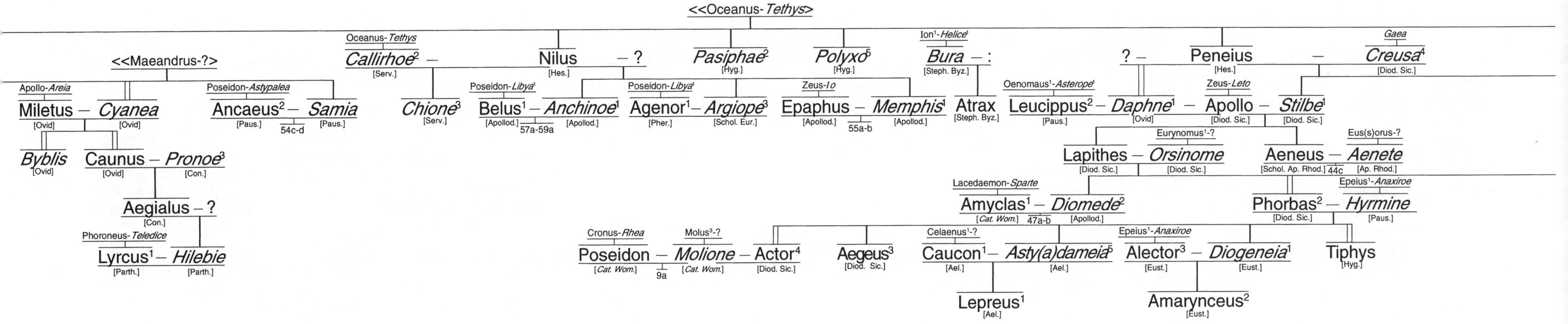

<<Oceanus-Tethys>
<<Maeandrus-?>
Apollo-Areia
Miletus – Cyanea
[Ovid] [Ovid]
Byblis [Ovid]
Caunus – Pronoe3
[Ovid] [Con.]
Aegialus – ?
[Con.]
Phoroneus-Teledice
Lyrcus1 – Hilebie
[Parth.] [Parth.]
Poseidon-Astypalea
Ancaeus2 – Samia
[Paus.] 54c-d [Paus.]
Oceanus-Tethys
Callirhoe2 –
[Serv.]
Chione3
[Serv.]
Nilus – ?
[Hes.]
Poseidon-Libya1
Belus1 – Anchinoe1
[Apollod.] 57a-59a [Apollod.]
Poseidon-Libya1
Agenor1 – Argiope3
[Pher.] [Schol. Eur.]
Zeus-Io
Epaphus – Memphis1
[Apollod.] 55a-b [Apollod.]
Pasiphae2
[Hyg.]
Polyxo5
[Hyg.]
Ion1-Helice1
Bura – :
[Steph. Byz.]
Atrax
[Steph. Byz.]
? – Peneius – Creusa4
[Hes.]
Gaea
[Diod. Sic.]
Oenomaus1-Asterope1
Leucippus2 – Daphne1 – Apollo – Stilbe1
[Paus.] [Ovid] [Diod. Sic.] [Diod. Sic.]
Zeus-Leto
Eurynomus1-?
Lapithes – Orsinome
[Diod. Sic.] [Diod. Sic.]
Eus(s)orus-?
Aeneus – Aenete
[Schol. Ap. Rhod.] 44c [Ap. Rhod.]
Lacedaemon-Sparte
Amyclas1 – Diomede2
[Cat. Wom.] 47a-b [Apollod.]
Epeius1-Anaxiroe
Phorbas2 – Hyrmine
[Diod. Sic.] [Paus.]
Cronus-Rhea
Poseidon – Molione – Actor4
[Cat. Wom.] 9a [Cat. Wom.] [Diod. Sic.]
Molus3-?
Aegeus3
[Diod. Sic.]
Celaenus1-?
Caucon1 – Asty(a)dameia5
[Ael.] [Ael.]
Lepreus1
[Ael.]
Epeius1-Anaxiroe
Alector3 – Diogeneia1
[Eust.] [Eust.]
Amarynceus2
[Eust.]
Tiphys
[Hyg.]

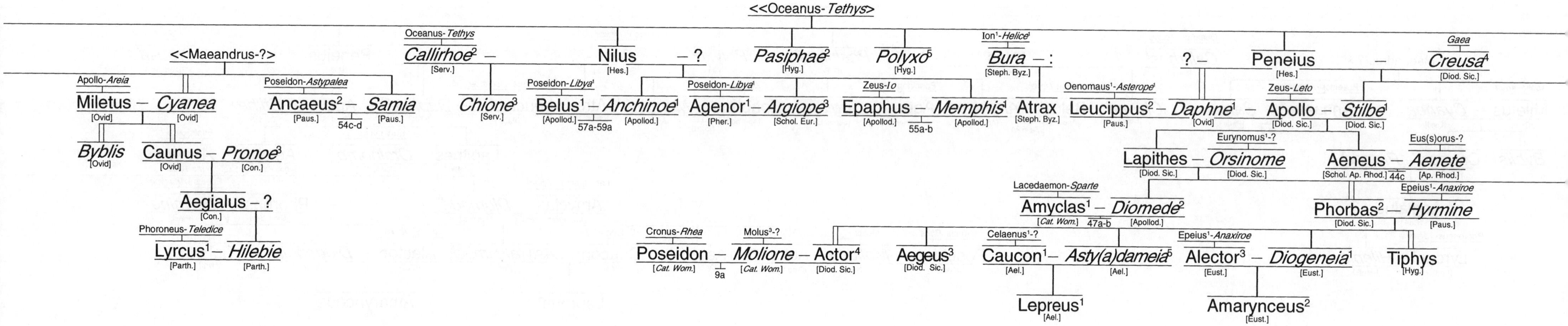
<<Oceanus-Tethys>
<<Maeandrus-?>
Oceanus-Tethys
Callirhoe² –
[Serv.]
Nilus – ?
[Hes.]
Pasiphae²
[Hyg.]
Polyxo⁵
[Hyg.]
Ion¹-Helice¹
Bura – :
[Steph. Byz.]
? – Peneius – Creusa⁴
[Hes.]
Gaea
[Diod. Sic.]
Apollo-Areia
Miletus – Cyanea
[Ovid] [Ovid]
Poseidon-Astypalea
Ancaeus² – Samia
[Paus.] 54c-d [Paus.]
Chione³
[Serv.]
Poseidon-Libya¹
Belus¹ – Anchinoe¹
[Apollod.] 57a-59a [Apollod.]
Poseidon-Libya¹
Agenor¹ – Argiope³
[Pher.] [Schol. Eur.]
Zeus-Io
Epaphus – Memphis¹
[Apollod.] 55a-b [Apollod.]
Atrax
[Steph. Byz.]
Oenomaus¹-Asterope¹
Leucippus² – Daphne¹ – Apollo – Stilbe¹
[Paus.] [Ovid] [Diod. Sic.] [Diod. Sic.]
Zeus-Leto
Byblis
[Ovid]
Caunus – Pronoe³
[Ovid] [Con.]
Eurynomus¹-?
Lapithes – Orsinome
[Diod. Sic.] [Diod. Sic.]
Eus(s)orus-?
Aeneus – Aenete
[Schol. Ap. Rhod.] 44c [Ap. Rhod.]
Aegialus – ?
[Con.]
Lacedaemon-Sparte
Amyclas¹ – Diomede²
[Cat. Wom.] 47a-b [Apollod.]
Epeius¹-Anaxiroe
Phorbas² – Hyrmine
[Diod. Sic.] [Paus.]
Phoroneus-Teledice
Lyrcus¹ – Hilebie
[Parth.] [Parth.]
Cronus-Rhea
Poseidon – Molione – Actor⁴
[Cat. Wom.] 9a [Cat. Wom.] [Diod. Sic.]
Molus³-?
Aegeus³
[Diod. Sic.]
Celaenus¹-?
Caucon¹ – Asty(a)dameia⁵
[Ael.] [Ael.]
Epeius¹-Anaxiroe
Alector³ – Diogeneia¹
[Eust.] [Eust.]
Tiphys
[Hyg.]
Lepreus¹
[Ael.]
Amarynceus²
[Eust.]

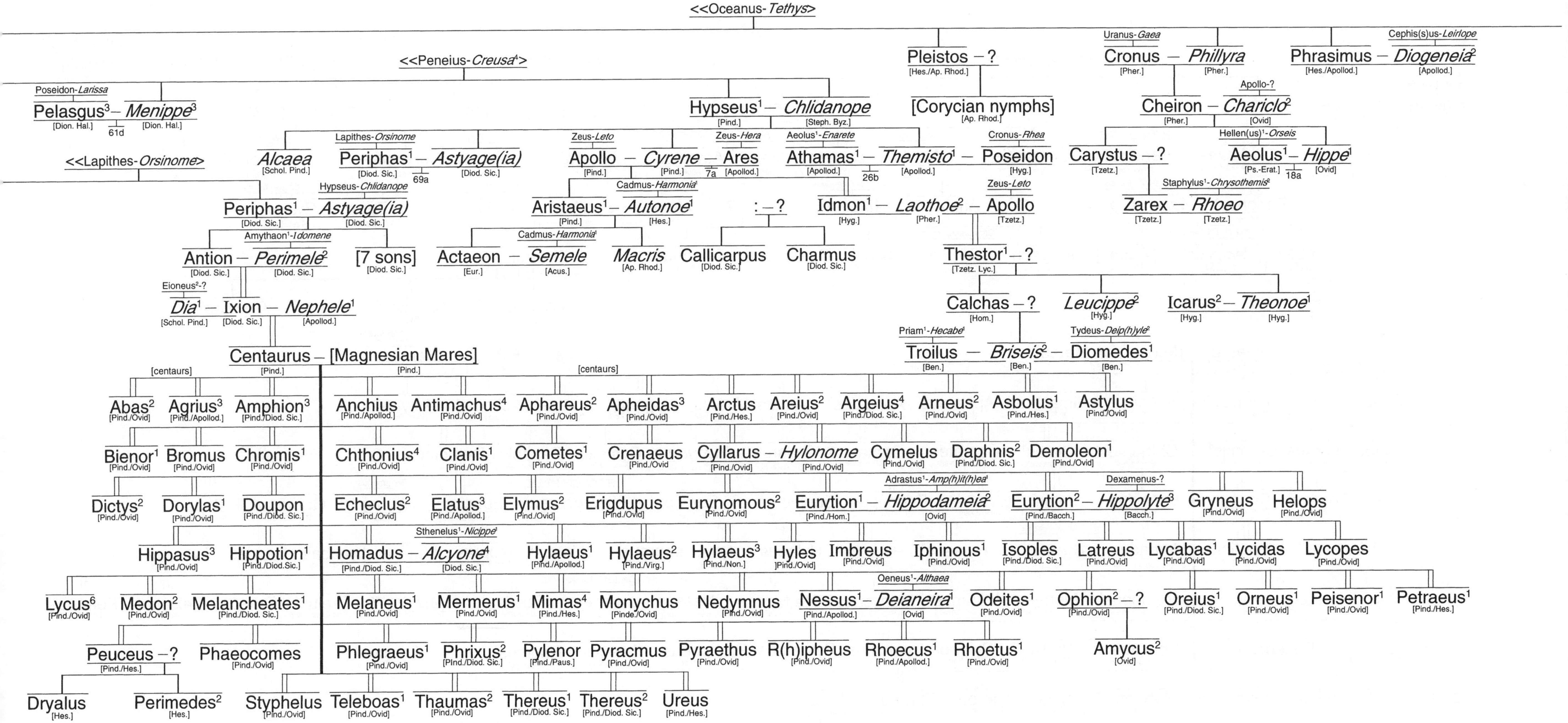

<<Oceanus-Tethys>
<<Peneius-Creusa[4]>
Pleistos – ?
[Hes./Ap. Rhod.]
Uranus-Gaea
Cronus – Phillyra
[Pher.] [Pher.]
Cephis(s)us-Leirlope
Phrasimus – Diogeneia[2]
[Hes./Apollod.] [Apollod.]
Poseidon-Larissa
Pelasgus[3] – Menippe[3]
[Dion. Hal.] 61d [Dion. Hal.]
Hypseus[1] – Chlidanope
[Pind.] [Steph. Byz.]
[Corycian nymphs]
[Ap. Rhod.]
Apollo-?
Cheiron – Chariclo[2]
[Pher.] [Ovid]
<<Lapithes-Orsinome>
Alcaea
[Schol. Pind.]
Lapithes-Orsinome
Periphas[1] – Astyage(ia)
[Diod. Sic.] 69a [Diod. Sic.]
Zeus-Leto
Apollo – Cyrene – Ares
[Pind.] [Pind.] 7a [Apollod.]
Zeus-Hera
Aeolus[1]-Enarete
Athamas[1] – Themisto[1] – Poseidon
[Apollod.] 26b [Apollod.] [Hyg.]
Cronus-Rhea
Carystus – ?
[Tzetz.]
Hellen(us)[1]-Orseis
Aeolus[1] – Hippe[1]
[Ps.-Erat.] 18a [Ovid]
Hypseus-Chlidanope
Periphas[1] – Astyage(ia)
[Diod. Sic.] [Diod. Sic.]
Cadmus-Harmonia[1]
Aristaeus[1] – Autonoe[1]
[Pind.] [Hes.]
: – ?
Zeus-Leto
Idmon[1] – Laothoe[2] – Apollo
[Hyg.] [Pher.] [Tzetz.]
Staphylus[1]-Chrysothemis[2]
Zarex – Rhoeo
[Tzetz.] [Tzetz.]
Amythaon[1]-Idomene
Antion – Perimele[2]
[Diod. Sic.] [Diod. Sic.]
[7 sons]
[Diod. Sic.]
Cadmus-Harmonia[1]
Actaeon – Semele
[Eur.] [Acus.]
Macris
[Ap. Rhod.]
Callicarpus
[Diod. Sic.]
Charmus
[Diod. Sic.]
Thestor[1] – ?
[Tzetz. Lyc.]
Eioneus[2]-?
Dia[1] – Ixion – Nephele[1]
[Schol. Pind.] [Diod. Sic.] [Apollod.]
Calchas – ?
[Hom.]
Leucippe[2]
[Hyg.]
Icarus[2] – Theonoe[1]
[Hyg.] [Hyg.]
Priam[1]-Hecabe[1]
Tydeus-Deip(h)yle[2]
Troilus – Briseis[2] – Diomedes[1]
[Ben.] [Ben.] [Ben.]
Centaurus – [Magnesian Mares]
[Pind.] [Pind.]
[centaurs]
[centaurs]
Abas[2] [Pind./Ovid]
Agrius[3] [Pind./Apollod.]
Amphion[3] [Pind./Diod. Sic.]
Anchius [Pind./Apollod.]
Antimachus[4] [Pind./Ovid]
Aphareus[2] [Pind./Ovid]
Apheidas[3] [Pind./Ovid]
Arctus [Pind./Hes.]
Areius[2] [Pind./Ovid]
Argeius[4] [Pind./Diod. Sic.]
Arneus[2] [Pind./Ovid]
Asbolus[1] [Pind./Hes.]
Astylus [Pind./Ovid]
Bienor[1] [Pind./Ovid]
Bromus [Pind./Ovid]
Chromis[1] [Pind./Ovid]
Chthonius[4] [Pind./Ovid]
Clanis[1] [Pind./Ovid]
Cometes[1] [Pind./Ovid]
Crenaeus [Pind./Ovid
Cyllarus – Hylonome
[Pind./Ovid] [Pind./Ovid]
Cymelus [Pind./Ovid]
Daphnis[2] [Pind./Diod. Sic.]
Demoleon[1] [Pind./Ovid]
Dictys[2] [Pind./Ovid]
Dorylas[1] [Pind./Ovid]
Doupon [Pind./Diod. Sic.]
Echeclus[2] [Pind./Ovid]
Elatus[3] [Pind./Apollod.]
Elymus[2] [Pind./Ovid]
Erigdupus [Pind./Ovid]
Eurynomous[2] [Pind./Ovid]
Adrastus[1]-Amp(h)it(h)ea[1]
Eurytion[1] – Hippodameia[2]
[Pind./Hom.] [Ovid]
Dexamenus-?
Eurytion[2] – Hippolyte[3]
[Pind./Bacch.] [Bacch.]
Gryneus [Pind./Ovid]
Helops [Pind./Ovid]
Hippasus[3] [Pind./Ovid]
Hippotion[1] [Pind./Diod.Sic.]
Sthenelus[1]-Nicippe[1]
Homadus – Alcyone[4]
[Pind./Diod. Sic.] [Diod. Sic.]
Hylaeus[1] [Pind./Apollod.]
Hylaeus[2] [Pind./Virg.]
Hylaeus[3] [Pind./Non.]
Hyles [Pind./Ovid]
Imbreus [Pind./Ovid]
Iphinous[1] [Pind./Ovid]
Isoples [Pind./Diod. Sic.]
Latreus [Pind./Ovid]
Lycabas[1] [Pind./Ovid]
Lycidas [Pind./Ovid]
Lycopes [Pind./Ovid]
Lycus[6] [Pind./Ovid]
Medon[2] [Pind./Ovid]
Melancheates[1] [Pind./Diod. Sic.]
Melaneus[1] [Pind./Ovid]
Mermerus[1] [Pind./Ovid]
Mimas[4] [Pind./Hes.]
Monychus [Pind./Ovid]
Nedymnus [Pind./Ovid]
Oeneus[1]-Althaea
Nessus[1] – Deianeira[1]
[Pind./Apollod.] [Ovid]
Odeites[1] [Pind./Ovid]
Ophion[2] – ?
[Pind./Ovid]
Oreius[1] [Pind./Diod. Sic.]
Orneus[1] [Pind./Ovid]
Peisenor[1] [Pind./Ovid]
Petraeus[1] [Pind./Hes.]
Peuceus – ?
[Pind./Hes.]
Phaeocomes [Pind./Ovid]
Phlegraeus[1] [Pind./Ovid]
Phrixus[2] [Pind./Diod. Sic.]
Pylenor [Pind./Paus.]
Pyracmus [Pind./Ovid]
Pyraethus [Pind./Ovid]
R(h)ipheus [Pind./Ovid]
Rhoecus[1] [Pind./Apollod.]
Rhoetus[1] [Pind./Ovid]
Amycus[2] [Ovid]
Dryalus [Hes.]
Perimedes[2] [Hes.]
Styphelus [Pind./Ovid]
Teleboas[1] [Pind./Ovid]
Thaumas[2] [Pind./Ovid]
Thereus[1] [Pind./Diod. Sic.]
Thereus[2] [Pind./Diod. Sic.]
Ureus [Pind./Hes.]

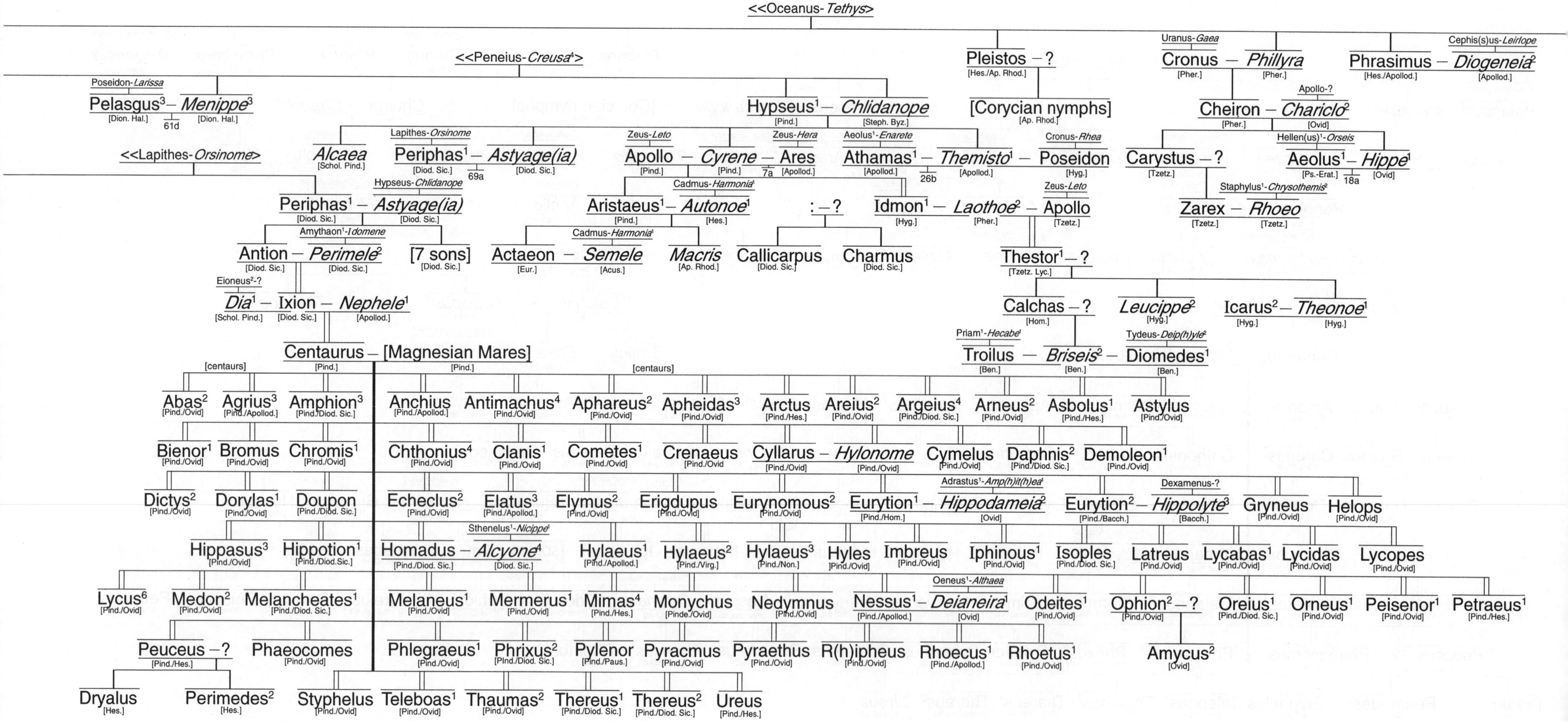

<<Oceanus-Tethys>
<<Peneius-Creusa[4]>
Pleistos – ?
[Hes./Ap. Rhod.]
Uranus-Gaea
Cronus – Phillyra
[Pher.] [Pher.]
Phrasimus – Diogeneia[2]
[Hes./Apollod.] [Apollod.]
Cephis(s)us-Leirlope
Poseidon-Larissa
Pelasgus[3] – Menippe[3]
[Dion. Hal.] 61d [Dion. Hal.]
Hypseus[1] – Chlidanope
[Pind.] [Steph. Byz.]
[Corycian nymphs]
[Ap. Rhod.]
Apollo-?
Cheiron – Chariclo[2]
[Pher.] [Ovid]
<<Lapithes-Orsinome>
Alcaea
[Schol. Pind.]
Lapithes-Orsinome
Periphas[1] – Astyage(ia)
[Diod. Sic.] 69a [Diod. Sic.]
Zeus-Leto
Apollo – Cyrene – Ares
[Pind.] [Pind.] 7a [Apollod.]
Zeus-Hera
Aeolus[1]-Enarete
Athamas[1] – Themisto[1] – Poseidon
[Apollod.] 26b [Apollod.] [Hyg.]
Cronus-Rhea
Carystus – ?
[Tzetz.]
Hellen(us)[1]-Orseis
Aeolus[1] – Hippe[1]
[Ps.-Erat.] 18a [Ovid]
Hypseus-Chlidanope
Periphas[1] – Astyage(ia)
[Diod. Sic.] [Diod. Sic.]
Cadmus-Harmonia[1]
Aristaeus[1] – Autonoe[1]
[Pind.] [Hes.]
: – ?
Zeus-Leto
Idmon[1] – Laothoe[2] – Apollo
[Hyg.] [Pher.] [Tzetz.]
Staphylus[1]-Chrysothemis[2]
Zarex – Rhoeo
[Tzetz.] [Tzetz.]
Amythaon[1]-Idomene
Antion – Perimele[2]
[Diod. Sic.] [Diod. Sic.]
[7 sons]
[Diod. Sic.]
Cadmus-Harmonia[1]
Actaeon – Semele
[Eur.] [Acus.]
Macris
[Ap. Rhod.]
Callicarpus
[Diod. Sic.]
Charmus
[Diod. Sic.]
Thestor[1] – ?
[Tzetz. Lyc.]
Eioneus[2]-?
Dia[1] – Ixion – Nephele[1]
[Schol. Pind.] [Diod. Sic.] [Apollod.]
Calchas – ?
[Hom.]
Leucippe[2]
[Hyg.]
Icarus[2] – Theonoe[1]
[Hyg.] [Hyg.]
Priam[1]-Hecabe[1]
Tydeus-Deip(h)yle[2]
Troilus – Briseis[2] – Diomedes[1]
[Ben.] [Ben.] [Ben.]
Centaurus – [Magnesian Mares]
[Pind.] [Pind.]
[centaurs]
[centaurs]
Abas[2]
[Pind./Ovid]
Agrius[3]
[Pind./Apollod.]
Amphion[3]
[Pind./Diod. Sic.]
Anchius
[Pind./Apollod.]
Antimachus[4]
[Pind./Ovid]
Aphareus[2]
[Pind./Ovid]
Apheidas[3]
[Pind./Ovid]
Arctus
[Pind./Hes.]
Areius[2]
[Pind./Ovid]
Argeius[4]
[Pind./Diod. Sic.]
Arneus[2]
[Pind./Ovid]
Asbolus[1]
[Pind./Hes.]
Astylus
[Pind./Ovid]
Bienor[1]
[Pind./Ovid]
Bromus
[Pind./Ovid]
Chromis[1]
[Pind./Ovid]
Chthonius[4]
[Pind./Ovid]
Clanis[1]
[Pind./Ovid]
Cometes[1]
[Pind./Ovid]
Crenaeus
[Pind./Ovid]
Cyllarus – Hylonome
[Pind./Ovid] [Pind./Ovid]
Cymelus
[Pind./Ovid]
Daphnis[2]
[Pind./Diod. Sic.]
Demoleon[1]
[Pind./Ovid]
Dictys[2]
[Pind./Ovid]
Dorylas[1]
[Pind./Ovid]
Doupon
[Pind./Diod. Sic.]
Echeclus[2]
[Pind./Ovid]
Elatus[3]
[Pind./Apollod.]
Elymus[2]
[Pind./Ovid]
Erigdupus
[Pind./Ovid]
Eurynomous[2]
[Pind./Ovid]
Adrastus[1]-Amp(h)it(h)ea[1]
Eurytion[1] – Hippodameia[2]
[Pind./Hom.] [Ovid]
Dexamenus-?
Eurytion[2] – Hippolyte[3]
[Pind./Bacch.] [Bacch.]
Gryneus
[Pind./Ovid]
Helops
[Pind./Ovid]
Hippasus[3]
[Pind./Ovid]
Hippotion[1]
[Pind./Diod.Sic.]
Stenelus[1]-Nicippe[1]
Homadus – Alcyone[4]
[Pind./Diod. Sic.] [Diod. Sic.]
Hylaeus[1]
[Pind./Apollod.]
Hylaeus[2]
[Pind./Virg.]
Hylaeus[3]
[Pind./Non.]
Hyles
[Pind./Ovid]
Imbreus
[Pind./Ovid]
Iphinous[1]
[Pind./Ovid]
Isoples
[Pind./Diod. Sic.]
Latreus
[Pind./Ovid]
Lycabas[1]
[Pind./Ovid]
Lycidas
[Pind./Ovid]
Lycopes
[Pind./Ovid]
Lycus[6]
[Pind./Ovid]
Medon[2]
[Pind./Ovid]
Melancheates[1]
[Pind./Diod. Sic.]
Melaneus[1]
[Pind./Ovid]
Mermerus[1]
[Pind./Ovid]
Mimas[4]
[Pind./Hes.]
Monychus
[Pind./Ovid]
Nedymnus
[Pind./Ovid]
Oeneus[1]-Althaea
Nessus[1] – Deianeira[1]
[Pind./Apollod.] [Ovid]
Odeites[1]
[Pind./Ovid]
Ophion[2] – ?
[Pind./Ovid]
Oreius[1]
[Pind./Diod. Sic.]
Orneus[1]
[Pind./Ovid]
Peisenor[1]
[Pind./Ovid]
Petraeus[1]
[Pind./Hes.]
Peuceus – ?
[Pind./Hes.]
Phaeocomes
[Pind./Ovid]
Phlegraeus[1]
[Pind./Ovid]
Phrixus[2]
[Pind./Diod. Sic.]
Pylenor
[Pind./Paus.]
Pyracmus
[Pind./Ovid]
Pyraethus
[Pind./Ovid]
R(h)ipheus
[Pind./Ovid]
Rhoecus[1]
[Pind./Apollod.]
Rhoetus[1]
[Pind./Ovid]
Amycus[2]
[Ovid]
Dryalus
[Hes.]
Perimedes[2]
[Hes.]
Styphelus
[Pind./Ovid]
Teleboas[1]
[Pind./Ovid]
Thaumas[2]
[Pind./Ovid]
Thereus[1]
[Pind./Diod. Sic.]
Thereus[2]
[Pind./Diod. Sic.]
Ureus
[Pind./Hes.]

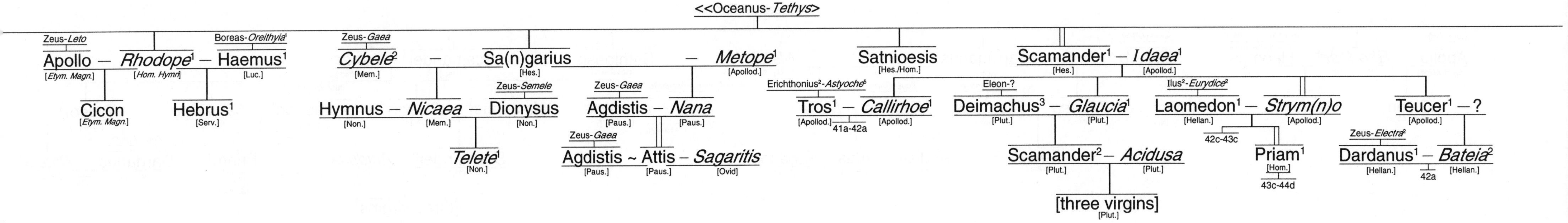

<<Oceanus-*Tethys*>
Zeus-*Leto*
Apollo – *Rhodope*[1] – Haemus[1]
[*Etym. Magn.*]
[*Hom. Hymn*]
Boreas-*Oreithyia*[1]
[Luc.]
Cicon
[*Etym. Magn.*]
Hebrus[1]
[Serv.]
Zeus-*Gaea*
Cybele[2] – Sa(n)garius – *Metope*[1]
[Mem.]
[Hes.]
[Apollod.]
Hymnus – *Nicaea* – Dionysus
[Non.]
[Mem.]
Zeus-*Semele*
[Non.]
Telete[1]
[Non.]
Zeus-*Gaea*
Agdistis – *Nana*
[Paus.]
[Paus.]
Zeus-*Gaea*
Agdistis ~ Attis – *Sagaritis*
[Paus.]
[Paus.]
[Ovid]
Satnioesis
[Hes./Hom.]
Scamander[1] – *Idaea*[1]
[Hes.]
[Apollod.]
Erichthonius[2]-*Astyoche*[5]
Tros[1] – *Callirhoe*[1]
[Apollod.]
41a-42a
[Apollod.]
Eleon-?
Deimachus[3] – *Glaucia*[1]
[Plut.]
[Plut.]
Scamander[2] – *Acidusa*
[Plut.]
[Plut.]
[three virgins]
[Plut.]
Ilus[2]-*Eurydice*[2]
Laomedon[1] – *Strym(n)o*
[Hellan.]
[Apollod.]
42c-43c
Priam[1]
[Hom.]
43c-44d
Teucer[1] – ?
[Apollod.]
Zeus-*Electra*[2]
Dardanus[1] – *Bateia*[2]
[Hellan.]
42a
[Hellan.]

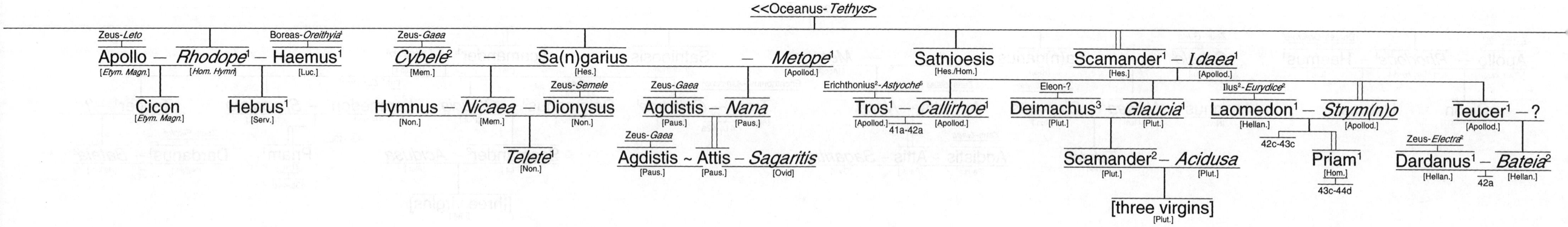
<<Oceanus-Tethys>
Zeus-Leto
Apollo – Rhodope¹ – Haemus¹
[Etym. Magn.]
[Hom. Hymn]
[Luc.]
Boreas-Oreithyia¹
Cicon
[Etym. Magn.]
Hebrus¹
[Serv.]
Zeus-Gaea
Cybele² – Sa(n)garius – Metope¹
[Mem.]
[Hes.]
[Apollod.]
Zeus-Semele
Hymnus – Nicaea – Dionysus
[Non.]
[Mem.]
[Non.]
Telete¹
[Non.]
Zeus-Gaea
Agdistis – Nana
[Paus.]
[Paus.]
Zeus-Gaea
Agdistis ~ Attis – Sagaritis
[Paus.]
[Paus.]
[Ovid]
Satnioesis
[Hes./Hom.]
Erichthonius²-Astyoche⁵
Tros¹ – Callirhoe¹
[Apollod.]
41a-42a
[Apollod.]
Scamander¹ – Idaea¹
[Hes.]
[Apollod.]
Eleon-?
Deimachus³ – Glaucia¹
[Plut.]
[Plut.]
Scamander² – Acidusa
[Plut.]
[Plut.]
[three virgins]
[Plut.]
Ilus²-Eurydice²
Laomedon¹ – Strym(n)o
[Hellan.]
[Apollod.]
42c-43c
Priam¹
[Hom.]
43c-44d
Teucer¹ – ?
[Apollod.]
Zeus-Electra²
Dardanus¹ – Bateia²
[Hellan.]
42a
[Hellan.]

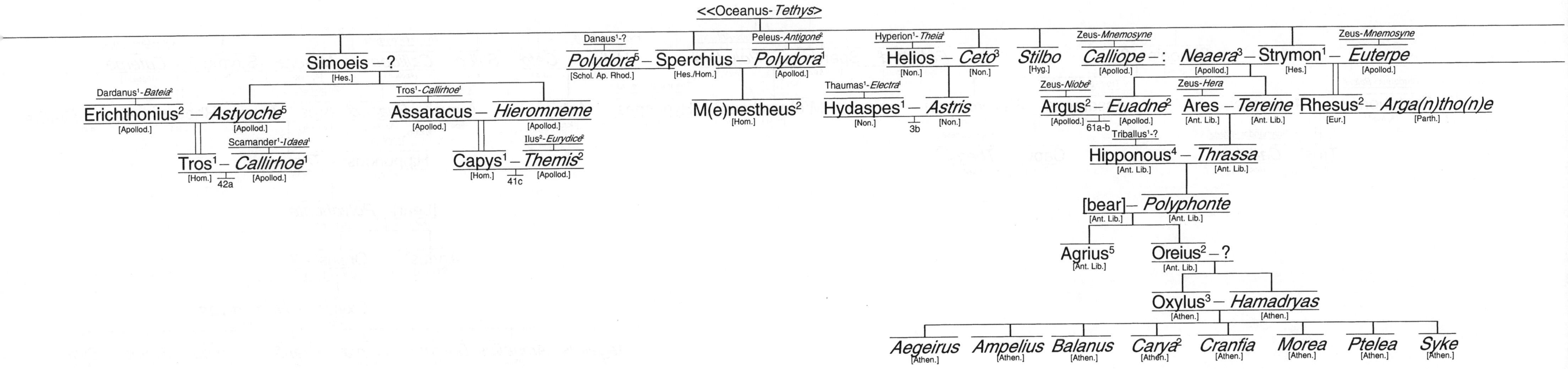

<<Oceanus-Tethys>
Simoeis – ?
[Hes.]
Dardanus¹-Bateia²
Erichthonius² – Astyoche⁵
[Apollod.]
[Apollod.]
Scamander¹-Idaea¹
Tros¹ – Callirhoe¹
[Hom.]
42a
[Apollod.]
Tros¹-Callirhoe¹
Assaracus – Hieromneme
[Apollod.]
[Apollod.]
Ilus²-Eurydice³
Capys¹ – Themis²
[Hom.]
41c
[Apollod.]
Danaus¹-?
Polydora⁵ – Sperchius – Polydora¹
[Schol. Ap. Rhod.]
[Hes./Hom.]
Peleus-Antigone³
[Apollod.]
M(e)nestheus²
[Hom.]
Hyperion¹-Theia¹
Helios – Ceto³
[Non.]
[Non.]
Thaumas¹-Electra¹
Hydaspes¹ – Astris
[Non.]
3b
[Non.]
Stilbo
[Hyg.]
Zeus-Mnemosyne
Calliope – :
[Apollod.]
Zeus-Niobe³
Argus² – Euadne²
[Apollod.]
61a-b
[Apollod.]
Triballus¹-?
Hipponous⁴ – Thrassa
[Ant. Lib.]
[Ant. Lib.]
[bear] – Polyphonte
[Ant. Lib.]
[Ant. Lib.]
Agrius⁵
[Ant. Lib.]
Oreius² – ?
[Ant. Lib.]
Oxylus³ – Hamadryas
[Athen.]
[Athen.]
Aegeirus [Athen.]
Ampelius [Athen.]
Balanus [Athen.]
Carya² [Athen.]
Cranfia [Athen.]
Morea [Athen.]
Ptelea [Athen.]
Syke [Athen.]
Neaera³ – Strymon¹ – Euterpe
[Apollod.]
[Hes.]
[Apollod.]
Zeus-Mnemosyne
Zeus-Hera
Ares – Tereine
[Ant. Lib.]
[Ant. Lib.]
Rhesus² – Arga(n)tho(n)e
[Eur.]
[Parth.]

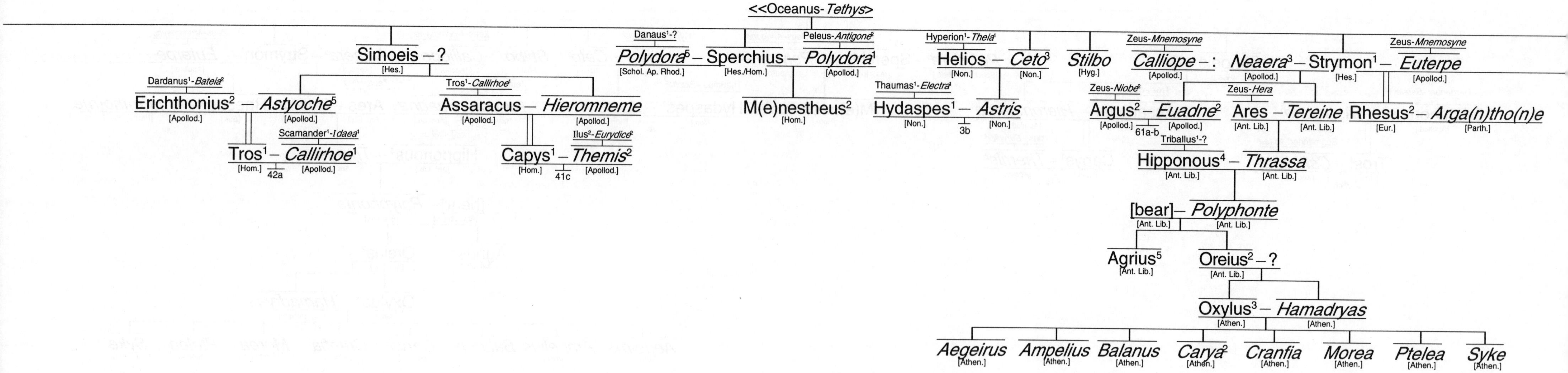

<<Oceanus-Tethys>
Simoeis – ?
[Hes.]
Dardanus¹-Bateia²
Erichthonius² – Astyoche⁵
[Apollod.] [Apollod.]
Scamander¹-Idaea¹
Tros¹ – Callirhoe¹
[Hom.] 42a [Apollod.]
Tros¹-Callirhoe¹
Assaracus – Hieromneme
[Apollod.] [Apollod.]
Ilus²-Eurydice²
Capys¹ – Themis²
[Hom.] 41c [Apollod.]
Danaus¹-?
Polydora⁵ – Sperchius – Polydora¹
[Schol. Ap. Rhod.] [Hes./Hom.] [Apollod.]
Peleus-Antigone²
M(e)nestheus²
[Hom.]
Hyperion¹-Theia¹
Helios – Ceto³
[Non.] [Non.]
Thaumas¹-Electra¹
Hydaspes¹ – Astris
[Non.] 3b [Non.]
Stilbo
[Hyg.]
Zeus-Mnemosyne
Calliope – : Neaera³ – Strymon¹ – Euterpe
[Apollod.] [Apollod.] [Hes.] [Apollod.]
Zeus-Mnemosyne
Zeus-Niobe²
Argus² – Euadne²
[Apollod.] 61a-b [Apollod.]
Zeus-Hera
Ares – Tereine
[Ant. Lib.] [Ant. Lib.]
Rhesus² – Arga(n)tho(n)e
[Eur.] [Parth.]
Triballus¹-?
Hipponous⁴ – Thrassa
[Ant. Lib.] [Ant. Lib.]
[bear] – Polyphonte
[Ant. Lib.] [Ant. Lib.]
Agrius⁵
[Ant. Lib.]
Oreius² – ?
[Ant. Lib.]
Oxylus³ – Hamadryas
[Athen.] [Athen.]
Aegeirus [Athen.]
Ampelius [Athen.]
Balanus [Athen.]
Carya² [Athen.]
Cranfia [Athen.]
Morea [Athen.]
Ptelea [Athen.]
Syke [Athen.]

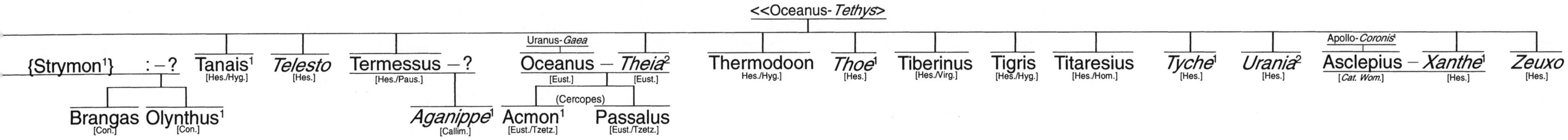

<<Oceanus-*Tethys*>
{Strymon[1]} : –?
Brangas [Con.]
Olynthus[1] [Con.]
Tanais[1] [Hes./Hyg.]
Telesto [Hes.]
Termessus –? [Hes./Paus.]
Aganippe[1] [Callim.]
Uranus-*Gaea*
Oceanus [Eust.] – *Theia*[2] [Eust.]
(Cercopes)
Acmon[1] [Eust./Tzetz.]
Passalus [Eust./Tzetz.]
Thermodoon Hes./Hyg.]
Thoe[1] [Hes.]
Tiberinus [Hes./Virg.]
Tigris [Hes./Hyg.]
Titaresius [Hes./Hom.]
Tyche[1] [Hes.]
Urania[2] [Hes.]
Apollo-*Coronis*[4]
Asclepius [*Cat. Wom.*] – *Xanthe*[1] [Hes.]
Zeuxo [Hes.]

Guide to the Index

1. The Index shows the location of each of the figures on the 72 segments of the Complete Chart and also provides descriptive information about them and a citation to an authoritative ancient source. Names of figures and of groups of figures are shown in the same manner as on the Complete Chart: male names are in roman type, *e.g.*, Zeus; female names are in italic type, *e.g.*, *Hera*; figures with the same name are distinguished by a numerical superscript, *e.g.*, Lycus[1], Lycus[2], Lycus[3]; and principal spelling variations are indicated by placing in parentheses the letter or syllable that some mythographers use in spelling the name, *e.g.*, *Asty(a)dameia*[1], Bellerophon(tes).

2. The entry for each figure includes seven types of information, in the following order:

First, alternate names of the figure, shown in parentheses, *e.g.*,

Heracles[1] (Alcides) (Aloides) (Melampyges) (Menoeceus[3])

All alternate names are also included in the alphabetical listing in the Index, cross-referenced to the figure's principal name, *e.g.*,

Alcides — see Heracles[1]

Second, descriptive information about the figure, shown in brackets, *e.g.*,

Acrisius [King of Argos]
Aloeus[1] [giant]
Amycus[2] [centaur]
Calais [Argonaut]
Calliope [epic poetry] [one of the Muses]
Polyneices [one of the Seven against Thebes]

Third, the primary relationship of the figure, *i.e.*, the names of the figure's parents, if known; otherwise, the names of the figure's principal spouse or paramour, *e.g.*,

Achilles, son of Peleus and *Thetis*
Boline, paramour of Apollo

Fourth, a citation to an authoritative ancient source in which the figure's parentage or other relationships are set forth. The citation is enclosed in angle brackets, with an abbreviated reference to the writer, the work, the book, and the section, verse, or line, *e.g.*,

Achilles, son of Peleus <Hom. *Il.* I.1> and *Thetis* <Hom. *Il.* I.414>

to indicate that an authoritative citation for Achilles as the son of Peleus is Homer's *Iliad*, book I, verse 1, and an authoritative citation for Achilles as the son of *Thetis* is Homer's *Iliad*, book I, verse 414. The abbreviations used in the citations are explained at the end of this guide.

Fifth, one or more alternate versions of the parentage of the figures, each with a citation to an authoritative ancient source reporting the alternate parentage. Alternate versions are listed in alphabetical order, except that the father shown on the chart is listed first with alternative versions of the mother. The alternative versions that have been listed do not purport to include all the various versions known to exist. In some of the alternative versions, the cited source identifies the name of a parent but does not indicate which of several figures with that same name is the parent. This uncertainty is reflected by a superscript question mark after the name, *e.g.*,

Argus[1], son of Arestor[1] <Ap. Rhod. *Arg.* 1.113> and *Mycene*
alternate parentage:
Polybus[?] and *Argeia*[?] <Hyg. *Fab.* 14>

to indicate that the cited source does not indicate which Polybus or which *Argeia* are the parents of Argus[1] according to an alternate version.

Sixth, the location on each segment of the Complete Chart where the figure appears in some relationship to another figure, whether as child, parent, spouse, or paramour. The system for numbering the locations is explained in detail in numbered paragraphs 6-12 of this guide.

Seventh, an identification of all the figures with whom the principal figure has a marital, extramarital, or homosexual relationship, with a citation to an authoritative ancient source reporting the relationship, *e.g.*,

Zeus [god] [supreme god], son of Cronus and *Rhea*
<Hes. *Theog.* 457>
— and *Hera* <Hes. *Theog.* 921>
— and *Leda* <Eur. *Hel.* 259>
— and Ganymede(s) <Eur. *Iph. at Aulis* 1049-53>

to indicate that Zeus has a marital relationship with *Hera*, an extramarital relationship with *Leda*, and a homosexual relationship with Ganymede(s). The Index entries do not distinguish between spouses and paramours.

3. Two citations are given where one source reports the parentage of a *group* of offspring, and a second, later source reports the *name* of the offspring, *e.g.*,

Aegle[1] [one of the Hesperides], daughter of *Nyx* <Hes. *Theog.* 213;
named, Apollod. *Bibl.* 2.5.11>

to indicate that Hes. *Theog.* 213 reports that the Hesperides are the daughters of *Nyx*, and Apollod. *Bibl.* 2.5.11, reports that *Aegle*[1] is one of the Hesperides.

4. In a few instances, two relationships of a figure are shown, *e.g.*,:

Macello, daughter of Damon; sister of *Dexithea*

This occurs where the figure's parent is not a descendant of other known figures and therefore appears on the Complete Chart only in small type, above the figure's name; listing an additional relative of the figure in the Index, *e.g.*, a sister, who appears on the Complete Chart in full size type, should assist the reader in locating the figure on the Complete Chart.

5. The Index includes an entry for the *name* of a group of figures, shown in parentheses, *e.g*, (Atlantiades), (Heliades^{1}), and the *designation* of a group of figures, shown in brackets, *e.g.*, [gods and goddesses], [Seven against Thebes], [Sibyls], [Titans].

6. All locations of a figure on the Complete Chart in each relationship with another figure (as parent, child, spouse, or paramour) are indicated by a segment number (the large-type number in the upper right-hand corner of each segment) and a letter (a, b, c, or d). The letters correspond to the four quadrants of a segment, *viz.*,

a	b
c	d

For example, in the entry:

Zeus, son of Cronus and *Rhea,* 5a

the location 5a indicates that Zeus appears in the upper left-hand quadrant of segment 5 in his relationship as the son of Cronus and *Hera. No lines appear on the segments to divide them into the four quadrants; the reader will have to visualize the quadrants.*

7. For figures whose parents are known, the one or sometimes two locations listed indicate where the figure appears in his or her parental chains. The first location, in roman type, indicates where the figure appears in his or her *paternal* chain; the second location, in italic type, indicates where the figure appears in his or her *maternal* chain, *e.g.*,

Achilles, son of Peleus and *Thetis*, 24c, *65c*

to indicate that Achilles appears in the lower left-hand quadrant of segment 24 in his paternal chain (*i.e.*, where Peleus appears as the son of *his* parents) and again in the lower left-hand quadrant of segment 65 in his maternal chain (*i.e.*, where *Thetis* appears as the daughter of *her* parents).

8. For figures whose parents are not known, the one location listed indicates where the figure appears in his or her primary relationship, usually as a spouse or paramour, *e.g.*,

Phthia^{4}, paramour of Apollo, 11d

to indicate that *Phthia*^{4}, whose parents are not known, appears in the lower right-hand quadrant of segment 11 as the paramour of Apollo.

9. A figure's spouses and paramours are usually shown at two locations: first at the location where the figure appears in his paternal chain, or (because of space limitations) in his maternal chain, and again at the location where the spouse or paramour appears in *her* parental chain. For example, *Aegina* appears as a paramour of Zeus in quadrant 5a, where Zeus appears in his parental chain, and she also appears in quadrant 66a, where she appears in her parental chain, with Zeus appearing in that quadrant as her paramour.

10. The entry for each figure includes the location of all of the figure's spouses or paramours, *e.g.*:

Autolycus^{1}, son of Hermes and *Chione*^{1}, 46b, *13a*
— and *Amphithea*^{2}, (13a)
— and *Mestra*, 34c
— and *Neaera*^{2}, 62d

The location for a figure's relation to a spouse or paramour is usually the location where the figure appears in relation to the spouse or paramour in *her* parental chain. Thus, Autolycus^{1} appears in the lower left-hand quadrant of segment 34 in a marital or extramarital relationship with *Mestra*, who appears at that location in *her* parental chain.

He also appears in the lower right-hand quadrant of segment 62 in an additional extramarital relationship with *Neaera*^{2}, who appears at that location in *her* parental chain. He also appears in the upper left-hand quadrant of segment 13 in a marital relationship with *Amphithea*^{2}. The location 13a is placed in parentheses because the parents of *Amphithea*^{2} are not known, and the location only repeats the location where Autolycus^{1} appears in one of his parental chains (in this instance, his maternal chain).

11. For figures with numerous paramours, *e.g.*, Apollo, Ares, Hermes, Poseidon, and Zeus, the parents of many of their paramours are unknown (or, if known, are not connected in their ancestral chains), and the location of such figures will often be on the left-hand edge of a segment (in the figure's own parental chain) with the paramour appearing in a different quadrant of that segment. The exact location of the paramour on that segment is always shown at the index entry for the paramour.

12. In those few instance where a figure's relationship to another figure is listed in the Index *only as a parent*, the listing indicates the segment number and quadrant in the usual manner, but the reader should be alert to the fact that the name appears at the indicated location in small type and will therefore be more difficult to locate than figures appearing in full size type, *e.g.*,

Clytius^{5}, father of *Pheno*, <Paus. 2.6.5>, 11b

to indicate that Clytius^{5} appears in the upper right-hand quadrant of segment 11, but because the parents of Clytius^{5} are not known, his name appears in this quadrant in small type, *viz.*,

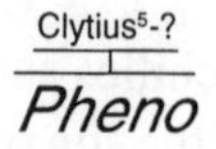

Figures identified in the Index only as a parent will be easier to locate on a segment of the Complete Chart by checking the Index entry for the child, noting the segment and quadrant where the child appears, and looking in that quadrant for the child's name (in full size type) and the parent's name immediately above.

13. In a few instances a figure is listed in the Index with an asterisk instead of a segment and quadrant location; this occurs where the figure has the same name as one or more figures who appear on the Complete Chart, but the figure is not related to any figure on the Complete Chart. The listing is given to distinguish the figure from others of the same name, *e.g.*,

Amphimachus[4], son of Nomion[1], *

to indicate that Amphimachus[4] is a different figure from Amphimachus[1], Amphimachus[2], and Amphimachus[3], but is not related to any figure on the Complete Chart and therefore is not shown on the Complete Chart.

14. In a few instances, a citation includes a parenthetical explanation to indicate that the cited source provides only a circumstance from which the listed relationship may be inferred, *e.g.*,

Meriones[2], son of Aeson and *Polymede* <Poly. *Strat.* 6, 1
(inferred because he is brother of Jason)>

to indicate that the listing of Meriones[2] as a son of Aeson and *Polymede* is an inference from the circumstances that Meriones[2] is identified in Poly. *Strat.* 6, 1 as a brother of Jason, and, at his entry, Jason is identified as the son of Aeson and *Polymede.*

Abbreviations Used in Citations

Acus. -- Acusilaus
Ael. -- Aelian
— *Var. Narr. -- Various Narrations*
— *De Nat. Anim. -- De Natura Animalium*
Aesch. -- Aeschylus
— *Agam. -- Agamemnon*
— *Eum. -- Eumenides*
— *Prom. Bound -- Prometheus Bound*
— *Sev. -- The Seven against Thebes*
— *Supp. -- The Suppliant Maidens*
Agath. -- Agathyllus
Akest. -- Akestorus
Alc. -- Alcaeus
— *Poet. Lesb. -- Poetarum Lesbiorum Fragmenta*
Alc. Sic. -- Alcaeus Siculus
Alciph. -- Alciphron
Alcm. -- Alcman
Andr. Hall. -- Andron of Hallicarnassus
Anti. -- Antimachus
Ant. Lib. -- Antoninus Liberalis
— *Met. -- Metamorphoses*
Apollod. -- Apollodorus
— *Bibl. -- Biblioteca*
— *Epit. -- Epitome*
Ap. Rhod. -- Apollonius Rhodius
— *Arg. -- Argonautica*
Apul. -- Apuleius
— *Met. -- Metamorphoses*
Arat. -- Aratus
— *Phaen. -- Phaenomena*
Aris. -- Aristotle
— *On Marv. Works Heard -- On Marvelous Works Heard*
Aristoph. -- Aristophanes
Arr. -- Arrian
— *Ind. -- Indica*
Asclep. -- Asclepiades
Athen. -- Athenaeus
Bacch. -- Bacchylides
Ben. -- Benoit
Ber. Pap. -- Berlin Papers
Callim. -- Callimachus
Cast. -- Castor
Cat. Wom. -- Catalogue of Women
Cerc. -- Cercops
Choer. -- Choerilus of Athens
Cic. -- Cicero
— *De Nat. Deor. -- De Natura Deorum Academica*
Cin. -- Cinaethon
Clem. Alex. -- Clement of Alexandria
— *Exhor. -- Exhortation to the Greeks*
— *Misc. -- Miscellanies*
— *Strom. -- Stromateis*
Con. -- Conon
— *Narr. -- Narrations*
Corn. -- Cornutus
— *De. Nat. Deor. -- De Natura Deorum*
Corp. Inscr. Gr. -- Corpus Inscriptionum Graecorum
Cyp. -- Cypria
Dem. Scep. -- Demetrius of Scepsis
Dicaearch. -- Dicaearchus
Dict. Cret. -- Dictys Cretensis
Diod. Sic. -- Diodorus Siculus
Diog. Laert. -- Diogenes Laertius
— *Lives -- Lives of Eminent Philosophers*
Dion. Hal.-- Dionysius of Hallicarnassus
— *Rom. Ant. -- Roman Antiquities*
Dion. Per. -- Dionysius Periegetes
Epich. -- Epicharmus
Epim. -- Epimenides
— *Theog. -- Theogony*
Erot. Scrip. Gr. -- Erotici Scriptores Graeci
Etym. Magn. -- Etymologicum Magnum
Euan. -- Euanthius
Eug. -- Eugammon
— *Tel. -- Telegony* (Epic Cycle)
Eum. -- Eumelus
Euphor. -- Euphorion
Eur. -- Euripides
— *Alc. -- Alcestis*
— *Andr. -- Andromache*
— *Ant. -- Antigone*
— *Bacc. -- The Bacchantes*
— *Cycl. -- The Cyclops*
— *Elec. -- Electra*
— *Hec. -- Hecuba*
— *Hel. -- Helen*
— *Her. -- Heracles*
— *Heracl. -- Heraclidae*
— *Hipp. -- Hippolytus*
— *Iph. in Aulis -- Iphigeneia in Aulis*
— *Iph. Taur. -- Iphigeneia among the Tauri*
— *Med. -- Medea*
— *Or. -- Orestes*
— *Phoen. Maid. -- Phoenician Maidens*
— *Rhes. -- Rhesus*
— *Supp. Wom. -- The Suppliants*
— *Tro. Wom. -- The Trojan Women*
Eust. -- Eustathius
— *Comm. Dion. Per. -- Commentaria in Dionysium Periegetam*
Fab. Pict. -- Fabius Pictor
Fest. -- Festus
— *De Verb. Sign. -- De Verborum Significatione*
F. Gr. H. -- Die Fragmente der Griechischen Historiker
F.H.G. -- Fragmenta Historicum Graecorum
Frag. Hes. -- Fragmenta Hesiodea
frg. -- fragment
Geopon. -- Geoponica
Gr. Ehoiai -- Great Ehoiai
Greg. Cor. -- Gregorius Corinthus
Hec. -- Hecataeus
Heg. -- Hegisinous
Heges. -- Hegesander
Hellan. -- Hellanicus
Heraclid. -- Heraclides
Herm. Col. -- Hermesianax of Colophon
Herm. Cyp. -- Hermesianax of Cyprus
Hermip. -- Hermippus
Herod. -- Herodotus
— *Hist. -- History*
Herodor. -- Herodorus
Hes. -- Hesiod

— *Shield* -- *Shield of Heracles (Scutum)*
— *Theog.* -- *Theogony*
Hes.—Hom. Hymns & Hom. -- *Hesiod—the Homeric Hymns and Homerica*
Hesyc. -- Hesychius of Alexandria
— *Lex.* -- *Lexicon*
Hesyc. Mil. -- Hesychius of Miletus
Hom. -- Homer
— *Il.* -- *The Iliad*
— *Od.* -- *The Odyssey*
Hom. Hymn -- *Homeric Hymn*
Hor. -- Horace
Hyg. -- Hyginus
— *Fab.* -- *Fabulae*
— *Poet. Astr.* -- *Poetica Astronomica*
Ibyc. -- Ibycus
Ist. -- Ister
Isyl. -- Isyllus
— *Lyr.* -- *Lyricus*
Lesch. -- Lesches
Lon. -- Longus
Luc. -- Lucian
— *Dial. Sea-Gods* -- *Dialogue of the Sea-Gods*
Lyc. -- Lycophron
— *Alex.* -- *Alexandra*
Mem. -- Memnon of Heraclea
Mene. Tyr. -- Menecrates of Tyre
Merk. & West -- Merkelbach, R., & West, M. L.
Mimn. -- Mimnermus
Nic. Eug. -- Nicetas Eugenianus
Nicand. -- Nicander
Non. -- Nonnus
— *Dion.* -- *Dionysiaca*
Opp. -- Oppian
— *Hal.* -- *Halieutica*
Orpheus
— *Arg.* -- *Argonauts*
Ovid
— *Fast.* -- *Fasti*
— *Her.* -- *Heroides*
— *Met.* -- *Metamorphoses*
Pal. -- Palaephatus
Parth. -- Parthenius
— *Love Stor.* -- *Love Stories*
Paus. -- Pausanias
Paus. Damasc. -- Pausanius of Damascus
P.E.G. -- *Poetae Epici Graeci*
Pher. -- Pherecydes (of Athens)
Pher. Syr. -- Pherecydes (of Syros)
Phil. -- Philostratus
— *Her.* -- *Heracles*
Phil. Bybl. -- Philon Byblus
Philoch. -- Philochorus
Philocr. -- Philocrates
Phot. -- Photius
— *Bibl.* -- *Biblioteca*
— *Lex.* -- *Lexicon*
Pind. -- Pindar
— *Isth.* -- *Isthmian Odes*
— *Nem.* -- *Nemean Odes*
— *Olym.* -- *Olympian Odes*
— *Pyth.* -- *Pythian Odes*
Plato
— *Crit.* -- *Critias*
— *Rep.* -- *Republic*
— *Tim.* -- *Timaeus*
P.L.F. -- *Poetae Lyrici Graeci*
P.L.F. -- *Poetarum Lesbiorum Fragmenta*
Pliny
— *Nat. His.* -- *Naturalis Historia*
Plut. -- Plutarch
— *Alcib.* -- *Alcibiades*
— *Aris.* -- *Aristides*
— *Brav. Wom.* -- *Bravery of Women*
— *Gr. and Rom. Par. Stor.* -- *Greek and Roman Parallel Stories*
— *Gr. Quest.* -- *Greek Questions*
— *Mor.* -- *Moralia*
— *Pyrr.* -- *Pyrrhus*
— *Rom.* -- *Romulus*
— *Sert.* -- *Sertorius*
— *Them.* -- *Themistocles*
— *Thes.* -- *Theseus*
P.M.G. -- *Poetae Melici Graeci*
Poll. -- Pollux
— *Onom.* -- *Onomasticon*
Poly. -- Polyaenus
— *Strat.* -- *Strategemata*
Pomp. Mela -- Pomponius Mela
— *De Sit. Orb.* -- *De Situ Orbis*
Proc. -- Proclus
— *Plat. Tim.* -- *Plato Timaeus*
Prop. -- Propertius
— *Eleg.* -- *Elegies*
Prax. -- Praxilla
Prob. -- Probus
Prox. -- Proxenos
Ptol. -- Ptolemaeus Hephaestion
Ps.-Erat. -- Pseudo-Eratosthenes
— *Cat.* -- *Catasterismi*
Ps.-Plut. -- Pseudo-Plutarch
— *De Fluv.* -- *De Fluvia*
Quint. Smyr. -- Quintus Smyrnaeus
— *Posthom.* -- *Posthomerica*
Schol. -- Scholia
Serv. -- Servius
— *Virg. Aen.* -- *Virgil's Aeneid*
— *Virg. Ecl.* -- *Virgil's Eclogues*
Sil. Ital. -- Silius Italicus
Simon. -- Simonides
Sol. -- Solinus
— *Coll. Rer. Mem.* -- *Collectanea Rerum Memorabilium*
Soph. -- Sophocles
— *Ant.* -- *Antigone*
— *Elec.* -- *Electra*
— *Oed. at Col.* -- *Oedipus at Colonus*
— *Oed. Tyr.* -- *Oedipus Tyrannus (the King)*
— *Phil.* -- *Philoctetes*
— *Trach. Wom.* -- *Trachinian Women*
Stat. -- Statius
— *Theb.* -- *Thebaid*
Steph. Byz. -- Stephanus Byzantium
Stes. -- Stesichorus
Strab. -- Strabo
Suid. -- Suidas
Teles. -- Telesilla
T.G.F. -- *Tragicorum Graecorum Fragmenta*
Theocr. -- Theocritus
Theopomp. -- Theopompus
Thuc. -- Thucydides
Tryph. -- Tryphiodorus
— *Tak. Ilium* -- *The Taking of Ilium*
Tzetz. -- Tzetzes
— *Antehom.* -- *Antehomerica*
— *Chil.* -- *Historiarum Variarum Chiliades*
— *Exeg. Il.* -- *Exegesis in Iliadem*
— on Lyc. -- on Lycophron
— *Posthom.* -- *Posthomerica*
Val. Flac. -- Valerius Flaccus
Virg. -- Virgil
— *Aen.* -- *Aeneid*
— *Ecl.* -- *Eclogues*
— *Geo.* -- *Georgics*
Xena. -- Xenagoras
Zen. -- Zenobius
— *Soph.* -- *Sophist*

Index

(A guide to this index is located at pages 159-162)

Abarbarea, paramour of Bucolion[2] <Hom. *Il.* VI.22>, 42c
Abas[1] [King of Argos], son of Lynceus[2] <Schol. on Pind. *Pyth.* 8.77> and *Hyperm(n)estra*[1] <Apollod. *Bibl.* 2.2.1>, *57d*
— and *Aglaia*[3] <Apollod. *Bibl.* 2.2.1>, (57d)
Abas[2] [centaur], offspring of Centaurus and a Magnesian Mare <Pind. *Pyth.* 2.50; named as centaur, Ovid *Met.* 12.306>, 69c
alternate parentage:
Ixion and *Nephele*[1] <Diod. Sic. 4.69.5>
Abas[3] [King of Euboea], son of Poseidon <Eust. on Hom. *Il.* 281> and *Arethusa*[3] <Hyg. *Fab.* 157>, 8b, *35a*
Abas[4], son of Melampus[1] <Apollod. *Bibl.* 1.9.13> and *Iphianassa*[1], 31d
Abas[5], son of Eurydamas[5] <Hom. *Il.* V.149>,*
Abas[6], father of Argus[7] <Stat. *Theb.* 9.758>, *
Abas[7], comrade of Diomedes[1] <Ovid *Met.* 14.494>, *
Abas[8], killed by Lausus <Virg. *Aen.* 10.429-29>, *
Abas[9], killed Pelates <Ovid *Met.* 5.123-26>, *
Abas[10], killed by Sthenelus[2] <Quint. Smyr. 11, 81>, *
Abderus, son of Hermes <Apollod. *Bibl.* 2.5.8>, 46d
— and Heracles[1] <Apollod. *Bibl.* 2.5.8>, 61d
Abia, daughter of Glenus <Paus. 4.30.1>, 60c
Abrote (*Habrote*), daughter of Onchestus[1] <Plut. *Gr. Quest.* 16.295> and *Oenope*, 9d, *34d*
— and Nisus[2] <Plut. *Gr. Quest.* 16.295>, 50d
[abstractions], offspring of *Eris* (see *Algea, Amphillogiai, Androktasiai, Ate, Dysnomia,* Horcus, Hysminai, *Lethe*[1], Limus, Logoi, Machai, *Neikea,* Phonoi, Ponus, *Pseudea*), *1a*
offspring of *Nyx* (see *Apate, Cer, (Ceres),* Geras, Hypnos, *Lyssa,* Momus, Mor(u)s, *Nemesis,* Oizys, *Oneiroi, Philotes,* Thanatus), *1a-b*
Absyrtus — see Apsyrtus
Acacalle — see *Acacallis*[1]
Acacallis[1] (*Acacalle*) (*Acalle*), daughter of Minos I and *Pasiphae*[1] <Apollod. *Bibl.* 3.1.2 (she is called *Acalle*)>, 53d
alternate parentage:
Minos I and *Crete*[1] <Asclep. in Apollod. *Bibl.* 3.1.2>
— and Apollo <Ap. Rhod. *Arg.* 4.1450-56>, 11a
— and Hermes <Paus. 8.53.4>, 46a
Acacallis[2] [nymph], paramour of Apollo <Paus. 10.16.3>, 11a
Acalanthis, daughter of Pierus[2] <Nicand. in Ant. Lib. *Met.* 9> and *Euippe*[2] <Ovid *Met.* 5.300 ff.>, 15a
Acallaris, daughter of Eumedes[4] and paramour of Tros[1] <Dion. Hal. *Rom. Ant.* 1.62.2>, 42a
Acalle — see *Acacallis*[1]
Acamantis —see [fifty daughters of Danaus[1]] (alternate version)
Acamas[1] [King of Melos], son of Theseus <Eur. *Heracl.* 11 (inferred because he is called brother of Demophon)> and *Phaedra* <Apollod. *Epit.* 1.18>, 51d
— and *Laodice*[1] <Parth. *Love Stor.* 16.2>, 43c
Acamas[2], son of Antenor[1] <Hom. *Il.* XI.60> and *Theano*[2] <Apollod. *Epit.* 3.33>, *45c*
Acamas[3], son of Eus(s)orus; brother of *Aenete* <Hom. *Il.* VI.8>, 44d
Acamas[4], suitor of *Penelope*[1] (from Dulichium) <Apollod. *Epit.* 7. 27>, *
Acamas[5], Aetolian soldier <Stat. *Theb.* 7.589>, *
Acamas[6], killed by Tydeus[1] <Stat. *Theb.* 3.173>, *
Acamas[7] [one of the dogs of Actaeon] <Hyg. *Fab.* 181>, *
Acarnan (Acarnas), son of Alcmaeon[1] and *Callirhoe*[4] <Apollod. *Bibl.* 3.7.6>, 32d
Acarnas — see Acarnan
Acaste[1], daughter of Oceanus and *Tethys* <Hes. *Theog.* 356>, 50a
Acaste[2], nurse for daughters of Adrastus[1] <Stat. *Theb.* 1.530>, *
Acastus [King of Iolcus] [Argonaut], son of Pelias[1] <*Cat. Wom., Frag. Hes.* frg. 37, Merk. & West> and *Anaxibia*[2] <Apollod. *Bibl.* 1.9.10>, 28c
alternate parentage:
Pelias and *Phylomache* <Apollod. *Bibl.* 1.9.10>
— and *Hippolyte*[2] <Pind. *Nem.* 5.25-30>, 33a
Aceles, son of Heracles[1] and *Malis* <Hellan. in *F.H.G.* 1.58, frg. 102, Müller>, 60d
Acerbas — see Sychaeus
Acesidas — see Idas[3]
Acesis (*Aceso*) [remedy], daughter of Asclepius and *Epeione* <Suid. "Epeione">, 19c
Aceso — see *Acesis*
Acessamenus, father of *Periboea*[6] <Hom. *Il.* XXI.143>, 67a
Acestes — see Aegestes
Achaeus[1], son of Xuthus[1] and *Creusa*[3] <*Cat. Wom., Hesiodi* frg. 10(a).20-24, Merk. & West (O.C.T.)>, 17b, *51b*
Achaeus[2], son of Poseidon and *Larissa*[1] <Dion. Hal. *Rom. Ant.* 1.17.3>, 8c, *61d*
Achelois — see [Muses] (alternate version)
Achelous [river], son of Oceanus and *Tethys* <Hes. *Theog.* 340>, 65b
alternate parentage:
Oceanus and a naiad <Ps.-Plut. *De Fluv.* 22>
Helios and *Gaea* <Acus. in *F.H.G.* 1.101, frg. 11a, Müller>
— and *Melpomene* <Apollod. *Bibl.* 1.3.4>, 6b
— and *Perimede*[1] <*Cat. Wom., Hesiodi* frg. 10(a).34-35 Merk. & West (O.C.T.)>, 29a
Achemone — see *Philonoe*
Acheron [river], son of Oceanus and *Tethys* <Hes. *Theog.* 367-68; named as river, Hom. *Od.* 10.513>, 50a
— and *Gorgyra* <Apollod. *Bibl.* 1.5.3>, (50a)
Achilles (Ligyron) [King of Myrmidons], son of Peleus <Hom. *Il.* I.1> and *Thetis* <Hom. *Il.* I.414>, 24c, *65c*
— and *Briseis*[1] <Hom. *Il.* I.184-92>, (24c)
— and *Deidameia*[1] <Apollod. *Bibl.* 3.13.8>, 11d
— and *Diomede*[1] <Hom. *Il.* IX.665>, (24c)
— and *Helen*[1] <Paus. 3.19.13>, 48d
— and *Hemithea*[1] <Tzetz. on Lyc. 232>, 43c
— and Patroclus[1] <Apollod. *Bibl.* 3.13.8>, 22d
— and *Peisidice*[4] <Parth. *Love Stor.* 21.2>, (24c)
— and *Pentheseleia* <*Etym. Magn.* "Kaystros" (inferred because she is called mother of Achilles' son, Cayst(ri)us)>, 7c
— and *Polyxena*[1] <Eur. *Tro. Wom.* 261-66>, 43c
— and Troilus <Schol. on Lyc. 307>, 43d
Achiroe — see *Anchinoe*[1]
Acidalia — see *Aphrodite*
Acidusa, wife of Scamander[2] <Plut. *Gr. Quest.* 41>, 70b
Acis, son of Faunus[1] and *Simaethis* <Ovid *Met.* 13.750>, (64a)
— and *Galateia*[1] <Ovid *Met.* 13.719-897>, 64a
Acmon[1] (Eurybatus[1]) (Sillus) [one of the Cercopes], son of Oceanus and *Theia*[2] <Eust. on Hom. *Od.* 1864.34; named, Tzetz. *Chil.* 5.77.94>, *72a*
Acmon[2], son of Socus and *Combe*[1] <Non. *Dion.* 13.143 >, *66c*

alternate parentage:
Apollo and *Rhetia* <Pher. in *F. Gr. H.* 3 F 48 (unnamed)>
Acmon[3], son of Manes <Steph. Byz. "Acmonia"> and *Callirhoe*[2], *51b*
Acmon[4], comrade of Diomedes[1] <Ovid *Met.* 14.494>, *
Acmon[5], comrade of Aeneas <Virg. *Aen.* 10.126>, *
Acmonides — see Arges
Acontes, son of Lycaon[1] <Apollod. *Bibl.* 3.8.1>, 62a
Acraea, daughter of Asterius[1] <Paus. 2.17.1>, 51a
Acragas, son of Zeus and *Asterope*[3] <Steph. Byz. "Acragantes">, 5a, *51a*
Acrisius [King of Argos], son of Abas[1] <Bacch. 11.66-69> and *Aglaia*[3] <Apollod. *Bibl.* 2.2.1>, 58d
— and *Aganippe*[2] <Hyg. *Fab.* 155>, (58d)
— and *Eurydice*[6] <*Cat. Wom., Frag. Hes.* frg. 129, Merk. & West>, 47b
Actaea[1], daughter of Nereus and *Doris*[1] <Hes. *Theog.* 249>, *63a*
Actaea[2], daughter of Danaus[1] and *Pieria*[1] <Apollod. *Bibl.* 2.1.5>, 57c
— and Periphas[3] <Apollod. *Bibl.* 2.1.5>, (57c)
Actaeon, son of Aristaeus[1] and *Autonoe*[1] <Eur. *Bacc.* 1226>, 69a
— and *Semele* <Acus. in *F. Gr. H.* 2 F 33>, 56c
Actaeus[1] [one of the Telchines], son of Pontus and *Gaea* <Tzetz. *Chil.* 12.836>, 2a
alternate parentage:
Tartarus and *Nemesis* <Bacch. frg. 52, Snell & Maehler>
Thalatta <Diod. Sic. 5.55.1>
Actaeus[2], son of Istrus[2] <Tzetz. *Antehom.* 274>, 54b
Actaeus[3] [King of Athens], husband of *Glauce*[1] <Pher. in *F. Gr. H.* 3 F 60>, 66b
Acte [one of the hours], daughter of Zeus and *Themis*[1] <Hyg. *Fab.* 83>, 6d
Actis, son of Helios and *Rhode*[1] <Hellan. in *F.H.G.* 1.59, frg. 107 Müller>, 14a
Actor[1] [King of Phthia], son of Myrmidon and *Peisidice*[1] <*Cat. Wom., Hesiodi* frg. 10a.101, Merk. & West (O.C.T.)>, 5d
— and *Polyboea*[3] <Eust. on Hom. *Il.* 321>, (5d)
Actor[2], son of Poseidon and *Agamede*[1] <Hyg. *Fab.* 157>, 8a, *63c*
Actor[3], son of Deion[1] and *Diomede*[3] <Apollod. *Bibl.* 1.9.4>, 22b
— and *Aegina* <Pind. *Olym.* 9.73>, 66a
Actor[4] [King of the Eleans], son of Phorbas[2] <Diod. Sic. 4.69.2> and *Hyrmine* <Paus. 5.1.11>, 68b
alternate parentage:
Eleius[1] <Apollod. *Bibl.* 2.7.2 (inferred because he is the brother of Augeias)>
— and *Molione* <*Cat. Wom., Frag. Hes.* frg. 17, Merk. & West>, (9a), (68b)
Actor[5], son of Acastus <Schol. on Lyc. 901> and *Hippolyte*[2], 28c
Actor[6], son of Azeus <Hom. *Il.* II.514>, 26c
Actor[7], son of Hippasus[9] <Apollod. *Bibl.* 1.8.16>, *
Actor[8], son of Oenops and brother of Hyperbius[2] <Aesch. *Sev.* 504, 555>, *
Actor[9], father of Sthenelus[6] <Ap. Rhod. *Arg.* 2.911>, *
Actor[10], warrior with Aeneas <Virg. *Aen.* 9.500>, *
Actor[11], warrior at Thebes <Stat. *Theb.* 8.135>, *
Acusilaus, son of Odysseus and *Penelope*[1] <Eug. *Tel.* (Epic Cycle) 2, Evelyn-White>, 13d
Adamas, son of Asius[2] <Hom. *Il.* XII.140>, 44c
Adherbas — see Sychaeus
Adiante, daughter of Danaus[1] and *Herse*[2] <Apollod. *Bibl.* 2.1.5>, 57d
— and Diaphron[2] <Apollod. *Bibl.* 2.1.5>, (57d)
Adite, daughter of Danaus[1] and *Pieria*[1] <Apollod. *Bibl.* 2.1.5>, 57c
— and Menalces[1] <Apollod. *Bibl.* 2.1.5>, (57c)
Admete[1], daughter of Eurystheus <Apollod. *Bibl.* 2.5.9> and *Antimache*, 58d
Admete[2], daughter of Oceanus and *Tethys* <Hes. *Theog.* 349>, 50a
Admetus[1] [King of Pherae] [Argonaut], son of Pheres[1] <Eur. *Alc.* 10> and *Periclymene*, 29c
alternate parentage:
Augeias <Paus. 10.25.2>
— and *Alcestis* <Hom. *Il.* II.714-15>, 28d
Admetus[2], killed by Philoctetes <Paus. 10.27.1>, *
Adonis, son of Cinyras[1] <Bion 1.93> and *Myrr(h)a* <Ovid *Met.* 10.503>, *11c*
alternate parentage:
Cinyras[1] and *Metharme* <Apollod. *Bibl.* 3.14.3>
Phoenix[2] and *Alphesiboea*[4] <*Cat. Wom., Frag. Hes.* frg. 139, Merk. & West>
Theias and *Smyrna* <Panyasis in Apollod. *Bibl.* 3.14.4>
— and *Aphrodite* <Apollod. *Bibl.* 3.14.4>, 5a
— and *Erinoma* <Serv. on Virg. *Ecl.* 10.18>, (11c)
— and *Persephone*[1] <Apollod. *Bibl.* 3.14.4>, 10a
Adramys, father of *Thebe*[4] <Diceaearch. in *F.H.G.* 2.238, frg. 11, Müller>, 60d
Adrasteia[1] — see *Nemesis*
Adrasteia[2], daughter of Melisseus[2] <Apollod. *Bibl.* 1.1.7> and *Amaltheia*[2] <Callim. *Hymn* 1.46 ff.>, *
Adrastine — see *Aegiale*
Adrastus[1] [King of Sicyon] [one of the Seven against Thebes (per Eur. *Phoen. Maid.* 160)], son of Talaus <Pind. *Nem.* 9.14> and *Lysimache*[1] <Apollod. *Bibl.* 1.9.13>, 30c
alternate parentage:
Talaus and *Eurynome*[5] <Hyg. *Fab.* 70>
Talaus and *Lysianassa*[2] <Paus. 2.6.6>
— and *Amphithea*[1] <Apollod. *Bibl.* 1.9.13>, 31d
Adrastus[2], father of *Eurydice*[2] <Apollod. *Bibl.* 3.12.3>, 42a
Adrastus[3], son of Merops[3] <Hom. *Il.* II.830>, 44c
Adrastus[4], son of Polyneices <Paus. 2.30.4> and *Argeia*[1], 55c, *30c*
Aea, pursued by Phasis[2] <Val. Flac. 5.426>, 62b
Aeacus [King of Aegina], son of Zeus <Hom. *Il.* XXI.189> and *Aegina* <Eur. *Iph. in Aulis* 695-99>, 5a, *23c*, *66a*
— and *Endeis* <Pind. *Nem.* 5.12>, 39a, 66b
— and *Psamathe*[1] <Hes. *Theog.* 1004-05>, 65a
Aeantides, son of Ajax[1] and *Glauce*[6] <Dict. Cret. 5.16>, 23c
Aeas [river], son of Oceanus and *Tethys* <Hes. *Theog.* 367-68; named as river, Ovid *Met.* 1.575>, 50a
Aechmagoras, son of Heracles[1] and *Phialo* <Paus. 8.12.3>, 60d
Aechmodicus, paramour of *Amphissa*[2] <Schol. on Hom. *Od.* 18.84>, 31d
Aeclus, son of Ion[1] and *Helice*[1] <Strab. 10.1.3>, 51b
Aedes — see Hades
Aedon, daughter of Pandareus[1] <Hom. *Od.* 19.518> and *Harmothoe*[1] <Schol. on Hom. *Od.* 19.518>, 66d
— and Polytechnus <Ant. Lib. *Met.* 11.2-4>, (66d)
— and Zethus <Hom. *Od.* 19.518-19>, (66d)
Aedoneus — see Hades
Aeetes [King of Colchis], son of Helios and *Perse(is)* <Hes. *Theog.* 957>, 14c
alternate parentage:
Helios and *Antiope*[4] <Eum. frg. 3.*P.E.G.*>
Helios and *Ephyra* <Epim. 3 B 13>
— and *Asterodia*[3] <Ap. Rhod. *Arg.* 3.243>, 51a
— and *Eidyia* <Hes. *Theog.* 959>, 53a
— and *Hecate* <Diod. Sic. 4.45.3>, 12a
— and *Neaera*[5] <Schol. on Ap. Rhod. *Arg.* 3.241>, (14c)
Aeetias — see *Medea*
Aeetine — see *Medea*
Aeetis — see *Medea*
Aega — see *Aex*

Aegaeon[1] — see Briareus
Aegaeon[2], son of Lycaon[1] <Apollod. *Bibl.* 3.8.1>, 62b
Aegaeus [river], son of Oceanus and *Tethys* <Hes. *Theog.* 367-68; named as river, Ap. Rhod. *Arg.* 4.543>, 50a
Aegeirus [poplar tree], daughter of Oxylus[3] and *Hamadryas* <Athen. 3.78b>, 71d
Aegeoneus, son of Priam[1] <Apollod. *Bibl.* 3.12.5>, 43d
Aegesta (*Segesta*), daughter of Hippotes[2] <Serv. on Virg. *Aen.* 1.550>, 67a
— and Crimisus[1] <Serv. on Virg. *Aen.* 1.550>, (67a)
Aegestes (Acestes), son of Crimisus[1] and *Aegesta* <Lyc. 960 ff.>, 67a
— and *Entella* <Tzetz. on Lyc. 953>, (67a)
Aegesus — see Aesepus
Aegeus[1] [King of Athens], son of Pandion II <Eur. *Medea* 663> and *Pylia* <Apollod. *Bibl.* 3.15.5>, 51a
alternate parentage:
Pandion II and *Creusa*[3] <Bacch. 18.15>
Scyrius <Apollod. *Bibl.* 3.15.5>
— and *Aethra*[1] <Eur. *Supp.* 5>, 38b
— and *Autochte* <Tzetz. on Lyc. 494>, 59d
— and *Chalciope*[3] <Apollod. *Bibl.* 3.15.6>, (51a)
— and *Medea* <Eur. *Medea* 1385>, 14c
— and *Meta* <Apollod. *Bibl.* 3.15.6>, 52a
Aegeus[2], son of Oeolycus <Herod. 4.149>, 55d
Aegeus[3], son of Phorbas[2] <Diod. Sic. 4.69.2> and *Hyrmine*, 68b
Aegiale (*Adrastine*), daughter of Adrastus[1] <Hom. *Il.* V.412> and *Amphithea*[1] <Apollod. *Bibl.* 1.9.13>, 30c
— and Cometes[3] <Apollod. *Epit.* 6.10>, 58c
— and Diomedes[1] <Hom. *Il.* V.414> 17d
Aegialeus[1] [one of the Epigoni], son of Adrastus[1] <Hellan. in *F. Gr. H.* 4 F 100> and *Amphithea*[1] <Apollod. *Bibl.* 1.9.13>, 30c
Aegialeus[2], son of Inachus and *Melia*[1] <Apollod. *Bibl.* 2.1.1>, 61a
alternate parentage:
Aeetes and *Hecate* <Diod. Sic. 4.41.3>
Phoroneus <Schol. Eur. 932>
Aegialeus[3] — see Apsyrtus
Aegialus, son of Caunus and *Pronoe*[3] <Con. *Narr.* 2>, 68a
Aegicerus, son of Aegipan and *Aex* <Ps.-Erat. *Cat.* 27>, 46d, *7d*
Aegicores, son of Ion[1] and *Helice*[1] <Eur. *Ion*>, 51b
Aegicorus [one of the Pans], son of Pan <Non. *Dion.* 14.75>, 64d
Aegimius [King of Doris], son of Dorus[1] <*Cat. Wom., Hesiodi* frg. 10a, Merk. & West (O.C.T.)>, 17b
Aegina, daughter of Asopus <Pind. *Isth.* 8.17 ff.> and *Metope*[2] <Apollod. *Bibl.* 3.12.6>, 66a
— and Actor[3] <Pind. *Ol.* 9.73>, 22b
— and Zeus <Pind. *Nem.* 8.6>, 5a, 23a
Aeginetes[1], son of Dereites <Paus. 7.18.5>, 47c
Aeginetes[2] [King of Arcadia], son of Pompus (descended from Bucolion[1], but not shown on segment 62c) <Paus. 8.5.9>, *
Aegipan, son of Zeus and *Aex* <Hyg. *Poet. Astr.* 2.13>, 5a, *46c*
alternate parentage:
Zeus and *Boetis* <Hyg. *Fab.* 155>
— and *Aex* <Ps.-Erat. *Cat.* 27>, 7d
Aegisthus [King of Mycenae], son of Thyestes[1] <Aesch. *Agam.* 1605-06> and *Pelopeia*[2] <Ael. *Var. Narr.*>, 39a, *39b*
— and *Clytemnestra* <Hom. *Od.* 3.264-73>, 48c
Aegius, son of Aegyptus[1] and [a Phoenician woman] <Apollod. *Bibl.* 2.1.5>, 57d
— and *Mnestra* <Apollod. *Bibl.* 2.1.5>, (57d)
Aegle[1] [one of the Hesperides], daughter of *Nyx* <Hes. *Theog.* 213; named, Apollod. *Bibl.* 2.5.11>, *1a*
alternate parentage:
Atlas and *Hesperis*[1] <Diod. Sic. 4.27.2>
Hesperus[1] <Paus. 5.17.2; 6.19.8>
Aegle[2] [one of the Heliades[2]], daughter of Helios and *Clymene*[1] <Ovid *Met.* 2.333-40; named, Hyg. *Fab.* 154>, 14a
alternate parentage:
Helios and *Rhode*[1] <Schol. on Hom. *Od.* 17.208>
Aegle[3], daughter of Panopeus[1] <*Cat. Wom., Frag. Hes.* frg. 147, Merk. & West>, 23c
— and Theseus <*Cat. Wom., Frag. Hes.* frg. 147, Merk. & West>, 51b
Aegle[4] (*Aglaia*[2]), daughter of Asclepius and *Epeione* <*Paean Erythr.* T. 592, Edelstein>, 19d
alternate parentage:
Asclepius and *Lampetia* <Hermip. frg 1, West>
Aegle[5] — see *Aglaia*[1]
Aegle[6], nurse of Dionysus <Non. *Dion.* 14.221>, *
Aegyptus[1] [King of Arabia and Egypt], son of Belus[1] <Aesch. *Supp.* 318 ff.> and *Anchinoe*[1] <Apollod. *Bibl.* 2.1.4>, 58a
— and [an Arabian woman] <Apollod. *Bibl.* 2.1.5>, (57c), (58c)
— and *Argyphia* <Apollod. *Bibl.* 2.1.5>, (57c), (58a)
— and *Caliadne* <Apollod. *Bibl.* 2.1.5>, (57c), (58a), (58c)
— and *Gorgo*[1] <Apollod. *Bibl.* 2.1.5>, (57c), (58a)
— and *Hephaestine* <Apollod. *Bibl.* 2.1.5>, (57d), (58a), (58c)
— and [a Phoenician woman] <Apollod. *Bibl.* 2.1.5>, (57d), (58c)
— and *Tyria* <Apollod. *Bibl.* 2.1.5>, (57c), (58a)
Aegyptus[2], son of Aegyptus[1] and *Gorgo*[1] <Apollod. *Bibl.* 2.1.5>, 57c
— and *Dioxippe*[1] <Apollod. *Bibl.* 2.1.5>, (57c)
Aegyrus, son of Thelxion <Paus. 2.5.7>, 61c
Aelius, son of Pelops[1] and *Hippodameia*[1] <Schol. on Eur. *Or.* 5>, *36a*
Aello[1] (*Nicothoe*) [storm wind] [one of the Harpuiai], daughter of Thaumas[1] and *Electra*[1] <Hes. *Theog.* 267>, 3a
alternate parentage:
Thaumas[1] and *Ozomene* <Hyg. *Fab.* 14>
Boreas <Pher. Syr. 7 B 5>
Oceanus and *Gaea* <Epim. *Theog.* 3 B 7>
Aello[2] [one of the dogs of Actaeon], Ovid *Met.* 3.221>, *
Aemathion[1] (Emathion[1]) [King of Arabia], son of Tithonus and *Eos* <Hes. *Theog.* 986>, 43c
Aemathion[2] (Emathion[2]), son of Zeus and *Electra*[2] <Non. *Dion.* 3.186-87>, 5c, *42a*
Aemathion[3] (Emathion[3]), father of Atymnius[3] <Quint. Smyr. 3.300-01>, *
Aemathion[4] — see Romus (alternate version)
Aemathion[5] (Emathion[4]), killed by Chromis[7] <Ovid *Met.* 5.98-103>, *
Aemilia, daughter of Aeneas[1] and *Lavinia*[2] <Plut. *Rom.* 2.3>, 41c
Aeneas[1], son of Anchises and *Aphrodite* <Hom. *Il.* II.819-20>, 41c
— and *Anthemone* <Agath. in Dion. Hal. *Rom. Ant.* 1.49.3>, 41(c)
— and *Codone*[1] <Agath. in Dion. Hal. *Rom. Ant.* 1.49.3>, 41(c)
— and *Creusa*[2] <Virg. *Aen.* 2.739>, 43c
— and *Dido* <Virg. *Aen.* 1.170-73>, (41c)
— and *Eurydice*[4] <Lesch. in Paus. 10.26.1>, (41c)
— and *Lavinia*[2] <Plut. *Rom.* 2.3>, 13d
Aeneas[2] (Silvius[2]), son of Silvius[1] <Diod. Sic. 7.5.9>, 41c
Aenete (*Aenippe*), daughter of Eus(s)orus; mother of Cyzicus <Ap. Rhod. *Arg.* 1.948 ff.>, 44c
— and Aeneus <Ap. Rhod. *Arg.* 1, 951>, 68b
Aenetus, son of Deion[1] and *Diomede*[3] <Apollod. *Bibl.* 1.9.4>, 22b
Aeneus [King of Doliones], son of Apollo and *Stilbe*[1] <Schol. on Ap. Rhod. *Arg.* 1.948>, 11c, *68b*
— and *Aenete* <Ap. Rhod. *Arg.* 1.948>, 44c
Aenippe — see *Aenete*
Aeolia, daughter of Amythaon[1] <Apollod. *Bibl.* 1.7.7> and *Idomene*, 31c

— and Calydon[1] <Apollod. *Bibl.* 1.7.7>, 15d
Aeolis — see *Canace*
Aeolus[1] [King of Thessaly], son of Hellen(us)[1] <*Cat. Wom., Frag. Hes.* frg. 9, Merk. & West> and *Orseis* <Apollod. *Bibl.* 1.7.3>, 18a
alternate parentage:
Zeus <Eur. *Ion* 64>
— and *Enarete* <Apollod. *Bibl.* 1.7.3>, (18a)
— and *Hippe*[1] <Ps.-Erat. *Cat.* 18>, 69b
Aeolus[2] [King of Aeolia] [keeper of the winds], son of Hippotes[4] <Hom. *Od.* 10.2> and *Melanippe*[5] <Diod. Sic. 4.67.3>, 18a, *18a*
— and *Cyane* <Diod. Sic. 5.7.6>, 13c
Aeolus[3], son of Poseidon and *Arne*[1] <Diod. Sic. 4.67.4 (Aeolus[3] might be the same as Aeolus[2], in which case *Arne*[1] would be the same as *Melanippe*[5])>, 8a, *18c*
Aeolus[4], father of Clytius[10] <Virg. *Aen.* 9.774>, *
Aeolus[5], a defender of Thebes <Stat. *Theb.* 9.765>, *
Aepytus[1] [King of Arcadia], son of Elatus[1] <Pind. *Olym.* 6.33 ff.> and *Laodice*[2], 62d
Aepytus[2], son of Hippothous[2] <Paus. 8.5.4>, 62c
Aepytus[3] (Cresphontes[2]) (Telephontes) [King of Messenia], son of Cresphontes[1] and *Merope*[2] <Apollod. *Bibl.* 2.8.5>, 60c, *62c*
Aepytus[4], son of Neleus[2] <Paus. 7.2.7>, 27d
Aepytus[5], defender of Thebes <Stat. *Theb.* 10.400>, *
Aero — see *Merope*[3]
Aerope[1] (*Europe*[5]), daughter of Catreus <*Cat. Wom., Frag. Hes.* frg. 195, Merk. & West>, 52c
— and Atreus <Eur. *Helen* 391-92>, 36b
— and Pleisthenes[1] <Apollod. *Bibl.* 3.2.2>, 37b
— and Thyestes <Hyg. *Fab.* 86>, 39a
Aerope[2] — see *Sterope*[3]
Aerope[3] — see *Merope*[3]
Aeropus, son of Cepheus[2] <Paus. 8.5.1>, 64c
alternate parentage:
Ares and *Sterope*[3] <Paus. 8.44.7>
Phegeus <Herod. 9.26>
Aesacus[1], son of Priam[1] and *Arisbe*[1] <Apollod. *Bibl.* 3.12.5, 44c
alternate parentage:
Priam[1] and *Alexirhoe* <Serv. on Virg. *Aen.* 254>
— and *Asterope*[4] <Apollod. *Bibl.* 3.12.5>, 67a
Aesacus[2] [horned centaur] <Non. *Dion.* 14.190>, *
Aeschreis, daughter of Thespius <Apollod. *Bibl.* 2.7.8> and *Megamede* <Apollod. *Bibl.* 2.4.10>, 50a
— and Heracles[1] <Apollod. *Bibl.* 2.7.8>, (50a)
Aesepus[1] [river], son of Oceanus and *Tethys* <Hes. *Theog.* 342>, 50b
Aesepus[2] (Aegesus), son of Bucolion[2] and *Abarbarea* <Hom. *Il.* VI.21-22>, 42c
Aesimus, son of Autolycus[1] and *Amphithea*[2] <Schol. on Lyc. 344>, 13a
Aeson [King of Thessaly], son of Cretheus[1] and *Tyro* <Hom. *Od.* 11.258-59>, 33a
— and *Polymede* <*Cat. Wom., Frag. Hes.* frg. 38, Merk. & West (she is called *Polymele*)>, 13a
Aesyetes, father of Alcathous[2] <Hom. *Il.* XIII.429>, 41c, and Antenor <Dict. Cret. 4.22>, 45c
— and *Cleomestra* <Dict. Cret. 4.33>, (41c), (45c)
Aesyle — see *Phaesyle*
Aethalides[1] (Pythagoras[1]) [Argonaut], son of Hermes <Heraclid. in Diog. Laert. *Lives* 8.4> and *Eupoleme(ia)* <Ap. Rhod. *Arg.* 1.54>, 46c, *5d*
Aethalides[2], sailor turned into a dolphin <Hyg. *Fab.* 134>, *
Aether [sky], son of Erebus and *Nyx* <Hes. *Theog.* 124-25>, 1a
alternate parentage:
Chaos <Hyg. *Fab.* pref.>
Chronus (Proc. *Plat. Tim.*> (Orphic theogony)
Aetheria [one of the Heliades[2]], daughter of Helios and *Clymene*[1] <Ovid *Met.* 2.333-40; named, Hyg. *Fab.* 154>, 14a
alternate parentage:
Helios and *Rhode*[1] <Schol. on Hom. *Od.* 17.208>
Aethiolas, son of Menelaus <Schol. on Hom. *Il.* III.175> and *Helen*[1] <Eust. on Hom. *Il.* 400.72>, 37a
Aethlius, son of Zeus <*Cat. Wom., Frag. Hes.* frg. 245, Merk. & West> and *Protogeneia*[1] <Apollod. *Bibl.* 1.7.3>, 6d, *15b*
alternate parentage:
Aeolus[1] <Paus. 5.8.2>
— and *Calyce*[1] <*Cat. Wom., Hesiodi* frg. 10(a).58-59, Merk. & West (O.C.T.)>, 27a
Aethon[1], son of Deucalion[2] <Hom. *Od.* 19.180-84>, 54c
Aethon[2], father of *Hyperm(n)estra*[3] <Ant. Lib. *Met.* 17.5>, *
Aethon[3] [one of the dogs of Actaeon] <Hyg. *Fab.* 181>, *
Aethon[4] [one of the horses of Hector[1]] <Hom. *Il.* VIII.185>, *
Aethon[5] [one of the horses of Helios] <Ovid *Met.* 2.153>, *
Aethon[6] [one of the horses of Pallas[4]] <Virg. *Aen.* 11.89>, *
Aethra[1], daughter of Pittheus <Hom. *Il.* III.144>, 38b
— and Aegeus[1] <Eur. *Supp.* 5>, 51a
— and Poseidon <Bacch. 17.34-36>, 8c
Aethra[2] — see *Pleione*
Aethra[3], wife of Phalanthus <Paus. 10.10.8>, *
Aethusa (*Arethusa*[4]), daughter of Poseidon and *Alcyone*[2] <Apollod. *Bibl.* 3.10.1>, 8a, *35a*
— and Apollo <Apollod. *Bibl.* 3.10.1>, 11a
Aethylla (*Anthia*), daughter of Laomedon[1] <Apollod. *Epit.* 6.15c> and *Strym(n)o*, 42c
Aetius [King of Troezen], son of Anthas <Paus. 2.30.7>, 35a
Aetne, daughter of Uranus and *Gaea* <Alc. Sic. in *F.H.G.* 4.296, frg. 2, Müller>, 4a
Aetolus[1] [King of Elis and Aetolia], son of Endymion <*Cat. Wom., Hesiodi* frg. 10(a).60-63, Merk. & West (O.C.T.)> and *Iphianassa*[2] <Apollod. *Bibl.* 1.7.6>, 15b
alternate parentage:
Endymion and *Hyperippe*[1] <Paus. 5.1.4>
Endymion and *Chromia* <Paus. 5.1.4>
— and *Pronoe*[1] <Apollod. *Bibl.* 1.7.7>, (15b)
Aetolus[2], son of Oxylus[2] and *Pieria*[2] <Paus. 5.4.4>, 16d
Aex (*Aega*), daughter of Olenus[1] <Hyg. *Poet. Astr.* 2.13> and *Lethaea*, 7d
— and Aegipan <Ps.-Erat. *Cat.* 27>, 46d
— and Pan <Hyg. *Poet. Astr.* 2.13>, 46a
— and Zeus <Hyg. *Poet. Astr.* 2.13>, 5a
Aezieus [King in the Peloponnesus], father of Lycaon[4] <Dion. Hal. *Rom. Ant.* 1.11.2>, 62b
Agamede[1], daughter of Augeias <Hom. *Il.* XI.739>, 63c
— and Mulius[1] <Hom. *Il.* IX.739>, (63c)
— and Poseidon <Hyg. *Fab.* 157>, 8a
Agamede[2], daughter of *Macaria* <Steph. Byz. "Agamede">, *60a*
Agamedes[1], son of Erginus[1] <*Hom. Hymn* 3 (to Pythian Apollo), 296>, 26c
Agamedes[2] [King of Arcadia], son of Stymphalus[1] <Paus. 8.4.8>, 62c
Agamedidas [King of Cleonai], father of Thersander[3] <Paus. 3.16.6>, 60d
Agamemnon [King of Mycenae], son of Atreus <Hom. *Il.* I.24> and *Aerope*[1] <Eur. *Helen* 391-92>, 36a
alternate parentage:
Endymion and *Hyperippe*[1] <Paus. 5.1.4>
Endymion and *Chromia* <Paus. 5.1.4>
— and Argynnus <Athen. 13.603d>, 20d
— and *Briseis*[1] <Hom. *Il.* I.319-56>, (36a)
— and *Cassandra*[1] <Eur. *Tro. Wom.* 246-51>, 43d
— and *Chryseis*[1] <Virg. *Aen.* 1.112>, (36a)
— and *Clytemnestra* <Aesch. *Agam.* 602>, 48c
Agamestor — see Cleitus[5]

Aganippe[1], daughter of Termessus <Callim. in Serv. on Virg. *Ecl.* 10.12>, 72a
Aganippe[2], paramour of Acrisius <Hyg. *Fab.* 155>, 58d
Aganus, son of Paris and *Helen*[1] <*P.E.G.* frg. 12>, 43c
Agapenor [King of Tegea in Arcadia], son of Ancaeus[1] <Hom. *Il.* II.609>, 64c
Agaptolemus, son of Aegyptus[1] and [a Phoenecian woman] <Apollod. *Bibl.* 2.1.5>, 57d
— and *Peirene*[1] <Apollod. *Bibl.* 2.1.5>, (57d)
Agassamenus [King of Naxos], son of Hecetorus <Parth. *Love Stor.* 19>, 34c
— and *Pancratis* <Diod. Sic. 5.50.6>, (34c)
Agasthenes [King of Elis], son of Augeias <Hom. *Il.* II.624>, 63c
— and *Peloris* <Hyg. *Fab.* 97>, (63c)
Agatho(n), son of Priam[1] <Hom. *Il.* XXIV.249>, 43d
Agathyrnus, son of Aeolus[2] and *Cyane*[1] <Hom. *Od.* 10.2-6; named, Diod. Sic. 5.8.1>, 18c
Agathyrsus, son of Heracles and *Echidna* <Herod. 4.9-10>, 60c
Agave[1], daughter of Cadmus and *Harmonia*[1] <Hes. *Theog.* 976>, 55d
— and Echion[1] <Eur. *Bacch.* 229>, 7d
— and Lycotherses <Hyg. *Fab.* 240>, (55d)
Agave[2], daughter of Danaus[1] and *Europe*[3] <Apollod. *Bibl.* 2.1.5>, 57d
— and Lycus[9] <Apollod. *Bibl.* 2.1.5>, (57d)
Agave[3], daughter of Nereus and *Doris*[1] <Hes. *Theog.* 247>, *63a*
Agave[4] [Amazon] <Hyg. *Fab.* 163>, *
Agavus, son of Priam[1] <Dict. Cret. 4.7>, 43d
Agdistis/*Cybele*[2], hermaphrodite son/daughter of Zeus and *Gaea* <Paus. 7.17.5 (called Agdistis) (born from seed of Zeus dropped on earth)>, 5c, *2b*; as Agdistis, 70a; as *Cybele*[2], 2b, 2d
— and Attis <Paus. 7.17.5>, 70a
— and *Nana* <Paus. 7.17.5>, 70a
Agelaus[1], son of Damastor[1] <Hom. *Od.* 20.321>, 52d
Agelaus[2], son of Heracles and *Omphale* <Apollod. *Bibl.* 2.7.8>, 60c
Agelaus[3], son of Oeneus[1] and *Althaea* <*Cat. Wom., Frag. Hes.* frg. 25.15, Merk. & West>, 17c
Agelaus[4], son of Stymphalus[1] <Paus. 8.35.9>, 62c
Agelaus[5], son of Temenus[1] <Apollod. *Bibl.* 2.8.5>, 60d
Agelaus[6], son of Maeon[2] <Quint. Smyr. 3.229>, *
Agelaus[7], son of Phradmon <Hom. *Il.* VIII.259>, *
Agelaus[8], son of Hippasus[8] <Quint. Smyr. 1.279>, *
Agelaus[9], father of Antheus[2] <Non. *Dion.* 35.382-84>, *
Agelaus[10], servant of Priam[1] <Apollod. *Bibl.* 3.12.5>, *
Agelaus[11], killed by Hector <Hom. *Il.* XI.303>, *
Agelus, son of Poseidon <Ion in Paus. 7.4.8>, 9c
Agenor[1] [King of Phoenicia], son of Poseidon <Apollod. *Bibl.* 2.1.4> and *Libya*[1] <Aesch. *Supp. Maid.* 322>, 8c, *55b*
— and *Argiope*[3] <Pher. in *F. Gr. H.* 3 F 21>, 68a
— and *Damno* <Pher. in *F. Gr. H.* 3 F 21>, 59a
— and *Telephassa* <Apollod. *Bibl.* 2.1.1>, (55b)
Agenor[2] [King of Argos], son of Ecbasus <Apollod. *Bibl.* 2.1.2>, 61b
Agenor[3], son of Phegeus[1] <Apollod. *Bibl.* 3.7.6>, 59b
Agenor[4] [King of Pleuron and Calydon], son of Pleuron <*Cat. Wom., Hesiodi* frg. 10(a).64-65, Merk. & West (O.C.T.)> and *Xanthippe*[1] <Apollod. *Bibl.* 1.7.7>, 15b
— and *Epicaste*[3] <Apollod. *Bibl.* 1.7.7>, (15b)
Agenor[5], son of Amphion[1] and *Niobe*[1] <Apollod. *Bibl.* 3.5.6>, 66c
Agenor[6] [King of Argos], son of Triop(a)s[2] and *Sois* <Hellan. in Schol. on Hom. *Il.* III.75>, 61d
Agenor[7], son of Antenor[1] <Hom. *Il.* IX.59> and *Theano*[2], *45c*
Agenor[8], son of Aegyptus[1] and [an Arabian woman] <Apollod. *Bibl.* 2.1.5>, 57d
— and *Cleopatra*[4] <Apollod. *Bibl.* 2.1.5>, (57d)
Agenor[9], son of Areus[1] <Paus. 7.18.5>, 47c
Agenor[10] — see Phineus[2]
Agenor[11], brother of Tages <Stat. *Theb.* 9.270-72>, *
Agenor[12], suitor of *Penelope*[1] (from Dulichium) <Apollod. *Epit.* 7.27>, *
Agenor[13], suitor of *Penelope*[1] (from Zacynthus) <Apollod. *Epit.* 7.29>, *
Agenor[14], killed by Neoptolemus <Quint. Smyr. 13.217>, *
Agis[1], son of Eurysthenes[1] <Herod. 7.204> and *Anaxandra*, 60d
Agis[2], soldier with Aeneas <Virg. *Aen.* 10.750>, *
Aglaia[1] (*Aegle*[5]) (*Charis*) (*Pasithea*[1]) [splendor] [one of the Graces], daughter of Zeus and *Eurynome*[1] <Hes. *Theog.* 909>, 5d
alternate parentage:
Dionysus and *Coronis*[5] <Non. *Dion.* 48.555-56>
Dionysus <Non. *Dion.* 15.91> and *Hera* <Non. *Dion.* 31.185>
Helios and *Aegle*[1] <Anti. in Paus. 9.35.5>
— and Hephaestus <Hes. *Theog.* 945 (in Hom. *Il.* XVIII.380, she is called *Charis*)>, 7b
— and Hypnos <Hom. *Il.* XIV.269-75 (she is called *Pasithea*)>, 1a
Aglaia[2] — see *Aegle*[4]
Aglaia[3] (*Ocaleia*), daughter of Mantineus[1] <Apollod. *Bibl.* 2.2.1>, 57d
— and Abas[1] <Apollod. *Bibl.* 2.2.1>, (57d)
Aglaia[4], daughter of Thespius <Apollod. *Bibl.* 2.7.8> and *Megamede* <Apollod. *Bibl.* 2.4.10>, 50a
— and Heracles[1] <Apollod. *Bibl.* 2.7.8>, (50a)
Aglaia[5] — see Bias[1] (alternate version)
Aglaia[6], wife of Charopus <Hom. *Il.* II.672>, *
Aglaope (*Aglaopheme*) (*Aglaophonus*) [one of the Sirens], daughter of Achelous and *Melpomene* <Apollod. *Epit.* 7.18>, 65b
alternate parentage:
Achelous and *Sterope*[2] <Apollod. *Bibl.* 1.7.10>
Achelous and *Terpsichore* <Ap. Rhod. *Arg.* 4.893>
Aglaopheme — see *Aglaope*
Aglaophonus — see *Aglaope*
Aglaurus[1] (*Agraulus*[1]), daughter of Actaeus[3] <Apollod. *Bibl.* 3.14.2> and *Glauce*[1], 66b
— and Cecrops I <Apollod. *Bibl.* 3.14.1>, (66b)
Aglaurus[2] (*Agraulus*[2]), daughter of Cecrops I <Herod. 8.53> and *Aglaurus*[1] <Apollod. *Bibl.* 3.14.2>, *66b*
— and Ares <Hellan. in *F. Gr. H.* 4 F 38>, 7a
Aglaurus[3], daughter of Erechtheus II and *Procris*[1] <Hyg. *Fab.* 153>, 51a
Aglaus, son of Thyestes[1] <Apollod. *Epit.* 2.13> and *Laodameia*[5] <Schol. on Eur. *Or.* 4>, 39b
Agorius, son of Damasius <Paus. 5.4.3>, 36d
Agraeus[1], son of Temenus[1] <Paus. 2.28.3>, 60d
Agraeus[2], son of Eulaeus <Non. *Dion.* 26.45>, *
Agraulus[1] — see *Aglaurus*[1]
Agraulus[2] — see *Aglaurus*[2]
Agreus[1] — see Aristaeus
Agreus[2], son of Hermes and *Sose* <Non. *Dion.* 14.91>, 46d
Agreus[3], soldier from Epidaurus <Stat. *Theb.* 6.912>, *
Agreus[4], soldier from Pylus <Stat. *Theb.* 10.682>, *
Agrinome — see *Laonome*[3]
Agriope[1] — see *Telephassa*
Agriope[2] — see *Eurydice*[1]
Agrius[1] [King of Calydon], son of Portheus[1] <Hom. *Il.* XIV.115-16> and *Euryte*[1] <Apollod. *Bibl.* 1.7.10>, 16d
— and *Dia*[4] <Schol. on Hom. *Il.* II.212>, (16d)
Agrius[2] [giant], son of *Gaea* (and the blood of Uranus) <Hes. *Theog.* 180-86; named as giant, Apollod. *Bibl.* 1.6.2>, *4a*
Agrius[3] [centaur], offspring of Centaurus and a Magnesian Mare <Pind. *Pyth.* 2.50; named as centaur, Apollod. *Bibl.* 2.5.4>, 69c

alternate parentage:
Ixion and *Nephele*[1] <Diod. Sic. 4.69.5>
Agrius[4], son of Odysseus and *Circe* <Hes. *Theog.* 1013>, 13c
Agrius[5], son of [a bear] and *Polyphonte* <Ant. Lib. *Met.* 21.3>, *71b*
Agrius[6], suitor of *Penelope*[1] (from Dulichium) <Apollod. *Epit.* 7.27>, *
Agrius[7] [one of the dogs of Actaeon] <Hyg. *Fab.* 181>, *
Agron[1], son of Ninus <Herod. 1.7>, 61c
Agron[2], son of Eumelus[3] <Ant. Lib. Met. 15.1>, *
Agryphia — see *Argyphia*
Agylleus, son of Heracles[1] <Stat. *Theb.* 10.249>, 61c
Aias[1] — see Ajax[1]
Aias[2] — see Ajax[2]
Aimylus, son of Ascanius[1] and *Roma*[2] <Fest. *De Sign. Verb.* "Aemilian">, 41c
Ajax[1] (Aias[1]) [King of Megara], son of Telamon <Hom. *Il.* II.528> and *Periboea*[2] <Soph. *Ajax* 569 (she is called *Eriboea*)>, 23d, *40a*
— and *Glauce*[6] <Dict. Cret. 5.16>, (23d)
— and *Lyside* <Steph. Byz. "Philaidai">, 8a
— and *Tecmessa*[1] <Soph. *Ajax* 206>, 63d
Ajax[2] (Aias[2]), son of Oileus[1] <Hom. *Il.* II.527> and *Eriopis*[3] <Schol. on. Hom. *Il.* 13.697>, 15c
alternate parentage:
Oileus[1] and *Rhene* <Hyg. *Fab.* 97>
Oileus[1] and *Alcimache* <Schol. on Hom. *Il.* XV.332>
— and *Cassandra*[1] <Eur. *Tro. Wom.* 70>, 43d
Alabando, son of Car[1] and *Callirhoe*[6] <Steph. Byz. "Alabanda">, 61a, *67b*
Alalcomenia, daughter of Ogygus[1] <Paus. 9.33.4>, 16c
Alastor[1], son of Neleus[1] and *Chloris*[2] <*Cat. Wom., Frag. Hes.* frg. 33(a), Merk. & West>, 27c
— and *Harpalyce*[2] <Parth. *Love Stor.* 13.2>, 26d
Alastor[2], father of Tros[2] <Hom. *Il.* XX.463>, *
Alastor[3], comrade of Teucer[2] <Hom. *Il.* VIII.333>, *
Alazygus, son of Halirrhothius[2] <*Cat. Wom., Frag. Hes.* frg. 49, Merk. & West>, 25a
Alcaea, daughter of Hypseus[1] and *Chlidanope* <Schol. on Pind. 31>, 69a
Alcaeus[1], son of Androgeus <Apollod. *Bibl.* 2.5.9>, 53d
Alcaeus[2] (Cleolaus[1]), son of Perseus[1] and *Andromeda* <*Cat. Wom., Frag. Hes.* frg. 135, Merk. & West>, 59c
— and *Asty(a)dameia*[4] <*Cat. Wom., Frag. Hes.* frg. 190, Merk. & West>, 36a
— and *Laonome*[2] <Apollod. *Bibl.* 2.4.5>, (59c)
Alcaeus[3], son of Heracles[1] and a slave girl <Herod. 1.7>, 61c
Alcaeus[4], original name of Heracles[1] <Diod. Sic. 4.10.1>, *
Alcaeus[5], one of Oenopion's generals <Diod. Sic. 5.79.2>, *
Alcaeus[6], son of Margasus and *Phyllis*[2] <Quint. Smyr. 10.138>, *
Alcanor[1], husband of *Iaera*[2]; father of Bitias[1] <Virg. *Aen.* 9.672-73>, 41d
Alcanor[2], brother of Maeon[2] and Numitor <Virg. *Aen.* 10.336>, *
Alcathoe (*Alcithoe*) (*Iris*[2]), daughter of Minyas and *Euryanassa*[2] <Nicand. in Ant. Lib. *Met.* 10>, 20d
Alcathous[1] [King of Megara], son of Pelops[1] <Apollod. *Bibl.* 3.12.7> and *Axioche*, *40a*
— and *Euaechme*[1] <Paus. 1.43.4>, 9a
— and *Pyrgo*[1] <Paus. 1.43.4>, (40a)
Alcathous[2], son of Aesyetes <Hom. *Il.* XIII.429> and *Cleomestra*; husband of *Hippodameia*[5] <Hom. *Il.* XIII.431>, 41c
Alcathous[3], son of Portheus[1] and *Euryte*[1] <*Cat. Wom., Hesiodi* frg. 10a.52, Merk. & West (O.C.T.)>, 15d
Alcathous[4], killed by Caedicus <Vir. *Aen.* 10.747>, *
Alcathous[5], killed by Amphiaraus <Stat. *Theb.* 7.718>, *
Alcathous[6], killed by Achilles <Quint. Smyr. 3.158>, *
Alce[1], daughter of Olympus[3] and *Cybele*[2] <Diod. Sic. 5.49.3>, *2d*
Alce[2] [one of the dogs of Actaeon] <Ovid *Met.* 220>, *
Alcemon — see Acmon[1]
Alces, son of Aegyptus[1] and [an Arabian woman] <Apollod. *Bibl.* 2.1.5>, 57d
— and *Glauce*[3] <Apollod. *Bibl.* 2.1.5>, (57d)
Alceste — see *Alcestis*
Alcestis (*Alceste*), daughter of Pelias[1] <Hom. *Il.* II.715> and *Anaxibia*[2] <Apollod. *Bibl.* 1.9.10>, 28d
alternate parentage:
Pelias and *Phylomache* <Apollod. *Bibl.* 1.9.10>
— and Admetus[1] <Hom. *Il.* II.714-15>, 29c
Alcidameia, paramour of Hermes <Paus. 2.3.8>, 46a
Alcides — see Heracles[1]
Alcidice, daughter of Aleus <Diod. Sic. 4.68> and *Neaera*[2], 63c
— and Salmoneus <Apollod. *Bibl.*1.9.8>, 27b
Alcimache, daughter of Aeacus <Schol. on Hom. *Il.* XIII.694> and *Endeis*, 23d
alternate parentage:
Phylacus <Schol. on Hom. *Il.* XIII.694> and *Clymene*[4]
— and Oileus[1] <Schol. on Hom. *Il.* XIII.694>, 15c
Alcimede[1] (*Phylaceis*), daughter of Phylacus[1] <Ap. Rhod. *Arg.* 1.47> and *Clymene*[4] <Stes. in Schol. on Ap. Rhod. *Arg.* 1.230>, 22c
Alcimede[2], daughter of Cydimus <Stat. *Theb.* 5.227-36>, *
Alcimedon[1], father of *Phialo* <Paus. 8.12.3>, 60d
Alcimedon[2], sailor turned into a dolphin <Hyg. *Fab.* 134>, *
Alcimedon[3], son of Laerceus <Hom. *Il.* XVI.197>, *
Alcimene — see *Philonoe*
Alcimenes[1], son of Jason and *Medea* <Diod. Sic. 4.54.1>, 33c
Alcimenes[2] — see Deliades
Alcinoe[1] — see *Alcyone*[4]
Alcinoe[2], daughter of Polybus[3] <Parth. *Love Stor.* 27.1>, *
Alcinoe[3], a nurse of Zeus <Paus. 8.47.3>, *
Alcinous [King of Phaecians], son of Nausithous[1] <Hom. *Od.* 7.63>, 9a
alternate parentage:
Phaeax[1] <Diod. Sic. 4.72.2>
— and *Arete* <Hom. *Od.* 7.65-66>, 9c
Alcinus, son of Hippocoon[1] <Apollod. *Bibl.* 3.10.5>, 47c
Alcippe[1], daughter of Ares and *Aglaurus*[2] <Hellan. in *F. Gr. H.* 4 F 38>, 7a
— and Eupalamus <Apollod. *Bibl.* 3.15.8>, 49b
— and Halirrhothius[1] <Apollod. *Bibl.* 3.14.2>, 8d
Alcippe[2], daughter of Oenomaus[1] <Plut. *Gr. and Rom. Par. Stor.* 40> and *Asterope*[1], 7c, *39a*
— and Euenus[1] <Plut. *Gr. and Rom. Par. Stor.* 40 (she is called mother of *Marpessa*)>, 15c
Alcippe[3], daughter of Alcyoneus[1] <Heges. in *F.H.G.* 4.422 frg. 46, Müller>, 4a
Alcippe[4] [Amazon] <Diod. Sic. 4.16.3>, *
Alcippe[5], sister of Astraeus[3] <Ps.-Plut. *De Fluv.* 21>, *
Alcippe[6], servant of *Helen*[1] <Hom. *Od.* 4.124>, *
Alcithoe — see *Alcathoe*
Alcmaeon[1] [one of the Epigoni], son of Amphiaraus <Hom. *Od.* 15.248> and *Eriphyle* <Apollod. *Bibl.* 3.7.2>, 32d
— and *Arsinoe*[2] <Apollod. *Bibl.* 3.7.5>, 59b
— and *Callirhoe*[4] <Apollod. *Bibl.* 3.7.5>, 29a, 65a
— and *Manto*[1] <Apollod. *Bibl.* 3.7.7>, (32d)
Alcmaeon[2], son of Sillus[1] <Paus. 2.18.8>, 27d
Alcmaeon[3], son of Thestor[2] <Hom. *Il.* XI.394>, *
Alcmene (*Eurymede*[2]) (*Lysidice*[3]), daughter of Electryon[1] <Hes. *Shield* 1 ff.> and *Anaxo*[1] <Apollod. *Bibl.* 2.4.5>, 59d
alternate parentage:
Electryon[1] and *Lysidice*[1] <Plut. *Thes.* 7.1>
Electryon[1] and *Eurydice*[11] <Diod. Sic. 4.9.1>
Pelops[1] <Eur. *Heracl.* 210-11>
— and Amphitryon <Hom. *Od.* 11.266>, 59c
— and Rhadamanthys <Apollod. *Bibl.* 3.1.2>, 52c
— and Zeus <Hom *Il.* XIV.324>, 5a

Alcmenor, son of Aegyptus[1] and [an Arabian woman] <Apollod. *Bibl.* 2.1.5>, 57d

— and *Hippomedusa* <Apollod. *Bibl.* 2.1.5>, (57d)

Alcon[1], son of Hippocoon[1] <Apollod. *Bibl.* 3.10.5>, 47c

Alcon[2], son of Ares <Hyg. *Fab.* 173>, 7c

Alcon[3], son of Erechtheus II <Prox. in Schol. on Ap. Rhod. *Arg.* 1.97-100> and *Praxithea*[2], 49a

Alcon[4], son of Hephaestus and *Cabeira* <Non. *Dion.* 14.22>, 7b

Alcon[5], son of Megacles <Quint. Smyr. 308-09>, *

Alcon[6], maker of the bowl Aeneas gave to Anius <Ovid *Met.* 13.678-83>, *

Alcon[7], a defender of Thebes <Stat. *Theb.* 9.121>, *

Alcyone[1] (*Halcyone*[1]), daughter of Aeolus[1] <*Cat. Wom., Hesiodi* frg. 10(d).1, Merk. & West (O.C.T.)> and *Enarete* <Apollod. *Bibl.* 1.7.3>, 23b

alternate parentage:

Aeolus[1] and *Aegiale* <Hyg. *Fab.* 65>

— and Ceyx[1] <*Cat. Wom., Hesiodi* frg. 10(d).1, Merk. & West O.C.T.)>, 13b

Alcyone[2] (*Halcyone*[2]), daughter of Atlas <*Cat. Wom., Frag. Hes.* frg. 169, Merk. & West> and *Pleione* <Apollod. *Bibl.* 3.10.1>, 35a

— and Poseidon <Apollod. *Bibl.* 3.10.1>, 8a

Alcyone[3] — see *Cleopatra*[2]

Alcyone[4] (*Alcinoe*[1]) (*Halcyone*[4]), daughter of Sthenelus[1] and *Nicippe*[1] <Apollod. *Bibl.* 2.4.5>, 58d

— and Homadus <Diod. Sic. 4.12.7>, 69c

Alcyone[5] — see *Marpessa*

Alcyone[6], wife of Perieres[1] <*Cat. Wom., Frag. Hes.* frg. 49, Merk. & West>, 25a

Alcyone[7], wife of Chalcadon[2] <Apollod. *Epit.* 3.11>, 8b

Alcyone[8], priestess at Argos <Dion. Hal. *Rom. Ant.* 1.22.3>, *

Alcyoneus[1] [giant], son of *Gaea* (and the blood of Uranus) <Hes. *Theog.* 180-86; named as giant, Apollod. *Bibl.* 1.6.2>, *4a*

Alcyoneus[2] — see Ischys

Alcyoneus[3], son of Diemus and *Meganeira*[3] <Ant. Lib. *Met.* 8>, *

Alcyoneus[4], warrior with Memnon <Quint. Smyr. 2.364>, *

(Alcyonides), daughters of Alcyoneus[1] (see *Alcippe*[3], *Anthe*, *Asteria*[7], *Drimo*, *Methone*[2], *Pallene*[2], *Phthonia*), 4a-b

Alebion — see Ialebion

Alector[1] [King of Argos], son of Anaxagoras <Paus. 2.18.5>, 58c

Alector[2], father-in-law of Megapenthes[1] <Hom. *Od.* 4.10>, 37c

Alector[3] [King of Elis], son of Epeius[1] and *Anaxiroe* <Eust. on Hom. *Il.* 303> 16c

— and *Diogeneia*[1] <Eust. on Hom. *Il.* 303>, 68b

Alector[4] — see Electryon[2]

Alector[5], son of Magnes[2] and *Meliboea*[3] <Eust. on Hom. *Il.* 338>, 21b

Alectryon — see Electryon[2]

Alegenor, son of Itonus[2] <Diod. Sic. 4.67.7>, 18c

Alesus (Halesus[1]), son of Poseidon <Serv. on Virg. *Aen.* 8.285>, 9c

Aletes[1] [King of Mycenae], son of Aegisthus <Hyg. *Fab.* 122>, 39b

Aletes[2], son of Icarius[2] and *Periboea*[5] <Apollod. *Bibl.* 3.10.6>, 47c

Aletes[3] [King of Corinth], son of Hippotes[3] <Con. *Narr.* 26>, 55d

Aletes[4], a friend of Aeneas <Virg. *Aen.* 1.120>, *

Aletes[5], an elderly Theban <Stat. *Theb.* 3.178>, *

Alethia [truth], daughter of Zeus <Pind. *Olym.* 10.4>, 6c

Aleus [King of Tegea in Arcadia], son of Apheidas[1] <Apollod. *Bibl.* 3.9.1>, 63c

— and *Neara*[2] <Apollod. *Bibl.* 3.9.1>, 62d

Alexander[1] — see Paris

Alexander[2], son of Eurystheus <Apollod. *Bibl.* 2.8.1> and *Antimache*, 58d

Alexander[3], son of Pyrrhus[3] <Paus. 4.35.3>, *

Alexandra — see *Cassandra*[1]

Alexanor, son of Machaon <Paus. 2.11.6> and *Anticleia*[3], 19c

Alexiares (Alexiraes), son of Heracles[1] and *Hebe* <Apollod. *Bibl.* 2.7.8>, 60c

Alexiraes — see Alexiares

Alexirhoe, daughter of Granicus <Ovid *Met.* 11.763>, 67b

— and Dionysus <Ps.-Plut. *De Fluv.* 7.5>, 56c

— and Mygdon(us)[1] <Ps.-Plut. *De Fluv.* 12.1>, 8d

— and Priam[1] <Serv. on Virg. *Aen.* 4.354>, 43d

Algea [pains] [abstraction], offspring of *Eris* <Hes. *Theog.* 227>, *1a*

Aliartus — see Haliartus

Alistra, paramour of Poseidon <Tzetz. on *Lyc.* 1206>, 8a

Alithersus, son of Ancaeus[2] and *Samia* <Paus. 7.4.2>, 54c

Al(l)ecto [one of the Furies], daughter of *Gaea* (and the blood of Uranus) <Hes. *Theog.* 185; named, Apollod. *Bibl.* 1.1.4>, 4a

alternate parentage:

Cronus <Epim. *Theog.* 3 B 19>

Nyx <Aesch. *Eum.* 416>

Almo(n)[1] [river], son of Oceanus and *Tethys* <Hes. *Theog.* 367-68; named as river Apollod. *Bibl.* 3.12.5>, 50b

Almo[2], son of Tyrrheus <Virg. *Aen.* 7.495-96>, *

Almus (Halmus) (Olmus) [King of Orchomenus], son of Sisyphus <Paus. 2.4.3> and *Merope*[1], 19b

(Aloadae) [sons of Poseidon and *Iphimedeia*; step-sons of Aloeus[1]] — see Ephialtes[2], Otus[1]

Aloeus[1] [giant], son of Poseidon and *Canace* <Apollod. *Bibl.* 1.7.4>, 8a, *34a*

— and *Eeriboea* <Hom. *Il.* V.389>, (34a)

— and *Iphimedeia* <Apollod. *Bibl.* 1.7.4>, 34c

Aloeus[2] [King of Asopia], son of Helios and *Antiope*[4] <Tzetz. on Lyc. 175>, 14a

Aloides — see Heracles[1]

Alope, daughter of Cercyon[1] <Pher. in *F. Gr. H.* 3 F 147>, 9d

— and Poseidon <Hellan. in *F. Gr. H.* 4 F 43>, 8b

Alopius, son of Heracles[1] and *Antiope*[5] <Apollod. *Bibl.* 2.7.8>, *50c*

Alpheius [river], son of Oceanus and *Tethys* <Hes. *Theog.* 338>, 65b

— and *Arethusa*[2] <Paus. 5.7.2>, (65b)

— and *Telegone* <Paus. 4.30.2>, 46d

Alphenor, son of Amphion[1] and *Niobe*[1] <Ovid *Met.* 6.248>, 66c

Alphesiboea[1] — see *Arsinoe*[2]

Alphesiboea[2], daughter of Bias[1] and *Pero*[1] <Pher. in *F.H.G.* 1.89, frg. 75, Müller>, 30c

Alphesiboea[3], paramour of Dionysus <Herm. Cyp. in *F.H.G.* 4.428 frg. 3, Müller>, 56c

Alphesiboea[4], paramour of Phoenix[2] <*Cat. Wom., Frag. Hes.* frg. 139, Merk. & West>, 53b

Alpus [giant], son of *Gaea* (and the blood of Uranus) <Hes. *Theog.* 180-86; named as giant, Non. *Dion.* 25.238>, *4a*

Altes [King of the Leleges], father of *Laothoe*[1] <Hom. *Il.* XXI.85>, 43d

Althaea, daughter of Thestius <Bacch. 5.137> and *Eurythemis(te)* <Apollod. *Bibl.* 1.7.10>, 15c

alternate parentage:

Thestius and *Laophonte* <Pher. in *F. Gr. H.* 3 F 9>

Dionysus and *Deianeira*[1] <Apollod. *Bibl.* 1.8.1>

— and Ares <Apollod. *Bibl.* 1.8.2>, 7a

— and Dionysus <Hyg. *Fab.* 129>, 56c

— and Oeneus[1] <*Cat. Wom., Frag. Hes* . frg. 25, Merk. & West>, 17c

Althaemenes, son of Catreus <Apollod. *Bibl.* 3.2.2>, 52d

Althaepus [King of Oraea], son of Poseidon and *Leis* <Paus. 2.30.6>, 8c

Alxion — see Oenomaus[1] (alternate version)

Alycus, son of Sciron[2] <Plut. *Thes.* 32.5>, 39a

Alyzeus, son of Icarius[2] <Strab. 2.7.7> and *Periboea*[5], 47d

alternate parentage:

Icarius[2] and *Polycaste*[2] <Strab. 10.2.24>

Amaleus, son of Amphion[1] and *Niobe*[1] <Eust. on Hom. *Od.* 1875>,

66c

Amaltheia[1] — see *Deiphobe*

Amaltheia[2], daughter of Haemonius <Apollod. *Bibl.* 2.7.5>, *

Amaltheia[3] [Naiad], Zeus's nurse, who suckled him with her she-goat <Ovid *Fast.* 5.115>, *

Amaltheia[4], she-goat whose skin became the Aegis (Zeus's shield) <Hyg. *Poet. Astr.* 2.13>, *

Amarynceus[1], son of Pyttius <Paus. 5.1.10>, 17d

Amarynceus[2], son of Alector[3] and *Diogeneia*[1] <Eust. on Hom. *Il.* 303>, 16c, *68b*

Amarynceus[3], son of Onesimachus <Hyg. *Fab.* 97>, *

Amata, wife of Latinus[1] <Fab. Pict. in *F.H.G.* 3.93 frg. 23, Müller>, 13d

Amatheia, daughter of Nereus <Hom. *Il.* XVIII.48> and *Doris*[1] <Hyg. *Fab.* pref.>, *63a*

Amathus, son of Macedon and *Oreithyia*[2] <Schol. on Hom. *Il.* 14.226>, 15a

Ambracia[1], daughter of Augeias <Steph. Byz. "Ambracia">, 63d

Ambracia[2], daughter of Phorbas[5] <Steph. Byz. "Dexamenae">, 14c

Ambracia[3], daughter of Melaneus[2] <Ant. Lib. *Met.* 4> and *Stratonice*[2], 11d, *15d*

Ambrax, son of Dexamenus <Dion. Hal. *Rom. Ant.* 1.32>, 14c

Ambrosia [one of the Hyades], daughter of Atlas and *Pleione* <Hyg. *Fab.* 192>, 44b
alternate parentage:
Hyas and *Boeotia* <Hyg. *Poet. Astr.* 2.21>

Ameirace — see *Penelope*

Amestrius, son of Heracles[1] and *Eone* <Apollod. *Bibl.* 2.7.8>, *50c*

Ammon[1] (Jupiter Ammon), father of Iarbas <Virg. *Aen.* 4.197-201>, 41d
— and a [Garamantian nymph] <Virg. *Aen.* 4.197-201>, (41d)

Ammon[2], brother of Broteas[2] <Ovid *Met.* 5.107>, *

Ammon[3], an Ethiopian oracle <Apollod. *Bibl.* 2.4.3>, *

Ampelius [vine], daughter of Oxylus[3] and *Hamadryas* <Athen. 3.78b>, 71d

Ampelus, companion of Dionysus <Ovid *Fast.* 3.407>, 56c

Amphalces, son of Antiphates[2] and *Zeuxippe*[3] <Diod. Sic. 4.68.5>, 32c

Ampheres — see [five sets of twins]

Amphialus[1], son of Neoptolemus and *Andromache* <Hyg. *Fab.* 123>, 24c

Amphialus[2], son of Polyneus <Hom. *Od.* 8.114>, *

Amphialus[3], sailed with Menelaus <Paus. 10.25.3>, *

Amphialus[4], suitor of *Penelope*[1] (from Ithaca) <Apollod. *Epit.* 7.30>, *

Amphianax[1] — see Iobates

Amphianax[2], son of Antimachus[6] <Paus. 3.25.10>, *

Amphiaraus (Amphiorax) [one of the Seven against Thebes (per Aesch. *Sev.* 485-87)], son of Oicle(u)s <Hom. *Od.* 15.244> and *Hyperm(n)estra*[2] <*Cat. Wom., Frag. Hes.* frg. 25.34-35, Merk. & West>, 32d
alternate parentage:
Apollo and *Hyperm(n)estra* <Hyg. *Fab.* 70>
— and *Eriphyle* <Pind. *Nem.* 9.16-17>, 31c

Amphibia — see *Nicippe*[1]

Amphicles, son of Agis[1] <Paus. 3.16.9>, 60d

Amphicomone —see [fifty daughters of Danaus[1]] (alternate version)

Amphictyon [King of Athens], son of Deucalion[1] and *Pyrrha*[1] <Theopomp. in *F.H.G.* 1.291 frg. 80, Müller>, 16a
alternate version of parentage:
autochthonous <Apollod. *Bibl.* 3.14.6>
— and *Chthonopatra* <Eust. on Hom. *Il.* 277>, (16a)
— and *Cranae*[1] <Apollod. *Bibl.* 3.14.5>, (16a)

Amphictyone, wife of Elatus[1] <Pher. in *F.H.G.* 1.71 frg. 8, Müller>, 62c

Amphidamantus — see *Amphiria* (alternate version)

Amphidamas[1] [King of Tegea] [Argonaut], son of Aleus <Ap. Rhod. *Arg.* 1.161-62> and *Neaera*[2], 63d
alternate parentage:
Aleus and *Cleobule*[1] <Hyg. *Fab.* 14>
Lycurgus[4] and *Cleophyle* <Apollod. *Bibl.* 3.9.2>
Lycurgus[4] and *Eurynome*[5] <Apollod. *Bibl.* 3.9.2>

Amphidamas[2] (Iphidamas[2]), son of Busiris[1] <Pher. in *F.H.G.* 1.78 frg. 33, Müller>, 8d

Amphidamas[3], father of Clesonymus <Hellan. in *F.H.G.* 1.52 frg. 51, Müller>; spelled Clitonymus <Apollod. *Bibl.* 3.13. 8>, *

Amphidamas[4] [from Cythera], received a helmut from Autolycus[1] and gave it to Molus[1] <Hom. *Il.* X, 265-71>, *

Amphidamas[5], a warrior who hid in the Trojan horse <Tryph. *Tak. Ilium* 182>, *

Amphidicus (Asphodicus), son of Astacus <Apollod. *Bibl.* 3.6.8>, 9b

Amphidocus, son of Orchomenus[2] <*Cat. Wom., Frag. Hes.* frg. 77, Merk. & West>, 20c

Amphillogiai [disputes] [abstraction], offspring of *Eris* <Hes. *Theog.* 229>, *1a*

Amphilochus[1] [one of the Epigoni], son of Amphiaraus <Hom. *Od.* 15.248> and *Eriphyle* <Apollod. *Bibl.* 3.7.2>, 33c

Amphilochus[2], son of Alcmaeon and *Manto*[1] <Eur. in *T.G.F.* 479 ff., Nauck>, 32d

Amphilochus[3], son of Dryas[6] <Parth. *Love Stor.* 27>, *

Amphimachus[1], son of Cteatus <Hom. *Il.* II.621> and *Theronice* <Paus. 5.2.3>, 9a

Amphimachus[2], son of Polyxenus[1] <Paus. 5.3.4>, 63c

Amphimachus[3], son of Electryon[1] and *Lysidice*[1] <*Cat. Wom., Frag. Hes.* frg. 193, Merk. & West>, 59d, *38a*
alternate parentage:
Electryon[1] and *Anaxo*[1] <Apollod. *Bibl.* 2.4.5>

Amphimachus[4], son of Nomion[1] <Hom. *Il.* II.871>, *

Amphimachus[5], suitor of *Penelope*[1] (from Dulichium) <Apollod. *Epit.* 7.27>, *

Amphimachus[6], suitor of *Penelope*[1] (from Ithaca) <Apollod. *Epit.* 7.30>, *

Amphimarus, son of Poseidon <Paus. 9.29.3>, 9c
— and *Urania*[1] <Paus. 9.29.3>, 6b

Amphimede, wife of Pterelaus <Schol. on Hom. *Od.* 17.207>, 58d

Amphinome[1], daughter of Nereus <Hom. *Il.* XVIII.44> and *Doris*[1] <Hyg. *Fab.* pref.>, *63a*

Amphinome[2], daughter of Pelias[1] <Diod. Sic. 4.53.2> and *Anaxibia*[2], 28d
— and Andraemon[3] <Diod. Sic. 4.53.2>, (28d)

Amphinome[3] — see Jason (alternate version)

Amphinome[4], wife of Arizelus <Quint. Smyr. 10.75>, *

Amphinomous[1], father of *Thyria* <Ant. Lib. *Met.* 12.1>, 11d

Amphinomous[2], son of Diomedes[1] and *Euippe*[1] <Ant. Lib. *Met.* 37.3>, 17d

Amphinomous[3], son of Nisus[3] <Hom. *Od.* 16.396>, 47d
— and *Penelope*[1] <Apollod. *Epit.* 7.40>, (47d)

Amphion[1] [King of Thebes], son of Zeus and *Antiope*[1] <Hom. *Od.* 11.260-65>, 5a, *66d*
— and *Niobe*[1] <*Cat. Wom., Frag. Hes.* frg. 183, Merk. & West>, 41a

Amphion[2] [King of Orchomenus], son of Iasus[2] and *Persephone*[2] <Hom. *Od.* 11.281 ff.>, 20c
alternate parentage:
Iasius[2] <Paus. 9.36.8> (unless this is a spelling variation of Iasus[2])
— and *Persephone*[2] <Schol. on Hom. *Od.* 11.281 ff.>, 20c

Amphion[3] [centaur], offspring of Centaurus and a Magnesian Mare <Pind. *Pyth.* 2.50; named as centaur, Diod. Sic. 4.12.7>, 69c
alternate parentage:
Ixion and *Nephele*[1] <Diod. Sic. 4.69.5>

Amphion[4] [Argonaut], son of Hyperasius <Ap. Rhod. *Arg.* 1.174> and *Hypso*, 61d
Amphion[5], commanded the Epeans <Hom. *Il.* XIII.691>, *
Amphion[6], killed by Aeneas <Quint. Smyr. 10.111>, *
Amphiorax — see Amphiaraus
Amphirho, daughter of Oceanus and *Tethys* <Hes. *Theog.* 360>, 50b
Amphiria (*Antibia*), daughter of Pelops[1] <Schol. on Hom. *Il.* XIX.116> and *Hippodameia*[1], *36a*
alternate parentage:
Amphidamantus <Schol. on Hom. *Il.* XIX.116>
Amphissa[1] — see *Isse*
Amphissa[2], daughter of Echetus <Schol. on Hom. *Od.* 18.84>, 31d
— and Aechmodicus <Schol. on Hom. *Od.* 18.84>, (31d)
Amphissus, son of Apollo and *Dryope*[2] <Ovid *Met.* 9.356 ff.>, 11c, *11d*
Amphithea[1] (*Demonassa*[3]) (*Iphitea*), daughter of Pronax <Apollod. *Bibl.* 1.9.13>, 31d
— and Adrastus[1] <Apollod. *Bibl.* 1.9.13>, 30c
— and Dion <Serv. on Virg. *Ecl.* 8.29>, (31d)
Amphithea[2], wife of Autolycus[1] <Hom. *Od.* 19.414>, 13a
Amphithea[3] — see *Eurydice*[3]
Amphithemis[1] (Garamas), son of Apollo and *Acacallis*[1] <Ap. Rhod. *Arg.* 4.1495>, 11a, *53d*
— and a nymph of Triton <Ap. Rhod. *Arg.* 4.1496>, 63b
Amphithemis[2] [horned centaur] <Non. *Dion.* 14.191>, *
Amphithoe, daughter of Nereus <Hom. *Il.* XVIII.42> and *Doris*[1] <Hyg. *Fab.* pref.>, *63b*
Amphitrite, daughter of Nereus <Hes. *Theog.* 243> and *Doris*[1] <Apollod. *Bibl.* 1.2.7>, *63b*
alternate parentage:
Oceanus and *Tethys* <Apollod. *Bibl.* 1.2.2>
— and Poseidon <Hes. *Theog.* 930>, 8b
Amphitryon [King of Tiryns], son of Alcaeus[2] <Hes. *Shield* 26> and *Asty(a)dameia*[4] <Apollod. *Bibl.* 2.4.5>, 59c
alternate parentage:
Alcaeus[2] and *Hipponome* <Apollod. *Bibl.* 2.4.5>
Alcaeus[2] and *Laonome*[2] <Apollod. *Bibl.* 2.4.5>
— and *Alcmene* <Hom. *Od.* 11.266>, 59d
Amphius[1], son of Merops[3] <Hom. *Il.* II.830>, 44c
Amphius[2], son of Selagus <Hom. *Il.* V.612>, *
Amphoterus[1], son of Alcmaeon[1] and *Callirhoe*[4] <Apollod. *Bibl.* 3.7.6>, 32d
Amphoterus[2], killed by Patroclus[1] <Hom. *Il.* XVI.417>, *
Amphrysus [river], son of Oceanus and *Tethys* <Hes. *Theog.* 367-68; named as river, Ovid *Met.* 1.575>, 50b
Ampycus[1] — see Ampyx[2]
Ampycus[2], seer of Demeter <Ovid *Met.* 5.109>, *
Ampyx[1], son of Pelias[2] <Paus. 7.18.5>, 47c
Ampyx[2] (Ampycus[1]), father of Mopsus[2] <Hes. *Shield* 182>, *
Ampyx[3], fought Perseus <Ovid *Met.* 5.184>, *
Ampyx[4], fought the centaur Echeclus[2] <Ovid *Met.* 12.451>, *
Amyce, daughter of Salaminus <Paus. Damasc. in *F.H.G.* 4.469 frg. 4, Müller>, 59a
— and Casus <Paus. Damasc. in *F.H.G.* 4.469 frg. 4, Müller>, (59a)
Amyclas[1] [King of Sparta], son of Lacedaemon and *Sparte* <Apollod. *Bibl.* 3.10.3>, 47a
— and *Diomede*[2] <*Cat. Wom., Frag. Hes.* frg. 171, Merk. & West>, 68b
Amyclas[2], son of Amphion[1] and *Niobe*[1] <Paus. 2.21.9>, 66c
Amycus[1] [giant] [King of Bebryces], son of Poseidon <Apollod. *Bibl.* 1.9.20> and *Melia*[2] <Ap. Rhod. *Arg.* 2.2-3>, 8d
Amycus[2] [centaur], offspring of Ophion[2] <Ovid *Met.* 12.244>, 69d
Amycus[3], husband of *Theano*[4] <Virg. *Aen.* 10.704>, *
Amycus[4], brother of Diores[3] <Virg. *Aen.* 12.509>, *
Amycus[5], killed by Turnus <Virg. *Aen.* 9.771>, *
Amymone[1], daughter of Danaus[1] and *Europe*[3] <Pher. in *Schol.* on Ap. Rhod. *Arg.* 4.1091>, 57c, 57c
— and Enceladus[2] <Apollod. *Bibl.* 2.1.5>, (57c)
— and Poseidon <Pher. in *F. Gr. H.* 3 F 4>, 8b
Amymone[2] — see *Beroe*[1]
Amyntor[1] [King of Dolopians in Thessaly], son of Ormenus[1] <Hom. *Il.* IX.448>, 24d
— and *Hippodameia*[3] <Schol. A on Hom. *Il.* IX.448>, (24d)
— and *Clytie*[2] <Schol. A on Hom. *Il.* 9.448>, (24d)
Amyntor[2] [King of Pelasgians in Thessaly], son of Phrastor[1] <Hellan. Lesb. in *F.H.G.* 1.83 frg. 45, Müller>, 61d
Amyntor[3], father of Teutamides <Dion. Hal. *Rom. Ant.* 28.3>, *
Amyntor[4] — see [fifty sons of Aegyptus[1]] (alternate version)
Amythaon[1], son of Cretheus[1] and *Tyro* <Hom. *Od.* 11.258-59>, 30b
— and *Idomene* <Apollod. *Bibl.* 1.9.11>, 29d
Amythaon[2], Lemnian man <Val. Flac. 2.162>, *
Anactor, son of Electryon[1] and *Anaxo*[1] <Apollod. *Bibl.* 2.4.5>, 59d
Anadyomene — see *Aphrodite*
Ananke [necessity] — see (Moirae) (alternate parentage)
Anaphlystus, son of Troezen[1] <Paus. 2.30.9>, 39b
Anatole [one of the hours], daughter of Zeus and *Themis*[1] <Hyg. *Fab.* 183>, 6d
Anax [giant], son of *Gaea* (and the blood of Uranus) <Hes. *Theog.* 180-86; named as giant, Eust. on Hom. *Il.* XXI.24>, *4a*
Anaxagoras [King of Argos], son of Megapenthes[2] <Diod. Sic. 4.68.4>, 58c
alternate parentage:
Argeius[6] <Paus. 2.18.4>
Anaxandra, daughter of Thersander[3] <Paus. 3.16.6>, 61c
— and Eurysthenes[1] <Paus. 3.16.6>, 60d
Anaxibia[1] (*Astyoche*[6]) (*Astyocheia*) (*Cydragora*), daughter of Atreus and *Aerope*[1] <Paus. 2.29.4>, 37a
alternate parentage:
Pleisthenes[1] and *Cleola* <*Frag. Hes.* frg. 194, Merk. & West>
— and Strophius[1] <Paus. 2.29.4>, 23c
Anaxibia[2], daughter of Bias[1] <Apollod. *Bibl.* 1.9.10> and *Lysippe*[1], 30c
— and Pelias[1] <Apollod. *Bibl.* 1.9.10>, 28c
Anaxibia[3], daughter of Danaus[1] and [an Ethiopian woman] <Apollod. *Bibl.* 2.1.5>, 58c
— and Archelaus[5] <Apollod. *Bibl.* 2.1.5>, (58c)
Anaxibia[4], daughter of Cratieus <Apollod. *Bibl.* 1.9.9>, 27d
— and Nestor <Apollod. *Bibl.* 1.9.9>, (27d)
Anaximene — see *Anaximenia*
Anaximenia (*Anaximene*), wife of Mygdon(us)[2] <Serv. on Virg. *Aen.* 2.341>, 43d
Anaxiroe, daughter of Coronus[2] <Paus. 5.1.6>, 16a
— and Epeius[1] <Paus. 5.1.6>, (16a)
Anaxis — see Anogon
Anaxo[1], daughter of Alcaeus[2] and *Asty(a)dameia*[4] <Apollod. *Bibl.* 2.4.5>, 59c
alternate parentage:
Alcaeus[2] and *Laonome*[2] <Apollod. *Bibl.* 2.4.5>
Alcaeus[2] and *Hipponome* <Apollod. *Bibl.* 2.4.5>
— and Electryon[1] <Apollod. *Bibl.* 2.4.5>, 59d
Anaxo[2], paramour of Theseus <Plut. *Thes.* 29.1>, 51b
Ancaeus[1] [Argonaut], son of Lycurgus[4] and *Cleophyle* <Apollod. *Bibl.* 3.9.2>, 64c
alternate parentage:
Lycurgus[4] and *Eurynome*[5] <Apollod. *Bibl.* 3.9.2>
Ancaeus[2] [King of Leleges] [Argonaut], son of Poseidon and *Astypalaea* <Paus. 7.4.2>, 8a, *54d*
alternate parentage:
Poseidon and *Althaea* <Hyg. *Fab.* 14>
— and *Samia* <Paus. 7.4.2>, 68a
Anchiale[1], paramour of Apollo <Serv. on Virg. *Ecl.* 1.65>, 11a
Anchiale[2], daughter of Iapetus <Steph. Byz. "Anchiale">, 16a

Anchinoe[1] (*Achiroe*) (*Side*[2]), daughter of Nilus <Apollod. *Bibl.* 2.1.4>, 68a
— and Belus[1] <Apollod. *Bibl.* 2.1.4>, 57b
Anchinoe[2], wife of Proteus[1] <Steph. Byz. "Cabiria">, 9c
Anchiroe[1], daughter of Chremetes <Non. *Dion.* 13.380>, 52a
— and Psyllus <Non. *Dion.* 13.381>, (52a)
Anchiroe[2], daughter of Erasinus <Ant. Lib. 40>, 53b
Anchiroe[3] [nymph] <Paus. 8.31.4>, *
Anchises [King of Dardania], son of Capys[1] <Hom. *Il.* XX.239> and *Themis*[2] <Apollod. *Bibl.* 3.12.2 (she is called *Themiste*)>, 41c
alternate parentage:
Capys[1] and *Hieromneme* <Dion. Hal. *Rom. Ant.* 1.62.2>
— and *Aphrodite* <Hom. *Il.* II.819>, 5a
Anchius [centaur], offspring Centaurus and a Magnesian Mare <Pind. *Pyth.* 2.50; named as centaur, Apollod. *Bibl.* 2.5.4>, 69c
alternate parentage:
Ixion and *Nephele*[1] <Diod. Sic. 4.69.5>
Anchurus, son of Midas[1] <Plut. *Gr. and Rom. Par. Stor.* 5>, 2d
— and *Timothea* <Plut. *Gr. and Rom. Par. Stor.* 5>, (2d)
Ancyor, son of Lycaon[1] <Apollod. *Bibl.* 3.8.1>, 62b
Andraemon[1] [King of Calydon], husband of *Gorge*[1] <Apollod. *Bibl.* 1.8.1>, 16d
Andraemon[2], son of Oxylus[2] <Ant. Lib. *Met.* 32.3> and *Pieria*[2], 16d
— and *Dryope*[2] <Ovid *Met.* 9.332-37>, 11d
Andraemon[3], wife of *Amphinome*[2] <Diod. Sic. 4.53.2>, 28d
Andraemon[4], son of Codrus[1] <Paus. 7.3.2>, 27c
Andraemon[5], founder of Colophon <Mimn. in Strab. 14.1.3>, *
Andraemon[6], suitor of *Penelope*[1] (from Dulichium) <Apollod. *Epit.* 7.27>, *
Andreus[1], son of Orchomenus[2] <*Cat. Wom., Frag. Hes.* frg. 70, Merk. & West>, 20c
alternate parentage:
Peneius <Paus. 9.34.5> and *Creusa*[4]
— and *Euippe*[4] <Paus. 9.34.9>, 26d
Andreus[2], general of Oenopion[1] <Diod. Sic. 5.79.2>, *
Androcles[1], son of Aeolus[2] and *Cyane*[1] <Hom. *Od.* 10.2-6; named, Diod. Sic. 5.8.1>, 18c
Androcles[2], son of Phintas <Paus. 4.4.4>, *
Androclus[1], son of Codrus[1] <Pher. in Strab. 14.1.3>, 27c
Androclus[2], son of Androclus[1] <Paus. 7.2.4>, 27c
Androdamas, son of Phlias and *Chthonophyle* <Paus. 2.6.3>, 56d, *49b*
Androgeneia, paramour of Minos I <Non. *Dion.* 13.225-26>, 54c
Androgeus [King of Paros], son of Minos I <*Cat. Wom., Frag. Hes.* frg. 145, Merk. & West> and *Pasiphae*[1] <Apollod. *Bibl.* 3.1.2>, 53d
alternate parentage:
Minos I and *Crete*[1] <Apollod. *Bibl.* 3.1.2>
Androktasiai [manslaughters] [abstraction], offspring of *Eris* <Hes. *Theog.* 228>, *1a*
Andromache, daughter of Eetion[1] <Hom. *Il.* VI.395>, 24c, 43c, 43c
— and Hector[1] <Hom. *Il.* VI.395>, (43c)
— and Helenus[1] <Paus. 1.11.1>, (43c)
— and Neoptolemus <Eur. *Andr.* 16>, 24c
Andromeda, daughter of Cepheus[1] and *Cassiopeia*[1] <Apollod. *Bibl.* 2.4.3>, 58d
— and Perseus[1] <*Cat. Wom., Frag. Hes.* frg. 135, Merk. & West>, 58d
— and Phineus[2] <Apollod. *Bibl.* 2.4.3>, 58d
Andropompus[1] [King of Messenia], son of Borus[2] <Paus. 2.18.8>, 27d
Andropompus[2], founder of Lebedus <Strab. 14.1.3>, *
Andrus, son of Anius and *Dorippe* <Ovid *Met.* 13.651-52>, 56d
Anemone — see Adonis
Angcinoes, paramour of Ares <Schol. on Lyc. 583>, 7a
Angitia — see *Medea*
Anicetus (Anticetus), son of Heracles[1] and *Hebe* <Apollod. *Bibl.* 2.7.8>, 60c
Anioche[1] — see *Henioche*[1]
Anioche[2] — see *Henioche*[2]
Anippe — see Busirus[1] (alternate version)
Anius [King of Delos], son of Apollo and *Rhoeo* <Diod. Sic. 5.61, 2>, 11c, *56d*
alternate parentage:
Apollo and *Creusa*[3] <Con. *Narr.* 41>
— and *Dorippe* <Tzetz. on Lyc. 570, 581>, (56d)
Anna Perenna, daughter of Belus[3] <Ovid *Fast.* 3.523-60>, 41d
Anogon (Anaxis), son of Castor[1] and *Hilaeira* <Apollod. *Bibl.* 3. 11.2>, 48d, *25d*
Antaeus[1] [giant], son of Poseidon <Apollod. *Bibl.* 2.5.11>, 9c
alternate parentage:
Gaea <Hyg. *Fab.* 31>
— and *Iphinoe*[4] <Pher. in *F. Gr. H.* 3 F 76>, (9c)
— and *Tinge* <Plut. *Sertorius*>, (9c)
Antaeus[2] [King of Irasa], father of *Alceis* <Pind. *Pyth.* 9.108>, *
Antaeus[3], killed by Aeneas <Virg. *Aen.* 10.561>, *
Antagoras[1], son of Eurypylus[2] <*Frag. Hes.* frg. 43a.60, Merk. & West>, 34c
Antagoras[2], a shepherd who wrestled Heracles[1] <Plut. *Gr. Quest.* 58>, *
Anteia — see *Stheneboea*
Anteias, son of Odysseus and *Circe* <Xena. in Dion. Hal. *Rom. Ant.* 1.72.5>, 13c
Antenor[1], son of Aesyetes and *Cleomestra* <Dict. Cret. 4.22>, 45c
— and *Theano*[2] <Hom. *Il.* VI.298-99>, (45c)
Antenor[2], suitor of *Penelope*[1] (from Zacynthus) <Apollod. *Epit.* 7.30>, *
Anterus [passion], son of Ares and *Aphrodite* <Cic. *De Nat. Deor.* 3.23.59>, 7a
Anthas [King of Troezen], son of Poseidon and *Alcyone*[2] <Paus. 2.30.8>, 8a, *35a*
Anthe, daughter of Alcyoneus[1] <Eust. on Hom. *Il.* 776>, 4a
Anthea, daughter of Thespius <Apollod. *Bibl.* 2.7.8> and *Megamede* <Apollod. *Bibl.* 2.4.10>, 50a
— and Heracles[1] <Apollod. *Bibl.* 2.7.8>, (50a)
Anthelia, daughter of Danaus[1] and *Polyxo*[3] <Apollod. *Bibl.* 2.1.5>, 57d
— and Cisseus[2] <Apollod. *Bibl.* 2.1.5>, 57d
Anthemone, paramour of Aeneas <Agath. in Dion. Hal. *Rom. Ant.* 1.49.2>, 41c
Antheus[1], son of Antenor[1] <Schol. on Lyc. 132> and *Theano*[2], *45c*
— and Paris <Lyc. 134>, 43c
Antheus[2], son of Agelaus[9] <Non. *Dion.* 35.382-84>, *
Antheus[3], son of Nomion[2] <Ant. Lib. *Met.* 5.1>, *
Antheus[4], fought with Seven Against Thebes <Stat. *Theb.* 10. 544>, *
Antheus[5], comrade of Aeneas <Virg. *Aen.* 1.512>, *
Anthia — see *Aethylla*
Anthippe, daughter of Thespius <Apollod. *Bibl.* 2.7.8> and *Megamede* <Apollod. *Bibl.* 2.4.10>, 50a
— and Heracles[1] <Apollod. *Bibl.* 2.7.8>, (50a)
Antiades, son of Heracles[1] and *Aglaia*[4] <Apollod. *Bibl.* 2.7. 8>, *50c*
Antianeira[1] (*Meneteis*), daughter of Menetes <Ap. Rhod. *Arg.* 1.57>, 46a
— and Hermes <Ap. Rhod. *Arg.* 1.57>, (46a)
Antianeira[2] [Amazon] <Mimn. frg. 21a, Gerber>, *
Antibia — see *Amphiria*
Anticetus — see Anicetus
Anticleia[1], daughter of Autolycus[1] and *Amphithea*[2] <Hom. *Od.* 19.394-95, 416>, 13a
— and Laertes <Hom. *Od.* 11.85>, 5c
— and Sisyphus <Hyg. *Fab.* 200>, 18b

Anticleia[2], paramour of Hephaestus <Apollod. *Bibl.* 2.16.1>, 7b
Anticleia[3], daughter of Diocles[1] <Paus. 4.30.3>, 65b
— and Machaon <Paus. 4.30.3>, 19d
Anticleia[4] — see *Philonoe*
Antigone[1], daughter of Oedipus <Aesch. *Sev.* 861 (she is called brother of Eteocles)> and *Jocasta* <Eur. *Phoen. Wom.* 59>, 55c
alternate parentage:
Oedipus and *Euryganeia* <Pher. frg. 52, Sturz>
— and Haemon[1] <Soph. *Ant.* 571-73, 629>, 55d
Antigone[2] (*Philomela*[3]), daughter of Eurytion[3] <Apollod. *Bibl.* 3.13.1>, 22d
— and Peleus <Apollod. *Bibl.* 3.13.1>, 24a
Antigone[3], daughter of Laomedon[1] <Ovid *Met.* 6.93> and *Strym(n)o*, 42c
Antigone[4], daughter of Pheres[1] <Hyg. *Fab.* 14> and *Periclymene,* 29d
— and Cometes[4] <Hyg. *Fab.* 14>, (29d)
Antileon, son of Heracles[1] and *Procris*[2] <Apollod. *Bibl.* 2.7.8>, *50c*
Antilochus (Archilochus[2]), son of Nestor <Hom. *Il.* V.565> and *Anaxibia*[4] <Apollod. *Bibl.* 1.9.9>, 27c
alternate parentage:
Nestor and *Eurydice*[7] (inferred because she is wife of Nestor) <Hom. *Od.* 3.453>
Antimache, daughter of Amphidamas[1] <Apollod. *Bibl.* 3.9.2>, 63c
— and Eurystheus <Apollod. *Bibl.* 3.9.2>, 58d
Antimachus[1], son of Heracles[1] and *Nicippe*[2] <Apollod. *Bibl.* 2.7.8>, *51c*
Antimachus[2], son of Thrasyanor <Paus. 2.19.1>, 60c
Antimachus[3], son of Hippodamas[1] <*Cat. Wom., Hesiodi* frg. 10a.45-47, Merk. & West (O.C.T.)>, 65a
Antimachus[4] [centaur], offspring of Centaurus and a Magnesian Mare <Pind. *Pyth.* 2.50; named as centaur, Ovid *Met.* 12.460>, 69c
alternate parentage:
Ixion and *Nephele*[1] <Diod. Sic. 4.69.5>
Antimachus[5], father of Hippolochus[3] <Hom. *Il.* XI.122>, *
Antimachus[6], father of Amphianax[2] <Paus. 3.25.10>, *
Antimachus[7] — see [fifty sons of Aegyptus[1]] (alternate version)
Antimachus[8], suitor of *Penelope*[1] (from Dulichium) <Apollod. *Epit.* 7.28>, *
Antimachus[9], killed by Aeneas <Quint. Smyr. 6.622>, *
Antimenes[1], son of Deiphon(tes)[2] and *Hyrnetho* <Paus. 2.28.3>, 60c
Antimenes[2] (Eurymenes[1]), son of Neleus[1] and *Chloris*[2] <*Cat. Wom., Frag. Hes.* frg. 33(a), Merk. & West>, 27c
Antinoe[1] — see *Cleophyle*
Antinoe[2], daughter of Pelias[1] <Paus. 8.11.2> and *Anaxibia*[2], 28d
Antinous, paramour of *Penelope*[1] <Apollod. *Epit.* 7.38>, 47d
Antioche[1] — *see Antiope*[6]
Antioche[2] [Amazon] <Hyg. *Fab.* 163>, *
Antiochus[1], son of Pterelaus <Apollod. *Bibl.* 2.4.5> and *Amphimede*, 58d
Antiochus[2], son of Heracles[1] <Apollod. *Bibl.* 8.2.3> and *Mideia*[3] <Paus. 1.5.2>, 60c
Antiochus[3], son of Melas[3] <Apollod. *Bibl.* 1.8.5>, 16d
Antiochus[4], son of Phintas <Paus. 4.44>, *
Antiochus[5] — see [fifty sons of Aegyptus[1]] (alternate version)
Antion, son of Periphas[1] and *Astyage(ia)* <Diod. Sic. 4.69.3>, 69a
— and *Perimele*[2] <Diod. Sic. 4.69.3>, 31d
Antiope[1], daughter of Asopus and *Metope*[2] <Hom. *Od.* 11.260-65>, 66d
alternate parentage:
Nycteus and *Polyxo*[2] <Apollod. *Bibl.* 3.10.1>
— and Epopeus[1] <Paus. 2.6.2>, 34b
— and Lycus[1] <Hyg. *Fab.* 7>, 35b
— and Phocus[2] <Paus. 9.17.4>, 18c
— and Zeus <Hom. *Od.* 11.262>, 5a
Antiope[2], wife of Laocoon[1] <Serv. on Virg. *Aen.* 2.201>, 45c
Antiope[3] — see *Hippolyte*[1]
Antiope[4], paramour of Helios <Tzetz. on Lyc. 175>, 14a
Antiope[5], daughter of Thespius <Apollod. *Bibl.* 2.7.8> and *Megamede* <Apollod. *Bibl.* 2.4.10>, 50a
— and Heracles[1] <Apollod. *Bibl.* 2.7.8>, 50a
Antiope[6] (*Antioche*[1]), daughter of Pylo(n)[1] <Hyg. *Fab.* 14>, 11d, 15d, 60b
— and Eurytus[2] <*Cat. Wom., Frag. Hes.* frg. 26, Merk. & West>, 11d, 15d, (60b)
Antiope[7] —see *Euippe*[2]
Antiope[8] — see *Melanippe*[4]
Antiope[9] [Amazon], daughter of Ares and *Otrere* <Paus. 1.41.7 (she is called sister of *Hippolyte*[1])>, 7c
Antiope[10], paramour of Poseidon <Hyg. *Fab.* 157>, 8b
Antiophemus — see Musaeus (alternate parentage)
Antiphantes (Antiphas) (Ethron), son of Laocoon[1] <Hyg. *Fab.* 135> and *Antiope*[2], 45c
Antiphas — see Antiphantes
Antiphateia, daughter of Naubolus[1] <Schol. on Eur. 33>, 52d
— and Crisus <Schol. on Eur. 33>, 23c
Antiphates[1], son of Sarpedon[1] <Virg. *Aen.* 9.698-700>, 52c
Antiphates[2], son of Melampus[1] <Hom. *Od.* 15.242 ff.> and *Iphianassa*[1] <Pher. in *F. Gr. H.* 3 F 115>, 32c
alternate parentage:
Melampus[1] and *Iphianeira*[2] <Diod. Sic. 4.68.4-5>
— and *Zeuxippe*[3] <Diod. Sic. 4.68.5>, 47c
Antiphates[3] [giant] [King of the Laestrygonians] <Apollod. *Epit.* 7.12>, *
Antiphates[5], a warrior who hid in the Trojan horse <Tryph. *Tak. Ilium* 180>, *
Antiphates[4], killed by Leonteus <Hom *Il.* XII.191>, *
Antiphonus, son of Priam[1] <Hom. *Il.* XXIV.250>, 43d
Antiphus[1], son of Priam[1] <Hom. *Il.* XI.101> and *Hecabe*[1] <Apollod. *Bibl.* 3.11.5>, 43c
Antiphus[2], son of Thessalus[2] <Hom. *Il.* II.678>, 60b
alternate parentage:
Thessalus[2] and *Chalciope*[2] <Hyg. *Fab.* 97>
Antiphus[3], son of Myrmidon and *Peisidice*[1] <*Cat. Wom., Hesiodi* frg. 10a.101, Merk. & West (O.C.T.)>, 5d
Antiphus[4], son of Heracles[1] and *Laothoe*[3] <Apollod. *Bibl.* 2.7.8>, *50c*
Antiphus[5], son of Aegyptius <Hom. *Od.* 2.15-17>,*
Antiphus[6], son of Talaemenes <Hom. *Il.* II.864-65>, *
Antiphus[7], friend of Odysseus <Hom. *Od.* 17.68>, *
Antiphus[8], killed by Apollo <Stat. *Theb.* 7.755>, *
Antiphus[9], killed by Eurypylus[1] <Quint. Smyr. 6.615>, *
Aoede [song] [one of the Boeotian Muses], daughter of Uranus <Paus. 9.29.2> and *Gaea*, 6b
alternate parentage:
"the second Jupiter" (son of Caelus) <Cic. *De Nat. Deor.* 3.54-55>
Aon, son of Poseidon <Schol. on Stat. *Theb.* 1.33>, 9c
Aoris[1] — see *Chloris*[2]
Aoris[2], son of Aras; brother of *Araethyrea* <Paus. 2.12.5>, 56d
Apate [deception] [abstraction], offspring of *Nyx* <Hes. *Theog.* 224>, *1a*
Apemosyne, daughter of Catreus <Apollod. *Bibl.* 3.2.1>, 52d
— and Hermes <Apollod. *Bibl.* 3.2.1>, 46a
Aphaea — see *Britomartis*
Aphare(u)s, son of Thestius <Bacch. 5.128-29 (inferred because he is called brother of *Althaea*)> and *Eurythemis(te)*, 15d
Aphareus[1] [King of Messene], son of Perieres[1] and *Gorgophone*[1] <Apollod. *Bibl.* 1.9.3>, 25b
— and *Arene* <Apollod. *Bibl.* 3.10.1>, 47d
Aphareus[2] [centaur], offspring of Centaurus and a Magnesian Mare <Pind. *Pyth.* 2.50; named as centaur Ovid *Met.* 12.340>,

69c
alternate parentage:
Ixion and *Nephele*[1] <Diod. Sic. 4.69.5>
Aphareus[3], son of Caletor[2] <Hom. *Il.* XIII.541>, *
Apheidas[1], son of Arcas[1] and *Chrysopeleia* <Apollod. *Bibl.* 3.9.1>, 63c
alternate parentage:
Arcas[1] and *Erato*[2] <Paus. 8.4.2>
Arcas[1] and *Leaneira* <Apollod. *Bibl.* 3.9.1>
Arcas[1] and *Meganeira*[1] <Apollod. *Bibl.* 3.9.1>
Apheidas[2] [King of Athens], son of Oxyntes <Nicand. in *F.H.G.* 3.386 frg. 50, Müller>, 51c
Apheidas[3] [centaur], offspring of Centaurus and a Magnesian Mare <Pind. *Pyth.* 2.50; named as centaur, Ovid *Met.* 12.318>, 69c
alternate parentage:
Ixion and *Nephele*[1] <Diod. Sic. 4.69.5>
Apheidas[4], son of Polypemon[2]; father of Eperitus, alias initially used by Odysseus to his father upon his return <Hom. *Od.* 24.302-07>, *
Aphrodite (*Acidalia*) (*Anadyomene*) (*Cythereia*) [goddess] [beauty], daughter of Zeus <Hom. *Il.* III.374> and *Dione*[1] <Hom. *Il.* V.371>, 5a, *53a*
alternate parentage:
Cronus <Epim. *Theog.* 3 B 19>
Uranus (from his genitals) and the Sea <Hes. *Theog.* 188-96>
— and Adonis <Apollod. *Bibl.* 3.14.4>, 11c
— and Anchises <Hom. *Il.* II.819>, 41c
— and Ares <Hes. *Theog.* 934>, 7a
— and Butes[1] <Diod. Sic. 4.83.1>, 53a
— and Dionysus <Paus. 9.31.2>, 56c
— and Hephaestus <Hom. *Od.* 8.266-358>, 7b
— and Hermes <Ovid *Met.* 4.287>, 46a
— and Phaethon[2] <Hes. *Theog.* 987-90>, 46c
— and Poseidon <Serv. on Virg. *Aen.* 1.570>, 8b
Apidanus [river], son of Oceanus and *Tethys* <Hes. *Theog.* 367-68; named as river, Ovid *Met.* 1.575>, 50b
Apis[1] [King of Argos], son of Phoroneus and *Teledice* <Apollod. *Bibl.* 2.1.1>, 61a
alternate parentage:
Phoroneus and *Cinna* <Hyg. *Fab.* 145>
Apis[2] [King of Sicyon], son of Telchis <Paus. 2.5.7>, 61a
Apis[3], son of Jason <Paus. 5.1.8> and *Medea*, 33c
Apis[4], son of Apollo <Aesch. *Supp. Maid.* 252-53>, 11c
Apis[5], the sacred ox who appeared in a dream of *Telethusa* <Ovid *Met.* 9.691>, *
Apisaon[1], son of Hippasus[4] <Hom. *Il.* XVII.348>, 44d
Apisaon[2], son of Phausias <Hom. *Il.* XI.577>, *
Apollo (Phoebus) [god] [music], son of Zeus and *Leto* <Hes. *Theog.* 919>, 5c, *11a*
alternate parentage:
Dionysus and *Isis* <Herod. 2.156>
Oceanus ("from whom all we gods proceed") <Hom. *Il.* XIV.202>)
— and *Acacallis*[1] <Ap. Rhod. *Arg.* 4.1450-56>, 53d
— and *Acacallis*[2] <Paus. 10.16.3>, (11a)
— and *Aethusa* <Apollod. *Bibl.* 3.10.1>, 35a
— and *Anchiale*[1] <Serv. on Virg. *Ecl.* 1.65>, (11a)
— and *Areia* <Apollod. *Bibl.* 3.1.2>, (11a)
— and *Arsinoe*[1] <*Cat. Wom., Frag. Hes.* frg. 50, Merk. & West>, 25c
— and *Boline* <Paus. 7.23.3>, (11a)
— and Branchus[1] <Con. *Narr.* 33>, (11a)
— and *Calliope* <Asclep. in *F. Gr. H.* 12 F 6>, 6a
— and Carn(e)us <Prax. in *P.L.G.* 3.568 frg. 7, Bergk>, 5c
— and *Castalia* <Schol. on Eur. *Or.* 1094>, 65b
— and *Celaeno*[3] <Paus. 10.6.2>, 17a
— and *Chione*[1] <Ovid *Met.* 11.311>, 13b
— and *Chrysorthe* <Paus. 2.5.5>, 8d
— and Cinyras[1] <Pind. *Pyth.* 2.15>, 11c
— and *Cleobula*[3] <Hyg. *Fab.* 161>, (11a)
— and *Cleopatra*[2] <Hom. *Il.* IX.562-63>, 25d
— and *Coronis*[1] <*Hom. Hymn* 16 (to Asclepius) 1-3>, 19d
— and *Corycia* <Paus. 10.6.3>, (11a)
— and *Creusa*[3] <Eur. *Ion* 70-76>, 51b
— and Cyparissus[2] <Ovid *Met.* 10.106-42>, 60a
— and *Cyrene* <Pind. *Pyth.* 9.5-70>, 69a
— and *Daphne*[1] <Ovid *Met.* 1.493-568>, 68b
— and *Dia*[3] <Tzetz. on Lyc. 480>, 64b
— and *Dryope*[2] <Ovid *Met.* 9.334>, 11d
— and *Euadne*[3] <Pind. *Olym.* 6.42>, 9a
— and Hyacinthus[1] <Apollod. *Bibl.* 1.3.3>, 47b
— and Hyman(aeus)[1] <Ant. Lib. *Met.* 23.2>, 56c
— and Ileus <*Cat. Wom., Frag. Hes.* frg. 235, Merk. & West>, 11d
— and *Isse* <Ovid *Met.* 6.122-23>, 14a
— and *Laothoe*[2] <Tzetz. on Lyc. 427>, 69b
— and *Lycia* <Serv. on Virg. *Aen.* 3.332>, (11c)
— and *Marpessa*[1] <Hom *Il.* IX.557>, 15c
— and *Melaena* <Paus. 10.6.2>, 49b
— and *Melia*[1] <Paus. 9.10.5>, 61a
— and *Ocyrrhoe*[2] <Ap. Rhod. in Athen. 7.283d>, (11c)
— and *Othreis* <Ant. Lib. *Met.* 13.1>, (11c)
— and *Paphos* <Schol. on Pind. *Pyth.* 27>, (11c)
— and *Parthenope*[3] <Paus. 7.4.2>, 54d
— and *Phthia*[4] <Apollod. *Bibl.* 1.7.6>, (11c)
— and *Psamathe*[2] <Paus. 1.43.7>, 61c
— and *Rhetia* <Pher. in Strab. 10.3.21>, (11c)
— and *Rhodope*[1] <*Etym. Magn.* 513.36>, 70a
— and *Rhoeo* <Diod. Sic. 5.62.1>, 56d
— and *Sinope* <Diod. Sic. 4.72.2>, 66b
— and *Stilbe*[1] <Diod. Sic. 4.69.1>, 68b
— and *Syllis* <Paus. 2.6.3>, (11c)
— and *Themisto*[2] <Steph. Byz. "Galeotai">, (11c)
— and *Thero*[1] <*Gr. Ehoiai, Frag. Hes.* frg. 252, Merk. & West>, 55d
— and *Thyia*[2] <Paus. 10.6.4>, (11c)
— and *Thyria* <Ant. Lib. *Met.* 12.1>, (11c)
Apriate, paramour of Trambelus <Parth. *Love Stor.* 26.1>, 23d
Apsuedes, daughter of Nereus <Hom. *Il.* XVIII.44> and *Doris*[1], *63b*
Apsyrtus (Absyrtus) (Aegialeus[3]) (Phaethon[3]) [King of Colchis], son of Aeetes and *Asterodeia*[3] <Ap. Rhod. *Arg.* 3.242-43>, 14c
alternate parentage:
Aeetes and *Eidyia* <Cic. *De. Nat. Deor.* 3.19.48>
Apterus, husband of *Eulimene*[1] <Parth. *Love Stor.* 35.1>, 53d
[Arabian woman], paramour of Aegyptus[1] <Apollod. *Bibl.* 2.1.5>, 57c, 58c
Arabs — see Arabus
Arabus, son of Hermes and *Thronia* <*Cat. Wom., Frag. Hes.* frg. 137, Merk. & West>, 46c, *59c*
alternate parentage:
Apollo and *Babylone* <Pliny 7.197>
Araethyrea, daughter of Aras <Paus. 2.12.5>, 56d
— and Dionysus <Paus. 2.12.6>, (56d)
Aras, father of *Aoris*[2] and *Araethyrea* <Paus. 2.12.5>, 56d
Aratus, son of Asclepius and *Aristodeme*[2] <Paus. 2.10.3>, 19c
Arbelus, son of Aegyptus[1] and *Hephaestine* <Apollod. *Bibl.* 2.1.5>, 57d
— and *Oeme* <Apollod. *Bibl.* 2.1.5>, (57d)
Arcadia[1], wife of Nyctimus <Plut. *Gr. and Rom. Par. Stor.* 36>, 63a
Arcadia[2] —see [fifty daughters of Danaus[1]] (alternate version)
Arcas[1] [King of Arcadia], son of Zeus and *Callisto*[1] <Apollod. *Bibl.*

3.8.2>,5b, *62c*
alternate version:
Pan and *Callisto* <Ps.-Erat. *Cat.* 1>
— and *Chrysopeleia* <Eum. in Apollod. *Bibl.* 3.9.1>, (62c)
— and *Erato*[2] <Paus. 8.4.2>, (62c)
— and *Leaneira* <Paus. 10.9.3>, 47b
— and *Meganeira*[1] <Apollod. *Bibl.* 3.9.1>, 46d
Arcas[2] [one of the dogs of Actaeon] <Hyg. *Fab.* 181>, *
Arce, daughter of Thaumas[1] <Ptol. 6> and *Electra*[1], 3b
Arceisius, son of Zeus <Ovid *Met.* 13.147> and *Euryodia* <Eust. on Hom. *Od.* 1796>, 5c
alternate parentage:
Cephalus and *Procris*[1] <Hyg. *Fab.* 189>
— and *Chalcomedusa* <Eust. on Hom. *Od.* 1796>, (5c)
Arcelaus, son of Archilycus <Diod. Sic. 4.67.7> and *Theobula*[1] <Hyg. *Fab.* 97>, 18c
Archander, son of Achaeus[1] <Paus. 2.6.2>, 17b
alternate parentage:
Phthius <Herod. 2.98>
— and *Scaea* <Paus. 7.1.3>, 57d
Archebates, son of Lycaon[1] <Apollod. *Bibl.* 3.8.1>, 62b
Archedicus, son of Heracles[1] and *Eurypyle*[1] <Apollod. *Bibl.* 2.7.8>, *50d*
Archedius, son of Tegeates and *Maera*[2] <Paus. 8.53.3>, 63d
Archelaus[1] — see Echelas
Archelaus[2], son of Electryon[1] and *Anaxo*[1] <Apollod. *Bibl.* 2.4.5>, 59d
Archelaus[3], son of Maeandrus <Ps.-Plut. *De Fluv.* 9.1>, 67b
Archelaus[4], son of Temenus[1] <Hyg. *Fab.* 219>, 60d
Archelaus[5], son of Aegyptus[1] and [a Phoenician woman] <Apollod. *Bibl.* 2.1.5>, 58c
— and *Anaxibia*[3] <Apollod. *Bibl.* 2.1.5>, 58c
Archelaus[6], son of Agesilaus <Paus. 3.2.5>, *
Archemachus[1], son of Priam[1] <Apollod. *Bibl.* 3.12.5>, 43d
Archemachus[2], son of Heracles[1] and *Patro* <Apollod. *Bibl.* 2.7.8>, *50c*
Archemorus — see Opheltes[1]
Archenor, son of Amphion[1] and *Niobe*[1] <Hyg. *Fab.* 11>, 66d
Archilochus[1], son of Antenor[1] <Hom. *Il.* II.822-23> and *Theano*[2] <Apollod. *Epit.* 3.32>, *45c*
Archilochus[2] — see Antilochus
Archilycus (Areilycus[1]), son of Itonus[2] <Diod. Sic. 4.67.7>, 18c
— and *Theobula*[1] <Hyg. *Fab.* 97>, (18c)
Archippe — see *Nicippe*[1]
Architeles[1], son of Achaeus[1] <Paus. 2.6.2>, 17b
— and *Automate* <Paus. 7.1.3>, 57d
Arctus [centaur], offspring of Centaurus and a Magnesian Mare <Pind. *Pyth* 2, 50; named as centaur, Hes. *Shield* 186>, 69d
alternate parentage:
Ixion and *Nephele*[1] <Diod. Sic. 4.69.5>
Ardalus, son of Hephaestus <Paus. 2.31.4>, 7d
Ardeias, son of Odysseus and *Circe* <Xena. in Dion. Hal. *Rom. Ant.* 1.72.5>, 13c
Ardescus [river], son of Oceanus and *Tethys* <Hes. *Theog.* 345>, 50b
Aregonis — see *Chloris*[2]
Areia (*Deione*[2]), daughter of Cleochus <Apollod. *Bibl.* 3.1.2>, 11b
— and Apollo <Apollod. *Bibl.* 3.1.2>, (11b)
Areilycus[1] — see Archilycus
Areicylus[2], killed by Patroclus[1] <Hom. *Il.* XVI.309>, *
Areius[1] [Argonaut], son of Bias[1] and *Pero*[1] <Ap. Rhod. *Arg.* 1.119-20>, 30c
Areius[2] [centaur], offspring of Centaurus and a Magnesian Mare <Pind. *Pyth.* 2.50; named as centaur, Ovid *Met.* 12.311>, 69c
alternate parentage:
Ixion and *Nephele*[1] <Diod. Sic. 4.69.5>
Areius[3] [King of Teuthranis], killed by Pergamus <Paus. 1.11. 1>, *
Arene (*Polydora*[4]), daughter of Oebalus[1] <Apollod. *Bibl.* 3.10.3> and *Bateia*[1], 47d
— and Aphareus[1] <Apollod. *Bibl.* 3.10.3>, 25b
Ares (Enyalius) [god] [war], son of Zeus and *Hera* <Hom. *Il.* V.892, 896>, 7a
alternate parentage:
Oceanus ("from whom all we gods proceed") <Hom. *Il.* XIV.202>
— and *Aglaurus*[2] <Hellan. in *F. Gr. H.* 4 F 38>, *66b*
— and *Althaea* <Apollod. *Bibl.* 1.8.2>, 15d
— and *Angcinoes* <Schol. on Lyc. *Alex.* 583>, (7a)
— and *Aphrodite* <Hes. *Theog.* 934>, 5a
— and *Astynome*[3] <Ps.-Plut. 22.4>, 30d
— and *Astyoche*[1] <Hom. *Il.* II.512>, 26c
— and *Callirhoe*[7] <Steph. Byz. "Bistonia">, (7a)
— and *Chryse*[1] <Paus. 9.36.1>, 19c
— and *Critobule* <Ps.-Plut. *De Fluv.* 3.2>, (7a)
— and *Cyrene* <Apollod. *Bibl.* 2.5.8>, 69a
— and *Demodice*[2] <Apollod. *Bibl.* 1.7.7>, 15c
— and *Dotis* <Apollod. *Bibl.* 3.5.5>, 62c
— and *Enyo*[2] <Hom. *Il.* V.594>, (7c)
— and *Eos* <Apollod. *Bibl.* 1.4.4-5>, 12b
— and *Harmonia*[2] <Ap. Rhod. *Arg.* 2.990>, (7a)
— and *Harpinna* <Diod. Sic. 4.73.1>, 66b
— and Meleager <*Cat. Wom., Frag. Hes.* frg. 25, Merk. & West>, 17c
— and *Ossa* <Con. *Narr.* 10>, (7a)
— and *Otrere* <Hyg. *Fab.* 30>, (7c)
— and *Pelopeia*[1] <Apollod. *Bibl.* 2.7.7>, 28d
— and *Phylonome*[1] <Plut. *Gr. and Rom. Par. Stor.* 36>, 63c
— and *Protogeneia*[2] <Apollod. *Bibl.* 1.7.7>, 15d
— and *Pyrene*[2] <Apollod. *Bibl.* 2.5.11>, (7c)
— and *Sterope*[3] <Paus. 8.44.7>, 64c
— and *Tereine* <Ant. Lib. *Met.* 21.1>, 71b
— and *Theogone* <Ps.-Plut. *De Fluv.* 7.5>, (7c)
— and *Triteia* <Paus. 7.22.5>, 63b
Arestor[1], husband of *Mycene* <Paus. 2.16.4>, 55a
Arestor[2], father of Opheltes[5] <Non. *Dion.* 35.379>, *
Arestorides, son of Peiras[1] and *Callirhoe*[5] <Hyg. *Fab.* 145>, 61a
Arete [virtue], daughter of Rhexenor[1] <Hom. *Od.* 7.65-66>, 9c
— and Alcinous <Hom. *Od.* 7.65-66>, 9a
Arethusa[1] [one of the Hesperides], daughter of *Nyx* <Hes. *Theog.* 215; named, Apollod. *Bibl.* 2.5.11>, *1a*
alternate parentage:
Atlas and *Hesperis*[1] <Diod. Sic. 4.27.2>
Hesperus <Paus. 5.17.2, 6.19.8>
Arethusa[2], paramour of Alpheius <Paus. 5.7.2>, 65b
Arethusa[3], daughter of Hyperes[1] <*Cat. Wom., Hesiodi* frg. 188A, Merk. & West (O.C.T.)>, 35a
— and Poseidon <*Cat. Wom., Hesiodi* frg. 188A, Merk. & West (O.C.T.)>, 8b
Arethusa[4] — see *Aethusa*
Arethusa[5], daughter of Nereus and *Doris*[1] <Hyg. *Fab*, pref.>, *63b*
Arethusa[6], wife of Thersander[4] <Quint. Smyr. 10.79-82>, *
Arethusa[7] [one of the dogs of Actaeon] <Hyg. *Fab.* 181>, *
Aretus[1], son of Nestor <Hom. *Od.* 3.414> and *Anaxibia*[4] <Apollod. *Bibl.* 1.9.9>, 27c
alternate parentage:
Nestor and *Eurydice*[7] (inferred because she is wife of Nestor) <Hom. *Od.* 3.453>
Aretus[2], son of Priam[1] <Apollod. *Bibl.* 3.12.5>, 43d
Aretus[3], soldier with King Deriades <Non. *Dion.* 26.250>, *
Aretus[4], killed by Clytius[3] <Ap. Rhod. *Arg.* 2.117>, *
Aretus[5], killed by Deriades <Non. *Dion.* 32.188>, *
Areus[1], son of Ampyx[1] <Paus. 7.18.5>, 47c
Areus[2], son of Acrostatus[1] <Paus. 3.6.4>, *

Areus[3], son of Acrostatus[2] <Paus. 3.6.6>, *
Argades, son of Ion[1] <Eur. *Ion* 1574> and *Helice*[1], 51b
Argalus [King of Sparta], son of Amyclas[1] and *Diomede*[2] <Paus. 3.1.3>, 47a
Arga(n)tho(n)e, wife of Rhesus[2] <Parth. *Love Stor.* 36.1>, 6b, 71b
Argeia[1], daughter of Adrastus[1] <*Cat. Wom., Frag. Hes.* frg. 192, Merk. & West> and *Amphithea*[1] <Apollod. *Bibl.* 1.9.13>, 30c
— and Polyneices <Eur. *Supp.* 133-38; named, Apollod. *Bibl.* 3.6.1>, 55c
Argeia[2], daughter of Oceanus and *Tethys* <Hyg. *Fab.* 143>, 50b
— and Inachus <Hyg. *Fab.* 143>, 55a
Argeia[3], daughter of Autesion[1] <Apollod. *Bibl.* 2.8.3>, 55c
— and Aristodemus <Herod. 6.52>, 60d
Argeius[1], son of Megapenthes[2] <Paus. 2.18.4>, 58c
Argeius[2], son of Licymnius <Apollod. *Bibl.* 2.7.7> and *Perimede*[2], 59c
Argeius[3], son of Pelops[1] <Schol. on Hom. *Od.* 22> and *Hippodameia*[1] <Schol. on Eur. 5>, *36a*
alternate parentage:
Pelops[1] and *Hegesandra* <Schol. on Hom. *Od.* 22>
— and *Hegesandra* <Pher. in *F. Gr. H.* 3 F 132>, 47a
Argeius[4] [centaur], offspring of Centaurus and a Magnesian Mare <Pind. *Pyth.* 2.50; named as centaur, Diod. Sic. 4.12.7>, 69c
alternate parentage:
Ixion and *Nephele*[1] <Diod. Sic. 4.69.5>
Argeius[5], suitor of *Penelope*[1] (from Dulichium) <Apollod. *Epit.* 7.27>, *
Argele, daughter of Thespius <Apollod. *Bibl.* 2.7.8> and *Megamede* <Apollod. *Bibl.* 2.4.10>, 50a
— and Heracles[1] <Apollod. *Bibl.* 2.7.8>, (50a)
Argennus [one of the Pans], son of Pan <Non. *Dion.* 14.75>, 64d
Arges (Acmonides) (Pyracmon) [thunderbolt] [one of the Uranian Cyclopes], son of Uranus and *Gaea* <Hes. *Theog.* 140>, 4b
Argestes [Northwest wind], son of Astraeus[1] and *Eos* <Hes. *Theog.* 378-79; named as wind, Ap. Rhod. *Arg.* 2.958>, 12b
Argiope[1], paramour of Philammon <Apollod. *Bibl.* 1.3.3>, 13b
Argiope[2], daughter of Teuthras <Diod. Sic. 4.33.12>, 60a
— and Telephus <Diod. Sic. 4.33.12>, (60a)
Argiope[3], daughter of Nilus <Schol. on Eur. *Phoen. Maid.* 5>, 68b
— and Agenor[1] <Pher. in *F. Gr. H.* 3 F 21>, 55b
Argiope[4] — see *Eurydice*[1]
Argiope[5], paramour of Branchus[2] <Apollod. *Epit.* 1.3>, *
Argius, son of Aegyptus[1] and [a Phoenician woman] <Apollod. *Bibl.* 2.1.5>, 58c
— and *Euippe*[7] <Apollod. *Bibl.* 2.1.5>, (58c)
Argus[1] [builder of the Argo], son of Arestor[1] <Ap. Rhod. *Arg.* 1.113> and *Mycene*, *55a*
alternate parentage:
Danaus[2] <Hyg. *Fab.* 14>
Dongus <Hyg. *Fab.* 14>
Polybus[7] and *Argeia*[7] <Hyg. *Fab.* 14>
Argus[2] [King of Argos], son of Zeus and *Niobe*[2] <Apollod. *Bibl.* 2.1.1>, 6c, *61b*
— and *Euadne*[2] <Apollod. *Bibl.* 2.1.2>, 71b
Argus[3] (Panoptes), son of Agenor[2] <Apollod. *Bibl.* 2.1.2>, 61d
alternate parentage:
autochthonous <Aesch. *Prom. Bound* 567>
— and *Ismene*[2] <*Frag. Hes.* frg. 294, Merk. & West>, 66b
Argus[4], son of Phrixus[1] <Apollod. *Bibl.* 1.9.1> and *Chalciope*[1] <Hyg. *Fab.* 21>, 26c
— and *Perimele*[3] <Ant. Lib. *Met.* 23.1>, 29c
Argus[5], son of Peiras[1] and *Callirhoe*[5] <Hyg. *Fab.* 145>, 61a
Argus[6] [one of the Pans], son of Pan <Non. *Dion.* 14.86>, 64d
Argus[7], son of Abas[6] (killed by Parthenopaeus) <Stat. *Theb.* 9. 758>, *
Argus[8], killed by Hypseus[7] <Stat. *Theb.* 8.445>, *
Argus[9], dog of Odysseus <Hom. *Od.* 17.290-94>, *
Argynnus, son of Copreus[2] and *Peisidice*[5] <Prop. 3.7.22 (Camps' note)>, 20d
— and Agamemnon <Athen. 13.603d>, 36b
— and Hymen(aeus)[1] <Athen. 13.603d>, 56c
Argyphia (Agryphia), wife of Aegyptus[1] <Apollod. *Bibl.* 2.1.5>, 58a, 57c
Ariadne, daughter of Minos I <Hom. *Od.* 11.322-23> and *Pasiphae*[1] <Apollod. *Bibl.* 3.1.2>, 53c
alternate parentage:
Minos I and *Crete*[1] <Apollod. *Bibl.* 3.1.2>
— and Dionysus <Hes. *Theog.* 947>, 56c
— and Glaucus[3] <Athen. 7.296b>, 62a
— and Oenarus <Plut. *Thes.* 20.1>, (53c)
— and Theseus <Plut. *Thes.* 19.1>, 51a
Arion[1] [horse], offspring of Poseidon and *Demeter* <Apollod. *Bibl.* 3.6.8>, 8c
alternate parentage:
Poseidon and one of the Erinyes <Schol. on Hom. *Il.* XXIII. 346>
Arion[2], [King of Miletus], paramour of *Theaneira* <Euphor. *F.H.G.* 4.335 frg. 21, Müller>, 23d
Arisbe[1], daughter of Merops[3] <Apollod. *Bibl.* 3.12.5>, 44c
— and Hyrtacus <Apollod. *Bibl.* 3.12.5>, (44c)
— and Priam[1] <Apollod. *Bibl.* 3.11.5>, (44c)
Arisbe[2] — see *Bateia*[2]
Arisbe[3], daughter of Macar(eus)[3] <Eust. on Hom. *Il.* 894>, 43c
— and Paris <Eust. on Hom. *Il.* 894>, 43c
Aristaechme, daughter of Hyllus[1] <*Cat. Wom., Hesiodi*, frg. 71A, Merk. & West (O.C.T.) and *Gr. Ehoiai, Frag. Hes.* frg. 251a, Merk. & West> and *Iole*, 60c
— and Polycaon[2] <*Gr. Ehoiai, Frag. Hes.* frg. 251a, Merk. & West>, 9d
Aristaeus[1] (Agreus[1]) (Nomus), son of Apollo and *Cyrene* <Pind. *Pyth.* 9.5-70>, 11a, *69a*
— and *Autonoe*[1] <Hes. *Theog.* 977>, 55d
Aristaeus[2], son of Paeon[6] <Pher. in *F. Gr. H.* 3 F 44>, *
Aristas, son of Parthaon[2] <Paus. 8.24.1>, 63d
Aristodeme[1], daughter of Priam[1] <Apollod. *Bibl.* 3.12.5>, 43d
Aristodeme[2], paramour of Asclepius <Paus. 2.10.3>, 19c
Aristodemus, son of Aristomachus[1] <Herod. 7.204>, 60d
— and *Argeia*[3] <Herod. 6.52>, 55c
Aristomache, daughter of Priam[1] <Paus. 10.26.1>, 43d
— and Critolaus <Paus. 10.26.1>, 42d
Aristomachus[1], son of Cleodaeus <Herod. 6.52>, 60c
Aristomachus[2], son of Talaus and *Lysimache*[1] <Apollod. *Bibl.* 1.9.13>, 30d
Arnacia — see *Penelope*[1]
Arnaea — see *Penelope*[1]
Arnaeus — see Irus[2]
Arne[1] (*Melanippe*[2]), daughter of Aeolus[2] <Diod. Sic. 4.67.4>, 18c
alternate parentage:
Aeolus[1] <Paus. 9.40.5>
— and Metapontus <Hyg. *Fab.* 186>, 19a
— and Poseidon <Diod. Sic. 4.67.4>, 8a
Arne[2], princess of Paros <Ovid *Met.* 7.464>, *
Arneus[1], father of *Megamede* <Apollod. *Bibl.* 2.4.10>, 50a
Arneus[2] [centaur], offspring of Centaurus and a Magnesian Mare <Pind. *Pyth.* 2.50; named as centaur, Ovid *Met.* 12.311>, 69d
alternate parentage:
Ixion and *Nephele*[1] <Diod. Sic. 4.69.5>
Arpoxais, son of Targitaus <Herod. 4.5>, 6d
Arrhon[1], son of Clymenus[1] <Paus. 9.37.1> and *Budeia*, 26c
Arrhon[2], son of Erymanthus[3] <Paus. 8.24.1>, *

Arripe, paramour (victim) of Tmolus <Ps.-Plut. *De Fluv.* 7.5>, 7c
Arsalte —see [fifty daughters of Danaus[1]] (alternate version)
Arsinoe[1], daughter of Leucippus[1] <*Cat. Wom., Frag. Hes.* frg. 50, Merk. & West> and *Philodice*, 25d
— and Apollo <*Cat. Wom., Frag. Hes.* frg. 50, Merk. & West>, 11a
Arsinoe[2] (*Alphesiboea*[1]), daughter of Phegeus[1] <Apollod. *Bibl.* 3.7.5>, 59b
— and Alcmaeon[1] <Apollod. *Bibl.* 3.7.5>, 32d
Arsinoe[3] — see *Arsippe*
Arsinoe[4] — see *Epeione*
Arsinoe[5] — see (Hyades) (alternate version)
Arsinoe[6], nurse of Orestes <Pind. *Pyth.* 11.17>, *
Arsinoe[7], daughter of Nicocreon <Ant. Lib. *Met.* 39>, *
Arsinous[1], father of *Hecamede* <Hom. *Il.* XI.625>, 27d
Arsinous[2], father of Chromius[4] and Ennomus <Apollod. *Epit.* 3.35>, *
Arsippe (*Arsinoe*[3]), daughter of Minyas <Nicand. in Ant. Lib. *Met.* 10> and *Euryanassa*[2], 20d
Artemis [goddess] [hunting], daughter of Zeus and *Leto* <Hes. *Theog.* 919>, 5c, *11b*
alternate parentage:
Demeter <Paus. 8.37.6>
Dionysus and *Isis* <Herod. 2.156>
Oceanus ("from whom all we gods proceed") <Hom. *Il.* XIV.202>
Asbolus[1] [centaur], offspring of Centaurus and a Magnesian Mare <Pind. *Pyth* 2.50; named as centaur, Hes. *Shield* 185>, 69d
alternate parentage:
Ixion and *Nephele*[1] <Diod. Sic. 4.69.5>
Asbolus[2] [one of the dogs of Actaeon] <Ovid *Met.* 3.221>, *
Ascalaphus[1] [King of Orchomenus], son of Ares and *Astyoche*[1] <Hom. *Il.* II.512, 513>, 7b
alternate parentage:
Lycus[10] and *Pernis* <Hyg. *Fab.* 97>
Ascalaphus[2], son of Acheron and *Gorgyra* <Apollod. *Bibl.* 1.5.3>, 50a
alternate parentage:
Acheron and *Orphnea* <Ovid. *Met.* 5.539>
Ascanius[1] (Ilus[4]) (Iulus[1]), son of Aeneas[1] <Plut. *Rom.* 2.1> and *Creusa*[2], 41c
— and *Roma*[3] <Plut. *Rom.* 2.1>, 13d
Ascanius[2] (Iulus[2]), son of Priam[1] <Apollod. *Bibl.* 3.12.5>, 43d
Ascanius[3], son of Aretaon <Apollod. *Epit.* 3.35>, *
Asclepius (Asculapius) (Paeon[3]) [healing], son of Apollo and *Coronis*[1] <*Hom. Hymn* 16 (to Asclepius), 1-3>, 11b, *19d*
alternate parentage:
Apollo and *Arsinoe*[1] <*Cat. Wom., Frag. Hes.* frg. 50, Merk. & West>
— and *Aristodeme*[2] <Paus. 3.10.3>, (19d)
— and *Epeione* <Paus. 2.29.1>, (19d)
— and *Xanthe*[1] <*Cat. Wom., Frag. Hes.* frg. 53, Merk. & West>, 72b
Ascra, paramour of Poseidon <Heg. in Paus. 9.29.1>, 8a
Asculapius — see Asclepius
[ash tree nymph], paramour of Silenus <Apollod. *Bibl.* 2.5.4>, 46c
Asia[1], daughter of Oceanus and *Tethys* <Hes. *Theog.* 359>, 51a
— and Iapetus <Apollod. *Bibl.* 1.2.4>, 16b
— and Prometheus[1] <Herod. 4.45.3>, 16a
Asia[2], daughter of Nereus and *Doris*[1] <Hyg. *Fab.* pref.>, *63b*
Asies, son of Cotys[1] <Herod. 4. 45.3> and *Halia*[3] <Dion. Hal. *Rom. Ant.* 1.27.3>, 51b
Asiexa, daughter of Oceanus and *Tethys* <Hes. *Theog.* 359>, 51a
Asine, daughter of Lacedaemon <Steph. Byz. "Asine"> and *Sparte*, 47b
— and Himerus[1] <Ps.-Plut. *De Fluv.* 17>, (47b)
Asius[1] [King of Phrygia], son of Dymas[1] and *Telecleia* <Eur. in Eust. on Hom. *Il.* 188>, 17d, *41d*
Asius[2] [King of Percote], son of Hyrtacus <Hom. *Il.* II.837> and *Arisbe*[1], 44c
Asius[3], son of Imbrasus <Virg. *Aen.* 10.124>, *
Asopis[1], daughter of Asopus and *Metope*[2] <Diod. Sic. 4.72.1>, 66a
Asopis[2], daughter of Thespius <Apollod. *Bibl.* 2.7.8> and *Megamede* <Apollod. *Bibl.* 2.4.10>, 50a
— and Heracles[1] <Apollod. *Bibl.* 2.7.8>, (50a)
Asopo — see [Muses] (alternate version)
Asopus [river], son of Oceanus and *Tethys* <Hes. *Theog.* 367-68; named as river, Apollod. *Bibl.* 3.12.6>, 66a
alternate parentage:
Poseidon and *Celusa* <Paus. 2.12.4>
Poseidon and *Pero* <Acus. frg. 22, Sturz>
Zeus and *Eurynome*[1] <Apollod. *Bibl.* 3.12.6>
— and *Metope*[2] <Apollod. *Bibl.* 3.12.6>, 54b
Asphodicus — see Amphidicus
Aspledon[1], son of Poseidon and *Mideia*[1] <Paus. 9.37.6>, 8c
alternate parentage:
Presbo and *Sterope*[6] <Schol. on Hom. *Il.* II.511>
Aspledon[2], son of Orchomenus[2] <*Cat. Wom., Frag. Hes.* frg. 77, Merk. & West>, 20d
Assaon — see *Niobe*[1] (alternate version)
Assaracus [King of Troy], son of Tros[1] <Hom. *Il.* XX.232> and *Callirhoe*[1] <Apollod. *Bibl.* 3.12.2>, 41a
alternate parentage:
Tros[1] and *Acallaris* <Dion. Hal. *Rom. Ant.* 1.62.2>
— and *Clytodora*[2] <Dion. Hal. *Rom. Ant.* 1.62.2>, 42d
— and *Hieromneme* <Apollod. *Bibl.* 3.12.2>, 71a
Astacus, son of Poseidon and *Olbia* <Steph. Byz. "Astacus">, 9b
Asteria[1], daughter of C(o)eus and *Phoebe*[1] <Hes. *Theog.* 409>, 12a
— and Perses[2] <Hes. *Theog.* 409-10>, (12a)
— and Zeus <Cic. *De Nat. Deor.* 3.42>, 5a
Asteria[2] — see *Asterope*[1]
Asteria[3] — see *Asterodia*[2]
Asteria[4], daughter of Hydis <Steph. Byz. "Hydissus">, 18d
— and Bellerophon(tes) <Steph. Byz. "Hydissus">, (18d)
Asteria[5], daughter of Teucer[2] and *Eune* <Tzetz. on Lyc. 447>, 23d
Asteria[6], daughter of Danaus[1] and *Atlantia* or *Phoebe* <Apollod. *Bibl.* 2.1.5>, 57d
— and Chaetus <Apollod. *Bibl.* 2.1.5>, (57d)
Asteria[7], daughter of Alcyoneus[1] <Eust. on Hom. *Il.* 776>, 4a
Asteria[8] [Amazon] <Diod. Sic. 4.16.3>, *
Asterie — *Astris*
Asterion[1] — see Asterius[1]
Asterion[2] — see Asterius[7]
Asterion[3] — see Asterius[5]
Asterion[4] — see Asterius[4]
Asterion[5], servant of Astraeus[1] <Non. *Dion.* 58-66>, *
Asterius[1] (Asterion[1]) [river], son of Oceanus and *Tethys* <Hes. *Theog.* 367-68; named as river, Paus. 2.17.2>, 51a
Asterius[2] — see Catreus
Asterius[3], son of Neleus[1] and *Chloris*[2] <*Cat. Wom., Frag. Hes.* frg. 33(a), Merk. & West>, 27c
Asterius[4] (Asterion[4]) [King of Crete], son of Tectamus and a daughter of Cretheus <Diod. Sic. 4.60.2>, 17a, *32d*
alternate parentage:
Minos I and *Androgeneia* <Non. *Dion.* 13.222-52>
— and *Europe*[1] <Diod. Sic. 4.60.2>, 53d
Asterius[5] (Asterion[3]) [Argonaut], son of Cometes[4] <Ap. Rhod. *Arg.* 1.35> and *Antigone*[4] <Hyg. *Fab.* 14>, *29d*
alternate parentage:
Hyperasius <Hyg. *Fab.* 14>
Asterius[6] [giant], son of Anax <Paus. 7.2.3>, 4a
Asterius[7] (Asterion[2]) [Minotaur], offspring of [the Cretan Bull] and *Pasiphae*[1] <Apollod. *Bibl.* 3.1.4>, 54c
Asterius[8] (Deucalion[3]) [Argonaut], son of Hyperasius <Ap. Rhod. *Arg.* 1.174> and *Hypso*, 61d

Asterius[9], son of Minos I and *Androgeneia* <Non. *Dion.* 13.221-25>, 54c
Asterius[10] — see [fifty sons of Aegyptus[1]] (alternate version)
Asterodeia[1], wife of Endymion <Paus. 5.1.4>, 15b
Asterodeia[2] (*Asteria*[3]) (*Asteropeia*[2]), daughter of Deion[1] and *Diomede*[3] <Apollod. *Bibl.* 1.9.4>, 22a
— and Phocus[1] <Tzetz. on Lyc. 53.939>, 23c
Asterodeia[3] (*Eurylyte*), daughter of Oceanus and *Tethys* <Schol. on Ap. Rhod. 3.242-44>, 51a
— paramour of Aeetes <Ap. Rhod. *Arg.* 3.243>, 14c
Asteropaeus, son of Pelegon <Hom. *Il.* XXI.140-41>, 67a
Asterope[1] (*Asteria*[2]) (*Sterope*[1]), daughter of Atlas <*Cat. Wom., Frag. Hes.* frg. 169, Merk. & West> and *Pleione* <Apollod. *Bibl.* 3.10.1>, 39a
— and Oenomaus[1] <Apollod. *Bibl.* 3.10.1>, 7c
Asterope[2], wife of Hippal(cy)mus[2] <Hyg. *Fab.* 97>, 18d
Asterope[3], daughter of Oceanus <Steph. Byz. "Acragantes"> and *Tethys*, 51a
— and Zeus <Steph. Byz. "Acragantes">, 5a
Asterope[4] (*Hesperia*[2]), daughter of Cebrenus <Apollod. *Bibl.* 3.12.5>, 67a
— and Aesacus <Apollod. *Bibl.* 3.12.5>, 44c
Asteropeia[1], daughter of Pelias[1] <Paus. 8.11.2> and *Anaxibia*[2], 28d
Asteropeia[2] — see *Asterodia*[2]
Astioche — see *Axioche*
Astraea, daughter of Zeus and *Themis*[1] <Hes. in Hyg. *Poet. Astr.* 2.25>, 6c, *10b*
Astraeus[1], son of Crius[1] and *Eurybia*[1] <Hes. *Theog.* 376>, 12a
— and *Eos* <Hes. *Theog.* 376>, (12a)
Astraeus[2] [satyr], son of Selinus <Non. *Dion.* 14.99> and [an ash tree nymph], 46c
Astraeus[3], brother of *Alcippe*[5] <Ps.-Plut. *De Fluv.* 21>, *
Astris (*Asterie*), daughter of Helios and *Ceto* <Non. *Dion.* 26.353-54>, 14a, *71b*
— and Hydaspes[1] <Non. *Dion.* 26.352-53>, 3b
Asty(a)dameia[1], daughter of Amyntor[1] <Apollod. *Bibl.* 2.7.8> and *Hippodameia*[3], 24d
alternate parentage:
Ormenus[1] <Diod. Sic. 4.37.4>
— and Heracles[1] <Apollod. *Bibl.* 2.7.8>, 60a
Asty(a)dameia[2] — see *Hippolyte*[2]
Asty(a)dameia[3], daughter of Strophius[1] <Schol. on Eur. *Or.* 33> and *Anaxibia*[1], 23c, *37a*
Asty(a)dameia[4], daughter of Pelops[1] <*Cat. Wom., Frag. Hes.* frg. 190, Merk. & West> and *Hippodameia*[1] <Apollod. *Bibl.* 2.4.5>, *36a*
— and Alcaeus[2] <*Cat. Wom., Frag. Hes.* frg. 190, Merk. & West>, 59c
Asty(a)dameia[5], daughter of Phorbas[2] <Ael. *Var. Narr.* 1.24> and *Hyrmine*, 68b
— and Caucon[1] <Ael. *Var. Narr.* 1.24>, 3b
Astyage(ia), daughter of Hypseus[1] <Diod. Sic. 4.69.3> and *Chlidanope*, 69a
— and Periphas[1] <Diod. Sic. 4.69.3>, 69a
Astyanax[1] (Scamandrius[1]), son of Hector[1] and *Andromache* <Hom. *Il.* VI.402>, 43c
Astyanax[2], son of Heracles[1] and *Epilais* <Apollod. *Bibl.* 2.7.8>, *50c*
Astyanax[3], descendant of Arcas[1] <Paus. 8.38.5>, *
Astybies, son of Heracles[1] and *Calametis* <Apollod. *Bibl.* 2.7.8>, *50c*
Astycrateia[1], daughter of Polyidus[1] <Paus. 1.43.5> and *Eurydameia*, 31d, *63d*
Astycrateia[2], daughter of Amphion[1] and *Niobe*[1] <Apollod. *Bibl.* 3.5.6>, 66d
Astygonus, son of Priam[1] <Apollod. *Bibl.* 3.12.5>, 43d
Astylus [centaur], offspring of Centaurus and a Magnesian Mare <Pind. *Pyth.* 2.50; named as centaur, Ovid *Met.* 12.307>, 69c
alternate parentage:
Ixion and *Nephele*[1] <Diod. Sic. 4.69.5>
Astymedusa — see *Medusa*[3]
Astynome[1] — see *Chryseis*[1]
Astynome[2], daughter of Amphion[1] and *Niobe*[1] <Hyg. *Fab.* 69>, 66d
Astynome[3], daughter of Talaus <Hyg. *Fab.* 70> and *Lysimache*[1], 30d
— and Ares <Ps.-Plut. 22.4>, 7b
— and Hipponous[1] <Hyg. *Fab.* 70>, 58c
Astynous[1], son of Phaethon[2] <Apollod. *Bibl.* 3.14.2>, 46c
Astynous[2], son of Proteaon <Hom *Il.* XV.454>, *
Astynous[3], killed by Diomedes[1] <Hom. *Il.* V.144>, *
Astyoche[1], daughter of Actor[6] <Hom. *Il.* II.512>, 26c
— and Ares <Hom. *Il.* II.512>, 7b
Astyoche[2], daughter of Phylas[4] <Apollod. *Bibl.* 2.7.8>, 60b
— and Heracles[1] <Hom. *Il.* II.659>, (60b)
Astyoche[3], daughter of Laomedon[1] and *Strym(n)o* <Apollod. *Bibl.* 3.12.3>, 42c
alternate parentage:
Laomedon[1] and *Leucippe*[8] <Apollod. *Bibl.* 3.12.3>
Laomedon[1] and *Placia* <Apollod. *Bibl.* 3.12.3>
— and Telephus <Quint. Smyr. 6.135>, 60a
Astyoche[4], daughter of Amphion[1] and *Niobe*[1] <Apollod. *Bibl.* 3.5.6>, 66c
Astyoche[5], daughter of Simoeis <Apollod. *Bibl.* 3.12.2>, 71a
— and Erichthonius[2] <Apollod. *Bibl.* 3.12.1>, 42a
Astyoche[6] — see *Anaxibia*[1]
Astyoche[7] (*Diomedeia*), wife of Iphiclus[2] <Hyg. *Fab.* 103 (she is called *Diomedeia*)>, 22c
Astyoche[8], mother of Pentheus[2] <Stat. *Theb.* 3.171>, *
Astyocheia — see *Anaxibia*[1]
Astyochus, son of Aeolus[2] and *Cyane*[1] <Hom. *Od.* 10.2-6; named, Diod. Sic. 5.8.1>, 18c
Astypalaea, daughter of Phoenix[2] and *Perimede*[3] <Paus. 7.4.2>, 54d
— and Poseidon <Apollod. *Bibl.* 2.7.1>, 8a
Atalanta[1], daughter of Iasus[4] and *Clymene*[4] <Apollod. *Bibl.* 3.9.2>, 64d, *20c*
alternate parentage:
Maenalus[2] <Eur. in Apollod. *Bibl.* 3.9.2>
— and Melanion <Apollod. *Bibl.* 3.9.2>, 63d
— and Meleager <Hyg. *Fab.* 99>, 17c
Atalanta[2], daughter of Schoeneus[1] <*Cat. Wom., Frag. Hes.* frgs. 72-76, Merk. & West>, 26d
— and Hippomenes[1] <Ovid *Met.* 10.560-680>, 9b
Atalantia, paramour of Danaus[1] <Apollod. *Bibl.* 2.1.5>, 57b
Atas, son of Priam[1] <Apollod. *Bibl.* 3.12.5>, 43d
Ate [ruin] [abstraction], offspring of *Eris* <Hes. *Theog.* 230>, *1a*
alternate parentage:
Zeus <Hom. *Il.* XIX.92>
Athamas[1] [King of Orchomenus], son of Aeolus[1] <*Cat. Wom., Frag. Hes.* frg. 10, Merk. & West> and *Enarete* <Apollod. *Bibl.* 1.7.3>, 26a
— and *Ino* <Apollod. *Bibl.* 1.9.1>, 55b
— and *Nephele*[2] <*Cat. Wom., Frag. Hes.* frg. 68, Merk. & West (she is called mother of Phrixus[1] and *Helle*)>, (26a)
— and *Themisto*[1] <Apollod. *Bibl.* 1.9.2>, 69b
Athamas[2], son of Minyas and *Phanosyra* <Schol. on Ap. Rhod. *Arg.* 1.230>, 20c
Athamas[3], son of Oenopion[1] <Paus. 7.4.6> and *Helice*[4], 56c
Athamas[4] — see [fifty sons of Aegyptus[1]] (alternate version)
Athamas[5], descendant of Athamas[1] <Paus. 7.3.3>, *
Athene (*Atrytone*) (*Pallas Athene*) (*Tritogeneia*[1]) [goddess] [wisdom], daughter of Zeus <Hom. *Il.* II.156-57> and *Metis*[1] <Hes. *Theog.* 888-89>; emerged from the head of Zeus <*Hom. Hymn* 28 (to *Athena*)>, 5d, *61b*
alternate parentage:

Zeus alone <Aesch. *Eum.* 736-38 ("no mother")>
Oceanus ("from whom all we gods proceed") <Hom. *Il.* XIV.202>
Poseidon and [Tritonian Lake] <Herod. 4.180>
— and Hephaestus <Apollod. *Bibl.* 3.14.6>, 7b
Athis, son of *Limnaee* <Ovid *Met.* 5.50>, *54a*
Atlantia, paramour of Danaus <Apollod. *Bibl.* 2.1.5>, 57b, 57c
(Atlantiades), children of Atlas and *Pleione* (see *Alcyone*[2], *Asterope*[1], *Calypso*[1], Canethus[1], *Celeano*[1], *Dione*[3], *Electra*[2], (Hyades), Hyas, *Maera*[2], *Maia*, *Merope*[1], *Taygete*), 35a-47b
Atlas [giant], son of Iapetus and *Clymene*[1] <Hes. *Theog.* 509>, 35b, *52a*
alternate parentage:
Iapetus and *Asia* <Apollod. *Bibl.* 1.2.4>
Poseidon and *Cleito*[1] <Plato *Crit.* 113d (in this version, twin brother of Eumelus[5])>
Uranus <Diod. Sic. 3.60.1>
— and *Hesperis*[1] <Diod. Sic. 4.27.2>, 18b
— and *Pleione* <Apollod. *Bibl.* 3.10.1>, 63a
Atrax, son of Peneius and *Bura* <Steph. Byz. "Atrax">, 68b, *51b*
Atreus [King of Mycenae], son of Pelops[1] <Apollod. *Bibl.* 2.4.6> and *Hippodameia*[1] <Hyg. *Fab.* 85>, 41a, *36b*
— and *Aerope*[1] <Eur. *Hel.* 391-92>, 52c
— and *Cleola* <Schol. on Eur. *Or.* 4>, 37b
— and *Pelopeia*[2] <Hyg. *Fab.* 88>, 39b
Atromus, son of Heracles[1] and *Stratonice*[3] <Apollod. *Bibl.* 2.7.8>, *50d*
Atropos [one of the Moirae], daughter of Zeus and *Themis*[1] <Hes. *Theog.* 901-05>, 6c
alternate parentage:
Nyx <Hes. *Theog.* 217-18>
Atrytone — see *Athene*
Atthis, daughter of Cranaus and *Pedias* <Apollod. *Bibl.* 3.14.5>, 16a
Attis, son of Agdistis and *Nana* <Paus. 7.17.5 (conceived when *Nana* became pregnant from the nuts of the almond tree that grew from the severed male organs of Agdistis)>, 70a
alternate version:
Calaus[2] <Herm. Col. in Paus. 7.17.5>
— and Agdistis <Paus. 7.17.9>, (70a)
— and *Sagaritis* <Ovid *Fast.* 4.225-33>, (70a)
Atymnius[1], son of Zeus and *Cassiopeia*[1] <Apollod. *Bibl.* 3.1.2>, 5b
Atymnius[2], son of Amisodorus <Hom. *Il.* XVI.317, 328>, *
Atymnius[3], son of Aemathion[3] and *Pegasis* <Quint. Smyr. 3.300-01>, *
Atys[1] [King of Lydia], son of Manes <Herod. 1.94> and *Callirhoe*[2], 51b
alternate parentage:
Cotys[1] and *Halia*[3] <Dion. Hal. *Rom. Ant.* 1.27.1>
— and *Callithea* <Dion. Hal. *Rom. Ant.* 1.27.2>, (51b)
Atys[2], son of Croesus <Herod. 1.34>, *
Atys[3], friend of Iulus[7] <Virg. *Aen.* 5.567-69>, *
Atys[4], killed by Tydeus[2] <Stat. *Theb.* 8.554-86>, *
Auge[1], daughter of Aleus and *Neaera*[2] <Apollod. *Bibl.* 3.9.1>, 63d
— and Heracles[1] <*Cat. Wom., Frag. Hes.* frg. 165, Merk. & West>, 60a
— and Teuthras <Apollod. *Bibl.* 3.9.1>, (63d)
Auge[2] [one of the hours], daughter of Zeus and *Themis*[1] <Hyg. *Fab.* 183>, 6d
Augeias [King of Elis] [Argonaut], son of Helios <Apollod. *Bibl.* 2.5.5> and *Nausidame* <Hyg. *Fab.* 14>, 14b, *63d*
alternate parentage:
Eleius[1] <Paus. 5.1.9>
Phorbas[2] <Apollod. *Bibl.* 2.5.5>
Poseidon <Apollod. *Bibl.* 2.5.5>
Auges, son of Helios <Non. *Dion.* 14.44-45>, 14c
Aulis, daughter of Ogygus[1] <Paus. 9.19.5>, 16a
Aulon, son of Tlesimenus <Paus. 3.12.9>, 64d
Aura[1], daughter of Lelas and *Periboea*[7] <Non. *Dion.* 48.241-48>, *62b*
— and Dionysus <Non. *Dion.* 48.621-44>, 56c
Aura[2] [mare of Pheidolas] <Paus. 6.13.9>, *
Aura[3] [one of the dogs of Actaeon] <Hyg. *Fab.* 181>, *
Auson, son of Odysseus and *Calypso*[1] <Suid. *Lex.* "Ausonion">, 13c, *40b*
alternate parentage:
Odysseus and *Circe* <Eust. on Hom. *Od.* 1379>
Autesion[1] [King of Thebes], son of Tisamenus[2] <Paus. 9.5.8>, 55c
Autesion[2], killed by Corymbasus <Non. *Dion.* 28.92-112>, *
Autochte, daughter of Perseus[1] <Tzetz. on Lyc. 494> and *Andromeda*, 59d
— and Aegeus[1] <Tzetz. on Lyc. 494>, 51a
Autochthon — see [five sets of twins]
Autodice —see [fifty daughters of Danaus[1]] (alternate version)
Autolaus, son of Arcas[1] <Paus. 8.4.2>, 62c
Autolycus[1], son of Hermes <Apollod. *Bibl.* 1.9.16> and *Chione*[1] <Ovid *Met.* 11.312>, 46b, *13a*
alternate parentage:
Hermes and *Philonis*[1] <Pher in *F. Gr. H.* 3 F 120>
Hermes and *Stilbe*[2] <Schol. on Hom. *Il.* X.266-67>
Daedalion <Paus. 8.4.6>
— and *Amphithea*[2] <Hom. *Od.* 19.414>, (13a)
— and *Mestra* <Ovid *Met.* 8.738>, 34c
— and *Neaera*[2] <Paus. 8.4.6>, 62d
Autolycus[2], son of Deimachus[5] <Ap. Rhod. *Arg.* 2.954>, *
Autolyte, paramour of Metapontus <Diod. Sic. 4.67.5>, 19a
Automate, daughter of Danaus[1] and *Europe*[3] <Apollod. *Bibl.* 2.1.5>, 57c, 57d
— and Architeles[1] <Paus. 7.1.3>, 17b
— and Busiris[2] <Apollod. *Bibl.* 2.1.5>, (57c)
Automedusa, daughter of Alcathous[1] <Apollod. *Bibl.* 2.4.11> and *Euaechme*[1], 40a
— and Iphicles <Apollod. *Bibl.* 2.4.11>, 59d
Autonoe[1], daughter of Cadmus <Apollod. *Bibl.* 3.4.2> and *Harmonia*[1] <Hes. *Theog.* 977>, 55d
— and Aristaeus[1] <Hes. *Theog.* 977>, 69a
Autonoe[2], daughter of Danaus[1] and *Polyxo*[2] <Apollod. *Bibl.* 2.1.5>, (57c)
— and Eurylochus[2] <Apollod. *Bibl.* 2.1.5>, 57c
Autonoe[3], daughter of Nereus and *Doris*[1] <Hes. *Theog.* 258>, *63b*
Autonoe[4], daughter of Peireus <Apollod. *Bibl.* 2.7.8>, 60b
— and Heracles[1] <Apollod. *Bibl.* 2.7.8>, (60b)
Autonoe[5], servant of *Penelope* <Hom. *Od.* 18.182>, *
Auxo[1] — see *Dike*
Auxo[2] — see (Charites) (alternate version)
Axenus [river], son of Oceanus and *Tethys* <Hes. *Theog.* 367-68; named as river, Hyg. *Fab.* pref.>, 51a
Axioche (*Astioche*), paramour of Pelops[1] <Schol. on Pind. *Olym.* 1.144>, 39b, 40a, 41a
Axion[1], son of Priam[1] <Paus. 10.27.1>, 43d
Axion[2], son of Phegeus[1] <Paus. 8.24.10>, 59b
Axiothea — see *Pronoea*
Axius [river], son of Oceanus and Tethys <Hes. *Theog.* 367-68; named as river, Hom. *Il.* II.850>, 67a
— and *Periboea*[6] <Hom. *Il.* XXI.143>, (67a)
Azaes — see [five sets of twins]
Azan [King of Azania, Arcadia], son of Arcas[1] and *Erato*[2] <Paus. 10.9.3>, 62c
Azeus, son of Clymenus[1] <Paus. 9.37.1> and *Budeia*, 26c

Babylon, son of Belus[1] and *Anchinoe*[1] <Phil. Bybl. in *F.H.G.* 3. 575 frg. 17, Müller>, 58b
Babylonian Sibyl — see *Sabbe*
Babys, son of Oeagrus and *Calliope* <Zen. *Soph.* 3.30 (inferred

because he is called brother of Marsyas)>, *6a*
Bacchus — see Dionysus
alternate parentage:
Dionysus <Non. *Dion.* 48.954>
Balanus [oak-nut tree], daughter of Oxylus[3] and *Hamadryas* <Athen. 3.78b>, 71d
Balius[1] [one of Achilles' horses], offspring of Zephyrus and *Podarge* <Hom. *Il.* XVI.145-47>, 12a, *3b*
Balius[2] [one of the dogs of Actaeon] <Hyg. *Fab.* 181>, *
Bargasus, son of Heracles[1] and *Barge* <Steph. Byz. "Bargasa">, 60b
Barge, paramour of Heracles[1] <Steph. Byz. "Bargasa">, 60b
Basilus, son of Lyrcus[1] and *Molpadia*[1] <Parth. *Love Stor.* 1.3>, 61a, *56d*
Bateia[1] (*Nicostrate*[2]), wife of Oebalus[1] <Apollod. *Bibl.* 3.10.4>, 47a
Bateia[2] (*Arisbe*[2]) (*Myrine*[2]), daughter of Teucer[1] <Hellan. in *F. Gr. H.* 4 F 24>, 70b
— and Dardanus[1] <Hellan. in *F. Gr. H.* 4 F 24>, 42a
Bayard [stallion], offspring of Boreas and [Sithonian Harpy] <Non. *Dion.* 37.157-59>, 12b
[bear], mate of *Polyphonte* <Ant. Lib. *Met.* 31.1>, 71b
Bebryce — see *Bryce*
Bebryclus (Bebryx), father of *Pyrene*[1] <Sil. Ital. 3.420 ff.>, 60d
Bebryx — see Bebryclus
Bellerophon(tes) (Hipponous[2]) [King of Lycia], son of Glaucus[1] <Hom. *Il.* VI.155> and *Eurynome*[2] <Apollod. *Bibl.* 1.9.3 (mother is called *Eurymede*)>, 18d
alternate parentage:
Poseidon <*Cat. Wom., Frag. Hes.* frg. 43a, Merk. & West> and *Eurynome*[2] <Hyg. *Fab.* 57>
Poseidon and *Mestra* <Schol. on Hom. *Il.* VI.191>
— and *Asteria*[4] <Steph. Byz. "Hydissus">, (18d)
— and *Philonoe* <Tzetz. on Lyc. 17>, (18d)
Belus[1], son of Poseidon <Apollod. *Bibl.* 2.1.4> and *Libya*[1] <Aesch. *Supp.* 319>, 8c, *57b*
— and *Anchinoe*[1] <Apollod. *Bibl.* 2.1.4>, 68a
Belus[2] (Mutto) [King of Tyre], father of *Dido* <Virg. *Aen.* 1.620>, Pygmalion[2] <Virg. *Aen.* 1.350>, and *Anna Perenna* <Ovid *Fast.* 3.523-60>, 41d
Belus[3], son of Alcaeus[3] <Herod. 1.7>, 61c
Belus[4] [King of Babylon], father of Theias <Ant. Lib. *Met.* 34>, *
Belus[5] — see Heracles[7]
Benthesicyme, daughter of Poseidon and *Amphitrite* <Apollod. *Bibl.* 3.15.4>, *63b*
Beres, son of Macedon <Steph. Byz. "Beres"> and *Oreithyia*[2], 15a
Beroe[1] (*Amymone*[2]), daughter of Adonis and *Aphrodite* <Non. *Dion.* 41.143-84 (mother is called *Cythereia*)>, 11c
— and Poseidon <Non. *Dion.* 43.394-98>, 8a
Beroe[2], daughter of Oceanus <Virg. *Geo.* 4.339>, and *Tethys*, 51b
Beroe[3], daughter of Nereus and *Doris*[1] <Hyg. *Fab.* pref.>, 63b
Beroe[4], wife of Doryclus[4] <Virg. *Aen.* 5.619-20>, *
Beroe[5], nurse of *Semele* <Ovid *Met.* 3.281>, *
Bia [force], daughter of Pallas[1] and *Styx* <Hes. *Theog.* 385>, 12a
Biadice — see *Demodice*
Bianor — see Ocnus
Biantes — see Promachus[1]
Bias[1] [King of Argos], son of Amythaon[1] and *Idomene* <Apollod. *Bibl.* 1, 9, 11>, 30c
alternate parentage:
Amythaon[1] and *Aglaia*[5] <Diod. Sic. 4.68.3>
Rhodope[2] <Schol. Theo. 3.43>
— and *Lysippe*[1] <Apollod. *Bibl.* 2.2.2>, 57d
— and *Pero*[1] <*Cat. Wom., Frag. Hes.* frg. 33, Merk. & West>, 27d
Bias[2], son of Priam[1] <Apollod. *Bibl.* 3.12.5>, 43d
Bias[3], son of Melampus[1] and *Iphianeira*[2] <Diod. Sic. 4.68.4-5>, 32d
Bias[4], father of Dardanus[2] and Laogonus <Hom. *Il.* XX.460>, *
Bias[5], suitor of *Penelope*[1] (from Dulichium), Apollod. *Epit.* 7.27>, *
Bias[6], killed by Pylas <Apollod. *Bibl.* 3.15.5>, *
Biblis — see *Byblis*
Bienor[1] [centaur], offspring of Centaurus and a Magnesian Mare <Pind. *Pyth.* 2.50; named as centaur, Ovid *Met.* 12.345>, 69c
alternate parentage:
Ixion and *Nephele*[1] <Diod. Sic. 4.69.5>
Bienor[2], killed by Agamemnon <Hom. *Il.* XI.93>, *
Bienor[3], son of Pyrnus <Val. Flac. 3.112>, *
Bisaltes [King of Thrace], father of *Theophane* <Hyg. *Fab.* 188>, 9b
Biston, son of Ares and *Callirhoe*[7] <Steph. Byz. "Bistonia">, 7a
Bithynia, daughter of Zeus and *Thrace* <Steph. Byz. "Bithynia">, 55a
Bitias[1], son of Alcanor[1] and *Iaera*[2] <Virg. *Aen.* 9.672-73>, 41d
— and *Dido* <Virg. *Aen.* 1.739>, (41d)
Bitias[2], son of *Cydippe*[4] <Hyg. *Fab.* 254>, *
Boagrius [river], son of Oceanus and *Tethys* <Hes. *Theog.* 367-68; named as river, Hom. *Il.* II.535>, 67a
Boeotia, paramour of Hyas <Hyg. *Poet. Astr.* 2.21>, 44b
(Boeotian Muses), daughters of Uranus and *Gaea*, 6b — see *Aoede*, *Melete*, *Mneme*
Boeotus[1], son of Poseidon and *Arne*[1] <Diod. Sic. 4.67.4>, 8a, *18c*
alternate parentage:
Poseidon and *Antiope*[10] <Hyg. *Fab.* 157>
Boeotus[2], son of Itonus[1] and *Melanippe*[6] <Paus. 9.1.1 (he might be the same as Boeotus[1], since both are said to be the source of the name of the Boeotian people <Paus. 9.1.1; Diod. Sic. 4.67.6>, but Bell, *Women,* "Melanippe (3)," p. 298, suggests they are different persons)>, 16a
Bolbe, paramour of Heracles[1] <Athen. 8.334e>, 60b
Boline, paramour of Apollo <Paus. 7.23.3>, 11a
Boreas[1] [North wind], son of Astraeus[1] and *Eos* <Hes. *Theog.* 379>, 12b
— and [Mares of Erichthonius[2]] <Hom. *Il.* XX.220-28>, (12b)
— and *Oreithyia*[1] <Herod. 7.189>, 51a
— and *Pitys* <*Geopon.* 11, 12>, (12b)
— and [Sithonian Harpy] <Non. *Dion.* 37.157-59>, (12b)
Boreas[2] [one of the dogs of Actaeon] <Hyg. *Fab.* 181>, *
Borus[1], son of Perieres[1] <Apollod. *Bibl.* 3.13.1> and *Gorgophone*[1], 25a
— and *Polydora*[1] <Hom. *Il.* XVI.175-79>, 22d, 24c
Borus[2], son of Penthilus[2] <Paus. 2.18.8>, 27d
Borus[3], father of Phaestus[2] <Hom. *Il.* V.43> *
Borythenes, father of paramour of Zeus <Herod. 4.5>, 6d
Braesia, daughter of Cinyras[1] and *Metharme* <Apollod. *Bibl.* 3.14.3>, 11c
Branchus[1], son of Smicrus <Con. *Narr.* 33>, 11a
— and Apollo <Con. *Narr.* 33>, (11a)
Branchus[2], paramour of *Argiope*[5] <Apollod. *Epit.* 1.3>, *
Brangas, son of Strymon <Con. *Narr.* 4>, 72a
Bretannus, father of *Celtine* <Parth. *Love Stor.* 30.1>, 60b
Briareus (Aegaeon[1]) [one of the Hecatoncheires], son of Uranus and *Gaea* <Hes. *Theog.* 149>, 4b
— and *Cymopoleia* <Hes. *Theog.* 819>, 9c
Brimo — see *Hecate*
Briseis[1] (*Hippodameia*[4]), daughter of Brise(u)s <Hom. *Il.* I.184, 392>, 24c
— and Achilles <Hom. *Il.* I.184, 392>, (24c)
— and Agamemnon <Hom. *Il.* I.319-56>, 36a
— and Mynes <Hom. *Il.* XIX.296>, 51d
Briseis[2] (*Cressida* in medieval myth), daughter of Calchas <Ben. *Le Roman de Troie* 4 (she is called Briseida)>, 69d
— and Diomedes[1] <Ben. *Le Roman de Troie* 20-21>, 17d

— and Troilus <Ben. *Le Roman de Troie* 8>, 43d
Brise(u)s, father of *Briseis*[1] <Hom. *Il.* I.392>, 24c, 36a, 51d
Britomartis (*Aphaea*) (*Dictynna*) (*Laphria*), daughter of Zeus and *Carme* <Ant. Lib. *Met.* 40.1>, 5b
— and Minos I <Paus. 2.30.3>, 54c
Bromie[1] — see (Hyades) (alternate version)
Bromie[2] [one of the Bacchae] <Non. *Dion.* 21.88>, *
Bromius[1] — see Dionysus
Bromius[2], son of Aegyptus[1] and *Caliadne* <Apollod. *Bibl.* 2.1.5>, 57d
— and *Erato*[3] <Apollod. *Bibl.* 2.1.5>, (57d)
Bromus [centaur], offspring of Centaurus and a Magnesian Mare <Pind. *Pyth.* 2.50; named as centaur, Ovid *Met.* 12.459>, 69c
alternate parentage:
Ixion and *Nephele*[1] <Diod. Sic. 4.69.5>
Brontes[1] [thunder] [one of the Uranian Cyclopes], son of Uranus and *Gaea* <Hes. *Theog.* 140>, 4b
Brontes[2], killed by Jason <Val. Flac. 3.152>, *
Broteas[1], son of Tantalus[1] <Paus. 3.22.4> and *Dione*[3], 41a
alternate parentage:
Tantalus[1] and *Euryanassa*[1] <Schol. on Eur. *Or.* 5>
Broteas[2], brother of Ammon[2] <Ovid *Met.* 5.107>, *
Broteas[3], fought the centaurs <Ovid *Met.* 12.262>, *
Broteas[4], a hunter <Apollod. *Epit.* 2.2 (may be same as Broteas[1], per Frazier's note)>, *
Bryce (*Bebryce*), daughter of Danaus[1] and *Polyxo*[3] <Apollod. *Bibl.* 2.1.5>, 58c
— and Chthonius[2] <Apollod. *Bibl.* 2.1.5>, (58c)
Bucetus — see Echetus (alternate version)
Bucolion[1] [King of Arcadia], son of Holaeas <Paus. 8.5.7>, 62c
Bucolion[2], son of Laomedon[1] <Hom. *Il.* VI.21 ff.> and *Calybe*[1] <Apollod. *Bibl.* 3.12.3>, 42c
— and *Abarbarea* <Hom. *Il.* VI.22>, (42c)
Bucolion[3], son of Lycaon[1] <Apollod. *Bibl.* 3.8.1>, 62b
Bucolion[4], killed by Eurypylus[1] <Quint. Smyr. 6.615>, *
Bucolus[1], son of Hippocoon[1] <Apollod. *Bibl.* 3.10.5>, 47c
Bucolus[2], son of Heracles[1] and *Marse* <Apollod. *Bibl.* 2.7.8>, *50b*
Bucolus[3] — see Daphnis[1]
Budeia (*Byzyge*), wife of Clymenus[1] <Eust. on Hom. *Il.* 1076.26>, 26d
Buleus, son of Heracles[1] and *Elachia* <Apollod. *Bibl.* 2.7.8>, *50d*
Bunicus — see Bunomus
Bunomus (Bunicus), son of Paris and *Helen*[1] <Dict. Cret. 5.5>, 43c
Bunus [King of Corinth], son of Hermes and *Alcidameia* <Paus. 2.3.8>, 46a
Buphagus — see Oxeater
Bura, daughter of Ion[1] and *Helice*[1] <Paus. 7.25.5>, 51b
— and Peneius <Steph. Byz. "Atrax">, 68b
Busiris[1] [King of Egypt], son of Poseidon and *Lysianassa*[1] <Apollod. *Bibl.* 2.5.11>, 8d
alternate parentage:
Poseidon and *Anippe* <Plut. *Gr. and Rom. Par. Stor.* 38>
Busiris[2], son of Aegyptus[1] <Apollod. *Bibl.* 2.1.5>, 57c
— and *Automate* <Apollod. *Bibl.* 2.1.5>, (57c)
Butes[1] [Argonaut], son of Teleon <Ap. Rhod. *Arg.* 4.912-13> and *Zeuxippe*[4] <Hyg. *Fab.* 14>, *53a*
— and *Aphrodite* <Diod. Sic. 4.83.1>, 5a
Butes[2], son of Boreas[1] <Diod. Sic. 5.50.2>, 12b
— and *Coronis*[4] <Diod. Sic. 5.50.5>, (12b)
Butes[3], son of Pandion I and *Zeuxippe*[1] <Apollod. *Bibl.* 3.14.8>, 49a
alternate parentage:
Poseidon <*Cat. Wom., Frag. Hes.* frg. 223, Merk. & West>
— and *Chthonia*[1] <Apollod. *Bibl.* 3.15.1>, 50b
Butes[4], son of Poseidon <*Cat. Wom., Frag. Hes.* frg. 223, Merk. & West>, 9d
Butes[5], armor-bearer for Anchises <Virg. *Aen.* 9.647-49>, *
Butes[6], killed by *Camilla* <Virg. *Aen.* 11.689-91>, *
Butes[7], killed by Dares <Virg. *Aen.* 5.372>, *
Butes[8], killed by Haemon[1] <Stat. *Theb.* 8.484>, *
Byblis (*Biblis*), daughter of Miletus and *Cyanea* <Ovid *Met.* 9.450-54>, *68a*
alternate parentage:
Miletus and *Tragasia* <Nicaenetus in Parth. *Love Stor.* 11.2>
Byzas, son of Poseidon and *Ceroessa* <Steph. Byz. "Byzantium">, 8c, *55b*
— and *Phidaleia* <Hesyc. Mil. in *F.H.G.* 4.149 frg. 17, Müller>, (8c), (55b)
Byzyge — see *Budeia*

Caanthus, son of Oceanus <Paus. 9.10.5> and *Tethys*, 51b
Cabeira, daughter of Proteus[1] and *Anchinoe*[2] <Steph. Byz. "Cabiria">, 9c
— and Hephaestus <Acus. in Strab. 10.3.21>, 7b
(Cabeiri), children of Ca(d)millus <Acus. in Strab. 10.3.21>, 9c
alternate parentage:
Hephaestus and *Cabeira* <Pher. in *F. Gr. H.* 3 F 48>
Cabye — see *Cambyse*
Caca, daughter of Hephaestus <Serv. on Virg. *Aen.* 8.190>, 7d
Cacus [monster], son of Hephaestus <Virg. *Aen.* 8.195-99 (father is called Vulcan)>, 7d
[Cadmean Dragon], offspring of Ares <Apollod. *Bibl.* 3.4.1>, 7d
alternate parentage:
Ares and *Tilphose* <Schol. on Eur. *Ant.* 126>
Ca(d)millus, son of Hephaestus and *Cabeira* <Acus. in Strab. 10. 3.21>, 7b, *9c*
Cadmus [King of Thebes], son of Agenor[1] <Pher. in *F. Gr. H.* 3 F 21> and *Telephassa* <Apollod. *Bibl.* 3.1.1>, 55a
alternate parentage:
Agenor[1] and *Argiope*[3] <Pher. in *F. Gr. H.* 3 F 21>
Phoenix[2] and *Argiope*[3] <Schol. on Ap. Rhod. *Arg.* 3.1186>
— and *Harmonia*[1] <Hes. *Theog.* 975-76>, 7a
Caecinus [river], son of Oceanus and *Tethys* <Hes. *Theog.* 367-68; named as river, Paus. 6.6.5>, 51b
Caeculus, son of Hephaestus <Virg. *Aen.* 7.678-81>, 7d
Caeneus[1] — see *Caenis*/Caeneus[1]
Caeneus[2], son of Coronus[3] <Apollod. *Bibl.* 1.9.16>, 8a
Caeneus[3], killed by Haemus <Stat. *Theb.* 7.644>, *
Caeneus[4], killed by Turnus <Virg. *Aen.* 9.573>, *
Caenis/Caeneus[1], daughter/son of Elatus[2] <Ovid *Met.* 12.190> and *Hippeia*, 8a
alternate parentage:
as *Caenis*, daughter of Atrax <Ant. Lib. *Met.* 17.4>
— and Poseidon <*Cat. Wom., Frag. Hes.* frg. 87, Merk. & West>, (8a)
Caicus[1] [river], son of Oceanus and *Tethys* <Hes. *Theog.* 343>, 51b
Caicus[2], comrade of Aeneas <Virg. *Aen.* 1.183>, *
Caicus[3], killed by Lexanor <Val. Flac. 6.686-88>, *
Caistrus — see Cayst(ri)us
Calais [Argonaut], son of Boreas[1] and *Oreithyia*[1] <Acus. in *F. Gr. H.* 2 F 30>, 12b
Calametis, daughter of Thespius <Apollod. *Bibl.* 2.7.8> and *Megamede* <Apollod. *Bibl.* 2.4.10>, 50a
— and Heracles[1] <Apollod. *Bibl.* 2.7.8>, (50a)
Calamus, son of Maeandrus <Serv. on Virg. *Ecl.* 5.48>, 67b
— and Carpus <Serv. on Virg. *Ecl.* 5.48>, 12a
Calaus[1] — see Callileon
Calaus[2] — see Attis
Calchas, son of Thestor[1] <Hom. *Il.* I.69>, 69b
Calchinia, daughter of Leucippus[3] <Paus. 2.5.7>, 61c
— and Poseidon <Paus. 2.5.5>, 8b
Cale — see *Thaleia*[2]

Caletor[1], son of Clytius[1] <Hom. *Il.* XV.419-20>, 42c
Caletor[2], father of Aphareus[2] <Hom. *Il.* XIII.541>, *
Caliadne, paramour of Aegyptus[1] <Apollod. *Bibl.* 2.1.5>, 57c, 58a
Callianassa, daughter of Nereus <Hom. *Il.* XVIII.44> and *Doris*[1], *64a*
Callianeira, daughter of Nereus <Hom. *Il.* XVIII.43> and *Doris*[1], *64a*
Calliarus, son of Odeodochus and *Laonome*[3] <Steph. Byz. "Calliarus">, 15c
Callias, son of Temenus[1] <Apollod. *Bibl.* 2.8.5>, 60d
Callicarpus, son of Aristaeus[1] <Diod. Sic. 4.82.4>, 69a
Callidice[1] [Queen of Thesprotia], paramour of Odysseus <Apollod. *Epit.* 7.35>, 13c
Callidice[2], daughter of Danaus[1] and *Crino* <Apollod. *Bibl.* 2.1.5>, 57d
— and Pandion[4] <Apollod. *Bibl.* 2.1.5>, (57d)
Callidice[3], daughter of Celeus[1] <*Hom. Hymn* 2 (to *Demeter*) 108> and *Metaneira*, 46b
Callileon (Calaus[1]), son of Thyestes[1] <Apollod. *Epit.* 2.13> and *Laodameia*[5] <Schol. on Eur. *Or.* 4>, 39b
Calliope [epic poetry] [one of the Muses], daughter of Zeus and *Mnemosyne* <Hes. *Theog.* 79>, 6a
— and Apollo <Asclep. in *F. Gr. H.* 12 F 6>, 11a
— and Oeagrus <Apollod. *Bibl.* 3.1.2>, (6a)
— and Strymon[1] <Apollod. *Bibl.* 1.3.4>, 71b
Callipolis, son of Alcathous[1] <Paus. 1.42.7> and *Euaechme*[1], 40a
Callirhoe[1], daughter of Scamander[1] <Apollod. *Bibl.* 3.12.2> and *Idaea*[1], 70b
— and Tros[1] <Apollod. *Bibl.* 3.12.2>, 42a
Callirhoe[2], daughter of Oceanus and *Tethys* <Hes. *Theog.* 351>, 51b
— and Chrysaor <Hes. *Theog.* 979-980>, 2b
— and Manes <Dion. Hal. *Rom. Ant.* 1.27>, (51b)
— and Nilus <Serv. on Virg. *Aen.* 4.250>, 68a
Callirhoe[3], daughter of Lycus[11] <Plut. *Gr. and Rom. Par. Stor.* 23>, 17d
— and Diomedes[1] <Plut. *Gr. and Rom. Par. Stor.* 23>, (17d)
Callirhoe[4], daughter of Achelous <Apollod. *Bibl.* 3.7.5> and *Perimede*[1], 65a, *29a*
— and Alcmaeon[1] <Apollod. *Bibl.* 3.7.5>, 32d
Callirhoe[5], wife of Peiras[1] <Hyg. *Fab.* 145>, 61a
Callirhoe[6], daughter of Maeandrus <Steph. Byz. "Alabanda">, 67b
— and Car[1] <Steph. Byz. "Alabanda">, 61a
Callirhoe[7], daughter of Nestus <Steph Byz. "Bistonia">, 7a
— and Ares <Steph. Byz. "Bistonia">, (7a)
Callirhoe[8], paramour of Coresus <Paus. 7.21.1>, *
Callirhoe[9], daughter of Phocus[4] <Plut. *Love Stor.* 4 .774-75>, *
Callisto[1] (*Helice*[2]) (*Themisto*[3]), daughter of Lycaon[1] <*Cat. Wom., Frag. Hes.* frg. 163, Merk. & West>, 62a
alternate parentage:
Ceteus[1] <Pher. in *F. Gr. H.* 3 F 157>
Nycteus[2] <Apollod. *Bibl.* 3.8.2>
— and Zeus <Eur. *Helen* 375-76>, 5b
Callisto[2] (*Phace*), daughter of Laertes and *Anticleia*[1] <Athen. 4. 158c (inferred because she is called sister of Odysseus)>, 5c, *13c*
Callisto[3], daughter of Celtius and *Stilbe*[2] <Schol. on Eur. *Or.* 1646>, *
Callisto[4], a priestess at Troy <Tzetz. *Posthom.* 776>, *
Callithea, daughter of Choraeus <Dion. Hal. *Rom. Ant.* 1.27.2>, 51b
— and Atys[1] <Dion. Hal. *Rom. Ant.* 1.27.2>, (51b)
Callithoe, daughter of Celeus[1] <*Hom. Hymn* 2 (to *Demeter*), 109> and *Metaneira*, 46b
Calus — see Perdix[2]
Calybe[1], paramour of Laomedon[1] <Apollod. *Bibl.* 3.12.3>, 42c
Calybe[2], priestess of *Juno* <Virg. *Aen.* 7.419-20>, *
Calybe[3] [one of the Bacchae] <Non. *Dion.* 29.270>, *
Calyce[1], daughter of Aeolus[1] <*Cat. Wom., Hesiodi* frg. 10(a), Merk. & West (O.C.T.)> and *Enarete* <Apollod. *Bibl.* 1.7.3>, 27a
— and Aethlius <*Cat. Wom., Hesiodi* frg. 10(a), Merk. & West (O.C.T.)>, 15b
Calyce[2], daughter of Hecaton <Hyg. *Fab.* 157>, 8b
— and Poseidon <Hyg. *Fab.* 157>, 8b
Calyce[3], one of the nurses of Dionysus <Non. *Dion.* 14.222>, *
Calydon[1] [King of Calydon], son of Aetolus[1] <*Cat. Wom., Hesiodi* frg. 10(a), Merk. & West (O.C.T.)> and *Pronoe*[1] <Apollod. *Bibl.* 1.7.7>, 15b
— and *Aeolia* <Apollod. *Bibl.* 1.7.7>, 31a
Calydon[2], son of Thestius <Ps.-Plut. *De Fluv.* 22.4> and *Eurythemis(te)*, 15d
Calydon[3], son of Ares and *Astynome*[3] <Ps.-Plut. *De Fluv.* 22.4>, 7b
Calypso[1], daughter of Atlas <Hom. *Od.* 7.245> and *Pleione* <Hyg. *Fab.* pref.>, 40b
— and Odysseus <Hom. *Od.* 7.245>, 13c
Calypso[2], daughter of Oceanus and *Tethys* <Hes. *Theog.* 359>, 51b
Calypso[3], daughter of Nereus and *Doris*[1] <Apollod. *Bibl.* 1.2.7>, *64a*
Cambyse (*Cabye*), daughter of Opus[1] <Pind. *Ol.* 9.65>, 15a
— and Locrus[2] <Plut. *Gr. Quest.* 15>, 16a
— and Zeus <Pind. *Ol.* 9.65>, 5b
Cameiro (*Cleodora*[2]) (*Cleothera*), daughter of Pandareus[1] <Paus. 10.30.1> and *Harmothoe*[1], 66d
Cameirus, son of Cercaphus[1] and *Cydippe*[1] <Diod. Sic. 5.57.8>, 14a
Camiro — see *Cameira*
Canace (*Aeolis*), daughter of Aeolus[1] <*Cat. Wom., Hesiodi* frg. 10(a).34, Merk. & West (O.C.T.)> and *Enarete* <Apollod. *Bibl.* 1.7.3>, 34a
— and Macar(eus)[1] <Ovid *Her.* 11>, (34a)
— and Poseidon <*Cat. Wom., Frag. Hes.* frg. 10(a).102-02, Merk. & West (O.C.T.)>, 8a
Candalus, son of Helios and *Rhode*[1] <Diod. Sic. 5.56.5>, 14a
Canes, son of Cephalus[2] <Diod. Sic. 4.53.2> and *Procris*[1], 22c
— and *Euadne*[4] <Diod. Sic. 4.53.2>, 28d
Canethus[1] (Canthus) [Argonaut], son of Abas[3] <Ap. Rhod. *Arg.* 1.77>, 8b
Canethus[2], son of Lycaon[1] <Apollod. *Bibl.* 3.8.1>, 62b
Canethus[3], husband of *Henioche*[2] <Plut. *Thes.* 25.4>, 38b
Canthus — see Canethus[1]
Capaneus [one of the Seven against Thebes (per Aesch. *Sev.* 423)], son of Hipponous[1] <Apollod. *Bibl.* 3.6.3> and *Astynome*[3] <Hyg. *Fab.* 70>, 58c
— and *Euadne*[1] <Eur. *Supp.* 984>, 58c
Caphaurus (Cephalion), son of Amphithemis[1] and a nymph, daughter of Triton <Ap. Rhod. *Arg.* 4.1496>, 53d, *63b*
Capheira, daughter of Oceanus <Diod. Sic. 5.55.1> and *Tethys*, 52a
Capylus, son of Heracles[1] and *Hippo*[1] <Apollod. *Bibl.* 2.7.8>, *50c*
Capys[1], son of Assaracus <Hom. *Il.* XX, 239> and *Hieromneme* <Apollod. *Bibl.* 3.12.2>, 41c
alternate parentage:
Assaracus and *Clytodora*[2] <Dion. Hal. *Rom. Ant.* 1.62>
— and *Themis*[2] <Apollod. *Bibl.* 2.12.2 (she is called *Themiste*)>, (41c)
Capys[2], son of Epytus <Ovid *Fast.* 4.44-45>, *
Car[1] [King of Megara], son of Phoroneus and *Teledice* <Paus. 1.39. 6>, 61a
— and *Callirhoe*[6] <Steph. Byz. "Alabanda">, 67b
Car[2], son of Atys[1] <Herod. 1.171.6 (inferred because he is called brother of Lydus)> and *Callithea*, 51b
Caresus [river], son of Oceanus and Tethys <Hes. *Theog.* 367-68; named as river, Hom. *Il.* XII.20>, 67a
Carmanor, son of Dionysus and *Alexirhoe* <Ps.-Plut. *De Fluv.* 7.

5>, 56c, *67b*
Carme, daughter of Eubulus <Paus. 2.20.3>, 56c
alternate parentage:
Phoenix[2] and *Cassiopeia*[1] <Ant. Lib. *Met.* 40.1>
— and Zeus <Ant. Lib. *Met.* 40.1>, 5b
Carmentis — see *Nicostrate*[1]
Carn(e)us, son of Zeus and *Europe*[1] <Prax. in Paus. 3.13.5>, 5c
— and Apollo <Prax. in *P.L.G.* 3.568 frg. 7, Bergk>, 11a
Carpo — see *Eirene*[1]
Carpus, son of Zephyrus <Serv. on Virg. *Ecl.* 5.48> and *Chloris*[4], 12a
— and Calamus < Serv. on Virg. *Ecl.* 5.48>, 67b
Carteron, son of Lycaon[1] <Apollod. *Bibl.* 3.8.1>, 62b
Carthago, daughter of Heracles[3] <Cic. *De Nat. Deor.* 3.42>, 5a
Carya[1], daughter of Dion and *Amphithea*[1] <Serv. on Virg. *Ecl.* 8.29>, 31d
— and Dionysus <Serv. on Virg. *Ecl.* 8.29>, 56d
Carya[2] [walnut tree], daughter of Oxylus[3] and *Hamadryas* <Athen. 3.78b>, 71d
Carystus, son of Cheiron <Tzetz. on Lyc. 580> and *Chariclo*[2], 69b
Cassandra[1] (*Alexandra*), daughter of Priam[1] <Hom. *Il.* XIII.363> and *Hecabe*[1] <Eur. *Tro. Wom.* passim>, 43d
— and Agamemnon <Eur. *Tro. Wom.* 246-51>, 36b
— and Ajax[2] <Eur. *Tro. Wom.* 70>, 15c
— and Coroebus[1] <Paus. 10.27.1>, 43d
Cassandra[2] — see *Philonoe*
Cassiopeia[1] (*Iope*[2]), daughter of Arabus <*Cat. Wom., Frag. Hes.* frg. 138, Merk. & West>, 46c
— and Cepheus[1] <Apollod. *Bibl.* 2.4.3>, 58b
— and Phoenix[2] <*Cat. Wom., Frag. Hes.* frg. 138, Merk. & West>, 53b
— and Zeus <Apollod. *Bibl.* 3.1.2>, 5b
Cassiopeia[2] — see *Memphis*[1]
Cassiphone, daughter of Odysseus and *Circe* <Schol. on Lyc. 808>, 13c
— and Telemachus <Schol. on Lyc. 808>, 13c
Castalia, daughter of Achelous <Paus. 10.8.5> and *Calliope*, 65b
— and Apollo <Schol. on Eur. *Or.* 1094>, 11a
Castalius, father of *Thyia*[2] <Paus. 10.6.4>, 11d
Castianeira, paramour of Priam[1] <Hom. *Il.* VIII.303-05>, 43d
Castor[1] [one of the Dioscuri] [Argonaut], son of Tyndareus and *Leda* <Hom. *Od.* 11.300>, 48d
alternate parentage:
Zeus and *Leda* <*Hom. Hymn* 17 (to the Dioscuri)>
— and *Hilaeira* <Apollod. *Bibl.* 3.11.2>, 25d
Castor[2], comrade of Aeneas <Virg. *Aen.* 10.124>, *
Casus, son of Inachus and *Melia*[1] <Paus. Damasc. in *F.H.G.* 4.469 frg. 4. Müller>, 59a
— and *Amyce* <Paus. Damasc. in *F.H.G.* 4.469 frg. 4, Müller>, (59a)
Catillus, son of Amphiaraus <Sol. *Coll. Rer. Mem.* 2.7> and *Eriphyle*, 33c
Catinus, son of Catillus <Sol. *Coll. Rer. Mem.* 2.7>, 33c
Catis — see Melas[5]
Catreus (Asterius[2]) (Crateus) [King of Crete], son of Minos I and *Pasiphae*[1] <Apollod. *Bibl.* 3.1.2>, 52d
alternate parentage:
Minos I and *Crete*[1] <Asclep. in Apollod. *Bibl.* 3.1.2>
Caucon[1], son of Celaenus <Paus. 4.1.5>, 68b
— and *Asty(a)dameia*[5] <Ael. *Var. Narr.* 1.24>, (68b)
Caucon[2], son of Lycaon[1] <Apollod. *Bibl.* 3.8.1>, 62b
Caunus, son of Miletus and *Cyanea* <Ovid *Met.* 9.450-54>, *68a*
alternate parentage:
Miletus and *Tragasia* <Nicaenetus in Parth. *Love Stor.* 11. 2>
— and *Pronoe*[3] <Con. *Narr.* 2>, (68a)
Cayst(ri)us (Caistrus), son of Achilles <Serv. on Virg. *Aen.* 11.661> and *Pentheseleia* <*Etym. Magn.* "Kaystros">, 24c, *7c*
Caystrus [river], son of Oceanus and *Tethys* <Hes. *Theog.* 367-68; named as river, Paus. 7.2.7>, 52a
Cebrenus [river], son of Oceanus and *Tethys* <Hes. *Theog.* 367-68; named as river, Apollod. *Bibl.* 3.12.5>, 67a
Cebriones, son of Priam[1] <Hom. *Il.* XVI.738>, 43d
Cecrops I [King of Athens] [man/serpent], autochthonous; husband of *Aglaurus*[1] <Apollod. *Bibl.* 3.14.1>, 66b
alternate parentage:
Gaea <Hyg. *Fab.* 148>
Cecrops II [King of Athens], son of Erechtheus II and *Praxithea*[2] <Apollod. *Bibl.* 3.15.1>, 50a
alternate parentage:
Hephaestus <Hyg. *Fab.* 148>
— and *Metiadusa* <Apollod. *Bibl.* 3.15.5>, 49b
Ceisus (Cissus[1]) (Creisus), son of Temenus[1] <Paus. 2.19.1>, 60d
Celaene, daughter of Proetus[1] <Ael. *Var. Narr.* 3.41> and *Stheneboea*, 57d
Celaeneus[1], son of Electryon[1] and *Lysidice*[1] <*Cat. Wom., Frag. Hes.* frg. 193, Merk. & West>, 59d, *38a*
alternate parentage:
Electryon[1] and *Anaxo*[1] <Apollod. *Bibl.* 2.4.5>
Celaeneus[2] [one of the Pans], son of Pan <Non. *Dion.* 14.74>, 64d
Celaeneus[3], Indian warrior <Non. *Dion.* 14.324>, *
Celaeno[1], daughter of Atlas <*Cat. Wom., Frag. Hes.* frg. 169, Merk. & West> and *Pleione* <Apollod. *Bibl.* 3.10.1>, 40b
alternate parentage:
Ergeus <Hyg. *Fab.* 157>
— and Poseidon <Apollod. *Bibl.* 3.10.1>, 8b
— and Prometheus[1] <Tzetz. on Lyc. 132>, 16a
Celaeno[2] [dark clouds] [one of the Harpuiai], daughter of Thaumas[1] and *Electra*[1] <Hyg. *Fab.* pref.>, 3a
alternate parentage:
Thaumas[1] and *Ozomene* <Hyg. *Fab.* 14>
Boreas <Pher. Syr. 7 B 5>
Oceanus and *Gaea* <Epim. *Theog.* 3 B 7>
Celaeno[3], daughter of Hyamus <Paus. 10.6.3> and *Melantho*[1], 17a
— and Apollo <Paus. 10.6.2>, 11b
Celaeno[4], daughter of Danaus[1] and *Crino* <Apollod. *Bibl.* 2.1.5>, 58c
— and Hyperbius[1] <Apollod. *Bibl.* 2.1.5>, (58c)
— and Poseidon <Strab. 12.8.18>, 8b
Celaeno[5] [Amazon] <Diod. Sic. 4.16.3>, *
Celaenus[1], son of Phlyus <Paus. 4.1.5>, 3b
Celaenus[2], son of Poseidon and *Celaeno*[4] <Strab. 12.8.18>, 8b
Celeus[1] [King of Eleusis], son of Eleusis <*Hom. Hymn* 2 (to *Demeter*), 106> and *Cothone*, 46b
— and *Metaneira* <*Hom. Hymn* 2 (to *Demeter*), 233-34>, (46b)
Celeus[2], entered cave of Zeus seeking honey <Ant. Lib. *Met.* 19>, *
Celeustanor, son of Heracles[1] and *Iphis*[4] <Apollod. *Bibl.* 2.7.8>, *50c*
Celeutor, son of Agrius[1] <Apollod. *Bibl.* 1.8.6> and *Dia*[4], 16d
Celmis — see (Dactyls) (alternate version)
Celtine, daughter of Bretannus <Parth. *Love Stor.* 30.1>, 60b
— and Heracles[1] <Parth. *Love Stor.* 30.1>, (60b)
Celtus[1], son of Heracles[1] and *Celtine* <Parth. *Love Stor.* 30.2>, 60b
Celtus[2], son of *Asterope*[1] <*Etym. Magn.* "Keltoi">, 39a
Celtus[3], son of Meges[3] and *Periboea*[8] <Quint. Smyr. 7.605-11>, *
Celtus[4], suitor of *Penelope*[1] (from Zacynthus) <Apollod. *Epit.* 7.30>, *
Celusa — see Asopus (alternate version)
Cenchreis, wife of Cinyras[1] <Ovid *Met.* 10.453>, 11c
Cenchreus — see Cenchrias
Cenchrias (Cenchreus), son of Poseidon and *Peirene*[2] <Paus. 2.2. 3>, 9b, *66a*
Cenchris, daughter of Pierus[2] <Nicand. in Ant. Lib. *Met.* 9>

and *Euippe*[2] <Ovid *Met.* 5.300 ff.>, 15a
[centaurs], offspring of Centaurus and [Magnesian Mares] <Pind. *Pyth.* 2.50>, 69c-d
Centaurus, son of Ixion and *Nephele*[1] <Pind. *Pyth.* 2.50>, 69a
alternate parentage:
Apollo and *Stilbe* <Diod. Sic. 4.69.2>
— and [Magnesian Mares] <Pind. *Pyth.* 2.48-49>, (69a)
Cephalion — see Caphaurus
Cephalus[1], son of Hermes and *Herse*[1] <Apollod. *Bibl.* 3.14.3>, 46c
alternate parentage:
Hermes and *Creusa*[3] <Hyg. *Fab.* 160>
Pandion? <Hyg. *Fab.* 270>
— and *Eos* <Hes. *Theog.* 987>, 12b
Cephalus[2], son of Deion[1] <Hellan. in *F. Gr. H.* 3 F 34> and *Diomede*[3] <Apollod. *Bibl.* 1.9.4>, 22a
— and *Clymene*[4] <Paus. 10.29.6>, 20c
— and *Procris*[1] <Hellan. in *F. Gr. H.* 3 F 34>, 51a
Cepheus[1] [King of Ethiopia], son of Belus[1] <Herod. 7.61> and *Anchinoe*[1], 58b
alternate parentage:
Agenor[1] <Schol. on Eur. *Phoen. Maid.*>
— and *Cassiopeia*[1] <Apollod. *Bibl.* 2.4.3>, 46c
Cepheus[2] [King of Tegea in Arcadia] [Argonaut], son of Aleus and *Neaera*[2] <Apollod. *Bibl.* 3.9.1>, 64c
alternate parentage:
Aleus and *Cleobule*[5] <Hyg. *Fab.* 14>
Cepheus[3], son of Lycurgus[4] <Apollod. *Bibl.* 1.8.2> and *Cleophyle*, 64c
Cephis(s)us [river], son of Oceanus and *Tethys* <Hes. *Theog.* 366-67; named as river, Hom. *Il.* II.523>, 49b
— and *Leiriope* <Ovid *Met.* 3.344-45>, 55b
Cer [destruction] [abstraction], offspring of *Nyx* <Hes. *Theog.* 211>, *1b*
Cerambus, son of Euseirus and *Eidothea*[3] <Ant. Lib. *Met.* 22>, 9d
Ceramus, son of Dionysus and *Ariadne* <Paus. 1.3.1>, 56c
Cerberus[1] [dog of Hades], offspring of Typhon and *Echidna* <Hes. *Theog.* 311>, 1b
Cerberus[2], entered cave of Zeus seeking honey <Ant. Lib. *Met.* 19>, *
Cerberus[3], suitor of *Penelope*[1] (from Same) <Apollod. *Epit.* 7. 28>, *
Cerbia — see *Cydippe*[1]
Cercaphus[1], son of Helios and *Rhode*[1] <Diod. Sic. 5.56.5>, 14a
— and *Cydippe*[1] <Diod. Sic. 5.57.7>, 14b
Cercaphus[2], son of Aeolus[1] <Dem. Scep. in Strab. 9.5.18> and *Enarete*, 24b
Cerceis, daughter of Oceanus and *Tethys* <Hes. *Theog.* 355>, 52a
Cercetes, son of Aegyptus[1] and [a Phoenician woman] <Apollod. *Bibl.* 2.1.5>, 57d
— and *Dorius* <Apollod. *Bibl.* 2.1.5>, (57d)
(Cercopes), sons of Oceanus and *Theia*[2] (see Acmon[1] and Passalus), 72a
(their names are also suggested to be Eurybatus[1] and Phrynondas, or Syllus and Triballus[2], in <Schol. on Luc., p. 181, "*Alexandros*" 4.4>)
Cercyon[1] [King of Eleusis], son of Poseidon and a daughter of Amphictyon (possible *Atthis*) <Choer. in Paus. 1.14.3>, 9d
alternate parentage:
Hephaestus <Hyg. *Fab.* 38, 158>
Branchus[2] and *Argiope*[4] <Apollod. *Epit.* 1.37>
Cercyon[2], son of Agamedes[2] <Paus. 8.5.4>, 62c
Cercyra — see *Corcyra*
Cerdo, paramour of Phoroneus <Paus. 1.21.1>, 61a
Cerebia, paramour of Poseidon <Tzetz. on Lyc. 838>, 8b
(Ceres) [abstractions], offspring of *Nyx* <Hes. *Theog.* 217>, *1b*
Ceroessa, daughter of Zeus and *Io* <Steph. Byz. "Byzantium", 5d, *55b*
— and Poseidon <Steph. Byz. "Byzantium">, 8c
Certhe, daughter of Thespius <Apollod. *Bibl.* 2.7.8> and *Megamede* <Apollod. *Bibl.* 2.4.10>, 50c
— and Heracles[1] <Apollod. *Bibl.* 2.7.8>, (50c)
Cerynes, son of Temenus[1] <Diod. Sic. 7.13.1>, 60d
Ceryx, son of Hermes and *Pandrosos* <Schol. on Hom. *Il.* I.334>, 46d
alternate parentage:
Hermes and *Aglaurus*[2] <Paus. 1.38.3>
Hermes and *Herse*[1] <Marcellus of Side, *Inscriptiones Graecae* 14.1389>
Eumolpus <Paus. 1.38.3>
Cestrinus, son of Helenus[1] and *Andromache* <Paus. 1.11.1>, 43c
Ceteus[1] — see [fifty sons of Lycaon[1]] (alternate version)
Ceteus[2] [horned centaur] <Non. *Dion.* 14.188>, *
Ceto[1], daughter of Pontus and *Gaea* <Hes. *Theog.* 238>, 2b
— and Phorcus[1] <Hes. *Theog.* 270>, (2b)
Ceto[2], daughter of Nereus and *Doris*[1] <Apollod. *Bibl.* 1.2.7>, *64a*
Ceto[3], daughter of Oceanus <Non. *Dion.* 26.355> and *Tethys*, 71b
— and Helios <Non. *Dion.* 26.354-55>, 14a
Ceyx[1], son of Phosphor(us) <*Cat. Wom., Hesiodi* frg. 10(d), Merk. & West (O.C.T.)> and *Philonis*[2] <Hyg. *Fab.* 65>, 13b
— and *Alcyone*[1] <*Cat. Wom., Hesiodi* frg. 10(d), Merk. & West (O.C.T.)>, 23b
Ceyx[2] [King of Trachis], father of *Themistonoe* <Hes. *Shield* 350-56>, 7d
Chaeresileus, son of Iasius[2] <Paus. 9.20.2>, 35a
— and *Stratonice*[4] <Plut. *Gr. Quest.* 37>, (35a)
Chaetus, son of Aegyptus[1] and [an Arabian woman] <Apollod. *Bibl.* 2.1.5>, 57d
— and *Asteria*[6] <Apollod. *Bibl.* 2.1.5>, (57d)
Chairon, son of Apollo and *Thero*[1] <*Gr. Ehoiai, Frag. Hes.* frg. 252, Merk. & West>, 11d, *55d*
Chalciope[1] (*Euenia*) (*Iophassa*), daughter of Aeetes <Paus. 9.34.5> and *Asterodeia*[3], 14c
alternate parentage:
Aeetes and *Eidyia* <Ap. Rhod. *Arg.* 3.249>
— and Phrixus[1] <Apollod. *Bibl.* 1.9.1>, 26a
Chalciope[2], daughter of Eurypylus[2] <Apollod. *Bibl.* 2.7.8>, 34c
— and Heracles[1] <Apollod. *Bibl.* 2.7.8>, 60b
Chalciope[3], daughter of Rhexenor[2] <Apollod. *Bibl.* 3.15.6>, 51a
— and Aegeus[1] <Apollod. Bibl. 3.15.6>, (51a)
Chalciope[4], daughter of Phalerus[1] <Schol. on Ap. Rhod. *Arg.* 1.97>, 49a
Chalcis — see *Combe*[1]
Chalcodon[1], son of Aegyptus[1] and [an Arabian woman] <Apollod. *Bibl.* 2.1.5>, 57c
— and *Rhodeia* <Apollod. *Bibl.* 2.1.5>, (57c)
Chalcodon[2] [King of Abantes, in Euboea], son of Abas[3] <Eust. on Hom. *Il.* 281>, 8b
— and *Alcyone*[7] <Apollod. *Epit.* 3.11>, (8b)
Chalcodon[3], wounded Heracles[1] <Apollod. *Bibl.* 2.7.1>, *
Chalcomedusa, wife of Arceisius <Eust. on Hom. *Od.* 17.96>, 5c
Chalcon[1], son of Eurypylus[2] <*Cat. Wom., Frag. Hes.* frg. 43a, 60, Merk. & West>, 34c
Chalcon[2], father of Bathycles <Hom. *Il.* XVI.595>, *
Chaon, son of Priam[1] <Serv. on Virg. *Aen.* 3.297 (inferred because he is called brother of Helenus)>, 43d
Chaos, "came into being" (without parentage) <Hes. *Theog.* 116>, 1a
alternate parentage:
Chronus <Proc. *Plat. Tim.*> (Orphic theogony)
Chariclo[1], wife of Eueres[3] <Apollod. *Bibl.* 3.6.7>, 32d
Chariclo[2], daughter of Apollo <Schol. on Pind. *Pyth.* 4.182>, 11d
— and Cheiron <Ovid *Met.* 2.636>, 69b
Chariclo[3], daughter of Cychreus <Plut. *Thes.* 10.3>, 66b
— and Sciron[2] <Plut. *Thes.* 10.3>, 39a
Charis — see *Aglaia*[1]

(Charites) [Graces], daughters of Zeus and *Eurynome*[1] <Hes. *Theog.* 909> (see *Aglaia*[1], *Euphrosyne*, *Thaleia*[2]), 5d

others:

named in <Paus. 9.35.2>: *Auxo*[2], *Cleta*[2], *Hegemone*, *Phaenna*

named in <Herm. Col. in Paus. 9.35.5>: *Peitho*[5]

alternate parentage:

Dionysus and *Coronis*[5] <Non. *Dion.* 48.555>

Charmus, son of Aristaeus[1] <Diod. Sic. 4.82.4>, 69b

Charops[1], father of Oeagrus <Diod. Sic. 3.65.6>, 6a

Charops[2], son of Hippasus[4] <Hom. *Il.* XI.426>, 44d

Charops[3] [one of dogs of Actaeon] <Hyg. *Fab.* 181>, *

Charybdis [monster], offspring of Poseidon and *Gaea* <Serv. on Virg. *Aen.* 3.420>, 8c

Cheirobie, daughter of Deriades and *Orsiboe* <Non. *Dion.* 34.170-71>, 3b

— and Morrheus[1] <Non. *Dion.* 34.179>, (3b)

Cheiron [centaur], offspring of Cronus <Pher. in *F. Gr. H.* 3 F 50> and *Phillyra* <Hes. *Theog.* 1001-02>, *69b*

— and *Chariclo*[2] <Ovid *Met.* 2.636>, 11c

Chelidon, daughter of Pandareus <Ant. Lib. *Met.* 11.2-4> and *Harmothoe*[1], 66d

— and Polytechnus <Ant. Lib. *Met.* 11.5>, (66d)

Chersidamas[1], son of Priam[1] <Apollod. *Bibl.* 3.12.5>, 43d

Chersidamas[2], son of Pterelaus <Apollod. *Bibl.* 2.4.5> and *Amphimede*, 58d

Chesias, mother of *Ocyrrhoe*[2] <Ap. Rhod. in Athen. 7.283d>, 11d

— and Imbrasus[1] <Ap. Rhod. in Athen. 7.283d>, (11d)

Chias, daughter of Amphion[1] <Hyg. *Fab.* 69> and *Niobe*[1], 66c

[child (unnamed)] of Tantalus[2] and *Clytemnestra* <Eur. *Iph. in Aulis* 1150>, 39a

Childanope — see *Chlidanope*

Chimaera[1] [monster], offspring of Typhon and *Echidna* <Hes. *Theog.* 319>, 1b

alternate parentage:

Lernaean Hydra <Hes. *Theog.* 319 (referent of "she" is uncertain)>

— and Orth(r)us <Hes. *Theog.* 327>, 1b

Chimaera[2], paramour of Daphnis[1] <Serv. on Virg. *Ecl.* 8.68>, 46c

Chimaereus, son of Prometheus[1] and *Celaeno*[1] <Tzetz. on Lyc. 132>, 16a, *40b*

Chione[1] (*Philonis*[1]), daughter of Daedalion <Ovid *Met.* 11.301>, 13b

alternate parentage:

Deion[1] <Pher. in *F. Gr. H.* 3 F 120 (she is called *Philonis*)> and *Diomede*[1]

— and Apollo <Ovid *Met.* 11.311>, 11b

— and Hermes <Ovid *Met.* 11.308>, 46b

Chione[2], daughter of Boreas[1] and *Oreithyia*[1] <Apollod. *Bibl.* 3.15.2>, 13a

— and Poseidon <Apollod. *Bibl.* 3.15.8>, 8c

Chione[3], daughter of Nilus and *Callirhoe*[2] <Serv. on Virg. *Aen.* 4.250>, 68a, *51b*

Chione[4], paramour of Dionysus <Schol. Theo. 1.21>, 56d

Chirimachus, son of Electryon[1] and *Anaxo*[1] <Apollod. *Bibl.* 2.4.5>, 59d

Chius, son of Poseidon and a nymph <Ion in Paus. 7.4.6>, 9d

Chlidanope (*Childanope*) (*Tricca*), daughter of Peneius <Steph. Byz. "Tricce" (she is called Tricca)> and *Creusa*[4], 69b

— wife of Hypseus[1] <Schol. on Pind. *Pyth.* 9.31>, (69b)

Chloris[1] — see *Meliboea*[2]

Chloris[2] (*Aoris*[1]) (*Aregonis*), daughter of Amphion[2] <Hom. *Od.* 11.281-83> and *Persephone*[2] <Hom. *Od.* 11.281>, 20c

— and Neleus[1] <Hom. *Od.* 11.281-83>, 27c

Chloris[3], daughter of Teiresias <Schol. on Pind. *Nem.* 9.57a>, 32d

— and Poseidon <Schol. on Pind. *Nem.* 9.57a>, 8c

Chloris[4], wife of Zephyrus <Ovid *Fast.* 5.195-207>, 12a

Chloris[5], daughter of Pierus[2] <Nicand. in Ant. Lib. *Met.* 9> and *Euippe*[2] <Ovid *Met.* 5.300 ff.>, 15a

Chloris[6], paramour of Ampyx[2] and mother of Mopsus[2] <Tzetz. on Lyc. 881>, *

Choraeus, father of *Callithea* <Dion. Hal. *Rom. Ant.* 1.27>, 51b

Choricus [King of Arcadia], father of *Palaestra* <*Etym. Magn.* "Pale" 648.2-3>, 46d

Chremetes [river], son of Oceanus and *Tethys* <Hes. *Theog.* 367-68; named as river, Non. *Dion.* 13.380>, 52a

Chromia (*Neis*[3]), daughter of Itonus[1] <Paus. 5.1.4> and *Melanippe*[6], 16a

— and Endymion <Paus. 5.1.4>, 15b

Chromis[1] [centaur], offspring of Centaurus and a Magnesian Mare <Pind. *Pyth.* 2.50; named as centaur, Ovid *Met.* 12.331>, 69c

alternate parentage:

Ixion and *Nephele*[1] <Diod. Sic. 4.69.5>

Chromis[2], son of Heracles[1] <Stat. *Theb.* 6.346>, 61c

Chromis[3], a shepherd <Virg. *Ecl.* 6.16>, *

Chromis[4], killed by Camilla <Virg. *Aen.* 11.679>, *

Chromis[5], a Mysian captain in the Trojan War <Hom. *Il.* II. 858>, *

Chromis[6], son of *Dryope*[4] <Stat. *Theb.* 2.614-15>, *

Chromis[7], killed Aemathion[4] <Ovid *Met.* 5.98-103>, *

Chromis[8], killed by Amphiaraus <Stat. *Theb.* 7.691-714>, *

Chromis[9], killed by Tydeus[1] <Stat. *Theb.* 8.472-76>, *

Chromis[10], killed by Antiphus <Stat. *Theb.* 9.252>, *

Chromius[1], son of Neleus[1] and *Chloris*[2] <Hom. *Od.* 11.286>, 27c

Chromius[2], son of Pterelaus <Apollod. *Bibl.* 2.4.5> and *Amphimede*, 58d

Chromius[3], son of Priam[1] <Hom. *Il.* V.159>, 43d

Chromius[4], son of Arsinous[2] <Apollod. *Epit.* 3.35>,*

Chromius[5], killed by Teucer[2] <Hom. *Il.*VIII.273-74>, *

Chronus [time] — see Chaos (alternate version)

Chryasus — see Criasus[1]

Chrysaor, son of Poseidon and *Medusa*[1] <Hes. *Theog.* 281>, 8d, *2a*

— and *Callirhoe*[2] <Hes. *Theog.* 979-80>, 51b

Chryse[1], daughter of Almus <Paus. 9.36.1>, 19d

— and Ares <Paus. 9.36.1>, 7a

Chryse[2], daughter of Pallas[3] <Dion. Hal. *Rom. Ant.* 1.61.2>, 63d

— and Dardanus[1] <Dion. Hal. *Rom. Ant.* 1.61.2>, 42b

Chryse[3], guarded by a snake <Soph. *Phil.* 1327-28>, *

Chryseis[1] (*Astynome*[1]), daughter of Chryses[2] <Hom. *Il.* I.13>, 36b

— and Agamemnon <Hom. *Il.* I.112>, (36b)

Chryseis[2], daughter of Thespius <Apollod. Bibl. 2.7.8> and *Megamede* <Apollod. *Bibl.* 2.4.10>, 50c

— and Heracles[1] <Apollod. *Bibl.* 2.7.8>, (50c)

Chryseis[3], daughter of Oceanus and *Tethys* <Hes. *Theog.* 359>, 52a

Chryses[1], son of Poseidon and *Chrysogeneia* <Paus. 9.36.3>, 8c, *20c*

Chryses[2], father of *Chryseis*[1] <Hom. *Il.* I.13, 111>, 36b

Chryses[3], son of Agamemnon and *Chryseis*[1] <Hyg. *Fab.* 121>, 36b

Chryses[4], son of Minos I and *Pareia* <Apollod. *Bibl.* 3.1.2>, 54c

Chrysippe[1], daughter of Danaus[1] and *Memphis*[2] <Apollod. *Bibl.* 2.1.5>, 57c

— and Chrysippus[2] <Apollod. *Bibl.* 2.1.5>, (57c)

Chrysippe[2], daughter of Irus[1] <Steph. Byz. "Hellas"> and *Demonassa*[1], 22d

Chrysippus[1], son of Pelops[1] <Apollod. *Bibl.* 3.5.5> and *Axioche* <Schol. on Pind. 1.144>, 40a

alternate parentage:

Pelops[1] and *Danais* <Plut. *Gr. and Rom. Par. Stor.* 33>

— and Laius[1] <Apollod. *Bibl.* 3.5.5>, 55c

Chrysippus[2], son of Aegyptus[1] and *Tyria* <Apollod. *Bibl.* 2.1.5>, 57c

— and *Chrysippe*[1] <Apollod. *Bibl.* 2.1.5>, (57c)

Chrysogeneia (*Chrysogone*), daughter of Almus <Paus. 9.36.1, 3>, 20d

— and Poseidon <Paus. 9.36.3>, 8c
Chrysogone — see *Chrysogeneia*
Chrysonoe, daughter of Cleitus[2] <Con. *Narr.* 32> and *Pallene*[1]*, 7c*
— and Proteus[1] <Con. *Narr.* 32>, 9c
Chrysopeleia, wife of Arcas[1] <Eum. in Apollod. *Bibl.* 3.9.1>, 62c
Chrysorthe, daughter of Orthopolis <Paus. 2.5.5>, 8d
— and Apollo <Paus. 2.5.5>, 11b
Chrysothemis[1], daughter of Agamemnon <Hom. *Il.* IX.145> and *Clytemnestra* <Soph. *Elec.* passim>, 36a
Chrysothemis[2], wife of Staphylus[1] <Diod. Sic. 5.62.1>, 56d
Chrysothemis[3] —see [fifty daughters of Danaus[1]] (alternate version)
Chrysothemis[4], son of Carmanor <Paus. 10.7.2>, 56c
Chthonia[1] (*Othonia*), daughter of Erechtheus II and *Praxithea*[2] <Apollod. *Bibl.* 3.15.1>, 50b
— and Butes[3] <Apollod. *Bibl.* 3.15.1>, 49a
Chthonia[2], daughter of Phoroneus <Paus. 2.35.3 (she is called sister of Clymenus[2])> and *Teledice*, 61b
alternate parentage:
Colontas <Paus. 2.35.3>
Chthonia[3] — see *Melinoe*
Chthonius[1] [one of the (Spartoi) [sown men]], sprang from teeth of [Cadmean Dragon] <Apollod. *Bibl.* 3.4.2>, 7d
Chthonius[2], son of Aegyptus[1] and *Caliadne* <Apollod. *Bibl.* 2.1.5>, 58c
— and *Bryce* <Apollod. *Bibl.* 2.1.5>, (58c)
Chthonius[3], son of Poseidon and *Syme* <Diod. Sic. 5.53.1>, 9b
Chthonius[4] [centaur], offspring of Centaurus and a Magnesian Mare <Pind. *Pyth.* 2.50; named as centaur, Ovid *Met.* 12.441>, 69c
alternate parentage:
Ixion and *Nephele*[1] <Diod. Sic. 4.69.5>
Chthonius[5] [giant], son of *Gaea* (and the blood of Uranus) <Hes. *Theog.* 180-86; named as giant, Non. *Dion.* 48.21>, *4a*
Chthonius[6], defender of Thebes <Stat. *Theb.* 3.169>, *
Chthonopatra, wife of Amphictyon <Eust. on Hom. *Il.* 277>, 16a
Chthonophyle, daughter of Sicyon and *Zeuxippe*[2] <Paus. 2.6.3>, 49a
— and Hermes <Paus. 2.6.3>, 46b
— and Phlias <Ap. Rhod. *Arg.* 1.115-18>, (49a), 56d
Cicon, son of Apollo and *Rhodope*[1] <*Etym. Magn.* 513.36>, 11c, *70a*
Cilix, son of Agenor[1] <Herod. 7.9.1> and *Telephassa* <Apollod. *Bibl.* 3.1.1>, 56a
alternate parentage:
Phoenix[2] and *Cassiopeia*[1] <Pher. in *F. Gr. H.* 3 F 86>
Cilla[1] — see *Eurydice*[2]
Cilla[2], daughter of Cisseus[1] <Schol. on Lyc. 319> and *Telecleia*, 45d
alternate parentage:
Laomedon[1] and *Leucippe*[8] <Apollod. *Bibl.* 3.12.3>
Laomedon[1] and *Placia* <Apollod. *Bibl.* 3.12.3>
Laomedon[1] and *Strym(n)o* <Apollod. *Bibl.* 3.12.3>
— and Priam[1] <Schol. on Lyc. 319>, 43d
— and Thymoetes[2] <Schol. on Lyc. 319>, 43c
Cinna, wife of Phoroneus <Hyg. *Fab.* 145>, 61a
Cinyras[1] [King of Cyprus], son of Apollo <Schol. on Pind. *Pyth.* 27> and *Paphos* <Ovid *Met.* 10.298>, 11c
alternate parentage:
Sandocus and *Pharnace* <Apollod. *Bibl.* 3.14.3>
— and Apollo <Pind. *Pyth.* 2.15>, 11b
— and *Cenchreis* <Ovid *Met.* 10.453>, (11c)
— and *Metharme* <Apollod. *Bibl* 3.14.3>, (11c)
— and *Myrr(h)a* <Ovid *Met.* 10.462-68>, 11c
Cinyras[2], a chieftain of Liguria <Virg. *Aen.* 10.186>, *
Circe, daughter of Helios and *Perse(is)* <Hes. *Theog.* 957>, 14d
alternate parentage:
Helios and *Asterope*[?] <Orph. *Arg.* 1216>
Aeetes and *Hecate* <Diod. Sic. 4.45.3>
— and Odysseus <Hes. *Theog.* 1010>, 13c
— and Telemachus <Eust. on Hom. *Od.* 1796>, 13c
Cissa, daughter of Pierus[2] <Nicand. in Ant. Lib. *Met.* 9> and *Euippe*[2] <Ovid *Met.* 5.300 ff.>, 15a
Cisseis — see (Hyades) (alternate version)
Cisseus[1] [King of Thrace], husband of *Telecleia* <Schol. on Eur. *Hec.* 3>, 41d, 44c
Cisseus[2], son of Aegyptus[1] and *Caliadne* <Apollod. *Bibl.* 2.1.5>, 57d
— and *Anthelia* <Apollod. *Bibl.* 2.1.5>, (57d)
Cisseus[3], son of Melampus[3] <Virg. *Aen.* 10.320-24>, *
Cisseus[4] [King of Macedonia], killed by Archelaus[4] <Hyg. *Fab.*>, *
Cissus[1] — see Ceisus
Cissus[2] [satyr] <Non. *Dion.* 10.401>, *
Cladeus [river], son of Oceanus and *Tethys* <Hes. *Theog.* 367-68; named as river, Paus. 5.10.7>, 52a
Clanis[1] [centaur], offspring of Centaurus and a Magnesian Mare <Pind. *Pyth.* 2.50; named as centaur, Ovid *Met.* 12.381>, 69c
alternate parentage:
Ixion and *Nephele*[1] <Diod. Sic. 4.69.5>
Clanis[2], killed by Perseus[1] <Ovid *Met.* 5.141>, *
Clarus, son of Euander[2] <Virg. *Aen.* 10.126 (inferred because he is called brother of Sarpedon[2])> and *Laodameia*[2], 52c
Cleeia — see (Hyades) (alternate version)
Cleio[1] [history] [one of the Muses], daughter of Zeus and *Mnemosyne* <Hes. *Theog.* 77>, 6a
— and Pierus[1] <Apollod. *Bibl.* 1.3.3>, 21b
Cleio[2], daughter of Nereus and *Doris*[1] <Hyg. *Fab.* pref.>, *64a*
Cleio[3] —see [fifty daughters of Danaus[1]] (alternate version)
Cleio[4], daughter of Oceanus <Virg. *Geo.* 4.339-40> and *Tethys*, 52a
Cleisidice, daughter of Celeus[1] <*Hom. Hymn* 2 (to *Demeter*) 109> and *Metaneira*, 46b
Cleisithera (*Cleisithyra*), daughter of Idomeneus[2] and *Meda*[1] <Lyc. 1214-25>, 54c
Cleisithyra — see *Cleisithera*
Cleite[1], daughter of Merops[3] <Ap. Rhod. *Arg.* 1.974>, 44c
— and Cyzicus <Ap. Rhod. *Arg.* 1.974>, (44c)
Cleite[2], daughter of Danaus[1] and *Memphis*[2] <Apollod. *Bibl.* 2.1.5>, 57c
— and Cleitus[3] <Apollod. *Bibl.* 2.1.5>, (57c)
Cleite[3] [one of the Bacchae] <Non. *Dion.* 21.77>, *
Cleite[4], wife of Erylaus <Quint. Smyr. 8.121>, *
Cleito[1], daughter of Euenor and *Leucippe*[5] <Plato, *Crit.* 113d>, 8d
— and Poseidon <Plato, *Crit.* 113d>, (8d)
Cleito[2], mother of Hellus <Quint. Smyr. 11.67-69>, *
Cleitonymus, son of Amphidamas[1] <Apollod. *Bibl.* 3.13.8>, 63c
Cleitor[1], son of Azan <Paus. 8.4.4>, 62c
Cleitor[2], son of Lycaon[1] <Apollod. *Bibl.* 3.8.1>, 62b
Cleitor[3], father of *Eurymedusa*[1] <Clem. Alex. *Exhor.* 2.34>, 5d
Cleitus[1], son of Mantius <Hom. *Od.* 15.249>, 32c
— and *Eos* <Hom. *Od.* 15.248-49>, 12b
Cleitus[2], husband of *Pallene*[1] <Parth. *Love Stor.* 6.6>, 7c
Cleitus[3], son of Aegyptus[1] and *Tyria* <Apollod. *Bibl.* 2.1.5>, 57c
— and *Cleite*[2] <Apollod. *Bibl.* 2.1.5>, (57c)
Cleitus[4], son of Peisenor[3] <Hom. *Il.* XV.445>, *
Cleitus[5], son of Agamestor and [a nymph] <Quint. Smyr. 6.464-65>, *
Cleoboea[1], daughter of Criasus[1] and *Melantho*[2] <Schol. on Eur. *Or.* 932>, 61a
Cleoboea[2] — see *Eurythemis(te)*
Cleoboea[3], wife of Phobius <Parth. *Love Stor.* 14.1>, *
Cleobula[1] — see *Hippodameia*[3]
Cleobula[2] — see *Cleopatra*[1]

Cleobula[3], paramour of Apollo <Hyg. *Fab.* 161>, 11b
Cleobula[4] (*Clytie*[5]) (*Theobula*[2]), daughter of Aeolus[1] <Tzetz. on Lyc. 156, 162> and *Enarete*, 21a
— and Hermes <Tzetz. on Lyc. 156, 162>, 46b
Cleobule[1] — see Amphidamas[1] (alternate version)
Cleobule[2] — see Clonius[2] (alternate version)
Cleochareia (*Peridia*[1]), wife of Lelex[1] <Apollod. *Bibl.* 3.10.3>, 61c
Cleochus[1], father of *Areia* <Apollod. *Bibl.* 3.1.2>, 11b
Cleochus[2], warrior with Dionysus <Non. *Dion.* 40.227>, *
Cleodaeus, son of Hyllus[1] <Herod. 6.52> and *Iole*, 60c
alternate parentage:
Heracles[1] and [a slave] <Diod. Sic. 4.31.8>
Cleodameia, daughter of Danaus[1] and *Atlantia* or *Phoebe*[4] <Apollod. *Bibl.* 2.1.5>, 57d
— and Diocorsytes <Apollod. *Bibl.* 2.1.5>, (57d)
Cleodice, daughter of Lacedaemon <Ps.-Plut. *De Fluv.* 17> and *Sparte*, 47a
Cleodora[1], paramour of Poseidon <Paus. 10.6.1>, 8d
— and Cleopompus <Paus. 10.6.1>, (8d)
Cleodora[2] — see *Cameiro*
Cleodora[3], daughter of Danaus[1] and *Polyxo*[3] <Apollod. *Bibl.* 2.1.5>, 57d
— and Lixus <Apollod. *Bibl.* 2.1.5>, (57d)
Cleodoxa, daughter of Amphion[1] and *Niobe*[1] <Apollod. *Bibl.* 3.5.6>, 66c
Cleogenes, son of Silenus <Paus. 6.1.4> and [an ash tree nymph], 46c
Cleola, daughter of Dias <Schol on Eur. *Or.* 4>, 37b
— and Atreus <Schol. on Eur. *Or.* 4>, 36b
Cleolaus[1] — see Alcaeus[2]
Cleolaus[2], son of Heracles[1] and *Argele* <Apollod. *Bibl.* 2.7.8>, *50c*
Cleolaus[3], killed by Paris <Quint. Smyr. 6.631-34>, *
Cleomestra, mother of Alcathous[2] <Dict. Cret. 4.22>, 41c, and Antenor <Dict. Cret. 4.22>, 45c
— and Aesyetes <Dict. Cret. 4.22>, (41c), (45c)
Cleon, son of Pelops[1] and *Hippodameia*[1] <Schol. on Eur. *Or.* 4>, *36b*
Cleone, daughter of Asopus and *Metope*[2] <Diod. Sic. 4.72,1>, 66a
alternate parentage:
Pelops[1] <Paus. 2.15.1>
Cleonymus, son of Pelops[1] and *Hippodameia*[1] <Pher. in *F. Gr. H.* 3 F 20>, *36b*
Cleopatra[1] (*Cleobula*[2]) [Queen of Salmydessus], daughter of Boreas[1] and *Oreithyia*[1] <Apollod. *Bibl.* 3.15.2>, 13a
— and Phineus[1] <Ap. Rhod. *Arg.* 2.240>, 42a, 53d
Cleopatra[2] (*Alcyone*[3]) (*Halcyone*[3]), daughter of Idas[1] and *Marpessa*[1] <Hom. *Il.* IX.556-58>, 25d
— and Apollo <Hom. *Il.* IX.562-63>, 11b
— and Meleager <Hom. *Il.* IX.556-58>, 17c
Cleopatra[3], daughter of Tros[1] and *Callirhoe*[1] <Apollod. *Bibl.* 3.12.2>, 41b
Cleopatra[4], daughter of Danaus[1] and *Atlantia* or *Phoebe*[4] <Apollod. *Bibl.* 2.1.5>, 57d
— and Agenor[8] <Apollod. *Bibl.* 2.1.5>, (57d)
Cleopatra[5], daughter of Danaus[1] and *Polyxo*[3] <Apollod. *Bibl.* 2.1.5>, 57c
— and Hermus[1] <Apollod. *Bibl.* 2.1.5>, (57c)
Cleopatra[6], one of first two girls sent to Troy by the Locrians <Apollod. *Epit.* 6.21>, *
Cleophema, daughter of Malus and *Erato*[6] <Isyl. *Lyr.* 3.43>, 19d
— and Phlegyas[1] <Isyl. *Lyr.* 3.43>, (19d)
Cleophyle (*Antinoe*[1]), daughter of Cepheus[2] <Paus. 8.9.5 (she is called *Antinoe*)>, 64c
— and Lycurgus[4] <Apollod. *Bibl.* 3.8.2>, 64d
Cleopompus, husband of *Cleodora*[1] <Paus. 10.6.1>, 8d
Cleopus —see Cnopus
Cleothera — see *Cameiro*
Cleso, daughter of Cleson <Paus. 1.42.7>, 59c
Cleson (Cteson) [King of Megara], son of Lelex[2] <Paus. 1.42.8>, 59a
Cleta[1], wife of Eurotas <Schol. on Eur. 626>, 61c
Cleta[2] — see (Charites) (alternate version)
Clonia[1], wife of Hyrieus <Apollod. *Bibl.* 3.10.1>, 35b
Clonia[2] [Amazon] <Quint. Smyr. *Posthom.* 1.42>, *
Clonius[1], son of Priam[1] <Apollod. *Bibl.* 3.12.5>, 43d
Clonius[2], son of Alegenor <Diod. Sic. 4.67.7>, 18c
alternate parentage:
Lacritus and *Cleobule*[2] <Hyg. *Fab.* 97>
Clonius[3], killed by Tydeus <Stat. *Theb.* 8.697>, *
Clonius[4], killed by Turnus <Virg. *Aen.* 9.571-72>, *
Clonius[5], killed by Messapus <Virg. *Aen.* 10.750>, *
Clotho [one of the Moirae], daughter of Zeus and *Themis*[1] <Hes. *Theog.* 901-05>, 6c
alternate parentage:
Nyx <Hes. *Theog.* 217-18>
Clyanthus (Cylanthus), son of Leos[1] <*Suda* "Leokorion," Adler>, 6a
Clymene[1], daughter of Oceanus and *Tethys* <Hes. *Theog.* 351>, 52b
— and Helios <Ovid *Met.* 1.766-71>, 14a
— and Iapetus <Hes. *Theog.* 510>, 16b
— and Merops[2] <Ovid *Met.* 1.764>, (52b)
— and Prometheus[1] <Schol. on Hom. *Od.* 10.2>, 16a
Clymene[2], daughter of Nereus <Hom. *Il.* XVIII.45> and *Doris*[1], *64a*
Clymene[3], wife of Parthenopaeus <Hyg. *Fab.* 71>, 64d
Clymene[4] (*Neaera*[1]), daughter of Minyas and *Euryanassa*[2] <Schol. on Hom. *Od.* 11.236>, 20c
— and Cephalus[2] <Paus. 10.29.6>, 22a
— and Iasus[4] <Apollod. *Bibl.* 3.9.2>, 64d
— and Phylacus[1] <Schol. on Hom. *Od.* 11.326>, 22a
Clymene[5], daughter of Catreus <Apollod. *Bibl.* 3.2.1>, 52d
— and Nauplius[1] <Apollod. *Bibl.* 3.2.2>, (52d)
Clymene[6] — see *Periclymene*
Clymene[7] [Amazon] <Hyg. *Fab.* 163>, *
Clymene[8], handmaiden of *Helen*[1] <Hom. *Il.* III.144-45>, *
Clymenus[1] [King of Orchomenus], son of Presbon[1] <Paus. 9.37.1>, 26c
— and *Budeia* <Eust. on Hom. *Il.* 1076.26>, (26c)
Clymenus[2], son of Phoroneus <Paus. 2.35.3> and *Teledice*, 61b
Clymenus[3], son of Oeneus[1] and *Althaea* <*Cat. Wom., Frag. Hes.* frg. 25.16, Merk. & West>, 17c
Clymenus[4], son of Schoeneus[1] <Hyg. *Fab.* 206>, 26d
alternate parentage:
Teleus <Parth. *Love Stor.* 13.1>
— and *Epicaste*[4] <Parth. *Love Stor.* 13.1>, (26d)
— and *Harpalyce*[2] <Hyg. *Fab.* 206>, 26d
Clymenus[5], son of Orchomenus[2] <*Cat. Wom., Frag. Hes.* frg. 77, Merk. & West>, 20d
Clymenus[6], son of Helios <Hyg. *Fab.* 154>, 14c
— and *Merope*[4] <Hyg. *Fab.* 154>, 61b
Clymenus[7], son of Phylacus[1] and *Clymene*[4] <Val. Flac. 1.369-70 (he is called brother of Iphiclus[2])>, 22c
Clymenus[8], son of Cardys <Paus. 5.8.1>, *
Clymenus[9], suitor of *Penelope*[1] (from Dulichium) <Apollod. *Epit.* 7.27>, *
Clymenus[10], killed Hodites[3] <Ovid *Met.* 5.96-97>, *
Clytemnestra, daughter of Tyndareus <Hom. *Od.* 24.199> and *Leda* <Aesch. *Agam.* 914>, 48c
— and Aegisthus <Hom. *Od.* 3.264-73>, 39a
— and Agamemnon <Aesch. *Agam.* 602>, 36a
— and Tantalus[2] <Eur. *Iph. in Aulis* 1150>, 39a
Clytie[1], daughter of Oceanus and *Tethys* <Hes. *Theog.* 352>, 52b
Clytie[2] (*Phthia*[3]), paramour of Amyntor[1] <Schol. A on Hom. *Il.* 9.448>, 24d

— and Phoenix[1] <Schol. A on Hom. *Il.* 9.448>, 24d
Clytie[3] (*Merope*[6]), daughter of Pandareus <Paus. 10.30.1> and *Harmothoe*[1], 66d
Clytie[4], paramour of Helios <Ovid *Met.* 4.236-37>, 14a
Clytie[5] — see *Cleobule*[4]
Clytippe, daughter of Thespius <Apollod. *Bibl.* 2.7.8> and *Megamede* <Apollod. *Bibl.* 2.4.10>, 50c
— and Heracles[1] <Apollod. *Bibl.* 2.7.8>, (50c)
Clytius[1], son of Laomedon[1] <Hom. *Il.* XX.238> and *Strym(n)o* <Apollod. *Bibl.* 3.12.3>, 42d
alternate parentage:
Laomedon[1] and *Leucippe*[8] <Apollod. *Bibl.* 3.12.3>
Laomedon[1] and *Placia* <Apollod. *Bibl.* 3.12.3>
Clytius[2], son of Alcmaeon[1] and *Arsinoe*[2] <Paus. 6.17.6>, 32d, *59b*
Clytius[3] [Argonaut], son of Eurytus[2] <Ap. Rhod. *Arg.* 2.1040> and *Antiope*[6] <Hyg. *Fab.* 14>, 60b
Clytius[4] [giant], son of *Gaea* (and the blood of Uranus) <Hes. *Theog.* 180-86; named as giant, Apollod. *Bibl.* 1.6.2>, *4a*
Clytius[5], father of *Pheno* <Paus. 2.6.5>, 11b
Clytius[6], father of Piraeus <Hom. *Od.* 15.540>, *
Clytius[7], suitor of *Penelope*[1] (from Dulichium) <Apollod. *Epit.* 7.27>, *
Clytius[8], suitor of *Penelope*[1] (from Same) <Apollod. *Epit.* 7.29>, *
Clytius[9], suitor of *Penelope*[1] (from Zacynthus) <Apollod. *Epit.* 7. 29>, *
Clytius[10], son of Aeolus[4] <Virg. *Aen.* 9.774>, *
Clytius[11], killed by Turnus <Virg. *Aen.* 9.740-74>, *
Clytius[12], killed by Corambasus <Non. *Dion.* 28.63-66>, *
Clytius[13], killed by Perseus[1] <Ovid *Met.* 5.141>, *
Clytodora[1], paramour of Minyas <Schol. on Ap. Rhod. 1.230>, 20d
Clytodora[2], daughter of Laomedon[1] <Dion. Hal. *Rom. Ant.* 1.62.2> and *Strym(n)o*, 42d
— and Assaracus <Dion. Hal. *Rom. Ant.* 1.62.2>, 41a
Clytonaeus[1], son of Alcinous <Hom. *Od.* 8.119> and *Arete* <Hom. *Od.* 7.67>, 9c
Clytonaeus[2] [King of Nauplia], son of Naubolus[1] <Ap. Rhod. *Arg.* 1.134>, 52d
Clytus[1] — see [fifty sons of Aegyptus[1]] (alternate version)
Clytus[2], killed by Perseus[1] <Ovid *Met.* 5.87>, *
Cnopus (Cleopus), son of Codrus[1] <Strab. 14.1.3>, 27c
Cnossia, paramour of Menelaus <Apollod. *Bibl.* 3.11.1>, 37c
Cocytus [river], son of Oceanus and *Tethys* <Hes. *Theog.* 367-68; named as river, Hom. *Od.* 10.514>, 50a
Codone[1], paramour of Aeneas <Agath. in Dion. Hal. *Rom. Ant.* 1. 49.2>, 41c
Codone[2] [one of the Bacchae] <Non. *Dion.* 30.213>, *
Codrus[1] [King of Athens], son of Melanthus[2] <Herod. 1.147.1>, 27d
Codrus[2], husband of *Eurynome*[7] <Val. Flac. 2.136>, *
Coeranus[1], son of Abas[4] <Paus. 1.43.5>, 31d
Coeranus[2], son of Iphitus[5] <Ovid *Met.* 134, 257>, *
Coeranus[3], killed by Hector[1] <Hom. *Il.* XVII.611-14>, *
Coeron, brother of Croco(n) <Suid. "Kyronidai">, 46d
C(o)eus [Titan], son of Uranus and *Gaea* <Hes. *Theog.* 134>, 11b
— and *Phoebe*[1] <Hes. *Theog.* 404>, (11b)
Colaxais (Colaxes), son of Targitaus <Herod. 4.5>, 6d
alternate parentage:
Zeus and *Hora* <Val. Flac. 6.48-49>
Colaxes — see Colaxais
Colymbas, daughter of Pierus[2] <Nicand. in Ant. Lib. *Met.* 9> and *Euippe*[2] <Ovid *Met.* 5.300 ff.>, 15c
Comaetho[1], daughter of Pterelaus <Apollod. *Bibl.* 2.4.7> and *Amphimede*, 58d
Comaetho[2], wife of Cydnus[2] <Non. *Dion.* 40.143-44>, 52b
Comaetho[3], paramour of Melanippus[7] <Paus. 7.19.2>, *
Combe[1] (*Chalcis*), daughter of Asopus and *Metope*[2] <Diod. Sic. 4. 72.1 (she is called Chalcis)>, 66c
— and Socus[2] <Non. *Dion.* 13.144-46>, (66c)
Combe[2], daughter of Ophis[2] <Ovid *Met.* 7.382>, *
Cometes[1] [centaur], offspring of Centaurus and a Magnesian Mare <Pind. *Pyth.* 2.50; named as centaur, Ovid *Met.* 12.283>, 69c
alternate parentage:
Ixion and *Nephele*[1] <Diod. Sic. 4.69.5>
Cometes[2], son of Thestius <Paus. 8.45.2> and *Eurythemis(te)*, 15d
Cometes[3], son of Sthenelus[2] <Apollod. *Epit.* 6.10>, 58c
— and *Aegiale* <Apollod. *Epit.* 6.10>, 30c
Cometes[4], father of Asterius[5] <Ap. Rhod. *Arg.* 1.35>, 29d
— and *Antigone*[4] <Hyg. *Fab.* 14 (inferred because she is mother of Asterius[5])>, (29d)
Cometes[5], son of Tisamenus[1] <Paus. 7.5.2>, 36c
Coon, son of Antenor[1] <Hom. *Il.* XI.248-49> and *Theano*[2], *45c*
Copreus[1], son of Pelops[1] <Apollod. *Bibl.* 2.5.1> and *Hippodameia*[1], *37a*
Copreus[2], grandson of Orchomenus[2] <*Cat. Wom., Frag. Hes.* frg. 70 (critical apparatus, citing Bartoletti's restoration) Merk. & West>, 20d
— and *Peisidice*[5] <*Cat. Wom., Frag. Hes.* frg. 70, Merk. & West>, (20d)
Coras, son of Catillus <Sol. *Coll. Rer. Mem.* 2.7>, 33c
Corax [King of Sicyon], son of Coronus[1] <Paus. 2.5.5>, 11b
Corcyra (*Cercyra*), daughter of Asopus and *Metope*[2] <Diod. Sic. 4.72.1>, 66a
— and Poseidon <Diod. Sic. 4.72.2>, 8c
Core — see *Persephone*[1]
Corethon, son of Lycaon[1] <Apollod. *Bibl.* 3.8.1>, 62b
Corinthus[1] [King of Corinth], son of Marathon[1] <Paus. 2.1.1>, 34d
— and *Gorge*[3] <*Etym. Magn.* "Eschatiotis" 384.39-40>, (34d)
Corinthus[2], son of Pelops[1] and *Hippodameia*[1] <Schol. on Eur. *Or.* 5>, *37a*
Coroebus[1], son of Mygdon(us)[2] and *Anaxamenia* <Eur. *Rhes.* 534>, 43d
— and *Cassandra*[1] <Paus. 10.27.1>, (43d)
Coroebus[2], a defender of Thebes <Stat. *Theb.* 9.745>, *
Coroebus[3], killed Vengeance <Paus. 1.43.7>, *
Coroneus, father of *Coronis*[2] <Ovid *Met.* 2.550>, 8c
(Coronides), daughters of Orion (see *Menippe*[2], *Metioche*), 53c
Coronis[1], daughter of Phlegyas[1] <*Hom. Hymn* 16 (to Asclepius), 1-5> and *Cleophema* <Isyl. *Lyr.* 3.43>, 19d
alternate parentage:
Azan <*Hom. Hymn* 3 (to Pythian Apollo), 211>
— and Apollo <*Hom. Hymn* 16 (to Asclepius), 1-3>, 11b
— and Ischys <*Cat. Wom., Frag. Hes.* frg. 60, Merk. & West>, 62d
Coronis[2], daughter of Coroneus <Ovid *Met.* 2.550>, 8c
— and Poseidon <Ovid *Met.* 2.550>, (8c)
Coronis[3] [one of the Hyades], daughter of Atlas and *Pleione* <Hyg. *Fab.* 192>, 44b
alternate parentage:
Hyas and *Boeotia* <Hyg. *Poet. Astr.* 2.21>
Coronis[4], paramour of Butes[2] <Diod. Sic. 5.50.5>, 12b
Coronis[5] — see (Charites) (alternate version)
Coronus[1] [King of Sicyon], son of Apollo and *Chrysorthe* <Paus. 2. 5.5>, 11b, *8d*
Coronus[2], father of *Anaxiroe* <Paus. 5.1.6>, 16a
Coronus[3] [Argonaut], son of Caeneus[1] <Hom. *Il.* II.746>, 8a
Coronus[4], son of Thersander[2] <Paus. 9.34.5>, 19c
(Corybantes), sons of Socus and *Combe* (see Acmon[2], Damneus, Ideaeus[3], Melisseus[1], Mimas[2], Ocythous, Prymneus), 66c
alternate parentage:
Apollo and *Rhetia* <Pher. in *F. Gr. H.* 3 F 48>
Corybas, son of Iasion and *Cybele*[2] <Diod. Sic. 5.49.2>, 42b
— and *Thebe*[3] <Diod. Sic. 5.49.3>, 56c
Corycia, paramour of Apollo <Paus. 10.6.3>, 11a
[Corycian nymphs], daughters of Pleistos <Ap. Rhod. *Arg.* 2.710>,

69b
Corynetes — see Periphetes[1]
Corythus[1], son of Zeus <Serv. on Virg. *Aen.* 3.167-70>, 6c
— and *Electra*[2] <Serv. on Virg. *Aen.* 7.207>, 42b
Corythus[2], son of Paris and *Helen*[1] <Nicand. in Parth. *Love Stor.* 34.2>, 43c
alternate parentage:
Paris and *Oenone*[1] <Parth. *Love Stor.* 34.1>
Corythus[3], wounded Pelates <Ovid *Met.* 5.123-25>, *
Corythus[4], king who named Telephus <Diod. Sic. 4.33.11>, *
Corythus[5], killed by Rhoetus[1] <Ovid *Met.* 12.283-89>, *
Cothone, wife of Eleusis <Hyg. *Fab.* 147>, 46b, 52b
Cothus, son of Ion[1] and *Helice*[1] <Strab. 10.1.3>, 51b
alternate parentage:
Xuthus[1] <Plut. *Gr. Quest.* 22>
Cottus [one of the Hecatoncheires], son of Uranus and *Gaea* <Hes. *Theog.* 149>, 4a
Cotys[1] [King of Maeonia], son of Manes and *Callirhoe*[2] <Dion. Hal. *Rom. Ant.* 1.27.1>, 51b
— and *Halia*[3] <Dion. Hal. *Rom. Ant.* 1.27.1>, (51b)
Cotys[2], killed by the Argonauts <Val. Flac. 3.112>, *
Cragaleus, son of Dryops[2] <Ant. Lib. *Met.* 4.1>, 64d
Cragasus (Traga(na)sus), father of *Philonome*[2] <Paus. 10.14.2>, 43c
Crambis — see Plexippus[2]
Cranae[1], daughter of Cranaus and *Pedias* <Apollod. *Bibl.* 3.14.5>, 16a
— and Amphictyon <Apollod. *Bibl.* 3.14.5>, (16a)
Cranae[2], paramour of Janus <Ovid *Fast.* 6.107, 124>, *
Cranaechme, daughter of Cranaus and *Pedias* <Apollod. *Bibl.* 3.14.5>, 16a
Cranaus [King of Athens], father of *Att(h)is*, *Cranae*, and *Cranaechme* <Apollod. *Bibl.* 3.14.5>, 16a
— and *Pedias* <Apollod. *Bibl.* 3.14.5>, 51d
Cranfia [cornel tree], daughter of Oxylus[3] and *Hamadryas* <Athen. 3.78b>, 71d
Cranon, son of Pelasgus[3] <Steph. Byz. "Cranon"> and *Menippe*[3], 61d
Cranto, daughter of Nereus and *Doris*[1] <Apollod. *Bibl.* 1.2.7>, *64a*
Crataegonus, son of Psyllus and *Anchiroe*[1] <Non. *Dion.* 13.378>, 52a
Crataeis[1], paramour of Phorcus[1] <Hom. *Od.* 12.127 (inferred because she is called mother of *Scylla*[2]) (called *Hecate* in Ap. Rhod. *Arg.* 4.828)>, 2b
Crataeis[2] [river], son of Oceanus and *Tethys* <Hes. *Theog.* 367-68; named as river, Hyg. *Fab.* 199>, 52b
Crateus — see Catreus
Cratieus, father of *Anaxibia*[3] <Apollod. *Bibl.* 1.9.9>, 27d
Cratus [power], son of Pallas[1] and *Styx* <Hes. *Theog.* 385>, 12a
Creisus — see Ceisus
Crenaeus[1] [centaur], offspring of Centaurus and a Magnesian Mare <Pind. *Pyth.* 2.50; named as centaur, Ovid *Met.* 12.313>, 69c
alternate parentage:
Ixion and *Nephele*[1] <Diod. Sic. 4.69.5>
Crenaeus[2], son of Faunus and *Ismenis* <Stat. *Theb.* 9.319-20>, *
Crenaeus[3], killed by Idmon[1] <Val. Flac. 3.175-78>, *
Crenaeus[4], killed by *Myrmidone* <Stat. *Theb.* 5.221-24>, *
Creneis, daughter of Nereus and *Doris*[1] <Hyg. *Fab.* pref.>, *64a*
Creon[1] [King of Corinth], son of Lycaethus[1] <Schol. on Eur. *Med.*>, 33b
Creon[2] [King of Thebes], son of Menoeceus[1] <Soph. *Ant.* 156-57>, 55d
— and *Eurydice*[9] <Soph. *Ant.* 1180>, (55d)
Creon[3], son of Heracles[1] <Apollod. *Bibl.* 2.7.8>, 51c
Creontiades, son of Heracles[1] and *Megara* <Apollod. *Bibl.* 2.4.11>, 60d
Cresphontes[1] [King of Messenia], son of Aristomachus[1] <Apollod. *Bibl.* 2.8.2-4>, 60c
— and *Merope*[2] <Apollod. *Bibl.* 2.8.5>, 62c
Cresphontes[2] — see Aepytus[3]
Cressida — see *Briseis*[2]
[Cretan Bull], father of Asterius[7] [Minotaur] <Apollod. *Bibl.* 3.1.4>, 54c
— and *Pasiphae*[1] <Apollod. *Bibl.* 3.1.4>, (54c)
Crete[1], daughter of Asterius[4] <Apollod. *Bibl.* 3.1.2> and *Europe*[1], 17c
— and Minos I <Asclep. in Apollod. *Bibl.* 3.1.2>, 54c
Crete[2], daughter of Deucalion[1] <Apollod. *Bibl.* 3.2.3> and *Pyrrha*[1], 16b
Crete[3] — see *Perse(is)*
Crete[4], daughter of one of the Curetes <Diod. Sic. 3.71.3>, *
Cretheis — see *Asty(a)dameia*[2]
Cretheus[1] [King of Iolcus], son of Aeolus[1] <Hom. *Od.* 11.235 ff.> and *Enarete* <Apollod. *Bibl.* 1.7.3>, 30a
alternate parentage:
Poseidon <Paus. 4.2.5>
— and *Demodice*[1] <Hyg. *Poet. Astr.* 2.20>, (30a)
— and *Tyro* <Hom. *Od.* 11.240>, 27b, 63c
Cretheus[2], killed by Turnus <Virg. *Aen.* 9.74>, *
Cretheus[3], killed by Hippomedon[1] <Stat. *Theb.* 9.307>, *
Crethon, son of Diocles[1] <Hom. *Il.* V.542>, 65b
Cretus, son of Zeus <Eust. *Comm. Dion. Per.* 498>, 6c
Creusa[1] — see *Glauce*[2]
Creusa[2], daughter of Priam[1] and *Hecabe*[1] <Apollod. *Bibl.* 3.11.5>, 43c
— and Aeneas[1] <Virg. *Aen.* 2.739>, 41c
Creusa[3], daughter of Erechtheus II <*Cat. Wom., Hesiodi* frg. 10(a).20-21, Merk. & West (O.C.T.)> and *Praxithea*[2] <Apollod. *Bibl.* 3.15.1>, 51b
— and Apollo <Eur. *Ion* 70-76>, 11a
— and Xuthus[1] <*Cat. Wom., Hesiodi* frg. 10(a).20, Merk. & West (O.C.T.)>, 17b
Creusa[4], daughter of *Gaea* <Pind. *Pyth.* 9.13>, *2a*
— and Peneius <Diod. Sic. 4.69.1>, 68b
Creusa[5], wife of Cassandrus <Quint. Smyr. 8.81>, *
Criasus[1] (Chryasus) [King of Argos], son of Argus[2] and *Euadne*[2] <Apollod. *Bibl.* 2.1.2>, 61b
— and *Melantho*[2] <Schol. on Eur. *Or.* 932>, (61b)
Criasus[2], killed by Deriades <Non. *Dion.* 32.186>, *
Crimisus[1] (Crinisus) [river], son of Oceanus and *Tethys* <Hes. *Theog.* 367-68; named as river, Virg. *Aen.* 5.39>, 67a
— and *Aegesta* <Serv. on Virg. *Aen.* 1.550>, (67a)
Crimisus[2], killed by Deriades <Non. *Dion.* 32.234>, *
Crinacus, son of Hyrieus <Schol. on Hom. *Il.* XXIV.544>, 35a
alternate parentage:
Poseidon and *Alcyone*[2] <*Cat. Wom., Frag. Hes.* frg. 184, Merk. & West>
Zeus <Diod. Sic. 5.81.4>
Crinisus — see Crimisus[1]
Crino[1], daughter of Antenor[1] and *Theano*[2] <Paus. 10.27.1>, (45c)
Crino[2], paramour of Danaus[1] <Apollod. *Bibl.* 2.1.5>, 57b, 57d
Crisus, son of Phocus[1] <Paus. 2.29.4> and *Asterodeia*[2], 23c
— and *Antiphateia* <Schol. on Eur. 33>, 52d
Critobule, paramour of Ares <Ps.-Plut. *De Fluv.* 3.2>, 7a
Critolaus, son of Hicetaon[1] <Paus. 10.26.1>, 42d
— and *Aristomache* <Paus. 10.26.1>, 43d
Critomedeia —see [fifty daughters of Danaus[1]] (alternate version)
Crius[1] [Titan], son of Uranus and *Gaea* <Hes. *Theog.* 134>, 12a
— and *Eurybia*[1] <Hes. *Theog.* 376>, 3a
Crius[2], son of Theocles <Paus. 13.1.3>, *
Croco(n), husband of *Saesara* <Paus. 1.38.2>, 46d
[Crommyon Sow] — see *Phaea*
Cromus[1], son of Poseidon <Paus. 4.1.3>, 9d
Cromus[2] — see [fifty sons of Lycaon[1]] (alternate version)

Cronius[1], son of Zeus and *Himalia* <Diod. Sic. 5.55.5>, 5c
Cronius[2], killed by Oenomaus[1] <Paus. 6.21.11>, *
Cronus [Titan] [time], son of Uranus and *Gaea* <Hes. *Theog.* 137>, 5a
alternate parentage:
Oceanus and *Tethys* <Plato *Tim.* 40e>
— and *Phillyra* <Pher. in *F. Gr. H.* 3 F 50>, 69b
— and *Rhea* <Hes. *Theog.* 453>, (5a)
— and *Thrace* <Steph. Byz. "Bithynia">, 55a
Crotopus [King of Argos], son of Agenor[6] <Paus. 2.16.1>, 61d
Crotus, son of Pan and *Eupheme*[1] <Hyg. *Fab.* 224>, 46c
Cteatus, son of Poseidon <Hom. *Il.* II, 621> and *Molione* <*Cat. Wom., Frag. Hes.* frg. 17, Merk. & West>, 9a
alternate parentage:
Actor[4] and *Molione* <Paus. 8.14.9>
— and *Theronice* <Paus. 5.3.3>, 14d
Ctesippus[1], son of Heracles[1] and *Asty(a)dameia*[1] <Apollod. *Bibl.* 2. 7.8>, 60a
Ctesippus[2], son of Heracles[1] and *Deianeira*[1] <*Cat. Wom., Frag. Hes.* frg. 25.19, Merk. & West>, 60a
Ctesippus[3], son of Polytherses <Hom. *Od.* 22.285-86>, *
Ctesippus[4], suitor of *Penelope*[1] (from Same) <Apollod. *Epit.* 7. 28>, *
Ctesippus[5], suitor of *Penelope*[1] (from Ithaca) <Apollod. *Epit.* 7. 30>, *
Cteson — see Cleson
Ctimene, daughter of Laertes and *Anticleia*[1] <Hom. *Od.* 15.364>, 5c, *13c*
— and Eurylochus[1] <Eust. on Hom. *Od.* 1784>, (5c), (13c)
Ctimenus — see Eurydamas[1] (alternate veresion)
[Cumaean Sibyl] — see *Deiphobe*
(Curetes) — see (Dactyls)
Cyane[1], daughter of Liparus <Diod. Sic. 5.7.6>, 13c
— and Aeolus[2] <Diod. Sic. 5.7.6>, 18a
Cyane[2] — see *Cyanea*
Cyane[3], paramour of Anapis <Ovid *Met.* 5.410-11>, *
Cyanea (*Cyane*[2]) (*Eidothea*[1]) (*Idothea*[1]), daughter of Maeandrus <Ovid *Met.* 9.450-54>, 68a
alternate parentage:
Eurytus[7] <Ant. Lib. *Met.* 30.2 (she is called *Eidothea*)>
— and Miletus <Ovid *Met.* 9.449-52>, 11b
Cyanippus[1] [King of Argos] [one of the Epigoni], son of Adrastus[1] and *Amphithea*[1] <Apollod. *Bibl* 1.9.13>, 30c
alternate parentage:
Aegialeus[1] <Paus. 2.18.4>
Cyanippus[2], son of Pharax <Parth. *Love Stor.* 10.1>, *
Cyaretus — see Cydrelus
Cybele[1] — see *Rhea*
Cybele[2]/Agdistis (*Dindymene*) [Phrygian Mother of the Gods], hermaphrodite daughter/son of Zeus and *Gaea* <Paus. 7.17.5 (called Agdistis) (born from seed of Zeus dropped on earth)>, 5a, *2b*, *2d*
alternate parentage:
(as *Cybele*) Meion and *Dindyme* <Diod Sic. 3.58.1>
— and Gordius <Hyg. *Fab.* 274>, (2d)
— and Iasion <Diod. Sic. 5.49.2>, 42b
— and Olympus[3] <Diod. Sic. 5.49.3>, (2d)
— and Sa(n)garius <Mem. in *F. Gr. H.* 434 F 1, 28, 29>, 70a
Cychreus (Cynchreus) [King of Salamis], son of Poseidon and *Salamis* <Apollod. *Bibl.* 3.12.7>, 9b, *66b*
(Cyclopes), sons of Uranus and *Gaea* (see Arges, Brontes, Steropes), 4a-b
Cycnus[1], son of Ares <Eur. *Alc.* 502-03> and *Pelopeia*[1] <Apollod. *Bibl.* 2.7.7>, 7d, *28d*
— and *Themistonoe* <Hes. *Shield* 350-56>, (7d)
Cycnus[2] [King of Colona], son of Poseidon <Paus. 10.14.2> and *Calyce*[2] <Hyg. *Fab.* 157>, 8b
alternate parentage:
Poseidon and *Scamandrodice* <Schol. on Pind. *Olym.* 2. 147>
— and *Philonome*[2] <Paus. 10.14.2>, 43c
— and *Procleia* <Paus. 10.14.2>, 43c
Cycnus[3], son of Apollo and *Thyria* <Ant. Lib. *Met.* 12.1>, 11d
Cycnus[4] [King in Macedonia], son of Ares and *Pyrene*[2] <Apollod. *Bibl.* 2.5.11>, 7c
Cycnus[5], father of *Glauce*[6] <Dict. Cret. 2.13>, 23c
Cycnus[6] [King of Ligurians], son of Sthenelus[5] <Ovid *Met.* 2. 367>, *
Cycnus[7], son of Ocytus and *Aurophites* <Hyg. *Fab.* 97>, *
Cycnus[8], suitor of *Penelope*[1] (from Dulichium) <Apollod. *Epit.* 7. 27>, *
Cydippe[1] (*Cyrbia*) (*Lysippe*[3]), daughter of Ochimus and *Hegetoria* <Diod. Sic. 5.57.7>, 14b
— and Cercaphus <Diod. Sic. 5.57.7>, 14a
Cydippe[2], daughter of Nereus and *Doris*[1] <Hyg. *Fab.* pref.>, *64a*
Cydippe[3], wife of Acontius <Ovid *Her.* 20.21>, *
Cydippe[4], mother of Bitias[2] and Cleops <Hyg. *Fab.* 254> (called Biton and Cleobis <Herod. 1.31>), *
Cydnus [river], son of Oceanus and *Tethys* <Hes. *Theog.* 367-68; named as river, Non. *Dion.* 2.144>, 52b
alternate parentage:
Anchiale[2] <Steph. Byz. "Anchiale">
— and *Comaetho*[2] <Non. *Dion.* 40.143-44>, (52b)
Cydon[1], son of Hermes and *Acacallis*[1] <Paus. 8.53.4>, 46a, *53d*
alternate parentage:
Apollo and *Acacallis*[1] <Steph. Byz. "Cydonia">
Tegeates and *Maera*[2] <Paus. 8.53.4>
Cydon[2], killed by Aeneas <Virg. *Aen.* 10.324>, *
Cydon[3], killed by Tydeus[1] <Stat. *Theb.* 2.623>, *
Cydon[4], killed by Lemnian women <Stat. *Theb.* 5.220>, *
Cydon[5], killed by Hippomedon[1] <Stat. *Theb.* 9.127>, *
Cydon[6], killed by Parthenopaeus <Stat. *Theb.* 9.759>, *
Cydon[7] [horse ridden by Hippodamus] <Stat. *Theb.* 6.465>, *
Cydragora — see *Anaxibia*[1]
Cydrelus (Cyaretus), son of Codrus[1] <Strab. 14.1.3>, 27c
Cylanthus — see Clyanthus
Cylarabes (Cylasabis) [King of Argos], son of Sthenelus[2] <Paus. 2. 18.4>, 58c
Cylasabis — see Cylarabes
Cylindrus — see Cytis(s)orus
Cyllarus[1] [centaur], offspring of Centaurus and a Magnesian Mare <Pind. *Pyth.* 2.50; named as centaur, Ovid *Met.* 12.393-417>, 69c
alternate parentage:
Ixion and *Nephele*[1] <Diod. Sic. 4.69.5>
— and *Hylonome* <Ovid *Met.* 12.393-408>, (69c)
Cyllarus[2], son of Brongus <Non. *Dion.* 26.220>, *
Cyllen, son of Elatus[1] <Paus. 8.4.4> and *Laodice*[2], 62d
Cyllene[1], paramour of Pelasgus[1] <Apollod. *Bibl.* 3.8.1>, 62b
— and Lycaon[1] <Dion. Hal. *Rom. Ant.* 11.13.1>, 62b
Cyllene[2], daughter and paramour of Menephron <Hyg. *Fab.* 253>, *
Cyllenus — see (Dactyls) (alternate version)
Cymatolege, daughter of Nereus and *Doris*[1] <Hes. *Theog.* 253>, *64b*
Cymelus [centaur], offspring of Centaurus and a Magnesian Mare <Pind. *Pyth.* 2.50; named as centaur, Ovid *Met.* 12.455>, 69d
alternate parentage:
Ixion and *Nephele*[1] <Diod. Sic. 4.69.5>
Cymo, daughter of Nereus and *Doris*[1] <Hes. *Theog.* 255>, *64b*
Cymodoce, daughter of Nereus and *Doris*[1] <Hes. *Theog.* 254>, *64b*
Cymopoleia, daughter of Poseidon <Hes. *Theog.* 819>, 9d
— and Briareus <Hes. *Theog.* 819>, 4b
Cymothoe, daughter of Nereus and *Doris*[1] <Hes. *Theog.* 245>, *64b*

Cymothon, son of Oeagrus and *Calliope* <Tzetz. on Lyc. 831>, *6a*
Cynaethus, son of Lycaon[1] <Apollod. *Bibl.* 3.8.1>, 63a
Cynchreus — see Cychreus
Cynna, mother of *Eurydice*[1] <Athen. 4.155a>, 6a
Cynortas — see Cynortes
Cynortes (Cynortas) [King of Sparta], son of Amyclas[1] and *Diomede*[2] <Apollod. *Bibl.* 3.10.3>, 47a
Cynorus — see Cynosurus
Cynosurus (Cynorus), son of Pelops[1] and *Hippodameia*[1] <Schol. on Eur. 5>, *37b*
Cynurus, son of Perseus[1] <Paus. 3.2.2> and *Andromeda*, 58d
Cynus, son of Opus[2] <Eust. on Hom. *Il.* 277>, 15a
Cyparissus[1], son of Minyas <Schol. on Hom. *Il.* II.519>, and *Euryanassa*[2], 20d
Cyparissus[2], son of Telephus and *Argiope*[2] <Serv. on Virg. *Aen.* 3.680>, 60a
— and Apollo <Ovid *Met.* 10.106-42>, 11a
Cypselus[1] [King of Arcadia], son of Aepytus[2] <Paus. 8.5.6>, 62c
— and *Herodice* <Athen. 13.609f>, (62c)
Cypselus[2], son of Eetion[3] and *Labda* <Herod. 5.92>; father of Periander <Paus. 2.28.3>, 60d
(Cyrbantes), children of Apollo and *Rhetia* <Pher. in Strab. 10.3.21>, 11c
Cyrbia — see *Cydippe*[1]
Cyrene, daughter of Hypseus[1] <Pind. *Pyth.* 9.3-17> and *Chlidanope* <Schol. on Pind. 13>, 69a
— and Apollo <Pind. *Pyth.* 9.5-7>, 11a
— and Ares <Apollod. *Bibl.* 2.5.8>, 7a
Cyrianassa — see *Iphianassa*[1]
Cythereia — see *Aphrodite*
Cytis(s)orus (Cylindrus), son of Phrixus[1] and *Chalciope*[1] <Apollod. *Bibl.* 1.9.1>, 26c
Cytus, son of Zeus and *Himalia* <Diod. Sic. 5.55.5>, 5c
Cyzicus [King of the Doliones], son of Aeneus and *Aenete* <Ap. Rhod. *Arg.* 1.951>, 44c
alternate parentage:
Eus(s)orus <Hyg. *Fab.* 16>
— and *Cleite*[1] <Ap. Rhod. *Arg.* 1.974>, (44c)
— and *Laris(s)a*[2] <Parth. *Love Stor.* 23.1>, (44c)

(Dactyls) (Curetes), children of *Anchiale*[1] (see Epimedes, Heracles[2], Iasius[1], Idas[3], Paeonaeus, and five female Dactyls), 11a-b
other Dactyls, children of *Anchiale*[1]:
Cyllenus and Titias[1] <Ap. Rhod. *Arg.* 1.1126>
Celmis, Damnameneus[2], and Delas (Scythes[2]) <Clem. *Strom.* i.16.75 in *Hes.—Hom. Hymns and Hom.*, "Idaean Dactyls," Evelyn-White>
other Dactyls, children of *Ida*[4]:
Ledas, Meidas, Midas[2], Oidas, and Pheidas <*Etym. Magn.* "Dactyls">
Daedalion, son of Phosphor(us) <Ovid *Met.* 11.295-96>, 13b
Daedalus, son of Eupalamus and *Alcippe*[1] <Apollod. *Bibl.* 3.15.8>, 49b
alternate parentage:
Eupalamus and *Merope*[5] <Plut. *Thes.* 19.5>
Metion and *Iphinoe*[5] <Pher. in *F. Gr. H.* 3 F 146>
Palamaon <Paus. 9.3.2>
— and [a Cretan woman] <Strab. 6.3.3>, (49b)
— and *Naucrate* <Apollod. *Epit.* 1.12>, (49b)
Daeira, daughter of Oceanus and *Tethys* <Paus. 1.38.7>, 52b
— and Hermes <Paus. 1.38.7>, 46b
Daeto, daughter of Pelops[1] <Tzetz. on Lyc. 212> and *Hippodameia*[1], *37b*
— and Thyestes[1] <Tzetz. on Lyc. 212>, 39a
Daimenus, son of Tisamenus[1] <Paus. 7.5.2>, 36c
Daiphron[1], son of Aegyptus[1] <Apollod. *Bibl.* 2.1.5>, 57d
— and *Scaea* <Apollod. *Bibl.* 2.1.5>, (57d)
Daiphron[2], son of Aegyptus[1] and *Hephaestine* <Apollod. *Bibl.* 2.1.5>, 57d
— and *Adiante* <Apollod. *Bibl.* 2.1.5>, (57d)
Damaethus, father of *Syrna* <Steph. Byz. "Syrna">, 19d
Damaphon, son of Thoas[4] <Paus. 2.4.3>, 18c
Damascus, son of Hermes and *Halimede* <Steph. Byz. "Damascus">, 46c
Damasen [giant], son of *Gaea* (and the blood of Uranus) <Hes. *Theog.* 180-86; named as giant, Non. *Dion.* 25.453-54>, *4a*
Damasias, son of Penthilus[1] <Paus. 7.5.2>, 36d
Damasichthon[1], son of Amphion[1] and *Niobe*[1] <Apollod. *Bibl.*3.5.6>, 66c
Damasichthon[2], son of Opheltes[2] <Paus. 9.5.16>, 18d
Damasichton[3], son of Codrus[1] <Paus. 7.3.1>, 27d
Damasippus, son of Icarius[2] and *Periboea*[5] <Apollod. *Bibl.* 3.10.5>, 47c
Damastes — see Polypemon
Damastor[1], son of Nauplius[1] <Schol. on Ap. Rhod. 4.1091>, 52d
Damastor[2], suitor of *Penelope*[1] (from Dulichium) <Apollod. *Epit.* 7.27>, *
Damasus[1], son of Codrus[1] <Paus. 7.3.6>, 27d
Damasus[2], killed by Polypoetes[1] <Hom. *Il.* XII.183>, *
Damasus[3], killed by Haemon[?] <Stat. *Theb.* 8.494>, *
Damnameneus[1] — see (Telchines) (alternate version)
Damnameneus[2] — see (Dactyls) (alternate version)
Damnameneus[3], paramour of *Melis* <Non. *Dion.* 33.324-26>, *
Damneus, son of Socus and *Combe*[1] <Non. *Dion.* 13.144>, *66c*
alternate parentage:
Apollo and *Rhetia* <Pher. in *F. Gr. H.* 3 F 48 (unnamed)>
Damno, daughter of Belus[1] <Pher. in *F. Gr. H.* 3 F 21>, and *Anchinoe*[1], 59a
— and Agenor[1] <Pher. in *F. Gr. H.* 3 F 21>, 55a
Damocrateia, daughter of Actor[3] and *Aegina* <Schol. on Pind. *Olym.* 9.106b>, 22d
Damon, father of *Dexithea*[1] and *Macello* <Nicand. in Schol. on Ovid *Ibis* 477>, 54d
Damone —see [fifty daughters of Danaus[1]] (alternate version)
Danae, daughter of Acrisius <Hom. *Il.* XIV.319> and *Eurydice*[6] <Pher. frg. 2, Sturz>, 58d
alternate parentage:
Acrisius and *Aganippe*[2] <Hyg. *Fab.* 155>
— and Polydectes[1] <Pind. *Pyth.* 12.14-15>, 15c
— and Proetus[1] <Apollod. *Bibl.* 2.4.1>, 57d
— and Zeus <Hom. *Il.* XIV.319>, 5b
(Danaides) — see [fifty daughters of Danaus[1]]
Danais — see Chrysippus[1] (alternate version)
Danaus[1] [King of Lybia and later Argos], son of Belus[1] and *Anchinoe*[1] <Pher. in *Schol.* on Ap. Rhod. *Arg.* 3.1185>, 57a
— and *Atlantia* (or *Phoebe*[4]) <Apollod. *Bibl.* 2.1.5>, (57a), (57c), (58c)
— and *Crino*[2] <Apollod. *Bibl.* 2.1.5>, (57a), (57c), (58c)
— and *Elephantis* <Apollod. *Bibl.* 2.1.5>, (57a), (57c)
— and [an Ethiopian woman] <Apollod. *Bibl.* 2.1.5>, (57c), (58c)
— and *Europe*[3] <Apollod. *Bibl.* 2.1.5>, (57a), (57c)
— and *Herse*[2] <Apollod. *Bibl.* 2.1.5>, (57a), (57c)
— and *Memphis*[2] <Apollod. *Bibl.* 2.1.5>, (57a), (57c)
— and *Pieria*[1] <Apollod. *Bibl.* 2.1.5>, (57a), (57c)
— and *Polyxo*[3] <Apollod. *Bibl.* 2.1.5>, (57a), (57c)
Danaus[2], father of Argus[1] (alternate version) <Hyg. *Fab.* 14>, *
Danaus[3], father of Phocus[5] <Hyg. *Fab.* 97>, *
Danaus[4], soldier at Thebes <Stat. *Theb.* 10.315>, *
Daphne[1], daughter of Peneius <Ovid *Met.* 1.493-507>, 68b
alternate parentage:
Amyclas <Plut. *Agis* 9>
Ladon[1] and *Gaea* <Pal. 49>
— and Apollo <Ovid *Met.* 1.493-568>, 11a

— and Leucippus[2] <Paus. 8.20.2>, 7c, 40a
Daphne[2] — see *Manto*[1]
Daphnis[1] (Bucolus[3]), son of Hermes and *Thronia* <Diod. Sic. 4.84. 4>, 46c
— and *Chimaera*[2] <Serv. on Virg. *Ecl.* 8.68>, (46c)
— and *Echenais* <Parth. *Love Stor.* 29>, (46c)
— and *Pi(m)pleia* <Serv. on Virg. *Ecl.* 8.68>, (46c)
Daphnis[2] [centaur], offspring of Centaurus and a Magnesian Mare <Pind. *Pyth.* 2.50; named as centaur, Diod. Sic. 4.12.7>, 69d
alternate parentage:
Ixion and *Nephele*[1] <Diod. Sic. 4.69.5>
Daphnis[3], child, suckled by a goat, and raised by Lamo and *Myrtale* <Lon. *Daphnis and Chloe* 1.2-3>, *
Daphnis[4], shepherd of Mt. Ida <Ovid *Met.* 4.278>, *
Daphnis[5], nymph, prophetess for *Gaea* <Paus. 10.5.5>, *
Daphoeneus [one of the Pans], son of Pan <Non. *Dion.* 14.80>, 64d
Daplidice —see [fifty daughters of Danaus[1]] (alternate version)
Dardanus[1] [King of Troy and Dardania], son of Zeus <Hom. *Il.* XX.215-16> and *Electra*[2] <Apollod. *Bibl.* 3.12.1>, 5c, *42b*
— and *Bateia*[2] <Hellan. in *F. Gr. H.* 4 F 24>, 70b
— and *Chryse*[2] <Dion. Hal. *Rom. Ant.* 1.61>, 63d
— and *Neso*[1] <Tzetz. on Lyc. 1465>, (42b)
Dardanus[2], son of Bias[4] <Hom. *Il.* XX.460>, *
Dascylus[1] [King of the Mariandyni], son of Tantalus[1] <Schol. on Ap. Rhod *Arg.* 2.752 (inferred because Lycus[5] is grandson of Tantalus[1])> and *Dione*[3], *41a*
Dascylus[2], son of Lycus[5] <Ap. Rhod. *Arg.* 2.803>, 41a
Dascylus[3], father of Gyges[2] <Herod. 1.8>, *
[daughter (unnamed)] of Aeneas and *Anethemone* <Dion. Hal. *Rom. Ant.* 1.49.2>, 41c
[daughter (unnamed)] of Aeneas and *Codone*[1] <Dion. Hal. *Rom. Ant.* 1.49.2>, 41c
Daunius [King of Apulia], son of Lycaon[1] (alternate version) <Ant. Lib. *Met.* 31.1> and father of *Euippe*[1] <Ant. Lib. *Met.* 37.3>, 17d
Deianeira[1], daughter of Oeneus[1] and *Althaea* <*Cat. Wom., Frag. Hes.* frg. 25, 17, Merk. & West>, 16d
alternate parentage:
Dionysus and *Althaea* <Apollod. *Bibl.* 1.8.1>
— and Heracles[1] <*Cat. Wom., Frag. Hes.* frg. 25, 17-18, Merk. & West>, 60a
— and Nessus[1] <Ovid *Met.* 9.102-25>, 69d
Deianeira[2] — see *Hippolyte*[3]
Deianeira[3], daughter of Lycaon[4] <Dion. Hal. *Rom. Ant.* 1.11.2>, 62b
— and Pelasgus[1] <Dion. Hal. *Rom. Ant.* 1.11.2>, (62b)
Deianeira[4] [Amazon] <Diod. Sic. 4.16.3>, *
Deicoon[1] (Deion[2]), son of Heracles[1] and *Megara* <Apollod. *Bibl.* 2. 7.8>, 60d
Deicoon[2], son of Pergasus <Hom. *Il.* 5.535>, *
Deidameia[1], daughter of Lycomedes[1] <Apollod. *Bibl.* 3.13.8>, 11d
— and Achilles <Apollod. *Bibl.* 3.13.8>, 24c
Deidameia[2] — see *Eurythemis(te)*
Deidameia[3] — see *Laodameia*[2]
Deidameia[4] — see *Hippodameia*[2]
Deidameia[5], daughter of Pyrrhus[4] <Paus. 4.35.3>, *
Deimachus[1], son of Neleus[1] and *Chloris*[2] <*Cat. Wom., Frag. Hes.* frg. 33(a), Merk. & West>, 27c
Deimachus[2], father of *Enarete* <Apollod. *Bibl.* 1.7.3>, 18a
Deimachus[3], son of Eleon <Plut. *Gr. Quest.* 41>, 70b
— and *Glaucia*[1] <Plut. *Gr. Quest.* 41>, (70b)
Deimachus[4], son of Electryon[1] and *Lysidice*[1] <*Cat. Wom., Frag. Hes.* frg. 193, Merk. & West>, 59d, *38a*
Deimachus[5], father of Autolycus[2], Deileon, and Phlogius <Ap. Rhod. *Arg.* 2.954>, *
Deimas, son of Dardanus[1] and *Chryse*[2] <Dion. Hal. *Rom. Ant.* 1. 61>, 42b
Deimus [terror], son of Ares and *Aphrodite* <Hes. *Theog.* 934>, 7a
Deino [one of the Graeae], daughter of Phorcus[1] and *Ceto*[1] <Pher. in *F. Gr. H.* 3 F 11>, 2a
Deion[1] (Deioneus[1]) [King of Phocis], son of Aeolus[1] <*Cat. Wom., Frag. Hes.* frg. 58, Merk. & West> and *Enarete* <Apollod. *Bibl.* 1.7.3>, 22a
— and *Diomede*[3] <Apollod. *Bibl.* 1.9.4>, 17b
Deion[2] — see Deicoon[1]
Deione[1] — see *Persephone*
Deione[2] — see *Areia*
Deioneus[1] — see Deion[1]
Deion(eus)[2], son of Eurytus[2] <Plut. *Thes.* 8.3> and *Antiope*[6], 60b
— and *Perigune* <Plut. *Thes.* 8.3>, 34d
Deioneus[3] — see Eioneus[2]
Deioneus[4], killed by Philoctetes <Quint. Smyr. 10.167>, *
Deiope, daughter of Triptolemus <Paus. 1.14.1>, 46d
— and Musaeus <Aris. *On Marv. Works Heard* 131.3-5>, 6b
Deiopeia[1], daughter of Nereus and *Doris*[1] <Hyg. *Fab.* pref.>, *64b*
Deiopeia[2], nymph offered to Aeolus[2] if he would help sink the fleet of Aeneas[1] <Virg. *Aen.* 1.65-75>, *
Deiopites, son of Priam[1] <Apollod. *Bibl.* 3.12.5>, 43d
Deiphilus — see Nebrophonus
Deiphobe (*Amaltheia*[1]) (*Demo*[2]) (*Demophile*[1]) (*Herophile*[2]) [Cumaean Sibyl], daughter of Glaucus[3] <Virg. *Aen.* 6.34>, 62a
Deiphobus[1], son of Priam[1] <Hom. *Il.* XII.94> and *Hecabe*[1] <Apollod. *Bibl.* 3.11.5>, 43c
— and *Helen*[1] <Tzetz. on Lyc. 143>, 48d
Deiphobus[2], son of Hippolytus[1] <Apollod. *Bibl.* 2.6.2>, 51c
Deiphontes[1] — see Demophoon[1]
Deiphontes[2] [King of Argos], son of Antimachus[2] <Paus. 2.19.1>, 60c
— and *Hyrnetho* <Paus. 2.19.1>, 60c
Deiphyle[1] — see *Leipephilene*
Deiphyle[2], daughter of Adrastus[1] <Eur. *Supp.* 133-38; named, Apollod. *Bibl.* 1.9.13> and *Amp(h)it(h)ea*[1] <Apollod. *Bibl.* 1.9.13>, 30d
— and Tydeus <Eur. *Supp.* 133-38; named, Apollod. *Bibl.* 3.6. 1>, 17d
Deipylus[1], son of Jason and *Hypsipyle* <Hyg. *Fab.* 140>, 33d
Deipylus[2], son of Polym(n)estor[1] and *Ilione* <Hyg. *Fab.* 109>, 43d
Delas (Scythes[2]) — see (Dactyls) (alternate version)
Deliades (Alcimenes[2]) (Peiren), son of Glaucus[1] <Apollod. *Bibl.* 2. 3.1> and *Eurynome*[2], 18d
Delphus, son of Apollo and *Celaeno*[3] <Paus. 10.6.3>, 11a, *17a*
alternate parentage:
Apollo and *Melaena* <Paus. 10.6.4>
Apollo and *Thyia*[2] <Paus. 10.6.4>
Poseidon and *Melantho*[1] <Tzetz. on Lyc. 208>
Delphyne — see *Pytho(n)*
Demeter [goddess] [agriculture], daughter of Cronus and *Rhea* <Hes. *Theog.* 454>, 10a
alternate parentage:
Oceanus ("from whom all we gods proceed") <Hom. *Il.* XIV.202>
— and Iasion <Hom. *Od.* 5.124-25>, 42b
— and Poseidon <Apollod. *Bibl.* 3.6.8>, 8c
— and Zeus <Hes. *Theog.* 912>, 5b
Demo[1], daughter of Celeus[1] <*Hom. Hymn* 2 (to *Demeter*) 109>, and *Metaneira*, 46b
Demo[2] — see *Deiphobe*
Democoon, son of Priam[1] <Hom. *Il.* IV.499>, 43d
Demodice[1] (*Biadice*), wife of Cretheus[1] <Hyg. *Poet. Astr.* 2.20>, 30a
Demodice[2] (*Demonice*), daughter of Agenor[4] <*Cat. Wom., Frag. Hes.* frg. 22, Merk. & West> and *Epicaste*[3] <Apollod. *Bibl.*

1.7.7>, 15c
— and Ares <Apollod. *Bibl.* 1.7.7>, 7b
Demoditas —see [fifty daughters of Danaus[1]] (alternate version)
Demoleon[1] [centaur], offspring of Centaurus and a Magnesian Mare <Pind. *Pyth.* 2.50; named as centaur, <Ovid *Met.* 12. 369>, 69d
alternate version:
Ixion and *Nephele*[1] <Diod. Sic. 4.69.5>
Demoleon[2], son of Antenor[1] <Hom. *Il.* XX.395> and *Theano*[2], *45c*
Demoleon[3], son of Phrixus[1] and *Chalciope*[1] <Hyg. *Fab.* 14>, 26c
Demoleon[4], son of Hippasus[7] <Quint. Smyr. 10.119-20>, *
Demonassa[1], wife of Irus[1] <Hyg. *Fab.* 14>, 22d
Demonassa[2], daughter of Amphiaraus <Paus. 9.5.8> and *Eriphyle* <Paus. 5.17.7>, 32d
— and Thersander[1] <Paus. 9.5.8>, 30c, 55c
Demonassa[3] — see *Amphithea*[1]
Demonassa[4], wife of Hippolochus[1] <Schol. on Hom. *Il.* VI.206>, 18d
Demonassa[5] (*Methone*[3]), wife of Poeas <Hyg. *Fab.* 97>, 22c
Demonice — see *Demodice*[2]
Demophile[1] — see *Deiphobe*
Demophile[2] —see [fifty daughters of Danaus[1]] (alternate version)
Demophon[1] [King of Athens], son of Theseus <Eur. *Heracl.* 115> and *Phaedra* <Apollod. *Epit.* 1.18>, 51c
— and *Phyllis*[1] <Apollod. *Epit.* 6.16>, 7d
Demophon[2] [King of Elaeusa] <Hyg. *Poet. Astr.* 2.40>, *
Demophoon[1] (Deiphontes[1]), son of Celeus[1] and *Metaneira* <*Hom. Hymn* 2 (to *Demeter*) 232-33>, 46b
Demophoon[2], killed by *Camilla* <Virg. *Aen.* 11.658-74>, *
Dercetis[1] — see *Derceto*
Dercetis[2], mother of Alatreus <Stat. *Theb.* 7.298>, *
Derceto (*Dercetis*[1]), mother of *Semiramis* <Diod. Sic. 2.4.2-6>, 61c
Dercynus, son of Poseidon <Apollod. *Bibl.* 2.5.10>, 9c
Dereites, son of Harpalus[1] <Paus. 7.18.5>, 47a
Deriades, son of Hydaspes[1] and *Astris* <Non. *Dion.* 26.352-53>, 3b
Dero, daughter of Nereus and *Doris*[1] <Apollod. *Bibl.* 1.2.7>, *64b*
Despoena [the Mistress], daughter of Poseidon and *Demeter* <Paus. 8.37.8 (she is called "the Mistress")>, 8c
Deucalion[1] [King of Pherae], son of Prometheus[1] <*Cat. Wom., Frag. Hes.* frg. 2, Merk. & West> and an undetermined woman (sometimes said to be *Clymene, Hesione, Pandora,* or *Pronoea,* but thought by West to be unknown, M. L. West, *Hes. Cat. Wom.* 50-51), 16b
alternate parentage:
Prometheus and *Clymene*[1] <Schol. on Hom. *Od.* 10.2>
Prometheus and *Pandora*[1] <*Cat. Wom., Frag. Hes.* frg. 2, Merk. & West>
Prometheus and *Pronoea* <*Cat. Wom.*, frg. 1, in *Hes.—Hom. Hymns & Hom.*, Evelyn-White>
Prometheus and *Pryneia* <*Frag. Hes.* frg. 4, Merk. & West> (N.B., frg. 2, Merk. & West, and frg. 1, Evelyn-White, cite the same source, Schol. on Ap. Rhod. *Arg.*, but render the spelling of the wife of Prometheus differently, yielding the different transliterations *Pandora* and *Pronoea*)
— and *Pyrrha*[1] <*Cat. Wom., Frag. Hes.* frg. 2, Merk. & West>, (16b)
Deucalion[2] [King of Crete], son of Minos I <Hom. *Il.* XIII.451> and *Pasiphae*[1] <Apollod. *Bibl.* 3.1.2>, 54c
alternate parentage:
Minos I and *Crete*[1] <Asclep. in Apollod. *Bibl.* 3.1.2>
Deucalion[3] — see Asterius[8] (called Deucalion <Val. Flac. 1.366>)
Deucalion[4], killed by Achilles <Hom. *Il.* XX.472-79>, *
Dexamene, daughter of Nereus <Hom. *Il.* XVIII.42> and *Doris*[1], *64b*
Dexamenus [King of Olenus], son of Mesolas and *Ambracia*[2] <Steph. Byz. "Dexamenae">, 14c
alternate parentage:
Heracles[1] <Dion. Hal. *Rom. Ant.* 1.50.4>
Oeceus <Callim. *Hymn to Delos* 102>
Dexithea[1], daughter of Damon <Nicand. in Schol. on Ovid *Ibis* 477>, 54d
— and Minos I <Bacch. 1.114-19>, (54d)
Dexithea[2], daughter of Phorbas[4] <Plut. *Rom.* 2.2>, 41c
— and Aeneas[1] <Plut. *Rom.* 2.2>, (41c)
Dia[1], daughter of Eioneus[2] <Schol. on Pind. *Pyth.* 2.40b>, 69a
— and Ixion <Schol. on Pind. *Pyth.* 2.40b>, (69a)
— and Zeus <Hom. *Il.* XIV.319>, 5a
Dia[2] — see *Hebe*
Dia[3], daughter of Lycaon[1] <*Etym. Magn.* "Dryops">, 64b
— and Apollo <Tzetz. on Lyc. 480>, 11b
Dia[4], wife of Agrius[1] <Schol. on Hom. *Il.* II.212>, 16d
Dia[5] — see *Idaea*[2]
Diapreses — see [five sets of twins]
Dias, son of Pelops[1] <*Etym. Magn.* "Dias"> and *Hippodameia*[1] <Schol. on Eur. *Or.* 5(4)>, *37b*
Dicaeus, son of Poseidon <Con. *Narr.* 17 (inferred because he is called brother of Syleus)>, 9d
Dictynna — see *Britomartis*
Dictys[1] [King of Seriphus], son of Magnes[1] <*Cat. Wom., Frag. Hes.* frg. 8, Merk. & West> and [a Naiad] <Apollod. *Bibl.* 1. 9. 6>, 15c
alternate parentage:
Magnes[3] <*Cat. Wom., Frag. Hes.* frg. 8, Merk. & West>
Poseidon and *Agamede*[1] <Hyg. *Fab.* 157>
Poseidon and *Cerebia* <Tzetz. on Lyc. 838>
Dictys[2] [centaur], offspring of Centaurus and a Magnesian Mare <Pind. *Pyth.* 2.50; named as centaur, Ovid *Met.* 12.333>, 69c
alternate parentage:
Ixion and *Nephele*[1] <Diod. Sic. 4.69.5>
Dictys[3], sailor turned into a dolphin <Hyg. *Fab.* 134>, *
Didaeon, son of Eurytus[2] and *Antiope*[6] <*Cat. Wom., Frag. Hes.* frg. 26, Merk. & West>, 60b
Didnasus, father of Morrheus[1] <Non. *Dion.* 26.72-73>, 3b
Dido (*Elissa*) [Queen of Carthage], daughter of Belus[2] <Virg. *Aen.* 1.620>, 41d
— and Aeneas[1] <Virg. *Aen.* 1.170-73>, (41d)
— and Bitias[1] <Virg. *Aen.* 1.739>, (41d)
— and Iarbas <Vir. *Aen.* 4.198-201>, (41d)
— and Sichaeus <Virg. *Aen.* 1.341>, (41d)
Dike (*Auxo*[1]) [justice] [one of the Horae], daughter of Zeus and *Themis*[1] <Hes. *Theog.* 902>, 6c
Dindymene — see *Cybele*[2]
Diochthonde, daughter of Minyas and *Phanosyra* <Schol. on Ap. Rhod. *Arg.* 1.230>, 20d
Diocles[1], son of Orsilochus[2] <Hom. *Il.* V.546>, 65b
Diocles[2], son of Cleophantus <Plut. *Them.* 32.1>, *
Diocles[3] [King of Eleusis] <Plut. *Thes.* 10.3>, *
Diocorystes, son of Aegyptus[1] and [an Arabian woman] <Apollod. *Bibl.* 2.1.5>, 57d
— and *Cleodameia* <Apollod. *Bibl.* 2.1.5>, (57d)
Diodorus, son of Sophax <Plut. *Sert.*>, 61c
Diogeneia[1], daughter of Phorbas[2] <Eust. on Hom. *Il.* 303> and *Hyrmine*, 68b
— and Alector[3] <Eust. on Hom. *Il.* 303>, 16c
Diogeneia[2], daughter of Cephis(s)us <Apollod. *Bibl.* 3.15.1> and *Leiriope*, 49b
— and Phrasimus <Apollod. *Bibl.* 3.15.1>, 69b
Diogeneia[3], daughter of Celeus[1] <Paus. 1.38.3> and *Metaneira*, 46b
Diomede[1], daughter of Phorbas[1] <Hom. *Il.* IX.665>, 24d
— and Achilles <Hom. *Il.* IX.665>, (24d)
Diomede[2], daughter of Lapithes <Apollod. *Bibl.* 3.10.3> and

Orsinome, 68b
— and Amyclas[1] <*Cat. Wom., Frag. Hes.* frg. 171, Merk. & West>, 47a
Diomede[3], daughter of Xuthus[1] and *Creusa*[3] <*Cat. Wom., Hesiodi* frg. 10(a).20-24, Merk. & West (O.C.T.)>, 17b, *51b*
— and Deion[1] <Apollod. *Bibl.* 1.9.4>, 22b
Diomedeia — see *Astyoche*[7]
Diomedes[1] [King of Aetolia] [one of the Epigoni], son of Tydeus <Hom. *Il.* IV.365> and *Deiphyle*[2] <Hyg. *Fab.* 97>, 17d
— and *Aegiale* <Hom. *Il.* V.414>, 30c
— and *Briseis*[2] <Ben. *Le Roman de Troie* 20-21>, 69d
— and *Callirhoe*[3] <Plut. *Gr. and Rom. Par. Stor.* 23>, (17d)
— and *Euippe*[1] <Ant. Lib. *Met.* 37.3>, (17d)
Diomedes[2], son of Diomedes[1] and *Euippe*[1] <Ant. Lib. *Met.* 37.3>, 17d
Diomedes[3] [King of the Bistones, Thrace], son of Ares and *Cyrene* <Apollod. *Bibl.* 2.5.8>, 7a
— and *Hippodameia*[7] <*Etym. Magn.* "Iphthimos">, (7a)
Diomedes[4] — see Jason
Diomedes[5], sent Romus to Troy <Plut. *Rom.* 2.1>, *
Diomedia — see Iola(u)s (alternate version)
Diomeneia, daughter of Arcas[1] <Paus. 8.9.9>, 62c
Dion [King of Sparta], husband of *Amphithea*[1] <Serv. on Virg. *Ecl.* 8.29>, 31d
Dione[1] [Titan], daughter of Oceanus and *Tethys* <Hes. *Theog.* 353>, 53a
alternate parentage:
Uranus and *Gaea* <Apollod. *Bibl.* 1.1.3>
— and Zeus <Hom. *Il.* V.371>, 5a
Dione[2], daughter of Nereus and *Doris*[1] <Apollod. *Bibl.* 1.2.7>, *64b*
Dione[3], daughter of Atlas <Hyg. *Fab.* 83> and *Pleione*, 41a
— and Tantalus[1] <Hyg. *Fab.* 83>, (41a)
Dionysus (Bacchus) (Bromius[1]) (Iacchus[1]) [god] [wine], son of Zeus and *Semele* <Hes. *Theog.* 941>, 6d, *56c*
alternate parentage:
Zeus and *Demeter* <Diod. Sic. 3.62.6>
Oceanus ("from whom all we gods proceed") <Hom. *Il.* XIV.202>
— and *Alexirhoe* <Ps.-Plut. *De Fluv.* 7.5>, 67b
— and *Alphesiboea*[3] <Herm. Cyp. in *F.H.G.* 4.428 frg. 3, Müller>, (56c)
— and *Althaea* <Hyg. *Fab.* 129>, 15d
— and Ampelus <Ovid *Fast.* 3.407>, (56c)
— and *Aphrodite* <Paus. 9.31.2>, 5a
— and *Araethyrea* <Paus. 2.12.6>, (56c)
— and *Ariadne* <Hes. *Theog.* 947>, 53c
— and *Aura*[1] <Non. *Dion.* 48.472 ff.>, 62b
— and *Carya*[1] <Serv. on Virg. *Ecl.* 8.29>, 31c
— and *Chione*[4] <Schol. Theo. 1.21>, (56c)
— and *Erigone*[1] <Ovid *Met.* 6.123-24>, (56c)
— and *Nicaea* <Non. *Dion.* 16.75-403>, 70a
— and *Physcoa* <Paus. 5.16.7>, (56c)
Diopatra, paramour of Poseidon <Ant. Lib. *Met.* 22>, 8c
Diores[1], son of Aeolus[2] <Parth. *Love Stor.* 2.2>, 18c
— and *Polymela*[2] <Parth. *Love Stor.* 2.2>, (18c)
Diores[2], son of Amarynceus[1] <Hom. *Il.* II.622>; brother-in-law of *Periboea*[1], 17d
Diores[3], brother of Amyclas[4] <Virg. *Aen.* 12.509>, *
(Dioscuri), sons of *Leda* by Zeus and Tyndareus (see Castor and Polydeuces), 48d
Dioxippe[1], daughter of Danaus[1] and *Pieria*[1] <Apollod. *Bibl.* 2.1.5>, 57c
— and Aegyptus[2] <Apollod. *Bibl.* 2.1.5>, (57c)
Dioxippe[2] [one of the Heliades[2]], daughter of Helios and *Clymene*[1] <Ovid *Met.* 2.333-40; named, Hyg. *Fab.* 154>, 14a
alternate parentage:
Helios and *Rhode*[1] <Schol. on Hom. *Od.* 17.208>
Dioxippe[3] [Amazon] <Hyg. *Fab.* 163>, *
Dioxippe[4] [one of the dogs of Actaeon] <Hyg. *Fab.* 181>, *
Dipoenus, son of Daedalus <Paus. 2.15.1> and *Naucrate*, 49b
Dirce, daughter of Achelous <Eur. *Bacc.* 519-20>, 65a
alternate parentage:
Ismenus[1] <Non. *Dion.* 44.9-10>
— and Lycus[1] <Eur. *Her.* 7-8>, 35b
Dius[1], son of Priam[1] <Hom. *Il.* XXIV.251>, 43d
Dius[2], contested Oxylus[2] for control of Eleia <Paus. 5.4.1>, *
Dodon, son of Zeus and *Europe*[1] <Akest. in Steph. Byz. "Dodona">, 5c, *53d*
Dodone, daughter of Oceanus and *Tethys* <Steph. Byz. "Dodona">, 53a
[dog of Geryon(eus)] — see Orth(r)us
[dog of Hades] — see Cerberus
Dolion, son of Silenus and [an ash tree nymph (she is called *Melia*)] <Strab. 12.4.8>, 46c
Doloncus, son of Cronus and *Thrace* <Steph. Byz. "Bithynia">, 55a
Dolops[1], son of Lampus[1] <Hom. *Il.* XV.525-26>, 42d
Dolops[2], son of Clytius[1] <Hom. *Il.* XI.304>, 42d
Dolops[3], father of Iphimacus <Hyg. *Fab.* 102>, *
Dorceus — see Dorycleus
Dordoche — see *Periboea*[5]
Doridas, son of Propodas <Paus. 2.4.3>, 18d
Dorippe, wife of Anius <Tzetz. on Lyc. 570, 581>, 56d
Doris[1], daughter of Oceanus and *Tethys* <Hes. *Theog.* 350>, 64b
— and Nereus <Hes. *Theog.* 240-41>, 3a
Doris[2], daughter of Nereus and *Doris*[1] <Hes. *Theog.* 250>, *64a*
Dorius, daughter of Danaus[1] and [an Ethiopian woman] <Apollod. *Bibl.* 2.1.5>, 57d
— and Cercetes <Apollod. *Bibl.* 2.1.5>, (57d)
Dorus[1], son of Hellen(us)[1] <*Cat. Wom., Frag. Hes.* frg. 9, Merk. & West> and *Orseis* <Apollod. *Bibl.* 1.7.3>, 17a
alternate parentage:
Xuthus[1] and *Creusa*[3] <Eur. *Ion* 1582-83>
Dorus[2], son of Apollo and *Phthia*[4] <Apollod. *Bibl.* 1.7.6>, 11d
Dorus[3], son of Cleues <Strab. 13.1.3>, *
Dorycleus (Dorceus), son of Hippocoon[1] <Apollod. *Bibl.* 3.10.5>, 47c
Doryclus[1] — see Leontophon(us)
Doryclus[2], son of Priam[1] <Hom. *Il.* XI.490>, 43d
Doryclus[3], son of Phoenix[2] and *Cassiopeia*[1] <Pher. in *F. Gr. H.* 3 F 86>, 53d
Doryclus[4], husband of *Beroe*[4] <Virg. *Aen.* 5.619-20>, *
Doryclus[5], warrior with Dionysus <Non. *Dion.* 29.263>, *
Doryclus[6], from Lemnos <Val. Flac. 2, 149>, *
Doryclus[7], won Olympian boxing prize Pind. *Olym.* 10.67>, *
Dorylas[1] [centaur], offspring of Centaurus and a Magnesian Mare <Pind. *Pyth.* 2.50; named as centaur, Ovid *Met.* 12.381>, 69c
alternate parentage:
Ixion and *Nephele*[1] <Diod. Sic. 4.69.5>
Dorylas[2], killed by Halcyoneus <Ovid. *Met.* 5.129>, *
Dorylas[3], killed by Tydeus <Stat. *Theb.* 2.572>, *
Dotis, daughter of Elatus[1] and *Amphictyone* <Steph. Byz. "Dotium">, 62c
— and Ares <Apollod. *Bibl.* 3.5.5>, 7b
— and Ialysus <Athen. 7.296c>, 14a
Doto, daughter of Nereus and *Doris*[1] <Hes. *Theog.* 248>, *64a*
Doupon [centaur], offspring of Centaurus and a Magnesian Mare <Pind. *Pyth.* 2.50; named as centaur, Diod. Sic. 4.12.7>, 69c
alternate parentage:
Ixion and *Nephele*[1] <Diod. Sic. 4.69.5>
Dracontis, daughter of Pierus[2] <Nicand. in Ant. Lib. *Met.* 9> and *Euippe*[2] <Ovid *Met.* 5.300 ff.>, 15c
Drimo, daughter of Alcyoneus[1] <Eust. on Hom. *Il.* 776>, 4a

Dryalus [centaur], offspring of Peceus <Hes. *Shield* 187>, 69c
Dryas[1], son of Ares <Apollod. *Bibl.* 1.8.2>, 7c
alternate parentage:
Iapetus <Hyg. *Fab.* 173>
Dryas[2], son of Aegyptus[1] and *Caliadne* <Apollod. *Bibl.* 2.1.5>, 57c
— and *Eurydice*[8] <Apollod. *Bibl.* 2.1.5>, (57c)
Dryas[3], father of Lycurgus[5] <Hom. *Il.* VI.131>, *
Dryas[4], son of Lycurgus[5] <Apollod. *Bibl.* 3.5.1>, *
Dryas[5], father of Munichus <Ant. Lib. *Met.* 14.1>, *
Dryas[6], father of Amphilochus[3] <Parth. *Love Stor.* 27>, *
Dryas[7], a warrior at Thebes <Stat. *Theb.* 7.255>, *
Dryas[8], killed by Deiphobus[1] <Quint. Smyr. 11.87>, *
Dryas[9], killed by Cleitus[2] <Parth. *Love Stor.* 6.5>, *
Drymo, daughter of Nereus and *Doris*[1] <Hyg. *Fab.* pref.>, *64a*
Dryope[1], daughter of Dryops[2] <*Hom. Hymn* 19 (to Pan)>, 64d
— and Hermes <*Hom. Hymn* 19 (to Pan)>, 46a
Dryope[2], daughter of Eurytus[2] <Ovid *Met.* 9.335-36 (inferred because she is daughter of *Iole*'s father)>, 11d, 60b
— and Andraemon[2] <Ovid *Met.* 9.332-37>, 16d
— and Apollo <Ovid *Met.* 9.334>, (11d)
Dryope[3], mother of Tarquitus <Virg. *Aen.* 10.550-51>, *
Dryope[4], mother of Chromis[6] <Stat. *Theb.* 2.614-15>, *
Dryope[5], a Lemnian woman whose form Venus took <Val. Flac. 2. 174>, *
Dryops[1], son of Priam[1] <Apollod. *Bibl.* 3.12.5>, 43d
Dryops[2], son of Apollo <Paus. 4, 34, 11> and *Dia*[3] <Tzetz. on Lyc. 480>, 11a, *64d*
alternate parentage:
Sperchius and *Polydora*[5] <Ant. Lib. *Met.* 32.1>
Dryops[3], killed by Clausus <Virg. *Aen.* 10.346>, *
Dymas[1] [King of Phrygia], son of Aegimius <*Cat. Wom., Hesiodi* frg. 10a.6-7, Merk. & West (O.C.T.)>, 17b
— and *Telecleia* <Eur. in Eust. on Hom. *Il.* 188>, 41d
Dymas[2], a sea captain <Hom. *Od.* 6.22>, *
Dymas[3], a stranger who warned the Argonauts <Val. Flac. 4. 188>, *
Dymas[4], fought with Aeneas at Troy <Virg. *Aen.* 2.341>, *
Dymas[5], fought against Thebes <Stat. *Theb.* 10.348>, *
Dymas[6], killed by Aeneas <Quint. Smyr. 8.303>, *
Dyna — see *Lavinia*[1]
Dynamene, daughter of Nereus and *Doris*[1] <Hes. *Theog.* 248>, *64a*
Dynastes, son of Heracles[1] and *Erato*[4] <Apollod. *Bibl.* 2.7.8>, *50d*
Dyrrachius, son of Poseidon and *Melissa*[4] <Steph. Byz. "Dyrrachium">, 8c
Dysaules — see Triptolemus (alternate version)
Dysis [one of the hours], daughter of Zeus and *Themis*[1] <Hyg. *Fab.* 183>, 6d
Dysnomia [lawlessness] [abstraction], offspring of *Eris* <Hes. *Theog.* 230>, *1a*
Dysponteus, son of Oenomaus[1] <Paus. 6.22.4> and *Asterope*[1], 7c, *39a*

Ecbasus, son of Argus[2] and *Euadne*[2] <Apollod. *Bibl.* 2.1.2>, 61b
Echecles, son of Actor[1] <Hom. *Il.* XVI.187> and *Polyboea*[3], 5d
— and *Polymela*[1] <Hom. *Il.* XIV.181>, (5d)
Echeclus[1], son of Agenor[7] <Paus. 10.27.1>, 45c
Echeclus[2] [centaur], offspring of Centaurus and a Magnesian Mare <Pind. *Pyth.* 2.50; named as centaur Ovid *Met.* 12>, 69c
alternate parentage:
Ixion and *Nephele*[1] <Diod. Sic. 4.69.5>
Echeclus[3], killed by Patroclus[1] <Hom. *Il.* XVI.694>, *
Echeclus[4], killed by Ancaeus[2] <Val. Flac. 3.138>, *
Echelas (Archelaus[1]), son of Penthilus[1] <Paus. 3.2.1>, 36d
Echemmon[1], son of Priam[1] <Hom. *Il.* V.159>, 43d
Echemmon[2], killed by Eurypylus[1] <Quint. Smyr. 6.580>, *
Echemus [King of Tegea in Arcadia], son of Aeropus <Herod. 9. 26>, 64c
— and *Timandra*[1] <*Cat. Wom., Frag. Hes.* frg. 23(a).31-33, Merk. & West>, 48c
Echenais, paramour of Daphnis[1] <Parth. *Love Stor.* 29.1>, 46c
Echephron[1], son of Nestor <Hom. *Od.* 3.413> and *Anaxibia*[4] <Apollod. *Bibl.* 1.7.7>, 27c
alternate parentage:
Nestor and *Eurydice*[7] <Hom. *Od.* 3.453 (inferred because she is wife of Nestor)>
Echephron[2], son of Priam[1] <Apollod. *Bibl.* 3.12.5>, 44c
Echephron[3], son of Heracles[1] and *Psophis*[1] <Paus. 8.24.2>, 60d, *53a*
Echepolus[1], son of Anchises <Hom. *Il.* XXIII.296>, 41d
Echepolus[2], son of Thalysias <Hom. *Il.* IV.458>, *
Echestratus, son of Agis[1] <Herod. 7.204>, 60d
Echetus [King of Epeirus], son of Euchenor[1] and *Phlogea* <Schol. on Hom. *Od.* 18.84>, 31d
alternate parentage:
Bucetus <Schol. on Hom. *Od.* 18.84>
Echidna [monster], offspring of Phorcus[1] and *Ceto*[1] <Hes. *Theog.* 297>, 2a
alternate parentage:
Peiras[2] and *Sty* <Epim. *Theog.* 3 B 67>
Tartarus and *Gaea* <Apollod. *Bibl.* 2.1.2>
— and Heracles[1] <Herod. 4.9>, 60c
— and Typhon <Hes. *Theog.* 297>, 1b
Echion[1] [one of the (Spartoi) [sown men]], sprang from teeth of [Cadmean Dragon] <Eur. *Bacc.* 1274>, 7d
— and *Agave*[1] <Eur. *Bacc.* 229>, 55c
Echion[2] [Argonaut], son of Hermes <Pind. *Pyth.* 4.178-79> and *Antianeira*[1] <Ap. Rhod. *Arg.* 1.51>, 46a
alternate parentage:
Hermes and *Laothoe*[5] <Orph. *Arg.* 135-37>
Echion[3], son of Portheus[3] <Apollod. *Epit.* 5.20>, *
Echion[4], suitor of *Penelope*[1] (from Dulichium) <Apollod. *Epit.* 7. 27>, *
Echius, son of Damastor[1] <Hom. *Il.* XVI.416>, 52d
Echo, daughter of [mortal father] and [Naiad] <Lon. *Daphnis and Chloe*, 3.23>, 46a, 49b
— and Narcissus (whom she loved) <Ovid *Met.* 3.356-401>, (49b)
— and Pan <Tzetz. on Lyc. 310>, (46a)
Ecnominus — see [fifty sons of Aegyptus[1]] (alternate version)
Eeriboea, wife of Aloeus[1] <Hom. *Il.* V.389>, 34a
Eetion[1] [King of Thebe], father of *Andromache* <Hom. *Il.* VI.395> and seven sons <Hom. *Il.* VI.429>, 24c, 43c, 43c
Eetion[2] (from Imbrus), ransomed Lycaon[2] <Hom. XXI.34-43>, *
Eetion[3], father of Podes <Hom. *Il.* XVII.590>, *
Eetion[4], father of Cypselus[2] <Herod. 5.92>, *
Eetion[5], killed by Paris <Quint. Smyr. 6.639>, *
Eido — see *Eidothea*[2]
Eidothea[1] — see *Cyanea*
Eidothea[2] (*Eido*) (*Eurynome*[4]) (*Idothea*[2]) (*Theonoe*[2]), daughter of Proteus[3] <Hom. *Od.* 4.365> and *Psamathe*[1] <Eur. *Helen* 10-12 (she is called *Eido* and *Theonoe*)>, *65a*
Eidothea[3], paramour of Euseirus <Ant. Lib. *Met.* 22>, 9d
Eidothea[4] — see *Idaea*[2]
Eidothea[5], daughter of Eurytus[9] <Ant. Lib. *Met.* 30>, *
Eidyia (*Hipsea*) (*Hypsea*) (*Idyia*) (*Ipsea*), daughter of Oceanus and *Tethys* <Hes. *Theog.* 352>, 53a
— and Aeetes <Hes. *Theog.* 959>, 14c
Eileithyia (*Ileithyia*) [childbirth], daughter of Zeus and *Hera* <Hes. *Theog.* 922>, 5a
Eione, daughter of Nereus and *Doris*[1] <Hes. *Theog.* 255>, *64a*
Eioneus[1], son of Magnes[2] and *Philodice*[2] <Schol. on Eur. *Phoen. Maid.* 1760>, 21a
Eioneus[2] (Deioneus[3]), father of *Dia*[1] <Schol. on Pind. *Pyth.* 2. 40b>, 69a
Eioneus[3] — see Rhesus[2] (alternate version)

Eioenus[4], killed by Hector[1] <Hom. *Il.* VII.11>, *
Eioneus[5], killed by Neoptolemus <Paus. 10.27.1>, *
Eirene[1] (*Carpo*) (*Irene*) [peace] [one of the Horae], daughter of Zeus and *Themis*[1] <Hes. *Theog.* 902>, 6c
Eirene[2], daughter of Poseidon and *Melantheia*[2] <Plut. *Gr. Quest.* 19>, 8c, *65b*
Ekphas, father of *Eurycleia*[2] <Epim. in *F. Gr. H.* 3 B 15>, 55c
Elachia, daughter of Thespius <Apollod. Bibl. 2.7.8> and *Megamede* <Apollod. *Bibl.* 2.4.10>, 50c
— and Heracles[1] <Apollod. *Bibl.* 2.7.8>, (50c)
Elais [olive] [one of the (Oenotropae)], daughter of Anius <Apollod. *Epit.* 3.10> and *Dorippe*, 56d
Elara, daughter of Orchomenus[2] <*Cat. Wom., Frag. Hes.* frg. 78, Merk. & West>, 20d
— and Zeus <Apollod. *Bibl.* 1.4.1>, (5c)
Elasippus[1] — see [five sets of twins]
Elasippus[2], son of Haemon[6] <Quint. Smyr. 1.230>, *
Elatius — see Elatus[2]
Elatus[1] [King of Arcadia], son of Arcas[1] <Apollod. *Bibl.* 3.9.1> and *Chrysopeleia* <Eum. in Apollod. *Bibl.* 3.9.1>, 62c
alternate parentage:
Arcas and *Erato*[2] <Paus. 8.4.2>
Arcas and *Leaneira* <Apollod. *Bibl.* 3.9.1>
— and *Amphictyone* <Pher. in *F.H.G.* 1.71 frg. 8, Müller>, (62c)
— and *Laodice*[2] <Apollod. *Bibl.* 3.9.1>, 11c
Elatus[2] (Elatius) [King of Thessaly], father of *Caenis*/Caeneus[1] <Ovid *Met.* 12.190>, 8a, and Polyphemus[2] <Apollod. *Bibl.* 1.9.16>, 59d
— and *Hippeia* <Hyg. *Fab.* 14>, (8a), (59d)
Elatus[3] [centaur], offspring of Centaurus and a Magnesian Mare <Pind. *Pyth.* 2.50; named as centaur, Apollod. *Bibl.* 2.5.4>, 69c
alternate parentage:
Ixion and *Nephele*[1] <Diod. Sic. 4.69.5>
Elatus[4], father of Ampyx[2] <Hyg. *Fab.* 128 (he is called Ampycus), *
Elatus[5], suitor of *Penelope*[1] (from Same) <Apollod. *Epit.* 7.28>, *
Elatus[6], killed by Agamemnon <Hom. *Il.* 6.33>, *
Elector, husband of *Polycaste*[3] <*Cat. Wom., Hesiodi* frg. 10a.67, Merk. & West (O.C.T.)>, 27a
Electra[1], daughter of Oceanus and *Tethys* <Hes. *Theog.* 349>, 53a
— and Thaumas[1] <Hes. *Theog.* 265-66>, 3a
Electra[2], daughter of Atlas <*Cat. Wom., Frag. Hes.* frg. 169, Merk. & West> and *Pleione* <Apollod. *Bibl.* 3.10.1>, 42b
— and Corythus[1] <Serv. on Virg. *Aen.* 7.207>, 6c
— and Zeus <Hellan. in *F. Gr. H.* 4 F 19a>, 5c
Electra[3] (*Laodice*[3]), daughter of Agamemnon <Hom. *Il.* IX.145 (she is called *Laodice*)> and *Clytemnestra* <Apollod. *Epit.* 2.16>, 36a
— and Pylades <Eur. *Elec.* 1249>, 23c, 37a
Electra[4], daughter of Agenor[1] and *Telephassa* <Paus. 9.8.3>, 56a
Electra[5], daughter of Danaus[1] and *Polyxo*[3] <Apollod. *Bibl.* 2.1.5>, 57c
— and Peristhenes <Apollod. *Bibl.* 2.1.5>, (57c)
Electra[6], servant of Helen[1] <Paus. 10.25.4>, *
Electryon[1] [King of Mycenae], son of Perseus[1] and *Andromeda* <*Cat. Wom., Frag. Hes.* frg. 135, Merk. & West>, 59d
— and *Anaxo*[1] <Apollod. *Bibl.* 2.4.5>, 59c
— and *Eurydice*[11] <Diod. Sic. 4.9.1>, 38a
— and *Lysidice*[1] <*Cat. Wom., Frag. Hes.* frg. 193, Merk. & West>, 38a
— and *Mideia*[2] <Apollod. *Bibl.* 2.4.5>, (59d)
Electryon[2] (Alector[4]) (Alectryon), son of Itonus[2] <Diod. Sic. 4.67.7>, 18c
Electryo(ne), daughter of Helios and *Rhode*[1] <Diod. Sic. 5.56.5>, 14a
Elege, daughter of Proetus[1] <Ael. *Var. Narr.* 3.41> and *Stheneboea*, 57d
Eleius[1] [King of Elis], son of Poseidon and *Eurycyde* <Paus. 5, 1, 8>, 8d
Eleius[2] [King of Elis], son of Amphimachus[2] <Paus. 5.3.4>, 63d
Eleius[3], son of Cimon <Plut. *Pericles* 29.1>, *
Eleon, father of Deimachus[3] <Plut. *Gr. Quest.* 41>, 70b
Elephantis, paramour of Danaus[1] <Apollod. *Bibl.* 2.1.5>, 57b, 57c
Elephenor [King of Euboea], son of Chalcodon[2] <Hom. *Il.* IV.464> and *Alcyone*[7] <Apollod. *Epit.* 3.11>, 8b
alternate parentage:
Chalcodon[2] and *Imenarete* <Hyg. *Fab.* 97>
Elete (*Telete*) [one of the hours], daughter of Zeus and *Themis*[1] <Hyg. *Fab.* 183>, 6d
Eleusinus — see Eleusis
Eleusis (Eleusinus), son of Hermes and *Daeira* <Paus. 1.38.7>, 46b, *52b*
alternate parentage:
Ogygus[2] <Paus. 1.38.7>
— and *Cothone* <Hyg. *Fab.* 147>, (46b), (52b)
Eleuther[1], son of Apollo and *Aethusa* <Apollod. *Bibl.* 3.10.1>, 11a, *35a*
Eleuther[2] — see [fifty sons of Lycaon[1]] (alternate version)
Elissa — see *Dido*
Ellops, son of Ion[1] and *Helice*[1] <Strab. 10.1.3>, 52a
Elymus[1], son of Anchises <Serv. on Virg. *Aen.* 5.73>, 41c
Elymus[2] [centaur], offspring of Centaurus and a Magnesian Mare <Pind. *Pyth.* 2.50; named as centaur, Ovid *Met.* 460>, 69c
alternate parentage:
Ixion and *Nephele*[1] <Diod. Sic. 4.69.5>
Elymus[3], killed by *Gorge*[4] <Stat. *Theb.* 5.207>, *
(Emathides) — see (Pierides[2])
Emathion[1] — see Aemathion[1]
Emathion[2] — see Aemathion[2]
Emathion[3] — see Aemathion[3]
Emathion[4] — see Aemathion[4]
Emathion[5] — see Aemathion[5]
Enarete, daughter of Deimachus[2] <Apollod. *Bibl.* 1.7.3>, 18a
— and Aeolus[1] <Apollod. *Bibl.* 1.7.3>, (18a)
Enarophorus, son of Hippocoon[1] <Apollod. *Bibl.* 3.10.5>, 47c
Enceladus[1] [giant], son of *Gaea* (and the blood of Uranus) <Hes. *Theog.* 180-86; named as giant, Apollod. *Bibl.* 1.6.2>, *4a*
Enceladus[2], son of Aegyptus[1] <Apollod. *Bibl.* 2.1.5>, 57c
— and *Amymone*[1] <Apollod. *Bibl.* 2.1.5>, (57c)
Endeis, daughter of Sciron[2] <Apollod. *Bibl.* 3.12.6> and *Chariclo*[3] <Plut. *Thes.* 10.3>, 39a, *66b*
alternate parentage:
Cheiron <Schol. on Pind. *Nem.* 5.12> and *Chariclo*[3]
— and Aeacus <Pind. *Nem.* 5.12>, 23b, 66a
Endeus, son of Oicle(u)s and *Hyperm(n)estra*[2] <*Cat. Wom., Frag. Hes.* frg. 25.34-40, Merk. & West>, 32d
Endymion [King of Elis], son of Aethlius and *Calyce*[1] <*Cat. Wom., Hesiodi* frg. 10(a).60, Merk. & West (O.C.T.)>, 15b, *27a*
alternate parentage:
Zeus <Apollod. *Bibl.* 1.7.5>
— and *Asterodeia*[1] <Paus. 5.1.4>, (15b)
— and *Chromia* <Paus. 5.1.4>, 16a
— and *Hyperippe*[1] <Paus. 5.1.4>, 62d
— and *Iphianassa*[2] <Apollod. *Bibl.* 1.7.6>, (15b)
— and *Selene* <Paus. 5.1.4>, 14b
Enetus, son of Choricus; brother of *Palaestra* <Serv. on Virg. *Aen.* 8.138>, 46d
Enipeus [river], son of Oceanus and *Tethys* <Hes. *Theog.* 367-68; named as river, Hom. *Od.* 11.238-39>, 53a
— and *Tyro* <Hom. *Od.* 11.238>, 27b
Enodia — see *Hecate*
Enorches, son of Thyestes[1] and *Daeto* <Tzetz. on Lyc. 212>, 39a, *37b*
Entelides, son of Heracles[1] and *Menippis* <Apollod. *Bibl.* 2.7.8>,

50d
Entella, wife of Aegestes <Tzetz. on Lyc. 953>, 67a
Enudus, son of Ancaeus[2] and *Samia* <Paus. 7.4.2>, 54c
Enyalius — see Ares
Enyo[1] [one of the Graeae], daughter of Phorcus[1] and *Ceto*[1] <Hes. *Theog.* 273>, 2a
Enyo[2] [war], companion-in-arms of Ares <Hom. *Il.* V.594>, 7b
alternate relationships:
mother of Ares <Schol. on Hom. *Il.* V.333>
mother, daughter, or wet-nurse of Ares <Corn. *De Nat. Deor.* 21>
sister of Ares <Quint. Smyr. *Posthom.* 8.425 (he is called Polemos)>
Eone, daughter of Thespius <Apollod. *Bibl.* 2.7.8> and *Megamede* <Apollod. *Bibl.* 2.4.10>, 50c
— and Heracles[1] <Apollod. *Bibl.* 2.7.8>, 50c
Eos [dawn], daughter of Hyperion[1] and *Theia*[1] <Hes. *Theog.* 372>, 12b
alternate parentage:
Hyperion[1] and *Aether* <Hyg. *Fab.* pref.>
— and Ares <Apollod. *Bibl.* 1.4.4-5>, 7b
— and Astraeus[1] <Hes. *Theog.* 376>, (12b)
— and Cephalus[1] <Hes. *Theog.* 987>, 46c
— and Cleitus[1] <Hom. *Od.* 15.248-50>, 32c
— and Orion <Hom. *Od.* 5.121-22>, 53c
— and Tithonus <Hes. *Theog.* 986>, 43c
Eosphorus — see Phosphor(us)
Epaphus[1] [King of Egypt], son of Zeus and *Io* <Aesch. *Supp.* 266-68>, 5d, *55a*
— and *Memphis*[1] <Apollod. *Bibl.* 2.1.4>, 68b
Epaphus[2] — see Epopeus[1]
Epeione (*Arsinoe*[4]), daughter of Merops[1] <Schol. on Hom. *Il.* IV.195>, 19d
— and Asclepius <Paus. 2.29.1>, (19d)
Epeirus, daughter of Echion[1] <Parth. *Love Stor.* 32.4> and *Agave*[1], 7d, *55c*
Epeius[1] [King of Elis], son of Endymion and *Chromia* <Paus. 5.1.4>, 16a
— and *Anaxiroe* <Paus. 5.1.6>, (16a)
Epeius[2] [builder of the Wooden Horse], son of Panopeus[1] <Hom. *Il.* XXIII.666>, 23c
Ephesus, son of Caystus <Paus. 7.2.4>, 52a
Ephialtes[1] [giant], son of *Gaea* (and the blood of Uranus) <Hes. *Theog.* 180-86; named as giant, Apollod. *Bibl.* 1.6.2>, *4a*
Ephialtes[2] [giant] [one of the Aloidae], son of Poseidon and *Iphimedeia* <Hom. *Od.* 11.305-07>, 8c
alternate parentage:
Aloeus[1] and *Iphimedeia* <Hom. *Il.* V.385>
Ephialtes[3] — see [fifty sons of Aegyptus[1]] (alternate version)
Ephippus, son of Poemander <Plut. *Gr. Quest.* 37.299c> and *Tanagra*, 35c
Ephyra[1], daughter of Oceanus <Paus. 2.1.1> and *Tethys*, 53b
Ephyra[2], daughter of Nereus and *Doris*[1] <Hyg. *Fab.* pref.>, *64a*
Epicaste[1] — see *Jocasta*
Epicaste[2], daughter of Augeias <Apollod. *Bibl.* 2.7.8>, 63d
— and Heracles[1] <Apollod. *Bibl.* 2.7.8>, 60c
Epicaste[3], daughter of Calydon[1] and *Aeolia* <Apollod. *Bibl.* 1.7.7>, 15d
— and Agenor[4] <Apollod. *Bibl.* 1.7.7>, (15d)
Epicaste[4], wife of Clymenus[4] <Parth. *Love Stor.* 13.1>, 26d
Epidamnus, father of *Melissa*[4] <Steph. Byz. "Dyrrachium">, 8c
Epidaurus, son of Argus[2] and *Euadne*[2] <Apollod. *Bibl.* 2.1.2>, 61a
alternate parentage:
Apollo <Paus. 2.26.3>
Pelops[1] <Paus. 2.26.3>
(Epigoni) [sons of the Seven against Thebes] — see Alcmaeon[1], Amphilocus[1], Diomedes[1], Medon[5], Polydorus[1], Promachus[1], Sthenelus[2], Thersander[1] (also Aegialeus[1] if Adrastus[1] is listed among the Seven; Euryalus[3] if Mecisteus is listed among the Seven)
Epilais, daughter of Thespius <Apollod. *Bibl.* 2.7.8> and *Megamede* <Apollod. *Bibl.* 2.4.10>, 50c
— and Heracles[1] <Apollod. *Bibl.* 2.7.8>, (50c)
Epilaus[1], son of Neleus[1] and *Chloris*[2] <*Cat. Wom., Frag. Hes.* frg. 33(a), Merk. & West>, 27c
Epilaus[2], son of Electryon[1] and *Lysidice*[1] <*Cat. Wom., Frag. Hes.* frg. 193, Merk. & West>, 59d, *38a*
Epimedes [one of the Dactyls], son of *Anchiale*[1] <Ap. Rhod. *Arg.* 1128; named, Paus. 5.7.6>, *11a*
alternate origin:
born on Mt. Ida of uncertain parentage <Diod. Sic. 5. 64. 4>
Epimetheus, son of Iapetus and *Clymene*[1] <Hes. *Theog.* 511>, 16b, *52a*
alternate parentage:
Iapetus and *Asia* <Apollod. *Bibl.* 1.2.3-4>
— and *Pandora*[1] <Apollod. *Bibl.* 1.7.2>, (16b), (52a)
Epistrophus[1], son of Euenus[3] <Hom. *Il.* II.692-93>, 51d
alternate parentage:
Mecisteus[1] <Apollod. *Epit.* 3.35>
Epistrophus[2], son of Iphitus[3] <Hom. *Il.* II.517> and *Hippolyte*[4] <Hyg. *Fab.* 97>, 23c
Epochus, son of Lycurgus[4] and *Cleophyle* <Apollod. *Bibl.* 3.9.2>, 64d
alternate parentage:
Lycurgus[4] and *Eurynome*[7] <Apollod. *Bibl.* 3.9.2>
Epopeus[1] (Epaphus[2]) [King of Sicyon], son of Poseidon and *Canace* <Apollod. *Bibl.* 1.7.4>, 8a, *34b*
alternate parentage:
Aloeus[2] <Paus. 2.3.10>
— and *Antiope*[1] <Paus. 2.6.2>, 66d
Epopeus[2] [King of Lesbos], father and paramour of *Nyctimene* <Serv. on Virg. *Geo.* 1.403>, *
Epopeus[3], sailor turned into a dolphin <Hyg. *Fab.* 134>, *
Epopeus[4], killed by his mother <Stat. *Theb.* 5.225>, *
Erasinus [river], son of Oceanus and *Tethys* <Hes. *Theog.* 367-68; named as river, Paus. 2.24.6>, 53b
Erasippus, son of Heracles[1] and *Lysippe*[2] <Apollod. *Bibl.* 2.7.8>, *50d*
Erasus, son of Triphylus <Paus. 10.9.3>, 62c
Erato[1] [lyric poetry] [one of the Muses], daughter of Zeus and *Mnemosyne* <Hes. *Theog.* 78>, 6a
Erato[2], wife of Arcas[1] <Paus. 8.4.2>, 62c
Erato[3], daughter of Danaus[1] and *Polyxo*[3] <Apollod. *Bibl.* 2.1.5>, 57d
— and Bromius[2] <Apollod. *Bibl.* 2.1.5>, (57d)
Erato[4], daughter of Thespius <Apollod. *Bibl.* 2.7.8> and *Megamede* <Apollod. *Bibl.* 2.4.10>, 50d
— and Heracles[1] <Apollod. *Bibl.* 2.7.8>, (50c)
Erato[5], daughter of Nereus and *Doris*[1] <Hes. *Theog.* 246>, *64a*
Erato[6], mother of *Cleophema* <Isyl. *Lyr.* 3.43>, 19d
— and Malus <Isyl. *Lyr.* 3.43>, (19d)
Erato[7] — see (Hyades) (alternate version)
Erato[8] [a nymph of Nysa] <Hyg. *Fab.* 182>, *
Erebus [darkness], came from Chaos <Hes. *Theog.* 123>, 1a
— and *Nyx* <Hes. *Theog.* 125>, 1a
alternate parentage:
Chronus <Proc. *Plat. Tim.*> (Orphic theogony)
Erechtheus I — see Erichthonius[1]
Erechtheus II [King of Athens], son of Pandion I and *Zeuxippe*[1] <Apollod. *Bibl.* 3.14.8>, 49a
— and *Praxithea*[2] <Apollod. *Bibl.* 3.15.1>, (49a)
— and *Procris*[1] <Hyg. *Fab.* 153>, 51a
Ereuthalion[1], son of Criasus[1] and *Melantho*[2] <Schol. on Eur. *Phoen. Maid.* 1116>, 61b
Ereuthalion[2], father of Oeneus[5] <Non. *Dion.* 43.54-55>, *

Ereuthalion[3] <killed by Nestor <Hom *Il.* IV.319>, *
Ergeus — see *Celaeno*[1] (alternate version)
Erginus[1] [King of Orchomenus], son of Clymenus[1] <Paus. 9.37.1> and *Budeia*, 26c
Erginus[2] [Argonaut], son of Poseidon <Apollod. *Bibl.* 1.9.16>, 9d
Erginus[3], stole the Palladium <Plut. *Gr. Quest.* 48>, *
Erginus[4], killed by Hippomedon[1] <Stat. *Theb.* 9.305>, *
Eriboea[1] — *Periboea*[2]
Eriboea[2] [Amazon] <Diod. Sic. 4.16.3>, *
Erichthonius[1] (Erechtheus I) [monster] [King of Athens], son of Hephaestus <Apollod. *Bibl.* 3.14.6 (his sperm fell on the soil)>, 7d
alternate parentage:
Hephaestus and *Attis* <Apollod. *Bibl.* 3.14.6>
autochthonous <Hom. *Il.* II, 548>
— and *Praxithea*[1] <Apollod. *Bibl.* 3.4.6>, 49a
Erichthonius[2] [King of Troy and Dardania], son of Dardanus[1] <Hom. *Il.* XX.220> and *Bateia*[2] <Dion. Hal. *Rom. Ant.* 1.62.1>, 42a
alternate parentage:
Dardanus[1] and *Olizone* <Dict. Cret. 4.22>
— and *Astyoche*[5] <Apollod. *Bibl.* 3.12.1>, 71a
Eridanus [river], son of Oceanus and *Tethys* <Hes. *Theog.* 338>, 53a
Erigdupus [centaur], offspring of Centaurus and a Magnesian Mare <Pind. *Pyth.* 2.50; named as centaur, Ovid *Met.* 12.453>, 69c
alternate parentage:
Ixion and *Nephele*[1] <Diod. Sic. 4.69.5>
Erigone[1], daughter of Icarius[1] <Apollod. *Bibl.* 3.14.7> and *Phanothea* <Clem. Alex. *Misc.* 80.3 (she is called wife of Icarius)>, 56d
— and Dionysus <Ovid *Met.* 6.123-24>, (56d)
Erigone[2], daughter of Aegisthus and *Clytemnestra* <Apollod. *Epit.* 6.25>, 39c
— and Orestes[1] <Paus. 2.18.5>, 36b
Erigone[3], daughter of *Themis*[1] <Serv. on Virg. *Ecl.* 4.6>, *10b*
Erinoma, paramour of Adonis <Serv. on Virg. *Ecl.* 10.18>, 11c
(Erinyes) (Eumenides) (Semnai) [Furies], daughters of *Gaea* (and the blood of Uranus) <Hes. *Theog.* 185> (see *Al(l)ecto, Megaera, Tisiphone*[2]), 4b
alternate parentage:
Cronus <Epim. *Theog.* 3 B 19>
Nyx <Aesch. *Eum.* 416>
Eriopis[1], daughter of Jason and *Medea* <Paus. 2.3.7>, 33c
Eriopis[2], daughter of Apollo and *Arsinoe*[1] <Schol. on Pind. *Pyth.* 3.14>, 11a, *25d*
Eriopis[3], wife of Oileus[1] <Hom. *Il.* XII.697>, 15c
Eriphia — see (Hyades) (alternate version)
Eriphyle, daughter of Talaus and *Lysimache*[1] <Apollod. *Bibl.* 1.9.13>, 31c
— and Amphiaraus <Pind. *Nem.* 9.16-17>, 32d
Eris [strife], daughter of *Nyx* <Hes. *Theog.* 225>, *1a*
alternate parentage:
Zeus and *Hera* <Hom. *Il.* IV.441 (inferred because she is called the sister of Ares)>
Eros [love], came from Chaos (without parentage) <Hes. *Theog.* 120>, 1a
alternate parentage:
Aether and *Nyx* <Acus. in *F. Gr. H.* 2 F 6>
Ares and *Aphrodite* <Simon. in 575 *P.E.G.*>
Eileithyia <Olen in Paus. 9.27.2>
Erebus and *Nyx* <Acus. in *F. Gr. H.* 2 F 6>
Hermes and *Artemis* <Cic. *De Nat. Deor.* 3.23>
Uranus and *Aphrodite* <Sappho 198 *P.L.F*>
Uranus and *Gaea* <Sappho 198 *P.L.F.*>
Zephyrus and *Iris* <Alc. 327 *P.L.F.*>
Zeus <Eur. *Hipp.* 531>
— and *Psyche* <Apul. *Met.* 5.4 (he is called Cupid)>, (1a)
Ersa (*Herse*[3]), daughter of Zeus and *Selene* <Alc. in Plut. *Tab. Talk* 3.10>, 6d
Erybotes, son of Teleon <Ap. Rhod. *Arg.* 1.72> and *Zeuxippe*[4], *53a*
Erydameia, daughter of Tyndareus and *Leda* <Serv. on Virg. *Aen.* 8.130>, 48c
Erymanthus[1], son of Apollo <Ptol. 1>, 11c
Erymanthus[2], son of Arcas[1] <Paus. 8.24.1> and *Chrysopeleia*, 63c
Erymanthus[3], son of Aristas <Paus. 8.24.1>, *
Erysichthon[1], son of Triop(a)s[1] <Callim. *Hymn to Demeter*, 79-81> and *Hiscilla*, 34a
alternate parentage:
Myrmidon <Athen. 10.416b>
Erysichthon[2], son of Cecrops I and *Aglaurus*[1] <Apollod. *Bibl.* 3.14.2>, 66b
Erytheia[1] (*Erytheis*) [one of the Hesperides], daughter of *Nyx* <Hes. *Theog.* 215; named, Apollod. *Bibl.* 2.5.11>, *1a*
alternate parentage:
Atlas and *Hesperis*[1] <Diod. Sic. 4.27.2>
Hesperus[1] <Paus. 5.17.2; 6.19.8>
Erytheia[2], daughter of Geryon(eus) <Paus. 10.17.4>, 2b
— and Hermes <Paus. 10.17.4>, 46b
Erytheis — see *Erytheia*[1]
Erythras[1], son of Heracles[1] and *Exole* <Apollod. *Bibl.* 2.7.8>, *51c*
Erythras[2], son of Leucon[1] <Paus. 6.21.11>, 26d
[Erythrean Sibyl] — see *Herophile*[4]
Erythrion — see Erythrius
Erythrius (Erythrion), son of Athamas[1] and *Themisto*[1] <Apollod. *Bibl.* 1.9.2>, 26b
Erythrus, son of Rhadamanthys <Diod. Sic. 5.79.1>, 52d
Eryx[1] [King of Sicily], son of Butes[1] and *Aphrodite* <Diod. Sic. 4.83.1>, 53a
alternate parentage:
Poseidon <Apollod. *Bibl.* 2.5.10>
Eryx[2], turned into stone when he saw the head of *Medusa*[1] <Ovid *Met.* 5.196>, *
Eryx[3], killed by Hippomedon[1] <Stat. *Theb.* 9.128>, *
Eteocles[1] [King of Thebes], son of Oedipus <Aesch. *Sev.* 654-57> and *Jocasta* <Eur. *Phoen. Wom.* 55>, 55c
alternate parentage:
Oedipus and *Euryganeia* <Paus. 9.5.5>
Eteocles[2] [King of Orchomenus], son of Andreus[1] <*Cat. Wom., Frag Hes.* frg. 70, Merk. & West> and *Euippe*[4] <Paus. 9.34.9>, 20d
alternate parentage:
Cephis(s)us <Paus. 9.34.9>
— and *Euippe*[4] <*Cat. Wom., Frag. Hes.* frgs. 70, 71, Merk. & West>, (20d)
Eteoclus [one of the Seven against Thebes (per Aesch. *Sev.* 485-87)], son of Iphis[1] <Eur. *Supp.* 1037>, 58c
Eteoclymene, daughter of Minyas and *Clytodora*[1] <Schol. on Ap. Rhod *Arg.* 1.230>, 20d
[Ethiopian woman], paramour of Danaus[1] <Apollod. *Bibl.* 2.1.5>, 57d, 58c
Ethoda(ea) (*Neaera*[4]), daughter of Amphion[1] and *Niobe*[1] <Apollod. *Bibl.* 3.5.6>, 66c
Ethron — see Antiphantes
Etias, daughter of Aeneas[1] <Paus. 3.22.11> and *Creusa*[2], 41c
Euadne[1] (*Ianeira*), daughter of Iphis[1] <Eur. *Supp.* 984-85>, 58c
— and Capaneus <Eur. *Supp.* 984>, (58c)
Euadne[2] (*Peitho*[3]), daughter of Strymon[1] and *Neaera*[3] <Apollod. *Bibl.* 2.1.2>, 71b
— and Argus[2] <Apollod. *Bibl.* 2.1.2>, 61b
Euadne[3], daughter of Poseidon and *Pitane*[1] <Pind. *Olym.* 6.27-30>, 9a
— and Apollo <Pind. *Olym.* 6.35>, 11c
Euadne[4], daughter of Pelias[1] <Diod. Sic. 4.52.2> and *Anaxibia*[2],

28d
— and Canes <Diod. Sic. 4.53.2>, 22c
Euaechme[1], daughter of Megareus[1] <Paus. 1.43.4> and *Merope*[8], 9b
— and Alcathous[1] <Paus. 1.43.4>, 40a
Euaechme[2], daughter of Hyllus[1] <*Cat. Wom., Hesiodi* frg. 71A, Merk. & West (O.C.T.) and *Gr. Ehoiai, Frag. Hes.* frg. 251a, Merk. & West> and *Iole*, 60d
— and Polycreion <*Gr. Ehoiai, Frag. Hes.* frg. 251a, Merk. & West>, 9d
Euaemon[1], son of Ormenus[1] <Dem. Scep. in Strab. 9.5.18>, 24d
— and *Opis*[2] <Hyg. *Fab.* 97>, (24d)
Euaemon[2], son of Lycaon[1] <Apollod. *Bibl.* 3.8.1>, 63a
Euaemon[3] — see [five sets of twins]
Euagoras[1], son of Priam[1] <Apollod. *Bibl.* 3.12.5>, 44c
Euagoras[2], son of Neleus[1] and *Chloris*[2] <*Cat. Wom., Frag. Hes.* frg. 33(a), Merk. & West>, 27c
Euagore, daughter of Nereus and *Doris*[1] <Hes. *Theog.* 257>, *64a*
Euagoreis, daughter of Oceanus and *Tethys* <Hyg. *Fab.* pref.>, 53b
Euander[1], son of Hermes <Dion. Hal. *Rom. Ant.* 1.31> and *Nicostrate*[1] <Paus. 8.43.2>, 46c, *54b*
Euander[2] [King of Lycia], son of Sarpedon[1] <Diod. Sic. 5.79.3>, 52c
— and *Laodameia*[2] <Diod. Sic. 5.79.3 (she is called *Deidameia*)>, 18b
Euander[3], son of Priam[1] <Apollod. *Bibl.* 3.12.5>, 44c
Euanippe, wife of Hippomedon[1] <Hyg. *Fab.* 71>, 31c
Euanthes[1], son of Oenopion[1] <Paus. 7.4.6> and *Helice*[4], 56c
Euanthes[2], son of Dionysus <Paus. 7.4.8> and *Ariadne* <Schol. on Ap. Rhod. *Arg.* 3.997>, 56c
Euanthes[3], killed by Mezentius <Virg. *Aen.* 10.697>, *
Euarete, daughter of Acrisius <Hyg. *Fab.* 84> and *Eurydice*[6], 58d
— and Oenomaus[1] <Hyg. *Fab.* 84>, 7c
Euarne, daughter of Nereus and *Doris*[1] <Hes. *Theog.* 259>, *64a*
Euboea[1], daughter of Asterius[1] <Paus. 2.17.1>, 51a
Euboea[2], wife of Phorbas[3] <Schol. on Eur. *Or.* 932>, 61b
Euboea[3], daughter of Asopus <Eust. on Hom. *Il.* 278> and *Metope*[2], 66b
— and Poseidon <Hesyc. *Lex.* "Euboia">, 8c
Euboea[4], daughter of Thespius <Apollod. *Bibl.* 2.7.8> and *Megamede* <Apollod. *Bibl.* 2.4.10>, 50d
— and Heracles[1] <Apollod. *Bibl.* 2.7.8>, (50c)
Euboea[5], daughter of Larymnus <Athen. 7.296b>, 49a
— and Polybus[1] <Athen. 7.296b>, (49a)
Eubote, daughter of Thespius <Apollod. *Bibl.* 2.7.8> and *Megamede* <Apollod. *Bibl.* 2.4.10>, 50d
— and Heracles[1] <Apollod. *Bibl.* 2.7.8>, (50c)
Eubule[1], daughter of Leos[1] <Ael. *Var. Narr.* 12.28>, 6a
Eubule[2]—see [fifty daughters of Danaus[1]] (alternate version)
Eubuleus, son of Celeus[1] <Paus. 1.14.2> and *Metaneira*, 46b
alternate parentage:
Dysaules < Paus. 1.14.3>
Oceanus and *Gaea* <Musaeus in Paus. 1.14.2>
Trochilus[2] <Paus. 1.14.1>
Eubulus, son of Carmanor <Paus. 2.30.3>, 56c
alternate parentage:
Demeter <Diod. Sic. 5.76.3>
Euchenor[1], son of Polyidus[1] <Hom. *Il.* XIII.663> and *Eurydameia*, 31d, *63d*
alternate parentage:
Coeranus[1] <Paus. 1.43.6>
— and *Phlogea* <Schol. on Hom. *Od.* 18.84>, (31d), (63d)
Euchenor[2], son of Aegyptus[1] and [an Arabian woman] <Apollod. *Bibl.* 2.1.5>, 58c
— and *Iphimedusa* <Apollod. *Bibl.* 2.1.5>, (58c)
Eucleia, daughter of Heracles[1] and *Myrto* <Plut. *Aris.*>, 60c, *22d*
Eucra(n)te, daughter of Nereus and *Doris*[1] <Hes. *Theog.* 243>, *64a*
Eudora[1] [one of the Hyades], daughter of Atlas and *Pleione* <Hyg. *Fab.* 192>, 44b
alternate parentage:
Hyas and *Boeotia* <Hyg. *Poet. Astr.* 2.21>
Eudora[2], daughter of Nereus and *Doris*[1] <Hes. *Theog.* 244>, *64b*
Eudora[3], daughter of Oceanus and *Tethys* <Hes. *Theog.* 360>, 53b
Eudorus, son of Hermes and *Polymela*[1] <Hom. *Il.* XVI.179>, 46d
Eudoxa, daughter of Amphion[1] and *Niobe*[1] <Hyg. *Fab.* 11>, 66d
Euenia — see *Chalciope*[1]
Euenor[1], father of *Cleito*[1] <Plato *Crit.* 113d>, 8d
— and *Leucippe*[5] <Plato *Crit.* 113d>, (8d)
Euenor[2], father of Leiocritus <Hom. *Od.* 2.242>, *
Euenor[3], killed by Neoptolemus <Quint. Smyr. 11.33>, *
Euenor[4], killed by Paris <Quint. Smyr. 1.274>, *
Euenus[1] [King of Aetolia], son of Ares and *Demodice*[2] <Apollod. *Bibl.* 1.7.7>, 7a, *15c*
alternate parentage:
Ares and *Sterope*[1] <Plut. *Gr. and Rom. Par. Stor.* 40>
— and *Alcippe*[2] <Plut. *Gr. and Rom. Par. Stor.* 40 (inferred because she is called mother of *Marpessa*)>, 39a
Euenus[2] [river], son of Oceanus and *Tethys* <Hes. *Theog.* 345>, 53b
Euenus[3] [King of Lyrnessus], son of Selepus <Hom. *Il.* II.693>, 51d
Eueres[1], son of Pterelaus <Apollod. *Bibl.* 2.4.5> and *Amphimede*, 58d
Eueres[2], son of Heracles[1] and *Parthenope*[2] <Apollod. *Bibl.* 2.7.8>, 60d, *62c*
Eueres[3] (descendant of Udaeus), husband of *Chariclo*[1] <Apollod. *Bibl.* 3.6.7>, 32d
Eugeneius [one of the Pans], son of Pan <Non. *Dion.* 14.78>, 64d
Euhenus, son of Heracles[1] <Hyg. *Fab.* 162>, 61c
Euippe[1], daughter of Daunius <Ant. Lib. *Met.* 37.3>, 17d
— and Diomedes[1] <Ant. Lib. *Met.* 37.3>, (17d)
Euippe[2] (*Antiope*[7]), wife of Pierus[2] <Ovid *Met.* 5.305>, 15a
Euippe[3] — see *Hippe*[1]
Euippe[4], daughter of Leucon[1] <*Cat. Wom., Frag. Hes.* frg. 70, Merk. & West>, 26d
— and Andreus[1] <Paus. 9.34.8>, 20d
— and Eteocles[2] <*Cat. Wom., Frag. Hes.* frg. 70, Merk. & West>, 20d
Euippe[5], daughter of Danaus[1] and *Polyxo*[3] <Apollod. *Bibl.* 2.1.5>, 57d
— and Imbrus <Apollod. *Bibl.* 2.1.5>, (57d)
Euippe[6], daughter of Tyrimmas <Soph. in Parth. *Love Stor.* 3>, 13d
— and Odysseus <Soph. in Parth. *Love Stor.* 3>, (13d)
Euippe[7], daughter of Danaus[1] and [an Ethiopian woman] <Apollod. *Bibl.* 2.1.5>, 58c
— and Argius <Apollod. *Bibl.* 2.1.5>, (58c)
Euippus[1], son of Thestius and *Eurythemis(te)* <Apollod. *Bibl.* 1.7.10>, 15d
Euippus[2], son of Megareus[1] <Paus. 1.41.4> and *Merope*[8], 9a
Euippus[3], killed by Patroclus[1] <Hom. *Il.* XVI.417>, *
Eulimene[1], daughter of Cydon[1] <Parth. *Love Stor.* 35.1>, 53d
— and Apterus <Parth. *Love Stor.* 53.1>, (53d)
— and Lycastus[3] <Parth. *Love Stor.* 35.1>, (53d)
Eulimene[2], daughter of Nereus and *Doris*[1] <Hes. *Theog.* 247>, *64b*
Eumedes[1], son of Melas[3] <Apollod. *Bibl.* 1.8.5>, 16d
Eumedes[2], son of Heracles[1] and *Lyse* <Apollod. *Bibl.* 2.7.8>, *50c*
Eumedes[3], son of Hippocoon[1] <Paus. 3.14.6>, 47c
Eumedes[4], father of *Acallaris* <Dion. Hal. *Rom. Ant.* 1.62.2>, 42a
Eumedes[5] [a Herald], father of Dolon <Hom. *Il.* X.314>, *
Eumedes[6], son of Dolon <Virg. *Aen.* 12.346>, *
Eumelus[1] [King of Pherae], son of Admetus[1] and *Alcestis* <Hom. *Il.* II.714-15>, 29c
— and *Iphthime*[1] <Hom. *Od.* 4.796-98>, 47d
Eumelus[2] [King of Patrea], father of Antheias <Paus. 7.18.2>, *
Eumelus[3], son of Merops[5] <Ant. Lib. *Met.* 15.1>, *
Eumelus[4], son of Eugnotus <Ant. Lib. *Met.* 18.1>, *

Eumelus[5] — see [five sets of twins]
Eumelus[6], suitor of *Penelope*[1] (from Same) <Apollod. *Epit.* 7. 29>, *
Eumelus[7], reported the burning of Aeneas's fleet <Virg. *Aen.* 5.665>, *
(Eumenides) — see (Erinyes)
Eumetes, son of Lycaon[1] <Apollod. *Bibl.* 3.8.1>, 63a
Eumolpe, daughter of Nereus and *Doris*[1] <Apollod. *Bibl.* 1.2.7>, *64b*
Eumolpus[1] [King of Thrace], son of Poseidon and *Chione*[2] <Apollod. *Bibl.* 3.15.4>, 8c, *13a*
— and unnamed daughter of *Benthesicyme* <Apollod. *Bibl.* 3.15.4>, 63b
Eumolpus[2] (Molpus), flute player called by *Philonome*[2] as her witness <Apollod. *Epit.* 3.24-25>, *
Eumon, son of Lycaon[1] <Apollod. *Bibl.* 3.8.1>, 63a
Eune, daughter of Cinyras[1] <Tzetz. on Lyc. 450 (her father is identified as "Cyperos" (likely "King of Cyprus," which Cinyras[1] was at the time of the Trojan War, according to Theopomp. in *F.H.G.* 1.295, frg. 11b, Müller)> and *Metharme*, 11c
— and Teucer[2] <Tzetz. on Lyc. 450>, 23d
Euneice, daughter of Nereus and *Doris*[1] <Hes. *Theog.* 246>, *64b*
Euneus[1] [King of Lemnos], son of Jason and *Hypsipyle* <Hom. *Il.* VII.468-69>, 33d
Euneus[2], son of Clytius[10] <Virg. *Aen.* 11.666>, *
Euneus[3], brother of Thoas[8] <Plut. *Thes.* 26.3>, *
Eunomia[1] (*Thallo*) [order] [one of the Horae], daughter of Zeus and *Themis*[1] <Hes. *Theog.* 902>, 6c
Eunomia[2] — see *Eurynome*[1]
Eupalamus, son of Metion[1] <Apollod. *Bibl.* 3.15.8>, 49b
alternate parentage:
Erechtheus II <Diod. Sic. 4.74.1>
— and *Alcippe*[1] <Apollod. *Bibl.* 3.15.8>, 7a
— and *Merope*[5] <Plut. *Thes.* 19.5>, 49a
— and *Pharismede* <Schol. on Plato *Rep.* 7.529>, (49b)
Eupheme[1], paramour of Pan <Hyg. *Fab.* 224>, 46a
Eupheme[2]—see [fifty daughters of Danaus[1]] (alternate version)
Euphemus[1] [Argonaut], son of Poseidon and *Europe*[2] <Ap. Rhod. *Arg.* 1.177-79>, 8d
alternate parentage:
Poseidon and *Celaeno*[3] <Hyg. *Fab.* 157>
Poseidon and *Mecionice* <*Gr. Eoiae*, frg. 6, in *Hes.—Hom. Hymns & Hom.*, Evelyn-White>
Poseidon and *Oris* <Tzetz. *Chil.* 2.43>
— and *Lamache* <Schol. on Pind. *Pyth.* 4.55>, (8d)
— and *Laonome*[1] <Tzetz. on Lyc. 886>, 59d
Euphemus[2], son of Troezen[3] <Hom. *Il.* II.846-47>, *
Euphemus[3], father of Eurybatus <Ant. Lib. *Met.* 8>, *
Euphorion, son of Achilles and *Helen*[1] <Ptol. 4.1>, 24c, *48d*
Euphrates [river], son of Oceanus and *Tethys* <Hes. *Theog.* 367-68; named as river, Hyg. *Fab.* pref.>, 53b
Euphrosyne [gladness] [one of the Graces], daughter of Zeus and *Eurynome*[1] <Hes. *Theog.* 909>, 5d
alternate parentage:
Dionysus and *Coronis*[5] <Non. *Dion.* 48.555-56>
Helios and *Aegle*[1] <Anti. in Paus. 9.35.5>
Eupinytus, son of Amphion[1] and *Niobe*[1] <Apollod. *Bibl.* 3.5.6>, 66d
Eupoleme(ia), daughter of Myrmidon <Ap. Rhod. *Arg.* 1.55> and *Peisidice*[1], 5d
— and Hermes <Ap. Rhod. *Arg.* 1.51-55>, 46c
Eupompe, daughter of Nereus and *Doris*[1] <Hes. *Theog.* 261>, *64b*
Euporie [one of the hours], daughter of Zeus and *Themis*[1] <Hyg. *Fab.* 183>, 6d
Euripedes, son of Apollo and *Cleobula*[3] <Hyg. *Fab.* 161>, 11b
Europe[1], daughter of Phoenix[2] <Hom. *Il.* XIV.321> and *Perimede*[3] <Paus. 7.4.1>, 53d
alternate parentage:
Agenor[1] and *Argiope*[3] <Hyg. *Fab.* 178>
Agenor[1] and *Telephassa* <Apollod. *Bibl.* 3.1.1>
— and Asterius[4] <Diod. Sic. 4.60.2>, 17a
— and Zeus <Hom. *Il.* XIV.321>, 5c
Europe[2] (*Machionassa*), daughter of Tityus <Ap. Rhod. *Arg.* 1. 178>, 3b
— and Poseidon <Ap. Rhod. *Arg.* 1.178>, 8d
Europe[3], wife of Danaus[1] <Apollod. *Bibl.* 2.1.5>, 57a, 57c
Europe[4], daughter of Oceanus and *Tethys* <Hes. *Theog.* 357>, 53b
Europe[5] — see *Aerope*[1]
Europome —see [fifty daughters of Danaus[1]] (alternate version)
Europs, son of Aegialeus[2] <Paus. 2.5.6>, 61a
alternate version:
Phoroneus <Paus. 2.34.5>
Europus, son of Macedon and *Oreithyia*[2] <Steph. Byz. "Europus">, 15a
Eurotas [King of Laconia], son of Lelex[1] and *Cleochareia* <Apollod. *Bibl.* 3.10.3>, 61c
alternate parentage:
Myles <Paus. 3.1.1>
— and *Cleta*[1] <Schol. on Eur. 626>, (61c)
Eurus [East wind], son of Astraeus[1] <Non. *Dion.* 6.28-38> and *Eos*, 12b
Euryale[1] [one of the Gorgons], daughter of Phorcus[1] and *Ceto*[1] <Hes. *Theog.* 276>, 2b
alternate parentage:
Gorgon (son of Typhon and *Echidna*) and *Ceto*[1] <Hyg. *Fab.* pref.>
Euryale[2], daughter of Minos I <*Cat. Wom., Frag. Hes.* frg. 148(a), Merk. & West> and *Pasiphae*[1], 53c
— and Poseidon <*Cat. Wom., Frag. Hes.* frg. 148(a), Merk. & West>, 8d
Euryale[3] [Amazon] <Val. Flac. 5.611>, *
Euryalus[1], son of Odysseus and *Euippe*[6] <Soph. in Parth. *Love Stor.* 3.1>, 13d
Euryalus[2], son of Melas[3] <Apollod. *Bibl.* 1.8.5>, 16d
Euryalus[3] [one of the Epigoni], son of Mecisteus[1] <Hom. *Il.* II. 566>, 31c
Euryalus[4], son of Opheltes[3] <Virg. *Aen.* 9.196-201>, 44c
— and Nisus[1] <Virg. *Aen.* 9.177-84>, (44c)
Euryalus[5], son of Naubolus[4] <Hom. *Od.* 8.111>, *
Euryalus[6] [one of the Cyclopes] <Non. *Dion.* 14.59>, *
Euryalus[7], suitor of *Penelope*[1] (from Dulichium) <Apollod. *Epit.* 7.27>, *
Euryalus[8], suitor of *Penelope*[1] (from Zacynthus) <Apollod. *Bibl.* 7. 29>, *
Euryalus[9], killed by Oenomaus[1] <Paus. 6.21.10>, *
Euryanassa[1], daughter of Pactolus <Tzetz. on Lyc. 52>, 5c
— and Tantalus[1] <Tzetz. on Lyc. 52>, (5c)
Euryanassa[2], daughter of Hyperphas <Schol. on Hom. *Il.* XI.326>, 20d
— and Minyas <Nicand. in Ant. Lib. *Met.* 10>, (20d)
Eurybates[1] — see (Cercopes) (alternate version)
Eurybates[2], a herald of Odysseus <Hom. Od. 19.247>, *
Eurybia[1], daughter of Pontus and *Gaea* <Hes. *Theog.* 239>, 3a
— and Crius[1] <Hes. *Theog.* 376>, 12a
Eurybia[2], daughter of Thespius <Apollod. *Bibl.* 2.7.8> and *Megamede* <Apollod. *Bibl.* 2.4.10>, 50d
— and Heracles[1] <Apollod. *Bibl.* 2.7.8>, 50d
Eurybia[3] [Amazon] <Diod. Sic. 4.16.3>, *
Eurybius[1], son of Eurystheus <Apollod. *Bibl.* 2.8.1> and *Antimache*, 59c
Eurybius[2], son of Neleus[1] and *Chloris*[2] <*Cat. Wom., Frag. Hes.* frg. 33(a), Merk. & West>, 27c
Eurybius[3], son of Electryon[1] and *Lysidice*[1] <*Cat. Wom., Frag. Hes.* frg. 193, Merk. & West>, 59d, *38a*

Eurybius[4], a commander of the horned centaurs <Non. *Dion.* 14. 187>, *

Eurycapys, son of Heracles[1] and *Clytippe* <Apollod. *Bibl.* 2.7.8>, *50c*

Eurycleia[1], daughter of Athamas[1] and *Ino* <Mene. Tyr. in *F.H.G.* 1.86 frg. 6, Müller>, 26a

— and Melas[5] <Pher. in *F.H.G.* 1.86 frg. 55, Müller>, 26c

Eurycleia[2], daughter of Ekphas <Epim. in *F. Gr. H.* 3 B 15>, 55c

— and Laius[1] <Epim. in *F. Gr. H.* 3 B 15>, (55c)

Eurycleia[3], daughter of Ops <Hom. *Od.* 1.429>, *

Eurycleia[4], nurse of Odysseus <Hom. *Od.* 19.352-58>, *

Eurycyde, daughter of Endymion and *Chromia* <Paus. 5.1.4>, 15b

— and Poseidon <Paus. 5.1.8>, 8d

Eurydamas[1] [Argonaut], son of Irus[1] and *Demonassa*[1] <Hyg. *Fab.* 14>, 22d

alternate parentage:

Ctimenus <Ap. Rhod. *Arg.* 1.68>

Eurydamas[2], son of Aegyptus[1] and [a Phoenician woman] <Apollod. *Bibl.* 2.1.5>, 57d

— and *Phartis* <Apollod. *Bibl.* 2.1.5>, (57d)

Eurydamas[3], son-in-law of Antenor[1] <Quint. Smyr. 13.178-79>, 45d

Eurydamas[4], son of Pelias[1] <Tryph. *Tak. Ilium* 180> and *Anaxibia*[2], 28c

Eurydamas[5], father of Abas[5] and Polyidus[2] <Hom. *Il.* V.149>, *

Eurydamas[6], suitor of *Penelope*[1] <Hom. *Od.* 18.296>, *

Eurydameia, daughter of Phyleus[1] <Pher. in *F.H.G.* 4.638 frg. 24a, Müller> and *Timandra*[1], 63d

— and Polyidus[1] <Pher. in *F.H.G.* 4.638 frg. 24a, Müller>, 31d

Eurydice[1] (*Agriope*[2]) (*Argiope*[4]), daughter of *Cynna* <Athen. 4. 155a>, *6a*

— and Orpheus <Apollod. *Bibl.* 1.3.2>, (6a)

Eurydice[2] (*Cilla*[1]), daughter of Adrastus[2] <Apollod. *Bibl.* 3.11.3>, 42a

— and Ilus[2] <Apollod. *Bibl.* 3.11.3>, (42a)

Eurydice[3] (*Amphithea*[3]), wife of Lycurgus[1] <Apollod. *Bibl.* 1. 9.14>, 29d

Eurydice[4], paramour of Aeneas[1] <Lesch. in Paus. 10.26.1>, 41c

Eurydice[5], daughter of Amphiaraus and *Eriphyle* <Paus. 5.17.6>, 33c

Eurydice[6], daughter of Lacedaemon <Pher. in *F. Gr. H.* 3 F 10> and *Sparte* <Apollod. *Bibl.* 3.10.3>, 47b

— and Acrisius <*Cat. Wom., Frag. Hes.* frg. 129, Merk. & West>, 58d

Eurydice[7], daughter of Clymenus[1] <Hom. *Od.* 3.451-52> and *Budeia*, 26d

— and Nestor <Hom. *Od.* 3.453>, 27d

Eurydice[8], daughter of Danaus[1] and *Polyxo*[3] <Apollod. *Bibl.* 2.1. 5>, 57c

— and Dryas[2] <Apollod. *Bibl.* 2.1.5>, (57c)

Eurydice[9] (*Henioche*[3]), wife of Creon[2] <Soph. *Ant.* 1180>, 55d

Eurydice[10], daughter of Actor[3] <Schol. on Hom. *Il.* XVI.175> and *Aegina*, 22d

— and Peleus <Schol. on Hom. *Il.* XVI.175>, 24a

Eurydice[11], daughter of Pelops[1] <Diod. Sic. 4.9.1> and *Hippodameia*[1], *38a*

— and Electryon[1] <Diod. Sic. 4.9.1>, 59d

Eurydice[12], daughter of Nereus and *Doris*[1] <Hyg. *Fab.* pref.>, *64b*

Eurydomene — see *Eurynome*[1]

Euryganeia, daughter of Hyperphas <Apollod. *Bibl.* 3.5.8>, 55c

— and Oedipus <Paus. 9.5.5>, (55c)

Eurygyes, son of Minos I <*Cat. Wom., Frag. Hes.* frg. 146, Merk. & West> and *Pasiphae*, 52d

Euryleon, son of Aeneas[1] and *Creusa*[2] <Schol. on Lyc. 1263>, 41c

Eurylochus[1], husband of *Ctimene* <Eust. on Hom. *Od.* 1784>, 5c, 13c

Eurylochus[2], son of Aegyptus[1] and *Caliadne* <Apollod. *Bibl.* 2.1. 5>, 57c

— and *Autonoe*[2] <Apollod. *Bibl.* 2.1.5>, (57c)

Eurylochus[3], suitor of *Penelope*[1] (from Zacynthus) <Apollod. *Epit.* 7.29>, *

Eurylyte — see *Asterodeia*[3]

Eurymachus[1], son of Antenor[1] and *Theano*[2] <Paus. 10.27.1>, *45d*

Eurymachus[2], son of Polybus[6] <Hom. *Od.* 1.399>, *

Eurymachus[3], suitor of *Hippodameia*[1] <Paus. 6.21.10>, *

Eurymachus[4], killed by Polydamas <Quint. Smyr. 11.60>, *

Eurymede[1] — see *Eurynome*[2]

Eurymede[2] — see *Alcmene*

Eurymede[3], daughter of Oeneus[1] and *Althaea* <Ant. Lib. *Met.* 2.1>, 17c

Eurymedon[1] [giant], father of *Periboea*[4] <Hom. *Od.* 7.58-59>, 9a

Eurymedon[2], son of Minos I and *Pareia* <Apollod. *Bibl.* 3.1.2>, 54c

Eurymedon[3], son of Hephaestus and *Cabeira* <Non. *Dion.* 14.22>, 7b

Eurymedon[4], son of Dionysus and *Ariadne* <Hyg. *Fab.* 14>, 56c

Eurymedon[5], son of Ptolemaeus <Hom. *Il.* IV.228>, *

Eurymedon[6], charioteer of Agamemnon <Paus. 2.16.6>, *

Eurymedon[7], son of Faunus <Stat. *Theb.* 7.262>, *

Eurymedusa[1], daughter of Cleitor[3] <Clem. Alex. *Exhor.* 2.34>, 5d

— and Zeus <Serv. on Virg. *Aen.* 2.7>, (5d)

Eurymedusa[2], nurse for *Nausicaa* <Hom. *Od.* 7.8-12>, *

Eurymenes[1] — see Antimenes[2]

Eurymenes[2], killed by Meges[1] <Quint. Smyr. 10.98>, *

Eurynome[1] (*Eunomia*[2]) (*Eurydomene*), daughter of Oceanus and *Tethys* <Hes. *Theog.* 358>, 53b

— and Ophion <Ap. Rhod. *Arg.* 1.501>, (53b)

— and Zeus <Hes. *Theog.* 909>, 5d

Eurynome[2] (*Eurymede*[1]), daughter of Nisus[2] <*Cat. Wom., Frag. Hes.* frg. 43a, Merk. & West> and *Abrote*, 50d, *34d*

— and Glaucus[1] <Apollod. *Bibl.* 1.9.3 (she is called *Eurymede*)>, 18b

Eurynome[3], mother of *Leucothoe*[1] <Ovid *Met.* 4.208 ff.>, 14a

— and Orchamus <Ovid *Met.* 4.208 ff.>, (14a)

Eurynome[4] — see *Eidothea*[2]

Eurynome[5], paramour of Lycurgus[4] <Apollod. *Bibl.* 3.9.2>, 64c

Eurynome[6], daughter of Iphitus[4] <Hyg. *Fab.* 70>, 30d

— and Talaus <Hyg. *Fab.* 70>, (30d)

Eurynome[7] — see Amphidamas[1] (alternate version)

Eurynome[8], servant of *Penelope*[1] <Hom. *Od.* 17.496>, *

Eurynome[9], wife of Codrus[2] <Val. Flac. 2.136>, *

Eurynomus[1], son of Magnes[2] and *Philodice*[2] <Schol. on Eur. *Phoen. Maid.* 1760>, 21a

Eurynomus[2] [centaur], offspring of Centaurus and a Magnesian Mare <Pind. *Pyth.* 2.50; named as centaur, Ovid *Met.* 12.311>, 69c

alternate parentage:

Ixion and *Nephele*[1] <Diod. Sic. 4.69.5>

Eurynomus[3], son of Aegyptius <Hom. *Od.* 2.15-21>, *

Eurynomus[4] [demonic spirit in Hades] <Paus. 10.28.4>, *

Eurynomus[5], killed by Ajax[1] <Quint. Smyr. 1.530>, *

Euryodia, paramour of Zeus <Eust. on Hom. *Od.* 1796>, 5c

Euryopes, son of Heracles[1] and *Terpsicrate* <Apollod. *Bibl.* 2.7. 8>, *50d*

Euryphaessa — see *Theia*[1]

Eurypon, son of Sous <Paus. 3.7.1>, 60d

alternate parentage:

Procles[1] <Strab. 8.5.5>

Eurypyle[1], daughter of Thespius <Apollod. *Bibl.* 2.7.8> and *Megamede* <Apollod. *Bibl.* 2.4.10>, 50d

— and Heracles[1] <Apollod. *Bibl.* 2.7.8>, (50d)

Eurypyle[2] [one of the Bacchae] <Non. *Dion.* 30.222>, *

Eurypylus[1] [King of Moesia], son of Telephus <Apollod. *Epit.* 5.11> and *Astyoche*[3] <Acus. in Schol. on Hom. *Od.* 11. 250>, 60a, *42c*

Eurypylus[2] [King of Cos], son of Poseidon and *Mestra* <*Cat. Wom.,*

Frag. Hes. frg. 43a, Merk. & West>, 8c, *34c*
alternate parentage:
Poseidon and *Astypalaea* <Apollod. *Bibl.* 2.7.1>
Eurypylus[3], son of Temenus[1] <Apollod. *Bibl.* 2.7.5>, 60c
Eurypylus[4], son of Heracles[1] and *Eubote* <Apollod. *Bibl.* 2.7.8>, *50d*
Eurypylus[5], son of Poseidon and *Celaeno*[1] <Schol. on Ap. Rhod. *Arg.* 4.1561>, 8b, *40b*
Eurypylus[6], son of Thestius and *Eurythemis(te)* <Apollod. *Bibl.* 1. 7.10>, 15d
Eurypylus[7], son of Euaemon[1] <Hom. *Il.* V.76> and *Opis*[2] <Hyg. *Fab.* 97>, 24d
Eurypylus[8], son of Dexamenus <Paus. 7.19.9>, 14c
Eurypylus[9], suitor of *Penelope*[1] (from Dulichium) <Apollod. *Epit.* 7.27>, *
Eurysaces [King of Salamis], son of Ajax[1] <Soph. *Ajax* 544-74> and *Tecmessa*[1] <Soph. *Ajax* 785-812> 23d, *63d*
Eurysthenes[1] [King of Sparta], son of Aristodemus <Herod. 7. 204> and *Argeia*[3] <Apollod. *Bibl.* 2.8.3>, 60d
— and *Anaxandra* <Paus. 3.16.6>, 61c
Eurysthenes[2] — see [fifty sons of Aegyptus[1]] (alternate version)
Eurystheus [King of Argos, Mycenae, and Tiryns], son of Sthenelus[1] <Hom. *Il.* XIX.123> and *Nicippe*[1] <Apollod. *Bibl.* 2.4.5>, 58d
— and *Antimache* <Apollod. *Bibl.* 3.9.2>, 63c
Euryte[1], daughter of Hippodamas[1] <*Cat. Wom., Hesiodi* frg. 10a.45-49, Merk. & West (O.C.T.)>, 65a
— and Portheus[1] <*Cat. Wom., Hesiodi* frg. 10a.49-50, Merk. & West (O.C.T.)>, 15d
Euryte[2], paramour of Poseidon <Apollod. *Bibl.* 3.14.2>, 8d
Eurytele, daughter of Thespius <Apollod. Bibl. 2.7.8> and *Megamede* <Apollod. *Bibl.* 2.4.10>, 51c
Eurythemis(te) (*Deidameia*[2]) (*Leucippe*[6]), daughter of Portheus[1] and *Laothoe*[4] <*Cat. Wom., Frag. Hes.* frg. 26.9, Merk. & West>, 15d
alternate parentage:
Cleoboea[2] <Apollod. *Bibl.* 1.7.10>
Xanthus[7] <Schol. on Eur. *Or.* 11>
— and Tantalus[1] <Schol. on Eur. *Or.* 11>, (15d)
— and Thestius <*Cat. Wom., Frag. Hes.* frg. 10a.35, Merk. & West; named Apollod. *Bibl.* 1.7.10>, 15d
Eurytia — see *Idaea*[2]
Eurytion[1] (Eurytus[5]) [centaur], offspring of Centaurus and a Magnesian Mare <Pind. *Pyth.* 2.50; named as centaur, Hom. *Od.* 21.299>, 69d
alternate parentage:
Ixion and *Nephele*[1] <Diod. Sic. 4.69.5>
— and *Hippodameia*[2] <Ovid *Met.* 12.224 (he is called Eurytus)>, 30d
Eurytion[2] [centaur], offspring of Centaurus and a Magnesian Mare <Pind. *Pyth.* 2.50; named as centaur, Bacch. frg. 44, Snell & Maehler>, 69d
alternate parentage:
Ixion and *Nephele*[1] <Diod. Sic. 4.69.5>
— and *Hippolyte*[3] <Bacch. frg. 44, Snell & Maehler>, 14c
Eurytion[3] (Eurytus[3]) [King of Phthia] [Argonaut], son of Irus[1] <Ap. Rhod. *Arg.* 1.72> and *Demonassa*[1] <Hyg. *Fab.* 14>, 22b
alternate parentage:
Actor[1] <Apollod. *Bibl.* 1.8.2>
Eurytion[4], son of Lycaon[4] <Virg. *Aen.* 5.495-96 (inferred because he is called brother of Pandarus[2])>, *
Eurytion[5], herdsman of Geryon(eus) <Apollod. *Bibl.* 2.5.10>, *
Eurytion[6], killed by Parthenopaeus <Stat. *Theb.* 9.749>, *
Eurytus[1] [Argonaut], son of Hermes <Pind. *Pyth.* 4.178-79> and *Antianeira*[1] <Ap. Rhod. *Arg.* 1.51>, 46a
Eurytus[2] [King of Oechalia], son of Melaneus[2] and *Stratonice*[2] <*Cat. Wom., Frag. Hes.* frg. 26, Merk. & West>, 11d, *15d*
alternate parentage:
Melaneus[2] and *Oechalia* <Paus. 4.3.10>
— and *Antiope*[6] <Hyg. *Fab.* 14>, 60b
Eurytus[3] — see Eurytion[3]
Eurytus[4], son of Poseidon <Hom. *Il.* II.621> and *Molione* <*Cat. Wom., Frag. Hes.* frg. 17, Merk. & West>, 9a
alternate parentage:
Actor[4] and *Molione* <Paus. 8.14.9>
Augeias <Diod. Sic. 4.33.3>
— and *Theraephone* <Paus. 5.3.3>, 14c
Eurytus[5] — see Eurytion[1]
Eurytus[6], son of Hippocoon[1] <Apollod. *Bibl.* 3.10.5>, 47c
Eurytus[7] [giant], son of *Gaea* (and the blood of Uranus) <Hes. *Theog.* 180-86; named as giant, Apollod. *Bibl.* 1.6.2>, *4a*
Eurytus[8], father of Clonus <Virg. 10.499>, *
Eurytus[9] [King of Caria], father of *Eidothea*[5] <Ant. Lib. *Met.* 30>, *
Eurytus[10], killed by Eurypylus[1] <Quint. Smyr. 8.109-11>, *
Euseirus, son of Poseidon <Ant. Lib. *Met.* 22>, 9d
— and *Eidothea*[3] <Ant. Lib. *Met.* 22>, (9d)
Eus(s)orus, father of *Aenete* <Ap. Rhod. *Arg.* 1.948 ff.> and Acamas[3], 44c
Eustyoche — see *Timandra*[1]
Euterpe [music] [one of the Muses], daughter of Zeus and *Mnemosyne* <Hes. *Theog.* 77>, 6b
— and Strymon <Apollod. *Bibl.* 1.3.4>, 71b
Euthymus[1], son of Caecinus <Paus. 6.6.4>, 51b
alternate parentage:
Astycles <Paus. 6.6.4>
Euthymus[2], fought Polites <Strab. 6.1.5>, *
Eutiches, son of Hippocoon[1] <Apollod. *Bibl.* 3.10.5>, 47c
Euxanthius, son of Minos I and *Dexithea* <Bacch. 1.125>, 54d
Exole, daughter of Thespius <Apollod. Bibl. 2.7.8> and *Megamede* <Apollod. *Bibl.* 2.4.10>, 51c
— and Heracles[1] <Apollod. *Bibl.* 2.7.8>, (51c)

[Fates] — see (Moirae)
Faunus[1], father of Acis <Ovid *Met.* 13.750>, 64a
— and *Simaethis* <Ovid *Met.* 13.750>, (64a)
Faunus[2] [King in Italy], son of Hermes <Plut. *Gr. and Rom. Par. Stor.* 38>, 46d
[fifty daughters of Danaus[1]] <Apollod. *Bibl.* 2.1.5> (see *Actaea*[2], *Adiante*, *Adite*, *Agave*[2], *Amymone*, *Anaxibia*[3], *Anthelia*, *Asteria*[6], *Automate*, *Autonoe*[2], *Bryce*, *Callidice*[2], *Celaeno*[4], *Chrysippe*[1], *Cleite*[2], *Cleodameia*, *Cleodora*[3], *Cleopatra*[4], *Cleopatra*[5], *Dioxippe*[1], *Dorius*, *Electra*[5], *Erato*[3], *Euippe*[5], *Euippe*[7], *Eurydice*[8], *Glauce*[3], *Glaucippe*, *Gorge*[2], *Gorgophone*[2], *Hippodameia*[6], *Hippodice*, *Hippomedusa*, *Hyperippe*[2], *Hyperm(n)estra*[1], *Iphimedusa*, *Mnestra*, *Nelo*, *Ocypete*[2], *Oeme*, *Peirene*[1], *Phartis*, *Podarce*, *Pylarge*, *Rhode*[2], *Rhodeia*[2], *Scaea*, *Sthenele*[2], *Stygne*, *Theano*[3]), 57c-58c
others:
named in <Hyg. *Fab.* 170>: *Acamantis*, *Amphicomone*, *Arcadia*[2], *Arsalte*, *Autodice*, *Chrysothemis*[3], *Cleio*[3], *Critomedeia*, *Damone*, *Daplidice*, *Demoditas*, *Demophile*[2], *Eubule*[2], *Eupheme*[2], *Europome*, *Hecabe*[2], *Helice*[5], *Helicta*, *Hero*[3], *Hipparete*, *Hippothoe*[5], *Hyale*[1], *Itea*, *Mideia*[4], *Monuste*, *Myrmidone*, *Phila*, *Philomela*[5], *Polybe*, *Polyxena*[2], *Pyrante*, *Pyrantis*, *Scylla*[3] *Themistagora*, *Trite*,
named in <Schol. on Ap. Rhod. *Arg.* 1.230>: *Hesione*[4]
named in <Hesyc. *Lex.* "Hippe">: *Hippe*[4]
[fifty daughters (unnamed)], children of Endymion and *Selene* <Paus. 5.1.4>, 14b, *15a*
[fifty sons of Aegyptus[1]] <Apollod. *Bibl.* 2.1.5> (see Aegius, Aegyptus[2], Agaptolemus, Agenor[8], Alces, Alcmenor, Arbelus, Archelaus[5], Argeius[5], Bromius[2], Busiris[2],

Cercetes, Chaetus, Chalcodon[1], Chrysippus[2], Chthonius[2], Cisseus[2], Cleitus[3], Daiphron[1], Daiphron[2], Diocorystes, Dryas[2], Enceladus[2], Euchenor[2], Eurydamas[2], Eurylochus[2], Hermus[1], Hippocorystes[1], Hippolytus[3], Hippothous[4], Hyperbius[1], Idas[2], Idmon[2], Imbrus, Istrus[1], Lampus[2], Lixus, Lycus[9], Lynceus[2], Menalces, Menemachus, Oenus[3], Pandion[4], Periphas[3], Peristhenes, Phantes, Polyctor[2], Potamon, Proteus[2], Sthenelus[4]), 57c-58c

others:

named in <Hyg. *Fab.* 170 (called those killed by daughters of Danaus[1])>: Amyntor[4], Andromachus, Antimachus[7], Antiochus[5], Antipaphus, Aristonoos, Armoasbus, Asterides, Asterius[10], Athamas[4], Athletes, Canthus, Cassus, Clytus[1], Demarcus, Dolichus, Ecnominus, Ephilates[3], Eudaemon, Eurysthenes[2], Hyperantus, Iltonomus, Midanus, Mineus, Niauius, Obrimus, Pamphilus, Panthius, Perius, Philinus, Plexippus[4], Podasimus, Polydector, Protheon, Pugno, Xanthus[9]

[Fifty sons of Lycaon[1]] <Apollod. *Bibl.* 3.8.1 (49 named)> (see Acontes, Aegaeon[2], Ancyor, Archebates, Bucolion[3], Canethus[2], Carteron, Caucon[2], Cleitor[2], Corethon, Cynauthus, Euaemon[2], Eumetes, Eumon, Genetor, Haemon[4], Halipherus, Harpaleus, Harpalycus[2], Helix, Heraeeus, Hopleus[2], Horus, Leon, Linus[4], Lycius[1], Macar(eus)[2], Macednus, Maenalus, Mantineus[2], Mecisteus[2], Melaenus, Nyctimus, Orchomenus[1], Pallas[3], Peucetius, Phassus, Phineus[3], Phthius[2], Physius, Plato, Polichus, Portheus[2], Prothous[1], Socleus, Stymphalus[2], Tegeates (named by Paus.), Teleboas[2], Thresprotus, Titanas), 62a-64d

others:

named in <Paus. 8.3.1-5; 8.6.6>: Acacus, Alipherus, Aseatas, Chareseus, Cromus[2], Daseates, Hellison, Hypsus, Oenotrus, Orestheus[2], Peraethus, Phigalus, Sumateus, Thocnus, Thyraeus, Trapezeus, Tricolonus[1]

named in <Plut. *Gr. Quest.* 39>: Eleuther[2], Lebadus

named in <Hyg. *Poet. Astr.* 2.6>: Ceteus[1]

named in <Ant. Lib. *Met.* 31>: Daunius and Iapyx[2]

named in <Dion. Hal. *Rom. Ant.* 1.11.2-3>: Oenotrus

named in <Steph. Byz. "Psophis">: Psophis[3]

[fifty sons (unnamed)], children of Pallas[6] <Apollod. *Epit.* 1.11>, 51a

[five daughters, Dactyls (unnamed)], children of *Anchiale* <Ap. Rhod. *Arg.* 1.1128 (referred to by Soph. in Strab. 3.10. 22)>, *11b*

alternate parentage:

born on Mt. Ida of uncertain parentage <Diod. Sic. 5.64.4>

[five sets of twins], children of Poseidon and *Cleito*[1] <Plato *Crit.* 113d-114b> (Atlas and Eumelus[5], Ampheres and Euaemon[3], Mneseus and Autochthon, Elasippus[1] and Mestor[4], Azaes and Diareses), 8c-d

[Furies] — see (Erinyes)

Gaea (*Ge*) [earth], came from Chaos <Hes. *Theog.* 117>, 2b

alternate parentage:

Aether and *Hemera* <Hyg. *Fab.* pref.>

— and Oceanus <Pher. in Apollod. *Bibl.* 1.5.2>, 55a

— and Pontus <Hes. *Theog.* 234>, 2b

— and Poseidon <Serv. on Virg. *Aen.* 3.420>, 8c

— and Tartarus[1] <Hes. *Theog.* 821-22>, 1b

— and Uranus <Hes. *Theog.* 133>, 4b

— and Zeus <Paus. 7.17.5>, 5c

Galanthis — see *Historis*

Galateia[1], daughter of Nereus and *Doris*[1] <Hes. *Theog.* 250>, *64a*

— and Acis <Ovid *Met.* 13.739-897>, (64a)

— and Polyphemus[1] <Ovid *Met.* 13.739-897>, 2b, 9c

Galateia[2] [statue brought to life], wife of Pygmalion[1] <Ovid *Met.* 10.247-97>, 11c

Galateia[3], daughter of Eurytius <Ant. Lib. *Met.* 17.1>, *

Gala(te)s, son of Heracles[1] <Diod. Sic. 5.24.3>, 61c

Galaxaure, daughter of Oceanus and *Tethys* <Hes. *Theog.* 353>, 54a

Galene, daughter of Nereus and *Doris*[1] <Hes. *Theog.* 244>, *64a*

Galeotes, son of Apollo and *Themisto*[2] <Steph. Byz. "Galeotai">, 11d

Ganges [river], son of Oceanus and *Tethys* <Hes. *Theog.* 367-68; named as river, Ovid *Met.* 5.51> and *Tethys*, 54a

alternate parentage:

Indus and *Calauria* <Ps.-Plut. *De Fluv.* 4.1>

Ganymede — see *Hebe*

Ganymede(s), son of Tros[1] <Hom. *Il.* XX.233> and *Callirhoe*[1] <Apollod. *Bibl.* 3.12.1>, 41b

alternate parentage:

Assarcus <Hyg. *Fab.* 224>

Erichthonius[1] <Hyg. *Fab.* 271>

— and Zeus <Eur. *Iph. in Aulis* 1049-53>, 5c

[Garamantian nymph], mother of Iarbas <Virg. *Aen.* 4.197-201>, 41d

— and Ammon[1] <Virg. *Aen.* 4.197-201>, (41d)

Garamas — see Amphithemis[1]

Ge — see *Gaea*

Gelanor [King of Argos], son of Sthenelas <Paus. 2.16.1>, 61d

Geleon, son of Ion[1] <Eur. *Ion* 1574> and *Helice*[1], 52a

Gelonus, son of Heracles[1] and *Echidna* <Herod. 4.9>, 60c

Genetor, son of Lycaon[1] <Apollod. *Bibl.* 3.8.1>, 63a

Geras [old age] [abstraction], offspring of *Nyx* <Hes. *Theog.* 225>, *1b*

Geryon(eus) [King of Erythia] [monster], offspring of Chrysaor and *Callirhoe*[2] <Hes. *Theog.* 982>, 2b

[giants], sons of *Gaea* (and the blood of Uranus) <Hes. *Theog.* 185> (see Agrius[2], Alcyoneus[1], Alpus, Anax, Chthonius[5], Clytius[4], Damasen, Enceladus[1], Ephialtes[1], Eurytus[7], Gration, Hippolytus[2], Hopladamus, Mimas[1], Pallas[2], Peloreus, Polybotes, Porphyrion[1], Rhoetus[2], Thoas[7], Thoon[1], Thurius, Typhoeus[2]), 4a

Gigas, son of Hermes and *Hiera*[2] <Tzetz. on Lyc. 42>, 46c

Glauce[1], daughter of Cychreus <Pher. in *F. Gr. H.* 3 F 60>, 66b

— and Actaeus[3] <Pher. in *F. Gr. H.* 3 F 60>, (66b)

— and Telamon <Diod. Sic. 4.72.7>, 23c

Glauce[2] (*Creusa*[1]), daughter of Creon[1] <Eur. *Medea* 19; named, Apollod. *Bibl.* 1.9.28)>, 33d

— and Jason <Eur. *Medea* 19; named, Apollod. *Bibl.* 1.9.28)>, (33d)

Glauce[3], daughter of Danaus[1] and *Atlantia* or *Phoebe*[4] <Apollod. *Bibl.* 2.1.5>, 57d

— and Alces <Apollod. *Bibl.* 2.1.5>, (57d)

Glauce[4], daughter of Nereus and *Doris*[1] <Hes. *Theog.* 244>, *64a*

Glauce[5] — see *Hippolyte*[1]

Glauce[6], daughter of Cycnus[5] <Dict. Cret. 2.13>, 23c

— and Ajax[1] <Dict. Cret. 5.15>, 23c, 40c

Glauce[7], wife of Upis <Cic. *De Nat. Deor.* 3.23>, *

Glauce[8], Arcadian nymph <Paus. 8.47.3>, *

Glaucia[1], daughter of Scamander[1] <Plut. *Gr. Quest.* 41> and *Idaea*[1], 70b

— and Deimachus[3] <Plut. *Gr. Quest.* 41>, (70b)

Glaucia[2] — see (Pleiades) (alternate version)

Glaucia[3], daughter of *Hippo*[3] <Callim. frg. 693, Pfeiffer>, *

Glaucippe, daughter of Danaus[1] and *Polyxo*[3] <Apollod. *Bibl.* 2.1. 5>, 57d

— and Potamon <Apollod. *Bibl.* 2.1.5>, (57d)

Glauconome, daughter of Nereus and *Doris*[1] <Hes. *Theog.* 256>, *64a*

Glaucus[1] (Taraxippus[2]) [King of Ephyra], son of Sisyphus <Hom. *Il.* VI.154> and *Merope*[1] <Apollod. *Bibl.* 1.9.3>, 18b

— and *Eurynome*[2] <Apollod. *Bibl.* 1.9.3>, 34d, 50d
— and *Mestra* <*Cat. Wom., Frag. Hes.* frg. 43a, Merk. & West>, 34c
— and *Pantidyia* <Schol. on Ap. Rhod. 1.146>, (18b)
Glaucus[2] [King of Lycia], son of Hippolochus[1] <Hom. *Il.* VI.206> and *Demonassa*[4] <Schol. on Hom. *Il.* VI.206>, 18d
Glaucus[3], son of Poseidon and [a Naiad] <Athen. 7.296 (citing Euan.)>, 9a, *62a*
alternate parentage:
Anthedon and *Alcyone*[7] <Athen. 7.296b (citing Mnaseas)>
Polybus[1] and *Euboea*[5] <Athen. 7.296b>
— and *Ariadne* <Athen 7.296b>, 53d
— and *Hydne* <Athen. 7.296e (citing Aeschrion of Samos)>, 49d
— and Melicertes <Athen. 7.297 (citing Hedylus of Samos)>, 26b
— and Nereus <Athen. 7.296f (citing Nicand.)>, 64b
— and *Scylla*[2] <Ovid *Met.* 13.899-968>, 2b
— and *Syme* <Athen. 7.296c>, 14a
Glaucus[4], son of Minos I and *Pasiphae*[1] <Apollod. *Bibl.* 3.1.2>, 53c
alternate parentage:
Minos I and *Crete* <Asclep. in Apollod. *Bibl.* 3.1.2>
Glaucus[5] [King of Messenia], son of Aepytus[3] <Paus. 4.3.9>, 60c
Glaucus[6], son of Antenor[1] <Apollod. *Epit.* 5.21> and *Theano*[2], *45d*
Glaucus[7], son of Priam[1] <Apollod. *Bibl.* 3.12.5>, 44c
Glaucus[8] [one of the Pans], son of Pan <Non. *Dion.* 14.82>, 64d
Glaucus[9], son of Aretus[4] and *Laobia* <Non. *Dion.* 250-56>, *
Glaucus[10], son of Imbrasus <Virg. *Aen.* 12.343>, *
Glaucus[11], suitor of *Penelope*[1] (from Dulichium) <Apollod. *Epit.* 7.27>, *
Glaucus[12], killed by Jason <Val. Flac. 3.153>, *
Glenus, son of Heracles[1] and *Deianeira*[1] <*Cat. Wom., Frag. Hes.* frg. 25.19, Merk. & West>, 60a
Glyphius, pursuer of *Teiresias* <Eust. on Hom. *Od.* 1665.48 ff.>, 32d
[gods and goddesses] — see *Aphrodite*, Apollo, Ares, *Artemis*, *Athene*, *Demeter*, Dionysus, Hephaestus, *Hera*, Hermes, Poseidon, Zeus (the twelve on the Parthenon frieze), and Helios, *Hestia*, *Selene*, Uranus,
[Golden Ram], offspring of Poseidon and *Theophane* <Hyg. *Fab.* 188>, 9b
Golgos, son of Adonis and *Aphrodite* <Schol. on Theo. 15.100>, 11c
Gordius [King of Phrygia], paramour of *Cybele*[2] <Hyg. *Fab.* 274 (inferred because she is the mother of Midas, son of Gordius)>, 2b
Gorgasus, son of Machaon and *Anticleia*[3] <Paus. 4.30.3>, 19c
Gorge[1], daughter of Oeneus[1] and *Althaea* <*Cat. Wom., Frag. Hes.* frg. 25.17, Merk. & West>, 16d
— and Andraemon[1] <Apollod. *Bibl.* 1.8.1>, (16d)
Gorge[2], daughter of Danaus[1] and *Atlantia* or *Phoebe*[4] <Apollod. *Bibl.* 2.1.5>, 58c
— and Hippothous[4] <Apollod. *Bibl.* 2.1.5>, (58c)
Gorge[3], daughter of Megareus[3] <*Etym. Magn.* "Eschatiotis" 384.39-40>, 34d
— and Corinthus[1] <*Etym. Magn.* "Eschatiotis" 384.39-40>, (34d)
Gorge[4], Lemnian woman who killed Elymus[3] <Stat. *Theb.* 5.207>, *
Gorge[5] [one of the Bacchae] <Non. *Dion.* 29.266>, *
Gorgo[1], paramour of Aegyptus[1] <Apollod. *Bibl.* 2.1.5>, 57c, 58a
Gorgo[2] [one of the dogs of Actaeon] <Hyg. *Fab.* 181>, *
(Gorgons), daughters of Phorcus[1] and *Ceto*[1] <Hes. *Theog.* 276> (see *Euryale*[1], *Medusa*[1], *Sthen(n)o*), 2b
Gorgophone[1], daughter of Perseus[1] and *Andromeda* <*Cat. Wom., Frag. Hes.* frg. 135, Merk. & West>, 59c
— and Oebalus[1] <Paus. 2.21.8>, 47a
— and Perieres[1] <Apollod. *Bibl.* 2.4.5>, 25b
Gorgophone[2], daughter of Danaus[1] and *Elephantis* <Apollod. *Bibl.* 2.1.5>, 57c
— and Proteus[2] <Apollod. *Bibl.* 2.1.5>, (57c)
Gorgophonus, son of Electryon[1] and *Lysidice*[1] <*Cat. Wom., Frag. Hes.* frg. 193, Merk. & West>, 59d, *38a*
alternate parentage:
Electryon[1] and *Anaxo*[1] <Apollod. *Bibl.* 2.4.5>
Gorgyra (*Orphne*), wife of Acheron <Apollod. *Bibl.* 1.5.3>, 50a
Gorgythion, son of Priam[1] and *Castianeira* <Hom. *Il.* VIII.303-05>, 43d
Gortys[1], son of Rhadamanthys <Paus. 8.53.4>, 52d
alternate parentage:
Tegeates <Paus. 8.53.4>
Gortys[2], son of Stymphalus[1] <Paus. 8.4.8>, 62c
[Graces] — see (Charites)
(Graeae), daughters of Phorcus[1] and *Ceto*[1] (see *Deino*, *Enyo*[1], *Pe(m)phredo*), 2a
Graecus, son of Zeus and *Pandora*[3] <*Cat. Wom., Frag. Hes.* frg. 5, Merk. & West>, 6c, *16b*
Granicus [river], son of Oceanus and *Tethys* <Hes. *Theog.* 342>, 67b
Gras, son of Echelas <Paus. 3.2.1>, 36d
Gration [giant], son of *Gaea* (and the blood of Uranus) <Hes. *Theog.* 180-86; named as giant, Apollod. *Bibl.* 1.6.2>, *4a*
Gryneus [centaur], offspring of Centaurus and a Magnesian Mare <Pind. *Pyth.* 2.50; named as centaur, Ovid *Met.* 12.257>, 69d
alternate parentage:
Ixion and *Nephele*[1] <Diod. Sic. 4.69.5>
Grynus, son of Euryplus[1] <Serv. on Virg. *Ecl.* 3.63>, 60a
Guneus[1], father of *Laonome*[2] <Apollod. *Bibl.* 2.4.5>, 59c
Guneus[2] [King of Cyphus], son of Ocytus <Apollod. *Epit.* 3.14>, *
Gy(g)es[1] [one of the Hecatoncheires], son of Uranus and *Gaea* <Hes. *Theog.* 149>, 4a
Gyges[2], son of Dascylus[3] <Herod. 1.8> and father of Myrsus[2] <Herod. 3.122>, *
Gyges[3], killed by Turnus <Virg. *Aen.* 9.762>, *
Gymnastica [one of the hours], daughter of Zeus and *Themis*[1] <Hyg. *Fab.* 183>, 6d
Gyrton, son of Ares and *Chryse*[1] <Steph. Byz. "Gyrton" (he is called brother of Phlegyas)>, 7a, *19c*
Gyrtone, daughter of Phlegyas <Schol. on Ap. Rhod. *Arg.* 1.57>, 19c

Habrote — see *Abrote*
Hades (Aedes) (Aedoneus) (Pluto(n)) [underworld], son of Cronus and *Rhea* <Hes. *Theog.* 455>, 10a
— and *Leuce* <Serv. on Virg. *Ecl.* 7.61>, 55b
— and *Minthe* <Opp. *Hal.* 3, 486 (he is called Aidoneus)>, 50a
— and *Persephone*[1] <Hes. *Theog.* 914>, 10a
Haemon[1], son of Creon[2] <Soph. *Ant.* 572-73> and *Eurydice*[9] <Soph. *Ant.* 1181>, 55d
— and *Antigone*[1] <Soph. *Ant.* 571-73, 629>, 55c
Haemon[2], son of Pelasgus[3] <Schol. on Ap. Rhod. 3.1090> and *Menippe*[3], 61d
Haemon[3] [King of Aetolia], son of Thoas[6] <Paus. 5.3.6>, 16d
Haemon[4], son of Lycaon[1] <Apollod. *Bibl.* 3.8.1>, 63a
Haemon[5], son of Magnes[2] and *Meliboea*[3] <Eust. on Hom. *Il.* 338>, 21b
Haemon[6], father of Elasippus[2] <Quint. Smyr. 1.230>, *
Haemon[7], son of Mavors <Virg. *Aen.* 9.685>, *
Haemon[8], father of Thessalus[4] <Strab. 9.5.23>, *
Haemon[9] (Haemus[3]), human turned into mountain <Ovid *Met.* 6.83>, *
Haemon[10] [one of the dogs of Actaeon] <Hyg. *Fab.* 181>, *
Haemus[1], son of Boreas[1] and *Oreithyia*[1] <Steph. Byz. "Aemus">,

12b
— and *Rhodope*[1] <Luc. *Dance* 51>, 70a
Haemus[2], son of Ares <Tzetz. *Antehom.* 273>, 7c
Haemus[3] — see Haemon[9]
Haemus[4], a defender of Thebes <Stat. *Theb.* 7.644>, *
Haero — see *Merope*[3]
Hagnias — see Tiphys (alternate version)
Halaesus, son of Agamemnon <Virg. *Aen.* 7.723>, 36b
Halcyone[1] — see *Alcyone*[1]
Halcyone[2] — see *Alcyone*[2]
Halcyone[3] — see *Cleopatra*[2]
Halcyone[4] —see *Alcyone*[4]
Halcyone[5] — see *Marpessa*
Halesus[1] — see Alesus
Halesus[2], killed by Latreus <Ovid *Met.* 12.462>, *
Halia[1] (*Leucothea*[1]), daughter of Pontus and *Gaea* <Diod. Sic. 5.55.4 (inferred because *Halia*[1] is called sister of the Telchines)>, 3a
alternate parentage:
Thalatta <Diod. Sic. 5.55.4>
— and Poseidon <Diod. Sic. 5.55.4>, 8c
Halia[2], daughter of Nereus and *Doris*[1] <Hes. *Theog.* 245>, *64a*
Halia[3], daughter of Tyllus <Dion. Hal. *Rom. Ant.* 1.27.1>, 51b
— and Cotys[1] <Dion. Hal. *Rom. Ant.* 1.27.1>, (51b)
Haliacmon [river], son of Oceanus and *Tethys* <Hes. *Theog.* 341>, 54a
Haliartus (Aliartus), son of Thersander[2] <Paus. 9.34.5>, 19c
Halimede, daughter of Nereus and *Doris*[1] <Hes. *Theog.* 255>, *64a*
— and Hermes <Steph. Byz. "Damascus">, 46c
Halipherus, son of Lycaon[1] <Apollod. *Bibl.* 3.8.1>, 64a
Halirrhothius[1], son of Poseidon and *Euryte*[2] <Apollod. *Bibl.* 3.14. 2>, 8d
alternate parentage:
Poseidon and *Aglaurus*[2] <Hellan. in *F. Gr. H.* 4 F 38>
— and *Alcippe*[1] <Apollod. *Bibl.* 3.14.2>, 7a
Halirrhothius[2], son of Perieres[1] and *Alcyone*[6] <*Cat. Wom., Frag. Hes.* frg. 49, Merk. & West>, 25a
Halius[1], son of Alcinous <Hom. *Od.* 8.119> and *Arete* <Hom. *Od.* 7.67>, 9c
Halius[2], suitor of *Penelope*[1] (from Zacynthus)] <Apollod. *Epit.* 7. 29>, *
Halius[3], killed by Odysseus <Hom. *Od.* 5.678>, *
Halius[4], killed by Turnus <Virg. *Aen.* 9.767>, *
Halmus — see Almus
Halocrates, son of Heracles[1] and *Olympusa* <Apollod. *Bibl.* 2.7. 8>, *51c*
Halys[1] [river], son of Oceanus and *Tethys* <Hes. *Theog.* 367-68; named as river, Herod. 1.103>, 54a
Halys[2], killed by Turnus <Virg. *Aen.* 9.765>, *
Halys[3], killed by Jason <Val. Flac. 1.157>, *
Halys[4], killed by Tydeus[1] <Stat. *Theb.* 2.574>, *
Hamadryas, daughter of Oreius[2] <Athen. 3.78b>, 71b
— and Oxylus[3] <Athen. 3.78b>, (71b)
Harmonia[1] (*Hermionea*), daughter of Ares and *Aphrodite* <Hes. *Theog.* 936>, 7a
alternate parentage:
Zeus and *Electra*[2] <Hellan. in *F. Gr. H.* 4 F 23>
— and Cadmus <Hes. *Theog.* 975-76>, 55d
Harmonia[2], paramour of Ares <Ap. Rhod. *Arg.* 2.990>, 7a
Harmonia[3] [nurse of the world] <Non. *Dion.* 41.314>, *
Harmonide, daughter of Polypheides <Schol. on Hom. *Od.* 15. 223>, 32c
Harmothoe[1], wife of Pandareus <Eust. on Hom. *Od.* 1875.31>, 66d
Harmothoe[2] [Amazon] <Quint. Smyr. 1. 44>, *
Harpaleus, son of Lycaon[1] <Apollod. *Bibl.* 3.8.1>, 64a
Harpalus[1], son of Amyclas[1] and *Diomede*[2] <Paus. 7.18.5>, 47a
Harpalus[2] [one of the dogs of Actaeon] <Hyg. *Fab.* 181>, *
Harpalyce[1], daughter of Harpalycus[1] <Hyg. *Fab.* 193>, 46d
Harpalyce[2], daughter of Clymenus[4] <Hyg. *Fab.* 206> and *Epicaste*[4], 26d
— and Alastor[1] <Parth. *Love Stor.* 13.2>, 27c
— and Clymenus[4] <Hyg. *Fab.* 206>, (26d)
Harpalyce[3], paramour of Iphiclus[3] <Athen. 14.619e>, 15d
Harpalycus[1] [King of Thrace], son of Hermes <Theocr. *Idylls* 24.115-16>, 46d
Harpalycus[2], son of Lycaon[1] <Apollod. *Bibl.* 3.8.1>, 64a
Harpalycus[3], killed by *Camilla* <Virg. *Aen.* 11.675>, *
[Harpies] — see (Harpuiai)
Harpinna, daughter of Asopus and *Metope*[2] <Diod. Sic. 4.73.1>, 66b
— and Ares <Diod. Sic. 4.73.1>, 7a
(Harpuiai) [Harpies], daughters of Thaumas[1] and *Electra*[1] (see *Aello*, *Celeano*[2], *Ocypete*[1], *Podarge*), 3a-b
alternate parentage:
Boreas <Pherecydes of Syros 7 B 5>
Oceanus and *Gaea* <Epim. *Theog.* 3 B 7>
Hebe (*Dia*[2]) (*Ganymede*) [cup-bearer of the gods], daughter of Zeus and *Hera* <Hes. *Theog.* 922>, 5a
— and Heracles[1] <Hom. *Od.* 11.604>, 60c
Hebrus[1], son of Haemus[1] and *Rhodope*[1] <Serv. on Virg. *Aen.* 1. 317>, 12b, *70a*
Hebrus[2], son of Dolichaon <Virg. *Aen.* 10.697>, *
Hebrus[3], killed by Polydeuces <Val. Flac. 3.149>, *
Hebrus[4], killed by Jason <Val. Flac. 6.618>, *
Hebrus[5], killed by Danaus[3] <Stat. *Theb.* 10.315>, *
Hecabe[1], daughter of Cisseus[1] <Eur. *Hec.* 3> and *Telecleia*, 43d
alternate parentage:
Dymas[1] <Hom. *Il.* XVI.718-19 (inferred because she is called brother of Asius)> and *Eunoe*
Sa(n)garius and *Metope*[1] <Apollod. *Bibl.* 3.12.5>
— and Odysseus <Eur. *Tro. Wom.* 274-78>, 13d
— and Priam[1] <Hom. *Il.* XXIV.283-99>, (43d)
Hecabe[2] —see [fifty daughters of Danaus[1]] (alternate version)
Hecaerge, daughter of Boreas[1] <Callim. *Hymn to Delos* 292-93>, and *Oreithyia*[1], 12b
Hecamede, daughter of Arsinous[1] <Hom. *Il.* XI.625>, 27d
— and Nestor <Hom. *Il.* XI.625>, (27d)
Hecate (*Brimo*) (*Crataeis*[1]) (*Enodia*), daughter of Perses[2] and *Asteria*[1] <Hes. *Theog.* 411>, 12a
alternate parentage:
Aristaeus[2] <Pher. in *F. Gr. H.* 3 F 44>
Persaeus <*Hom. Hymn* 2 (to *Demeter*)>
Zeus and *Asteria*[1] <Musaeus 2 B 16>
Zeus and *Demeter* <Call. frg. 466, Pfeiffer>
— and Aeetes <Diod. Sic. 4.45.3>, 14c
— and Phorbas[7] <*Gr. Ehoiai, Frag. Hes.* frg. 262, Merk. & West> (Evelyn-White renders the name Phoebus from the same fragment <*Gr. Eoiae*, frg. 13, in *Hes.—Hom. Hymns & Hom.*, Evelyn-White>), (12a)
— and Phorcus[1] <Ap. Rhod. *Arg.* 4.828 (she is called *Crataeis*)>, 2b
Hecaterus, husband of a daughter of Phoroneus (probably *Niobe*[2]) <Hes. in Strab. 10.3.19>, 61b
Hecaton, father of *Calyce*[2] <Hyg. *Fab.* 157>, 8b
(Hecatoncheires), sons of Uranus and *Gaea* (see Briareus, Cottus, Gy(g)es[1]), 4a
Hecetorus, father of Agassamenus and Scellis <Parth. *Love Stor.* 19>, 34a
Hector[1], son of Priam[1] <Hom. *Il.* II.816-17> and *Hecabe*[1] <Apollod. *Bibl.* 3.11.5>, 43c
alternate parentage:
Apollo <Stes. in *P.M.G.* 224>
— and *Andromache* <Hom. *Il.* VI.395>, (43c)
Hector[2] [King of Chios] <Paus. 7.4.9>, *
Hegeleus, son of Tyrrhenus <Paus. 2.21.3> and *Sardo*[1], 51b

Hegemone — see (Charites) (alternate version)
Hegesandra, daughter of Amyclas[1] <Pher. in *F. Gr. H.* 3 F 132> and *Diomede*[2], 47a
— and Argeius[3] <Pher. in *F. Gr. H.* 3 F 132>, 36a
Hegetoria, wife of Ochimus <Diod. Sic. 5.57.7>, 14b
Heleius, son of Perseus[1] and *Andromeda* <Apollod. *Bibl.* 2.4.5>, 58d
Helen[1], daughter of Zeus <Hom. *Il.* III.426> and *Leda* <Apollod. *Bibl.* 3.10.7>, 5c, *16c*, *48d*
alternate parentage:
Zeus and *Nemesis* <Apollod. *Bibl.* 3.10.7>
Zeus and [an Oceanid] <*Cat. Wom., Frag. Hes.* frg. 24, Merk. & West>
Tyndareus and *Leda* <*Cat. Wom., Frag. Hes.* frg. 23a, 38, Merk. & West>
— and Achilles <Paus. 3.19.13>, 24c
— and Deiphobus[1] <Tzetz. on Lyc. 143>, 43c
— and Menelaus <Hom. *Od.* 4.10; 15.53-54>, 37a
— and Paris <Hom. *Il.* III.425-36>, 43c
— and Theseus <Plut. *Thes.* 29.2>, 51b
Helen[2], daughter of Paris and *Helen*[1] <Ptol. 4>, 43c
Helen[3], daughter of Aegisthus and *Clytemnestra* <Phot. *Lib.* 149.14>, 39a
Helen[4], daughter of Faustulus <Ptol. 4>, *
Helenus[1], son of Priam[1] <Hom. *Il.* VI.75> and *Hecabe*[1] <Apollod. *Bibl.* 3.11.5>, 43c
— and *Andromache* <Paus. 1.11.1>, (43c)
Helenus[2], son of Oenops <Hom. *Il.* V.707>, *
Helenus[3], suitor of *Penelope*[1] (from Ithaca) <Apollod. *Epit.* 7.30>, *
(Heliades[1]), children of Helios and *Rhode*[1] <Diod. Sic. 5.56.3> (see Actis, Candalus, Cercaphus, *Electryo(ne)*, Macar(eus)[4], Ochimus, Tenages), 14a-b
(Heliades[2]) (Phaeontides), daughters of Helios and *Clymene*[1] <Ovid *Met.* 2.340; named, Hyg. *Fab.* 154> (see *Aegle*[2], *Aetheria*, *Dioxippe*[2], *Helie*, *Merope*[9], *Phoebe*[5]), 14a-b
Helicaon[1], son of Antenor[1] <Hom. *Il.* III.123> and *Theano*[2], *45d*
— and *Laodice*[1] <Hom. *Il.* III.123-24>, 43c
Helicaon[2], warrior with Dionysus <Non. *Dion.* 43.57>, *
Helice[1], daughter of Selinus <Paus. 7.1.2>, 9d
— and Ion[1] <Paus. 7.1.2>, 17b, 51b
Helice[2] — see *Callisto*[1]
Helice[3], daughter of Olenus[1] <Hyg. *Poet. Astr.* 2.13> and *Lethaea*, 7d
Helice[4], wife of Oenopion[1] <Parth. *Love Stor.* 20.1>, 56c
Helice[5] —see [fifty daughters of Danaus[1]] (alternate version)
Heliconis, daughter of Thespius <Apollod. *Bibl.* 2.7.8> and *Megamede* <Apollod. *Bibl.* 2.4.10>, 51c
— and Heracles[1] <Apollod. *Bibl.* 2.7.8>, (51c)
Helicta —see [fifty daughters of Danaus[1]] (alternate version)
Helie [one of the Heliades[2]], daughter of Helios and *Clymene*[1] <Ovid *Met.* 2.333-40; named, Hyg. *Fab.* 154>, 14a
alternate parentage:
Helios and *Rhode*[1] <Schol. on Hom. *Od.* 17.208>
Helios [god] [sun], son of Hyperion[1] and *Theia*[1] <Hes. *Theog.* 371>, 14a
alternate parentage:
Oceanus ("from whom all we gods proceed") <Hom. *Il.* XIV.202>
— and *Antiope*[4] <Tzetz. on Lyc. 175>, (14a)
— and *Ceto*[3] <Non. *Dion.* 26.354-55>, 71b
— and *Clymene*[1] <Ovid *Met.* 1.766-71>, 52b
— and *Clytie*[4] <Ovid *Met.* 4.236-37>, (14a)
— and *Leocothoe*[1] <Ovid *Met.* 4.208 ff.>, (14a)
— and *Nausidame* <Hyg. *Fab.* 14>, 63d
— and *Neaera*[1] <Hom. *Od.* 12.132>, (14a)
— and *Ocyrrhoe*[3] <Ps.-Plut. *De Fluv.* 5.1>, 62a
— and *Perse(is)* <Hes. *Theog.* 956>, 62b
— and *Rhode*[1] <Apollod. *Bibl.* 1.4.5>, 3a
Helix[1], son of Lycaon[1] <Apollod. *Bibl.* 3.8.1>, 64a
Helix[2], killed by Nestor <Val. Flac. 6.570>, *
Helle, daughter of Athamas[1] <Apollod. *Bibl.* 1.9.1> and *Nephele*[2] <*Cat. Wom., Frag. Hes.* frg. 68, Merk. & West>, 26a
— and Poseidon <Hyg. *Poet. Astr.* 2.20>, 8c
Hellen(us)[1] [King of Phthia], son of Deucalion[1] and *Pyrrha*[1] <*Cat. Wom., Frag. Hes.* frg. 2, Merk. & West>, 17b
alternate parentage:
Zeus and *Pyrrha*[1] <Apollod. *Bibl.* 1.7.2>
— and *Orseis* <Apollod. *Bibl.* 1.7.3>, (17b)
Hellen[2], son of Poseidon and *Antiope*[10] <Hyg. *Fab.* 157>, 8b
Hellison — see [fifty sons of Lycaon[1]] (alternate version)
Helops[1] [centaur], offspring of Centaurus and a Magnesian Mare <Pind. *Pyth.* 2.50; named as centaur, Ovid *Met.* 12.333>, 69d
alternate parentage:
Ixion and *Nephele*[1] <Diod. Sic. 4.69.5>
Helops[2], killed by Theseus <Stat. *Theb.* 12.746>, *
Helorus, son of Istrus[2] <Tzetz. *Antehom.* 274>, 54b
Hemera [day], daughter of Erebus and *Nyx* <Hes. *Theog.* 124-25, 1a
alternate parentage:
Chaos <Hyg. *Fab.* pref.>
— and Phaethon[2] <Paus. 1.3.1>, 46c
Hemithea[1], daughter of Cycnus[2] and *Procleia* <Paus. 10.14.2>, *43c*
— and Achilles <Tzetz. on Lyc. 232>, 24d
Hemithea[2] — see *Molpadia*[1]
Henioche[1], daughter of Creon[2] and *Eurydice*[9] <Paus. 9.10.3>, 55d
Henioche[2], daughter of Pittheus <Plut. *Thes.* 25.4>, 38b
— and Canethus[3] <Plut. *Thes.* 25.4>, (38b)
Henioche[3] — see *Eurydice*[9]
Henioche[4], nurse of *Medea* <Val. Flac. 5.357>, *
Hephaestine, paramour of Aegyptus[1] <Apollod. Bibl. 2.1.5>, 57d-58c, 58a
Hephaestus [god] [fire], son of Zeus and *Hera* <Hom. *Il.* I.571-72, 578>, 7b
alternate parentage:
Hera <Hes. *Theog.* 927>
Oceanus ("from whom all we gods proceed") <Hom. *Il.* XIV.202>
Talus[3] <Cin. in Paus. 8.53.5>
— and *Aglaia*[1] <Hes. *Theog.* 945>, 5d
— and *Anticleia*[2] <Apollod. *Bibl.* 3.16.1>, (7b)
— and *Aphrodite* <Hom. *Od.* 8.266-358>, 5b
— and *Athene* <Apollod. *Bibl.* 3.14.6>, 5d, 61b
— and *Cabeira* <Acus. in Strab. 10.3.21>, 9c
— and *Charis* <Hom. *Il.* XVIII.382>, (7b)
— and Lernus's wife <Ap. Rhod. *Arg.* 1.202>, 7d
— and *Ocresia* <Ovid *Fast.* 6.628-29 (he is called Vulcan)>, (7b)
Heptapore — see [Muses] (alternate version)
Heptaporus [river], son of Oceanus and *Tethys* <Hes. *Theog.* 341>, 54a
Hera [goddess] [childbirth] [heaven], daughter of Cronus <Hom. *Il.* IV.59> and *Rhea* <Hes. *Theog.* 454>, 5a
alternate parentage:
Oceanus ("from whom all we gods proceed") <Hom. *Il.* XIV.202>
— and Zeus <Hes. *Theog.* 921>, 5a
Heracles[1] (Alcides) (Aloides) (Melampyges) (Menoeceus[3]) [Argonaut], son of Zeus and *Alcmene* <Hom. *Il.* XIV.324>, 5a, *59d*
— and Abderus <Apollod. *Bibl.* 2.5.8>, 46d
— and *Aeschreis* [one of the Thespiades] <Apollod. *Bibl.* 2.7.8>, 50a
— and *Aglaia*[4] [one of the Thespiades] <Apollod. *Bibl.* 2.7.8>,

50a
— and *Anthea* [one of the Thespiades] <Apollod. *Bibl.* 2.7.8>, 50a
— and *Anthippe* [one of the Thespiades] <Apollod. *Bibl.* 2.7. 8>, 50a
— and *Antiope*[5] [one of the Thespiades] <Apollod. *Bibl.* 2.7.8>, 50a
— and *Argele* [one of the Thespiades] <Apollod. *Bibl.* 2.7.8>, 50a
— and *Asopis*[2] [one of the Thespiades] <Apollod. *Bibl.* 2. 7. 8>, 50a
— and *Asty(a)dameia*[1] <Apollod. *Bibl.* 2.7.8>, 24d
— and *Astyoche*[2] <Hom. *Il.* II.659>, (60a)
— and *Auge*[1] <*Cat. Wom., Frag. Hes.* frg. 165, Merk. & West>, 63d
— and *Autonoe*[4] <Apollod. *Bibl.* 2.7.8>, (60a)
— and *Barge* <Steph. Byz. "Bargasa">, (60a)
— and *Bolbe* <Athen. 8.334e>, (60a)
— and *Calametis* [one of the Thespiades] <Apollod. *Bibl.* 2.7. 8>, 50a
— and *Celtine* <Parth. *Love Stor.* 30.1>, (60a)
— and *Certhe* [one of the Thespiades] <Apollod. *Bibl.* 2.7.8>, 50c
— and *Chalciope*[2] <Apollod. *Bibl.* 2.7.8>, 34c
— and *Chryseis*[2] [one of the Thespiades] <Apollod. *Bibl.* 2.7. 8>, 50c
— and *Clytippe* [one of the Thespiades] <Apollod. *Bibl.* 2.7. 8>, 50c
— and *Deianeira*[1] <*Cat. Wom., Frag. Hes.* frg. 25.17-18, Merk. & West>, 16d
— and *Echidna* <Herod. 4.9>, 2a
— and *Elachia* [one of the Thespiades] <Apollod. *Bibl.* 2.7. 8>, 50c
— and *Eone* [one of the Thespiades] <Apollod. *Bibl.* 2.7. 8>, 50c
— and *Epicaste*[2] <Apollod. *Bibl.* 2.7.8>, 63d
— and *Epilais* [one of the Thespiades] <Apollod. *Bibl.* 2.7.8>, 50c
— and *Erato*[4] [one of the Thespiades] <Apollod. *Bibl.* 2.7.8>, 50c
— and *Euboea*[4] [one of the Thespiades] <Apollod. *Bibl.* 2.7. 8>, 50c
— and *Eubote* [one of the Thespiades] <Apollod. *Bibl.* 2.7.8>, 50c
— and *Eurybia*[2] [one of the Thespiades] <Apollod. *Bibl.* 2.7. 8>, 50c
— and *Eurypyle*[1] [one of the Thespiades] <Apollod. *Bibl.* 2.7. 8>, 50c
— and *Eurytele* [one of the Thespiades] <Apollod. *Bibl.* 2.7. 8>, 51c
— and *Exole* [one of the Thespiades] <Apollod. *Bibl.* 2.7.8>, 51c
— and *Hebe* <Hom. *Od.* 11.604>, 5a
— and *Heliconis* [one of the Thespiades] <Apollod. *Bibl.* 2.7. 8>, 51c
— and *Heychia*[2] [one of the Thespiades] <Apollod. *Bibl.* 2.7. 8>, 50c
— and *Hippo*[1] [one of the Thespiades] <Apollod. *Bibl.* 2.7.8>, 50c
— and *Hippocrate* [one of the Thespiades] <Apollod. *Bibl.* 2. 7.8>, 50c
— and Hylas <Apollod. *Bibl.* 1.9.19>, 64d
— and *Iole* <Soph. *Trach. Wom.* 427>, 60a
— and *Iphinoe*[4] <Pher. in *F. Gr. H.* 3 F 76>, (60c)
— and *Iphis*[4] [one of the Thespiades] <Apollod. *Bibl.* 2.7.8>, 50c
— and *Laothoe*[3] [one of the Thespiades] <Apollod. *Bibl.* 2.7. 8>, 50c
— and *Lavinia*[1] <Dion. Hal. *Rom. Ant.* 1.32>, 46c
— and *Lyse* [one of the Thespiades] <Apollod. *Bibl.* 2.7.8>, 50c
— and *Lysidice*[2] [one of the Thespiades] <Apollod. *Bibl.* 2.7. 8>, 50c
— and *Lysippe*[2] [one of the Thespiades] <Apollod. *Bibl.* 2.7. 8>, 50c
— and *Malis* <Hellan. in *F.H.G.* 1.58 frg. 102, Müller>, (60c)
— and *Marse* [one of the Thespiades] <Apollod. *Bibl.* 2.7.8>, 50c
— and *Megara* <Eur. *Her.* 69>, 55d
— and *Meline* [one of the Thespiades] <Apollod. *Bibl.* 2.7.8>, 50c
— and *Melite*[2] <Ap. Rhod. *Arg.* 4.538>, (60c)
— and *Menippis* [one of the Thespiades] <Apollod. *Bibl.* 2.7. 8>, 50c
— and *Mideia*[3] <Paus. 1.5.2>, (60c)
— and *Myrto*[1] <Plut. *Aris.* 20.6>, 22d
— and *Nicippe*[2] [one of the Thespiades] <Apollod. *Bibl.* 2.7. 8>, 51c
— and *Nike*[2] [one of the Thespiades] <Apollod. *Bibl.* 2.7.8>, 51c
— and *Olympusa* [one of the Thespiades] <Apollod. *Bibl.* 2.7. 8>, 51c
— and *Omphale* <Dion. Hal. *Rom. Ant.* 1.28.1>, (60c)
— and *Oreia* [one of the Thespiades] <Apollod. *Bibl.* 2.7.8>, 50c
— and *Pallantia* <Serv. on Virg. *Aen.* 8.51 (citing Varro)>, 46c
— and *Panope*[2] [one of the Thespiades] <Apollod. *Bibl.* 2.7. 8>, 50c
— and *Parthenope*[2] <Apollod. *Bibl.* 2.7.8>, 62c
— and *Patro* [one of the Thespiades] <Apollod. *Bibl.* 2.7.8>, 50c
— and *Phialo* <Paus. 8.12.3>, (60c)
— and *Phyleis* [one of the Thespiades] <Apollod. *Bibl.* 2.7.8>, 50c
— and *Praxithea*[3] [one of the Thespiades] <Apollod. *Bibl.* 2. 7.8>, 50c
— and *Procris*[2] [one of the Thespiades] <Apollod. *Bibl.* 2.7. 8>, 50c
— and *Psophis*[1] <Paus. 8.24.2>, 53a
— and *Pyrene*[1] <Sil. Ital. 3.420 ff.>, (60c)
— and *Pyrippe* [one of the Thespiades] <Apollod. *Bibl.* 2.7. 8>, 50c
— and [a slave girl] <Herod. 1.7>, (61c)
— and Sostratus <Paus. 7.17.8>, (61c)
— and *Stratonice*[3] [one of the Thespiades] <Apollod. *Bibl.* 2. 7.8>, 50c
— and *Terpsicrate* [one of the Thespiades] <Apollod. *Bibl.* 2. 7.8>, 50c
— and *Thebe*[4] <Dicaearch. in *F.H.G.* 2.238 frg. 11, Müller>, (60c)
— and *Tinge* <Plut. *Sertorius* 9>, (61c)
— and *Tiphyse* [one of the Thespiades] <Apollod. *Bibl.* 2.7. 8>, 50c
— and *Toxicrate* [one of the Thespiades] <Apollod. *Bibl.* 2.7. 8>, 50c
— and *Tyrus* <Poll. *Onom.* 1.45>, (61c)
— and *Xanthis* [one of the Thespiades] <Apollod. *Bibl.* 2.7. 8>, 50c
Heracles[2] [one of the Dactyls], son of *Anchiale*[1] <Ap. Rhod. *Arg.* 1128; named, Paus. 5.7.6>, *11a*
alternate parentage:
born on Mt. Ida of uncertain parentage <Diod. Sic. 5.64.4>
Heracles[3], son of Zeus and *Asteria*[1] <Cic. *De Nat. Deor.* 3.42>,

5a, *12a*
Heracles[4], son of Zeus and *Lysithoe* (said by Cicero to be an earlier Zeus) <Cic. *De Nat. Deor.* 3.42>, *
Heracles[5] (of Thasus), father of Theagenes by Timosthenes' wife <Paus. 6.11.2>, *
Heracles[6], son of Nilus <Cic. *De Nat. Deor.* 3.42>, *
Heracles[7] (Belus[5]) [from India], father and paramour of *Pandaea* <Arr. *Ind.* 9.3-4>, *
Heraeeus, son of Lycaon[1] <Apollod. *Bibl.* 3.8.1>, 64a
Hermaphroditus, son of Hermes and *Aphrodite* <Diod. Sic. 4.6. 5>, 46a
— and *Salmacis* <Ovid *Met.* 4.288-391>, (46a)
Hermes [god] [messenger of the gods], son of Zeus and *Maia* <Hes. *Theog.* 938>, 5c, *46a*
alternate parentage:
Oceanus ("from whom all we gods proceed") <Hom. *Il.* XIV.202>
— and *Acacallis*[1] <Paus. 8.53.4>, 53d
— and *Alcidameia* <Paus. 2.3.8>, (46a)
— and *Antianeira*[1] <Ap. Rhod. *Arg.* 1.57>, (46a)
— and *Apemosyne* <Apollod. *Bibl.* 3.2.1>, 52d
— and *Aphrodite* <Ovid *Met.* 4.287>, 5b
— and *Chione*[1] <Ovid *Met.* 11.308>, 13a
— and *Chthonophyle* <Paus. 2.6.3>, 49a
— and *Cleobula*[4] <Hyg. *Fab.* 224 (she is called *Theobula*)>, 21a
— and *Daeira* <Paus. 1.38.7>, 52b
— and *Dryope*[1] <*Hom. Hymn* 19 (to Pan)>, 64d
— and *Erytheia*[2] <Paus. 10.17.4>, 2b
— and *Eupolome(ia)* <Ap. Rhod. *Arg.* 1.51-55>, 5d
— and *Halimede* <Steph. Byz. "Damascus">, 64a
— and *Herse*[1] <Apollod. *Bibl.* 3.14.3>, 66b
— and *Hiera*[2] <Tzetz. on Lyc. 42>, (46c)
— and *Iphthime*[2] <Non. *Dion.* 14.114-15>, 17a
— and *Isse* <Steph. Byz. "Issa">, 14a
— and *Laothoe*[5] <Orph. *Arg.* 135-37>, (46c)
— and *Lara(nda)* <Ovid *Fast.* 2.613-15>, (46c)
— and *Libya*[2] <Hyg. *Fab.* 160>, 52d
— and *Nicostrate*[1] <Paus. 8.43.2>, 54b
— and *Palaestra* <*Etym. Magn.* "Pale" 648.2-3>, (46c)
— and *Pandrosos* <Schol. on Hom. *Il.* I.334>, 66b
— and *Penelope*[2] <Non. *Dion.* 14.93>, (46c)
— and *Phylodameia* <Paus. 4.30.2>, 57b
— and *Polymela*[1] <Hom. *Il.* XVI.182-87>, (46c)
— and *Rhene*[2] <Diod. Sic. 5.48.1>, (46c)
— and *Sose* <Non. *Dion.* 14.89>, (46d)
— and *Stilbe*[2] <Schol. on Hom. *Il.* X.266-67>, 13b
— and *Thronia* <*Cat. Wom., Frag. Hes.* frgs. 137-38, Merk. & West>, 59a
Hermion, son of Europs <Paus. 2.34.5>, 61a
Hermione, daughter of Menelaus and *Helen*[1] <Hom. *Od.* 4.10>, 37a
— and Orestes[1] <Eur. *Or.* 1654-77>, 36a
— and Neoptolemus <Hom. *Od.* 4.10>, 24c
Hermionea — see *Harmonia*
Hermus[1], son of Aegyptus[1] and *Caliadne* <Apollod. *Bibl.* 2.1. 5>, 57c
— and *Cleopatra*[5] <Apollod. *Bibl.* 2.1.5>, (57c)
Hermus[2] [river], son of Oceanus and *Tethys* <Hes. *Theog.* 343>, 54a
Hero[1], daughter of Priam[1] <Hyg. *Fab.* 90>, 44c
Hero[2], paramour of Lyander <Ovid *Her.* 18; 19>, *
Hero[3] —see [fifty daughters of Danaus[1]] (alternate version)
Herodice, wife of Cypselus[1] <Athen. 13.609f>, 62c
Herophile[1] [Libyan Sibyl], daughter of Zeus and *Lamia*[1] <Paus. 10.12.1>, 5d
Herophile[2] [Cumaean Sibyl] — see *Deiphobe*
Herophile[3] [Trojan Sibyl]— see *Sibylla*
Herophile[4] [Erythrean Sibyl], daughter of Theodorus and a nymph <Paus. 10.12.7>, *
Herophile[5] [Marpessan Sibyl], daughter of a mortal man and a nymph on Mt. Ida <Paus. 10.12.1>, *
Herse[1], daughter of Cecrops I and *Aglaurus*[1] <Apollod. *Bibl.* 3. 14.2>, *66b*
— and Hermes <Apollod. *Bibl.* 3.14.3>, 46c
Herse[2], paramour of Danaus[1] <Apollod. *Bibl.* 2.1.5>, 57b, 57d
Herse[3] — see *Ersa*
Hesione[1], daughter of Laomedon[1] <Soph. *Ajax* 1299-1303; named, Apollod. *Bibl.* 3.12.3> and *Strym(n)o* <Apollod. *Bibl.* 3.12.3>, 42d
alternate parentage:
Laomedon[1] and *Leucippe*[8] <Apollod. *Bibl.* 3.12.3>
Laomedon[1] and *Placia* <Apollod. *Bibl.* 3.12.3>
— and Telamon <Soph. *Ajax.* 1299-1303; named, Apollod. *Bibl.* 2.6.4>, 23d
Hesione[2], daughter of Oceanus and *Tethys* <Aesch. *Prom. Bound* 560>, 54a
— and Prometheus[1] <Aesch. *Prom. Bound* 560>, 16b
Hesione[3], wife of Nauplius[1] <Cerc. in Apollod. *Bibl.* 2.1.5>, 52d
Hesione[4] — see [fifty daughters of Danaus[1]] (alternate version)
Hespera — see *Hesperia*[1]
Hesperethusa — see *Hesperia*[1]
Hesperia[1] (*Hespera*) (*Hesperethusa*) [one of the Hesperides], daughter of *Nyx* <Hes. *Theog.* 215; named, Apollod. *Bibl.* 2.5.11>, *1a*
alternate parentage:
Atlas and *Hesperis*[1] <Diod. Sic. 4.27.2>
Hesperus[1] <Paus. 5.17.2; 6.19.8>
Hesperia[2] — see *Asterope*[4]
(Hesperides), daughters of *Nyx* <Hes. *Theog.* 213> (see *Aegle*[1], *Arethusa*[1], *Erytheia*[1], *Hesperia*[1]), *1a*
alternate parentage:
Atlas and *Hesperis*[1] <Diod. Sic. 4.27.2>
Hesperus[1] <Paus. 5.17.2; 6.19.8>
Hesperis[1], daughter of Hesperus[1] <Diod. Sic. 4.27.2>, 18b
— and Atlas <Diod. Sic. 4.27.2>, 35b
Hesperis[2] [one of the hours], daughter of Zeus and *Themis*[1] <Hyg. *Fab.* 183>, 6d
Hesperus[1] [evening star], son of Iapetus and *Clymene* <Diod. Sic. 4.27.1 (inferred because he is called brother of Atlas)>, 18b, *52b*
alternate parentage:
Atlas <Diod. Sic. 3.60.1>
Hesperus[2] — see Phosphor(us)
Hestia [goddess] [fire], daughter of Cronus and *Rhea* <Hes. *Theog.* 454>, 10b
alternate parentage:
Oceanus ("from whom all we gods proceed") <Hom. *Il.* XIV.202>
Hesychia[1] [tranquility], daughter of *Dike* <Pind. *Pyth.* 8.1>, *6c*
Hesychia[2], daughter of Thespius <Apollod. *Bibl.* 2.7.8> and *Megamede* <Apollod. *Bibl.* 2.4.10>, 50c
— and Heracles[1] <Apollod. *Bibl.* 2.7.8>, (50c)
Hicetaon[1], son of Laomedon[1] <Hom. *Il.* II.238> and *Strym(n)o* <Apollod. 3.12.3>, 42d
alternate parentage:
Laomedon[1] and *Leucippe*[8] <Apollod. *Bibl.* 3.12.3>
Laomedon[1] and *Placia* <Apollod. *Bibl.* 3.12.3>
Hicetaon[2], killed by Achilles <Parth. *Love Stor.* 21.3>, *
Hiera[1], wife of Telephus <Tzetz. on Lyc. 1249>, 60a
Hiera[2], paramour of Hermes <Tzetz. on Lyc. 42>, 46c
Hiera[3] — see *Iaera*[2]
Hieromneme, daughter of Simois <Apollod. *Bibl.* 3.12.2>, 71a
— and Assaracus <Apollod. *Bibl.* 3.12.1>, 41a
Hilaeira (*Talaira*), daughter of Leucippus[1] <Apollod. *Bibl.* 3.10.

3> and *Philodice*[1], 25d
alternate parentage:
Apollo <Paus. 3.16.1 (citing poet of the *Kypria*)>
— and Castor[1] <Apollod. *Bibl.* 3.11.2>, 48c
Hilebie, daughter of Aegialus[2] <Parth. *Love Stor.* 1.1>, 68a
— and Lyrcus[1] <Parth. *Love Stor.* 1.1>, 61a
Himalia, paramour of Zeus <Diod. Sic. 5.55.5>, 5c
Himerus[1], son of Lacedaemon <Ps.-Plut. *De Fluv.* 17> and *Sparta*, 47b
— and *Asine* <Ps.-Plut. *De Fluv.* 17>, (47b)
Himerus[2] [desire], accompanied *Aphrodite* <Hes. *Theog.* 201>, *
Himmaradus, son of Eumolpus[1] <Paus. 1.5.2>, 13a
Hippal(cy)mus[1], son of Pelops[1] and *Hippodameia*[1] <Schol. on Pind. *Olym.* 1.144>, *37b*
Hippal(cy)mus[2], son of Itonus[2] <Diod. Sic. 4.27.2>, 18c
— and *Asterope*[2] <Hyg. *Fab.* 97>, (18c)
Hipparete —see [fifty daughters of Danaus[1]] (alternate version)
Hippasus[1], son of Pelops[1] and *Hippodameia*[1] <Schol. on Eur. 5>, *37b*
Hippasus[2], son of *Leucippe*[1] <Nicand. in Ant. Lib. *Met.* 10>, *20d*
Hippasus[3] [centaur], offspring of Centaurus and a Magnesian Mare <Pind. *Pyth.* 2.50; named as centaur, Ovid *Met.* 12. 350>, 69d
alternate parentage:
Ixion and *Nephele*[1] <Diod. Sic. 4.69.5>
Hippasus[4], son of Priam[1] <Hyg. *Fab.* 190>, 44d
Hippasus[5], son of Eurytus[2] <Hyg. *Fab.* 173> and *Antiope*[6], 60b
Hippasus[6], son of Ceyx[2] <Apollod. *Bibl.* 2.7.7>, 7d
Hippasus[7], father of Demoleon[4] <Quint. Smyr. 10.119-20>, *
Hippasus[8], father of Agelaus[8] <Quint. Smyr. 1.279>, *
Hippasus[9], father of Actor[7] <Apollod. *Bibl.* 1.8.16>, *
Hippasus[10], father of Euphranor <Paus. 2.13.2>, *
Hippasus[11] — see Naubolus[2] (alternate version)
Hippasus[12], killed by Agenor[14] <Quint. Smyr. 11.87>, *
Hippe[1] (*Euippe*[3]) (*Melanippe*[1]) (*Ocyrrhoe*[1]), daughter of Cheiron and *Chariclo*[2] <Ovid *Met.* 2.636 (she is called *Ocyrrhoe*)>, 69b
— and Aeolus[1] <Ps.-Erat. *Cat.* 18>, 18a
Hippe[2], wife of Theseus <*Cat. Wom., Frag. Hes.* frg. 298, Merk. & West>, 51d
Hippe[3] — see *Hippeia*
Hippe[4] — see [fifty daughters of Danaus[1]] (alternate version)
Hippe[5], a nymph of Mt. Tmolus <Orph. *Hymns* 48.4>, *
Hippeia (*Hippe*[3]), mother of *Caenis*/Caeneus[1] <Ovid *Met.* 12. 190>, 8a, and Polyphemus[2] <Apollod. *Bibl.* 1.9.16>, 59d
— and Elatus[2] <Hyg. *Fab.* 14>, (8a), (59d)
Hippeus, son of Heracles[1] and *Procris*[2] <Apollod. *Bibl.* 2.7.8>, *50c*
Hippo[1], daughter of Thespius <Apollod. *Bibl.* 2.7.8> and *Megamede* <Apollod. *Bibl.* 2.4.10>, 50c
— and Heracles[1] <Apollod. *Bibl.* 2.7.8>, (50c)
Hippo[2], daughter of Oceanus and *Tethys* <Hes. *Theog.* 351>, 54a
Hippo[3] [queen of the Amazons] <Callim. *Hymn* III (to Artemis) 2.239, 266>, *
Hippo[4], daughter of Scedasus <Paus. 9.13.3>, *
Hippoclus, son of Copreus[2] and *Peisidice*[5] <*Cat. Wom., Frag. Hes.* frg. 70, Merk. & West>, 20d
Hippocoon[1] [King of Sparta], son of Oebalus[1] and *Bateia*[1] <Apollod. *Bibl.* 3.10.5>, 47c
alternate parentage:
Oebalus[1] and *Nicostrate* <Schol. on Eur. *Or.* 457>
Hippocoon[2], son of Hyrtacus <Virg. *Aen.* 5.492> and *Ida*[2], 44c
Hippocoon[3] — see Neleus[1] (alternate version)
Hippocoon[4], counsellor of the Thracians <Hom. *Il.* X.518>, *
Hippocorystes[1], son of Aegyptus[1] and *Hephaestine* <Apollod. *Bibl.* 2.1.5>, 58c
— and *Hyperippe*[2] <Apollod. *Bibl.* 2.1.5>, (58c)
Hippocorystes[2], son of Hippocoon[1] <Apollod. *Bibl.* 3.10.5>, 47c
Hippocrate, daughter of Thespius <Apollod. *Bibl.* 2.7.8> and *Megamede* <Apollod. *Bibl.* 2.4.10>, 50c
— and Heracles[1] <Apollod. *Bibl.* 2.7.8>, (50c)
Hippocratus — see Hippotes[2]
Hippodamas[1], son of Achelous and *Perimede*[1] <Apollod. *Bibl.* 1. 7.3>, 65a, *29a*
Hippodamas[2], son of Priam[1] <Apollod. *Bibl.* 3.12.5>, 44c
Hippodamas[3] — see *Perimede*[1] (alternate version)
Hippodameia[1], daughter of Oenomaus[1] <Pind. *Olym.* 1.67 ff.> and *Asterope*[1] <Paus. 5.10.6>, 7c, *39a*
alternate parentage:
Oenomaus[1] and *Euarete* <Hyg. *Fab.* 84>
— and Oenomaus[1] <Hyg. *Fab.* 253>, 7c
— and Pelops[1] <Eur. *Iph. in Taur.* 3-4, 824>, 41b
Hippodameia[2] (*Deidameia*[4]) (*Ischomache*), daughter of Adrastus[1] <Hyg. *Fab.* 33> and *Amphithea*[1], 30d
alternate parentage:
Atrax <Steph. Byz. "Atrax">
Butes[2] <Diod. Sic. 4.69.3>
— and Eurytion[1] <Ovid *Met.* 12.224>, 69d
— and Peirithous[1] <Diod. Sic. 4.70.3>, (30d)
Hippodameia[3] (*Cleobula*[1]), wife of Amyntor[1] <Schol. A on Hom. *Il.* IX.448>, 24d
Hippodameia[4] — see *Briseis*[1]
Hippodameia[5], daughter of Anchises and *Aphrodite* <Hom. *Il.* XIII.429>, 41c
— and Alcathous[2] <Hom. *Il.* XIII.431>, (41c)
Hippodameia[6], daughter of Danaus[1] and *Atlantia* or *Phoebe*[4] <Apollod. *Bibl.* 2.1.5>, 57c
— and Istrus[1] <Apollod. *Bibl.* 2.1.5>, (57c)
Hippodameia[7], wife of Diomedes[3] <*Etym. Magn.* "Iphthimos," 480.44>, 7a
Hippodameia[8], servant of *Penelope* <Hom. *Od.* 18.182>, *
Hippodameia[9], wife of Autonous <Ant. Lib. *Met.* 7>, *
Hippodameia[10], accompanied Theseus on his return from Crete <*Corp. Inscr. Gr.* 8185b>, *
Hippodamus[1], son of Oenomaus[1] <Stat. *Theb.* 6.346-47> and *Asterope*[1], 7c
Hippodamus[2], killed by Odysseus <Hom. *Il.* XI.335>, *
Hippodice, daughter of Danaus[1] and *Herse*[2] <Apollod. *Bibl.* 2.1. 5>, 57d
— and Idas[2] <Apollod. *Bibl.* 2.1.5>, (57d)
Hippodromus, son of Heracles[1] and *Anthippe* <Apollod. *Bibl.* 2. 7.8>, *50c*
Hippolochus[1], son of Bellerophon(tes) and *Philonoe* <Hom. *Il.* VI.197>, 18d
— and *Demonassa*[4] <Schol. on Hom. *Il.* VI.206>, (18d)
Hippolochus[2], son of Antenor[1] <Tzetz. on Lyc. 874> and *Theano*, *45c*
Hippolochus[3], son of Antimachus[5] <Hom. *Il.* XI.122>, *
Hippolyte[1] (*Antiope*[3]) (*Glauce*[5]) [Queen of the Amazons], daughter of Ares and *Otrere* <Hyg. *Fab.* 30>, 7c
— and Soloon <Plut. *Thes.* 26.3 (she is called *Antiope*)>, 51c
— and Theseus <Plut. *Thes.* 26.1 (she is called *Antiope*)>, 51c
Hippolyte[2] (*Asty(a)dameia*[2]) (*Cretheis*), daughter of Cretheus[1] <Pind. *Nem.* 5.25-26> and *Tyro*, 33a
— and Acastus <Pind. *Nem.* 5.25-30>, 28c
— and Peleus <Pind. *Nem.* 5.25-33>, 24a
Hippolyte[3] (*Deianeira*[2]) (*Mnesimache*), daughter of Dexamenus <Diod. Sic. 4.33.1>, 14c
— and Azan <Diod. Sic. 4.33.1>, 62c
— and Eurytion[2] <Bacch. frg. 44, Snell & Maehler>, 69d
Hippolyte[4], wife of Iphitus[3] <Hyg. *Fab.* 97>, 23c
Hippolyte[5], daughter of Aeson <Ibyc. in *PMG* 301> and *Polymede*, 33c
Hippolytus[1] [King of Troezen], son of Theseus <Eur. *Hipp.*

10> and *Hippolyte*[1] <Eur. *Hipp.* 11; named, Apollod. *Epit.* 5.2>, 51c
— and *Phaedra* <Apollod. *Epit.* 1.16-18>, 53c
Hippolytus[2] [giant], son of *Gaea* (and the blood of Uranus) <Hes. *Theog.* 180-86; named as giant, Apollod. *Bibl.* 1.6. 2>, *4a*
Hippolytus[3], son of Aegyptus[1] and [an Arabian woman] <Apollod. *Bibl.* 2.1.5>, 58c
— and *Rhode*[2] <Apollod. *Bibl.* 2.1.5>, (58c)
Hippolytus[4], son of Rhopalus <Paus. 2.6.7>, 61d
Hippomachus, father of *Perineice* <Schol. on Ap. Rhod. *Arg.* 1.207-10>, 23c
Hippomedon[1] [one of the Seven against Thebes (per Aesch. *Sev.* 485-87)], son of Talaus <Soph. *Oed. at Col.* 1317-18> and *Lysimache*[1], 31c
alternate parentage:
Aristomachus[2] <Apollod. *Bibl.* 3.6.3>
Mnesimachus and *Metidice* <Hyg. *Fab.* 70>
— and *Euanippe* <Hyg. *Fab.* 71>, (31c)
Hippomedon[2], son of Hippasus[11] and *Ocyone* <Quint. Smyr. 11.36-37>, *
Hippomedon[3], killed by Neoptolemus <Quint. Smyr. 8.86>, *
Hippomedusa, daughter of Danaus[1] and *Atlantia* or *Phoebe*[4] <Apollod. *Bibl.* 2.1.5>, 57d
— and Alcmenor <Apollod. *Bibl.* 2.1.5>, (57d)
Hippomenes[1], son of Megareus[1] and *Merope*[8] <Hyg. *Fab.* 185>, 9b
— and *Atalanta*[2] <Ovid *Met.* 10.560-680>, 26d
Hippomenes[2], comrade of Teucer[2] <Quint. Smyr. 8.311>, *
Hipponoe[1], daughter of Nereus and *Doris*[1] <Hes. *Theog.* 251>, *64b*
Hipponoe[2] — see *Iphinoe*[1]
Hipponome, daughter of Menoeceus[1] <Apollod. *Bibl.* 2.4.5>, 55d
Hipponous[1] [King of Olenus], son of Anaxagoras <Schol. on Eur. *Phoen. Maid.* 180>, 58c
— and *Astynome*[3] <Hyg. *Fab.* 70>, 30d
Hipponous[2] — see Bellerophon(tes)
Hipponous[3], son of Priam[1] and *Hecabe*[1] <Apollod. *Bibl.* 3.11.5>, 43d
Hipponous[4], son of Triballus[1] <Ant. Lib. *Met.* 21.1>, 71b
— and *Thrassa* <Ant. Lib. *Met.* 21.1>, (71b)
Hipponous[5], son of Adrastus[1] <Hyg. *Fab.* 242> and *Amphithea*[1], 30d
Hipponous[6], killed by Hector[1] <Hom. *Il.* XI.303>, *
Hippostratus, son of Amarynceus[1] <*Cat. Wom., Frag. Hes.* frg. 12, Merk. & West>, 17d
— and *Periboea*[1] <*Cat. Wom., Frag. Hes.* frg. 12, Merk. & West>, (17d)
Hippotas[1] — see Hippotes[3]
Hippotas[2] — see Hippotes[5]
Hippotas[3] (Hippotes[5]), father of Amastrus <Virg. *Aen.* 11. 676>, *
Hippotes[1], son of Creon[1] <Diod. Sic. 4.55.6>, 33d
Hippotes[2] (Hippocratus), father of *Aegesta* <Serv. on Virg. *Aen.* 1.550>, 67a
Hippotes[3] (Hippotas[1]), son of Phylas[2] <*Gr. Ehoiai* frg. 252, Merk. & West> and *Leipephilene* <Paus. 9.40.6>, *55d*
Hippotes[4], son of Mimas[3] <Diod. Sic. 4.67.3>, 18a
— and *Melanippe*[5] <Diod. Sic. 4.67.3>, 18a
Hippotes[5] — see Hippotas[2]
Hippothoe[1], daughter of Mestor[1] and *Lysidice*[1] <Apollod. *Bibl.* 2.4.5>, 58d, *38a*
— and Poseidon <Apollod. *Bibl.* 2.4.5>, 8c
Hippothoe[2], daughter of Pelias[1] and *Anaxibia*[2] <Apollod. *Bibl.* 1. 9.10>, 28d
alternate parentage:
Pelias[1] and *Phylomache* <Apollod. *Bibl.* 1.9.10>
Hippothoe[3], daughter of Nereus and *Doris*[1] <Hes. *Theog.* 251>, *64b*
Hippothoe[4] [Amazon] <Quint. Smyr. *Posthom.* 1.42>, *
Hippothoe[5] —see [fifty daughters of Danaus[1]] (alternate version)
Hippothoon (Hippothous[7]) [King of Eleusis], son of Poseidon and *Alope* <Hellan. in *F. Gr. H.* 4 F 43>, 8b, *9d*
Hippothous[1], son of Pelasgus[3] and *Menippe*[3] <Apollod. *Epit.* 3.35>, 61d
Hippothous[2], son of Cercyon[2] <Paus. 8.5.4>, 62c
Hippothous[3], son of Priam[1] <Hom. *Il.* XXIV.251>, 44c
Hippothous[4], son of Aegyptus[1] and [an Arabian woman] <Apollod. *Bibl.* 2.1.5>, 58c
— and *Gorge*[2] <Apollod. *Bibl.* 2.1.5>, (58c)
Hippothous[5], son of Aleus and *Neaera*[2] <Hyg. *Fab.* 244>, 64c
Hippothous[6], son of Hippocoon[1] <Apollod. *Bibl.* 3.10.5>, 47c
Hippothous[7] — see Hippothoon
Hippothous[8], son of Lethus <Hom. *Il.* XVII.288>, *
Hippotion[1] [centaur], offspring of Centaurus and a Magnesian Mare <Pind. *Pyth.* 2.50; named as centaur, Diod. Sic. 4.12.7>, 69c
alternate parentage:
Ixion and *Nephele*[1] <Diod. Sic. 4.69.5>
Hippotion[2], killed by Meriones <Hom. *Il.* XIV.514>, *
Hippozygus, son of Heracles[1] and *Hippocrate* <Apollod. *Bibl.* 2. 7.8>, 50c
Hipsea — see *Eidyia*
Hiscilla, daughter of Myrmidon <Hyg. *Poet. Astr.* 2.14> and *Peisidice*[1], 5d
— and Triop(a)s[1] <Hyg. *Poet. Astr.* 2.14>, 34a
Historis (*Galanthis*), daughter of Teiresias <Paus. 9.11.2>, 32d
Hixibius — see Hyperbius
Hodeodochus — see Odeodochus
Hodites[1] — see Odeites[1]
Hodites[2] — see Oneites
Hodites[3], killed by Clymenus[8] <Ovid *Met.* 5.96-97>, *
Hodoedochus — see Odeodochus
Holaeas, son of Cypselus[1] <Paus. 8.5.7> and *Herodice*, 62c
Homadus [centaur], offspring of Centaurus and a Magnesian Mare <Pind. *Pyth.* 2.50; named as centaur, Diod. Sic. 4.12.7>, 69c
alternate parentage:
Ixion and *Nephele*[1] <Diod. Sic. 4.69.5>
— and *Alcyone*[4] <Diod. Sic. 4.12.7>, 58d
Homoleus, son of Amphion[1] <Schol. on Eur. *Phoen. Maid.* 1119> and *Niobe*[1], 66d
Homolippus, son of Heracles[1] and *Xanthis* <Apollod. *Bibl.* 2.7. 8>, *51c*
Hopladamus [giant], son of *Gaea* (and the blood of Uranus) <Hes. *Theog.* 180-86; named as giant, Paus. 8.32.6>, *4a*
Hoples, son of Ion[1] <Eur. *Ion* 1574> and *Helice*[1], 52a
Hopleus[1], son of Poseidon and *Canace* <Apollod. *Bibl.* 1.7.4>, 8a, *34a*
Hopleus[2], son of Lycaon[1] <Apollod. *Bibl.* 3.8.1>, 64a
Hopleus[3], fought against the centaurs <Hes. *Shield* 180>, *
Hopleus[4], killed by Aepytus[5] <Stat. *Theb.* 10.400>, *
Hora — see Colaxais (alternate version)
(Horae) [seasons], daughters of Zeus and *Themis*[1] <Hes. *Theog.* 902> (see *Dike*, *Eirene*[1], *Eunomia*[1]; at Athens, *Carpo* and *Thallo* <Paus. 9.35.1>, 6c
Horcus [oath] [abstraction], offspring of *Eris* <Hes. *Theog.* 231>, *1a*
Hormenus [one of the Telchines], son of Pontus and *Gaea* <Tzetz. *Chil.* 12.836>, 2a
alternate parentage:
Tartarus and *Nemesis* <Bacch. frg. 52, Snell & Maehler>
Thalatta <Diod. Sic. 5.55.1>

[Horses of Achilles], offspring of Zephyrus and *Podarge* <Hom. *Il.* XVI.145-47> (see Balius[1] and Xanthus[1]), 12a
Horus, son of Lycaon[1] <Apollod. *Bibl.* 3.8.1>, 64a
[hours], daughters of Zeus and *Themis*[1] <Hyg. *Fab* 183> (see *Acte*, *Anatole*, *Auge*[2], *Dysis*, *Elete*, *Euporie*, *Gymnastica*, *Hesperis*[2], *Mesembria*, *Musica*, *Nymphe*[1], *Orthosie*, *Pherusa*[2], *Sponde*), 6d
Hyacinthus[1], son of Amyclas[1] and *Diomede*[2] <Apollod. *Bibl.* 3. 10.3>, 47a
alternate parentage:
Pierus[1] and *Cleio* <Apollod. *Bibl.* 1.3.3>
— and Apollo <Apollod. *Bibl.* 1.3.3>, 11c
— and Thamyris[1] <Apollod. *Bibl.* 1.3.3>, 13b
Hyacinthus[2], father of *Aegleis, Antheis, Lytaea*, and *Orthaea* (Hyacinthides) <Apollod. *Bibl.* 3.15.8>, *
(Hyades) daughters of Atlas and *Pleione* <Hyg. *Fab.* 192 (named for their brother Hyas)> (see *Ambrosia*, *Coronis*[3], *Eudora*[1], *Phaesyle*, *Polyxo*[4]), 44b
alternate parentage:
Hyas and *Boeotia* <Hyg. *Poet. Astr.* 2.21>
others:
named in <Hyg. *Fab.* 182>: *Arsinoe*[5], *Bromie*, *Cisseis*, *Erato*[7], *Eriphia*, *Nysa*, *Polyhymno*
named in <*Cat. Wom., Frag. Hes.* frg. 291, Merk. & West>: *Cleeia*, *Phaeo*
named in <Hyg. *Poet. Astr.* 2.21>: *Pedile*, *Phyto*[1], *Thyone*[2]
Hyagnis — see Marsyas (alternate version)
Hyale[1] —see [fifty daughters of Danaus[1]] (alternate version)
Hyale[2], a nymph <Ovid *Met.* 3.171>, *
Hyamus, son of Lycorus <Paus. 10.6.3>, 17a
— and *Melantho*[1] <Schol. on Eur. 1097>, (17a)
Hyanthidas, son of Propadas <Paus. 2.4.3>, 18d
Hyapate, daughter of Onnes and *Semiramis* <Diod. Sic. 2.5.1>, 61c
Hyas, son of Atlas <Ovid *Fast.* 5, 181> and *Pleione* <Hyg. *Fab.* 192>, 44b
— and *Boeotia* <Hyg. *Poet. Astr.* 2.21>, (44b)
Hybris (*Thymbris*[1]), paramour of Zeus <Apollod. *Bibl.* 1.4.1>, 5d
Hydaspe, daughter of Onnes and *Semiramis* <Diod. Sic. 2.5.1>, 61c
Hydaspes[1] [river], son of Thaumas[1] and *Electra*[1] <Non. *Dion.* 26.359-62>, 3b
— and *Astris* <Non. *Dion.* 26.352-53>, 14a, 71b
Hydaspes[2], killed by Sacrator <Vir. *Aen.* 10.748>, *
Hydis, father of *Asteria*[4] <Steph. Byz. "Hydissus">, 18d
Hydissus, son of Bellerophon(tes) and *Asteria*[4] <Steph. Byz. "Hydissus">, 18b
Hydne, daughter of Scyllis <Paus. 10.19.1>, 49d
— and Glaucus[3] <Athen. 7.296e (citing Aeschrion of Samos)>, 62a
Hydra — see [Lernaean Hydra]
Hygieia [health], daughter of Asclepius and *Epeione* <*Paean Erythr.*, T. 592>, 19d
Hylaeus[1] [centaur], offspring of Centaurus and a Magnesian Mare <Pind. *Pyth* 2.50; named as centaur, Apollod. *Bibl.* 3.9.2 (killed by *Atalanta*[1])>, 69c
alternate parentage:
Ixion and *Nephele*[1] <Diod. Sic. 4.69.5>
Hylaeus[2] [centaur], offspring of Centaurus and a Magnesian Mare <Pind. *Pyth* 2.50; named as centaur, Virg. *Aen.* 8.294 (killed by Heracles[1])>, 69c
alternate parentage:
Ixion and *Nephele*[1] <Diod. Sic. 4.69.5>
Hylaeus[3] [centaur], offspring of Centaurus and a Magnesian Mare <Pind. *Pyth* 2.50; named as centaur, Non. *Dion.* 17.200 (killed by Orontes)>, 69c
alternate parentage:
Ixion and *Nephele*[1] <Diod. Sic. 4.69.5>
Hylaeus[4] [one of the dogs of Actaeon] <Ovid *Met.* 3.217>, *
Hylas [Argonaut], son of Theiodamas[1] <Apollod. *Bibl.* 1.9.19> and *Menodice* <Hyg. *Fab.* 14>, 64d
alternate parentage:
Ceyx[2] <Ant. Lib. *Met.* 26.1>
— and Heracles[1] <Apollod. *Bibl.* 1.9.19>, 61d
— and a nymph of the spring of Pegai <Ap. Rhod. *Arg.* 1. 1220-35>, (64d)
Hyles [centaur], offspring of Centaurus and a Magnesian Mare <Pind. *Pyth* 2.50; named as centaur, Ovid *Met.* 12.379>, 69c
alternate parentage:
Ixion and *Nephele*[1] <Diod. Sic. 4.69.5>
Hyllus[1], son of Heracles[1] and *Deianeira*[1] <*Cat. Wom., Frag. Hes.* frg. 25.19, Merk. & West>, 60a
alternate parentage:
Heracles[1] and *Melite*[2] <Ap. Rhod. *Arg.* 4.539>
Heracles[1] and *Omphale* <Paus. 1.35.8>
— and *Iole* <Apollod. *Bibl.* 2.8.2>, (60a)
Hyllus[2], son of *Gaea* <Paus. 1.35.8>, 2b
Hyllus[3], son of Thersander[4] and *Arethusa*[6] <Quint. Smyr. 10.80-82>, *
Hyllus[4], killed by Turnus <Virg. *Aen.* 12.535>, *
Hyllus[5], killed by Ajax[1] <Quint. Smyr. 1.529>, *
Hylonome [centaur], offspring of Centaurus and a Magnesian Mare <Pind. *Pyth.* 2.50; named as centaur, Ovid *Met.* 12, 404>, 69d
alternate parentage:
Ixion and *Nephele*[1] <Diod. Sic. 4.69.5>
— and Cyllarus[1] <Ovid *Met.* 12.393-408>, (69d)
Hymen(aeus)[1] [marriage], son of Dionysus and *Aphrodite* <Serv. on Virg. *Aen.* 4.127>, 56c
alternate parentage:
Magnes[3] <Ant. Lib. *Met.* 23.1>
Terpsichore <Alciph. 1.13>
Urania <Non. *Dion.* 24.87>
— and Apollo <Ant. Lib. *Met.* 23.2>, 11c
— and Argynnus <Athen. 13.603d>, 20d
Hymen(aeus)[2], son of Phlegyas[1] <Non. *Dion.* 29.31>, 19c
Hymnus, paramour of *Nicaea* <Non. *Dion.* 16.204-369>, 70a
Hyperantus — see [fifty sons of Aegyptus[1]] (alternate version)
Hyperasius, son of Pellen <Ap. Rhod. *Arg.* 1.176>, 61d
— and *Hypso* <Val. Flac. 1.366 (inferred because she is mother of his children)>, (61d)
Hyperbius[1] (Hixibius), son of Aegyptus[1] and *Hephaestine* <Apollod. *Bibl.* 2.1.5>, 58c
— and *Celaeno*[4] <Apollod. *Bibl.* 2.1.5>, (58c)
Hyperbius[2], son of Oenops <Aesch. *Sev.* 503-04>, *
Hyperenor[1] [one of the (Spartoi) [sown men]], sprang from teeth of [Cadmean Dragon] <Apollod. *Bibl.* 3.4.2>, 7d
Hyperenor[2] — see Hyperes[1]
Hyperenor[3], son of Panthous <Schol. on Hom. *Il.* XVII.23a> and *Phrontis*[3], *
Hyperenor[4], killed by Haemon[1] <Stat. *Theb.* 8.493>, *
Hyperenor[5], suitor of *Penelope* (from Same) <Apollod. *Epit.* 7.28>, *
Hyperes[1] (Hyperenor[2]) [King of Troezon], son of Poseidon and *Alcyone*[2] <Paus. 2.30.8>, 8a, *35a*
Hyperes[2], son of Melas[5] and *Eurycleia*[1] <Pher. in *F.H.G.* 1.86 frg. 55, Müller>, 26c
Hyperia — see *Hyperippe*[2]
Hyperion[1] [Titan], son of Uranus and *Gaea* <Hes. *Theog.* 134>, 13b
— and *Theia*[1] <Hes. *Theog.* 374>, (13b)
Hyperion[2], son of Priam[1] <Apollod. *Bibl.* 3.12.5>, 44d

Hyperippe[1], daughter of Arcas[1] and *Chrysopeleia* <Paus. 5.1.4>, 62d
— and Endymion <Paus. 5.1.4>, 15b
Hyperippe[2] (*Hyperia*), daughter of Danaus[1] and *Crino* <Apollod. *Bibl.* 2.1.5>, 58c
— and Hippocorystes <Apollod. *Bibl.* 2.1.5>, (58c)
Hyperippe[3], daughter of Leucon[1] <*Cat. Wom., Frag. Hes.* frg. 70.9, Merk. & West>, 26d
Hyperippe[4], daughter of Munichus and *Lelante* <Ant. Lib. *Met.* 14>, *
Hyperlaus, son of Mylas[3] <Apollod. *Bibl.* 1.8.5>, 16d
Hyperm(n)estra[1], daughter of Danaus[1] and *Elephantis* <Apollod. *Bibl.* 2.1.5>, 57c, 57d
— and Lynceus[2] <Apollod. *Bibl.* 2.1.5>, (57c), (57d)
Hyperm(n)estra[2], daughter of Thestius and *Eurythemis(te)* <Apollod. *Bibl.* 1.7.10>, 16c
— and Oicle(u)s <*Cat. Wom., Frag. Hes.* frg. 25.34-35, Merk. & West>, 32d
Hyperm(n)estra[3], daughter of Aethon[2] <Ant. Lib. *Met.* 17.5>, *
Hyperochus[1], son of Priam[1] <Apollod. *Bibl.* 3.12.5>, 44d
Hyperochus[2], son of Magnes[2] and *Meliboea*[3] <Eust. on Hom. *Il.* 338>, 21b
Hyperphas, father of *Euryanassa*[2] <Schol. on Hom. *Il.* XI.326>, 20d, and *Euryganeia* <Apollod. *Bibl.* 3.5.8>, 55c
Hypnos [sleep] [abstraction], offspring of *Nyx* <Hes. *Theog.* 212>, *1a*
alternate parentage:
Erebus and *Nyx* <Hyg. *Fab.* pref.>
— and *Aglaia*[1] <Hom. *Il.* XIV.269-75 (called *Pasithea*)>, 5d
Hypsea — see *Eidyia*
Hypseus[1] [King of Lapiths], son of Peneius and *Creusa*[4] <Pind. *Pyth.* 9.13 ff.>, 69a
— and *Chlidanope* <Schol. on Pind. *Pyth.* 9.31>, (69a)
Hypseus[2], killed by Perseus[1] <Ovid *Met.* 5.98>, *
Hypseus[3], killed by Capaneus <Stat. *Theb.* 9.540-49>, *
Hypsipyle [Queen of Lemnos], daughter of Thoas[1] <Apollod. *Bibl.* 1.9.16> and *Myrine*[1], 56d, *32d*
— and Jason <Apollod. *Bibl.* 1.9.17>, 33d
Hypso, wife of Hyperasius <Val. Flac. 1.366 (inferred because she is mother of his children)>, 61d
Hypsus — see [fifty sons of Lycaon[1]] (alternate version)
Hyria — see *Thyria*
Hyrieus [King of Hyria, Boeotia], son of Poseidon and *Alcyone*[2] <Apollod. *Bibl.* 3.10.1>, 8a, *35b*
— and *Clonia*[1] <Apollod. *Bibl.* 3.10.1>, (35b)
Hyrmine, daughter of Epeius[1] and *Anaxiroe* <Paus. 5.1.6>, 16c
— and Phorbas[2] <Paus. 5.1.11>, 68b
Hyrnetho, daughter of Temenus[1] <Apollod. *Bibl.* 2.8.5>, 60c
— and Deiphontes[2] <Paus. 2.19.1>, 60c
Hyrtacus [King of Arisbe in the Troad], husband of *Arisbe*[1] <Apollod. *Bibl.* 3.12.5>, 44c
— and *Ida*[2] <Virg. *Aen.* 9.177-79>, (44c)
Hysminai [battles] [abstraction], offspring of *Eris* <Hes. *Theog.* 228>, *1a*

Iacchus[1] — see Dionysus
Iacchus[2], son of Zeus <Eur. *Bacc.* 725>, 6c
Iacchus[3] — see Zagreus
Iache, daughter of Oceanus and *Tethys* <*Hom. Hymn* 2 (to *Demeter)* 417>, 54b
Iaera[1], daughter of Nereus <Hom. *Il.* XVIII.41> and *Doris*[1], *64b*
Iaera[2] (*Hiera*[3]), mother of Bitias[1] <Virg. *Aen.* 9.672-73>, 41d
— and Alcanor[1] <Virg. *Aen.* 9.672-73>, (41d)
Ialebion (Alebion), son of Poseidon <Apollod. *Bibl.* 2.5.10>, 9c
Ialemus — see Linus[3]
Ialmenus[1] [King of Orchomenus], son of Ares and *Astyoche*[1] <Hom. *Il.* II.512-13>, 7b
alternate parentage:
Lycus[7] and *Pernis* <Hyg. *Fab.* 97>
Ialmenus[2], killed by Agylleus <Stat. *Theb.* 10.305-08>, *
Ialysus, son of Cercaphus[1] and *Cydippe*[1] <Diod. Sic. 5.57.8>, 14a
— and *Dotis* <Athen. 7.296c>, 62c
Iambe, daughter of Pan and *Echo* <*Etym. Magn.* "Iambe" 465. 24>, 46c
Iamus, son of Apollo and *Euadne*[3] <Pind. *Olym.* 6.42>, 11c, *9a*
Ianassa, daughter of Nereus <Hom. *Il.* XVIII, 46> and *Doris*[1], *64b*
Ianeira[1] — see *Euadne*[1]
Ianeira[2], daughter of Oceanus and *Tethys* <Hes. *Theog.* 356>, 54b
Ianeira[3], daughter of Nereus <Hom. *Il.* XVIII.46> and *Doris*[1] <Apollod. *Bibl.* 1.2.7>, *64b*
Ianiscus[1] [King of Sicyon], son of Asclepius and *Epeione* <Schol. on Aristoph. *Plutus* 701>, 19d
Ianiscus[2], descendant of Clytius[1] <Paus. 2.6.6>, *
Ianthe[1], daughter of Oceanus and *Tethys* <Hes. *Theog.* 349>, 54b
Ianthe[2], daughter of Telestes <Ovid *Met.* 9.670-797>, *
— and Iphis[6] <Ovid *Met.* 9.670-79>, *
Iapetus [Titan], son of Uranus and *Gaea* <Hes. *Theog.* 134>, 16b
— and *Asia*[1] <Apollod. *Bibl.* 1.2.4>, 51a
— and *Clymene*[1] <Hes. *Theog.* 510>, 52a
— and *Thornax(e)* <Paus. 8.27.17>, (16b)
Iapyx[1], son of Daedalus and [a Cretan woman] <Strab. 6.3.2>, 49b
Iapyx[2] — see [fifty sons of Lycaon[1]] (alternate version)
Iapyx[3], killed by Theseus <Stat. *Theb.* 12.746>, *
Iarbas, son of Ammon[1] and a Garamantian nymph <Virg. *Aen.* 4.198-201>, 41d
— and *Dido* <Virg. *Aen.* 4.198-201>, (41d)
Iardanus [King of Lydia], father of *Omphale* <Apollod. *Bibl.* 2. 6.3>, 60c
Iasion (Iasus[5]), son of Zeus and *Electra*[2] <Apollod. *Bibl.* 3.12. 1>, 5c, *42b*
alternate parentage:
Ilithius <Hyg. *Fab.* 270>
Thuscus <Hyg. *Poet. Astr.* 2.4>
— and *Cybele*[2] <Diod. Sic. 5.49.2>, 2b
— and *Demeter* <Hom. *Od.* 5.124-25>, 10a
Iasius[1] [one of the Dactyls], son of *Anchiale*[1] <Ap. Rhod. *Arg.* 1128; named, Paus. 5.7.6>*, 11b*
alternate parentage:
born on Mt. Ida of uncertain parentage <Diod. Sic. 5.64. 4>
Iasius[2], son of Eleuther[1] <Paus. 9.20.1>, 35a
Iasius[3], won a horse-race at Olympia <Paus. 8.48.1>, *
Iaso [cure], daughter of Asclepius and *Epeione* <*Paean Erythr.*, T. 592>, 19d
alternate parentage:
Asclepius and *Lampetia* <Hermip. frg. 1, West>
Iason — see Jason
Iasus[1] [King of Argos], son of Triop(a)s[2] and *Sois* <Schol. on Eur. *Or.* 932>, 61d
Iasus[2] [King of Minyae], paramour of *Persephone*[2] <Schol. on Hom. *Od.* 11.281 ff.>, 20c
Iasus[3], son of Argus[3] and *Ismene*[2] <Apollod. *Bibl.* 2.1.3>, 61d, *66b*
Iasus[4] [King of Arcadia], son of Lycurgus[4] and *Cleophyle* <Apollod. *Bibl.* 3.9.2>, 64d
alternate parentage:
Lycurgus[4] and *Eurynome*[7] <Apollod. *Bibl.* 3.9.2>
— and *Clymene*[4] <Apollod. *Bibl.* 3.9.2>, 20c
Iasus[5] — see Iasion

Iasus[6], son of Sphelus <Hom. *Il.* XV.337-39>, *
Iasus[7], father of Palinurus <Virg. *Aen.* 5.843>, *
Iasus[8], father of Dmetor <Hom. *Od.* 17.443>, *
Icadius, son of Apollo and *Lycia* <Serv. on Virg. *Aen.* 3.332>, 11d
Icarius[1], father of *Erigone*[1] <Apollod. *Bibl.* 3.14.7>, 56d
— and *Phanothea* <Clem. Alex. *Misc.* 80.3>, (56d)
Icarius[2], son of Oebalus[1] and *Bateia*[1] <Apollod. *Bibl.* 3.10.5>, 47d
alternate parentage:
Perieres[1] and *Gorgophone*[1] <Apollod. *Bibl.* 1.9.5>
— and *Periboea*[5] <Schol. on Hom. *Od.* 15.15>, (47d)
— and *Polycaste*[2] <Strab. 10.2.24>, (47d)
Icarus[1], son of Daedalus and *Naucrate* <Apollod. *Epit.* 1.12>, 49b
Icarus[2] [King of Caria], husband of *Theonoe*[1] <Hyg. *Fab.* 190>, 69b
Icelus (Phobetor) [terror] [abstraction], offspring of Hypnos <Ovid *Met.* 11.575-670>, 1a
Ida[1], daughter of Corybas and *Thebe*[3] <Diod. Sic. 4.60.3>, 42b
— and Lycastus[1] <Diod. Sic. 4.60.3>, 54c
Ida[2] [nymph], paramour of Hyrtacus <Virg. *Aen.* 9.177-79>, 44c
Ida[3] (*Melissa*[3]), daughter of Melisseus[2] <Apollod. *Bibl.* 1.1.7>, *
Ida[4], mother of Idaean Dactyls <*Etym. Magn.* "Dactyls">, *
Ida[5], a Theban mother <Stat. *Theb.* 3.134>, *
Idaea[1], wife of Scamander[1] <Apollod. *Bibl.* 3.12.1>, 70b
Idaea[2] (*Dia*[5]) (*Eidothea*[4]) (*Eurytia*), daughter of Dardanus[1] <Apollod. *Bibl.* 3.15.3> and *Bateia*[2], 42a
— and Phineus[1] <Apollod. *Bibl.* 3.15.3>, 13a, 53d
Idaeus[1], son of Dardanus[1] and *Chryse*[2] <Dion. Hal. *Rom. Ant.* 1. 61.2>, 42b
Idaeus[2], son of Paris and *Helen*[1] <Dict. Cret. 5.5>, 43c
Idaeus[3], son of Socus and *Combe*[1] <Non. *Dion.* 13.144>, *66c*
alternate parentage:
Apollo and *Rhetia* <Pher. in *F. Gr. H.* 3 F 48 (unnamed)>
Idaeus[4], son of Priam[1] <Ptol. 5>, 44d
Idaeus[5], son of Dares <Hom. *Il.* V.9-11>, *
Idaeus[6], chariot driver for Priam[1] <Hom. *Il.* XXIV.328>, *
Idas[1] [Argonaut], son of Aphareus[1] <Pind. *Nem.* 10.65> and *Arene* <Apollod. *Bibl.* 3.10.3>, 25d
alternate parentage:
Poseidon <Simon. in *P.M.G.* 563>
— and *Marpessa*[1] <Hom. *Il.* IX.557>, 15c
Idas[2], son of Aegyptus[1] and *Hephaestine* <Apollod. *Bibl.* 2.1.5>, 57d
— and *Hippodice* <Apollod. *Bibl.* 2.1.5>, (57d)
Idas[3] (Acesidas) [one of the Dactyls], son of *Anchiale*[1] <Ap. Rhod. *Arg.* 1.1128; named, Paus. 5.7.6>, *11b*
alternate parentage:
born on Mt. Ida of uncertain parentage <Diod. Sic. 5.64.4>
Idas[4], son of Clymenus[4] and *Epicaste*[4] <Parth. *Love Stor.* 13.1>, 26d
Idas[5], a youth from Pisa <Stat. *Theb.* 6.553>, *
Idas[6], comrade of Diomedes[1] <Ovid *Met.* 14.494>, *
Idas[7], killed by Phineus <Ovid *Met.* 5.90>, *
Idas[8], killed by Turnus <Virg. *Aen.* 9.575>, *
Idas[9], killed by Tydeus[1] <Stat. *Theb.* 8.466>, *
Idmon[1] [Argonaut], son of Apollo <Pher. in *F.H.G.*, 1.88 frg. 70, Müller> and *Cyrene* <Hyg. *Fab.* 14>, 11a, *69b*
alternate parentage:
Apollo and *Antianeira* <Orpheus *Arg.* 189>
Apollo and *Asteria*[1] <Pher. in *F. Gr. H.* 3 F 108>
Abas[4] <Ap. Rhod. *Arg.* 2.816>
— and *Laothoe*[2] <Pher. in *F.H.G.* 1.88 frg. 70, Müller>, (69b)
Idmon[2], son of Aegyptus[1] and *Gorgo*[1] <Apollod. *Bibl.* 2.1.5>, 57d
— and *Pylarge* <Apollod. *Bibl.* 2.1.5>, (57d)
Idmon[3], father of *Arachne* <Ovid *Met.* 6.8-10>, *
Idmon[4], a herald for Turnus <Virg. *Aen.* 12.75>, *
Idomene, daughter of Pheres[1] <Apollod. *Bibl.* 1.9.11> and *Periclymene*, 29d
alternate parentage:
Abas[?] <Apollod. *Bibl.* 2.2.2>
— and Amythaon[1] <Apollod. *Bibl.* 1.9.11>, 30b
Idomeneus[1], son of Priam[1] <Apollod. *Bibl.* 3.12.5>, 44d
Idomeneus[2] [King of Crete], son of Deucalion[2] <Hom. *Il.* XII. 117>, 54c
— and *Meda*[1] <Lyc. 1214-25>, (54c)
Idothea[1] — see *Cyanea*
Idothea[2] — see *Eidothea*[2]
Idyia — see *Eidyia*
Ileithyia — see *Eileithyia*
Ileus, son of Apollo and *Urea*[2] <Hyg. *Fab.* 161>, 11d
— and Apollo <*Cat. Wom., Frag. Hes.* frg. 235, Merk. & West>, 11c
Ilia — see Romulus, Remus[1] (alternate versions)
Ilione, daughter of Priam[1] <Virg. *Aen.* 1.653> and *Hecabe*[1], 43d
— and Polym(n)estor[1] <Hyg. *Fab.* 109>, (43d)
Ilioneus[1], son of Phorbas[1] <Hom. *Il.* XIV.489-90>, 24d
Ilioneus[2], son of Amphion[1] and *Niobe*[1] <Ovid *Met.* 6.255-71>, 66c
Ilioneus[3], comrade of Aeneas <Virg. *Aen.* 1.120>, *
Ilioneus[4], killed by Diomedes[1] <Quint. Smyr. 13.181>, *
Ilithius — see Iasion (alternate version)
Illyrius, son of Cadmus <Apollod. *Bibl.* 3.5.4> and *Harmonia*[1], 56c
Ilus[1] (Za(n)cynthus), son of Dardanus[1] <Hom. *Il.* XI.372> and *Bateia*[2] <Apollod. *Bibl.* 3.12.2>, 42a
Ilus[2] [King of Troy], son of Tros[1] <Hom. *Il.* XX.233> and *Callirhoe*[1] <Apollod. *Bibl.* 3.12.2>, 42a
— and *Eurydice*[2] <Apollod. *Bibl.* 3.11.3>, (42a)
Ilus[3] [King of Ephyre], son of Mermerus[3] <Hom. *Od.* 1.259>, 33c
Ilus[4] — see Ascanius[1]
Ilus[5], ally of Turnus <Virg. *Aen.* 10.400>, *
Imbrasus[1], husband of *Chesias*; father of *Ocyrrhoe*[2] <Ap. Rhod. in Athen. 7.283d>, 11d
Imbrasus[2], father of Peirous <Hom. *Il.* IV.520>, *
Imbrasus[3], father of Asius <Virg. *Aen.* 10.123>, *
Imbreus [centaur], offspring of Centaurus and a Magnesian Mare <Pind. *Pyth.* 2.50; named as centaur, Ovid *Met.* 12. 312>, 69c
alternate parentage:
Ixion and *Nephele*[1] <Diod. Sic. 4.69.5>
Imbrius, son of Mentor[2] <Hom. *Il.* XIII.170>, 44c
— and *Medisicaste*[2] <Hom. *Il.* XIII.170-73>, 44c
Imbrus, son of Aegyptus[1] and *Caliadne* <Apollod. *Bibl.* 2.1.5>, 57d
— and *Euippe*[5] <Apollod. *Bibl.* 2.1.5>, (57d)
Imenarete — see Elephenor (alternate version)
Imeusimus, son of Icarius[2] and *Periboea*[5] <Apollod. *Bibl.* 3.10. 6>, 47d
alternate parentage:
Icarius[2] and *Polycaste*[2] <Strab. 10.2.24>
Immaradus — see Ismarus[2]
Inachus [King of Argos], son of Oceanus and *Tethys* <Apollod. *Bibl.* 2.1.1>, 55a
— and *Argeia*[2] <Hyg. *Fab.* 143>, 50b
— and *Melia*[1] <Apollod. *Bibl.* 2.1.1>, 61a
Indus[1] [river], son of Oceanus and *Tethys* <Hes. *Theog.* 367-68; named as river, Hyg. *Fab.* pref.>, 54b
Indus[2] [King in Scythia] <Hyg. *Fab.* 274>, *
Indus[3], autochthonous ancestor of Indians <Non. *Dion.*18. 271>, *

Ino (*Leucothoe*[2]), daughter of Cadmus <Hom. *Od.* 5.332> and *Harmonia*[1] <Hes. *Theog.* 976>, 55d
— and Athamas[1] <Apollod. *Bibl.* 1.9.1>, 26a
Io, daughter of Inachus <Aesch. *Prom. Bound* 590> and *Melia*[1], 55b
alternate parentage:
Inachus and *Argeia*[2] <Hyg. *Fab.* 145>
Iasus[3] <Apollod. *Bibl.* 2.1.3>
Peiren <*Cat. Wom., Frag. Hes.* frg. 124, Merk. & West>
— and Telegonus[3] <Apollod. *Bibl.* 2.1.3>, (55b)
— and Zeus <Steph. Byz. "Byzantium">, 5d
Iobates [King of Lycia], father of *Philonoe* <Apollod. *Bibl.* 2.3.2>, 18d
Iobes, son of Heracles[1] and *Certhe* <Apollod. *Bibl.* 2.7.8>, *50c*
Iocastus, son of Aeolus[2] and *Cyane*[1] <Hom. *Od.* 10.2-6; named, Diod. Sic. 5.8.1>, 18c
Iodama, daughter of Itonus[1] <Tzetz. on Lyc. 355> and *Melanippe*[6], 16a
— and Zeus <Tzetz. on Lyc. 1206>, 5d
Iola(u)s, son of Iphicles and *Automedusa* <Apollod. *Bibl.* 2.4.11>, 59c, *40a*
alternate parentage:
Iphicles and *Diomedia* (father is called Iphiclus) <Hyg. *Fab.* 103>
— and *Megara* <Apollod. *Bibl.* 2.6.1>, 55d
Iole, daughter of Eurytus[2] <Soph. *Trach. Wom.* 420> and *Antiope*[6], 60a
— and Heracles[1] <Soph. *Trach. Wom.* 427>, 60c
— and Hyllus[1] <Soph. *Trach. Wom.* 1224>, (60a)
Ion[1], son of Xuthus[1] and *Creusa*[3] <*Cat. Wom., Hesiodi* frg. 10(a).20-24, Merk. & West (O.C.T.)>, 17b, *51b*
alternate parentage:
Apollo and *Creusa*[3] <Eur. *Ion* 70-76>
— and *Helice*[1] <Paus. 7.1.2>, 9d
Ion[2], son of Gargettus <Paus. 6.22.7>, *
Ion[3], killed by Chromis[10] <Stat. *Theb.* 9.252>, *
Ione[1], daughter of Nereus and *Doris*[1] <Apollod. *Bibl.* 1.2.7>, *64b*
Ione[2], a nurse of Dionysus <Non. *Dion.*14.221>, *
Iope[1], daughter of Iphicles <Plut. *Thes.* 29.1> and *Automedusa*, 59d, *40a*
— and Theseus <Plut. *Thes.* 29.1>, 51b
Iope[2] — see *Cassiopeia*[1]
Iophassa — see *Chalciope*[1]
Ioxus, son of Melanippus[5] <Plut. *Thes.* 8.3>, 51d
Iphianassa[1] (*Cyrianassa*), daughter of Proetus[1] <*Cat. Wom., Frag. Hes.* frg. 129, Merk. & West> and *Stheneboea* <Apollod. *Bibl.* 2.2.2>, 57d
— and Melampus[1] <Pher. in *F. Gr. H.* 3 F 114>, 32c
Iphianassa[2], wife of Endymion <Apollod. *Bibl.* 1.7.6>, 15b
Iphianassa[3] (*Iphimede*) (she is called *Iphigeneia* by tragedians, but the *Cypria*, frg. 24, *P.E.G.*, identifies her as a different person), daughter of Agamemnon <Hom. *Il.* IX. 145> and *Clytemnestra*, 36a
Iphianassa[4], daughter of Nereus <Luc. *Dial. Sea-Gods* 14> and *Doris*[1], 64b
Iphianassa[5], wife of Medon[10] <Quint. Smyr. 8.295-96>, *
Iphianeira[1], daughter of Oicle(u)s and *Hyperm(n)estra*[2] <*Cat. Wom., Frag. Hes.* frg. 25.34-39, Merk. & West>, 32d
Iphianeira[2], daughter of Megapenthes[2] <Diod. Sic. 4.68.4>, 58d
— and Melampus[1] <Diod. Sic. 4.68.4>, 32d
Iphiboe — see *Nausidame*
Iphicles (Iphiclus[1]), son of Amphitryon and *Alcmene* <Apollod. *Bibl.* 2.4.8>, 59d
— and *Automedusa* <Apollod. *Bibl.* 2.4.11>, 40a
— and *Megara* <Hom. *Od.* 11.268>, 55d
Iphiclus[1] — see Iphicles
Iphiclus[2] [King of Phylace] [Argonaut], son of Phylacus[1] <Hom. *Il.* II.705> and *Clymene*[4], 22c
alternate parentage:
Cephalus[2] and *Clymene*[4] <Paus. 10.29.6>
— and *Astyoche*[7] <Hyg. *Fab.* 103 (she is called *Diomedeia*)>, (22c)
Iphiclus[3] [Argonaut], son of Thestius <Bacch. 5.128-29> and *Eurythemis(te)* <Apollod. *Bibl.* 1.7.10>, 15d
— and *Harpalyce*[3] <Athen. 14.619e>, (15d)
Iphiclus[4], son of Idomeneus[2] and *Meda*[1] <Tzetz. on Lyc. 1217>, 54c
Iphidamas[1], son of Antenor[1] and *Theano*[2] <Hom. *Il.* XI.221>, *45c*
— and unnamed daughter of Cisseus[1] <Hom. *Il.* XI.221-29> and *Telecleia*, (45c)
Iphidamas[2] — see Amphidamas[2]
Iphidamas[3], suitor of *Penelope*[1] (from Dulichium) <Apollod. *Epit.* 7.27>, *
Iphidamas[4], a warrior who hid in the Trojan horse <Tryph. *Tak. Ilium* 181>, *
Iphigeneia, daughter of Agamemnon <*Cyp.* frg. 24, *P.E.G.* (tragedians use her name for the third daughter of Agamemnon whom Homer called *Iphianassa*, Hom. *Il.* IX.144, but the *Cypria* identifies her as a fourth daughter)> and *Clytemnestra* <Eur. *Iph. in Aulis* 417>, 36a
alternate parentage:
Theseus and *Helen*[1] <Ant. Lib. *Met.* 27.1>
Iphimede — see *Iphianassa*[3]
Iphimedeia, daughter of Triop(a)s[1] <Apollod. *Bibl.* 1.7.4> and *Hiscilla*, 34c
— and Aloeus[1] <Apollod. *Bibl.* 1.7.4>, 34a
— and Poseidon <Hom. *Od.* 11.305-06>, 8c
Iphimedon, son of Eurystheus <Apollod. *Bibl.* 2.8.1> and *Antimache*, 59c
Iphimedusa, daughter of Danaus[1] and *Atlantia* or *Phoebe*[4] <Apollod. *Bibl.* 2.1.5>, (58c)
— and Euchenor[2] <Apollod. *Bibl.* 2.1.5>, 58c
Iphinoe[1] (*Hipponoe*[2]) (*Ipponoe*), daughter of Proetus[1] <*Cat. Wom., Frag. Hes.* frg. 129, Merk. & West> and *Stheneboea* <Apollod. *Bibl.* 2.2.2>, 57d
Iphinoe[2], daughter of Alcathous[1] <Paus. 1.43.4> and *Euaechme*[1], 40a
Iphinoe[3], daughter of Nisus[2] <Paus. 1.39.5> and *Abrote*, 50d, *34d*
— and Megareus[1] <Paus. 1.39.5>, 9b
Iphinoe[4], wife of Antaeus[1] <Pher. in *F. Gr. H.* 3 F 76>, 9c
— and Heracles[1] <Pher. in *F. Gr. H.* 3 F 76>, 60c
Iphinoe[5], wife of Metion[1] <Pher. in *F. Gr. H.* 3 F 146>, 49b
Iphinoe[6], sister of Eetion[1] <Schol. B on Hom. *Il.* III.366>, *
Iphinoe[7], a woman from Lemnos <Ap. Rhod. *Arg.* 1.703>, *
Iphinous[1] [centaur], offspring of Centaurus and a Magnesian Mare <Pind. *Pyth.* 2.50; named as centaur, Ovid *Met.* 12. 381>, 69d
alternate parentage:
Ixion and *Nephele*[1] <Diod. Sic. 4.69.5>
Iphinous[2], son of Dexius <Hom. *Il.* VII.16>, *
Iphinous[3], killed by Amphiaraus <Stat. *Theb.* 7.714>, *
Iphis[1] [King of Argos], son of Alector[1] <Apollod. *Bibl.* 3.6.2>, 58c
Iphis[2], son of Sthenelus[1] and *Nicippe*[1] <Schol. on Ap. Rhod. *Arg.* 4.223-30>, 58d
Iphis[3], paramour of Patroclus[1] <Hom. *Il.* IX.666-67>, 22d
Iphis[4], daughter of Thespius <Apollod. *Bibl.* 2.7.8> and *Megamede* <Apollod. *Bibl.* 2.4.10>, 50c
— and Heracles[1] <Apollod. *Bibl.* 2.7.8>, (50c)
Iphis[5], suitor of *Anaxarete* <Ovid *Met.* 14.700-761>, *
Iphis[6]/Iphis[6], daughter/son of Ligdus and *Telethusa* <Ovid *Met.* 9.670-79>, *

Iphis[7], an Argonaut <Val. Flac. 1.441>, *
Iphis[8], killed by Acamas[5] <Stat. *Theb.* 8.447>, *
Iphitea — see *Amphithea*[1]
Iphitus[1], son of Eurytus[2] <Hom. *Od.* 21.14> and *Antiope*[6] <Hyg. *Fab.* 14>, 60b
Iphitus[2], son of Haemon[3] <Paus. 5.4.6>, 16d
alternate parentage:
Praxonides <Paus. 5.4.6>
Iphitus[3] [King of Phocis] [Argonaut], son of Naubolus[2] <Hom. *Il.* II.518> and *Perineice*, 23c
alternate parentage:
Hippasus[9] <Hyg. *Fab.* 14>
— and *Hippolyte*[4] <Hyg. *Fab.* 97>, (23c)
Iphitus[4], father of *Eurynome*[6] <Hyg. *Fab.* 70>, 30d
Iphitus[5], father of Archeptolemus <Hom. *Il.* VIII.128>, *
Iphitus[6], father of Coeranus[2] <Ovid *Met.* 13.257>, *
Iphitus[7], killed by Copreus <Apollod. *Bibl.* 2.5.1>, *
Iphthime[1], daughter of Icarius[2] <Hom. *Od.* 4.796-98> and *Periboea*[5], 47d
— and Eumelus[1] <Hom. *Od.* 4.796-98>, 29c
Iphthime[2], daughter of Dorus[1] <*Cat. Wom., Hesiodi* frg. 10a.13, Merk. & West (O.C.T.)>, 17a
— and Hermes <Non. *Dion.* 14.114-15>, 46c
Ipponoe — see *Iphinoe*[1]
Ipsea — see *Eidyia*
Irene — see *Eirene*
Iris[1] [rainbow], daughter of Thaumas[1] and *Electra*[1] <Hes. *Theog.* 266>, 3b
— and Zephyrus <Alc. *Poet. Lesb.* frg. 327>, 12a
Iris[2] — see *Alcathoe*
Iris[3] [one of the horses of Admetus[1]] <Stat. *Theb.* 6.461>, *
Irus[1], son of Actor[3] <Ap. Rhod. *Arg.* 1.73> and *Aegina*, 22d
— and *Demonassa*[1] <Hyg. *Fab.* 14>, (22d)
Irus[2] (Arnaeus), a beggar who wrestled with Odysseus <Hom. *Od.* 18.1-7>, *
Isaie, daughter of Agenor[1] and *Damno* <Pher. in *F. Gr. H.* 3 F 21>, 59c
Isander (Peisander[1]), son of Bellerophon(tes) and *Philonoe* <Hom. *Il.* VI.197>, 18b
Ischenus (Taraxippus[1]), son of Gigas <Tzetz. on Lyc. 42>, 46c
Ischepolis, son of Alcathous[1] <Paus. 1.42.6> and *Euaechme*[1], 40a
Ischomache — see *Hippodameia*[2]
Ischys (Alcyoneus[2]), son of Elatus[1] <*Hom. Hymn* 3 (to Pythian Apollo), 212> and *Laodice*[2], 62d
alternate parentage:
Elatus[2] (inferred because he is brother of Caeneus[1]) <Apollod. *Bibl.* 3.10.3>
— and *Coronis*[1] <*Cat. Wom., Frag. Hes.* frg. 60, Merk. & West>, 19d
Isis — see *Artemis* (alternate version)
Ismarus[1], son of Astacus <Apollod. *Bibl.* 3.6.8>, 9b
Ismarus[2] (Immaradus), son of Eumolpus[1] <Apollod. *Bibl.* 3.15.4>, 13a
Ismarus[3] — see Ismenus[1]
Ismarus[4], comrade of Aeneas <Virg. *Aen.* 10.141>, *
Ismene[1], daughter of Oedipus <Aesch. *Sev.* 861 (inferred because she is called sister of Eteocles[1])> and *Jocasta* <Eur. *Phoen. Wom.* 57>, 55c
alternate parentage:
Oedipus and *Euryganeia* <Paus. 9.5.5>
— and Periclymenus[3] <Mimn frg. 21, Gerber>, (55c)
Ismene[2], daughter of Asopus <Apollod. *Bibl.* 2.1.1> and *Metope*[2], 66b
— and Argus[3] <*Cat. Wom., Frag. Hes.* frg. 294, Merk. & West>, 61d
Ismenus[1] (Ismarus[3]), son of Apollo and *Melia*[1] <Paus. 9.10.5>, 11d
Ismenus[2], son of Asopus and *Metope*[2] <Apollod. *Bibl.* 3.12.6>, 66a
alternate parentage:
Oceanus and *Tethys* <Hyg. *Fab.* pref.>
Ismenus[3], son of Amphion[1] and *Niobe*[1] <Apollod. *Bibl.* 3.5.6>, 66c
Ismenus[4], [river], son of Oceanus and *Tethys* <Hes. *Theog.* 367-68; named as river, Hyg. *Fab.* pref.>, 54b
Isoples [centaur], offspring of Centaurus and a Magnesian Mare <Pind. *Pyth.* 2.50; named as centaur, Diod. Sic. 4.12.7>, 69d
alternate parentage:
Ixion and *Nephele*[1] <Diod. Sic. 4.69.5>
Isse (*Amphissa*[1]), daughter of Macar(eus)[4] <Ovid *Met.* 6.124>, 14a
— and Apollo <Ovid *Met.* 6.122-23>, 11d
— and Hermes <Steph. Byz. "Issa">, 46c
Ister — see Istrus[2]
Isthmius[1], son of Temenus[1] <Paus. 4.3.8>, 60d
Isthmius[2] [King of Messenia], son of Glaucus[5] <Paus. 4.3.10>, 60c
Istrus[1], son of Aegyptus[1] and [an Arabian woman] <Apollod. *Bibl.* 2.1.5>, 57c
— and *Hippodameia*[6] <Apollod. *Bibl.* 2.1.5>, (57c)
Istrus[2] (Ister) [river], son of Oceanus and *Tethys* <Hes. *Theog.* 339>, 54b
Isus, son of Priam[1] <Hom. *Il.* XI.101>, 44d
Italus, son of Telegonus[1] and *Penelope*[1] <Hyg. *Fab.* 127>, 13d
— and *Leucaria* <Dion. Hal. *Rom. Ant.* 1.72.6>, 13d
Itea —see [fifty daughters of Danaus[1]] (alternate version)
Ithacus[1], son of Pterelaus and *Amphimede* <Schol. on Hom. *Od.* 17.207>, 58d
Ithacus[2], suitor of *Penelope*[1] (from Same) <Apollod. *Epit.* 7.28>, *
Itone, daughter of Lyctius <Diod. Sic. 4.60.3>, 54c
— and Minos I <Diod. Sic. 4.60.3>, (54c)
Itonus[1], son of Amphictyon <Paus. 9.34.1> and *Cranae*[1], 16a
— and *Melanippe*[6] <Paus. 9.1.1>, (16a)
Itonus[2], son of Boeotus[1] <Diod. Sic. 4.67.7>, 18c
Itylus, son of Zet(h)us and *Aedon* <Hom. *Od.* 19.522>, 66d
alternate parentage:
Polytechnus and *Aedon* <Ant. Lib. *Met.* 11.2-4>
Itys[1] — see Itylus
Itys[2], son of Tereus[1] and *Procne* <Apollod. *Bibl.* 3.14.8>, 49a
Itys[3], killed by Castor[1] <Val. Flac. 3.189>, *
Itys[4], killed by Parthenopaeus <Stat. *Theb.* 7.642>, *
Itys[5], killed by Turnus <Virg. *Aen.* 9.574>, *
Iulius, son of Ascanius[1] <Diod. Sic. 7.5.8> and *Roma*[2], 41c
Iulus[1] — see Ascanius[1]
Iulus[2] — see Ascanius[2]
Ixion [King of Thessaly], son of Antion and *Perimele*[2] <Diod. Sic. 4.69.2>, 69a, *31b*
alternate parentage:
Leonteus[3] <Hyg. *Fab.* 62>
Phlegyas <Schol. A on Hom. *Il.* I.268>
Zeus <Schol. on Hom. *Od.* 21.303>
— and *Dia*[1] <Schol. on Pind. *Pyth.* 2.40b>, (69a)
— and *Nephele*[1] <Apollod. *Epit.* 1.20>, (69a)
Iynx[1], daughter of Pierus[2] <Nicand. in Ant. Lib. *Met.* 9> and *Euippe*[2] <Ovid *Met.* 5.300 ff.>, 15c
Iynx[2], daughter of Pan and *Echo* <Tzetz. on Lyc. 310>, 46c

Jason (Diomedes[4]) (Iason) [King of Iolcus] [Argonaut], son of Aeson <Hes. *Theog.* 992-1000> and *Polymede* <*Cat. Wom., Frag. Hes.* frg. 38, Merk. & West (she is called *Polymele*)>, 33d
alternate parentage:

Aeson and *Alcimede*[1] <Ap. Rhod. *Arg.* 1.234>
Aeson and *Amphinome*[3] <Diod. Sic. 4.50.2>
— and *Glauce*[2] <Eur. *Medea* 19 (named, Apollod. *Bibl.* 1.9.28)>, (33d)
— and *Hypsipyle* <Apollod. *Bibl.* 1.9.16>, 32d, 56d
— and *Medea* <Hes. *Theog.* 958-61, 992-1002>, 14c
Jocasta (*Epicaste*[1]), daughter of Menoeceus[1] <Eur. *Phoen. Wom.* 11>, 55d
— and Laius[1] <Soph. *Oed. Tyr.* 708-14>, 55c
— and Oedipus <Aesch. *Sev.* 752-57; Jocasta named, Soph. *Oed. Tyr.* 639>, 55c
Jupiter Ammon — see Ammon

Labdacus [King of Thebes], son of Polydorus[2] <Eur. *Phoen. Wom.* 8-9> and *Nycteis* <Apollod. *Bibl.* 3.5.5>, 55c
Labotas — see Lebotas
Lacedaemon [King of Sparta], son of Zeus and *Taygete* <Apollod. *Bibl.* 3.10.3>, 6c, *47b*
— and *Sparte* <Apollod. *Bibl.* 3.10.3>, 61c
Lacestades [King of Sicyon], son of Hippolytus[4] <Paus. 2.6.7>, 61d
Lachesis [one of the Moirae], daughter of Zeus and *Themis*[1] <Hes. *Theog.* 901-05>, 6d
alternate parentage:
Nyx <Hes. *Theog.* 217-18>
Lacritus — see Clonius[2] (alternate version)
Ladocus — see Laodochus[4]
Ladon[1] [river], son of Oceanus and *Tethys* <Hes. *Theog.* 344>, 54b
Ladon[2] (Ophis[1]) [serpent], offspring of Phorcus[1] and *Ceto*[1] <Hes. *Theog.* 334; named, Ap. Rhod. *Arg.* 4.1396>, 2a
alternate parentage:
Gaea <Ap. Rhod. *Arg.* 4.1396>
Ladon[3], comrade of Aeneas <Virg. *Aen.* 10.413>, *
Ladon[4] [one of the dogs of Actaeon] <Ovid *Met.* 3.219>, *
Laertes [King of Ithaca], son of Arceisius <Hom. *Od.* 16.118> and *Chalcomedusa* <Eust. on Hom. *Od.* 1796>, 5c
— and *Anticleia*[1] <Hom. *Od.* 11.85>, 13a
Laestrygon, son of Poseidon <*Cat. Wom.*, appx. frg. 40A, in *Hom. Hymns and Homerica*, Evelyn-White>, 9d
Laias [King of Elis], son of Oxylus[2] and *Pieria*[2] <Paus. 5.4.4>, 16d
Laius[1] [King of Thebes], son of Labdacus <Soph. *Oed. Tyr.* 226>, 55c
— and Chrysippus[1] <Apollod. *Bibl.* 3.5.5>, 40a
— and *Eurycleia*[2] <Epim. in *F. Gr. H.* 3 B 15>, (55c)
— and *Jocasta* <Soph. *Oed. Tyr.* 708-14>, 55d
Laius[2], entered cave of Zeus seeking honey <Ant. Lib. *Met.* 19>, *
Lala — see *Lara(nda)*
Lamache (*Malache*), paramour of Euphemus[1] <Schol. on Pind. *Pyth.* 4.55>, 8d
Lamadia — see *Laomedeia*
Lamedon [King of Sicyon], son of Coronus[1] <Paus. 2.5.5>, 11b
— and *Pheno* <Paus. 2.6.5>, (11b)
Lamia[1], daughter of Poseidon <Paus. 10.12.1>, 9d
— and Zeus <Paus. 10.12.1>, 5d
Lamia[2] (*Sybaris*[1]) [monster], killed by Eurybatus <Ant. Lib. *Met.* 8>, *
Lamon — see Lamus[2]
Lampethusa — see *Lampetia*
Lampetia (*Lampethusa*), daughter of Helios and *Neaera*[1] <Hom. *Od.* 12.132>, 14b
alternate parentage:
Helios and *Rhode*[1] <Schol. on Hom. *Od.* 17.208>
Helios and *Clymene*[1] <Ovid *Met.* 2.334-48>
Clymenus[6] and *Merope*[4] <Hyg. *Fab.* 154>
Lampon — see Lampus[1]
Lampus[1] (Lampon), son of Laomedon[1] <Hom. *Il.* XX.239> and *Strym(n)o* <Apollod. *Bibl.* 3.12.3>, 42d
alternate parentage:
Laomedon[1] and *Leucippe*[8] <Apollod. *Bibl.* 3.12.3>
Laomedon[1] and *Placia* <Apollod. *Bibl.* 3.12.3>
Lampus[2], son of Aegyptus[1] and *Gorgo*[1] <Apollod. *Bibl.* 2.1.5>, 57c
— and *Ocypete*[2] <Apollod. *Bibl.* 2.1.5>, (57c)
Lampus[3], son of Prolaus and *Lysippe*[6] <Paus. 5.2.4>, *
Lampus[4], killed by Tydeus[1] <Stat. *Theb.* 2.623>, *
Lampus[5], killed by Amphiaraus <Stat. *Theb.* 7.759>, *
Lampus[6], one of the horses of Hector[1] <Hom. *Il.* VIII.185>, *
Lampus[7], one of the horses of *Eos* <Hom. *Od.* 23.246>, *
Lampus[8], one of the dogs of Actaeon <Hyg. *Fab.* 181>, *
Lamus[1] (Lamon), son of Heracles[1] and *Omphale* <Diod. Sic. 4.31.8>, 60c
Lamus[2], son of Zeus <Non. *Dion.* 9.28-29>, 6d
Lamus[3] [King of Laestrygonians] <Hom. *Od.* 10.82-83>, *
Lamus[4], killed by Nisus[1] <Virg. *Aen.* 9.334>, *
Lamus[5], killed by Thoas[6] <Quint. Smyr. 11.90>, *
Lamus[6], killed by Parthenopaeus <Stat. *Theb.* 9.764>, *
Lanassa (*Leonassa*), daughter of Cleodaeus <Plut. *Pyrr.* 1.2>, 60c
— and Neoptolemus (Plut. *Pyrrhus* (he is called Pyrrhus)>, 24c
Laocoon[1], son of Antenor[1] <Schol. on Lyc. 347> and *Theano*[2], *45c*
— and *Antiope*[2] <Serv. on Virg. *Aen.* 2.201>, (45c)
Laocoon[2] [Argonaut], son of Portheus[1] <Ap. Rhod. *Arg.* 1.192> and *Euryte*[1] <Hyg. *Fab.* 14 (inferred because he is called brother of Oeneus[1])>, 17c
alternate parentage:
Portheus[1] and [a servant] <Ap. Rhod. 1.192>
Laocoon[3], a seer <Apollod. *Epit.* 5.17>, *
Laodamas[1], son of Alcinous <Hom. *Od.* 7.170> and *Arete* <Hom. *Od.* 7.67>, 9c
Laodamas[2], son of Antenor[1] and *Theano*[2] <Hom. *Il.* XV.517>, *45d*
Laodamas[3] [King of Thebes], son of Eteocles[1] <Apollod. *Bibl.* 3.7.3>, 55c
Laodamas[4], son of Hector[1] and *Andromache* <Dict. Cret. 6.12>, 43c
Laodamas[5], killed by Neoptolemus <Quint. Smyr. 11.20>, *
Laodameia[1], daughter of Acastus <Ovid *Her.* 13.25> and *Hippolyte*[2], 28c
— and Protesilaus <Ovid *Her.* 13.25>, 22c
Laodameia[2] (*Deidameia*[3]), daughter of Bellerophon(tes) and *Philonoe* <Hom. *Il.* VI.197>, 18b
— and Euander[2] <Diod. Sic. 5.79.3 (she is called *Deidameia*)>, 52c
— and Zeus <Hom. *Il.* VI.198-99>, 5d, 52c
Laodameia[3] — see *Leaneira*
Laodameia[4], daughter of Alcmaeon[1] <Schol. A on Hom. *Il.* XVI.175>, 32d
— and Peleus <Schol. A on Hom. *Il.* XVI.175>, 24b
Laodameia[5], paramour of Thyestes[1] <Schol. on Eur. *Or.* 4>, 39b
Laodameia[6], nurse of Orestes <Schol. on Pind. *Pyth.* 11.25>, *
Laodice[1], daughter of Priam[1] and *Hecabe*[1] <Hom. *Il.* VI.252>, 43c
— and Acamas[1] <Parth. *Love Stor.* 16.2>, 51d
— and Helicaon[1] <Hom. *Il.* III.123-24>, 45d
— and Telephus <Hyg. *Fab.* 101>, 60a
Laodice[2], daughter of Cinyras[1] <Apollod. *Bibl.* 3.9.1> and *Metharme*, 11c
— and Elatus[1] <Apollod. *Bibl.* 3.9.1>, 62d
Laodice[3] — see *Electra*[3]
Laodice[4], daughter of Iphis[1] <Schol. on Eur. *Phoen. Maid.* 180>,

58c
Laodice[5], daughter of Agapenor <Paus. 8.53.7>, 64c
Laodice[6], Hyperborean maiden <Herod. 2.33>, *
Laodochus[1], son of Antenor[1] and *Theano*[2] <Hom. *Il.* IV.87>, *45d*
Laodochus[2], son of Apollo and *Phthia*[4] <Apollod. *Bibl.* 1.7.6>, 11d
Laodochus[3] (Leodocus) [Argonaut], son of Bias[1] and *Pero*[1] <Ap. Rhod. *Arg.* 1.120>, 30c
Laodochus[4], son of Echemus and *Timandra*[1] <*Cat. Wom., Frag. Hes.* frg. 23(a).34, Merk. & West>, 64c, *48c*
Laodochus[5], son of Priam[1] <Apollod. *Bibl.* 3.12.5>, 44c
Laogore, daughter of Cinyras[1] and *Metharme* <Apollod. *Bibl.* 3. 14.3>, 11c
Laomedeia (*Lamadia*), daughter of Nereus and *Doris*[1] <Hes. *Theog.* 257>, *64b*
Laomedon[1] [King of Troy], son of Ilus[2] <Hom. *Il.* XX.236> and *Eurydice*[2] <Apollod. *Bibl.* 3.11.3>, 42c
alternate parentage:
Ilus[2] and *Leucippe*[4] <Hyg. *Fab.* 250>
— and *Calybe*[1] <Apollod. *Bibl.* 3.12.3>, (42c)
— and *Leucippe*[8] <Apollod. *Bibl.* 3.12.3>, (42c)
— and *Placia* <Apollod. *Bibl.* 3.12.3>, (42c)
— and *Strym(n)o* <Hellan. in *F. Gr. H.* 4 F 139>, 70b
— and *Zeuxippe*[5] <Schol. on Hom. *Il.* III.250>, (42c)
Laomedon[2], son of Heracles[1] and *Meline* <Apollod. *Bibl.* 2.7. 8>, *50d*
Laomedon[3], suitor of *Penelope*[1] (from Zathyncus) <Apollod. *Epit.* 7.29>, *
Laomedon[4], killed by Thrasymedes[1] <Quint. Smyr. 2.293-94>, *
Laomenes, son of Heracles[1] and *Oreia* <Apollod. *Bibl.* 2.7.8>, *50c*
Laonome[1], daughter of Amphitryon and *Alcmene* <Schol. on Ap. Rhod. *Arg.* 1.1241>, *59d*
— and Euphemus[1] <Tzetz. on Lyc. 886>, 8d
— and Polyphemus[2] <Schol. on Ap. Rhod. *Arg.* 1.1241>, (59d)
Laonome[2], daughter of Guneus <Apollod. *Bibl.* 2.4.5>, 59c
— and Alcaeus[2] <Apollod. *Bibl.* 2.4.5>, (59c)
Laonome[3] (*Agrinome*), daughter of Perseon <Hyg. *Fab.* 14>, 15c
— and Odeodochus <Hyg. *Fab.* 14>, (15c)
Laonytus, son of Oedipus and *Jocasta* <Pher. in *F. Gr. H.* 3 F 95>, 55c
Laophonte, daughter of Pleuron and *Xanthippe*[1] <Apollod. *Bibl.* 1.7.7>, 15c
Laothoe[1], daughter of Altes <Hom. *Il.* XXI.85>, 43d
— and Priam[1] <Hom. *Il.* XXI.85>, (43d)
Laothoe[2], wife of Idmon[1] <Pher. in *F.H.G.* 1.88 frg. 70, Müller>, 69b
— and Apollo <Tzetz. on Lyc. 427>, 11d
Laothoe[3], daughter of Thespius <Apollod. *Bibl.* 2.7.8> and *Megamede* <Apollod. *Bibl.* 2.4.10>, 50c
— and Heracles[1] <Apollod. *Bibl.* 2.7.8>, (50c)
Laothoe[4], paramour of Portheus[1] <*Cat. Wom., Frag. Hes.* frg. 26.5-7, Merk. & West>, 15d
Laothoe[5], paramour of Hermes <Orph. *Arg.* 135-37>, 46c
Laphria — see *Britomartis*
Lapithes [King of Thessaly], son of Apollo and *Stilbe*[1] <Diod. Sic. 4.69.2>, 11c, *68b*
— and *Orsinome* <Diod. Sic. 4.69.2>, 21c
Lapithus, son of Aeolus[2] <Diod. Sic. 5.81.6>, 18c
Lara(nda) (*Lala*), daughter of Almo(n)[1] <Ovid *Fast.* 2.599>, 50b
— and Hermes <Ovid *Fast.* 2.613-15>, 46c
(Lares), twin sons of Hermes and *Lara(nda)* <Ovid *Fast.* 2.615-16>, 46c
Larissa[1], daughter of Pelasgus[2] <Paus. 2.23.9>, 61d
— and Poseidon <Dion. Hal. *Rom. Ant.* 1.17>, 8c
Laris(s)a[2], daughter of Piasus <Parth. *Love Stor.* 23.1>, 44c
— and Cyzicus <Parth. *Love Stor.* 23.1>, (44c)
Larymna, daughter of Cynus <Paus. 9.23.4>, 15a
Larymnus, father of *Euboea*[5] <Athen. 7.296b>, 49a
Lathria, daughter of Thersander[3] <Paus. 3.16.6>, 60d
— and Procles[1] <Paus. 3.16.6>, (60d)
Latinus[1] [King of Latinum], son of Odysseus and *Circe* <Hes. *Theog.* 1013>, 13d
alternate parentage:
Odysseus and *Calypso*[1] <Apollod. *Epit.* 7.24>
Faunus and *Marica* <Virg. *Aen.* 7.46-48>
Heracles[1] and a Hyperborean girl <Dion. Hal. *Rom. Ant.* 1.43.1>
Telemachus and *Circe* <Hyg. *Fab.* 127>
— and *Amata* <Fab. Pict. in *F.H.G.* 3.93 frg. 23, Müller>, (13d)
Latinus[2], son of Silvius <Ovid *Fast.* 4.43>, 41c
Latramis, daughter of Dionysus and *Ariadne* <Schol. on Ap. Rhod. *Arg.* 3.997>, 56c
Latreus [centaur], offspring of Centaurus and a Magnesian Mare <Pind. *Pyth.* 2.50; named as centaur, Ovid *Met.* 12.487>, 69d
alternate parentage:
Ixion and *Nephele*[1] <Diod. Sic. 4.69.5>
Lavinia[1] (*Dyna*), daughter of Euander[1] <Dion. Hal. *Rom. Ant.* 1. 32.1>, 46c
— and Heracles[1] <Dion. Hal. *Rom. Ant.* 1.32.1>, 60d
Lavinia[2] (*Laurina*), daughter of Latinus[1] <Diod. Sic. 7.5.8> and *Amata* <Virg. *Aen.* 7.342, 356-58, 605>, 13d
— and Aeneas[1] <Plut. *Rom.* 2.3>, 41c
Lavinia[3], daughter of Anius <Dion. Hal. *Rom. Ant.* 1.59.3> and *Dorippe*, 56d
Leades, son of Astacus <Apollod. *Bibl.* 3.6.8>, 9b
Leagore (*Liagore*), daughter of Nereus and *Doris*[1] <Hes. *Theog.* 257>, *64b*
Leandre — see *Leaneira*
Leaneira (*Laodameia*[3]) (*Leandre*), daughter of Amyclas[1] <Apollod. *Bibl.* 3.9.1> and *Diomede*[2], 47b
— and Arcas[1] <Apollod. *Bibl.* 3.9.1>, 62c
Learchus, son of Athamas[1] and *Ino* <Apollod. *Bibl.* 1.9.1>, 26a
Lebadus — see [fifty sons of Lycaon[1]] (alternate version)
Lebes, father of Rhacius <Schol. on Ap. Rhod. 1.308>, 32d
Lebotas (Labotas) (Leobotas), son of Echestratus <Herod. 7. 204>, 60d
Leches, son of Poseidon and *Peirene*[2] <Paus. 2.2.3>, 9b, *66a*
Leda, daughter of Thestius and *Eurythemis(te)* <Apollod. *Bibl.* 1.7.10>, 16c
alternate parentage:
Thestius and *Laophonte* <Pher. in *F. Gr. H.* 3 F 9>
Glaucus[1] and *Pantidyia* <Eum. frg. 7.*P.E.G.*>
— and Tyndareus <Hom. *Od.* 11, 300>, 48d
— and Zeus <Eur. *Hel.* 259>, 5c
Leimon, son of Tegeates <Paus. 8.53.4> and *Maera*[2], 63d
Leipephilene (*Deip(h)yle*[1]), daughter of Iola(u)s <*Gr. Ehoiai, Frag. Hes.* frg. 252, Merk. & West> and *Megara*, 59c, *55d*
— and Phylas[2] <*Gr. Ehoiai, Frag. Hes.* frg. 252, Merk. & West>, 60c
Leiriope, daughter of Oceanus and *Tethys* <Ovid *Met.* 3.343 (she is called a river nymph)>, 55b
— and Cephis(s)us <Ovid *Met.* 3.344-45>, 49b
Leis, daughter of Orus[1] <Paus. 2.30.6>, 8c
— and Poseidon <Paus. 2.30.6>, (8c)
Leitus, son of Electryon[2] <Hom. *Il.* XVII.604 (father is called Alectryon)>, 18c
Lelantus — see Lelas

Lelas (Lelantus), paramour of *Periboea*[7] <Non. *Dion.* 48.247-48>, 62b
Lelex[1], father of Polycaon[1] <Paus. 3.1.1>, 61c
— and *Cleochareia* <Apollod. *Bibl.* 3.10.3>, (61c)
Lelex[2] [King of Megara], son of Poseidon and *Libya*[1] <Paus. 1. 44.3>, 8c, *59a*
Lelex[3], grandfather of Teleboas[4] <Aris. in Strab. 7.1.2>, *
Leneus [satyr], son of Silenus <Non. *Dion.* 14.99> and [ash tree nymph], 46c
Leobotes — see Lebotes
Leocritus[1], son of Euenor[1] <Hom. *Od.* 2.242> and *Leucippe*[5], 8b
Leocritus[2], son of Polydamas <Paus. 10.27.1>, *
Leodocus — see Laodochus[3]
Leon[1], son of Lycaon[1] <Apollod. *Bibl.* 3.8.1>, 64b
Leon[2], one of the dogs of Actaeon <Hyg. *Fab.* 181>, *
Leonassa — see *Lanassa*
Leonteus[1], son of Coronus[3] <Hom. *Il.* II.746>, 8b
Leonteus[2], brother of Andraemon[3] <Diod. Sic. 4.53.2>, 28d
Leonteus[3] — see Ixion (alternate version)
Leonteus[4], killed by Hippomedon[1] <Stat. *Theb.* 9.133-36>, *
(Leontides), daughters of Leos (see *Eubule*, *Praxithea*[4], *Theope*), 6a
Leontomenes, son of Tisamenus[1] <Paus. 7.6.2>, 36c
Leontophon(us) (Doryclus[1]), son of Odysseus and the daughter of Thoas[6] <Apollod. *Epit.* 7.40>, 13d, *16d*
Leos[1], son of Orpheus <Phot. *Lex.* "Leokorion">, 6a
Leos[2], a herald from Agnus <Plut. *Thes.* 13.2>, *
Lepreus[1], son of Caucon[1] and *Asty(a)dameia*[5] <Ael. *Var. Narr.* 1.24>, 68b
Lepreus[2], son of Pyrgeus <Paus. 5.5.4>, *
[Lernaean Hydra], offspring of Typhon and *Echidna* <Hes. *Theog.* 313>, 1b
Lernus[1], son of Proetus[2] <Ap. Rhod. *Arg.* 1.134>, 52d
— and unnamed wife, paramour of Hephaestus <Ap. Rhod. *Arg.* 1.202>, 7d
Lernus[2], husband of *Amphiale* <Quint. Smyr. 10.221-22>, *
Lernus[3], killed by *Pentheseleia* <Quint. Smyr. 1.228>, *
Lesbus, son of Lapithus <Diod. Sic. 5.81.6>, 18c
— and *Methymna* <Diod. Sic. 5.81.6>, 14a
Lethaea, paramour of Olenus[1] <Ovid *Met.* 10.68>, 7d
Lethe[1] [forgetfulness] [abstraction], offspring of *Eris* <Hes. *Theog.* 227>, *1a*
Lethe[2] [river], daughter of Oceanus and *Tethys* <Hes. *Theog.* 366-67; named as river, Paus. 1.35.4>, 50a
Leto, daughter of C(o)eus and *Phoebe*[1] <Hes. *Theog.* 406>, 11b
— and Tityus <Hom. *Od.* 11.576-80>, 3b
— and Zeus <Hes. *Theog.* 918>, 5c
Letreus, son of Pelops[1] <Paus. 6.22.8> and *Hippodameia*[1], *37b*
Leucadius, son of Icarius[2] <Strab. 2.7.7> and *Periboea*[5], 47d
alternate parentage:
Icarius[2] and *Polycaste*[2] <Strab. 10.2.24>
Leucaria, daughter of Latinus[1] <Dion. Hal. *Rom. Ant.* 1.72.6>, 13d
— and Italus <Dion. Hal. *Rom. Ant.* 1.72.6>, 13d
Leuce, daughter of Oceanus <Serv. on Virg. *Ecl.* 7.61> and *Tethys*, 55b
— and Hades <Serv. on Virg. *Ecl.* 7.61>, 10b
Leucippe[1] (*Leucone*[1]), daughter of Minyas <Nicand. in Ant. Lib. *Met.* 10.1> and *Euryanassa*[2], 20d
Leucippe[2], daughter of Thestor[1] <Hyg. *Fab.* 190>, 69b
Leucippe[3] (*Lysippe*[4]), mother of Teuthras <Ps.-Plut. *De Fluv.* 21. 3 (she is called *Lysippe*)> and Tyres <Virg. *Aen.* 10.402-03 (this son is called brother of Teuthras)>, 63d
Leucippe[4] — see Laomedon[1] (alternate version)
Leucippe[5], mother of *Cleito*[1] <Plato *Crit.* 113d> and Leocritus[1] <Hom. *Od.* 2.242 (inferred because he is son of Euenor)>, 8d
— and Euenor <Plato *Crit.* 113d>, (8d)
Leucippe[6] — see *Eurythemis(te)*
Leucippe[7], daughter of Oceanus and *Tethys* <*Hom. Hymn* 2 (to *Demeter*), 416>, 61a
Leucippe[8], paramour of Laomedon[1] <Apollod. *Bibl.* 3.12.3>, 42c
Leucippe[9] — see *Nicippe*[1]
Leucippus[1] [King of Messenia], son of Perieres[1] and *Gorgophone*[1] <Apollod. *Bibl.* 1.9.5>, 25a
— and *Philodice*[1] <Tzetz. on Lyc. 511>, 55a
Leucippus[2], son of Oenomaus[1] <Paus. 8.20.2> and *Asterope*[1], 7c, *40a*
— and *Daphne*[1] <Paus. 8.20.2>, 68b
Leucippus[3] [King of Sicyon], son of Thurimachus <Paus. 2.5. 7>, 61c
Leucippus[4], son of Poemander <Plut. *Gr. Quest.* 37.299c> and *Tanagra*, 35c
Leucippus[5], son of Heracles[1] and *Eurytele* <Apollod. *Bibl.* 2.7. 8>, *51c*
Leucippus[6], son of Naxus <Diod. Sic. 5.51.3>, 15d
Leucippus[7]/*Leucippus*[7], son/daughter of Lamprus and *Galateia*[3] <Ant. Lib. *Met.* 17.3>, *
Leucippus[8], son of Xanthius <Parth. *Love Stor.* 5.1> *
Leucippus[9], sent by Macar(eus)[4] to Rhodes <Diod. Sic. 5.81. 8>, *
Leucon[1], son of Athamas[1] and *Themisto*[1] <*Cat. Wom., Hesiodi* frg. 10a.64, Merk. & West (O.C.T.)>, 26b
Leucon[2] [one of the dogs of Actaeon] <Ovid *Met.* 3.220>, *
Leucone[1], daughter of Apheidas[1] <Paus. 8.44.8>, 63c
Leucone[2], wife of Cyanippus[2] <Parth. *Love Stor.* 10.1>, *
Leucones, son of Heracles[1] and *Aeschreis* <Apollod. *Bibl.* 2.7. 8>, *50c*
Leuconoe[1] — see *Leucippe*[1]
Leuconoe[2], daughter of Poseidon and *Themisto*[2] <Hyg. *Fab.* 157>, 9b
Leuconoe[3], daughter of Lucifer <Hyg. *Fab.* 161>, *
Leucopeus, son of Portheus[1] and *Euryte*[1] <Apollod. *Bibl.* 1.7. 10>, 17c
Leucophanes, son of Euphemus[1] and *Lamache* <Schol. on Pind. *Pyth.* 4.55>, 8d
Leucosia[1] — see [Sirens]
Leucosia[2], cousin of Aeneas <Dion. Hal. *Rom. Ant.* 1.53.2>, *
Leucothea[1] — see *Halia*[1]
Leucothea[2], paramour of Zeus <Ps.-Plut. *De Fluv.* 7.1>, 5c
Leucothoe[1], daughter of Orchamus and *Eurynome*[3] <Ovid *Met.* 4.208 ff.>, 14a
— and Helios <Ovid *Met.* 4.208 ff.>, (14a)
Leucothoe[2] — see *Ino*
Leucothoe[3], daughter of Nereus and *Doris*[1] <Hyg. *Fab.* pref.>, *65a*
Leucus[1], son of Talaus <Schol. on Hom. *Il.* II.649> and *Lysimache*[1], 31c
— and *Meda*[1] <Apollod. *Epit.* 6.10>, 54c
Leucus[2], a singer from Lesbos <Non. *Dion.* 24.231>, *
Leucus[3], killed by Antiphus[1] <Hom. *Il.* IV.491>, *
Liagore — see *Leagore*
Libya[1], daughter of Epaphus[1] <Aesch. *Supp.* 318> and *Memphis*[1] <Apollod. *Bibl.* 2.1.4>, 55b
— and Poseidon <Apollod. *Bibl.* 2.1.4>, 8c
Libya[2], daughter of Palamedes <Hyg. *Fab.* 160>, 52d
— and Hermes <Hyg. *Fab.* 160>, 46c
[Libyan Sibyl] — see *Herophile*[1]
Libys[1], son of Hermes and *Libya*[2] <Hyg. *Fab.* 160>, 46c, *52d*
Libys[2], sailor turned into a dolphin <Ovid *Met.* 3.615>, *
Licymnius, son of Electryon[1] and *Mideia*[2] <Apollod. *Bibl.* 2. 4. 5>, 59c
— and *Perimede*[2] <Apollod. *Bibl.* 2 .5.6>, (59c)
Ligeia[1] — see [Sirens]
Ligeia[2], daughter of Nereus and *Doris*[1] <Hyg. *Fab.* pref.>, *65a*

Ligyron — see Achilles
Ligys, son of Poseidon <Tzetz. on Lyc. *Alex.* 649 (inferred because he is called brother of Alebion)>, 9c
Lilaea, daughter of Cephis(s)us <Paus. 10.33.2> and *Leiriope*, 49b
Limnaee (*Limniace*), daughter of Ganges <Ovid *Met.* 5.51>, 54a
Limniace — see *Limnaee*
Limnoreia, daughter of Nereus <Hom. *Il.* XVIII, 40> and *Doris*[1] <Apollod. *Bibl.* 1.2.7>, *65a*
Limus [famine] [abstraction], offspring of *Eris* <Hes. *Theog.* 227>, *1a*
Lindus, son of Cercaphus[1] and *Cydippe*[1] <Diod. Sic. 5.57.8>, 14a
Linus[1] (Oitolinos), son of Amphimarus and *Urania*[1] <Paus. 9. 29.6>, *6b*
alternate parentage:
Apollo and *Urania*[1] <Hyg. *Fab.* 161>
Linus[2], son of Apollo and *Psamathe*[2] <Paus. 2.19.7>, 11d, *61c*
Linus[3] (Ialemus), son of Oeagrus and *Calliope* <Apollod. *Bibl.* 1.3.2>, *6a*
alternate parentage:
Apollo and *Calliope* <Apollod. *Bibl.* 1.3.2>
Linus[4], son of Lycaon[1] <Apollod. *Bibl.* 3.8.1>, 64b
Linus[5], killed by Hypseus[3] <Stat. *Theb.* 9.254>, *
Liparus, son of Auson <Diod. Sic. 5.7.5>, 13c
Lipoxais, son of Targitaus <Herod. 4.5>, 6d
(Litae) [prayers], daughters of Zeus <Hom. *Il.* IX.502-16>, 6d
Lityerses, son of Midas[1] <Theocr. in Hesyc. *Lex.* "Lityerses" X. 41>, 2d
Lixus, son of Aegyptus[1] and *Caliadne* <Apollod. *Bibl.* 2.1.5>, 57d
— and *Cleodora*[3] <Apollod. *Bibl.* 2.1.5>, (57d)
Locrus[1], son of Zeus and *Maera*[1] <Plut. *Gr. and Rom. Par. Stor.* 36>, 5c, *19c*
Locrus[2], son of Physcus <Eust. on Hom. *Il.* 277>, 16a
— and *Cambyse* <Plut. *Gr. Quest.* 15>, 15a
Logoi [lies] [abstraction], offspring of *Eris* <Hes. *Theog.* 229>, *1a*
Lotis, paramour of Priapus <Ovid *Fast.* 1.415-40>, 56c
Loxo, daughter of Boreas <Callim. *Hymn to Delos* 292-93> and *Oreithyia*[1], 13a
Lycabas[1] [centaur], offspring of Centaurus and a Magnesian Mare <Pind. *Pyth.* 2.50; named as centaur, Ovid *Met.* 12, 303>, 69d
alternate parentage:
Ixion and *Nephele*[1] <Diod. Sic. 4.69.5>
Lycabas[2], sailor turned into a dolphin <Ovid *Met.* 3.622>, *
Lycabas[3], killed by Perseus[1] <Ovid *Met.* 5.59-73>, *
Lycaethus[1], father of Creon[1] <Schol. on Eur. *Med.*>, 33b
Lycaethus[2], son of Hippocoon[1] <Apollod. *Bibl.* 3.10.5>, 47c
Lycaethus[3], suitor of *Penelope*[1] (from Same) <Apollod. *Epit.* 7. 29>, *
Lycaeus — see Phleias (alternate version)
Lycaon[1] [King of Arcadia], son of Pelasgus[1] <Hes. in Strab. 5.2. 4> and *Meliboea*[1] <Apollod. *Bibl.* 3.8.1>, 62a
alternate parentage:
Pelasgus[1] and *Cyllene* <Apollod. *Bibl.* 3.8.1>
Pelasgus[1] and *Deianeira*[3] <Dion. Hal. *Rom. Ant.* 1.11.2>
autochthonous <Ant. Lib. *Met.* 31.1>
— and *Cyllene*[1] <Dion. Hal. *Rom. Ant.* 1.13.1>, (62a)
— and *Nonacris* <Paus. 8.17.6>, (62a)
Lycaon[2], son of Priam[1] <Hom. *Il.* XX.81-82> and *Laothoe*[1] <Hom. *Il.* XXII.46 ff.>, 43d
Lycaon[3], son of Ares <Eur. *Alc.* 501-02> and *Pelopeia*[1], 7d
Lycaon[4], son of Aezeius <Dion. Hal. *Rom. Ant.* 1.11.2>, 62b
Lycaon[5] [King of Zeleia in Lycia], father of Eurytion[4] and Pandarus[2] <Hom. *Il.* II.826>, *
Lycaon[6], father of Daunus <Ant. Lib. *Met.* 31.1>, *
Lycaon[7], from Crete <Virg. *Aen.* 9.304>, *
Lycastus[1] [King of Crete], son of Minos I and *Itone* <Diod. Sic. 4.60.3>, 54c
— and *Ida*[1] <Diod. Sic. 4.60.3>, 42b
Lycastus[2], son of Ares and *Phylonome* <Plut. *Gr. and Rom. Par. Stor.* 36>, 7c, *63c*
Lycastus[3], paramour of *Eulimene*[1] <Parth. *Love Stor.* 35.1>, 53d
Lycia, paramour of Apollo <Serv. on Virg. *Aen.* 3.332>, 11d
Lycidas [centaur], offspring of Centaurus and a Magnesian Mare <Pind. *Pyth.* 2.50; named as centaur, Ovid *Met.* 12.311>, 69d
alternate parentage:
Ixion and *Nephele*[1] <Diod. Sic. 4.69.5>
Lycius[1], son of Lycaon[1] <Apollod. *Bibl.* 3.8.1>, 64b
Lycius[2], son of Cleinis and *Harpa* <Ant. Lib. *Met.* 20.3>, *
Lyco, daughter of Dion and *Amphithea*[1] <Serv. on Virg. *Ecl.* 8.29>, *31d*
Lycomedes[1] [King of Scyros], son of Apollo and *Parthenope*[3] <Paus. 7.4.2>, 11d, *54d*
Lycomedes[2], son of Creon[2] <Hom. *Il.* IX.84> and *Eurydice*[9], 55d
Lycopes [centaur], offspring of Centaurus and a Magnesian Mare <Pind. *Pyth.* 2.50; named as centaur Ovid *Met.* 12.350>, 69d
alternate parentage:
Ixion and *Nephele*[1] <Diod. Sic. 4.69.5>
Lycopeus, son of Agrius[1] <Apollod. *Bibl.* 1.8.6> and *Dia*[4], 16d
Lycophron[1], son of Periander and *Melissa*[2] <Herod. 3.50.3>, *60d*
Lycophron[2], son of Mastor <Hom. *Il.* XV.430-38>, *
Lycorias, daughter of Nereus and *Doris*[1] <Hyg. *Fab.* pref.>, *65a*
Lycorus, son of Apollo and *Corycia* <Paus. 10.6.3>, 11a
Lycotherses [King of Illyria], husband of *Agave*[1] <Hyg. *Fab.* 240>, 55d
Lyctius, father of *Itone* <Diod. Sic. 4.60.3>, 54c
Lycurgus[1] [King of Nemea], son of Pheres[1] <Apollod. *Bibl.* 1.9. 14> and *Periclymene*, 29d
— and *Eurydice*[3] <Apollod. *Bibl.* 1.9.14>, (29d)
Lycurgus[2], son of Heracles[1] and *Toxicrate* <Apollod. *Bibl.* 2.7. 8>, 50d
Lycurgus[3], son of Pronax <Apollod. *Bibl.* 1.9.13>, 31d
Lycurgus[4] [King of Tegea in Arcadia], son of Aleus and *Neaera*[2] <Apollod. *Bibl.* 3.9.1>, 64c
— and *Cleophyle* <Apollod. *Bibl.* 3.8.2>, (64c)
Lycurgus[5], son of Boreas[1] <Diod. Sic. 5.50.2>, 12b
Lycurgus[6] [King of Edonians], son of Dryas[4] <Hom. *Il.* VI. 130>, *
Lycurgus[7], law-giver in the reign of Agesilaus <Paus. 3.2.4>, *
Lycurgus[8], killed by Oenomaus[1] <Paus. 6.21.10>, *
Lycus[1] [King of Boeotia and Thebes], son of Hyrieus and *Clonia*[1] <Apollod. *Bibl.* 3.10.1>, 35b
alternate parentage:
Chthonius[1] <Apollod. *Bibl.* 3.5.5>
— and *Antiope*[1] <Hyg. *Fab.* 7>, 66d
— and *Dirce* <Eur. *Her.* 7-8>, (35b)
Lycus[2], son of Lycus[1] <Eur. *Her.* 26-31> and *Dirce*, 35b
Lycus[3] [one of the Telchines], son of Pontus and *Gaea* <Tzetz. *Chil.* 12.836>, 2b
alternate parentage:
Tartarus and *Nemesis* <Bacch. frg. 52, Snell & Maehler>
Thalatta <Diod. Sic. 5.55.1>
Lycus[4], son of Pandion II and *Pylia* <Apollod. *Bibl.* 3.15.5>, 50d
Lycus[5] [King of the Mariandyni], son of Dascylus[1] <Ap. Rhod. *Arg.* 2.776>, 41a
Lycus[6] [centaur], offspring of Centaurus and a Magnesian Mare <Pind. *Pyth.* 2.50; named as centaur, Ovid *Met.* 12.331>, 69d

alternate parentage:
Ixion and *Nephele*[1] <Diod. Sic. 4.69.5>

Lycus[7], son of Poseidon and *Celaeno*[1] <Hellan. in *F. Gr. H.* 4 F 19>, 8b, *40b*
alternate parentage:
Prometheus[1] and *Celaeno*[1] <Tzetz. on Lyc. 132>

Lycus[8], son of Ares <Hyg. *Fab.* 159>, 7c

Lycus[9], son of Aegyptus[1] <Apollod. *Bibl.* 2.1.5>, 57c
— and *Agave*[2] <Apollod. *Bibl.* 2.1.5>, (57d)

Lycus[10] — see Ascalaphus[1] (alternate version)

Lycus[11] [King of Lycia], father of *Callirhoe*[3] <Plut. *Gr. and Rom. Par. Stor.* 23>, 17d

Lycus[12] [satyr], son of Hermes and *Iphthime*[2] <Non. *Dion.* 14. 112-14>, *17a*

Lycus[13] — see (Telchines) (alternate version)

Lycus[14], son of Aretus[1] and *Laobia* <Non. *Dion.* 250-56>, *

Lycus[15], one of the lost comrades of Aeneas <Virg. *Aen.* 1. 221>, *

Lycus[16], a defender of Thebes <Stat. *Theb.* 9.106-07>, *

Lycus[17], comrade of Diomedes[1] <Ovid *Met.* 14.494>, *

Lycus[18], killed by Turnus <Virg. *Aen.* 9.544-59>, *

Lydus [King of Maconia], son of Atys[1] <Herod. 1.7> and *Callithea*, 51b

Lygaeus, father of *Polycaste*[2] <Strab. 10.2.24>, 47d

Lyncaeus, son of Heracles[1] and *Tiphyse* <Apollod. *Bibl.* 2.7.8>, 50d

Lynceus[1] [Argonaut], son of Aphareus[1] <Pind. *Nem.* 10.65> and *Arene* <Apollod. *Bibl.* 3.10.3>, 25d

Lynceus[2] [King of Argos], son of Aegyptus[1] and *Argyphia* <Apollod. *Bibl.* 2.1.5>, 57c
— and *Hyperm(n)estra*[1] <Apollod. *Bibl.* 2.1.5>, (57c)

Lynceus[3] [King of Thrace], husband of *Laethusa* <Hyg. *Fab.* 45>, *

Lynceus[4], killed by Turnus <Virg. *Aen.* 9.768>, *

Lynceus[5], one of the dogs of Actaeon <Hyg. *Fab.* 181>, *

Lyrcus[1], son of Phoroneus <Parth. *Love Stor.* 1.1> and *Teledice*, 61a
— and *Hilebie* <Parth. *Love Stor.* 1.1>, 68a
— and *Molpadia*[1] <Parth. *Love Stor.* 1.3>, 56d

Lyrcus[2], son of Abas[1] <Paus. 2.25.5>, 57d

Lyrus, son of Anchises and *Aphrodite* <Apollod. *Bibl.* 3.12.2>, 41d

Lyse, daughter of Thespius <Apollod. *Bibl.* 2.7.8> and *Megamede* <Apollod. *Bibl.* 2.4.10>, 50c
— and Heracles[1] <Apollod. *Bibl.* 2.7.8>, (50c)

Lysianassa[1], daughter of Epaphus[1] <Apollod. *Bibl.* 2.5.11> and *Memphis*[1], 55a
— and Poseidon <Apollod. *Bibl.* 2.5.11>, 8d

Lysianassa[2], daughter of Polybus[1] <Paus. 2.6.3>, 49c
— and Talaus <Paus. 2.6.3>, 30d

Lysianassa[3], daughter of Nereus and *Doris*[1] <Hes. *Theog.* 258>, *65a*

Lyside, daughter of Coronus[3] <Steph. Byz. "Philaidai">, 8b
— and Ajax[1] <Steph. Byz. "Philaidai">, 23c, 40a

Lysidice[1], daughter of Pelops[1] <*Cat. Wom., Frag. Hes.* frg. 193, Merk. & West> and *Hippodameia*[1] <Plut. *Thes.* 7.1>, *38a*
— and Electryon[1] <*Cat. Wom., Frag. Hes.* frg. 193, Merk. & West>, 59d
— and Mestor[1] <Apollod. *Bibl.* 2.4.5>, 58d

Lysidice[2], daughter of Thespius <Apollod. *Bibl.* 2.7.8> and *Megamede* <Apollod. *Bibl.* 2.4.10>, 50d
— and Heracles[1] <Apollod. *Bibl.* 2.7.8>, (50d)

Lysidice[3] — see *Alcmene*

Lysimache[1], daughter of Abas[4] <Apollod. *Bibl.* 1.9.13>, 31d
alternate parentage:
Polybus[1] <Schol. Pind. *Nem.* 9.30>
— and Talaus <Apollod. *Bibl.* 1.9.13>, 30d

Lysimache[2], daughter of Priam[1] <Apollod. *Bibl.* 3.12.5>, 44c

Lysinomus, son of Electryon[1] and *Anaxo*[1] <Apollod. *Bibl.* 2.4. 5>, 59d

Lysippe[1], daughter of Proetus[1] <*Cat. Wom., Frag. Hes.* frg. 129, Merk. & West> and *Stheneboea* <Apollod. *Bibl.* 2.2.2>, 57d
— and Bias[1] <Apollod. *Bibl.* 2.2.2>, 30c

Lysippe[2], daughter of Thespius <Apollod. *Bibl.* 2.7.8> and *Megamede* <Apollod. *Bibl.* 2.4.10>, 50d
— and Heracles[1] <Apollod. *Bibl.* 2.7.8>, (50d)

Lysippe[3] — see *Cydippe*[1]

Lysippe[4] — see *Leucippe*[3]

Lysippe[5] [Amazon], mother of Tanais[2] <Ps.-Plut. *De Fluv.* 14>, *

Lysippe[6], mother of Lampus[3] <Paus. 5.2.4>, *

Lysithous, son of Priam[1] <Apollod. *Bibl.* 3.12.5>, 44c

Lyssa [madness] [abstraction], offspring of *Nyx* (and the blood of Uranus) <Eur. *Her.* 844>, 1b

Macar(eus)[1], son of Aeolus[1] <*Hom. Hymn* 3 (to Delian Apollo), 38-39> and *Enarete* <Hyg. *Fab.* 238>, 34a
— and *Canace* <Ovid *Her.* 11>, (34a)

Macar(eus)[2], son of Lycaon[1] <Apollod. *Bibl.* 3.8.1>, 64b

Macar(eus)[3], father of *Arisbe*[3] <Eust. on Hom. *Il.* 894>, 43c

Macar(eus)[4] [King of Lesbos], son of Helios and *Rhode*[1] <Diod. Sic. 5.56.5>, 14a
alternate parentage:
Crinacus <Diod. Sic. 5.81.4>

Macar(eus)[5] — see Mermerus[2]

Macar(eus)[6], companion of Odysseus <Ovid *Met.* 14.159 (he is called Ulysses)>, *

Macaria, daughter of Heracles[1] and *Deianeira*[1] <Paus. 1.32.5>, 60a

Macednus, son of Lycaon[1] <Apollod. *Bibl.* 3.8.1>, 64b

Macedon, son of Zeus and *Thyia*[1] <*Cat. Wom., Frag. Hes.* frg. 7, Merk. & West>, 6c, *15a*
alternate parentage:
Magnes[3] and *Cleio* <Tzetz. on Lyc. 831>
Osiris <Diod. Sic. 1.18.1>
— and *Oreithyia*[2] <Steph. Byz. "Europus">, 50a

Macello, daughter of Damon; sister of *Dexithea* <Nicand. in Schol. on Ovid *Ibis* 475>, 54d

Machai [quarrels] [abstraction], offspring of *Eris* <Hes. *Theog.* 228>, *1a*

Machaon, son of Asclepius <Hom. *Il.* II.731-32; IV.194> and *Epeione* <Schol. on Pind. *Pyth.* 3.14>, 19c
alternate parentage:
Asclepius and *Arsinoe*[7] <Schol. on Hom. *Il.* IV.195>
Asclepius and *Coronis*[1] <Hyg. *Fab.* 97>
Asclepius and *Lampetia* <Hermip. frg. 1, West>
Asclepius and *Xanthe*[1] <*Cat. Wom., Frag. Hes.* frg. 53, Merk. & West>
— and *Anticleia*[3] <Paus. 4.30.3>, 65b

Machionassa — see *Europe*[2]

Macistus, son of Athamas[1] and *Nephele*[2] <Steph. Byz. "Macistus" (inferred because he is called brother of Phrixus)>, 26a

Macris, daughter of Aristaeus[1] <Ap. Rhod. *Arg.* 4.1130> and *Autonoe*[1], 69a

Maeandrus [river], son of Oceanus and *Tethys* <Hes. *Theog.* 339>, 67b

Maenalus[1], son of Lycaon[1] <Apollod. *Bibl.* 3.8.1>, 64c

Maenalus[2] — see *Atalanta*[1] (alternate version)

Maenalus[3], killed by Odysseus <Quint. Smyr. 3.299>, *

Maeon[1], son of Haemon[1] <Hom. *Il.* IV.394> and *Antigone*[1] <Schol. on Soph. *Ant.* 1350>, 55d, *55c*

Maeon[2], father of Agelaus[6] <Quint. Smyr. 3.229>, *

Maeon[3], killed by Aeneas <Virg. *Aen.* 10.336>, *
Maera[1], daughter of Proetus[3] <Paus. 10.30.2>, 19c
alternate parentage:
Proetus[1] and *Stheneboea* <Schol. on Hom. *Od.* 11.326 (mother is called *Anteia*)>
— and Zeus <Plut. *Gr. and Rom. Par. Stor.* 36>, 5c
Maera[2], daughter of Atlas <Paus. 8.12.7> and *Pleione*, 45b
— and Tegeates <Paus. 8.48.6>, 63b
Maera[3], daughter of Nereus <Hom. *Il.* XVIII.46> and *Doris*[1], *65a*
Maera[4], daughter of Erasinus <Ant. Lib. *Met.* 40>, 53b
Maera[5], dog of Icarius[1] <Hyg. *Poet. Astr.* 2.4>, *
Maera[6], priestess of *Aphrodite* <Stat. *Theb.* 8.477>, *
Magnes[1], son of Zeus and *Thyia*[1] <*Cat. Wom., Frag. Hes.* frg. 7, Merk. & West>, 6c, *15a*, *15c*
— and [a Naiad] <Apollod. *Bibl.* 1.9.6>, (15c)
Magnes[2], son of Aeolus[1] and *Enarete* <Apollod. *Bibl.* 1.7.3>, 21b
alternate parentage:
Aeolus[1] and *Philodice*[2] <Schol. on Eur. *Phoen. Maid.* 1760>
— and *Meliboea*[3] <Eust. on Hom. *Il.* 338>, (21b)
— and *Philodice*[2] <Schol. on Eur. *Phoen. Maid.* 1760>, (21c)
Magnes[3], son of Argus[4] and *Perimele*[3] <Ant. Lib. *Met.* 23.1>, 26c, *29c*
Magnes[4], suitor of *Penelope*[1] (from Zacynthos) <Apollod. *Epit.* 7.29>, *
[Magnesian Mares], mates of Centaurus <Pind. *Pyth.* 2.48-49>, 69c
Maia, daughter of Atlas <*Cat. Wom., Frag. Hes.* frg. 169, Merk. & West> and *Pleione* <Apollod. *Bibl.* 3.10.1>, 46a
alternate parentage:
Hippo[3] <Callim. frg. 693, Pfeiffer>
— and Zeus <Hes. *Theog.* 938>, 5c
[Maiden] — see *Persephone*[1]
Malache — see *Lamache*
Malis, paramour of Heracles[1] <Hellan. in *F.H.G.* 1.58 frg. 102, Müller>, 60d
Malus, father of *Cleophema* <Isyl. *Lyr.* 3.43>, 19d
— and *Erato*[6] <Isyl. *Lyr.* 3.43>, (19d)
Manes [King of Paeonia], son of Zeus and *Gaea* <Dion. Hal. *Rom. Ant.* 1.27.1>, 5c, *2b*
— and *Callirhoe*[2] <Dion. Hal. *Rom. Ant.* 1.27.1> 51b
Mantineus[1], father of *Aglaia*[3] <Apollod. *Bibl.* 2.2.1>, 57b
Mantineus[2], son of Lycaon[1] <Apollod. *Bibl.* 3.8.1>, 64c
Mantius, son of Melampus[1] <Hom. *Od.* 15.242> and *Iphianassa*[1], 32c
Manto[1] (*Daphne*[2]), daughter of Teiresias <Apollod. *Bibl.* 3.7.4>, 32d
— and Alcmaeon[1] <Apollod. *Bibl.* 3.7.7>, (32d)
— and Rhacius <Paus. 7.3.1>, (32d)
Manto[2], daughter of Polyidus[1] <Paus. 1.43.5> and *Eurydameia*, 31d, *63d*
Manto[3], daughter of Melampus[1] <Diod. Sic. 4.68.4-5> and *Iphianassa*[1], 32c
alternate parentage:
Melampus[1] and *Iphianeira*[2] <Diod. Sic. 4.68.4-5>
Manto[4], mother of Ocnus <Virg. *Aen.* 10.198-99>, *
Maraphius, son of Menelaus and *Helen*[1] <Schol. on Hom. *Il.* I. 147 ff.>, 37b
Marathon[1], son of Epopeus[1] <Paus. 2.1.1> and *Antiope*[1], 34d
Marathon[2], son of Deucalion[1] and *Pyrrha*[1] <Hec. in *F. Gr. H.* 1 F 13>, 16b
[Mares of Erichthonius[2]], mates of Boreas[1] <Hom. *Il.* XX.220-28>, 12b
Mariandynus, son of Phineus[1] and *Idaea*[2] <Schol. on Ap. Rhod. *Arg.* 140>, *42a*
Marica — see Latinus[1] (alternate version)
Maron[1], son of Euanthes[1] <Hom. *Od.* 9.197>, 56c
alternate parentage:
Dionysus <Eur. *Cycl.* 141-44>
Maron[2] [satyr], son of Silenus <Non. *Dion.* 14.99> and [ash tree nymph], 46c
Marpessa[1] (*Alcyone*[5]) (*Halcyone*[5]), daughter of Euenus[1] <Hom. *Il.* IX.557> and *Alcippe*[2], 15c
— and Apollo <Hom. *Il.* IX.557>, 11d
— and Idas[1] <Hom. *Il.* IX.557>, 25d
Marpessa[2], betrothed to Phylleus <Stat. *Theb.* 3.172-73>, *
[Marpessan Sibyl] — see *Herophile*[5]
Marse, daughter of Thespius <Apollod. *Bibl.* 2.7.8> and *Megamede* <Apollod. *Bibl.* 2.4.10>, 50d
— and Heracles[1] <Apollod. *Bibl.* 2.7.8>, (50d)
Marsyas, son of Oeagrus <Hyg. *Fab.* 165> and *Calliope*, *6a*
alternate parentage:
Hyagnis <Non. *Dion.* 1.4.2>
Olympus[1] <Apollod. *Bibl.* 1.4.2>
Mecionice — see Euphemus[1] (alternate version)
Mecisteus[1] [one of the Seven Against Thebes (per Apollod. *Bibl.* 3.6.3)], son of Talaus <Hom. *Il.* II.566> and *Lysimache*[1] <Apollod. *Bibl.* 1.9.13>, 31c
Mecisteus[2], son of Lycaon[1] <Apollod. *Bibl.* 3.8.1>, 64c
Mecisteus[3], father of Epistrophus and Odius <Apollod. *Epit.* 3.35>, *
Mecisteus[4], son of Echius <Hom. *Il.* VIII.333>, *
Mecisteus[5], suitor of *Penelope*[1] (from Dulichium) <Apollod. *Epit.* 7.27>, *
Meda[1], wife of Idomeneus[2] <Lyc. 1214-25>, 54c
— and Leucus[1] <Apollod. *Epit.* 6.10>, 31c
Meda[2] — see *Mideia*[3]
Mede — see *Periboea*[5]
Medea (*Aeetias*) (*Aeetine*) (*Aeetis*) (*Angitia*), daughter of Aeetes and *Eidyia* <Hes. *Theog.* 961>, 14c
alternate parentage:
Aeetes and *Hecate* <Diod. Sic. 4.45.3>
— and Aegeus[1] <Eur. *Medea* 1385>, 51a
— and Jason <Hes. *Theog.* 958-61, 992-1002>, 33d
Medeius (Medus[1]) (Polyxenus[2]), son of Jason and *Medea* <Hes. *Theog.* 1001>, 33c
alternate parentage:
Aegeus[1] and *Medea* <Apollod. *Bibl.* 1.9.28>
Medesicaste[1], daughter of Laomedon[1] <Apollod. *Epit.* 7.15c> and *Strym(n)o*, 42d
Medesicaste[2], daughter of Priam[1] <Hom. *Il.* XIII.173>, 44c
— and Imbrius <Hom. *Il.* XIII.170-73>, (44c)
Medon[1], son of Pylades and *Electra*[3] <Paus. 2.16.5>, 23c, *36c*
Medon[2] [centaur], offspring of Centaurus and a Magnesian Mare <Pind. *Pyth.* 2.50; named as centaur, Ovid *Met.* 12.302>, 69d
alternate parentage:
Ixion and *Nephele*[1] <Diod. Sic. 4.69.5>
Medon[3], son of Oileus[1] and *Rhene*[1] <Hom. *Il.* II.727-28>, 15c
alternate parentage:
Oileus[1] and *Alcimache* <Schol. on Hom. *Il.* XIII.694>
Medon[4], son of Ceisus <Paus. 2.19.2>, 60d
Medon[5] [one of the Epigoni], son of Eteoclus <Schol. (Townley) on Hom. *Il.* IV.406>, 58c
Medon[6], son of Antenor[1] <Virg. *Aen.* 6.482>, *45d*
Medon[7] [King of Athens], son of Codrus[1] <Paus. 7.2.1>, 27d
Medon[8], sailor turned into a dolphin <Ovid *Met.* 3.670-91>, *
Medon[9], herald who warned *Penelope* <Hom. *Od.* 4.678>, *
Medon[10], husband of *Iphianassa*[5] <Quint. Smyr. 8.295-96>, *
Medon[11], suitor of *Penelope*[1] (from Dulichium) <Apollod. *Epit.* 7.27>, *
Medon[12], killed by the Argonauts <Val. Flac. 3.118>, *
Medus[1] — see Medeius

Medus[2], son of Dionysus and *Alphesiboea*[3] <Ps.-Plut. *De Fluv.* 24.1>, 56c
Medusa[1] [one of the Gorgons], daughter of Phorcus[1] and *Ceto*[1] <Hes. *Theog.* 276>, 2b
alternate parentage:
Gorgon (son of Typhon and *Echidna*) and *Ceto*[1] <Hyg. *Fab.* pref.>
— and Poseidon <Hes. *Theog.* 278>, 8d
Medusa[2], daughter of Priam[1] <Apollod. *Bibl.* 3.12.5>, 44c
Medusa[3] (*Astymedusa*), daughter of Sthenelus[1] and *Nicippe*[1] <Apollod. *Bibl.* 2.4.5>, 58d
— and Oedipus <Pher. in *F. Gr. H.* 3 F 95>, 55c
Medusa[4], daughter of Pelias[1] <*Cat. Wom., Frag. Hes.* frg. 37, Merk. & West> and *Anaxibia*[2], 28d
Megaera [one of the Furies], daughter of *Gaea* (and the blood of Uranus) <Hes. *Theog.* 185; named, Apollod. *Bibl.* 1.4. 4>, 4b
alternate parentage:
Nyx <Aesch. *Eum.* 416>
Megalesius [one of the Telchines], son of Pontus and *Gaea* <Tzetz. *Chil.* 12.836>, 2b
alternate parentage:
Tartarus and *Nemesis* <Bacch. frg. 52, Snell & Maehler>
Thalatta, Diod. Sic. 5.55.1>
Megamede, daughter of Arnaeus[1] <Apollod. *Bibl.* 2.4.10>, 50a
— and Thespius <Apollod. *Bibl.* 2.4.10>, (50a)
Meganeira[1], daughter of Croco(n) <Apollod. *Bibl.* 3.9.1> and *Saesara*, 46d
— and Arcas[1] <Apollod. *Bibl.* 3.9.1>, 62d
Meganeira[2] — see *Metaneira*
Meganeira[3], mother of Alcyoneus[3] <Ant. Lib. *Met.* 8>, *
Megapenthes[1], son of Menelaus <Hom. *Od.* 4.11> and *Pieris* <Apollod. *Bibl.* 3.11.1>, 37c
alternate parentage:
Menelaus and *Tereis* <Acus. in Apollod. *Bibl.* 3.11.1>
— and an unnamed daughter of Alector[2] <Hom. *Od.* 4.14>, (37c)
Megapenthes[2] [King of Argos], son of Proetus[1] and *Stheneboea* <Apollod. *Bibl.* 2.2.2>, 58c
Megara, daughter of Creon[2] <Hom. *Od.* 11.268-69> and *Eurydice*[9], 55d
— and Heracles[1] <Eur. *Her.* 69>, 60d
— and Iola(u)s <Apollod. *Bibl.* 2.6.1>, 40a, 59c
— and Iphicles <Hom. *Od.* 11.268>, 55d
Megareus[1] [King of Megara], son of Poseidon <Paus. 1.39.5> and *Oenope* <Hyg. *Fab.* 157>, 9b
alternate parentage:
Hippomenes[1] <Apollod. *Bibl.* 3.15.8>
Onchestus[1] <Plut. *Gr. Quest.* 295a>
— and *Iphinoe*[3] <Paus. 1.39.5>, 34d, 50d
— and *Merope*[8] <Hyg. *Fab.* 185>, (9b)
Megareus[2], son of Creon[2] <Aech. *Sev.* 474> and *Eurydice*[9], 55d
alternate parentage:
Aegeus[1] <Steph. Byz. "Megara">
Megareus[3], father of *Gorge*[3] <*Etym. Magn.* "Eschatiotis," 384. 39-40>, 34d
Megarus[1], son of Zeus and [a Sithnidian nymph] <Paus. 1.40.1>, 6d
Megarus[2], son of Apollo <Steph. Byz. "Megara">, 11d
Megassares, father of *Pharnace* <Apollod. *Bibl.* 3.14.3>, 46c
Meges[1] [King of Dulichium], son of Phyleus[1] <Hom. *Il.* II.627-28> and *Timandra*[1], 63d
Meges[2], son of Dymas[1] <Quint. Smyr. 7.606-07> and *Telecleia*, 17d
Meges[3], father of Polymnius <Quint. Smyr. 2.292>, *
Meges[4], a defender of Thebes <Stat. *Theb.* 10.19>, *
Melaena, daughter of Cephis(s)us <Paus. 10.6.2> and *Leiriope*, 49b
— and Apollo <Paus. 10.6.2>, 11d
Melaeneus, son of Lycaon[1] <Apollod. *Bibl.* 3.8.1>, 64c
Melampus[1] [King of Argos], son of Amythaon[1] and *Idomene* <Apollod. *Bibl.* 1.9.11>, 32c
alternate parentage:
Amythaon[1] and *Aglaia*[5] <Diod. Sic. 4.68.3>
Rhodope[2] <Schol. Theo. 3.43>
— and *Iphianassa*[1] <Pher. in *F. Gr. H.* 3 F 114>, 57d
— and *Iphianeira*[2] <Diod. Sic. 4.68.4>, 58d
Melampus[2], father of Cisseus[3] and Gyas <Virg. *Aen.* 10.320-24>, *
Melampus[3] [one of the dogs of Actaeon] <Ovid *Met.* 3.202>, *
Melampyges — see Heracles[1]
Melancheates[1] [centaur], offspring Centaurus and a Magnesian Mare <Pind. *Pyth.* 2.50; named as centaur, Diod. Sic. 4. 12.7>, 69c
alternate parentage:
Ixion and *Nephele*[1] <Diod. Sic. 4.69.5>
Melancheates[2] [one of the dogs of Actaeon] <Hyg. *Fab.* 181>, *
Melaneus[1] [centaur], offspring of Centaurus and a Magnesian Mare <Pind. *Pyth.* 2.50; named as centaur, Ovid *Met.* 12.306>, 69c
alternate parentage:
Ixion and *Nephele*[1] <Diod. Sic. 4.69.5>
Melaneus[2] [King of Oechalia], son of Apollo <Paus. 4.2.2>, 11d
— and *Oechalia* <Paus. 4.2.3>, (11d)
— and *Stratonice*[2] <*Cat. Wom., Frag. Hes.* frg. 26.9-25, Merk. & West>, 15d
Melaneus[3], son of Aretus[1] and *Laobia* <Non. *Dion.* 26.250-56>, *
Melaneus[4], father of Autonous <Ant. Lib. *Met.* 7>, *
Melaneus[5], father of Amphimedon <Hom. *Od.* 24.1045>, *
Melaneus[6], son of Alexinomous <Quint. Smyr. 8.77>, *
Melaneus[7], an Indian who warned Astraeis <Non. *Dion.* 14. 302>, *
Melaneus[8] [one of the dogs of Actaeon] <Ovid *Met.* 3.224>, *
Melanion, son of Amphidamas[1] <Apollod. *Bibl.* 3.9.2>, 63d
— *Atalanta*[1] <Apollod. *Bibl.* 3.9.2>, 20c, 64d
Melanippe[1] — see *Hippe*[1]
Melanippe[2] — see *Arne*
Melanippe[3], daughter of Oeneus[1] and *Althaea* <Ant. Lib. *Met.* 2. 1>, 17c
Melanippe[4] (*Antiope*[8]) [Amazon], daughter of Ares <Ap. Rhod. *Arg.* 2.996> and *Otrere*, 7c
Melanippe[5], daughter of Aeolus[1] and *Hippe*[1] <Greg. Cor. *Rhetoric*, vol. 7, p. 1313>, 18a
— and Hippotes[4] <Diod. Sic. 4.67.3>, 18a
Melanippe[6] [nymph], paramour of Itonus[1] <Paus. 9.1.1>, 16a
Melanippus[1], son of Astacus <Apollod. *Bibl.* 3.6.8>, 9b
Melanippus[2], son of Ares and *Triteia* <Paus. 7.22.5>, 7c, *63b*
Melanippus[3], son of Hicetaon[1] <Hom. *Il.* XV.546-47>, 42d
Melanippus[4], son of Priam[1] <Apollod. *Bibl.* 3.12.5>, 44c
Melanippus[5], son of Theseus and *Perigune* <Plut. *Thes.* 8.3>, 51d
Melanippus[6], son of Agrius[1] <Apollod. *Bibl.* 1.8.6> and *Dia*[4], 16d
Melanippus[7], paramour of *Comaetho*[3] <Paus. 7.19.2>, *
Melanippus[8], killed by Teucer[2] <Hom. *Il.* VIII.273-77>, *
Melanippus[9], killed by Patroclus[1] <Hom. *Il.* XVI.593-96>, *
Melantheia[1] — see *Melantho*[1]
Melantheia[2], daughter of Alpheius <Plut. *Gr. Quest.* 19> and *Telegone*, 65b
— and Poseidon <Plut. *Gr. Quest.* 19>, 8c
Melantho[1] (*Melantheia*[1]), daugher of Deucalion[1] <Tzetz. on Lyc. 208> and *Pyrrha*[1], 17a
— and Hyamus <Schol. on Eur. 1097>, (17a)
— and Poseidon <Ovid *Met.* 6.117>, 8d

Melantho[2], wife of Criasus[1] <Schol. on Eur. *Or.* 932>, 61b
Melantho[3], daughter of Dolius <Hom. *Od.* 18.321-22>, *
Melanthus[1] — see Thymbraeus[1]
Melanthus[2] [King of Athens], son of Andropompus[1] <Paus. 2.18.8>, 27d
Melanthus[3], sailor turned into a dolphin <Ovid *Met.* 3.615>, *
Melanthus[4], killed by Telamon <Val. Flac. 3.203>, *
Melas[1], son of Poseidon <Ion in Paus. 7.4.8>, 9c
Melas[2], son of Heracles[1] and *Omphale* <Schol. on Hom. *Il.* XVIII.219>, 60c
Melas[3], son of Portheus[1] <Hom. *Il.* XIV.115-17> and *Euryte*[1] <Apollod. *Bibl.* 1.7.10>, 16d
Melas[4], son of Licymnius <Apollod. *Bibl.* 2.7.8> and *Perimede*[2], 59c
Melas[5] (Catis), son of Phrixus[1] and *Chalciope*[1] <Apollod. *Bibl.* 1.9.1>, 26c
— and *Eurycleia*[1] <Pher. in *F.H.G.* 1.86 frg. 55, Müller>, 26a
Melas[6], son of Oenopion[1] <Paus. 7.4.6> and *Helice*[4], 56c
Melas[7], son of Antasus <Paus. 5.18.7>, *
Melas[8], son of Ops <Paus. 8.28.4>, *
Melas[9], sailor turned into a dolphin <Hyg. *Fab.* 134>, *
Meleager [Argonaut], son of Oeneus[1] and *Althaea* <Hom. *Il.* IX. 543-55>, 17c
alternate parentage:
Ares and *Althaea* <Apollod. *Bibl.* 1.8.2>
— and Ares <*Cat. Wom., Frag. Hes.* frg. 25, Merk. & West>, 7a
— and *Atalanta*[1] <Hyg. *Fab.* 99>, 20c, 64d
— and *Cleopatra*[2] <Hom. *Il.* IX.556-58>, 25d
Melete [practice] [one of the Boeotian Muses], daughter of Uranus <Paus. 9.29.2> and *Gaea*, 6b
alternate parentage:
"the second Jupiter" (son of Caelus) <Cic. *De Nat. Deor.* 3.54-55>
Melia[1] (*Melissa*[1]), daughter of Oceanus and *Tethys* <Apollod. *Bibl.* 2.1.1>, 61a
— and Apollo <Paus. 9.10.5>, 11d
— and Inachus <Apollod. *Bibl.* 2.1.1>, 55b
Melia[2], paramour of Poseidon <Ap. Rhod. *Arg.* 2.2-3>, 8d
Melia[3], daughter of Agenor[1] and *Damno* <Pher. in *F. Gr. H.* 3 F 21>, 59c
(Meliades) [ash tree nymphs], daughters of *Gaea* (and the blood of Uranus) <Hes. *Theog.* 187>, 4b
Meliboea[1], daughter of Oceanus and *Tethys* <Hes. *Theog.* 354>, 61a
— and Pelasgus[1] <Apollod. *Bibl.* 3.8.1>, 62b
Meliboea[2] (*Chloris*[1]), daughter of Amphion[1] and *Niobe*[1] <Teles. in Apollod. *Bibl.* 3.5.6>, 66c
Meliboea[3], wife of Magnes[2] <Eust. on Hom. *Il.* 338>, 21b
Meliboea[4], wife of Alexis <Serv. on Virg. *Aen.* 1.720>, *
Melicertes (Palaemon[1]) [ports], son of Athamas[1] and *Ino* <Apollod. *Bibl.* 1.9.1>, 26b
— and Glaucus[3] <Athen. 7.297 (citing Hedylus)>, 62a
Meline, daughter of Thespius <Apollod. *Bibl.* 2.7.8> and *Megamede* <Apollod. *Bibl.* 2.4.10>, 50d
— and Heracles[1] <Apollod. *Bibl.* 2.7.8>, (50d)
Melinoe (*Chthonia*[3]), daughter of Zeus and *Persephone*[1] <Orph. *Hymns* 71>, 6c
Melissa[1] — see *Melia*[1]
Melissa[2], daughter of Procles[1] <Paus. 2.28.4> and *Lathria*, 60d
— and Periander <Paus. 2.28.4>, (60d)
Melissa[3] — see *Ida*[2]
Melissa[4], daughter of Epidamnus <Steph. Byz. "Dyrrachium">, 8c
— and Poseidon <Steph. Byz. "Dyrrachium">, (8c)
Melisseus[1], son of Socus and *Combe*[1] <Non. *Dion.* 13.143>, *66c*
alternate parentage:
Apollo and *Rhetia* <Pher. in *F. Gr. H.* 3 F 48 (unnamed)>
Melisseus[2] [King of Crete], father of *Adrastia* and *Ida*[2] <Apollod. *Bibl.* 1.1.7>, *
Melisseus[3] [King in Caria] <Diod. Sic. 5.61.1>, *
Melite[1], daughter of Nereus and *Doris*[1] <Hes. *Theog.* 247>, *65a*
Melite[2], daughter of Aegaeus <Ap. Rhod. *Arg.* 4.542>, 60c
— and Heracles[1] <Ap. Rhod. *Arg.* 4.452>, (60c)
Melite[3] — see *Meta*
Melite[4], daughter of Oceanus and *Tethys* <*Hom. Hymn* 2 (to *Demeter*), 417>, 61b
Melite[5], daughter of Erasinus <Ant. Lib. *Met.* 40>, 53b
Melite[6], daughter of Myrmex <*Cat. Wom., Frag. Hes.* frg. 225, Merk. & West>, *
Meliteus, son of Zeus and *Othreis* <Ant. Lib. *Met.* 23.1>, 6c
Melobosis, daughter of Oceanus and *Tethys* <Hes. *Theog.* 354>, 61b
Melphis, wife of Molus[1] <Hyg. *Fab.* 97>, 54c
Melpomene [tragedy] [one of the Muses], daughter of Zeus and *Mnemosyne* <Hes. *Theog.* 77>, 6b
— and Achelous <Apollod. *Bibl.* 1.3.4>, 65b
Melus, son of Rhacius and *Manto*[1] <Steph. Byz. "Malloeis">, *32d*
Memnon [King of Ethiopia], son of Tithonus and *Eos* <Hes. *Theog.* 984>, 43c
Memphis[1] (*Cassiopeia*[2]), daughter of Nilus <Apollod. *Bibl.* 2.1.4 (she is called daughter of the Nile)>, 68b
— and Epaphus[1] <Apollod. *Bibl.* 2.1.4>, 55b
Memphis[2], paramour of Danaus[1] <Apollod. *Bibl.* 2.1.5>, 57b, 57c
Menalces[1] (Metalces), son of Aegyptus[1] and *Gorgo*[1] <Apollod. *Bibl.* 2.1.5>, 57c
— and *Adite* <Apollod. *Bibl.* 2.1.5>, (57c)
Menalces[2], son of Medon[10] <Quint. Smyr. 8.294>, *
Menalippus, son of Acastus <Dict. Cret. 6.8> and *Hippolyte*[2], 28c
Mendeis, paramour of Sithon <Con. *Narr.* 10>, 7d
Mene — see *Selene*
Menelaus [King of Sparta], son of Atreus <Hom. *Il.* IV.115> and *Aerope*[1] <Eur. *Helen* 391-92>, 37a, 37c
alternate parentage:
Pleisthenes[1] and *Cleola* <*Cat. Wom., Frag. Hes.* frg. 194, Merk. & West>
Pleisthenes[1] and *Eriphyle* <Schol. on Eur. 4>
Pleisthenes[1] and *Aerope*[1] <Apollod. *Bibl.* 3.2.2>
— and *Cnossia* <Apollod. *Bibl.* 3.11.1>, (37c)
— and *Helen*[1] <Hom. *Od.* 4.10; 15.53-54>, 48d
— and *Pieris* <Apollod. *Bibl.* 3.11.1>, (37c)
Menemachus, son of Aegyptus[1] and [a Phoenician woman] <Apollod. *Bibl.* 2.1.5>, 58c
— and *Nelo* <Apollod. *Bibl.* 2.1.5>, (58c)
M(e)nestheus[1] [King of Athens], son of Peteus <Hom. *Il.* IV. 327>, 49a
M(e)nestheus[2], son of Sperchius <Hom. *Il.* XVI.173-74> and *Polydora*[1] <Apollod. *Bibl.* 3.13.4-5>, 71b, *22d, 24c*
M(e)nestheus[3], son of Clytius[10] <Virg. *Aen.* 10.129>, *
Menestho, daughter of Oceanus and *Tethys* <Hes. *Theog.* 357>, 61b
Meneteis — see *Antianeira*
Menetes, father of *Antianeira* <Ap. Rhod. *Arg.* 1.57>, 46a
Menippe[1] — see *Nicippe*[1]
Menippe[2], daughter of Orion <Ant. Lib. *Met.* 25.1>, 53c
Menippe[3], daughter of Peneius <Dion. Hal. *Rom. Ant.* 1.28.3> and *Creusa*[4], 69a
— and Pelasgus[3] <Dion. Hal. *Rom. Ant.* 1.28.3>, 61d
Menippe[4], daughter of Nereus and *Doris*[1] <Hes. *Theog.* 260>, *65a*
Menippe[5], daughter of Oceanus and *Tethys* <Hyg. *Fab.* pref.>, 61b

Menippe[6], daughter of Thamyris[1] <Tzetz. on *Chil.* 1.12>, 13d
Menippe[7] [Amazon] <Val. Flac. 6.377>, *
Menippis, daughter of Thespius <Apollod. *Bibl.* 2.7.8> and *Megamede* <Apollod. *Bibl.* 2.4.10>, 50d
— and Heracles[1] <Apollod. *Bibl.* 2.7.8>, (50d)
Menodice, daughter of Orion <Hyg. *Fab.* 14>, 53d
— and Theiodamas[1] <Hyg. *Fab.* 14>, 64d
Menoeceus[1], son of Oclasus <Schol. on Eur. *Phoen. Maid.* 942>, 55d
Menoeceus[2], son of Creon[2] <Eur. *Phoen. Maid.* 908-18> and *Eurydice*[9], 55d
Menoeceus[3] — see Heracles[1]
Menoetius[1], son of Iapetus and *Clymene*[1] <Hes. *Theog.* 510>, 16b, *52b*
Menoetius[2] [Argonaut], son of Actor[3] <Hom. *Il.* XVI.14> and *Aegina* <Pind. *Olym.* 9.73>, 22d, *66a*
alternate parentage:
Aeacus <*Cat. Wom., Frag. Hes.* frg. 212(a), Merk. & West>
— and *Sthenele*[1] <Apollod. *Bibl.* 3.13.8>, 28c
Menoetius[3], killed by Eurypylus[1] <Quint. Smyr. 8.111>, *
Menon(es) — see Onnes
Mentha — see *Minthe*
Mentor[1], son of Eurystheus <Apollod. *Bibl.* 2.8.1> and *Antimache*, 58d
Mentor[2], father of Imbrius <Hom. *Il.* XIII.170>, 44c
Mentor[3], son of Heracles[1] and *Asopis*[2] <Apollod. *Bibl.* 2.7.8>, *50c*
Mentor[4], son of Alcimous <Hom. *Od.* 22.234>, *
Meriones[1], son of Molus[1] <Hom. *Il.* X.270> and *Melphis* <Hyg. *Fab.* 97>, 54c
Meriones[2], son of Aeson and *Polymede* <Poly. *Strat.* 6.1 (inferred because he is brother of Jason)>, 33c
Mermerus[1] [centaur], offspring of Centaurus and a Magnesian Mare <Pind. *Pyth.* 2.50; named as centaur <Ovid *Met.* 12.304>, 69c
alternate parentage:
Ixion and *Nephele*[1] <Diod. Sic. 4.69.5>
Mermerus[2] (Macar(eus)[5]), son of Jason and *Medea* <Apollod. *Bibl.* 1.9.28>, 33c
Mermerus[3], son of Pheres[2] <Eust. on Hom. *Od.* 1416.2-3>, 33c
Mermerus[4], killed by Antilochus <Hom. *Il.* XIV.513>, *
Merope[1], daughter of Atlas <*Cat. Wom., Frag. Hes.* frg. 169, Merk. & West> and *Pleione* <Apollod. *Bibl.* 3.10.1>, 47a
— and Sisyphus <Pher. in *F. Gr. H.* 3 F 119>, 18a
Merope[2], daughter of Cypselus[1] <Paus. 4.6.6> and *Herodice*, 62c
— and Cresphontes[1] <Apollod. *Bibl.* 2.8.5>, 60c
— and Polyphontes[1] <Apollod. *Bibl.* 2.8.5>, (62c)
Merope[3] (*Aero*) (*Aerope*[3]) (*Haero*), daughter of Oenopion[1] <Apollod. *Bibl.* 1.4.3> and *Helice*[4] <Parth. *Love Stor.* 20.1>, 56c
— and Orion <Apollod. *Bibl.* 1.4.3>, 53c
Merope[4], daughter of Oceanus and *Tethys* <Hyg. *Fab.* 154>, 61b
— and Clymenus[6] <Hyg. *Fab.* 154>, 14c
Merope[5], daughter of Erechtheus II <Plut. *Thes.* 19.5> and *Praxithea*[2], 49a
— and Eupalamus <Plut. *Thes.* 9.5>, (49a)
Merope[6] — see *Clytie*[3]
Merope[7], daughter of Autolycus[1] <Schol. on Lyc. 344> and *Amphithea*[2], 13a
Merope[8], wife of Megareus[1] <Hyg. *Fab.* 185>, 9b
Merope[9], [one of the Heliades[2]], daughter of Helios and *Clymene*[1] <Ovid *Met.* 2.333-40; named, Hyg. *Fab.* 154>, 14a
alternate parentage:
Helios and *Rhode*[1] <Schol. on Hom. *Od.* 17.208>
Merope[10] (*Periboea*[3]), paramour of Polybus[3] <Soph. *Oed. Tyr.* 990>, *
Merops[1], father of *Epeione* <Schol. on Hom. *Il.* IV.195>, 19d
Merops[2] [King of Ethiopians], husband of *Clymene*[1] <Ovid *Met.* 1.764; 11.184>, 52b
Merops[3] [King of Percote], father of Adrastus[3] and Amphius[1] <Hom. *Il.* II.828-30>, *Arisbe*[1] <Apollod. *Bibl.* 3.12.5>, and *Cleite*[1] <Ap. Rhod. *Arg.*>, 44c
Merops[4] [King of Miletus], father of Pandareus[1] <Ant. Lib. *Met.* 36.2>, 66d
Merops[5] [King of Cos], father of Eumelus[3] <Ant. Lib. *Met.* 15.1> and *Cos* <Hyg. *Poet. Astr.* 2.16>, *
Mesembria [one of the hours], daughter of Zeus and *Themis*[1] <Hyg. *Fab.* 183>, 6d
Mesolas, husband of *Ambracia*[2] <Steph. Byz. "Dexamenae">, 14c
Messapus [King of Etruria], son of Poseidon <Serv. on Virg. *Aen.* 7.691>, 9d
Messene, daughter of Triop(a)s[2] <Paus. 4.1.1> and *Sois*, 61c
— and Polycaon[1] <Paus. 4.1.1>, (61c)
Mestor[1], son of Perseus[1] and *Andromeda* <Apollod. *Bibl.* 2.4.5>, 58d
— and *Lysidice*[1] <Apollod. *Bibl.* 2.4.5>, 38a
Mestor[2], son of Pterelaus <Apollod. *Bibl.* 2.4.5> and *Amphimede*, 58d
Mestor[3], son of Priam[1] <Hom. *Il.* XXIV.257>, 44d
Mestor[4] — see [five sets of twins]
Mestra (*Metra*), daughter of Erysichton[1] <*Cat. Wom., Frag. Hes.* frg. 43a, Merk. & West>, 34c
— and Autolycus[1] <Ovid *Met.* 8.738>, 13b
— and Glaucus[1] <*Cat. Wom., Frag. Hes.* frg. 43a, Merk. & West>, 18b
— and Poseidon <*Cat. Wom., Frag. Hes.* frg. 43a, Merk. & West>, 8c
Meta, daughter of Hoples <Apollod. *Bibl.* 3.15.6>, 52a
— and Aegeus[1] <Apollod. *Bibl.* 3.15.6>, 51a
Metalces — see Menalces
Metanastes, son of Archander and *Scaea* <Paus. 7.1.6>, 17d
Metaneira (*Meganeira*[2]), wife of Celeus[1] <*Hom. Hymn* 2 (to *Demeter*), 232-33>, 46b
Metapontus [King of Icaria], son of Sisyphus <Steph. Byz. "Metapontum" (he is called a stranger from Metapontium, Diod. Sic. 4.67.4)> and *Merope*[1], 19a
— and *Arne*[1] <Hyg. *Fab.* 186>, 18c
— and *Autolyte* <Diod. Sic. 4.67.5>, (19a)
— and *Theano*[1] <Hyg. *Fab.* 186>, (19a)
Metharme, daughter of Pygmalion[1] <Apollod. *Bibl.* 3.14.3> and *Galateia*[2], 11c
— and Cinyras[1] <Apollod. *Bibl.* 3.14.3>, (11c)
Methone[1] — see *Metope*[2]
Methone[2], daughter of Alcyoneus[1] <Eust. on Hom. *Il.* 776>, 4a
Methone[3] — see *Demonassa*[5]
Methymna, daughter of Macar(eus)[4] <Diod. Sic. 5.81.7>, 14b
— and Lesbus <Diod. Sic. 5.81.6>, 18c
Metiadusa, daughter of Eupalamus <Apollod. *Bibl.* 3.15.5> and *Alcippe*[1], 49b
— and Cecrops II <Apollod. *Bibl.* 3.15.5>, 50b
Metidice (*Mythidice*), daughter of Talaus <Hyg. *Fab.* 70> and *Lysimache*[1], 31d
— and Mnesimachus <Hyg. *Fab.* 70>, (31d)
Metioche[1], daughter of Orion <Ant. Lib. *Met.* 25.1>, 53c
Metioche[2], a woman captured at Troy <Paus. 10.26.2>, *
Metion[1], son of Erechtheus II <Pher. in *F. Gr. H.* 3 F 146> and *Praxithea*[2] <Apollod. *Bibl.* 3.15.1>, 49b
alternate parentage:
Eupalamus <Diod. Sic. 4.76.1>
— and *Iphinoe*[5] <Pher. in *F. Gr. H.* 3 F 146>, (49b)

Metion[2], father of Phorbas[8] <Ovid *Met.* 5.73>, *
Metis[1] [wisdom], daughter of Oceanus and *Tethys* <Hes. *Theog.* 358>, 61b
— and Zeus <Hes. *Theog.* 886>, 5d
Metis[2] — see *Procne*
Metope[1], wife of Sa(n)garius <Apollod. *Bibl.* 3.12.5>, 70a
Metope[2] (*Methone*[1]) (*Parnassa*), daughter of Ladon[1] <Apollod. *Bibl.* 3.12.6>, 54b
— and Asopus <Apollod. *Bibl.* 3.12.6>, 66b
Metope[3], daughter of Asopus and *Metope*[2] <Schol. on Pind. *Isth.* 8.37>, 66a
Metra — see *Mestra*
Midanus — see [fifty sons of Aegyptus[1]] (alternate version)
Midas[1] [King of Phrygia], son of Gordius <Paus. 1.4.5> and *Cybele*[2] <Hyg. *Fab.* 274>, 2b
Midas[2] — see (Dactyls) (alternate version)
Mideia[1], paramour of Poseidon <Paus. 9.37.6>, 8c
Mideia[2], paramour of Electryon[1] <Apollod. *Bibl.* 2.4.5>, 59c
Mideia[3] (*Meda*[2]), daughter of Phylas[1] <Paus. 1.5.2>, 60c
— and Heracles[1] <Paus. 1.5.2>, (60c)
Mideia[4] —see [fifty daughters of Danaus[1]] (alternate version)
Miletus, son of Apollo and *Areia* <Apollod. *Bibl.* 3.1.2>, 11b
alternate parentage:
Apollo and *Acacallis*[1] <Ant. Lib. *Met.* 30.1>
Apollo and *Deione* <Ovid *Met.* 9.493>
Asterius[2] <Non. *Dion.* 13.546-47>
— and *Cyanea* <Ovid *Met.* 9.449-52>, 68a
— and Minos I <Apollod. *Bibl.* 3.1.2>, 54d
— and Sarpedon[1] <Apollod. *Bibl.* 3.1.2>, 52c
Mimas[1] [giant], son of *Gaea* (and the blood of Uranus) <Hes. *Theog.* 180-86; named as giant, Apollod. *Bibl.* 1.6.2>, *4a*
Mimas[2], son of Socus and *Combe*[1] <Non. *Dion.* 13.141>, *66c*
alternate parentage:
Apollo and *Rhetia* <Pher. in *F. Gr. H.* 3 F 48 (unnamed)>
Mimas[3], son of Aeolus[1] <Diod. Sic. 4.67.3>, 18a
Mimas[4] [centaur], offspring of Centaurus and a Magnesian Mare <Pind. *Pyth* 2.50; named as centaur, Hes. *Shield* 186>, 69c
alternate parentage:
Ixion and *Nephele*[1] <Diod. Sic. 4.69.5>
Mimas[5], son of Amycus[3] and Theano[4] <Virg. *Aen.* 10.704>, *
Mimas[6], killed by Polydeuces <Ap. Rhod. *Arg.* 2.105>, *
Mimas[7], killed by Idomeneus[2] <Quint. Smyr. 13.212>, *
Mimas[8], killed by Hippomedon[1], <Stat. *Theb.* 9.290>, *
Mineus — see [fifty sons of Aegyptus[1]] (alternate version)
Minos I [King of Crete], son of Zeus and *Europe*[1] <Hom. *Il.* XIV.322>, 5c, *54c*
— and *Androgeneia* <Non. *Dion.* 13.225-26>, (54c)
— and *Britomartis* <Paus. 2.20.3>, 5b
— and *Crete*[1] <Asclep. in Apollod. *Bibl.* 3.1.2>, 17c
— and *Dexithea*[1] <Apollod. *Bibl.* 3.1.2>, (54c)
— and *Itone* <Diod. Sic. 4.60.3>, (54c)
— and Miletus <Apollod. *Bibl.* 3.1.2>, 11b
— and *Pareia* <Apollod. *Bibl.* 3.1.2>, (54c)
— and *Pasiphae*[1] <Apollod. *Bibl.* 1.9.1>,14d
— and *Procris*[1] <Ant. Lib. *Met.* 41.4>, 51a
— and *Scylla*[1] <Apollod. *Bibl.* 3.15.8>, 34d, 50d
Minos II [King of Crete], son of Lycastus[1] and *Ida*[1] <Diod. Sic. 4.60.3>, 54c, *42b*
[Minotaur] — see Asterius[7]
Minthe (*Mentha*), daughter of Cocytus <Opp. *Hal.* 3.486>, 50a
— and Hades <Opp. *Hal.* 3.486 (he is called Aidoneus)>, 10a
(Minyades), daughters of Minyas and *Euryanassa*[2] <Nicand. in Ant. Lib. *Met.* 10> (see *Alcathoe*, *Arsippe*, *Leucippe*[1]), 20d
Minyas [King of Orchomenus], son of Chryses[1] <Paus. 9.36.3>, 20c
alternate parentage:
Olmos <Schol. on Hom. *Il.* II.11>
Orchomenus[7] <Ant. Lib. *Met.* 10.1>
Poseidon and *Euryanassa*[2] <Schol. on Hom. *Od.* 11.326>
— and *Clytodora*[1] <Schol. on Ap. Rhod. 1.230>, (20c)
— and *Euryanassa*[2] <Nicand. in Ant. Lib. *Met.* 10>, (20c)
— and *Phanosyra* <Schol. on Ap. Rhod. 1.230>, (20c)
Minyeius [river], son of Oceanus and Tethys <Hes. *Theog.* 367-68; named as river, Hom. *Il.* XI.721>, 67b
Misenus, son of Aeolus[1] <Virg. *Aen.* 6.163> and *Enarete*, 21b
Mnasinous — see Mnesileus
Mneme [memory] [one of the Boeotian Muses], daughter of Uranus <Paus. 9.29.2> and *Gaea*, 6b
Mnemosyne [Titan] [memory], daughter of Uranus and *Gaea* <Hes. *Theog.* 135>, 10b
— and Zeus <Hes. *Theog.* 76-79>, 6a
Mneseus — see [five sets of twins]
Mnesileus (Mnasinous), son of Polydeuces and *Phoebe*[2] <Apollod. *Bibl.* 3.11.2>, 48d, *25c*
Mnesimache — see *Hippolyte*[3]
Mnesimachus, husband of *Metidice* <Hyg. *Fab.* 70>, 31c
Mnestra, daughter of Danaus[1] and [an Ethiopian woman] <Apollod. *Bibl.* 2.1.5>, (57d)
— and Aegius <Apollod. *Bibl.* 2.1.5>, 57d
(Moirae) [Fates], daughters of Zeus and *Themis*[1] <Hes. *Theog.* 901-05> (see *Atropos*, *Clotho*, *Lachesis*), 6c-d
alternate parentage:
Ananke <Plato *Rep.* 617c>
Cronus <Epim. *Theog.* 3 B 19>
Nyx <Hes. *Theog.* 217-18>
Molion[1], son of Eurytus[2] <Diod. Sic. 4.37.5> and *Antiope*[6], 60b
Molion[2], squire of Odysseus <Hom. *Il.* XI.322>, *
Molion[3], killed by *Pentheseleia* <Quint. Smyr. 1.227>, *
Molione, daughter of Molus[3] <Eust. on Hom. *Il.* 882>, 9a, 68a
— and Actor[4] <*Cat. Wom., Frag. Hes.* frg. 17, Merk. & West>, (68a)
— and Poseidon <*Cat. Wom., Frag. Hes.* frg. 17, Merk. & West>, (9a)
Molossus, son of Neoptolemus and *Andromache* <Eur. *Andr.* 309>, 24c
Molpadia[1] (*Hemithea*[2]), daughter of Staphylus[1] and *Chrysothemis*[2] <Diod. Sic. 5.62.1>, 56d
— and Lyrcus[1] <Parth. *Love Stor.* 1.3>, 61a
Molpadia[2] [Amazon] <Paus. 1.2.1>, *
Molpe — see [Sirens]
Molpus — see Eumolpus[2]
Molus[1], son of Deucalion[2] <Apollod. *Bibl.* 3.2.3>, 54c
— and *Melphis* <Hyg. *Fab.* 97>, (54c)
Molus[2], son of Ares and *Demodice*[2] <Apollod. *Bibl.* 1.7.7>, 7b, *15c*
Molus[3], father of *Molione* <Eust. on Hom. *Il.* 882>, 9a, 68a
Molus[4], killed by Agenor[12] <Quint. Smyr. 6.624>, *
Momus [blame] [abstraction], offspring of *Nyx* <Hes. *Theog.* 213>, *1b*
Monuste —see [fifty daughters of Danaus[1]] (alternate version)
Monychus [centaur], offspring of Centaurus and a Magnesian Mare <Pind. *Pyth.* 2.50; named as centaur Ovid *Met.* 12. 501>, 69c
alternate parentage:
Ixion and *Nephele*[1] <Diod. Sic. 4.69.5>
Mopsus[1], son of Rhacius and *Manto*[1] <Paus. 7.3.1>, *32d*
alternate parentage:
Apollo and *Manto*[1] <Apollod. *Epit.* 6.3>
Mopsus[2] [Argonaut], son of Ampyx[2] <Hes. *Shield* 182> and *Chloris*[6] <Tzetz. on Lyc. 881>, *
Mopsus[3], a shepherd <Virg. *Ecl.* 5, passim>, *
Mopsus[4], son of Nicodamas and *Oenoe*[4] <Ant. Lib. *Met.* 16.1-

2>, *
Mopsus[5], killed by Hippomedon[1] <Stat. *Theb.* 11.126>, *
Morea [mulberry tree], daughter of Oxylus[3] and *Hamadryas* <Athen. 3.78b>, 71d
Morpheus [dreams] [abstraction], offspring of Hypnos <Ovid *Met.* 11.575-690>, 1a
Morrheus[1], son of Didnasus <Non. *Dion.* 26.72-73>, 3b
— and *Cheirobie* <Non. *Dion.* 34.179>, (3b)
Morrheus[2], one of the earsleepers <Non. *Dion.* 26.98-100>, *
Mor(u)s [doom] [abstraction], offspring of *Nyx* <Hes. *Theog.* 211>, *1b*
Mothone, daughter of Oeneus[1] <Paus. 4.35.1> and *Althaea*, 17d
Mulius[1], husband of *Agamede*[1] <Hom. *Il.* IX.739>, 63c
Mulius[2], servant of Amphinomous[3] <Hom. *Od.* 18.423>, *
Mulius[3], killed by Patroclus[1] <Hom. *Il.* XVI.696>, *
Mulius[4], killed by Achilles <Hom. *Il.* XX.472>, *
Munippus, son of Priam[1] and *Cilla*[2] <Schol. on Lyc. 319>, 43d, *45d*
alternate parentage:
Thymoetes[2] and *Cilla*[2] <Schol. on Lyc. 319>
Munitus, son of Acamas[1] and *Laodice*[1] <Parth. *Love Stor.* 16.3>, 51d, *43c*
Musaeus, son of Orpheus <Diod. Sic. 4.25.1>, 6a
alternate parentage:
Antiophemus <Paus. 10.12.6>
— and *Deiope* <Aris. *On Marv. Works Heard* 131.3-5>, 46d
[Muses] (*Pierides*[1]), daughters of Zeus and *Mnemosyne* <Hes. *Theog.* 77-79> (see *Calliope, Cleio*[1], *Erato*[1], *Euterpe, Melpomene, Polymnia, Terpsichore*[1], *Thaleia*[1], *Urania*[1]), 6a-b
others:
named in <Epich., *Testimonios Frg.* 38>: *Achelois, Asopo, Heptapore, Neilo(s), Rhodia*[2], *Titoplous*, and *Tritone*
Musica [one of the hours], daughter of Zeus and *Themis*[1] <Hyg. *Fab.* 183>, 6d
Mutto — see Belus[3]
Mutunus — see Priapus
Mycene, daughter of Inachus <Paus. 2.16.4> and *Melia*[1], 55a
— and Arestor[1] <Paus. 2.16.4>, (55a)
Myceneus, son of Sparton[2] <Acus. in Paus. 2.16.4 (although Pausanias discredits this relationship)>, 61b
Mygdon(us)[1] [King of the Bebryces], son of Poseidon <Apollod. *Bibl.* 2.5.9 (inferred because he is called brother of Amycus[1])> and *Melia*[2], 8d
— and *Alexirhoe* <Ps.-Plut. *De Fluv.* 12.1>, 67b
Mygdon(us)[2] [King of Phrygia], father of Coroebus[1] <Paus. 10. 27.1>, 43d
— and *Anaxamenia* <Serv. on Virg. *Aen.* 2.341>, (43d)
Myles [King of Laconia], son of Lelex[1] <Paus. 3.1.1> and *Cleochareia*, 61c
Mylius, son of Priam[1] <Apollod. *Bibl.* 3.12.5>, 44d
Mynes [King of Lyrnessus], son of Euenus[3] <Hom. *Il.* II.692-93>, 51d
— and *Briseis*[1] <Hom. *Il.* XIX.296>, (51d)
Myrine[1], daughter of Cretheus[1] <Schol. on Ap. Rhod. *Arg.* 1.604> and *Tyro*, 32b
— and Thoas[1] <Schol. on Ap. Rhod. *Arg.* 1.60>, 56d
Myrine[2] — see *Bateia*[2]
Myrine[3] [Libyan Amazon] <Diod. Sic. 3.53.2>, *
Myrmidon, son of Zeus <Eust. on Hom. *Il.* 112.44>, and *Eurymedusa*[1] <Serv. on Virg. *Aen.* 2.7>, 5d
— and *Peisidice*[1] <*Cat. Wom., Hesiodi* frg. 10(a).99-100, Merk. & West (O.C.T.)>, 28b
Myrmidone —see [fifty daughters of Danaus[1]] (alternate version)
Myrr(h)a (*Smyrna*[1]), daughter of Cinyras[1] <Ovid *Met.* 10.337> and *Cenchreis* <Hyg. *Fab.* 58>, 11c
alternate parentage:
Theias <Apollod. *Bibl.* 3.14.4> and *Oreithyia*[5] <Ant. Lib. *Met.* 34>
— and Cinyras[1] <Ovid *Met.* 10.462-68>, 11c
Myrtilus, son of Hermes <Apollod. *Epit.* 2.6> and *Cleobula*[4] <Tzetz. on Lyc. 156, 162>, 46b, *21a*
alternate parentage:
Hermes and *Clytie*[7] <Hyg. *Poet. Astr.* 2.13>
Hermes and *Phaethusa*[2] <Schol. on Ap. Rhod. *Arg.* 1.752>
Myrto[1], daughter of Menoetius[2] <Plut. *Aris.* 20.6> and *Sthenele*[2], 22d
— and Heracles[1] <Plut. *Aris.* 20.6>, 60c
Myrto[2] [Amazon] <Schol. on Ap. Rhod. *Arg.* 1.752>, *
Myrto[3] [one of the Bacchae] <Non. *Dion.* 29.270>, *
Mysus, son of Atys[1] <Herod. 1.171.6 (inferred because he is called brother of Lydus)> and Callithea, 51b
Mythidice — see *Metidice*
Mytilene[1], daughter of Macar(eus)[4] <Diod. Sic. 5.81.7>, 14b
— and Poseidon <Steph. Byz. "Mytilene">, 9a
Mytilene[2] [Libyan Amazon] <Diod. Sic. 3.55.7>, *
Myton, son of Poseidon and *Mytilene*[1] <Steph. Byz. "Mytilene">, 9a, *14b*

[Naiad], daughter of Oceanus and *Tethys* <Euan. in Athen. 7.296>, 62a
— paramour of Poseidon <Euan. in Athen. 7.296>, 9a
[Naiads], daughters of Zeus <Hom. *Od.* 13.257>, 6d
Nana, daughter of Sa(n)garius <Paus. 7.17.5> and *Metope*[1], 70a
— and Agdistis <Paus. 7.17.5>, (70a)
Nanas, son of Teutamides <Hellan. in Dion. Hal. *Rom. Ant.* 1.28.3>, 61d
Naoclus — see Nauclus
Narcaeus, son of Dionysus and *Physcoa* <Paus. 5.16.7>, 56d
Narcissus, son of Cephis(s)us and *Leiriope* <Ovid *Met.* 3.343-48>, 49b
— and *Echo* (who loved him) <Ovid *Met.* 3.356-401>, (49b)
Nasamon, son of Amphithemis[1] and [a nymph of Triton] <Ap. Rhod. *Arg.* 4.1496>, 53d, *63b*
Naubolus[1] [King of Tanagra], son of Lernus[1] <Ap. Rhod. *Arg.* 1. 132>, 52d
Naubolus[2] [King of Phocis], son of Phocus[1] <Paus. 10.33.10> and *Asterodeia*[2], 23c
alternate parentage:
Hippasus[11] <Stat. *Theb.* 7.355>
Ornytus <Ap. Rhod. *Arg.* 1.207>
— and *Perineice* <Schol. on Ap. Rhod. *Arg.* 1.207-10>, (23c)
Naubolus[3], father of Pylon <*Cat. Wom., Frag. Hes.* frg. 26, Merk. & West (inferred because he is grandfather of *Antiope*[6])>, 60b
Naubolus[4], father of Euryalus[5] <Hom. *Od.* 8.111>, *
Nauclus (Naoclus), son of Codrus[1] <Strab. 14.1.3>, 27d
Naucrate, paramour of Daedalus <Apollod. *Epit.* 1.12>, 49b
Naupiadame — see *Nausidame*
Nauplius[1], son of Poseidon and *Amymone* <Apollod. *Bibl.* 2.1. 5>, 8b, *57c*
— and *Clymene*[5] <Apollod. *Bibl.* 2.1.5>, 52d
— and *Hesione*[3] <Cerc. in Apollod. *Bibl.* 2.1.5>, (57c)
— and *Philyra* <Apollod. *Bibl.* 2.1.5 (quoting author of *The Returns*)>, (57c)
Nauplius[2] [King of Nauplia] [Argonaut], son of Clytonaeus[2] <Ap. Rhod. *Arg.* 1.132>, 52d
Nausicaa, daughter of Alcinous <Hom. *Od.* 6.17> and *Arete* <Hom. *Od.* 7.67>, 9c
— and Telemachus <Hellan. in *F. Gr. H.* 4 F 156>, 13c
Nausidame (*Iphiboe*) (*Naupiadame*), daughter of Amphidamas[1] <Hyg. *Fab.* 14>, 63d

— and Helios <Hyg. *Fab.* 14>, 14b
Nausimedon, son of Nauplius[1] and *Clymene*[5] <Apollod. *Bibl.* 2.1.5>, 52d
alternate parentage:
Nauplius[1] and *Hesione*[3] <Apollod. *Bibl.* 2.1.5>
Nauplius[1] and *Philyra* <Apollod. *Bibl.* 2.1.5>
Nauplius[2] <Grimal "Nauplius">
Nausinous, son of Odysseus and *Calypso*[1] <Hes. *Theog.* 1017>, 13c, *40b*
Nausithoe, daughter of Nereus and *Doris*[1] <Apollod. *Bibl.* 1.2.7>, *65a*
Nausithous[1] [King of Phaeacians], son of Poseidon and *Periboea*[4] <Hom. *Od.* 7.56-57>, 9a
Nausithous[2], son of Odysseus and *Calypso*[1] <Hes. *Theog.* 1018>, 13c, *40b*
alternate parentage:
Odysseus and *Circe* <Hyg. *Fab.* 125>
Nausithous[3], the pilot of Theseus's ship <Philoch. in Plut. *Thes.* 17.6>, *
Naxus, son of Endymion <Steph. Byz. "Naxus"> and *Chromia*, 15b
alternate parentage:
Polemon <Diod. Sic. 5.51.3>
Neaera[1], paramour of Helios <Hom. *Od.* 12.132>, 14b
Neaera[2], daughter of Pereus <Apollod. *Bibl.* 3.9.1>, 62d
— and Aleus <Apollod. *Bibl.* 3.9.1>, 63c
— and Autolycus[1] <Paus. 8.4.6>, 13b
Neaera[3], wife of Strymon <Apollod. *Bibl.* 2.1.2>, 71b
Neaera[4] — see *Ethoda(ea)*
Neaera[5], wife of Aeetes <Schol. on Ap. Rhod. *Arg.* 3.241>, 14d
Neaera[6], wife of Hypsicreon <Parth. *Love Stor.* 18.3>, *
Neaera[7], paramour of Theiodamas[2] <Quint. Smyr. 1.292>, *
Neaera[8], a Lemnian woman <Val. Flac. 2.141>, *
Nebrophonus[1] (Deiphilus) (Thoas[2]) [King of Lemnos], son of Jason and *Hypsipyle* <Apollod. *Bibl.* 1.9.17>, 33d
Nebrophonus[2] [one of the dogs of Actaeon] <Hyg. *Fab.* 181>, *
Nedymnus [centaur], offspring of Centaurus and a Magnesian Mare <Pind. *Pyth.* 2.50; named as centaur, Ovid *Met.* 12.350>, 69c
alternate parentage:
Ixion and *Nephele*[1] <Diod. Sic. 4.69.5>
Neikea [grievances] [abstraction], offspring of *Eris* <Hes. *Theog.* 229>, *1a*
Neilos[1] — see Nilus
Neilo(s)[2] — see [Muses] (alternate version)

Neis[1], son of Zethus and *Aedon*[1] <Paus. 9.8.3>, 66d
Neis[2], daughter of Amphion[1] and *Niobe*[1] <Schol. on Eur. *Phoen. Maid.* 1104>, 66c
Neis[3] — see *Chromia*
Neleus[1] [King of Pylos], son of Poseidon and *Tyro* <Hom. *Od.* 11.235-54>, 9c, *27c*
alternate parentage:
Cretheus[1] <Paus. 4.2.5> and *Tyro*
Hippocoon[3] <Hyg. *Fab.* 10>
— and *Chloris*[2] <Hom. *Od.* 11.281-83>, 20c
Neleus[2], son of Codrus[1] <Paus. 7.2.1>, 27d
Nelo, daughter of Danaus[1] and [an Ethiopian woman] <Apollod. *Bibl.* 2.1.5>, 58c
— and Menemachus <Apollod. *Bibl.* 2.1.5>, (58c)
Nemea, daughter of Asopus <Paus. 2.15.3> and *Metope*[2], 66a
[Nemean Lion], offspring of Orth(r)us and *Chimaera*[1] <Hes. *Theog.* 326-27>, *1b*
alternate parentage:
Orth(r)us and *Echidna* <Hes. *Theog.* 326-27 (referent of "she" is unclear)>
Nemertes, daughter of Nereus and *Doris*[1] <Hes. *Theog.* 261>, *65a*
Nemesis (Adrasteia[1]*)* [retributive justice] [abstraction], offspring of *Nyx* <Hes. *Theog.* 223>, *1b*
alternate parentage:
Oceanus <Paus. 1.33.3>
Zeus <Eur. *Rhes.* 344>
Neomeris, daughter of Nereus and *Doris*[1] <Apollod. *Bibl.* 1.2.7>, *65a*
Neoptolemus (Pyrrhus[1]), son of Achilles <Hom. *Il.* XIX.326-28> and *Deidameia*[1] <Apollod. *Epit.* 6.13>, 24c
alternate parentage:
Achilles and *Euryganeia* <Lyc. 324>
— and *Andromache* <Eur. *Andr.* 16>, (24c)
— and *Hermione* <Hom. *Od.* 4.10>, 37a
— and *Lanassa* <Plut. *Pyrr.*>, 60c
Nephalion, son of Minos I and *Pareia* <Apollod. *Bibl.* 3.1.2>, 54c
Nephele[1] [cloud], paramour of Ixion <Apollod. *Epit.* 1.20>, 69a
Nephele[2], wife of Athamas[1] <*Cat. Wom., Frag. Hes.* frg. 68, Merk. & West (inferred because she is called mother of Phrixus[1] and *Helle*)>, 26a
Nephele[3] [nymph] <Ovid *Met.* 3.171>, *
Nephus, son of Heracles[1] and *Praxithea*[3] <Apollod. *Bibl.* 2.7.8>, *50c*
(Nereids), daughters of Nereus and *Doris*[1] (see *Actaea*[1], *Agave*[3], *Amatheia*, *Amphinome*[1], *Amphitoe*, *Amphitrite*, *Apsuedes*, *Arethusa*[5], *Asia*[2], *Autonoe*[3], *Beroe*[3], *Callianassa*, *Callianeira*, *Calypso*[3], *Ceto*[2], *Cleio*[2], *Clymene*[2], *Cranto*, *Creneis*, *Cydippe*[2], *Cymatolege*, *Cymo*, *Cymodoce*, *Cymothoe*, *Deiopeia*[1], *Dero*, *Dexamene*, *Dione*[2], *Doris*[2], *Doto*, *Drymo*, *Dynamene*, *Eione*, *Ephyra*[2], *Erato*[5], *Euagore*, *Euarne*, *Eucra(n)te*, *Eudora*[2], *Eulimene*[2], *Eumolpe*, *Euneice*, *Eupompe*, *Eurydice*[12], *Galateia*[1], *Galene*, *Glauce*[4], *Glauconome*, *Halia*[2], *Halimede*, *Hipponoe*[1], *Hippothoe*[3], *Iaera*[1], *Ianassa*, *Ianeira*[3], *Ione*[1], *Iphianassa*[4], *Laodameia*, *Leagore*, *Leucothoe*[3], *Ligeia*[2], *Limnoreia*, *Lycorias*, *Lysianassa*[3], *Maera*[3], *Melite*[1], *Menippe*[4], *Nausithoe*, *Nemertes*, *Neomeris*, *Nesaea*, *Neso*[2], *Opis*[3], *Oreithyia*[4], *Panope*[1], *Pasithea*[2], *Pherusa*[1], *Phyllodoce*, *Plexaure*[2], *Ploto*, *Polynoe*, *Polynome*, *Pontemedusa*, *Pontoporeia*, *Pronoe*[2], *Proto*, *Protomedeia*, *Psamathe*[1], *Sao*, *Speio*, *Thaleia*[3], *Themisto*[4], *Thetis*, *Thoe*[2], *Xantho*), *63a-65d*
Nereus, son of Pontus and *Gaea* <Hes. *Theog.* 234>, 3a
— and *Doris*[1] <Hes. *Theog.* 240-41>, 64b
— and Glaucus[3] <Athen. 7.296f (citing Nicand.)>, 62a
Nerites, son of Nereus and *Doris*[1] <Ael. *De Nat. Anim.* 14.18>, *65a*
— and Poseidon <Ael. *De Nat. Anim.* 14.18>, 9b
Neritus, son of Pterelaus and *Amphimede* <Schol. on Hom. *Od.* 17.207>, 58d
Nesaea, daughter of Nereus and *Doris*[1] <Hes. *Theog.* 249>, 65a
Neso[1], paramour of Dardanus[1] <Tzetz. on Lyc. 1465>, 42b
Neso[2], daughter of Nereus and *Doris*[1] <Hes. *Theog.* 261>, *65a*
Nessa, daughter of Pierus[2] <Nicand. in Ant. Lib. *Met.* 9> and *Euippe*[2] <Ovid *Met.* 5.300 ff.>, 15c
Nesson, son of Thessalus[2] <Strab. 9.5.23>, 60b
Nessus[1] [centaur], offspring of Centaurus and a Magnesian Mare <Pind. *Pyth.* 2.50; named as centaur, Apollod. *Bibl.* 2.5.4>, 69d
alternate parentage:
Ixion and *Nephele*[1] <Diod. Sic. 4.69.5>
— and *Deianeira*[1] <Ovid *Met.* 9.102-25>, 16d
Nessus[2] [river], son of Oceanus and *Tethys* <Hes. *Theog.* 341>, 62a
Nessus[3], killed by Ajax[1] <Quint. Smyr. 3.231>, *
Nestor [King of Pylos], son of Neleus[1] and *Chloris*[2] <Hom. *Od.* 11.286>, 27d
— and *Anaxibia*[4] <Apollod. *Bibl.* 1.9.9>, (27d)
— and *Eurydice*[7] <Hom. *Od.* 3.453>, 26d
— and *Hecamede* <Hom. *Il.* XI.625>, (27d)
Nestus, father of *Callirhoe*[7] <Steph. Byz. "Bistonia">, 7a
Nicaea, daughter of Sa(n)garius and *Cybele*[2] <Mem. in *F. Gr. H.*

434 F 1.28.29>, 70a
— and Dionysus <Non. *Dion.* 16.75-403>, 56d
— and Hymnus <Non. *Dion.* 16.204-369>, (70a)
Nicippe[1] (*Amphibia*) (*Archippe*) (*Leucippe*[9]) (*Menippe*[1]), daughter of Pelops[1] <*Cat. Wom., Frag. Hes.* frg. 190, Merk. & West> and *Hippodameia*[1] <Apollod. *Bibl.* 2.4.5>, *38b*
— and Sthenelus[1] <*Cat. Wom., Frag. Hes.* frg. 190, Merk. & West>, 58d
Nicippe[2], daughter of Thespius <Apollod. *Bibl.* 2.7.8> and *Megamede* <Apollod. *Bibl.* 2.4.10>, 51c
— and Heracles[1] <Apollod. *Bibl.* 2.7.8>, (51c)
Nicodromus, son of Heracles[1] and *Nike*[2] <Apollod. *Bibl.* 2.7.8>, *51c*
Nicomachus[1], son of Machaon and *Anticleia*[3] <Paus. 4.30.3>, 19d
Nicomachus[2], suitor of *Penelope*[1] (from Dulichium) <Apollod. *Epit.* 7.28>, *
Nicostrate[1] (*Carmentis*) (*Themis*[3]), daughter of Ladon[1] <Paus. 8. 43.2 (called *Carmentis*, Virg. *Aen.* 8.335)>, 54b
— and Hermes <Paus. 8.43.2>, 46c
Nicostrate[2] — see *Bateia*[1]
Nicostratus, son of Menelaus and *Helen*[1] <Schol. on Soph. *Elec.* 539>, 37b
alternate parentage:
Menelaus and *Pieris* <Paus. 2.18.5>, 45c
Nicothoe — see *Aello*[1]
Nike[1] [victory], daughter of Pallas[1] and *Styx* <Hes. *Theog.* 384>, 12a
Nike[2], daughter of Thespius <Apollod. *Bibl.* 2.7.8> and *Megamede* <Apollod. *Bibl.* 2.4.10>, 51c
— and Heracles[1] <Apollod. *Bibl.* 2.7.8>, (51c)
Nile — see Nilus
Nilus (Nile) [river], son of Oceanus and *Tethys* <Hes. *Theog.* 338>, 68a
— and *Callirhoe*[2] <Serv. on Virg. *Aen.* 4.250>, 51b
Ninus, son of Belus[3] <Herod. 1.7>, 61c
— and *Semiramis* <Diod. Sic. 2.4.1>, (61c)
Ninyas, son of Ninus and *Semiramis* <Diod. Sic. 2.7.1>, 61c
Niobe[1], daughter of Tantalus[1] <*Cat. Wom., Frag. Hes.* frg. 183, Merk. & West> and *Dione*[3] <Hyg. *Fab.* 83>, *41a*
alternate parentage:
Tantalus[1] and *Euryanassa*[1] <Schol. on Eur. *Or.* 5>
Assaon <Parth. *Love Stor.* 33>
— and Amphion[1] <*Cat. Wom., Frag. Hes.* frg. 183, Merk. & West>, 66d
— and Philottus <Parth. *Love Stor.* 33>, (41a)
Niobe[2], daughter of Phoroneus and *Teledice* <Apollod. *Bibl.* 2.1.1>, 61b
alternate parentage:
Phoroneus and *Cinna* <Hyg. *Fab.* 145>
— and Hecaterus <Hes. in Strab. 10.3.19>, (61b)
— and Zeus <Apollod. *Bibl.* 2.1.1>, 6c
Nireus[1], son of Poseidon and *Canace* <Apollod. *Bibl.* 1.7.4>, 8a, *34b*
Nireus[2], son of Charopus and *Aglaia*[2] <Diod. Sic. 5.53.2>, *
Nisus[1], son of Hyrtacus and *Ida*[2] <Virg. *Aen.* 9.177-79>, 44c
— and Euryalus[4] <Virg. *Aen.* 9.177-84>, (44c)
Nisus[2] [King of Megara], son of Pandion II <*Cat. Wom., Frag. Hes.* frg. 43a, Merk. & West> and *Pylia* <Apollod. *Bibl.* 3.15.5>, 50d
alternate parentage:
Ares <Hyg. *Fab.* 198>
Deion[1] <Hyg. *Fab.* 198>
— and *Abrote* <Plut. *Gr. Quest.* 16.295>, 9d, 34d
Nisus[3], son of Aretias; father of Amphinomous[3] <Hom. *Od.* 16.394>, 47d
Nomia[1] — see *Pi(m)pleia*
Nomia[2] [Arcadian nymph] <Paus. 10.31.10>, *
Nomion[1], father of Amphimachus[4] <Hom. *Il.* II.871>, *
Nomion[2], father of Anetheus[3] <Ant. Lib. *Met.* 5.1>, *
Nomius[1], son of Hermes and *Penelope*[2] <Non. *Dion.* 14.92>, 46d
Nomius[2], son of Electryon[1] and *Lysidice*[1] <*Cat. Wom., Frag. Hes.* frg. 193, Merk. & West>, 59d, *38b*
Nomius[3], killed by Hippomedon[1] <Stat. *Theb.* 9.290>, *
Nomus — see Aristaeus
Nonacris, wife of Lycaon[1] <Paus. 8.17.6>, 62a
Norax, son of Hermes and *Erytheia*[2] <Paus. 10.17.4>, 46b, *2b*
Notus [South wind], son of Astraeus[1] and *Eos* <Hes. *Theog.* 380>, 12b
Nycteis, daughter of Nycteus[1] <Apollod. *Bibl.* 3.5.3> and *Polyxo*[2], 35b
— and Polydorus[2] <Apollod. *Bibl.* 3.5.3>, 55c
Nycteus[1] [King of Thebes], son of Hyrieus and *Clonia*[1] <Apollod. *Bibl.* 3.10.1>, 35b
alternate parentage:
Chthonius[1] <Apollod. *Bibl.* 3.5.5>
— and *Polyxo*[2] <Apollod. *Bibl.* 3.10.1>, (35b)
Nycteus[2], son of Poseidon and *Celaeno*[1] <Hyg. *Fab.* 157>, 8b
Nycteus[3], comrade of Diomedes[1] <Ovid *Met.* 14.504>, *
Nyctimus [King of Arcadia], son of Lycaon[1] <Apollod. *Bibl.* 3.8. 1>, 63a
— and *Arcadia*[1] <Plut. *Gr. and Rom. Par. Stor.* 36>, (63a)
Nymphe[1] [one of the hours], daughter of Zeus and *Themis*[1] <Hyg. *Fab.* 183>, 6d
Nymphe[2], paramour of Zeus <Diod. Sic. 5.48.1>, 6c
Nysa — see (Hyades) (alternate version)
Nyx [night], came from Chaos <Hes. *Theog.* 123>, 1a
— and Erebus <Hes. *Theog.* 125>, 1a

Oaxus, son of Apollo and *Anchiale*[1] <Serv. on Virg. *Aen.* 1.65>, 11a
Obriareus, paramour of *Thrace* <Steph. Byz. "Trieres">, 55a
Ocaleia — see *Aglaia*[3]
(Oceanids), daughters of Oceanus and *Tethys* (see *Acaste, Admete*[2], *Amphirho, Argeia*[2], *Asia*[1], *Asiexa, Asterodeia*[3], *Asterope*[3], *Beroe*[2], *Callirhoe*[2], *Calypso*[2], *Capheira, Cerceis, Ceto*[3], *Chryseis*[3], *Cleio*[4], *Clymene*[1], *Clytie*[1], *Daeira, Dione*[1], *Dodone, Doris*[1], *Eidyia, Electra*[1], *Ephyra*[1], *Euagoreis, Eudora*[3], *Europe*[4], *Eurynome*[1], *Galaxaure, Hesione*[2], *Hippo*[2], *Iache, Ianeira*[2], *Ianthe*[2], *Leiriope, Leuce, Leucippe*[7], *Melia*[1], *Meliboea*[1], *Melite*[4], *Melobosis, Memestho, Menippe*[5], *Merope*[4], *Metis, Ocyrrhoe*[3], *Ouranie, Pasiphae*[2], *Pasithoe, Peitho*[2], *Periboea*[7], *Perse(is), Petraea, Phaeno, Phillyra, Pleione, Plexaure*[1], *Pluto*[1], *Polydora*[3], *Polyxo*[5], *Prymno, Rhodeia*[1], *Rhodope*[1], *Stilbo, Telesto, Theia*[2], *Thoe*[1], *Tyche*[1], *Urania*[2], *Xanthe*[1], *Zeuxo*), 50a-72b
Oceanus [Titan] [ocean stream], son of Uranus and *Gaea* <Hes. *Theog.* 133>, 55a
— and *Gaea* <Pher. in Apollod. *Bibl.* 1.5.2>, 2b
— and *Parthenope*[4] <Andr. Hall. in *F.H.G.* 2.349 frg. 1, Müller>, (55a)
— and *Tethys* <Hes. *Theog.* 337>, (55a)
— and *Theia*[2] <Eust. on Hom. *Od.* 1864>, 72a
Ochimus, son of Helios and *Rhode*[1] <Diod. Sic. 5.56.5>, 14b
— and *Hegetoria* <Diod. Sic. 5.57.7>, (14b)
Oclasus, son of Pentheus[1] <Schol. on Eur. *Phoen. Maid.* 942>, 55d
Ocresia, paramour of Hephaestus <Ovid *Fast.* 6.628-29 (he is called Vulcan)>, 7b
Ocypete[1] (*Ocypode*) (*Ocythoe*) [swift flying] [one of the Harpuiai], daughter of Thaumas[1] and *Electra*[1] <Hes. *Theog.* 267>, 3a
alternate parentage:
Thaumas[1] and *Ozomene* <Hyg. *Fab.* 14>
Boreas <Pher. Syr. 7 B 5>
Oceanus and *Gaea* <Epim. *Theog.* 3 B 7>
Ocypete[2], daughter of Danaus[1] and *Pieria*[1] <Apollod. *Bibl.* 2.1.5>,

57c
— and Lampus[2] <Apollod. *Bibl.* 2.1.5>, (57c)
Ocypete[3] [one of the dogs of Actaeon] <Hyg. *Fab.* 181>, *
Ocypode — see *Ocypete*[1]
Ocyrrhoe[1] — see *Hippe*[1]
Ocyrrhoe[2], daughter of Imbrasus[1] and *Chesias* <Ap. Rhod. in Athen. 7.283d>, 11d <Diod. Sic. 3.65.6>, 11d
alternate parentage:
Ares <Non. *Dion.* 13.428>
— and Apollo <Ap. Rhod. in Athen. 7.283d>, (11d)
Ocyrrhoe[3], daughter of Oceanus and *Tethys* <Hes. *Theog.* 360>, 62a
— and Helios <Ps.-Plut. *De Fluv.* 5.1>, 14b
Ocythoe — see *Ocypete*[1]
Ocythous[1], son of Socus and *Combe*[1] <Non. *Dion.* 13.142>, *66c*
alternate parentage:
Apollo and *Rhetia* <Pher. in *F. Gr. H.* 3 F 48 (unnamed)>
Ocythous[2], killed by Ajax[1] <Quint. Smyr. 3.230>, *
Ocythous[3] [one of the dogs of Actaeon] <Hyg. *Fab.* 181>, *
Odeites[1] (Hodites[1]) [centaur], offspring of Centaurus and a Magnesian Mare <Pind. *Pyth.* 2.50; named as centaur, Ovid *Met.* 12.457>, 69d
alternate parentage:
Ixion and *Nephele*[1] <Diod. Sic. 4.69.5>
Odeites[2] — see Oneites
Odeodochus (Hodeodochus) (Hodoedochus), son of Cynus <Eust. on Hom. *Il.* 277>, 15c
— and *Laonome*[3] <Hyg. *Fab.* 14>, (15c)
Odysseus [King of Ithaca], son of Laertes <Hom. *Il.* III.200> and *Anticleia*[1] <Hom. *Od.* 11.85>, 5c, *13c*
alternate parentage:
Sisyphus <Eur. *Cycl.* 104> and *Anticleia*[1]
— and *Callidice*[1] <Apollod. *Epit.* 7.35>, (13c)
— and *Calypso*[1] <Hom. *Od.* 7.245>, 40b
— and *Circe* <Hes. *Theog.* 1010>, 14d
— and *Euippe*[6] <Apollod. *Epit.* 7.40>, (13c)
— and *Hecabe*[1] <Eur. *Tro. Wom.* 274-78>, 43d
— and *Penelope*[1] <Hom. *Od.* 11.247>, 47d
— and *Polymela*[2] <Parth. *Love Stor.* 2.1>, 18c
— and unnamed daughter of Thoas[6] <Apollod. *Epit.* 7.40>, (13c)
Oeager — see Oeagrus
Oeagrus (Oeager) [King of Thrace], son of Charops[1] <Diod. Sic. 3. 65.6>, 6a
alternate parentage:
Ares <Non. *Dion.* 13.428>
— and *Calliope* <Apollod. *Bibl.* 1.3.2>, (6a)
Oeax, son of Nauplius[2] and *Clymene*[5] <Apollod. *Bibl.* 2.1.5>, 52d
alternate parentage:
Nauplius[1] and *Hesione*[3] <Apollod. *Bibl.* 2.1.5>
Nauplius[1] and *Philyra* <Apollod. *Bibl.* 2.1.5>
Nauplius[1] <Grimal "Nauplius">
Oebalus[1] [King of Sparta], son of Cynortes <Paus. 3.1.4>, 47a
alternate parentage:
Perieres[1] <Apollod. *Bibl.* 3.10.4>
— and *Bateia*[1] <Apollod. *Bibl.* 3.10.4>, (47a)
— and *Gorgophone*[1] <Paus. 2.21.8>, 59c
Oebalus[2], son of Telon and *Sebethis* <Virg. *Aen.* 7.733-34>, *
Oebalus[3], a Spartan warrior <Stat. *Theb.* 10.498>, *
Oechalia, wife of Melaneus[2] <Paus. 4.2.3>, 11d
Oecles — see Oicle(u)s
Oedipus [King of Thebes], son of Laius[1] <Soph. *Oed. Tyr.* 714-22> and *Jocasta* <Hom. *Od.* 11.271 (she is called *Epicaste*)>, 55c
alternate parentage:
Laius[1] and *Eurycleia*[4] <"Epimenides" in *F. Gr. H.* 3 B 15>
— and *Euryganeia* <Paus. 9.5.5>, (55c)
— and *Jocasta* <Aesch. *Sev.* 752-57; Jocasta named, Soph. *Oed. Tyr.* 639>, 55d
— and *Medusa*[3] <Pher. in *F. Gr. H.* 3 F 95>, 58d
Oeme, daughter of Danaus[1] and *Crino* <Apollod. *Bibl.* 2.1.5>, 57d
— and Arbelus <Apollod. *Bibl.* 2.1.5>, (57d)
Oenarus, husband of *Ariadne* <Plut. *Thes.* 20.1>, 53d
Oeneus[1] [King of Pleuron and Calydon], son of Portheus[1] <Hom. *Il.* XIV.115-17> and *Euryte*[1] <Apollod. *Bibl.* 1.7.10>, 17c
alternate parentage:
Phytius <Hec. in Athen. 2.3>
— and *Althaea* <*Cat. Wom., Frag. Hes.* frg. 25, Merk. & West>, 15c
— and *Periboea*[1] <*Cat. Wom., Frag. Hes.* frg. 12, Merk. & West>, (17c)
Oeneus[2], son of Pandion II <Paus. 1.5.2>, 50c
Oeneus[3], son of Aegyptus[1] and *Gorgo*[1] <Apollod. *Bibl.* 2.1.5>, 57c
— and *Podarce* <Apollod. *Bibl.* 2.1.5>, (57c)
Oeneus[4], father of *Perimede*[3] <Paus. 7.4.2 (might be the same as Oeneus[1])>, 53b
Oeneus[5], son of Ereuthalion[2] <Non. *Dion.* 43.54-55>, *
Oenia — see *Ornia*
Oeno [one of the Oenotropae] [wine], daughter of Anius <Apollod. *Epit.* 3.10> and *Dorippe*, 56d
Oenoe[1], wife of Thoas[1] <Ap. Rhod. *Arg.* 1.625>, 56d
Oenoe[2], sister of Epochus <Paus. 1.33.7>, *
Oenoe[3], nurse of Zeus <Paus. 8.47.3>, *
Oenoe[4], wife of Nicodamas <Ant. Lib. *Met.* 16.2>, *
Oenomaus[1] [King of Pisa in Elis], son of Ares <Paus. 5.1.6> and *Harpinna* <Paus. 5.22.6>, 7c, *66b*
alternate parentage:
Ares and *Asterope*[1] <Hellan. in *F. Gr. H.* 4 F 19>
Alxion <Paus. 5.1.6>
— and *Asterope*[1] <Apollod. *Bibl.* 3.10.1>, 39a
— and *Euarete* <Hyg. *Fab.* 84>, 58d
— and *Hippodameia*[1] <Hyg. *Fab.* 253>, 39a
Oenomaus[2], father of Oenopion[2] <Non. *Dion.* 43.60>, *
Oenomaus[3], killed by Ares and Hector[1] <Hom. *Il.* V.706>, *
Oenomaus[4], killed by Idomeneus[2] <Hom. *Il.* XIII.506>, *
Oenomaus[5], killed by Corymbasus <Non. *Dion.* 28.96-102>, *
Oenone[1], daughter of Cebrenus <Apollod. *Bibl.* 3.12.6>, 67a
— and Paris <Apollod. *Bibl.* 3.12.6>, 43c
Oenone[2], a follower of Dionysus <Non. *Dion.* 29.252>, *
Oenone[3], mother of Melantheus <Non. *Dion.* 43.62>, *
Oenope, daughter of Epopeus[1] <Hyg. *Fab.* 157> and *Antiope*[1], 34d
— and Onchestus[1] <Plut. *Gr. Quest.* 16.295>, 9d
— and Poseidon <Hyg. *Fab.* 157>, 9b
Oenopion[1] [King of Chios], son of Dionysus and *Ariadne* <Apollod. *Epit.* 1.9>, 56c
alternate parentage:
Theseus and *Ariadne* <Ion of Chios in Plut. *Thes.* 20.2>
— and *Helice*[4] <Parth. *Love Stor.* 20.1>, (56c)
Oenopion[2], son of Oenomaus[2] <Non. *Dion.* 43.60>, *
(Oenotropae) [wine growers], daughters of Anius and *Dorippe* <Apollod. *Epit.* 3.10> (*Elais*, *Oeno*, *Spermo*), 56d
Oeoclus, son of Poseidon and *Ascra* <Heg. in Paus. 9.29.1>, 8a
Oeolycus, son of Theras <Paus. 3.15.6>, 55d
Oeonus, son of Licymnius <Paus. 3.15.4> and *Perimede*[2], 59c
Oeroe, daughter of Asopus <Herod. 9.51> and *Metope*[2], 66b
Oestrobles, son of Heracles[1] and *Hesychia*[2] <Apollod. *Bibl.* 2.7.8>, *50c*
Ogygia, daughter of Amphion[1] and *Niobe*[1] <Apollod. *Bibl.* 3.5.6>, 66d
Ogygus[1] [King of Eleusis], son of Poseidon and *Alistra* <Tzetz. on Lyc. 1206>, 8a
alternate parentage:
Calypso <Eust. on Hom. *Od.* 1393.31>
autochthonous <Paus. 9.5.1>
— and *Thebe*[2] <Tzetz. on Lyc. 1206>, 5d, 16a

Ogygus[2] — see Eleusis (alternate version)
Oicle(u)s (Oecles) [King of Arcadia], son of Antiphates[2] <Hom. *Od.* 15.243> and *Zeuxippe*[3], 32d
alternate parentage:
Mantius <Paus. 6.17.6>
Amphiaraus <Diod. Sic. 4.32.3>
— and *Hyperm(n)estra*[2] <*Cat. Wom., Frag. Hes.* frg. 25.34-35, Merk. & West>, 16c
Oileus[1] [King of Locris] [Argonaut], son of Odeodochus and *Laonome*[3] <Eust. on Hom. *Il.* 227>, 15c
— and *Alcimache* <Schol. on Hom. *Il.* XIII.694>, 23d
— and *Eriopis*[3] <Hom. *Il.* XIII.697>, (15c)
— and *Rhene*[1] <Hom. *Il.* II.727-28>, (15c)
Oileus[2], killed by Agamemnon <Hom. *Il.* XI.92-94>, *
Oitolinus — see Linus[1]
Oizys [pain] [abstraction], offspring of *Nyx* <Hes. *Theog.* 213>, *1b*
Olbia, paramour of Poseidon <Steph. Byz. "Astacus">, 9b
Olenias, son of Oeneus[1] <Apollod. *Bibl.* 1.8.5 (inferred because he is called brother of Tydeus)> and *Periboea*[1], 17d
Olenus[1], son of Hephaestus <Hyg. *Poet. Astr.* 2.13>, 7d
alternate parentage:
Zeus and *Anaxithea* <Steph. Byz. "Olenus">
— and *Lethaea* <Ovid *Met.* 10.68>, (7d)
Olenus[2], father of Tectaphus <Ovid *Met.* 12.433>, *
Olenus[3], father of Phoceus <Val. Flac. 3.204>, *
Olmus — see Almus
Olympus[1], son of Marsyas <Hyg. *Fab.* 273>, 6a
Olympus[2], son of Heracles[1] and *Euboea*[4] <Apollod. *Bibl.* 2.7.8>, *50d*
Olympus[3], paramour of *Cybele*[2] <Diod. Sic. 5.49.3>, 2d
Olympus[4], son of Cres <Phot. *Bibl.* 147b.37>, *
Olympusa, daughter of Thespius <Apollod. *Bibl.* 2.7.8> and *Megamede* <Apollod. *Bibl.* 2.4.10>, (51c)
— and Heracles[1] <Apollod. *Bibl.* 2.7.8>, 51c
Olynthus[1], son of Strymon <Con. *Narr.* 4>, 72a
Olynthus[2], son of Heracles[1] <Steph. Byz. "Olynthus"> and *Bolbe* <Athen. 8.334e>, 60b
Omester [one of the Pans], son of Pan <Non. *Dion.* 14.80>, 64d
Omphale [Queen of Lydia], daughter of Iardanus <Apollod. *Bibl.* 2.6.3>, 60c
— and Heracles[1] <Dion. Hal. *Rom. Ant.* 1.28.1>, (60c)
— and Tmolus <Apollod. *Bibl.* 2.6.3>, 7c
Onchestus[1], son of Poseidon <Paus. 9.26.3>, 9d
alternate parentage:
Boeotus[1] <*Cat. Wom., Frag. Hes.* frg. 219, Merk. & West>
— and *Oenope* <Plut. *Gr. Quest.* 16.295>, 34d
Onchestus[2], son of Agrius[1] <Apollod. *Bibl.* 1.8.6> and *Dia*[4], 16d
Oncius [King of Thelpusa], son of Apollo <Paus. 8.25.4>, 11d
[One thousand sons], children of Hypnos <Ovid *Met.* 1.633>, 1a
Oneiroi [dreams] [abstraction], offspring of *Nyx* <Hes. *Theog.* 212>, *1b*
Oneites (Hodites[1]) (Odeites[2]), son of Heracles[1] and *Deianeira*[1] <*Cat. Wom., Frag. Hes.* frg. 25.19, Merk. & West>, 60a
Onesippus, son of Heracles[1] and *Chryseis*[2] <Apollod. *Bibl.* 2.7.8>, *50c*
Onnes (Menon(es)), paramour of *Semiramis* <Diod. Sic. 2.5.1>, 61c
Opheltes[1] (Archemorus), son of Lycurgus[1] and *Eurydice*[3] <Apollod. *Bibl.* 1.9.14>, 29d
Opheltes[2], son of Peneleus <Paus. 9.5.16>, 18d
Opheltes[3], father of Euryalus[4] <Virg. *Aen.* 9.196-201>, 44c
Opheltes[4], sailor turned into a dolphin <Ovid *Met.* 3.641-68>, *
Opheltes[5], son of Arestor[2] <Non. *Dion.* 35.379>, *
Opheltes[6], killed by Telamon <Val. Flac. 1.198>, *
Ophion[1], paramour of *Eurynome*[1] <Ap. Rhod. *Arg.* 1.501>, 53b
Ophion[2] [centaur], offspring of Centaurus and a Magnesian Mare <Pind. *Pyth.* 2.50; named as centaur, Ovid *Met.* 12.245>, 69d
alternate parentage:
Ixion and *Nephele*[1] <Diod. Sic. 4.69.5>
Ophis[1] — see Ladon[2]
Ophis[2], father of *Combe*[2] <Ovid *Met.* 7.383>, *
Ophites, son of Heracles[1] and *Megara* <Hyg. *Fab.* 72>, 60d
Opis[1] [Hyperborean maiden], paramour of Orion <Apollod. *Bibl.* 1.4.5>, 53c
Opis[2], wife of Euaemon[1] <Hyg. *Fab.* 97>, 24d
Opis[3], daughter of Nereus and *Doris*[1] <Hyg. *Fab.* pref.>, *65a*
Opis[4], attendant of Artemis <Virg. *Aen.* 11.533>, *
Opus[1] [King of Elis], son of Zeus and *Protogeneia*[1] <Schol. on Pind. *Olym.* 9.87a-b>, 6d, *15a*
Opus[2], son of Zeus and *Cambyse* <Pind. *Olym.* 9.63>, 5b, *15a*
alternate parentage:
Locrus[2] and *Cambyse* <Eust. on Hom. *Il.* 277>
Orchamus [King of Persia], father of *Leucothoe*[1] <Ovid *Met.* 4.208 ff.>, 14a
— and *Eurynome*[3] <Ovid *Met.* 4.208 ff.>, (14a)
Orchomenus[1], son of Lycaon[1] <Apollod. *Bibl.* 3.8.1>, 63b
Orchomenus[2] [King of Orchomenus], son of Minyas <*Cat. Wom., Frag. Hes.* frg. 70.35, Merk. & West> and *Phanosyra* <Schol. on Ap. Rhod. 1.230>, 20d
Orchomenus[3], son of Thyestes[1] <Apollod. *Epit.* 2.13> and *Laodameia*[5] <Schol. on Eur. *Or.* 4>, 39b
Orchomenus[4], son of Athamas[1] and *Themisto*[1] <Hyg. *Fab.* 1>, 26b
Oreaside — see *Sois*
Oreia, daughter of Thespius <Apollod. *Bibl.* 2.7.8> and *Megamede* <Apollod. *Bibl.* 2.4.10>, (50c)
— and Heracles[1] <Apollod. *Bibl.* 2.7.8>, 50c
Oreithyia[1], daughter of Erechtheus II <Herod. 7.189> and *Praxithea*[2] <Apollod. *Bibl.* 3.15.1>, 51a
— and Boreas[1] <Herod. 7, 189>, 12b
Oreithyia[2], daughter of Cecrops II <Steph. Byz. "Europus"> and *Metiadusa*, 50a
— and Macedon <Steph. Byz. "Europus">, 15a
Oreithyia[3] — see *Otrere*
Oreithyia[4], daughter of Nereus <Hom. *Il.* XVIII.46> and *Doris*[1], *65b*
Oreithyia[5] — see *Myrr(h)a* (alternate version)
Oreius[1] [centaur], offspring of Centaurus and a Magnesian Mare <Pind. *Pyth.* 2.50; named as centaur, Diod. Sic. 4.12.7>, 69d
alternate parentage:
Ixion and *Nephele*[1] <Diod. Sic. 4.69.5>
Oreius[2], son of [a bear] and *Polyphonte* <Ant. Lib. *Met.* 21.3>, *71b*
Oreius[3], killed by Gryneus <Ovid *Met.* 12.262>, *
Orestes[1] [King of Argos, Mycenae, and Sparta], son of Agamemnon <Hom. *Od.* 1.30> and *Clytemnestra* <Soph. *Elec.* passim>, 36a
— and *Erigone*[2] <Paus. 2.18.5>, 39a
— and *Hermione* <Eur. *Or.* 1654-77>, 37a
Orestes[2], son of Achelous and *Perimede*[1] <Apollod. *Bibl.* 1.7.3>, 65b, *29a*
Orestes[3] [satyr], comrade of Dionysus <Non. *Dion.* 14.106>, *
Orestes[4], killed by Hector[1] <Hom. *Il.* V.704-05>, *
Orestes[5], killed by Leonteus[1] <Hom. *Il.* XII.185-93>, *
Orestheus[1], son of Deucalion[1] <Hec. in *F. Gr. H.* 1 F 13> and *Pyrrha*[1], 16b
Orestheus[2] — see [fifty sons of Lycaon[1]] (alternate version)
Orion [giant], son of Poseidon and *Euryale*[2] <*Cat. Wom., Frag. Hes.* frg. 148(a), Merk. & West>, 8d, *53c*
alternate parentage:
Hyrieus <Ant. Lib. *Met.* 25.1> and *Clonia*
— and *Eos* <Hom. *Od.* 5.121-22>, 12b
— and *Merope*[3] <Apollod. *Bibl.* 1.4.3>, 56c
— and *Opis*[1] <Apollod. *Bibl.* 1.4.5>, (53c)
— and *Pleione* <Hyg. *Poet. Astr.* 2.21>, 63a

— and *Side*[1] <Apollod. *Bibl.* 1.4.3>, (53c)
Oris, daughter of Orion <Tzetz. on *Chil.* 2.43>, 53c
— and Poseidon <Tzetz. on *Chil.* 2.43>, 9b
Ormenus[1], son of Cercaphus[2] <Dem. Scep. in Strab. 9.5.18>, 24b
Ormenus[2] [King of Syrie], father of Ctesius <Hom. *Od.* 15. 414>, *
Ormenus[3], suitor of *Penelope*[1] (from Zacynthus) <Apollod. *Epit.* 7.30>, *
Ormenus[4], killed by Teucer[2] <Hom. *Il.* VIII.274>, *
Ormenus[5], killed by Polypoetes[1] <Hom. *Il.* XII.187>, *
Orneus[1] [centaur], offspring of Centaurus and a Magnesian Mare <Pind. *Pyth.* 2.50; named as centaur, Ovid *Met.* 12.302>, 69d
alternate parentage:
Ixion and *Nephele*[1] <Diod. Sic. 4.69.5>
Orneus[2], son of Erechtheus II <Plut. *Thes.* 32.1> and *Praxithea*[2], 49a
Ornia (*Oenia*), daughter of Asopus and *Metope*[2] <Diod. Sic. 4.72. 1>, 66b
Ornytion, son of Sisyphus <Paus. 2.4.3> and *Merope*[1], 18a
Ornytus — see Naubolus[2] (alternate version)
Orontes[1], husband of *Protonoe* <Non. *Dion.* 34.179>, 3b
Orontes[2] [river], son of Oceanus and *Tethys* <Hes. *Theog.* 367-68; named as river, Hyg. *Fab.* pref.>, 62a
Orontes[3], comrade of Aeneas <Virg. *Aen.* 1.113>, *
Orphe, daughter of Dion and *Amphithea*[1] <Serv. on Virg. *Ecl.* 8.29>, 31d
Orpheus [Argonaut], son of Oeagrus and *Calliope* <Apollod. *Bibl.* 1.3.2>, *6a*
alternate parentage:
Oeagrus and *Polymnia* <Schol. on Ap. Rhod. *Arg.* 1.23>
Apollo and *Calliope* <Asclep. in *F. Gr. H.* 12 F 6>
Menippe[6] <Tzetz. on *Chil.* 1.12>
an unnamed daughter of Pierus <Paus. 9.30.4>
— and *Eurydice*[1] <Apollod. *Bibl.* 1.3.2>, (6a)
Orphne — see *Gorgyra*
Orphnea — see Ascalaphus[2] (alternate version)
Orsedice, daughter of Cinyras[1] and *Metharme* <Apollod. *Bibl.* 3. 14.3>, 11d
Orseis (*Ortheis*), paramour of Hellen(us)[1] <Apollod. *Bibl.* 1.7.3>, 17b
Orsiboe, wife of Deriades <Non. *Dion.* 40.91-101>, 3b
Orsilochus[1], son of Idomeneus[2] <Hom. *Od.* 13.259-60> and *Meda*[1], 54c
Orsilochus[2], son of Alpheius <Hom. *Il.* V.546> and *Telegone*, 65b
Orsilochus[3], son of Diocles[1] <Hom. *Il.* V.542>, 65b
Orsilochus[4], inventor of the four-horse chariot <Hyg. *Poet. Astr.* 2. 13>, *
Orsilochus[5], killed by Teucer[2] <Hom. *Il.* VIII.273-74>, *
Orsilochus[6], killed by *Camilla* <Virg. *Aen.* 11.690>, *
Orsinome, daughter of Eurynomus[1] <Diod. Sic. 4.69.2>, 21c
— and Lapithes <Diod. Sic. 4.69.2>, 68b
Orsobia, daughter of Deiphontes[2] and *Hyrnetho* <Paus. 2.28.3>, 60c
— and Pamphylas <Paus. 2.28.6>, 17b
Ortheis — see *Orseis*
Orthopolis, son of Plemnaeus <Paus. 2.5.5>, 8b
Orthosie [one of the hours], daughter of Zeus and *Themis*[1] <Hyg. *Fab.* 183>, 6d
Orth(r)us [dog of Geryon(eus)], offspring of Typhon and *Echidna* <Hes. *Theog.* 309>, 1b
— and *Chimaera*[1] <Hes. *Theog.* 327>, 1b
Orus[1] [King of Troezen], father of *Leis* <Paus. 2.30.5>, 8c
Orus[2], killed by Hector[1] <Hom. *Il.* XI.303>, *
Oryithus — see Pandion[3]
Osiris — see Macedon (alternate version)
Ossa, paramour of Ares <Con. *Narr.* 10>, 7b
Othreis, paramour of Zeus <Ant. Lib. *Met.* 13.1>, 6c
— and Apollo <Ant. Lib. *Met.* 13.1>, 11c
Otrere (*Oreithyia*[3]) [Amazon], paramour of Ares <Hyg. *Fab.* 30>, 7c
Otreus[1], father of *Placia* <Apollod. *Bibl.* 3.12.3>, 42c
Otreus[2], son of Dascylus <Val. Flac. 4.162 (inferred because he is called brother of Lycus[5], note 1, p. 198)>, 41a
Otus[1] [giant] [one of the Aloidae], son of Poseidon and *Iphimedeia*[1] <Hom. *Od.* 11.305-07>, 8c
alternate parentage:
Aloeus[1] and *Iphimedeia*[1] <Hom. *Il.* V.385>
Otus[2], killed by Polydamas <Hom. *Il.* XV.518>, *
Oudaeus — see Udaeus
Ouranie, daughter of Oceanus and *Tethys* <Hes. *Theog.* 350>, 62a
Oxeater (Buphagus), son of Iapetus and *Thornax(e)* <Paus. 8.27. 17>, 16a
— and *Promne* <Paus. 8.14.9 (her paramour is called Buphagus)>, (16a)
Oxylus[1], son of Ares and *Protogeneia*[2] <Apollod. *Bibl.* 1.7.7>, 7c, *15d*
Oxylus[2] [King of Elis and Aetolia], son of Haemon[3] <Paus. 5.3.6>, 16d
alternate parentage:
Andraemon[2] <Apollod. *Bibl.* 2.8.3>
— and *Pieria*[2] <Paus. 5.4.4>, (16d)
Oxylus[3], son of Oreius[2] <Athen. 3.78b>, 71b
— and *Hamadryas* <Athen. 3.78b>, (71b)
Oxyntes [King of Athens], son of Demophon[1] <Tzetz. *Chil.* 1.182>, 51c
Oxyporus, son of Cinyras[1] and *Metharme* <Apollod. *Bibl.* 3.14.3>, 11d
Ozomene — see *Aello*[1], *Celaeno*[2] (alternate versions)

Pactolus [river], son of Zeus and *Leucothea*[2] <Ps.-Plut. *De Fluv.* 7. 1>, 5c
Paeon[1], son of Endymion and *Chromia* <Paus. 5.1.4>, 16a
Paeon[2], son of Antilochus <Paus. 2.18.8>, 27c
Paeon[3] — see Asclepius
Paeon[4] (Edonus), son of Poseidon and *Helle* <Hyg. *Poet. Astr.* 2. 20>, 8c
Paeon[5], father of Agastrophus <Hom. *Il.* XI.340>, *
Paeon[6], father of Aristaeus[2] <Pher. in *F. Gr. H.* 3 F 44>, *
Paeonaeus [one of the Dactyls], son of *Anchiale*[1] <Ap. Rhod. *Arg.* 1.1128; named, Paus. 5.7.6>, *11b*
alternate parentage:
born on Mt. Ida of uncertain parentage <Diod. Sic. 5.64.4>
Palaechthon — see Pelasgus[1] (alternate version)
Palaemon[1] — see Melicertes
Palaemon[2] (Palaemonius) [Argonaut], son of Hephaestus <Ap. Rhod. *Arg.* 1.202-04> and the wife of Lernus[1], 7d
alternate parentage:
Aetolus[1] <Apollod. *Bibl.* 1.9.16>
Lernus[1] <Hyg. *Fab.* 14>
Palaemon[3], son of Heracles[1] and *Autonoe*[4] <Apollod. *Bibl.* 2.7.8>, 60b
Palaemon[4], a warrior at Thebes <Stat. *Theb.* 8.135>, *
Palaemonius — see Palaemon[2]
Palaestra, daughter of Choricus <*Etym. Magn.* "Pale" 648.2-3>, 46d
— and Hermes <*Etym. Magn.* "Pale" 648.2-3>, (46d)
Palamaon — see Daedalus (alternate version)
Palamedes, son of Nauplius[1] and *Clymene*[5] <Apollod. *Bibl.* 2.1. 5>, 52d
alternate parentage:
Nauplius[1] and *Hesione*[3] <Apollod. *Bibl.* 2.1.5>
Nauplius[1] and *Philyra* <Apollod. *Bibl.* 2.1.5>
Nauplius[2] <Grimal "Nauplius">

Pale, daughter of *Palaestra* <*Etym. Magn.* "Pale" 648.2-3>, *46d*
(Palici), sons of Zeus and *Thaleia*[4] <Steph. Byz. "Paliki">, 6c, *7d*
Pallantia, daughter of Euander[1] <Serv. on Virg. *Aen.* 8.51 (citing Varro)>, 46d
— and Heracles[1] <Serv. on Virg. *Aen.* 8.51 (citing Varro)>, 60d
Pallas[1], son of Crius[1] and *Eurybia*[1] <Hes. *Theog.* 376>, 12a
— and *Styx* <Hes. *Theog.* 384>, 50a
Pallas[2] [giant], son of *Gaea* (and the blood of Uranus) <Hes. *Theog.* 180-86; named as giant, Apollod. *Bibl.* 1.6.2>, *4a*
Pallas[3], son of Lycaon[1] <Apollod. *Bibl.* 3.8.1>, 63b
Pallas[4], son of Euander[1] <Virg. *Aen.* 8.1104>, 46d
Pallas[5], son of Heracles[1] and *Lavinia*[1] <Dion. Hal. *Rom. Ant.* 1.32>, 60d, *46c*
Pallas[6], son of Pandion II and *Pylia* <Apollod. *Bibl.* 3.15.5>, 51a
Pallas[7], daughter of Triton <Apollod. *Bibl.* 3.11.3>, 63b
Pallas[8], son of Megamedes <*Hom. Hymn* 4 (to Hermes), 100>, *
Pallas Athene — see *Athene*
Pallene[1], daughter of Sithon <Parth. *Love Stor.* 6.1> and *Mendeis* <Con. *Narr.* 10>, 7d
— and Cleitus[2] <Parth. *Love Stor.* 6.6>, (7d)
Pallene[2], daughter of Alcyoneus[1] <Eust. on Hom. *Il.* 776>, 4a
Pammerope, daughter of Celeus[1] <Paus. 1.38.3> and *Metaneira*, 46b
Pammon[1], son of Priam[1] <Hom. *Il.* XXIV.250> and *Hecabe*[1] <Apollod. *Bibl.* 3.12.5>, 43d
Pammon[2], son of Hippasus[8] <Quint. Smyr. 6.562>, *
Pamphylus [King of Doris], son of Aegimius <*Cat. Wom., Hesiodi* frg. 10a.6-7, Merk. & West (O.C.T.)>, 17b
— and *Orsobia* <Paus. 2.28.6>, 60c
Pan, son of Hermes and *Dryope*[1] <*Hom. Hymn* 19 (to Pan), 1.33>, 46a, *64d*
alternate parentage:
Hermes and *Penelope*[1] <Apollod. *Epit.* 7.39>
Apollo and *Penelope*[1] <Pind. frg.100, Snell & Maehler>
Zeus and *Hybris* <Apollod. *Bibl.* 1.4.1>
— and *Aex* <Hyg. *Poet. Astr.* 2.13>, 7d
— and *Echo* <Tzetz. on Lyc. 310>, (46a)
— and *Eupheme*[1] <Hyg. *Fab.* 224>, (46a)
— and *Pitys* <Prop. *Eleg.* 1.18.20 (she is called *Pinus*)>, (46a)
— and *Selene* <Virg. *Geo.* 3.393-95>, 14b
— and *Syrinx* <Ovid *Met.* 1.690>, (46a)
Panaceia[1] [peace], daughter of Asclepius and *Epeione* <*Paean Erythr.* T. 592>, 19d
alternate parentage:
Asclepius and *Lampetia* <Hermip. frg. 1,West>
Panaceia[2], mother of Proteus[4] <Quint. Smyr. 3.301-03>, *
Pancratis, daughter of Aloeus[1] and *Iphimedeia* <Diod. Sic. 5.50. 6>, 34c
— and Agassamenus <Diod. Sic. 5.50.6>, (34c)
Pandareus, son of Merops[4] <Ant. Lib. *Met.* 36.2>, 66d
— and *Harmothoe*[1] <Eust. on Hom. *Od.* 1875.31>, (66d)
Pandarus[1], son of Alcanor[1] and *Iaera*[2]; brother of Bitias[1] <Virg. *Aen.* 9.672-73>, 41d
Pandarus[2], son of Lycaon[4] <Hom. *Il.* II.826>, *
Pandeia, daughter of Zeus and *Selene* <*Hom. Hymn* 32 (to *Selene*), 15>, 6d
Pandion I [King of Athens], son of Erichthonius[1] and *Praxithea*[1] <Apollod. *Bibl.* 3.14.6>, 49a
— and *Zeuxippe*[1] <Apollod. *Bibl.* 3.14.8>, (49a)
Pandion II [King of Athens and Megara], son of Cecrops II and *Metiadusa* <Apollod. *Bibl.* 3.15.5>, 50b
— and *Pylia* <Apollod. *Bibl.* 3.15.5>, 59c
Pandion[3] (Oryithus) (Parthenius[1]), son of Phineus[2] and *Cleopatra*[1] <Apollod. *Bibl.* 3.15.3>, 13a
Pandion[4], son of Aegyptus[1] and *Hephaestine* <Apollod. *Bibl.* 2.1. 5>, 57d
— and *Callidice*[2] <Apollod. *Bibl.* 2.1.5>, (57d)
Pandion[5], father of Lamprus <Parth. *Love Stor.* 17.1>, *
Pandora[1] [first mortal woman, molded from clay by Hephaestus], wife of Epimetheus <Hes. *Works and Days* 79-89>, 16b, 52a
Pandora[2], daughter of Erechtheus II <Suid. *Lex.* "Parthenoi"> and *Praxithea*[2], 51a
Pandora[3], daughter of Deucalion[1] <*Cat. Wom., Frag. Hes.* frg. 5, Merk. & West> and *Pyrrha*[1], 16b
— and Zeus <*Cat. Wom., Frag. Hes.* frg. 5, Merk. & West>, 6c
Pandorus, son of Erechtheus II and *Praxithea*[2] <Apollod. *Bibl.* 3. 15.1>, 50b
Pandrosos, daughter of Cecrops I and *Aglaurus*[1] <Apollod. *Bibl.* 3. 14.2>, *66b*
— and Hermes <Schol. on Hom. *Il.* I. 334>, 46d
Pangarus, son of Ares and *Critobule* <Ps.-Plut. *De Fluv.* 3.2>, 7a
Panope[1], daughter of Nereus and *Doris*[1] <Hes. *Theog.* 250>, *65b*
Panope[2], daughter of Thespius <Apollod. *Bibl.* 2.7.8> and *Megamede* <Apollod. *Bibl.* 2.4.10>, 50c
— and Heracles[1] <Apollod. *Bibl.* 2.7.8>, (50c)
Panopeus[1] (Pharoteus), son of Phocus[1] <Paus. 2.29.4> and *Asterodeia*[2], 23c
Panopeus[2], killed at Thebes <Stat. *Theb.* 10.497>, *
Panoptes — see Argus[3]
[Pans] [horned rock-dwellers] sons of Pan <Non. *Dion.* 14.70-86> (see Aegicorus, Argennus, Argus[6], Celaeneus[2], Daphoeneus, Eugeneius, Glaucus[8], Omester, Philamnus, Phobus[2], Phorbas[6], Xanthus[7]), 64d
sons of Hermes <Non. *Dion.* 14.92-95> (see Agreus[2], Nomius[1]), 46d
Pantidyia, wife of Thestius <Schol. on Ap. Rhod. 1.146>, 15d
— and Glaucus[1] <Schol. on Ap. Rhod. 1.146>, 18b
Paphos, daughter of Pygmalion[1] <Ovid *Met.* 10.296 (the child is sometimes called a son)> and *Galateia*[2], 11c
— and Apollo <Schol. on Pind. *Pyth.* 27>, (11c)
Pareia, wife of Minos I <Apollod. *Bibl.* 2.1.3>, 54c
Parias, son of Philomelus[1] <Hyg. *Poet. Astr.* 2.4>, 42b
Paris (Alexander[1]), son of Priam[1] and *Hecabe*[1] <Hom. *Il.* XXIV. 249>, 43c
— and Antheus[1] <Lyc. 134>, 45c
— and *Arisbe*[3] <Eust. on Hom. *Il.* 894>, (43c)
— and *Helen*[1] <Hom. *Il.* III.425-36>, 48d
— and *Oenone*[1] <Apollod. *Bibl.* 3.12.6>, 67a
Parnassa — see *Metope*[2]
Parnassus, son of Poseidon and *Cleodora*[1] <Paus. 10.6.1>, 8d
Parrhasius, son of Ares and *Phylonome* <Plut. *Gr. and Rom. Par. Stor.* 36>, 7c, *63c*
Parthaon[1] — see Portheus[1]
Parthaon[2] (Porthaon[2]), son of Periphetes[3] <Paus. 8.24.1>, 63d
Parthenia[1], wife of Samus <Schol. on Ap. Rhod. *Arg.* 1.187>, 54d
Parthenia[2] — see (Pleiades) (alternate version)
Parthenia[3] [Mare of Marmax] <Paus. 6.21.7>, *
Parthenia[4], daughter of *Hippo*[3] <Callim. frg. 693, Pfeiffer>, *
Parthenius[1] — see Pandion[3]
Parthenius[2] [river], son of Oceanus and *Tethys* <Hes. *Theog.* 344>, 62a
Parthenius[3], killed by Rapo <Virg. *Aen.* 10.748>, *
Parthenopaeus [one of the Seven against Thebes (per Aesch. *Sev.* 524-48)], son of Melanion <Apollod. *Bibl.* 3.9.2> and *Atalanta*[1] <Soph. *Oed. at Col.* 1319-23>, 63d, *64d*
alternate parentage:
Ares and *Atalanta*[1] <Apollod. *Bibl.* 3.9.2>
Meleager and *Atalanta*[1] <Hyg. *Fab.* 99>
Talaus and *Lysimache*[1] <Apollod. *Bibl.* 1.9.13>
— and *Clymene*[3] <Hyg. *Fab.* 71>, (64d)
Parthenope[1] — see [Sirens]
Parthenope[2], daughter of Stymphalus[1] <Apollod. *Bibl.* 2.7.8>, 62d
— and Heracles[1] <Apollod. *Bibl.* 2.7.8>, 60d
Parthenope[3], daughter of Ancaeus[2] and *Samia* <Paus. 7.4.2>, 54d

— and Apollo <Paus. 7.4.2>, 11d
Parthenope[4], paramour of Oceanus <Andr. Hall. in *F.H.G.* 2.349 frg. 1, Müller>, 55a
Parthenos, daughter of Staphylus[1] and *Chrysothemis*[2] <Diod. Sic. 5.62.1>, 56d
alternate parentage:
Apollo and *Chrysothemis*[2] <Hyg. *Poet. Astr.* 2.25>
Pasidice (*Peisidice*[3]), daughter of Pelias[1] and *Anaxibia*[2] <*Cat. Wom., Frag. Hes.* frg. 37, Merk. & West>, 28d
alternate parentage:
Pelias and *Phylomache* <Apollod. *Bibl.* 1.9.10>
Pasiphae[1], daughter of Helios and *Perse(is)* <Apollod. *Bibl.* 1.9.1>, 14d
alternate parentage:
Helios and *Crete*[1] <Diod. Sic. 4.60.4>
— and [the Cretan Bull] <Apollod. *Bibl.* 3.1.4>, 54c
— and Minos I <Apollod. *Bibl.* 1.9.1>, 54c
Pasiphae[2], daughter of Oceanus and *Tethys* <Hyg. *Fab.* pref.>, 68a
Pasiphae[3], oracle at Thalamae <Plut. *Agis*>, *
Pasithea[1] — see *Aglaia*[1]
Pasithea[2], daughter of Nereus and *Doris*[1] <Hes. *Theog.* 246>, *65b*
Pasithoe, daughter of Oceanus and *Tethys* <Hes. *Theog.* 352>, 62b
Passalus (Phrynondas) (Triballus[2]) [one of the Cercopes], son of Oceanus and *Theia*[2] <Eust. on Hom. *Od.* 1864.34; named, Tzetz. *Chil.* 5.77.94>, *72a*
Patreus, son of Preugenes <Paus. 7.18.5>, 47c
Patro, daughter of Thespius <Apollod. *Bibl.* 2.7.8> and *Megamede* <Apollod. *Bibl.* 2.4.10>, 50c
— and Heracles[1] <Apollod. *Bibl.* 2.7.8>, (50c)
Patroclus[1], son of Menoetius[2] <Hom. *Il.* I.307> and *Sthenele*[1] <Apollod. *Bibl.* 3.13.8>, 22d
alternate parentage:
Menoetius[2] and *Periopis* <Apollod. *Bibl.* 3.13.8>
Menoetius[2] and *Philomela*[4] <Hyg. *Fab.* 97>
Menoetius[2] and *Polymela*[4] <Philocr. in Apollod. *Bibl.* 3.13.8>
— and Achilles <Apollod. *Bibl.* 3.18.8>, 24d
— and *Iphis*[3] <Hom. *Il.* IX.666-67>, (22d)
Patroclus[2], son of Heracles[1] and *Pyrippe* <Apollod. *Bibl.* 2.7.8>, *50d*
Pedaeus, son of Antenor[1] <Hom. *Il.* V.69>, 45c
Pedasus[1], son of Bucolion[2] and *Abarbarea* <Hom. *Il.* VI.21-22>, 42c
Pedasus[2], mortal horse of Achilles <Hom. *Il.* XVI.467>, *
Pedias, daughter of Mynes <Apollod. *Bibl.* 3.14.5> and *Briseis*[1] (or possibly daughter of a different Mynes than the son of Euneus[3]), 51d
— and Cranaus <Apollod. *Bibl.* 3.14.5>, 16a, 51d
Pedile — see (Hyades) (alternate version)
Pegasus [winged horse], son of Poseidon and *Medusa*[1] <Hes. *Theog.* 281>, 8d, *2b*
Peiranthus — see Peiras[1]
Peiras[1] (Peiranthus) (Peirasus), son of Argus[2] and *Euadne*[2] <Apollod. *Bibl.* 2.1.2>, 61a
— and *Callirhoe*[5] <Hyg. *Fab.* 145>, (61a)
Peiras[2], paramour of *Styx* <Epim. in Paus. 8.18.2>, 50a
Peirasus — see Peiras
Peiren — see Deliades
Peirene[1], daughter of Danaus[1] and [an Ethiopian woman] <Apollod. *Bibl.* 2.1.5>, 57d
— and Agaptolemus <Apollod. *Bibl.* 2.1.5>, (57d)
Peirene[2], daughter of Asopus and *Metope*[2] <Diod. Sic. 4.72.1>, 66a
alternate parentage:
Achelous <Paus. 2.2.3>
Oebalus <Paus. 2.2.3>
— and Poseidon <Diod. Sic. 4.72.1>, 9b
Peireus, father of *Autonoe*[4] <Apollod. *Bibl.* 2.7.8>, 60b
Peirithous[1] [King of the Lapiths], son of Zeus and *Dia*[1] <Hom. *Il.* XIV.319 (*Dia*[1] is identified as wife of Ixion)>, 5a
alternate parentage:
Ixion and *Dia*[2] <Diod. Sic. 4.69.2>
— and *Hippodameia*[2] <Diod. Sic. 4.70.3>, 30d
Peirithous[2], son of Aepytus[1] <*Cat. Wom., Frag. Hes.* frg. 166, Merk. & West>, 62d
Peisander[1] — see Isander
Peisander[2], son of Antimachus[2] <Hom. *Il.* XI.122>, *
Peisander[3], son of Maemalus <Hom. *Il.* XVI.193-94>, *
Peisander[4], son of Polyctor[3] <Hom. *Od.* 18.299>, *
Peisander[5], father of Maenalus[3] <Quint. Smyr. 3.298-99>, *
Peisander[6], killed by Menelaus <Hom. *Il.* XIII.601>, *
Peisenor[1] [centaur], offspring of Centaurus and a Magnesian Mare <Pind. *Pyth.* 2.50; named as centaur, Ovid *Met.* 12.303>, 69d
alternate parentage:
Ixion and *Nephele*[1] <Diod. Sic. 4.69.5>
Peisenor[2], father of Ops <Hom. *Od.* 1.439>, *
Peisenor[3], father of Cleitus[4] <Hom. *Il.* XV.445>, *
Peisenor[4], a herald <Hom. *Od.* 2.38>, *
Peisenor[5], suitor of *Penelope*[1] (from Same) <Apollod. *Epit.* 7.28>, *
Peisidice[1], daughter of Aeolus[1] <*Cat. Wom., Hesiodi* frg. 10(a).100-03, Merk. & West (O.C.T.)> and *Enarete* <Apollod. *Bibl.* 1.7.3>, 28b
— and Myrmidon <*Cat. Wom., Hesiodi* frg. 10(a).99-100, Merk. & West (O.C.T.)>, 5d
Peisidice[2], daughter of Nestor and *Anaxibia*[4] <*Cat. Wom., Frag. Hes.* frg. 35, Merk. & West>, 27c
alternate parentage:
Nestor and *Eurydice*[7] <Hom. *Od.* 3.453 (inferred because she is wife of Nestor)>
Peisidice[3] — see *Pasidice*
Peisidice[4], paramour of Achilles <Parth. *Love Stor.* 21.2>, 24c
Peisidice[5], daughter of Leucon[1] <*Cat. Wom., Frag. Hes.* frg. 70, Merk. & West>, 20d
— and Copreus[2] <*Cat. Wom., Frag. Hes.* frg. 70, Merk. & West>, (20d)
Peisinoe[1] [one of the Sirens], daughter of Achelous and *Melpomene* <Apollod. *Epit.* 7.18>, 65b
alternate parentage:
Achelous and *Sterope*[2] <Apollod. *Bibl.* 1.7.10>
Achelous and *Terpsichore* <Ap. Rhod. *Arg.* 4.893>
Peisinoe[2], shape of the girl assumed by *Aphrodite* <Non. *Dion.* 4.72>, *
Peisistratus[1], son of Nestor <Hom. *Od.* 3.36> and *Anaxibia*[4] <Apollod. *Bibl.* 1.9.9>, 27c
alternate parentage:
Nestor and *Eurydice*[7] <Hom. *Od.* 3.453 (inferred because she is wife of Nestor)>
Peisistratus[2], son of Peisistratus[1] <Paus. 2.18.8>, 27d
Peisistratus[3], son of Hippocrates <Herod. 1.59.6>, *
Peisus[1], son of Apollo <Serv. on Virg. *Aen.* 10.179>, 11d
Peisus[2] [King of Pisa in Elis], son of Aphareus[1] and *Arene* <Apollod. *Bibl.* 3.10.3>, 25d
alternate parentage:
Perieres[1] <Paus. 5.17.9>
Peitho[1] [persuasion], daughter of *Ate* <Aesch. *Agam.* 387>, *1a*
Peitho[2], daughter of Oceanus and *Tethys* <Hes. *Theog.* 349>, 62b
Peitho[3] — see *Euadne*[2]
Peitho[4] — see *Teledice*
Peitho[5] — see (Charites) (alternate version)
Pelagon[1], son of Asopus and *Metope*[2] <Apollod. *Bibl.* 3.12.6>, 66a
Pelagon[2], friend of Sarpedon[1] <Hom. *Il.* V.695>, *
Pelagon[3], attacked by a boar <Ovid *Met.* 8.360>, *
Pelagon[4], killed by Oenomaus[1] <Paus. 6.21.11>, *
Pelasgus[1] [King of Arcadia], son of Zeus and *Niobe*[2] <Acus. in

Apollod. *Bibl.* 2.1.1>, 6c, *62a*
alternate parentage:
Palaechthon <Aesch. *Supp.* 250>
autochthonous <*Cat. Wom., Frag. Hes.* frg. 160, Merk. & West>
— and *Cyllene*[1] <Apollod. *Bibl.* 3.8.1>, (62a)
— and *Deianeira*[3] <Dion. Hal. *Rom. Ant.* 1.11.2>, (62a)
— and *Meliboea*[1] <Apollod. *Bibl.* 3.8.1>, 61a
Pelasgus[2], son of Triop(a)s[2] and *Sois* <Schol. on Eur. *Or.* 932>, 61d
Pelasgus[3], son of Poseidon and *Larissa*[1] <Dion. Hal. *Rom. Ant.* 1. 17.3>, 8c, *61d*
— and *Menippe*[3] <Dion. Hal. *Rom. Ant.* 1.28.3>, 69a
Pelasgus[4], son of Asopus and *Metope*[2] <Diod. Sic. 4.71.1>, 66a
Pelegon, son of Axius and *Periboea*[6] <Hom. *Il.* XXI.140>, 67a
Peleus [King of Myrmidons] [Argonaut], son of Aeacus <Hom. *Il.* XVI.15> and *Endeis* <Apollod. *Bibl.* 3.12.6>, 24c
— and *Antigone*[2] <Apollod. *Bibl.* 3.13.1>, 22d
— and *Eurydice*[10] <Schol. A on Hom. *Il.* XVI.175>, 22d
— and *Hippolyte*[2] <Pind. *Nem.* 5.25-33>, 33a
— and *Laodameia*[4] <Schol. A on Hom. *Il.* XVI.175>, 32d
— and *Polymela*[3] <Eust. on Hom. *Il.* 321>, 23c
— and *Thetis* <Hes. *Theog.* 1006>, 65a
Pelia — see *Pylia*
(Peliades), daughters of Pelias and *Anaxibia*[2] (see *Alcestis*, *Amphinome*[2], *Antinoe*[2], *Asteropeia*[1], *Euadne*[4], *Hippothoe*[2], *Medusa*[4], *Pasadice*, *Pelopeia*[1]), 28d
Pelias[1] [King of Iolchus], son of Poseidon and *Tyro* <Hom. *Od.* 11. 235-54>, 9c, *28c*
alternate parentage:
Cretheus and *Tyro* <Hyg. *Fab.* 12>
— and *Anaxibia*[2] <Apollod. *Bibl.* 1.9.10>, 30c
— and *Phylomache* <Apollod. *Bibl.* 1.9.10>, 66c
Pelias[2], son of Aeginetes[1] <Paus. 7.18.5>, 47c
Pelias[3], wounded by Odysseus <Virg. *Aen.* 2.435-36>, *
Pellen, son of Phorbas[3] <Paus. 7.26.5> and *Euboea*[2], 61d
Pelopeia[1], daughter of Pelias[1] and *Anaxibia*[2] <Apollod. *Bibl.* 1.9. 10>, 28d
alternate parentage:
Pelias[1] and *Phylomache* <Apollod. *Bibl.* 1.9.10>
— and Ares <Apollod. *Bibl.* 2.7.7>, 7d
Pelopeia[2], daughter of Thyestes[1] <Hyg. *Fab.* 87>, 39b
— and Atreus <Hyg. *Fab.* 88>, 36b
— and Thyestes[1] <Hyg. *Fab.* 87>, 39a
Pelopeia[3], daughter of Amphion[1] and *Niobe*[1] <Apollod. *Bibl.* 3.5. 6>, 66d
Pelops[1] [King of Pisa in Elis], son of Tantalus[1] <Eur. *Iph. in Taur.* 1> and *Dione*[3] <Hyg. *Fab.* 83>, *41a*
alternate parentage:
Tantalus[1] and *Clytie*[7] <Pher. in *F. Gr. H.* 3 F 40>
Tantalus[1] and *Euryanassa*[1] <Schol. on Eur. *Or.* 5>
Tantalus[1] and *Eurythemis(te)* <Schol. on Eur. *Or.* 11>
— and *Axioche* <Schol. on Pind. *Olym.* 1.144>, 39a, 40a, 41a
— and *Hippodameia*[1] <Eur. *Iph. in Taur.* 3-4, 824>, 39a
Pelops[2], son of Agamemnon and *Cassandra*[1] <Paus. 2.16.5>, 36b
Pelops[3], son of Pelops[1] <Schol. on Pind. *Olym.* 1.144> and *Hippodameia*[1], *38b*
Peloreus [giant], son of *Gaea* (and the blood of Uranus) <Hes. *Theog.* 180-86; named as giant, Non. *Dion.* 48.39>, *4a*
Peloris, wife of Agasthenes <Hyg. *Fab.* 97>, 63c
Pelor(us) [one of the Spartoi [sown men]], sprang from teeth of the Cadmean Dragon <Apollod. *Bibl.* 3.4.2>, 7d
Pemon — see Polypemon
Pe(m)phredo [one of the Graeae], daughter of Phorcus[1] and *Ceto*[1] <Hes. *Theog.* 273>, 2a
Peneius [river], son of Oceanus and *Tethys* <Hes. *Theog.* 343>, 68b
— and *Bura* <Steph. Byz. "Atrax">, 51b
— and *Creusa*[4] <Diod. Sic. 4.69.1>, 2a
Peneleus, son of Hippal(cy)mus[2] <Diod. Sic. 4.67.7> and *Asterope*[2] <Hyg. *Fab.* 97>, 18d
Penelope[1] (*Ameirace*) (*Arnacia*) (*Arnaea*), daughter of Icarius[2] <Hom. *Od.* 1.328> and *Periboea*[5] <Apollod. *Bibl.* 3.10.6>, 47d
alternate parentage:
Icarius[2] and *Polycaste*[2] <Strab. 10.2.24>
— and Amphinomous[3] <Apollod. *Epit.* 7.40>, (47d)
— and Antinous <Apollod. *Epit.* 7.38>, (47d)
— and Odysseus <Hom. *Od.* 11.247>, 13c
— and Telegonus[1] <Hyg. *Fab.* 127>, 13d
Penelope[2], paramour of Hermes <Non. *Dion.* 14.93>, 46d
Penthesileia [Amazon], daughter of Ares and *Otrere* <Apollod. *Epit.* 5.1>, 7c
— and Achilles <*Etym. Magn.* "Kaystros" (inferred because she is called mother of Achilles' son, Cayst(ri)us[1])>, 24c
Pentheus[1] [King of Thebes], son of Echion[1] and *Agave*[1] <Eur. *Bacc.* 507>, 7d, *55d*
Pentheus[2], son of *Astyoche*[8] <Stat. *Theb.* 3.170>, *
Penthilus[1] [King of Argos and Sparta], son of Orestes[1] and *Erigone*[2] <Paus. 2.18.5>, 36d
Penthilus[2], son of Periclymenus[1] <Paus. 2.18.8>, 27d
Peparethus, son of Dionysus and *Ariadne* <Apollod. *Bibl. Epit.* 1. 9>, 56c
Peratus, son of Poseidon and *Calchinia* <Paus. 2.5.5>, 8b
Perdix[1], daughter of Eupalamus and *Alcippe*[1] <Apollod. *Bibl.* 3.15. 8 (inferred because she is sister of Daedalus)>, 49b
alternate parentage:
Eupalamus and *Merope*[5] <Plut. *Thes.* 19.5>
Metion and *Iphinoe*[5] <Pher. in *F. Gr. H.* 3 F 146>
Palamaon <Paus. 9.3.2> (all versions inferred because she is sister of Daedalus)
Perdix[2] (Calus) (Talus[1]), son of *Perdix*[1] <Apollod. *Bibl.* 3.15.8 (called Talus)>, 49b
Pereus, son of Elatus[1] and *Laodice*[2] <Apollod. *Bibl.* 3.9.1>, 62d
Pergamus, son of Neoptolemus and *Andromache* <Paus. 1.11.1 (father is called Pyrrhus)>, 24d
Perialces, son of Bias[1] and *Pero*[1] <Eust. on Hom. *Od.* 1685>, 30c
Periander (Pyranthus), son of Cypselus[2] <Paus. 2.28.8>, 60d
— and *Melissa*[2] <Paus. 2.28.8>, (60d)
Periboea[1], daughter of Hipponous[1] <*Cat. Wom., Frag. Hes.* frg. 12, Merk. & West> and *Astynome*[3], 58c
— and Hippostratus <*Cat. Wom., Frag. Hes.* frg. 12, Merk. & West>, 17d
— and Oeneus[1] <*Cat. Wom., Frag. Hes.* frg. 12, Merk. & West>, 17d
Periboea[2] (*Eriboea*[1]), daughter of Alcathous[1] <Apollod. *Bibl.* 3. 12.7> and *Euaechme*[1], 40a
— and Telamon <Soph. *Ajax* 569 (inferred because she is mother of Ajax[1])>, 23d
— and Theseus <Plut. *Thes.* 29.1>, 51d
Periboea[3] — see *Merope*[10]
Periboea[4], daughter of Eurymedon[1] <Hom. *Od.* 7.56-58>, 9a
— and Poseidon <Hom. *Od.* 7.56-58>, (9a)
Periboea[5] (*Dordoche*) (*Mede*), wife of Icarius[2] <Schol. on Hom. *Od.* 15.15>, 47d
Periboea[6], daughter of Acessamenus <Hom. *Il.* XXI.143>, 67a
— and Axius <Hom. *Il.* XXI.143>, (67a)
Periboea[7], daughter of Oceanus <Non. *Dion.* 48.248> and *Tethys*, 62b
— and Lelas <Non. *Dion.* 48.247-48>, (62b)
Periboea[8], wife of Meges[3] <Quint. Smyr. 7.605-10>, *
Periboea[9], one of first two girls sent to Troy by the Locrians <Apollod. *Epit.* 6.21>, *
Periclymene (*Clymene*[6]), daughter of Minyas and *Clytodora*[1] <Schol. on Ap. Rhod. *Arg.* 1.230>, 20d
— and Pheres[1] <Hyg. *Fab.* 14>, 29b
Periclymenus[1] [Argonaut], son of Neleus[1] and *Chloris*[2] <Hom. *Od.*

11.286>, 27d
Periclymenus[2], son of Poseidon and *Chloris*[3] <Schol. on Pind. *Nem.* 9.57a>, 8c, *32d*
alternate parentage:
Poseidon and *Astypalea* <Hyg. *Fab.* 157>
Periclymenus[3] (Theoclymenus[4]), paramour of *Ismene*[1] <Mimn. frg. 21, Gerber>, 55c
Periclymenus[4], suitor of *Penelope*[1] (from Zacynthus) <Apollod. *Epit.* 7.30>, *
Peridia[1] — see *Cleochareia*
Peridia[2], mother of Onites <Virg. *Aen.* 12.514>, *
Perieres[1] [King of Messena], son of Aeolus[1] <*Cat. Wom., Frag. Hes.* frg. 10, Merk. & West> and *Enarete* <Apollod. *Bibl.* 1.7.3>, 25b
alternate parentage:
Cynortes <Apollod. *Bibl.* 1.9.5>
— and *Alcyone*[6] <*Cat. Wom., Frag. Hes.* frg. 49, Merk. & West>, (25b)
— and *Gorgophone*[1] <Apollod. *Bibl.* 2.4.5>, 59c
Perieres[2], charioteer of Menoeceus[1] <Apollod. *Bibl.* 2.4.11>, *
Perigune, daughter of Sinis <Plut. *Thes.* 8.2>, 34d
— and Deion(eus)[2] <Plut. *Thes.* 8.3>, 60b
— and Theseus <Plut. *Thes.* 8.3>, 51d
Perila(u)s[1], son of Ancaeus[2] and *Samia* <Paus. 7.4.2>, 54d
Perilaus[2], son of Icarius[2] and *Periboea*[5] <Apollod. *Bibl.* 3.10.6>, 47d
Perilaus[3], killed by Neoptolemus <Quint. Smyr. 8.293>, *
Perimede[1] (*Perimele*[1]), daughter of Aeolus[1] <*Cat. Wom., Hesiodi* frg. 10(a).34, Merk. & West (O.C.T.)> and *Enarete* <Apollod. *Bibl.* 1.7.3>, 29a
alternate parentage:
Hippodamas[3] <Ovid. *Met.* 8.593 (she is called *Perimele*)>
— and Achelous <*Cat. Wom., Hesiodi* frg. 10(a).34-35, Merk. & West (O.C.T.)> , 65a
Perimede[2], daughter of Alcaeus[2] and *Asty(a)dameia*[4] <Apollod. *Bibl.* 2.5.6 (inferred because she is called sister of Amphitryon)>, 59c
— and Licymnius <Apollod. *Bibl.* 2.5.6>, (59c)
Perimede[3], daughter of Oeneus[4] <Paus. 7.4.2>, 53b
— and Phoenix[2] <Paus. 7.4.2>, (53b)
Perimedes[1], son of Eurystheus <Apollod. *Bibl.* 2.8.1> and *Antimache*, 59c
Perimedes[2] [centaur], offspring of Peuceus <Hes. *Shield* 186>, 69c
Perimedes[3], killed by Neoptolemus <Quint. Smyr. 8.291>, *
Perimedes[4], suitor of *Penelope*[1] (from Same) <Apollod. *Epit.* 7.29>, *
Perimele[1] — see *Perimede*[1]
Perimele[2], daughter of Amythaon[1] <Diod. Sic. 4.69.3> and *Idomene*, 31d
— and Antion <Diod. Sic. 4.69.3>, 69a
Perimele[3], daughter of Admetus[1] <Ant. Lib. *Met.* 23.1> and *Alcestis*, 29d
— and Argus[4] <Ant. Lib. *Met.* 23.1>, 26c
Perineice, daughter of Hippomachus <Schol. on Ap. Rhod. *Arg.* 1.207-10>, 23c
— and Naubolus[2] <Schol. on Ap. Rhod. *Arg.* 1.207-10>, (23c)
Periopis, daughter of Pheres[1] <Apollod. *Bibl.* 3.13.8> and *Periclymene*, 29d
Periphas[1] [King of Thessaly], son of Lapithes and *Orsinome* <Diod. Sic. 4.69.2>, 69a
— and *Astyage(ia)* <Diod. Sic. 4.69.3>, (69a)
Periphas[2], son of Oeneus[1] and *Althaea* <*Cat. Wom., Frag. Hes.* frg. 25, Merk. & West>, 17d
Periphas[3], son of Aegyptus[1] and *Gorgo*[1] <Apollod. *Bibl.* 2.1.5>, 57c
— and *Actaea*[2] <Apollod. *Bibl.* 2.1.5>, (57c)
Periphas[4], son of Aretus[1] and *Laobia* <Non. *Dion.* 250-56>, *
Periphas[5], son of Epytus <Hom. *Il.* XVII.324-25>, *
Periphas[6], son of Ochesius <Hom. *Il.* V.842>, *
Periphas[7], autochthonous <Ant. Lib. *Met.* 6.1>, *
Periphas[8], suitor of *Penelope*[1] (from Zacynthus) <Apollod. *Epit.* 7.30>, *
Periphas[9], killed by Tydeus[1] <Stat. *Theb.* 2.631>, *
Periphas[10], killed by Menoeceus[2] <Stat. *Theb.* 7.641>, *
Periphetes[1] (Corynetes), son of Hephaestus and *Anticleia*[2] <Apollod. *Bibl.* 3.16.1>, 7b
alternate parentage:
Poseidon <Hyg. *Fab.* 38 (he is called Corynetes)>
Periphetes[2], son of Copreus[1] <Hom. *Il.* XV.638-39>, 37a
Periphetes[3], son of Nyctimus <Paus. 8.24.1>, 63d
Periphetes[4], killed by Teucer[1] <Hom. *Il.* XIV.515>, *
Peristhenes, son of Aegyptus[1] and *Caliadne* <Apollod. *Bibl.* 2.1.5>, 57c
— and *Electra*[5] <Apollod. *Bibl.* 2.1.5>, (57c)
Pernis — see Ascalaphus[1] (alternate version)
Pero[1], daughter of Neleus[1] and *Chloris*[2] <Hom. *Od.* 11.287>, 27d
— and Bias[1] <*Cat. Wom., Frag. Hes.* frg. 33, Merk. & West>, 30c
Pero[2], paramour of Poseidon <Acus. in Apollod. *Bibl.* 3.12.5>, 9a
Persaeus — see Perses[2]
Perse(is) (*Crete*[3]), daughter of Oceanus and *Tethys* <Hes. *Theog.* 356>, 62b
— and Helios <Hes. *Theog.* 956>, 14c
Perseon, father of *Laonome*[3] <Hyg. *Fab.* 14 (she is called *Agrinome*)>, 15c
Persephone[1] (*Core*) (*Deione*[1]) [the Maiden], daughter of Zeus and *Demeter* <Hes. *Theog.* 912>, 5b, *10a*
alternate parentage:
Zeus and *Styx* <Apollod. *Bibl.* 1.3.1>
— and Adonis <Apollod. *Bibl.* 3.14.4>, 11c
— and Hades <Hes. *Theog.* 913-14>, 10a
— and Zeus <Non. *Dion.* 5.566-67>, 6c
Persephone[2], daughter of Minyas <Schol. on Hom. *Od.* 11.281 ff.>, 20c
— and Amphion[2] <Schol. on Hom. *Od.* 11.281 ff.>, 20c
— and Iasus[2] <Schol. on Hom. *Od.* 11.281 ff.>, (20c)
Persep(t)olis (Ptoliporthus[2]), son of Telemachus and *Polycaste*[1] <*Cat. Wom., Frag. Hes.* frg. 221, Merk. & West>, 13d, *27d*
Perses[1], son of Perseus[1] and *Andromeda* <Herod. 7.61>, 58d
Perses[2] (Persaeus) [Titan], son of Crius[1] and *Eurybia*[1] <Hes. *Theog.* 377>, 12a
— and *Asteria*[1] <Hes. *Theog.* 409-10>, (12a)
Perses[3], son of Helios and *Perse(is)* <Diod. Sic. 4.45.1>, 14c
Perseus[1] [King of Mycenae and Tiryns], son of Zeus and *Danae* <Hom. *Il.* XIV.319>, 5b, *58d*
alternate parentage:
Proetus[1] and *Danae* <Apollod. *Bibl.* 2.4.1>
— and *Andromeda* <*Cat. Wom., Frag. Hes.* frg. 135, Merk. & West>, 58d
Perseus[2], son of Nestor <Hom. *Od.* 3.413> and *Anaxibia*[4] <Apollod. *Bibl.* 1.9.9>, 27c
alternate parentage:
Nestor and *Eurydice*[7] <Hom. *Od.* 3.453 (inferred because she is wife of Nestor)>
Perseus[3], governor of Dardanus <Parth. *Love Stor.* 16>, *
Peteus [monster], son of Orneus[2] <Plut. *Thes.* 32.1>, 49a
Petraea (*Petrea*), daughter of Oceanus and *Tethys* <Hes. *Theog.* 357>, 62b
Petraeus[1] [centaur], offspring of Centaurus and a Magnesian Mare <Pind. *Pyth.* 2.50; named as centaur, Hes. *Shield* 186>, 69d
alternate parentage:
Ixion and *Nephele*[1] <Diod. Sic. 4.69.5>
Petraeus[2], a leader of the horned satyrs <Non. *Dion.* 14.109>, *
Petraeus[3], a captain of the horned centaurs <Non. *Dion.* 14.189>, *
Petrea — see *Petraea*

Peucetius, son of Lycaon[1] <Apollod. *Bibl.* 3.8.1>, 64c
Peuceus [centaur], offspring of Centaurus and a Magnesian Mare <Pind. *Pyth.* 2.50; named as centaur, Hes. *Shield* 186>, 69c
alternate parentage:
Ixion and *Nephele*[1] <Diod. Sic. 4.69.5>
Phace — see *Callisto*[2]
Phaea [Crommyon Sow], offspring of Typhon and *Echidna* <Apollod. *Epit.* 1.1-2>, 1b
Phaeax[1] [King of Corfu], son of Poseidon and *Corcyra* <Diod. Sic. 4.72.3>, 8c, *66a*
Phaeax[2], the look-out for the ship of Theseus <Plut. *Thes.* 17.6>, *
Phaedimus[1], son of Amphion[1] and *Niobe*[1] <Apollod. *Bibl.* 3.5.6>, 66d
Phaedimus[2] [King of the Sidonians] <Hom. *Od.* 4.617>, *
Phaedimus[3], son of Pentheus[2] <Stat. *Theb.* 2.575>, *
Phaedra, daughter of Minos I and *Pasiphae*[1] <Apollod. *Bibl.* 3.1. 2>, 53c
alternate parentage:
Minos I and *Crete*[1] <Asclep. in Apollod. *Bibl.* 3.1.2>
— and Hippolytus[1] <Apollod. *Epit.* 1.16-18>, 51c
— and Theseus <Eur. *Hipp.* 27>, 51c
Phaenna — see (Charites) (alternate version)
Phaeno, daughter of Oceanus and *Tethys* <*Hom. Hymn* 2 (to *Demeter*) 416>, 62b
Phaenops, son of Asius[2] <Hom. *Il.* XVII.583>, 44c
Phaeo — see (Hyades) (alternate version)
Phaeocomes [centaur], offspring of Centaurus and a Magnesian Mare <Pind. *Pyth.* 2.50; named as centaur, Ovid *Met.* 12. 430>, 69c
alternate parentage:
Ixion and *Nephele*[1] <Diod. Sic. 4.69.5>
(Phaeontides) — see (Heliades[2])
Phaestus[1] [King of Sicyon], son of Heracles[1] <Paus. 2.6.6>, 61c
alternate parentage:
Rhopalus <Steph. Byz. "Phaestos">
Phaestus[2], son of Borus[3] <Hom. *Il.* V.43>, *
Phaesyle (*Aesyle*) [one of the Hyades], daughter of Atlas and *Pleione* <Hyg. *Fab.* 192>, 44b
alternate parentage:
Hyas and *Boeotia* <Hyg. *Poet. Astr.* 2.21>
Phaethon[1], son of Helios and *Clymene*[1] <Ovid *Met.* 1.759-79>, 14a
alternate parentage:
Helios and *Prote* <Tzetz. on *Chil.* 4.363>
Helios and *Rhode*[1] <Schol. on Hom. *Od.* 17.208>
Clymenus[6] and *Merope*[4] <Hyg. *Fab.* 154>
Phaethon[2], son of Cephalus[1] and *Eos* <Hes. *Theog.* 987>, 46c
alternate parentage:
Cephalus[1] and *Hemera* <Paus. 1.3.1>
Tithonus <Apollod. *Bibl.* 3.14.3>
— and *Aphrodite* <Hes. *Theog.* 987-90>, 5b
— and *Hemera* <Paus. 1.3.1>, 1a
Phaethon[3] — see Apsyrtus
Phaethon[4] [one of the steeds of *Eos*] <Hom. *Od.* 23.246>, *
Phaethusa[1], daughter of Helios and *Neaera*[1] <Hom. *Od.* 12.132>, 14b
alternate parentage:
Helios and *Clymene*[1] <Ovid *Met.* 2.334-48>
Helios and *Rhode*[1] <Schol. on Hom. *Od.* 17.208>
Clymenus[6] and *Merope*[4] <Hyg. *Fab.* 154>
Phaethusa[2], daughter of Danaus[1] <Schol. on Ap. Rhod. *Arg.* 1. 752>, 57a
Phagrus, son of Apollo and *Othreis* <Ant. Lib. *Met.* 13.1>, 11c
Phalces[1] [King of Sicyon], son of Temenus[1] <Paus. 2.11.2>, 60d
Phalces[2], comrade of Perses[3] <Val. Flac. 6.88.554>, *
Phalces[3], killed by Antilochus <Hom. *Il.* XIV.413>, *
Phalerus[1] [Argonaut], son of Alcon[3] <Ap. Rhod. *Arg.* 1.94>, 49a
Phalerus[2], killed by Neoptolemus <Quint. Smyr. 8.291-93>, *
Phalias, son of Heracles[1] and *Heliconis* <Apollod. *Bibl.* 2.7. 8>, *51c*
Phanosyra, paramour of Minyas <Schol. on Ap. Rhod. 1.230>, 20d
Phanothea, mother of *Erigone*[1] <Clem. Alex. *Misc.* 80.3 (inferred because she is wife of Icarius[1])>, 56d
— and Icarius[1] <Clem. Alex. *Misc.* 80.3>, (56d)
Phantasus [fantasy] [abstraction], offspring of Hypnos <Ovid *Met.* 575-690>, 1a
Phantes, son of Aegyptus[1] and *Caliadne* <Apollod. *Bibl.* 2.1.5>, 57c
— and *Theano*[3] <Apollod. *Bibl.* 2.1.5>, (57c)
Phanus, son of Dionysus <Apollod. *Bibl.* 1.9.16> and *Ariadne*, 56d
Phaola — see *Phaeo*
Phares, son of Hermes and *Phylodameia* <Paus. 7.22.3>, 46d, *57b*
Pharismede, paramour of Eupalamus <Schol. on Plato *Rep.* 7. 529>, 49b
Pharnace, daughter of Megassares <Apollod. *Bibl.* 3.14.3>, 46c
— and Sandocus <Apollod. *Bibl.* 3.14.3>, (46c)
Pharoteus — see Panopeus[1]
Phartis, daughter of Danaus[1] and [an Ethiopian woman] <Apollod. *Bibl.* 2.1.5>, 57d
— and Eurydamas[2] <Apollod. *Bibl.* 2.1.5>, (57d)
Phasis[1], son of Helios and *Ocyrrhoe*[3] <Ps.-Plut. *De Fluv.* 5.1>, 14b
Phasis[2] [river], son of Oceanus and *Tethys* <Hes. *Theog.* 340>, 62b
— and *Aea* <Val. Flac. 5.426>, (62b)
Phasis[3], killed by Neoptolemus <Quint. Smyr. 10.84-89>, *
Phasithea — see *Praxithea*[4]
Phassus, son of Lycaon[1] <Apollod. *Bibl.* 3.8.1>, 64c
Phegeus[1] (Phlegeus) [King of Phegea], son of Inachus and *Melia*[1] <Steph. Byz. "Phegea" (inferred because he is called brother of Phoroneus)>, 59b
alternate parentage:
Alpheius <Hyg. *Fab.* 244>
Phegeus[2], son of Dares <Hom. *Il.* V.9-11>, *
Phegeus[3], messenger for Theseus <Stat. *Theb.* 12.596>, *
Phegeus[4], killed by Turnus <Virg. *Aen.* 5.740-55>, *
Phegeus[5], killed by Tydeus <Stat. *Theb.* 2.587-609>, *
Phegeus[6], killed by Agreus[3] <Stat. *Theb.* 8.441-42>, *
Pheidippus, son of Thessalus[2] <Hom. *Il.* II.678>, 60b
Pheme [rumour], daughter of *Gaea* <Virg. *Aen.* 4.170-80>, 3b
Pheneus, son of Melas[3] <Apollod. *Bibl.* 1.8.5>, 16d
Pheno, daughter of Clytius[5] <Paus. 2.6.5>, 11b
— and Lamedon <Paus. 2.6.5>, (11b)
Pheraemon, son of Aeolus[2] and *Cyane*[1] <Hom. *Od.* 10.2-6; named, Diod. Sic. 5.8.1>, 18c
Phereboea, paramour of Theseus <Plut. *Thes.* 29.1>, 51d
Pheres[1], son of Cretheus[1] and *Tyro* <Hom. *Od.* 11.258-59>, 29b
— and *Periclymene* <Hyg. *Fab.* 14>, 20d
Pheres[2], son of Jason and *Medea* <Apollod. *Bibl.* 1.9.28>, 33c
Pheres[3] (Phereus[1]), son of Oeneus[1] and *Althaea* <*Cat. Wom., Frag. Hes.* frg. 25.15, Merk. & West>, 17c
Pheres[4], a defender of Thebes <Stat. *Theb.* 9.106>, *
Pheres[5], killed by Halaesus <Virg. *Aen.* 10.411-13>, *
Pheres[6], killed by Aeneas <Quint. Smyr. 6.622>, *
Pherespondus [satyr], son of Hermes and *Iphthime*[2] <Non. *Dion.* 14.112-14>, *17a*
Phereus[1] — see Pheres[3]
Phereus[2], a leader of the horned satyrs <Non. *Dion.* 14.106>, *
Phereus[3], fought at Troy <Quint. Smyr. 2.279>, *
Pherusa[1], daughter of Nereus and *Doris*[1] <Hes. *Theog.* 248>, *65b*
Pherusa[2] [one of the hours], daughter of Zeus and *Themis*[1] <Hyg. *Fab.* 183>, 6d
Phialo (Phillo(ne)), daughter of Alcimedon[1] <Paus. 8.12.3>, 60d
— and Heracles[1] <Paus. 8.12.3>, (60d)
Phidaleia, wife of Byzas <Hesyc. Mil. in *F.H.G.* 4.149 frg. 17, Müller>, 8c, 55b
Phila —see [fifty daughters of Danaus[1]] (alternate version)
Philaemon, son of Priam[1] <Apollod. *Bibl.* 3.12.5>, 44d

Philaeus[1], son of Ajax[1] <Herod. 6.35.1> and *Lyside* <Steph. Byz. "Philaidai">, 23d, *8a*
alternate parentage:
Eurysaces <Paus. 1.35.2>
Philaeus[2], son of Munichus and *Lelante* <Ant. Lib. *Met.* 14.1>, *
Philammon, son of Apollo and *Chione*[1] <Ovid *Met.* 11.315>, 11b, *13b*
alternate parentage:
Apollo and *Leuconoe*[3] <Hyg. *Fab.* 161>
Apollo and *Philonis*[1] <Pher. in *F. Gr. H.* 3 F 120>
Hephaestus <Hyg. *Fab.* 158>
— and *Argiope*[1] <Apollod. *Bibl.* 1.3.3>, (13b)
Philamnus [one of the Pans], son of Pan <Non. *Dion.* 14.81>, 64d
Philander, son of Apollo and *Acacallis*[2] <Paus. 10.16.3>, 11a
Philanthus, son of Agelaus[4] <Paus. 8.33.9>, 62c
Phillo(ne) — see *Phialo*
Phillyra, daughter of Oceanus <Pher. in *F. Gr. H.* 3 F 50> and *Tethys*, 69b
— and Cronus <Pher. in *F. Gr. H.* 3 F 50>, 5a
Philoctetes, son of Poeas <Hom. *Od.* 3.190> and *Demonassa*[5] <Hyg. *Fab.* 97>, 22c
Philodice[1], daughter of Inachus and *Melia*[1] <Tzetz. on Lyc. *Alex.* 511>, 55a
— and Leucippus[1] <Tzetz. on Lyc. *Alex.* 511>, 25b
Philodice[2], paramour of Magnes[2] <Schol. on Eur. *Phoen. Maid.* 1760>, 21a
Philolaus, son of Minos I and *Pareia* <Apollod. *Bibl.* 3.1.2>, 54c
Philomela[1], daughter of Pandion I and *Zeuxippe*[1] <Apollod. *Bibl.* 3.14.8>, 49a
— and Tereus[1] <Apollod. *Bibl.* 3.14.8>, 7c, (49a)
Philomela[2], daughter of Actor[3] <Schol. on Ap. Rhod. *Arg.* 2.558> and *Aegina*, 22d
Philomela[3] — see *Antigone*[2]
Philomela[4] — see Patroclus[1] (alternate version)
Philomela[5] —see [fifty daughters of Danaus[1]] (alternate version)
Philomelus[1], son of Iasion and *Demeter* <Hyg. *Poet. Astr.* 2.4>, 42b
Philomelus[2], son of Theotimus <Paus. 10.2.1>, *
Philonis[1] — see *Chione*[1]
Philonis[2], wife of Phospor(us) <Hyg. *Fab.* 65>, 13b
Philonoe (*Achemone*) (*Alcimene*) (*Anticleia*[4]) (*Cassandra*[2]), daughter of Iobates <Apollod. *Bibl.* 2.3.2>, 18d
— and Bellerophon(tes) <Tzetz. on Lyc. 17>, (18d)
Philonome, daughter of Cragasus <Paus. 10.14.2>, 43c
— and Cycnus[2] <Paus. 10.14.2>, 8b, (43c)
Philotes [affection] [abstraction], offspring of *Nyx* <Hes. *Theog.* 224>, *1b*
Philottus, paramour of *Niobe*[1] <Parth. *Love Stor.* 33>, 41a
Philyra, wife of Nauplius[1] <Apollod. *Bibl.* 2.1.5 (quoting author of *The Returns*)>, 57c
Phineus[1] [King of Thrace], son of Phoenix[2] and *Cassiopeia*[1] <*Cat. Wom., Frag. Hes.* frg. 138, Merk. & West>, 53d
alternate parentage:
Agenor[1] <Hellan. in *F. Gr. H.* 4 F 95>
Poseidon <Apollod. *Bibl.* 1.9.21>
— and *Cleopatra*[1] <Ap. Rhod. *Arg.* 2.240>, 13a, 42a
— and *Idaea*[2] <Apollod. *Bibl.* 3.15.3>, 13a, 42a
Phineus[2] (Agenor[10]), son of Belus[1] and *Anchinoe*[1] <Apollod. *Bibl.* 2.1.4>, 58b
— and *Andromeda* <Apollod. *Bibl.* 2.4.3>, 58d
Phineus[3], son of Lycaon[1] <Apollod. *Bibl.* 3.8.1>, 64c
Phisadie, daughter of Zeus and *Dia*[1] <Hyg. *Fab.* 79 (inferred because she is called sister of Peirithous[1])>, 5a
Phix [Theban Sphinx], offspring of Orth(r)us and *Chimaera*[1] <Hes. *Theog.* 326>, *1b*
alternate parentage:
Orth(r)us and *Echidna* <Hes. *Theog.* 326-27 (referent of "she" is unclear)>
Typhon and *Echidna* <Apollod. *Bibl.* 3.5.8>
Phlegethon [river], son of Oceanus and *Tethys* <Hes. *Theog.* 367-68>; named as river, Hom. *Il.* X.514 (he is called Pyriphlegethon)>, 63a
Phlegius — see Phegeus[1]
Phlegraeus[1] [centaur], offspring of Centaurus and a Magnesian Mare <Pind. *Pyth.* 2.50; named as centaur, Ovid *Met.* 12. 379>, 69c
alternate parentage:
Ixion and *Nephele*[1] <Diod. Sic. 4.69.5>
Phlegraeus[2], a leader of the horned satyrs <Non. *Dion.* 14.107>, *
Phlegyas[1] [King of Orchomenus], son of Ares and *Chryse*[1] <Paus. 9.36.1>, 7a, *19d*
alternate parentage:
Ares and *Dotis* <Apollod. *Bibl.* 3.5.5>
autochthonous <Non. *Dion.* 29.31>
— and *Cleophema* <Isyl. *Lyr.* 3.43>, (19d)
Phlegyas[2], killed by Perseus[1] <Ovid *Met.* 5.87-88>, *
Phlegyas[3], killed by Heracles[1] <Val. Flac. 3.125>, *
Phlegyas[4], killed by Amphiaraus <Stat. *Theb.* 3.79>, *
Phlegyas[5], killed by Tydeus[1] <Stat. *Theb.* 8.688>, *
Phlias (Phliasus) [Argonaut], son of Dionysus and *Araethyrea* <Ap. Rhod. *Arg.* 1.115-18>, 56d
alternate parentage:
Dionysus and *Ariadne* <Hyg. *Fab.* 14>
Ceisus <Paus. 2.12.6>
Lycaeus <Val. Flac. 1.411-12>
— and *Chthonopyle* <Ap. Rhod. *Arg.* 1.115-18>, 49b
Phliasus — see Phlias
Phlogea, wife of Euchenor[1] <Schol. on Hom. *Od.* 18.84>, 31d, 63d
Phlyus, son of *Gaea* <Paus. 4.1.5>, 3b
Phobetor — see Icelus
Phobus[1] [panic], son of Ares and *Aphrodite* <Hes. *Theog.* 934>, 7a
Phobus[2] [one of the Pans], son of Pan <Non. *Dion.* 14.81>, 64d
Phocus[1], son of Aeacus and *Psamathe*[1] <Hes. *Theog.* 1004-05>, 23c
— and *Asterodeia*[2] <Tzetz. on Lyc. 53, 939>, 22a
Phocus[2], son of Ornytion <Paus. 2.4.3>, 18c
alternate parentage:
Poseidon <Paus. 2.4.3>
— and *Antiope*[1] <Paus. 9.17.4>, 66d
Phocus[3], son of Caeneus[1] <Hyg. *Fab.* 14>, 8a
Phocus[4], father of *Callirhoe*[10] <Plut. *Love Stor.* 4.774-75>, *
Phocus[5], son of Danaus[3] <Hyg. *Fab.* 97>, *
Phoebe[1] [Titan], daughter of Uranus and *Gaea* <Hes. *Theog.* 136>, 11b
— and C(o)eus <Hes. *Theog.* 404>, (11b)
Phoebe[2], daughter of Leucippus[1] <Apollod. *Bibl.* 3.10.3> and *Philodice*[1], 25c
alternate parentage:
Apollo <Paus. 3.16.1 (citing poet of the *Kypria*)>
— and Polydeuces <Apollod. *Bibl.* 3.11.2>, 48d
Phoebe[3], daughter of Tyndareus and *Leda* <Eur. *Iph. at Aulis* 50>, 48c
Phoebe[4], paramour of Danaus[1] <Apollod. *Bibl.* 2.1.5>, 57c
Phoebe[5] [one of the Heliades[2]], daughter of Helios and *Clymene*[1] <Ovid *Met.* 2.333-40; named, Hyg. *Fab.* 154>, 14a
alternate parentage:
Helios and *Rhode*[1] <Schol. on Hom. *Od.* 17.208>
Phoebe[6] [Amazon] <Diod. Sic. 4.16.3>, *
Phoebus — see Apollo
Phoenice, daughter of Phoenix[2] and *Telephe* <Schol. Eur. *Phoen. Maid.* 5>, 53d
[Phoenician woman], paramour of Aegyptus[1] <Apollod. *Bibl.* 2.1. 5>, 57d, 58c
Phoenix[1] [King of Dolopes], son of Amyntor[1] <Hom. *Il.* IX.449> and *Hippodameia*[3] <Schol. A on Hom. *Il.* IX.448>, 24d
— and *Clytie*[3] <Schol. on Hom. *Il.* IX.448>, (24d)

Phoenix[2] [King of Phoenicia], son of Agenor[1] <*Cat. Wom., Frag. Hes.* frg. 138, Merk. & West> and *Telephassa* <Apollod. *Bibl.* 3.1.1>, 53b
alternate parentage:
Agenor[1] and *Damno* <Pher. in *F. Gr. H.* 3 F 21>
Belus[1] <Non. *Dion.* 3.296>
— and *Alphesiboea*[4] <*Cat. Wom., Frag. Hes.* frg. 139, Merk. & West>, (53b)
— and *Cassiopeia*[1] <*Cat. Wom., Frag. Hes.* frg. 138, Merk. & West>, 46c
— and *Perimede*[3] <Paus. 7.4.2>, (53b)
— and *Telephe* <Schol. Eur. *Phoen. Maid.* 5>, (53b)
Phoenix[3], guardian of Hymenaeus[2] <Non. *Dion.* 13.85-86>, *
Pholus[1] [centaur], offspring of Silenus and an [ash tree nymph] <Apollod. *Bibl.* 2.5.4>, 46c
Pholus[2], killed by Turnus <Virg. *Aen.* 12.341>, *
Pholus[3], killed by Tydeus[1] <Stat. *Theb.* 8.476>, *
Phonoi [murders] [abstraction], offspring of *Eris* <Hes. *Theog.* 228>, *1a*
Phorbas[1], father of Ilioneus[1] <Hom. *Il.* XIV.490-91> and *Diomede*[1] <Hom. *Il.* IX.665-66>, 24d
Phorbas[2] [King of Thessaly], son of Lapithes and *Orsinome* <Diod. Sic. 4.69.2>, 68b
alternate parentage:
Triop(a)s[1] <*Hom. Hymn* 3 (to Pythian Apollo) 213>
— and *Hyrmine* <Paus. 5.1.11>, 16c
Phorbas[3] [King of Argos], son of Criasus[1] and *Melantho*[2] <Schol. on Eur. *Or.* 932>, 61b
alternate parentage:
Argus[2] <Paus. 2.16.1> and *Euadne*[2]
— and *Euboea*[2] <Schol. on Eur. *Or.* 932>, (61b)
Phorbas[4], father of *Dexithea*[2] <Plut. *Rom.* 2.2>, 41c
Phorbas[5], son of Helios <Steph. Byz. "Dexamenae">, 14c
Phorbas[6] [one of the Pans], son of Pan <Non. *Dion.* 14.94>, 64d
Phorbas[7], paramour of *Hecate* <*Gr. Ehoiai, Frag. Hes.* frg. 262, Merk. & West>, 12a
Phorbas[8], son of Metion[2] <Ovid *Met.* 5.73>, *
Phorbas[9], captained the cavalry of Erechtheidae <Eur. *Supp. Wom.* 680>, *
Phorbas[10], attendant of *Antigone*[1] <Stat. *Theb.* 7.253>, *
Phorbas[11], boxer killed by Apollo <Schol. on Hom. *Il.* XXIII. 660>, *
Phorbus, father of *Pronoe*[1] <Apollod. *Bibl.* 1.7.7>, 15b
Phorcus[1], son of Pontus and *Gaea* <Hes. *Theog.* 237>, 2b
alternate parentage:
Eidoethea[2] <Acus. in *F. Gr. H.* 2 F 11>
Oceanus and *Tethys* <Plato *Tim.* 40e>
— and *Ceto*[1] <Hes. *Theog.* 270>, (2b)
— and *Crataeis*[1] <Hom. *Od.* 12.127 (inferred because she is called mother of *Scylla*[2])>, (2b)
— and *Hecate* <Ap. Rhod. *Arg.* 4.828>, 12a
Phorcus[2], son of Phaenops <Hom. *Il.* XVII.312>, 44c
(Phorcydes), daughters of Phorcus[1] and *Ceto*[1] — see (Gorgons), (Graeae)
Phoroneus [King of Argos], son of Inachus and *Melia*[1] <Apollod. *Bibl.* 2.1.1>, 61a
alternate parentage:
Inachus and *Argeia*[2] <Hyg. *Fab.* 143>
— and *Cerdo* <Paus. 1.21.1>, (61a)
— and *Cinna* <Hyg. *Fab.* 145>, (61a)
— and *Teledice* <Apollod. *Bibl.* 2.1.1>, (61a)
Phosphor(us) (Eosphorus) (Hesperus[2]) [morning star], son of Astraeus and *Eos* <Hes. *Theog.* 381>, 13b
alternate parentage:
Cephalus[1] and *Eos* <Hyg. *Poet. Astr.* 2.42 (he is called Hesperus)>
— and *Philonis*[2] <Hyg. *Fab.* 65>, (13b)
Phrasimus [river], son of Oceanus and *Tethys* <Hes. *Theog.* 366-67; named as river, Apollod. *Bibl.* 3.15.1>, 69b
— and *Diogeneia*[2] <Apollod. *Bibl.* 3.5.1>, 49b
Phrasius[1] — see Thrasius[1]
Phrasius[2] (Rhadius), alternate version of son of Neleus[1] and *Chloris*[2] <Apollod. *Bibl.* 1.9.9>, *
Phrasius[3], killed by Deriades <Non. *Dion.* 32.229-34>, *
Phrastor[1], son of Pelasgus[3] and *Menippe*[3] <Dion. Hal. *Rom. Ant.* 1. 28>, 61d
Phrastor[2], son of Oedipus and *Jocasta* <Pher. in *F. Gr. H.* 3 F 95>, 55c
Phrixus[1], son of Athamas[1] <Apollod. *Bibl.* 1.9.1> and *Nephele*[2] <*Cat. Wom., Frag. Hes.* frg. 68, Merk. & West>, 26a
— and *Chalciope*[1] <Paus. 1.9.1>, 14c
Phrixus[2] [centaur], offspring of Centaurus and a Magnesian Mare <Pind. *Pyth.* 2.50; named as centaur, Diod. Sic. 4.12.7>, 69c
alternate parentage:
Ixion and *Nephele*[1] <Diod. Sic. 4.69. 5>
Phrixus[3], comrade of Perses[3] <Val. Flac. 6.70>, *
Phrontis[1], son of Phrixus[1] and *Chalciope*[1] <Apollod. *Bibl.* 1.9.1>, 26c
Phrontis[2], son of Onetor <Hom. *Od.* 3.282>, *
Phrontis[3], wife of Panthous <Hom. *Il.* XVII.41>, *
Phrynondas — see Passalus
Phthia[1], paramour of Zeus <Serv. on Virg. *Aen.* 1.242>, 6c
Phthia[2], daughter of Amphion[1] and *Niobe*[1] <Apollod. *Bibl.* 3.5.6>, 66c
Phthia[3] — see *Clytie*[2]
Phthia[4], paramour of Apollo <Apollod. *Bibl.* 1.7.6>, 11d
Phthius[1], son of Poseidon and *Larissa*[1] <Dion. Hal. *Rom. Ant.* 1.17. 3>, 8c, *61d*
Phthius[2], son of Lycaon[1] <Apollod. *Bibl.* 3.8.1>, 64d
Phthonia, daughter of Alcyoneus[1] <Eust. on Hom. *Il.* 776>, 4a
Phylaceis — see *Alcimede*
Phylacides, son of Apollo and *Acacallis*[2] <Paus. 10.16.3>, 11a
Phylacus[1] [King of Phylace], son of Deion[1] and *Diomede*[3] <Apollod. *Bibl.* 1.9.4>, 22a
— and *Clymene*[4] <Hyg. *Fab.* 14>, 20c
Phylacus[2], killed by Leitus <Hom. *Il.* VI.34-35>, *
Phylas[1] [King of Dryopes], father of *Mideia*[3] <Paus. 1.5.2>, 60c
Phylas[2], son of Antiochus[2] <Apollod. *Bibl.* 2.8.3>, 60c
— and *Leipephilene* <*Gr. Ehoiai, Frag. Hes.* frg. 252, Merk. & West>, 55d, 59c
Phylas[3], father of *Polymela*[1] <Hom. *Il.* XVI.182>, 5d, 46d
Phylas[4] (Phyleus[2]) [King of Ephyra], father of *Astyoche*[2] <Apollod. *Bibl.* 2.7.8>, 60b
Phyleis, daughter of Thespius <Apollod. *Bibl.* 2.7.8> and *Megamede* <Apollod. *Bibl.* 2.4.10>, 50c
— and Heracles[1] <Apollod. *Bibl.* 2.7.8>, (50c)
Phyleus[1] [King of Elis and Dulichium], son of Augeias <Apollod. *Bibl.* 2.5.5>, 63d
— and *Timandra*[1] <*Cat. Wom., Frag. Hes.* frg. 176, Merk. & West>, 48c
Phyleus[2] — see Phylas[4]
Phyleus[3], killed by Amphiaraus <Stat. *Theb.* 7.7112>, *
Phyleus[4], killed by Theseus <Sat. *Theb.* 12.745>, *
Phyllis[1], daughter of Sithon <Serv. on Virg. *Ecl.* 5.10> and *Mendeis*, 7d
— and Demophon[1] <Apollod. *Epit.* 6.16>, 51c
Phyllis[2], wife of Margasus <Quint. Smyr. 10.143>, *
Phyllodoce, daughter of Nereus and *Doris*[1] <Hyg. *Fab.* pref.>, *65a*
Phylodameia, daughter of Danaus[1] <Paus. 4.30.2>, 57b
— and Hermes <Paus. 4.30.2>, 46d
Phylomache, daughter of Amphion[1] <Apollod. *Bibl.* 1.9.10> and *Niobe*[1], 66c
— and Pelias[1] <Apollod. *Bibl.* 1.9.10>, 28c
Phylonoe, daughter of Tyndareus and *Leda* <*Cat. Wom., Frag.*

Hes. frg. 23(a), 10, Merk. & West>, 48c
Phylonome, daughter of Nyctimus and *Arcadia*[1] <Plut. *Gr. and Rom. Par. Stor.* 36>, 63c
— and Ares <Plut. *Gr. and Rom. Par. Stor.* 36>, 7c
Phylonomous, son of Electryon[1] and *Anaxo*[1] <Apollod. *Bibl.* 2.4. 5>, 59d
Physcoa, paramour of Dionysus <Paus. 5.16.7>, 56d
Physcus, son of Amphictyon and *Chthonopatra* <Eust. on Hom. *Il.* 277>, 16a
Physius, son of Lycaon[1] <Apollod. *Bibl.* 3.8.1>, 64d
Phytius, son of Orestheus[1] <Hec. in Athen. 2.3>, 16b
Phyto[1] — see (Hyades) (alternate version)
Phyto[2] [Samian Sibyl] <Lydus *De Mensibus* 4.47>, *
Piasus, father of *Laris(s)a*[2] <Parth. *Love Stor.* 23.1>, 44c
Pielus, son of Neoptolemus and *Andromache* <Paus. 1.11.1 (father is called Pyrrhus)>, 24d
Pieria[1], wife of Danaus[1] <Apollod. *Bibl.* 2.1.5>, 57b, 57c
Pieria[2], wife of Oxylus[2] <Paus. 5.4.4>, 16d
Pieria[3], daughter of Pythes and *Iapygia* <Plut. *Brav. of Wom.* 16>, *
(Pierides[1]) — see [Muses]
(Pierides[2]) (Emathides), daughters of Pierus[2] <Nicand. in Ant. Lib. *Met.* 9> and *Euippe*[2] <Ovid *Met.* 300 ff.> (see *Acalanthis*, *Cenchris*, *Chloris*[5], *Cissa*, *Colymbas*, *Dracontis*, *Iynx*[1], *Nessa*, *Pipo*), 15a, 15c
Pieris, paramour of Menelaus <Apollod. *Bibl.* 3.11.1>, 37c
Pierus[1] [King of Pella], son of Magnes[2] <Apollod. *Bibl.* 1.3.3> and *Meliboea*[3], 21b
— and *Cleio*[1] <Apollod. *Bibl.* 1.3.3>, 6a
Pierus[2] [King of Macedonia], son of Macedon <Schol. on Hom. *Il.* XIV.226b> and *Oreithyia*[2], 15a
alternate parentage:
Apollo <Serv. on Virg. *Geo.* 7.21>
Eleuther <Schol. on Hom. *Il.* XIV.226c>
— and *Euippe*[2] <Ovid *Met.* 5.305>, (15a)
Pi(m)pleia (*Nomia*[1]), paramour of Daphnis[1] <Serv. on Virg. *Ecl.* 8. 68>, 46c
Pipo, daughter of Pierus[2] <Nicand. in Ant. Lib. *Met.* 9> and *Euippe*[2] <Ovid *Met.* 5.300 ff.>, 15c
Pitane[1], paramour of Poseidon <Pind. *Olym.* 6.28-30>, 9a
Pitane[2] [Libyan Amazon] <Diod. Sic. 3.55.6>, *
Pithys — see Pitys
Pitocamptes — see Sinis
Pittheus [King of Troezen], son of Pelops[1] <Eur. *Medea* 684> and *Hippodameia*[1] <Plut. *Thes.* 7.1>, *38b*
Pityocamptes — see Sinis
Pitys (*Pithys*), paramour of Pan <Non. *Dion.* 2.118>, 46a
— and Boreas[1] <*Geopon.* 11.12>, 12b
Placia, daughter of Otreus[1] <Apollod. *Bibl.* 3.12.3>, 42c
— and Laomedon[1] <Apollod. *Bibl.* 3.12.3>, (42c)
Plataea, daughter of Asopus <Paus. 9.1.2> and *Metope*[2], 66a
Plato, son of Lycaon[1] <Apollod. *Bibl.* 3.8.1>, 64c
(Pleiades), daughters of Atlas and *Pleione* (see *Alcyone*[2], *Asterope*[1], *Calypso*[1], *Celaeno*[1], *Dione*[3], *Electra*[2], *Maera*[2], *Maia*, *Merope*[1], *Taygete*), 35a-47b
others:
named in <Schol. Theo. 13.25>: *Glaucia*[2], *Parthenia*, *Protis, Stonychia*
Pleione (*Aethra*[2]), daughter of Oceanus <Apollod. *Bibl.* 3.10.1> and *Tethys* <Ovid *Fast.* 5.81-83>, 63a
— and Atlas <Apollod. *Bibl.* 3.10.1>, 35b, 52a
— and Orion <Hyg. *Poet. Astr.* 2.21>, 53c
Pleisthenes[1] [King of Argos], son of Atreus <Schol. on Eur. *Or.* 4> and *Cleola* <Schol. on Eur. *Or.* 4>, *37b*
alternate parentage:
Atreus and *Aerope*[1] <*Cat. Wom., Frag. Hes.* frg. 194, Merk. & West>
Pelops[1] and *Hippodameia*[1] <Schol. on Pind. *Olym.* 1.144>
— and *Aerope*[1] <Apollod. *Bibl.* 3.2.2>, 52c
Pleisthenes[2], son of Thyestes[1] <Hyg. *Fab.* 88> and *Aerope*[1] <Hyg. *Fab.* 246>, 39a
Pleisthenes[3], son of Acastus and *Hippolyte*[2] <Dict. Cret. 6.8>, 28c
Pleisthenes[4], son of Menelaus and *Helen*[1] <*Cyp.* frg. 12, *P.E.G.*>, 37b
Pleistos [river], son of Oceanus and *Tethys* <Hes. *Theog.* 367-68; named as river, Ap. Rhod. *Arg.* 2.710>, 69b
Plemnaeus, son of Peratus <Paus. 2.5.5>, 8b
Pleuron [King of Pleuron], son of Aetolus[1] <*Cat. Wom., Hesiodi* frg. 10(a).63-64, Merk. & West (O.C.T.)> and *Pronoe*[1] <Apollod. *Bibl.* 1.7.7>, 15d
— and *Xanthippe*[1] <Apollod. *Bibl.* 1.7.7>, 17a
Plexaure[1], daughter of Oceanus and *Tethys* <Hes. *Theog.* 352>, 63a
Plexaure[2], daughter of Nereus and *Doris*[1] <Apollod. *Bibl.* 1.2.7>, *65a*
Plexippus[1], son of Thestius and *Eurythemis(te)* <Apollod. *Bibl.* 1. 7.10>, 16c
Plexippus[2] (Crambis), son of Phineus[1] and *Cleopatra*[1] <Apollod. *Bibl.* 3.15.3>, 13a
Plexippus[3], son of Choricus and brother of *Palaestra* <Serv. on Virg. *Aen.* 8.138>, 46d
Plexippus[4] — see [fifty sons of Aegyptus[1]] (alternate version)
Ploto, daughter of Nereus and *Doris*[1] <Hes. *Theog.* 243>, *65a*
Pluto[1], daughter of Oceanus and *Tethys* <Hes. *Theog.* 355>, 63a
Pluto[2], daughter of Cronus <Schol. on Pind. *Olym.* 3.41> and *Rhea*, 5b
alternate parentage:
Himas <Hyg. *Fab.* 155>
— and Zeus <Paus. 2.22.4>, 6d
Pluto(n) — see Hades
Plutus [wealth], son of Iasion and *Demeter* <Hes. *Theog.* 969>, 42b
Podaleirius [King of Ethone], son of Asclepius <Hom. *Il.* II.731-32> and *Epeione* <Schol. on Pind. *Pyth.* 3.14>, 19d
alternate parentage:
Ascelpius and *Lampetia* <Hermip. frg 1, West>
— and Syrna <Steph. Byz. "Syrna">, (19d)
Podarce, daughter of Danaus[1] and *Pieria*[1] <Apollod. *Bibl.* 2.1.5>, 57c
— and Oeneus[3] <Apollod. *Bibl.* 2.1.5>, (57c)
Podarces[1] — see Priam[1]
Podarces[2], son of Iphiclus[2] <Hom. *Il.* II.704-05> and *Astyoche*[7], 22c
Podarces[3], one of the horses of Nebrophonous <Stat. *Theb.* 6.466 (he is called Thoas)>, *
Podarge [swift foot] [one of the Harpuiai], daughter of Thaumas[1] and *Electra*[1] <Hyg. *Fab.* pref.; named, Hom. *Il.* XVI.150>, 3b
alternate parentage:
Boreas <Pher. Syr. 7 B 5>
Oceanus and *Gaea* <Epim. *Theog.* 3 B 7>
— and Zephyrus <Hom. *Il.* XVI.145-47>, 12a
Poeas, son of Phylacus <Eust. on Hom. *Il.* 323> and *Clymene*[4], 22c
alternate parentage:
Thaumacus <Apollod. *Bibl.* 1.9.16>
— and *Demonassa*[5] <Hyg. *Fab.* 97>, (22c)
Poemander, son of Chaeresileus <Paus. 9.20.2> and *Stratonice*[4] <Plut. *Gr. Quest.* 37>, 35c
— and *Tanagra* <Paus. 9.20.2>, 34b
Polemocrates, son of Machaon <Paus. 2.38.6> and *Anticleia*[3], 19d
Polichus, son of Lycaon[1] <Apollod. *Bibl.* 3.8.1>, 64c
Poliporthes (Ptoliporthes[1]), son of Odysseus and *Penelope*[1] <Apollod. *Epit.* 7.35>, 13d
Polites[1], son of Priam[1] <Hom. *Il.* II.791> and *Hecabe*[1] <Apollod. *Bibl.* 3.11.5>, 43d
Polites[2], companion of Odysseus <Hom. *Od.* 10.224>, *
Polites[3], a member of the crew of Menelaus <Paus. 10.25.3>, *

Polites[4], killed by Amphiaraus and Apollo <Stat. *Theb.* 7.757>, *
Polites[5], killed by Haemon[1] <Stat. *Theb.* 8.491>, *
Polites[6], killed by Hippomedon[1] <Stat. *Theb.* 9.125>, *
Pollux — see Polydeuces
Poltys, son of Poseidon <Apollod. *Bibl.* 2.5.9>, 9c
Polybe —see [fifty daughters of Danaus[1]] (alternate version)
Polyboea[1], daughter of Amyclas[1] and *Diomede*[2] <Paus. 3.19.4>, 47b
Polyboea[2], daughter of Oicle(u)s and *Hyperm(n)estra*[2] <Diod. Sic. 4.68.5>, 32d
Polyboea[3], wife of Actor[1] <Eust. on Hom. *Il.* 321>, 5d
Polybotes [giant], son of *Gaea* (and the blood of Uranus) <Hes. *Theog.* 180-86; named as giant, Apollod. *Bibl.* 1.6.2>, *4a*
Polybus[1] [King of Sicyon], son of Hermes and *Chthonophyle* <Paus. 2.6.3>, 46b, *49a*
— and *Euboea*[5] <Athen. 7.296b>, (49a)
Polybus[2], son of Antenor[1] <Hom. *Il.* XI.59> and *Theano*[2], *45d*
Polybus[3] [King of Corinth] [raised Oedipus], paramour of *Merope*[9] <Soph. *Oed. Tyr.* 990>, *
Polybus[4] [King of Thebes, Egypt], husband of *Alcandre* <Hom. *Od.* 4.126>, *
Polybus[5], father of Eurymachus[2] <Hom. *Od.* 1.399>, *
Polybus[6], suitor of *Penelope*[1] (from Zacynthus) <Apollod. *Epit.* 7. 30>, *
Polybus[7], Phaeacian craftsman <Hom. *Od.* 8.373>, *
Polycaon[1], son of Lelex[1] <Paus. 4.1.1> and *Cleochareia*, 61c
— and *Messene* <Paus. 4.1.1>, (61c)
Polycaon[2], son of Butes[4] <*Gr. Ehoiai, Frag. Hes.* frg. 251a, Merk. & West>, 9d
— and *Aristaechme* <*Gr. Ehoiai, Frag. Hes.* frg. 251a, Merk. & West>, 60c
Polycaste[1], daughter of Nestor <Hom. *Od.* 3. 464-65> and *Anaxibia*[4] <Apollod. *Bibl.* 1.9.9>, 27d
alternate parentage:
Nestor and *Eurydice*[7] <Hom. *Od.* 3.453 (inferred because she is wife of Nestor)>
— and Telemachus <*Cat. Wom., Frag. Hes.* frg. 221, Merk. & West>, 13d
Polycaste[2], daughter of Lygaeus <Strab. 10.2.24>, 47d
— and Icarius[2] <Strab. 10.2.24>, (47d)
Polycaste[3], daughter of Aethlius and *Calyce*[1] <*Cat. Wom., Hesiodi* frg. 10a.58-66, Merk. & West (O.C.T.)>, 27a
— and Elector <*Cat. Wom., Hesiodi* frg. 10a.66-67, Merk. & West (O.C.T.)>, (27a)
Polycreion, son of Butes[4] <*Gr. Ehoiai, Frag. Hes.* frg. 251a, Merk. & West>, 9d
— and *Euaechme*[2] <*Gr. Ehoiai, Frag. Hes.*, frg. 251a, Merk. & West>, 60d
Polyctor[1], son of Pterelaus and *Amphimede* <Schol. on Hom. *Od.* 17.207>, 58d
Polyctor[2], son of Aegyptus[1] and *Caliadne* <Apollod. *Bibl.* 2.1.5>, 58c
— and *Stygne* <Apollod. *Bibl.* 2.1.5>, (58c)
Polyctor[3], father of Peisander[4] <Hom. *Od.* 18.299>, *
Polydamas[1], son of Antenor[1] and *Theano*[2] <Serv. on Virg. *Aen.* 1. 242-480>, *45d*
Polydamas[2], son of Panthous <Hom. *Il.* XIV.450> and *Phrontis*[3], *
Polydectes[1] [King of Seriphus], son of Magnes[1] <*Cat. Wom., Frag. Hes.* frg. 8, Merk. & West> and [a Naiad] <Apollod. *Bibl.* 1.9.6>, 15c
alternate parentage:
Magnes[3] <*Cat. Wom., Frag. Hes.* frg. 8, Merk. & West>
Poseidon and *Cerebia* <Tzetz. on Lyc. 838>
— and *Danae* <Pind. *Pyth.* 12.14-15>, 58d
Polydectes[2], son of Eunomus[2] <Paus. 3.7.3>, *
Polydeuces (Pollux) [one of the Dioscuri] [Argonaut], son of Tyndareus and *Leda* <Hom. *Od.* 11.298-301>, 48d
alternate parentage:
Zeus and *Leda* <*Hom. Hymn* 17 (to the Dioscuri)>
— and *Phoebe*[2] <Apollod. *Bibl.* 3.11.2>, 25c
Polydora[1], daughter of Peleus <Hom. *Il.* XVI.175> and *Antigone*[2] <Schol. on Hom. *Il.* XVI.115>, 24c, *22d*
alternate parentage:
Peleus and *Thetis* <*Cat. Wom., Frag. Hes.* frg. 213, Merk. & West>
— and Borus[1] <Hom. *Il.* XVI.175-79>, 25a
— and Sperchius <Hom. *Il.* XVI.175-76>, 71b
Polydora[2], daughter of Meleager and *Cleopatra*[2] <Paus. 4.2.7>, 17d, *25d*
— and Protesilaus <Paus. 4.2.7>, 22c
Polydora[3], daughter of Oceanus and *Tethys* <Hes. *Theog.* 354>, 63b
Polydora[4] — see *Arene*
Polydora[5], daughter of Danaus[1] <Ant. Lib. *Met.* 32.1>, 57a
— and Sperchius <Schol. on Ap. Rhod. 1.1212-19a>, 71a
Polydora[6] [Amazon] <Hyg. *Fab.* 163>, *
Polydorus[1] [one of the Epigoni], son of Hippomedon[1] <Paus. 2.20. 4> and *Euanippe* <Hyg. *Fab.* 71>, 31c
Polydorus[2] [King of Thebes], son of Cadmus and *Harmonia*[1] <Hes. *Theog.* 978>, 55c
— and *Nycteis* <Apollod. *Bibl.* 3.5.3>, 35b
Polydorus[3], son of Priam[1] <Hom. *Il.* XX.407> and *Laothoe*[1] <Hom. *Il.* XXII.46 ff.>, 43d
alternate parentage:
Priam[1] and *Hecabe* <Eur. *Hec.* 4>
Polydorus[4], suitor of *Penelope*[1] <from Zacynthus) <Apollod. *Epit.* 7.29>, *
Polydorus[5], killed by Odysseus <Quint. Smyr. 11.79>, *
Polygonus, son of Proteus[1] <Apollod. *Bibl.* 2.5.9>, 9c
Poly(hy)mnia —see *Polymnia*
Polyhymno —see (Hyades) (alternate version)
Polyidus[1], son of Coeranus[1] <Apollod. *Bibl.* 3.3.1>, 31d
— and *Eurydameia* <Pher. in *F.H.G.* 4.638 frg. 24a, Müller>, 63d
Polyidus[2], son of Eurydamas[5] <Hom. *Il.* V.149>, *
Polyidus[3], suitor of *Penelope*[1] (from Dulichium) <Apollod. *Epit.* 7. 27>, *
Polylaus, son of Heracles[1] and *Eurybia*[2] <Apollod. *Bibl.* 2.7.8>, *50d*
Polymede (*Polymela*[5]), daughter of Autolycus[1] <Apollod. *Bibl.* 1. 9.16> and *Amphithea*[2], 13b
— and Aeson <*Cat. Wom., Frag. Hes.* frg. 38, Merk. & West (she is called *Polymele*)>, 33a
Polymedon, son of Priam[1] <Apollod. *Bibl.* 3.12.5>, 44d
Polymela[1], daughter of Phylas[3] <Hom. *Il.* XVI.181>, 5d
— and Echecles <Hom. *Il.* XVI.181>, (5d)
— and Hermes <Hom. *Il.* XVI.182-87>, 46d
Polymela[2], daughter of Aeolus[2] <Parth. *Love Stor.* 2.2>, 18c
— and Diores[1] <Parth. *Love Stor.* 2.2>, (18c)
— and Odysseus <Parth. *Love Stor.* 2.1>, 13d
Polymela[3], daughter of Actor[3] and *Aegina* <Eust. on Hom. *Il.* 321>, 23c
— and Peleus <Eust. on Hom. *Il.* 321>, 24c
Polymela[4], daughter of Peleus <Apollod. *Bibl.* 3.13.8> and *Polymela*[3], 24c, *23c*
Polymela[5] — see *Polymede*
Polym(n)estor[1] [King of Thrace], husband of *Ilione* <Hyg. *Fab.* 109>, 43d
Polym(n)estor[2], son of Aeginetes[2] <Paus. 8.5.9>, *
Polymnia [sacred poetry] [one of the Muses], daughter of Zeus and *Mnemosyne* <Apollod. *Bibl.* 1.3.1>, 6b
Polyneices [King of Thebes] [one of the Seven against Thebes (per Aesch. *Sev.* 632-32)], son of Oedipus and *Jocasta* <Eur. *Phoen. Maid.* 56>, 55c

alternate parentage:
Oedipus and *Euryganeia* <Paus. 9.5.5>
— and *Argeia*[1] <Eur. *Supp*. 133-38; named, Apollod. *Bibl*. 3.6. 1>, 30c
Polynoe, daughter of Nereus and *Doris*[1] <Hes. *Theog*. 258>, *65a*
Polynome, daughter of Nereus and *Doris*[1] <Apollod. *Bibl*. 1.2.7>, *65a*
Polypemon[1] (Damastes) (Pemon) (Procrustes), son of Poseidon <Hyg. *Fab*. 38 (he is called Procrustes)>, 9d
— and *Sylea* <Apollod. *Bibl*. 3.16.2>, 34d
Polypemon[2], father of Apheidas[3] and grandfather of Eperitus (alias initially used by Odysseus to his father upon his return) <Hom. *Od*. 24.302-07>, *
Polypheides, son of Mantius <Hom. *Od*. 15.249>, 32c
Polyphemus[1] [cyclops], son of Poseidon and *Thoosa* <Hom. *Od*. 1. 70-74>, 9c, *2b*
— and *Galateia*[1] <Ovid *Met*. 13.739-897>, 64a
Polyphemus[2] [Argonaut], son of Elatus[2] <Apollod. *Bibl*. 1.9.16> and *Hippeia* <Hyg. *Fab*. 14>, 59d
— and *Laonome*[1] <Schol. on Ap. Rhod. *Arg*. 1.1241>, (59d)
Polyphonte, daughter of Hipponous[4] and *Thrassa* <Ant. Lib. *Met*. 21.1>, 71b
— and [a bear] <Ant. Lib. *Met*. 21, 1>, (71b)
Polyphontes[1] [King of Messenia], wife of *Merope*[2] <Apollod. *Bibl*. 2.8.5>, 60c, 62c
Polyphontes[2], son of Autophonus <Hom. *Il*. IV.395>, *
Polyphontes[3], killed by Oedipus <Apollod. *Bibl*. 3.5.7>, *
Polypoetes[1], son of Peirithous and *Hippodameia*[2] <Hom. *Il*. II. 742>, *30d*
Polypoetes[2], son of Apollo and *Phthia*[4] <Apollod. *Bibl*. 1.7.6>, 11d
Polypoetes[3] [King of Thesprotia], son of Odysseus and *Callidice*[1] <Apollod. *Epit*. 7.35>, 13c
Polypoetes[4], suitor of *Penelope*[1] (from Dulichium) <Apollod. *Epit*. 7.28>, *
Polyporthis — see Ptoliporthus[1]
Polytechnus, husband of *Aedon* <Ant. Lib. *Met*. 11.2-4>, 66d
— and *Chelidon* <Ant. Lib. *Met*. 11.5>, (66d)
Polyxena[1], daughter of Priam[1] and *Hecabe*[1] <Eur. *Hec*. 40.76>, 43c
— and Achilles <Eur. *Tro. Wom*. 261-66>, 24c
Polyxena[2] —see [fifty daughters of Danaus[1]] (alternate version)
Polyxenus[1], son of Agasthenes <Hom. *Il*. II.624-25> and *Peloris*, 63c
Polyxenus[2] — see Medeius
Polyxenus[3] [King of the Eleans] <Apollod. *Bibl*. 2.4.6>, *
Polyxo[1], wife of Tlepolemus[1] <Paus. 3.19.9>, 60b
Polyxo[2], wife of Nycteus[1] <Apollod. *Bibl*. 3.10.1>, 35b
Polyxo[3], paramour of Danaus[1] <Apollod. *Bibl*. 2.1.5>, 57b, 57c
Polyxo[4] [one of the Hyades], daughter of Atlas and *Pleione* <Hyg. *Fab*. 192>, 44b
alternate parentage:
Hyas and *Boeotia* <Hyg. *Poet. Astr*. 2.21>
Polyxo[5], daughter of Oceanus and *Tethys* <Hyg. *Fab*. pref.>, 68b
Polyxo[6], mother of Actorionus <Callim. *Hymn to Demeter* 77-78>, *
Polyxo[7], nurse of *Hypsipyle* <Ap. Rhod. *Arg*. 1.668>, *
Pontomedusa, daughter of Nereus and *Doris*[1] <Apollod. *Bibl*. 1.2. 7>, *65a*
Pontoporeia, daughter of Nereus and *Doris*[1] <Hes. *Theog*. 256>, *65a*
Pontus [sea], son of *Gaea* <Hes. *Theog*. 132>, *2b*
alternate parentage:
Aether and *Hemera* <Hyg. *Fab*. pref.>
— and *Gaea* <Hes. *Theog*. 234>, 2b
Ponus [hardship] [abstraction], offspring of *Eris* <Hes. *Theog*. 226>, *1a*
Porphyrion[1] [giant], son of *Gaea* (and the blood of Uranus) <Hes. *Theog*. 180-86; named as giant, Apollod. *Bibl*. 1.6.2>, *4a*
Porphyrion[2], son of Athamas[1] and *Themisto*[1] <Non. *Dion*. 9.317>, 26b
Porthaon[1] — see Portheus[1]
Porthaon[2] — see Parthaon[2]
Portheus[1] (Parthaon[1]) (Porthaon[1]) [King of Calydon], son of Agenor[4] <*Cat. Wom., Hesiodi* frg. 10a.50, Merk. & West (O.C.T.)> and *Epicaste*[3] <Apollod. *Bibl*. 1.7.7>, 15d
alternate parentage:
Ares <Ant. Lib. *Met*. 2.1>
— and *Euryte*[1] <*Cat. Wom., Hesiodi* frg. 10a.49-50, Merk. & West (O.C.T.)>, 65a
— and *Laothoe*[4] <*Cat. Wom., Frag. Hes*., frg. 26.5-7>, (15)
Portheus[2], son of Lycaon[1] <Apollod. *Bibl*. 3.8.1>, 64c
Portheus[3], father of Echion[3] <Apollod. *Epit*. 5.20>, *
Poseidon [god] [sea], son of Cronus and *Rhea* <Hes. *Theog*. 456>, 8a
alternate parentage:
Oceanus ("from whom all we gods proceed") <Hom. *Il*. XIV.202>
— and *Aethra*[1] <Bacch. 17.34-36>, 38b, 51a
— and *Agamede*[1] <Hyg. *Fab*. 157>, 63c
— and *Alcyone*[2] <Apollod. *Bibl*. 3.10.1>, 35a
— and *Alistra* <Tzetz. on Lyc. 1206>, (8a)
— and *Alope* <Hellan. in *F. Gr. H*. 4 F 43>, 9d
— and *Amphitrite*[1] <Hes. *Theog*. 930>, 63b
— and *Amymone*[1] <Pher. in *F. Gr. H*. 3 F 4>, 57c
— and *Aphrodite* <Serv. on Virg. *Aen*. 1.570>, 5b
— and *Arethusa*[3] <*Cat. Wom., Hesiodi* frg. 188a, Merk. & West (O.C.T.)>, 35a
— and *Arne*[1] <Diod. Sic. 4.67.4>, 18c
— and *Ascra* <Heg. in Paus. 9.29.1>, (8a)
— and *Astypalaea* <Apollod. *Bibl*. 2.7.1>, 54d
— and *Beroe*[1] <Non. *Dion*. 43.394-98>, 11c
— and *Caenis* <*Cat. Wom., Frag. Hes*. frg. 87, Merk. & West>, (8a)
— and *Calchinia* <Paus. 2.5.5>, 61c
— and *Calyce*[2] <Hyg. *Fab*. 157>, (8a)
— and *Canace* <*Cat. Wom., Hesiodi* frg. 10(a).34, Merk. & West (O.C.T.)>, 34a
— and *Celaeno*[1] <Apollod. *Bibl*. 3.10.1>, 40b
— and *Celaeno*[4] <Strab. 12.8.18>, (8a)
— and *Cerebia* <Tzetz. on Lyc. 838>, (8a)
— and *Ceroessa* <Steph. Byz. "Byzantium">, 55b
— and *Chione*[2] <Apollod. *Bibl*. 3.15.8>, 13a
— and *Chloris*[3] <Schol. on Pind. *Nem*. 9.57a>, 32d
— and *Chrysogeneia* <Paus. 9.36.3>, 20c
— and *Cleito*[1] <Plato *Crit*. 113d>, (8c)
— and *Corcyra* <Diod. Sic. 4.72.2>, 66a
— and *Coronis*[2] <Ovid *Met*. 2.550>, (8c)
— and daughter of Amphictyon <Choer. in Paus. 1.14.1>, (9c)
— and *Demeter* <Apollod. *Bibl*. 3.6.8>, 10a
— and *Diopatra* <Ant. Lib. *Met*. 22>, (8c)
— and *Euboea*[3] <Hesyc. *Lex*. "Euboia">, 66b
— and *Europe*[2] <Ap. Rhod. *Arg*. 1.178>, 3b
— and *Euryale*[2] <*Cat. Wom., Frag. Hes*. frg. 148(a), Merk. & West>, 53c
— and *Eurycyde* <Paus. 5.1.8>, 15b
— and *Euryte*[2] <Apollod. *Bibl*. 3.14.2>, (8c)
— and *Gaea* <Serv. on Virg. *Aen*. 3.420>, 2b
— and *Halia*[1] <Diod. Sic. 5.55.4>, 3a
— and *Helle* <Hyg. *Poet. Astr*. 2.20>, 26a
— and *Hippothoe*[1] <Apollod. *Bibl*. 2.4.5>, 38a, 58d
— and *Iphimedeia* <Hom. *Od*. 11.305-06>, 34a
— and *Larissa*[1] <Dion. Hal. *Rom. Ant*. 1.17>, 61d
— and *Leis* <Paus. 2.30.6>, (8c)
— and *Libya*[1] <Apollod. *Bibl*. 2.1.4>, 55b
— and *Lysianassa*[1] <Apollod. *Bibl*. 2.5.11>, 55a
— and *Medusa*[1] <Hes. *Theog*. 278>, 2b

— and *Melantheia*[2] <Plut. *Gr. Quest.* 19>, 65b
— and *Melantho*[1] <Ovid *Met.* 6.117>, 17a
— and *Melia*[2] <Ap. Rhod. *Arg.* 2.2-3>, (8c)
— and *Melissa*[4] <Steph. Byz. "Dyrrachium">, (8c)
— and *Mestra* <*Cat. Wom., Frag. Hes.* frg. 43a, Merk. & West>, 34c
— and *Mideia*[1] <Paus. 9.37.6>, (8c)
— and *Molione* <*Cat. Wom., Frag. Hes.* frg. 17, Merk. & West>, (9a), 68a
— and *Mytilene*[1] <Steph. Byz. "Mytilene">, 14b
— and [a Naiad (mother of Glaucus[3])] <Euan. in Athen. 7.296>, 62a
— and Nerites <Ael. *De Nat. Anim.* 14.18>, 65a
— and *Oenope* <Hyg. *Fab.* 157>, 34d
— and *Olbia* <Steph. Byz. "Astacus">, (9a)
— and *Oris* <Tzetz. *Chil.* 2.43>, 53c
— and *Peirene*[2] <Diod. Sic. 4.72.1>, 66a
— and *Periboea*[4] <Hom. *Od.* 7.56-58>, (9a)
— and *Pero*[2] <Acus. in Apollod. *Bibl.* 3.12.5, (9a)
— and *Pitane*[1] <Pind. *Olym.* 6.28-30>, (9a)
— and *Salamis* <Apollod. *Bibl.* 3.12.7>, 66b
— and *Scamandrodice* <Schol. on Pind. *Olym.* 2.147>, (9a)
— and *Scylla*[2] <Serv. on Virg. *Aen.* 3.420>, 2b
— and *Syme* <Diod. Sic. 5.53.1>, 14a
— and *Themisto*[1] <Hyg. *Fab.* 157>, 69b
— and *Theophane* <Hyg. *Fab.* 188>, (9a)
— and *Thoosa* <Hom. *Od.* 1.71-72>, 2b
— and *Tritogeneia*[2] <Tzetz. on Lyc. 874>, 34b
— and *Tyro* <Hom. *Od.* 11.240>, 27b, 63c
Potamon, son of Aegyptus[1] and *Caliadne* <Apollod. *Bibl.* 2.1.5>, 57d
— and Glaucippe <Apollod. *Bibl.* 2.1.5>, (57d)
Pothos [desire], daughter of Zephyrus and *Iris*[1] <Non. *Dion.* 47. 341-42>, 12a
Prax, grandson of Pergamus <Paus. 3.20.8>, 24d
(Praxidicae), daughters of Ogygus[1] (see *Alalcomenia, Aulis, Thelxionoea*), 16c
Praxithea[1], daughter of [a river nymph] <Apollod. *Bibl.* 3.14.6>, 49a
— and Erichthonius[1] <Apollod. *Bibl.* 3.14.6>, 7d, (49a)
Praxithea[2], daughter of Cephis(s)us <Eur. *Erechtheus* 349-70 in *T.G.F.* 464 ff., Nauck> and *Leiriope*, 49b
alternate parentage:
Phrasimus and *Diogeneia*[2] <Apollod. *Bibl.* 3.15.1>
— and Erechtheus II <Apollod. *Bibl.* 3.15.1>, (49b)
Praxithea[3], daughter of Thespius <Apollod. *Bibl.* 2.7.8> and *Megamede* <Apollod. *Bibl.* 2.4.10>, 50c
— and Heracles[1] <Apollod. *Bibl.* 2.7.8>, (50c)
Praxithea[4] (*Phasithea*), daughter of Leos[1] <Ael. *Var. Narr.* 12. 28>, 6a
Presbon[1], son of Phrixus[1] and *Chalciope*[1] <Paus. 9.34.5>, 26c
Presbon[2], son of Minyas and *Clytodora*[1] <Schol. on Ap. Rhod. 1. 230>, 20d
Preugenes, son of Agenor[9] <Paus. 7.18.5>, 47c
Priam[1] (Podarces[1]) [King of Troy], son of Laomedon[1] <Hom. *Il.* III. 250> and *Strym(n)o* <Hellan. in *F. Gr. H.* 4 F 139>, 43c, *70b*
alternate parentage:
Laomedon[1] and *Leucippe*[8] <Apollod. *Bibl.* 3.12.3>
Laomedon[1] and *Placia* <Apollod. *Bibl.* 3.12.3>
Dardanus[1] and *Zeuxippe*[5] <Alcm. in *P.M.G.* 71>
— and *Alexirhoe* <Serv. on Virg. *Aen.* 4.354>, 67a
— and *Arisbe*[1] <Apollod. *Bibl.* 3.11.5>, (44c)
— and *Castianeira* <Hom. *Il.* VIII.303-05>, (43c)
— and *Cilla*[2] <Schol. on Lyc. 319>, 45d
— and *Hecabe*[1] <Hom. *Il.* XXIV.283-99>, (43c)
— and *Laothoe*[1] <Hom. *Il.* XXI.85>, 43c
Priam[2], son of Polites[1] <Virg. *Aen.* 5.563-64>, 43d
Priapus (Mutunus) [fertility], son of Dionysus and *Aphrodite* <Diod. Sic. 4.6.1>, 56c
alternate parentage:
Dionysus and *Chione*[4] <Schol. Theo. 1.21>
Hermes <Hyg. *Fab.* 160>
— and *Lotis* <Ovid *Fast.* 1.415-40>, (56c)
Priasus[1], son of Caeneus[1] <Hyg. *Fab.* 14>, 8a
Priasus[2], a captain of the Phrygians <Non. *Dion.* 13.521>, *
Priolaus, son of Dascylus[1] <Ap. Rhod. *Arg.* 2.779>, 41a
Procleia, daughter of Laomedon[1] <Apollod. *Epit.* 3.24> and *Strym(n)o*, 43c
alternate parentage:
Clytius[1] <Paus. 10.14.2>
— and Cycnus[2] <Paus. 10.14.2>, 8b, (43c)
Procles[1] [King of Sparta], son of Aristodemus and *Argeia*[3] <Apollod. *Bibl.* 2.8.3>, 60d
— and *Lathria* <Paus. 3.16.6>, (60d)
Procles[2], son of Pityreus <Paus. 7.4.3>, *
Procles[3], father of *Melissa* <Paus. 2.28.8>, *
Procne (*Metis*[2]), daughter of Pandion I and *Zeuxippe*[1] <Apollod. *Bibl.* 3.14.8>, 49a
— and Tereus[1] <Apollod. *Bibl.* 3.14.8>, 7c, (49a)
Procris[1], daughter of Erechtheus II <Hellan. in *F. Gr. H.* 3 F 34> and *Praxithea*[2] <Apollod. *Bibl.* 3.15.1>, 51a
— and Cephalus[2] <Hellan. in *F. Gr. H.* 3 F 34>, 22a
— and Erechtheus II <Hyg. *Fab.* 153>, 49a
— and Minos I <Ant. Lib. *Met.* 41.4>, 54c
— and Pteleon <Apollod. *Bibl.* 3.15.1>, (51a)
Procris[2], daughter of Thespius <Apollod. *Bibl.* 2.7.8> and *Megamede* <Apollod. *Bibl.* 2.4.10>, 50c
— and Heracles[1] <Apollod. *Bibl.* 2.7.8>, (50c)
Procrustes — see Polypemon
(Proetides), daughters of Proetus[1] and *Stheneboea* (see *Celaene, Elege, Iphianassa*[1], *Iphinoe*[1], *Lysippe*[1]), 57d
Proetus[1] [King of Tiryns], son of Abas[1] and *Aglaia*[3] <Bacch. 11.66-69>, 57d
— and *Danae* <Apollod. *Bibl.* 2.4.1>, 58d
— and *Stheneboea* <Hom. *Il.* VI.157 (she is called *Anteia*)>, 63d
Proetus[2], son of Nauplius[1] <Ap. Rhod. *Arg.* 1.135>, 52d
Proetus[3], son of Thersander[2] <Paus. 10.30.2>, 19c
Proetus[4] [of Thebes], father of Galinthi(a)s <Ant. Lib. *Met.* 29. 1>, *
Promachus[1] (Biantes) (Stratolaus) [one of the Epigoni], son of Parthenopaeus <Apollod. *Bibl.* 1.9.13> and *Clymene*[3] <Hyg. *Fab.* 71>, 64d
Promachus[2], son of Heracles[1] and *Psophis*[1] <Paus. 8.24.2>, 60d, *53a*
Promachus[3], son of Aeson and *Polymede* <Apollod. *Bibl.* 1.9.27>, 33c
Promachus[4], son of Alegenor <Hom. *Il.* XIV.503>, 18c
Promachus[5], suitor of *Penelope*[1] (from Ithaca) <Apollod. *Epit.* 7. 30>, *
[Promethean Eagle], offspring of Typhon and *Echidna* <Pher. in *F. Gr. H.* 3 F 7>, 1b
Prometheus[1] [Titan], son of Iapetus and *Clymene*[1] <Hes. *Theog.* 510>, 16b, *52b*
alternate parentage:
Eurymedon and *Hera* <Schol. on Hom. *Il.* XIV.295>
Gaea <Aesch. *Prom. Bound* 209-10>
Iapetus and *Asia* <Apollod. *Bibl.* 1.2.3-4>
Themis[1] <Aesch. *Prom. Bound* 18>
— and *Asia*[1] <Herod. 4.45.3>, 51a
— and *Celaeno*[1] <Tzetz. on Lyc. 132>, 40b
— and *Clymene*[1] <Schol. on Hom. *Od.* 10.2>, 52b
— and *Hesione*[2] <Aesch. *Prom. Bound* 560>, 54a
Prometheus[2], son of Codrus[1] <Paus. 7.3.3>, 27d

Prometheus[3], father of Aetnaeus <Paus. 9.25.6>, *
Promne, wife of Oxeater <Paus. 8.14.9 (he is called Buphagus)>, 16a
Pronax, son of Talaus and *Lysimache*[1] <Apollod. *Bibl.* 1.9.13>, 31d
Pronoe[1], daughter of Phorbus <Apollod. *Bibl.* 1.7.7>, 15b
— and Aetolus[1] <Apollod. *Bibl.* 1.7.7>, (15b)
Pronoe[2], daughter of Nereus and *Doris*[1] <Hes. *Theog.* 261>, *65b*
Pronoe[3], wife of Caunus <Con. *Narr.* 2>, 68a
Pronoe[4], daughter of Melampus[1] <Diod. Sic. 4.68.4-5> and *Iphianassa*[1], 32c
alternate parentage:
Melampus[1] and *Iphianeira*[2] <Diod. Sic. 4.68.4-5>
Pronoe[5], mother of Lassus <Quint. Smyr. 6.469>, *
Pronoea — see Deucalion[1] (alternate version)
Pronomus[1] [satyr], son of Hermes and *Iphthime*[2] <Non. *Dion.* 14. 112-14>, *17a*
Pronomus[2], suitor of *Penelope*[1] (from Zacythus) <Apollod. *Epit.* 7. 29>, *
Pronous[1], son of Phegeus[1] <Apollod. *Bibl.* 3.7.6>, 59b
Pronous[2], son of Deucalion[1] and *Pyrrha*[1] <Hec. in *F. Gr. H.* 1 F 13>, 16b
Pronous[3], suitor of *Penelope*[1] <Apollod. *Epit.* 7.30>, *
Pronous[4], killed by Patroclus[1] <Hom. *Il.* XVI.399>, *
Propodas, son of Damaphon <Paus. 2.4.3>, 18d
Prosymna, daughter of Asterius[1] <Paus. 2.17.1>, 51a
Protesilaus [King of Thessaly], son of Iphiclus[2] <Hom. *Il.* II.707-10 (inferred because he is called brother of Podarces[2])> and *Astyoche*[7], 22c
alternate parentage:
Actor[3] <*Cat. Wom., Frag. Hes.* frg. 62, Merk. & West>
— and *Laodameia*[1] <Ovid *Her.* 13.25>, 28c
— and *Polydora*[2] <Paus. 4.2.7>, 17c, 25d
Proteus[1], son of Poseidon <Apollod. 2.5.9>, 9c
— and *Anchinoe*[2] <Steph. Byz. "Cabiria">, (9c)
— and *Chrysonoe* <Con. *Narr.* 32>, 7c
Proteus[2], son of Aegyptus[1] and *Agryphia* <Apollod. *Bibl.* 2.1.5>, 57c
— and *Gorgophone*[2] <Apollod. *Bibl.* 2.1.5>, (57c)
Proteus[3] [King of Egypt], husband of *Psamathe*[1] <Eur. *Hel.* 7>, 65a
Proteus[4], father of *Panaceia*[2] <Quint. Smyr. 3.301-03>, *
Prothoenor[1], son of Archilycus <Diod. Sic. 4.67.> and *Theobula*[1] <Hyg. *Fab.* 97>, 18c
Prothoenor[2], killed by Hypseus[1] <Ovid *Met.* 5.98>, *
Prothous[1], son of Lycaon[1] <Apollod. *Bibl.* 3.8.1>, 64c
Prothous[2], son of Thestius <Paus. 8.45.6> and *Eurythemis(te)*, 16c
Prothous[3], son of Agrius[1] <Apollod. *Bibl.* 1.8.6> and *Dia*[4], 16d
Prothous[4], son of Tenthredon <Hom. *Il.* II.756>, 21d
Prothous[5], drew the lots for places in the chariot race <Stat. *Theb.* 6.389-91>, *
Prothous[6], suitor of *Penelope*[1] (from Same) <Apollod. *Epit.* 7. 29>, *
Prothous[7], killed by Tydeus[2] <Stat. *Theb.* 8.540>, *
Protis — see (Pleaides) (alternate version)
Proto, daughter of Nereus and *Doris*[1] <Hes. *Theog.* 248>, *65b*
Protogeneia[1], daughter of Deucalion[1] <Pher. in *F. Gr. H.* 3 F 23> and *Pyrrha*[1] <Apollod. *Bibl.* 1.7.1>, 15a
— and Zeus <Apollod. *Bibl.* 1.7.3>, 6d
Protogeneia[2], daughter of Calydon[1] and *Aeolia* <Apollod. *Bibl.* 1. 7.7>, 15d
— and Ares <Apollod. *Bibl.* 1.7.7>, 7c
Protogeneia[3], daughter of Erechtheus II <Suid. in *F. Gr. H.* 325 F. 4> and *Praxithea*[2], 51a
Protomedeia, daughter of Nereus and *Doris*[1] <Hes. *Theog.* 249>, *65b*
Protonoe, daughter of Deriades and *Orsiboe* <Non. *Dion.* 34.179>, 3b
— and Orontes[1] <Non. *Dion.* 34.179>, (3b)
Prylis, son of Hermes and *Isse* <Tzetz. on Lyc. 219>, 46c, *14a*
Prymneus[1], son of Socus and *Combe*[1] <Non. *Dion.* 13.141>, *66c*
alternate parentage:
Apollo and *Rhetia* <Pher. in *F. Gr. H.* 3 F 48 (unnamed)>
Prymneus[2], a competitor in the games to honor Odysseus <Hom. *Od.* 8.111>, *
Prymno, daughter of Oceanus and *Tethys* <Hes. *Theog.* 350>, 63b
Psamathe[1], daughter of Nereus and *Doris*[1] <Hes. *Theog.* 260>, *65a*
— and Aeacus <Hes. *Theog.* 1004-05>, 23c, 66a
— and Proteus[3] <Eur. *Hel.* 7>, (65a)
Psamathe[2], daughter of Crotopus <Paus. 1.43.7>, 61d
— and Apollo <Paus. 1.43.7>, 11d
Pseudea [lies] [abstraction], offspring of *Eris* <Hes. *Theog.* 229>, *1a*
Psophis[1], daughter of Eryx[1] <Paus. 8.24.2>, 53a
— and Heracles[1] <Paus. 8.24.2>, 60d
Psophis[2], daughter of Xanthus[5] <Paus. 8.24.1>, 63c
Psophis[3] — see [fifty sons of Lycaon[1]] (alternate version)
Psophis[4], son of Arrhon[2] <Paus. 8.24.1>, *
Psyche, paramour of Eros <Apul. *Met.* 5.4 (he is called Cupid)>, 1a
Psyllus, husband of *Anchiroe*[1] <Non. *Dion.* 13.381>, 52a
Ptelea [elm tree], daughter of Oxylus[3] and *Hamadryas* <Athen. 3. 78b>, 71d
Pteleon, paramour of *Procris*[1] <Apollod. *Bibl.* 3.15.1>, 51a
Pterelaus, son of Taphius <Apollod. *Bibl.* 2.4.5>, 58d
alternate parentage:
Poseidon and *Hippothoe*[1] <Herodor. in *F. Gr. H.* 31 F 15>
— and *Amphimede* <Schol. on Hom. *Od.* 17.207>, (58d)
Ptolemaeus[1], son of Damasichthon[2] <Paus. 9.5.16>, 18d
Ptolemaeus[2], son of Peiraeus < Hom. *Il.* IV.228>, *
Ptolemaeus[3], son of Alexander[3] <Paus. 4.35.3>, *
Ptoliporthes[1] — see Poliporthes
Ptoliporthes[2] — see Perseptolis
Ptous, son of Athamas[1] and *Themisto*[1] <Apollod. *Bibl.* 2.1.5>, 26b
Pygmalion[1] [King of Cyprus], father of *Metharme* <Apollod. *Bibl.* 3.14.3>, 11c
— and *Galateia*[2] <Ovid *Met.* 10.247-97>, (11c)
Pygmalion[2], son of Belus[3] <Virg. *Aen.* 1.350 (inferred because he is called brother of *Dido*)>, 41d
Pygmalion[3], son of Poseidon <Hyg. *Fab.* 56 (inferred because he is called brother of Busiris)> and *Lysianassa*[1], 8d
Pylades, son of Strophius[1] <Eur. *Iph. Taur.* 915-18> and *Anaxibia*[1] <Paus. 2.29.4>, 23c, *37a*
— and *Electra*[3] <Eur. *Elec.* 1249>, 36a
Pylaon, son of Neleus[1] and *Chloris*[2] <*Cat. Wom., Frag. Hes.* frg. 33(a), Merk. & West>, 27d
Pylarge, daughter of Danaus[1] and *Pieria*[1] <Apollod. *Bibl.* 2.1.5>, 57d
— and Idmon[2] <Apollod. *Bibl.* 2.1.5>, (57d)
Pylas [King of Megara], son of Cleson <Paus. 4.36.1>, 59c
Pylenor [centaur], offspring of Centaurus and a Magnesian Mare <Pind. *Pyth.* 2.50; named as centaur, Paus. 5.5.10>, 69c
alternate parentage:
Ixion and *Nephele*[1] <Diod. Sic. 4.69.5>
Pyleus, son of Clymenus[1] <Paus. 9.37.1> and *Budeia*, 26d
Pylia (*Pelia*), daughter of Pylas <Apollod. *Bibl.* 3.15.5>, 59c
— and Pandion II <Apollod. *Bibl.* 3.15.5>, 50b
Pylo(n)[1], father of *Antiope*[6] <Hyg. *Fab.* 14>, 60b
Pylo(n)[2], killed by Polypoetes[1] <Hom. *Il.* XII.187>, *
Pylus[1], son of Ares and *Demodice*[2] <Apollod. *Bibl.* 1.7.7-8>, 7b, *15c*
Pylus[2], son of Portheus[1] and *Euryte*[1] <*Cat. Wom., Hesiodi* frg. 10a.50-54, Merk. & West (O.C.T.)>, 17c
Pyracmon — see Arges
Pyracmus [centaur], offspring of Centaurus and a Magnesian Mare <Pind. *Pyth.* 2.50; named as centaur, Ovid *Met.* 12.460>, 69c
alternate parentage:

Ixion and *Nephele*[1] <Diod. Sic. 4.69.5>
Pyraethus [centaur], offspring of Centaurus and a Magnesian Mare <Pind. *Pyth* 2.50; named as centaur, Ovid *Met.* 12.459>, 69c
alternate parentage:
Ixion and *Nephele*[1] <Diod. Sic. 4.69.5>
Pyrante —see [fifty daughters of Danaus[1]] (alternate version)
Pyranthus — see Periander
Pyrantis —see [fifty daughters of Danaus[1]] (alternate version)
Pyrene[1], daughter of Bebryclus <Sil. Ital. 3.420 ff.>, 60d
— and Heracles[1] <Sil. Ital. 3.420 ff.>, (60d)
Pyrene[2], paramour of Ares <Apollod. *Bibl.* 2.5.11>, 7c
Pyrgo[1], wife of Alcathous[1] <Paus. 1.43.4>, 40a
Pyrgo[2], nurse of the children of Priam[1] <Virg. *Aen.* 5.644>, *
Pyrippe, daughter of Thespius <Apollod. *Bibl.* 2.7.8> and *Megamede* <Apollod. *Bibl.* 2.4.10>, 50d
— and Heracles[1] <Apollod. *Bibl.* 2.7.8>, (50d)
Pyrodes, son of Cilix <Pliny *Nat. Hist.* 7.99>, 56c
Pyrrha[1], daughter of Epimetheus and *Pandora*[1] <Apollod. *Bibl.* 1. 7.2>, 16b
— and Deucalion[1] <*Cat. Wom., Frag. Hes.* frg. 2, Merk. & West>, (16b)
Pyrrha[2], daughter of Creon[2] <Paus. 9.10.3> and *Eurydice*[9], 55d
Pyrrhus[1] — see Neoptolemus
Pyrrhus[2], son of Neoptolemus and *Lanassa* <Plut. *Pyrr.* 1.2>, 24c
Pyrrhus[3], father of Alexander[3] <Paus. 4.35.3>, *
Pyrrhus[4], son of Ptolemaeus[3] and father of *Deidameia*[5] <Paus. 4. 35.3>, *
Pyrrhus[5], son of Aeacides <Paus. 1.11.1>, *
Pythaeus, son of Apollo <Paus. 2.35.2>, 11d
Pythagoras[1] — see Aethalides[1]
Pythagoras[2], son of Mnesarchus <Paus. 2.13.2>, *
Pythes, son of Delphus <Paus. 10.6.4>, 17a
Pytho(n) (*Delphyne*) [dragon], offspring of *Gaea* <Hyg. *Fab.* 140>, *2b*
Pyttius, father of Amaryncеus[1] <Paus. 5.1.10>, 17d

Raidne — see [Sirens]
Rarus — see Triptolemus (alternate version)
Remus[1], son of Aeneas[1] and *Dexithea*[2] <Plut. *Rom.* 2.2>, 41c
alternate parentage:
Ares and *Aemilia* <Plut. *Rom.* 2.3>
Ares and *Ilia* <Virg. *Aen.* 6.776-77>
Latinus[1] and *Roma*[2] <Plut. *Rom.* 2.3>
an apparition and handmaid of Tarchetius <Plut. *Rom.* 2.5>
Remus[2], a comrade of Turnus <Virg. *Aen.* 9.330>, *
Rhacius, son of Lebes <Schol. on Ap. Rhod. 1.308>, 32d
— and *Manto*[1] <Paus. 7.3.1>, (32d)
Rhadamanthys, son of Zeus and *Europe*[1] <Hom. *Il.* XIV.322>, 5c, *52d*
alternate parentage:
Hephaestus <Cin. in Paus. 8.53.5>
— and *Alcmene* <Apollod. *Bibl.* 3.1.2>, 59d
Rhadius — see Phrasius[2]
Rhea (*Cybele*[1]) [Titan] [earth], daughter of Uranus and *Gaea* <Hes. *Theog.* 135>, 5a
alternate parentage:
Oceanus and *Tethys* <Plato *Tim.* 40e>
— and Cronus <Hes. *Theog.* 453>, (5a)
Rhegnidas, son of Phalces[1] <Paus. 2.13.1>, 60d
Rhene[1], paramour of Oileus[1] <Hom. *Il.* II.727-28>, 15c
Rhene[2], paramour of Hermes <Diod. Sic. 5.48.1>, 46d
Rhenus [river], son of Oceanus and Tethys <Hes. *Theog.* 367-68; named as river, Non. *Dion.* 43.410>, 63b
Rhesus[1] [river], son of Oceanus and *Tethys* <Hes. *Theog.* 340>, 63b
Rhesus[2] [King of Thrace], son of Strymon[1] <Eur. *Rhes.* 274-80> and *Euterpe* <Apollod. *Bibl.* 1.3.4>, 71b, *6a*
alternate parentage:
Strymon[1] and *Calliope* <Apollod. *Bibl.* 1.3.4>
Eioneus[3] <Hom. *Il.* X.435>
— and *Arga(n)tho(n)e* <Parth. *Love Stor.* 36.1>, (71b)
Rhetia, paramour of Apollo <Pher. in Strab. 10.3.21>, 11c
Rhexenor[1], son of Nausithous[1] <Hom. *Od.* 7.63>, 9a
Rhexenor[2], father of *Chalciope*[3] <Apollod. *Bibl.* 3.15.6>, 51a
Rhexenor[3], comrade of Diomedes[1] <Ovid *Met.* 14.504>, *
R(h)ipheus [centaur], offspring of Centaurus and a Magnesian Mare <Pind. *Pyth.* 2.50; named as centaur, Ovid *Met.* 12. 351>, 69d
alternate parentage:
Ixion and *Nephele*[1] <Diod. Sic. 4.69.5>
Rhode[1] (*Rhodus*), daughter of Poseidon and *Halia*[1] <Diod. Sic. 5. 55.5 (she is called *Rhodus*)>, 8c, *3a*
alternate parentage:
Poseidon and *Amphitrite* <Apollod. *Bibl.* 1.4.5>
Asopus <Schol. on Hom. *Od.* 17.208>
— and Helios <Apollod. *Bibl.* 1.4.5>, 14a
Rhode[2], daughter of Danaus[1] and *Atlantia* or *Phoebe*[4] <Apollod. *Bibl.* 2.1.5>, 58c
— and Hippolytus[3] <Apollod. *Bibl.* 2.1.5>, (58c)
Rhode[3], one of the nurses of Dionysus <Non. *Dion.* 14.223>, *
Rhodeia, daughter of Oceanus and *Tethys* <Hes. *Theog.* 351>, 63b
Rhodia[1], daughter of Danaus[1] and *Atlantia* or *Phoebe*[4] <Apollod. *Bibl.* 2.1.5>, 57d
— and Chalcodon[1] <Apollod. *Bibl.* 2.1.5>, (57d)
Rhodia[2] — see [Muses] (alternate version)
Rhodius [river], son of Oceanus and *Tethys* <Hes. *Theog.* 341>, 63b
Rhodope[1], daughter of Oceanus and *Tethys* <*Hom. Hymn* 2 (to Demeter) 420 (inferred because she is listed with a group of daughters of Oceanus and *Tethys*); named, Hyg. *Fab.* pref.>, 70a
— and Apollo <*Etym. Magn.* 513.36>, 11c
— and Haemus[1] <Luc. *Dance* 51>, 12b
Rhodope[2] — see Bias[1] and Melampus[1] <alternate version>
Rhodope[3], paramour of Euthynicus <Nic. Eug. in *Erot. Scrip. Gr.* 3.263-91>, *
Rhodus — see *Rhode*[1]
Rhoecus[1] [centaur], offspring of Centaurus and a Magnesian Mare <Pind. *Pyth* 2.50; named as centaur, Apollod. *Bibl.* 3.9.2>, 69d
alternate parentage:
Ixion and *Nephele*[1] <Diod. Sic. 4.69.5>
Rhoecus[2] — see Rhoetus[2]
Rhoeo, daughter of Staphylus[1] and *Chrysothemis*[2] <Diod. Sic. 5. 62.1>, 56d
— and Apollo <Diod. Sic. 5.62.1>, 11c
— and Zarex <Tzetz. on Lyc. 580>, 69b
Rhoeteia, daughter of Sithon <Tzetz. on Lyc. 1161> and *Mendeis*, 7d
Rhoetus[1] [centaur], offspring of Centaurus and a Magnesian Mare <Pind. *Pyth.* 2.50; named as centaur, Ovid *Met.* 12.269>, 69d
alternate parentage:
Ixion and *Nephele*[1] <Diod. Sic. 4.69.5>
Rhoetus[2] (Rhoecus[2]) [giant], son of Uranus (from his blood) and *Gaea* <Hes. *Theog.* 185; named as giant, Hor. *Odes* 2.19. 23>, 4a
Rhoetus[3], a comrade of Turnus <Virg. *Aen.* 9.343>, *
Rhoetus[4], killed by Perseus[1] <Ovid *Met.* 5.38>, *
Rhome — see *Roma*[1]
Rhopalus, son of Phaestus[1] <Paus. 2.6.7>, 61d
[Rivers of Hell], children of Oceanus and *Tethys* (see Acheron, Cocytus, *Lethe*[2], *Styx*), 50a
Roma[1], mother of *Roma*[2] <Plut. *Rom.* 2.3>, 13d
Roma[2], daughter of *Roma*[1] <Plut. *Rom.* 2.3>, 13d

— and Latinus[1] <Plut. *Rom.* 2.3>, (13d)
Roma[3], daughter of Italus and *Leucaria* <Plut. *Rom.* 2.1>, 13d
alternate parentage:
Euander[1] <Serv. on Virg. *Aen.* 1.273>
Odysseus and *Circe* <Serv. on Virg. *Aen.* 1.273>
Telemachus <Serv. on Virg. *Aen.* 1.273>
Telephus <Plut. *Rom.* 2.1>
— and Aeneas <Plut. *Rom.* 2.1>, 41c
— and Ascanius[1] <Plut. *Rom.* 2.1>, 41c
Romanus, son of Odysseus and *Circe* <Plut. *Rom.* 2.1>, 13d
Romulus, son of Aeneas[1] and *Dexithea*[2] <Plut. *Rom.* 2.2>, 41c
alternate parentage:
Ares and *Aemilia* <Plut. *Rom.* 2.3>
Ares and *Ilia* <Virg. *Aen.* 6.776-77>
Latinus[1] and *Roma*[2] <Plut. *Rom.* 2.3>
an apparition and handmaid of Tarchetius <Plut. *Rom.* 2. 5>
Romus, son of Aeneas[1] <Dion. Hal. *Rom. Ant.* 1.72.1 (citing Cephalon of Gorgis)> and *Lavinia*[2], 41c
alternate parentage:
Aemathion[5] <Dion. Hal. *Rom. Ant.* 1.72.6>
Odysseus and *Circe* <Xena. in Dion. Hal. *Rom. Ant.* 1.72.5>

Sabbe [Babylonian Sibyl], daughter of Berosus and *Erymanthe* <Paus. 10.12.5>, *
Saesara, daughter of Celeus[1] <Paus. 1.38.2> and *Metaneira*, 46d
— and Croco(n) <Paus. 1.38.2>, (46d)
Sagaris[1], son of Mygdon(us)[1] and *Alexirhoe* <Ps.-Plut. *De Fluv.* 12. 1>, 8d, *67b*
Sagaris[2], killed by Turnus <Virg. *Aen.* 9.570-75>, *
Sagaritis (*Sa(n)garitis*), paramour of Attis <Ovid *Fast.* 4.225-33> 70a
Salagus, son of Oenopion[1] <Paus. 7.4.6> and *Helice*[4], 56c
Salaminus [King of Cyprus], father of *Amyce* <Paus. Damasc. in *F.H.G.* 4.469 frg. 65, Müller>, 59a
Salamis, daughter of Asopus <Apollod. *Bibl.* 3.12.7> and *Metope*[2] <Diod. Sic. 4.72.1>, 66b
— and Poseidon <Apollod. *Bibl.* 3.12.7>, 9b
Salmacis, paramour of Hermaphroditus <Ovid *Met.* 4.288-391>, 46a
Salmoneus [King of Elis], son of Aeolus[1] <*Cat. Wom., Frag. Hes.* frg. 10, Merk. & West> and *Enarete* <Apollod. *Bibl.* 1.7. 3>, 27b
— and *Alcidice* <Apollod. *Bibl.* 1.9.8>, 63c
— and *Sidero* <Apollod. *Bibl.* 1.9.8>, (27b)
Samia, daughter of Maeandrus <Paus. 7.4.2>, 68a
— and Ancaeus[2] <Paus. 7.4.2>, 54d
Samon — see Saon[1]
Samus, son of Ancaeus[2] and *Samia* <Paus. 7.4.2>, 54d
— and *Parthenia*[1] <Schol. on Ap. Rhod. *Arg.* 1.187>, (54d)
Sandocus, son of Astynous[1] <Apollod. *Bibl.* 3.14.3>, 46c
— and *Pharnace* <Apollod. *Bibl.* 3.14.3>, (46c)
Sa(n)garitis — see *Sagaritis*
Sa(n)garius [river], son of Oceanus and *Tethys* <Hes. *Theog.* 344>, 70a
— and *Cybele*[2] <Mem. in *F. Gr. H.* 434 F 1, 28, 29>, 2d
— and *Metope*[1] <Apollod. *Bibl.* 3.12.5>, (70a)
Sao, daughter of Nereus and *Doris*[1] <Hes. *Theog.* 243>, *65a*
Saon[1] (Samon), son of Hermes and *Rhene*[2] <Diod. Sic. 5.48.1>, 46d
alternate parentage:
Zeus and *Nymphe*[2] <Diod. Sic. 5.48.1>
Saon[2], an envoy from Acraephnium <Paus. 9.40.2>, *
Sardo[1], wife of Tyrrhenus <Schol. on Plato *Tim.* 25b>, 51b
Sardo[2], daughter of Sthenelus[7] <Hyg. *Fab.* 275>, *
Sarpedon[1], son of Zeus and *Europe*[1] <*Cat. Wom., Frag. Hes.* frgs. 140-41, Merk. & West>, 5c, *52c*
— and Miletus <Apollod. *Bibl.* 3.1.2>, 11b
Sarpedon[2] [King of Lycia], son of Zeus and *Laodameia*[2] <Hom. *Il.* VI. 198-99>, 5d, *18d*
alternate parentage:
Euander[2] and *Laodameia*[2] <Diod. Sic. 5.79.3 (mother is called *Deidameia*)>
(or same as Sarpedon[1])
Sarpedon[3], son of Poseidon <Apollod. *Bibl.* 2.5.9>, 9c
Satnioesis [river], son of Oceanus and Tethys <Hes. *Theog.* 367-68; named as river, Hom. *Il.* XXI.87>, 70b
Satyria, daughter of Minos I <Serv. on Virg. *Aen.* 1.533>, 54d
— and Taras <Prob. on Virg. *Geo.* 2.197>, 9d
[satyrs], offspring of Hermes and *Iphthime*[2] <Non. *Dion.* 14.105-16>, *17a*
Scaea, daughter of Danaus[1] and *Europe*[3] <Apollod. *Bibl.* 2.1.5>, 57d, 57d
— and Archander <Paus. 7.1.3>, 17b
— and Diaphron[1] <Apollod. *Bibl.* 2.1.5>, (57d)
Scaeus, son of Hippocoon[1] <Apollod. *Bibl.* 3.10.5>, 47c
Scamander[1] (Xanthus[2]) [river], son of Oceanus and *Tethys* <Hes. *Theog.* 345>, 70b
alternate parentage:
Zeus <Hom. *Il.* XXI.2-3 (river is called Xanthus)>
— and *Idaea*[1] <Apollod. *Bibl.* 3.12.1>, (70b)
Scamander[2], son of Deimachus[3] and *Glaucia*[1] <Plut. *Gr. Quest.* 41>, *70b*
— and *Acidusa* <Plut. *Gr. Quest.* 41>, (70b)
Scamandrius[1] — see Astyanax[1]
Scamandrius[2], son of Strophius[3] <Hom. *Il.* V.50>, *
Scamandrodice, paramour of Poseidon <Schol. on Pind. *Olym.* 2. 147>, 9b
Scellis, son of Hecetorus <Parth. *Love Stor.* 19>, 34c
Scelmis — see (Telchines) (alternate version)
Scephrus, son of Tegeates <Paus. 8.53.4> and *Maera*[2], 63d
Schedius[1], son of Perimedes[1] <Hom. *Il.* XV.515>, 59c
Schedius[2] [King of Phocis], son of Iphitus[3] <Hom. *Il.* XVII.306-07> and *Hippolyte*[4] <Hyg. *Fab.* 97>, 23c
Schedius[3], suitor of *Penelope*[1] (from Dulichium) <Apollod. *Epit.* 7. 27>, *
Schedius[4], killed by Neoptolemus <Quint. Smyr. 10.84-87>, *
Schoeneus[1] [King of Boeotia], son of Athamas[1] and *Themisto*[1] <Apollod. *Bibl.* 1.9.2>, 26b
Schoeneus[2], son of Autonoos and *Hippodameia*[9] <Ant. Lib. *Met.* 7>, *
Sciron[1], son of Pylas <Paus. 1.39.6>, 59c
— and an unnamed daughter of Pandion II and *Pylia* <Paus. 1.39. 6>, 50b
Sciron[2], son of Pelops[1] <Apollod. *Epit.* 1.2> and *Hippodameia*[1], *39a*
alternate parentage:
Canethus[3] and *Henioche*[2] <Plut. *Thes.* 25.4>
Poseidon <Apollod. *Epit.* 1.2>
— and *Chariclo*[3] <Plut. *Thes.* 10.3>, 66b
Scylla[1], daughter of Nisus[2] <Apollod. *Bibl.* 3.15.8> and *Abrote*, 50d, *34d*
— and Minos I <Apollod. *Bibl.* 3.15.8>, 54c
Scylla[2] [nymph, then monster], daughter of Phorcus[1] and *Crataeis*[1] <Ap. Rhod. *Arg.* 4.825-26>, 2b
alternate parentage:
Phorcus[1] and *Hecate* <Acus. in *F. Gr. H.* 2 F 42>
Lamia[2] <Schol. on Ap. Rhod. 4.825-31>
Phorbas[7] and *Hecate* <*Gr. Ehoiai, Frag. Hes.* frg. 262, Merk. & West> (Evelyn-White renders the father Phoebus from the same fragment <*Gr. Eoiae*, frg. 13, in *Hes.—Hom. Hymns & Hom.*, Evelyn-White>)
Trienus and *Crataeis*[1] <Apollod. *Epit.* 7.20>
Triton <Eust. on Hom. *Od.* 1714>
Typhon <Hyg. *Fab.* 125>
— and Glaucus[3] <Ovid *Met.* 13.899-968>, 62a

— and Poseidon <Serv. on Virg. *Aen.* 3.420>, 9b
Scylla[3] —see [fifty daughters of Danaus[1]] (alternate version)
Scyllis, son of Daedalus and *Naucrate* <Paus. 2.15.1>, 49b
Scyrius — see Aegeus[1] (alternate version)
Scythes[1], son of Heracles[1] and *Echidna* <Herod. 4.10>, 60c
alternate parentage:
Zeus <Diod. Sic. 2.43.3>
Scythes[2] — see Delas
[seasons] — see (Horae)
Sebrus — see Tebrus
Segesta — see *Aegesta*
Selene (*Mene*) [goddess] [moon], daughter of Hyperion[1] and *Theia*[1] <Hes. *Theog.* 371>, 14b
alternate parentage:
Hyperion[1] and *Aether* <Hyg. *Fab.* pref.>
Pallas[8] <*Hom. Hymn* 4 (to Hermes) 100>
— and Endymion <Paus. 5.1.4>, 15a
— and Pan <Virg. *Geo.* 3.393-95>, 46a
— and Zeus <*Hom. Hymn* 32 (to Selene)>, 6d
Selepus, father of Soloon <Hom. *Il.* II.693>, 51d
Selinus [King of Aegialia], son of Poseidon <Steph. Byz. "Helice">, 9d
Semele (*Thyone*[1]), daughter of Cadmus and *Harmonia*[1] <Hes. *Theog.* 976>, 56c
— and Actaeon <Acus. in *F. Gr. H.* 2 F 33>, 69a
— and Zeus <Hes. *Theog.* 940-41>, 6d
Semiramis, daughter of [a Syrian] and *Derceto* <Diod. Sic. 2.4.3>, 61c
— and Ninus <Diod. Sic. 2.4.1>, (61c)
— and Onnes <Diod. Sic. 2.5.1>, (61c)
(Semnai) — see (Erinyes)
Semus, son of Halirrhothius[2] <*Cat. Wom., Frag. Hes.* frg. 49, Merk. & West>, 25a
[Seven against Thebes] — see Amphiaraus, Capaneus[1], Eteoclus, Hippomedon[1], Parthenopaeus, Polyneices, Tydeus <Aesch. *Sev.* 370-633>
other lists:
omits Eteoclus and includes Adrastus[1] <Eur. *Phoen. Maid.*>
omits Polyneices and Tydeus and includes Adrastus[1] and Mecisteus <Apollod. *Bibl.* 3.6.3>
names Creon[2], Dryas[8], Eteocles[1], Eurymedon[7], Haemon[1], Hypseus[3], and Menoeceus[2] <Stat. *Theb.* 8.353-57>
[seven sons], children of Eetion[1] <Hom. VI.420>, 24c
[seven sons], children of Periphas[1] and *Astyage(ia)* <Diod. Sic. 4. 69.3>, 69a
Sibylla (*Herophile*[3]) [Trojan Sibyl], daughter of Dardanus[1] and *Neso*[1] <Tzetz. on Lyc. 1465>, 42b
[sibyls] — see the following:
[Babylonian Sibyl] — see *Sabbe*
[Cumaean Sibyl] — see *Deiphobe*
[Erythrean Sibyl] — see *Herophile*[4]
[Libyan Sibyl] — see *Herophile*[1]
[Marpessan Sibyl] — see *Herophile*[5]
[Samian Sibyl] — see *Phyto*[2]
[Trojan Sibyl] — see *Sibylla*
Sicharbas — see Sychaeus
Sicinus, son of Thoas[1] and *Oenoe*[1] <Ap. Rhod. *Arg.* 1.624>, 56d
Sicyon [King of Sicyon], son of Metion <Paus. 2.6.3>, 49a
alternate parentage:
Erechtheus II <*Cat. Wom., Frag. Hes.* frg. 224, Merk. & West>
Marathon <Paus. 2.1.1>
Pelops[1] <Ibyc. in *P.M.G.* 308>
— and *Zeuxippe*[2] <Paus. 2.6.2>, 11d
Side[1], wife of Orion <Apollod. *Bibl.* 1.4.3>, 53c
Side[2] — see *Anchinoe*[1]
Side[3], daughter of Danaus[1] <Paus. 3.22.11>, 57a
Side[4], daughter of Mentaurus <Steph. Byz. "Side">, *
Side[5], committed suicide and became a bird to avoid her father's advances <Dion. Per. *On Birds* 1.7>, *
Sidero, paramour of Salmoneus <Apollod. *Bibl.* 1.9.8>, 27b
Silenus [King of Nysa], son of Pan <Serv. on Virg. *Ecl.* 6.13>, 46c
alternate parentage:
autochthonous <Non. *Dion.* 14.96>
born from drops of blood that fell from the sky <Serv. on Virg. *Ecl.* 6.13>
— and [ash tree nymph] <Apollod. *Bibl.* 2.5.4>, (46c)
Sillus[1], son of Thrasymedes[1] <Paus. 2.18.8>, 27d
Sillus[2] — see Acmon[1]
Silvius[1], son of Aeneas[1] and *Lavinia*[2] <Diod. Sic. 7.5.8>, 41c
Silvius[2] — see Aeneas[2]
Simaethis, mother of Acis <Ovid *Met.* 13.750>, 64a
— and Faunus[1] <Ovid *Met.* 13.750>, (64a)
Simoeis [river], son of Oceanus and *Tethys* <Hes. *Theog.* 342>, 71a
Sinis (Pitocamptes) (Pityocamptes), son of Polypemon[1] and *Sylea* <Apollod. *Bibl.* 3.16.2>, 34d
alternate parentage:
Canethus[3] and *Henioche*[2] <Plut. *Thes.* 25.5>
Poseidon <Bacch. 18.19-22>
Sinon, son of Aesimus <Schol. on Lyc. 344>, 13c
Sinope, daughter of Asopus <Ap. Rhod. *Arg.* 2.947> and *Metope*[2] <Diod. Sic. 4.72.1>, 66b
— and Apollo <Diod. Sic. 4.72.2>, 11c
Sipylus, son of Amphion[1] and *Niobe*[1] <Apollod. *Bibl.* 3.5.6>, 66d
[Sirens], daughters of Achelous and *Melpomene* <Apollod. *Epit.* 7.18> (see *Aglaope*, *Peisinoe*[1], *Thelxiepeia*), 65b
other lists:
Leucosia[1], *Ligeia*[1], *Parthenope*[1] <Tzetz. on Lyc. 712>
Aglaophonus, *Molpe*, *Thelxiope* <Schol. on Ap. Rhod. *Arg.* 4.882>
Molpe, *Raidne*, *Thelxiope*, *Teles*[2] <Hyg. *Fab.* pref.>
Sisyphus [King of Corinth], son of Aeolus[1] <Hom. *Il.* VI.154> and *Enarete* <Apollod. *Bibl.* 1.7.3>, 18a
— and *Anticleia*[1] <Hyg. *Fab.* 200>, 13a
— and *Merope*[1] <Pher. in *F. Gr. H.* 3 F 119>, 47a
— and *Tyro* <Hyg. *Fab.* 60>, 27b
[Sithnidian nymph], paramour of Zeus <Paus. 1.40.1>, 6d
Sithon [King of Thrace], son of Ares and *Ossa* <Con. *Narr.*>, 7d
alternate parentage:
Ares and *Angcinoes* <Schol. on Lyc. *Alex.* 583>
— and *Mendeis* <Con. *Narr.* 10>, (7d)
[Sithonian Harpy], paramour of Boreas <Non. *Dion.* 37.158-59>, 12b
[six daughters (unnamed)], children of Aeolus[2] and *Cyane*[1] <Hom. *Od.* 10.2-6>, 18c
[six sons (unnamed)], children of Peleus and *Thetis* <Lyc. 177-79>, 24c
[six sons (unnamed)], children of Poseidon and *Halia*[1] <Diod. Sic. 5.55.5>, 8c, *3a*
[slave girl], paramour of Heracles[1] <Herod. 1.7>, 61c
Smerdius, son of Leucippus[6] <Diod. Sic. 5.51.3>, 15d
Smicrus, father of Branchus[1] <Con. *Narr.* 33>, 11a
Smyrna[1] — see *Myrr(h)a*
Smyrna[2] [Amazon] <Strabo 14.1.4>, *
[snake], offspring of Heracles[1] and *Pyrene* <Syl. Ital. 3.420 ff.>, 60d
Socleus, son of Lycaon[1] <Apollod. *Bibl.* 3.8.1>, 64c
Socus[1], son of Hippasus[4] <Hom. *Il.* XI.427>, 44d
Socus[2], husband of *Combe*[1] <Non. *Dion.* 13.146-48>, 66c
Sois (*Oreaside*), wife of Triop(a)s[2] <Hellan. in Schol. on Hom. *Il.* III.75>, 61d
Soloon, son of Selepus< Hom. *Il.* II.693>, 51d
— and *Hippolyte*[1] <Plut. *Thes.* 26.3 (called *Antiope*)>, 7c
Solymus[1], son of Ares <*Etym. Magn.* "Solymus" 721.43>, 7d

Solymus[2], a comrade of Aeneas <Ovid *Fast.* 4.79>, *
[son (unnamed)] of Clymenus[4] and *Harpalyce*[2] <Hyg. *Fab.* 206>, 26d
[son (unnamed)] of Tantalus[2] <Apollod. *Epit.* 2.16> and *Clytemnestra* <Eur. *Iph. in Aulis* 1150>, 48c
Sophax, son of Heracles and *Tinge* <Plut. *Sert.* 9>, 61c
Sosana, daughter of Ninus <Diod. Sic. 2.6.9>, 61c
Sose, paramour of Hermes <Non. *Dion.* 14.89>, 46d
Sostratus, companion of Heracles[1] <Paus. 7.17.8>, 61c
Sous, son of Procles[1] <Paus. 3.7.1> and *Lathria*, 60d
[sown men] — see (Spart(o)i)
Spartaeus, son of Zeus and *Himalia* <Diod. Sic. 5.55.5>, 5d
Sparte, daughter of Eurotas <Apollod. *Bibl.* 3.10.3> and *Cleta*[1] <Schol. on Eur. 626>, 61c
— and Lacedaemon <Apollod. *Bibl.* 3.10.3>, 47b
(Spartoi) [sown men], sprang from teeth of [Cadmean Dragon] (see Chthonius[1], Echion[1], Hyperenor[1], Pelor(us), Udaeus), 7d
Sparton[1], son of Tisamenus[1] <Paus. 7.5.2>, 36c
Sparton[2], son of Phoroneus <Acus. in Paus. 2.16.4 (although Pausanias discredits this relationship)> and *Teledice*, 61b
Sparton[3], father of Eurytius <Ant. Lib. *Met.* 17.1>, *
Speio, daughter of Nereus and *Doris*[1] <Hes. *Theog.* 245>, *65a*
Sperchius [river], son of Oceanus and *Tethys* <Hes. *Theog.* 367-68; named as river, Hom. *Il.* XVI.174>, 71a
— and *Polydora*[1] <Hom. *Il.* XVI.175-76>, 22d, 24c
— and *Polydora*[5] <Schol. on Ap. Rhod. *Arg.* 1.1212-19a>, 57a
Spermo [one of the (Oenotropae)] [seed], daughter of Anius <Apollod. *Epit.* 3.10> and *Dorippe*, 56d
Sphettus, son of Troezen[1] <Paus. 2.30.9>, 39b
Sphincius, son of Athamas[1] and *Themisto*[1] <Hyg. *Fab.* 243>, 26b
[Sphinx] — see *Phix*
Sphyrus, son of Machaon <Paus. 2.23.4> and *Anticleia*[3], 19d
Sponde [one of the hours], daughter of Zeus and *Themis*[1] <Hyg. *Fab.* 183>, 6d
Staphylus[1], son of Dionysus and *Ariadne* <Apollod. *Epit.* 1.9>, 56d
alternate parentage:
Theseus and *Ariadne* <Ion of Chios in Plut. *Thes.* 20.2>
— and *Chrysothemis*[2] <Diod. Sic. 5.62.1>, (56d)
Staphylus[2], [King of Assyria], husband of *Methe* <Non. *Dion.* 18.124>, *
Staphylus[3], son of Oenomaus[2] <Non. *Dion.* 43.60>, *
[stars], offspring of Astraeus and *Eos* <Hes. *Theog.* 383>, 13b
Sternops, son of Melas[3] <Apollod. *Bibl.* 1.8.5>, 16d
Sterope[1] — see *Asterope*[1]
Sterope[2], daughter of Portheus[1] and *Laothoe*[4] <*Cat. Wom., Frag. Hes.* frg. 26.9, Merk. & West>, 15d
alternate parentage:
Portheus[1] and *Euryte*[1] <Apollod. *Bibl.* 1.7.10>
Sterope[3] (*Aerope*[2]), daughter of Cepheus[2] <Apollod. *Bibl.* 2.7.3>, 64c
— and Ares <Paus. 8.44.7>, 7c
Sterope[4], daughter of Pleuron and *Xanthippe*[1] <Apollod. *Bibl.* 1.7.7>, 15d
Sterope[5], daughter of Acastus <Apollod. *Bibl.* 3.13.3> and *Hippolyte*[2], 28c
Sterope[6] — see Aspledon[1] (alternate version)
Sterope[7] [one of the Bacchae] <Non. *Dion.* 30.222>, *
Sterope[8] [one of the horses of Helios] <Hyg. *Fab.* 183>, *
Steropes [lightning] [one of the Uranian Cyclopes], son of Uranus and *Gaea* <Hes. *Theog.* 140>, 4b
Stetheboea —see *Stheneboea*
Stheneboea (Anteia) (*Stetheboea*), daughter of Apheidas[1] <*Cat. Wom., Frag. Hes.* frg. 129, Merk. & West>, 63d
alternate parentage:
Amphianax <Apollod. *Bibl.* 2.2.>
Iobates <Apollod. *Bibl.* 2.2.1>
— and Proetus[1] <Hom. *Il.* VI.157 (she is called *Anteia*)>, 57d
Sthenelas [King of Argos], son of Crotopus <Paus. 2.16.1>, 61d
Sthenelaus[1], son of Melas[3] <Apollod. *Bibl.* 1.8.5>, 16d
Sthenelaus[2], son of Ithaemenes <Hom. *Il.* XVI.586>, *
Sthenele[1], daughter of Acastus <Apollod. *Bibl.* 3.13.8> and *Hippolyte*[2], 28c
— and Menoetius[2] <Apollod. *Bibl.* 3.13.8>, 22d, 66a
Sthenele[2], daughter of Danaus[1] and *Memphis* <Apollod. *Bibl.* 2.1.5>, 57c
— and Sthenelus[4] <Apollod. *Bibl.* 2.1.5>, (57c)
Sthenelus[1] [King of Mycenae], son of Perseus[1] <Hom. *Il.* XIX.116> and *Andromeda* <Apollod. *Bibl.* 2.4.5>, 58d
— and *Nicippe*[1] <*Cat. Wom., Frag. Hes.* frg. 190, Merk. & West>, 38b
Sthenelus[2] [King of Argos] [one of the Epigoni], son of Capaneus <Hom. *Il.* II.564> and *Euadne*[1] <Hyg. *Fab.* 97>, *58c*
Sthenelus[3], son of Androgeus <Apollod. *Bibl.* 2.5.9>, 53d
Sthenelus[4], son of Aegyptus[1] and *Tyria* <Apollod. *Bibl.* 2.1.5>, 57c
— and *Sthenele*[2] <Apollod. *Bibl.* 2.1.5>, (57c)
Sthenelus[5] [King of Ligurians], father of Cycnus[6] <Ovid *Met.* 2.367>, *
Sthenelus[6], son of Actor[9] <Ap. Rhod. *Arg.* 2.911>, *
Sthenelus[7], father of Sardo[2] <Hyg. *Fab.* 275>, *
Sthenelus[8], killed by Turnus <Virg. *Aen.* 12.341>, *
Sthen(n)o [one of the Gorgons], daughter of Phorcus[1] and *Ceto*[1] <Hes. *Theog.* 276>, 2b
alternate parentage:
Gorgon (son of Typhon and *Echidna*) and *Ceto*[1] <Hyg. *Fab.* pref.>
Stilbe[1], daughter of Peneius and *Creusa*[4] <Diod. Sic. 4.69.1>, 68b
— and Apollo <Diod. Sic. 4.69.1>, 11c
Stilbe[2], daughter of Phosphor(us) <Schol. on Hom. *Il.* X.266-67 (he is called Eosphorus)>, 13b
— and Hermes <Schol. on Hom. *Il.* X.266-67>, 46d
Stilbe[3], paramour of Celtius <Schol. on Eur. *Or.* 1646>, *
Stilbo, daughter of Oceanus and *Tethys* <Hyg. *Fab.* pref.>, 71b
Stonychia — see (Pleiades) (alternate version)
Strambelus — see Trambelus
Stratichus — see Stratius[1]
Stratius[1] (Stratichus), son of Nestor <Hom. *Od.* 3.413> and *Anaxibia*[4] <Apollod. *Bibl.* 1.9.9 (Apollod. calls him Stratichus)>, 27d
alternate parentage:
Nestor and *Eurydice*[7] <Hom. *Od.* 3.453 (inferred because she is wife of Nestor)>
Stratius[2], son of Clymenus[1] <Paus. 9.37.1> and *Budeia*, 26d
Stratius[3], suitor of *Penelope*[1] (from Zacynthus) <Apollod. *Epit.* 7.29>, *
Stratobates, son of Electryon[1] and *Anaxo*[1] <Apollod *Bibl.* 2.4.5>, 59d
Stratolaus — see Promachus[1]
Stratonice[1], daughter of Pleuron and *Xanthippe*[1] <Apollod. *Bibl.* 1.7.7>, 15d
Stratonice[2], daughter of Portheus[1] and *Laothoe*[4] <*Cat. Wom., Frag. Hes.* frg. 26.9, Merk. & West>, 15d
— and Melaneus[2] <*Cat. Wom., Frag. Hes.* frg. 26.25, Merk. & West>, 11d
Stratonice[3], daughter of Thespius <Apollod. *Bibl.* 2.7.8> and *Megamede* <Apollod. *Bibl.* 2.4.10>, 50d
— and Heracles[1] <Apollod. *Bibl.* 2.7.8>, (50d)
Stratonice[4], wife of Chaerisilaus <Plut. *Gr. Quest.* 37 (inferred because she is called mother of Poemander)>, 35a
Strombus, son of Poseidon and *Ceroessa* <Hesyc. Mil. in *F.H.G.* 4.149 frg. 20, Müller (inferred because he is called brother of Byzas)>, 8c, *55b*
Strophius[1] [King of Phocis], son of Crisus <Paus. 2.29.4> and *Antiphateia*, 23c
— and *Anaxibia*[1] <Paus. 2.29.4>, 37a

Strophius[2], son of Pylades and *Electra*[3] <Paus. 2.16.5>, 23c, *36c*
Strophius[3], father of Scamandrius[2] <Hom. *Il.* V.50>, *
Strophius[4], father of Phlogius <Non. *Dion.* 30.108>, *
Strophius[5], a member of the crew of Menelaus <Paus. 10.25.3>, *
Strym(n)o (*Thym(n)o*), daughter of Scamander[1] <Apollod. *Bibl.* 3.12.3> and *Idaea*[1], 70b
alternate parentage:
Otreus <Apollod. *Bibl.* 3.11.3 (she is called *Placia*)>
— and Laomedon[1] <Hellan. in *F. Gr. H.* 4 F 139>, 42c
Strymon[1] [river], son of Oceanus and *Tethys* <Hes. *Theog.* 339>, 71b
— and *Calliope* <Apollod. *Bibl.* 1.3.4>, 6a
— and *Euterpe* <Apollod. *Bibl.* 1.3.4>, 6a
— and *Neaera*[3] <Apollod. *Bibl.* 2.1.2>, (71b)
Strymon[2], killed by Caresus <Val. Flac. 6.193>, *
Strymon[3] [one of the horses of Chromis[2]] <Stat. *Theb.* 6.464>, *
Stygne, daughter of Danaus[1] and *Polyxo*[3] <Apollod. *Bibl.* 2.1.5>, 58c
— and Polyctor[2] <Apollod. *Bibl.* 2.1.5>, (58c)
Stymphalus[1] [King of Arcadia], son of Elatus[1] and *Laodice*[2] <Apollod. *Bibl.* 3.9.1>, 62c
Stymphalus[2], son of Lycaon[1] <Apollod. *Bibl.* 3.8.1>, 64c
Styphelus [centaur], offspring of Centaurus and a Magnesian Mare <Pind. *Pyth.* 2.50; named as centaur, Ovid *Met.* 12.460>, 69c
alternate parentage:
Ixion and *Nephele*[1] <Diod. Sic. 4.69.5>
Styx [river], daughter of Oceanus and *Tethys* <Hes. *Theog.* 361>, 50a
alternate parentage:
Erebus and *Nyx* <Hyg. *Fab.* pref.>
— and Pallas[1] <Hes. *Theog.* 384>, 12a
— and Peiras[2] <Epim. in Paus. 8.18.21>, (50a)
— and Zeus <Apollod. *Bibl.* 1.3.1>, 6d
Swiftfoot [mare], offspring of Boreas and [Sithonian Harpy] <Non. *Dion.* 37.157-59>, 12b
Sybaris[1] — see *Lamia*[2]
Sybaris[2], killed by Turnus <Virg. *Aen.* 12.363>, *
Sybaris[3], killed by Hippomedon[1] <Stat. *Theb.* 7.642>, *
Sychaeus (Acerbas) (Adherbas) (Sicharbas) (Sychreus), paramour of *Dido* <Virg. *Aen.* 1.345>, 41d
Sychreus — see Sychaeus
Syke [fig tree], daughter of Oxylus[3] and *Hamadryas* <Athen. 3.78b>, 71d
Sylea, daughter of Corinthus[1] <Apollod. *Bibl.* 3.16.2>, 34d
— and Polypemon[1] <Apollod. *Bibl.* 3.16.2>, (34d)
Syleus, son of Poseidon <Con. *Narr.* 17>, 9d
Syllis, paramour of Apollo <Paus. 2.6.3>, 11c
Syllus — see (Cercopes) (alternate version)
Sylvius — see Aeneas[2]
Syme, daughter of Ialysus <Steph. Byz. "Syme"> and *Dotis* <Athen. 7.296c>, 14a
— and Glaucus[3] <Athen. 7.296c>, 62a
— and Poseidon <Diod. Sic. 5.53.1>, 9b
Syrinx, paramour of Pan <Ovid *Met.* 1.690>, 46a
Syrna, daughter of Damaethus <Steph. Byz. "Syrna">, 19d
— and Podaleirius <Steph. Byz. "Syrna">, (19d)
Syrus[1], son of Apollo and *Sinope* <Diod. Sic. 4.72.2>, 11c, *66b*
alternate parentage:
Agenor[1] <Eust. *Comm. Dion. Per.* 899>
Syrus[2] [one of the dogs of Actaeon] <Hyg. *Fab.* 181>, *

Talaira — see *Hilaeira*
Talaus [King of Argos] [Argonaut], son of Bias[1] and *Pero*[1] <*Cat. Wom., Frag. Hes.* frg. 37, Merk. & West>, 30d
alternate parentage:
Cretheus[1] <Paus. 8.25.9> and *Tyro*
— and *Eurynome*[6] <Hyg. *Fab.* 70>, (30d)
— and *Lysianassa*[2] <Paus. 2.6.3>, 49c
— and *Lysimache*[1] <Apollod. *Bibl.* 1.9.13>, 31d
Taleus, son of Adonis and *Erinoma* <Serv. on Virg. *Geo.* 10.18>, 11c
Talus[1] — see Perdix[2]
Talus[2], son of Oenopion[1] <Paus. 7.4.6> and *Helice*[4], 56d
Talus[3], son of Cres <Kinaithon in Paus. 8.53.5>, *
Talus[4], killed by Aeneas <Virg. *Aen.* 12.513>, *
Tanagra, daughter of Aeolus[1] and *Enarete* <Paus. 9.20.2>, 34b
alternate parentage:
Asopus and *Metope*[2] <Diod. Sic. 4.72.1>
— and Poemander <Paus. 9.20.2>, 35c
Tanais[1] [river], son of Oceanus and *Tethys* <Hes. *Theog.* 366-67; named as river, Hyg. *Fab.* pref.>, 72a
Tanais[2], son of *Lysippe*[7] <Ps.-Plut. *De Fluv.* 14>, *
Tanais[3], killed by Aeneas <Virg. *Aen.* 12.513>, *
Tantalus[1] [King of Sipylus], son of Zeus <Eur. *Iph. in Aulis* 504> and *Pluto*[2] <Paus. 2.22.3>, 6d
alternate parentage:
Tmolus <Schol. on Eur. *Or.* 5> and *Pluto*[2] <Schol. on Eur. *Or.* 4>
— and *Dione*[3] <Hyg. *Fab.* 83>, 41a
— and *Euryanassa*[1] <Tzetz. on Lyc. 52>, 5c
— and *Eurythemis(te)* <Schol. on Eur. *Or.* 11>, 15d
Tantalus[2], son of Thyestes[1] <Apollod. *Epit.* 2.16> and *Aerope*[1] <Hyg. *Fab.* 246>, 39a
— and *Clytemnestra* <Eur. *Iph. in Aulis* 1150>, 48a
Tantalus[3], son of Amphion[1] and *Niobe*[1] <Apollod. *Bibl.* 3.5.6>, 66d
Taphius [King of Taphos], son of Poseidon and *Hippothoe*[1] <Apollod. *Bibl.* 2.4.5>, 8c, *58d*
alternate parentage:
Pterlaus <Herodor. in *F. Gr. H.* 31 F 15>
Taras, son of Poseidon <Paus. 10.10.8>, 9d
— and *Satyria* <Prob. on Virg. *Geo.* 2.197>, 54d
Taraxippus[1] — see Ischenus
Taraxippus[2] — see Glaucus[1]
Tarchon, son of Telephus and *Hiera*[1] <Tzetz. on Lyc. 1249>, 60a
Targitaus, son of Zeus and daughter of Borysthenes <Herod. 4.5>, 6d
Tartara — see Typhon (alternate version)
Tartarus[1], came from Chaos <Hes. *Theog.* 119>, 1b
— and *Gaea* <Hes. *Theog.* 821-22>, 2b
Tartarus[2], killed by Astygityes <Ant. Lib. *Met.* 13.3-4>, *
Tauropolis[1], daughter of Cleson <Paus. 1.42.7>, 59c
Tauropolis[2], son of Dionysus and *Ariadne* <Schol. on Ap. Rhod. *Arg.* 3.997>, 56d
Taurus[1], son of Neleus[1] and *Chloris*[2] <*Cat. Wom., Frag. Hes.* frg. 33(a), Merk. & West>, 27d
Taurus[2], a general of Minos II <Plut. *Thes.* 16.1>, *
Taygete, daughter of Atlas <*Cat. Wom., Frag. Hes.* frg. 169, Merk. & West> and *Pleione* <Apollod. *Bibl.* 3.10.1>, 47b
— and Zeus <Apollod. *Bibl.* 3.10.3>, 6c
Tebrus (Sebrus), son of Hippocoon[1] <Apollod. *Bibl.* 3.10.5>, 47c
Tecmessa[1], daughter of Teuthras <Soph. *Ajax* 206 (her father is called *Teleutas*)>, 63d
— and Ajax[1] <Soph. *Ajax* 206>, 23d, 40a
Tecmessa[2] [Amazon] <Diod. Sic. 4.16.3>, *
Tectamus [King of Crete], son of Dorus[1] <Diod. Sic. 4.60.2>, 17a
— and a daughter of Cretheus <Diod. 4.60.2>, 32b
Tegeates, son of Lycaon[1] <Paus. 8.3.4>, 63b
— and *Maera*[2] <Paus. 8.48.6>, 45b
Tegyrius [King of Thrace], father-in-law of Ismarus[2] <Apollod. *Bibl.* 3.15.4>, 13a
Teiresias/Teiresias, daughter/son of Eueres[3] and *Chariclo*[1] <Apollod. *Bibl.* 3.6.7>, 32d
— pursued by Glyphius <Eust. on Hom. *Od.* 1665.48 ff.>, (32d)
Telamon [King of Salamis] [Argonaut], son of Aeacus and *Endeis*

<Bacch. 13.96-99>, 23d
alternate parentage:
Actaeus[3] and *Glauce*[1] <Pher. in *F. Gr. H.* 3 F 60>
— and *Glauce*[1] <Diod. Sic. 4.72.7>, 66b
— and *Hesione*[1] <Soph. *Ajax* 1299-1303; named, Apollod. *Bibl.* 2.6.4>, 42d
— and *Periboea*[2] <Soph. *Ajax* 569 (inferred because she is mother of Ajax[1])>, 40a
— and *Theaneira* <Ist. in *F. Gr. H.* 334 F 57>, 23d
(Telchines), sons of Pontus and *Gaea* <Tzetz. *Chil.* 12.836> (see Actaeus[1], Hormenus, Lycus[3], Megalesius), 2a
alternate parentage:
Tartarus and *Nemesis* <Bacch. frg. 52, Snell & Maehler>
Thalatta <Diod. Sic. 5.55.1>
others:
Damnameneus[1], Lycus[13], Scelmis, sons of Poseidon <Non. *Dion.* 14.36-40>
Telchis [King of Sicyon], son of Europs <Paus. 2.5.7>, 61a
Teleboas[1] [centaur], offspring of Centaurus and a Magnesian Mare <Pind. *Pyth.* 2.50; named as centaur, Ovid *Met.* 12.441>, 69c
alternate parentage:
Ixion and *Nephele*[1] <Diod. Sic. 4.69.5>
Teleboas[2], son of Lycaon[1] <Apollod. *Bibl.* 3.8.1>, 64c
Teleboas[3], son of Poseidon <Athen. 11.498c> and *Hippothoe*[1], 8c, *58d*
alternate parentage:
Pterelaus <Herodor. in *F. Gr. H.* 31 F 15>
Teleboas[4], grandson of Lelex[3] <Aris. in Strab. 7.1.2>, *
Telecleia, daughter of Ilus[2] <Schol. on Eur. *Hec.* 3> and *Eurydice*[2], 41d
— and Cisseus[1] <Schol. on Eur. *Hec.* 3>, 44d
— and Dymas[1] <Eur. in Eust. on Hom. *Il.* 188>, 17b
Teledamus[1], son of Agamemnon and *Cassandra*[1] <Paus. 2.16.5>, 36b
Teledamus[2] — see Telegonus[1]
Teledice (*Cerdo*) (*Peitho*[4]), paramour of Phoroneus <Apollod. *Bibl.* 2.1.1>, 61a
Telegone, daughter of Phares <Paus. 4.30.2>, 46d
— and Alpheius <Paus. 4.30.2>, 65b
Telegonus[1] (Teledamus[2]), son of Odysseus and *Circe* <Hes. *Theog.* 1014>, 13d
alternate parentage:
Odysseus and *Calypso*[1] <Eug. *Tel.* 2 (Epic Cycle) in *Hes.—Hom. Hymns and Hom.*, Evelyn-White>
Latinus[1] and *Roma*[2] <Dion. Hal. *Rom. Ant.* 1.72.5>
— and *Penelope*[1] <Hyg. *Fab.* 127>, 47d
Telegonus[2], son of Proteus[1] <Apollod. *Bibl.* 2.5.9>, 9c
Telegonus[3] [King of Egypt], husband of *Io* <Apollod. *Bibl.* 2.1.3>, 55b
Telemachus, son of Odysseus <Hom. *Il.* IV.354> and *Penelope*[1] <Hom. *Od.* 17.100-07>, 13c
— and *Cassiphone* <Schol. on Lyc. 808>, 13c
— and *Circe* <Eust. on Hom. *Od.* 1796>, 14d
— and *Nausicaa* <Hellan. in *F. Gr. H.* 4 F 156>, 9c
— and *Polycaste*[1] <*Cat. Wom., Frag. Hes.* frg. 221, Merk. & West>, 27d
Teleon, husband of *Zeuxippe*[4] <Hyg. *Fab.* 14>, 53a
Telephassa (*Agriope*[1]), wife of Agenor[1] <Apollod. *Bibl.* 2.1.1>, 55b
Telephe, daughter of *Epimedusa* <Schol. Eur. *Phoen. Maid.* 5>, 53b
— and Phoenix[2] <Schol. Eur. *Phoen. Maid.* 5>, (53b)
Telephontes — see Aepytus[3]
Telephus [King of Teuthrania in Mysia], son of Heracles[1] and *Auge*[1] <*Cat. Wom., Frag. Hes.* frg. 165, Merk. & West>, 60a
— and *Argiope*[2] <Diod. Sic. 4.33.12>, (60a)
— and *Astyoche*[3] <Quint. Smyr. 6.135>, 42c
— and *Hiera*[1] <Tzetz. on Lyc. 1249>, (60a)
— and *Laodice*[1] <Hyg. *Fab.* 101>, 43c
Teles[1], son of Heracles[1] and *Lysidice*[2] <Apollod. *Bibl.* 2.7.8>, *50d*
Teles[2] — [see Sirens] (alternate version)
Telestas, son of Priam[1] <Apollod. *Bibl.* 3.12.5>, 44d
Telesto, daughter of Oceanus and *Tethys* <Hes. *Theog.* 358>, 72a
Telete[1], daughter of Dionysus and *Nicaea* <Non. *Dion.* 16.395-402>, 56d, *70a*
Telete[2] — see *Elete*
Teleutagoras, son of Heracles[1] and one of the Thespiades (*Eury . . .*) <Apollod. *Bibl.* 2.7.8>, *51c*
Teleutas — see Teuthras
Tellis, son of Tisamenus[1] <Paus. 7.5.2>, 36d
Telphousa — see *Thelpousa*
Temenus[1] [King of Argos], son of Aristomachus[1] <Apollod. Bibl. 2.8.2>, 60c
alternate parentage:
Heracles[1] <Hyg. *Fab.* 219>
Temenus[2] [King of Stymphalus], son of Pelasgus[1] <Paus. 8.22.2> and *Meliboea*[1], 62b
Temenus[3], son of Phegeus[1] <Paus. 8.24.1>, 59b
Tenages, son of Helios and *Rhode*[1] <Diod. Sic. 5.56.5>, 14b
Tenerus, son of Apollo and *Melia*[1] <Paus. 9.10.5>, 11d
alternate parentage:
Zeus <Steph. Byz. "Taenerus">
Ten(n)es [King of Tenedos], son of Cycnus[2] and *Procleia* <Paus. 10.14.2>, *43c*
alternate parentage:
Apollo <Apollod. *Epit.* 3.23>
Tenthredon, son of Magnes[2] and *Meliboea*[3] <Eust. on Hom. *Il.* 338>, 21b
Tereine, daughter of Strymon[1] <Ant. Lib. *Met.* 21.1> and *Neaera*[3], 71b
— and Ares <Ant. Lib. *Met.* 21.1>, 7c
Tereis — see Megapenthes[1] (alternate version)
Tereus[1] [King of Thrace], son of Ares <Apollod. *Bibl.* 3.14.8>, 7c
— and *Philomela*[1] <Apollod. *Bibl.* 3.14.8>, 49a
— and *Procne* <Apollod. *Bibl.* 3.14.8>, 49a
Tereus[2], killed by *Camilla* <Virg. *Aen.* 11.675>, *
Termessus [river], son of Oceanus and *Tethys* <Hes. *Theog.* 366-67; named as river, Paus. 9.29.3>, 72a
Terpsichore[1] [dance] [one of the Muses], daughter of Zeus and *Mnemosyne* <Hes. *Theog.* 78>, 6b
Terpsichore[2] [one of the Bacchae] <Non. *Dion.* 29.237>, *
Terpsicrate, daughter of Thespius <Apollod. *Bibl.* 2.7.8> and *Megamede* <Apollod. *Bibl.* 2.4.10>, 50d
— and Heracles[1] <Apollod. *Bibl.* 2.7.8>, (50d)
Tethys [Titan], daughter of Uranus and *Gaea* <Hes. *Theog.* 136>, 55a
— and Oceanus <Hes. *Theog.* 337>, (55a)
Teucer[1] [King of Phrygia], son of Scamander[1] and *Idaea*[1] <Apollod. *Bibl.* 3.12.1>, 70b
Teucer[2] (Teucras), son of Telamon <Hom. *Il.* VIII.281> and *Hesione*[1] <Apollod. *Bibl.* 3.12.7>, 23d
— and *Eune* <Tzetz. on Lyc. 450>, 11c
Teucras — see Teucer[2]
Teutamides, son of Amyntor[2] <Hellan. in Dion. Hal. *Rom. Ant.* 1.28.3>, 61d
Teuthras[1] (Teleutas) [King of Phrygia], son of *Leucippe*[3] <Ps.-Plut. *De Fluv.* 21.3 (his mother is called *Lysippe*)>, *63d*
— and *Auge*[1] <Apollod. *Bibl.* 3.9.1>, (63d)
Teuthras[2], brother of Tyres[1] <Virg. *Aen.* 10.403>, *
Teuthras[3], killed by Ares and Hector[1] <Hom. *Il.* V.705>, *
Thalassa — see *Thalatta*
Thalatta (*Thalassa*), daughter of Aether and *Hemera* <Hyg. *Fab.* pref.> (not shown on chart because these parents are also

reported by the same source as an alternate version of the parents of *Gaea* and Uranus), *
Thaleia[1] [comedy] [one of the Muses], daughter of Zeus and *Mnemosyne* <Hes. *Theog.* 77>, 6b
Thaleia[2] (*Cale*) [festivity] [one of the Graces], daughter of Zeus and *Eurynome*[1] <Hes. *Theog.* 909>, 5d
alternate parentage:
Dionysus and *Coronis*[5] <Non. *Dion.* 48.555-56>
Helios and *Aegle*[1] <Anti. in Paus. 9.35.5>
Thaleia[3], daughter of Nereus <Hom. *Il.* XVIII.41> and *Doris*[1], *65a*
Thaleia[4], daughter of Hephaestus <Steph. Byz. "Paliki">, 7d
— and Zeus <Steph. Byz. "Paliki">, 6c
Thallo — see *Eunomia*[1]
Thalpius, son of Eurytus[4] <Hom. *Il.* II.621> and *Theraephone* <Paus. 5.2.3>, 9a, *14c*
Thamyris[1], son of Philammon and *Argiope*[1] <Apollod. *Bibl.* 1.3.3>, 13b
— and Hyacinthus[1] <Apollod. *Bibl.* 1.3.3>, 47a
Thamyris[2], killed by Actor[11] <Stat. *Theb.* 10.314>, *
Thanatus [death] [abstraction], offspring of *Nyx* <Hes. *Theog.* 212>, *1b*
Thasius, son of Anius <Hyg. *Fab.* 247>, 56d
Thasus, son of Agenor[1] <Schol. on Eur. *Phoen. Maid.* 217> and *Telephassa*, 56b
alternate parentage:
Cilix <Pher. in Apollod. *Bibl.* 3.1.1>
Poseidon <Apollod. *Bibl.* 3.1.1>
Thaumacus — see Poeas (alternate version)
Thaumas[1], son of Pontus and *Gaea* <Hes. *Theog.* 237>, 3a
— and *Electra*[1] <Hes. *Theog.* 265-66>, 53a
Thaumas[2] [centaur], offspring of Centaurus and a Magnesian Mare <Pind. *Pyth.* 2.50; named as centaur, Ovid *Met.* 12.303>, 69c
alternate parentage:
Ixion and *Nephele*[1] <Diod. Sic. 4.69.5>
Theaneira, paramour of Telamon <Ist. in *F. Gr. H.* 334 F 57>, 23d
— and Arion[2] <Euphor. in *F.H.G.* 4.335 frg. 21, Müller>, (23d)
Theano[1], wife of Metapontus <Hyg. *Fab.* 186>, 19a
Theano[2], daughter of Cisseus[1] <Hom. *Il.* VI.297-98> and *Telecleia*, 45d
— and Antenor[1] <Hom. *Il.* VI.298-99>, (45d)
Theano[3], daughter of Danaus[1] and *Polyxo*[3] <Apollod. *Bibl.* 2.1.5>, 57c
— and Phantes <Apollod. *Bibl.* 2.1.5>, (57c)
Theano[4], wife of Amycus[3] <Virg. *Aen.* 10.704>, *
Theano[5], daughter of Menon <Plut. *Alcaeus* 22.4>, *
[Theban Sphinx] — see *Phix*
Thebe[1], daughter of Asopus and *Metope*[2] <Herod. 5.80>, 66a
— and Zethus <Apollod. *Bibl.* 3.5.6>, 66d
Thebe[2], daughter of Zeus and *Iodama* <Tzetz. on Lyc. 1206>, 5d, *16a*
— and Ogygus[1] <Tzetz. on Lyc. 1206>, 8a
Thebe[3], daughter of Cilix <Diod. Sic. 5.49.4>, 56c
— and Corybas <Diod. Sic. 5.49.3>, 42b
Thebe[4], daughter of Adramys <Dicaearch. in *F.H.G.* 2.238 frg. 11, Müller>, 60d
— and Heracles[1] <Dicaearch. in *F.H.G.* 2.238 frg. 11, Müller>, (60d)
Thebe[5], daughter of Prometheus[1] <Steph. Byz. "Thebe">, 16a
Theia[1] (*Euryphaessa*) [Titan], daughter of Uranus and *Gaea* <Hes. *Theog.* 135>, 13b
— and Hyperion[1] <Hes. *Theog.* 374>, (13b)
Theia[2], daughter of Oceanus and *Tethys* <Eust. on Hom. *Od.* 1864.34>, 72a
— Oceanus <Eust. on Hom. *Od.* 1854>, 55a
Theias — see Adonis (alternate version) and *Myrr(h)a* (alternate version)
Theiodamas[1] [King of Dryopes], son of Dryops[2] <Schol. on Ap. Rhod. *Arg.* 1.131>, 64d
— and *Menodice* <Hyg. *Fab.* 14>, 53d
Theiodamas[2], father of Dresaeus <Quint. Smyr. 1.292>, *
Thelpousa (*Telphousa*), daughter of Ladon[1] <Paus. 8.25.2>, 54b
Thelxiepeia (*Thelxinoe*[1]) (*Thelxiope*) [one of the Sirens], daughter of Achelous and *Melpomene* <Apollod. *Epit.* 7.18>, 65b
alternate parentage:
Achelous and *Sterope*[2] <Apollod. *Bibl.* 1.7.10>
Achelous and *Terpsichore* <Ap. Rhod. *Arg.* 4.893>
Thelxinoe[1] — see *Thelxiepeia*
Thelxinoe[2], an attendant of *Semele* <Non. *Dion.* 8.195>, *
Thelxion, son of Apis[2] <Paus. 2.5.7>, 61a
Thelxionoea, daughter of Ogygus[1] <Suid. "Praxidike">, 16c
alternate parentage:
"the second Jupiter" (son of Caelus) <Cic. *De Nat. Deor.* 3. 54-55>
Thelxiope — see *Thelxiepeia*
Themis[1] [Titan] [justice], daughter of Uranus and *Gaea* <Hes. *Theog.* 135>, 10b
alternate parentage:
Titanis <Hyg. *Fab.* 183 (Hyginus might mean "of Titans")>
— and Zeus <Hes. *Theog.* 901>, 6c
Themis[2] (*Themiste*), daughter of Ilus[2] <Apollod. *Bibl.* 3.12.2> and *Eurydice*[2], 41c
— and Capys[1] <Apollod. *Bibl.* 3.12.2>, (41c), 71a
Themis[3] — see *Nicostrate*[1]
Themistagora —see [fifty daughters of Danaus[1]] (alternate version)
Themiste — see *Themis*[2]
Themisto[1], daughter of Hypseus[1] <Apollod. *Bibl.* 1.9.2> and *Chlidanope*, 69b
— and Athamas[1] <Apollod. *Bibl.* 1.9.2>, 26b
— and Poseidon <Hyg. *Fab.* 157>, 9b
Themisto[2], daughter of Zabius <Steph. Byz. "Galeotai">, 11d
— and Apollo <Steph. Byz. "Galeotai">, (11d)
Themisto[3] — see *Callisto*
Themisto[4], daughter of Nereus and *Doris*[1] <Hes. *Theog.* 261>, *65a*
Themistonoe, daughter of Ceyx[2] <Hes. *Shield* 350-56>, 7d
— and Cycnus[1] <Hes. *Shield* 350-56>, (7d), 28d
Themon, son of Euander[2] <Virg. *Aen.* 10.126 (inferred because he is called brother of Sarpedon[2])> and *Laodameia*[2], 52c
Theobula[1], wife of Archylocus <Hyg. *Fab.* 97 (he is called Areilycus)>, 18c
Theobula[2] — see *Cleobula*[4]
Theoclymenus[1], son of Polypheides <Hom. *Od.* 15.252-56>, 32c
alternate parentage:
Thestor[1] <Hyg. *Fab.* 88>
Theoclymenus[2] [King of Egypt], son of Proteus[3] and *Psamathe*[1] <Eur. *Hel.* 4-9>, *65a*
Theoclymenus[3], son of Tmolus <Ps.-Plut. *De Fluv.* 7.5> and *Omphale*, 7c
Theoclymenus[4] — see Periclymenus[3]
Theoclymenus[5], helped sacrifice the Delphian cow <Non. *Dion.* 5. 11>, *
Theogone, paramour of Ares <Ps.-Plut. *De Fluv.* 7.5>, 7c
Theonoe[1], daughter of Thestor[1] <Hyg. *Fab.* 190>, 69b
— and Icarus[2] <Hyg. *Fab.* 190>, (69b)
Theonoe[2] — see *Eidothea*[2]
Theope[1], daughter of Leos[1] <Ael. *Var. Narr.* 12.28>, 6a
Theope[2] [one of the Bacchae] <Non. *Dion.* 21.86>, *
Theophane, daughter of Bisaltes <Hyg. *Fab.* 188>, 9b
— and Poseidon <Hyg. *Fab.* 188>, (9b)
Thera, daughter of Amphion[1] <Hyg. *Fab.* 69> and *Niobe*[1], 66d
Theraephone, daughter of Dexamenus <Paus. 5.3.3>, 14c
— and Eurytus[4] <Paus. 5.3.3>, 9a
Therager, son of Clymenus[4] and *Epicaste*[4] <Parth. *Love Stor.* 13. 1>, 26d

Therapne, daughter of Lelex[1] <Paus. 3.15.6> and *Cleochereia*, 61c
Theras, son of Autesion[1] <Paus. 3.19.9>, 55d
Thereus[1] [centaur], offspring of Centaurus and a Magnesian Mare <Pind. *Pyth.* 2.50; named as centaur, Diod. Sic. 4.12.7 (killed by Heracles[1])>, 69c
alternate parentage:
Ixion and *Nephele*[1] <Diod. Sic. 4.69.5>
Thereus[2] [centaur], offspring of Centaurus and a Magnesian Mare <Pind. *Pyth.* 2.50; named as centaur, Ovid *Met.* 12.353 (killed by Theseus)>, 69c
alternate parentage:
Ixion and *Nephele*[1] <Diod. Sic. 4.69.5>
Therimachus, son of Heracles[1] and *Megara* <Apollod. *Bibl.* 2.4. 11>, 60d
Thermius, son of Haemon[3] <Paus. 5.3.7 (inferred because he is called brother of Oxylus[2])>, 16d
Thermodoon [river], son of Oceanus and *Tethys* <Hes. *Theog.* 367-68; named as river, Hyg. *Fab.* pref.>, 72a
Thero[1], daughter of Phylas[2] and *Leipephilene* <*Gr. Ehoiai, Frag. Hes.* frg. 252, Merk. & West>, 55d
— and Apollo <*Gr. Ehoiai, Frag. Hes.* frg. 252, Merk. & West>, 11d
Thero[2], nurse of Ares <Paus. 3.19.8>, *
Theronice, daughter of Dexamenus <Paus. 5.3.3>, 14d
— and Cteatus <Paus. 5.3.3>, 9a
Thersander[1] (Tisandrus[2]) [King of Thebes] [one of the Epigoni], son of Polyneices <Pind. *Ol.* 2.42-43> and *Argeia*[1] <Serv. on Virg. *Aen.* 261>, 55c, *30c*
— and *Demonassa*[2] <Paus. 9.5.8>, 32d
Thersander[2], son of Sisyphus <Paus. 2.4.3> and *Merope*[1], 19a
Thersander[3], son of Agamedidas <Paus. 3.16.6>, 60d
Thersander[4], husband of *Arethusa*[6] <Quint. Smyr. 10.79-82>, *
Thersilochus[1], son of Antenor[1] <Virg. *Aen.* 6.482> and *Theano*[2], *45d*
Thersilochus[2], suitor of *Penelope*[1] (from Dulichium) <Apollod. *Epit.* 7.27>, *
Thersilochus[3], killed by Turnus <Virg. *Aen.* 12.363>, *
Thersippus — see Thersites
Thersites (Thersippus), son of Agrius[1] <Apollod. *Bibl.* 1.8.6> and *Dia*[4] <Schol. on Hom. *Il.* II.212>, 16d
Theseus [King of Athens], son of Aegeus[1] <Hom. *Il.* VI.297-98> and *Aethra*[1] <Eur. *Supp.* 4>, 51a, *38b*
alternate parentage:
Pandion II <Bacch. 17.15-16>
Poseidon and *Aethra*[1] <Bacch. 17.57-59>
— and *Aegle*[3] <*Cat. Wom., Frag. Hes.* frg. 298, Merk & West>, 23c
— and *Anaxo*[2] <Plut. *Thes.* 29.1>, (51a)
— and *Ariadne* <Plut. *Thes.* 19.1>, 53c
— and *Helen*[1] <Plut. *Thes.* 29.2>, 48d
— and *Hippe*[2] <*Cat. Wom., Frag. Hes.* frg. 298, Merk. & West>, (51a)
— and *Hippolyte*[1] <Apollod. *Epit.* 5.2>, 7c
— and *Iope*[1] <Plut. *Thes.* 29.1>, 40a, 59d
— and *Periboea*[2] <Plut. *Thes.* 29.1>, 40a
— and *Perigune* <Plut. *Thes.* 8.3>, 34d
— and *Phaedra* <Eur. *Hipp.* 27>, 53c
— and *Phereboea* <Plut. *Thes.* 29.1>, (51c)
Thespeia, daughter of Asopus and *Metope*[2] <Diod. Sic. 4.72.1>, 66a
(Thespiades), daughters of Thespius <Apollod. *Bibl.* 2.7.8> and *Megamede* <Apollod. *Bibl.* 2.4.10> (see *Aeschreis, Aglaia*[4]*, Anthea, Anthippe, Antiope*[5]*, Argele, Asopis*[2]*, Calametis, Certhe, Chryseis*[2]*, Clytippe, Elachia, Eone, Epilais, Erato*[4]*, Euboea*[4]*, Eubote, Eurybia*[2]*, Eurypyle*[1]*, Eurytele, Exole, Heliconis, Hesychia*[2]*, Hippo*[1]*, Hippocrate, Iphis*[4]*, Laothoe*[3]*, Lyse, Lysidice*[2]*, Lysippe*[2]*, Marse, Meline, Menippis, Nicippe*[2]*, Nike*[2]*, Olympusa, Oreia, Panope*[2]*, Patro, Phyleis, Praxithea*[3]*, Procris*[2]*, Pyrippe, Stratonice*[3]*, Terpsicrate, Tiphyse, Toxicrate, Xanthis*, and two unnamed daughters), 50a-51c
Thespius [King of Thespiae], son of Erechtheus II <Diod. Sic. 4. 29.2> and *Praxithea*[2], 50a
— and *Megamede* <Apollod. *Bibl.* 2.4.10>, (50a)
Thesprotus[1], son of Lycaon[1] <Apollod. *Bibl.* 3.8.1>, 64d
Thesprotus[2] [King in area of Lake Avernus] <Hyg. *Fab.* 88>, *
Thessalus[1] [King of Iolcus], son of Jason and *Medea* <Diod. Sic. 4. 54.1>, 33d
Thessalus[2] (Thettalus) [King of Thessaly], son of Heracles[1] and *Chalciope*[2] <Apollod. *Bibl.* 2.7.8 (he is called Thettalus)>, 60b, *34c*
Thessalus[3], son of Cimon <Plut. *Alcib.* 19.2>, *
Thessalus[4], son of Haemon[8] <Strab. 9.5.23>, *
Thestalus, son of Heracles[1] and *Epicaste*[2] <Apollod. *Bibl.* 2.7.8>, 60c, *63d*
Thestius [King of Pleuron], son of Ares and *Demodice*[2] <Apollod. *Bibl.* 1.7.7-8>, 7b, *15d*
alternate parentage:
Agenor[4] <Paus. 3.13.8>
— and *Eurythemis(te)* <*Cat. Wom., Frag. Hes.* frg. 10a.35, Merk. & West; named, Apollod. *Bibl.* 1.7.10>, 15d
— and *Pantidyia* <Schol. on Ap. Rhod. *Arg.* 1.146>, (15d)
Thestor[1], son of Apollo <Tzetz. on Lyc. 427> and *Laothoe*[2], 11d, *69b*
alternate parentage:
Apollo and *Attala* <Tzetz. on Lyc. 427>
Idmon[1] and *Laothoe*[2] <Pher. in *F.H.G.* 1.88 frg. 70, Müller>
Thestor[2], son of Enops <Hom. *Il.* XVI.400>, *
Thetis, daughter of Nereus and *Doris*[1] <Hes. *Theog.* 244>, *65a*
— and Peleus <Hes. *Theog.* 1006>, 24c
Thettalus — see Thessalus[2]
Thiodamas, son of Melampus[1] <Stat. *Theb.* 8.278-79>, 32c
Thoas[1] [King of Lemnos], son of Dionysus <Ap. Rhod. *Arg.* 4.425-26> and *Ariadne* <Apollod. *Epit.* 1.9>, 56d
alternate parentage:
Borysthenes <Ant. Lib. *Met.* 27.3>
— and *Myrine*[1] <Schol. on Ap. Rhod. *Arg.* 1.604>, 32b
— *Oenoe*[1] <Ap. Rhod. *Arg.* 1.625>, (56d)
Thoas[2] — see Nebrophonus
Thoas[3], son of Selepus <Hom. *Il.* II.693>, 51d
Thoas[4], son of Ornytion <Paus. 2.4.3>, 18c
Thoas[5], son of Icarius[2] and *Periboea*[5] <Apollod. *Bibl.* 3.10.6>, 47d
Thoas[6] [King of Aetolia], son of Andraemon[1] <Hom. *Il.* VII.168> and *Gorge*[1] <Apollod. *Epit.* 3.12>, *16d*
Thoas[7] [giant], son of *Gaea* (and the blood of Uranus) <Hes. *Theog.* 180-86; named as giant, Apollod. *Bibl.* 1.6.2>, *4a*
Thoas[8], brother of Euneus[3] <Plut. *Theseus* 26.3>, *
Thoas[9], suitor of *Penelope*[1] (from Dulichium) <Apollod. *Epit.* 7.27>, *
Thoas[10], killed by Tydeus[1] <Stat. *Theb.* 8.696>, *
Thoe[1], daughter of Oceanus and *Tethys* <Hes. *Theog.* 354>, 72b
Thoe[2], daughter of Nereus and *Doris*[1] <Hes. *Theog.* 245>, *65b*
Thoe[3] [Amazon] <Val. Flac. 6.375>, *
Thoe[4] [one of the horses of Admetus[1]] <Stat. *Theb.* 6.462>, *
Thoon[1] [giant], son of *Gaea* (and the blood of Uranus) <Hes. *Theog.* 180-86; named as giant, Apollod. *Bibl.* 1.6.2>, *4a*
Thoon[2], son of Phaenops <Hom. *Il.* V.152>, 44c
Thoon[3], competed in the games that honored Odysseus <Hom. *Od.* 8.111>, *
Thoon[4], killed by Odysseus <Hom. *Il.* XI.422>, *
Thoon[5], killed by Antilochus <Hom. *Il.* XIII.545>, *
Thoon[6], killed by Corymbasus <Non. *Dion.* 28.112>, *
Thoosa, daughter of Phorcus[1] <Hom. *Od.* 1.71-72> and *Ceto*[1], 2b
— and Poseidon <Hom. *Od.* 1.71-72>, 9c
Thornax(e), wife of Iapetus <Paus. 8.27.17>, 16a

Thrace, daughter of Oceanus and *Parthenope*[4] <Andr. Hall. in *F.H.G.* 2.349 frg. 1, Müller>, 55a
— and Cronus <Steph. Byz. "Bithynia">, 5b
— and Obriareus <Steph. Byz. "Trieres">, (55a)
— and Zeus <Steph. Byz. "Bithynia">, 6c
Thrasius[1] (Phrasius[1]), son of Pygmalion[3] <Hyg. *Fab.* 56 (inferred because father is called brother of Busiris)>, 8d
Thrassa, daughter of Ares and *Tereine* <Ant. Lib. *Met.* 21.1>, 7c, *71b*
— and Hipponous[4] <Ant. Lib. *Met.* 21.1>, (71b)
Thrasyanor, son of Ctesippus[2] <Paus. 2.18.8>, 60a
Thrasymedes[1], son of Nestor <Hom. *Il.* IX.81> and *Anaxibia*[4] <Apollod. *Bibl.* 1.9.9>, 27d
alternate parentage:
Nestor and *Eurydice*[7] <Hom. *Od.* 3.453 (inferred because she is wife of Nestor)>
Thrasymedes[2], son of Philomelus[1] <Poly. *Strat.* 5.14.1>, 42b
Thrasymedes[3], suitor of *Penelope*[1] (from Dulichium) <Apollod. *Epit.* 7.27>, *
[three thousand daughters], children of Oceanus and *Tethys* <Hes. *Theog.* 364>, 49b
[three thousand sons], children of Oceanus and *Tethys* <Hes. *Theog.* 367-68>, 49b
[three virgins], daughters of Scamander[2] <Plut. *Gr. Quest.* 41> and *Acidusa*, 70b
Threpsippas, son of Heracles[1] and *Panope*[2] <Apollod. *Bibl.* 2.7.8>, *50c*
(Thriai), daughters of Zeus <Pher. in *F. Gr. H.* 3 F 49>, 6d
Thrinax, son of Helios <Non. *Dion.* 14.44>, 14c
Thronia, daughter of Belus[1] <*Cat. Wom., Frag. Hes.* frg. 137, Merk & West> and *Anchinoe*[1], 59a
— and Hermes <*Cat. Wom., Frag. Hes.* frg. 137, Merk. & West>, 46c
Thurimachus, son of Aegyrus <Paus. 2.5.7>, 61c
Thurius [giant], son of *Gaea* (and the blood of Uranus) <Hes. *Theog.* 180-86; named as giant, Paus. 3.18.11>, *4a*
Thuscus — see Iasion (alternate version)
Thyestes[1] [King of Mycenae], son of Pelops[1] <Apollod. *Bibl.* 2.4.6> and *Hippodameia*[1] <Hyg. *Fab.* 85>, *39a*
— and *Aerope*[1] <Hyg. *Fab.* 86>, 52c
— and *Daeto* <Tzetz. on Lyc. 212>, 37b
— and *Laodameia*[5] <Schol. on Eur. *Or.* 4>, (39a)
— and *Pelopeia*[2] <Hyg. *Fab.* 87>, 39b
Thyestes[2], an attendant for Cadmus <Non. *Dion.* 5.13>, *
Thyia[1], daughter of Deucalion[1] <*Cat. Wom., Frag. Hes.* frg. 7, Merk. & West> and *Pyrrha*[1], 15a
alternate parentage:
Uranus and *Gaea* <Apollod. *Bibl.* 1.1.3>
— and Zeus <*Cat. Wom., Frag. Hes.* frg. 7, Merk. & West>, 6c
Thyia[2], daughter of Castalius <Paus. 10.6.4>, 11d
alternate parentage:
Cephissus <Herod. 7.178>
— and Apollo <Paus. 10.6.4>, (11d)
Thymbraeus[1] (Melanathus[1]), son of Laocoon[1] <Hyg. *Fab.* 135> and *Antiope*[2], 45c
Thymbraeus[2], a warrior with Aeneas <Virg. *Aen.* 12.458>, *
Thymbris[1] — see *Hybris*
Thymbris[2], a comrade of Aeneas <Virg. *Aen.* 10.124>, *
Thym(n)o — see *Strym(n)o*
Thymoetes[1] [King of Athens], son of Oxyntes <Paus. 2.18.9>, 51d
Thymoetes[2], son of Laomedon[1] <Diod. Sic. 3.67.5> and *Strym(n)o*, 43c
— and *Cilla*[2] <Schol. on Lyc. 319>, 45d
Thymoetes[3], son of Thymoetes[3] <Diod. Sic. 3.67.5>, 43c
Thymoetes[4], son of Hicetaon[1] <Virg. *Aen.* 10.125>, 42d
Thynus, son of Phineus[1] and *Idaea*[2] <Schol. on Ap. Rhod. *Arg.* 140>, *42a*
Thyone[1] — see *Semele*
Thyone[2] — see (Hyades) (alternate version)
Thyreus, son of Oeneus[1] <Apollod. *Bibl.* 1.8.1> and *Althaea*, 17c
Thyria (*Hyria*), daughter of Amphinomous[1] <Ant. Lib. *Met.* 12.1>, 11d
— and Apollo <Ant. Lib. *Met.* 12.1>, (11d)
Tiasa, daughter of Eurotas <Paus. 3.18.6> and *Cleta*[1], 61c
Tiburinus [river], son of Oceanus and Tethys <Hes. Theog. 367-68; named as river, Virg. *Aen.* 8.32>, 72b
Tiburnus — see Tiburtus
Tiburtus (Tiburnus), son of Catillus <Sol. *Coll. Rer. Mem.* 2.7>, 33c
Tigasis, son of Heracles[1] and *Phyleis* <Apollod. *Bibl.* 2.7.8>, *50c*
Tigris [river], son of Oceanus and *Tethys* <Hes. *Theog.* 367-68; named as river, Hyg. *Fab.* pref.>, 72b
Tilphose — see [Cadmean Dragon] (alternate version)
Timalcus, son of Megareus[1] <Paus. 1.41.4> and *Merope*[8], 9b
Timandra[1] (*Eustyoche*), daughter of Tyndareus and *Leda* <*Cat. Wom., Frag. Hes.* frg. 23(a), 9, Merk. & West>, 48c
— and Echemus <*Cat. Wom., Frag. Hes.* frg. 23(a), 31-33, Merk. & West>, 64c
— and Phyleus[1] <*Cat. Wom., Frag. Hes.* frg. 176, Merk. & West>, 63d
Timandra[2], mother of Neophron <Ant. Lib. *Met.* 5.2>, *
Timandra[3], paramour of Alcibiades <Plut. *Alcib.* 39.1>, *
Timeas, son of Polyneices <Paus. 2.20.4> and *Argeia*[1], 55c, *30c*
Timolus — see Tmolus
Timothea, wife of Anchurus <Plut. *Gr. and Rom. Par. Stor.* 5>, 2d
Tinge, wife of Antaeus[1] <Plut. *Sert.* 9>, 9c
— and Heracles[1] <Plut. *Sert.* 9>, 61c
Tiphys [Argonaut], son of Phorbas[2] and *Hyrmine* <Hyg. *Fab.* 14>, 68b
alternate parentage:
Hagnias <Apollod. *Bibl.* 1.9.16>
Tiphyse, daughter of Thespius <Apollod. *Bibl.* 2.7.8> and *Megamede* <Apollod. *Bibl.* 2.4.10>, 50d
— and Heracles[1] <Apollod. *Bibl.* 2.7.8>, (50d)
Tiryns, son of Argus[2] <Paus. 2.25.7> and Euadne[2], 61a
Tisamenus[1] [King of Sparta and Argos], son of Orestes[1] <Apollod. *Bibl.* 2.8.2> and *Hermione* <Apollod. *Epit.* 6.28>, 36c
Tisamenus[2] [King of Thebes], son of Thersander[1] and *Demonassa*[2] <Paus. 9.5.8>, 55c
Tisandrus[1], son of Jason and *Medea* <Diod. Sic. 4.54.2>, 33d
Tisandrus[2] — see Thersander[1]
Tisiphone[1], daughter of Alcmaeon[1] and *Manto*[1] <Apollod. *Bibl.* 3.7.7>, 32d
Tisiphone[2] [one of the Furies], daughter of *Gaea* (and the blood of Uranus) <Hes. *Theog.* 185; named, Apollod. *Bibl.* 1.1.4>, 4b
alternate parentage:
Nyx <Aesch. *Eum.* 416>
Tisiphone[3], daughter of Antimachus[5] <Quint. Smyr. 1.406>, *
Titan, son of Hyperion[1] and *Theia*[1] <Paus. 2.11.5 (this name is also applied to some of the Titans)>, 14b
Titanas, son of Lycaon[1] <Apollod. *Bibl.* 3.8.1>, 64d
[Titanidae] — see *Mnemosyne*, *Phoebe*[1], *Rhea*, *Tethys*, *Theia*[1], *Themis*[1] (some mythographers include *Dione*[1])
Titanis — see *Themis*[1] (alternate version)
[Titans] — see C(o)eus, Crius, Cronus, Hyperion[1], Iapetus, Oceanus (some mythographers include Atlas, Epimetheus, Helios, Pallas[1], Prometheus)
Titaresius [river], son of Oceanus and Tethys <Hes. *Theog.* 367-68; named as river, Hom. *Il.* II.751>, 72b
Tithonus, son of Laomedon[1] <Hom. *Il.* XX.238> and *Strym(n)o* <Apollod. *Bibl.* 3.12.3>, 43c
alternate parentage:
Laomedon[1] and *Leucippe*[8] <Apollod. *Bibl.* 3.12.3>
Laomedon[1] and *Placia* <Apollod. *Bibl.* 3.12.3>

Cephalus and *Eos* <Apollod. *Bibl.* 3.14.3>
— and *Eos* <Hes. *Theog.* 386>, 12b
Titias[1] — see (Dactyls) (alternate version)
Titias[2], a Mysian boxer <Ap. Rhod. *Arg.* 2.783>, *
Titoplous — see [Muses] (alternate version)
Tityus [giant], son of *Gaea* <Hom. *Od.* 11.576>, *3b*
alternate parentage:
Zeus <Pher. in *F. Gr. H.* 3 F 55> and *Elara* <*Cat. Wom., Frag. Hes.* frg. 78, Merk. & West>
— and *Leto* <Hyg. *Fab.* 55>, 11b
Tlepolemus[1] (Tleptomelus) [King of Rhodes], son of Heracles[1] and *Astyoche*[2] <Hom. *Il.* II.658>, 60b
alternate parentage:
Heracles[1] and *Asty(a)dameia*[1] <*Cat. Wom., Frag. Hes.* frg. 232, Merk. & West>
— and *Polyxo*[1] <Paus. 3.19.9>, (60b)
Tlepolemus[2], son of Damastor[1] <Hom. *Il.* XVI.416>, 52d
Tleptolemus — see Tlepolemus
Tlesenor, son of Aepytus[1] <*Cat. Wom., Frag. Hes.* frg. 166, Merk. & West>, 62d
Tlesimenes — see Tlesimenus
Tlesimenus (Tlesimenes), son of Melanion <Paus. 3.12.9>, and *Atalanta*[1], 63d, *64d*
alternate parentage:
Parthenopaeus <Paus. 3.2.9>
Tmolus (Timolus) [King of Lydia], son of Ares and *Theogone* <Ps.-Plut. *De Fluv.* 7.5>, 7c
— and *Arripe* <Ps.-Plut. *De Fluv.* 7.5>, (7c)
— and *Omphale* <Apollod. *Bibl.* 2.6.3>, (7c)
Toxeus[1], son of Eurytus[2] <Diod. Sic. 4.37.4> and *Antiope*[6], 60b
Toxeus[2], son of Oeneus[1] and *Althaea* <*Cat. Wom., Frag. Hes.* frg. 25.16, Merk. & West>, 17c
Toxeus[3], son of Thestius <Ovid *Met.* 8.429-42>, 16c
Toxicrate, daughter of Thespius <Apollod. *Bibl.* 2.7.8> and *Megamede* <Apollod. *Bibl.* 2.4.10>, 50d
— and Heracles[1] <Apollod. *Bibl.* 2.7.8>, (50d)
Traga(na)sus — see Cragasus
Tragasia — see Caunus (alternate version)
Trambelus (Strambelus) [King of Leleges], son of Telamon <Parth. *Love Stor.* 26.1> and *Theaneira*, 23d
alternate parentage:
Telamon and *Hesione*[1] <Ist. in *F. Gr. H.* 334 F 57>
— and *Apriate* <Parth. *Love Stor.* 26>, (23d)
Triballus[1], father of Hipponous[4] <Ant. Lib. *Met.* 21.1>, 71b
Triballus[2] — see (Cercopes) (alternate version)
Tricca — see *Chlidanope*
Tricolonus[1] — see [fifty sons of Lycaon[1]] (alternate version)
Tricolonus[2], descendant of Triclonus[1], killed by Oenomaus[1] <Paus. 6.21.10>, *
Trienus — see *Scylla*[2] (alternate version)
Trierus, son of Obriareus and *Thrace* <Steph. Byz. "Trieres">, 55a
Trigoneia — see *Tritogeneia*[2]
Triop(a)s[1] [King of Thessaly], son of Poseidon and *Canace* <Apollod. *Bibl.* 1.7.4>, 8a, *34a*
alternate parentage:
Helios and *Rhode*[1] <Diod. Sic. 5.56.5>
Lapithes and *Stilbe* <Diod. Sic. 5.61.3>
— and *Hiscilla* <Hyg. *Poet. Astr.* 2.14>, 5d
Triop(a)s[2] [King of Argos], son of Phorbas[3] <Diod. Sic. 4.58.7> and *Euboea*[2], 61d
alternate parentage:
Peranthus <Hyg. *Fab.* 124>
— and *Sois* <Hellan. in Schol. on Hom. *Il.* III.75>, (61d)
Triop(a)s[3], son of Peiras[1] and *Callirhoe*[5] <Hyg. *Fab.* 145>, 61a
Triphylus, son of Arcas[1] and *Leaneira* <Paus. 10.9.3>, 62c, *47b*
Triptolemus, son of Celeus[1] <Paus. 1.14.2> and *Metaneira*, 46d
alternate parentage:
Deiope <Aris. *On Marv. Works Heard* 131.3-5>
Dysaules <Paus. 1.14.2>
Eleusinus and *Cothonea* <Hyg. *Fab.* 147>
Eleusis and *Metaneira* <Apollod. *Bibl.* 1.5.2>
Icarius[2] <Schol. on Virg. *Geo.* 1.19>
Oceanus and *Gaea* <Apollod. *Bibl.* 1.5.2>
Rarus and a daughter of Amphictyon (possibly *Atthis*) <Choer. in Paus. 1.14.3>
Trochilus[2] <Paus. 1.14.2>
Trite —see [fifty daughters of Danaus[1]] (alternate version)
Triteia, daughter of Triton <Paus. 7.22.5>, 63b
— and Ares <Paus. 7.22.5>, 7c
Tritogeneia[1] — see *Athene*
Tritogeneia[2], daughter of Aeolus[1] <Tzetz. on Lyc. 874> and *Enarete*, 34b
— and Poseidon <Tzetz. on Lyc. 874>, 9c
Triton, son of Poseidon and *Amphitrite* <Hes. *Theog.* 931>, *63b*
Tritone — see [Muses] (alternate version)
Trochilus[1], son of *Io* <Schol. on Arat. *Phaen.* 161 (mother is called *Callithea*, the name of *Io* in her capacity as priestess of *Hera*)>, *55b*
Trochilus[2], a priest <Paus. 1.14.1>, *
Troezen[1] [King of Troezen], son of Pelops[1] <Paus. 2.30.8> and *Hippodameia*[1], *39b*
Troezen[2], brother of Dimoetes and father of *Euopis* <Parth. *Love Stor.* 31.1>, *
Troezen[3], son of Ceos <Hom. *Il.* II.846-47>, *
Troilus, son of Priam[1] <Hom. *Il.* XXIV.257> and *Hecabe*[1], 43d
alternate parentage:
Apollo and *Hecabe*[1] <Apollod. *Bibl.* 3.12.5>
— and Achilles <Schol. on Lyc. 307>, 24d
— and *Briseis*[2] <Ben. *Le Roman de Troie* 8>, 69d
[Trojan Sibyl] — see *Sibylla*
Trophonius, son of Erginus[1] <*Hom. Hymn* 3 (to Pythian Apollo), 296>, 26d
alternate parentage:
Apollo <Paus. 9.37.3>, 26d
Tros[1] [King of Troy], son of Erichthonius[2] <Hom. *Il.* XX.230> and *Astyoche*[5] <Apollod. *Bibl.* 3.12.2>, 42a, *71a*
alternate parentage:
Erichthonius[2] and *Callirhoe*[1] <Dion. Hal. *Rom. Ant.* 1.62.2>
Teucer[1] <*Cat. Wom., Frag. Hes.* frg. 179, Merk. & West>
— and *Acallaris* <Dion. Hal. *Rom. Ant.* 1.62.2>, (42a)
— and *Callirhoe*[1] <Apollod. *Bibl.* 3.12.2>, 70b
Tros[2], son of Alastor[2] <Hom. *Il.* XX.463>, *
Tullius [King of Rome], son of Hephaestus and *Ocresia* <Ovid *Fast.* 6.628-29 (father is called Vulcan)>, 7b
[twelve colts], offspring of Boreas and [Mares of Erichthonius[2]] <Hom. *Il.* XX.220-28>, 12b
[twelve sons] of Neleus[1] and *Chloris*[2] <*Cat. Wom., Frag. Hes.* frg. 33a, Merk. & West and Hom. *Od.* 11.286> (see Alastor[1], Antimenes[2], Asterius[3], Chromius[1], Deimachus[1], Epilaus[1], Euagoras[2], Eurybius[2], Nestor, Periclymenus[1], Pylaon, Taurus[1]), 27c-d
other list:
includes Phrasius[2] and omits Antimenes[2] <Apollod. *Bibl.* 1.9.9>
[twenty sons (unnamed)] of Cepheus[2] <Diod. Sic. 4.33.6>, 64c
[twin sons (unnamed)] of Dionysus and *Aura*[1] <Non. *Dion.* 48.855>, 56c, *62b*
[two children (unnamed)] of Iphicles <Apollod. *Bibl.* 2.4.12> and *Automedusa*, 59d, *40a*
[two sons (unnamed)] of Cresphontes[1] and *Merope*[2] <Apollod. *Bibl.* 2.8.5>, 60c
[two sons (unnamed)] of Metapontus and *Theano*[1] <Hyg. *Fab.* 186>, 19c
[two sons (unnamed)] of Sisyphus and *Tyro* <Hyg. *Fab.* 60>,

18a
Tyche[1], daughter of Oceanus and *Tethys* <Hes. *Theog.* 360>, 72b
Tyche[2] [luck], daughter of Zeus <Pind. *Olym.* 12.1-2>, 6d
Tychius, son of Poseidon and *Euboea*[3] <Hesych. *Lex.* "Euboia">, 8c, *66b*
Tydeus [King of Calydon] [one of the Seven against Thebes (per Aesch. *Sev.* 376)] [Argonaut], son of Oeneus[1] <Hom. *Il.* V.813> and *Periboea*[1] <Apollod. *Bibl.* 1.8.5>, 17d
alternate parentage:
Oeneus[1] and *Gorge*[1] <Pisander in Apollod. *Bibl.* 1.8.5>
— and *Deiphyle*[2] <Eur. *Supp.* 133-38; named, Apollod. *Bibl.* 3.6.1>, 30c
Tyllus, father of *Halia*[3] <Dion. Hal. *Rom. Ant.* 1.27.1>, 51b
Tyndareus [King of Sparta], son of Oebalus[1] <*Cat. Wom., Frag. Hes.* frg. 199, Merk. & West> and *Bateia*[1] <Apollod. *Bibl.* 3.10.4>, 48d
alternate parentage:
Oebalus[1] and *Gorgophone*[1] <Paus. 3.1.4>
Perieres[1] and *Gorgophone*[1] <Apollod. *Bibl.* 1.9.5>
— and *Leda* <Hom. *Od.* 11.300>, 16c
Typhoeus[1] — see Typhon
Typhoeus[2] [giant], son of *Gaea* (and the blood of Uranus) <Hes. *Theog.* 180-86; named as giant, Non. *Dion.* 48.77>, *4a*
Typhon (Typhoeus[1]) [monster], offspring of Tartarus[1] and *Gaea* <Hes. *Theog.* 821-22>, 1b
alternate parentage:
Tartarus and *Tartara* <Hyg. *Fab.* 152>
Gaea <Nicand. in Ant. Lib. *Met.* 28>
Hera <Hom. *Hymn* 3 (to Pythian Apollo) 305-07>
autochthonous <Aesch. *Prom. Bound* 351-72>
— and *Echidna* <Hes. *Theog.* 297>, 2a
Tyrannus, son of Pterelaus <Apollod. *Bibl.* 2.4.5> and *Amphimede*, 58d
Tyria, paramour of Aegyptus[1] <Apollod. *Bibl.* 2.1.5>, 58a, 57c
Tyrimmas, father of *Euippe*[6] <Soph. in Parth. *Love Stor.* 3>, 13d
Tyro, daughter of Salmoneus <Hom. *Od.* 11.235-36> and *Alcidice* <Apollod. *Bibl.* 1.9.8>, 27b, *63c*
— and Cretheus[1] <Hom. *Od.* 11.240>, 30a
— and Enipeus <Hom. *Od.* 11.238>, 53a
— and Poseidon <Hom. *Od.* 11.240>, 9c
— and Sisyphus <Hyg. *Fab.* 60>, 18a
Tyrrhenus (Tyrsenus), son of Atys[1] <Herod. 1.94> and *Callithea*, 51b
alternate parentage:
Heracles[1] and *Omphale* <Dion. Hal. *Rom. Ant.* 1.28.1>
— and *Sardo*[1] <Schol. on Plato *Tim.* 25b>, (51b)
Tyrsenus — see Tyrrhenus
Tyrus, paramour of Heracles[1] <Poll. *Onom.* 1.45>, 61c

Udaeus (Oudaeus) [one of the (Spart(o)i) [sown men]], sprang from teeth of [Cadmean Dragon] <Apollod. *Bibl.* 3.4.2>, 7d
Urania[1] [astronomy] [one of the Muses], daughter of Zeus and *Mnemosyne* <Hes. *Theog.* 78>, 6b
— and Amphimarus <Paus. 9.29.3>, 9c
Urania[2], daughter of Oceanus and *Tethys* <Hes. *Theog.* 350>, 72b
Urania[3] [one of the dogs of Actaeon] <Hyg. *Fab.* 181>, *
[Uranian Cyclopes], sons of Uranus and *Gaea* <Hes. *Theog.* 140> (see Arges, Brontes[1], Steropes), 4b
Uranus [heaven], son of *Gaea* <Hes. *Theog.* 127>, *4a*
alternate parentage:
Aether and *Hemera* <Hyg. *Fab.* pref.>
original being <Apollod. *Bibl.* 1.1.1>
— and *Gaea* <Hes. *Theog.* 133>, 2b
Urea[1] [hills], daughter of *Gaea* <Hes. *Theog.* 129>, *4b*
Urea[2], daughter of Poseidon <Hyg. *Fab.* 161>, 6d
— and Apollo <Hyg. *Fab.* 161>, 11d
Ureus [centaur], offspring of Centaurus and a Magnesian Mare <Pind. *Pyth.* 2.50; named as centaur, Hes. *Shield* 186>, 69c
alternate parentage:
Ixion and *Nephele*[1] <Diod. Sic. 4.69.5>

[winds], children of Astraeus[1] and *Eos* <Hes. *Theog.* 378-79> (see Boreas[1], Notus, Zephyrus[1]; Argestes, named in Ap. Rhod. *Arg.* 2, 958; Eurus, named in Non. *Dion.* 6, 28-38), 12a-b
[wine growers] — see (Oenotropae)
[winged horse] — see Pegasus

Xanthe[1], daughter of Oceanus and *Tethys* <Hes. *Theog.* 356>, 72b
— and Asclepius <*Cat. Wom., Frag. Hes.* frg. 53, Merk. & West>, 19d
Xanthe[2] [Amazon] <Hyg. *Fab.* 163>, *
Xanthippe[1], daughter of Dorus[1] <Apollod. *Bibl.* 1.7.7>, 17a
— and Pleuron <Apollod. *Bibl.* 1.7.7>, 15d
Xanthippe[2], daughter of Mycon <Hyg. *Fab.* 254>, *
Xanthippus[1], son of Melas[3] <Apollod. *Bibl.* 1.8.5>, 16d
Xanthippus[2], son of Deiphontes[2] and *Hyrnetho* <Paus. 2.28.3>, 60c
Xanthis, daughter of Thespius <Apollod. *Bibl.* 2.7.8> and *Megamede* <Apollod. *Bibl.* 2.4.10>, 51c
— and Heracles[1] <Apollod. *Bibl.* 2.7.8>, (51c)
Xantho, daughter of Nereus and *Doris*[1] <Hyg. *Fab.* pref.>, *65b*
Xanthus[1] [one of the horses of Achilles], offspring of Zephyrus[1] and *Podarge* <Hom. *Il.* XVI.145-47>, 12a, *3b*
Xanthus[2] — see Scamander[1] (alternate version)
Xanthus[3], son of Phaenops <Hom. *Il.* V.152>, 44c
Xanthus[4] [King of Pelasgians], son of Triop(a)s[2] <Diod. Sic. 5.81.2> and *Sois*, 61d
Xanthus[5], son of Erymanthus[2] <Paus. 8.24.1>, 63c
Xanthus[6], son of Ptolemaeus[1] <Paus. 9.5.16>, 18d
Xanthus[7] [one of the Pans], son of Pan <Non. *Dion.* 14.82>, 64d
Xanthus[8], paramour of *Alcinoe*[2] <Parth. *Love Stor.* 27>, *
Xanthus[9] — see [fifty sons of Aegyptus[1]] (alternate version)
Xanthus[10] [King of Termera] <Parth. *Love Stor.* 35>, *
Xanthus[11] [one of the horses of Hector[1]] <Hom. *Il.* VIII. 185>, *
Xanthus[12] [one of the horses of Diomedes[3]] <Hyg. *Fab.* 30>, *
Xenia — see *Nomia*
Xenodamus, son of Menelaus amd *Cnossia* <Apollod. *Bibl.* 3.11.1>, 37c
Xenodice[1], daughter of Minos I and *Pasiphae*[1] <Apollod. *Bibl.* 3.1.2>, 54c
alternate parentage:
Minos I and *Crete* <Asclep. in Apollod. *Bibl.* 3.1.2>
Xenodice[2], a Trojan woman <Paus. 10.26.1>, *
Xenodoce, daughter of Syleus <Apollod. *Bibl.* 2.6.3>, 9d
Xuthus[1] [King of Athens], son of Hellen(us)[1] <*Cat. Wom., Frag. Hes.* frg. 9, Merk. & West> and *Orseis* <Apollod. *Bibl.* 1.7.3>, 17b
alternate parentage:

Aeolus[1] <Eur. *Ion* 300>
— and *Creusa*[3] <Eur. *Ion* 57>, 51b
Xuthus[2], son of Aeolus[2] and *Cyane*[1] <Hom. *Od.* 10.2-6; named, Diod. Sic. 5.8.1>, 18c

Zabius, father of *Themisto*[2] <Steph. Byz. "Galeotai">, 11d
Zagreus (Iacchus[3]), son of Zeus <Aesch. frg. 5 (from *Aegyptioi*, p. 4)> and *Persephone*[1] <Non. *Dion.* 5.566-67>, 6c, *10a*
Za(n)cynthus — see Ilus[1]
Zarex, son of Carystus <Tzetz. on Lyc. 580>, 69b
— and *Rhoeo* <Tzetz. on Lyc. 580>, 56d
Zelus [rivalry], son of Pallas[1] and *Styx* <Hes. *Theog.* 384>, 12a
Zephyrus[1] [West wind], son of Astraeus[1] and *Eos* <Hes. *Theog.* 379>, 12a
— and *Chloris*[4] <Ovid *Fast.* 5.195-207>, (12a)
— and *Iris*[1] <Alc. *Poet. Lesb.* frg. 327>, 3b
— and *Podarge* <Hom. *Il.* XVI.145-47>, 3b
Zephyrus[2] [one of the dogs of Actaeon] <Hyg. *Fab.* 181>, *
Zethes [Argonaut], son of Boreas[1] and *Oreithyia*[1] <Acus. in *F. Gr. H.* 2 F 30>, 13a
Zethus [King of Thebes], son of Zeus and *Antiope*[1] <Hom. *Od.* 11.260-65>, 5a, *66d*
— and *Aedon*[1] <Hom. *Od.* 19.518-19>, (66d)
— and *Thebe*[1] <Apollod. *Bibl.* 3.5.6>, 66a
Zeus [god] [supreme god], son of Cronus and *Rhea* <Hes. *Theog.* 457>, 5a
alternate parentage:
Oceanus ("from whom all we gods proceed") <Hom. *Il.* XIV.202>
— and *Aegina* <Pind. *Nem.* 8.6>, 23a, 66a
— and *Aex* <Hyg. *Poet. Astr.* 2.13>, 7d, 46a
— and *Alcmene* <Hom. *Il.* XIV.324>, 59d
— and *Antiope*[1] <Hom. *Od.* 11.262>, 66d
— and *Asteria*[1] <Cic. *De Nat. Deor.* 3.42>, 12a
— and *Asterope*[3] <Steph. Byz. "Acragantes">, 51a
— and *Callisto*[1] <Eur. *Helen* 375-76>, 62a
— and *Cambyse* <Pind. *Olym.* 9.65>, 15a
— and *Carme* <Ant. Lib. *Met.* 40.1>, 56c
— and *Cassiopeia*[1] <Apollod. *Bibl.* 3.1.2>, 46c
— and *Danae* <Hom. *Il.* XIV.319>, 58d
— and *Demeter* <Hes. *Theog.* 912>, 10a
— and *Dia*[1] <Hom. *Il.* XIV.319>, (5a)
— and *Dione*[1] <Hom. *Il.* V.371>, 53a
— and *Elara* <Apollod. *Bibl.* 1.4.1>, 20d
— and *Electra*[2] <Hellan. in *F. Gr. H.* 4 F 19a>, 42b
— and *Europe*[1] <Hom. *Il.* XIV.321>, 53d
— and *Eurymedusa*[1] <Serv. on Virg. *Aen.* 2.7>, (5c)
— and *Eurynome*[1] <Hes. *Theog.* 909>, 53b
— and *Euryodia* <Eust. on Hom. *Od.* 1796>, (5c)
— and *Gaea* <Paus. 7.17.5>, 2b
— and Ganymede(s) <Eur. *Iph. in Aulis* 1049-53>, 41b
— and *Hera* <Hes. *Theog.* 921>, (5a)
— and *Himalia* <Diod. Sic. 5.55.5>, (5c)
— and *Hybris* <Apollod. *Bibl.* 1.4.1>, (5c)
— and *Io* <Steph. Byz. "Byzantium">, 55b
— and *Iodama* <Tzetz. on Lyc. 1206>, 16a
— and *Lamia*[1] <Paus. 10.12.1>, (5c)
— and *Laodameia*[2] <Hom. *Il.* VI.198-99>, 18b, 52c
— and *Leda* <Eur. *Hel.* 259>, 16c, 48b
— and *Leto* <Hes. *Theog.* 918>, 11b
— and *Leucothea*[2] <Ps.-Plut. *De Fluv.* 7.1>, (5c)
— and *Maera*[1] <Plut. *Gr. and Rom. Par. Stor.* 36>, 19c
— and *Maia* <Hes. *Theog.* 938>, 46a
— and *Metis*[1] <Hes. *Theog.* 886>, 61b
— and *Mnemosyne* <Hes. *Theog.* 76-79>, 10b
— and *Niobe*[2] <Apollod. *Bibl.* 2.1.1>, 61b
— and *Nymphe* <Diod. Sic. 5.48.1>, (6c)
— and *Othreis* <Ant. Lib. *Met.* 13.1>, (6c)
— and *Pandora*[3] <*Cat. Wom., Frag. Hes.* frg. 5, Merk. & West>, 16b
— and *Persephone*[1] <Non. *Dion.* 5.566-67>, 10a
— and *Phthia*[1] <Serv. on Virg. *Aen.* 1.242>, (6c)
— and *Pluto*[2] <Paus. 2.22.3>, (6c)
— and *Protogeneia*[1] <Apollod. *Bibl.* 1.7.3>, 15a
— and *Selene* <*Hom. Hymn* 32 (to *Selene*)>, 14b
— and *Semele* <Hes. *Theog.* 940-41>, 56c
— and [Sithnidian nymph] <Paus. 1.40.1>, (6c)
— and *Styx* <Apollod. *Bibl.* 1.3.1>, 50a
— and *Taygete* <Apollod. *Bibl.* 3.10.3>, 47b
— and *Thaleia*[4] <Steph. Byz. "Paliki">, 7d
— and *Themis*[1] <Hes. *Theog.* 901>, 10b
— and *Thrace* <Steph. Byz. "Bithynia">, 55a
— and *Thyia*[1] <*Cat. Wom., Frag. Hes.* frg. 7, Merk. & West>, 15a
Zeuxippe[1], daughter of a river nymph <Apollod. *Bibl.* 3.14.8 (inferred because she is sister of *Praxithea*[1])>, 49a
— and Pandion I <Apollod. *Bibl.* 3.14.8>, 49a
Zeuxippe[2], daughter of Lamedon and *Pheno* <Paus. 2.6.2>, 11d
— and Sicyon <Paus. 2.6.2>, 49a
Zeuxippe[3], daughter of Hippocoon[1] <Diod. Sic. 4.68.5>, 47c
— and Antiphates[2] <Diod. Sic. 4.68.5>, 32d
Zeuxippe[4], daughter of Eridanus <Hyg. *Fab.* 14>, 53a
— and Teleon <Hyg. *Fab.* 14>, (53a)
Zeuxippe[5], paramour of Laomedon[1] <Schol. on Hom. *Il.* III.250>, 42d
Zeuxippus [King of Sicyon], son of Apollo and *Syllis* <Paus. 2.6.7>, 11c
Zeuxo, daughter of Oceanus and *Tethys* <Hes. *Theog.* 352>, 72b

Bibliography

Ancient Sources

Aelian, *De Natura Animalium*, Schofield, A. S., ed., Harvard Univ., Cambridge, Mass. (1959)

— *Various Narrations*, Dilts, M. R., ed., Teubner, Leipzig (1974)

Aeschylus, *Agamemnon, Eumenides, Prometheus Bound, The Seven Against Thebes, The Suppliant Maidens*, Cookson, G. M., trans., Univ. of Chicago, Chicago (1952)

Alcaeus in *Poetarum Lesbiorum Fragmenta*, Lobel, E., and Page, D. L., eds., Clarendon, Oxford (1955)

Alciphron, *Letters*, Benner, A. R., and Fobes, F. H., eds., Harvard Univ. (Loeb), Cambridge, Mass. (1949)

Antoninus Liberalis, *Les Metamorphoses*, Papathomopoulos, M., trans., Societé d'Edition "Les Belles Lettres," Paris (1968)

Apollodorus, *Apollodorus: The Library*, Frazer, J. G., trans., 2 vols., Harvard Univ. (Loeb), Cambridge, Mass. (1921)

— *Gods and Heroes of the Greeks: The Library of Apollodorus (Bibliotheca*, including *Epitome)*, Simpson, M., trans., Univ. of Massachusetts, Amherst, Mass. (1976)

Apollonius of Rhodes, *Jason and The Golden Fleece (The Argonautica)*, Hunter, R., trans., Clarendon, Oxford (1993)

Apuleius, *Metamorphoses*, Hanson, A. A., ed. and trans., Harvard (Loeb), Cambridge, Mass. (1989)

Aristotle, *On Marvelous Works Heard* in *Minor Works*, Hett, W. S., ed., Harvard Univ. (Loeb), Cambridge, Mass. (1936)

Arrian, *Indica*, Brunt, P. A., trans., Harvard Univ. (Loeb), Cambridge, Mass. (1976)

Athenaeus, *The Deipnosophists*, Gulick, C. B., ed., 7 vols., Harvard Univ. (Loeb), Cambridge, Mass. (1951)

Bacchylides, *Carmina cum fragmentis*, Snell, B., and Maehler, H., eds., Teubner, Leipzig (1970)

Benoit de St.-Maure, *Le Roman de Troie* in *The Story of Troilus*, Gordon, R. K., and Dent, J. M., trans., Dent, London (1934)

Bion in *Greek Bucolic Poets* (Theocritus, Bion, Moschus), Edmonds, J. M., ed. and trans., Harvard Univ. (Loeb), Cambridge, Mass. (1912)

Callimachus, *Callimachus*, Pfeiffer, R., ed., Clarendon, Oxford (1949)

Catalogue of Women (Ehoiai) (Gunaikon Katalogos), fragments in *Fragmenta Hesiodea*, Merkelbach, R. and West, M. L., eds., Clarendon, Oxford (1967); in *Hesiodi Theogonia, Opera et Dies, Scutum*, Solmsen, F., ed., and *Fragmenta Selecta*, Merkelbach, R., and West, M. L., eds., Oxford Univ. (O.C.T.), New York (3d ed. 1990); and in *Homeric Hymns and Homerica,* Evelyn-White, H. G., trans., Harvard Univ. (Loeb), Cambridge, Mass. (1982)

Cicero, *De Natura Deorum Academica*, Rackham, H., trans., Harvard Univ. (Loeb), Cambridge, Mass. (1933)

Clement of Alexandria, *Stromateis*, Ferguson, J., ed., Catholic Univ., Wash., D.C. (1991)

Conon, *Narrations* in *Historiae Poeticae Scriptores Antiqui*, Gale, T., ed., Muguet-Scott, Paris (1675)

Cypria in *Poetae Epici Graeci*, Bernabé, A., ed., Teubner, Leipzig (1987)

Dictys Cretensis, *Ephemeris Belli Troiani*, Meister, F., ed., Teubner, Leipzig (1872)

Diodorus Siculus, *The Library of History*, Oldfather, C. H., trans., 3 vols., Harvard Univ. (Loeb), Cambridge, Mass. (1939)

Diogenes Laertius, *Lives of Eminent Philosophers*, Hicks, R. D., ed., Harvard Univ. (Loeb), Cambridge, Mass. (1928)

Dionysius of Halicarnassus, *Roman Antiquities*, Cary, E., ed. and trans., Harvard Univ. (Loeb), Cambridge, Mass. (1937)

Dionysus Periegetes, *On Birds*, Garzya, A., ed., Teubner, Leipzig (1963)

Epicharmus, *Testimonios y fragmentos*, Rodriguez-Noriega Guillen, L., ed., Universidad de Oviedo (1996)

Epimenides in *Die Fragmente der Vorsokratiker*, Diels, H., and Kranz, W., eds., Weidmann, Berlin (6th ed. 1951)

Eratosthenes, *Catasterismi* (*Pseudo-Eratosthenis Catasterismi*), Oliveri, A., ed., Teubner, Leipzig (1897)

Euripides, *Alcestis*, *Andromache*, *The Bacchantes, The Cyclops, Electra*, *Hecuba*, *Helen*, *Heracles, Hippolytus, Ion*, *Iphigenia at Aulis*, *Iphigenia Among the Tauri, Medea*, *Orestes, The Phoenician Maidens, Rhesus, The Suppliants*, *The Trojan Women,* Coleridge, Edward P., trans., Univ. of Chicago, Chicago (1952)

Eustathius, *Commentaria in Dionysium Periegetam* in *Geographi Graeci Minores, II*, Bernhardy, G., ed., Teubner, Leipzig (1828)

— *Commentarii ad Homeri Iliadem*, van der Valk, M., ed., Brill, Leiden (1971)

— *Commentarii ad Homeri Odysseam*, Weiger, J. A., ed., Teubner, Leipzig (1825)

Festus, Sextus Pompeius, *De Verborum Significatione*, Valpy, London (1826)

Great Ehoiai (Megalai Ehoiai), fragments in *Fragmenta Hesiodea*, Merkelbach, R. and West, M. L., eds., Clarendon, Oxford (1967)

Gregorius Corinthus, *Rhetoric* in *Tragicorum Graecorum Fragmenta*, p. 509, Nauck, A., ed., Teubner, Leipzig (2d ed. 1889)

Hermippus, fragments in *Delectus ex Iambis et Elegis Graecis*, West, M. L., ed., Clarendon (O.C.T.), New York (1980)

Herodotus, *The History*, Grene, D., trans., Univ. of Chicago, Chicago (1987)

Hesiod, *Fragmenta Hesiodea* (including fragments from *The Catalogue of Women* and *The Great Ehoiai*), Merkelbach, R., and West, M. L., eds., Clarendon, Oxford (1967) (The *Catalogue* is sometimes attributed to Hesiod but, in Prof. West's view, was written by a later poet; see West, M. L., *The Hesiodic Catalogue of Women*, pp. 127-30.)

— *Hesiodi Carmina*, Rzach, A., ed., Teubner, Leipzig (1908)

— *Hesiodi Theogonia, Opera et Dies, Scutum*, Solmsen, F., ed., and *Fragmenta Selecta*, Merkelbach, R., and West, M. L., eds. (including fragments from *The Catalogue of Women* and *The Great Ehoiai*), Oxford Univ. (O.C.T.), New York (3d ed. 1990)

— *Homeric Hymns and Homerica* (including fragments from *The Catalogue of Women* and *The Epic Cycle*), Evelyn-White, H. G., trans., Harvard Univ. (Loeb), Cambridge, Mass. (1982)
— *Theogony*, West, M. L., trans., ed., and comm., Oxford Univ., Oxford (1988)
— *Works and Days*, West, M. L., trans., ed. and comm., Oxford Univ., Oxford (1988)
Hesychius of Alexandria, *Lexicon*, Latte, K., ed., Hauniae, Munksgaard, Copenhagen (1953)
Homer, *Homeri Opera*, Monro, D. B., and Allen, T. W., eds., 5 vols., Clarendon, Oxford (3d ed. 1969)
— *The Iliad*, Butler, S., trans., Univ. of Chicago, Chicago (1952)
— *The Odyssey*, Butler, S., trans., Univ. of Chicago, Chicago (1952)
Homeric Hymns in *Hesiod, The Homeric Hymns and Homerica*, Evelyn-White, H. G., trans., Harvard Univ. (Loeb), Cambridge, Mass. (1982)
Horace, *Odes and Epodes*, Bennett, C. E., trans., Harvard Univ. (Loeb), Cambridge, Mass. (1939)
Hyginus, *The Myths of Hyginus (Hygini Fabulae*, including *Poetica Astronomica)*, Grant, M., trans. and ed., Univ. of Kansas, Lawrence, Kansas (1960)
Isyllus, *Lyricus III* in *Collectanea Alexandrina*, Powell, J. U., ed., Clarendon, Oxford (1925)
Lactantius Placidus, *Commentarios in Statii Thebaida*, Janke, R., ed., Teubner, Leipzig (1898)
Longus, *Daphnis and Chloe*, Thornley, G., trans., Edmonds, J. M., ed., Harvard Univ. (Loeb), Cambridge, Mass. (1989)
Lucian, *Dance* in *Luciani Samosatensis Opera*, Dindorf, W., ed., Firmin-Didot, Paris (1884)
— *Dialogue of the Sea-Gods*, Harmon, A. M., trans., Harvard Univ. (Loeb), Cambridge, Mass. (1913)
Lycophron, *Lycophronis Alexandra*, Mascialino, L., ed., Teubner, Leipzig (1964)
Mimnermus, *Testimonia* and *Fragments* in *Greek Elegiac Poetry*, Gerber, D. E., ed. and trans., Harvard Univ. (Loeb), Cambridge, Mass. (1999)
Nonnos, *Dionysiaca*, Lind, L. R., ed., Rouse, W. H. D., trans., 3 vols., Harvard Univ. (Loeb), Cambridge, Mass. (1940)
Oppian, *Halieutica*, Mair, A. W., ed. and trans., Putnam, New York (1928)
Orphic Argonautica, Dottin, G., ed. and trans., Société d'édition "Les belles lettres," Paris (1930)
Orphic Hymns, Quandt, W., ed., Weidmann, Berlin (1955)
Ovid, *Fasti*, Frazier, J. G., ed. and trans., Harvard Univ. (Loeb), Cambridge, Mass. (2d ed. 1989)
— *Heroides* and *Amores*, Showerman, G., ed. and trans., Harvard Univ. (Loeb), Cambridge, Mass. (1963)
— *Metamorphoses*, Miller, F. J., trans., Harvard Univ. (Loeb), Cambridge, Mass. (1921)
Palaephatus, *Mythographi Graeci*, Festa, N., ed., Teubner, Leipzig (1902)
Parthenius, *The Love Romances (Love Stories) (Erotikon Pathematon)*, Gaselee, S., trans., Harvard Univ. (Loeb), Cambridge, Mass. (1989)
Pausanias, *Guide to Greece*, Levi, P., trans., 2 vols., Penguin Books, London (1971)
— *Pausaniae Graeciae Descriptio*, Rocha-Pereira, M. H., ed. and trans., Teubner, Leipzig (1973)
— *Pausanias's Description of Greece*, Fraser, J. G., ed. and trans., 6 vols., Biblo and Tannen, New York (1965)
Pherecydes, *Pherecydis Fragmenta*, Sturz, F. G., ed., Cnobloch, Leipzig (1824)
Photius, *Bibliotheca*, Bekker, I., ed., Reimer, Berlin (1824)
Pindar, *Odes of Pindar*, Sandys, J., trans., Harvard Univ. (Loeb), Cambridge, Mass. (1915)
— *Pindari Carmina cum fragmentis*, Snell, B., and Maehler, H., eds., Teubner, Leipzig (4th ed. 1975)
Plato, *Platonis Opera*, Burnet, J., ed., 5 vols., Clarendon (O.C.T.), Oxford (1900)
Pliny (the elder), *Naturalis Historia*, Rackham, H., trans., Harvard Univ. (Loeb), Cambridge, Mass. (1938-80)
Plutarch, *Alcibiades, Aristides, Pyrrhus, Romulus, Sertorius, Themistocles, Theseus* in *Plutarch's Lives*, Perrin, B., trans., 10 vols., Macmillan (Loeb), New York (1914)
— *Greek and Roman Parallel Stories* in *Moralia of Plutarch*, Vol. IV, Babbitt, F. C., ed. and trans., Harvard Univ. (Loeb), Cambridge, Mass. (1962)
— *Greek Questions* in *Moralia of Plutarch*, Vol. IV, Babbitt, F. C., ed. and trans., Harvard Univ. (Loeb), Cambridge, Mass. (1962)
— *Roman Questions* in *Moralia of Plutarch*, Vol. IV, Babbitt, F. C., ed. and trans., Harvard Univ. (Loeb), Cambridge, Mass. (1962)
— *Table Talk* in *Moralia of Plutarch,* vol. VIII, Clement, P. A., and Hoffleit, H. B., trans., Harvard Univ. (Loeb) Cambridge, Mass. (1969)
Pollux, *Onomasticon*, Bekker, E., ed., Niocolai, Berlin (1846)
Polyaenus, *Strategematon Libri Octo*, Woelfflin, E., ed., Teubner, Leipzig (1887)
Pomponius Mela, *Chorographia*, Frick, C., ed., Teubner, Leipzig (1880)
Proclus, *In Platonis Timaeum Commentaria*, Diehl, E., ed., 3 vols., Hakkert, Amsterdam (1965)
Propertius, *Elegies*, Camps, W. A., ed., Cambridge Univ., Cambridge (1967)
Pseudo-Eratosthenes, see Eratosthenes
Pseudo-Plutarch, *De Fluvius* in *Geographi Graeci Minores*, Müller, K., ed., Firmin-Didot, Paris (1861)
Ptolemaeus Hephaestion, *Nova Historia* in *Historiae Poeticae Scriptores Antiqui*, Gale, T., ed., Muguet-Scott, Paris (1675)
Quintus Smyrnaeus, *The Fall of Troy*, Way, A. S., trans., Harvard Univ. (Loeb), Cambridge, Mass. (1913)
Servius, *On Virgil's Aeneid*, *Servi Grammatici Qui Feruntur in Vergilii Carmina Commentarii*, Thilo, G., and Hagen, H., eds., Teubner, Leipzig (1881)
— *On Virgil's Eclogues* and *Georgics*, *Commentarii in Vergili Bucolica et Georgica*, Thilo, G., ed., Teubner, Leipzig (1887)
Silius Italicus, *Punica*, Bauer, L., ed., Teubner, Leipzig (1890)
Solinus, *Collectanea Rerum Memorabilium*, Mommsen, T., ed., Weidmann, Berlin (1895)
Sophocles, *Ajax, Antigone, Electra, Oedipus the King, Oedipus at Colonus, Philoctetes, Trachinian Women* in *The Complete Plays of Sophocles*, Jebb, R. C., trans., Bantam, New York (1967)
— *The Fragments of Sophocles*, Pearson, A. C., ed., 3 vols., Hakkert, Amsterdam (1963)
Statius, *Silvae* and *Thebiad*, Mozley, J. H., trans., 2 vols., Harvard Univ. (Loeb), Cambridge, Mass. (1928)
Stephanus Byzantium, *Ethnika kat epitomen*, Berkel, A. and Gronovius, J., eds., Haaring, Leiden (1694)
Strabo, *Geography*, Jones, H. L., trans. and ed., Putnam, New York (1924)
Suidas (Suda), *Suidae Lexikon*, Bernhardy, G., ed., Schwetschke, Halle (1843-1853); *Suidae Lexicon*, Adler, A., ed., Teubner, Leipzig (1933)
Thucydides, *The Peloponnesian War*, Hobbes, T., trans., Grene, D. ed., Univ. of Chicago, Chicago (1989)

Tryphiodorus, Livera, E., ed., Teubner, Leipzig (1982)
Tzetzes, Johannes, *Antehomerica, Homerica, Posthomerica*, Lehrs, F. S., ed., Firmin-Didot, Paris (1878)
— *Exegesis in Iliadem* in *Der Unbekannte Teil, der Ilias-Exegesis des I. Tzetzes*, Lolos, A., ed., Hain, Konistein (1981)
— *Historiarum Variarum Chiliades*, Kiesslingius, T., ed., Vogelius, Leipzig (1826)
— On Hesiod's *Theogony* and on Hesiod's *Works and Days* in *Hesiodi Ascraei, Opera Quae Quidem Extant*, Brickmann, J., trans., Basileia, Cologne (1542)
— On Lycophron (*Commentaria in Lycophronis Alexandram*), Pettelo, J., ed., E Theatro Sheldoniano, Oxford (1697)
Valerius Flaccus, *Argonautica*, Mozley, J. H., trans., Harv. Univ. (Loeb), Cambridge, Mass. (1934)
Virgil, *The Aeneid, The Eclogues, The Georgics,* Rhoades, J., trans., Univ. of Chicago, Chicago (1952)
Zenobius, *Sophist*, cited in *Crusius's commentary*, *Plutarchi de Proverbiis Alexandrinorum*, Crusius, O., ed., Teubner, Leipzig (1887)

Scholia

Scholia in Apollonium Rhodium Vetera, Wendel, C., ed., Weidmann, Berlin (1935)
Scholia in Aratum Vetera, Martin, J., ed., Teubner, Stuttgart (1974)
Scholia in Euripidem, Schwartz, E., ed., 2 vols., Reimer, Berlin (1887-91)
Scholia Graeca in Euripidis Tragoedias, Dindorf, W., ed., Typographeo Academico, Oxford (1863)
Scholia Graeca in Homeri Iliadem, Dindorf, W., ed., 6 vols., Typographeo Clarendoniano, Oxford (1875)
Scholia Graeca in Homeri Odysseam, Dindorf, W., ed., 2 vols., Typographeo Academico, Oxford (1855)
Scholia in Lucianum, Rabe, H., ed., Teubner, Stuttgart (1971)
Scholia Lycophronis Alexandra (includes scholia), Kinkel, G., ed., Teubner, Leipzig (1880)
Scholia Vetera in Pindari Carmina, Drachman, A. B., ed., 3 vols.,Teubner, Leipzig (1903-27)
Scholia Platonica, Greene, W. C., ed., American Philological Society, Haverford, Pa. (1938)
Scholia in Theocritum Vetera, Wendel, C., ed., Teubner, Stuttgart (1967)

Collections of Ancient Sources

Bergk, T., ed., *Poetae Lyrici Graeci*, 3 vols.,Teubner, Leipzig (1914)
Bernabé, A., ed., *Poetae Epici Graeci*, Teubner, Leipzig (1987)
Bernhardy, G., ed., *Geographi Graeci Minores, II*, Teubner, Leipzig (1828)
Curtis, E., and Kirchoff, A., eds., *Corpus Inscriptionum Graecarum*, Berlin (1877)
Diels, H., and Kranz, W., eds., *Die Fragmente der Vorsokratiker*, Weidmann, Berlin (6th ed. 1951)
Edelstein, E. J., and Edelstein, L., eds., *Asclepius: A Collection and Interpretation of the Testimonies*, Johns Hopkins Univ., Baltimore (1945)
Edmonds, J. M., ed. and trans., *Greek Bucolic Poets* (Theocritus, Bion, Moschus), Harvard Univ. (Loeb), Cambridge, Mass. (1912)
Evelyn-White, H. G., trans., *Hesiod—the Homeric Hymns and Homerica,* Harvard Univ. (Loeb), Cambridge, Mass. (1982)
Firmin-Didot, ed., *Erotica Scriptores Graeci*, Firmin-Didot, Paris (1885)
Fowler, R. L., ed., *Early Greek Mythography*, Vol. 1, Oxford Univ., New York (2000)
Fritsch, C., ed., *Geoponica, Geoponicorum Sive De Re Rustica*, 4 vols., Teubner, Leipzig (1781)
Gale, T., ed., *Historiae Poeticae Scriptores Antiqui*, Muguet-Scott, Paris (1675)
Gerber, D. E., ed. and trans., *Greek Elegiac Poetry*, Harvard Univ. (Loeb), Cambridge, Mass. (1999)
Jacoby, F., ed., *Die Fragmente der Griechischen Historiker*, 2 vols., Brill, Leiden (1923-58)
Lobel, E. and Page, D. L., eds., *Poetarum Lesbiorum Fragmenta*, Clarendon, Oxford (1955)
Müller, K., ed., *Fragmenta Historicorum Graecorum*, 5 vols., Firmin-Didot, Paris (1848-74)
Nauck, A., ed., *Tragicorum Graecorum Fragmenta*, Teubner, Leipzig (2d ed. 1889)
Page, D. L., ed., *Poetae Melici Graeci*, Clarendon, Oxford (1962)
Powell, J. U., *Collectanea Alexandrina*, ed., Clarendon, Oxford (1925)
West, M. L., ed., *Delectus ex Iambis et Elegis Graecis*, Clarendon (O.C.T.), Oxford (1980)

Commentaries, Dictionaries, Encyclopedias, and Handbooks

Bell, R. E., *Women of Classical Mythology*, Oxford Univ., New York (1993)
Boardman, J., ed., *Iconographicum Mythologiae Classicae*, 10 vols., Artemis, Zurich (1981-1999)
Bulfinch, T., *Bulfinch's Mythology: The Age of Fable*, New American Library, New York (1962)
Gantz, T., *Early Greek Myth*, Johns Hopkins Univ., Baltimore (1993)
Grant, M., and Hazel, J., *Who's Who in Classical Mythology*, Oxford Univ., New York (1993)
Graves, R., *The Greek Myths*, Penguin Books, Ltd., Middlesex, England (1955)
Grimal, P., *The Dictionary of Classical Mythology*, Presses Universitaire de France, Paris (1951); Maxwell-Hyslop, A. R., trans., Blackwell, Oxford (1986)
Gruppe, O., *Griechische Mythologie und Religionsgeschichte*, Beck, Munich (1906)
Hamilton, E., *Mythology, Timeless Tales of Gods and Heroes*, Little Brown & Co., New York (1940)
Harvey, P., *The Oxford Companion to Classical Literature*, Oxford Univ., Oxford (1984)
Hemberg, B., *Die Kabiren*, Uppsala (1950)
Hornblower, S. & Spawforth, A., eds., *Oxford Classical Dictionary*, Oxford Univ., New York (3d ed. 1996)
Howe, G., and Harper, G. A., *A Handbook of Classical Mythology*, Oracle, Royston, England (1996)
Kerényi, C., *The Gods of the Greeks*, Thames & Hudson, London (1951)
Kravitz, D., *Who's Who in Greek and Roman Mythology*, Clarkson N. Potter, Inc., New York (1975)
Lempriere, J., *Classical Dictionary*, (1788); Wright, F.A., rev., Routledge & Kegan Paul Ltd., London (1949)
Murray, A., *Who's Who in Mythology*, Crescent Books, New York (1988)
Oswalt, S. G., *Concise Encyclopedia of Greek and Roman Mythology*, Collins, London (1969)
Parada, C., *Genealogical Guide to Greek Mythology*, Forlag, Jonsered, Sweden (1993)
Pauly-Wissowa, *Realencyclopaedie der Classischen Altertumswissenschaft*, Metler, J. B., ed., 24 vols., 1st series, 10 vols., 2nd series, Metzler, Stuttgart (1894-1972)
Preller, L., and Preller, C. R., *Griechische Mythologie*, Weidmann, Berlin (1964)
Roscher, W. H., *Lexikon der Graesche und Romishe Mythologie*, Teubner, Leipzig (1884-1937)
Rose, H. J., *A Handbook of Greek Mythology*, Methuen, London (1928)
Schwab, G., *Gods and Heroes*, Pantheon, New York (1946)
Shapiro, M. S., and Hendricks, R. A., *A Dictionary of Mythologies*, Paladin, London (1981)

Smith, W. G., *Dictionary of Greek and Roman Biography and Mythology*, 3 vols., Murray, London (1880)

Stapleton, M., *The Illustrated Dictionary of Greek and Roman Mythology*, Bedrick, New York (1986)

Tripp, E., *The Meridian Handbook of Classical Mythology*, New American Library, New York (1970)

Sylburgius, F., ed., *Etymologicum Magnum*, Weigel, Leipzig (1816)

West, M. L., *The Hesiodic Catalogue of Women*, Oxford Univ., New York (1985)

Zimmerman, J. E., *Dictionary of Classical Mythology*, Harper & Row, New York (1964)

Internet Sites

Classical Mythology Online <www.oup-usa.org/sc/0195143388>

Greek Mythology <greekmythology.com >

Greek Mythology Link <homepage.mac.com/cparada/GML/>

Mythology <www.princeton.edu/~rhwebb/myth.html>

Perseus Digital Library <www.perseus.tufts.edu>

Source Guide—Bibliography for Greek & Roman Myth <www.theoi.com/SourceGuide.htm>

Appendix A

Greek Mythological Figures and their Roman Counterparts

Aias — Ajax
Alethia — Veritas
Amphitrite — Salacia
Ananke — Necessitas
Apeliotes — Solanus
Aphrodite — Erycina, Venus
Ares — Mars
Argestes — Corus
Ariadne — Libera
Artemis — Diana
Asclepius — Aesculapius
Athene — Minerva
Atropis — Morta
Boreas[1] — Aquila
Castor — Castores
(Charites) — (Gratiae)
Chloris[4] — Flora
Circe — Angitia
Clotho — Nona
Cronus — Saturn
Demeter — Ceres
Dike —Justitia
Dionysus — Bacchus, Liber
Eileithyia — Lucina
Eirene[1] — Pax
Enyo[2] — Bellona
Eos — Aurora, Mater Matuta
Eosphorus — Lucifer
(Erinyes) — (Dirae), (Furiae)
Eris — Discordia
Eros — Amor, Cupid
Eurus — Vulturus
Gaea — Tellus, Terra
Ganymede(s) — Catamitus
Hades — Dis, Orcus, Pluto
Hebe — Juventas
Hecabe[1] — Hecuba
Hecate — Trivia
(Hecatoncheires) — (Centimani)
Helios — Sol
Hephaestus — Mulciber, Vulcan
Hera — Juno
Heracles[1] — Hercules
Hermes — Mercury
Hesperus — Vesper
Hestia — Vesta
Hippolytus[1] — Virbius
Hygeia — Salus
Hypnos — Somnus
Lachesis — Decuma
Lara(nda) — Tacita
Leto — Latona
Leucothoe[2] — Matuta
(Moirae) — (Fatae), (Parcae)
[Muses] — (Camenae)
Nephele[1] — Nebula
Nicostrate[1] — Carmenta
Nike[1] — Victoria
Notus — Auster
Odysseus — Ulysses
Ossa — Fama
Pan — Faunus
Peitho — Suada, Suadela
Persephone — Averna, Proserpina
Phosphor(us) — Lucifer
Polydeuces — Pollux
Poseidon — Neptune
Rhea — Bona Dea, Ops
Selene — Luna
Solanus — Lips
Thanatos — Mors
Tyche — Fortuna
Uranus — Coelus
Zephyrus — Caurus, Favonius
Zeus — Jove, Jupiter

Appendix B

Roman Mythological Figures and their Greek Counterparts

Aesculapius — Asclepius
Ajax — Aias
Amor — Eros
Angitia — Circe
Aquilo — Boreas[1]
Aurora — Eos
Auster — Notus
Averna — Persephone
Bacchus — Dionysus
Bellona — Enyo[2]
Bona Dea — Rhea
(Camenae) — [Muses]
Carmenta — Nicostrate[1]
Castores — Castor
Catamitus — Ganymede(s)
Caurus — Zephyrus
(Centimani) — (Hecatoncheires)
Ceres — Demeter
Coelus — Uranus
Corus — Argestes
Cupid — Eros
Decuma — Lachesis
Diana — Artemis
(Dirae) — (Erinyes)
Dis — Hades
Discordia — Eris
Erycina — Aphrodite
Fama — Ossa
(Fatae) — (Moirae)
Faunus — Pan
Favonius — Zephyrus
Flora — Chloris[4]
Fortuna — Tyche
(Furiae) — (Erinyes)
(Gratiae) — (Charites)
Hecuba — Hebabe[1]
Hercules — Heracles[1]
Lucifer — Eosphorus
Jove — Zeus
Juno — Hera
Jupiter — Zeus
Justitia — Dike
Juventas — Hebe
Latona — Leto
Liber — Dionysus
Libera — Ariadne
Lips — Solanus
Lucifer — Phosphor(us)
Lucina — Eileithyia
Luna — Selene
Mars — Ares
Mater Matuta — Eos
Matuta — Leucothoe[2]
Mercury — Hermes
Minerva — Athene
Mors — Thanatos
Morta — Atropis
Mulciber — Hephaestus
Nebula — Nephele[1]
Necessitas — Ananke
Neptune — Poseidon
Nona — Clotho
Ops — Rhea
Orcus — Hades
(Parcae) — (Moirae)
Pax — Eirene[1]
Pluto — Hades
Pollux — Polydeuces
Proserpina — Persephone
Salacia — Amphitrite
Salus — Hygeia
Saturn — Cronus
Sol — Helios
Solanus — Apeliotes
Somnus — Hypnos
Suada — Peitho
Suadela — Peitho
Tacita — Lara(nda)
Tellus — Gaea
Terra — Gaea
Trivia — Hecate
Ulysses — Odysseus
Venus — Aphrodite
Veritas — Alethia
Vesper — Hesperus
Vesta — Hestia
Victoria — Nike[1]
Virbius — Hippolytus[1]
Vulcan — Hephaestus
Vulturnus — Eurus

Appendix C

Chronology of Principal Sources

Listed by Author

Acusilaus — 5th century B.C.
Aelian — born circa 165 A.D.
Aeschylus — 525 - 456 B.C.
Alcaeus — born circa 625 B.C.
Alciphron — 2nd-3rd century A.D.
Alcman — 7th century B.C.
Andron of Hallicarnassus — 5th century B.C.
Antimachus — 5th century B.C.
Antoninus Liberalis — 2nd century A.D.
Apollodorus — circa 180 - 120 B.C. (but the works attributed to him, incorrectly, are 1st or 2nd century A.D.)
Apollonius Rhodius — 295 - 215 B.C.
Apuleius — born 125 A.D.
Aratus — 3rd century B.C.
Aristophanes — born circa 460 B.C.
Aristotle — 384-322 B.C.
Arrian — born 86 A.D.
Asclepiades — 4th century B.C.
Athenaeus — 3rd century A.D.
Bacchylides — born circa 520 B.C.
Bion -- died 241 B.C.
Callimachus — born 310 B.C.
Castor — 1st century B.C.
Catalogue of Women — circa 580 - 520 B.C.
Cercops — 6th century B.C.
Choerilus — 6th century B.C.
Cicero — 106 - 43 B.C.
Cinaethon — 6th century B.C.
Clement of Alexandria — 150 - 211 A.D.
Conon — born 36 B.C.
Cornutus — 1st century A.D.
Demetrius of Scepsis — born 214 B.C.
Dichaearchus — 4th century B.C.
Diodorus Siculus — circa 44 B.C.
Diogenes Laertius — 3rd century A.D.
Dionysius of Hallicarnassus — circa 25 B.C.
Dionysius Periegetes — 2nd century A.D.
Epicharmus — 5th century B.C.
Epimenides — 7th century B.C.
Eratosthenes — circa 276 - 196 B.C.
Euanthius — 4th century A.D.
Eugammon — 6th century B.C.
Eumelus — 8th century B.C.
Euphorion — born 275 A.D.
Euripides — 480 - 406 B.C.
Eustathius — 12th century A.D.
Fabius Pictor — 3rd century B.C.
Hecataeus — 360 - 290 B.C.
Hegesander — 2nd century B.C.
Hellanicus — 480 - 395 B.C.
Heraclides — born 388 B.C.
Hermippus — 3rd century B.C.
Herodotus — 484 - 425 B.C.
Hesiod — 8th century B.C.
Hesychius of Alexandria — 5th century A.D.
Hesychius of Miletus — 6th century A.D.
Homer — 8th century B.C.
Horace — 65 - 8 B.C.
Hyginus — 64 B.C. - 17 A.D.
Ibycus — 6th century B.C.
Ion of Chios — 5th century B.C.
Ister — 3rd century B.C.
Isyllus — 4th century B.C.
Juvenal — 60-140 A.D.
Lesches — 7th century B.C.
Longus — 2nd-3rd century A.D.
Lucanus — 39 - 65 A.D.
Lycophron — 3rd century B.C.
Lydus — 490 - 560 A.D.
Memnon of Heraclea — 2nd century A.D.
Menecrates — born 340 B.C.
Mimnermus — 7th century B.C.
Nicander — born 137 B.C.
Nonnus — 5th century A.D.
Oppian — 2nd century A.D.
Ovid — 43 B.C. - 18 A.D.
Parthenius — 1st century B.C.
Pausanias — circa 170 A.D.
Pherecydes of Athens — 5th century B.C.
Pherecydes of Syros — 5th century B.C.
Philochorus — 3rd century B.C.
Philocrates — 4th century B.C.
Philon Byblus —circa 70 - 160 A.D.
Philostratus — 3rd century A.D.
Photius — born 810 A.D.
Pindar — born 521 B.C.
Plato — 427 - 348 B.C.
Pliny (the Elder) — 23 - 79 A.D.
Plutarch — born 46 A.D.
Pollux — 2nd century A.D.
Pomponius Mela — 1st century A.D.
Praxilla — 5th century B.C.
Proclus — 410 - 485 A.D.
Propertius — 50 - 16 B.C.
Ptolemaeus Hephaestion — 1st century A.D.
Quintus Smyrnaeus — 4th century A.D.
Servius — circa 400 A.D.
Silius Italicus — 26 - 102 A.D.
Simonides — 6th century B.C.
Solinus — 3rd century A.D.
Sophocles — 496 - 406 B.C.
Statius — 40 - 96 A.D.
Stephanus of Byzantium — 6th century A.D.
Stesichorus — circa 600 - 550 B.C.
Strabo — 64 B.C. - 19 A.D.
Suidas — 10th century A.D.
Telesilla — 5th century B.C.
Theocritus — circa 270 B.C.
Theopompus — born 376 B.C.
Thucydides – circa 460 - 400 B.C.
Tryphiodorus — 6th century A.D.
Tzetzes — circa 1110 - 1180 A.D.
Valerius Flaccus — 1st century A.D.
Virgil — 70 - 19 B.C.
Xenagoras — 2nd century B.C.
Zenobius — 2nd century A.D.

Listed by Chronology

Hesiod — 8th century B.C.
Homer — 8th century B.C.
Eumelus — 8th century B.C.
Alcman — 7th century B.C.
Epimenides — 7th century B.C.
Mimnermus — 7th century B.C.
Cercops — 6th century B.C.
Choerilus — 6th century B.C.
Cinaethon — 6th century B.C.
Eugammon — 6th century B.C.
Ibycus — 6th century B.C.
Lesches — 6th century B.C.
Simonides — 6th century B.C.
Alcaeus — born circa 625 B.C.
Stesichorus — circa 600 - 550 B.C.
Catalogue of Women — circa 580-520 B.C.
Aeschylus — 525 - 456 B.C.
Pindar — born 521 B.C.
Bacchylides — born circa 520 B.C.
Acusilaus — 5th century B.C.
Andron of Hallicarnassus — 5th century B.C.
Antimachus — 5th century B.C.
Epicharmus — 5th century B.C.
Ion of Chios — 5th century B.C.
Pherecydes of Athens — 5th century B.C.
Pherecydes of Syros — 5th century B.C.
Praxilla — 5th century B.C.
Telesilla — 5th century B.C.
Sophocles — 496 - 406 B.C.
Herodotus — 484 - 425 B.C.
Hellanicus — 480 - 395 B.C.
Euripides — 480 - 406 B.C.
Aristophanes — born circa 460 B.C.
Thucydides — circa 460-400 B.C.
Plato — 427 - 348 B.C.
Asclepiades — 4th century B.C.
Dichaearchus — 4th century B.C.

Isyllus — 4th century B.C.
Philocrates — 4th century B.C.
Heraclides — born 388 B.C.
Aristotle — 384-322 B.C.
Theopompus — born 376 B.C.
Hecataeus — 360 - 290 B.C.
Menecrates — born 340 B.C.
Callimachus — born 310 B.C.
Aratus — 3rd century B.C.
Fabius Pictor — 3rd century B.C.
Hermippus — 3rd century B.C.
Ister — 3rd century B.C.
Lycophron — 3rd century B.C.
Philochorus — 3rd century B.C
Apollonius Rhodius — 295 - 215 B.C.
Eratosthenes — circa 276 - 196 B.C.
Theocritus — circa 270 B.C.
Demetrius of Scepsis — born 214 B.C.
Bion -- died 241 B.C.
Apollodorus — circa 180 - 120 B.C. (but the works attributed to him, incorrectly, are 1st or 2nd century A.D.)
Nicander — born 137 B.C.
Hegesander — 2nd century B.C.
Xenagoras — 2nd century B.C.
Parthenius — 1st century B.C.
Castor — 1st century B.C.
Cicero — 106 - 43 B.C.
Virgil — 70 - 19 B.C.
Horace — 65 - 8 B.C.
Hyginus — 64 B.C. - 17 A.D.
Strabo — 64 B.C. - 19 A.D.
Propertius — 50 - 16 B.C.
Diodorus Siculus — circa 44 B.C.
Ovid — 43 B.C. - 18 A.D.
Conon — born 36 B.C.
Dionysius of Hallicarnassus — circa 25 B.C.
Cornutus — 1st century A.D.
Pomponius Mela —1st century A.D.
Ptolemaeus Hephaestion — 1st century A.D.
Valerius Flaccus — 1st century A.D.
Zenobius — 1st century A.D.
Pliny (the Elder) — 23 - 79 A.D.
Silius Italicus —26 - 102 A.D.
Lucanus — 39 - 65 A.D.
Statius — 40 - 96 A.D.
Plutarch — born 46 A.D.
Juvenal — 60 -140 A.D.
Philon Byblus —circa 70 - circa 160 A.D.
Arrian — born 86 A.D.
Apuleius — born 125 A.D.
Clement of Alexandria — 150 - 211 A.D.
Aelian — born circa 165 A.D.
Pausanias — circa 170 A.D.
Antoninus Liberalis — 2nd century A.D.
Dionysius Periegetes — 2nd century A.D.
Memnon of Heraclea — 2nd century A.D.
Oppian — 2nd century A.D.
Pollux — 2nd century A.D.
Zenobius — 2nd century A.D.
Alciphron — 2nd-3rd century A.D.
Longus — 2nd-3rd century A.D.
Euphorion — born 275 A.D.
Athenaeus — 3rd century A.D.
Diogenes Laertius — 3rd century A.D.
Philostratus — 3rd century A.D.
Solinus — 3rd century A.D.
Euanthius — 4th century A.D.
Quintus Smyrnaeus — 4th century A.D.
Servius — 4th century A.D.
Hesychius of Alexandria — 5th century A.D.
Nonnus — 5th century A.D.
Proclus — 410 - 485 A.D.
Lydus — 490 - 560 A.D.
Hesychius of Miletus — 6th century A.D.
Stephanus of Byzantium — 6th century A.D.
Tryphiodorus — 6th century A.D.
Photius — 810-93 A.D.
Suidas — 10th century A.D.
Tzetzes — circa 1110 - 1180 A.D.
Eustathius — 12th century A.D.